oestreol

# THE COMPANION TO
# IRISH TRADITIONAL MUSIC

# THE COMPANION TO IRISH TRADITIONAL MUSIC

*edited by*
Fintan Vallely

CORK UNIVERSITY PRESS

*Dedicated to Jim and Mary Vallely*

First published in 1999 by
Cork University Press
Crawford Business Park
Crosses Green
Cork
Ireland

© The editor and contributors 1999

All rights reserved. No part of this book may be reprinted or reproduced or utilized in any electronic, mechanical or other means, now known or hereafter invented, including photocopying and recording or otherwise, without either the prior written permission of the Publishers or a licence permitting restricted copying in Ireland issued by the Irish Copyright Licensing Agency Ltd, The Irish Writers' Centre, 19 Parnell Square, Dublin 1.

British Library Cataloguing in Publication Data
A CIP catalogue record for this book is available from the British Library.

ISBN 1 85918 148 1

Music setting by Leading Note, Millstreet
Typeset by Phototypeset Ltd, Dublin
Printed by MPG Books Ltd, Cornwall

# Contents

| | |
|---|---|
| *Acknowledgements* | vii |
| *Contributors* | ix |
| *Abbreviations* | xiv |
| Introduction | xv |
| A–Z ENTRIES | 1 |
| Chronology | 440 |
| Select Bibliography | 443 |
| Select Discography | 463 |

# Acknowledgements

The *Companion* is the product of all the contributors whose research, analysis, working and editing was typically done to pressing schedules. Some are owed gratitude in greater measure than others, and special appreciation is due to those who contributed pieces which due to overlaps of material, editorial considerations and time restrictions, could regrettably not be used. In particular the various advice, example, provocativeness, critique, patience, promptness, inadvertent revelation and conscious prompting of the following are noted: Eamon Coyne, Paul Brock, George Henderson, Róisín White, John Loesberg, Eileen O'Doherty, Dónal Ó Móráin, Terry Moylan, Muiris Ó Róchain, Nóirín Ní Riain, Pat Ahern, John Moulden, Paula Dundon, Hammy Hamilton, Hugh Shields, Liam McNulty, Joan McDermott, Glen Comiskey and the Conradh na Gaeilge office. Antaine Ó Faracháin is thanked for photographic assistance, Tomás Ó Canainn for prompt inspiration, Claire O'Loughlin for music setting, Catriona McEniry and Desi Wilkinson for résumés, précis and synopses, Naomh Parsons for computer work, Tom Sherlock for equipment, Steve Chambers for time and exquisite pedantry of accuracy, Barra Ó Seaghdha for translation, Hamish Moore for consultation, Labhrás Ó Murchú for CCÉ information; Joe Burke for East Galway photographs, Olga at The Living Tradition, Liam Mac Con Iomaire for exhaustive biographical work, Diarmuid Ó Muirithe for working in trying circumstances, Anina and Don Meade for bearing the pressure. Above all these however thanks must be extended to Nicholas Carolan and Maeve Gebruers of the Irish Traditional Music Archive for exceptional co-operation and use of resources and consulting media. But it is to Evelyn Conlon and Trevor that deepest appreciation must ultimately be extended for the unpredictable disruption to life, the blending of day and night to greyness, the levelling of the week to seven-day clockwork that compilation of this work at times entailed.

Several hundred books, journals and magazines have been consulted in compiling and checking these articles. In particular the editor acknowledges the material sourced, referenced and checked through *Treoir* magazine, *Bliain-Iris* (vol. 1, no. 2), *Bunreacht* and other books (CCÉ), *An Píobaire, Ceol na hÉireann* and *The Man and His Music* (NPU), *Folk Music and Dances of Ireland* and *Dancing in Ireland* (Breathnach), *Irish Minstrels and Musicians* and *Irish Folk Music – a Fascinating Hobby* (O'Neill), Armagh Pipers' Club publications, Siemens Nixdorf Feis Ceoil programme 1997, *Carolan* (O'Sullivan), *The Hedge Schools of Ireland* (P.J. Dowling), *The Waltz* (Carner), *Irish Music in America – Continuity and Change* (Moloney), *Blooming Meadows* (Vallely, Piggott, Nutan), *Dal gCais* (Hughes and Ó Róchain), *Exploring Irish Music and Dance* (Boullier), *Irish Music* magazine, *Folk Roots*, *The World of Percy French* (O'Dowda), *The Guinness Who's Who of Folk Music* (ed. Larkin), *The Roche Collection* (Ossian), *The Northern Fiddler* (O'Doherty, Feldman), *Here's a Health* (Seán Corcoran), *Chronology of Irish History* (J.E. Doherty and D.J. Hickey), *Traditional Music in Ireland* (Ó Canainn), sleeve notes, articles and documentary by Harry Bradshaw, Jackie Small, Robin Morton, Finbar Boyle, Máire O'Keeffe, Tom Sherlock, Séamus Mac Mathúna, Don Meade, Earl Hitchner, Tony MacMahon, Claddagh Records and Topic Records.

Synopsis usage of many works and, in some instances, consultation with their authors is here also acknowledged, in particular: *Repossessions* by Seán Ó Tuama, *May I Have the Pleasure* by Belinda Quirey, *The Irish Harp* by Joan Rimmer, *O'Farrell's* and *Ryan's Mammoth* collections (Patrick Sky), *The Wexford Carol* by Diarmuid Ó Muirithe, *The Broadside Ballad* by

Leslie Shepard, *Short Bibliography of Irish Folk Song* by Hugh Shields, *A Short Discography of Irish Folk Music*, and *A Collection of the Most Celebrated Irish Tunes* by Nicholas Carolan, and Eugene O'Curry research by Muiris Ó Róchain.

Permission is gratefully acknowledged to those who allowed reproduction of music notation, illustrations and diagrams, the sources of which are given with each item. The publishers particularly appreciate the opportunity to include original © research material on harp and modes by Máire Ní Chathasaigh; on harp by Ann Heymann; bibliography by Maeve Gebruers; dance bibliography by John Cullinane, and Goodman biography by Hugh Shields.

# Contributors

The contributors to this volume come mainly from within the traditional music community, and all have been involved in research, writing, collecting and comment on various aspects of traditional music, song and dance. All articles are credited by the author's initials appearing at the end of the piece. Such initials apply only to the connected paragraphs immediately above. Unaccredited items or paragraphs separated from credited material by line spaces are by the editor.

**Ahern, Pat.** Guitarist, member of Four Star Trio, and traditional music columnist with *The Examiner* newspaper. (PAA)

**Bazin, Fenella.** Performer and chronicler of Manx music at the Centre for Manx Studies. (FEB)

**Bennett, Margaret.** Singer and Research Fellow at Glasgow University, from a long line of Skye singers and pipers. (MAB)

**Berry, Phil.** Singer and songwriter, an authority on the songs of Wexford, and organiser of the Wexford singers' festival. (PAB)

**Boydell, Barra.** Lecturer in music at the NUI, Maynooth, he researches musical instruments and history of music in Ireland. (BAB)

**Bradshaw, Harry.** Radio producer, researcher, record producer with RTÉ from 1968, his Viva Voce label markets re-mastered 78s. (HAB)

**Brennan-Corcoran, Helen.** Dance researcher and teacher, her MA research is on the sean-nós dance style. (HEB).

**Browne, Peter.** Uilleann piper and radio producer. (PEB)

**Buckley, Ann.** Writer and researcher on the history of music in Ireland, medieval studies, iconography and the anthropology of music. (ANB)

**Carroll, Barry.** Hammer dulcimer player, from Lisburn, Co. Antrim. (BAC)

**Clarke, Tom.** From Letterkenny, an uilleann piper, he administers the 'Jigtime' programme in Belfast. (TOC)

**Comiskey, Glen.** From Co. Armagh, he is a piper, and archivist at the ITMA. (GLC)

**Cotter, Geraldine.** Piano player and music teacher, from Ennis, Co. Clare, author of tutors on tin whistle and piano in Irish music. (GEC)

**Cranford, Paul.** Fiddler and publisher on Cape Breton Island, Nova Scotia, he publishes local music through Cranford Publications. (PAC)

**Cranitch, Matt.** Fiddler, teacher, and author of *The Irish Fiddle Book*, he is researching the Sliabh Luachra fiddle tradition. (MAC)

**Crowley, Jimmy.** Singer, songwriter, bouzouki player, he is researching Cork urban song. (JIC)

**Cullinane, John.** Dance researcher and archivist, he has published extensively on Irish step dancing. (JOC).

**Cummins, Verena.** Currently researching East Galway style at UL. (VEC)

**Cunningham, Eric.** Flute and whistle player, from Headford, Co. Galway, he is researching the bodhrán at UL. (ERC)

**Daly, Gregory.** A flute player influenced by Packie Duignan and Jim Donoghue, an authority on South Sligo players and music. (GRD)

**de Búrca, Angela.** Lecturer in Irish at UCD, her song research has included work on 'Caoineadh na dTrí Mhuire'. (AND)

**de Grae, Paul.** Author of the first guitar tutor in traditional music, he has recorded with Jackie Daly and Smoky Chimney. (PAD)

**Dillane, Aibhlín.** She has been engaged in research into the piano in Irish traditional music at UL. (AID)

**Doherty, Liz.** Fiddler, from Buncrana, she lectures in traditional music at UCC, and is editor of the revised O'Neill collection. (LID)

**Douglas, Sheila.** From Perth, Scotland, a singer, storyteller and song editor, she teaches at the RSAMD in Glasgow. (SHD)

**Dowling, Martin.** Fiddler, born in Chicago of Irish parents, he is the ACNI's traditional arts officer. (MAD)

**Dromey, Paul.** Columnist with the *Evening Echo* since 1987, he writes for *The Examiner* and *Irish Music*. (PAD)

**Duffy, Paddy.** From Castleblayney, Co. Monaghan, he is Associate Professor of Geography, at NUI Maynooth. (PDU)

**Foley, Catherine.** Dancer, musician and Irish step dance teacher, she is director of the ethnochoreology programme at UL. (CAF)

**Garvin, Wilbert.** Writer, uilleann piper and bagpiper, he is author of *The Irish Bagpipe*. (WIG)

**Gebruers, Maeve.** A harp player, she is an archivist with the ITMA. (MAG)

**Graham, Len.** Singer and song-collector, an authority on song of Ulster. (LED)

**Gunn, Douglas.** Recorder player, teacher, composer and choral conductor, leader of the Douglas Gunn Ensemble. (DOG)

**Hamilton, Colin (Hammy).** Flute-player and maker, traditional music researcher and writer. (HAH)

**Hammond, David.** Singer, raconteur, film producer, known widely for his BBC radio production, *As I Roved Out*. (DAH)

**Hannan, Robbie.** Uilleann piper, director of the music section of the Ulster Folk and Transport Museum in Co. Down. (ROH)

**Harte, Frank.** Singer, collector, broadcaster. Born in Dublin, he is an authority on the song tradition. (FRH)

**Hastings, Gary.** Flute player, born in Belfast, living in Westport, he is an authority on Lambeg drum and fife. (GAH)

**Henigan, Julie.** Singer and researcher, from Missouri, USA, specialist in traditional Irish song and southern American folk music. (JUH)

**Hessian, Carl.** Pianist and keyboard player, he works with Moving Cloud and many leading performers. (CAH)

**Heymann, Ann.** Cláirseach performer and recording artist, writer and researcher, she is author of *Secrets of the Gaelic Harp*. (ANH)

**Hitchner, Earle.** Writer and radio broadcaster, he covers Irish and other musics for *The Wall Street Journal* and *Irish Echo*. (EAH)

**Keily, Brendan.** A journalist and researcher. (BRK)

**Kinnaird, Alison.** Harper, teacher and writer, she has published extensively on the Scottish harp. (ALK)

**Kinney, Phyllis.** From the US, she studied at the Juilliard School of Music in NY, and has published in English and Welsh. (PHK)

**Kinsella, Mick.** A leading harmonica player. (MIK)

**Ó Liatháin, Dónal.** Singer and songwriter, he is an authority on the lore and music of West Cork. (DOL)

**Mac Con Iomaire Liam.** Singer, journalist, and broadcaster, from Casla, Connemara Gaeltacht. (LIM)

**Mac Aoidh, Caomhín.** Fiddler, writer, teacher and founder member of Cairdeas na bhFidléirí, he specialises in Donegal fiddling. (CAM)

**MacGabhann, Antóin.** Fiddler, music organiser, teacher, he specialises in Cavan music. (AMG)

**MacIsaac, Ellen.** Born Ottawa, Canada, she is researching newly composed songs in the Anglo-Irish singing tradition. (ELM)

**Madden, Angela.** From Toomebridge, Co. Antrim, she is an authority on lilting in Ireland. (AMA)

**Matthews, Ceri.** A piper, he lives and plays in Wales. (CEM)

**McBride, Jimmy.** Singer, collector. He formed the Inishowen Traditional Singers' Circle and directs its annual seminar. (JIM)

**McCann, Anthony.** Writer, singer, bodhrán player. His PhD research at UL is on copyright in traditional music. (ANM)

**McCarthy, Johnny.** Flute and fiddle player, music teacher, he plays with Four Star Trio, and is researching Sliabh Luachra music. (JMC)

**McCullagh, L. E.** Tin whistle player, writer, researcher, he was born in Indianapolis, and is an authority on Irish music in Chicago. (LAM)

**McGettrick, Paul.** Flute player and teacher. He was a key worker on the Fleischmann project and teaches music technology at DIT. (PAM)

**McNamara, Brian.** Uilleann piper, flute player and specialist in the music of Leitrim. (BRM)

**Meade, Don.** Harmonica player and fiddler, organiser of New York's Eagle Tavern gigs, he writes in *The Irish Voice* newspaper. (DOM)

**Meek, Bill.** Singer, journalist. For many years a columnist on traditional music. (BIM)

**Mercier, Mel.** Bodhrán and bones player, he lectures in Irish music and ethnomusicology at UCC. (MEM)

**Mitchell, Mary.** Accordionist and uilleann piper, she is an archivist and music tutor at

UCC and has researched repertoire and style. (MAM)

**Moloney, Colette.** Director of Maoin Cheoil an Chláir in Ennis, her research on the Bunting manuscripts is published by the ITMA. (COM)

**Moloney, Mick.** Singer, banjo and mandolin player. Born in Galway he lives in Philadelphia; his PhD is in Irish music in the US. (MIM)

**Moulden, John.** Singer, researcher, lecturer and writer. He publishes and distributes material relating to Ulster song. (JOM)

**Moylan, Terry.** Uilleann piper, set dancer, writer, and a founder of Brook's Academy. (TEM)

**Munnelly, Tom.** Singer, song collector. Born in Dublin, he is now based in Clare where he collects and researches for UCD. (TOM)

**Murphy, Pat.** Set dancer and teacher, from Tipperary, he is based in Dublin. (PAM)

**Murphy, Seán.** A researcher living in Dublin. (SEM)

**Ní Chathasaigh, Máire.** Harp player, singer, born in Bandon, Co. Cork, she is an authority on harp, and its leading exponent. (MAN)

**Ní Chonaráin, Siobhán.** A flute player, she is researching sources of Irish music, and is working on a collection of slow airs. (SIN)

**Ní Shúilleabháin, Eilís.** A singer, from Cúil Aodha, Co. Cork, she is researching songs and singers of Gaeltacht Mhúscraí. (EIN)

**Ó Bróithe, Éamonn.** Uilleann pipes, singer. An authority on songs of the Déise area, and those of Eoghan Rua Ó Súilleabháin. (EAO)

**Ó Dubhghaill, Aodán.** Fiddler, producer and sound engineer with RTÉ, author of a discography of Irish traditional music in 1986. (AOO)

**Ó hAllmhuráin, Gearóid.** Co. Clare concertina player, historian, lecturer, anthropologist and ethnomusicologist living in California. (GEO)

**O'Boyle, Colm.** From Armagh, he is currently Professor of Celtic at Aberdeen University. (COO)

**O'Brien-Moran, Jimmy.** Uilleann pipes, saxophone. From Tramore, Co. Waterford, he teaches traditional music at WIT. (JIO)

**Ó Conluain, Proinnsias.** Radio producer and scriptwriter, he produced many documentaries on traditional music figures. (PRO)

**O'Connor, Mick.** Uilleann piper and flute player, he was in the Castle Céilí Band and has produced many books for CCÉ. (MIO)

**O'Doherty, Eamonn.** Flute player, architect and sculptor. From Derry, he is joint author of *The Northern Fiddler*. (EOD)

**O'Keeffe, Máire.** Fiddle player, radio presenter. She is researching the accordion in Irish traditional music at UL. (MAO)

**Ó Laoire, Lillis.** Singer, collector and lecturer, he was raised in Donegal; his research is in Irish-language song. (LIO)

**Ó Muirithe, Diarmuid.** He has lectured in Irish at UCD, published on dialectology, and his major research is on macaronic song. (DIO)

**O'Regan, John.** Journalist specialising in Irish music, he contributes to many publications, including *Irish Music* magazine. (JOO)

**Ó Riada, Peadar.** Concertina player, singer, composer. He has been the director of Cóir Chúil Aodha since 1971. (PEO)

**Ó Snodaigh, Pádraig.** Publisher, writer and former president of Conradh na Gaeilge. (PAO)

**Olsen, Ian A.** Singer and lecturer, editor of the *Aberdeen University Review*, he is an authority on north east Scottish music and song. (IAO)

**Quinn, Bob.** Writer, film-maker, photographer and member of Aosdána. He is a member of the RTÉ Authority. (BOQ)

**Quinn, Seán.** Accordion player. A founder of the Antrim Glens Traditions Group, he has written extensively for *Treoir*. (SEQ)

**Rees, Stephen.** He is attached to the University of North Wales at Bangor. (STR)

**Robb, Martha.** She is a graduate of the NCAD and author of *Irish Dance Costumes*. (MAR)

**Robinson, Andrew.** Teacher and writer. Former director of Maoin Cheoil an Chláir. (ANR)

**Schiller, Rina.** Born in Berlin, her BA research at QUB was on gender and traditional music; her MA was on Lambeg and bodhrán. (RIS)

**Sherlock, Tom.** Production manager with Claddagh Records (1982–97), he was involved with the Tradition Club in the 1980s. (TOS)

**Shields, Hugh.** Singer, collector, researcher, his major works are *Narrative Singing in Ireland* and *Tunes of the Munster Pipers*. (HUS)

**Small, Jackie.** Uilleann piper and accordion player, broadcaster and archivist, he is editor of *CRÉ 4*. (JAS)

**Smith, Graeme.** Accordion player and ethnomusicologist, he writes on Irish music for academic publications in Australia. (GRS)

**Smith, Jimmy.** From Co. Clare, he specialises in the collection and research of sporting songs. (JIS)

**Smith, Thérèse.** Ethnomusicologist, lecturer at UCD. Her research and publications cover Irish traditional and African American musics. (THS)

**Sommers Smith, Sally.** A fiddler, from Michigan, she is a student of the history and growth of Irish music. (SAS)

**Sproule, Dáithí.** A singer, from Derry, he is one of traditional music's leading guitarists. (DAS)

**Trew, Joanne.** A fiddler from Montreal, of Irish parents, she researches the music of the predominantly Irish-settled Ottawa Valley. (JOT)

**Tubridy, Michael.** Flute player and set dancer, he formerly played with the Chieftains, and in Ceoltóirí Chualann. (MIT)

**Ua Súilleabháin, Seán.** Singer, lecturer. From Inniscarra, Co. Cork, he lectures in the Department of Modern Irish at UCC. (SEU)

**Uí Ógáin, Ríonach.** Archivist/collector with the Department of Irish Folklore, UCD. (RIO)

**Vallely, Eithne.** From Donegal, a fiddle player, she was a founder of Armagh Pipers' Club and joint author of its many instrument tutors. (EIV)

**Viitanen, K. Johanna.** Traditional musician and journalist, writing on Irish music for Finnish music and other magazines. (VIK)

**Wilkinson, Desi.** A flute and bagpipe player, he has researched flute styles, and is an authority on Breton music. (DEW)

**Yeats, Gráinne.** Harpist, singer, researcher. She has written much on wire-strung harp, and has made several recordings on it. (GRY)

(AID) Dillane, Aibhlín
(ALK) Kinnaird, Alison
(AMA) Madden, Angela
(AMG) Mac Gabhann, Antóin
(AND) De Burca, Angela
(ANH) Heymann, Ann
(ANM) McCann, Anthony
(ANR) Robinson, Andrew
(AOO) Ó Dubhghaill, Aodhan
(BAB) Boydell, Barra
(BAC) Carroll, Barry
(BIM) Meek, Bill
(BOQ) Quinn, Bob
(BRK) Kiely, Brendan
(BRM) McNamara, Brian
(CAF) Foley, Catherine
(CAH) Hessian, Carl
(CAM) MacAoidh, Caomhín
(CEM) Matthews, Ceri
(COM) Moloney, Colette
(COO) O'Boyle, Colm
(DAH) Hammond, David
(DAS) Sproule, Dáithí
(DEW) Wilkinson, Desi
(DIO) Ó Muirithe, Diarmuid
(DOG) Gunn, Douglas
(DOL) Ó Liatháin, Dónal
(EAH) Hitchner, Earle
(EAO) Ó Bróithe, Eamon
(EOD) O'Doherty, Eamon
(EDI) Editor - Vallely, Fintan
(EIN) Ní Shúilleabháin, Eilís
(EIV) Vallely, Eithne
(ELM) MacIsaac, Ellen
(ERC) Cunningham, Eric
(FEB) Bazin, Fenella
(FRH) Harte, Frank
(GAH) Hastings, Gary
(GEC) Cotter, Geraldine
(GEO) Ó hAllmhuráin, Gearóid
(GLC) Comiskey, Glen
(GRD) Daly, Gregory
(GRY) Yeats, Grainne
(HAB) Bradshaw, Harry

(HEB) Brennan Corcoran, Helen
(HAH) Hamilton, Colin
(HUS) Shields, Hugh
(IAO) Olsen, Ian, A.
(JAS) Small, Jackie
(JIC) Crowley, Jimmy
(JIM) McBride, Jimmy
(JIO) O'Brien-Moran, Jimmy
(JIS) Smith, Jimmy
(JMC) McCarthy, Johnny
(JOC) Cullinane, John
(JOM) Moulden, John
(JOO) O'Regan, John
(JOT) Trew, Johanne
(JUH) Henigan, Julie
(LAM) McCullagh, Laurence P.
(LEG) Graham, Len
(LID) Doherty, Liz
(LIM) Mac Con Iomaire, Liam
(LIO) Ó Laoire, Lillis
(MAB) Bennett, Margaret
(MAC) Cranitch, Matt
(MAD) Dowling, Martin
(MAG) Gebruers, Maeve
(MAM) Mary Mitchell
(MAN) Ní Chathasaigh, Máire
(MAO) O'Keeffe, Máire
(MAR) Robb, Martha
(MEM) Mercier, Mel
(MIK) Kinsella, Mick
(MIM) Moloney, Mick
(MIO) O'Connor, Mick

(MIT) Tubridy, Michael
(PAA) Ahern, Pat
(PAC) Cranford, Paul
(PDG) De Grae, Paul
(PAD) Dromey, Paul
(PMG) McGettrick, Paul
(PAM) Murphy, Pat
(PAO) Ó Snodaigh, Pádraig
(PDU) Duffy, Paddy
(PEB) Browne, Peter
(PEO) Ó Riada, Peadar
(PHB) Phil Berry
(PHK) Kinney, Phyllis
(PRO) Ó Conluain, Proinnsias
(RIS) Schiller, Rina
(RIU) Uí Ógáin, Ríonach
(ROH) Hannan, Robbie
(SAS) Sommers-Smith, Sally
(SEM) Murphy, Sean
(SEQ) Quinn, Sean
(SEU) Ua Súilleabháin, Seán
(SHD) Douglas, Sheila
(SIN) Ní Chonaráin, Sinéad
(STR) Rees, Stephen
(TEM) Moylan, Terry
(THS) Smith, Thérèse
(TOC) Clarke, Tom
(TOM) Munnelly, Tommy
(TOS) Sherlock, Tom
(VEC) Cummins, Verena
(VIK) Viitanen, K., Johanna
(WIG) Garvin, Wilbert

# Abbreviations

2RN – Irish national radio (1926–38)
ACE – An Comhairle Ealaíon, The Arts Council of Ireland
ACNI – Arts Council of Northern Ireland
AOH – Ancient Order of Hibernians
APC – Armagh Pipers' Club
C4 – Channel Four television (Britain)
C&W – Country and western music
CBC – Crosbhealach an Cheoil conference, 1996 (and proceedings, 1999)
CBÉ – Comhairle Bhéaloideas Éireann (Folklore of Ireland Council)
CCÉ – Comhaltas Ceoltóirí Éireann
CRÉ (1, 2, 3 and 4) – *Ceol Rince na hÉireann* (Breathnach)
CRC – Cairde Rince Céilí na hÉireann
CRG – An Coimisiún le Rincí Gaelach (Irish Dancing Commission)
DCU – Dublin City University
DII – *Dancing In Ireland* (Breathnach)
DIT – Dublin Institute of Technology
EEOT – European Ethnic Oral Traditions (research publication)
EFDSS – English Folk Dance and Song Society
FÁS – employment and training scheme
FMJ – *Folk Music Journal* (of the EFDSS)
FMSI – Folk Music Society of Ireland
GAA – Gaelic Athletic Association
IFC – Irish Folklore Commission
IFMS – Irish Folk Music Studies
IMM – *Irish Minstrels and Musicians* (O'Neill)
IMRO – Irish Music Rights Organisation
ITMA – Irish Traditional Music Archive
IWMC – Irish World Music Centre, University of Limerick
LOL – (Loyal) Orange Lodge
LSAD – Limerick School of Art and Design
NCAD – National College of Art and Design (Dublin)
NI – Northern Ireland
NLI – National Library of Ireland
NMAJ – *North Munster Archaeology Journal*
NUI – National University of Ireland
NUU – New University of Ulster (Coleraine, Co. Derry)
OBU – Outside Broadcast Unit of RÉ and RTÉ
PBS – Public Broadcasting Service (US)
PLC – Post Leaving Certificate (courses other than third-level)
PRO – Public Relations Officer
QUB – Queen's University, Belfast
RBÉ – Roinn Béaloideas Éireann (Dept. Irish Folklore, UCD)
RÉ – Raidió Éireann (Irish national radio, 1938–66)
RIA – Royal Irish Academy
RIAM – Royal Irish Academy of Music
RnaG – Raidió na Gaeltachta (Irish language radio station)
RSAMD – Royal Scottish Academy of Music and Drama, Glasgow
RTC – Regional Technical College, third-level college outside the university structure
RTÉ – Raidió Teilifís Éireann (Irish national radio and television from 1966)
SPD – St Patrick's Teacher Training College, Drumcondra, Dublin
TMSA – Traditional Music and Song Association of Scotland
TnaG – Teilifís na Gaeilge (Irish language TV station)
TTCT – Teastas i dTeagasc Ceolta Tíre (lit. 'certificate in teaching folk music')
TUI – Teachers' Union of Ireland
UCC – University College, Cork
UCD – University College, Dublin
UCG – University College, Galway
UL – University of Limerick
WIT – Waterford Institute of Technology

# Introduction

IRISH TRADITIONAL MUSIC is now a sophisticated *listening* music, and no longer a medium only for dancing. Within it are players of many degrees of competence, understanding and sensitivity. Its popular image accommodates everything from the *Riverdance* big-stage spectacular to street-side busking, and although played more in towns than in the country, its performance retains a comfortable rural ethos and is everywhere still an easy-entry social occasion. There is a staggering variety of traditional music activity in Ireland as we enter the twenty-first century. Throughout the island there are more than fifteen hundred music 'sessions' weekly, many in some way commercial, with half of them running throughout the year. There are at least one hundred and sixty different cultural, commercial and artistic organisations involved in the music, and some fifty major performance venues where the top players can be heard often. There are more than seven hundred music and dance classes weekly. Multinationals Sony and JVC have invested in promoting the music abroad, and there are close on a thousand specialised albums available, mostly from established labels. These range from 'straight', solo, old-style playing to modernist fusions with jazz, rock, classical and various folk musics. There are one hundred and forty instrument makers and repairers involved, over a hundred businesses supplying instruments, and more than fifty music shops selling albums and books. All this is considerable commercial interest in the indigenous music of an island of approximately five million people.

In the 1960s a player might be jeered at in the street for carrying a fiddle-case, joked about for playing uilleann pipes, or clichéd for persisting with the harp. At the end of that decade the country had fifty uilleann pipers and the harp was in limbo. One could either not afford a proper instrument or get one repaired. There were few major music events and only a handful of albums available to listen to or learn from. Now, at the turn of the new century, there are more than five hundred pipers in Ireland, another three hundred abroad, all highly-organised. There are two major harping organisations and a network of harp schools. Instruments are accessible to most aspirants, and there is a network of services for them. There are both large-scale commercial and part-time grapevine festival interests in Irish music all over Europe and the US, and embryonically in Japan. These can keep professional players in constant demand. In Ireland the year does not have enough weekends to accommodate the volume of commemorative, fleadh and festival music activity. There is an overwhelming choice of available recorded material, and it is difficult not to know of someone who is involved in the music.

In the midst of all this *doing* there is also a considerable literature. Supreme among it are Breathnach's *Folk Music and Dances of Ireland,* and Ó Cannain's *Traditional Music in Ireland*. There are many other studies, collections of written music, anecdotal publications, windows on other lives and eras, cameos of revered players, and analyses of the music dating back over two hundred years. Some small amount of this material is visible on music-shop shelves, but most is either inaccessible except to the specialist scholar, or out of print. What is the worth of O'Neill's magnificent compilations and biographies, Roche's illuminating introductions, Breathnach's polemicising and observation, Tom Munnelly's collecting,

Ríonach Uí Ógáin's analysis, Hugh Shields' sorting and deduction, if one does not know what has been done? What value are the Irish Traditional Music Archive, the Comhaltas Ceoltóirí Éireann collections and the university archives if one does not know what they contain, or that they exist? This book is an introduction to all of these. It adds to the information already available within music organisations, draws on many of the topics covered in much of the presently available literature, and adds its own skein of analysis to their store.

When the *Companion to Irish Traditional Music* proposal was first mooted in 1996, the very idea of an A–Z reference work seemed absurd. Common sense had up to then dictated that all publications be either chronological, or at least structured in discrete categories. But as the *Companion*'s potential-topics list developed in tandem with its conceptual form, it gradually became clear that such a format was ideally-suited to a subject that, treated otherwise, is now so vast as to be potentially unwieldy, or tedious to those already familiar with it. All publications in this field are burdened by the pressure to cover everything that needs to be known – most recently Fleischmann's mammoth collection magnificently strove to get all the pre-1855 'in-print' tunes into one volume. The *Companion* offers a different approach. It presents together selections from and summaries of the interpretations, observations, compilations and research of those who have been involved in traditional music's scholarship, analysis and comment during the process of its self-definition through the twentieth century.

Accordingly some one hundred and fifty commentators were considered and approached to be contributors. Many obvious researchers are not represented in this text, and some who are might be expected to have contributed more. But this kind of work is demanding and uncompromising towards ongoing research schedules and bread-and-butter issues. So perhaps it is a comment on the business of traditional music's academic and research scene that not everyone who was requested could oblige. Involving the present one hundred and eight people was an intense labour – commissioning articles, issuing reminders, studying draft copies, editing, approval, correction and repeated re-correction – these all absorb enormous energy, demand extreme patience on all sides, eat into time and generate endless communication costs. Any piece included has involved phone-calls, faxes, letters, disks or emails; often the shorter the entry the greater the difficulties. The topics list swelled from a projected seven hundred in 1996 to almost a thousand by publication, four hundred of these concentrating on individuals and involving 300,000 words (yet still the volume could easily be doubled). As topics and people are reduced to hard information, necessary editing to size and style may have compromised individual turns of phrase, liberal prose and superlative ratings. But the central thread of writers' articles has hopefully been kept in focus.

This is a book which ideally should have been done by a properly financed editorial team. But as things presently are, no such support could conceivably be available in this small country. Despite the high commercial and artistic profile of traditional music, the collective third-level education establishment does not yet recognise its intellectual content as fit for undergraduate degree status; nor yet the second-level system, which provides general music education in only twenty-five per cent of schools, and has almost no provision for teaching the traditional music option available within that. Postgraduate students who wish to explore the music further are restricted by the consequent inadequacy, priority policies and tight purse-strings of college libraries. Casualties at the bottom of this scale, the public, have few resources at all beyond the handful of well-worn texts that might be found on local library shelves, hidden among faith-healing, calligraphy and Celtic crosses.

In this climate the *Companion* emerges initially as the editorial fruit of one mind, but from a consciousness that has been conditioned by playing music in Ireland and abroad through much of the modern revival period, and by practical, journalistic and academic experience. The work in these pages has benefited in equal measure from both salve and caustic. It has been aided too by the precise summary and reference information demanded by teaching, this refined by the challenge of working at third-level with inadequate resources. Comment from and debate with writers and readers also vitally chiseled the volume to a crisp profile, and buffed it to a comfortable texture. Great generosity of spirit jostled at times with debilitating suspicion, but every system of thinking is objectively constructive, its own concerns a route to a common end.

Because the *Companion to Irish Traditional Music* has sought to avoid the detail of material covered adequately in excellent extant publications, not every important and relevant person or topic is included here. While in many instances this was simply not feasible within editorial restrictions, the coverage of major figures for appropriate meritous or commendatory reasons may have obstructed the objective value of the work. A full spectrum of players past and present would amount to a directory, or a bible-sized 'who's who?', neither of which is the intention. Space and the sheer work involved prohibit the inclusion of many influential, generous and thoroughly stylish players such as Denis McMahon, Paddy Cronin, Paddy Killoran, or Frank Jordan who are not dealt with by name. Nor are Denis Ryan, Catherine McEvoy, Patsy Hanley, Richard and Finbar Dwyer, Seamus Egan, Colm Murphy, Eileen Ivers, Ringo McDonough, Patsy Broderick, P.J. Crotty, Yvonne Griffin and Liz Kane, among the younger 'masters'. And indeed, many families which have been central to traditional music are not present, among them the Moynihans of Cork, McNamaras of Tulla, O'Briens of Portglenone, Burns of Newry, McMahons of Ennis, Smiths of Mayo, Dinkens of Monaghan, O'Briens and Crehans of Dublin, Droneys and Lewises of Clare, McSherrys of Belfast, the McAuliffes of Kerry and the Binghams of Comber. What is in these pages is but a considered sample of the realm of traditional music. Perhaps it can be expanded for future editions, and to that end biographical, critical review and other suggestions are encouraged and welcomed; in particular, comment and correction would be appreciated on dates, name and place spellings, all of which have been a minefield of near impossibility in dealing with so many writers and sources.

Absence from this text therefore does not indicate considered inferior status, nor does a lengthy article necessarily indicate superiority. In a book like this there may well be less to be said about Michael Coleman in the remoteness of the opening decades of the twentieth century than about a researcher of the output and calibre of Jackie Small in its closing score of years. Musicians too are very often people of carefully-metered words, their stories are warm and anecdotal, most comfortably presented in the secure expansiveness of journals and radio interviews. If treatments seem uneven, it should be borne in mind that the policy was to avoid unduly bothering any of the biographees for personal information: already existing sources, if adequate, were used wherever possible.

The *Companion to Irish Traditional Music* is also new to traditional music in that it departs from the format of previous analyses by covering cultures which, while peripheral to the Irish island, are related to and are historically important for a full understanding of Irish music. Thus Scotland, Cape Breton and Canada are explored not only for Irish overlap or ingredient, but also for the familiarity of their playing practice and repertoire; Wales is dealt with in some detail, Isle of Man is introduced, and influential English song is examined both indirectly and through the media of collections and organisations. Brittany is covered as a culture which has adopted much confidence from Irish music revival, and for its perception as a sister 'Celtic nation' which supports many travelling Irish musicians. Finland is an example of a country where Irish music has carved out a cultural niche and established an active playing and listening community. And since so much of Irish music activity hinges around its retention and recording in the US, that country is dealt with extensively.

Among the instruments detailed, most intensively covered is the harp. Indigenous, and the oldest music device we have, it has generated the greatest volume of scholarship. Song too is covered in depth, both sean-nós and that in the English language, this section departing from a strictly alphabetic arrangement to more coherently muster its variety. Dance is dealt with in its most popular manifestations, while folkloric and other aspects of the 'traditional arts' are merely referenced in proportion to their connection to the process of music-making. An appendix seemed the most useful home for what is loosely-termed 'chronology', a data-assembly which places books and events in a time-scale that reveals the historical, if not political patterning of traditional music revivals. The bibliography pays tribute to the great volume of academic, amateur and functional scholarship and discourse within the music, and a selected discography gives some idea of the scale of production of the music, and its enormous diversity of styles.

The *Companion* sets traditional music in a panorama of people, instruments, music and history. But in the end this is a book, and the music is best described in the playing.

Fintan Vallely, April 1999

# A

**accordion.** Bellows-operated, free-reed, diatonic instrument on which the melody notes are articulated by buttons or keys operated by the fingers of the right hand, bass notes by those on the left. Depressing one of these in tandem with closing and opening the bellows directs air through a particular tuned 'reed' or set of 'reeds'. Reeds produce sound as a result of vibration generated by the air pressure. The accordions used in Irish music are known as melodeon, button accordion and piano accordion.

*button accordion.* Each button is designed to activate one or more reeds, the note to be played may normally – but depending on the instrument and model – involve from two to four reeds. These are known as voices. In an instrument with two reeds per note, one of these is usually tuned slightly sharper than the other. Smaller accordions will have two reeds per note, larger ones like the typical 'two coupler' Paolo Soprani accordion will have four, most Paolo Sopranis made in the 1940s will have three. The more reeds in play the richer the tone, the fewer in play the lighter the tone and the less dominant the instrument. In an accordion with three reeds per note, one may be tuned exactly to pitch, one slightly above, and one below.

Alternatively, the 'three-stop' Saltarelle or Serrenellini instruments have two reeds tuned to the same octave (one slightly sharp), the third tuned to the octave below. Larger accordions also have 'couplers' (switches) that can increase volume by bringing in another set of reeds tuned the same way, but often an octave lower. In Irish music at the present time, some players adjust the reeds to suit their personal tastes, and in this way have altered, and improved, accordion style and appreciation. For instance, the small Hohner 'Black Dot' accordion with two reeds per note is very popular, but since the ideal now in Irish music is to have a clear but non-aggressive melody, one fashion is to tune each reed in a pair the same, as in concertina.

*melodeon.* Best known today as an early form of button accordion (diatonic accordion), the melodeon was made popular in the US by the German American John Kimmel, his contacts with Irish Americans helped popularise it in Ireland. The simple, basic instrument comes in various keys – e.g. in D and in G – and has ten buttons all in one row, these giving a fixed scale that denotes the key of the instrument. The melodeon was largely replaced by the chromatic button accordion after the 1930s, but is still treasured for dance playing where its choppy, push and pull action is highly rhythmic. Present-day players include Paul Brock, Bobby Gardiner, P.J. Hernon, Johnny Connolly, Tom Doherty, Breandán Begley. The single-row, diatonic, D-melodeon scale:

```
PUSH  F#  A   D   F#  A   D   F#  A   D   F#
PULL  A   C#  E   G   B   C#  E   G   B   C#
```

Two-row button accordion   (EDI)

*melodeon and accordion differences.* The colloquial term for all melodeons and accordions is simply 'melodeon', regardless of construction. But in any case, the button accordion and melodeon are basically the same instrument: both use button fingering, both are single-action (different note on push and pull). However, the term 'accordion' in Ireland usually means 'two-row' accordion. Melodeon and accordion are distinguished by style, nationality of construction and use of terminology. The melodeon is 'German' style, the accordion is 'Viennese' style. The melodeon normally has one, but in the past has had two or three rows of melody buttons, and it can come in different pitches. The accordion may alternatively have piano keys, and two or more rows of buttons; the more buttons, the greater the playing potential and range of possibilities. Stylistically the melodeon is 'open action' – its mechanism is often visible, sometimes decorated, and its left-hand bass notes will be attached externally on a box. The accordion is modestly 'closed in' and streamlined, a grille covers the levers, and its left-hand bass notes are built in, hidden from view. The melodeon generally has reed-engaging 'stops' on top, the accordion generally not. Melodeons as used in Irish music are usually style eschewing and rudimentary, utilitarian in construction and appearance – a 'poor-person's instrument'. Accordions traditionally have been as impressive as their power is commanding: highly decorative veneers and plastics, chrome grilles and name-badges, sometimes sequinned, boldly proclaiming either the manufacturer's name (in the manner of motor cars and designer clothing) or (in the US) that of the player.

*button accordion structure.* The typical accordion has two rows of buttons set in a flat keyboard. All have lowest notes at the top, twelve buttons on the outer row, eleven on the inner. There is a semitone interval between the button-rows (those for the continental and English markets are a fourth apart, or otherwise). The 'flat' keyboard facilitates the decoration favoured in traditional music – rolling – the 'stepped' keyboard found on continental accordions favours a different style of playing. The button-rows are described by the home key of each row – e.g. B/C, C#/D, etc. The standards in Ireland for playing most conveniently in concert pitch are B/C and C#/D, but there are different fashions depending on player, and sometimes area. Each of the two major styles of playing use the button rows differently. In B/C playing the player picks the note conveniently, smoothly playing 'across the rows'. In the C#/D style (also known as 'press and draw') the player will work on one row, thus demanding much in-and-out bellows work and so a 'choppy' style. Depending on the instrument used in this style the player can choose either the inner or outer row as the main playing row, hence the expressions 'inside out' (C#/D) and 'outside in' (D/D#).

Melodeon (EDI)

*Freeman's Journal* advertisement for accordions, 22 December 1855

*manufacturers.* Today the instruments played in traditional music are made mostly in Italy, Germany, Czechoslovakia and China (and, latterly, in Ireland and England, but using Italian reed-plates and other components). In this century it is the Italian and German models that have been of most significance in Irish music. The most widespread use of button accordions is in folk musics of Europe and the Americas. Hohner of Germany, after 1905, were the mass producers but there are now many specialised craft makers manufacturing instruments designed specially for the demands of faster, more intricate playing of Irish, Cajun, Italian, French and Newfoundland musics. Hohner make and supply their own reeds, French and Italian accordions use Italian reeds, and around the town of Castelfidardo, near Ancona, Italy, are concentrated perhaps fifty or more accordion and reed-plate makers. Paolo Soprani (oldest Italian maker, began in the 1850s, but now only a brand-name of the Menghini company), Mengascini, Baffetti (who make Saltarelle) and Castagnari are located in Recanati; Serrenellini is further south at Loreto. In the 1940s the grey, Paolo Soprani, two-row button-accordion became the standard instrument in Ireland. By the mid-1950s the red-coloured model (internally different) had taken over. With its button rows starting with B/C, C/C#, C#/D, D/D# and G/G#, it offered great flexibility and adventure to curious and skilled players. A three-row accordion – the Hohner 'Shand' Marino – was produced for Scottish dance band leader Jimmy Shand but made only a brief impact in Ireland. (EDI)

See bandoneon; Burke, Joe; concertina; Cooley, Joe; Daly, Jackie; Derrane, Joe; free reeds; harmonica; Kimmel, John; O'Brien, Paddy; O'Leary, Johnny.

*Ireland.* The 'ten-key' accordion or 'melodeon' appeared in Ireland in the second half of the nineteenth century. The adoption of the instrument into Irish traditional music coincided with both the decline of the pipes and with the spread of set dancing. By the turn of the century in Ireland the instrument with ten buttons had become known as a 'melodeon'. It was played in the 'push and draw' system which gave the player two notes on each button and created a staccato, bouncy phrasing because of the articulation achieved from the bellows-work. Often referred to as 'the poor man's pipes', the melodeon quickly became popular as an instrument played for dancers, this for several reasons: it was new and modern and easy to carry; its reeds would hold their tuning for longer than the pipes during inclement weather; it had a bright clear tone, and enough volume to cut through loud crowd noise in pre-amplification days.

The first evidence we have of the sound of the accordion is from the early cylinder and disc recordings made in America at the start of this century. The first person to be recorded playing Irish dance music on it was John J. Kimmel. One of the first Irish-born players to record in America was Peter J. Conlon whose prolific output of recordings between 1917 and 1930 shows exceptional performance. During the early decades of the 1900s, the instrument came into its own in the Irish emigrant dance halls of America where it was one of the dominant instruments in the early dance bands, its powerful volume and consistency guaranteeing it favour. At this time instruments which could withstand the pressures of playing seven nights a week in humid, hot, noisy dance halls were developed, with some single-row models having up to six sets of reeds for extra loudness. Baldoni-Bartoli and F. H. Walters were two of the most popular New York manufacturers of these.

By the late 1920s fully chromatic two-row accordions were common in Irish traditional music, and by the 1930s in Ireland two very distinct playing styles were emerging on instruments pitched in keys of C/C#, C#/D, D/D# and G/G#. The 'press and draw' style was still used, but with the addition of the second button row the accordion had changed from a diatonic to a chromatic instrument. The musician usually played on the inside row and moved to the outside for necessary semitones and descriptive notes such as C natural and F natural. In America the 'outside in' system was used – where the musician played on the outside row and moved to the inside row for the semitones. Boston accordion player, Joe Derrane, is one of the best-known exponents of this.

## FULL B—C KEYBOARD

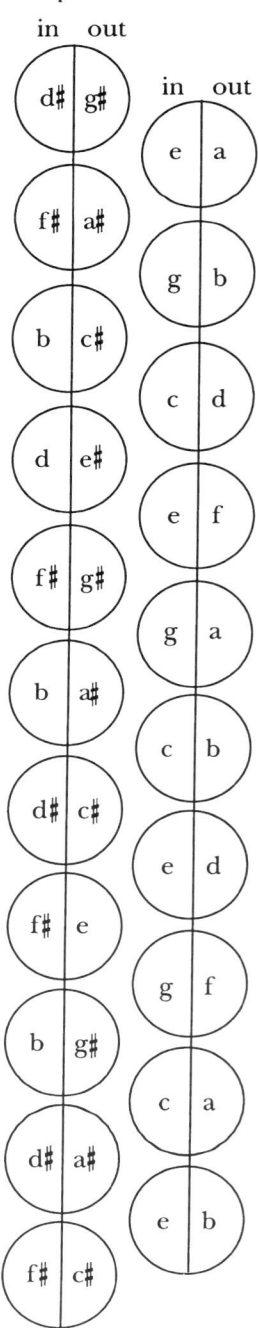

Button system on diatonic accordion     (Ossian)

In Ireland Joe Cooley played the 'press and draw' style on a D/D# accordion and is credited with advancing the popularity of the instrument through the 1950s and '60s.

*playing styles.* In recent decades the accordion pitched in B and C has been the most popular of the many instruments in this family. In use in Ireland since the late 1920s, popular among the B/C players were Michael Grogan (one of the first to be recorded by Regal Zonophone when they began recording in Ireland in the early 1930s) and Sonny Brogan (who played with Seán Ó Riada in Ceoltóirí Chualann). The name most associated with the B/C style however is Paddy O'Brien from Newtown near Nenagh, Co. Tipperary who developed a method which became the standard during the 1960s, one of its most renowned current exponents being Joe Burke. The B/C system requires less bellows-work than the old 'push and draw' system and allows for a much more legato style. But the 'push and draw' system is much closer to the older rhythmic melodeon style and is therefore preferred by set dancers. Among the noted 'push and draw' players are Jackie Daly, Máirtín O'Connor, Charlie Harris, Paul Brock, Tony MacMahon and Johnny O'Leary. Some musicians use both systems, playing B and C on a two-row accordion as well as also using the 'press and draw' system on a single-row melodeon. Among these are Bobby Gardiner and P. J. Hernon.

The 'sound' of the accordion in Irish music has undergone major changes since the mid-1970s. Prior to then, a two-row instrument produced a 'wet' sound – this the result of the reeds in each note-group being 'widely' tuned, so creating a vibrato tone. Jackie Daly has been credited with introducing a 'dry' sound, achieved by tuning the reeds in each note-group to the same pitch, making the sound close to that of a concertina. This was first heard on *Jackie Daly agus Séamus Creagh* in 1977, and numerous variations on it can be heard among today's younger players.

From the early 1980s the accordion has been a main feature in many of the most prominent groups playing traditional music, such as De Dannan, Patrick Street, Buttons and Bows, Altan, Arcady, Four Men and a Dog and the Sharon Shannon Band. Many different makes of accordion are in use: Hohner and Paolo Soprani are still used, but Saltarelle and Castagnari are becoming popular. Accordions are now also being manufactured in Ireland in recent years by 'Cáirdín' in Co. Tipperary, and 'Kincora' in Ennis, Co. Clare.

See Kimmell, John. (MAO)

Piano-key accordion (EDI)

*piano accordion*. Accordion with piano-key-operation, using double action (same note on push and draw). This has been used in Irish céilí bands in the past, but like modern-day, electronic 'keyboards' and their immediate predecessor the electronic accordion (Cordovox etc.), the piano-appearance is not favoured in present-day traditional music. Invented by Bouton of Paris in 1852 and greatly improved in the 1920s, there are both short and long keyboard piano accordions, the former less domineering. The piano accordion's note production is not, however, favoured in what is the well-defined current aesthetic in Irish music. The piano accordion is the standard in Scottish music, however, a legacy from fiddle-orchestras and 1940s–50s dance bands perhaps,

but like the five-row 'continental' instrument, and despite the existence of top-class players (e.g. Alan Kelly, Séamus Meehan, Karen Tweed), it remains of peripheral interest in the south of Ireland.

Northern counties have produced many piano- and button-accordion players, making the instrument somewhat emblematic there, the piano-key instrument more favoured in past years. This was due to the dominance of the instrument in céilí bands, and to the popularity of céilí dancing in Northern nationalist culture. Indeed in the 1950s and '60s Donegal brothers Richie and Barney Fitzgerald's band won a national poll run by Mitchelstown Creameries as the favourite band in Ireland. The Fred Hanna (Portadown), Malachy Doris (Cookstown) and Vincent Lowe (Newry) 'céilí' bands influenced many through BBC broadcasts and recordings. But all played mainly for ballroom dancing, and Irish music for them was a sideline. The same was partly true of five-row player Jackie Hearst (Newry), although he did for a time participate in a 'tunes' band, The International, with piano-accordionist Fintan Callan. Seán O'Neill's Aughnacloy, Co. Tyrone, Inis Fáil Céilí Band produced two LPs for Ember records in the 1960s and toured the USA frequently. They recorded in the 1980s and '90s (*40 Irish Accordion Favourites*, *40 Irish Pub Songs*, etc.). From Antrim there was Wilcil McDowell (All-Ireland champion) and Leslie Craig. Francie Murphy of Fivemiletown played with the prize-winning Pride of Erin Céilí Band; Tommy Maguire from Lisnaskea, Fermanagh, played both the two-row and five-row accordions.

Accordion is particularly strong in Fermanagh and its older exponents include Larry Hoy (Derrygonnelly) and John McGurran (Garrison), the latter long-time chairman of Belfast CCÉ. Tyrone is strong on accordion too – Billy Rushe of Drumquin, John O'Neill from Donaghmore (who led the Old Cross Céilí Band), Patsy Farrell of Ballygawley, and Seán McCusker of Dromore. Tommy John Quinn from Derrylaughin, Coalisland (accordion and melodeon) has been a well-known session player all over Ireland. Johnny Pickering from Markethill, Co. Armagh was also leader of a famous band which featured regularly on broadcasts from Raidió Éireann. In

Antrim there was Dan Doherty (Loughguile), while James McElheran (Cushendun) plays for set dancing, and Ronnie Bamber of Cullybackey is an instrument repairer as well as player. Today there are many younger players, notably Gerry Lappin of Armagh, John Hendry, Co. Derry and Damien McKee of Dunloy, Co. Antrim, Jim McGrath of Monea and Annette Owens Tempo. Accordion remains a significant element in traditional music in the northern part of Ireland. (SEQ)

**'ac Dhonncha, Seán.** (1919–96). Sean-nós singer. Third youngest of ten children from Carna, Connemara, close to the birthplace of life-long friend Joe Heaney. Encouraged by teacher Bríd Ní Fhlatharta in Aird National School to sing and learn old Irish songs and their background, he won a scholarship to a preparatory college for teachers, and qualified as a primary teacher in St Patrick's College, Drumcondra, Dublin in 1940. He taught in Cashel National School, Connemara from 1943 where he established a friendship with Séamus Ennis who was collecting songs and music locally. He taught in Co. Cavan from 1947 and won a county medal with Mullahoran football team in 1949. Twenty-five years followed as principal in Ahascragh National School near Ballinasloe, Co. Galway. One of the first traditional singers to record on the Gael-Linn label, he won a gold medal at the 1953 Oireachtas and received Gradam Shean-nós Cois Life in 1995. On his seventy-fifth birthday in 1994, Cló Iar-Chonnachta issued a special CD selection of his songs in Irish and in English, *Seán 'ac Dhonncha: An Spailpín Fánach*. His songs are also available on Gael-Linn, Columbia, Claddagh and Topic. (LIM)

**acetate disks.** See reproduction of music, acetate discs.

**acoustic.** The term used to describe non-electric/electronic instruments. It is also used to describe a performance which does not use microphone amplification. All traditional music instruments are 'acoustic', but in band situations and sophisticated solo performances, electronic keyboards and electric bass are often used. Such, and other electronic interventions, are also usually part of studio recordings. 'Session' playing is by definition without PA, and so is described as 'acoustic'. A venue may also be described as having a good or bad acoustic.

**aerophone.** Literally 'instrument the tone of which is produced by wind'. Aerophones are sub-divided according to how the sound is produced: 1. flutes, 2. trumpets and 3. reeds and reed-pipes.

*flutes*. The sound is made by directing a stream of wind against a sharp edge, the resultant turbulence producing an 'edge tone'; the pitch of the note is regulated by the position of finger-holes, as in a flute, or by the length of individual pipes, as in pan-pipes. The stream of air may be made directly at the lips (as in concert flute, or East Europe 'kaval', etc.), or it may be focused by a narrow channel in the mouthpiece of the instrument (as in tin whistle, recorder, etc.). Flutes may be blown from the mouth, or the nose, they may be long and slender (tin whistle), or globular (ocarina); they may be end-blown or side-blown.

*trumpets*. The sound is made by setting up a vibration with pursed lips (as in trumpet, or ancient-Irish horns, 'adharc', 'dord', etc.) Blown animal horns – used still in many African countries – had some currency in ancient Ireland. One of these, preserved for many years in a wall at Coolea, Co. Cork, and stolen from a car in Dublin in the 1970s, was attributed to Ó Súilleabháin Béara; it was of the kind described as 'barra bua' in the tales of the Fianna. Today some Irish-music players use Australian didgeridoo to produce a fixed-pitch drone with tongue, vibrato and mouth-cavity effects. Trumpet notes are achieved by a combination of 'overblowing' harmonics (adharc, hunting horn) and/or shortening and lengthening the air column in the instrument (with a 'slide' in trombone, with valves in trumpet).

*reeds and reed-pipes*. The sound is made by air vibrating a metal or wood 'reed'. Reeds may be 1. single idioglot (as in uilleann pipe drones), 2. double (as in uilleann pipe chanters and regulators), 3. free (as in accordions, concertinas, melodeons), or 4. single tongue (as in clarinet, saxophone). Among the ancient

Irish wind instruments listed by O'Curry are cuisle and pipai, these likely relating to reed instruments.

See medieval Ireland; *Musical Instruments of the Ancient Irish*; O'Curry, Eugene.

**air.** Often used to describe the melody of a tune, how the tune goes – as in 'What is the air of The Merry Blacksmith?' Also used as 'an air', abbreviation for 'slow air'.

See slow air.

**aisling.** Plural aislingí. The aisling, or 'vision poem', is an Irish poetic form with an ancient lineage which was utilised as the vehicle *par excellence* for the expression of political and social disaffection among the 'dispossessed poets' of the eighteenth century. Subsequently, it has become a popular folksong genre. Two distinct sub-groups of the aisling preceded the eighteenth-century form. 1. The early medieval 'love' or 'fairy' aisling, in which the narrator – while lying either asleep or newly wakened on his bed – is visited by a fairy woman, who enraptures him with her beauty. Similar too is the equally ancient prophecy aisling, in which the poet receives a prophetic vision (often of success in battle), which may or may not be delivered by a woman. 2. The allegorical aisling which did not emerge as a distinct genre until the eighteenth century – its origins remaining a matter of speculation. Whatever its genesis, this form depicts an encounter not unlike that of the love or prophecy aisling; however, the 'spéirbhean' ('woman from heaven') it presents is typically neither fairy nor mortal but an allegorical personification of Ireland, who tends to appear to the sleeping poet not as he lies on his bed, but most often, as Gerard Murphy notes, 'in outdoor surroundings, beneath trees, or on a hillside, or beside a river'. The poet interrogates her, asking if she is any one of a number of mythological beauties (Venus, Deirdre, or Helen, for example), but she reveals herself to be none other than crownless Ireland awaiting the return of the Stuart king, then prophesies success for the Jacobite cause (Gerard Murphy, 'Notes on Aisling Poetry', *Éigse* 1, 1939). Not all eighteenth-century aislingí follow this pattern precisely, some omitting the dream premise or the interrogation, and others the allegorical or political inferences. (Indeed, some scholars dispute whether the latter are even true aislingí.) But whether more or less to type (the pattern most closely associated with Eoghan Rua Ó Súilleabháin), the eighteenth-century aisling was indisputably a well-established and much-exploited genre. Its widespread popularity probably owed much to the poets' practice of setting their lyrics to well-known folk melodies of the period, facilitating the entry of aislingí into the popular song repertoire, whence they also influenced Anglo-Irish folksong. Examples of the genre include 'An Spealadóir' and 'Ceo Draíochta' (Eoghan Rua Ó Súilleabháin, 1748–84, its most famous exponent), 'Úirchill an Chreagáin' (Art Mac Cumhaigh, d. 1773), 'Go Moch Is Mé im Aonar' (Eoghan an Mhéirín), and 'Gile na Gile' (Aogán Ó Rathaille). (JUH)

While having many antecedents in Gaelic and French literature, the composing of political aislingí was firmly established by Aogán Ó Rathaille (1675–1728) as a literary fashion. After Eoghan Rua the genre goes into decline, although examples were composed concerning the United Irishmen, Bonaparte and Daniel O'Connell. Aislingí remain an important part of the Gaelic song repertoire of Munster. A distinctive tradition of aisling composition thrived in south-east Ulster and examples by Art Mac Cumhaigh in particular are still popular among Irish-speakers throughout Ulster. (EAO)

See song, Jacobite.

**All-Ireland.** The All-Ireland Fleadh Cheoil, Fleadh Cheoil na hÉireann. 'Going to the All-Ireland' indicates attending the event, 'Winning the All-Ireland' usually means achieving first place in the senior (over-eighteen) competition category, up to the 1980s the highest (visible) level of achievement, recognition or honour in the music.

See fleadh cheoil.

**Altan.** Inspired by a 1983 album duet of Frankie Kennedy and Mairéad Ní Mhaonaigh *(Ceol Aduaidh)*, by the late 1990s this group was the beacon among 'straight' traditional music bands. With flute (the late Frankie Kennedy),

Altan: Daithí Sproule, Ciarán Curran, Mairéad Ní Mhaonaigh, Dermot Byrne, Ciarán Tourish (Nutan)

fiddles (Mairéad Ní Mhaonaigh, Ciarán Tourish and originally Paul O'Shaughnessy), accordion (Dermot Byrne), cittern (Ciarán Curran) and guitar (Mark Kelly, Daithí Sproule) they did not utilise the rock ethos of other '80s groups in order to gain profile. Typically their material comprises structured arrangements of jigs, reels, Highlands, Germans and hornpipes, built around Ní Mhaonaigh's traditional song. Defying sceptics, without resort to synthesised sound, they have carved a niche for themselves in the awareness broken open by the Chieftains, particularly in the USA. A major achievement has also been their basing themselves largely in the once-unfashionable medium of Donegal music. They have recorded five albums for the Green Linnet label, *Blackwaterside* and *Runaway Sunday* for Virgin.

**America.** See USA.

**amhrán.** Literally 'song', used particularly in reference to Irish-language song.
See sean-nós.

**Anglo-Irish folksong.** Songs of Irish provenance composed in the English language.
See ballads; song.

**Antrim and Derry Fiddlers' Association.** The Counties Antrim and Derry Country Fiddlers' Association was inaugurated on 14 May 1953 with the objectives: 'To preserve the art of country fiddling in as pure a form as possible, free from commercialism, and to encourage juveniles to take up and carry on this art, as did their fathers before them. The Association, as a body to be absolutely non-political and non-sectarian. To foster public interest in folk music generally and country fiddling in particular. To protect country fiddlers from exploitation and give them, as an organisation, a very large measure of control of programmes which their committee decide to contribute in aid of charity. Active membership not to be confined to the counties Antrim and Derry, but open to all who are genuine country fiddlers and wish to enroll. To become a strong and real brotherhood in the real sense of the word in keeping alive one of the very few remaining arts by which the executants make their own entertainment and at the same time give great pleasure to their countless admirers.' There was a further rule: 'An active member on attaining the age of 70 (that is to say a fiddler who has been performing regularly up to that age) shall become an honorary member. Thus we wish to encourage the young and honour the old.' Most members were from Co. Antrim with some from Derry and a few from Down. Founder members included Alex Kerr (Newtown Crommelin) and Mickey McIlhatton (Glenravel). Drawing its membership from both religious traditions it gave performances in aid of charity in Catholic and Protestant church halls and in Hibernian and Orange halls. It is still in existence but due to the 'troubles' meets now in the Tullymore House Hotel in Broughshane, Co. Antrim. (JOM)

**Appalachian dulcimer.** Popularised by singer/broadcaster Jean Ritchie who learnt to play it from her grandfather, it is associated mostly with accompaniment of W. Virginia/Kentucky,

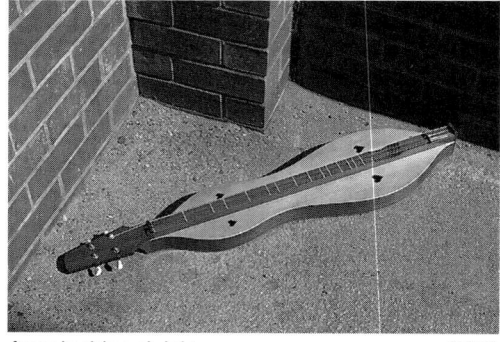

Appalachian dulcimer (EDI)

Appalachian mountain song. Most likely developed from European prototypes it is made and played still as a popular 'folk' instrument. With a double pear-shaped sound box topped by a string-carrying 'beam', it is played flat across the knees. It uses three strings (or paired sets of strings) – the one nearest the player is fretted and used for melody, the others are drones, all are sounded using either a plectrum or finger-picks. It is usually encountered as accompaniment to singing.

**appoggiatura.** Classical music term for an ornamenting note placed before an essential melodic note. Referred to in Irish music as a cut, tip, etc.

See ornament.

**archives.** One of the more urgent matters on the agenda of the late Breandán Breathnach was the establishment of a national traditional music archive. This was not achieved in his lifetime. However, 'The Irish Traditional Music Archive'/'Taisce Cheol Dúchais Éireann' at 63 Merrion Square, Dublin was established in 1987. Other publicly accessible archives are at An Roinn Bhéaloideas Éireann (Dept. of Irish Folklore, UCD), the Ulster Folk and Transport Museum, Co. Down, and Comhaltas Ceoltóirí Éireann's Cultúrlann at Belgrave Square, Monkstown, Co. Dublin. The National Sound Archive of the British Library has much Irish material in London, BBC Northern Ireland has recordings of traditional music and song, as has RTÉ in Dublin. In the US, in Boston, there is the Burns Library Irish Music Archive, in Indiana the University of Notre Dame has Francis O'Neill's library. Regionally, in Ireland the Coleman Heritage Centre has a South Sligo archive, Muckross House in Killarney has an archive, CCÉ intends to have material accessible in its various existing and planned regional centres, and bodies like Siamsa Tíre in Tralee have material appropriate to their function. Dance is catered for by the ITMA, but a specific private collection is held in the Cullinane Archive Collection of Irish Dance in Cork. The Irish World Music Centre of the University of Limerick is also building an archive – this related to dance also – and the Music Dept. at University College Cork has its own collection. Many researchers and music lovers also have substantial private collections of books and recorded material.

See under individual titles.

**Armagh Pipers' Club.** Founded in 1966 by a group of traditional music enthusiasts motivated by painter and piper Brian Vallely and his wife Eithne. Affiliated to no national body, it set itself up to revive and promote the playing of the uilleann pipes and traditional music in general. From the beginning it taught classes in Armagh city and Markethill, later in Coalisland, Co. Tyrone, then in Monaghan. The majority of its members play flutes, whistles, fiddles and pipes, some play concertinas and accordions. Their members have taken part in Fleadh, Slógadh, Scór and other competitions over the years, many achieving the highest of honours. Concert performances have been done all over Europe. Desiring traditional music to be community based, it currently has eighteen children's classes and four for adults. It has an instrument loan scheme and runs weekly sessions all year round and monthly children's sessions. From 1980–85 it hosted the week-long Bunting summer school at Benburb, Co. Tyrone. Its major festival is William Kennedy Festival of Piping, held annually in November; in 1998 it hosted an international folk dance festival. Since 1972 it has been publishing a series of tutor books – for tin whistle, fiddle, uilleann pipes, and children's singing.

**ASCAP (American Society of Composers, Authors and Publishers).** Established in 1914, ASCAP is the largest performing rights collection agency in the world in terms of constituency, licence fee collections, and performance royalty payments. It is the USA's equivalent of IMRO. (ANM)

See copyright.

*As I Roved Out.* A programme series broadcast weekly on BBC radio from 1951 to *c.* 1960. The collectors were chiefly Seán O'Boyle, Séamus Ennis and Peter Kennedy. Recordings are catalogued and available in the BBC Northern Ireland archives. These include songs and music from many groups and individuals including the McPeakes, Maggie and Sarah Chambers, Liam Andrews, the Dorans, Tom Turkington, Mickey Doherty, R. L. O'Mealy, Tom McGinley.

**assonance.** In song, vowel rhyming.

See Ó Súilleabháin, Eoghan Rua; song, metres.

*Atlantean.* See sean-nós.

Aughrim Slopes Céilí Band (Paddy Fahy and Paddy Kelly are in centre at back) (CCÉ)

**Aughrim Slopes Céilí Band.** Begun under the direction of musician Jack Fahy of Killaghbeg House, Kilconnell, Co. Galway (father of composer, fiddler Paddy Fahy). As a trio, fiddlers Paddy Kelly and Jack Mulcaire, with accordionist Joe Mills auditioned in 1927 for 2RN radio as the Aughrim Slopes Trio, with the signature tune 'Lament after the Battle of Aughrim' (in reference to the local battle site). This was hugely popular – broadcasts were noticed in the Co. Galway press and locally those with wireless sets placed them on windowsills to share the music. Records were made in 1928 and 1933, and the group also won first prize at the 1934 Thomond Feis of Limerick. Joined by garda Jim Drury on fiddle, they broadcast again, this leading to a contract to record three 78s, now with teacher Josie Halloran on piano. A request to him by Fr Cummins of Ballinasloe for them to provide music for a céilí to open a Scouts' club led to the formation of a band. An engagement followed at the Old Ground Hotel in Ennis, and thereafter they played all over Ireland from Kerry to Donegal, broadcasting weekly on Raidió Éireann, by 1940 having a full year's engagement diary. In 1945 they toured England, Scotland and Wales, playing to emigrant audiences of up to 2,000. They won an All-Ireland in 1953 and in 1956 recorded for HMV. Different personnel joined and left over the years, emigration broke the band up, but its hallmark sound remains a nostalgic, but vivid, landmark in the music. They recorded an album *Jigs and Reels: The Aughrim Slopes Céilí Band*.

**aulos.** Sometimes used as a poetic term for 'flute', but in its original form it is still found in the Mediterranean as a pair of reed instruments (sometimes attached) held in the mouth, played simultaneously, each fingered by separate hands. Depictions of its use in ancient Greece show players with puffed cheeks, suggesting the use of circular breathing. The instrument is similar to the Sardinian launeddas, and to the 'triple pipe' depicted in Ireland – most impressively on the tenth-century Cross of the Scriptures at Clonmacnoise, Co. Tipperary.

**aural education.** Music is an aural experience, it is not a visual one. Traditional music in most cultures was learned by 'ear', and the ability to learn and teach the music aurally is still greatly valued. Much school time was devoted a generation ago to the memorising of songs and poems, tables, maths formulae, long passages of Shakespeare etc., so that learning music in the same way was perfectly natural. Recent educational changes place less emphasis on such rote learning and memorising, and more on understanding – using calculators, computers, TV, etc. In the world of classical music, aural learning plays a very tiny part – Grade 8 Standard performance can be achieved without learning anything by ear, or having memorised a single piece of music. Nowadays a vast amount of traditional music can be found in books. The traditional musician recognises this as a valuable source of new tunes and knows how to add the embellishments and variations that can make the written page come alive as real traditional music. But more often than not, players learn from each other, from mentors and from field and commercial recordings. (EIV)

See music notation; reproduction of music; scale.

**Austin Stack Céilí Band.** Founded by Leo Redmond and featured frequently on early Raidió Éireann, named so after playing a function for the Austin Stack Camogie Club. Essentially a string band, the principal members were Edith Cross Moore (fiddle), Seán Fitzpatrick (fiddle), Pat Maguire (fiddle), Pat Greene (drums and wire brush), Tommy Breen (piccolo) and Leo Redmond (piano). By the early 1950s the band was featured on the Mitchelstown Creameries' Raidió Éireann 'sponsored programmes' and in the mid-decade was an integral part of the Annual Dress Céilí on St Patrick's Night at the UCD Aula Maxima, Newman House, Dublin.

**Australia.** Irish emigrants and their descendants in Australia are estimated as being 20 to 30 per cent of the Australian population. No other region has as much Irish emigrant ancestry. The first Irish to arrive were convicts, between 1793 and *c.* 1850, but the biggest portion of the emigrants are likely to have been on assisted passage schemes between 1850 and 1870, yet more arrived in the 1950s, 1960s, and again in the 1980s.

Irish and Irish-style music use and distribution in Australia follows the same patterns as in America or Britain, but the history of Australian-Irish immigration has an additional distinctive effect. Central to this is the Australian nationalist ideology which asserts a rural and working-class core to Australian identity, often attributing putative Australian characteristics of rebelliousness and independence to Irish convict and settler influence. Thus many Australians, even those with little direct contact with Ireland, have no difficulty in imagining an affective link to the place, its culture and its music.

*song*. Much of the corpus of nineteenth-century vernacular song identified as 'Australian folk song' (such as the mid-1800s' songs of Irish convict-poet Frank McNamara) displays Irish-style features. Most famous is the convict's lament 'Moreton Bay', based on the 'Youghal Harbour' melodic model, complete with internal assonances of Gaelic prosody. There is, however, almost no evidence of the survival of Irish language song, though many immigrants were Irish speakers. Narrative ballads of outlawry and bushranging extol the exploits of nineteenth-century social bandits, from convict 'bolters' like Bold Jack Donahue to later figures such as Ned Kelly. Being composed from the first decades of European occupation, many of these show Irish origins in their come-all-ye format, fourteen-syllable lines, gapped melodic modes and ABBA structure. Since such attributes are found variously in English and Scottish eighteenth- to nineteenth-century ballads, the exact extent of the Irish character is difficult to ascertain. In vernacular balladry, song-styles associated with the nineteenth-century stage-Irish theatrical figure were also important: the comic 'The Days they Taught them French at Killalloo' is a model for several Australian traditional songs, notably 'Drover's Dream'. Echoes of Irish song models are to be found also in the hillbilly-style songmaking of Australian country music bush balladists like Slim Dusty and Buddy Williams, popular after the 1940s.

*dance music*. The repertoire of Australian social dance music is less influenced by specifically Irish forms and playing styles, and among older rural players of fiddle, accordion or concertina, jigs and reels are likely to be limited to a few widely known tunes. However, a large body of Varsovienna, Mazurka and Schottische comparable to those played in Ireland have been collected, but are closely linked to nineteenth-century European popular dance styles. Music in Irish-Australian communities is usefully looked at in three periods.

1. Nineteenth-century to World War II. Irish Australians then felt excluded from institutions of power, and for Catholic Irish it was their church and its allied institutions which facilitated their ethnic cohesion. In this period St Patrick's day celebrations in major population centres of Australia aired two contrasting public musics: the genteel and sentimental ballads (Moore's melodies and parlour ballads) were reserved for 'national' evening concerts, whereas step dancing and its accompanying music took their place with athletic events in the 'national' day sports events and picnics. These represent both emblematic and recreational music expressions of Irishness. Gaelic League influence favoured Irish pipe bands too, hosting them in Melbourne, Perth and Sydney around

the turn of the century, they also favoured Irish music and dance. Adelaide Irish music enthusiast Patrick O'Leary, active over the period 1890 to 1920, corresponded with Francis O'Neill, and a number of prominent nineteenth-century Irish-Australian musicians are noted in O'Neill's *Irish Musicians and Minstrels*. Most significant of these was 'The Australian Piper' John Coughlan, an active public performer since his arrival in the colony of Victoria in 1884, and at least one of his pupils, a violin player, continued as a locally influential teacher up to the 1930s.

Throughout the first half of the twentieth century, as generations of Irish-born were replaced by Irish-Australians with no direct experience of Ireland, music and dance representations of Irishness came to mirror the ordered constructions utilised in Ireland. Step dancing changed from a male athletic pursuit to a cultural one practised primarily by children. But the changes did indicate that Irish dance music was gaining greater acceptance as a national cultural symbol – even if becoming less 'popular'.

2. World War II to 1980. The early-1950s' Irish immigrants were initially mostly male, rural construction workers. They socialised with Irish music and dance, often associated with GAA clubs who with Irish pipers' associations and the like organised public dances. Amongst these immigrants were instrumentalists, usually accordion players who usually played for local céilí bands and in CCÉ activities and had some status in their community. The first Australian branch of CCÉ was organised in Melbourne in 1970 by recently arrived Vincent Loughnane and Kerry sean-nós singer Eileen Begley. Its popularity generated branches in other capital cities over the next decade, but these were often unstable due to the difficulty of accommodating the roles of immigrant social club, national cultural organisation and music interest group. Other bodies, like the Adelaide-based Celtic Musicians' Association (1971), have enjoyed more constancy.

3. 1970 to 1999. Running parallel, and symbiotically, were the 1970s' Australian folk movement's folk-rock style 'bush bands' and the 'session' scene. Bush bands became a pathway for Irish music to move beyond immigrant subculture: the Wild Colonial Boys, the Bushwhackers and the Cobbers in the early 1970s developed a masculinist vernacular Australian balladry linked with predominantly Irish dance tunes, a performance format informed by both the Dubliners' style and céilí band expertise. The style moved from pub-rock to cross generational entertainment, and through the 1980s became integrated into Australian country music. 'Sessions' have become institutionalised in the folk music movement, these held in pubs favoured by Irish immigrants, who for the players provide an appreciative audience and appropriate validation; in Melbourne alone five public sessions were happening weekly at the end of the 1990s. Such local growth of Irish music has stimulated the development of specialist styles in the Australian folk movement, and some of the social patterns of session playing have been adopted in other genres.

A new wave of Irish immigrants after 1985 provided yet more contexts, audiences and performers in Irish music. Relatively well-educated young adults – eager consumers of pub entertainment – inspired the establishment of ballad and celtic rock bands playing in styles from Irish-popular to Pogues, all mixed with bush band. Following a 1996 Guinness 'Irish Pub' promotion campaign, the many Irish-theme bars that opened (Melbourne had ten in 1997) hosted everything from traditional sessions to 'covers' of Irish rock groups. These have influenced new non-Irish-Australian bands to adopt the celtic rock/new-age labels that reflect the influence of the Irish-based music models.

*dance*. Irish dance styles in Australia also shifted from popular recreation to national emblem. Nineteenth-century Irish step dancing in Australia was common both on the popular stage, and in vernacular recreation; young men had danced it competitively to hornpipe-style tunes at 'cellar flap' dances. After the turn of the twentieth century Irish dancing teachers applied the aesthetic of 'national' culture, and, as in Ireland, introduced regulations. Dance styles for instance using features common to Scottish dance that had been eliminated by the rule-books in Ireland lingered however up to the 1950s. Since then the Irish dance commission's influence has obscured older styles. Irish dance associations are now organised throughout Australia, teaching thousands of children of both Irish immigrants and of Irish-Australians and maintaining a cultural link to Ireland. They take part in the annual national competitions of the Australian Irish Dancing Association, and in international competitions.

Social dances sanctioned by the Gaelic League were being held in Australia by 1908, and were used at celebratory occasions up to World War II. Post-war immigrants generally indulged in mainstream popular dances, with a couple of céilí dances performed half-way through the evening. Irish sporting clubs still follow this format. A set-dance revival in Australia has followed that in Ireland; begun in the late 1980s, the dances are now learnt and performed in groups in Melbourne, Sydney and Adelaide. Major professional Irish musicians are promoted in Australia by Guinness tours, CCÉ, folk festivals and other groups. Short-term resident teachers such as Brendan Mulkere and Máire O'Keeffe have had, since the mid-'80s, a strong influence on playing standards. The current popularity of Irish-based music reflects both the world-wide fashion, and the legacy of personal and affective contact between Ireland and Australia. (GRS)

Ref. 'The Genesis of the Bush Band' in Margaret Kartomi and Stephen Blum (eds.), *Music-Cultures in Contact: Convergences and Collisions* (1994); 'Irish Music in Melbourne, 1850–1980', in Phillip Bull (ed.) *Papers from the Sixth Irish-Australian Conference* (1990).

**authenticity.** See style and authenticity, regional style.

# B

**bagpipe.** A reed instrument on which melody is played on a 'chanter', accompanied by one or more drones; air is provided through a blowing pipe, supplied either by the player's lungs or a bellows. All 'pipes' have a bag reservoir which also controls wind supply.

*history.* Some form of 'pipes' has been documented as far back as 1,000 BC in Syria. Certainly the Romans used them as an instrument of war. They were either introduced to these islands by them, or earlier by Celtic culture after 500 BC. All bagpipes produce their tones with what is called a 'reed', this being activated by air pressure. The simplest form of reed-pipes have no bag – the Breton 'bombarde', Italian 'ciaramella' and Sardinian 'launeddas'. The launeddas is blown by 'circular breathing', a technique in which the player uses the swollen cheeks as a kind of air reservoir to facilitate continuous playing while taking a fresh breath through the nose.

The first attempt at having an external air reservoir was the 'bladder pipe' in thirteenth-century Europe; the pipe was blown via a bladder filled with air from the mouth, the elastic contraction-tension of the swollen bag giving the player some respite to take a breath. The idea of a larger bag followed not long after – a stitched-up sheep- or goat-skin held under the arm, and with pressure controlled by the elbow – it gave the player a reserve supply of air and a chance to take a rest from blowing. By the Middle Ages the bagpipe was popular all over Europe. Associated with the shepherd, bagpipes played by country people at weddings are painted by Peter Breughel; David Teniers has people dancing to a bagpipe; Hans Holbein the Younger has dancing to both bladder pipe and bagpipe. In the 1549 *Complaynt of Scotland* the bladder-pipe and bagpipe are described too. The bagpipe became an instrument of the English court from the fourteenth to the sixteenth centuries (Henry VIII had five sets) and was the main provider of music for festivals and weddings. In fifteenth-century Scotland, James I was a bagpipe player.

The idea of using bellows in place of the lungs as an air-supply is as old as piping itself – the first organ was constructed in 246 BC in ancient Greece and by 228 AD bellows were being used in organs in Hungary; in 826 AD the first Western European organ was built in Aachen. In first-century Rome, Nero favoured the organ, but was also known for his ability on some form of 'bag and pipe'. There is no actual literary reference to 'bagpipes' until the tenth century, and from then until the fourteenth century they were the loud, outdoor, celebratory or marshalling instrument. The bass drone was already being used in France in 1280, but hitching a bellows to pipes was only first recorded in drawings from Ferrara in 1521 (Marcuse, 1975, *Survey of Musical Instruments*). The bellows was established in France by 1577, where the 'musette' was to become a popular instrument of court in the 1600s and 1700s; bellows were well established on Irish pipes by 1770.

Bladder pipes are still to be found in Poland where they can have one or two bladders held against the chest. In Albania, Siberia, Turkey, Brittany and Sicily they are often used too, but as a toy. Most nationalities in Europe and the Islamic world have bagpipes: Poland has its 'koziol' (= goat), Arabic Africa has its 'jirbah', Galicia has its 'gaita', Bulgaria has the 'gaida', Brittany has 'biniou', southern France has 'chabreta', Belarus has 'duduk'. Asia and Central Europe have many versions.

*kinds of bagpipe.* The first record of some sort of 'pipe' in Ireland is at the eleventh-century Aonach Carman. The next is with soldiers at Crecy in 1346, then in a fifteenth-century wood carving from Woodstock Castle, Co. Kilkenny. The father of the astronomer Galileo praised the versatility of the Irish bagpipes' emotional appeal in 1581; there were pipes on both sides at the battles of Boyne and Aughrim in the seventeenth century, and at Fontenoy in

BAGPIPE, BRIAN BORÚ BAGPIPES

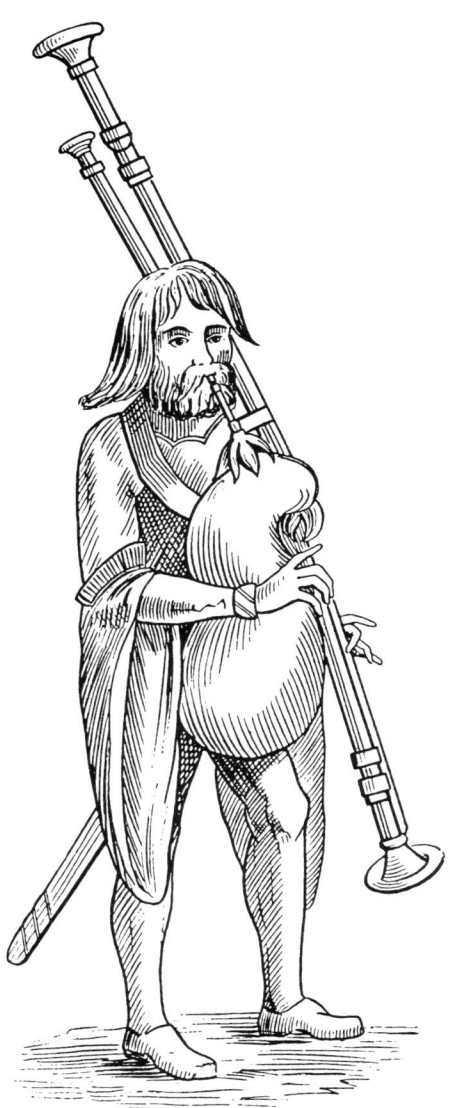

Irish war piper (from Derricke's *Image of Irelande*, 1581)

1745. In Ireland, prohibitory statutes in the eighteenth century may have pushed the old mouth-blown bagpipe into decline, but if they did, then that contributed to the development in the same period of the uilleann pipes. A revival of the old Irish mouth-blown bagpipes in the great surge of national symbolism at the turn of the twentieth century produced the 'Brian Ború' pipes. A keyed chanter ultimately developed out of that, but still, the uilleann pipes remain the only indigenous pipes that have been played with any degree of continuity in Ireland. There are several kinds of English pipes: Lincolnshire, Leicestershire, Cornwall, Northumbrian, etc., but the only one of those that has remained in playing circulation is the bellows-blown Northumbrian, which has a solidly established tradition, repertoire and fund of expertise. Billy Pigg, Pauline Cato and Kathryn Tickell have been among the best-known exponents through the twentieth century. Scotland has five types of bagpipe.

A Scottish version of the uilleann pipes – a concert-pitch, bellows-blown pipes – also existed in the last century; it survives only in the museum and by reference in a tutor book. (EDI)

*Brian Ború bagpipes*. The name applied to an Irish, mouth-blown bagpipe that is basically similar to the Highland/Scottish bagpipe except that the chanter is fitted with keys which extend the range of the chanter by three notes – two above and one below – giving a range of twelve notes instead of nine. The chanter notes range from bottom to top thus: E F# G# A B C# D E F# G# A B. The music is, however, written in the key of A, as with the highland bagpipe. Of these, the notes G# A B C# D E F# G# represent the holes. The two notes below which use keys are E and F#, the two above using keys are A and B. This extra range of the chanter enables many more popular and dance tunes to be played in stricter tune than is possible with the highland pipes. To achieve this scope, in place of the usual bottom note-hole a key is operated with the little finger of the right hand to give F#; this, when moved slightly further down, can operate a second key which gives E. Since however the normal bottom note (G on the highland chanter) cannot be played directly with the little finger, the ornamentation which is so characteristic of the highland pipe chanter cannot be achieved. One of the 'top' keys is operated with the index finger of the left hand while the back hole is open, the other top key is operated by the thumb of the left hand – the keys are mounted on 'pillars' as on the flute. The pipe has three drones like the highland pipes, but with the usual (middle) tenor drone replaced by a baritone – an idea probably drawn from the uilleann pipes. The instrument's tone is slightly more mellow than that of the highland pipes. The idea of extending the range of the chanter came from a William O'Duane from Dungannon, Co. Tyrone, his first (unsuccessful) effort known as the 'Dungannon' bagpipe. It was developed by the London flutemaker, Henry Starck, and became known as the 'Brian Ború bagpipe'. The pipes were formerly used by the London Irish Rifles Band, and the Royal Irish Fusiliers; the Royal Enniskillen Fusiliers Band also played them for many years, as did the Field Marshall Montgomery Pipe Band in Belfast up to the mid-1950s. Perfected around 1910, enthusiasm for such a pipe was generated in part by desire for an 'Irish', mouth-blown bagpipe. Such had been referenced graphically in Derricke's 1581 travelogue 'Image of Irelande', but while the notion was complementary to both the late Victorian and Irish senses of 'national' symbolism, enhancing the potential of bagpipes undoubtedly was the compelling reason for the innovation. (WIG)

*sixteenth and seventeenth centuries.* Researcher Seán Donnelly's work has pointed to a chronology of bagpipe activity in Ireland beginning only in the mid 1500s. Much of this information relates to what are known as 'pardons' to pipers from the English monarchy. In 1572 Sir Henry Sidney complained of O'Mores and O'Connors raiding Kildare and the Pale accompanied by bagpipes; in 1589 Piers Butler names two pipers supposedly killed by himself. Irish language literature from the sixteenth century refers to cuisleanna/cuisleannaigh, the one reference to 'píopa' is ambiguous. The English play *Captain Thomas Stukely* (referring to 1566) mentions a bagpiper.

In the seventeenth century Fynes Moryson describes an attack by Hugh O'Neill's forces on a military camp near Armagh in 1601 as involving bagpipes and drums, the killing of a piper in the same year indicating that they were considered important to military morale, this verified again during the 'Wars of the Confederation' (1641–52). (Donnelly, *Ceol*, V, 11, 1982).

*highland bagpipe.* (Scottish). Invented probably simultaneously in places as diverse as India, China, Italy, Greece and even Scotland and Ireland. Scotland's earliest depiction was at Melrose Abbey, possibly dating to 1136, another is at Roslyn Chapel (1440). Originally an instrument connected with the clans system, for the last 150 years pipers have been more popularly associated with regimental bands, with 'pibroch' music giving it artistic dimension. The instrument has a blow pipe, a skin bag as air reservoir, a chanter for melody, and three drones. Usually associated with the outdoors, it is played standing or sitting, the drones up over the player's shoulder. Originally with one drone, a second is supposed to have been added around 1500, and the bass drone possibly around 1800. Originally the chanter was pitched to A, but in the present day it is sharp of Bb, a gradual rise in pitch dictated by fashion in brightness and volume. It has a lower G, and has nine notes in an individual scale – G A B C# D E F# G# A' – in which the C is not quite C#, the D is slightly sharp, high G# is slightly flat, this leading to difficulties in playing with other instruments. Designed to play solo or in unison, the bagpipe is intended to harmonise only with its own drones. It has two tenor drones tuned to the A' of the chanter, and a bass drone tuned to A in the octave below. (EDI)

*bagpipes in Irish art.* Bagpipes, as distinct from uilleann pipes, are rare in Irish painting. This reflects both the minor role played by the war pipes in Irish music and the limited occasions when Irish artists painted scenes of music-making in other cultures in which bagpipes might have occurred. Despite their occurrence in European contexts from the thirteenth century, bagpipes are only first depicted in an Irish scene in the sixteenth century. A set of warpipes is shown in Derricke's 'Image of Irelande' (1581); although the accuracy of the pipes themselves cannot be relied on, their use for marching into battle is well documented. The modern use of the Scottish bagpipes as a marching instrument is reflected in 'A piper of the Irish Fusiliers' (crayon on paper) by the Belfast artist William Conor (1881–1968, Ulster Museum). (BAB)

*Cornish pipes.* Extinct for some 200 years, reconstructed in the 1980s from images in literature, in stone and in paintings. Like the

Allan MacDonald of Glenuig with Highland pipes (BRV)

Italian 'zampogna' (bagpipe) these are mouth blown, have one drone, and use two chanters with flared, bell ends. Research into the instrument and possible repertoire continues.

*Scottish bagpipes.* Bagpipes in Scotland have been made in different varieties, these roughly divided into Highland and Lowland:

1. Highland pipes, which can be subdivided into three types:
(a) the great highland pipe (as described above), with a loud, conical-bore chanter. Originally a folk instrument, this was adopted by the military in the late eighteenth century with the formation of the Scots regiments in the British army, and has been associated with them and with competitions ever since.
(b) the highland 'small pipe' or 'chamber pipe', either mouth or bellows blown, using a more mellow, parallel-bore chanter. It became increasingly popular after 1746 in response to the Act of Proscription's outlawing of pipes – it could be played quietly indoors for recreational purposes. A major revival of this instrument, centred around pipemaker Hamish Moore, has been in vogue since the early 1980s.
(c) the 'reel' pipe, used for dance music. With a conical chanter in the key of A, this is louder, and may be either mouth or bellows blown.

Music for the highland bagpipe is divided into 1. Ceol Mór (or Piobaireachd), a sophisticated art-form music, and 2. Ceol Beag – the dance music of reel, jig, strathspey, etc., the music too played by the pipe bands. Piobaireachd structure could be described as a suite with theme and variation, it has numerous parts; writer Francis Collinson (1966) summarises them as 1. the Urlár (ground, a slow melody, decorated); 2. the Siúbhal (literally 'walk', with doubling or trebling, a speeding up of the Urlár melody); 3. the Taorluath (a falling-note figure, related to practice in older harp music), and 4. the Crunluath (a 'crowning', completing movement).

The highland pipes and their highly standardised, printed-music repertoire have now become the standard marching-band instrument in Ireland, and all over the world, even in for instance, India, which has its own form of bagpipe, or Brittany, whose indigenous bagpipe is the *biniou*. In Scotland however, the bagpipe is currently undergoing a cultural renaissance, as artistically aware, able players (Allan MacDonald, Fred Morrison, Gordon Duncan, etc.) attempt to break out of the disciplinarian, literate code that has been imposed over centuries on the instrument's practice and image by army bandmasters. All three varieties of Scottish pipes can be heard on Hamish Moore's *Dannsa'air an Drochaid*.

2. 'Lowland' pipes, mouth and (mostly) bellows blown, with a different repertoire to that of the highland instrument. These are subdivided into:
(a) 'border' pipes, with three drones. Quieter, they are used for dance music also, and may have a bellows. They have a conical chanter. Players on these were once employed by border towns to sound morning call and evening curfew.

(b) 'small' pipes, like Northumbrian pipes, and with the same fingering, chanter in the key of F or G, and similarly are played with a closed fingering system. Developed in the eighteenth century, but almost extinct by the turn of the twentieth, the 'small' pipes were revived and played by Hamish Moore. With a very mellow tone, their scale runs F G A B C D E F# G', the drones are pitched FCF. The pipes' repertoire draws on dance music and paced airs.

Kathryn Tickell playing Northumbrian pipes (BRV)

*Northumbrian pipes.* Associated with Northumbria in the north-east of England, particularly with the Tyneside area. Bellows blown, they are similar to the Scottish 'small' pipes but differ in having a closed-end chanter. This delicately toned instrument has four drones and a chanter with double reed. Staccato fingering is the typical style – a 'pipping' sound – and the chanter has seven finger holes, and also up to seven keys. The drones have individual, sliding on-off controls; three of them are used at a time, depending on the key of the melody. The instrument dates as far back as the seventeenth century and may be a copy of the French 'musette'. The pipes can be heard on Kathryn Tickell's *Borderlands*, and Pauline Cato's *By Land and Sea*. (EDI)

*Welsh bagpipes.* ('pibgod' or 'pibau cwd'). It is certain that bagpipes were known and played in Wales from the Middle Ages onwards. Whether there was such a thing as an identifiably Welsh bagpipe is less easy to establish. There is some iconographical evidence from before the seventeenth century: fifteenth-century carvings in Llaneilian church in Anglesea depict two mouth-blown instruments, one with a double chanter and the other with a single chanter, each with a single drone; a sixteenth-century manuscript in the British Library (Add. MS 15036) shows two mouth-blown sets, one with double chanter and no drone, the other with single chanter and single drone. Moreover, a six-hole double chanter is preserved at the Museum of Welsh Life in St Fagan's, near Cardiff; it is dated 1701, and is said to have come from North Wales. Its Welsh origin has been disputed, but the horn bells at the lower end clearly resemble extant examples of the Welsh pibgorn.

Nevertheless, poems and antiquarian accounts from the eighteenth and nineteenth centuries mention the use of bagpipes, especially in the context of weddings. Most refer to events in South Wales, particularly in Carmarthen, the Vale of Neath, and Breconshire. But the music historian Robert Griffith recalled that as a child he heard a Welshman playing bagpipes 'on at least two occasions' at the fair in Llanrwst in North Wales during the 1850s. There are no descriptions of any of the instruments. (STR)

Both single and double-chanter Welsh pipes have been revived in recent years, made by Julian Goodacre of Edinburgh and Jonathan Shorland of Cardiff. Current exponents of Welsh piping include Peter Stacey (of the group Aberjaber), Jonathan Shorland and Ceri Rhys Matthews (Saith Rhyfeddod, Fernhill).

See crwth; pibgorn; Wales.

**ballad.** The term 'ballad' derived originally from the South of France and described a song performed by solo and chorus to dancing, but only in occasional cases narrative. The English term applies today to a narrative lyric song which flourished through Europe from the late Middle Ages under different names and persists unevenly in the modern European tradition. This old international genre is verbally characterised by the functional propriety of its oral style. In Ireland the ballad (*bailéad*) enters with Anglo-Scottish settlement in the seventeenth century and is normally in English, though rare examples have gone into Irish and some have influenced songs in Irish or been influenced by them. Such influences are difficult to establish; one may say, for example, that the ballad 'Barbara Allen' and the song in Irish 'Snaidhm an Ghrá' (the love knot), treat the same theme of love and death though their relationship remains uncertain.

None of these old ballads was composed in Ireland, though many, like the 'Lass of Aughrim', 'Lord Gregory', have a long history in the island. Perhaps their rarity in Irish is partly explained by the already existing native genre of the 'lay' (*laoi*), substantially also a narrative one. As poetry, the old ballads were edited by F. J. Child. As song, they are made accessible by Bertrand H. Bronson, who has shown how well and how widely versions of their tunes have been transmitted through the English-speaking world – but not usually, it seems, across language frontiers. For their part the stories told in these songs were quite adaptable to new languages. The English ballad of 'Lady Isabel and the Elf Knight' and its continental counterparts have given rise to much comparative research.

The old ballad is generally believed to have been a product of the common people, despite its fondness for regal and aristocratic characters, and to have been verbally composed without the aid of literacy. Its detached perspective in the third person is enlivened by direct discourse, usually between two persons; gaps interrupt its sequential storytelling leaving only the essentials of the story. With such effects its poetry is decidedly literary, and the story is fiction, not – like the poetry of lyric song in Irish – decidedly historical or true-to-life. Yet the singing practices of the two languages have produced hybrids of the most interesting diversity.

The term 'ballad' also describes later kinds of narrative song more diverse than the old genre and variously labelled as the 'vulgar', the 'street', the 'broadside', the 'new' etc. ballad, thus alluding respectively to its public, its place of performance, printed text, and temporal relation to the *old* ballad. These songs profited by the invention of printing and the spread of literacy. They became commercial and by the eighteenth century were copiously printed in Dublin – the first surviving sheet in 1626 – and in Cork. The nineteenth century was their heyday, the twentieth a time of varied printed formats and a profusion of media, audio and visual. The songs themselves found varied formats and storytelling in them merged with description, lyric effects etc. Still they were called 'ballads', which really brings back the past since 'ballads' in popular (not learned) usage were simply 'good old familiar songs to sing', as they still are today.

Alongside these commercially viable songs (which of course could also be sustained in domestic and similar practice without financial motive), there survive from the early nineteenth century onwards many local songs of familiar character. These allude to the environment or to known individuals, using well-known Irish airs, sometimes in pastiche form, and often by a known author, but not achieving fame in print and probably the better for it. Whereas the old ballads tended to stick to airs of some antiquity that are also used outside Ireland, the more recent traditional songs, whether local and domestic or urban and commercial, adopted many native Irish airs. The local songs are the most thoroughly Irish but to leave an impression of the older ballads (from a description of their features) as thoroughly foreign would be regrettable. Borrowed songs of other nations cannot fail to acquire features of the borrowers, and the old ballads in Ireland have acquired a strongly Irish idiom. (HUS)

See ballad sheets; broadsheets.

**ballad groups.** The Irish ballad group boom began in the early 1960s in Dublin. From an historical perspective one can see it as an offshoot of the American urban folk revival which had preceded it by several years. There were also strong connections with the English Folk Revival which was spearheaded by Ewan McColl and A. L. Lloyd. The whole idea of arranging Irish folk songs for group performance began in New York's Greenwich Village at the heart of the folk revival when Liam, Tom and Paddy Clancy came together with Tommy Makem and created a new approach to the music with a distinctive hybrid sound of lusty vocals accompanied by guitar and five-string banjo.

In Ireland the first major 'ballad group' was the Dubliners. Whereas the Clancy Brothers and Tommy Makem were clean cut, if a tad on the boisterous side, the Dubliners were a bearded, hard-drinking, hard-living crew, who quickly became adopted by the Dublin working class and then went on to became favourites among college and Bohemian audiences in Ireland and England, Ronnie Drew and Luke Kelly becoming household names. Kieran Burke played the tin whistle, John Sheehan played the fiddle and Barney McKenna popularised Irish music on the tenor banjo. The Clancys and Tommy Makem and the Dubliners set the prototype for the ballad group craze.

The boom developed in the context of the improving national economy in the early 1960s and intensified as the country prepared for membership of the European Economic Community. Irish society began to experience rapid social, political and economic changes. Young men and women who in previous generations would have emigrated or worked for subsistence on small farms now became wage earners. Lounge bars developed in response, and with the new music of the Clancy Brothers and Dubliners sweeping the country there was employment for ballad groups.

New groups were formed almost weekly. Some of these were Clancy Brothers and Dubliner clones belting out the hits of the day to a boozy backdrop of raucously participating punters. Others developed their own repertoires and styles. There were solo performers such as Danny Doyle, Paddy Reilly and Bob Lynch. There were duos like Ann Byrne and Jesse Owens, the Corcoran Brothers, the Byrne Brothers (the Spiceland Folk), Terry Woods and Gay Corcoran, Finbar and Eddie Furey and trios like the Ludlows, the Spailpín Folk, the Emmet Folk, the Grehan Sisters, the McKenna Folk and the Johnstons. Some of the groups had four or more members: the Wolfe Tones, the Pavees, We Four, the Parnell Folk and of course the Chieftains who played every Wednesday night in the Chariot Inn in Ranelagh (it would be some years before they were to go on to become international luminaries and the standard bearers for Irish traditional music around the world). They too cut their teeth in the ballad boom.

The travelling musician Pecker Dunne was a colourful addition to the scene and his 'Sullivan's John' became a staple song within it for years. Margaret Barry trod a similar course in London playing in the pubs with Sligo fiddler Michael Gorman. Men mostly dominated the ballad scene but there were a few women performers too including Ann Byrne, Maeve Mulvaney, Gay Corcoran and the Grehan and Johnston sisters.

Many of the groups were named after patriots: Wolfe Tone, Robert Emmet, Charles Stuart Parnell, James Connolly. The Emmet Folk and the Parnell Folk played in noisy pubs like the Castle Inn and Maher's of Moore Street in Dublin. People talked away with the poorly amplified sound providing a comforting backdrop to a babble of animated conversation which intensified as it got closer to closing time. But there were always attentive audiences in Dublin's folk clubs of that time – the Old Triangle in Leeson Street, the Universal in Parnell Square and later in the 95 Folk Club in Harcourt Street. The 95 Club moved to Slattery's of Capel Street where it ran for for over a decade.

The guitar was mandatory in ballad groups. Almost anybody could buy a cheap one, learn a few rudimentary chords and then they would be in 'business'. Banjos – either tenor or five-string – were prominent too as were mandolins but they demanded more skill and commitment. The Dubliners had John Sheehan on fiddle and other groups also had a fiddler, but while some traditional tunes were played now and again, by and large the groups concentrated on vocal material. Most of the songs were Irish but there were English and Scottish ones too and a sprinkling of American songs. New songs written by composers like Dominic

Behan, Ewan McColl and Cyril Tawney were favourites.

Johnny Moynihan of Sweeny's Men introduced the bouzouki to Irish music in 1967 after a trip to the continent, creating the distinctive mandolin/bouzouki counterpoint so characteristic of Sweeny's Men and Planxty. This was an almost bizarre time in the commercial Irish music scene with folk recordings regularly hitting the top of the hit parade. The Ludlows, the Johnstons, Sweeny's Men, the Dubliners, Danny Doyle, Paddy Reilly shared ranking in the Irish charts with the Beatles and the Rolling Stones.

On the fringe of the scene were traditional musicians such as Seán Keane, Tommy Peoples, Séamus Ennis, Willie Clancy, Finbar and Eddie Furey, Ted Furey, the Keenans, Liam Óg Ó Floinn and Matt Molloy. These rubbed shoulders with singers like Christy Moore and Andy Irvine, a collaboration which in time would result in the emergence of Planxty and the Bothy Band. Many of these musicians went on to become seminal figures in top Irish music groups in the 1970s and '80s – Donal Lunny, Andy Irvine, Johnny Moynihan, Terry Woods and Christy Moore.

After audience tastes changed in Ireland many performers from the ballad group scene left for the US in the 1970s. The era fizzled out almost as quickly as it had begun. It had always more enthusiasm and energy than sophistication, and audiences were tiring of the formula as its musical limitations became exposed. Emigrant balladeers ended up performing in US Irish bars in the 1980s and '90s, joined by refugees from the Irish showband scene, now also moribund in the homeland. Today the ballad-group tradition lingers on in Ireland, Europe and the US. There is still a modicum of part-time work in Ireland, but more so in hundreds of Irish-American bars in the US. Performers sing in Ireland as in the US for drinking audiences who like 'singalong' material that they are familiar with, frequently performed in a style modelled after the Clancy Brothers and Tommy Makem. In Ireland as in the US, this is often the introduction to Irish music for many people.

Ground-breaking and classic among ballad groups were the Clancy Brothers and Tommy Makem, now reissued on TCD 1002. (MIM)

**ballad sheets.** Single-sheet song tracts, imported to Ireland from Britain after the late 1500s, but being printed in Ireland from the 1570s. Known popularly as 'broadsides', 'broadsheets' and 'ballets', they were sold by street vendors ('patterers') who might sing the contents of their song-sheets. Ballad singers, like other itinerant musicians, were obliged to have a licence for such performance, and for sale of their song sheets.

See ballad; broadsheet.

Old Ballinakill Céilí Band, c. 1929 with (left) piper Neilus Cronin, and (right) piper Leo Rowsome (Moloney Family)

**Ballinakill Traditional Dance Players.** The parish of Ballinakill lies between Woodford and Loughrea in Co. Galway. In 1926 the Ballinakill Traditional Dance Players were assembled by curate Fr Larkin to provide music for dancing in the local school. Original members were Tommy Whyte and Jerry Moloney (fiddles), Stephen Moloney and Tommy Whelan (flutes), Anna Rafferty (piano). They broadcast on 2RN after Séamus Clandillon had heard them playing at a feis in Athlone in 1928. Known as the Ballinakill Céilí Band, they then went on to record nine 78s during the 1930s, toured Ireland, England and America, disbanding in 1943. Their LPs include *St Patrick's Night in Dublin* (Capitol T10201) and *Leprechauns*. (VEC)

**bandoneon.** A German version of the accordion, invented in 1846. Favoured in South America, it has been the mainstay of tango music there. It uses parallel-sided steel reeds – like the German concertina which has a similar tone. It is found occasionally as an exotic instrument in Irish and 'folk' musics.

See accordion; concertina; free reeds.

**Bangor set dancers.** Based in Bangor, Co. Down, they specialise in quadrilles, lancers and Caledonian as still danced locally at the pace traditional to the area, in a manner likely the same as when these dances were first introduced to this island in the 1800s.

See Donnan, Jackie; set dance.

Tenor banjo with wood-back resonator    (EDI)

**banjo.** A plucked fretted lute in which the sound is amplified by the tensioning of its strings over a bridge seated on a fine skin diaphragm stretched over a circular metal frame. The early origins of the instrument are obscure. That its precursors came from Africa to America, probably via the West Indies, is by now well established. Yet, the multitude of African peoples, languages, and musics makes it very difficult to associate the banjo with any specific African prototype. From various historical references, however, it can be deduced that the banjar, bangie, banjer, banza, or banjo was played in early seventeenth-century America by Africans in slavery who constructed their instruments from gourds, wood, and tanned skins, using hemp or gut for strings. This prototype was eventually to lead to the evolution of the modern banjo in the late eighteenth and early nineteenth centuries. Until about 1800 the banjo remained essentially an African American instrument, and although at times there was considerable interaction between whites and African Americans enjoying music and dance, whites usually participated as observers. What brought the instrument to the attention of the nation, however, was a grotesque representation of African American culture by white performers in black-face 'minstrel' shows which toured Ireland just before the Famine. Percy French played banjo in such a format *c.* 1880.

The banjo they introduced was most likely the five-string banjo of the minstrels and not the earlier three- or four-string variety which was common on the plantations. This is supported by a nineteenth-century sketch in Captain Francis O'Neill's *Irish Minstrels and Musicians* of piper Dick Stephenson and banjoist John Dunne, where the fifth string and peg on Dunne's banjo are clearly visible. By this time the banjo had undergone several transformations of a technological nature. Instead of tacking the skin head directly to the wooden hoop or gourd body, banjo-makers added a thin metal band which sat on top of the wooden rim over the head, this secured by hooks and nuts which fastened through 'shows' mounted around the side of the body. The tension of the skin could thus be adjusted. Factory-made gut strings replaced the old home-made strings and round wooden hoops were used as frames, instead of hollow gourds, this giving the instrument more durability.

The minstrel banjo lacked frets, and as a result, playing above the fifth string peg position posed severe intonation problems. It wasn't until 1878 that frets were added to the commercially produced banjo, a development credited to Henry Dobson of New York State. It took three decades of animated controversy for the idea to catch on. Some opponents deemed the innovation as sacrilegious as putting frets on a violin.

The earliest Irish banjos then were certainly

fretless. Up to the turn of the nineteenth century banjos were plucked and strummed by the fingers. So the evidence, though circumstantial, would indicate that originally the banjo was used in Ireland for rudimentary accompaniment of songs and tunes with perhaps some of the simpler melodies being plucked out by the fingers.

This all changed dramatically at the turn of the century when steel strings were invented. Influenced by the use of the plectrum in mandolin playing, banjo players started to experiment with different plectral playing styles. The idea of tuning the banjo in fifths, just like the mandolin, caught on around this time as well. Many players began to remove the short fifth string from the banjo, and before long four-string banjos, originally called 'plectrum' banjos, were being manufactured. These were full-sized 22-fret banjos just like today's five-string instrument but without the fifth string. Then around 1915 the tango or tenor banjo was invented, coinciding with the popularity in America of the new exotic dance form imported from Latin America, which was sweeping the nation at the time. The tenor banjo had seventeen or nineteen frets, a shorter neck tuned in fifths just like the mandolin or fiddle, though not at the same pitch and was played with a plectrum. The plectrum and tenor banjos became the preferred form of the instrument in vaudeville, dixieland jazz, ragtime and swing. In fact the five-string banjo languished for years, except in Appalachia, until it was restored to popularity through bluegrass, the 1960s folk revival and the revival of old-time traditional mountain music.

The first Irish banjo player to record commercially was James Wheeler, who was featured along with accordion player Eddie Herborn in a Columbia recording in 1916. The most famous Irish banjo player of the 1920s and '30s was Mike Flanagan, born in County Waterford in 1898, who emigrated to the United States with his family at the age of ten. Like many of the Irish banjo players of that era, he started on the mandolin and was self-taught. In essence he invented his own style of playing. He played for decades in the Irish dance halls in New York City with his brother Joe, a virtuoso accordionist. The banjo/accordion combination was

The Pecker Dunne, singer and banjo player (Derek Spiers/Report)

ideal for the non-amplified, non-air conditioned dance halls of the day. The duo was known as the Flanagan Brothers and they recorded prodigiously between the early 1920s and the late 1930s. Other banjo players to record in America in the 1920s and '30s included Jimmy McDade of the Four Provinces Orchestra in Philadelphia, Michael Gaffney in New York and Neil Nolan, originally from Prince Edward Island, who recorded with Dan Sullivan's Shamrock Band in Boston. There was great life and exuberance in these early recordings, in part because the music was designed for lively dancing, but also because at that time the banjo was traditionally tuned higher than nowadays – still in fifths but in the standard tenor banjo tuning where the top string was pitched at C. There are a few players in America who still favour this tuning, most notably Jimmy Kelly in Boston. Most of the young players however favour the GDAE tuning which is now 'standard' for Irish traditional banjo players.

It's not hard to pinpoint when this 'standardisation' occurred. Before 1960 a number of styles and instruments co-existed in the modest fraternity of banjo players in Ireland. Some players favoured the five-string, some the banjo-mandolin, while others favoured varieties of the four-string instrument. Some players used a pick, while others used a thimble, most notably a member of the famous Dunne family of travelling musicians from Limerick who played outside the Augustinian Church in O'Connell Street in Limerick every weekend in the 1960s.

In the early 1960s too, the rise to commercial success of the Dubliners in the Irish and English folk revival was to have a profound effect on the fortunes of the tenor banjo in Irish music. Barney McKenna's skill helped bring scores of new devotees to the instrument, almost all tuning like him to GDAE, an octave below the fiddle. There are now hundreds of accomplished tenor banjo players in Ireland, England and America. Many individual and virtuoso styles of playing are emerging with every passing year. The instrument has come of age in Irish music. (MIM)

**bards.** The hereditary, professional, literary caste which flourished in the Gaelic and Gaelicised lordships of Ireland (and in Gaelic Scotland) from the time of the Anglo–Norman conquest to the final destruction of Gaelic society (*c.* 1200–1650). 'Bardic Poetry' refers to the poetry they produced. Usually of one of the great bardic clans such as Ó Dálaigh, Mac Con Midhe, Ó Gnímh, Ó hEodhasa, Ó hUiginn, Mac an Bháird, the bard received a thorough and intensive education in grammar, poetry, Gaelic literature, historical, genealogical and topographical lore, and much else besides, in one of the bardic 'schools'. The bards' primary social function was to eulogise and elegise the nobility in verse, a task for which they were generously recompensed. This afforded many of them wealth in accordance with their high status and prestige. Much of this 'official' poetry – composed by and for a society with very different tastes and values to those of the present day – is of limited attraction to the modern reader. A small number of poems of a more personal nature (personal tragedies, love poetry, personal observations on contemporary events, religious poetry etc.) have survived and are generally of greater interest and appeal.

Among the bards who earned an enduring reputation in the Gaelic literary tradition are Muireadhach Albanach and Donnchadh Mór Ó Dálaigh, Giolla Bhríde Mac Con Midhe (thirteenth century), Gofraidh Fionn Ó Dálaigh (fourteenth century), Tadhg Óg Ó hUiginn (fifteenth century) and Tadhg Dall Ó hUiginn (sixteenth century). As an integral part of, and vested interest in, a distinctive native culture and socio-political system, the bards were always considered inimical to the spread of English 'civility'. Consequently, control – or elimination – of them was an important part of the Tudor conquest in the sixteenth century.

The bards mainly practised a form of poetry known as 'dán díreach' ('straight verse') where the amount of syllables in each line (as opposed to the number of stresses, as in song metres), and the number of syllables in the last word in each line, are the predominant features. 'Dán díreach' also included intricate and strict rules involving alliteration, rhyme, assonance etc. To compose well required great skill and erudition, and convention demanded ritual sensory deprivation, perhaps echoing the spiritual austerities of their pre-Christian predecessors. With the gradual disappearance of the bardic schools, the necessary training could not be provided, and the practice of syllabic poetry declined during the seventeenth century, although examples are found from as late as the mid-eighteenth century. Its practice in Scotland continued with the survival of bardic schools in Gaelic Scotland into the eighteenth century.

The performance of a newly composed bardic panegyric was an important occasion – the bard sitting with the lord, and the poem chanted or sung by a 'reacaire' (reciter) accompanied by a harper. There is little evidence concerning the musical delivery of the poetry. When the repertoire of the old harpers was first examined in Granard and Belfast in the latter half of the eighteenth century, it was found to consist mostly of song airs, very unlikely to have been used to provide dramatic accompaniment to the chanting of syllabic poetry. The literary tradition bestowed on the oral tradition a relaxed form of syllabic poetry in the form of 'laoithe Fiannaíochta', narrative poems concerning the adventures of Fionn Mac Cumhail and his warrior comrades.

These first gained widespread popularity during bardic times, but survived in Ireland into the present century, and a few are still sung today in the Western Isles of Scotland. The manner of their singing was perhaps not dissimilar to the art of the reacaire. While the bards regarded the more popular song metres as inappropriate for more formal work, it seems probable that they conceded to popular taste on occasions of less importance or formality. Certainly, when song metres begin to displace syllabic poetry as the literary medium, they emerge in very developed forms implying a long, established tradition of composition. As early as the beginning of the seventeenth century, Seathrún Céitinn (1570–1644) was composing with impressive skill assonantal rhymes corresponding to the stresses in each line. With the adoption by the literary tradition of song as the medium for their art, the poets bequeathed to the folk-song repertoire a considerable corpus of songs that have aptly been described as 'folk-songs by destination but not by origination'. Particularly where the literary tradition was maintained throughout the eighteenth century in Munster and South-East Ulster, this fact influenced in a general way the style, tastes and vocabulary of purer folk-song composition. (EAO)

**barn dance.** A form of 'round the hall' social dance most popular up to the 1950s. It was generally performed to hornpipe time (4/4), but, related to marching practice, danced to 6/8 time in north Co. Antrim.

**Barron, Pat.** Last of the travelling dancing-masters to teach in West Clare in the 1930s.

**Barry, Margaret.** (1917–89). Banjo player and singer. Born Peter Street, Cork, her father and uncle played banjo, her mother the harp. At age sixteen, following the death of her mother, 'Maggie' went on the road, singing at fairs, markets, football matches and other gatherings all over Ireland, but concentrating on the area between Dundalk, Newry, Armagh and Forkhill. Self-taught, and having learnt her songs by ear, some of her lyrics can be jumbled and 'sound-alike', her sources are eclectic: she got 'The Factory Girl' from Alan Lomax while he was collecting in Ireland, 'My Lagan Love' was picked up through eavesdropping at the open door of a record shop. Strongest and best known of her repertoire were 'The Blarney Stone', 'The Hills of Donegal', 'The Wild Colonial Boy', 'The Flower of Sweet Strabane', 'The Turf Man from Ardee', 'The Galway Shawl', 'She Moved Through the Fair' and 'Eileen McMahon' – all popular, as opposed to 'traditional' Irish song of her times, her taste reflecting attitudes typical of street singers everywhere.

Lomax took her to London to make a recording; there she played in sessions with many Irish musicians, teaming up with Michael Gorman, fiddler, from Tubbercurry, Co. Sligo, who had settled there in the mid-1940s. Recordings spread her fame, and with him she was able to fill London's Albert Hall and New York's Carnegie Hall. They played together until his death in 1969, renowned for their interpretation of 'Lord Gordon', and for the complex jig 'Stray-away Child', reputedly composed by her in memory of her younger life, but usually attributed to him. Another tune 'The Drunken Hens' was composed in memory of the disposal method she used as a result of a failed poteen-making attempt. Her last decade was spent in Banbridge, Co. Down. Occasional trips were made to play in folk clubs such as that in Armagh where she once memorably entertained the Church of Ireland's bishop, Dr George Otto Simms.

**bars, Irish.** See Irish bars.

**Basker, Tommy.** (1923–99). Cape Breton harmonica player whose attitudes to life and music have influenced many younger musicians both in Cape Breton and in Ireland. He learned from his father, Alex Basker, and first recorded on 78 discs with fiddler Johnny Wilmot (1952). He recorded a solo CD, *The Tin Sandwich* (1994). Although many modern harmonica players use blues techniques (tonguing and single note) this player makes his embellishments with throat more so than tongue. (PAC)

**BBC Sound Archive.** This contains recorded material covering a period of over sixty years. The BBC began its radio activities in 1922 but initial broadcasts were live and few were recorded for posterity. The earliest surviving BBC recording of an Irish traditional performer that we know of dates to 1943 and is of the Westmeath-born piper R. S. O'Mealy. However, in the late 1940s the BBC undertook the responsibility of systematically recording what was believed to remain of the indigenous folk music of England, Ireland, Scotland and Wales. As part of this project performers of Irish traditional music, song and dance were documented both in Ireland and among areas of Irish settlement in Britain.

The project was initiated by Brian George, a Donegal man who had emigrated to England and risen in the ranks of the BBC in London. As part of a pilot scheme, he travelled in 1947 to Ireland to look at the possibility of intensive collection of Irish traditional music. Here he met Séamus Ennis who had at that time just finished working for the Irish Folklore Commission. It was the singers and musicians with whom Ennis put George in contact who convinced the Donegal man of the viability of the proposed venture. Ennis, who was to shortly begin employment with Raidió Éireann, was ironically given as his first assignment the job of assisting George and the BBC in their collecting activities in Ireland. After a further pilot scheme in 1949, collecting began in earnest in the summer of 1952. Ennis was by then in the full-time employment of the BBC. Engaged as a collector he made occasional forays into the northern part of Ireland but it was in the more southern counties that his activities concentrated.

The job of collecting material from Ulster was given to two men: Peter Kennedy, an Englishman in the employ of the English Folk Dance and Song Society, and Belfast-born Seán O'Boyle. Kennedy had been involved with the folk community in England for a number of years and was seconded to the BBC by the EFDSS on the strength of his previous experience. O'Boyle was engaged not only due to his knowledge of the Irish language but also because of his own personal interest in and knowledge of many of the traditional performers eventually documented in their travels. During the summer months of 1952–54 both men made a series of highly successful collecting trips across the North. It was between these years that the bulk of what we now consider to be the BBC Folk Music Collection of Irish traditional music was amassed. Collecting was done on both disc and reel-to-reel tape formats, although the BBC eventually transferred all recordings to coarse and micro-groove discs, the preferred archive storage medium at that time. In all, the three main collectors documented over 1,500 individual performances of Irish traditional music, totalling well over one hundred hours of original material. Much of this includes English song, Irish song, keening, lilting/jigging, solo, duet and all manner of instrumental groupings, as well as dancing, speech, folklore and local custom. Selections were broadcast on the BBC radio show *As I Roved Out*. Both Ennis and Kennedy were to continue their collecting work in Britain, albeit on a smaller scale, well into the late 1950s.

Until recently, copies of this material existed in disc form in the BBC archives in London, among other BBC regional archives, and with the English Folk Dance and Song Society. In 1996 disc copies which had been given to the National Sound Archive, a branch of the British Library, were transferred to digital format in a joint venture between the BBC and the Irish Traditional Music Archive. These copies are now available for consultation with full computer indexes at the premises of the Irish Traditional Music Archive in Dublin. (GLC)

**Begley family.** A family of nine brothers and sisters, musicians and singers, from the Dingle peninsula, Co. Kerry. Their father was a singer and played melodeon, their mother also a singer, and her father too. The Begley household was known for song in the 1950s, both traditional and the eclectic available repertoire of that time. House parties were frequent, sometimes the local emigrant wakes (ball nights) were held there. Eldest of the family is Máire (Ní Bheaglaíoch), singer and accordion player, also a broadcaster with Radio Kerry where she co-hosts a traditional music show *Kingdom Céilí*. Séamus (accordion, of 'Begley and Cooney') picked up his earliest tunes from her, and like youngest brother Breandán (button accordion and melodeon, of the group Beginish), learnt considerable professional style playing jigs, polkas, slides, airs and hornpipes in the family's dance hall at Muiríoch. Sister Eibhlín sings, and while in Melbourne in 1970 was instrumental in setting up the first Australian branch of CCÉ. Singer and concertina player Jós is a founder member of the all-women group Macalla and works with Raidió na Gaeltachta: guitarist Galvin Ralston is her son, while Caitlín's son, Aogán Lynch plays concertina. Between them the Begleys have several recordings.

**Belfast.** From its cultural heyday in the late eighteenth century it quickly became an industrial centre and during the nineteenth century established shipyards, ropeworks, tobacco factories and a linen trade that developed into the biggest in the world. The hundreds of thousands who flocked there in search of work brought their own music with them. The Falls Road became the focus of the people from the shores of Lough Neagh; the Shankhill became a home for those who moved in from Co. Antrim. The people who worked in the shipyards and ropeworks of Ballymacarret came from the Hollywood hills, and Sandy Row was populated by mill workers from the Lagan Valley. They all had different origins, cultures and traditions, features that often clashed and collided. A new culture evolved in the city streets and rows of redbrick houses, sometimes with a backward glance towards rural themes, but with the urgent staccato bustle of an urban pressure. The immigrant workers from Clyde shipyards and Lancashire mills, added to the new culture so that the songs, verses and music are a fascinating mixture of the Irish, the Scots and the English, along with the exuberant and gawky elements of the mission hall and the music hall. Hugh Quinn first collected this rich material, and in later years, David Hammond and Maurice Leydon. (DAH)

Political/religious segregation of society influences and highlights music as an identity marker but this is constantly being renegotiated. The inter-community, cross-community, and transnational communicative powers of traditional music leave Belfast a strong music scene rooted in numerous small-scale venues in pubs, clubs and hotels. Local sessions occur weekly, often four or five simultaneously in different venues; fiddle is the most popular instrument, flute is next, both played to a high standard. Fiddles and flutes are made in the city (Rab Cherry and Sam Murray respectively). Ballad singing is a lot less popular than instrumental music, set dancing is strong and political 'party' songs are to be heard in suburban social clubs. Harp events throughout the year are organised by the Belfast Harp Foundation.

There are twenty or so regular sessions in the city, and there are also sessions occasionally in GAA clubs, and those run monthly by CCÉ. Crescent Arts Centre (University Road) and An Cultúrlann (Falls Road), have regular music and dance classes and also present stage concerts; An Cultúrlann concentrates on Irish-language events. Set-dancing classes and céilís have had increasing popularity through the 1990s; some are community/club-based, others (notably in South Belfast/Queen's University area) attract participation from a wider culture and class spread. (RIS)

**Belfast Folk Festival.** Begun 1980 as a City Hall sponsored project. Its major event then was an open-air concert in the Botanic Gardens with Ralph McTell, Danny Thompson, Donovan and Freddy White. Practically every well-known band played at the festival over the years – among them the Dubliners, the Chieftains and De Dannan. Abandoned since 1994, the festival in later years shifted its emphasis to non-'headliner' groups, and garnered financial support from Guinness, Laganside Development, the Arts Council of Northern Ireland, the Northern Ireland Tourist Board and the Arts Council in Dublin.

**Belfast Folk Song Club.** Formed *c.* 1963 on the model of similar clubs in Scotland and England. Probably the first of its kind on the island of Ireland, certainly in the North, it met on Sunday evenings (an innovation in the Belfast of the time). Most of the performances were of songs learned from books or from recordings of English and Scottish singers, notably Ewan MacColl, Robin Hall and Jimmy MacGregor, A. L. Lloyd or Americans like Woody Guthrie and Pete Seeger. Few participants had any knowledge of Irish traditional singing; many were youth hostellers whose experience had been of community sing-songs in hostels, hence the norm was for a song to be accompanied and for audiences to be encouraged to join choruses. Among those involved were Leslie Bingham, Robin Morton and John Moulden. The club collapsed after some five years as a result of disagreements among the organisers over 'purism'. The club influenced many others, some more popularly oriented than others, especially the Ulster Folk Music Society, which moved towards an experience of traditional form. Other clubs and session venues of about the same time were the Pike Folk Song Club, The Old House, Pat's Bar, Ulster Folk Song Society, Ulster Folk Music Society, Queen's Folk Song Society, Salisbury Street, Antrim Road and Victoria Square. (JOM)

**Belfast Set Dancing Society.** Organised primarily by Mary Fox, this co-ordinates and oversees set-dance workshops, seminars, céilithe, schools and adult classes involving teachers from all over the island.

**Bell, Derek.** (1935– ). Harper and multi-instrumentalist. Born in Belfast and exhibiting outstanding musical ability as a child, he was awarded a scholarship in composition to the Royal College of Music, London. He is known best for harp (a late vocation) but is an exceptional player on the oboe, cor anglais, dulcimer, and piano. He studied piano with Rosina Lovinne. He has appeared as a soloist with symphony orchestras in Ireland and Britain and as far afield as Moscow, Budapest, Berlin, and USA. He resigned a position with the BBC Northern Ireland Orchestra in 1974 to become a full-time member of the Chieftains and has recorded five solo albums. (BIM)

**Bergin, Mary.** (1949– ). Whistle. From Shankhill, Co. Dublin, her mother played fiddle, her father melodeon. She picked up the whistle at nine, having heard Willie Clancy play in an Oireachtas concert in Dublin. Influenced by visiting musicians (Kathleen Harrington and Elizabeth Crotty in particular), and local fleadh sessions in the 1960s (in Blackrock with fiddlers Joe Liddy and Sean O'Dwyer), whistle player Terry Horan also informed her playing. She played too in the Claremen's Club in Church Street, Dublin and the Thomas Street Pipers' Club sessions. She worked for Raidió Éireann then CCÉ in Monkstown before moving to live in Spiddal where she now teaches the whistle. She plays with bouzouki player Alec Finn of De Dannan, and in the group Dordán. Brightly ornamented but uncluttered, her playing is distinctive with a crisp articulation, and has been the role model for two decades of whistle players. Her first solo album *Feadóg Stáin* in 1979 is still the definitive; a second came in 1989, and she has recorded also with Dordán.

**Blessing, John.** (1913–1993). Flute player, singer, storyteller. From Carrickavoher, Aughavas, Co. Leitrim, a key figure in the history of south Leitrim music. His style and repertoire were learned from his father Michael. Recorded in 1993.

See Leitrim, South.

**bodhrán.** A shallow, circular frame-drum with a skin of goat-hide, the form of which dates to 3,000 BC. Made of fish-skin in Lapland, widespread as the 'tar' all over north Africa, 'doira' in Afghanistan, and throughout Asia, it has become a phenomenal Irish music icon since the

Bodhrán player at Athea, Co. Limerick, 1946 (Caomhín Ó Danachair, CBÉ)

1960s. Folklore information is scarce; turn-of-the-century literature on Irish music does not mention it at all and historic pictorial and written records point to the music tradition in Ireland being primarily melodic. The 'madhouse of theorising' about the bodhrán's origins (the words of American researcher Janet McCrickard) wrongly ascribes it a mythic role as 'the traditional Irish percussion', or 'the heartbeat of Irish music'. John B. Keane, in his novel, *The Bodhrán Makers*, so invests the device with a romantic tradition which he invents from conflating its use in the new-year's 'wren' with the image of its very modern-day playing style. Brian Friel's play *Dancing at Lughnasa* incorrectly includes the bodhrán with a modern playing style in a scene that involves a 1930s' radio programme. The film *Titanic* farcically includes it in modern style as percussion among low-class (Irish emigrant) passengers.

The bodhrán was played artistically in Irish music only in certain areas prior to the 1960s. As Micheál Ó Súilleabháin said in his address to the 1996 Crossroads Conference: 'If you just go back a small bit, the bodhrán was played one day a year. All the old lads I talked to around 1970/71 told me "you take out the bodhrán any day of the year other than 26 December and you're mad. Its like wearing shamrock on the First of June".' The best efforts at sourcing it are in its original skin tray 'winnower' form, 'dallán', used here as late as the 1930s. That was not specific to Ireland. Called 'wecht' in England and Lowland Scotland, Janet McCrickard includes in her book both descriptions from Scottish literature and examples extant in the National Museum of Scotland. In Scots Gaelic it was called 'dallach'. There, a pierced version – for sieving – was called 'crerar', the winnower was 'windin' wecht', other versions were used for baking, and for storing haggis. There is only one suggestion of its use as a drum: in Nethertown, Fife, a drum belonging to the 1796 French-revolutionary Friends of the People was stored in 'Thresher Charlie's Garret'. Dinneen's 1927 Irish dictionary gives 'a shallow skin-bottomed vessel, a drum, a dildurn' as the meaning of 'bodhrán'. McCrickard deduces that 'dildurn' is from the Gaelic word 'dilder', meaning 'to make a rattling sound', similar to a Yorkshire word 'dildam'. Further, Dinneen describes the Irish 'dallán' as a 'winnowing fan, a sheephide, a "wight"'. McCrickard refers also to an obsolete Ulster word 'bull' meaning a 'skin drum', and to the old English word 'buller' meaning 'din'. Clearly there are inter-relationships between both devices and the descriptive words.

*the wren*. For the druids in Ireland prior to Christianity the wren was sacred, and a modern Christian tale involves St Stephen hiding in a whin gorse bush being betrayed by a wren. Based on this, on one day of the year the wren is killed: the 26th December wren hunt in Roscommon, Sligo, Kerry and other places takes ritual revenge, uses loud noise of drum and music to stun the bird (bodhrán = deafening). This is reminiscent of a similar symbolic practice, using fife and drum, which exists in France, which may have been adapted here in the eighteenth century, and which may in turn explain its customary use also in Sligo/Roscommon. In this sense alone, as in Nethertown, Fifeshire, the bodhrán may reflect another tradition, that of revolutionary France which produced the 1798 rebellion.

*use in Ireland*. The earliest evidence in Ireland is provided by Hamilton's *Irish Flute Player's Handbook*. Therein he reproduces a painting from *c*. 1842 which depicts a flute player playing in the company of a tambourine being played in the Islamic fashion with fingertips. The uniform and the features of the player suggest a non-national, and/or a military connection, or possibly a band connection. Since the Salvation Army bands (in Ireland since the 1870s) used tambourine, one can only speculate. Gerry Hallinan, born in Co. Roscommon (d. 1994 while dancing a set in Albany, NY), described how as children in the 1920s he and friends made drums from a bent sally (willow) branch over which they stretched a skin. Significantly, they nailed on pennies as jingles. Sonny Davey reports that Thomas McAuley, master bodhrán maker before him, would use the rim of a redundant sand-riddle for a frame, and would attach pot-menders (light, tinned-metal discs) as jingles. Both these cases suggest the copying of a manufactured, Islamic style instrument like that in the Hamilton picture. Further, Davey describes the older Pat Killoran as playing the bodhrán in an extrovert manner 'with runs and graces, from skin middle out to the rim, using the tips of his fingers and nails'. Willie Reynolds in his autobiography describes Paddy Kelly of Ballymore: 'he could hit it off the top of his head and also off his elbow', and says that most players used fingers. All of this suggests the Islam-influenced style currently prevalent on the continent – in 'Tarantella' music in Southern Italy, but particularly (Islamic influenced) folk music in Spain, i.e. tambourine technique. Kevin Danagher's 1949 photograph of a young bodhrán player from Kerry suggests the modern-day playing pose, but in the absence of a sound-recording it is hard to tell. However it came to Ireland, Seán Ó Riada certainly triggered the bodhrán's modern-day popularity by adapting it as a form of percussion for his radio ensemble Ceoltóirí Chualann. Willie Reynolds recalls that in his young days, players were 'few and far between', that 'the Fleadhanna Ceoil brought it into popularity'.

*construction*. A frame is made from a steamed plywood plank bent into a circle. Over this is stretched a cured goatskin which, according to the skill of the maker, will be scraped down to provide a particular thickness and playing timbre. The skin is tacked or glued in place. That is the basic bodhrán. More sophisticated makers include a tuning device. This involves another, movable, plywood hoop fitted on guides inside the frame. It is operated up and down by a system of screws, Allen keys or wood wedges which adjust skin tension in order to alter instrument pitch, or to compensate for humidity and temperature changes. Playing is done either with both ends of a knobbed stick (cipín, tipper) or with the back of the fingers. In modern times the skin tension may be adjusted by the pressure of the left hand from the inside, giving a pitch-changing sensation. The top players have their own systems of aesthetics and techniques. Beating style has learned much from Indian tablas, Arabic tar and dumbeq; rhythm seems to be informed too by the footwork of step-dancers and expert set-dancers.

*manufacture*. It is made widely today, most profusely by Malachy and Anne Kearns' IDA-backed enterprise in Roundstone, Co. Galway. Other makers include Pádraig McNeela in Dublin who makes up to six hundred of the ornamental and a couple of hundred of the playable kind annually, these are sold at regular kerbside stalls at the Willie Clancy school and fleadhanna ceoil. Like the others, Charlie Byrne from Tipperary is a modern maker – he began only after his daughter had 'won the all-Ireland [fleadh championship] on it twenty-nine years ago'. Belfast maker Eamon Maguire began playing and making after hearing one in Doolin in the early '60s. Among the other makers are Frank McNamara in Ennistymon and Paddy Clancy in Limerick. Bodhráns are now also manufactured in England and Scotland and similar Pakistani drums are imported. (EDI)

*style*. Bodhrán performance cannot easily be categorised into different regional styles; it is more easily defined by referring to the manner of performance peculiar to an individual, or to a group of players. There are currently as many styles of playing in existence – in and outside of Ireland – as there are players to execute them. Some insist that the correct method involves following the rhythm of the tune, others hold that the melody of the tune (by way of tonal adjustment) must be followed. Some use both methods. Certain players make use of 'motor' rhythms or rhythmic patterns which are not so symbolically bound up with the melody, but rhythmically add a sympathetic accompaniment (Jim Higgins, Colm Murphy). In all bodhrán styles the player's rhythmic repertoire comprises 'down strokes', 'up strokes', 'doubling' or 'trebling' and combinations of each. It is the unique and individual grouping of these basic but indispensable strokes with other devices that differentiates between one style and another.

Syncopation, which is fundamental to jazz rhythm, is another method of varying time melodically and, more importantly, rhythmically. A basic reel rhythm would sound as follows:

(Where    D = down stroke and
          U = upstroke)

Basic jig rhythms consist of:

[musical notation: 6/8 time, D U D U D U]

[musical notation: 6/8 time, D D D D D U]

[musical notation: 6/8 time, D U D D U D]

The division of these groups of beats into smaller sub-divisions can lead to further stylistic differences between performers. The jig rhythm

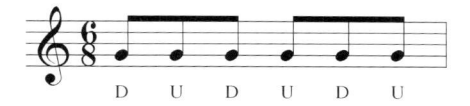

[musical notation: 6/8 time, D U D U D U]

can be enhanced for example to give

[musical notation: 6/8 time, D D U D U D U]

(a double down stroke on the first beat of each bar).

This stroke when suitably articulated is often referred to as 'doubling', 'trebling', the 'triplet' or the 'roll'. In the above example the additional down stroke is played between beats 1 and 2 but this itself is only one of the five possible placings within a bar of 6/8. The bodhrán player's style is also governed by the method with which the 'roll' or 'triplet' is executed.

The style of a bodhrán player is not only concerned with the manner in which the player personally chooses to articulate the rhythm but also in his or her preferred performance method. Bodhrán styles cannot be clearly classified according to easily defined divisions. The terminology used here is loosely applied, in fact each of the styles has common fundamental traits. The most common style of bodhrán performance is the 'two-sided stick style'; others include the 'one-sided stick style', the 'hand style', the 'brush style' and a very contemporary 'two-handed style'.

In the 'two-sided stick style' the stick is held similar to a pen but closer to one end than the mid-point. A less conventional method is to place the middle finger in a circular strap fixed to the middle of the stick, the fingers either side holding the stick in place. Noteworthy exponents of this style are Mel Mercier and Frank Torpey. In each case the bodhrán is held with the opposite hand placed on the skin dampening the overall effect. In only some exceptional cases is the bodhrán held by use of cross bars or chords attached to the back of the drum – this was a feature of the playing of Seán Ó Riada and Peadar Mercier in the 1960s.

In the hand technique, the bodhrán is more often held by the crossbars at the back, the tension of the skin being adjusted by use of the fingers on the same hand (Donal Lunny, Séamus Tansey, Ted McGowan, Josie McDonagh, Sonny Davey). With both these methods the bodhrán may only have a range of two or three tonal areas but this may be as effective or aesthetically satisfying to its performers and their audience if it has sufficient rhythmic interest. Nowadays most performers dampen the skin at the back with the hand giving rise to greater tonal possibilities.

In the 'one-sided stick style' the player often uses very similar rhythms to the 'two-sided stick style' but executing the same rhythms using only one end of the stick. The 'brush style' is also played in this fashion using a hairbrush, drum-kit brushes or something similar.

At present, certain bodhrán players are noted for particular performance practices that together with many other components fuse to give them an overall style. There is a very fertile cross-pollination of ideas between players. Some of these stylistic devices include: the 'rim shot', a rhythmic contrast between skin and wood sounds often found in the playing of Johnny 'Ringo' McDonagh. This echoes the use of wood-block as contrast by the snare drummer in a céilí band. 'Slapping' is a method of emphasising certain beats by use of the left hand hitting the skin open-handedly (Tommy Hayes). Some contemporary styles make use of tonally pronounced rhythmic runs from high to low pitch, not unlike a 'fill' on drum kit (John Joe Kelly). Others make use of non-Irish traditional rhythmic ideas such as Indian polyrhythmic structures (Mel Mercier) and African and Latin American rhythms. Conventional and unconventional elements stand side by side, and these rhythmic peculiarities are crafted into the music with imaginative effect and originality.

The hand style is possibly the more archaic, but is associated with the instrument's Northern region. John Joe Lowry from Tynagh, East Galway, won the All-Ireland competition in the early 1990s using it the same way as in Sligo/Roscommon. Junior Davey (from Sligo) is another All-Ireland winner. He uses stick, as does Mossy Griffin of Ennis. A male-ethos instrument in the past, many younger women play bodhrán today e.g. Cherish the Ladies, Cathy Jordan of Dervish and Aimée Leonard of the group Anam. (ERC)

**Bogside Fleadh.** Held in Derry, August 1969, in conjunction with the then barricading of the area. Called for by socialist Eamon McCann, the event is of interest because like 'Free Belfast' its agenda reflected the variety of cultural influences within its population, a communitas with religious/political focus. Formerly, it was Republican ballads which had always been associated with nationalist politics in Northern Ireland, but after the 1960s' Civil Rights era came a new coalition of interests, few of its ideologies being represented by glorious and sentimental militaristic song. It had indeed its own agitational songs, but also a strong commitment to creating an alternative culture. The traditional music revival movement and the 'Fleadh Cheoil' since the 1950s had already been established as an important focus of a new type of democratic, accessible, aesthetically oriented, Irish, music identity. Objectively this was related to neither religion nor political persuasion and involved both Protestants and Catholics. It was as much a reaction against the 'parlour-Irish' culture adopted by the new Catholic middle classes of the Republic and Northern Ireland as it was opposed to perceived destructive 'non-Irish', British and American popular cultural values. Hence the Fleadh appealed as a 'radical' format for celebration in the Bogside. A wide spectrum of liberal to nationalist traditional music and popular-ballad entertainers took part, emotionally involved by the infective vision of a city population under siege to unbending authority. Among them were Luke Kelly and the Dubliners, Tommy Makem, Liam O'Flynn, Armagh Pipers' Club, Eugene Lambert's Wanderly Wagon and young local dance-school step-dancers. Individual pipers, fiddle, flute and accordion players from counties Armagh, Antrim, Tyrone, Cavan, Leitrim and Roscommon arrived spontaneously and behaved much as at any other fleadh, doing spots on the 'official' lorry platform and playing casual tunes in groups in the street, but undoubtedly affected by the enormity of what was going on. In fact, this was not the local people's music at all, but in an atmosphere flavoured by the presence of numerous German and other 'revolutionary tourists', heightened by lorries packed with relief-provisions arriving from places like Galway, it all added to the camaraderie and the jolly, ecstatic mood. The organisation was casual and haphazard, the event slipped into history as possibly greater than it was. It was remembered by a 'commemorative' fleadh in 1994.

**Bogue, Bernard.** Born in Co. Fermanagh in 1860, joined the Royal Irish Constabulary in 1881 and on appointment had postings to counties Clare, Down, Antrim and Tyrone. Bogue played the fiddle and whistle and in his off-duty time wrote down tunes he heard. On his retirement he taught the fiddle in Co. Monaghan. In 1917, he was corresponding with another policeman/collector – Chief O'Neill in Chicago. His original ledgers with his impressive collection of several thousand reels, jigs, hornpipes, airs and songs have survived; several are included in the 1996, Vol. 4 of *Ceol Rince na hÉireann*. (HAB)

**bombarde.** A small oboe-like instrument with a penetrating sound. Used in Breton music, it is fingered like a tin whistle with an extra hole to allow one note below the stated key (usually B flat, sometimes C or D). Typically it is played in duet with Breton bagpipe the biniou, this pitched an octave above with its drone an octave below. Bombarde and biniou hocket – call and response, swapping parts; this originated in giving players the time to relax breathing in order to sustain playing for longer periods, but it is now a stylistic feature of playing practice.

See Brittany.

Bones (EDI)

**bones.** A pair of animal rib-bones held hanging loosely from the fingers of an upraised hand and impacted against each other in a castanet-like fashion to give a bright idiophonic accompaniment in modern-day traditional music. Used to the same effect as spoons, and the more casual coin-on-bottle impulsive time-keeping, these are the unique Irish idiophone. The only such instruments listed by O'Curry are 'crotals' and 'clocca' which were kinds of bell; no mention is made of bones. However, bones are referenced in his transcription of the verses on the ancient Fair of Carman: Pipes, fiddles, chainmen Bone-men and tube players (although this may indicate some kind of bone flute). While the bodhrán holds pride of place as the principal percussion instrument of Irish traditional music, the bones, although much less frequently heard, provide the distinctive idiophonic component of the sound of that tradition. In terms of their playing technique the bones have often been confused with the 'spoons', and the sound they produce is, at times, likened somewhat inaccurately to that of the Spanish castanets. The bones, as played in the Irish tradition, are in fact unique both in terms of the technique used to play them, and the timbral palate and rhythmic constructions they offer to the traditional percussionist. As with all other musical instruments the sounds produced by the bones, and the stylistic organisation of those sounds as music, are intimately related to the construction of the instrument itself and its playing technique.

The length and curvature of the bones chosen by any one performer depends on personal playing style and hand size. The two bones are generally of similar length, usually between four and eight inches long. Depending on the grip employed to hold the bones, however, there may be a preference for two bones of different length and girth.

*style*. There is evidence to suggest that the bones have played a part in music-making of various kinds throughout the world for centuries. This music of the bones has almost certainly never been notated in any form in the past. It is also extremely unlikely that the instrument ever had a mnemonic-based language similar to the Solkattu of south Indian percussion, for instance, or the drum languages of most African drumming traditions. If it had, it may have facilitated the oral transmission of the instrument's repertoire of rhythms down to the present day. Of the few extant traditions of bones playing, the two-handed style found principally in North America is one of the most significant. There the bones can be heard providing the rhythmic element in a variety of musics including Irish traditional music. It is especially interesting for the rhythmic possibilities inherent in the pairing of two sets, one set in each hand of a single performer. Cross-rhythm, counter rhythms, interlocking rhythms and sometimes polyrhythm characterise the style.

It is the single-handed style, however, which predominates within the Irish tradition. In the hand of a stylish virtuoso the subtle complexity of the bones, the gently modulated, linear articulation of time belies the simplicity of the instrument itself.

*construction.* Many players in the past fashioned their own instruments, most typically from the rib-bone of a cow or sheep. Two separate lengths of bone were cut from the rib or ribs, scraped clean and then dried in the sun or slowly in an oven. This process could take some time and the bones only became truly dried, clean and smooth after several months of playing and handling. Animal ribs are still preferred by bones players today but they can also be made from other materials such as some woods, plastics and even slate. A small market now exists for the instrument and machine-finished and manufactured sets are now readily available.

*playing technique.* Most players use one of two grips for holding the instrument in the playing position. In both cases a loose fist is formed with the heel of the hand facing the ground. It is the placement of the first bone which distinguishes one grip from the other. One end of this bone is held either between the thumb and forefinger or between the forefinger and index finger leaving the greater part of the bone to hang from the fist in a vertical manner. The second bone is almost invariably placed in a similar fashion between the index finger and ring finger. With the elbow bent to place the forearm at right angles to the body a smooth oscillation of the wrist from side to side causes the bones to beat together as they are held in this secure, but flexible, parallel position. This 'throwing' of the lower arm away from the body and its cyclic return cause the bones to sound their characteristic triplet motif, a rhythmic cell which, when mastered and played even as a simple ostinato, captures the essential gait of the reel, jig and hornpipe. This cell then, when manipulated, displaced, and punctuated by single strokes and flourishes, generates the syncopations and additive rhythms which characterise the bone-player's art.

A relatively recent innovation in playing technique is the application of tonal shading in performance: tightening or loosening the grip on the bones, gradually or suddenly, while maintaining the necessary wrist and arm motion, gives rise to slight changes in the tone produced by the instrument. The tonal range available is small yet the changes can be executed in a variety of interesting and effective ways which colour the rhythms and thus enhance the percussionist's ability to make more complex musical statements. More difficult independent finger manipulation techniques, again in the bones-playing hand, can be used to achieve similar results. Indeed, within the Irish tradition the non-playing hand has remained largely redundant thus far in the development of the style. It is not uncommon, however, to see the more flamboyant performer allow this free hand to be swept into spontaneous movement, bringing both hands into an eloquent dance born of the exhilaration, and the frustration of a body caught up in musical motion. Music becomes dance becomes music.

*history in Irish music.* The bones appeared on the national stage at about the same time as the bodhrán in Seán Ó Riada's ensemble arrangements of Irish traditional music for the group Ceoltóirí Chualann. The instrument had been used to accompany dance music before this, along with other unusual members of the idiophone family such as the fireside tongs and the ubiquitous coin and beer bottle combination. Ronnie McShane was the first bones player to perform with Ceoltóirí Chualann and Ó Riada wove his crisp and precise rhythms into the fabric of the new sound with a fine sensibility to orchestral colour. The relatively high 'pitch' of the bones made them a perfect foil for the lower tones of first Ó Riada's and then Peadar Mercier's bodhrán. Mercier brought both bones and bodhrán to the Chieftains. The combination of the two instruments, and in particular the juxtaposition of their contrasting timbres, has rarely been more effectively employed than in the Chieftains' arrangements of 'The Morning Dew' and 'The Battle of Aughrim'. The group still features this dramatic combination of instruments today with Martin Fay on bones and Kevin Conneff on bodhrán.

*players today.* Bones playing has continued to develop in several ways since the early Chieftains' performances. The best exponents now display greater virtuosity, rhythmic and timbral variety, syncopation and even implied polyrhythm in their playing. Stylists such as Tommy Hayes and Junior Davey, and younger players like Rossa Ó Snodaigh, playing a two-handed style, and Cork woman, Olga Barry, continue to explore new rhythmic territories with the instrument. However, it is probably still fair to suggest that as yet there is really only one bones-playing style within the Irish tradition. A variety of approaches to the striking of the bodhrán skin using a stick, knuckles or thumb has probably always characterised the playing of the Irish frame-drum and while we are beginning to witness the development of distinct modern styles of playing that instrument the same cannot be said of the bones. Yet as individual bones players continue to shape their own musical gestures within the slowly broadening sweep of a homogeneous style, diversification becomes inevitable and new distinct styles will emerge. (MEM)

See idiophone; wood block.

**bothy ballads.** A unique body of songs composed mainly in the farming areas of the north-east of Scotland between 1830 and 1890 and perhaps up to the First World War. They were precisely defined by the Aberdeenshire folk-song collector Gavin Greig (1856–1914) as follows: 'We apply the term . . . to that kind of ditty which recounts the experiences of a farm-servant while fulfilling his half-yearly engagements at some "toon" [farm unit]. Its form is largely stereotyped. It deals mainly in characterisations . . . the farm and the farmer, fellow servants, male and female, the horses, the work, and sometimes the food. Nor is this always done "in complimental mood". The references to the master especially are often quite caustic. Sometimes the food forms matter of sinister comment, in which case the cook or the housekeeper may get dragged in. Fellow servants of the male sex are usually handled by the singer in a kindly enough way. The treatment of the female members of the establishment varies a good deal. As a rule it does not err on the side of chivalry, sometimes the allusions may be altered or purged by those who would seek to introduce the ditties to modern readers or hearers.'

The anomaly about the term 'bothy ballad' is that, in the north-east of Scotland, farm workers were rarely housed in separate self-catering units – the 'bothy' system – but instead were given food, heat and light in the farm kitchen, retiring to primitive quarters (often just a loft above the horses), known as the 'chaumer', to sleep. This was known as the chaumer or 'kitchie' system, and paradoxically gave rise to the songs known as bothy ballads (for in the farms outside the north-east, where self-catering barracks or bothies were the rule, bothy ballads were scarce). Furthermore, the derivation of the word, 'bothy', is itself unclear. The Gaelic for such a primitive hut or outhouse is indeed 'bothán', but this has been pronounced without the 'th' being sounded ('bo-han') for centuries. It may derive from an Old English root from which comes the still-used word, 'booth' – as, for example, a fisherman's hut.

The term 'bothy ballad' is not recorded until the turn of the nineteenth century, and appears first referring to the sort of song sung by the lower class of men such as travellers and navvies. Early collectors used the term 'ploughman songs'. The agricultural revolution had transformed north-east farming. The old, democratic run-rig system was changed by creating larger farm units – the 'ferm touns', run by a farmer, his family, and if needed, hired labour known as 'farm servants'. These servants were young men and women from the neighbouring 'cottar' families; they had the ambition of owning or renting a farm of their own in turn, and expected kindly relations from their employers. When some of the bigger farmers began to ape the gentry, or were hit by hard times, the treatment of their workers could be harsh, and this could give rise to much resentment. Servants were hired for a six-month fee, usually at hiring fairs in the larger country towns. It was the heyday of the skilled horsemen, who worked the two-horse plough with pride, and regarded themselves as an élite. Many 'In Praise of Ploughmen' songs were the result. The vast majority of bothy ballads were composed and sung for pure entertainment – more often than not in the farmhouse itself where the farmers and their families would often join in with gusto. There was a particularly rich seam of comic songs, some very old such as (*c.* 1700) 'The Muckin' o' Geordie's Byre'. One important exponent at the turn of the century was George Bruce Thomson, a failed medical student and probable drug addict, who composed a number of songs in the Irish comic song tradition such as 'MacFarlan o' the Sprotts o' Burnieboosie' (a comic wooing song) which remain extremely popular to this day.

Only some fifty of the old bothy ballads have survived, many fragmentary, and are mostly recorded in the Greig-Duncan Folk Song Collection. The songs were extremely occasional in form, and, unless very catchy, or the singers migrated outside their farm area, they did not survive. Probably many thousands had a brief mayfly existence, and will never now be known. During the early twentieth century migration from the countryside to the towns increased, and performers appeared on the scene to entertain such exiles with music hall or concert hall songs – largely comic – celebrating the old country way of life. There were no references, of course, to the harshness and misery that had been part of life on the ferm touns, and this very popular, sanitised form of nostalgic comic song was promoted by concert performers such as George Morris and Will Kemp. They were also issued as gramophone recordings, and later broadcast on early radio. Soon not even the farms and chaumers were without a wind-up gramophone and weekly purchases of such recordings. Morris and Kemp, however, did sing half a dozen of the old songs, and it is only these few which have survived to the present day.

The concert-hall bothy ballad continues to thrive, and retains a vibrant contemporary writing and performing tradition. Many of the older songs were set to Gaelic-style airs. The still-popular 'Drumdelgie' was set to 'The Irish Jaunting Car', for example, and the 1843 'Bogie's Bonny Belle' was carried by the haunting air known as 'Eilean A' Cheo'. The Highlands of Scotland border the north-east, and may well have been the source, but the nineteenth century, which saw the rise of the bothy ballad, was also the time of massive construction in the north-east – roads, canals, railways – which brought in floods of migrant workers, especially Irish navvies. Unlike in other parts of the country, these navvies lived within the local communities where they mixed well (often settling) and it seems likely that the already musical north-east folk rapidly absorbed and took over Irish and other tunes and songs. (IAO)

**Bothy Band.** Formed in 1974, originally named Seachtair and assembled to play at a Gael-Linn sponsored show in Dublin. Original line-up consisted of Donal Lunny (bouzouki, guitar, bodhrán), Mícheál Ó Domhnaill (guitar, vocals), Tríona Ní Dhómhnaill (clavinet, vocals), Matt Molloy (flute, whistle), Paddy Keenan (uilleann pipes), Tony McMahon (accordion) and Paddy Glackin (fiddle). Without Glackin and McMahon the group became the Bothy Band, fancifully named after the bothies – migrant workers' huts in Scotland. Tommy Peoples (fiddle) from St Johnston, Co. Donegal, then joined; he had already played with Tríona in Brittany with Liam Weldon and the band 1691. The Bothy Band took tunes from mostly Irish, but also Scots sources, including songs in Scots Gaelic. Some of its Irish material had been learned from Neillí Ní Dhomhnaill in Rannafast. The band's first album, *The Bothy Band*, was recorded in 1975 for the Mulligan label, set up by Donal Lunny. Crisp powerful arrangement with a strong, unique group sound was their hallmark. They signed to Polydor for UK releases and played London's High Wycombe Town Hall late in 1975 to rapturous acclaim, so too the Cambridge Folk Festival in the summer of 1976 after which Kevin Bourke replaced Tommy Peoples. Their second album, *Old Hag You Have Killed Me*, was recorded in Wales, *Out of the Wind, Into the Sun* and *After Hours* were recorded live in Paris in 1978. The band disbanded in 1979 after appearing at Ballysodare Folk Festival in Co. Sligo. Paddy Keenan went on to play with Paddy Glackin on the album *Doublin*. Tríona went to the USA where she settled in Chapel Hill, North Carolina and formed Touchstone with Zan McCloud, Mark Roberts and Claudine Lnagille, later joined by Skip Parente. Mícheál and Kevin played together and recorded *Promenade* and *Portland* and Mícheál formed

Nightnoise with Billy Oskay; later Tríona and jazz flute player Brian Dunning joined. Burke recorded the album *Up Close* and joined Patrick Street and also formed his own band Open House. Lunny rejoined Planxty and later formed Moving Hearts. Molloy joined the Chieftains. (JOO)

**Boullier, Nigel and Dianna.** (Banjo/fiddle and fiddle). From Bangor, Co. Down, they learnt from local fiddlers and other musicians at sessions in Comber and Baloo House. Style and aesthetic draws on the music of elusive Shrigley fiddler Jackie Donnan, a meticulous archivist, with an extensive repertoire of Co. Down dance music. Their playing is influenced too by playing all over the island, particularly in Co. Clare. Dianna has written *Exploring Irish Music and Dance* (1998), an introduction to traditional music and instruments.

**bouzouki.** A typical long-neck lute with its original form dating to 3,000 BC, developed in Turkey as the 'saz' or 'baghalma'. It was adapted by the Greeks to become the heartbeat of the café/opium-den/brothel Greek Rembetika blues-style music which enjoyed edge-of-life popularity in seaports around the turn of the twentieth century. Polite society shunned it, composer Mikis Theodorakis rehabilitated its image with the soundtrack for the film *Zorba the Greek*. This, concurrent with the end of dictatorship in Greece in the 1970s, restored cultural significance to the 'music of the people', giving it identity in the café and orchestral music now familiar to millions of tourists. Originally with three double sets of strings, it progressed to four in the early 1950s. It was brought to Irish music in the mid-'60s by multi-instrumentalist Johnny Moynihan who played with Sweeny's Men, Planxty and De Dannan.

*Irish bouzouki*. The original Greek bouzouki has a teardrop-shaped, half-melon profile body and a long neck, strings tuned CFAD', but it was nativised by its pioneering Irish proponents Andy Irvine, Donal Lunny and Alec Finn, and now has four double, guitar-length, metal strings, and a more easily managed, flat back. Strings are tuned as the first four strings on guitar – there may be up to twenty-six fixed frets for forming the notes. Playing is, as guitar, melody picked with a plectrum, and/or strummed or plucked chords. Used mostly for accompaniment it is tuned GDAD and ADAD.

Irish bouzouki (EDI)

**bow.** Used to sound notes on the fiddle, it is constructed from horsehair stretched from end to end of a piece of light wood. It is used to sound fiddle strings by being pulled and pushed at right angles across them (sideways motion causes squeaking). Horsehair's microscopic structure of overlapping 'teeth' alternately pulls and releases the string, this 'dynamic tension' causing production of a note related to the length, thickness and tension of the string. The application of 'rosin' causes the bow to act in the same way in the reverse direction too. The pitch of the note played is not affected by the speed of bowing. White horsehair is favoured in the western world, but Hungarian and other fiddlers can be seen with dark bows. Older bows were arch-shaped, Baroque bows were almost horizontal, modern bows have an upward bend at the ends to distribute tension evenly and have a 'frog' mechanism at the handling end to adjust the hair tension. The bow is first depicted and written about in the tenth century and is assumed to have originated in Arabic countries in conjunction with horse-cultures. Some bowed zithers – for example in Korea – are sounded with a simple stick of fuschia wood.

See fiddle.

**box.** An abbreviation for 'squeezebox', the colloquial generic name for all such instruments, this coming from the push and pull action of accordions, melodeons and concertinas. Another such colloquial term is the use of 'melodeon' to denote all accordions, this probably stemming from the folk memory of the instrument originally popular here up until the 1930s.

See accordion; concertina; free reed; harmonica.

**Boyce, Jackie.** Singer, piper, instrument maker. From Comber, Co. Down, his background is bands, wherein his father's five brothers played Scottish pipes. His grandmother played melodeon and sang; their's was a céilí house. Meeting John Flanagan of Corofin sharpened an interest in singing; 1960s–70s sessions in the Castle Inn, Baloo House and Ma Boyce's developing his talent, and hearing Joe Holmes and Len Graham led him to collect local songs and Napoleonic ballads. His style is 'Ulster', and his (and Sinéad Cahir's) vilification through the partial, stylistic preferences of fleadh judges only reinforces this. He makes bagpipe, uilleann pipe and Northumbrian pipe bags and bellows, exporting them all over the world.

**Boys of the Lough.** Formed in 1967 by Robin Morton (song, concertina, bodhrán), Cathal McConnell (song, flute, whistle), and Tommy Gunn (song, fiddle, bones), the name was adopted for a television recording. Gunn left early in the band's history, and in 1968 Morton and McConnell joined with Shetland fiddler Aly Bain, and Mike Whelans who in 1972 was replaced by Dick Gaughan. In 1973 multi-strings instrumentalist Dave Richardson replaced Gaughan, Morton's place was taken by Tich Richardson in 1979, the latter's tragic death bringing in, in 1985, Rathcoole (Co. Dublin) piper and singer Christy O'Leary (pipes, song). Cork guitarist/pianist John Coakley joined in the late 1980s, Chris Newman (guitar) also played with the band, and currently Breandán Begley (accordion, song) is a member. The group began with a local, regional Irish ethos, expanded to incorporate Scottish music, and currently are based more in Irish material. But McConnell's persona continues to define their ethos, his attitude to meaning in song, accent and repertoire a constant in three decades of professional playing.

**Bradshaw, Harry.** (1947–  ). Radio producer, researcher, record producer. Born Bray, Co. Wicklow. In 1965 took up employment in recording at Dublin's Eamon Andrews Studios, then at film and sound work, while taking night classes in telecommunications and electronics. He joined RTÉ in 1968, where he did sound for Mícheál Ó Súilleabháin's early RTÉ recordings, and Noirín Ní Riain's 1978 *Seinn Aililiú*. Associated with *The Long Note*, he became its producer in 1978, in this series devoting time to documentary features, such as that on nineteenth-century uilleann piper and composer, Johnny Patterson. He also produced *Folkland, Music of the People* and – his best-known achievement – *The Irish Phonograph* series, featuring 78 rpm recordings from the 1920s and '30s and presented by Nicholas Carolan. The two also collaborated on the 1986 *John McKenna – His Original Recordings*. His 1988 *Bunch of Keys* has the contents of nine acetate discs of uilleann piper Johnny Doran recorded in 1947; the 1990 *Gravel Walks* has Donegal fiddler Mickey Doherty. Both were published by Comhairle Bhéaloideas Éireann. In 1989 he started his own label Viva Voce to market re-mastered 78s, the *James Morrison – The Professor*, fiddle album was his first release, next was *Fluters of Old Erin*, and *Michael Coleman – 1891–1945*. Currently he works half time on a joint RTÉ/ITMA project which has transferred and catalogued the bulk of RTÉ radio's archive tape into a 300-CD catalogue designed to make the material easily accessible to the public. He is employed also by the 'Ceol' commercial music-heritage project in Smithfield, Dublin.

**brass fiddle.** See fiddle, tin/brass.

**Breathnach, Breandán.** (1912–85). Uilleann piper, collector, publisher, writer and organiser. Born 1912 in the Liberties, Dublin, his father, Pádraig Walsh, was a silk weaver. The single most important activist in Irish traditional music in the twentieth century, he became interested in highland pipes in his youth, and subsequently, through his acquaintance with the Potts family of the Coombe, took up the uilleann pipes. He worked as a civil servant and devoted his leisure hours to music. Out of the habit of noting down tunes from musicians, his life's work gradually evolved, and motivated by the need to identify collected tunes, he began an examination of all available collections. He invented an index system which allowed him to assign a unique code to any tune, and using this, he classified and ordered a huge body of Irish traditional dance music. In this, he was the first person ever to be in a position to realise the sheer extent of the material, and his own estimate, in the early 1980s, was that the Irish tradition included over 7,000 individual dance tunes. By identifying duplicates and variants he could find the earliest occurrences of tunes and trace their history through printed and manuscript collections and recordings. The index which he made of his material enabled him to identify unpublished items, and those that differed substantially from previously published versions. Collections of this material, starting in 1963, have been published in four volumes as *Ceol Rince na hÉireann*.

Such work began as a private hobby, but awareness of its importance saw him seconded from his post in the Department of Agriculture to the Department of Education where he could devote all his time to it: 'moving from pigs to jigs' as he put it. His project was then transferred to the Department of Irish Folklore in UCD. While engaged himself in the study of the dance music, he initiated a pilot scheme to send song collectors around the country to assess the extent of traditional song material still to be found. This resulted in the recording of the largest body of traditional songs ever collected in Ireland.

Prior to the publication of *Ceol Rince*, he initiated a tune-sheet *Tacar Port*, and in 1963 he started the magazine *Ceol,* which appeared intermittently until his death. It too usually carried transcriptions of music or songs from important sources. In 1971 he published *Folk Music and Dances of Ireland,* a handbook of Irish music with accompanying cassette, and started a recording label, Spól, which issued one EP of traditional music and one of a recording of the correct Cois Fharraige pronunciation of Irish. In 1968 he was instrumental in founding Na Píobairí Uilleann, of which he was chairman until his death, and in 1971, with Hugh Shields, Tom Munnelly and others, he founded the Folk Music Society of Ireland. Anticipating the explosion of interest which occurred in the 1980s, in 1978 or thereabouts he was enthusiastic about initiating set dancing in the Na Píobairí Uilleann premises at Essex Street in Dublin. In tandem with this activity he collected, lectured and contributed articles to a variety of publications, including the *Irish Times*, *An Píobaire* and *Soundpost*, with *Ceol* becoming a standard guide through the currents and eddies of the traditional music revival in the 1960s and '70s. His 1983 booklet *Dancing in Ireland* remains the outstanding reference-point in traditional dance, and his most thorough document on Irish music, *Ceol agus Rince na hÉireann*, was published posthumously in 1989.

Trenchant, outspoken criticism of what he regarded as phoney, shallow or inferior was a regular feature of such pieces, along with generous praise for anything he regarded as 'sound'; in everything he wrote he was direct, informative and often witty. The subjects he covered were as diverse as the use of notation in the transmission of Irish music, a comprehensive index of the tunes of Jackson the eighteenth-century Limerick piper and the works of Captain Francis O'Neill. His death in 1985 deprived his associates and the music world of an entertaining companion, a tireless organiser and facilitator and a brilliant scholar who was utterly generous in sharing his huge knowledge of Irish music. 'Sharing' was central to him – illustrated contrarily by his anecdote of the piper who called for his pipes upon his death-bed and, taking out the reeds, bit and destroyed them.

Breathnach inspired and encouraged many

others. The ground-breaking studies of Willie Clancy and Patsy Touhey and the first ever collections of Irish set-dances owe much to him, and many projects that he had envisaged or was promoting before his death have since been brought to completion by his associates. Such was the establishment of the Irish Traditional Music Archive, the publication of books *Ceol Rince na hÉireann IV*, *The Music of Johnny O'Leary*, the Goodman collection, the songs of Tom Lenihan, the *Séamus Ennis Tutor* and the *Music of Séamus Ennis*.

Listening to younger pipers, and pondering the lineage of their tunes or style, Breandán Breathnach might typically assess that the music – 'the thing' – would be 'safe for another sixty years'. With some 800 pipers playing in 1998, largely as a result of his insight, determination and promotion activity, 'the thing' has guaranteed secure passage well into its next millennium. (TEM)

See *Ceol Rince na hÉireann*; Na Píobairí Uilleann.

**Breathnach, Máire.** (1956– ). Fiddle, viola, whistle, keyboard, singer and composer. Born in Dublin to bilingual parents she was reared in a home with a strong music ethos. At the age of six she began taking violin lessons at the School of Music, and attendance at the all-Irish Scoil Mhuire placed her in a milieu of confident traditional players and group formation. She played with Cormac Breathnach and Niall Ó Callanáin as Meristem at the end of the 1980s, and a career break in 1990 after nine years lecturing at the College of Music led her to play and record with Mary Black, Sharon Shannon, Christy Moore, Donal Lunny, Dolores Keane, Ronnie Drew, Bill Whelan and for *Riverdance*. She recorded *Angels Candles* in 1993, *Voyage of Bran* in 1994 and *Celtic Lovers* in 1996. Mythically themed, these involve her own airs and dance tunes and utilise traditional instruments. Her material has been recorded by other players and she has made TV and radio signatures, much film and theatre music, some involving orchestra. This includes *In the Name of the Father* and *Rob Roy*.

**Brian Ború bagpipes.**
See bagpipes.

***Bringing It All Back Home.*** A television series in five one-hour parts, commissioned by the BBC in association with RTÉ in 1990, transmitted in 1991. Its thesis is that Irish traditional music influenced American rock, country and folk musics. This the programme established by tracing early emigration from Ireland to the USA. It also documented the ongoing influence of those genres on Irish music from the earliest migrations of the Irish in the eighteenth century to America and to Britain. Primarily a musical exploration, the programme is performance-driven, involving some seventy musicians, and edited down from as many hours of recording. It included Appalachian fiddler Ricky Skaggs playing with Paddy Glackin; De Dannan on stage with a New York Klezmer band; piper Davey Spillane and the Everly Brothers; Mary Black and Dolores Keane singing with Emmylou Harris; and an interview with the *avant garde* American composer John Cage about his work *Roaratorio* which used Irish traditional musicians. A one-hour cut, *Irish Music and America – A Musical Migration*, was broadcast in the US in 1994. An album, also entitled *Bringing It All Back Home*, contains selections from the series and a book of the same name by Nuala O'Connor was issued in 1991 by BBC Enterprises.

See King, Philip; O'Connor, Nuala.

**Brittany.** The peninsula of the French land-mass which juts out into the Atlantic with the bay of Biscay on its southern shores, the English channel to the north. Superficially, Brittany shares many of the social values, language and organisational structures of the rest of France (itself a highly diverse entity) but there are quite fundamental cultural differences which set it apart from France *per se*, most importantly the Breton language and the folk-music tradition within Brittany itself. Its most significant cultural division is based on the linguistic divide. In Basse Bretagne, Breton, a Celtic language is still spoken together with French. In Haute Bretagne, French, together with Gallo, is spoken. (Gallo is a Romance language akin to French, often described as a 'rural patois'.) The Breton language is indigenous only to the area known as Basse Bretagne but its continuing use is close to the hearts of many cultural activists throughout Brittany.

Although France is generally rich in different regional forms of traditional music, it is arguably only in Brittany that music is not a thing of folklore and remains, or has increasingly become, a popular part of everyday social activity. Traditional dance music, both vocal and instrumental, and the circle dance in the context of the festou noz (lit. 'night dances') are the most popular representations of Pan-Breton identity today.

*historical perspective.* Up until the 1940s vocal music was by far the most common accompaniment to dancing at any social gathering in Brittany, be it a *pardon* (pattern), a wedding, harvest festival or the more intimate context of a *veillée* or musical evening. Any form of ceremonial parade – notably a wedding procession – was usually led by one or two musicians. In Basse Bretagne this may have been the bombarde/biniou koz (old bagpipe) combination, a clarinet (Treujenn-gaol) or on rare occasions a fiddler. In Haute Bretagne the vielle or hurdy-gurdy was more likely. Bombarde and biniou duets, the oldest version of the *couple sonneurs*, are still in demand for weddings. Music and dance competitions provide targets of achievement and standards, and are popular both with the public and among musicians themselves. In all there are more than seventy each year, many of them annual events since 1949.

Younger people now know more traditional dances than the older generation. This is because of changes in lifestyle, greater ease of communication and a comparatively new perception of Breton music as a genre in itself. Folk-dance classes are held in practically every community in Brittany, teaching a pan-Breton repertoire of dances. They cater for an ever-increasing fest-noz-going public; this in turn encourages younger musicians. They also cater for older Bretons who had never before the opportunity to learn different dance steps from outside their own locality.

*singing for dancers.* Kan ha Diskan and other vocal *chant à repondre* are without doubt the basis of Breton traditional music. Still relatively popular, though under some pressure, this older way of leading the dance in Basse Bretagne and Haute Bretagne – by singing *rondes* or *dans-tro* for dancers – takes several different forms. Most Breton dances are originally intended to be danced in a ring, usually in a clockwise direction leading to the left. *Kan ha diskan* (literally singer and descant or counter-singer), functions as a verse/echo discourse. The lead singer is called the *kaner* and the singer (or sometimes singers) who reply to his or her refrain is/are called the *diskaner(s)*. The diskaner sings the *response chevauche* to the kaner, this means that s/he overlaps on the last phrase, which could be as little as one word. S/he sings the same words as the kaner, but may well improvise on the melody – good improvisations are usually mutually acknowledged. There are no breaks in the song, it is continually pushed forward with impressive momentum. The tunes used may be attractive, but they also have a distinctly functional role related to the dance itself.

There is a body of well-known tunes; dancers will recognise the genre of the dance immediately from the prelude which is a slow version of the dance tune played to invite people on to the floor. It has no rhythmic indicators and is an excellent vehicle for vocal improvisation. In times past most songs and tunes in the suite of dances were given names, just as in Ireland, but in recent decades musicians will describe their tunes as sets of a particular dance-genre only.

The contents of Kan ha Diskan are generally folk tales about market days, errant tailors and sailors and the like, but they can also be local social commentaries. Most singers of Kan ha Diskan are men, but a new generation of women is increasingly emerging – the legendary singers Soeurs Goadec, who were still active in the early 1980s, set a strong precedent for female Kan ha Diskan. Kan ha Diskan is performed in the Breton language and only with the genres which originate in the area known as Les Monts D'Arre.

*Kan ha Diskan and language activism.* Recent compositions tend to be mostly instrumental. This indicates a decline in spoken Breton in the Basse Bretagne region and is a cause of concern among Breton language activists. There are considerably more musicians than singers, the musicians being younger. In general the younger singers of Kan ha Diskan are committed Breton language activists. Their enthusiastic and energetic efforts mean that Kan ha Diskan is being taught to young people in *Diwan* schools (where the Breton language is the teaching medium), and the bi-lingual classes which are found in some schools in the private and public sector of L'Education Nationale.

*instrumental music.* Tunes are a mixture of recently composed and older melodies. All groups will play music from Basse Bretagne for the dancers, and stick to the Kan ha Diskan formula, emulating the power and drive of the voices. They are increasingly common at festou noz, this causing some chagrin; they have largely replaced the sonneurs and singers. This trend goes back to the 1960s and the influence of Alan Stivell. It is also influenced by groups from the other 'celtic' countries.

*instrumental style.* An understanding of the aesthetic values of the vocal tradition is regarded as essential to the ability to play instrumental dance music with authenticity and competence. The strident timbre of the voices and the use of a traditional vibrato known as a *chevrement* (goat-like sound) are essential guidelines for instrumentalists who wish their style to be 'traditional'. Musicians who speak the Breton language are favoured by language activists over those who do not. Players make a distinction between the purely instrumental tune repertoire (*airs à sonner*) and the older vocal repertoire (*airs à chanter*) even though these dance songs are also played as purely instrumental pieces.

*bombarde and biniou.* The word *sonneur* is used essentially for players of the bombarde and biniou koz – the *couple sonneurs* being the ultimate traditional dance musical ensemble in Brittany. The bombarde and biniou koz (old bagpipe) are the oldest form of musical accompaniment for the dance in Brittany. Some form of bombarde and biniou combination was in use in most parts of continental Europe until the seventeenth century at least, but Brittany has became a repository for it. The bombarde is a pastoral shawm which has a range of essentially two octaves and the biniou is a one-droned bagpipe. Both have a strident high-pitched sound and are ideal for leading the dance in outdoor situations, the bombarde taking the role of the kaner and the biniou the diskaner. Although the biniou plays continuously during the dance, it is always the bombarde player who introduces the melody and leads the refrain. In the 1950s the biniou braz (big biniou) or Scottish bagpipes (first introduced in early 1900s) supplanted the smaller instrument for a while, but this trend has been reversed in recent years with the bagpipes finding a permanent home with the *bagadou*, a typically Breton form of the pipe band founded in the 1950s.

*popular dance forms.* During the 1970s and '80s, individual researchers such as Jean-Michel Guilcher and organisations such as Les Cercles Celtiques and Dastum comprehensively documented well over a thousand regional dance forms, including local variants of widely popular dances. This verifies that up to and including the immediate post-war years most people in any given locality knew only one set of movements and steps, those of the local traditional dance. This does not apply to imported dances from metropolitan France and elsewhere, where people followed the fashions of their youth.

Although known 'good' dancers introduce variations on the theme, the general form of the *dans* (*tro* or *ronde*, literally dancing in a ring or round) is very old, and in many cases goes back to at least medieval times. There is much evidence to suggest that Breton traditional dances were adopted by the French court from the early middle ages until at least the reign of Louis IV. This challenges the idea that peasant dances are but impoverished versions of courtly dances.

During the past thirty years of resurgence in traditional music, certain forms have attained more widespread popularity. These are mostly those forms that were still in popular use up until the 1970s, and were the main sources of tune repertoire for both the bagadou (bombarde and bagpipe bands) and Celtic folk revivalists like Alan Stivell.

With the exception of key-note events to celebrate one particular dance form, or a truly local event, six dance types dominate in the average fest noz. These may differ in emphases or frequency of performance depending on whether the event is held in the Haute Bretagne or Basse Bretagne regions, but they are generally present at the majority of festou noz. These include the *suite gavotte*, the *suite plinn*, the *ronde Loudeac*, the *an dro* and *landdé*. All Breton dances are originally intended to be danced in a ring, but due to the huge numbers of people who attend the contemporary festou noz, space becomes a problem, and the dancers often form a twisting serpent. In addition, modern practice often ignores the older social etiquette of male-female balance.

All of the traditional dances currently popular in today's pan-Breton festou noz were originally regional or highly localised dance genres.

*modern trends.* Since the early days of the 1970s with the influence of Alan Stivel and the plethora of Irish groups visiting Brittany, Breton music has undergone some major changes in performance and treatment of the music. Every other form of music has flirted with the traditional 'raw bar' and many traditional musicians have in their turn flirted with other musical forms. But the most significant and tangible change is the group phenomenon, and the introduction of new instruments to the pool. Notable among these is the present use of the simple-system wooden flute – introduced from Irish traditional music. Brittany now has a number of virtuoso players such as Jean Michel Veillion, Herve Guillou, Stefan Morvan and Jean Luc Thomas. (DEW)

See bagad; bombarde; fest noz.

**broadsheet.** A single sheet of paper upon one side of which was a printed ballad – tales of the famous, war news, comic verse, political and satirical song, dramatic tales of crimes and trials in verse, the confessions of the condemned, last words to a loved one before execution, statements of being wronged or of innocence. These were sometimes fixed to walls of pubs, homes or workplaces. Sedentary occupations like weaving were associated with ballad broadsheets – they could be pinned or pasted up on or opposite a loom. Walls of country houses in Britain have been found to have as many as twenty layers of them; singer Eugene Judge from Garrison, Co. Fermanagh (born *c.* 1910), recalled his mother placing broadsheets on the bedroom walls to encourage her children to learn songs. The printer was often also the publisher, the sheets were sold in bulk to street pedlars – who may have done a round in rural areas – and to singer-sellers ('patterers') who might also sell through performing in the pubs, at fairs or in the street. The writers might be unlettered and professional, or sometimes

Irish ballad sellers (Carraig Books)

students in need of funds. From the eighteenth century comes a broadsheet of a hanging tale 'The Night before Larry was Stretched' – this was constantly reprinted over 200 years:

> The night before Larry was stretched
> The boys they all paid him a visit
> A bait in their sacks too they fetched
> They sweated their duds till they riz it
> For Larry was ever the lad
> When a boy was condemned to the squeezer
> Would fence all the duds that he had
> To help a poor friend in the squeezer

Another popular broadsheet song was 'The Rakes of Mallow' (also played as a single reel):

> Spending faster than it comes
> Beating waiters, bailiffs, duns
> Bacchus's true begotten sons
> Live the Rakes of Mallow

Broadsheets were known too as 'broadsides', this denoting the fact that they were printed on one side only; they might also be known as 'slip ballads', on account of the long, thin piece of paper upon which they were presented.

*history*. Broadside ballads were sold all over Europe – in Germany, France, Switzerland, Italy etc. They appeared in England in the early sixteenth century and their importation to Ireland in 1593 is referred to in an edict from Dublin Castle in relation to 'suspicious cargoes reaching Ireland by sea' (Shields, 1993). In Britain statistics show colossal sales – in 1849 the Rush and Manning murder ballads each sold 2.5 million copies, the 1840 'Courvoisier' and 'Greenacre' examples sold 1.65 million, and the earlier, 1828, Maria Marten piece sold 1.16 million. Late seventeenth-century London had more than 250 ballad publishers (Chappell, *Ballad Society*, vol. 2, pt. 1, 1872). Laws against them dating to 1543 relate to politico-religious orientation. Ballads are regarded as having come to maturity in the late seventeenth and early eighteenth centuries, belonging 'to the heroic or patriarchal age of capitalism, where every apprentice could aspire ... to be the Lord Mayor of London, and there was still little social distinction between wage-earner, shopkeeper, merchant and craftsman' (De Sola Pinto and Rodway, 1965). Their sales rose with the mechanisation of labour and mass production, they declined with the passing away of street, tavern and fair-day culture. They were an important focus of political agitation by the United Irish movement at the end of the eighteenth century. They were weakened by the new police forces' implementation of vagrancy laws after 1829; their journalistic function was challenged by competition from the rise of the press after 1855 when stamp duty charges were abolished, and their entertainment value was over-ridden by the rise of the music hall. Broadsheet ballads fulfilled journalistic, entertainment, popular fiction and religious and moralistic roles. They tended to be comic, realistic and unheroic. Their printing in Dublin is documented from 1571. They included already well-known ballads and popular song, and more topical new material that was written by scribes hired by the printers.

*language and style*. In Ireland the broadsheet songs were for the most part in the English language. Their format, its language and content were disliked by the Gaelic poets who, while possibly seeing in them a challenge both to their own art, and their occupation, like some English-language ballad singers in Ireland today, considered the printed word on a page to be cold and lifeless (Shields, 1995). By the end of the eighteenth century Irish forms of song – such as aisling poetry – were appearing in widely sold broadsheets. Hedge school teachers were often the authors of this material which was strongly nationalistic. Their songs were of the lavish, effusive eulogies which recruited classical mythology as a source of imagery. These songs often brought politics to the urban and rural lower classes and confirmed political identity in an age before popular newspapers, but the older songs – sometimes adjusted for local topicality – were frequently more popular. In his 1875 pamphlet 'Irish Street Ballads', James Hand speaks of a million copies of one edition being sold. Hundreds of new songs appeared in print each year; 20 per cent to 40 per cent of them were political (Zimmerman, 1967). The ballads were sold everywhere that crowds gathered:

> The announcement of a fair, a race or an election would call them to the roads, with a sheaf of ballads rolled in their hat or in the tail of their coat.

The scene painted is one of great bustle, and travel writers of the period were impressed:

> On these and similar occasions of popular excitement in Ireland the most remarkable objects are the ballad singers, who are in no country so numerous as here. In Kilkenny there were literally twice as many ballad-singers as lamp-posts standing in the street. Their usual stand is in the gutter which separates the footpath on which the foot-passengers walk from the carriage-way; and in this kennel they are perpetually strolling up and down. They are generally provided with a number of printed copies of the ballads which they sing, and their principal employment consists in the sale of these songs, which they are continually waving in the air, with a peculiar and stereotyped motion of the hand. ... Crowds of poor people, beggars and rabble, perseveringly swarm around them, follow them step by step, and listen to them with a degree of eagerness which may partly be attributed to the fact that the singers proclaim their own misfortune, which they have turned into verse, but still more to the great delight which the Irish take in music and singing, and in every thing new that passes in the streets. (Kohl, 1844, from Zimmerman, 1967)

The ballad singers and the broadside trade remained popular until the 1880s by which time they had been eclipsed by newspapers, and were being undermined in Ireland by other entertainment media such as gramophone records (after 1888) and cinema (1896). By the end of World War I they were scarce, but still around. They continued to be manufactured by provincial printers for sale at fairs and other gatherings until the late 1950s and some Dubliners will recall a seller of broadsheets whose stand was outside the Adelphi cinema in Middle Abbey Street until the early 1960s. In more recent times, broadsheet series and individual song sheets have been published by enthusiasts, but only in the context of the late-twentieth-century specialised singers' 'community'.

Ref. Leslie Shepard, *The Broadside Ballad* (1962, 1978).

**broadside.** See broadsheet.

**Brock, Paul.** (1944– ). Accordion, melodeon. Born in Athlone, Co. Westmeath, his parents encouraged him in music, and by the early 1950s he was playing a single-row melodeon, inspired by visits as a boy to his uncle's radio/music shop. Records (78s) and wireless programmes such as *Ceolta Tíre*, *As I Roved Out* and *A Job of Journeywork* were influential, complementing the strong Irish music tradition of the midland counties that had hosted the birth of CCÉ, the first of the All-Ireland music gatherings, and the second such fleadh at Athlone in 1953. Fiddler Frank Dolphin, originally from Ballisodare, Co. Sligo taught him his early repertoire and technique, and visits to his aunt's home in west Clare grounded Paul in Clare music too. He won All-Irelands in the latter half of the 1950s and was Hohner National Senior Champion also in 1960. Through the 1960s and 1970s he mastered the single-row, two-row, three-row and five-row button accordions, and his collaborations with Frankie Gavin resulted in their 1986 Gael-Linn recording *Omós do Joe Cooley*. In 1989, he formed Moving Cloud along with fiddle players Manus McGuire and Maeve Donnelly. Also featuring Kevin Crawford and Carl Hession, this has produced several recordings: *Moving Cloud* (1989, 1994), *Sound of Stone* (1993) and *Foxglove* (1998). *Mo Cháirdín* is his 1992 solo album.

**Broderick, Vincent.** (1920– ). Flute. Born at Carrowmore, Bullaun, Loughrea, Co. Galway. One of seven children, influenced by his mother Ann, he and brother Peter began playing on flutes given to them by a local priest. By their teens they were accomplished players, performing for house dances in their area, and often in the company of the Rolands, Paddy Carty, Kathleen Harrington, Joe Leary and Joe Cooley. A prolific composer, Vincent has made many tunes, and in 1954 won the All-Ireland flute with one of these – played on a copper-pipe flute he had also made himself. He moved to Dublin in the early 1950s where he played in the Pipers' Club and various bands – including the Kincora and the Eamonn Ceannt. A member of CCÉ, he has taken part in many tours abroad, and he teaches flute and whistle. His collection is published in *The Turoe Stone* (1992).

**Browne, Peter.** (1953– ). Born Ranelagh, Dublin. Uilleann piper, flute and tin whistle player, record producer, broadcaster, writer and lecturer on traditional music. From the age of six he has been a player of traditional music, numbering among his tutors Séamus Ennis, Willie Clancy and Leo Rowsome. He played in groups such as Raftery, 1691 and the Bothy Band and recorded two LPs in the 1980s with Philip King. He has toured extensively abroad, especially in France and Germany. As a broadcaster, he has produced and presented several radio programmes, e.g., *The Long Note*, *Airneán*, *Mo Cheol Thú*, *Ulster Folk*, *Teach a' Chéilidhe* and also a series of documentary tribute programmes on musicians, e.g., Pádraig O'Keeffe, Denis Murphy, Séamus Ennis, Liam Weldon, Tommy Potts, Johnny O'Leary, Paddy Keenan. He has also produced three CDs of rare recordings of traditional musicians from the RTÉ sound archives: *The Sliabh Luachra Fiddle-Master – Pádraig O'Keeffe*, *Denis Murphy – Music from Sliabh Luachra* and *Séamus Ennis – The Return from Fingal*. He has played as a session musician with such people as Mary Black, Paul Brady, Mick Hanley, the Dubliners and also as guest soloist with the RTÉ Concert Orchestra.

**Buckley, Ann.** Researcher, lecturer, writer. Her interests and publications involve history of music in Ireland, medieval studies, iconography, ethnomusicology and the anthropology of music; her main regional interests are Ireland and Central and Eastern Europe. She was the co-ordinator of a project on music in medieval Ireland at the University of Notre Dame, Indiana, she is founder member and co-ordinator of the International Research Group on Music in the Medieval Celtic Regions, is a member of editorial board of the journal, *Music in Art*, and is on the board of advisors at the Research Center for Music Iconography, City University of New York. She has lectured widely in these islands, in Europe, America and Canada, and has broadcast with RTÉ and the BBC World Service among others.

Her publications include: 'What was tiompán?' (*Jahrbuch für musikalische Volksund Völkerkunde* 9, 1977); 'Tiompán in Irish literature' (*Studia Instrumentorum Musicae Popularis* 5, 1977); 'Considerations in a stylistic analysis of uilleann piping' (*Studia Instrumentorum Musicae Popularis* 6, 1979); 'The relevance of literary sources in the archaeological investigation of musical instruments' (*Cambridge Music-archaeological Reports* 6); 'History and archaeology of Jew's harps in Ireland' (*North Munster Antiquaries Journal* 25, 1983); 'Jew's harps in Irish archaeology' (*Second Conference of the ICTM Study Group on Music Archaeology*, ed. Cajsa S. Lund); 'A Viking bow from eleventh-century Dublin' (*Archaeologia Musicalis* 1, 1986); 'Musical instruments from Medieval Dublin' (*The Archaeology of Early Music Cultures*, ed. E. Hickmann and D. Hughes, 1988); 'Musical instruments in Ireland from the ninth to the fourteenth century' (*Irish Musical Studies* 1, ed. G. Gillen and H. White, 1990); 'Harps and lyres on early medieval monuments' (*Harpa* 7 (3), 1992); 'Music in medieval Irish society' (*Harpa* 11 (3), 1993); 'An archaeological survey of musical instruments from medieval Ireland' (*Festschrift Tadeusz Malinowski*, 1995); 'Music as symbolic sound in medieval Irish society' (*Irish Musical Studies* 3, 1995). Dr Buckley is also the author of the forthcoming 'Music in ancient and medieval Ireland', in *A New History of Ireland* 1, gen. ed. Dáibhí Ó Cróinín (RIA, Dublin, Clarendon Press, Oxford). She has contributed entries on tiompán and Celtic chant to *The New Grove Dictionary of Musical Instruments*, and has books on *Music in Medieval Ireland*, and *Folk Music Instruments of Ireland* in progress. She is also guest editor and contributor to a special Irish issue of *Early Music* (May 2000).

**Bunting, Edward.** (1773–1843). An Armagh-born organist who was employed to notate the music played at the 1792 Belfast Harp Festival. There he lived with the McCracken family and associated with many of the members of the United Irish Society who had initiated the event. The purpose of the Harp Festival was to preserve the remnants of the Gaelic harp tradition for posterity. Bunting was so taken by the group of ageing harpers at the festival that he subsequently chose to devote a large proportion of his time to the collection and publication of Irish music. He toured Mayo in 1792 with Richard Kirwan, founder of the Royal Irish Academy, collecting a number of airs. In the same year he also gathered material in the counties Derry and Tyrone, visiting the harper Denis Hempson at his home in Magilligan. Bunting met Arthur O'Neill in Newry late in 1792 and visited Denis Hempson and Donal Black in 1795 or 1796. His first publication appeared in 1796 and contained sixty-six tunes.

Bunting was the first Irish collector that we know of to gather music from musicians 'in the field'. He also had some impressive ideas about publication – planning to print Irish texts with accompanying tunes and English translations. To that end Patrick Lynch, an Irish scholar, accompanied him on his 1802 tour of Connacht. Bunting later employed James Cody to collect both music and texts in Ulster. Bunting's plans to include the Gaelic texts were not successful however, as the 1809 publication contained seventy-seven airs, twenty of which were accompanied by English texts. Also, in making piano arrangements of tunes for publication Bunting provided versions of the tunes that lacked authenticity in relation to their original repertoire. He was aiming his publications at a particular market – the amateur musicians amongst the middle and upper classes. Certainly the printed music would have been of little use to the musically non-literate traditional musicians and harpers who were his sources.

After 1809 Bunting does not appear to have undertaken any major tour or collection. Most of his time was now devoted to arranging tunes he had already collected or that he received from correspondents. His final collection was published in 1840 and contained 151 tunes plus an elaborate introduction. Bunting wished to revise and re-edit his two earlier volumes, but, due to ill health, did not manage to do so. He died on 21 December 1843, and is buried in Mount St Jerome Cemetery in Dublin. (COM)

**Bunting's Manuscripts.** These are part of a collection of private papers and prints which belonged to Edward Bunting (1773–1843) and which are currently preserved in the Library of the Queen's University Belfast. The manuscripts consist of various volumes and unbound sheets containing musical notations and song texts. Besides his manuscripts Bunting is known for his three musical publications.

1. A General Collection of the ANCIENT IRISH MUSIC Containing a variety of Admired Airs never before published and also The Compositions of CONOLON and CAROLAN Collected from the Harpers &c in the different Provinces of IRELAND, and adapted for the Piano-Forte, with a Prefatory Introduction by EDWARD BUNTING (London, Dublin 1796).

2. A General Collection of the Ancient MUSIC OF IRELAND, Arranged for the Piano Forte; some of the most admired MELODIES are adapted for the VOICE, To Poetry chiefly translated from the Original Irish Songs, by Thomas Campbell Esqr. and OTHER eminent POETS: To which is prefixed A Historical & CRITICAL Dissertation on The Egyptian, British and Irish Harp by EDWARD BUNTING. Vol. 1 (London 1809).

3. THE ANCIENT MUSIC OF IRELAND, Arranged for the PIANOFORTE. To which is prefixed A DISSERTATION ON THE IRISH HARP AND HARPERS, including an account of the OLD MELODIES OF IRELAND by EDWARD BUNTING (Dublin 1840).

The Bunting collection was re-discovered in 1907 by Charlotte Milligan Fox who was then secretary of the Irish Folk Song Society. Dr Louis MacRory of Battersea, a grandson of Edward Bunting, entrusted Fox with certain papers which had belonged to his grandfather. On MacRory's recommendation she later retrieved additional papers from Lady Florence Deane, a granddaughter of Edward Bunting who lived in Dublin. Fox used the papers as the basis for a number of articles for the *Journal of the Irish Folk Song Society* and for her book *Annals of the Irish Harpers*. On her death in 1916 Fox bequeathed the Bunting papers to the Library of Queen's University Belfast. The library purchased a further selection of Bunting items from Lady Florence Deane in 1917.

*value of the collection.* The Bunting Manuscripts are an important source of music and lore from the Gaelic Harp music tradition. They provide information on harp structure, tuning, ornamentation, repertoire and playing technique as well as details and stories of the harpers and their lifestyle. Other musical genres are also present in the manuscripts, including Irish traditional music, military and art music, all of which help to provide an insight into the musical life of the time. In addition to this there are also a large number of song texts in both Irish and English. Although the Bunting collection is such a large and important source, very little of the music is readily accessible as only a relatively small number of the tunes can be found in the Bunting publications. There are still hundreds of items which remain unedited in the manuscripts. This perhaps is due to the fact that the Bunting Manuscripts are disorganised and are often only a collection of jumbled loose sheets from different sources and eras. The collection is termed the Bunting 'manuscripts' but there are approximately eighty different handwritings in evidence. Bunting appears to be the common denominator rather than the sole collector: he probably did gather much of the material himself but he was also the person for whom the copyists or collectors worked or to whom correspondents sent their contributions. The extant Bunting Manuscripts are incomplete: approximately half the tunes in the Bunting publications are not found in the manuscripts in draft notation form. As it is highly unlikely that only the tunes in the prints would have been lost it is impossible to quantify the total amount of material missing from the present collection. It is perhaps fanciful to hope that the missing material is still in existence and that it could be rediscovered. Such a discovery would undoubtedly provide further insights into musical life in Ireland in the eighteenth and nineteenth centuries. Ref. *The Ancient Music of Ireland* (Waltons, 1969). (COM)

**Burke, Joe.** (1939– ). Accordion. Born Kilnadeema, Loughrea, Co. Galway, he plays fiddle, pipes and concert flute, as well as being best known for his contribution to the style of playing Irish music on B/C accordion. His mentors were Paddy O'Brien, Kevin Keegan and Joe Cooley, but he has been influenced by the fiddle recordings of Michael Coleman and the playing of Paddy Fahy. Leader of the Leitrim (Co. Galway parish) Céilí Band which won the All-Ireland at the 1959 Fleadh Cheoil, he himself won the senior button accordion title in 1959 and 1960. He recorded the last 78s to be made in Ireland for Gael-Linn in 1959. From 1962 to 1965 he lived in America, playing professionally and regularly with Andy McGann, Catherine Brennan Grant, Larry Redican and Paddy Killoran. During this time he recorded 'A Tribute to Michael Coleman' with Andy McGann and Felix Dolan. On his return to Ireland he played with Seán Maguire, recording *Two Champions* (1971) with Josephine Keegan on piano. His first solo album *Galway's Own Joe Burke* followed in the same year. From 1988 to 1992 he lived again in the US, in St Louis. Other recordings include *Traditional Music of Ireland* (1973) with Charlie Lennon on piano; *The Funny Reel* (1979) with Andy McGann and Felix Doran; *The Tailor's Choice* (1983); *Happy to Meet and Sorry to Part* (1986); *The Leg of the Duck* (1992) and *The Bucks of Oranmore* (1996) with Charlie Lennon on piano. He now lives in his home place in Kilnadeema; he is married to accordion and guitar player Anne Conroy. (MAO)

**Burke, Kevin.** Fiddle. Born in London of Irish parents from Co. Sligo. He was taught first by a classical teacher at the age of eight, but was heavily influenced by parental choice of recordings played in the home – Coleman, Morrison and Killoran. His reputation in traditional music saw him replace Tommy Peoples in the Bothy Band, then with their demise in 1979 he and Mícheál Ó Domhnaill came together to record *Promenade* and *Portland*. He played and recorded with Paul Brady and Andy Irvine, presently he is the mainstay of Patrick Street, also with Irvine, and Arty McGlynn. He has played with Christy Moore and Arlo Guthrie, and his other band Open House mixes music genres – Irish, Appalachian, Central European and Latin-American with outstanding clog-dancer Sandy Silva.

**Burns Library Irish Music Archive.** Boston College, USA. Formed 1990 with materials from private donors, it houses recorded and printed Irish traditional music material. This important archive contains early Irish and Scottish 78s, out-of-print LPs, and US and Irish nineteenth-century sheet music, ballads, sean-nós songs, céilí band and solo instrumental recordings. It is accessible through Boston College online public catalogue (on-site and remote access) which also accesses Irish music items held by the O'Neill Library.

**Butcher, Eddie.** (1900–80). Singer, farm labourer and road worker from Aughil, Magilligan, Co. Derry. The most accomplished of four singing brothers from a singing family in a singing locality, his repertoire exceeded 100 songs, several of which he composed entirely and others in part. His life, singing style and songs have been documented by Hugh Shields in articles in *Ulster Folklife* and *Ceol*, in books *Shamrock Rose and Thistle* and *Narrative Singing in Ireland* and in broadcasts from Dublin and Belfast in the 1960s. These latter made him well known and towards the end of his life it was his delight to be visited by singers, who spent many hours listening, singing and learning. Among those whom he deeply influenced were Len Graham, Frank Harte and Andy Irvine and through them many others. Some of his recordings are still available. They allow us to hear a robust singer, accented in the almost Scottish way of North Derry; a style, deceptively simple, cloaking a voice of some range which is well controlled, and with a seemingly flat delivery which is nevertheless very dramatic. He is recorded on *Adam in Paradise: The Songs of Eddie Butcher*. (JOM)

# C

**Cairde na Cruite.** (lit. 'friends of the harp'). A harping organisation founded in 1960 at the suggestion of Cearbhall Ó Dálaigh (President of Ireland 1974–76). Its aims are to promote interest in the Irish harp through teaching, concerts, publishing arrangements of harp music, and commissioning works from Irish composers. Ó Dálaigh was its first cathaoirleach (chairperson), and Eibhlín Nic Chathailriabhaigh was rúnaí (secretary) for many years. Cáirde runs a harp-hire scheme, organises courses, workshops, and master classes throughout Ireland, and its members have set up harp schools in Derry (1970s) Wexford (1983), Nobber (1991) and Mullingar. Cáirde members adjudicate and teach also at the annual Pan Celtic, Keadue and Granard harp festivals – the society maintains close contact with Scotland and Wales – and play and teach world-wide.

'An Chúirt Chruitireachta' is Cáirde's major international annual summer-school, a residential, week-long course held in June at Termonfeckin, Co. Louth. Directed by Aibhlín McCrann, its workshops and concerts given by Irish and international artists attract students of many nationalities. They study technique, traditional ornamentation, session playing, the wire-strung harp, early harp music, and singing in Irish. Teachers have included Mercedes Bolger, Máire Ní Chathasaigh, Helen Davies, Áine Ní Dhubhghaill, Kim and Tracy Fleming, Kathleen Loughnane and Caitríona and Gráinne Yeats. While in 1963 Cáirde had difficulty in finding the necessary six harpers to perform its commissioned A. J. Potter piece *Teach Lán le Cruitirí*, by 1992 some forty were available for the bicentennial of the Belfast Harpers' Festival. The society has published *The Irish Harp Book* (ed. Sheila Larchet Cuthbert, 1975); *Sounding Harps*, Vols. I–IV (eds. Gráinne Yeats, Mercedes Bolger, 1990–98); *My Gentle Harp* (eds. Mercedes Bolger, Elizabeth Hannon, 1992). (GRY)

**Cairdeas na bhFidléirí.** A development organisation formed in the early 1980s with the aim of promoting the Donegal fiddle tradition. This it addresses through education which includes regular classes for all playing levels at venues throughout Donegal, weekend workshops and master classes, and an annual summer-school in Glencolmcille. An annual gathering is held at Glenties each October, which features classes, lectures and a concert. Cairdeas has produced a series of printed tutors as well as a series of CDs of Donegal fiddlers. Membership is free and open to all interested. The current committee includes fiddlers Rab Cherry, Róisín Harrigan, Caoimhín Mac Aoidh, Mairéad Ní Mhaonaigh, Martin McGinley and Paul O'Shaughnessy. (CAM)

See fiddle, Donegal.

**Caitlín Maude.** (1941–82). Sean-nós singer. Born Casla, Co. Galway, she took an Arts degree at University College, Galway in 1962 and, having spent one year teaching in England, she returned to Ireland and taught in various schools. A talented fiddle-player, playwright, actress and published poet, she is best remembered for her singing in Irish, and was largely responsible for establishing a traditional singers' club, An Bonnán Buí (The Yellow Bittern), in Dublin city. An LP of her singing entitled *Caitlín* was issued by Gael-Linn (Dublin, 1975). She was deeply committed to the Irish language and played a leading part in the civil rights movement in the Connemara Gaeltacht in the late 1960s. (RIU)

**Campbell, Thomas.** (1777–1844). Poet, songwriter, writer, author of 'The Wounded Huzzar' and other parlour style songs which have been assimilated by traditional music. Born in Glasgow, he was a contemporary of Bunting's and an ardent believer in political reform, in 1794 walking to Edinburgh and back to attend a trial of a political reformer, Joseph Gerald. He favoured Poland as a theme in his pursuit of justice, is known for *The*

*Pleasures of Hope* (1799), and his *A Philosophical Survey of the South of Ireland* (1778) is memorable for the line 'Tis distance lends enchantment to the view'. He was three times elected lord rector of Glasgow University – on the last occasion defeating Walter Scott. He retired to Boulogne in 1843 where he died.

**Canada.** Irish settlement began in Newfoundland in the early seventeenth century and spread west to Quebec and Ontario during the nineteenth century. By 1871 the Irish were the second-largest ethnic group (after the French) in the country, and today approximately four million Canadians claim at least partial Irish ancestry.

*instruments.* The fiddle is the predominant 'traditional' instrument across the country, usually accompanied by the piano or, particularly in Western Canada, by the guitar. The button accordion is very popular in Newfoundland and Quebec, and the diatonic harmonica and occasionally, the Jew's harp also feature in some parts. Rhythmic accompaniment may be provided by the use of the spoons, or in the case of French-Canadian fiddlers, by rhythmic patterns with their feet. Tune lilting, known as 'mouth music' in the Maritime provinces, and as 'turlutage' in Quebec, was standard practice when an instrument was unavailable. In the past, traditional instrumental music has been strongly linked with dance traditions, both the step dance and the square dance, but today it is sometimes difficult to find fiddlers or accordionists who are willing and able to accompany dancing.

*repertoire.* The primary influence on the traditional instrumental music repertoires of English and French Canada appears to have come from Irish and Scottish traditions. This is apparent in the tune types and melodies and, in some regions, in the style of performance. Canadian and American tunes also feature prominently. The reel is the most common tune type and there is a tendency to absorb related tune types such as hornpipes, played in 2/4 metre. In French-Canadian and native fiddling styles, it is common practice to cut a beat in the last bar of a phrase, thus propelling the music forward. The playing of slow airs is virtually unknown outside Cape Breton, but waltzes are played throughout the country, often as performance pieces intended for listening rather than dancing. Tunes are usually played in sets of the same tune type and are combined without regard for tune style or origin. Hence a single set may consist of Irish, Scottish, French-Canadian, and American tunes. There are conventions of combining different tune types into a set – for example the strathspey-reel set prevalent in Cape Breton, and the clog-jig-reel set popular in the Ottawa Valley.

*style, transmission, composition.* Tune composition is widespread and occurs in many styles, thus it is not uncommon for a French-Canadian player to compose a reel in convincing Irish style. Until the 1940s, the lumbercamps of Quebec, Ontario, New Brunswick and the Northeastern United States played an important role in the transmission of tunes, songs and dances. Even today, the transmission of tune repertoires is still primarily aural since many older players do not read music and few printed tune collections are widely available (except in Cape Breton). It is common practice to learn tunes from recordings, some from commercial sources and others privately taped at house parties or fiddle contests. In the past, instrumental teaching usually occurred in an informal setting and on an irregular basis, but now formal structured lessons are the norm. Students learn to read music and incorporate techniques from classical music practice.

The development of a pan-Canadian 'old time' style of fiddle playing has been largely attributed to Maritime fiddler Don Messer (1909–73), whose regular programmes on Canadian radio and television over a forty-year period had a tremendous impact on fiddlers nationwide. Quebecois fiddler Jean Carignan (1916–88), himself a devotee of the recordings of Michael Coleman and James Morrison, is well known for his blending of Irish and French-Canadian styles. Accordionist Philippe Bruneau (b. 1934) has been most influential in the popularisation of Quebec accordion style.

*festivals and organisations.* The principal venues for traditional music in Canada are dance halls, fiddle contests, agricultural fairs, house parties and local pubs. Folk festivals which feature contemporary folk music as well as traditional musics from many countries are annual events in many communities. Notable Irish festivals include: the Newfoundland Irish Festival; the Winnipeg Irish Fest; and the annual Irish festival held in Chatham, New Brunswick. In the cities of Montreal, Ottawa, Toronto and Vancouver, CCÉ operates branches which sponsor many events, including a monthly céilí. There are numerous Irish dance schools across Canada, and Irish dance feiseanna are held in many centres.

*song*. The impact of Irish song in Canada is evident in the large number of Irish ballads and songs in the English-language song repertoire, particularly in Newfoundland, Irish-settled areas of Quebec and Ontario, such as the Ottawa Valley and the Peterborough region, and in the Miramichi region of New Brunswick. Large numbers of Irish songs turn up in Canadian song collections and Canadian song texts set to Irish melodies are also common. The 'Come-all-ye' ballad, popular in Ireland, is the usual setting for Canadian songs and ballads about the sea, life in the lumbercamps, and tragic historical events. This song type consists of four-line stanzas with seven stressed syllables to each line and is most often in 6/8 metre with a structure of ABBA. Another borrowing from the Irish tradition is the speaking of the last word or phrase of a song, a convention characteristic of lumbercamp singers and also noted in Newfoundland. The singing style varies from region to region but in general employs little or no ornamentation. Quebec singer O. J. Abbott's recording, *Irish and British Songs from the Ottawa Valley*, is one of the finest examples of this style. The influence of Irish song is also evident in the compositions of contemporary Canadian songwriters such as Stan Rogers (1949–83). Notable collectors of Canadian English-language song have been: Helen Creighton (Maritime Provinces); Edith Fowke (Ontario); Edward D. Ives (New Brunswick); Elizabeth Greanleaf, Maud Karpeles, MacEdward Leach, and Anita Best (Newfoundland). (JOT)

See Cape Breton Island.

**Canny, Paddy.** (1919– ). Fiddler, from Glendree, Tulla, Co. Clare. Renowned for distinct East Clare style, his music has a characteristic 'lonesome' touch, something that he feels has developed in his own playing. One of three brothers, all of whom played fiddle, he was influenced by his father Pat and local fiddlers Pat McNamara and Martin Nugent. In his youth he was a popular player for house dances, and in 1946 he was one of founders of Tulla Céilí Band. He toured America with Dr Bill Loughnane, playing in Carnegie Hall. He made numerous live radio broadcasts from the late 1940s and 1950s; his playing of 'Trim the Velvet' was used as the signature tune for Ciarán Mac Mathúna's *Job of Journeywork* programme for several years and he made television appearances in the 1960s. In 1959 he recorded *All-Ireland Champions Violin* with Peter O'Loughlin, P. Joe Hayes and Bridie Lafferty. He left the Tulla band in 1967 and in 1997 recorded a solo album. (MAO)

**Cape Breton Island.** Part of the eastern Canadian province of Nova Scotia renowned for its unique style of fiddle playing. The area, originally inhabited by Mi'qmaq Indians and French Acadians, has become home to many ethnic groups over the years, the largest influx of immigrants being Highland Scots who settled in the island in the eighteenth and early nineteenth centuries. Family names such as MacDonald, MacNeil and Rankin remain common in Cape Breton and connections with Scotland are also immediately obvious from placenames such as Glencoe, Inverness and Iona. The Gaelic language, music, song and dance brought here by these Scottish settlers flourished in the isolation offered by Cape Breton Island.

*Scottish style.* In Scotland, however, at the source of the tradition, dramatic change was occurring as the music first declined in popularity and later was revived in a new context, dependent on its separation from the dance. Cape Breton thus existed as a 'marginal survival' (B. Nettl and H. Myers, *Folk Music in the United States: An Introduction*, Detroit, 1976), maintaining the tradition which had disappeared from the original centre in a distant geographic location. Inevitably the Cape Breton situation itself became susceptible to change as external influences began to infiltrate the tradition, most noticeably from the beginning of the twentieth century onwards. These changes bore little resemblance to those shaping the contemporary Scottish tradition, and so the musics of Scotland and Cape Breton, while stemming from a single past, developed as two distinct identities.

*pipes, fiddle and piano.* The fiddle and bagpipes were the two instruments transported to the island with the first settlers, both being used chiefly to provide music for the dance. The combination of solo fiddle with piano accompaniment, occasionally supplemented by guitar, is the representative sound of Cape Breton today. The fiddle quickly established itself as the preferred instrument as the pipes became associated with military styles and contexts. In recent times however there has been a return to the old style and repertory of piping, this promoted by people such as Alex Currie, Barry Shears, Paul MacNeil and Jamie MacInnis. The earliest fiddle style was believed to have been highly influenced by the piping and by the Gaelic language; indeed one of the greatest compliments given to fiddlers was that they 'had the Gaelic' in their music. The style, epitomised in the playing of individuals such as Mary 'Hughie' MacDonald and Donald Angus Beaton (1912–82), was characterised by a number of left-hand embellishments, the frequent use of drones and double stops, and various techniques involving the bow. The most common of these was the 'cut' – the division of a long note into several smaller values of the same note by replacing a single bow-stroke with several separate strokes. Many fiddlers chose to maximise on volume and drone potential by retuning the fiddle, often to E'AEA (known as high bass); others often performed in pairs or teams.

As the twentieth century progressed, the fiddle style began to change, in many ways to accommodate the developing piano-accompaniment style. The piano itself replaced the simple drone accompaniment provided by pump-organ which had become popular from the early 1900s. A basic chordal accompaniment gradually became more busy and complex so that the style today involves the entire range of the keyboard, much syncopation in the right hand, octave movement in the left hand, chromatic runs and glissandos. Subsequently the fiddle style became less involved, using fewer drones and embellishments in favour of a clearer tone, eliminating modal inflections to bring the tuning in line with the piano. Winston 'Scotty' Fitzgerald (1914–87) and Angus Chisholm (1908–79) were among the players responsible for introducing these new stylistic traits into the tradition. Their influence, and that of players such as Buddy MacMaster and Carl MacKenzie, is evident in the playing of many of today's younger fiddlers.

*repertoire.* The repertory of the Cape Breton fiddler is drawn from a wide variety of sources, old and new, oral and literate. In performance the integrity of the melodic line must be maintained at all times; tunes are performed 'correctly' and no practice of spontaneous variation is accepted. Traditionally many tunes were borrowed from the piping and 'puirt-a-beul' or mouth music traditions. The music of Scotland's 'Golden Age' (from fiddlers such as Neil Gow and William Marshall) forms a substantial part of the repertory. Local compositions are also highly significant – most fiddlers compose or 'make' tunes – and names such as Dan R. MacDonald, Jerry Holland and John Morris Rankin are known well beyond Cape Breton. In recent times the repertory has become markedly more eclectic with tunes from Shetland, French-Canada and the United States appearing alongside Scottish and Cape Breton tunes. Irish tunes are becoming increasingly popular.

*Irish influence.* While the Irish represent 30 per cent of the population make-up of the island, Irish music has mainly been associated with one small area known as 'The Northside'. This includes the town of North Sydney which is the entry point to North America for the ferry from Newfoundland, an area well known for its connections with Irish music. Players from the Northside such as Joe Confiant, Johnny Wilmot, Tommy Basker and Robert Stubbert have been important in promoting Irish music and passing it on to subsequent generations. Today, musicians such as Brenda Stubbert and the members of the Barra MacNeil family are legacy to that tradition. With the exception of double-jigs the Irish repertory and style were not hugely significant throughout the rest of Cape Breton until recent times. Contact firstly with Irish-American musicians and later Irish musicians through the festival circuit, along with increased performance opportunities in Ireland have led to a greater sharing of musical ideas. The first Irish celebration of Cape Breton music took place in 1993 at University College, Cork and was recorded on the CD, *Traditional Music from Cape Breton Island*. An organisation which promotes and encourage musical links between the two islands, The Cape Breton/Ireland Musical Bridge, is currently operated from the Music Department in UCC.

*dance*. The repertory, and to a large extent the style, of the Cape Breton fiddler, is dictated by the requirements of the dance. Dancing exists both as a solo tradition and at a social level where square dances are performed to groups of jigs and reels. For the solo step-dancer a strathspey and reel are required. This tune combination forms the core of the Cape Breton fiddlers' repertory even in the absence of a dancer. The strathspey, characterised by its dotted rhythms and Scotch snaps, gradually accelerates in tempo making the transition into the reel a seamless one. The strathspey and reel group is often augmented by other tune types such as the air, march or slow strathspey. These precede the strathspey proper so that the strathspey-reel combination culminates the medley. Traditionally the entire group of tunes was based around a single tonal centre; today's players often prefer to change key at some point.

*revival and current practice*. In 1971 the Canadian Broadcasting Corporation produced a documentary entitled *The Vanishing Cape Breton Fiddler* prophesying the demise of the local tradition. In reaction to this a number of events were organised in an effort to halt the decline and classes were established to encourage the younger generation to take up the music. The success of these ventures is still evident today. Scores of young players continue to play the fiddle and what was once primarily regarded as a male instrument now has many female exponents. Summer courses are offered annually at the Gaelic College at St Ann's, and more recently at the Céilidh Trail School of Celtic Music in Inverness. Besides catering to local students such courses also allow visitors to the island to experience the music first-hand.

The house-party or céilí remains the popular event for informal music-making and dancing in Cape Breton. Dances happen on a regular basis at various halls throughout the island such as Glencoe and West Mabou. A number of outdoor concerts are held throughout the summer months in communities such as Glendale, Big Pond, Broad Cove and Iona. Such events are highlights of each community's social calendar and are important homecoming occasions for the many Cape Bretoners who live in other parts of Canada and the United States. Typically the concerts feature mainly local Cape Breton talent – fiddlers, dancers, pipers and singers, representing both the local English-language song tradition and the Gaelic song tradition which is currently enjoying popularity as part of the wider language revival. The first important local celebration of Cape Breton music in a more international context was the Celtic Colours Festival held in October 1997 when Cape Breton fiddlers such as Natalie MacMaster and Ashley MacIsaac performed in a line-up that included performers from Ireland, Scotland and Quebec. These players, along with others such as the Rankin Family and the Barra MacNeils, have done much over the last decade to promote and popularise music from this area at an international level, and to establish it firmly within the commercial world of 'Celtic' music. In doing this, the intrinsic value of the music is rarely compromised although the visual and performance contexts are often dramatically different from what is familiar in Cape Breton. (LID)

See Basker, Tommy; Confiant, Joe; Fitzgerald, Winston Scotty; Fortune, Henry; Holland, Jerry; Stubbert, Robert; Tomas, Otis; Wilmot, Johnny.

**Carman, Fair of.** Detailed in O'Curry's *On The Manners and Customs of the Ancient Irish*. A mythic festival of sport, recreation and commerce reputedly initiated by the Tuatha De Dannan to celebrate Carman, mother of the sons of Dibad from Athens, whom they held as hostage to guarantee freedom from pillaging by her sons. Initiated upon her death, the event is said to have been running for 580 years by the time of Christ: 'On the Kalends of August they assembled there, and on the sixth of August they left it'. It was detailed in a seventy-nine-verse lyric (included in O'Curry) which contains references of interest to music:

> Pipes, fiddles, chainmen
> Bone-men and tube players
> A crowd of babbling, painted masks
> Roarers and loud bellowers.

It is from this fair that Wexford (Ir. Loch Garman) takes its name.

**carol.** French *carole*. Originally a song to accompany dancing, but later, by common usage, it came to refer to old, Christmas-season religious songs.

See song, sean-nós.

**Carolan, Mary Ann.** (1902–85). Singer, concertina player. Born at Tenure, Drogheda, Co. Louth, her father was Pat Usher, a concertina player. He played formidably even up to the time of his death in 1962 at age ninety-four; he also had a large song repertoire. Mary Ann's brother Pat played fiddle and also sang. Her repertoire had Irish and Scottish songs, the latter including some of the classic Child pieces, including 'Jock o' Hazeldean' which she sang in Scots dialect. She also sang the formidable 'Burns' Highland Mary', and local scribe Johnny Brodigan's scathingly satirical 'Wedding of Sweet Baltray'. She is recorded on Topic.

**Carolan, Nicholas.** (1946–   ). Archivist, researcher and collector, writer. Born at Drogheda, Co. Louth, he is co-founder and director of the Irish Traditional Music Archive in Dublin, and general editor of its publications. A former teacher he may be best known as researcher and presenter of the RTÉ radio series *The Irish Phonograph* (1983–86) and television series *Come West Along the Road* (1995–98). A frequent lecturer on Irish traditional music, from 1977 to 1992 he was secretary of the Folk Music Society of Ireland, and from 1985 has lectured on Irish traditional music in Trinity College Dublin. Among his published work is an edition of the first collection of Irish music *A Collection of the Most Celebrated Irish Tunes of 1724* (1986), *A Short Discography of Irish Folk Music* (1987), *A Harvest Saved: Francis O'Neill and Irish Music in Chicago* (1997), and the article on Irish traditional music in the *New Grove Dictionary of Music and Musicians* (1999 edition).

Turloch Carolan (from a painting by J. C. Turnbull, 1844)

**Carolan, Turloch.** (1670–1738). Harper, composer. Born Nobber, Co. Meath. Referred to variously as Turlough O'Carolan, Turloch O'Carolan, O Carolan, O'Carolan and (perhaps most commonly) Carolan. At age four he moved with parents to Alderford, Co. Roscommon, where his father worked for the Mac Dermott Roe family. Turloch was educated by them, and when he was blinded by smallpox at age eighteen, Mrs Mac Dermott Roe arranged for him to learn to play the harp. She supported him until age twenty-one when she provided for him a helper/guide, horse and stipend and he began his itinerant career in the manner of the times.

Carolan, like other harpers, was treated with respect and given hospitality in many of the 'big houses', both of native aristocracy and newer landowners. He appears to have been

## O'Rourke's Noble Feast (Ossian)

## George Brabazon (Ossian)

Two pieces by Turloch Carolan

considered an adequate, but not remarkable, harper, having come to the instrument at too late an age, but he quickly established a reputation as a composer. This gave him a status superior to his fellow harpers. After an eventful and musically prolific life, he died at Alderford.

*the music*. Carolan's music reflected the contemporary taste of his day, particularly the styles of Italian composers Gemienai and Corelli whose influence can be seen in his pieces. One collection of his music was published during his lifetime, but his reputation as composer continued to grow after his death. During the eighteenth century the following collections of his music, or in which his music featured prominently, were published: *A Collection of the most Celebrated Irish Tunes*, John and William Neale (Dublin, 1724); *Aria di Camera*, Dan. Wright (London, *c*.1730); *Compositions by Carolan* [title page missing] (Dublin, 1742 or later); *A Favourite Collection of the so much admired old Irish Tunes*, John Lee (Dublin, 1780); *The Hibernian Muse* (London, *c*.1780); *A General Collection of the Ancient Irish Music*, Edward Bunting (Dublin and London 1796). This trend continued in the nineteenth century, most notably with Edward Bunting's inclusion of Carolan pieces collected from harpers in 1809 and 1840. It continued into the twentieth century culminating in *Carolan, the Life, Times and Music of an Irish Harper* (2 vols.), Donal O'Sullivan (London, 1958, 1984). This included all the extant tunes known at that time. It is an indispensable and comprehensive work of considerable scholarship, but nevertheless is considered to be flawed in some aspects. It seems probable that most of Carolan's tunes were settings of words which he composed himself. The single exception was 'Pléaráca na Ruarcach' with words by poet Aodh Mac Gabhrain (Hugh MacGauran, d. 1710). According to O'Sullivan, the words of only seventy songs have survived. Most of these are included also in *Amhrain Chearbhalláin* (The Poems of Carolan), Tomás Ó Máille (Irish Texts Society, London, 1916) but while this is a useful source, it also contains much that is not by Carolan. The words as they have survived do not always match in a satisfactory way the tunes as they have survived. This, coupled with the the fact that many of the tunes have a very wide musical range, gives rise to the suggestion that the words may not have been sung but rather recited over the music. O'Sullivan included in his collection a total of 213 tunes.

*influences.* Three disparate influences coalesce in Carolan's music, producing a phenomenon unique in the history of Irish music: (i) the music of the Irish harping tradition, the roots of which descend to the depths of antiquity, and which was to die out by the end of the eighteenth century, (ii) the traditional songs and dance music, and, very importantly, (iii) the music by the great Italian composers of his day, in particular that of Arcangelo Corelli (1653–1713). Carolan therefore falls comfortably into no convenient musicological category and becomes an enigmatic and most interesting musical figure. It could be argued that his tremendous influence both on his contemporaries and later harpers contributed to the eventual demise of the itinerant harpers in Ireland. It is not known how Carolan or the other harpers played their music. Theirs was an entirely oral tradition being handed down from master to pupil. Nothing was ever committed to paper. All present-day performances of Carolan's music must therefore be in 'arrangements' of some kind or other. Carolan's tunes do not display pretentiousness, possessing, as O'Sullivan's book says, 'a kind of puckish joyousness . . . with here and there a sunbeam captured from the perennial sunshine of Italy'.

Carolan music played on baroque instruments can be heard on the Douglas Gunn Ensemble's *Carolan, Agus Ceolta Eile* and Carolan music played on various instruments can be heard on the compilation collection *The Legacy of Turlough O'Carolan*; also on Derek Bell's and Máire Ní Chathasaigh's recordings. (DOG)

**Carolan, William.** (1849–1937). Piper. Born at Corfad, Ballybay, Co. Monaghan. Moved to Doapey Mills in Aghabog in the early twentieth century where he remained until his death.

**Carroll, John.** (1835–1900). Piper. Born in the parish of Miltown Malbay, Co. Clare. He and his brother Michael were well known for their flute playing from an early age, and through his acquaintance with blind Inagh piper Garret Barry, John moved to the pipes. An associate of piper Tom Hehir, John played a Moloney set.

**Carroll, Liz.** (1956–  ) Fiddler, composer. Born in Chicago, her father, from Brocca,

Tullamore, Co. Offaly, played accordion. Her mother is from Ballyhahill, near Shanagolden, Co. Limerick, her own father Tom Cahill played fiddle. Liz started fiddle at nine, taught by Sr Francine at school. Her interest in Irish music was gleaned from her parents' involvement in the Irish American community. She had access to all the city session repertoire of players such as Kevin Keegan, Eleanor Neary, Johnny McGreevy and Joe Cooley. She step-danced as a child with the Dennehy school (Michael Flatley's alma mater), often visiting Ireland while playing fiddle for their dancing in competitions. Playing in Washington DC followed by a State Department tour to Africa in 1983 introduced her to professional music; she now teaches and performs, particularly with Billy McComiskey, and in the group Trian with McComiskey and Daithí Sproule. Equally known as a composer and an outstanding player, she has made some 150 tunes; her solo albums having a rare high percentage of 'own material'. In 1994 she received a National Endowment for the Arts National Heritage Award (previously won by Joe Heaney, Martin Mulvihill, Michael Flatley and Jack Coen).

**Carson, Ciaran.** (1948– ). Writer, organiser, flute-player. Born in Belfast, his father played airs on accordion and sang; Ciaran began playing with him on harmonica at the age of nine, moving on to whistle at twelve. His first experience of traditional music was in clubs like 'Salisbury Street' where the emphasis was on singing; this developed an interest in dance music, prompting his taking up flute and travelling to sessions and fleadhanna all over the island. This interest led to his position as Traditional Arts Officer with the Arts Council of Northern Ireland in 1975, succeeding poet Michael Longley's three years at the same work. In the course of this, over twenty-five years he established a credibility for the ACNI in traditional music: he was regarded by musicians and organisers as having a feel for the genuine in music, song and dance. Such sponsored events as Beleek, Portrush and Downpatrick singers' weekends became hallmark occasions which contributed significantly to recognition and valuing of a song tradition. The 'You and Yours' concert tours throughout his term brought musicians to diverse venues all over his jurisdiction, other grant aid to such as Forkhill and Derrytresk festivals boosted awareness and learning in singing, piping, and particularly in set-dancing. Under his direction the ACNI consistently contributed to music events south of the border which were felt to have importance for, and relevance to, northern counties, such as the Willie Clancy and south Sligo summer schools. One of Ireland's major poets, his 1986 *Pocket Guide to Irish Traditional Music* remains an important guide to the heart of music practice, and his 1996 *Last Night's Fun* carries this further in de-mystifying prose. He left his position in 1998 to concentrate on writing.

**Carthy, Tom.** (1799–1905). Uilleann piper. Born at Castle Green, Ballybunion, Co. Kerry, he acquired his mastery of the pipes at an early age. Seated near to his home playing music to all who felt moved to listen, he became almost a feature of the area over sixty-five years of the century. He died in 1905, his life spanning three centuries.

**Carty, John.** (1962– ). Fiddle, banjo, flute. Born in London, his main inspiration came from his father, Roscommon man John P. Carty (flute, fiddle, sax). He became involved from an early age with London Irish Music Circle, was taught by Clareman Brendan Mulkere in the early 1970s, and was exposed to a wide variety of musical styles. He returned to live permanently in Ireland in 1991. Increasingly drawn to the playing of an older generation of musicians mainly from the South Sligo area, his interpretation of their music is highly original. He has made numerous recordings for television and radio, and tours in Europe and America. Records include a CD of banjo music with Brian McGrath on piano, *The Cat that Ate the Candle* (1993), and a solo fiddle album (1996) featuring some of the classic selections of such musicians as Michael Coleman, Lad O'Beirne and Paddy Killoran. Considered a unique fiddle talent, he is popular in the US and tours with a Flanagan Brothers-style band, At the Racket. He teaches banjo and fiddle at summer schools and workshops. (GRD)

Paddy Carty. Note the keyed instrument (CCÉ)

**Carty, Paddy.** (1929–85). Flute player. Born at Rafford, Loughrea, Co. Galway, he was a most creative player whose music continues to inspire and influence. One of the first players to use a keyed flute, he began on a normal eight-key instrument with open holes, changed to a metal, keyed Boehm system, and eventually settled for a Radcliff Model with holed keys which incorporated characteristics of both, but enabled him to play in any key while keeping a fingering system akin to that of the simple-system flute with which he was already familiar. Self-taught, his music has an unhurried and lyrical 'Carty' flow which is untroubled by technical difficulty. He won several All-Ireland titles in the early 1960s, and continued to play regularly in and around the Loughrea area – particularly at Moylan's pub – until his death in 1985. He recorded *Paddy Carty, Traditional Irish Music* accompanied by Mick O'Connor on tenor banjo.

**Casey, Bobby.** (1926– ). Fiddle. Annagh, Miltown Malbay, Co. Clare. Self-taught under father's (John 'Scully' Casey) influence and tutored by Junior Crehan. He had all of Scully's music by age thirteen, and played house and crossroads dances, American wakes, sports meetings, parish concerts, céilís and in public houses on fair days. His contemporaries were John Joe Healy (concertina and fiddle), Paddy Galvin, Mike Downes (fiddle), John Fennell (flute), Paddy McNamara, Josie Mooney, Miko Doyle, Josie Hayes, Miko Reddan, Pat O'Brien, Martin Talty, Willie Clancy; also Paddy Canny, P. Joe Hayes, Martin Rochford, Dr Bill Loughnane, Seán Reid, the Prestons, McNamaras, Paddy O'Brien and Joe Cooley. Casey played in the early years with Willie Clancy (then fiddle and flute) and with him moved to Dublin where they played with John Kelly and Joe Ryan before going to London. Clancy returned to Clare but Casey remained, and married there in 1954. He played with piper and concertina player Tommy McCarthy all over England; their families were close, both living in Kentish Town. A pivotal stylist, Casey's music society in Camden Town included Michael Falsey, Paddy Taylor, Roger Sherlock, Martin Burns, Jimmy Power, Séamus Ennis, Seán McGuire, Maggie Barry, Brian Rooney, Michael Gorman, Andy Boyle, Jimmy Dunleavy, B. Mulhearn, Paddy Breen, Kit O'Connor, Tommy McGuire, Matt Regan, Raymond Roland, Lucy Farr, Jim Minogue, Liam Farrell, Julia Clifford, Danny Meehan, John Bowe, Brendan McGlinchey, P. J. Crotty, Kevin Taylor, Felix Doran, Mick O'Connor. He has a solo LP *Taking Flight*, and a tape *Casey in the Cowhouse* recorded in August 1959 in Junior Crehan's byre by Sta Crehan on a Grundig reel-to-reel. He can be heard also on *Paddy in the Smoke* and *Clare Fiddlers*. He played in London-based band the Thatch, and on *Bringing it All Back Home*.

**cassette tape.** See reproduction of music, tape recording.

**Cavan.** In common with the tradition in the rest of Ulster, the fiddle has been the most popular instrument here. Cavan style of music could be described as having a clean and crisp rhythm, clear emphasis on beat and matching the 'lifty' heel-toe style of dancing performed in the sets there. Old fiddle players used a lot of bow, rather than fingers; they liked intricate tunes. Most highly regarded of the Cavan fiddlers were Patsy Cooke (Mountnugent), Eugene Leddy (Butlersbridge), Packie Fay (Killeshandra), Francie McCaul (Doogary), Johnny Coyle and James Harry McInerney (Mullahoran). Among these, James Harry emigrated to New York where he made a cylinder recording of 'The Cavan Reel'. Dr Brian Galligan, one of CCÉ's founders, was perhaps the most dominant figure in Cavan music and dancing, but the best-known fiddler associated with the county is Seán Maguire whose father John was from Mullahoran parish, then rich in fiddle-playing. Ed Reavy is Cavan's other name in fiddling, one of traditional music's most prolific composers.

*Cavan musicians today.* Vincent Tighe, from Munterconnaught, first learned the fiddle from local players Peter Gibney and Michael Caldwell, and later took up the accordion. He spent some thirty-five years in England, mostly in Coventry, where he played at sessions and fleadhs, organised the Shannon Céilí Band and played at céilís in Irish centres all over England. He returned to Munterconnaught in 1978 where he now has the Carrick Céilí Band. Interested in accordions from an early age, he is a skilled repairer and tuner, teaches the instrument and leads monthly local sessions. Other Cavan players are Mattie Lynch (accordion), Jimmy McIntyre, Tommy Reilly, Michael Caldwell and Patsy Cooke, (fiddlers). Antóin Mac Gabhann is one of Cavan's best known fiddlers and is prominent in CCÉ. Martin Donohoe (accordion), from Cavan town, learned from John Donohoe, who taught the Breffni Boys Marching Band. Now with a strong individual style, he was introduced to traditional music by Pat McCabe of Monaghan and is currently researching the music of the Cavan/Fermanagh area under the auspices of their county councils and the Peace and Reconciliation Council. Pádraig McGovern of Ballymagovern, West Cavan, is an All-Ireland winner on the uilleann pipes, his family learned their music from teachers such as Frank Kelly of Ballinamore, Vincent Tighe, P. J. Flood and John Morrow. Tommy King is a noted flute player, perhaps better known as one of the top sean-nós dancers, and flute-player Paddy McDermott of Killeshandra has taught and brought forward a culture of musicians in the Cornafean area. Singer Séamus Fay of Drumconnick is a third-generation lilter, having learned from his mother, and she from her mother. Winner of four All-Ireland titles, he has a large repertoire of complex tunes which he can lilt at ease. P. J. Flood, Belturbet, learned uilleann pipes from Jack Wade in Clones. Playing a Keenan set with a Rowsome chanter he is an established and well-regarded teacher, with a dozen young pipers locally as well some 100 pupils on other instruments. He himself was influenced by fiddlers John P. Reilly, Tommy Geehan and Con McGerty. Peter Maguire (uilleann pipes), Mullahoran, learned from Matt Kiernan, himself having taught Brian and Ray McNamara from Co. Leitrim. Martin Gaffney (flute, accordion) from Killeshandra, learned from Cissie Fitzpatrick and Tommy Curran (a piccolo player who had a marching band); other influences were fiddlers Packie Fay, John P. Reilly and Bobby Hands. He plays with the Killeshandra Wrenboy Group, and has recorded with Gene Anderson of Carrick-on-Shannon. Philip Clarke (piano accordion, piano) Mullaghboy, Kilnaleck, teaches, and organises the Breffni Céilí Band. Eddie Clarke (harmonica player), one of Cavan's finest musicians and internationally known, has recorded with Clare/Drogheda fiddler Joe Ryan. Cavan still has several céilí bands, best known is Eugene Leddy's (Butlersbridge). Formed in the late 1930s and continuing until the '70s, it broadcast first from the GPO in 1942. With the Ballinamore Céilí Band they are featured on a live LP from a céilí in the Irish Club, Parnell Square, Dublin. Now eighty-five, Eugene Leddy is still playing. The Breffni Céilí Band was one of Cavan's other better-known dance groups, formed by Paddy Galligan in the 1950s. (AMG)

**CD.** See reproduction of music, new technologies.

**céilí.** 1. In Northern counties the term denotes a social visit, e.g. 'going on a kaley', kayleying, making one's kayley. 2. Throughout the country it means 'social dance' with what are taken to be indigenous, old-Irish dance forms, these compiled by a process of revival, reconstruction and composition in the years following the Gaelic Revival after 1897. 3. In Scotland the term indicates an on-stage concert or social night involving music, song and dance performance.

*history.* The first céilí was held on 30 October 1897 (Féile Samhain) in Bloomsbury Hall, London. In pursuit of new activities for the London Gaelic League, the Scottish céilí evenings in London were visited. It was decided to use the same term 'céilithe' for a London Irish social evening based on the structure of the Scottish evenings. The London Gaelic League were already using the term 'seilgí' for day-outings.

Based on what was believed to be an old tradition, it was a piper, Tomás Ó Gearacháin, who opened the proceedings at the céilí, followed by songs by Mícheál Ó Súilleabháin and Norma Borthwick, and Scottish and Welsh singers and musicians. M.C. Ó Fathaigh strictly controlled admission which was by invitation only. He also censored what songs were permissible; 'Phil the Fluter's Ball' was unacceptable as being 'stage Irish'. They were very conscious of 'breaking new ground' and the need to create a good image. Dancing consisted of 'Sets, Quadrilles and Waltzes to Irish music'. Those figure dances, now referred to as céilí dances, were not known at the time. Another landmark 'céilí' was the occasion of a performance by Frank Lee's 'Tara' céilí band at the Sarsfield Club, Notting Hill, London on St Patrick's Night, 1918.

The céilí phenomenon spread from London to Ireland and other countries. Subsequently the céilí became commercialised and came to consist more of figure dancing (known as céilí dances) and fewer songs and musical performances. The extreme popularity of the céilí gave rise to the need for specialist groups of musicians which became known as céilí bands. During the 1950s and '60s, céilí bands attracted such crowds of dancers as to fill the largest halls in Ireland, City Hall, Cork and Mansion House, Dublin being packed to capacity weekly.

**céilí bands.** A group of musicians organised together either on a permanent, professional, or an *ad hoc* basis, in order to provide music for céilí (Irish) social dancing, and/or (today) set dancing. The céilí band in the past might (in a community) be a large ensemble of varying composition, brought together occasionally, or, maybe a family grouping (such as the McCuskers). Instruments used were typically fiddle, flute, button accordion, piano, bass and snare drum with woodblock, banjo, sometimes double bass; uilleann pipes were sometimes played (Tulla), piccolo (McCuskers) also, and in some cases the saxophone (Gallowglass). The 1897 Gaelic League céilí in Bloomsbury Hall, London may have been the first céilí dance with the music provided by an *ad hoc* group of musicians, but from this landmark began the development of group-playing in pursuit of the louder volume required to fill larger venues. As dance venues expanded from kitchen to schoolhouse, to quaysides and crossroads, and finally to commercial and parochial halls, demand for louder music was created. Two circumstances are claimed as producing the term 'céilí band': 1. In 1918 Frank Lee organised musicians to play for a St Patrick's Day Céilí at Notting Hill, London. He called his grouping a 'céilí band', for other contemporary Irish dance-music groups had gone by such titles as 'The Ballinakill Traditional Dance Players', 'Paddy Killoran's Pride of Erin Orchestra', etc. 2. Following the Civil War in 1922, a group of Irish 'Free State' Army chiefs approached pipemaker and player William Rowsome with a request to get a group of musicians to play for their first céilí in the Hibernian School, Phoenix Park, Dublin, HQ of the military's Irish-speaking battalion. This was a difficult task in the social depression of the period, but the piper got his son Leo to bring together enough pipers and fiddlers for the night. This resulted in the army, GAA and Gaelic League collectively setting about organising cultural activities (CCÉ Bliain Iris, 1968). With pianist Leo Molloy, Leo Rowsome founded the Siamsa Gael Céilí band. At 14 Parnell Square, Dublin, the Dick Smyth Céilí Trio played for weekly dances at this time, and the Siamsa Gael played three nights a week at Clery's Ballroom. The second major band to get together was the

Colmcille Céilidhe, this prompting the starting of bands all over the country. Radio station 2RN, at the instigation of its director Séamus Clandillon, was the main promoter of these after 1926; the Ballinakill, Aughrim Slopes, Moate and Athlone bands were the first to broadcast, in a series that continued right throughout World War II.

Hundreds of bands proliferated all over the island, varying hugely in instrumentation, personnel, repertoire, music taste and professionalism. Some were entirely *ad hoc*, 'gather-ups' built around the personality of a leader or strong player, often an accordionist, but others had a fairly stable core, adjusted as the pressures of emigration, family commitments or work demanded. They had reached their zenith by the 1950s and into the 1960s those from the Northern counties tended to be stronger, this by dint of their mediation of political sentiment for nationalists. Bands often travelled huge distances – the McCuskers from Armagh might play in Kerry – many travelled on tours to Britain and the US, often entertaining in prestigious venues like New York's Carnegie Hall (Tulla, McCuskers). Of all the bands, several have been 'rated' as aesthetically tasteful and artistic – among these are Johnny Pickering's, the Tulla, Kilfenora and Aughrim Slopes. Bands like the McCuskers were noted for their specialised, local-flavour repertoires; the Laichtín Naofa and Tulla were highly regarded for the skill of some of their players. Others like the Gallowglass, from Naas, Co. Kildare, achieved almost 'pop' status. Many made records, particularly in the LP era, some of these are treasured musically and are scarce (*Coleman Country, Laichtín Naofa*). Others achieved popularity through repeated radio plays. Scottish accordion player Jimmy Shand, touring with his band in Ireland, introduced a tendency for some bands to aspire to a Scottish-style sound, this particularly towards the end of the popularity of the céilí band and its eclipse by the semi-pop, electric-guitar based 'showbands' in the 1960s. (EDI)

The major bands included the following: All-Star, Boston; Ardellis, Kildare, formed 1957; Assaroe, Donegal; Aughrim Slopes, Galway, founded 1934; Austin Stack, Dublin, 1930s; Avoca, Wicklow; Ballinahinch, Clare;

Rathaspeck Céilí group at Taghmon Feis, Co. Wexford, 1934 (CCÉ)

Ballinakill, Galway, formed 1928; Ballinamere; Tullamore, Co. Offaly; Ballinamore, Leitrim; Ballycar, Clare; Banba, Draperstown, Co. Derry; Banna Beola, Na; Banna Céilí CCÉ Dun Dealgan (Dundalk); Banna Céilí Cumann na bPíobairí Uilleann (Piper's Club), Dublin; Corcomroe, Clare; Banna Cheol na Coiribe (Corrib), Galway; Barrett's, Birmingham, formed 1963; Black Diamond, Leitrim; Belhavel Céilí Group; Blackthorn Céilidh Band, Down; Blarney, Cork; Boro, Wexford; Boyle CCÉ, Roscommon; Brendan Hogan and the Ballinakill, Galway; Brendan Mulhaire; Brian Boru; Bridge, Laois; Brophy Brothers, Dublin; Brophy, Dublin; Brosna, Kerry; Bunclody, Wexford; Castle, Dublin, formed 1963; Castleboro, Clonroche, Co. Wexford; Castlemore, Manchester; Cat Scan Céilí, Mayo; Charlie Kelly, Derry, 1940s/50s; Christy Gamble, Shandon, Cork; Clontarf, Dublin; Clune; Coleman Country, Sligo; Colmcille, London; Colmcille, New York; Connemara, Galway; Coolin; Country; Countryside, Sligo; Cuchulainn, Dundalk; Crossroads Céilí; Cuckoo Lane, Tralee; Daingean Castle, Co. Clare; Dawn; Dermot O'Brien and His, Louth, formed 1954; Desmond, Kerry; Dick Smith's, Dublin; Dick Smith's Star Céilidh Band, Dublin; Disirt Tola (formerly Inchicronan), Clare; Donal O'Martin; Donal Ring, Cork; Donegore; Doonaree; Dublin; Dublin Metropolitan Garda; Duhallow, Cork; Dun Aengus, Dublin, formed 1969; Dungarvan, Waterford; Dysart, Clare; Eamonn Ceannt, Dublin; Dundrum, Down; Eamonn O'Murray,

Monaghan; Earlsfield Boys, Sligo; Éire Óg; Emerald, Slane, Co. Meath, 1950s; Erne, Newtownbutler, Co. Fermanagh; Esker Riada; Eugene Leddy's Co. Cavan; Father Fielding's, Kilkenny; Feighroe (Fiach Roe), Clare; Ferns, Wexford; Fiach Rua, Clare, formed 1940; Fodhla, Dublin; Fortrill, Ardara; Four Courts; Foxford; Frank Lee's Tara, London, 1930s; Fred Hanna, 1940s/50s; Gallowglass, Kildare; Galway, formed 1939; Garda; Garrai Eoin; George McSweeney; Glenmona; Glenside, London; Glenview, Co. Sligo; Glincastle; Glinside; Golden Star, Kilfenora, Co. Clare; Gold Ring; Gorey, Wexford/Galway; Graiguenamanagh, Kilkenny; Green Cross; Green Linnet; Greens, Tipperary; Harp; Hughie Trainor's, Armagh; Inchicronan, Clare, formed 1979; Inis Cealltra; Inisfail; Innisfree, Sligo; Jack Barrett, Meath; Jackie Coogan; Jackie Hearst, Down; Jackie Hearst International, Down; Jim Lynn; Jimmy McNamara's, Armagh; Joe Burke's; Joe Cooley Céilí Group; Johnny Pickering, Charlemont, Co. Armagh; Keane's; Kearney; Kieran Kelly's, Westmeath; Kilbride, Co. Roscommon; Kilfenora, Co. Clare; Kilfenora Fiddle, Co. Clare; Killimer, Co. Galway; Killina; Killoran Memorial, Ballinasloe, Co. Galway; Kiltormer, Ballinasloe, Co. Galway; Kincora, Dublin, 1930s; Knocknagow, Tipperary; Laichtín Naofa, Miltown Malbay, Co. Clare; Leeds; Leitrim (Co.); Leitrim [parish] Co. Galway; Leo Casey, Westmeath, formed 1950; Liam Ivory; Liberty Boys, Dublin; Liverpool; Longridge, Offaly; Lough Arrow; Lough Derg, Tipperary; Lough Gowna, Dublin; Lough Lurgan, Galway; Lynch Brothers, Meath; McCoy; McCusker Brothers, Killcreevy, Co. Armagh; McElroy; McNiece; McSherry; Malachy Doris, Cookstown, Co. Tyrone; Malachy Sweeney's, Armagh; Matt Cunningham; Mayglass, Wexford; Michael Moran Shamrock, Longford/Dublin; Michael Sexton, Co. Clare; Mick Cronin; Miltown Malbay, Co. Clare; Moate, Co. Westmeath; Mooncoin, Co. Waterford; Mount View, Derrylin, Co. Fermanagh; Mrs Crotty's, Co. Clare; Moyglass, Co. Wexford; Muinebeag Melody Makers, Carlow; Naomh Éanna; Naomh Eoin, Ennis, Co. Clare; Nazareth House, Derry; New York; Noel Frost; Noel and Paul Frost; Noel Tuohy, Dublin; Noel Tuohy Radio, Dublin; Northern Province; Ó Dálaigh's; Old Cross; Orchard County, Armagh; Ormond, Tipperary; Ormond Star, Tipperary; Owenmore, Leitrim; Paddy O'Brien, Tipperary; Paul Duffy Céilí; Pride of Erin, Fermanagh/Tyrone; Pride of the North; Quidi Vidi; Quilty, Co. Clare; Raheny, Dublin; Raymond Smyth, Dublin; Richard Fitzgerald, Bundoran Co. Donegal; Roddy McCorley; Roisín Dubh, Gurteen, Co. Sligo; St Albans, London; St Brendan's; St Colmcille's, London; St Fachnan's, Kilfenora, Co. Clare; St Flannan's College, Co. Clare; St Peter's, Dungannon, Co. Tyrone; St Malachy's, Manchester; St Malachy's, Warrenpoint; St Mary's; St Michael's Junior, Thurles; St Rocks, Glasgow; Sanctuary; Seán Dunphy, Dublin; Seán Maguire, Belfast; Seán McDermott; Seán Norman, Edenderry, Offaly; Seán Ryan's, Tipperary/Drummond, Co. Laois; Seán Ryan and Don Coughlan, Tipperary; Shamrock; Shangarry; Shannonside; Shaskeen, Galway; Shannon Star, Drumshanbo, Co. Leitrim; Shop Street; Siamsa, Dundalk, 1960s; Siamsa Gaedhal; Silver Spear; Silver Star; Slieve Pheilim, Leitrim; Sonny Flynn's, Roscommon, South Sligo; Spailpín Mac Oireachtaigh Irish; Smith's, Mayo; Swallow's Tail, Sligo; Tadhg Kearney, Cork; Táin, Dundalk, 1990s; Tara, New York; Temple House, Dublin; Thatch, London; Tom Senier and his Céilidhe Orchestra; Tulla, Clare, formed 1947; Tulla Junior, Clare; Vincent Lowe's, late 1940s; Wee Electric; Western; West Clare, Kilrush, formed 1935. Many of these still survive in younger transformations; some, like the Tulla, having undergone almost complete transfusions of personnel, era and age-group. (MAG)

*set dance céilí bands.* The set-dance revival has seen the development of more specialised 'set-dance' bands, staffed by top musicians, who were familiar with set dances and sometimes worked with a dance 'caller', these also providing music for 'céilí' dancing. The revival movement of céilí dance in 1997/8 produced yet other bands, and gave the set-dance bands greater playing opportunity. Individual players among these groups will often be professional, many having other playing outlets in small-scale sessions. Among such bands currently are:

Emerald, Tyrone; Castleblaney, Monaghan; Ardmore; Cathal McNulty; Gold Ring; Marina, W. Cork; Michael Sexton, Clare; Killimer, Galway; Dan Herlihy, Kerry; Donie Nolan, Cork; Four Star Trio, Cork; Mountain Road Band, Fermanagh; John Gordon, Fermanagh; Green Isle; Gaoth Dobhair; Finvola; Fodhla, Louth; John Davey, Louth; Seán Norman; Móna Dubh, Westmeath; Glenside, Roscommon; Cahir Sound; Congers, Roscommon; Taylors Cross; Templehouse; Ard Erin; Matt Cunningham; Swallow's Tail; Shaskeen; West Clare Ramblers.

*'listening' céilí bands.* Other bands utilise the format of the céilí band as a structure for playing a nostalgic style of unison music (Moving Cloud, Swallow's Tail), using it as a showcase of the talents of their members. Their articulation of the music, and attention to the detail of solo instrumental 'voice', reflects awareness of the abiding principles of 'listening' groups, these more or less formalised by Ó Riada's Ceoltóirí Chualann. Modernist bands like 'Kips Bay Céilí Band' under US accordionist John Whelan use a céilí band format, but modern instrumentation, producing a sound closer to a 'Celtic Rock'. Their aim is to provide music for dance – hence the term 'céilí band' – with accordion and fiddle sound. Their use of the more solidly traditional reel and jig based material encompasses the ethos of 'Irishness' and 'traditional'.

*Belfast, 1950–90.* Best known of the period are the Banba, Ard Scoil, Liam Magee's, Séamus White's, Eddie Fagan's, Billy Burns, The Ó Cathain, the Northern Province, Johnny Maguire's, McPeake's, the Ros-na-Rí and the Ard-Rí. The Ard Scoil in Divis Street was a major centre for Irish language and culture and had its own céilí band. A member of that was accordion player Eddie Fagan who also took part in the Séamus White band and then went on to form his own band with Seán Quinn (accordion), and, at different times, John Bogues, Tom and Etta Hickland (fiddles), Tom Ginley (flute), Gerry Hobbs (drums), Brendan Fagan (bass) and Brian Fagan (piano). Billy Burns' band came to prominence through exposure on the early UTV programme *Fiddle and Flute*. The Ó Cathain Céilí Band included a number of musicians who had moved into Belfast from the country, among them Seán Rodgers and Fergus McTaggart (fiddles) and Billy Rush (accordion). The Northern Province was formed by some members of the Belfast CCÉ and included Alex Crawford, Fergus McTaggart and Denis Sweeney (fiddles), Tommy Maguire and Billy Rushe (accordions), Francie McCormick (drums) and Doris Crawford (piano). Johnny Maguire (flute), and son, Seán Maguire (fiddler), put together various bands as the occasion required, these including fiddlers Leo Ginley and Jim McKendry, Tom Ginley (flute) and accordionists Eddie Dornan and Tommy Maguire with drummer Gerry Hobbs. The McPeake piping family organised a céilí band which was resident in the Irish-speaking club Cumann Chluain Ard, off the Falls Road. 'Middle' Francie and 'young' Francie played the pipes, accordionists were Hilary Galway and Séamus McPeake, with James McMahon on flute, Jim McKendry and Tommy Gunn on fiddles, Tommy McCrudden (bass), Joe McCullough (drums) and Henry O'Prey (piano). Some members of the McPeake band (McKendry, McCullough and O'Prey) broke away in 1963 to form the Ard Rí band in collaboration with Seán Quinn and Dan McElroy (accordion) and Gus McElroy (fiddle) – all from the Co. Down Blackthorn Céilí Band. The Ard Rí also had piper Paddy McCaffrey, and played for a number of years with changing personnel including accordionists James McElheran and J. J. Carty. The Ros-na-Rí band was formed in 1962 by fiddlers Denis Sweeney and Davy Rice, with Cathal McCabe and later Olive Blaney on piano, Kieran Burke (accordion), Tony Scarisbrick (drums) and Sid Bates (ex-Jimmy Shand) on bass.

*decline.* Céilí dancing and the heyday of céilí bands in Belfast went into decline with the onset of the troubles in 1969, and by the 1980s, with no regular céilís, the bands disappeared. There was a small revival in the early 1990s which saw the re-emergence of a more compact Ard Rí band, but the golden era of céilí bands in Belfast is now a matter of history. During the period of 'the barricades' on the Falls Road from 1969–72, when small side-streets sealed themselves off, there was a blossoming of open-air 'street céilís' as an assertion of nationalist culture. A number of *ad hoc* céilí bands were created on occasion, one of these was the Jimmy O'Neill Band with Jimmy Cunningham on banjo and Séamus McCullough on drums. This band played on numerous street corners, remuneration was refreshments only. (SEQ)

**céilí dance.** In 1897, Irish figure (céilí) dances were unknown, so ironically, sets and quadrilles were performed at Irish language and other 'national' functions. In an effort to change this, Patrick Reidy, a London dance master who was familiar with figure dances from his native Co. Kerry was employed to teach these to the London Gaelic League, who subsequently promoted the newly discovered figure dances at their céilí events. Members of the London Gaelic League travelled to West Cork and Kerry to collect such figure dances, and these were published in two books in London: *A Handbook of Irish Dances* by O'Keeffe and O'Brien (1902), and *A Guide to Irish Dancing* by Sheehan. The figure dances were taught and performed with great discipline and so were more acceptable, image-wise, to the Gaelic League than the less-rigidly performed sets or quadrilles. Sets fell into disfavour, and were denounced in most Gaelic League circles as, in any case, 'un-Irish'. Initially, figure dances were viewed with scepticism. The 1901 Oireachtas set up a committee to investigate their origin and four- and eight-hand reels were disallowed at the Oireachtas up to 1913. In 1924 Elizabeth Burchenal, an American anthropologist published *National Dances of Ireland* in New York. Seán Óg Ó Ceallaigh was the first to use the term 'céilí dances' when he published figure-dance descriptions in a Dublin newspaper. The Irish Dancing Commission has published a description of thirty of these céilí dances in three parts of *Ár Rinncidhe Fóirne* (1939, 1943, 1969). (JOC)

*types of céilí dance.* Thirty of these are described by An Coimisiún le Rincí Gaelacha in its official hand book *Ár Rinncidhe Fóirne*. They were progressively published in three sections.

Book 1 (1939): Walls of Limerick, four-hand reel, eight-hand reel, Morris reel, high-cauled cap, sixteen-hand reel, eight-hand jig, harvest-time jig.

Book 2 (1943): rince fada, Bridge of Athlone, Siege of Carrick, Antrim reel, Glencar reel, Three Tunes (Co. Armagh), St Patrick's Day, Trip to the cottage (Co. Armagh), An rince mór.

Book 3 (1969): Hay maker's jig; Fairy reel, Duke Reel, Cross Reel, Waves of Tory, Rakes of Mallow, Gates of Derry, Sweets of May (Armagh), Bonfire dance.

The Céilí Dance revival movement is organised through Cáirde Rince Céilí na hÉireann, Charlestown, Ardee, Co. Louth.

See dance; set dancing.

**céirnín.** The Irish word for record. Céir = wax, céirnín = wax disc. Derived from Victor's record master-making process which involved electroplating a wax 'master' disc.

See reproduction of music.

**Celtic Flame music festival** 1997. Held in Dublin, Cork, Limerick and Galway, this was a major tourist-oriented event organised via the Tourism Council, by the Irish Tourist Board in London, in an effort to expand the season. More than a third of its £300,000 budget came from the Department for Tourism and Trade, £75,000 from the European Regional Development Fund, and the balance from Guinness and other sponsors. The artistes were assembled by MCD in Dublin, making it a thoroughly tourism/commerce music festival, part of a new genesis for Irish music. Headline performers included Paul Brady, Sharon Shannon, Mary Coughlan, Eddie Reader, Begley and Cooney, Altan, Frances Black, Dolores Keane, Donal Lunny, Brian Kennedy and Máirtín O'Connor. Parallel with it all were 'pub trail' and other acts that included Bumblebees, Nomos, Stockton's Wing, Tamalin and Kila.

**Celtic music.** Fanciful term which expresses a world-view or record-shelf category rather than actual links between music genres. 1. Indicates 'Irish' or 'Scottish' musics, but is increasingly used in Britain and the US to denote 'Irish', this suggesting discomfort with 'Irishness'. In Europe it may denote Breton or Galician music in addition to Irish, Scottish and Welsh. The music of Brittany is different to Irish music, but is within the playing and listening experience of many Irish traditional musicians. Isle of Man,

England and Wales are connected cultures, but Scotland has particularly strong linguistic and music links with Ireland, as has the Scots-Irish diaspora in Canada (Cape Breton, Newfoundland, etc.). 2. More superficially the term 'Celtic' has come to apply to an easy-listening, 'mood' music with dreamy, non-specific but Irish/Scots flavour, marketed as 'relaxing', 'evocative', etc. Such albums are legion, and enjoy a large sale in the US where the Narada company produces many compilation and re-licensed collections – including the playing of such as Máire Ní Chathasaigh, John Whelan and Joanie Madden – while the Mercury label's 'Secret Garden' features Davy Spillane. Traditional players sometimes use the term also, probably to appeal to the pre-formed audience (Seán O'Driscoll's solo album is titled *Celtic Music*, Shanachie's 90 per cent Irish song collection is *Celtic Love Songs*, Green Linnet's, with similar composition, is *Celtic Women in Music and Song*), but few players would describe themselves as playing anything other than 'traditional' or 'Irish' music.

See tradition.

**Ceol.** 1. Irish for music usually denoting instrumental music, and often indicating a session. 2. A journal of Irish music, published and edited by Breandán Breathnach. Begun in 1963, it was originally supported through private subscription and advertising, but in later years financial assistance was received from the Arts Council. Its aims were the promotion of Irish traditional instrumental and vocal music and the cultivation of their practice in a traditional manner. To this end *Ceol* published articles on every aspect of traditional music, featuring extensive tune and song transcriptions, biographies of noted performers with selections from their repertoire, and reviews of the then currently available commercial publications of traditional music, both recorded and printed. In all, eight volumes containing twenty-two numbers were issued. Publication ceased with the death of the journal's editor, the final volume having already been in preparation prior to his death. (GLC)

**Ceol Centre, Smithfield.** See Chief O'Neill Ceol Centre.

***Ceol Rince na hÉireann.*** The authoritative and prestigious series of published collections of Irish dance music from the greatest scholar and collector of traditional music of the twentieth century, Breandán Breathnach. The four volumes which have appeared to date have enjoyed unprecedented popularity, and the series has spawned numerous other publications. The *Ceol Rince* series, as it is known informally among musicians, is published by An Gúm, the Irish state publishing company, attached to the Department of Education. Breathnach – a lifelong civil servant – worked in the company at one time. He was an officer in the Department of Agriculture when he submitted his first collection to An Gúm in 1958, this published in 1963 as *Ceol Rince na hÉireann*. The music in the volume was collected from Breathnach's friends, musicians largely resident in Dublin in the 1950s. He recruited literate musicians to transcribe tunes, including fiddlers Seán Keane and Eithne Carey, paying them two shillings per tune. The book was a new departure in publications of Irish dance tunes in that the transcriptions presented in it showed a new respect for and insight into the styles of playing of the performers, reflecting Breathnach's 'insider' status as a performer himself, and perhaps also – if marginally – the influence of Bartok's seminal collections of folk music.

On the strength of this pioneering book, Breathnach launched a national campaign to collect traditional dance music, under the auspices of the Department of Education, in the mid-1960s. The first fruits of the large collection assembled during that campaign appeared in *Ceol Rince na hÉireann II* in 1976. After Breathnach's retirement from the civil service in 1977 he produced one further volume in the series, this time containing transcriptions from the commercial recordings which had appeared in considerable numbers in the folk music revival from the 1960s onward, a revival to which his first volume had been a notable contribution. This volume, *Ceol Rince na hÉireann III,* appeared in 1985, the year of Breathnach's death. In 1997 a further volume – the fourth in the series – appeared, edited from Breathnach's national collection by Jackie Small. This is devoted to music from a previously untapped source for publication –

## Bolton Street (Reel)

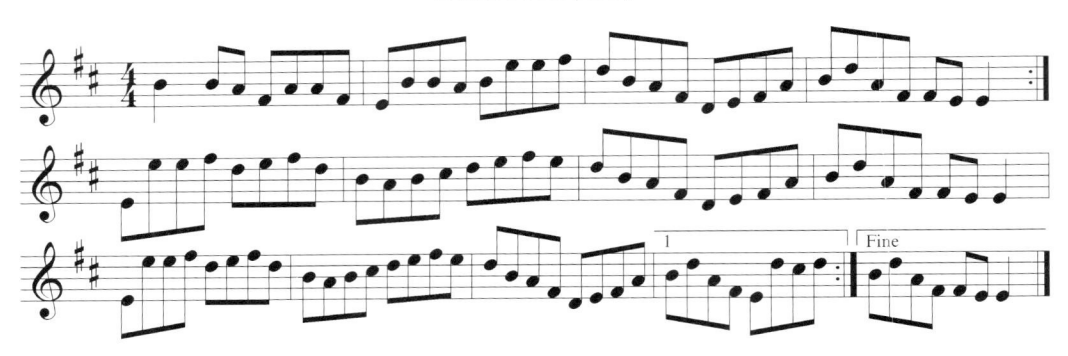

*Tune from CRÉ 4. It was sourced from the Grier collection* (An Gúm)

the manuscript collections of dance music held in private hands around the country. A fifth volume, drawn again (as was *Ceol Rince na hÉireann II*) largely from field recordings made during Breathnach's collecting campaign or donated to it, is due to appear in 1999, and yet further volumes are planned. (JAS)

**Ceolta Tíre.** Weekly radio programme which became synonymous with the growing popularity of traditional music from 1955–70. Presented by Ciarán MacMathúna and broadcasting much live material, it and *A Job of Journeywork* were hugely influential in an era where radio dominated communications and where there were few commercial recordings of traditional music. His field recording trips yielded notable performances by, and established national reputations for, musicians like Elizabeth Crotty, Junior Crehan, Fred Finn, Peter Horan and John Doherty. MacMathúna collected extensively in counties Clare, Galway, Kerry and Cork, and also in Leitrim, Sligo, Wexford, Donegal, Tyrone and Antrim. Thousands of these recordings, with others, have been remastered and indexed in a joint RTÉ Radio and Irish Traditional Music Archive project. (HAB)

See MacMathúna, Ciarán.

**Ceoltóirí Chualann.** This was the name adopted by musicians brought together initially to provide music for Brian McMahon's play *The Honey Spike* when Seán Ó Riada worked as musical director at the Abbey Theatre, Dublin, at the end of the 1950s. The musicians continued to meet for musical evenings at Ó Riada's home in Galloping Green in south Dublin where they adopted the local place-name 'Cualann' as a handle. They first came to national attention in 1961 when they were heard on two Raidió Éireann series *Fleadh Cheoil an Raidió* and *Reacaireact an Riadaigh*. Ó Riada's arrangements offered much new appreciation of traditional music sound. Ceoltóirí Chualann's music was well received, especially in more formal music circles, and with Ó Riada's determination this led to concert performances, a film soundtrack in 1961 for *The Playboy of the Western World* and an influential series of commercial recordings issued by Gael-Linn. The 1969 live recording *Ó Riada sa Gaiety* marked the zenith of the group's decade of achievement. Playing in the group were Seán Ó Riada (harpsichord and bodhrán), Seán Ó Sé (singer), John Kelly, Seán Keane and Martin Fay (fiddles), Paddy Moloney (uilleann pipes), Michael Tubridy (flute), Seán Potts (tin whistle), Ronnie McShane (bones and bodhrán – later replaced by Peadar Mercier), Sonny Brogan and Éamon de Buitléar (accordion). Other albums include *Ceol na nUasal* and *The Battle of Aughrim*. The group's final performance was at Cork City Hall in 1969. (HAB)

See Ó Riada, Seán.

**chanter.** The melody-producing part of all bagpipes.

See bagpipes; uilleann pipes.

**chapbook.** A simple pamphlet of twenty-four pages made up from two folded sheets of paper, upon which were densely printed adult and children's stories, anecdotes, short stories, woodcut images, verses and songs. These sold initially for a penny to readers uncritical of the quality of presentation or spelling; they were issued by printers eager to supply the mass market which existed for such productions – popular titles could sell thousands of copies.

**Chieftains, The.** Group. In 1963 Garech Browne, a member of the Guinness family, invited uilleann piper Paddy Moloney to form a group to record a once-off album for his company Claddagh Records. Moloney involved three of his colleagues from Ceoltóirí Chualann – Martin Fay (fiddle), Seán Potts (tin whistle) and Michael Tubridy (flute) – and Castletowngeoghan bodhrán player Davey Fallon. Poet John Montague, then a director of Claddagh, suggested a collective title 'The Chieftains'. Now in existence thirty-five years, the band has recorded almost fifty albums and film scores, with another thirty involving individuals and groupings of Chieftains members. The band is firmly established as a definitive and commanding sound in Irish music internationally.

Fallon was succeeded by the late Peadar Mercier on bodhrán, he in turn was replaced by Kevin Conneff. At different stages Seán Potts and Michael Tubridy resigned, Seán Keane (fiddle) joined in 1968, Derek Bell in 1974 and Matt Molloy in 1979. Today step dance performances typically augment the Chieftains' performance, and during one period dancer Michael Flatley was featured regularly on tours. Following the release of its first album the band increased its popular appeal through concerts and television appearances, leading to the recording of a second album in 1969. In 1970 they played support to Fairport Convention at the National Stadium, Dublin, achieving great acclaim. Despite difficult periods, the band has steadily developed its profile with a programme of touring abroad, this being particularly strong under the managership of impresario Jo Lustig. A successful 1975 concert in the Albert Hall, London directed the Chieftains down a full-time professional road, touring now involves the whole world. The Chieftains have a policy of engaging in some way with the music of their host nations, most notably with China in 1984. They have received major recording and entertainment awards. Activities of the band include concerts, recordings, radio and television; they have been featured in film, ballet, and theatre productions, these usually involving leader Moloney's arrangements and compositions. Association with well-known singers in other fields has been one of the Chieftains' best-known ventures – Chinese, rock, country, jazz, and orchestral. Particularly tenacious has been their 1990s' association with Galician music, notably that of piper Carlos Nunez. Yet the group consistently can be defined by having a solid and unchanging central core repertoire that evolved in the 1970s, thus identifying both continued demand for unadulterated Irish traditional music, and suiting the priorities and private musicianship of the band's talented individual members.

Awards: 1973: Golden disc for best album sold in Spain. 1975: *Melody Maker* 'Group of the Year'. 1993: Five Grammy nominations led to two awards. Further Grammys in 1994, 1996, 1997. (BIM)

**Chief O'Neill Ceol Centre.** Opened in 1999, and located at Smithfield, Dublin, this is a high-tech, multi-media facility giving both fixed-exhibit and audio-visual explanation of Irish traditional music. In various discrete departments it covers history, song and singing, instruments, dance and lore of the music. A 180-degree screen cinema features details of music and topography of the music regions. Harry Bradshaw has been the major consultant to the scheme.

**Child, Francis James.** (1825–96). Known for his monumental publication of *The English and Scottish Popular Ballads* between 1882 and 1898, in which he categorised what we would now call the 'great', 'classical' or 'traditional' ballads of Scotland and England, giving each category a 'Child' number used to this day, and relating his findings to ballads in over thirty different language sources. Although recent scholarship is rapidly altering the situation, comparatively little has been known about the wider aspects of a man who was described in his obituary in the *Boston Daily Globe* as America's 'most distinguished, scholarly master of the English language and of English literature'. Born in Boston the son of an impoverished sailmaker, he worked his way into Harvard College in 1842, graduating top of his year in 1846. After holding a number of tutoring posts he specialised in early English literature, studying in Europe during 1849–51, where he became acquainted with the works of the Brothers Grimm. The University of Göttingen was later to award him an honorary PhD in 1851, the year he returned to Harvard to take up the post of Boylston Professor of Rhetoric and Oratory. During this period he published *English and Scottish Ballads* (1857–9), a workmanlike enough collection, but was to be spurred on to higher things by the remarkable collection of Danish ballads, *Danmarks gamle Folkeviser* (1853–90), edited by Svend Grundtvig; this was to be both the model and inspiration for Child's own great work. The American Civil War, marriage and a family, together with heavy teaching duties, took up most of his time until 1876, when he became Harvard's first Professor of English (a post he held for the rest of his life), with time for research which he pursued in Chaucer, Rhetoric, Shakespeare, Anglo-Saxon and the Ballads.

Eventually he settled on a plan to publish a collection of all the popular ballads in the English language. It was to be comprehensive, giving every independent copy and variations, both in print and manuscript, having proper prefaces, and relating the ballads to those in other languages and traditions. In order to carry out this enormous task he not only built up a comprehensive collection of ballad books and manuscripts in all languages in Harvard library (where he happened to be Secretary of the Library Council) but also enlisted the willing cooperation of scholars from all over the world. By 1874 most of the preparatory work had been completed, together with his theory of popular ballads, based mainly on Grundtvig, the Brothers Grimm, and Herder. The end result was his *English and Scottish Popular Ballads* (1882–98), comprising five volumes issued in ten parts (although sadly, he did not live to see the final parts through the press).

Within these thoroughly researched and immaculately presented volumes were 305 individual ballads and their variants that he thought worthy of inclusion, each with a preface which not only discussed the ballad in question, its origin and 'historical' background, but related it to similar ballads in over thirty other languages.

Despite contemporary criticism his canon remains remarkably firm to this day, with only a handful of 'missing' ballads competing for late entry, and it remains the standard reference for all work in the field. Perhaps more serious is the claim that Child remained an 'arm-chair scholar' who was not only something of a romantic but held to a number of unjustifiable prejudices in a field of which he had no actual first-hand experience. The great north east of Scotland collector, Gavin Greig (1856–1914), was to complain in 1913, for example, that Child 'knows nothing of the inwardness, nor of the atmosphere of the ballad, and has to make up for his ignorance by perambulating the continent, telling us more about the ballad there than he can of it in Scotland', but even if the entire scholarly apparatus of *The English and Scottish Popular Ballads* comes one day to be discounted, his meticulous and painstaking collection of both printed and manuscript versions of virtually every ballad in existence in his day is an accomplishment which deserves both the admiration and gratitude of scholar and singer alike. Ref. Bertrand Bronson, *The Traditional Tunes of the Child Ballads* (1959–72). (IAO)

**chordophone.** Any stringed instrument wherein a note is produced by the agitation (by plucking, bowing or striking) of a stretched string. The pitch of the note produced is directly proportional to 1. the length of the string, 2. the diameter of the string, and 3. the tension of the string, e.g., the longer, thicker and looser the string, the lower the note. Strings may be made of metal or gut in Europe, but in Asia they are often of tightly wound silk, and in African countries may be of horse or other animal tail-hair, sisal or other plant fibre. The sound may or may not be amplified or modified by a sound-box. Chordophones are subdivided into 1. bows, 2. harps, 3. lyres,

4. lutes, and 5. zithers. 'Bows' are various kinds of simple hunting-bow-style plucked instruments held to the mouth and sounding like Jew's harp. Harps have their strings at an angle to the sound-box, while lyres have their strings parallel to the soundbox. Harps are important in Irish music history and lyres have been depicted in early Christian crosses in Ireland. In Asia and Europe the lyre developed a neck, and 'peg box' to hold the string ends, becoming 'lutes'. Plucked and bowed lutes include bouzouki, cittern, mandolin, guitar, banjo, fiddles etc. Zithers are played in many forms around the world; one branch of them developed into dulcimers, and then (when mechanised) into the piano, harpsichord, etc.

**chromatic.** Literally meaning 'coloured', suggesting that the notes on the diatonic scale are 'flavoured' or made more interesting by selective use of the accidentals (sharps and flats). The term is applied to the scale as used on piano where all the notes are 'regularly' separated by intervals of a semitone, this facilitating starting a scale on any note, and playing in different keys. Thus a chromatic scale has twelve notes:

D Eb E F nat. F# G G# A Bb B C nat. C#

The term is also used to describe an instrument's potential: two-row accordions have a fully chromatic scale, as do keyed concert flutes: the player can play notes and semitones in sequence. Tin whistle and one-row melodeon have 'diatonic' scales but fiddle has fully chromatic potential.

See diatonic; key; scale.

**Chruinnaght.** Manx traditional music festival, revived in the 1970s by Mona Douglas and central to local music revival.

See Manx traditional music.

**Church Street Club.** Probably the longest running 'session' in Ireland, the club was formed in Dublin in 1956 around a nucleus of Sligo/Leitrim musicians who had moved to Dublin. The MC at gatherings was generally John Egan who had played the flute in the Kincora Céilí Band from 1942 to 1947. Other regulars in the 1950s included flute players John Brennan and Dessie O'Connor, Leitrim fiddler Tom Mulligan, Bill Harte, John Ryan (concertina), John Kelly, Sonny Brogan and piper John Clarke. The musicians, particularly Egan, were dedicated to fostering the music through playing and learning at sessions, and visiting musicians were encouraged to play a solo or to join in. Many young musicians like Tony McMahon and Barney McKenna and even much younger individuals like Peter Browne were regular participants in the late '50s. The session was held in a room above a bookmakers in Church Street until the early 1960s when its popularity forced a move to the adjacent Boy's Brigade Hall. This was the height of the club's reputation, with the country's finest musicians stopping by and playing. There followed a peripatetic existence when the popularity of the session waned and the venue changed many times from Brú na Gael to the Midland Hotel to the Kings Inns Pub on Henrietta Street, and McGoverns of Smithfield (now the Cobblestone). The 'Church Street Session' eventually established itself in Hughes' of Chancery Street where John Egan presided with warmth and humour until his death in 1983. The session continues there on Tuesday evenings with the anchor position of John Egan now taken by fiddler Pearl O'Shaughnessy who continues a tradition of encouraging regulars and visitors to learn, to appreciate, or simply to enjoy themselves by participating. (EAO)

**Cinnamond, Robert.** (1884–1968). Singer. From near Lough Neagh in Co. Antrim this highly regarded source singer had a remarkably mixed repertoire – Child ballads, political song, local lyrics and Anglo-Irish love song – and an original, high-pitched singing style. He is recorded on *Ye Ramblin' Boys of Pleasure*.

**circular breathing.** A technique of breathing for wind instruments which allows continuous playing without pause for breath. It is used by many bagpipe players, but particularly by Sardinian 'launeddas' (triple pipe) players whose instrument does not have an air reservoir. Players using the technique can play for an hour or more without pause for normal breath. The musician breathes deeply before beginning playing, then re-breathes through the nose at semibreve intervals. Wind is 'stored' in the puffed-up cheeks and used to keep the instrument going while a fresh breath is taken through the nose. Glass-blowers also use the same technique.

**cittern.** A modern, Irish-music version of the cittern totally unlike either its original ancestor – the ancient Greek kithara – or the slender Renaissance-European forms known as English guitar and Portuguese guitar. 'Cittern', as we know it, is a term of convenience, like the uilleann pipes, an instrument-maker's adaptation to suit the music. Luthier Stefan Sobell of Northumberland developed for it a shorter neck than the bouzouki and a deep pear-shape like the Irish bouzouki, a stable, flat-back body like the guitar. Notes are formed by fingering spaced, raised frets with one hand, and plectrum-plucking strings with the other. It produces a deeper, bass-note sound like one of its ancestors, the Arabic *úd*, or lute, but shorter string length also gives it a sharper sound than bouzouki, and less after-note resonance. There are four or five pairs of strings tuned according to the preference of the player – GDAD/A, GDGD/G, GDAE/A, AEAE/A – and there is a range of two octaves over the open strings. The shorter neck and string length and its five sets of strings combine to make it suited to melody playing, while still retaining an accompaniment potential similar to the bouzouki. The bouzouki-guitar is another development of this which combines the familiarity of guitar shape, neck and fingering with tone of bouzouki. Ciarán Curran, Fintan McManus and Garry Ó Briain are leading players.

**Claddagh Records.** Founded in 1959 by nineteen-year-old Guinness heir Garech Browne along with Dublin medical doctor Ivor Browne (no relation) initially to produce a record of their uilleann pipes teacher Leo Rowsome. It was to become one of the most highly regarded traditional music record labels. Also involved in the early days of the company were New York-born poet and writer John Montague, and, for a short time, Dun Laoghaire-based record-shop owner Liam MacAlasdair. Claddagh's second release was the debut recording of the Chieftains, who took their name from John Montague's collection *Death of a Chieftain* (1965). Paddy Moloney, piper and leader of the Chieftains, worked as label manager for Claddagh from the mid-1960s on until his band turned professional in the early 1970s. With Moloney and Montague, Garech Browne pursued an adventurous recording policy throughout the 1960s, releasing ground-breaking albums by the traditional singers Sarah and Rita Keane, Dolly MacMahon, Máire Áine Ní Dhonnachdha and Seán 'ac Dhonncha. Sliabh Luachra fiddle players Denis Murphy and Julia Clifford were recorded for the seminal *The Star above the Garter*. London-based flute-player Paddy Taylor, Dublin fiddler Tommy Potts and Seán Ó Riada all featured on Claddagh releases. The commercial backbone of the label was provided by the increasingly popular Chieftains records of which Claddagh issued a total of thirteen originals. Two volumes of solo piping compilations (*The Drones and the Chanters*) were important in helping the growth of interest in the uilleann pipes; Donegal fiddle music was celebrated in the release of *The Brass Fiddle*; harp player Derek Bell recorded the music of Carolan. While traditional music was the main area of interest for Claddagh, it also released spoken word recordings of Irish and Scottish poets and some classical music albums (Ó Riada, Frederick May, John Field). In 1984 the company opened a retail outlet in Dublin's Temple Bar area and the shop continues to be a meeting place for traditional music enthusiasts. In 1997 chairman Garech Browne formed a second company Claddagh Media. Fronted by David Kavanagh, this co-exists with the original company which continues to be managed by Jane Bolton. (TOS)

**Cláirseoirí na hÉireann.** (The Harpers' Association), set up in 1987 by harper Janet Harbison. The organisation runs the annual Summer Harp School at Kilmore House, Glenariff, Co. Antrim, the eighteenth-century ancestral home of the MacDonnells of the Glens of which family Dr John was sponsor of the Belfast Harp Festival in 1792. Emphasis of the school is learning 'by ear', and session playing. The school also makes some attempt to improve skills for traditional music teachers, and provides tuition in uilleann pipes, flute, fiddle and set dancing.

**claisceadal.** In traditional singing, a cappella group, usually doing arranged songs in Irish, in unison. Best known is Cóir Chúil Aodha begun by Seán Ó Riada. An tOireachtas competitions for claisceadal brought together many names well known in Irish language activities in the past.

**Clancy Brothers and Tommy Makem.** ('The Clancys'). A seminal ballad-group, comprising Clancy brothers Tom (1923–90), Pat (1923–98) and Liam of Carrick-on-Suir, Co. Tipperary, and Tommy Makem (b. 1932) of Keady, Co. Armagh. Originally a Shakespearean actor, then a singer with Seán Healy's dance band, Tom Clancy joined the RAF with brother Pat during World War II. They emigrated to Canada in 1950, moved to Ohio and then New York. Both acting, one of their productions was O'Casey's *The Plough and the Stars*. Working by day in a factory, they gradually became interested in singing; Tom acted in television shows and newly arrived brother Liam played guitar. Liam had met Tommy Makem through helping with Diane Hamilton's song collection, and both emigrated to the US in 1955. While recuperating from an accident Tommy took up singing with Liam, Pat and Tom, this leading to the recording in 1959 of *The Rising of the Moon* – an album of republican songs – on Pat's new label Tradition Records. A tour in Chicago followed; their music skills were rudimentary – a few guitar chords, Pat playing harmonica, Makem's hand injury then prevented him playing whistle – but they found instant popularity by acting naturally. In New York they played at the Blue Angel where they were recruited to perform on the prestigious, nation-wide Ed Sullivan television show. This gave them coast-to-coast acclaim, and made them professional. Dressing in Aran sweaters, which became their hallmark, their song style was unison – they belted out songs with gusto, they were relaxed, informal, humorous.

The songs were a break from the old Irish-American standards – 'Jug of Punch', 'Shoals of Herring', 'Leaving of Liverpool' – attracting a new audience in both the US and in Ireland and bringing a new consciousness to Irish music: '. . . it became respectable again for so-called respectable people to sing working-class songs' (Liam Clancy). Chronichler Pete Hamill described the Clancys' treatment of song as turning negative feeling around, providing an alternative lifestyle that wasn't stifled by Victorian platitudes. This re-colonisation of Irish song found for the Clancys and Tommy Makem a large following in the folk movement in the US. Their success and image found sympathetic resonances in Ireland too in the revival period of traditional music, that synergy bringing them to the front stage of popular music-making. Their style and presentation has been mimicked by hundreds of groups in the years since. Peripheral as they might have been in their early years to the revival of traditional dance music, they became however the entry point to that music for explorative music minds, and many musicians today can attest to them as being their first introduction to traditional music. Liam left to follow a solo career in 1969, the group made sporadic comebacks for St Patrick's Day and such symbolic festivals, and sporadic 'final' tours in various forms up to the mid-1990s. They made numerous recordings.

**Clancy, Willie.** (1918–73). Piper. Born at Miltown Malbay, Co. Clare. His mother, Ellen Killeen, was from an Ennistymon singing family; she sang and played concertina (his versions of the 'Concertina Reel' and 'Lark in the Morning' came from her). His father, Gilbert, who came from Islandbawn, four miles east of Miltown, also sang and played concertina and flute and had learned much from the legacy of blind piper Garret Barry (d. 1900). Willie began on whistle at age five, then played flute until he lost his teeth. He learned step dancing from dance master, fiddler and tambourine-player Thady Casey, and had songs from his mother and father – these of great advantage to his air playing. Although familiar with the pipes through hearing his father speak of Barry, Willie first saw a set only when Johnny Doran played locally at the races of 1936. Two years later he got bag, bellows and a Leo Rowsome chanter from Felix Doran. He took advice from Hugh Curtin of Clochán Mór (also taught by Garret Barry), finally

Willie Clancy (EDI)

getting an 1830s' set of Kilrush-made Maloney Brothers pipes. He took tuition too from Leo Rowsome in Dublin, and would always cycle to hear Johnny Doran when he was in the area. Local Tom Looney got him a Coyne 'C' set in 1942, these he eventually traded in against a new Rowsome set. In the early 1940s he was influenced by pipers Séamus Ennis, Bro. Gildas, John Potts and Andy Conroy (all tight-fingering stylists) and by 1947 he was skilful enough to contemplate taking part in the Oireachtas competition in which he came first. A carpenter by trade, economic necessity saw him move to Dublin in 1951, then to London in 1953 where he renewed his acquaintance with Ennis. While there too he located a Coyne 'B' set for £5 in a junk shop, and returned to Miltown after the death of his father in 1957. In that year he recorded for Gael-Linn on a 'Bb' chanter belonging to Seán Reid, and later was to play on Reid's custom-made, narrow-bore drone Rowsome set. His marriage to Dóirín Healy in 1962 led to a musical honeymoon in the home of Seán 'ac Dhonncha in Ahascragh, Co. Galway. At the end of the decade he was involved in the setting up of Na Píobairí Uilleann. Tom Looney supplied him with his Taylor concert set of pipes in 1969. A skilled reed-maker, Willie had planned to begin making pipes and had acquired the necessary equipment just by the time of his death.

Willie Clancy's piping style was gay and lively, his approach was serious, always mindful of the lore of the music. A jocose singer, his repertoire included 'The Gander', 'The Family Ointment' and other quasi-sexual lyrics which matched his boyish humour. An avid learner, he studied recordings of the Kerry piper Micí Cumbá Ó Súilleabháin and was passionately interested in sean-nós singing and the Irish language. Piper Pat Mitchell noted and published 152 of his tune settings, these are published in the *Dance Music of Willie Clancy*.

See Scoil Samhradh Willie Clancy.

**Clandillon, Séamus.** (1878–1944). Born near Gort, Co. Galway, a mixed language area. He went to school at St Flannan's College, Ennis, then to UCD in 1899 where his interest in Irish matters was sparked by a friend starting a college Gaelic League branch. By 1901 Clandillon was teaching Irish classes with Patrick Pearse. At college he was interested in choral singing and at home in Gort he had always collected songs. An arranger and publisher of songs, he married Maighréad Ní Annagáin, a singer and Irish-speaker from An Déise, Co. Waterford and a prize-winner in the 1901 Oireachtas. In 1904 they published a song book *Londubh an Chairn* and later, *Songs of the Irish Gaels* (1927). In a critical review of *Londubh an Chairn* in the *Irish Statesman*, Donal O'Sullivan called it an insult to Irish music. Between October and November of 1928 this resulted in the longest libel case in Ireland up to then. The jury was divided, and each side was awarded its costs.

In 1911 Clandillon won an Oireachtas Gold Medal for song and was in demand as a singer who accompanied himself on piano and took part in many cultural events in the early years of the century, including the Mansion House concert for returning prisoners in 1916 when he sang 'Seanachúirt na nDéis'. It was he who brought the song 'The Palatine's Daughter' to public knowledge (sung later by Seán Ó Sé). In 1926, as director of 2RN, in cramped surroundings in Little Denmark Street, Dublin, lack of finance often saw him singing selections on air himself. He engaged musicians and early céilí bands to play live, so beginning a policy of promoting traditional music which 2RN's successor, Raidió Éireann, continued. In February 1934, he went to work for the Department of Health.

Clandillon made eleven 78 records for Parlophone and HMV, singing with piano accompaniment, this style being in tune with the ideas of the time.

**Clannad.** Comprised of Máire Brennan (harp, song), Pól Brennan (guitar, song, percussion, flute), Ciarán Brennan (guitar, bass, song), Padraig Duggan (guitar, song, mandolin) and Noel Duggan (guitar, song): 'Enya' Brennan, Máire's sister, joined in 1979. Formed in 1970 through playing at the Brennans' father's bar 'Leo's' at Gweedore, Co. Donegal, they began with local festivals, then moved to playing in Germany in 1975. Already very well known, respected and successful in Ireland and Europe, they gained a yet larger audience through their performing of the signature tune for the 1982 TV series *Harry's Game*, this reaching number five in the British record charts and gaining them an Ivor Novello award. Their 1984 *Robin of Sherwood* track gained a British Academy Award for best soundtrack. Enya went solo in 1982 but the group continues to play a quieter schedule. Clannad created a particular 'Celtic-hush' style of popular music that made great use of electronic enhancement, this adding a hallmark mystical quality to the band's interpretations and arrangements of original and traditional, Irish-language, Donegal song. The influence of this is heard in other performers' styles, notably that of Aoife Ní Fhearaigh and in many 'Celtic' style recordings today.

**Clare.** See song, Clare.

**Clarke, Eddie.** (1945– ). Harmonica. Born in Virginia, Co. Cavan, he learned to play in the 1950s as a result of a Hohner harmonica promotion in his school. His first tunes were marches, these played by the school group which led the parade at the first fleadh in Cavan in 1954. His father played fiddle and accordion, but Eddie's influences were *Ceolta Tíre* and *Job of Journeywork* on Raidió Éireann, and being exposed to playing for dancing. Not until 1965 did he expand his repertoire, when he finished teacher training in Drumcondra and took the time to follow traditional music. He played around the Pipers' Club, John Egan's Club, O'Donoghues (he knew about them from the radio), and meeting Seán Welsh from Donard, Co. Wicklow introduced him to technique, as did the late Paddy Bán Ó Broin. Like his mentor Paddy Bán he plays the chromatic instrument, holding the button in, and releasing it for semitones. He played with Joe Ryan and John Kelly, winning the Oireachtas duets twice with Ryan in the early 1970s. He took part in the 1976 USA Bicentennial music tour with fiddler Maeve Donnelly, singer Maighréad Ní Dhómhnaill and bouzouki player Seán Corcoran. Together they made the album *Sailing into Walpole's Marsh* and with Joe Ryan, Clarke also recorded *Crossroads*.

**classification of instruments.** All music instruments of the world – from ancient to pre-electronic – can be classified according to a system set out by Erich von Hornbostel and Curt Sachs in 1914. This breaks music-making devices down to four categories: 1. aerophones, 2. chordophones, 3. membranophones and 4. idiophones. A fifth category – electrophones – is often used to classify electronic instruments. Inside the system a code number can be allocated to any instrument, pinpointing fairly accurately what the instrument is and how it is played. The system applies mostly to countries like, say, India which has hundreds of different indigenous instruments. This system is quite different to the classical orchestral division of 'brass', 'wind', 'reed', 'strings', 'percussion', etc.

**clavichord.** A fifteenth-century key-action, plucked-string chordophone, similar to the virginal, but usually much more compact, its table-top design and general appearance evoking the modern keyboard. Its strings are parallel to the keyboard, two strings per note. It is played by Mícheál Ó Súilleabháin on 'Jockey to the Fair'. An electronic version, the clavinet, was played by Tríona Ní Dhomhnaill in the Bothy Band.

See chordophone; dulcimer; harpsichord; piano.

**Cleary, Nora.** (1927–88). Singer. The Hand, Mullagh, Co. Clare. Her cottage on the Miltown Malbay road was a renowned gathering place for singers and musicians. She sang a mixture of old ballads, broadsides, local and topical songs, some composed by herself. Her repertoire was recorded for the Department of Irish Folklore. (TOM)

See song, Clare.

**Clifford, Julia.** (1914–97). Fiddle. Born in Lisheen, Co. Kerry, Sliabh Luachra player Julia Clifford spent most of her life in England. Despite her exile, she kept in touch with and exercised a strong influence on the music of her native area, through recordings and regular visits. She was an inspiration to succeeding generations of musicians, and to women players in particular. Daughter of Bill 'The Weaver' Murphy, she and brother Denis Murphy were pupils of Pádraig O'Keeffe, the Sliabh Luachra fiddle master. She made a number of recordings: *Kerry Fiddles* with Pádraig and Denis, *Ceol as Sliabh Luachra*, *The Star of Munster Trio* with her husband Johnny Clifford on piano accordion, and their son Billy on flute. (PAA)

*Clinton's Gems of Ireland.* An 1840 collection of 200 tunes including airs, jigs, planxties, slip jigs and a small number of reels and hornpipes. Its cover proclaims: 'Gems of Ireland containing the most popular of Moore's melodies, all the national airs and the celebrated melodies of Carolan, Connolan & al., collected from the most authentic sources and arranged for the flute by J C Clinton . . .'. These include 'The Irish Washerwoman', 'St Patrick's Day', 'The Lamentation for Owen O'Neill', and 'Peter Street'. Arrangements involve many third octave notes. (SIC)

**Coen, Fr Charles.** (1933– ). Born Woodford, Co. Galway to a musical family, he emigrated to America in 1954 where he became a priest. In 1974 he was first in All-Ireland concertina, flute and tin whistle and in 1978 won the singing. 'Fr Charlie' has been an inspirational figure in the US music scene, and is now centred in Red Hook, New York.

**Coimisiún le Rincí Gaelacha** (Dance Commission).

See step dance.

**Cóir Chúil Aodha.** Choir founded by Seán Ó Riada in 1964, its original purpose was to sing at liturgical services in Cúil Aodha church. Shortly after its inception it started also to sing as a 'claisceadal' – traditional singing group – and some of the choir's first public performances were at An tOireachtas. In 1964, encouraged

Julia Clifford's Slide (Moylan, Lilliput)

and aided by an tAthair D. Ó Concubhair, Ó Riada began arranging the Mass for choir and organ (for congregational singing) as the Second Vatican council was ending. Outside Cúil Aodha, this was first performed in Maynooth College, Dr Tomás Ó Fiaich the celebrant, and later recorded in the Dominican Priory of Tallaght, Dublin. Since Ó Riada's death the choir has been directed by his son Peadar. Many illustrious names from the world of Irish sean-nós singing and poetry have been associated with Cóir Chúil Aodha, and it has presided over many occasions of historical importance. Recordings: *Aifrean 1*, 1967; *Aifrean 2*, 1976; *Go mBeannaíotar Duit*, 1987; *Ceol 's Cibeal*, 1974; *Ó Riada Retrospective*, 1987; *Bringing It All Back Home*, and *Amidst these Hills*, 1992; *Wind's Gentle Whisper*, 1995. (PEO)

**Coleman country.** The area of south Sligo, north Roscommon and north-east Mayo which contains the village of Killavil, close to which fiddler Michael Coleman was born. The area has had a strong expression in music for more than 150 years, involving fife and drum bands, fiddle playing for dancing, flute and tin whistle. In the 1950s there were two céilí bands – the Glenview and the Coleman Country, sometimes exchanging members. The Coleman Country had Peter Horan (flute, fiddle), Alfie Joe Dineen (accordion), Séamus Tansey (flute), Fred Finn (fiddle), Peg McGrath (flute), Tommy Flynn (whistle), Noel Tansey (drums) and often Mary Mulholland (piano). They recorded on Heritage. Another album from the area is *Music From the Coleman Country*, with, in addition to some of the above named players, Andrew Davey, John O'Gara, Jim Donoghue, John Joe Mooney (whistle), Bernie Finn (flute), Tommy Toolin (tambourine) and Oliver Killoran (guitar). Music is passing to a younger generation in the area, with Boyle flute player, music teacher and writer Bernard Flaherty being a mainstay. Musicians like Gregory Daly (flute) and John Carty (fiddle) live in the vicinity, this contributing to a music continuity which, for instance, saw Ted McGowan (bodhrán player) celebrate twenty-five years of weekly music sessions in his bar The Róisín Dubh in 1998.

See fiddle, Sligo; Finn, Fred; flute, Sligo style; Horan, Peter.

**Coleman, Michael.** (1891–1946). Fiddler. Born and brought up on a small farm in the Killavil district of south Sligo, his father, James, was a noted flute player and one of his brothers, Jim, was also well regarded locally as a fiddler. Highly talented from an early age, Michael learned from listening to the many fiddle players in the Killavil area whose distinctive local way of playing has become known as the Sligo style. After short spells working locally, then in the English midlands, he set out with five companions for America in October 1914 where he stayed with an aunt in Lowell near Boston before moving to New York where he spent the remainder of his life. His recording career began in 1921 and his reputation became established through his 78 rpm records made for several different labels. The financial crash of 1929 and the resultant Depression were a severe blow to his professional music career, but he was able to resume in 1936, and his final recordings were made for radio in January 1945, a year before his untimely death in New York. Coleman's records are now regarded as classics of their kind and are among the finest examples of recorded folk music in the early twentieth century. They were sent back to Ireland, where they gave inspiration to players; his style and repertoire were learnt and reproduced credibly by better players. Listened to all over the country, his articulation, phrasing, bowing and dynamics became a 'standard' style. Through his prowess he exercised direction on repertoire too; the effects of this can be heard today in that some of his particular combinations in tune sets are still being played. Indeed, his (and, of course, others') medium of the 78 rpm record itself has determined the duration of sets of tunes to this day: players still stick to the three-tune 'track' which would fill one 'side' on a standard 78. A collection of his recordings and a detailed account of his life were issued by Gael-Linn/Viva Voce. (HAB)

**Coleman Traditional Society.** Following Killavil fiddler Michael Coleman's death in 1945, a 'Coleman Memorial Fund' was first formed in Batty McDonough's of Ballymote in 1958. Dick O'Beirne, nephew of fiddler Lad, was the instigator and secretary, Peter Horan was also on the original committee, as was Paddy Maguire of Ballymote (original treasurer), father of fiddlers Séamus and Manus. All committee members put in £5, other money was raised by appeal and subscription in Ireland, Britain and the US. This resulted in a site for 'clubroom, library and museum' being bought at Killavil in 1959. This was not developed, and in the beginning of the 1970s the committee was re-started as the 'Coleman Traditional Society'. On 7 September 1974 a memorial slab to Michael Coleman was erected at Mount Irwin townland, close to the original Coleman home, and in the years following a commemoration ceremony involving a music tribute to famed and cherished local musicians was held at the site. Ever growing, and promoted in radio broadcasts by prominent local musicians, this event developed as a music weekend that involved the vigorous energy of local flute player Séamus Tansey. This took on significant commercial proportions and finished in 1981. The Coleman Traditional Society was again revived in 1991, when, on the advice of then parish priest Canon Towey, in pursuit of funding for a centre, the CTS changed its name to Michael Coleman Heritage Centre Ltd. A Coleman Festival was begun in 1992, a site for erection of a replica of Coleman's family's old home was purchased at Knockgrania, this completed in 1998. Parallel with this a Coleman Centre was planned for the nearby town of Gurteen, this envisaged as incorporating both local, regional and national music educational needs, and also the development of music-related tourism. Building of this was completed in 1990. Since 1991 the Coleman Heritage Centre has been actively organising classes and a summertime music performance programme. It has produced two albums of music by local players (see discography) and its pupils have begun to appear on All-Ireland winners' lists.

**Coleman, Willie.** (1910–82). Fiddler. Lived at Carnaree, Ballymote, Co. Sligo. Composer of 'Willie Coleman's Jig' and several reels.

**Cole's collections.** See Ryan's Mammoth Collection.

**collectors, collections.** (instrumental music). See Breathnach; Bunting; Clinton; Fleischman; Forde; Goodman; Grier; Hudson; Jackson; Joyce; O'Farrell; O'Neill; O'Sullivan [Donal]; Petrie; Roche; Ryan.

**Collins, Daniel Michael.** (1937–  ). Fiddler, record producer. Born in Harlem, New York, son of a Galway man who as a youngster took lessons from Kerry dancing teacher J. T. McKenna and Mayo fiddler John McGrath. Now based in New Jersey he is a founder of Shanachie records, instigator of its policy of recording 'authentic' performers, and has for many years been to the forefront of traditional music recording.

See Shanachie.

**Comacs.** Well-known Donaghmore, Co. Tyrone, music family who were to the forefront of playing in the 1940s–60s. Johnny, James and Malachy were well known at fleadhanna ceoil. Their family had a céilí band – the Phelim O'Neill – which toured all of Ireland and England. Johnny and James played fiddles, Malachy piccolo and flute, Mick accordion, Mary guitar, Tommy drums, Paddy banjo mandolin.

> When Johnny took the fiddle down
> How happy we did feel
> As his flying fingers graced the strings
> With hornpipe, jig and reel
> 
> (from the poem by Jim McGurk)

**come-all-ye.** Irish-composed narrative song in the English language, a song type so named from the typical opening line: 'Come all Ye . . . loyal sailors/fellow Irishmen/brisky young fellows/dry-land sailors/sprightly sporting youths' etc. The purpose of the expression is to obtain order to begin singing, to indicate who the song might be of interest to, and/or to set the cultural scene for the plot of the song. Come-all-yes are usually explicit; often revelling in gory detail, they deal with real people, places and events. They borrowed their plot structures from Britain, but gradually developed their own idioms. A form of early journalism, they typically will set a scene, introduce characters and plot, develop a plot and conclude, often with a moral. For example, 'The Maid of Agahadowey':

Come all ye young men inclined to ramble
To some strange country your friends to see
Come pay attention to what I mention
And soon you'll hear what has happened to me
I left the parish of Agahadowey
Which causes me here in grief to stand
And ponder deeply on the days I sported
Down by the banks of the bonny Bann.

**Comhaltas Ceoltóirí Éireann (CCÉ).** The largest body involved in the promotion of Irish traditional music. Its aims and objects are 1. to promote Irish traditional music in all its forms, 2. to restore the playing of the harp and uilleann pipes in the national life of Ireland, 3. to promote Irish traditional dancing, 4. to create a closer bond among all lovers of Irish music, 5. to co-operate with all bodies working for the restoration of Irish culture, 6. to establish branches throughout the country and abroad to achieve these. Its constitution directs that it is non-political and non-denominational and membership is open to all who sympathise with its aims and objectives (and who keep its rules). Membership is therefore open also to non-musicians.

*structure*. It is organised throughout Ireland and abroad in a network of local branches. The main tasks of the branch are to 1. enrol traditional musicians, singers and dancers (who support CCÉ's aims), and 2. to organise teaching facilities. In Ireland the branches are responsible to thirty-two county boards, their function being to supervise the countys' branches and their music activity, to form new branches, and to submit motions to annual congress. In turn these boards answer to four provincial councils; their task to control and direct all CCÉ activities and to oversee all manner of disputes within the province. They organise themselves through an annual convention.

This structure is based on the historic counties of the island of Ireland. Since CCÉ deals with music, song and dance among Irish emigrant or Irish-identifying people only, Britain, North America and Australia are treated as additional 'regions' or 'provinces' of Irish culture, rather than as separate countries. The organisation currently reports that it has 400 branches, and is represented in all counties of Ireland. Branches are named mostly after their host town, village or townland, but sometimes may be dedicated to a local patron or saint, and often to the memory of a respected, deceased organiser or musician.

Branches, county boards and provincial councils operate in a bottom-up pyramidal structure overseen by a central executive council. A county board is formed where more than three branches are active there; this is administered by annually-elected voluntary personnel: chair, vice-chair, secretary, treasurer, PRO and two delegates from each branch. The provincial council has also chair, vice-chair, treasurer, secretary, two auditors, and two delegates from each county board. As a higher authority, this has ultimate responsibility for running most events in the province, and can discipline a county board. The central executive council (CEC) in turn has a president, general secretary, five vice-chairpersons, national treasurer, national registrar, competitions officer, music officer, PRO and also two delegates from each provincial council. In addition it has the chairpersons of the provincial councils. The CEC appoints permanent trustees in whom is vested the organisation's property, and to whom falls the responsibility of instituting any necessary criminal or civil proceedings on behalf of the organisation. It meets three times each year to direct the policy of the organisation between annual congresses and to decide upon the venues for the All-Ireland fleadhanna. The grass roots of this democratic structure is the annual congress which is attended by the members of the central executive council, two delegates from each branch, and two from each county board.

Congress elects a president, treasurer, secretary and registrar, it considers amendments to the constitution and other policy and financial matters. Central to the organisation is its headquarters in An Cultúrlann, at Belgrave Square, Monkstown, Co. Dublin (opened in 1974). Here are located the central bureaucracy and archive, and from here are organised most major activities. CCÉ also has regional cultural premises: Cois na hAbhna, Ennis, Co. Clare; The Boathouse, Wicklow; An Ceolann, Lixnaw, Co. Kerry; Dún na Sí, Moate, Co. Westmeath; Brú Ború, Cashel, Co. Tipperary; Dún Uladh, Omagh, Co. Tyrone; Teach Cheoil, Dunloy,

Co. Antrim; Teach Cheoil, Ennistymon, Co. Clare; Teach Cheoil, Corofin, Co. Clare; Teach Cheoil an Chreagáin, Derry; Rockchapel, Co. Tipperary.

The organisation has a full-time director general (appointed, not elected – since 1968 this position has been held by Labhrás Ó Murchú) and for many years has had several other key staff: rúnaí oifigeach (general secretary, Kit Hodge), timire cheoil (music director, Séamus Mac Mathúna), administrator, and projects officers. The position of director general is permanent and is not explained or rule-bound in CCÉ's constitution. The incumbent may also stand for an elected office. Incomes were initially covered by state development funding begun in 1967; since then variously by organisational revenue generated from membership levies, fleadh cheoil and tours proceeds, promotions, grant-aid and fund-raising. CCÉ's 1999 grant aid of £210,000 came from the government's Irish language budget.

*socio-political interventions.* This democratic political structure has a strong centre whose full-time, waged staff may also be the elected executives of the organisation. Disagreements between these and the 'grass roots' on matters of a broader cultural/political nature have in the past led to internal dispute and resignations. This is no different to what prevails in political parties, but the flexibility of one of the points in CCÉ's constitution has precipitated political problems in the past: 'development of an environment conducive to the Aims and Objects of the organisation' (*Bunreacht*, introduction). While this covers the use of the various media, it is also interpreted broadly to include the social/political environment of 'Irish cultural ethos', this incorporating on occasions political ideals and opinions. Thus the organisation caused controversy when in 1971 it cancelled the All-Ireland fleadh as a protest against internment of nationalists in Northern Ireland, and again when it issued statements (and *Treoir* editorials) taking a stand in the national referendum on abortion in 1983. Director general, Labhrás Ó Murchú, concurrent with his employment by CCÉ, is presently also a senator for the Fianna Fáil political party, sharing with C&W promoter Paschal Mooney a portfolio of 'Spokesperson on Arts, Heritage, the Gaeltacht and the Islands'. Such a position is not felt by CCÉ to be compromising of its national cultural ideals, for under his directorship over almost thirty years, CCÉ has expanded its remit, successfully lobbying for state and other funding.

The only major study of CCÉ is *The Case for Ireland's Comhaltas Ceoltóirí Éireann* by Edward O'Henry (*Ethnomusicology*, vol. 33, no. 1, 1989). CCÉ's own (*c.* 1970) publication *Comhaltas – CCÉ* (*Bliain-Iris,* vol. 1, no. 2) gives historical background to personalities.

*history.* The political climate of the 1920s discouraged relaxed social life throughout Ireland, civil war disrupted organised activities, and in the early years of the new state legislation on dancing became one of the agencies which contributed to breaking the link between much local music-making and social dance. Radio and records brought different standards into music-making and other forms of music and dance were competitively available. Deprived of an active purpose in the community, traditional music declined.

Concerned individuals came together at various times, but the kernel of organisation was the Dublin Pipers' Club which had re-formed in 1936. After 1948 discussions that included Jim Seery, Jack Naughton and Leo Rowsome led to a decision being taken to meet in January, 1951 with the coiste (committee) of Feis Lár na hÉireann (Cáit Bean Uí Mhuineacháin and Éamonn Ó Muineacháin, Garda Supt. O'Sullivan), in order to set up a Pipers' Club there. This resulted in a meeting on 4 February, 1951 at the Midland Hotel in Mullingar which issued an invitation to musicians all over the country to attend a music gathering in conjunction with the feis on the following Whitsun weekend. Following the success of this, on 14 October of the same year, at Cumann na bPíobairí's premises – Árus Ceannt, 14 Thomas Street, Dublin – an organisation was formalised as Cumann Ceoltóirí Éireann. Those present for this meeting were the Ó Muineacháins, Willie Reynolds, Arthur Connick, Thomas Rowsome, Pádraig Ó Móinseall, Leo Rowsome, Jim Seery, Paddy McElvaney, Paddy Kelly, M. Mac Carthaigh, Willie Hope, Rev. Bro. Redmond, Jack Naughton and Eamon Murray. The new

CCÉ touring ensemble (CCÉ)

organisation changed its name to Comhaltas Ceoltóirí Éireann in 1952, the year in which the first actual fleadh cheoil was held in Monaghan town. A constitution was adopted at Mullingar on 15 September, 1956, in the same year Northern counties became involved, and in 1960 provincial councils were set up. The first committee of the organisation included Reynolds, McElvaney, the Rowsomes, Seery, Monsell, Connick and Cáit Bean Uí Mhuineacháin (its first president).

*assessment.* Idealism is central to CCÉ. It addresses itself to 'culture', this involving things other than music – in particular the Irish language, on foot of which CCÉ gets its major government funding – but traditional music remains central to its public image. As a pioneer body in relatively anti-traditional music years of the 1950s–60s it dealt at a national level with the indifference, dismissiveness, criticisms of 'inferiority' and hostility that unaffiliated musicians in many parts of the island were obliged to face in their everyday lives. Therefore it could offer focus, confidence and credibility to those then currently involved in the music. The atmosphere of its early years was urgent; 'revival' was seen as a mission to pass on valued traditions and to ensure their survival and enhancement for posterity.

CCÉ has always targeted young people as the key to keeping the music in circulation ('mol an óige agus tiocfaidh siad', 'praise the young and they will respond' is their motto). Consequently its branches endeavoured to organise instrumental classes (some 600 are claimed in 1999). Since the 1950s the fleadh cheoil competition structure has become CCÉ's merit scale, and striving for the recognition that this offers has improved general playing standards hugely and has also attracted new participants. CCÉ's programme of international concert tours (begun in 1972), publications and recordings have contributed to a professionalism throughout traditional music which is its major visible evidence today – players such as Paddy Glackin, Mary Bergin, Joe Burke, Mick O'Brien, Liz Carroll (for instance) all cut their teeth in CCÉ activity, won their trophies, and graduated to being independent spirits in the music business. This professionalism (compared to popular musics) in an indigenous music genre also contributes hugely to the international image of Ireland, and tourism promotions utilise it heavily.

CCÉ employs all the paraphernalia of the commercial-music world in pursuit of its aims: tours, television programmes, and summer schools, teacher training, PR, albums, videos, lecturers, seminars, and courses. Its journal *Treoir* is its internal information outlet and morale-booster. Some 3,000 hours of archive tape document the music collected from older players over the last thirty and more years. The Cultúrlann administrative base deals with PR, information, training, education and recording.

The fleadh cheoil has been, and remains, the organisation's most important public event. Between county, provincial and regional levels, forty-seven of these were held in 1999. The All-Ireland is the biggest, drawing in excess of 100,000 visitors and musicians. Dance is part of CCÉ activities too, organised through the *Coiste Rince* which runs courses, exhibitions and competitions.

CCÉ's expansion has occurred almost paradoxically in a time-frame that has seen great social change, and a population shift from mainly rural to urban. It survived the introduction of television and other mass-entertainment media, and weathered fundamental amendments to national legislation on social, moral and political affairs often believed to be inimical to the music. Its most recent development (1998) has been the joint introduction with the Royal Irish Academy of Music of a graded traditional Irish music examinations syllabus.

*fleadh cheoil*. The 1951 inaugural music event at Mullingar (not yet called a 'fleadh cheoil') was a small affair, opening with a conference that led to a concert and céilí dance; competitions were easily accommodated under one roof. The fleadh was subsequently planned as an annual event that would provide a platform for performance, and an occasion of listening to the music, each equally important. It developed both inspiration for younger players to learn, and a supportive, educated and appreciative audience which valued the 'traditional' style of the playing. By the time of the Ennis All-Ireland in 1956 today's familiar pattern had already emerged: thousands were attending, sessions were reported as spilling over from the venues on to the pavements and into the pubs, sets were danced on the streets late into the night.

*competition, sample statistics*. All-Ireland Fleadh, Clonmel, 1994 illustrates gender balances: there were 144 competitions involving 1,246 instrumental soloists, 162 singers, 45 céilí bands, 99 duets and trios, 31 marching bands, 45 music groups and 28 set-dance teams. As in previous years, females dominated in the age groups up to eighteen (57 per cent), but males took over in all the senior categories (68 per cent). Overall, 56 per cent of the participating singers were female, as were 51 per cent of instrumentalists. 72 per cent of (mixed) senior first prizes went to males. Of the 1,656 soloists and bands/groups entered, 77 per cent were from Ireland, 11 per cent from the US, 10 per cent from England, 2 per cent from Glasgow. There were single entrants from Canada, Germany, Australia and New Zealand.

All-Ireland Fleadh, Listowel, 1995 illustrates regional distribution of prizes. Of the 431 first, second and third-prize winning individuals and groups, 7 per cent (30) were from England, 1.6 per cent per cent (7) from Scotland, and 1.9 per cent (8) from the USA (Ireland 89.8 per cent). Breaking this down further: of the 144 first-prize winners, 7 per cent (10) were from England, 2 per cent (3) were from Scotland, 2 per cent (3) from the USA, (Ireland 89 per cent). Of the 144 second-prize winners 7 per cent came from England, 0.7 per cent (1) from Scotland, 2.7 per cent (4) from the US (Ireland 89.6 per cent). Among third placings 7 per cent were from England, 2 per cent from Scotland, 0.7 per cent (1) from the USA, (Ireland 90.3 per cent). It can be seen from these figures that a disproportionate number of prizes were won by English entrants compared to those from the USA. Also, a disproportionate number of prizes were won by Irish entrants overall. Only with Scotland (mostly Glasgow) is the number of prizes consistent with the number of entrants. This reflects both the communication of the Irish Scots with the 'homeland', and the fact of the Scottish cultural environment's recognition of Scottish music and song which is closely related, structurally and historically, to that in Ireland. At the adjudication level the All-Ireland's overall results suggest an acceptance of taste or standards applicable in Ireland as the standard of what is to be sought for in the expression and interpretation of traditional music. While it could also indicate a prejudice against American players (accent, in music, is likely of no less significance than in language), it may also reflect the different level of application of musicians in Ireland. One aspect of the latter is the easier, and more taken-for-granted availability of sessions, something which applies too in England and Scotland. Another aspect of this is the acculturating playing and listening opportunities such as radio and TV which exist in Ireland (and in Scotland). But results seem to indicate that: 1) Just as goes for accents in language, the political/geographical home base of the Irish Republic is important to the survival of what we know as traditional music. 2) Close proximity to the island, frequency of visiting, similarity of overall cultures (particularly TV culture), incidence of people of Irish descent in England and Scotland – all give greater access to traditional music and make it more a part of overall, everyday cultural life.

See Mac Mathúna, Séamus; Ó Murchú, Labhrás.

**comic song.** See song, comic and satirical.

**composers and composition.** Traditional musicians in the last half of the twentieth century have generally distinguished between two types of tunes in the repertoire: 'traditional' tunes and modern compositions. The individual composers of the great body of tunes handed down from the last century via oral transmission, early sound recordings, and published manuscript collections such as those of Roche and O'Neill, are now lost to history. The early to middle decades of the twentieth century – marked by war, economic crisis, and massive emigration – appear now to have been a time of collection and preservation of traditional music on both sides of the Atlantic. Beginning in the late 1950s, a sense of solidity and confidence about the survival of traditional music returned, and with it the freedom to innovate and compose. In the context of the rapid transmission of tunes in the growing fleadh cheoil milieu of the 1960s and '70s (considerably aided by radio broadcasts and cheap, portable tape recorders), the boundary between the traditional and modern repertoire was often blurred. In the typical modern-day informal music session, tunes are often transmitted from one player to another without any information regarding origin or attribution. The gap between the tune and its origins is widened further by the circulation of commercial recordings with minimal textual information (sometimes inaccurate or poorly researched) about the tunes recorded. The result has been that many of the compositions of important composers of the 1950s and 1960s such as Seán Ryan, Ed Reavy, and Paddy O'Brien were either not until recently properly attributed, or else were regarded as 'traditional'. The situation is not without its difficulties and ironies given commercially driven concerns about accurate copyright control. Composition of dance tunes is now widespread and it is more and more common to find dedicated practitioners who have penned at least one of their own. In the first instance, musicians compose by subjecting given tunes to improvisation, reinterpretation, and alteration. The key of the tune may be changed, for example, opening up new possibilities of phrasing and ornamentation. A tune might also be set in a new time signature, giving an old jig new life as a reel, a polka, an eastern European groove, or a military march or dance-hall waltz a traditional sensibility. Or again, a two-part tune may be ramified into a much longer four- or five-part concerto like the piping jig 'The Gold Ring' or the reel 'The Bucks of Oranmore'. This process is clear in the case of the reel 'Bonnie Kate', which survives as a simple two-part tune as well as in Michael Coleman's more lengthy and elaborate rendition. Most musicians compose tunes only rarely, often as the result of a half-conscious process. But a growing number today are devoting considerable energy towards cultivating the process and inventing new tunes. Generally, contemporary composers direct their creative energies toward the full melodic possibilities of the eight-bar structure of dance tunes, moving beyond the rhythmic emphasis and repetitiveness traditionally perceived to be required for dancing. Ed Reavy, one of the most prolific of recent composers, described this process as one of building on an interesting or unique succession of phrases towards a logically and aesthetically complete tune. Others, notably Leitrim fiddler Charlie Lennon, attempt to yoke the melodic innovation to traditional structures and practices so that, for example, the long-established bowing and phrasing strategies of north Connacht fiddling may be employed to good effect in the new tunes. Other composers are more concerned to explore the technical limits and possibilities of their instruments than with musical forms. The compositions of fiddlers Paddy Fahy (Loughrea, Co. Galway) and Liz Carroll (Chicago) often have a distinctly violinistic sensibility, for example. Pipes and flute players also have developed repertoires that are particularly, though not exclusively, suited to their instruments. By contrast, some composers are so fascinated with melodic possibility that they suspend the requirements of the eight-bar structure altogether. One thinks of Dublin fiddler Tommy Potts' rendition of the reel 'My Love is in America', which takes the simple statement of the first eight bars of the tune and expands it into an intricate, run-on sentence full of digressions and ramifications. Alternatively, Tyrone bouzouki player Fintan McManus's reel 'The Guns of the Magnificent Seven' misses a solitary beat in its third part and, by falling short of the required full eight bars, re-configures the relationship between melody and rhythm. This strategy is so provocative that in some circles the missing beat has been filled in to return the tune to a strict dance format. Another recent fashion has been to expand the context of phrasing beyond the traditional four or eight bars to some higher multiple of four, a strategy that allows for more grandiose thematic or dynamic development. Recent compositions by Mícheál Ó Súilleabháin, Bill Whelan, and Donal Lunny, working within the time signature and phrasing decorum of the slip jig, slide, or polka, bear the long lines and extended development more reminiscent of the music of Corelli, Vivaldi, and O'Carolan than of the modern dance tune. Finally, composers are often motivated by social rather than musical factors. Many compositions mark special occasions or particular circumstances, from weddings and birthdays to the purely accidental or uncanny happenings of life. Cuz Teahan was famous for composing tunes in honour of musical friends, attempting to match the tune to the personality. In the professional realm, the musical and commercial pressures of the recording studio and the concert stage have also become a strong impetus towards composition. With the CD market now saturated with recordings of traditional material, recording artists rely increasingly on their own creative abilities. Recent CDs by the groups Altan and Déanta, for example, feature tunes created specifically for the project, sometimes during the recording process itself. While composition has flourished, criticism and pedagogy of modern tune-making can hardly be said to exist. Communities of traditional musicians tend to vote collectively with their fingers. In a largely unspoken process of selection, a minority of tunes possessed of that special combination of playability and aesthetic interest gradually fold themselves into the traditional repertoire, while the vast majority of new compositions languish in printed collections, on commercial CDs, or in the repertoires of isolated practitioners. (MAD)

Anglo system concertina (EDI)

**concertina.** Hexagonal, button-operated, free-reed, bellows-blown instrument played with the fingers of both hands. It uses one reed per note. Developed out of the harmonica principle, the concertina was developed as the 'symphonium' in 1829 by Charles Wheatstone in England, the 'English' concertina. The result of intense technical experimentation, its typically hexagonal profile is a compromise on Wheatstone's ideal of a cylindrical shape. Eight- and twelve-sided models were tried too. The instrument so designed was the 'English' system (same note on push and pull), and because it could match the range of the violin, it became popular for upper-class, casual music-making, much music being published specifically for it. Around the same time Carl Uhlig in Germany designed a diatonic 'conzertina', called the 'German' system (different notes on push and pull). In the early 1850s, English makers improved the German instrument, conferring on it the term 'Anglo-German' and then 'Anglo' concertina. Mass-production was now feasible; the Lachenal company supplied a quarter million over its years up until the 1930s while German factories made great numbers of cheap instruments also. Charles Jeffries produced what were considered to be the better of the Anglo concertinas; his company operated up to the 1920s. Wheatstones (they made some 60,000) ran until the late 1960s, while the Crabb company continued up until 1989. A further system is found in concertina – the 'Duet' – this developed by one Prof. McCann for Wheatstone, and providing separate treble and bass button-systems. Other 'Duets' exist, notably the 'Crane' system adopted by salvation army bands, and for them re-named the 'Triumph'. Today, concertinas are made mostly in Italy, and some in China.

*action*. Nicknamed 'the squeeze-box' – for its playing action – as were its relatives the accordion and melodeon, like these, the concertina has free reeds which are activated by air, the flow of which is regulated by pressing buttons in tandem with pressing and drawing out the bellows. The main variety of concertina in use in Irish music is the 'Anglo'. It is 'single-action' – each button has a different note on press and draw (two notes per button) – thirty of them arranged in three rows of five on each side, all the melody notes divided up between the two hands. In England the 'English' concertina is more popular – it has forty-eight or fifty-six keys arranged in four rows on each side; it uses 'double action' – push and pull give the same note (only one note per button) – making its playing action more flowing, like piano accordion, and more suitable for accompanying song, but less tasty for the rhythm desired in Irish dance music.

Originally expensive, and by 1850 an upper-class recreational instrument, factory mass production eventually rendered it popularly affordable. Its spread was aided by its uncomplicated playing technique, its robustness and volume – all of which were important in crowded, noisy venues. By the 1870s it was widespread in the music hall, and concertina bands were popular all over working-class England. A specially tough version was made in 1884 to endure the rigorous, all-weather trials of temperance-seeking, Salvation Army Bands. Such 'common' usage contributed to its abandonment by polite society; it became for them an object of abuse. It had spread to Ireland by the century's end, in tandem with popular use in Britain; mass-produced models were insubstantial, but were cheap, easy to master for simple dance-rhythms – and loud. Like melodeons and accordions its fixed and dependable tuning, loud volume and tolerance of the damp climate led to its partially replacing the uilleann pipes for dance music. In the 1920s William J. Mullally was recorded in the US on 78s (he can be heard on the remastered Viva Voce recording, and on Shanachie's *Wheels of the World*, vol. 2). Concertina was originally popular all over the island – but probably more so in urban environments – and older players are documented in the Sperrin Mountains, Tyrone, in the 1960s, in the Midlands, and elsewhere. Concertina was eclipsed in its own turn by the accordion – possibly because of its lighter tone – but it remained popular in Co. Clare. (EDI)

*Clare*. The concertina arrived originally in Co. Clare in the late 1800s in a variety of ways:

1. River traffic to and from Limerick along the lower Shannon, one of the last ports of call for ships crossing the north Atlantic. Maritime chandlers stocked cheap German concertinas as part of their trade merchandise, and many of these were exchanged with river pilots and fishing communities on both sides of the Shannon in Clare, Limerick and Kerry;

---

AN ELEGANT CHRISTMAS OR NEW YEAR'S GIFT
(THE CONCERTINA)
MAY be seen in great variety at the Manufacturer's,
JOSEPH SCATES,
26, COLLEGE-GREEN,
Importer of Pianofortes, Harmoniums, Concertinas, by Wheetetone; Flutinas, Accordeons, and the new Bell-Metal Harmonica.

Concertina advertisement in *Freeman's Journal*, 23 December 1852.

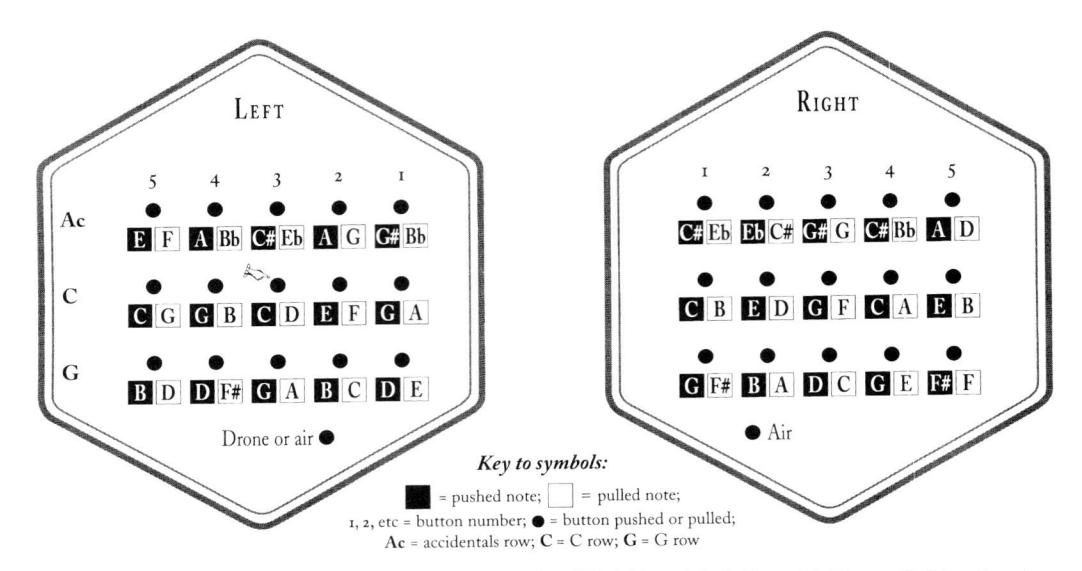

Push and pull note system on C & G Anglo concertina (Mick Bramich & Dave Mallinson Publications)

2. Between 1895 and World War I there was some interchange between British army band masters and local musicians in Clare, especially in areas adjacent to the garrison towns of Ennis, Kilrush and Ennistymon. This created inroads for emerging instruments like the concertina;

3. The instrument was also stocked by hardware stores, and women, with some income from egg and butter sales and other cottage industries, are described as being among its main patrons – concertina was in fact sometimes referred to as a 'bean chairdín' (female accordion);

4. During the 1930s many Clare immigrants in British cities sent concertinas home to families in remittance parcels. This source become particularly important in the 1950s when double-action, Anglo-German concertinas made by Jeffries, Wheatstone, Lachenal and Crabb became popular in rural Clare. Concertina had replaced the uilleann pipes as the popular instrument in rural Clare by the early 1900s.

Dialects and players: From 1890–1970, concertina playing in Clare developed within four musical 'dialects' corresponding for the most part to the set dancing 'dialects' of rural Clare.

1. That of south-west Clare was highly rhythmical, melodically simple, with single-row fingering technique on Anglo-German instruments. The plain set danced to polkas predominated in the area prior to the adoption of the Caledonian. Because of the influx of travelling teachers like fiddler George Whelan from Kerry, the music of the area was linked to the polka and slide repertoires of Kerry and west Limerick. Hence, older concertina players like Charlie Simmons, Solus Lillis, Elizabeth Crotty, Matty Hanrahan, Frank Griffin, John Kelly and Marty Purtill played a variety of archaic polkas and single reels. The Caledonian set however facilitated more complex double reels which were favoured by players like Tom Carey, Sonny Murray, Tommy McCarthy, Bernard O'Sullivan and Tommy MacMahon.

2. The concertina dialect of mid-west Clare, from the Fergus Valley in the east, to Quilty on the west coast, was shaped explicitly by the rhythmical complexities of Caledonian set dancing, as well as by the American 78 rpm recordings of William J. Mullally during the 1930s. Home to celebrated players like Noel Hill, Miriam Collins, Gerard Haugh, Gerdie Commane and the late Tony Crehan, the region still uses dancing master Pat Barron's steps and dance figures. That concertina style uses complex cross-row fingering, intense

melodic ornamentation and has a large repertoire of dance tunes. The most outstanding concertina master here in recent times was Paddy Murphy from Bealcragga, Connolly. Influenced by the recordings of Mullally, he pioneered a cross-row fingering system which facilitated the use of alternative scales for tunes in unfamiliar keys (many of which he and peers in the Fiach Roe Céilí Band learned orally from the fiddling of the local postman Hughdie Doohan who could 'read' the music from O'Neill's *1001 Gems*).

3. North Clare had three concertina communities situated along the perimeter of the Burren, Doolin, Bellharbour and Kilfenora/Kilnaboy. With the exception of Pakie Russell (whose innovative style also explored cross-row fingering), most of the older players in north Clare favoured melodically simple music and single-row fingering, accentuating the inside or G row of the Anglo-German concertina. The overriding feature of this dialect was its emphasis on rhythm for set dancers. This indigenous 'lift' was endemic in the music of Peadaí Pheaitín Ó Flannagáin, James Droney, Brody Kierse, Biddy McGrath and Michilín Connollan. It can still be heard today in the playing of Chris and Ann Droney, Máirtín Fahy and Mick Carrucan, all of whom are extolled by Clare set dancers.

4. East-Clare concertina was concentrated on the Clare-Galway border at Slieve Aughty, around Clooney and Feakle, and above the Shannon in Cratloe and Kilfentenan. German concertinas were popular here in the early 1900s, played mainly by women who seldom played beyond the confines of their own kitchens. The region's archaic repertoire and ethereal settings are found in the playing of John Naughton of Kilclaren, and in the recordings of Connie Hogan of Woodford. Mikey Donoghue, Bridget Dinan and Margaret Dooley represented a similar style around Tulla and Cratloe. Concertina music of Cratloe and Kilfentenan survived until recent times in the playing of Paddy Shaughnessy and John O'Gorman. The most prominent exponent of east Clare concertina music today is Mary McNamara who carries the style and repertoire of masters like John Naughton and Mikey Donoghue.

Clare concertina music has experienced a surge of interest since the 1980s, not least as a result of Scoil Samhraidh Willie Clancy, and Éigse Mrs Crotty which have created a forum for master performers and students. But in attracting large numbers of learners, they have failed to stem the decline of regional concertina dialects. Competitive performance and commercial recording have spurred the growth of a 'modernist' generic style and a meticulous imitation of professional performers. Emphasis on such technical accomplishment has generated prodigiously-ornamented tune settings and the introduction of non-local repertoires; it has also led to separation of 'performance' music from 'dance' music. Among those sustaining the older dialects of Clare are Jacqui McCarthy, Florence Fahy, Breeda Green, Louise Pyne and Francis Droney. Foremost among an innovative corps of 'modernist' performers are Noel Hill, Padraig Rynne, Hugh Healy and John MacMahon, whose technical genius has propelled the concertina music of Clare well beyond the limits of its former communal dialects. Despite this, like their predecessors in the early 1900s, women continue to dominate Clare concertina music. Among its celebrated female exponents are Yvonne and Lourda Griffin, Bríd and Ruth Meaney, Dympna Sullivan and Lorraine O'Brien. Longevity is common among female concertina players in Clare – Margaret Dooley and Bridget Dinan both lived well over one hundred years, and Susan Whelan of Islebrack celebrated her centenary in 1991 by playing a few tunes on a new Czechoslovakian concertina. The oldest musician in Clare today is Molly Carty (b. 1896) from Lissroe, Kilmaley who plays a Bastari concertina made in Italy.

**Confiant, Joe.** (1899–1986). Cape Breton Irish fiddler with unique settings of both Irish and Scottish tunes. With powerful tone, free bowhand, and profuse finger embellishments, he was renowned for spontaneous variation. He influenced both his nephew Johnny Wilmot and Robert (Bobby) Stubbert. Born on the Northside, he learned his fiddling from his uncles Henry and Billy Fortune. He played frequently with John Willie Morrison (piano) and Alex Basker (harmonica). (PAC)

**Connemara Quartet.** Mícheál Ó hEidhin (piano accordion), Tomás Ó Ceannabháin (uilleann pipes, Aird Mhóir, Carna), Pádraig Ó Ceannabháin (flute), Dónal Standún (Spiddal, banjo). This group recorded on CCÉ's first LP *Rambles of Kitty*, and won £500 prize for the Fiddler of Dooney's highly competitive group award in 1975.

**'Connerys, Na/The'.** Title of one of the big songs in the sean-nós tradition. It also has a version in English. The song takes its name from the Connery brothers – Patrick, James and John – born at the turn of the nineteenth century at Bohadoon, Sliabh gCua, Co. Waterford. Viewed by authorities as rebels, outlaws, faction fighters and convicts, they were from a distinguished family, but by 1829 their father had only a share in a small hilly farm. A dispute between one brother and Maurice Hackett – the steward of the land agent – resulted in the shooting of Hackett by two men dressed as women in 1831. John Connery was then implicated in two faction killings in 1833, but was acquitted after a constable was unable to translat e a death-bed statement from English back to its original Irish. When the land agent – Thomas Foley – evicted the Connerys, they promptly threatened his life and property, and in 1835, Foley, also an attorney, saw James Connery sentenced to transportation to New South Wales for life, damned by the evidence of Foley's brother William (grandfather of writer Arthur Conan Doyle). John Connery was acquitted when the crown witness developed amnesia. John and Patrick forcibly re-took their farm, but were convicted at the following assizes and sentenced to transportation for seven years. They escaped from Clogheen Bridewell, however, and threatened to kill the Foleys if the transportation verdict was not rescinded. This heroic action raised the possibility of widespread revolt, and the brothers had huge popular support which helped them evade capture for almost seven months during which they survived a gun-battle with police near Dungarvan. They arranged to go to America, but were betrayed by a Waterford city tailor tempted by the £50 government reward. Broken out of the city gaol by their sister Máire and an uncle in May 1836, they went underground and formally reappeared with the coronation of Queen Victoria in 1837, attempting to negotiate a pardon. Captured at Kilcloher in March 1838 after twenty-two months of freedom, they were convicted of jail breaking and sentenced to transportation for fourteen years. In a speech from the dock, John Connery identified the major cause of turmoil within Irish society as being the robbery of the poor by the rich. He further added that he had done nothing which would raise a blush on his forehead. The passion of the occasion caused a near riot as the brothers were removed from Waterford city for the last time. In New South Wales up until 1851, Patrick and John Connery were, as convicts, in charge of the Lachlan Swamp now better know as Sydney's Centennial Park. Through John's friendship with Minister James Fullerton, from Aghadowey, Co. Derry, he became a Presbyterian, and died in 1851. Patrick and James were later successful as contractors in Sydney, James dying in 1857, Patrick in 1880. The Connerys are important historical figures in pre-Famine Ireland for the manner in which they articulated, personalised and made explicit the whole tradition of agrarian dissent. They were potent symbols for the Irish speakers and small farmers of the uplands of Co. Waterford. Their epic and unequal struggle with the magistracy, police and courts earned them the title, as in the songs, of 'na sárfhir' (the great men). Although the Great Famine swept away the world of the Connerys it ironically helped to enhance their legendary status for they became a symbol of revolt and hope for better times. Traditional Irish music has cemented memory of the Connerys, for in three major songs they are portrayed as the ultimate role-models; no criticism of their action will be accepted:

> Is go bhfuil 'fhios ag gach aoinne nach rabhadar ciontach riamh in aon chor,
> Ach ag seasamh 'na gceart féineach is gan é acu le fáil.
> (Everyone knows they were above reproach,
> Fighting only for their rights which were denied).

Nioclás Tóibín sings of the Connerys on a 1977 Gael-Linn recording, and their life, trials and song lyrics are documented by Brendan Kiely in *The Connerys – The Making of a Waterford Legend*. (BRK)

**Connolly, Séamus.** (1944– ). Fiddler. Born at Killaloe, Co. Clare, he was the youngest winner ever of an All-Ireland senior fiddle title in the 1961 Fleadh Cheoil. First of ten All-Ireland solo awards, this led to the Sligo Fiddler of Dooney in 1967 and various Oireachtas duet titles, one with Peter O'Loughlin. He played with Joe Burke in the Leitrim Céilí Band in the late 1950s and early '60s, and also with Kitty Linnane in the Kilfenora. One of his most notable partners was Nenagh accordionist Paddy O'Brien with whom he recorded *The Banks of the Shannon*. He has two solo albums, *Notes from My Mind* (1988) and *Here and There* (1989). He is also to be heard on the 1991 Green Linnet album made from the March, 1990, Boston College Irish Fiddle Festival in conjunction with Mícheál Ó Súilleabháin. This led to his appointment to the college in 1990 where he teaches courses in Irish traditional fiddling. Widely known as a teacher and performer, he also organises a college concert and céilí programme with well-known Irish players, in addition to developing the new Irish archives for the Burns Library.

See Burns Library.

**Conradh na Gaeilge** (The Gaelic League). The main body promoting the Irish language. Set up in 1893, its headquarters are in Dublin. A classless organisation, it is by its nature educational and has been a widespread forum of adult education; its focus being the recapture of Ireland's past to make that a dynamic in the present and future; music and music heritage have always been within its remit. It was the instigator of, and still organises the annual Oireachtas competitive event. Begun in 1897, this featured the Dublin Musical Society enlarged with Gaelic Leaguers, performing choral song in Irish. Solo singing was featured from the start – with names such a Vincent O'Brien, Séamus Clandillon and Annie Patterson prominent in the early years. The pattern became varied and extended – thirteen competitions in the 1902 programme leading to the song-book series 'Cláirseach na nGael' under the editorship of Brendan Rogers and J. H. Lloyd, and in consultation with Hardebeck and Grattan Flood. Songs harmonised and arranged for 'chorus singing', by Robert Dwyer, were published as sung at the 1902 festival.

At the 1903 Conradh Ardfheis (annual conference) it was decided to take up sean-nós song in an organised way: 'that Traditional singing (old Irish Style) should be encouraged at future Oireachtas or Feiseanna'. Special conferences supported by Pearse, Alice Milligan, Edward Martyn et al. were organised in 1910 and 1911. The Feis Cheoil was almost coeval with the Oireachtas and the bigger feiseanna (Fr Matthew, Shligigh, etc.); all drew on a stream of consciousness released by An Conradh which led to smaller feiseanna being organised by its branches throughout the country. There was a certain tension between the sean-nós and the belcanto singing styles, and two separate traditions, and so almost two separate sets of competition evolved – Sorcha Ní Ghuairim, say, representing the former, Máire Ní Scolaí, the latter.

Competitions in composition were initiated at the 1901 Oireachtas and concerts were major points in the calendar of the Conradh itself, its branches and sub-organisations. Owen Lloyd had his 'Band of Harps' at the 1900 concert which also featured Tomás Rowsome on the pipes. They appeared along with the dancers who were coming to the fore since the first dancing competitions in 1898. The St Patrick's Day concerts, organised by branches of the League became showcases for all the best talent – John McCormack, for instance, being featured in 1907 (with A. P. Graves's 'When I Rose in the Morning') and Joseph O'Meara with 'The Foggy Dew'. Conradh na Gaeilge is administered from 6 Harcourt Street, Dublin and in 1999 its state funding was £205,000. (PAO)

See Oireachtas.

**Conway, Jim.** (1916– ). Fiddler. Born 1916 at Plumbridge, Co. Tyrone, he emigrated to New York where he settled in the Bronx. Best known of his family is son Brian – the 1986 All-Ireland senior fiddle winner – who was taught by Martin Wynne, and recorded *Apples in Winter* in 1981 with fiddler Tony DeMarco. Jim's daughter Rose has also recorded, with the 1985 album *Cherish the Ladies*.

**Conway, Ollie.** (1922–   ). Singer and dancer. Mullagh, Co. Clare. A dancer of great natural ability, both solo and in a set. The rhythm and fire of Conway's expertise is highly regarded in West Clare where he remains one of the county's most popular singers of traditional songs. He can be heard on *The Lambs on the Green Hills.* (TOM)

See song, Clare.

**Cooley, Joe.** (1924–73). Accordion. From Peterswell, Co. Galway, a builder by trade, he was a profoundly charismatic figure in traditional music – whether at home in Clare, in exile in Britain or the USA. Both his parents played the melodeon, and most of his older brothers were musicians. Growing up, the Cooley house was a popular gathering place – dances were held there almost every evening, the music provided by the family. His playing was deceptively simple and straightforward, but with a remarkable 'lonesome' quality which infatuated followers, inspired dancers and created a legend of the player in his own time. Always on the move, he worked in Clare, then London, and emigrated to the USA in 1954 where he went on to live in New York, Boston, Chicago and San Francisco. He played with Paddy O'Brien of Nenagh in the Tulla Céilí Band, later with him in New York, and much of his music-making over the years was with brother Séamus. Dancers were particularly drawn to Joe Cooley's music, Charlie Pigott recounting in the book *The Blooming Meadows* how, when leather and steel-clad shoes were worn, the dancers might loosen the toe-piece to create a buzzing which could be manipulated in the 'slide' motion to articulate grace notes and decoration in the tune being played. Joe Cooley returned to Ireland in 1972. Such was his power that his many admirers would travel from all over the country to hear him in the year prior to his death. The definitive (and only) collection of his music – *Cooley* – which contains a track with brother Séamus, was produced by Gael-Linn in 1975. Some tracks were recorded with brother Jack on bodhrán and Des Mulkere on banjo just three weeks before his death. Tony MacMahon, deeply touched by Joe Cooley's playing, recalls in the sleeve-notes the accordionist's travels: 'The two Joes [Cooley and fiddler Joe Leary] had played all over Clare and Galway in the early 1950s, travelling dusty, icy or rainy roads on a motorcycle, the fiddle slung over Cooley's back, the accordion tied to the fuel tank'.

*San Francisco.* Joe Cooley arrived in San Francisco in 1965 having spent much of the previous decade in Chicago. He played and taught until 1972, giving a valuable fillip to music in the area. Thirty years later his pupils Patricia Kennelly, Miliosa Lundy and John Lavel still sustain his East Galway style. His music associates were accordionist Kevin Keegan (Eyrecourt, Galway), flute player and fiddler Joe Murtagh (Miltown Malbay, Clare), harmonica player Larry Fitzgerald (Enniscorthy, Wexford), accordionist Maureen Costello (Tubber, Clare). Cooley, Keegan and Murtagh played at dances, fairs and festivals as the Gráinneog Céilí Band. Cooley appealed to a wide cross-section of music enthusiasts – many of them had no connection with Ireland or Irish America. His relaxed and uncluttered personality had enormous appeal to freedom-seeking hippies who formed part of California's cultural mosaic in the late 1960s. His death left a permanent void in San Francisco's Irish-music community. (GÓH)

**Cooley, Séamus.** (1929–97). Flute player, Galway, London, Chicago. Séamus Cooley was born into a famous music family in the Peterswell district, Co. Galway. By age ten he was playing tin whistle and concert flute, and largely self-taught he acknowledged Jim Fahey of Derrawee, Co. Galway as a mentor. But probably the greatest single influence on his music came from brother, Joe, with whom he played in a duet and in several famous céilí bands, including the Tulla which he joined at age sixteen. In 1949 he emigrated to London with Joe where he was a central figure in a milieu which included piper Willie Clancy, fiddlers Michael Gorman, Bobby Casey and Martin Byrnes, flute player Roger Sherlock and accordion players Eddie Bolger and Raymond Roland. In 1955, Séamus returned to Ireland, living at Longwood, Co. Meath where he played regularly with fiddler Jim O'Leary. In 1957, the two came first in duets at the Dungarvan All-Ireland Fleadh Cheoil where the Tulla band also took a first. All through this period, Séamus Cooley's association with the Tulla Céilí Band had continued; he was in their United States tour which followed in 1958, and recorded there with them. Remaining in the US, he joined brother Joe in Chicago, the two of them becoming fixtures there during the 1960s, playing regularly on radio, at Jack Hanley's House of Happiness and the Kerryman's Club. Together they founded the prize-winning Glenside Céilí Band, and over three consecutive years Séamus took firsts in senior flute at the Chicago Fleadh. In that city until the early 1980s he continued to be one of the most popular and active musicians in the Chicago Irish community, playing regularly for the Irish hour at Hoban's tavern on Sunday evenings and at céilís and concerts around Chicago. In the mid-1970s he performed at folk festivals with his wife, the former Mary McDonagh, a sean-nós singer from Leitirmór, Co. Galway, and with fiddler Johnny McGreevy. In 1975 Séamus recorded with McGreevy on the LP *McGreevy & Cooley* and as a soloist on *Hollow Poplar*. Séamus Cooley returned to Peterswell, Galway, in 1985 where he played in later years with accordionist Peter Gardiner.

**copyright.** A concept which describes the intellectual property-right that a composer or 'creator' has to their compositions. Copyright arises out of the idea that a music composition is unique, artistically and creatively original to the composer, as with books and other written texts. Copyright is paid for by 'royalties', and thereby provides a means of remuneration for composers when their original works are either played by other people, or performed on public broadcasts. This contributes to personal security by providing a structure for the material welfare of the composer, thereby encouraging and ensuring artistic and intellectual creation and cultural development. An original work is in copyright for seventy years after the end of the year in which the composer dies. Copyright gives composers or their heirs control over granting permission to use tunes or songs, so facilitating payment for their public performance by themselves and others. All music, including traditional music, is subject to copyright, and when this expires, all material becomes 'public domain'. Much of the old repertoire of traditional music is anonymously composed and 'public domain', therefore outside copyright control. However, in recognition of the individual variation ideally occurring in playing of such old tunes, Irish copyright practice regards the player as 'arranger', and so enables new performers of old works to claim 'Traditional Arrangement by the player' (Trad. Arr.), entitling them to a 100 per cent royalty for such performance and public broadcast. Owing to the inefficiency of large-scale self-administration of copyright, most composers exercise their rights collectively, through administrative societies like IMRO, ASCAP, PRS and MCPS. Copyright royalties are collected for all aspects of the listening/consumption of all musics. These are broken down to 1. live performance (gigs, concerts, festivals, etc.) and public broadcast (radio, TV, shops, etc.); 2. permissions given by composers to performers to record their material on albums, video, etc. (both of these are administered on behalf of, and benefit only, composers). 3. a broadcasting, 'record-performance' royalty that benefits the recording companies only. In Ireland three bodies administer all of this – IMRO, MCPS and PPI. For the purposes of applying copyright law in relation to music, a 'music user' is defined as the company, premises or organisation in whose premises or on whose network music is performed or broadcast. This includes live gig and concert venues, festivals and ambient-music performances. It includes radio and television companies, and also includes shops, shopping centres, public houses, buses, phone-lines etc., which use PA and other publicly heard playing of music. (ANM)

See ASCAP; IMRO; MCPS; PPI.

**Corcoran, Seán.** (1945– ). Bouzouki, singer, song collector. His singing was strongly influenced by local performers such as Mary Ann Carolan whom he began recording while still a schoolboy. Professionally he carried on this work for many years as a folk song collector, initially with Breandán Breathnach, with whom he was assistant editor of *Ceol*. He studied ethnomusicology with John Blacking at QUB, and in his fieldwork has covered every aspect of Irish traditions, including sean-nós, instrumental music, Orange drumming and fifing and traditional dancing. With a specialisation in vocal techniques and the importance of ideology in music, he is known internationally as a lecturer. He plays with the group Cran, and has recorded with them and also with Eddie Clarke. His collecting work for the ACNI resulted in the production in 1986 of the *Here's a Health* book and cassette document.

**Cork.** See song, Cork urban ballads; song, West Cork.

**Cork Pipers' Club.** Founded in 1898, centenary year of the 1798 rebellion, a year of great historic importance in which the country experienced a strong Gaelic 'revival'. Behind the club was John Smithwick ('Seán') Wayland, aided by Alderman William Phair, the first chairman. The first meeting was in 1898 at 10 Marlboro Street; all available city pipers were present. The club's aims were to promote Irish music and dance, language and culture. It sought to bring together musicians – especially pipers – and all those interested in its aims. Wayland and Phair sought out and introduced many pipers to the club, including Robert 'Bob' Thompson, Shane O'Neill, Jimmy Barry, and Michael 'Cumbaw' O'Sullivan. The club's activities included classes in uilleann piping, war piping and dance; these were held on several evenings each week. The piping tutors included Robert Thompson and Wayland; dance tutors included Theo Corkery and later Cormac Ó Caoimh. Annual concerts were held at the City Hall, Cork at which the club's own members were the chief performers along with invited guests. The Pioneer Quadrille Club on Tuesday, Thursday and Sunday nights was the club's social gathering. They started the Brian Boru Pipe Band, which performed all over the south-east, and in other parts of Ireland.

A feature of the Pipers' Club was its large number of female players – May McCarthy and Mollie Morrissey being the best known. Wayland's departure for Australia was the first in a sequence of events that led to the eventual wind-down of the club from 1930. Revived again in 1963, primarily due to the efforts of the late Mícheál Ó Riabhaigh, membership grew rapidly. Large numbers of young musicians attended classes and meetings each Saturday were followed by sessions. Activities included an annual concert held at the Cork School of Music, at which some of the great pipers of the time performed, including Leo

Liverpool Céilí Band. Eamonn Coyne is second from left, Charlie Lennon is third from right. (CCÉ)

Rowsome and Willie Clancy. An annual excursion to Tralibane, Bantry, Co. Cork, the birthplace of Captain Francis O'Neill was held, as well as visits to Mitchelstown and Cill na Martra. With the death of Mícheál Ó Riabhaigh in 1976, the club lost its chairman, teacher and founding member, but his students became the new organisers and promoters. One hundred years later the club still flourishes at 13 Dyke Parade, a tribute to teacher and pipe maker, the late Sylvester Ryan. (MAM)

**Coyne, Eamonn.** (1927–93). Fiddler. Born Co. Roscommon, he emigrated to Liverpool as a young man and remained there until his death. As a teenager in the late 1940s he began playing at céilís run by the local Gaelic League, and was one of the founding members of Liverpool CCÉ in 1957. He played with the Liverpool Céilí Band – formed to compete at fleadhanna and to play at the weekly céilíthe – and continued with it until his death. The band won Oireachtas titles in 1962, '63 and '64, the All-Ireland too in the latter two years. Eamon toured Ireland with them several times, adjudicated competitions all over Britain, taught with Liverpool CCÉ for several years, and was made its Honorary Life President. Father of a well-known music family, he was one of CCÉ's active organisers – regional delegate, a music sub-committee member in Britain and congress delegate. He is remembered by a Féile Cheoil in Liverpool.

**crack.** Uplifting and enjoyable conversation, fun. Often used to describe a combination of good music and drinking among a wide spread of friends not normally together – all in the circumstance of an occasion of great relaxation. Such might be a weekly session at the end of the working week, a chance bringing together at a reception or album launch, a funeral, or a regular annual music event. 'Having the crack', 'great crack', 'mighty crack', 'no crack at all' are how the word might be used in conversation. 'A cracker', in Belfast, might refer to an exceptional person, event, session or night.

**craic.** A modern-Gaelic, commercially exploited spelling of the English word 'crack', most typically found on Irish-bar posters linked by the word 'agus' to the word 'ceol', this indicating commercialisation of traditional music as a device in selling 'ól' (Caoimhín Mac Aoidh). Objection to the use of this spelling does not occur when it is used in writing in the Irish language, but it causes reaction when it appears as a 'borrowed' word in written English, because it is in fact originally an Old-English word which has been borrowed by the Irish language, and deductively translated (1977, Ó Dónaill) into Irish. The word 'crack' is in everyday use in Ulster, Scotland, England and the USA, and would appear to have become widespreadly popular in the southern part of Ireland only since the 1970s, where up until then the term 'geas' was the popular word for the same concept. The spelling 'craic' does not appear in Gaelic dictionaries until 1977; its converse does not appear in the 1904 Lane's or the 1959 de Bháldraithe English–Irish dictionaries. The spelling 'craic' is presumably deduced from the old Irish word 'cracaire' (jester, talker, Dineen 1927) but – controversially – slenderises its sound. It may also be linked, deductively, to the modern word 'craiceáil' (to drive crazy), but only by mischievous extrapolation to 'cráic' (the actual pronunciation in Belfast where the word is most popular) which in fact means 'buttock' or 'anus'. 'Crac' (conversation) is given in the modern Scots Gaelic dictionary (MacLennan, 1979) but not the inverse; 'cracaireachd' is translated as 'conversation' in the 1900 MacAlpine Scots Gaelic dictionary.

See crack.

**cran.** Decoration used in uilleann piping. A defining ornament, it is characteristically used to achieve a staccato low D of the chanter. It may also be used on low E. The effect is mimicked too on flute and fiddle, and is used also by some concertina and accordion players.

Cranning might be used on the low D notes on 'The Blackthorn Stick', p. 92.

## The Blackthorn Stick (Jig) (An Gúm)

**Crehan, Martin (Junior).** (1908–98). Fiddler, concertina player, singer, storyteller. Born Bonavilla, Mullach, Co. Clare, he began playing at the age of six, learning concertina first from his mother, later teaching himself fiddle with direction from Scully Casey. In his younger years he played with this 'master' for house and cross-roads dances, strawboy nights, wren balls, American wakes and 'swarrys'. He grew up among the last of the Gaelic speakers of west Clare, and learnt music from the last of the travelling players; at his most formal he played along with pipers Willie Clancy and Martin Talty in the Laichtín Naofa Céilí Band. Refusing to emigrate along with many of his contemporaries, his name eventually became synonymous with music revival, his home an open calling house to musicians and learners from all over the world. President and treasurer of Scoil Samhradh Willie Clancy – at which he taught for twenty-five years – in 1988 the Arts Council honoured his lifetime's contribution to the arts with the presentation of a portrait by Briain Bourke.

Junior Crehan was born into an era where music was an essential ingredient in the social fabric, he lived through its decline in challenging political and economic times, particularly clerical hostility and state dance-hall control; in his words: 'The Dance Halls' Act closed our schools of Tradition, and left us a poorer people'. He was with the music in its competitive struggles with the gramophone, radio and then television, and as a member first of CCÉ, and later the Willie Clancy Summer School he was active in its regeneration. He is noted for the composition of a dozen or so tunes, best known are 'Caisleán an Óir' (hornpipe), 'Farewell to Miltown' (reel), 'The Mist Covered Mountain' (jig), and the slow air 'Lament for the Country House Dance'. He was featured in many publications, notably *Dal gCais* and *Cara* magazines; he was the subject of an RTÉ radio documentary by Julian Vignoles in 1984, and recorded often on television. He had no solo recording, but can be heard on many compilations, among them *Fundúireacht An Riadaigh* album collection. He was well recognised in his own time – receiving presentations from the Arts Council on both his eightieth and ninetieth birthdays, and made 'Clareman of the Year' in 1989. *Dal gCais* vol. 3, 1977 carries a thorough interview with him; *Béaloideas* (1999, the journal of the

Folklore Department, UCD) has an extensive biography by Tom Munnelly.

**Crehan, Tony.** (1943–95). Concertina. Born at Mullach, Miltown Malbay. Son of renowned west Clare fiddler Junior Crehan, he had a style distinctive of West Clare. A composer of tunes, he was all his life involved in music organisation for CCÉ, and was chair of its Gorey, Co. Wexford branch. A teacher there, his pupils took many awards over the years, notably Pat Fitzpatrick on flute. With Thomas Keegan, Tony was part of the Gorey Céilí Band and broadcast on radio and television. He was the instigator of the Bobby Casey album *Casey in the Cowhouse*, compiled its notes and oversaw its production from his mother's tapes. He was buried during the Willie Clancy week of 1995.

**Crosbhealach an Cheoil** (Crossroads Conference, subtitled 'Tradition versus Change'). A conference on traditional music held at the Temple Bar Music Centre in Dublin over the weekend of 19–21 April, 1996. It was initiated by Fintan Vallely and Cormac Breatnach, and was planned and organised from the beginning by a committee which also included Liz Doherty, Colin Hamilton and Eithne Vallely. Each of the organisers was outside of traditional music's established organisational structures, all were musicians. The conference received the official patronage of President Mary Robinson, and was supported by An Chomhairle Ealaíon/The Arts Council; Arts Council of Northern Ireland; The Irish Music Rights Organisation; Music Departments in University College Dublin, National University of Ireland, Maynooth, University College Cork; School of Music, Trinity College Dublin; Irish World Music Centre at University of Limerick; Queen's University Belfast, Dept. of Ethnomusicology; The British Council.

Its argument, and call for papers read:

> The twentieth century is coming to an end, the Irish National/Romantic organisations – GAA and Gaelic League – are entering their second centuries. The setting up of Comhaltas Ceoltóirí Éireann approaches its fiftieth year, the Great Famine – with all its implications for music in exile – is at its 150th anniversary. 1798 – as a source of division which ultimately divides music in the popular mind, now approaches its 200th anniversary. The revolution of gramophone and electronic technology too, with its offshoots of redundancy and commoditisation in music-production, its effects on coalescence of styles, on preservation and revival movements, has now been with us for over 100 years. All of these have affected Irish traditional music. It seems timely that a conference around that music should be held.

Papers were called for on the topics of:
1. Tradition and change: who we are and the way we were, sensitivity toward and respect for the past, innovation and development, professionalism.
2. Education and organisations: state support, the music diaspora, political identity in music, gender in music practice, the oral tradition.
3. Commercialisation: history and myths, music fashions, revival and revitalisation, commoditisation.

Contributors were invited from 'within the music, song and dance community in Ireland and abroad, and from academics and specialists in other music fields.' Responses and opinions were anticipated as well. The final list of topics comprised: 1. Parallel traditions, 2. The song and instrumental traditions, 3. Culture and change, 4. Education-tradition-organisations, 5. Case studies and revival images, 6. Media, tradition and the industry, 7. Tradition and the notion of innovation.

Considering the debate generated by an RTÉ TV *Late Late Show* screening of a 'special' on *River of Sound* – particularly by the opinion of Tony MacMahon that its theme music didn't sound particularly Irish – it was decided to invite he and Mícheál Ó Súilleabháin to present forty-minute keynote addresses on an opening night, to be chaired by singer/writer/publisher Robin Morton.

Ó Súilleabháin's theme was 'Crossroads or Twin Track?' It raised a series of questions, it looked at change within traditional music and its community, cited the bodhrán and the music of Tommy Potts as case studies of change. It identified a process of change as having begun with the Revival in the 1950s, remarked on Potts' consideration of some of his playing as 'experimental'. Ó Súilleabháin held that traditional music could not recreate the music of the past masters because of their different era and mind-set, and he introduced the term 'trad-pop' as a final questioning of traditional music's commercial popularity today.

MacMahon perceived a superficiality in new-found interest in commercial traditional music. He illustrated in a lengthy audio excerpt from *River of Sound* what he felt was the remoteness of – in particular Ó Súilleabháin's – modern interpretation of the music. He introduced the term 'aural carpet' as questioning of the quantity of traditional music currently used and received un-artistically in Ireland, saw commercial music's modern interpretation as 'scrubbed clean' of historic voice to appeal to ignorant audiences, holding that technically brilliant younger musicians today often lacked basic feeling. He defended the uncredited components of traditional music artistry. His view was that traditional music was being mined for ideas by commercial music, and expressed concern that future generations would lose 'the way' in the economic, popular tumult.

Thirty-nine other speakers – almost all musicians and singers – addressed the gathering, Cathal Goan (Teilifís na Gaeilge) chaired the final open session, and Tom Munnelly gave the closing address. Impromptu sessions of music followed debate; organised music for set dancing also took place. Over the weekend 350 people took part.

Papers summary:

Ahern, Pat: 'Fiche Bliain ag Fás. A Personal Account of 20 Years of Tradition and Change', remarking on the explosion in the number of young people taking up traditional music – many of them urban-based with no previous links with the tradition.

Bazin, Fennella: 'Lessons from One Hundred Years Ago.' Examined two seminal collections of Manx music which were published 100 years ago, this in light of developments in the last twenty-five years.

Bennett, Margaret: 'From Kennedy Fraser to the Jimmy Shandrix Experience in Five Generations'. One of five generations of a music-making family, she looked at the process of transmission within it.

Boyes, Georgina: 'Unnatural Selection: Choice and Privileging in English Cultural Tradition'. Examined the ways in which specific types of singer and dancer, styles of performance etc. have been selected as suitable for display and transmission by organisations within the English Folk Revival.

Breatnach, Deasún: 'The influence of baroque music on O'Carolan, the traces of influences of French, southern English and Scottish music on the Irish.'

Burgess, Barry: 'Irish Music in Education – a Northern Ireland Perspective'. Viewed the issues which have influenced and restrained development of Irish traditional music in Northern Ireland education, including the two cultural identities, the NI curriculum and media.

Carolan, Nicholas: 'Irish Music to 1600: Traditions and Innovations'. Considered the evidence of innovation from before the sixteenth century using historical, literary and archaeological sources.

Corcoran, Seán: 'Whatever happened to Horse-whatsit?' Argued that the clamour for innovation is part of a post-colonial mind-set with parallels in other areas of Irish life; that it is the avant-garde of any period which always appears most dated in retrospect.

Cranitch, Matt: 'My mind will never be aisy'. Title of a tune in the 1907 *Dance Music of Ireland*, it has now evolved to become two slides in the present Sliabh Luachra repertoire. Pádraig O'Keeffe's and others' creative roles in this process of change was considered.

Curran, Catherine: 'Changing Audiences for Traditional Music 1956–96'. Changing perceptions of Irish culture within Ireland and abroad.

Dowling, Martin: 'Communities, Place and the Traditions of Irish Dance Music Today'. Considered the present breakdown of regional isolation and of stable locality-based communities, the relationship between performer and music-community.

Gaffney, Martin: 'DO judge a book by its cover'. An audio-video presentation examining the evolution of cover-style in Irish music records from the céilí band era through to the 1990s.

Gershen, Paulette: 'Tradition, Innovation and Identity. Ethnomusicological Reflections'. Innovation, authenticity and modernisation explored from some of the theoretical perspectives current in American ethnomusicology.

Hall, Reg: 'Heydays are Short Lived – Change in Music-making Practice in Rural Ireland 1850-1950'. Explored the social organisation of rural music-making in term of household, kinship and neighbours, community and trade; the shift from pre-famine, public space to private space in the late nineteenth century, back to public space in the 1930s.

Hammond, William: 'Traditional Music – Whose Copyright?' Looked at the relationship between traditional music, copyright and music rights.

Hannon, Robbie: 'Tradition and Innovation in Uilleann Piping'. Questioned the belief that the uilleann piping tradition is rigid and unchanging, suggesting that the top pipers balance their commitment to tradition with dynamism and innovation.

Harbison, Janet: 'Harpists, Harpers and Harpies'. The dilemma of the place and identity of the harp in Irish music-making.

Hensey, Áine: 'Michael Coleman's brother was a better fiddle player'. Looked at the real and perceived influences of the media, how it can both distort and enhance.

Hughes, Harry and Muiris Ó Róchain: 'The Willie Clancy Summer School'. Dealt with the history of this summer school.

Moloney, Mick: 'Acculturation, Assimilation and Revitalisation. Irish Music in Urban America 1960–96'. Looked at the dynamics of continuity and change in Irish music in America in the context of massive population displacement and social upheaval.

Larson-Skye, Cathy: 'Building Bridges – Challenges in Playing, Performing, and Teaching Irish Traditional Music in the American South'. Examined the problems of teaching and playing Irish music away from the supportive Irish community.

Mac Aoidh, Caoimhín: 'The Critical Role of Education in the Development of Traditional Music'. Argued that the foundation for progress in the development of traditional music demands the provision of an educational infrastructure.

Mac Góráin, Riobárd: 'Media, Tradition and the Industry'. Gael-Linn and its recording, distribution, successes and strengths world-wide since the 1950s.

McLaughlin, Dermot: 'Why Pay the Piper?' Looked at the structure and financial relations between the state and traditional music.

Moulden, John: 'Sing us a Folksong, Mouldy'. A perspective on the vocabulary of traditional music and song.

Munnelly, Tom: 'Black Pudding and Bottles of Smoke'. Argued that the events such as the Crossroads Conference itself are part of a cyclical response – in the long run their effects on the music are minimal.

Ó Cinnéide, Barra: 'The *Riverdance* Phenomenon'. Compared and contrasted the 'artistic freedom' experienced by the music since the establishment of CCÉ and the 'liberation' of dancing through *Riverdance*.

O'Donovan, Joe: 'Evolution and Innovation in 400 Years of Irish Dancing'. Outlined the major influences resulting in change, and looked towards the future of Irish dance.

O'Keeffe, Máire: 'Tradition and Change in the Irish Button Accordion'. An overview of the way in which a new instrument is adopted into an established musical tradition.

Ó Laoire, Lillis: 'Dearnad sa Bhrochán – Tradition and Change in Music in a Donegal Community, the music and song of Tory Island', showing that change generated within this community was seen essentially as a force for improvement.

Preston, Paschal: 'When Old Technologies Were New: The adoption, diffusion and impacts of recorded music in Ireland'. Focused on the period 1890–1940.

Schiller, Rina: 'Gender and Traditional Irish Music'. Investigated concepts of female performance in comparison to those associated with Western art music.

Smyth, Therese: 'The challenge of bringing oral tradition of music into an academic teaching environment'. Discussed the problems of integrating oral traditions of music – in particular Irish music – into a university music programme.

Sommers-Smyth, Sally: 'The Founder Effect: a Model of Traditional Music Evolution'. Discussed the differing standards of traditional music performance in Ireland and America.

Tansey, Séamus: 'Irish Traditional Music – the Melody of Ireland's Soul'. Explored the place of traditional music in his home culture, its evolution from the environment, the land and the people.

Topp-Fargion, Janet: 'Continuity, Change and the Forging of New Identities'. With special reference to the popular, urban music of South Africa and the Swahili Coast.

Trew, Johanne: 'Ethnicity and Identity: Music and Dance in the Ottawa Valley'. Discussed how Irish, Scots and French-Canadians over 200 years developed and maintained tradition and culture because of relative isolation.

Uí Ógáin, Ríonach: 'Camden Town go Ros a' Mhíl – Aspects of Change in the Connemara Song Tradition'. Examined development in the Connemara song tradition of a new type of song, and how this has become part of the repertoire of sean-nós.

Wilkinson, Desi: 'An Overview of Breton Traditional Dance Music'. How social and musical influences have been brought to bear on the performance of dance music forms in Brittany.

Full resumés and speaker profiles are published in *Crosbhealach an Cheoil – Clár* (1996, CBC); contributers' papers are published as *The Crossroads Conference* (1999, CBC).

**Cronin, Bess (Elizabeth).** (1876–1955). Daughter to Maighréad Ní Thuama and Seán Ó hIarlaithe, a school teacher in Barr d'Inse, Cúil Aodha, she was reared in her aunt's and uncle's house in An Ráth, in Réidh na nDoirí. Her family were noted for song and poetry, the inheritance of this made her an interesting source for collectors in the 1940s and '50s – among them Jean Ritchie, Alan Lomax, Robin Roberts, Brian George and Séamus Ennis – she featured regularly on BBC radio in the late 1940s and early 1950s. She did not give public performances but her repertoire ensured that she was widely influential. She had songs in both Irish and English, and was particularly known for the richness of her Irish. She married Seán Proinsias, son of Dónal Proinsias Ó Cróinín. Of her five sons Donnchadha was Professor of Irish at Carysfort Teacher Training College, Dublin, Seán was a folklore collector who wrote for the *Irish Press* and the *Kerryman* newspapers under various pen names. The untimely death of her only daughter Joan reputedly broke Bess's heart – she herself died the following year. But for her, it is believed that many older songs would have been lost – indeed the tune of 'Lord Gregory' comes from her, as does the comic song 'The Kangaroo'. She can be heard on OSS 15. (PEO, PAA)

**Crotty, Elizabeth.** (1885–1960). One of Co. Clare's most renowned concertina players, Elizabeth Markham was born in 1885, in Gower, two miles from Cooraclare on the Kilrush Road. She was the youngest of a large family. Her mother played fiddle and her older sister concertina. In 1914 'Lizzie' married close neighbour Miko Crotty and moved from her homeplace at Markham's Cross to Kilrush where they ran Crotty's pub in the square, which became a famous music 'house'. Mrs Crotty became a household name among traditional musicians through frequent airing on Ciarán MacMathúna's radio programmes in the 1950s – notably for the reels 'Wind that Shakes the Barley' and 'Reel with the Birl', these played on her Lachenal concertina. When Comhaltas Ceoltóirí Éireann was formed in Co. Clare in 1954, Mrs Crotty was elected president of the first County Board and held that position until her death. She is buried at Sharakyle cemetery, Kilrush. (MOK, MIT)

**Crowley, Jimmy.** (1950– ). Singer, songwriter, bouzouki player. Reared in Castletreasure, Co. Cork, his father was a wood machinist, his mother a weaver. He followed his father into the furniture trade as a cabinetmaker and later a carpenter. Influenced by local uilleann piper John Harris, and introduced to unaccompanied singing, his visits to Miltown Malbay and Dún Chaoin, Co. Kerry, in the late 1960s developed his interest, as did meeting Willie Clancy, Denis Murphy, Nioclás Tóibín, Séamus Ennis and Seán de hÓra. He formed a folk group, The Die-hards, with Michael Harris and Dee McCarthy and moved by the Folk Club at the Group Theatre, South Main Street, Cork, he formed Stokers Lodge to perform a Cork urban repertoire. He recorded 'The Boys of Fairhill', 'Camphouse Ballads', 'Some Things Never Change', and 'Jimí mo Mhíle Stór' (in Irish for Gael-Linn), more recently 'My Love is a Tall Ship'. Touring the world since 1977 led him to study his craft and culture, and to take an Irish and Léann Dúchais degree at UCC in 1997. He has written a ballad opera, 'Red Patriots', edited *Jimmy Crowley's Irish Songbook* (1986) and was a weekly columnist with *The Examiner* for seven years.

**cruitire.** (Lit. 'harper'.) Harper accompanying the reacaire as he delivered the words of the old Gaelic Court's *file*. The separate role survived until all three functions had gradually become merged in response to a combination of repression and social change, whereupon the harper became composer, poet and musician.

**crwth.** See Wales, crwth.

**Cullinane Archive Collection of Irish Dance Material, Cork.** A private collection started by John Cullinane in the 1960s. It contains 3,000 items of Irish dance material collected in Ireland, England, North America and Australasia and is the largest such archive in the world. It contains mixed hard copy and electronic media and has been the source of six books and some fifty articles on dance by Cullinane alone. It comprises: 600 original photographs dating from 1890, eighty recorded interviews dating from the 1970s; videos; feis programmes; a collection of early feis medals and certificates; early documents and manuscripts from the Irish Dancing Commission, including minutes and hand-written minute book from the 1930s as well as unpublished theses. It also has copies of 400 published articles on Irish dancing, and original copies of all major publications/books on the subject.

See bibliography.

**culture.** All aspects of any society constitute its culture. Ireland has many 'sub cultures' contained under the national mantle. Two interpretations of 'culture' are involved in traditional music. 1. beliefs, social structures, and material characteristics which define continuity in a racial, religious or social group, and 2. enlightenment and standards achievable through intellectual and aesthetic education: the intellectual and artistic content of civilisation.

Culture is not absolute, it is learned, it is seen most clearly when compared to other cultures. People claim and reject various 'cultural' artefacts in pursuit of defining their own culture – for instance, popular Northern Ireland Protestant/Unionist belief ascribes traditional music as 'Catholic culture' (despite the fact of its shared heritage).

Irish traditional music therefore means most to people on the island of Ireland; within this it means most to those who see themselves as Irish. People from abroad identify with the music for a variety of reasons: some on account of Irish ancestry, others because of its artistic merits, yet more because they experience the music as being fundamental and satisfying, removed from the self-absorbed and draining complexity of consumer-oriented, mass-produced commodity musics. Because of its readily identifiable 'sound', and ideologically bolstered by the prominence given to Irish music (and to song in particular as a carrier of language) by the early Gaelic League (the Gaelic Revival) in the nineteenth century, for most Irish people music, song and dance spring to mind as prime hallmarks of Irish 'culture'.

**Cumann Cheol Tíre Éireann.** See Folk Music Society of Ireland.

**Cumann Chluain Ard.** See céilí bands, Belfast.

**Curran, Murt.** (b. 1902). Step dancer and dance teacher. Born at Shambough, New Ross, Co. Wexford, he began work as a farmhand and learned Irish through the Mile Bush Sinn Féin Club around 1919. House dances at weekends introduced him to dance; the lancers and Wexford sets were the fare, music provided by melodeon and fiddle. A remarkable figure at 6'2" in size 12 shoes, his first performance was at a local hurling club concert. Interned in the Curragh Camp later, he taught dancing to his comrades and was himself taught fiddle. He began teaching formally in 1924, continuing in Crane St Studios, Liverpool, when he emigrated in 1926. He danced for Maud Gonne MacBride at the Irish Hall in Gay St, gave public exhibitions at the Argyle Theatre Music Hall in Birkenhead, eventually promoting his own concerts in church halls with céilí dances four nights a week. He became involved with Fianna Fáil in Liverpool, and returned to settle in Leighlinbridge, Co. Carlow in 1931 where he continued teaching dance. At this time he was teaching in Cloone parish in Co. Leitrim, and danced on radio with the Cloone Céilí Band. With the formation of the Irish Dancing Commission he was in popular demand as an adjudicator, but also worked at labouring in England to make a living, where he performed at Gaelic League functions. He danced on RTÉ television with Kerryman Liam Tarrant on *Bring Down the Lamp*, and on *Ag Déanamh Ceoil*, and later worked as an advertising model. His memoirs detail an eccentric and lonely life of interwoven dance, political incident, migration and travel.

**Curry, David** (d. 1971). Violinist, arranger, conductor with BBC Northern Ireland Orchestra. In 1938, Curry, a violinist with the BBC Northern Ireland Orchestra and a cousin of Charles Curry (a fiddler and one of the founders of the Antrim and Derry Country Fiddlers' Association), was asked to arrange traditional Irish dance tunes for a section of the orchestra. These were widely broadcast in Northern Ireland, in the UK *Light Programme* and BBC World Service in an extremely popular series of programmes called *Irish Rhythms*. In 1949 the BBC Northern Ireland Orchestra was re-formed following the Second World War and Curry, appointed its conductor, continued the series using full orchestra. For many, this slightly stilted example was their first introduction to Irish music. Some of it can be heard in the BBC Archive at the Ulster Folk and Transport Museum. David Curry's Irish Band recorded music in strict tempo for dancing on 78s published by the Columbia Company. Some of these were re-issued in the 1970s and as recently as 1990 on LP and cassette mainly with the title 'Irish Rhythms'. (JOM)

**Curtin, George.** See Ó Tuama, Mícheál.

**Custy, Frank.** Fiddle. Born Dysart, Co. Clare. A hurler in his younger years, he trained as a teacher in Dublin, and was introduced to tin whistle by a pupil – Seán Conway – in 1963. He learned, aided by colleague Mrs Connolly in Toonagh school, and by Seán Reid, Martin Mullins and Jack Mulkere. He then taught whistle in his school and began session and group playing in 1964, which produced the Dysart Céilí Band. A pioneer, he began teaching night classes in the Toonagh old school in 1964, branching further afield to Ennis and Kilfenora. The Dysart band's popularity, and their broadcasts on Raidió Éireann's *Céilí House*, helped form a new generation of players. He succeeded in establishing classes in Ennis VEC in 1969, and was involved with the award-winning St Flannan's College Céilí Band. A committed teacher, he has also been one of CCÉ's strongest activists in the revival of music in Co. Clare, founding the Toonagh branch in 1966, and starting the Bí Linn project with the GAA – this providing playing and dancing occasion for young musicians.

**cut.** A form of ornamentation of melody which involves separating two like notes by momentarily playing the higher note.
See grace note.

# D

**Dábh Scoil**. See song, West Cork.

***Dal gCais.*** Subtitled *Clare: its People and Culture.* This erratically-annual magazine was first published in 1972. Modelled on *The Capuchin Annual,* it drew somewhat on *Treoir*'s interview format and the analytical rigour of *Ceol*, seeing itself as addressing the national sphere of traditional music. It was started through private subscription and advertising, and set out to stimulate a positive appreciation of the past through its writings. To this end, contributions concentrated on local music, history, folklore, culture, politics, wildlife, archaeology and biography with occasional creative writing in the form of essays and poems. Traditional music, song and dance have been featured to some extent in every issue but more prominently from number three onwards. In later issues much of this type of material was drawn from the annual Scoil Samhraidh Willie Clancy/Willie Clancy Summer School. The bulk of articles were initially sourced locally but as the journal's profile heightened contributions from all parts of the country made up an increasing portion of each issue. The journal is heavily illustrated with both line drawings and photographs, many of which are of traditional musicians. *Dal gCais* is currently in its eleventh number with the twelfth presently in production. The editor is Harry Hughes of Miltown Malbay, one of the organisers of Scoil Samraidh Willie Clancy. (GLC)

**Daly, Jackie.** (1945–  ) Accordion, concertina. Born at Kanturk, Co. Cork, his mother sang and his father played melodeon, mostly polkas and waltzes, and only at weekends. At the age of seven Jackie began to play harmonica and tin whistle, then melodeon, learning his father's repertoire. At Knocknacolan crossroads Sunday evening platform dances – run by dancer Bill Sullivan – he heard accordion player Pat Cashman, and fiddlers Sean Lynch and Jim Keefe. From Ballydesmond, and a former pupil of Pádraig O'Keefe, the latter taught Jackie tunes and eventually he joined the players. Working in Holland took him out of music *c*. 1968–73, but back playing for a year he won the All-Ireland on accordion in 1974. Playing then with fiddler Séamus Creagh, their 1977 *Jackie Daly agus Séamus Creagh* became one of the most influential forces in the music of the 1970s. The Sliabh Luachra style's popularity outside its own area owes much to this duet. An exemplar of the 'press and draw', C#/D accordion style, his repertoire is rooted in the nearby Newmarket area of Co. Cork with slides and polkas dedicated to local, known players. He has been central to many of the most highly regarded players and groups in Irish music of recent years. He has played with such as Kevin Burke, De Dannan, Reel Union, Kinvara, Patrick Street, Buttons and Bows and Arcady, recording on four albums with De Dannan, six with Patrick Street, three with the Maguire brothers in Buttons and Bows, and one with Arcady. He has composed several tunes, and has two solo albums, *Jackie Daly* (1977, 1989), and *Many's The Wild Night* (1995). He has also recorded duet albums with fiddle players Séamus Creagh and Kevin Burke. (MAO)

**dance.**

*European history.* It is likely that dance was evolved before or independently of music as we know it today. The human body rhythms of heartbeat and breathing are echoed in the basic components of Western dance: a metrical beat mimics the pulse, the upper body responds to melodic phrases with 'the free-flowing arc of [the] breathing' (Quirey, 1976). Within historical time the melodic phrase has been the basis of European dance, not percussive beat. The earliest social dances were circular and linear chain dances, these dating to 1400–1200 BC Crete; of these the 'ring' dances – which used a sacred tree or stone as central focus – are most likely the oldest. By the middle ages, the chain dance was called the *carole*, this in two forms: linear dance called *farandole*, associated with the Mediterranean, which produced dance 'figures', and ring dances called *branle*, typically in Northern climes.

1. *farandole*. In early forms of dance the music was sung by the participants in simple, compound double or triple time, with a regular pulse. Done outdoors, the dance pattern at its most simple was indiscriminate, taking a labyrinthine course (as in 'leading a fine dance'). This developed to use (highly symbolic) three 'arched' figures with raised hands under which dancers passed: 'threading the needle', 'l'Escargot' and 'the arches' (all figures represented in contemporary European traditional and folk dances). These fell out of popularity in the fifteenth-century courts either because high head-dresses and pointed hats became fashionable, or for religious reasons, but remained popular in rural entertainment. The dance then became known as *hey* (hay, haye, heye or haye) with a changing of the dancers' location in relation to each other. This pattern is reflected in part of eightsome reel or Lancers.

2. *branle* (French: branler – to sway; English – braul, brawl). These were performed in an arc or circle, central to them was rhythm, the *branle double* related to the eight-bar phrase, the ballad metre, while the *branle simple* corresponds to a six-bar phrase. These and other branles became the basis of French folk dance by the sixteenth century and exhibited many regional variations.

*couple dances*. All this dance was, however, 'in line'. Couple dancing possibly arose first in twelfth-century Provence either as a break-up of the line into pairs in procession, and/or in response to the 'courtly-love' concept in the song of the period's Troubadours. By the fourteenth century, couple dance had been the norm in Northern Italy, and up to the late eighteenth century important upper-class dance was done in couples with other dancers looking on. This is considered to be 'Estampie', a transitional dance form which gave structure to dance – a beginning, middle and conclusion – but it also broke up the chain of community which earlier forms exercised. From this, 'court dance' emerged, as distinct from 'folk dance'. Those who had the leisure time to consider the arts of relaxation were more likely to be at court, and so it was there that 'development' in dance took place. In fifteenth-century Northern Italy, the facility of smooth floors in palaces had prompted the development of rise-and-fall footwork, a feature of many later dances up to modern times (Quirey, 1976). The addition of heels to shoes in the mid-seventeenth century had other effects, as had the French court fashion of walking with the toes turned out between the seventeenth and early twentieth centuries. Seventeenth-century Louis XIV's centralised court system kept an eye on courtiers through social pursuits like dance. He appointed dancing masters to develop a series of organised social/spatial dances; these drew on folk dance for inspiration and so developed the *minuet*. In this period English court balls involved French *branles* as well as English *country dances* (the latter spreading to France as the corruption *contredanse* and revived in the US in the 1980s as 'contra-dance'). French cotillions – a 'square' dance for four couples – moved to England, to America and to Ireland as did the later *quadrilles* ('sets'). English country dance revived under Henry VIII and Elizabeth I in England; it is reputed to have been brought to France by the exiled Charles II. On his return in 1660 he brought back French dance. Mary Queen of Scots is said to have brought French court dance to Scotland in 1561 but there were of course other traders and travellers. This ensured that throughout the seventeenth and eighteenth centuries masters of French dancing could be employed in England (Quirey, 1976).

*Ireland*. *Haye*, *rinnce fada*, and *rinnce mór* are the three names used to refer to dance in old literature: *haye* was a chain dance, *rinnce fada* had movements similar to English country dance (it is recorded as having been performed to welcome James I on his arrival at Kinsale in 1689), *rinnce mór*, or *trenchmore*, was a 'long dance' (noted by Playford in 1651). In 1265 a poem on New Ross's fortifications talks of 'carolling' (probably dancing to singing), and in 1413 dancing is described in relation to a Christmas visit by the Mayor of Waterford to the O'Driscoll seat at Baltimore, Co. Cork

(Breathnach, 1977). The first reference to dance in the Irish language is 1588, when Tomás Dubh, tenth Earl of Ormond, talks of: 'raingce timcheall teinne ag buidhin tseinbmhir treinneartmhuir' (a dance around fires by a slender, swift, vigorous company). The Irish words for dance, 'rinnce', first appears in 1609 and 'damhsa', ten years later. Descriptions of music and dance together come from 1602 at the court of Elizabeth I: 'We are at frolic here in court; much dancing in the privy chamber of Country dances before the queen's Majesty, who is exceedingly pleased therewith. Irish tunes are at this time much liked.'

'Country dances' were the form of that dance, but they were being done in court, and in England. Were these simply fashionable dances from the leisured classes at court who had time to organise choreographies? 'Withie' and 'sword' dances are recorded from 1669. But the common people in Ireland may have been dancing more free-form, simple dance, to fiddle and pipes. In 1670 Richard Head reports: 'Their Sunday is the most leisure day they have, in which they use all manner of sport; in every field a fiddle and the lasses footing it till they are all of a foam.' Jew's harp (or trump) were also used to make the music. In 1674 John Dunton reports of a wedding: 'a bagpiper and a blind harper that dinned us continually with their music, to which there was perpetual dancing'.

The 'cake dance', for couples, is mentioned in 1682 and continued into this century, but as well as courting and recreation, dance also had important social ritual functions, these exercised by forms of group dances derived from ancient chain and ring dances, similar to those done in other parts of Europe. Rinnce fada is described as being performed on May-eve and other occasions of celebration. Dancing was associated with important times of the year – Bealtaine, Lughnasa, Samhain, Imbolg – and with rituals of life – births, weddings, wakes. That Arthur Young in 1780 could report 'dancing is universal among the poor' is perhaps not surprising considering that the Irish population in the sixty-two years up to 1841 increased by 172 per cent to 8.18 million. Conclusions about pre-seventeenth-century dance in Ireland are speculative. But even though O'Curry notes that there is no Irish word for 'dance' (because the documentary evidence of dance is from the seventeenth century on), and because of its popularity depicted elsewhere by painters like Peter Breughel in sixteenth-century Holland (where bagpipes and dance are seen at weddings), it is reasonable to assume that it was practised similarly in Ireland.

*dancing masters.* The older style of dancing is solo step dance, and is found all over the country. This was taught by travelling dancing masters who were well established after the middle of the 1700s. They taught jig and reel steps and also devised round dances – for several couples – and 'set' dances (not to be confused with sets or set-dancing). These were display dances for themselves and their more talented pupils. Solo and group step dancing have been refined in the twentieth century into the costumed and choreographed kinds we see at competitions today, and in *Riverdance* and *Lord of the Dance*. In the competitions, dancers will be dressed in coloured costumes decorated with Celtic designs, these dating to the early twentieth century, their more elaborate forms initiated in the USA and Australia.

*politics of dance.* The Gaelic League favoured a de-Anglicisation policy in matters cultural. They progressively banned all surviving round, country and imported sets dances; they facilitated revival of older dances and the making of new dances. In 1939 Coimisiún an Rinnce (Irish Dancing Commission) published instruction for the approved choreographies, 'Siege of Ennis,' 'Walls of Limerick', 'Sweets of May', etc. Although sets were banned by the dancing commission they continued nevertheless, surviving to the present day in areas like North Kerry and Clare, boosted in the 1980s by revival, and in their original, courtly, form they are still danced with continuity in some Orange and parish halls in East Co. Down. Clerical opposition to dance was a European universal from the 1740s, and continued in the 1930s in Ireland in tandem with state desire for control, resulting in the 1935 Public Dance Halls Act. (EDI)

See céilí dance; Dance Halls Act; sean-nós dance; set dance; step dance.

**dance costumes.** These evolved from the desire to wear a distinctive Irish dress, an idea that had

Margaret Conneely of the McBride School of Dancing, Galway, in a costume featuring a box pleat and Celtic motifs (Tadhg Keady)

some vogue at the turn of the twentieth century under the influence of the 'Celtic Revival'. The wearing of Irish costume was encouraged as one manifestation of the growing spirit of national consciousness. At the height of this, 'Irish costume' might be worn on special occasions – such as the Gaelic League's annual Oireachtas exhibitions. Alongside the new interest in national costume, Irish dancing was also being revived, and soon it became customary to wear distinctively Irish costumes for dancing in competition. Such costumes were invented from knowledge gained from archaeological, philological and antiquarian research. One source was Eugene O'Curry's *Manners and Customs of the Ancient Irish*, which included descriptions of the 'léine' (a sleeveless, tunic-style linen garment) and the 'brat' (cloak) worn in early Christian Ireland. And so, from the turn of the twentieth-century, many female dancers have worn costumes derived from these. In support of Irish industry, such early dancing costumes were made in Irish fabrics – wool, linen, poplin and báinín (homespun, woven woollen cloth). Favoured colours were green, white and saffron. Celtic- or 'Kells'-style hand embroidery next became a feature of such dancing costumes, as did Irish lace collars and cuffs. Over the years, pleated and circular flare-style dresses have been popular, and in the first half of this century female dancers in some areas of Ireland wore kilts. Rural dress of the nineteenth and early twentieth centuries – which had much claim to be an Irish national costume – had some influence on the development of dancing costume, but not as much as might have been expected. Nationalist-minded people did not necessarily want to be associated with presentations of rural dress which were, even then, often regarded as being too 'stage Irish'.

Costumes currently appear in many colours, including black, red, purple, green, blue and white. Dresses with a 'box' or inverted pleat are favoured by dancers, and the brat has become a much smaller, neater accessory garment. Popular fabrics include synthetic velvet and Trevira. Machine embroidery and appliqué now decorate large areas of costumes, common motifs include Celtic interlace, birds, hounds, snakes, Irish harps, the 'Tara' brooch, the 'Claddagh' ring, torc neck-pieces, Celtic monograms, crests, round towers and shamrocks. Designs based on Irish legends have become increasingly popular. Other motifs include dancing shoes and musical instruments.

At the beginning of the century some male dancers wore long-tailed coats over shirts teamed with trousers. Knee-breeches – commonly worn by boys at the time – were used by many male dancers until the late 1930s and early 1940s. But since *Punch* magazine and comic postcards regularly featured 'Paddy' wearing knee-breeches, the Gaelic League discouraged the wearing of a form of dress in which the Irish were so negatively caricatured. During the Celtic Revival the kilt was popularised as a national costume for men. By the mid-1940s this, teamed with jacket, shirt, tie, knee-socks and brat became the usual outfit for male dancers competing at feiseanna. Such kilts and jackets were made in Irish tweed or wool, more recently gabardine has been used, velvet being popular too.

*Riverdance* has had considerable impact on the fashions, now making new concepts of costume design possible for dancers. Dresses in the new idiom are lighter than traditional costumes, popular fabrics include velvet and chiffon. Where embroidery is used, the motifs are less complicated, and decorate much smaller areas of the dress. The new fashion popular for male dancers consists of long trousers instead of kilts, with stylish shirts worn with or without a tie, and sometimes a cummerbund and/or a jacket or waistcoat. (MAR)

**Dance Halls Act.** (Public Dance Halls Act 1935). Houses and crossroads – where Irish music was played and sets danced – had been the main venues for social dance in Ireland prior to 1935. Indeed these still operated into the 1950s, especially for the 'wren' and American wakes. House dances were often fund-raisers – generally 'benefits' or for the fun of it, but sometimes for political groups – and they could be held in anyone's house, perhaps that of a host not favoured by church or law. Neither they nor cross-roads dancing could conveniently be morally or legally policed by clergy or Gardaí. However, they could not have generated so much antipathy as modern, popular music. For in addition, emigration and the beginnings of recorded (commercial/popular) music combined to give 'foreign' music genres like two-step, fox-trot and shimmy-shake a currency in Ireland. Private, commercial dance halls had been opened to capitalise on the new fashion but zealous Gaelic-Leaguers perceived this as undermining Irish culture. Catholic clergy damned 'all-night dances', and also saw these modern dances as 'imported from other countries and are, if not absolutely improper, on the borderline of Christian modesty' (*Irish Catholic Directory*, 1924), and more stridently 'importations from the vilest dens of London, Paris and New York, direct and unmistakable incitements to evil thoughts and evil desires'. In addition, there was also some concern among the authorities about the hazards of overcrowding in unsupervised premises, and about organisations such as the IRA running events to raise money. The issue became a battle for control. Religious and political forces combined to demand licensing of dancing. Intensely conservative lobbying was engaged in by the Church, this resulting in the Public Dance Halls Act, 1935. Under this, dancing required a licence, this would only be given to persons approved of by a district judge, and failure to comply was a criminal offence. Over-zealous, vigilante-style enforcement of the Act by some clergy destroyed social, non-commercial house dancing in many areas, and this, combined with the clergy opening their own halls for commercial, but morally supervised dancing, gradually shifted the social dance from private space to public. Many argue that this destroyed music, and terminally discouraged players. But it created the 'band', the céilí band in particular, as the mainstay of music for dancing in Ireland, so opening a new chapter in Irish music history. Demands of dancing in large spaces also altered the performance style of music: it did not require solo and duet playing, it sacrificed rhythm to beat, impersonalised the musicians, prioritised music-making over social occasion and obliged musicians to learn other forms of music demanded by the modern venue. Accordion became important, for volume, this diminishing the status of the subtlety inherent in, say, expert fiddle playing. Dancers were thus separated from the process of music-making, standards of appreciation declined, musicians lost local importance, became discouraged and many abandoned playing in a competitive era in which supply was greater than demand. This period was full of intense political passions in the country, and licensing decisions could be controversial, as could the hiring of particular céilí bands.

See céilí band; céilí dance; set dance; step dance.

**Davey, Andrew.** (1928– ). Fiddle. Born at Cloonagh, Gurteen, Co. Sligo. His father played fiddle, accordion and whistle and his mother, the accordion. Local musicians Benny Coughlan and James 'Sonny' Duffy were a big influence, this in an area with many fine players. He played in the late 1960s for the céilí band Celtic Cross with Séamus Tansey (flute) and Francis Grehan (song and guitar), then with Kevin Quigley's band. He played in duet with Séamus Tansey for many years in concert and on television, and is featured on *Music from Coleman Country* (1972). He has also recorded for national and local radio. His area is dominated by the legacy of Michael Coleman, James Morrison etc., yet he has developed and retained a most distinctive personal style. He plays with Declan Folan (fiddle), Noel Tansey (flute) and often with his son 'Junior', four times an All-Ireland bodhrán title winner. (GRD)

**Davey, Shaun.** (1948– ). Composer. He worked originally as an art historian but is known as composer since 1977. His major works include 'The Brendan Voyage', 'The Pilgrim', 'Granuaile' and 'The Relief of Derry', all of which used elements of traditional music. Much of his work has been enriched through sensitive collaboration with uilleann piper Liam O'Flynn; generally it augments orchestras with unusual features such as pipe bands, drum corps, folk ensembles and choral groups, solo traditional singers and musicians. Such dramatic presentation reflects the epic themes to which he seeks to give musical expression. Typically, his approach when scoring for full orchestra is to consider views of individual instrumentalists. Given the nature of his execution, Davey's work cannot be considered as falling within what is generally understood by the term 'traditional', yet he has contributed seriously to a broader musical ethos to which traditional roots are elementally essential. (BIM)

**Davey, Sonny (James).** (1909– ). Bodhrán maker. Born at Kiltycreen, Bunninadden, Ballymote, Co. Sligo, he was taught fiddle by his sister who had been taught by their uncle. A founder figure of bodhrán making, his is uniquely the area where it appears to have had an historic and consistent music role of some note. He made his first bodhrán at age twelve, having learnt curing 'from a Donegal man' and began making drums in the 1920s after a visitor offered him £4 for one, having heard him play it with fiddler Fred Finn in Bunninadden. He used nanny-goat hides and killed his own goats: 'Out of a big goat I got three bodhráns, from a medium one I got two, from a kid I'd get just one'. He played in groups at social gatherings, crossroads dances, and work meitheals. In the Rising Sun Céilí Band he played with Peter Horan, Séamus Tansey, Fred Finn and Mickey Hunt and made its snare and bass drums. He also played fife in Killavel fife and drum marching band (five or six fifes, two cymbals, a 'kettle' drum) during the 1920s and '30s, at 'flapper' sports, and for the 'wren' at New Year's.

See bodhrán.

**Davis, Thomas.** Essayist, songwriter, inspirational leader of the Young Ireland Movement.

See Young Irelanders.

**de Barra, Domhnall.** Accordion, whistle, flute, concertina, bodhrán player and singer. Born Athea, on the West Limerick-North Kerry border, he had music from both sides of his family. The music of his childhood was for set dancing, this colouring his rhythmic style and melodic fluency. He learnt whistle first at age eight from neighbour Dave Connors, then moved to accordion which left him in demand for local house dances. At nineteen he emigrated to Coventry where he played sessions, organised music classes, and started a céilí band. In his twenties he played with the Shannon Céilí Band in Coventry, and also in the Birmingham and Liverpool bands. He returned to Ireland in 1972, working as CCÉ regional organiser, teaching, and playing locally with musicians from the Athea/Carrigkerry area as Ceoltóirí Luimní. His Domhnall de Barra Céilí Band plays for céilís all over the South-West. Twice elected President of CCÉ, he recorded an LP of West Limerick tunes with Tuam guitarist Treasa Ní Cheannaigh, piper Eoin Ó Cionnaith and fiddler Séamus Glackin.

**De Dannan.** Next to the Bothy Band, one of the most significant groups of exceptional players to emerge in the late twentieth century. Led by fiddler Frankie Gavin, and with distinctive and pioneering bouzouki player Alec Finn, despite other personnel changes the band have maintained a unique, and unrivalled, 'clean' sound close to solo melody over twenty-five years. Formed in Spiddal, Co. Galway in 1974 out of session gatherings in Hughes' Pub, the original line-up had Frankie Gavin (fiddle), Johnny (Ringo) McDonagh (bodhrán), Alec

Finn (bouzouki), Charlie Piggott (bouzouki, banjo), Dolores Keane (vocals). Their first album *De Dannan* was produced by Donal Lunny in 1975. Keane was replaced by Andy Irvine in 1976; Johnny Moynihan replaced Irvine in 1977. On the 1978 album *Selected Jigs Reels and Songs*, Moynihan was replaced by Tim Lyons, later he by Jackie Daly, then Christy O'Leary in 1979. *Mist Covered Mountain* (1980) featured sean-nós singers Seán Ó Conaire and Tom Phaidín Tom. *Hey Jude* (1980) controversially adapted a Beatles song to traditional style. Other albums include *Star Spangled Molly* (1978) with Maura O'Connell and Irish-American vaudeville songs; *Ballroom* (1987) with Dolores Keane; *Song for Ireland* (1988) with Mary Black; *Half Set in Harlem* (1991) with klezmer music and American rock group gospel singers; *Hibernian Rhapsody* (1996) explored Queen's classic rock piece. Eleanor Shanley and Jimmy McCarthy have also sung with the band. Tim Lyons, Máirtín O'Connor and Aidan Coffey have played accordion, and currently Colm Murphy (bodhrán) and Derek Hickey (accordion) form part of the line-up. (JOO)

**Déise.** Historically 'the Déise' encompassed most of Co. Waterford and adjoining areas of Co. Tipperary. A distinctive indigenous song tradition is now largely confined to the parish of Rinn Ó gCuanach, the only remaining area in the region that is partly Irish-speaking. The singing style is also preserved and performed by a handful of enthusiasts elsewhere. Its present paucity of exponents and limited geographic spread, however, belie its cultural and historic importance. While much material has fallen into disuse, a wide area of Ossory and east Munster is represented in its still extensive repertoire. Though intrinsic parts of the Munster, Gaelic-singing tradition are represented elsewhere in the province, the Irish dialect of the Déise and the area's noticeable melodic strength afford it a distinctive regional identity. Many of the 'big' songs common to the Gaelic tradition elsewhere ('An Droighneán Donn', 'Domhnall Óg', etc.) are represented in the Déise tradition in unique and beautiful versions, but the area also has a substantial repertoire of unique, impressive songs, a signifying feature being the number that are of great historical interest. While the singing style has many features in common with other southern Gaeltacht areas the singing of Nioclás Tóibín has had a profound influence on the younger singers of the region; his vigorous and dynamic approach, his dramatic melodic ornamentation and relative restraint in the use of melismatic ornamentation has added much to the regional distinctiveness. Déise song is undergoing something of a revival through such singers as Áine Uí Cheallaigh, Áine Nic Mhurdhadha, Cárthach and Seán Mac Craith, Ciarán Ó Gealbháin and Sorcha Ní Chéilleachair. Representative recordings: Nioclás Tóibín (Gael-Linn, Cló Iar-Chonnachta), Áine Uí Cheallaigh (Gael-Linn). (EAO)

**Delaney, Dinny.** (1841–1919). Uilleann pipes. Born at Ballinasloe, Co. Galway and blind from infancy, he became a major reference point for Irish pipers. In his early days he played with and was reputedly taught by pipers Wills, Costello and Rainey, all of whom then circulated around Ballinasloe. From 1860 to 1890, in the pre-dance hall era, he travelled over a large area in an ass and cart, playing at house parties, fairs, crossroads céilís, festivals and weddings. He was also a regular competitor in feiseanna throughout Ireland in the early 1900s, winning more than twenty first prizes. In latter years he played on a Kenna set acquired in 1873. In 1916 he was arrested by the RIC at the Mountbellew fair for playing 'seditious tunes', this earning him the title thereafter of 'The Rebel Piper'. A professional, he also played for any members of the gentry willing to pay him. An Ediphone cylinder recording of his rollicking style was made at the third Feis Cheoil held in 1899.

**Dempsey, Seán.** (b. 1910). Uilleann pipes. Born in Co. Kildare, he lived at Firhouse, Tallaght, Co. Dublin. He played 'The Rakes of Kildare' with Leo Rowsome in *Irish Hearts*, the first Irish sound movie in 1934. Taught by Rowsome, he broadcast regularly throughout the 1940s, and often played abroad at festivals. He was passionately interested in flying and was the first Irish person to be Station Engineer at Shannon Airport (1941). He played at the World Folk Dance and Music festival at Berlin's Sports Palace in 1936 during the controversial

Olympics of that year. Rory O'Connor danced for him; a chair could not be found so he played while sitting on the back of one of Hitler's storm-troopers. 'Sent for' afterwards, his pipes were reputedly studied and admired by Hitler, Goering and Goebbels.

**Dennehy, Tim.** (1952– ). Singer, poet, broadcaster. Born in Ballinskelligs in Co. Kerry, raised there and in Cahersiveen. His parents inherited songs and stories in Irish, his mother, Nora Kelly from Cill Rialaigh sang constantly. Living in Dublin in 1979 he was one of the founding members of the Góilín traditional singing club. He presents traditional music programmes on Clare FM Radio. He has three albums *A Thimbleful of Song*, *A Winter's Tear* and *Farewell to Miltown Malbay*. (LIM)

**Derrane, Joe.** (1930– ). Accordion. Born Boston, Massachusetts to Irish parents (father, Patrick, from the Aran island of Inis Mór; mother, Helen, from the Four Roads area of Roscommon). A legendary figure among accordionists, especially D/C# players. The 78 rpm solo recordings he made as a teenager for the Copley label in 1946–47 were considered the pinnacle of Irish button-accordion playing in the US at that time. He also recorded several duets on the same label with his teacher and mentor, Jerry O'Brien (1899–1968) of Kinsale, Co. Cork, as well as a number of selections with the Irish All-Stars and the All-Star Céilí Band. From the 1940s to the mid-1950s, Derrane performed on the thriving ballroom scene along Dudley Street in Roxbury, Massachusetts, but when that started to wane he concentrated on piano accordion with mostly non-Irish bands. Almost thirty-five years passed before he made a comeback on the D/C# button accordion, at the 1994 Irish Folk Festival in Wolf Trap, Virginia. By then, his earlier solo recordings had enjoyed renewed popularity through their reissue on Rego Records, and within a year after his Wolf Trap performance, Derrane recorded *Give Us Another* for Green Linnet. He followed with *Return to Inis Mór* in 1996, and a third *The Tie That Binds*, with Shanachie in 1998. With his Longford-born wife, Anne, Derrane lives in Randolph, Massachusetts, where he teaches, composes, and maintains a busy performance schedule. (EAH)

**diatonic**. Literally 'two tones', this term refers to the major and minor scales in which there is an uneven progression of whole tones and semitones. This is in contrast to the 'chromatic' scale which has a note series based on semitones only. The term 'diatonic' is also used to describe an instrument's potential: melodeons, tin whistles and pipes have a diatonic scale, and can be played only in a limited number of keys. Thus, because the scale of D has F# and C#, a diatonic harmonica, or ten-button melodeon, in the key of D has the scale D E F# G A B C# D. Because it does not have notes F and C it can't be used to play tunes in the keys of C and G, but since a lot of dance music is in the key of D, the instrument is nevertheless very useful. Melodeons are also made in the keys of G (which has Cnat), and in C (which has Fnat and Cnat). The diatonic melodeon differs from the two-row, button accordion – called 'chromatic accordion' – which, like keyed flute, has a chromatic scale. Harmonicas follow the same pattern.

See chromatic; key; scale.

**diddley-dee.** Colloquial term used to denote (often dismissively) traditional music. It derives from the characteristic sound of the simplest form of lilting.

See lilting.

**Doherty, John.** (d. 1980). Fiddle. The Doherty family are the most popularly known fiddling family in Donegal and colloquially are known as 'The Simeys' – this a nickname from Simon, one of the patriarchs of the family. They were highly skilled tinsmiths and travelled throughout central and south-west Donegal making much-needed kitchen and farm utensils. At night, they also taught fiddle to interested children and provided music for house dances and other functions. Simon was a player of high repute, and his son Mickey (Mickey Mór) had an equal reputation. His bowing was legendary, folklore maintaining that when in good playing form the bow moved so quickly that the tip whistled. Mickey's children who survived childhood were all good fiddlers, but it was the youngest, John, who has become most widely

Johnny Doherty (EAO)

known. Born in Ardara, John's primary influence was his father, but he had a great admiration for the Scots fiddlers James Scott Skinner and to a lesser degree, William McKenzie Murdoch. John was playing in earnest by his early teens and had blossomed significantly by his mid-twenties. But even though for most of his adult life there was no great national interest in Donegal-style fiddle playing, he was nevertheless the most highly esteemed player for house dances along his travelling routes in the centre of the county. By the 1950s some collectors had visited him and reported on his prowess; by the 1970s his commercial recording had made him the most influential of all Donegal fiddlers. While his style may be considered as the archetypal Donegal fiddling, it is, however, curiously unique. It had many of the hallmarks of most of the sub-regional Donegal styles, but was highly complex and personal, and as he made clear, was consciously developed. Such was the impact of his dynamic playing that he remains the most influential Donegal fiddle player, and he is the credited source on many of the late twentieth-century flood of Donegal-style recordings. (CAM)

See Cairdeas na bhFidléirí; fiddle, Donegal.

**Donnan, Jackie.** Fiddle. East Co. Down player in a Protestant community with recreational pursuits peripheral to both mainstream regional life and typical traditional music society. He perceives his music as being in the rhythm of the dance, a quality picked up since he first began playing in the 1950s at socials that ran from 9 p.m. to 3 a.m. In his teenage years his area had a deep appreciation of the older music, played at harvest celebrations, and (as it still is) at regular weekly and fortnightly socials, notably at Ardmillan, where set dances are still danced and taught. The people of his hinterland of the Ballinahinch/Dromara area learnt their steps from a French dancing master known as Dr Albért, others carry on his teaching still: 'People's whole lives revolve around dancing'. He recalls Willie Savage (b. 1881, from a long line of fiddlers) and his son playing together several nights a week. Savage himself could describe his own grandfather playing with fiddler John Simpson (1830–1917) in earlier times for big-house servants' dances; Simpson's grandson Bobby Geddes played accordion for dancing until 1987. The matching of tunes to dances is held to be critical in Donnan's area and tradition; he dislikes the late twentieth-century fashion of 'hell for leather' reel playing, where players 'jump off one part of the tune on to the other'.

**Donnellan, Fr Luke.** (b. *c.* 1918). Collector. From Omeath, Co. Louth. Though living and working in America, he made annual summer visits to Omeath where he noted some 250 songs from the old, local Gaelic-speaking people of the area, recording also on Ediphone cylinders. One of his richest sources of song was Mary Harvessy, from whom he got Art McCooey's original 'Úirchill a Chreagáin' in 1918. His collection is housed in the Department of Folklore at UCD.

**Donnelly, Des.** (1933–73). Fiddle. A spirited and subtle fiddle player from Lacca, Fintona, Co. Tyrone, he spent many years playing in Manchester. A founder member of Manchester CCÉ, he won the All-Britain fiddle competition in 1972 and 1973 and is featured on the album entitled *Remember Des Donnelly*. He died tragically in an accident in 1973. His nephew,

Desi Donnelly, carries on as an outstanding professional traditional music player.

**Donnelly, Seán.** (1951– ) Piper, researcher, writer. Born in Ballyfermot, Dublin he learned highland pipes with the Fintan Lalor pipe band at the age of fifteen, and developed an interest in the uilleann pipes some years later. Learning to play these with NPU he met Breandán Breathnach, and under his influence began research into the pipes and the early history of Irish music. A graduate of Irish at Trinity College, Dublin, he is one of the foremost scholars in traditional music research. His work is published in a wide variety of journals, particularly *Ceol, Ceol na hÉireann, Common Stock* (journal of the Lowland and Borders Pipers' Association), *Piping Times* and various county historical societies' publications.

**Donoghue, Jim.** (1910–90). Tin whistle. Born at Drimacoo, Monasteraden, Co. Sligo, he was unique in his use of the Clarke 'C' whistle which he began to play at the age of ten. The tone he produced could be as strong as that of a concert flute, this achieved by his 'humouring' of the wooden fipple with a heated hack-saw blade. He was of the next generation to Michael Coleman and shared his repertory but was heavily influenced by Jim Coleman (fiddle) with whom he played for many years. He also cited musicians such as Paddy and Peter Sherlock, John Drury, Eugene Giblin and Peter Horan as influential as well as Fred Finn (fiddle). He recorded for television and radio in the 1980s, and is featured on *Music from Coleman Country* (1972). He was often partnered in his later years by bodhrán player and neighbour John Leyden, and could play bodhrán expertly in the local style himself. He was a major influence on the flute player, Séamus Tansey. (GRD)

**Doran, Felix.** (*c.* 1915–72). Brother to Johnny, and grandson of the famed John Cash. A travelling player, his original home was a horse-drawn caravan; he played at markets, fairs and races, he dealt in horses, then scrap metals, eventually ending up in the transport business in Manchester. A popular figure in Clare, he treasured meeting places where people could appreciate his fine legato style, repertoire and

Felix Doran and his son Michael playing on the Slaney at the 1967 All-Ireland fleadh at Enniscorthy (CCÉ)

finesse. A flamboyant executant of 'The Fox Chase', in 1963 he won the All-Ireland uilleann pipes in Mullingar. By then wealthy, he commissioned a set of all-silver pipes from a German engineer and at the end of the decade was a popular figure holding court with these, particularly at All-Ireland fleadhanna. He died in Manchester in 1972, and was buried in Rathnew, Co. Wicklow after an immense funeral. His son, Michael, and Neillídh Mulligan played at his graveside; the former and nephew John Rooney carry on his playing style. He is recorded on Topic – *The Last of the Travelling Pipers*.

**Doran, Johnny.** (1908–50). Uilleann pipes. One of the famous Doran family of travelling pipers and brother to Felix. Born at Rathnew, Co. Wicklow, his father was John Doran, also a piper, descendant of nineteenth-century Wexford piper John Cash. His parents lived for some time in England before settling off New Street in Dublin, which Johnny used as the hub of economic peregrinations in the 1930s. These took him through the Midlands to Clare and Donegal – among many other places – where he played at fairs, races, hurling and football games. World War II rationing confined him to Dublin again until 1945 when he resumed travel, working for some time as a bricklayers' assistant with Roscommon piper Andy Conroy. Wintering in Dublin over 1947–48 he was heard busking by Seán McBride who engaged him to play at a Clann na Poblachta election rally in Phoenix Hall, but his commitment to play at the party's final meeting in College Green was frustrated by the collapse of a wall on his caravan at Christchurch which seriously injured him. While paralysed in hospital, he was visited by John Kelly, Willie Clancy and Andy Conroy. They coaxed him to play the 'Fermoy Lasses' reel on the chanter while Clancy worked the bellows and Conroy the bag. Through John Kelly of Capel Street, he had been recorded by Kevin Danaher of the Folklore Commission in 1947, these recordings are the source of his album *The Bunch of Keys*. He resumed travelling after his release from hospital, but unable to walk and seriously weakened, he eventually died in 1950. His playing was regarded by Breandán Breathnach as intensely personal and emotional, highly skilled and utterly unselfconscious. This gave him a powerful charisma, his regulator playing being particularly impressive for its constant overlay of rhythms on chanter melody.

**double stopping.** A technique employed for ornamentation purposes, which involves the simultaneous sounding of more than one pitch (usually two), particularly at phrase endings. Originally associated with fiddle playing (the term itself referring specifically to the stopping of two strings with the fingers) it is now also popular with accordion and concertina players. (LID)

See fiddle.

**Douglas, Sheila.** (1932–  ). Born in Renfrew, she has been involved in the Folk Revival as a club organiser, singer, songwriter and through the Traditional Music and Song Association of Scotland, of which she is a past Chair. A teacher in Perth Academy from 1971–88 she took a PhD at Stirling University in 1986 for a research project on the storytelling traditions of the Stewart family whom she met in 1965. She has edited several song collections, including the Greig-Duncan, Vol. 7, and has published her own original prose and songs and a collection of stories based on her field recordings of the Stewarts called *The King of the Black Art*. She is a Scots language activist and teaches to Scottish music degree students at the Royal Scottish Academy of Music and Drama in Glasgow.

**Dowd, Dan.** (b. *c.* 1895). Piper, pipe maker. Born off Thomas Street, Dublin, he learned to play war pipes at the School of Music in Chatham Row, and joined his local James Connolly Pipe Band. While interned as a member of the Fianna under Seán McBride, he played these in Mountjoy jail, and in the Curragh camp, and led the prisoners as they marched from Kingsbridge Station on their release. In music school he first heard the sound of uilleann pipes in Leo Rowsome's class. With Jack Wade and Leo Purcell he went on to learn these from Billy Andrews at Essex Quay. In Donnycarney where he and his wife Mai worked with Clontarf CCÉ, their community included Jack Wade, the Rowsomes, Paddy

Moloney, Barney McKenna, John Sheehan and Ciarán O'Reilly. As a fireman, normal playing at socials was not available to him so he concentrated instead on reed- and pipe-making, working with Matt Kiernan. He was one of the key workers in Na Píobairí Uilleann, passing on to many his reed-making skills. The 1952 Egan pipes that he played were presented to him by fellow fireman Bill Crowe, at Tara St Fire Station.

**Dowling, Martin.** (1964– ). Fiddle, organiser. Born in Chicago, his father from Tullamore, Co. Offaly, his mother from Gurteen, Co. Sligo. As a child he heard albums of Seán Maguire, the Dubliners and the early Chieftains. From age seven to fourteen he took classical violin lessons and played in the Milwaukee Civic Youth Orchestra. His uncle – warpiper Christy Dowling – introduced him to O'Neill's book and Irish dance music, and he played for his sisters' Irish dancing. A break at age fourteen ended at twenty-one when poet and bodhrán player Michael Donaghy involved him in a band. Finishing a doctorate in history brought him to Dublin and Belfast from 1987–88, from 1989–93 he taught fiddle and played professionally in the US. He returned to live in Belfast in 1994. In 1998 he was appointed successor to Ciarán Carson as the Arts Council of Northern Ireland's traditional arts officer. He is married to flute player and singer Christine Plochman with whom he has recorded *A Thousand Farewells* (1997).

**draíocht.** A 'spell', or enchantment, the term is sometimes used in conjunction with music to impart a sense of skill, emotional expression or 'carrying away'. The concept is referred to usually as 'lonesome' – a suffusive, pleasurable pain evoked by the music, particularly by that of certain players. While the music of east Co. Clare and Galway – particularly the compositions of Paddy Fahy – may be described so, it is very often only the individual player who will be recognised as achieving it. The term 'lonesome' is used also in other areas – notably Co. Tyrone – and fiddler John Loughran aspired to it as his sense of aesthetic. It is generally associated with older players, and is used to describe the music of, say, Neillídh O'Boyle, Séamus Ennis, Joe Cooley and Ellen Galvin. Of it, Breandán Breathnach has written that it is most often associated with tunes in minor keys, but, again, skill and artistry are required to draw it out. Sliding into C-naturals and F-naturals may be part of the process, as indeed is subtle undercutting, 'micro' rolling and relaxed tempo – allowing the tune to lead the playing rather than the player 'driving' the melody. 'Caisleán An Óir' (hornpipe), 'Ballinasloe Fair' (reel) and 'Paddy Fahey's Jig' are tunes which facilitate this.

See harmony.

**drone.** A continuous tone which plays behind the melody, particularly on uilleann pipes and other bagpipes. Other instruments mimic this – the fiddle does so, often momentarily, by engaging the bow with a string which is not being utilised for melody; the flute can simulate the effect by constantly referencing, say, a low D; on the harp Máire Ní Chathasaigh pioneers a drone effect by at intervals striking an unused lower string, say E, and leaving it to resonate; accordion or concertina can use a held note so as a backing, particularly on airs.

**Dublin.** See song, Dublin.

**Dublin Pipers' Club.** Irish music, and particularly piping, has always survived and flourished well in inner-city Dublin, and there the Pipers' Club has been responsible for passing it on to the present day. The origins of club are tied up with the National Literary Revival which focused interest on all aspects of culture. This began during the closing decade of the nineteenth century and heralded the birth of the Gaelic League and the Feis Cheoil (Dublin). Examination of the Dublin Pipers' Club minute book (1900–04) reveals the cross-fertilisation of various interests coming together to promote Irish music. Many patrons had dual membership of the Gaelic League and later of the Irish Volunteers and many were Gaelic propagandists and ardent nationalists. Perhaps the most famous was Eamonn Ceannt – 1916 Proclamation signatory and leader of the Easter Rising – who was secretary of the Pipers' Club until he retired on his marriage to the treasurer, Áine Brennan.

It is through the Pipers' Club that the development of Irish music in Dublin can best be traced too over the entire twentieth century. It became defunct on a number of occasions; in 1906 it was in financial difficulties, and in 1911 was in a 'moribund' condition. The last entry signed in the second minute book of the Dublin Pipers' Club dated 14 October 1913 is a request from Pádraig Pearse via Eamonn Ceannt for pipers to play at a feis in aid of St Enda's Irish-language school. Also from the minute book we learn that greater political affairs had a profound effect on music.

From 15 January 1914 until 2 November 1921 there is no documentary evidence of the club's existence, but Breandán Breathnach established that it was reformed in Thomas Street in 1919, but put out of existence by the activities of the Black and Tans who raided it on one occasion. (Organisations and bands associated with Irish activities were frequently the target of the authorities.) The Fintan Lalor Pipe Band and the Cork Pipers' Club were raided during the same period, and William Keane, the Limerick piper, had his house burned by Black and Tans.

In an article, 'The Origin of Céilí Bands' (*Treoir*, 1968), Leo Rowsome states that after the 1916 insurrection, the Pipers' Club continued to meet at his father's house in Harold's Cross. A letter from the hon. secs. of the Irish Union Pipers' Club in November 1921 announced the resumption of its public activity at 132, Thomas Street and exhorted its members to support them. The letter was signed by Chas. J. B. Kenny and John Fleming (hon. sec.). A roll-book of this period, 1921–22, with a list of members is in the National Library. Rowsome also recalled that the Civil War put an end to all music gatherings, including the 'friendly sessions' of the Pipers' Club. It disrupted the Oireachtas competitions too; no instrumental competitions were held in 1922, and in 1923 there was a very limited number of events; in 1924 it was held in Cork with disappointing entries – no entries in the 'uilleann piper' or 'pipe-learner' competitions. Seán Ó Tuama has written that many people also felt that there was no longer a need for the Gaelic League or specialist music organisations at that time; people believed that in fact the country was in safe hands and culture would receive due recognition from a native government (*The Gaelic League Idea*, 1972, 1993, Mercier). The first flush of enthusiasm from the cultural revival had run its course.

From 1925 to 1936 the Pipers' Club in Dublin ceased to exist, but as with the situation after 1916, the music continued in the homes of musicians, notably those of William Rowsome and John Brogan (pipe maker, Harold's Cross), John Potts (the Coombe) and James Ennis of Finglas. In 1936 it was Leo Rowsome who brought things together again and revived the club from among thirty of his pupils in Schoolhouse Lane, off Molesworth Street, after a performance of the Siamsa Mór band in the Phoenix Park, 1936.

With Rowsome as its chair, Cumann na Píobairí was key to the setting up of 'Cumann Ceoltóirí na hÉireann' in 1951, then CCÉ. The Pipers' Club as a focus for organisation of traditional music was thereafter eclipsed by the rapid growth of CCÉ, but it continued its classes and sessions however, and through the 1960s it was the premier music venue in Dublin. With the opening in 1976 of CCÉ's 'Cultúrlann' at Belgrave Square, Monkstown, it moved again and is now a CCÉ branch – Craobh Leo Rowsome, Cumann na bPíobairí. The club continues to teach the uilleann pipes and other instruments.

But for the endeavours of the Gaelic League in founding the first Dublin Pipers' Club, and the early Oireachtas competitions for providing both a forum for playing and a challenge, the resurgence in the playing of the pipers and the revitalisation of the art of pipe making and reed making may not have materialised. In each decade of the twentieth century predictions were made in anticipation of the pipes following the fate of the harp. These have been proved wrong. Continuity with the old pipers was achieved through the Pipers' Club's first tutor Nicholas Markey, and through its mentor Leo Rowsome's family history. This has guaranteed the preservation and passing on of piping techniques and styles surviving from the nineteenth century. (MIO)

**Dubliners.** A seminal ballad-group formed from skilled musicians in O'Donoghue's bar, Dublin in 1962, the Dubliners were Barney

McKenna (banjo), Luke Kelly (1939–84, banjo), John Sheahan (fiddle), Ciarán Bourke and Ronnie Drew. Their professionalism, arrangements, Dublin-flavoured repertoire and singing ability made them popular players in Dublin and all over Ireland, and among Irish communities abroad by 1966. They were at once popular and traditional: with McKenna's banjo they gained respect from a 'traditional' audience, while Drew's uncompromising Dublin accent and 'iron-on-gravel' bass delivery, as well as the formidable power of Luke Kelly's passionate vocals, strongly identified the group with the city. They helped to bring Dublin into the picture of traditional music revival, and forced consideration of 'street song' as a valid part of Irish 'culture'. Their organised informality was iconoclastic, their irreverence for sacred cows embodied not only in delivery but song choice – 'Seven Drunken Nights', 'Black Velvet Band', 'Never Wed an Old Man', 'Take her up to Monto'. The Dubliners popularised the banjo and crossed class barriers, and it was through them that many of today's traditional players first witnessed the power of acoustic music-making.

**Dúchas.** Literally meaning 'tradition' and 'inheritance', 'nature'. It is the title of the renamed Masonic Hall at Edward Street, Tralee, Co. Kerry, a traditional arts centre administered by Co. Kerry CCÉ, the outcome of a project begun in 1976.

**Duignan, Packie.** (1922–92). Renowned flute player, dry humorist and popular local character born in Collier's Road, Arigna, Co. Roscommon. He worked in the coal mines of Arigna until the early 1970s. He began playing the Clarke whistle, particularly affected by the music of John McKenna, often playing selections of his 78 record tunes. His diaphragm-driven rhythm was classically associated with McKenna, but is popularly considered to reflect an indigenous style of flute playing. He recorded an album with fiddler Séamus Horan, made several radio and television broadcasts and played with the Shannon Star Céilí Band for about fifteen years after 1958. In later years he played mainly with Séamus Horan and Kieran Emmett. One of his casual groupings he referred to humorously as 'The Underprivileged Céilí Band'.

**dulcimer.** See hammer dulcimer.

**Dwyer, John.** (1933–   ). Fiddle. From Eyries, Castletownbere, Co. Cork, both his parents played accordion, his father the fiddle also. John learned fiddle at the age of eleven; brothers Richard, Michael and Finbar played accordion. Joining the Gardaí in 1955, in Dublin he attended the Church Street and Pipers' clubs where he was influenced by George Rawley, John Kelly, Tommy Potts, Sonny Brogan, Bill Harte, piper John Clarke and fiddler Jack Derwin. In 1959 he played in the Shannonside céilí band with Jim Masterson (father of piper, Declan), and from 1970–74 in the Castle céilí band. Based in Wexford after 1964, then Ring, Co. Waterford in 1972, he became chair first of the county board of CCÉ there, then of the Munster council. Now in New Ross, Co. Wexford, like his brothers he is a well-known composer. His tunes include 'The Fall of Dunloy', 'John Dwyer's Reel' and 'The Catha Mountains'.

**Dwyer, Michael.** (d. 1996). Tin whistle. Brother to John, Richard and Finbar, he played often at the Tradition Club in Dublin and was a highly regarded player, a prolific composer who made up to two hundred airs, reels and jigs, these currently being prepared for publication.

# E

**Early, James (Sgt).** Flute. From Carrickavoher, Aughavas, Co. Leitrim. A contemporary in Chicago of Francis O'Neill, and source of many of his collected tunes.

See Leitrim, South.

**East Galway style.** See Galway, East.

**ediphone.** See reproduction of music, ediphone.

**education.**
*second level*. The spread of the availability of formal music education in Ireland is uneven – Carlow, Cork, Galway, Kerry, Mayo and Westmeath being well served – and counties where traditional music is strong – such as Clare, Sligo, Roscommon and Leitrim – being poorly provided for.

An attempt was made in the 1980s by the Tara Irish Examining Board to formulate a grading system in traditional music, but it was not until 1998 that there was an Irish qualification in traditional music equivalent to the various 'grades' available in 'classical' music performance. Traditional musicians view such assessment with suspicion – seeing in it a contradiction between style and technical ability. Fleadh competition – almost exclusively restricted to childhood-to-early-twenties age groups – was the only competitive incentive until the advent in 1997 of the London College of Music scheme and then, in 1998, CCÉ/RIAM's syllabus. For the moment, fleadh ratings remain the major recognised qualification. However traditional music can be utilised in both parts of Ireland as a part of the second-level examination system – Junior and Leaving Certificates in the south, GCSE in the North. This despite the fact that in both areas there is no official, formal teacher-training in the subject. Further, there are no statistics available from the Irish Dept of Education on how many students take up the traditional music in the school option. Only 25 per cent of Ireland's 759 second-level schools offered any music as subject in 1997. Northern Ireland has 238 secondary schools, and all are obliged to teach music.

The London College of Music 'grades' system in Irish traditional music was a rather embarrassing situation for traditional music educators in Ireland, but it served to precipitate the (already planned) CCÉ/RIAM scheme.

The formal education music options provided are:

Leaving Certificate and Junior Certificate: Dept. of Education, Hawkins House, Dublin.
GCSE: NI Dept. of Education, Balloo Rd, Bangor, Co. Down.
London College of Music, Thames Valley Univ., St Mary's Rd, London W5 5RF, England.
Royal Irish Academy of Music, 36 Westland Row, Dublin 2.
Post Leaving Cert, Vocational Courses in Traditional music:
Ceoltóir, Senior College, Ballyfermot, Dublin.
Traditional, Folk, Performance, Senior College, Ballyfermot, Dublin.
Sound Engineering, Advanced Technology College, 19/20 Hogan Place 2, Dublin, Co. Dublin.
Sound Engineering, Sound Training Centre, Temple Bar Music Centre, Dublin 2, Dublin. (EDI)

*Northern Ireland*. Music became a compulsory subject in the Northern Ireland educational system with the introduction of the curriculum for four–sixteen year olds. Prior to this, some form of music was generally taught in the majority of primary schools from ages four–fourteen by class teachers, and in secondary schools by a music specialist. This teaching might vary from choral music to creative music, school band, school orchestra or traditional music, depending on the particular interest of the teacher. Most secondary schools have a qualified music teacher who looked after full-class teaching during the first three years,

O-Level music for years 4/5, A-Level music for years 6/7 – as well as having responsibility for the school choirs, band, orchestra, recorder ensembles etc., and directing the school musical.

O- and A-Level syllabi were entirely concerned with classical music. Education boards provided orchestral tuition by peripatetic teachers to selected pupils free of charge with a support system of Education Board bands and orchestras. The 1980s saw an examination of the music curriculum throughout the UK with a growing interest among music educationalists in 'ethnic' musics. When the GCSE exam was introduced in Northern Ireland in 1988, the syllabus was broadened to include traditional music (along with pop music, etc.). Prescribed set works over the next few years included recordings by the Chieftains, De Dannan, Sharon Shannon, etc.

This exam also included a performing, solo/ensemble and composing element, both of which could be in traditional music. Many schools now have traditional music ensembles, sometimes teacher-directed, at other times organised by the pupils themselves. Many schools employ traditional music teachers to provide tuition for pupils who choose to avail of it. At A-Level, traditional music is only in evidence in the general listening section of the exam which can embrace all forms of music. While students may perform traditional music, the emphasis in the exam is still firmly on art music as a basis for pupils to continue their music studies at university. (EIV)

*third level.* There is no undergraduate degree course currently available in Irish traditional music although one is planned to begin in the DIT School of Music in 1999. Most university music courses, however, incorporate it as a part of their overall programmes. It is found in this form in the following colleges:

UCC, Music Department, University College, Cork.
IWMC, University of Limerick, Plassey, Limerick.
Cork City VEC, Tramore Road, Cork, Co. Cork.
Cork School of Music, Union Quay, Cork, Co. Cork.
Waterford Institute of Technology, Waterford.
St Patrick's Training College, Drumcondra, Dublin 9.
NUI, Maynooth, Co. Kildare.
NUI, Galway.
University College, Dublin, Music Department, Belfield, Dublin 4.
Tralee Institute of Technology, School of Business and Social Studies, Clash, Tralee, Co. Kerry
Mary I., University of Limerick, South Circular Road, Limerick, Co. Limerick

*National University of Ireland, Cork.* Its Music Department has had a long and respected history in the teaching and promotion of Irish traditional music. Courses in Irish traditional music were first introduced by Carl Hardebeck as part of the Bachelor of Music degree in 1923. Annie Patterson – the first Irish woman to be awarded a PhD – took over the curriculum, followed in 1935 by Seán Neeson. Seán Ó Riada took up the post in 1963 and after his death, Tomás Ó Canainn continued the teaching until the appointment of Mícheál Ó Súilleabháin in 1975. Fiddler Liz Doherty was appointed full-time Irish music lecturer in 1997 after a three-year temporary position. Bodhrán player Mel Mercier lectures there in percussion and ethnomusicology. The Music Department offers teaching in Irish traditional music at both academic and practical levels. History courses cover topics ranging from the dance tradition, the song tradition, the development of group playing, the harp tradition, collectors and collections of Irish music, gender issues in Irish music, music from the Celtic countries, the creative process, to fieldwork in Irish music. A number of well-known music, song and dance performers tutor in the department on a regular basis. Courses in traditional music ensemble are also offered and workshops with well-known artists are a regular part of this. There is also a course in 'Celtic' fiddle styles and repertoires which has led to the formation of Fiddlesticks, a group of student fiddlers. Seminars concerning various aspects of traditional music are organised regularly and in 1996 the inaugural Seán Ó Riada International Conference was held. The Irish Traditional Music Society, organised by students, is an important and active part of musical life at UCC. It is responsible for weekly lunchtime concerts which over the years have featured important, recognised performers from Ireland,

Scotland, Cape Breton and Brittany. Sessions organised by the students are held regularly at pubs throughout the city. With the Music department, the society has been responsible for a number of festivals, the most recent being Trad on Campus. A series of five major weekend events under the banner of Éigse na Laoi was held between 1991 and 1995, these focusing separately on Donegal and Shetland, Irish music in America, Irish music in England, Cape Breton, and finally a celebration of Irish music worldwide. Recordings of these events were produced by Nimbus and Realworld. Triantan – the Irish Harp Society – is also operated from within the student body. The Music department houses a traditional music archive which is open to the public. The archive contains a large number of audio and video tapes, periodicals, photographs, under- and post-graduate student projects. It also has the Henebry wax cylinders – some of Ireland's oldest archival material. In conjunction with the Irish Traditional Music Society the archive publishes the annual Ó Riada memorial lectures. Traditional music is an integral part of the three-year BA degree and the four-year B. Mus. degree. All students in the Music department are exposed to Irish traditional music and much scope is allowed within the course structure for those who wish to specialise in the area. At post-graduate level traditional music may be studied for the degrees of MA, M.Mus., M.Phil and PhD. The department head is Prof. David Cox. (LID)

*National University of Ireland, Dublin.* The Music department offers courses in traditional music in the first and second years of the BA and B. Mus. degrees. The first-year course, 'History and Development of Irish Music', includes consideration of the structure of Irish music, its modes and scales; a study of some of the instruments, their history and their music; and an introduction to the principles of folk-music collecting. The second-year course, 'Irish Music', examines the history and practice of traditional music, including the fundamentals of traditional singing; basic methods of analysis and cataloguing; and study of the printed sources with special reference to the principal melodic types. Both of these courses may include an introduction to ethnomusicology. The Music Department Head is Prof. Harry White.

The NUI's Department of Irish Folklore is at UCD, Belfield. Its Folk Music Section is in Earlsfort Terrace, Dublin, and is open to the public. Irish folklore is offered to undergraduate second- and third-year students only; there is also a one-year higher diploma. The department's courses include lectures on Irish traditional music, song and dance. Lecture topics include instruments, instrumental music, song in English and Irish, music in Irish culture, history of Irish music, dance, collections in the department, collectors of music and song, etc. The Department Head is Prof. Séamas Ó Catháin.

*National University of Ireland, Galway.* The Department of Education offers a course in Irish traditional music in the context of the two-year diploma in Music Education. This course, which incorporates input from visiting lecturers as well as departmental personnel, varies somewhat in content. Topics generally covered include the instrumental tradition, the collectors, dance music, and song. Students who are themselves traditional musicians may, in second year, elect to specialise in their particular instrument. The Department Head is Dr John Marshall.

*National University of Ireland, Maynooth.* The B. Mus. course incorporates elements of traditional Irish music and ethnomusicology. In first year, a basic introduction to Irish music is offered by John O'Keefe. In second year all aspects of traditional music instrumentation, performance and style are covered by Fintan Vallely who also covers a third year ethnomusicology course based in organology, ethnomusicology concepts and selected regional studies. Department Head is Prof. Gerald Gillen.

*Queen's University, Belfast.* The college does not offer specific tuition in Irish traditional music, but may offer it as a course in its ethnomusicology programme which is located in the Department of Social Anthropology, School of Philosophical and Anthropological Studies. Since 1998 a 'Music of Europe' module is offered. This module uses case studies from the UK and Ireland, Scandinavia and Eastern Europe to examine the representation, transmission and performance of music in contemporary Europe. A performance ensemble associated with the module includes aspects of Irish traditional music. The Department Head is Prof. Hastings Donnan.

*School of Music, Cork*. The School of Music (Director, Dr Geoffrey Spratt), offers musicianship classes for Junior and Leaving Certificate students. In the context of the four-year B. Mus. degree course, a first-year course, 'A General Introduction to Irish Traditional Music', gives a brief historical overview of the tradition. Lecture topics include major traditional styles (with a concentration on Sliabh Luachra), instruments, singing tradition, dance tradition, as well as modern approaches to the tradition. Students may elect to play traditional instruments in ensembles, and degree students may take a traditional instrument as their second instrument. (THS)

*Trinity College, University of Dublin*. The department offers to general music students a course in Irish traditional music, lectured by Nicholas Carolan and Hugh Shields.

*University of Limerick*. The Irish World Music Centre is as a post-graduate research centre with special interests in Irish traditional music, dance studies and ethnomusicology. It offers MA courses of relevance to traditional music in ethnochoreology and ethnomusicology as well as a graduate diploma in education and music technology. Modular courses all involve history and theory, notation skills, international observation and practical performance or research. The teaching programmes are aimed at imparting classroom skills, education theory and planning, designed to deal with evolution and change. Ethnomusicology leans heavily on Irish music, provides a grounding in the subject's methods and research principles. The university's courses reference Irish traditional music as a base, but are placed in an international context. They are taught one-year programmes. Dr Mícheál Ó Súilleabháin is Professor, Dr John O'Connell covers ethnomusicology and Dr Catherine Foley is responsible for dance.

*Waterford Institute of Technology*. WIT offers a Bachelor of Arts in music. A new music facility was opened in 1997 as part of the College Street Campus. This has a concert hall, a music library, an electronic and computer music studio and a traditional music archive. Music studies courses are rooted in practical musicianship and performance, with a strong composition component. Public concerts are presented regularly and master-classes and external lectures in traditional music are arranged during the year. Tuition is available from specialist staff employed by the college for a wide range of orchestral and traditional instruments and for voice. The study of Irish traditional music is among the subjects taken in years 1, 2 and 4 under piper Jimmy O'Brien Moran; these include history and performance practices. The college also has an Irish traditional music archive which comprises a large collection of journals, music collections, albums and other material. (JIO)

*St Patrick's Teacher Training College, Dublin*. St Patrick's offers a course in Irish traditional music to both BA and BEd students. In the course of three years lecturer Fintan Vallely gives an introduction to all aspects of music, song and dance. The college has a strong performance focus and a Traditional Music Society which also involves non-music students. Department head is Marion Doherty.

*teacher training*. Teacher training courses are offered by the following:

TTCT, Teacher Training, Comhaltas Ceoltóirí Éireann, Belgrave Square, Monkstown, Dublin

IWMC, Graduate Diploma, Music Education, University of Limerick, Plassey, Limerick

Armagh Pipers' Club, Victoria Street, Armagh, Co. Armagh

Harp Foundation, 353 Crumlin Road, Belfast, Antrim BT14 7EA

*grades*.

1. CCÉ/RIAM Traditional Irish Music Examinations Syllabus. Introduced in December, 1998, this collaboration with the Royal Irish Academy aims at a non-competitive grading of music performance and theory. It is evaluated in three levels of an 'elementary cycle', through five levels of 'junior cycle' to four of a top 'senior cycle'. Knowledge of aspects of music other than performance is incorporated in the schedule, and emphasis is placed on learning by ear.

2. LCM (London College of Music) Irish Traditional Music Syllabus. Introduced in October, 1997, this offers three branches of

examination: solo instrumental, ensemble, and theoretical diploma by thesis. Instrumental music targets are graded as: preliminary, grades two, four, six and eight. It specifies the validity of regional styles, and emphasises memory performance; the students are obliged to have a developing knowledge of the music and their instrument.

**EFDSS.** See English Folk Dance and Song Society.

**Egan, John.** (1903– ). Flute. Born at Sooey, Co. Sligo. He learnt his first music from James Doyle, a flute player from Lacka, Riverstown, his local parish. In the early decades of the twentieth century his background was music-making and dancing each week in a neighbour's house. Sets, schottisches, barn dances and an occasional waltz would be danced; music was provided by flute players and fiddlers. While still a young man, he met John Joe Gardiner and became interested in the flute. Work took him to Donegal and London before he finally settled in Dublin in 1937. There he played with the members of the Kincora Band, and other Dublin-based musicians including Sonny Brogan, Bill Harte, Frank O'Higgins, John Kelly, John Stenson and Tom Mulligan. As a barman, however, he could not attend the normal Wednesday-night, music activity of the Pipers' Club in Thomas Street. Hence, with John Brennan, Tom Mulligan and others he established St Mary's Traditional Music Club in Church Street.

See Church Street Club.

**embouchure.** Term used in connection with flute-blowing to describe 1. the shape of the lips as employed in blowing, 2. the actual hole blown into on the flute.

See flute.

**emigration.** See song, emigration.

**English Folk Dance and Song Society.** (EFDSS). Founded in London as the Folk-Song Society on 16 May 1898. Its remit was 'the collection of Folk-Songs, Ballads and Tunes, and the publication of such of these as may be deemed advisable'. Rule X gave the committee 'the power to elect a limited number of Honorary members from amongst distinguished foreign authorities on the subject of Folk Music'. The first honorary secretary was Kate Lee, a professional singer and pivotal worker. She went on to 'discover' the Copper family. Lucy Broadwood, daughter of a well-known musical family, took over in 1904. Scots born, and with an intense affinity for all things Scottish and Gaelic, her appointment resulted in the *Journal of the Folk-Song Society* printing and discussing Scottish, Scots Gaelic, Irish, and Manx songs (as well as English, Canadian and French). There were, however, members who wanted the society to restrict its interests to 'English' folk-song, but attempts by Ralph Vaughan Williams and Cecil Sharp to implement this were rebuffed. Cecil Sharp, who had come on the scene relatively late compared to collecting pioneers such as Frank Kidson, Sabine Baring Gould and the Broadwoods (father and daughter), took up folk-song 'as a profession' and rushed out *English Folk-Song: Some Conclusions* in 1907. He was determined to use 'real' English folk-song to counter the tide of both trashy music-hall song and what was mistakenly called 'National Song', and especially to have it introduced into English schools. Influential members of the society saw him as pushy and opportunistic (he was particularly despised by Lucy Broadwood), and it is hardly surprising that in 1911 Sharp founded the English Folk Dance Society, dedicated purely to English dance. He kept it under strict control, following his personal orthodoxy, and fought bitterly with those he considered 'heretical' such as the 'evolutionary' Mary Neale, until his death in 1924. In 1930, the EFDS negotiated with the Folk-Song Society to amalgamate, but insisted that the word 'English' should be retained; thus the English Folk Dance and Song Society was formed in 1932. The first issue of its journal appeared the same year, but despite having 'English' in its title, the editor, Frank Howes, emphasised 'our belief in the value of the comparative method in all questions of folk-lore and in the international significance of national folk-art'. International dance festivals were held, and articles were to appear on a wide variety of British and European dances – Catalonian, Polish, Italian, Manx, etc. The

117

journal also continued to publish folk-song articles from outside England – Irish, Scottish (Lowland and Gaelic), Manx, Appalachian, Canadian, Maltese, Albanian, etc. This international thrust continued, and, significantly, the title of the journal was altered in 1965 simply to the *Folk Music Journal*. As will be clear, the society throughout its existence took a great interest in matters Gaelic and Irish, with major contributions from Lucy Broadwood onwards. Nos. 23, 24 and 25 (1920–21), for example, were devoted entirely to collections of Irish folk-songs, and such an interest continues to the present day. (IAO)

**Ennis, Séamus (Séamus Mac Aonghusa).** (1919–82). Uilleann piper and tin-whistle player, singer, story-teller, music collector, broadcaster. Born Jamestown, Finglas, Co. Dublin. One of the country's most important traditional music figures this century, his influence is seen widely and in varied ways. He inherited music from his father James Ennis, a civil servant with the Department of Agriculture, also a piper and a champion dancer from Naul. His mother was Mary McCabe from Co. Monaghan. Second-eldest of three brothers and three sisters he was educated at the Holy Faith Convent, Glasnevin, later at Belvedere College, then through Irish at Scoil Cholm Cille and Coláiste Mhuire; his Irish was perfected with visits to Rosmuc, Connemara. His father had learnt from Nicholas Markey of Meath (tutor to the Dublin Pipers' Club and pupil of Billy Taylor) and broadcast with the Fingal Trio for early Irish radio 2RN. Séamus's childhood was filled with their music-making. Visitors to the home included Dublin piper Liam Andrews, Drogheda player Pat Ward, fiddler Frank O'Higgins, flute player John Cawley. The young Ennis was given technical instruction and sight-reading tuition by his father, began playing on a Brogan set of pipes at age thirteen, and by his early twenties was extremely proficient. He sang in An Claisceadal, an Irish language choir directed by Colm Ó Lochlainn, and through him was introduced to Prof. Ó Duilearga of the Irish Folklore Commission. Following a commercial course he got a job with Colm Ó Lochlainn's Three Candles Press in Dublin from 1938–42, there becoming proficient at music transcription. He worked for the Irish Folklore Commission between 1942 and '47, moving to Raidió Éireann as Outside Broadcast Officer between 1947 and '51, where he produced documentary programmes, including some on sean-nós singing. In 1951 he teamed up with Brian George of the BBC as part of a collection scheme that covered Ireland, England, Scotland and Wales, this work taking him to London. For BBC Radio he collected and presented the pioneering Sunday-morning programme *As I Roved Out* (1951–c. 1960). Married in 1952 to Margaret Glynn, they had two children, Catherine and Christopher. He finished work with the BBC in 1958. Back in Ireland he freelanced with Raidió Éireann, travelled Ireland and abroad playing and lecturing. In the 1970s he played fiddle as part of the Halfpenny Bridge Quartet with Liam O'Flynn, Seán Keane and Tommy Grogan (accordion). In 1975 he moved to live on his grandfather's home farm at Naul, continuing his touring up to the time of his death in 1982. In all his endeavours in music he reached high standards, and his collections are a source heavily relied on by students of traditional music. He is regarded as an icon of modern piping, with a clean, crisp style structured by a finesse of technique that avoids obscuring the essential elements of the tune. His cran was distinctive, so too his 'ghost D' double-note illusion, and he could reach into the third octave on his chanter. His knowledge of the Irish language and of singing gave him a strong advantage in the playing of slow airs for which he was justly famous, his hallmark was the 'shiver' (fore-arm trill) on the high E and F. He is remembered in his prime as a tall, handsome man of independent character, witty, erudite and frequently charming. He made many recordings, possibly most representative being *The Return From Fingal*, produced by RTE in 1996. His uilleann pipe tutor was assembled posthumously from his notes by Wilbert Garvin and Robbie Hannan and published by NPU in 1998. (PEB) *the collector*. He worked as a full-time collector of music and song with the Irish Folklore Commission from 1942 to 1947, in west Munster, in counties Galway, Mayo, Cavan and Donegal, and in the Scottish Gaeltacht. Colm Ó Caodháin was one of his finest sources, giving Ennis over 200 items of song, music and lore. Elizabeth (Bess) Cronin of Baile Bhúirne, Co. Cork was another. Highly skilled at his job, Ennis could speak the dialect of Irish relevant to the particular area; his collection of songs is mostly in Irish. As a musician and singer himself he could establish a particularly good rapport with informants. The collection is now in the Department of Irish Folklore, National University of Ireland, Dublin; it consists of music notation, manuscript, text and sound recordings. (RIU)

**Ennis, Tom.** (1889– ). Piper. Born in Chicago, son of John Ennis, also a piper. A devotee of piper Pasty Tuohy, he fought in World War I and later ran a music business in New York. He made several recordings, some with James Morrison, most with piano backing.

**ethnomusicology.** The study of music in society. Alan Merriam's definition of 'music' is: 'a complex of activities, ideas and objects that are patterned into culturally meaningful sounds recognised to exist on a level different from secular communication' (*Anthropology of Music*, 1980). Ethnomusicology deals not only with the situations and the circumstances of where music is made, but also the academic and analytical world which tries to understand why and how music is produced. A by-product of world exploration and colonialism, it is a discipline which is implicitly 'White' in its original ethos, for it began by seeing itself as studying the music of non-Europeans. Its history is therefore burdened somewhat by being unobjective: it looked 'at' the music of the 'other'. Known as 'Comparative Musicology' in the beginning, it has changed hugely over the course of the last century. Now it takes all music as its territory – jazz and popular music studies are part of its remit, even classical music. Yet still, it is bound up with the notion of non-mainstream identities in music, and with the idea of 'tradition', and presently in Ireland many of those involved in the subject are concerned with Irish traditional music.

Initially, early music collectors – much in the manner of Bunting – were obliged to transcribe music and songs from their sources by hand. This was a flawed and subjective process, even if vital in its day. The invention of sound reproduction however made music recording and transcription potentially flawless, and made possible both scientific standards of analysis and second opinions. The first recordings in what is now ethnomusicology were made in 1889 by the American Walter Fewkes (of Passamaquoddy and Zuni Indian songs), four years after the British mathematician and philologist Alexander Ellis published a work titled 'On the musical scales of various nations', in which he dismissed the idea that there was only one 'natural' music scale.

When Darwinism in the 1880s was fashionably applied to musics of other peoples it tended to see either that Western music was highly developed and superior, or that the more 'underdeveloped' the people, the earlier the stage of evolution of the music, the closer to the ultimate truth in music, to the source of music. Such a utopian dream gradually dissipated as the idea of a 'world-wide diffusion' of music took over, and so a search for specific origins, in different areas, developed. This introduced the idea of studying music in society, the ethnological context: the circumstance in which it was played, not just what was being played. 'Ethnomusicology' resulted, involving ethnology and musicology, social process and sound, this bringing the social sciences together with the arts and science.

Typically an ethnomusicologist begins with an idea, then plans and designs research, gathers music and social data. These are studied and analysed, the information collated and tested against or compared with other studies. Ethnomusicology can 1. Supply information on technical production of sound. 2. Give information on behaviour in specific circumstances – hand and finger, diaphragm and body, how they are used, what tone they produce, rules for musicians, and rules for listeners. 3. It can relate the music to other social, political, economic, linguistic, religious, etc. behaviour.

If social life is about regulation of human behaviour in order to help a society survive, creative life, of which music is a major part, is to make the process of survival satisfying. Ethnomusicology acknowledges this overlap of interest; it is an analytical bridge between the social and the artistic.

# F

**Fahy, Paddy.** (1926– ). Fiddler, composer. Born at Kilconnell, Co. Galway, his father Jack was a noted fiddle-player and the initiator of the Aughrim Slopes Céilí Band. His mother could play accordion, the family had a great interest in music and gave their children access to all instruments. Paddy began playing at the age of five, specialising in fiddle, his sisters were prize-winning step dancers. A hurler of renown in his youth, he learnt a large repertoire rapidly, his interest benefiting greatly from music and set dancing in the large ballroom that was part of their home, Killaghbeg House. In later years the house was host to sessions among local musicians, this contributing to Fahy's reputation in the present day as the supreme tunesmith. Composer of some sixty pieces with a distinctive, profound lyricism, he is considered the doyen of east Galway style. His compositions are played widely, and greatly uncredited.

See Aughrim Slopes Céilí Band.

**Fallon, Joe.** (1935– ). Button accordion. Born at Collooney, Co. Sligo, he began to play the melodeon at age seven. He was taught by his father Michael (also a melodeon player) and his early influences were Frank Reilly (melodeon), Bernie Flynn (tin whistle), John Fallon (flute) and Danny Fallon (fiddle). He played with the Glenview Céilí Band during the 1960s, but later played regularly with Harry McGowan (flute), James Murray (flute/fiddle) and Jimmy Murphy (fiddle), from the 1970s to the early '80s, on two occasions in the US.

**Fallon, Martin.** (d. 1980). Fiddle, uilleann pipes. He began playing the tin whistle at the age of nine, and started playing with the Carroll family of Einlaghmore, out of which grew the Kilbride Céilí Band which took first in the 1945 and 1946 Roscommon Feiseanna. Moving to Clonaslee, Co. Laois in 1949 he formed new music associations – in the late 1950s playing pipes with Seán Ryan, Danny and Bernadette Coughlan, Dinny Lyons, John Brady, Maureen Kenny, Brendan McMahon, Tom Carey, Jim McGrath and Ellen Flanagan. Competitions, céilís and radio and television broadcasts followed for the band until its break-up in 1968. By 1963 Martin was mostly playing fiddle, and was adjudicating at all levels. In 1970, with Pat O'Meara (piano), Tom Ahearne (fiddle), Tony Coen (fiddle), Joe Smullen (flute) and Ellen Flanagan, Denis Ryan, Jim McGrath, Maura Connolly and Eugene Nolan, he formed the Bridge Céilí Band which won that year's All-Ireland, and also those in 1973 and 1974. More radio and television broadcasts followed, then an LP in 1976.

**famine.** See song, famine.

**Farr, Lucy.** (1912– ). Fiddle, song. Born Baunynauve, Ballinakill, Co. Galway, her father played melodeon and flute for house dances, her brother played flute and sang, an aunt played fiddle. A fiddle player in her youth, in her young adult years work and family took precedence over music-making, and she emigrated to London in the mid 1930s. In her fifties she returned to fiddle playing and singing, performing all over England with Reg Hall's 'Rakes'. A composer of several tunes, she was always present in the emergence of London's pub music scene and the revival of traditional music there in the 1960s. She continued to play, compose, and record traditional music up to the end of the 1990s. Her life is documented in *The Blooming Meadows* (1998), and she has a solo album *Stepping It Out*.

**Farrell, Patsy.** Ballygawley, Co. Tyrone. Singer, fiddler, tin whistle and accordion player from an early age. A composer of songs in a local, Tyrone style, his céilí band was widely known in the 1950s.

**fear an tí.** Literally 'man of the house', this is the 'master of ceremonies', the 'presenter' who typically introduces the performers in concerts. The role also extended to céilí dances where a singer may have to be introduced, a raffle run to raise funds, or announcements made. The role requires particular communication skills, and usually utilises a sense of humour. Different occasions demand different talents, thus storyteller John Campbell can keep an audience alive with humour between acts, others, like Muireann Daingean at the Scoil Samhraidh Willie Clancy all-star concert, require a more serious approach and an ability to give potted biographies which illuminate the performer and critically inform the audience.

**Féile Chomórtha Joe Éinniú.** Festival commemorating singer Joe Heaney. Begun at his homeplace in Carna, Co. Galway in June 1986, and organised by poet and teacher Mícheál Ó Cuaig and singer and lecturer Peadar Ó Ceannabháin.

**Féile na Bóinne.** Drogheda's occasional festival begun in 1976 as a focus for the town's traditional music, reflecting its diversity of cross-over Northern/Southern identity. It has featured players like John Kelly, Joe Ryan, Seán Corcoran, Sarah Ann O'Neill, Geordie Hanna, Nioclás Tóibín, Darach Ó Catháin, Paul Brady and Andy Irvine.

**feis.** (pl. feiseanna). Literally 'entertainment for the night', but in relation to music an abbreviation for 'feis cheoil', 'music festival involving competition'. Feiseanna may also involve Irish step dancing, and have been organised by local and regional branches of Conradh na Gaeilge to promote Irish-language related aspects of culture. The step dance organisations will also use the term 'feis' for their festivals; the first of these was held at Macroom, Co. Cork in 1899. The original Gaelic term 'feis' indicated an event which also celebrated politics and law-making, a usage still applied by Irish political parties for whom the annual congress is usually termed 'ard-fheis' (great gathering).

**feis cheoil.** A development of the Gaelic League (Conradh na Gaeilge), itself an 1986 product of the Irish National Literary Society whose president was then Douglas Hyde. The feis cheoil arose out of a gathering of people under the guidance of Dr Annie Patterson, its aim to 'promote the general cultivation of music in Ireland, with particular reference to Irish music'.

Songwriter P. J. McCall was one its leading figures, it also involved collector P. W. Joyce. Its offices at 19, Lincoln Place, Dublin organised the first feis cheoil in 1897 with a total of thirty-two competitions run over a week at the Rotunda Buildings; concerts were held each night at University College Dublin (now the National Concert Hall). The feis cheoil was held in Belfast in the years 1898 and 1900, and has run in Dublin without a break until the present time, interrupted only by the 1916 Easter Rising which caused a postponement of a few months. Other disruption was caused in 1913 when some of the executive committee resigned over the use of the word 'kiss' more than once in a choral piece.

Its performance/competition was inaugurated in furtherance of the promotion of the collection, preservation, study and advancement of old Irish music. In its first year the piping competition involved seven players, but the greatest interest for traditional musicians was the competition 'Discovery and vocal or instrumental performance of Ancient Irish Melodies hitherto unpublished'. These could be lilted, whistled, sung, played or noted in manuscript. From 1897–1900 some 10 per cent of these were recorded on wax cylinder for transcription from such as Brigid Kenny, Dublin ('The Independent Hornpipe'), Teresa Halpin, Limerick ('Death of Staker Wallace', air), Michael Daffy, Clare, ('Tullagh Reel' ['Paddy Ryan's Dream'], etc.), Daniel Markey, Drogheda ('Reilly From the Co. Cavan', air), John Ferguson, Wexford ('Drocketty's March'). Out of these collections, and amid competition (the desire being to avoid overlapping of material) with other works such as Petrie's, Joyce's, O'Neill's and Roche's collections, the feis cheoil collection of eighty-five tunes was published with source notes in 1914, republished as *The Darley & McCall Collection* in 1984. This early zealous effort to preserve disappeared by the 1920s, and despite the presence of a piping competition, the feis since then involves largely non-traditional music. The feis cheoil is now known as the Siemens Nixdorf Dublin Feis Cheoil. Currently its traditional music content is reduced to various competitions in harp. In his 1978 article on the event, Breathnach regards the competitors of 1897 to 1900 as the 'last in a line of professional performers. Then in their sixties and seventies, they would have acquired their skills and repertoire from musicians born in the previous century'. Although most of the recorded cylinders were re-used, a surviving forty-six given to the Folklore commission in 1955 (recorded 1899, half of useful quality) provide a narrow window to this era.

**Fermanagh.** By the time of the 1911 census this area's Co. Leitrim border still had a 10 per cent Gaelic-speaking population, and elsewhere in the county it was 1 per cent. It has been one of the outstanding regions of community practice of and respect for traditional music, song and dance. Turloch Carolan was patronised by some of the Big Houses of the 'Barony of Magheraboy' area in the seventeenth and eighteenth centuries; harpers, pipers and fiddlers were plentiful among the general population, so much so that in 1867 among the main pastimes as listed by an Enniskillen newspaper were fiddling and dancing. Flute playing was strong too. William Carroll, whose volume 'could blow the delft off a dresser', passed his repertoire and skills on to Eddie Duffy (d. 1986 at age ninety-three, still playing until shortly before his death). Particularly interesting are the dancers – Johnny and Pat Magee with the clap dance to the tune of 'Soldiers' Joy', and Vincent Duffy who, like Pat Magee, plays accordion. Duffy also plays fife and was part of the local mummers group. Fiddler Mick Hoy has been the exceptional figure in oral music culture here, but the area has many singers – like Rose and Tommy Johnson of Ardgart, whose house is an important institution for its 'kayleys'. Eugene Judge from Garrison, a prolific fund of songs, is also from a music family – his mother hung song broadsheets on the bedroom walls to encourage her children to learn songs. Ben 'Sketch' McGrath (d. 1986), so named for his wit and versatility in song for every occasion, was another outstanding raconteur with tales from his World War II service in North Africa and Italy. His son, accordionist Jim, carries this tradition on. Annie MacKenzie of Derrylin runs the Linnet Bar at Boho, a local session house. Her songs come from her mother and from migrant Leitrim men who came to the area to work. She re-organised the Boho Mummers some years ago, has made many local songs. Bridget Magee of Belcoo, from a family singing background also, is an authority on traditional dances, her sister Cassie Sheeran of Knockmore had also a large song repertoire, her style a complex of phrase, melody and rhythmic decoration variation. Jimmy Maguire – like Ben McGrath with his sisters Alice and Jane – 'chorused' with Eddie Stinson, the two also profound storytellers and wits. Much of this is visible in David Hammond's *Boho Singers* documentary (BBC NI), and can be heard on Seán Corcoran's (collected) *Here's a Health* (Arts Council of Northern Ireland, 1986). (Ref. Henry Glassie, *Passing the Time in Ballymenone.*)

See Hoy, Mick.

Fiddle (EDI)

**fiddle.** The earliest evidence of bowed instruments in Ireland is an eleventh-century bow excavated in Dublin. This is also the earliest example of a medieval bow anywhere in Europe. A twelfth-century carving in Co. Kerry depicts a bowed, six-string lyre. The earliest reference to the word 'fiddle' in Ireland is by O'Curry in relation to a seventh-century account of the Fair of Carman: 'Pipes, fiddles, chainmen, Bone-men and tube players'. The local predecessor of this kind of bowed instrument may have been the timpán, an Irish/Celtic instrument with from three to eight strings, sometimes also plectrum plucked. The eight-string 'ocht-tedach' psalterium or nabla was a Celtic instrument from the seventh to eleventh centuries. The cruit or crwth (Welsh) and crowde (English) is a small harp-lyre which was plucked, then later bowed; it had a neck, fingerboard and six strings – four fingered, two open – and was played on table or knee. *Cionnar cruit*, and *kinnor* are mentioned in a poem from 620 AD; with ten strings, played with a bow or plectrum, and like the cythara or canora of the middle ages it is an early relative of the guitar.

In 1674 Richard Head, writing on Ireland reported: 'in every field a fiddle, and the lasses footing it till they were all of a foam'; there is a late seventeenth-century Cork reference to teaching children fiddle. In 1721 an advertisement for John Neal's shop in Dublin began: 'There is fidles to be had . . .'. Old instruments were offered for sale by him, this indicating popularity. In 1742, Laurence Whyte wrote: 'In Beahan's days (our Governor for life), John played the Flute, and Billy played the Fife, Some play'd the fiddle, others vamped a base . . .'. The first Irish maker recorded was also John Neal, in 1729. Harper Arthur O'Neill mentions in his memoirs that fiddles were plentiful at Ardara, Co. Donegal in 1760, and in Fermanagh in 1770. In the 1750s there were 'plenty of pipers and fiddlers' in the Rosses, Co. Donegal, and that in 1782, at a music night he witnessed 'Gentlemen fiddlers 20'.

The modern-day violin – fiddle – has no connection with earlier described and excavated pre sixteenth-century forms. It emerged in Italy in 1550, the result of evolutionary experimentation with medieval fiddles. Mentioned in writing as *vyollon* from 1523, its depiction in familiar form appears in frescoes in Italy from 1530 at which time it is listed as a 'house-band' instrument. Originally it had three strings – like the present-day Hungarian 'folk' violin – and in other cultures may have had more. The Romanian 'folk' fiddle has five to seven extra sympathetic resonating strings, the Hungarian 'Gypsy' fiddle has an extra drone string, the Norwegian 'Hardanger' fiddle is smaller, and uses four 'sympathetic' resonating strings. The shape of the fiddle was arrived at by creating indents in its profile to permit the dipping of the bow on outside strings.

The standard violin is used in classical music in North Africa in Algeria and Morocco, sometimes played vertically on the knee. American folk fiddlers in Oklahoma, etc., play off the chest, or on the knee – this is adequate for the range of notes they utilise (in the 'first position') and is considered more comfortable and aesthetically 'correct'. In the 'first position' it is possible to move from low G to B" with the fiddle held by the hand gripping the fingerboard. The chin rest was introduced in 1820 to facilitate gripping the instrument with the chin, so freeing the hand to move into advanced positions to achieve a greater range of notes. Older Irish players may still play 'off the chest', and their fiddles will have no chin-rest, but most players today hold the fiddle under the chin. The instrument has four strings, tuned G D' A' E"; it is varnished to stop powdered bow-rosin affecting the wood and so dampening tone. It is played with a horsehair-strung bow impregnated with wood resin ('rosin').

The fiddle came before the uilleann pipes in Irish music, but after the bagpipes. It is extremely flexible for ornamentation, colour and articulation. The instrument has been wildly popular in Scotland since the seventeenth century where, with music technology leading the music, lavish strathspeys were developed to

Electric fiddle. The resonating box is replaced by an electronic pickup connected to an amplifier and/or 'effects' box. (EDI)

demonstrate virtuoso expertise. Reels were developed on it too and may have come to Ireland with the fiddle. Much Irish music has been composed on the instrument, but the compass of most tunes as played suggests that the uilleann pipes has been the standard for more than two centuries. (EDI)

*styles of playing.* The term 'style' means either the way in which one musician plays, as distinct from another, or alternatively, the distinguishing features of playing which identify musicians from a particular area. In the past, regional styles were confined primarily to their own geographic areas. However, with the advent of mass communication, recordings and competition, the differences between the regional styles may have become less obvious and the boundaries more diffuse. Since music in all styles is now readily available to everyone, a particular style may no longer be confined to its own specific region.

*elements of style.* Traditional music is essentially melodic, and relies for much of its character on the ornamentation of the melody line. On the fiddle, this is achieved by a combination of fingering ornamentation (normally with the left hand) and bowing ornamentation (normally with the right hand). In addition, the bowing itself is a fundamental feature of fiddle-playing. It is with the bow that particular note patterns and note sequences are grouped and played together, and that certain notes may be accentuated and emphasised. The bow has a significant effect on the sound produced by the fiddle, and also imparts to the music the appropriate rhythm and articulation, especially in the case of dance music.

Fingering ornamentation: The 'roll' is probably the most widely used ornament in fiddle-playing. Two auxiliary notes, one higher in pitch and one lower, decorate the main note, usually a dotted crotchet. All the notes in this sequence are usually played in the same bow stroke (Fig. 1). At normal playing tempo, the effect created by this ornament may be rhythmic as much as melodic, depending on the interpretation of the player.

Bowing ornamentation: Another major form of ornamentation is 'trebling'. Three notes of the same pitch, played in a triplet pattern, are used in place of a crotchet (Fig. 2). The notes,

Fig. 1

Trebling

Fig. 2

which are bowed separately, are played with very short bow-strokes, thereby creating an effect which is primarily rhythmic. Depending on the particular emphasis of the player, this ornament may have percussive qualities. (The use of the word 'treble' in this context differs completely from its use in the term 'treble clef'.)

The extent to which the various kinds of ornamentation are used, and the different ways in which the bow can create distinctive rhythmic nuances and colour, vary from player to player, and from one style of playing to another.

Repertoire can also be considered to be an element of style, in the sense that specific types of tunes and dance-rhythms may feature more prominently, or indeed only, in particular regions. The personality of the musician, the very soul of the performer, contributes much to the creative process, and so may also be regarded as having a major influence on the style of playing.

*regional styles.* The main regional fiddle-styles are generally considered to be those of Donegal, Sligo, Clare and Sliabh Luachra. These four areas are situated along a line from north to south, close to the western seaboard. It is impossible to be definitive in listing all the features of each style, because not every musician in a particular region plays the same way. Even within each region, there may be noticeable differences from one area to another. However, the styles of most of the players will have many similar features, so much so that such playing can be considered to constitute a regional style. In this regard, the analogy with spoken language may be helpful. Speakers in a particular dialect will not all speak in exactly the same way with identical accents and vocabulary. However, their speech will have many characteristics in common, and be recognisable as being the 'language' of a particular dialect and geographic area.

Donegal: A distinctive feature of the Donegal style is the use of single-note bowing, with short bow-strokes. Ornamentation is achieved primarily with the bow-hand, trebling being used to a much greater extent than rolls. The tempo is generally fast, which adds to the overall staccato-like effect of the style. One of the finest exponents of this music was John Doherty, whose recordings provide an excellent insight into this style of playing. The repertoire of the region includes a number of tune-types, such as highlands and strathspeys, not usually played elsewhere in Ireland, but having an obvious connection with Scotland.

Sligo: In the Sligo style, the pace is still fast, the playing is rhythmic with the bowing smoother. Rolls as well as trebles are features of the ornamentation. The fiddle music of this region is probably more widely known than any other, mainly from the playing of Michael Coleman, Paddy Killoran and James Morrison. Many of their 78 rpm recordings, made in New York in the 1920s, '30s and '40s, were sent home to Ireland by those who emigrated to America. The remarkable music on these records became a model of playing for many to try to emulate, and in a sense, this style became the 'standard'. The music of Coleman, in particular, has been a source of influence not only for fiddle players, but for others as well. His settings of tunes feature in the repertoire of many musicians.

Clare: The slower tempo of the Clare style allows the player to concentrate more on the melodic aspects of the music. The bowing is more fluid, and extensive use is made of left-hand ornamentation such as rolls. Frequently a distinction is made between the music from the west of the region and that from the east. The West Clare style is well represented by the fine playing of Bobby Casey, Junior Crehan, John Kelly, Patrick Kelly and Joe Ryan. The East Clare style is very much associated with the playing of Paddy Canny, whose wonderful music has been an inspiration to many, including those who play in other styles.

Sliabh Luachra: On the Cork/Kerry border near the source of the river Blackwater, Sliabh Luachra is renowned for slides and polkas. The direct and rhythmic style of playing these has influenced the playing of the other dance tunes. As the music is frequently played for the dancing of sets, it is lively and exuberant. Ornamentation is achieved mainly with the left hand, while the bow-hand provides the characteristic rhythm. A particular feature is the use of open strings to provide a drone-type rhythmic effect. To a greater extent than in the other regions, the repertoire of players here generally includes a number of slow airs. The recordings of Pádraig O'Keeffe, Denis Murphy and Julia Clifford all contain marvellous examples of this style of music.

Exceptions: Some areas do not fit into the general classification just outlined, and there are also players whose music may not belong to a particular regional style. For example, Paddy Cronin was a pupil of Pádraig O'Keeffe, but spent about forty years living in Boston. His distinctive music has elements of both the Sliabh Luachra style, which he learned at home, and the Sligo style, which was more prevalent in the United States during his time there. Seán McGuire has had a major influence on many fiddle players, because of the exceptional quality of his playing. His flamboyant style has many of the Sligo characteristics and much of its repertoire, but it is uniquely different at the same time. Tommy Potts, a native of Dublin, played music in a singularly personal way with a distinctly individual voice. His playing includes influences from outside the tradition as well as from within, as is exemplified by his unusual versions of tunes, combined with extraordinary interpretation.

*personal style.* For many musicians, their greatest sources of influence and inspiration are those whose music and playing they most admire. In the past, this usually meant local players, and perhaps a visiting fiddle master who taught in a particular area. However, with increased ease of travel and the widespread use of tape-recorders, sources of influence are no longer confined to the same locality. Also, the increased availability of commercially recorded music on CD, as well as on radio and television, has made music in all styles and genres, including those from outside the tradition, readily available to everyone.

These factors have contributed to the emergence of individual or personal styles of playing in which elements from some or all of the regional styles may be included. The result is a way of playing which is immediately recognisable as being that of a particular musician. Fiddle-players such as Kevin Burke, Liz Carroll, Séamus Connolly, Séamus Creagh, Frankie Gavin, Paddy Glackin, Martin Hayes, Seán Keane, James Kelly, Maeve Donnelly, Brendan McGlinchey, Connie O'Connell, Tommy Peoples, and many, many more, all have very distinctive, even unique, styles of playing. However, the influence of the various regional styles is audible to a greater or lesser extent in their music. (MAC)

*Donegal.* The distinctiveness of Donegal fiddle style can be summarised as a concurrence of Scottish influence, strong volume and bright ringing tone, staccato bowing with note for note bow-direction changes, and crisp triplets rather than rolls. Players such as Dinny McLaughlin of Inishowen and the late Jimmy Heuston of Drumkeen, Dermot McLaughlin of Derry as well as the Glackin brothers of Dublin all play with cracking triplets. Triplet playing indeed is highly developed by Tommy Peoples of St Johnston, East Donegal, who uses this ornament with an aggressive, almost explosive sound played both on beat and back beat. Rolls are popularly considered to be absent in Donegal fiddling, but in fact most of the Teelin players, and those in East Donegal, like the late Néillidh Boyle of Dungloe are prolific in their use. Despite the fact that all of these characteristics are recognised as being common in Donegal fiddling, the notion of a single 'Donegal Style' would still be accepted by very few, if any, Donegal players. It is more accurate to say that a number of sub-areas of the county – related to watersheds of physical geography which determined areas of socialisation prior to the relatively recent arrival of public transport – have local styles. All of these are still alive in an oral tradition, and older players are able to document generational changes and consistencies. The sub-regions of the county which are considered as having recognisable styles are Inishowen, East Donegal, Rosses and Gweedore, Croaghs, Teelin, Kilcar, Glencolmcille, Ballyshannon and Bundoran.

Up to the 1940s the house dance was the major form of entertainment in Donegal. Fiddle was the primary instrument for dance music; it and the fiddlers played an important social role. Players who were considered 'good' by dancers and listeners were held in high standing, and their services were sometimes called upon to help the needy with 'penny dances', and to subvert educational costs with 'schoolhouse dances'. From the 1950s onward, the music was being performed almost entirely for listening. Attention gradually came to focus on regional differences in styles, this leading to an almost competitive evaluation of them, some being perceived as 'better' than others. This has always caused tension over adjudication decisions in All-Ireland competitions, and leads to the conclusion that the favouring of 'an caighdeánach' ('Sligo' or 'Coleman' style) over, say, Donegal or Sliabh Luachra, is actively killing them off. In this atmosphere, only 'pride of place' can keep 'Donegal' or other national regional styles alive. The ascent of Altan's international popularity in the 1990s has hugely boosted confidence in Donegal style; acceptance elsewhere has given Donegal communities confidence in their basic fiddle 'accent'. With the re-emergence in the popularity of set dancing from the late 1980s, communities have moved a step further by also identifying and retrieving local dance customs. Consequently there has been a demand for fiddlers and other musicians who are conversant

Mickey Bán and Francie 'Dearg' O'Byrne, near Kilcar, Co. Donegal, 1977 (EAO)

**Rakish Paddy (Reel)**

Donegal version of the reel 'Rakish Paddy', also known in Scotland as 'Cabair Féigh' (LID)

with the local styles and rhythms which suit these.

Up to the mid-twentieth century, this county had some of the most influential players in Irish music. These have affected their succeeding generations both within and beyond the county (in particular the Glackin brothers), and internationally (through Altan). The county's many local styles of playing include from the north-west Néillidh Boyle (highly personalised and aggressive), Danny O'Donnell, Proinsias Ó Maonaigh and Mairéad Ní Mhaonaigh. The south-west has been a particularly strong area and home to the late Cassidy brothers Frank, Johnny and Paddy, to Con (their cousin), to Mick McShane, Connie Haughey, Jimmy Lyons, James Byrne, John Mhósaí McGinley, Frank McHugh, Francie-Dearg and Mickey-Bán O'Byrne. There are also John, Mickey and Simon Doherty, and their brothers Charlie and Hughie who are less well documented. Glencolmcille, Teelin, Carrick and Kilcar have produced John Gallagher and James Josie McHugh; The Croaghs has Vincent, Jimmy and Columba Campbell and their father, Peter. Younger players include Tommy Peoples, Séamus Gibson, Cathleen and Martin McGinley, Roisín and Damien Harrigan.

*tin/brass fiddles.* Travelling tinsmiths like the Dohertys, and their in-laws the McConnells, have been some of the most influential fiddlers in Co. Donegal for at least a century. Their skill in working with thin-gauge sheet metal – typically tinplate – in times of high demand for fiddles was recruited for fiddle construction too. A skilled maker could turn out a fiddle body in two hours, to it was fixed either a home-made neck and fingerboard, or more commonly, a discarded neck from a damaged timber fiddle. Two designs were used. For a more discerning customer, a metal fiddle would be made to the exact shape and dimensions of a full timber fiddle, with F-holes chiselled in the belly. For the less demanding, the body was the same general size as a full timber fiddle, but with a guitar or figure-eight profile, and circular sound holes drilled in the belly. Metal fiddles are typically dull in tone and low in volume – features that made them attractive for very small houses in the last century where playing a full-volume, timber instrument at night with an extended family all under one roof would not have been acceptable. They were also popular as the first instrument for a learner. Further, in a remote area like Donegal, there was poor access to expert repairers of wooden fiddles; robust, and insensitive to damp, a damaged tin fiddle could also be fixed conveniently. Many tin fiddles made by the Doherty, McConnell and Irwin families survive, and are prized by their owners. A single brass fiddle – that generally viewed as the icon of the Donegal fiddle tradition – was made, probably under the guidance of the Dohertys, by Frank and Paddy Cassidy from a drum recovered from the sea at the foot of Sliabh Liag near Teelin. While the 'tin fiddle' is quite likely to be unique to Donegal, or even to the Dohertys and their relatives in particular, a brass fiddle is nevertheless remembered in Co. Offaly. Since travelling tinsmiths were all over the island at the turn of the twentieth century, it seems possible that they were made elsewhere too. Brass and tin fiddles are made in the Magh Éna Fiddle School at Ballyshannon, Co. Donegal. (CAM)

*Tyrone.* It became increasingly difficult in the later part of the twentieth century to find specific regional styles of playing, as musicians modified their techniques through listening to records and the radio, and exchanged their repertoires of tunes at fleadhs and festivals around the country. Some areas, bypassed by main roads or otherwise geographically isolated, resisted this homogenisation and regional characteristics survived mainly among the older musicians. Among these were smaller pockets like the Newtowncashel area of Longford or Derrygonnelly in Fermanagh. Another such area was South Tyrone, particularly the mountainy area north of Ballygawley as far as Carrickmore and Pomeroy. Collecting for the Northern Ireland Arts Council in Tyrone in the mid-1970s, Allen Feldman and Eamon O'Doherty were led by Pomeroy fiddler John Loughran to a number of older musicians who were relatively unaffected by outside influences. Among these was Peter Turbit who had learnt his music from his uncle Ned not long after the beginning of this century. Turbit had many unusual tunes and an idiosyncratic style which was rustic and slow, 'a raw open fiddling' according to Loughran, though he also confirmed that the tempo conformed to that of the older dancing in that part of Tyrone. Feldman noted a remarkable similarity between Turbit's style and that of the Appalachian mountains in the US, but also had this to say 'One has to be careful in discussing diverse styles of fiddling within Counties Donegal and Tyrone due to the decimation of fiddlers through cultural change and death. One has to distinguish between what is a purely personal style of playing and what is a regional style – a fiddling aesthetic shared by several fiddlers in the same region. In Tyrone, due to the contemporary scarcity of accomplished fiddlers who play in the old style within each section of the county, these distinctions were almost impossible to make.' According to a number of musicians, a big influence on the music of the area had been the Carrickmore schoolteacher Master McDermott. One of the few remaining fiddlers taught by McDermott was John McKeown of Cappagh whose style was 'light and quick, utilising a long bow style and delicate harmonies reminiscent of Kerry fiddling'. Perhaps because of its inland location Tyrone was not given the same attention by collectors as the more scenically spectacular areas of the west coast, such as Kerry, Connemara and Donegal, and perhaps because of this remained relatively untouched. There is still a huge repertoire of tunes, even among the musicians who have been affected by media exposure, which are unique to the county.

Among the many noteworthy Tyrone musicians were blind John Loughran, whose infectious enthusiasm persuaded many older musicians who had put away their instruments to take to playing again. He was also a fund of

John Loughran, Pomeroy, Co. Tyrone, 1977 (EAO)

information and entertaining anecdote. His riotous verbatim interview in the *Northern Fiddler* shows an aware and crafted sense of understatement. Other Tyrone musicians playing in the 1950s and '60s included Johnny and Jimmy Comac from Donaghmore, and the Gallaghers from the other side of the county – Mickey who ran a pub in Mountfield, and Paddy who settled in Ederny, Co. Fermanagh. Younger players include Cathal Hayden of the group Four Men and a Dog. (EAO)

*teaching fiddle*. In traditional music this puts less emphasis on technique than on acquiring a fluid, relaxed but rhythmic sound. In the past, most fiddlers learned to play by watching and listening to another player, and working it out for themselves. Methods of holding the fiddle and bow were not regarded as important in themselves, and a wide range of possibilities existed.

Nowadays the influence of classical techniques on traditional fiddlers is very much more obvious as children are being taught in classes, and many traditional fiddlers have also studied classical music to some extent. After the tin whistle, the fiddle is the most accessible instrument for the learner – it is inexpensive, and unlike flute or uilleann pipes can be purchased in any music shop in a variety of sizes.

The characteristic features of Irish dance tunes make the fiddle a very suitable instrument. Cuts and rolls are easily executed, triplets can be bowed legato or singly to get the same effects as the pipes. Regional styles are often distinguished by bowing style. In general, Northern fiddlers favour a 'single' (one note per bow motion) bowing style, giving a strong rhythmic feel to the music; a smoother style with notes bowed in groups is popular in other areas. More influential than regional styles has been the music of individual fiddlers all over the country, foremost among these are Michael Coleman, Seán Maguire, John Doherty, Tommy Peoples, Paddy Canny, Martin Hayes, Frankie Gavin, etc.

Nowadays most fiddlers are taught in classes, progressing from simple airs, through polkas, jigs, hornpipes to reels. Teaching is either by ear with the pupil using a tape recorder to help them remember, or through some system of notation. Great emphasis is placed on listening in order to acquire what is not in the notation. Music must be memorised. Playing with other musicians (flute players, etc.), in a session situation helps playing, and also helps learners to extend their repertoire.

Initially the fiddle is one of the more difficult instruments to learn, as unlike most other instruments, the notes are not 'fixed'. Only by careful listening can the learner acquire the ability to play in tune. A beginner will find daunting the technical problems of fiddle and bow, learning tunes, and possibly learning to read music notation, all at the same time. A year or two of tin-whistle playing is considered a good preparation for fiddle.

*tuning*. In Irish music the standard tuning GDAE is generally used, though there have been exceptional cases of altered tuning e.g., AEAE to achieve drone effects, as in Patrick Kelly's recording of the 'Foxhunter's Reel'. Most of the music can be played in first position on the instrument, and the keys generally in use are G, D, and A – a related minor key, since fiddles play the same repertoire of tunes as flute, pipes, etc. However, there are some tunes in Bb, probably composed by fiddle or accordion players; these have an important place in traditional music repertoire. (EIV)

**Fiddler of Oriel.** Fiddle competition based in Monaghan town between 1969 and 1983. In that time it was won by some of the greatest names in traditional fiddling – Jim McKillop of Antrim, Tommy Peoples then in St Johnston, Joe Ryan from Meath, Tony Linnane from Clare, the late Martin Burns from Ahascragh, Co. Galway, Johnny Comac from Donaghmore, Co. Tyrone. In this early stage it was won twice by Antóin Mac Gabhann, now in Dunshaughlin, three times by Gerry O'Connor from Dundalk, and once – in its first year – by a woman, Kathleen Collins from Loughrea. Originally the concept of former Gael-Linn organiser Pádraig Ó Baoill, it was revived in 1996 as part of the 'Féile Oriel', offering £1,000 in prize money to the over-seventeen 'fiddler', £60 to the under-sixteen, and £100 to the under-seventeen. Prizes of £60 and £100 were also arranged for under-fourteen and under-seventeen singers in Irish and in English. The covering festival had fifty-seven free music-session events in public houses, most of them having no previous connection with traditional music. That year's competition was won by Co. Galway player, Liz Kane.

**Fiddlers Club.** See Church Street Club.

**fife.** Ancestor of the modern flute, forerunner of tin whistle with a parallel bore, six holes and no keys. It was played in most European/American armies up to the last century to accompany marching and signal orders. In Ireland, it is commonly made from elderberry (bourtry) or boxwood, and is often cigar shaped (thicker in the middle than at the ends), with metal ferrules. Associated in the twentieth century with the Orange Order and Ancient Order of Hibernians, and played in accompaniment to Lambeg drum, it previously had a wider politico-musical tradition throughout the country. The pitch of the lowest note is between Eb and Bb. Hard to blow, this dictates a staccato style which may have influenced an Ulster style of whistle playing, the ornamentation used is triplets and grace notes. A notable player is John Kennedy of Cullybackey, Co. Antrim. There was a similar repertoire among Orange and AOH players, except for small number of 'Party Tunes' (political). Dance tunes transposed to hornpipe time were exclusively used with Lambegs, and simplified to suit the limitations of the fife. The fife has been ousted by the whistle in the general musical tradition and is now moribund. In the marching tradition it has been marginalised by changing drumming traditions, and the rise of flute bands which use 'short' flutes pitched to B or Bb. The AOH fife tradition is now extinct and fifers are rare in all but the mid-Antrim area. However, in Connecticut, USA, fifing is hugely popular, and linked to period band revivals from the Civil War period. (GAH)

**fife and drum bands.** These, or others using small flutes and piccolos, were commonly associated with political organisations all over Ireland, particularly from the early 1800s until the 1930s. Their technology is relatively simple, the cost of construction or procurement low. The small flute which replaced the fife in the nineteenth century as the most accessible instrument for the rural people, was made of imported, hard, black wood and the tuning was more standardised – either in B, Bb or the slightly later and larger variant of F. These flutes are more easily blown, and the inclusion of several keys added the availability of accidentals. There are still many examples of these instruments around, but because of their pitch, they are generally not used for recreational playing. As do flute players today, John Blessing of Aughavas, Co. Leitrim, who recalled playing solo for a house céilí on a small flute, made a distinction between the usage of the small 'Bb' in the local marching band and the concert 'D' used by his father at house dances. Different genres of music were played on them. For instance, his bandmaster, a man called Fitzpatrick, taught him to play 'in the third octave using cross-fingering, Scottish marching tunes, harmonies and everything. But you needn't ask him to play a reel.'

Hear fife with Lambeg drum on the album *Lambeg Drums with Fife and Rattlys*. Fife and piccolo can be heard on *Flutes of Old Erin*.

See flute bands.

Mullaghduff Flute Band, Co. Donegal, 1996 (EDI)

**fill.** Term used to indicate getting a 'good tone' among older flute players. The suggestion is that the instrument must be 'filled' with wind, but of course this is not the case – clear flute tone is produced by good embouchure, a leak-proof instrument and, above all, either the player being totally familiar with its idiosyncrasies, or having a good-quality instrument to begin with. Still, 'filling' the flute persists as a term used to describe players' tones.

**Finland.**
*folk music and its organisation.* Western and Eastern cultures meet and mix in Finland, therefore its folk music combines styles and influences from different cultures and centuries. 'Pelimanni' is the Finnish word for traditional musician, 'Mestaripelimanni' is a title of honour and status given to master fiddlers, accordionists, singers and other musicians.

The music can be regarded as having two components: 1) the Eastern (Karelian) tradition (very old and mainly vocal), and 2) newer styles in the rest of the country, excluding Lappland (the Sami peoples of Lappland have their own distinct traditions).

Eastern tradition: Vocal and instrumental music similar to eastern Finland can be found in all neighbouring areas on the Baltic coast (in the present-day Republic of Karelia, Russia, Estonia, Lithuania and Latvia). Fiddling in this tradition is very strong along Finland's west coast. Centre to this is the town of Kaustinen with a traditional music institute engaged in research, concert promotion, teaching and publishing of recordings and books. The town and its environs are centre to dozens of mestaripelimannis, and here Finland's largest folk music festival is held annually. The folk music movement reflects the diverse origins of Finnish music, with some specialising in or borrowing from the Karelian tradition and its Baltic relatives, others immersed in the Finnish Swedish culture, and some in the music of Kaustinen itself. Most people, however, mix styles and tunes from these different cultures.

*folk music education.* The Sibelius Academy offers a degree in traditional music or dance, but ethnomusicology can be studied in the universities of Helsinki, Tampere and Jyväskylä. Some schools offer one- or several-year courses in traditional music (Kaustinen and Rääkkylä, famous folk music towns, both have their own schools). In some areas, kantele is played in primary schools. There are also primary and secondary schools that specialise in music, but their emphasis is on Western art music. Festivals run throughout the summer, the largest of these are Kaustinen Folk Music Festival, Kihaus in Rääkkylä, Pispalan Sottiisi in Tampere and Jutajaiset in Rovaniemi. The Sibelius Academy organises gigs and concerts bi-weekly throughout the winter months. Students at the Sibelius Academy's folk music department receive lessons in singing or in their main instrument, and one or more additional instruments. This has now some fifty students, eight full-time teachers and many part-timers. Degree courses usually take six to seven years, due to the emphasis on students' performance and work with their own music. During the first two years, group playing is compulsory, there are also lessons in traditional music theory, transcription, history, instrument-making and repair, sound system management and studio work. All subjects are taught from a traditional music base. Students have access to studios, and the department has its own traditional music CD series.

*instruments.* The native instrument is the kantele, a box zither, but most popular are the accordion (five-row, two-row and piano) and the fiddle. Just as accordion replaced the uilleann pipes for dance music in Ireland, so too in Finland. It and the fiddle have taken the place of the quieter, native 'kantele', but the kantele has become more popular too, with a strong culture of artists, groups and researchers who have dedicated their career to the instrument and its music. Many of these compose new music for the kantele. There have been many kinds of flutes and whistles in Finland, but that in use presently is the wooden, simple system instrument; this, as in Brittany, borrowed through influence from Irish music. Mandolin, clarinet, Jew's harp, harmonium, double bass, harmonica, Estonian bagpipes and jouhikko (jouhikantele) are also played. Groups and studios will use keyboards, synthesisers and samplers and there is a peripheral 'new-age' use of didgeridoo, marimba (thumb piano), djembe and úd.

Composition is strong in present-day folk music, with traditional music used as a base for personal and original music.

*tune types*. The non-eastern dance music has polska, menuetti, polkka, sottiisi, poloneesi, hambo, masurkka, marssi, valssi, jenkka. Karelian tradition has many types of songs and vocal music including the itkuvirsi (a kind of lament). The Lappish (Sami) culture has joiks.

*society*. Finnish traditional music has a very small audience, with perhaps a couple of dozen low-selling albums produced annually. Only Värttinä (Green Linnet), have successfully competed with popular/rock music. There are two bi-monthly, semi-commercial folk music magazines and several smaller, local publications. Revival began in the late 1970s, and in 1983, the Folk Music Department of the Sibelius Academy was established. Many of the best-known traditional bands have been formed in the academy. Popular and commercial revival of traditional music began in the late 1980s however, and traditional music has gained a small but stable conscious audience, with the average Finn being more aware of its existence than they might have been two decades ago.

*Irish music*. Interest in Irish music began to rise in the late 1960s, and the 1970s saw the first popular Finnish group playing Irish music. During the 1980s a Finnish–Irish music community was obvious, and at present Irish music in Finland is considered a component of cosmopolitan life. Performance is centred in the capital, Helsinki, in a few pub concert and session venues. It can be found too in similar venues in most of the largest towns – Turku, Tampere, Jyväskylä, and Oulu. Distribution is related to the presence or otherwise of a branch of the Finnish–Irish Society locally, and whether an area has folk music traditions of its own. The Irish-music community is small, but the music is of a reasonable standard, due to a combination of good teachers, availability of all Irish recordings and publications, and performance in Finland by the best Irish players at the Irish Festival and other folk festivals each year. Fiddle and guitar are the most popular instruments, the former related to traditional Finnish music which is dominated by fiddle and accordion. The guitar is the result of popular music and the influence of Finnish–Irish group, Korkkijalka, from 1979 until the late 1990s. Several of this group teach and one imports Irish pipes, flutes, bouzoukis and whistles. Flute, tin whistle and singing are popular; there are a few harpists, pipers, banjo and harmonica players. Much of the instrumental Irish music is based in Helsinki while in the provinces, guitar- and mandolin-backed ballad singing are more common.

The average Finnish player is aware of Ireland's regional music styles, and may be able to recognise some of them, but essentially their style is mixed. The Haapavesi Folk Institute is the main teacher of Irish music. Most teaching is by Irish players at a summer school; students of the Sibelius Academy and Conservatory of Kokkola can get tuition by request however. Otherwise, Irish music is learnt from recordings, tune collections such as O'Neills, and from other musicians. The influence of Kevin Burke and Matt Molloy is strong – Burke having left his imprint through playing live, Molloy through his recordings. The typical player of Irish music has a large collection of albums and will tape performances. They travel long distances to learn, and spend time in Ireland at sessions, concerts and fleadhs, and with musicians.

Typically, a Finnish-Irish music pub band will have a singer, guitar(s), bass, drums and one or more melody instruments. While there are no Irish-speaking Finnish singers, some do imitate the language as heard on recordings, and many of the popular pub-songs have been translated to Finnish. Groups will also play a mix of Celtic, or European styles and tunes. There are presently twenty or so such embryonic groups, perhaps a dozen competent enough to perform in public. Many Finnish traditional musicians play some Irish tunes or are interested in Irish music, but often this is done from sheet music and is misinterpreted, e.g., jigs appear as waltzes. Perhaps half of Finnish-Irish musicians also play Finnish music. Some players have neither formal music training nor interest in other cultures' traditional music. The influence of Finnish music can be heard in phrasing and emphasis; fiddlers with a strong classical background tend to over-use vibrato and classical bowing. Reels are the most popular tunes. The neighbouring cultures of Sweden and Estonia have also independent Irish-music communities, and there are folk music exchanges between these and Finland. But while the average Finn will recognise Irish music, they cannot distinguish between Finnish, Estonian and Swedish tunes. (JOV)

**Finn, Alec.** (1944– ). Bouzouki. Born in Yorkshire of Irish parents, his early interest was in blues and rock. He developed an interest in traditional music, moved to Dublin, then to Galway. A founder and current member of De Dannan he is noted for his playing of six-string Greek bouzouki and guitar. With Johnny Moynihan and Andy Irvine he is jointly credited with introducing bouzouki to Irish music. His solo album is *Blue Shamrock*.

**Finn, Fred.** (1919–86). Fiddle. Born Killavel, Co. Sligo, his father, Michael (fiddle) was a contemporary of Michael Coleman. Renowned for a humorous personality Fred drew much from the abundance of local fiddle players, but was also interested in flute and fiddle combination. Although his repertoire included all the great Coleman favourites, he did not allow his style to become an imitation of Coleman and his easy, relaxed playing is instantly recognisable. He played for many years with Peter Horan (flute) in a highly regarded duet. He made many recordings for radio and television in the 1970s and '80s. Records include an LP with Peter Horan (CCÉ 1988, posthumous) and *Coleman Country Céilí Band* (US 1972). He features on the LP *Music from Coleman Country* (1972) and was recorded for the UCC archives by Seán Ó Riada in 1969. (GRD)

**Fitzgerald, Winston 'Scotty'.** (1914–87). Born in White Point, a remote fishing village in northern Cape Breton. He was the most influential twentieth-century Cape Breton fiddler and recording artist, known for his 'clean' style, confidence, swing and impeccable settings of Scottish tunes. His father George was the grandson of a pioneer settler, James Fitzgerald from Ireland. His mother, Mary Paquette, came from Madeleine Island of Acadian (French) lineage. Recordings are still available and his tunes are published in *Winston Fitzgerald, A Collection of Fiddle Tunes* (1997). Hugely influential, his most recognised protegé is Jerry Holland.

**Flaherty, Bernard.** Flute, fiddle, writer. Born in Boyle, Co. Roscommon, he learned to play from his father, also Bernard. He teaches flute and fiddle, and is the author of *Trip to Sligo* (1990), the authoritative ethnography of south Sligo music and musicians, with a collection of 260 tunes played there.

**Flathouse dance board.** Set up in the summer of 1935 by members of the Flathouse Football Club at the gate lodge of Norman's Grove, Clonee, Co. Meath. The board itself was similar to the floor of a room and was kept standing by the hedge during the day and laid down on the grass on dance nights, Thursdays and Sundays. Musicians featured at the Flathouse included in 1935, John McAuley (fiddle), Willie Hobbs (melodeon), Seán Reilly (banjo, melodeon); 1936, John McAuley (fiddle), Jack Toole (fiddle), Paddy Manning (fiddle), Johnny Ward (melodeon), Peter Rooney (drums); 1937, Tom Keague (melodeon).

**Flatley, Michael.** Flute, step dance. Born in Chicago of Irish immigrant parents. His father Michael, from Gurteen, Co. Sligo, was an active promoter of traditional music in Chicago, and served in the 1970s as chairman of the Irish Musicians Association, based on the south-west side of the city. His mother, Eilish, and grandmother were noted step dancers from Co. Carlow. As a youth Flatley studied dance in the Dennis Dennehy school of Chicago, and on summer trips to Gurteen assimilated the distinctive style and repertoire of south Sligo flute-playing. In his teenage years he began to display his multifarious talents, winning dozens of regional and national dancing competitions and two all-Ireland flute awards. His dancing during this period was marked by athleticism and impeccable timing; his flute playing bore the distinctive trademarks made famous by Séamus Tansey and Matt Molloy: fast pace, embellishments featuring runs of triplets and frequent octave jumps, and overblowing. In the late 1970s and early 1980s he directed his own school of dance in Chicago. In the 1980s he became associated with the Chieftains, appearing regularly on their concert tours, and moved to Beverley Hills to pursue a career in film. Flatley gained European and world-wide popularity following a performance at the 1994 Eurovision Song Contest, which led to his starring role in the Broadway-style dance show *Riverdance*. This in turn prompted his creation of *Lord of the Dance*, a title shared by a dance piece of his old Dennehy School days in which he played a Jesus Christ role. (MAD)

**fleadh cheoil.** Literally 'feast of music', referred to generally as 'fleadh', plural 'fleadhanna ceoil', or, simply 'fleadhanna', and as a borrowed word in English, often 'fleadhs'. A non-commercial festival of traditional music, the first was held in Monaghan in 1952. Its purpose is to give those interested in playing and listening to traditional music a chance to do both in the favourable environment of a village or town, usually one which has a strong affinity to the music. The fleadh is largely spontaneous, but central to it are competitions in which young people of all ages compete in many instrumental, song and dance categories. Awards are trophies, medals and certificates. Solo and various multiple categories are catered to, the object being to provide a competitive edge and sufficient social interest to keep young people involved. Ideally, the pubs in the host town become centres for casual music-making sessions and in good weather these also take place on the street. While in the 1950s–'70s the fleadh was so hugely popular that it attracted unwelcome attention from alienated city and country youth, today it is a largely calm affair, with not even the biggest attracting unmanageable crowds. The year's major fleadh is the All-Ireland which can draw over 100,000 people on its August weekend each year. Provincial fleadhanna are titled by the name of their province, e.g. 'the Munster'.

See Comhaltas Ceoltóirí Éireann; fleadh cheoil.

**Fleadh Cheoil na hÉireann.** All-Ireland venues by year: 1951 Mullingar (not actually called a 'fleadh' but the template for such events that followed); 1952 Monaghan; 1953 Athlone; 1954 Cavan; 1955 Loughrea; 1956 Ennis; 1957 Dungarvan; 1958 Longford; 1959 Thurles; 1960 Boyle; 1961 Swinford; 1962 Gorey; 1963 Mullingar; 1964 Clones; 1965 Thurles; 1966 Boyle; 1967 Enniscorthy; 1968 Clones; 1969 Cashel; 1970 Listowel; 1971 fixed for Listowel, postponed due to the introduction of internment in August 1971. Competitions held in conjunction with the Fleadh Nua in Dublin in May 1972; 1972 Listowel; 1973 Listowel; 1974 Listowel; 1975 Buncrana; 1976 Buncrana; 1977 Ennis; 1978 Listowel; 1979 Buncrana; 1980 Buncrana; 1981 Listowel; 1982 Listowel; 1983 Kilkenny; 1984 Kilkenny; 1985 Listowel; 1986 Listowel; 1987 Listowel; 1988 Kilkenny; 1989 Sligo; 1990 Sligo; 1991 Sligo; 1992 Clonmel; 1993 Clonmel; 1994 Clonmel; 1995 Listowel; 1996 Listowel; 1997 Ballina; 1998 Ballina; 1999 Enniscorthy. (MAG)

**Fleischmann, Aloys.** (1910–92). Composer, professor, researcher. Born in Munich, raised in Ireland, and a graduate at UCC, he was professor of music there for forty-six years from age twenty-four in 1934. Founder of the Cork Symphony Orchestra and its conductor for fifty-six years (for this recorded in the *Guinness Book of Records*), and co-founder of the Cork Ballet, he was also deeply involved in the Cork Choral Society, and founded the Cork International Choral Festival. His interest in traditional music directed its inclusion in courses during his career, this involving first, Pilib Ó Laoghaire, then Seán Ó Riada and Mícheál Ó Súilleabháin. It also thematically conditioned his ballet and orchestral composition. A member of the RIA and of Aosdána his major project – and profound memorial – was the 'Sources of Irish Music' project, an attempt to catalogue every traditional tune recorded in Irish manuscript and printed collections. Begun *c.*1950, this appeared in print posthumously in 1999.

**fling.** A type of tune related to the hornpipe, deriving from the Scottish 'highland fling'. Such tunes were popular in dancing in the earlier part of the century but this use has now become redundant. Roche's collection is a useful source of these exotic pieces.

**flute.** Mouth-blown wind instrument which makes its basic music with an 'edge tone'. This is created by having a stream of air from the lips 'split' by a sharp edge, so generating turbulence

## Here Awa'

Highland fling from Cole's collection (compare with 'John Roche's Favourite' in the Roche collection)

and setting up sound waves in the air column in the body of the instrument. The simplest edge tone is produced in the panpipes and in the Eastern European 'kaval' type of instrument. In both of these, a wooden cylinder is pressed against the player's lips and a tone produced by blowing against the far rim – rather like making a note by blowing on a bottle neck.

More sophisticated is the standard concert flute where one blows against the sharp far side of a specially cut embouchure hole. In a tin whistle or flageolet the edge tone is produced by blowing down a duct which guides the air onto a sharp edge; the duct is created by almost filling the top of the tin whistle tube with a wooden plug, or else creating a channel in moulded plastic. Once such an edge tone is produced, the notes of a scale are made by opening or closing finger holes cut at precisely calculated distances. In panpipes, notes are produced by blowing on different lengths in a bundle of pipes – the longer the pipe, the lower the pitch, the shorter the pipe, the higher the pitch. On flutes and whistles such different lengths of pipes are simulated by having finger holes positioned at certain intervals, the position of the highest open hole on the instrument is the effective length of the instrument, and this length determines the pitch of the note. (EDI)

*history.* The history of the flute in western music is marked by two great revolutions in design. Up to the late seventeenth century, the flute had been a simple, one-piece, cylindrical-bore instrument with six finger holes and no keys of any type known as the renaissance flute. A group of wind instrument makers and players, many from the Hotteterre family who were associated with the French court, began around this time to improve the design of several types of wind instrument including the flute, the recorder and the oboe. The flute which they produced had several important features which set it apart from the renaissance instrument. It was now made in initially three, and then four pieces; the bore was now conical, tapering downwards from a cylindrical head joint. It also had a key on the footjoint, which provided the first semitone of the scale. These features improved the flute by giving it a much stronger and clearer tone, better tuning, an increased range, and with the aid of the key and a series of cross-fingerings it became a fully chromatic instrument. This type of flute, known as the baroque flute, was in general use until towards the end of the eighteenth century.

*keyed flutes.* Around this time, makers began to provide keys for the other semitones of the scale, which had previously been cross-fingered, and by the first decade of the nineteenth century, the eight-keyed flute, which had keys for all the semitones, and two keys to extend the range downwards to C, had become standard. This type of flute remained in vogue throughout much of the nineteenth century, but was eventually made obsolete by the second revolution in design, which was mainly the work of the German flautist and flute maker,

Fully-keyed concert flute played by Patti Bronson of Minneapolis        (David Aronow)

Theobald Böehm. Böehm's flute, which in its present form first appeared in 1847, was designed on acoustic principles. He changed the bore, making the head joint tapered, and the body cylindrical. He placed the tone holes in the scientifically correct places, and then designed the 'Böehm System' of keys to control them. This flute is now, with little modification, the standard flute for all kinds of music, from classical, through popular, to jazz.

Traditional and folk musicians, on the other hand, have always preferred the older, 'simple system' wooden flute in its various forms, and nowhere is this seen to greater effect than in Ireland. Irish players have always favoured the eight-keyed flute and, latterly, distinctly Irish adaptions of it.

*flute makers.* These fall into two distinct groups.
1. The pre-Böehm simple system flute and
2. The modern simple system flute.

1. The pre-Böehm flutes are in two categories.
(a) The German flute makers were a generally anonymous group who produced factory-made instruments of low to middle quality from about the last quarter of the nineteenth century to the early decades of the twentieth. There are no makers of note in this group, and the instruments generally carry no maker's stamp.
(b) The English makers have a much bigger reputation among Irish players. From about 1820 on, they began to produce flutes, which because of their design, incorporation of large finger holes and a fairly wide bore, had a 'big' sound, loud and with a clear but reedy tone. Best known of these makers were the London firm of Rudall and Rose who operated from 1820 until they were taken over by Boosey and Hawkes in 1955. There were many other makers in London in the same period who also produced excellent quality flutes but whose reputations have been somewhat overshadowed by Rudall and Rose.

From the traditional player's point of view, flutes from this period, even those by the best makers, have several drawbacks, most importantly that they were built to play in a different pitch. Since concert pitch in nineteenth-century England could be as high as A=455, this causes problems of tuning and tone when modern players try to play the instruments at today's lower frequency of A4=440. Tonally, however, they are unsurpassed. Some of these problems are solved by the slightly later English flutes, generally known as 'Pratten's Perfected', since the original design was sponsored by Robert Sydney Pratten, the leading flute player of his day. These flutes have bigger fingerholes and an even wider bore, and in general play slightly better at modern pitch and have much better tuning. They have an even bigger, more upfront sound.

2. The modern simple system flute. Since the type of flutes discussed above essentially ceased being made over a century ago it became very difficult for Irish traditional players to get hold of good instruments. This situation resulted, by the late 1970s, in the production in Ireland of flutes based on the old designs, and by the 1980s the balance had changed to the extent that newly made flutes were at least as popular with players as the best-quality old instruments. This process has continued in the 1990s and now the majority of players use newly made instruments. Initially these new makers produced copies of the older eight-keyed examples. At first these were keyless with the same capability for playing Irish music as the tin whistle, but soon fully keyed instruments were being made. These have become a standard instrument in the Irish tradition. Most modern makers today also offer flutes with up to the standard eight keys.

Although some makers still offer copies of 'classic flutes', many produce flutes to their own design, which are considered to be as good, if not better, than the best nineteenth-century instruments. The movement to produce new flutes based on the old simple system spread quickly from Ireland, where the first instruments were produced in 1977, initially to England and America, but eventually to France, where the increasing popularity of this type of flute in Breton traditional music encouraged their manufacture. The growing traditional music market has also led to the appearance of 'mass produced' simple system flutes generally manufactured in quantity in third-world factories. These are without exception of very poor quality.

*in Irish music.* The flute, as played in Irish traditional music, is an import with a relatively short history in this country. Fragments of flutes and whistles dating to the eleventh century have been excavated in Dublin, Cork and Waterford and sycamore fipple flutes have been recorded as being made by children in Antrim. There appears to have been no tradition of transverse flute making or playing in Ireland before the eighteenth century when the flute first began to appear in the hands of wealthy amateurs. During the eighteenth and much of the nineteenth centuries, the flute was an immensely popular instrument throughout Europe, and huge numbers of instruments were manufactured on the continent and in London. Although there are indications that it was already being played in traditional music by the late eighteenth century, it was not until the nineteenth that it became more widespread, and only quite late in that century did it become common. The flute was rarely if ever used by the professional players for accompanying dance.

Initially the cost of imported instruments would have dictated that only the more affluent amateurs could afford them, but this situation changed as the nineteenth century progressed. Firstly, a significant upturn in the economic conditions in Ireland from the middle of the century meant that more people were able to acquire instruments; secondly, and coincidentally, musical instruments of many types, including flutes, began to be mass produced around this time, rendering flutes available at reasonable cost to a population with more money to spend.

One of the imponderables in the history of the flute in Ireland is its strong association with certain parts of the country. Although it was, and is, played in every county, it has a very strong heartland in the mid-western counties of Sligo, Leitrim, and Roscommon, with South Fermanagh, East Galway, Clare and West Limerick also having a reputation. Now present in the tradition for over 200 years, the flute never achieved the same level of prestige or popularity as the pipes or fiddle, and this is reflected in the comparatively low number of recordings by flute players.

Since the beginning of the revival in the early 1950s, and in particular over the last twenty years, the flute has enjoyed somewhat of a surge in its reputation and popularity, and is now an immensely popular instrument throughout the country. This of course can in part be attributed to the effect of the recordings of virtuoso players such as Matt Molloy, Séamus Tansey, etc., but the rise of flute-making in Ireland is undoubtedly the major factor. (HAH)

*Leitrim style.* This is usually associated with flute player John McKenna of Arigna, near Drumshanbo who recorded extensively in the early part of the century. The prestigious nature of his records is best illustrated by a one-time neighbour, Tommy Gilmartin: 'Around his native area, no matter what the cost, if you were to sell the last cow, you'd buy one of his records . . . there would be no work done that day till it be heard' (Wilkinson, 1982). McKenna's music was learned from local flute players, and since he was almost a contemporary of Coleman, the present perceived Leitrim style of playing may pre-date the present popularly-perceived Sligo style. It is reminiscent of an older flute-playing aesthetic, likely at one time to be common to the whole Sligo/Leitrim region. Harry Bradshaw's research (1988) reveals that, unlike Sligo at the turn of the century where the fiddle was emerging, the flute was still the dominant instrument in Leitrim. When the local settings of tunes – then played with McKenna's idiosyncratic flare – began to arrive back in Leitrim on 78s, local pride ensured that the status of the instrument remained the same, or was elevated. McKenna has been, and largely continues to be the reference point for Leitrim's musical identity.

His was a driving, puffing, 'extrovert' style, comparatively sparing in the use of rolls. Variations are less elaborate than those which now characterise popular conceptions of Sligo music, but there was subtle lengthening of notes and short melodic phrasing, less ornate, legato rolling. This is suggestive of a more primal characteristic of the flute – as used for Irish dance music – than the continuous sound quality of a bowed instrument or pipes. Most north Leitrim flute players – such as Packie Duignan and Mick Woods – have cited McKenna as their major influence. The Leitrim player will push out notes with the diaphragm and articulate with the tip of the tongue. In the 1970s, both Duignan and Woods made records, further establishing the North Leitrim style. Another local player, John Blessing's style was described by Michael McNamara as a major source of music, a style unaided by reference to any commercial recordings. He describes his articulation of notes as: 'taken out with the nick of the tongue'. Going on to describe Blessing's father's playing he said: 'he could give a great furl o' wind to it, tongue and fingers' (1988). John Blessing had learned music informally from his father, and formally from a bandmaster, the latter's influence leading him to utilise third-octave notes. He and Michael McNamara both play with a great sense of urgency and unfettered wildness, they articulate notes with the tongue individually when coming to the end of a phrase, and even more emphatically at the end of a tune: this is fifing technique. McNamara describes this: 'We phrased short and emphasised the rolling' (1990). South Leitrim style, according to him, stems from the playing of John Blessing.

See McNamaras of Leitrim.

*Sligo style*. Particularly of interest to the history of music in Co. Sligo is the comment in Arthur O'Neill's memoirs of a music night spent in 1782 at the home of Jones Irwin of Streamstown, Co. Sligo. He records, in addition to the daughters of the house playing piano, 'Gentlemen flutes 6, Gentlemen violoncellos 2'. The particular style of Sligo presently stems from the influence of the emigrant fiddlers of the 1920s whose settings and arrangements of tunes were sent home on 78 rpm records to be learnt by the new generation of players. It was confident music, mirroring the America of its day, and it was listened to and learnt also by the era's older players. Sligo flute playing is heavily 'rolled', it is done at a fast pace, phrases tend to

Josie McDonough (left) plays bodhrán to Peter Horan, Killavel (centre) and Séamus Tansey, Gurteen, all of Co. Sligo                    (Nutan)

be long, and variations are introduced by subtle melody changes. Articulation is done both with the fingers and the tongue, but frontal articulation with the tongue is much less emphatic than in Leitrim playing. An emphatic puff from the diaphragm commonly accents each new phrase, most of the ornamentation is left to the fingers. Phrases are ornate, the tone smooth and even. These basic principles are best explained by listening to the great variety among players like Roger Sherlock, Matt Molloy, Peter Welsh, Harry McGowan, Josie McDermott, Peg Needham (McGrath), James Murray, Séamus Tansey, Peter Horan, Patsy Hanly, Jim Donoghue, Catherine McEvoy, Bernie Flaherty and many others. There is of course considerable individual interpretation – Séamus Tansey's playing is particularly florid and dramatic, making great use of a full-chest, pulsing dynamism – yet there is a general 'legato' feel to today's Sligo playing, with lots of descending rolls and triplets. Michael Coleman's national image was undoubtedly developed by his 78 rpm records which were played all over the country, but the establishment of the Coleman Country Céilí Band, radio broadcasts made from its recordings, and the Coleman Country festival, contributed hugely to the Sligo area's iconic status in traditional music. But because many of the principal musicians of the 1960s–'70s' revival were flute players, ironically the focus on the area then shifted from the fiddle to the flute, with which the area is now most associated. In those years too, and indeed in recent times, the area appears to have more flutes than any other instrument, but today the status of the instrument and its practitioners has been greatly enhanced – mainly through reflective professional players like Tansey and Molloy. However, flute's lowly image lingers, among older players in particular. Perhaps harking back to the status inherited from his childhood in the Coleman years, Peter Horan, for instance, who also plays fiddle, considers fiddle to be the superior instrument.

*fuarawn and status*. It is reasonably certain that flutes – whether side-blown or front-blown fipple whistles – have been a feature in rural Ireland for a considerable number of years. But they do not however feature significantly in any reference to travelling, professional performers in the last two centuries. This suggests that their status was unremarkable, or simply low, probably because of the sheer number of people involved in playing them. In an area of relative poverty, but with a vigorous culture such as that in the west of Ireland before the famine, one could deduce that a simply constructed instrument such as the 'bourtry' flute might be common currency among the people. Writing about the latter half of the nineteenth century, Francis O'Neill said of it in 1913: 'No one but a born musician, or one who had no other outlet for his musical instinct, was likely to learn to play the flute. The lame and blind, driven to the practice of music as a profession, invariably chose the union pipes or the fiddle as the most available instrument to touch the sensibilities of the people'. He added that fluters 'seldom took to the road, and that only "conspicuous excellence" would get them any notice'. The flute player had low status in a low-status profession.

But the flute's status did rise in the area in modern times. To understand its former low status however, it is useful to consider some of the more primitive flutes that are remembered. Both Josie McDermott and John Blessing could recall flutes made out of 'bourtry' (elder) and 'fuarawn' (hogweed – similar in growth structure to bamboo). According to them, this was a hit and miss operation: 'a bit of a gimmick to see if they would come right'. These were made by the older people and given to children as toys in order to encourage discovery of the rudiments of music-making (similar introductory practices are observed in other cultures also). The concert flute and Clarke's 'C' whistle were already familiar to both these men in their youth. McDermott describes the making of a 'fuarawn' flute, when and where it might be played:

> There was an ol' yoke that grows in the fields with a white flower on it . . . used to grow three or four feet high and there was sections in it, and when you cut into one section . . . you could make a rousing whistle out of it . . . You cut it at the notch, and leave the other end free, put four or six holes in it and one for blowing into. Sometimes the notch at the end . . . if you humoured it right, if you put the hole at the right distance away from it . . . it might work out. Usually you wouldn't get them long enough, I used to make them like an ol' fife, about the key of B or thereabouts, it could be slightly up or slightly down . . . they'd be false, it's seldom you'd get them pure right. It would be blown like a flute or a fife. That was the fuarawn. There was a fife and drum band in every parish at that time and teachers would be adding to them. All the young lads would go and some of them would learn nearly nothing and more of them would be fairly good. In the fields if you were out and there was a crowd at the hay, you'd be nearly bound to come across one flute player that could play a bit, so of course if you came across a suitable fuarawn, there'd be a flute made for him and that'd be it.

In living memory the bourtry flutes and fuarawn whistles respectively were sometimes modelled on the newly procured Clarke whistles pitched in C and the small flutes pitched in B or Bb. The suggestion that these types of primitive flutes made of native material were used to play dance music even before the eighteenth century cannot be dismissed, and this is of importance when looking at the development of a local aesthetic of flute-playing in Sligo, Roscommon and Leitrim. O'Neill writes, 'No musical instrument was in such common use among the Irish peasantry as the flute. From the "penny whistle" to the keyed instrument in sections it was always deservedly popular, for unlike the fiddle and the bagpipe it involved no expense beyond the purchase price.'

Bourtry flutes are made by reaming out the soft pith from a suitable length of elder wood with, for example, a knitting needle. The final result is a thin flute about ten inches long. If the spacing of the six holes is modelled on a standard tin whistle, and if soaked in water for a considerable period, it will sound a pleasing breathy and reedy note. This is the type of tone favoured by whistle player Jim Donoghue, and significantly he was regarded as a master musician by many Sligo players. He in fact used to adjust the wooden-fipple, Clarke C-whistle with a heated hacksaw blade in order to facilitate the production of a powerful reedy sound which he played in only one octave. While older flute players tended to revert to the whistle as they aged and 'lost power' (and teeth), Jim Donoghue became unique in being a specialist C-whistle player. Also related to a history of bourtry flutes is the common local practice of soaking timber concert flutes in water. While this is damaging to the wood, nevertheless by sealing any micro-cracks or leaks, the practice makes a flute easier to 'fill', and is the 'traditional method' of maintaining an instrument in good playing order. Further, flute players in the early years of revival eschewed the use of keys, even their presence was considered superfluous and it was common to see the key-holes bound up with tape: the aesthetic was to have a crude, keyless instrument, evocative of the bourtry flute. It is only in the last twenty years that there has been somewhat of 'technical renaissance', and in that time it has become prestigious to have a fully-keyed instrument and to use all the keys. This is the technical equivalent of 'shifting to the bridge' or using a chin rest in fiddle playing. (DEW)

**flute band.** Originating in eighteenth-century military practice, these were popular in political organisations all over Ireland in the latter half of the nineteenth century. Existing only on a small, mostly competition scale in the Republic (CCÉ has competitions for them), they are most popular now in Protestant society in Northern Ireland. There are two distinct kinds:

1. 'First Flute' bands. These use small Bb flutes with a tapered bore, simple system fingering, with one or more keys, accompanied by snare drums and bass drum. They are divided according to relative supremacy of music into (a) 'Melody' flute bands, with emphasis on flutes, simple musical arrangements, small compliment of drums; these are competition oriented; (b) 'Blood and Thunder Bands'/'Kick the Pope' bands, with a wilder style of playing, greater emphasis on drums; repertoire reflects a more political musical genre.

2. 'Part Bands'. Descended from 'First Flute' bands, perceived as more respectable with many sizes of flute (usually Böehm system), from Bb bass to Bb first flute, playing in complicated arrangements, the repertoire includes much classical material and demands a high degree of musical competence. Flute bands are historically important since they are the most likely vehicle for the introduction of flute into recreational music. (GAH)

See fife.

**Flynn, Patricia.** (1951– ). Singer. Born at Dromintee, Co. Armagh, her mother was a singer. She lived in England in the 1970s, returning to work in Portadown, Co. Armagh, then settling in 1980 at Mullaghbane. She began singing publicly in 1981, and draws on a repertoire of mostly local songs, many learnt from Mick Quinn. With a rich, 'round', passionate vocalisation, she has also absorbed much from Sarah Anne O'Neill, Róisín White and Geordie Hanna. Her solo album *Stray Leaves* came out in 1993.

**FMSI.** See Folk Music Society of Ireland.

**Foley, Catherine**. (1956– ). Dancer and musician, born in Cork city. She read music at UCC, her PhD research was in Irish traditional step dance in North Kerry. This she undertook at the Laban Centre for Movement and Dance at University of London's Goldsmiths College. A qualified Irish step-dance teacher (TCRG) and an associate of LAMDA in acting, she was the first person to document Irish step dance in the universal system known as Labanotation. She has undertaken considerable fieldwork in the area of Irish traditional music, song and dance, and is widely published in Irish dance studies media. Currently she is course director and lecturer on the masters programme in ethnochoreology at the IWMC, University of Limerick.

**folk club.** A forum for 'acoustic', participatory music and song in Britain, influenced by post World War II radicalism there and in the US, but based in a structure begun in the nineteenth century by such as Cecil Sharpe. The movement gained momentum after World War II; at its peak in the 1970s there were up to a thousand of these scattered all over England, Scotland and Wales. They represented many different interests, some conservative, but generally liberal or socialist – a political identification with 'the song of the people', the working people, both rural and urban. Typically a club might be started by a group of friends or close associates, they would negotiate a room in a local bar, meet weekly, or perhaps monthly, pay a small entrance fee, and sing or play for each other, perhaps together. Funds collected on the door and by the obligatory raffle generally allowed a professional performer to be paid once a month, this both created a professional cadre of performers, and contributed to the self-esteem and experience, and ultimately the standard of performance of the club's members. The earliest such club was set up in Bradford in 1956 (still running), others, like the Singers' Club in London, attracted huge followings. Out of them came a generation of British performers like Martin Carthy, Nic Jones, Dick Gaughan, Maddy Prior and Norma Waterson. As they declined, the 'Folk Festival' emerged, and although more about consumption, it has tended to fulfil the same function.

*Ireland*. Some folk clubs were formed in Ireland – in Dublin, Belfast, Armagh, Carrick-on-Shannon and Midleton for instance. In Dublin of the 1960s–'70s the ballad venues were pubs like the Castle Inn (Christchurch), and Maher's of Moore Street. Folk Clubs were the Old Triangle in Leeson Street, the Universal in Parnell Street, the 95 Folk Club in Harcourt Street. Drogheda song collector and singer (and member of the group Cran) Seán Corcoran, with Mick Moloney and Paddy McEvoy ran the latter, themselves playing as 'The Rakish Paddies'. When Moloney joined 'The Johnstons', Scottish singer Mary McGannon took his place; the 95 Club moved later to Slattery's of Capel Street. Folk clubs might often be more like a session, such as that in Armagh run by Matt Hughes, but unlike most sessions, always involved singing. As a movement this was never very extensive, and its peak did not last long – rather the Irish traditional movement had its own organisation, agenda, and annual calendar, most important among which was the 'session' as centre and the fleadh cheoil as festival. Irish folk clubs tended to be music based, the British scene was overwhelmingly song. While sessions continue to dominate in Ireland, with mostly music, British folk clubs still are song based, but many Irish players tour in them each year.

**folk festival.** Found throughout the western world, perhaps greatest in England, Wales and Scotland where it evolved out of the folk music movement and its organisations begun in the late nineteenth century. Fairport Convention, the Watersons, and many other groups made their names on this circuit which presently occupies most of the summer months. Festivals vary in policy. 'The National' is built around the 'small', important, stylistic and traditional singers, and for that is perhaps the most prestigious. Sidmouth is the largest; others, like Wadebridge, Whitby, Beverly, Farnham, Orkney, Shetland all having local flavour. The largest are organised professionally, catering for the floating community of those interested in folk and traditional musics who may travel hundreds of miles to attend. But most others are locally and voluntarily run, part of community cohesion. A major feature of these is the uniquely British Morris dancing in which scores of teams of gaily and outrageously bedecked dancers display on the streets for the duration of the events. The evening-time of most festivals features thousands of people (all age groups) taking part in one or more 'English country dancing' social dances (called a 'céilí', and visually very similar in its figures and movements to Irish céilí dance). Folk festivals in Ireland by contrast have all been organised around bigger professional groups – Chieftains, Boys of the Lough, De Dannan, etc. – and most are commercial. The voluntarily run fleadh cheoil is more the Irish equivalent of the folk festival.

**folk music.** 'Folk' music, song and dance are derived from the term 'folklore' first proposed by British antiquarian W. J. Thomas in 1846 to cover the culture and traditions of the common people. It stems from the awareness that industrialisation was obliterating old customs, attention having been drawn to this by Bishop Percy in the mid-eighteenth century. 'Folk' music has 1. continuity, in that it passes from generation to generation without great change; 2. it permits variation by the individual, but is controlled by the community, and 3. it utilises selection by the community as to what they wish to retain, or what they consider worthwhile. In Ireland the term 'traditional' is used in place of 'folk', this, the Irish Traditional Music Archive considers, emphasises transmission, rather than origin and circulation. Bruno Nettl (1965) emphasises the process of change: 'folk and traditional music . . . is music that is accepted by all or most of the people in a cultural group as their own . . . folk music is composed by individuals, but . . . subsequent to the original act of composition, many persons make changes', this he sees as 'communal re-creation'.

See traditional music.

**Folk Music Society of Ireland (Cumann Cheol Tíre Éireann).** Established in 1971 by Breandán Breathnach, Diarmuid Breathnach, Seóirse Bodley, Seán Ó Baoill, Hugh Shields, Tom Munnelly and Proinsias Ó Conluain 'to encourage an informed interest in traditional music, to preserve this music and to sustain its traditions, and to promote the study of traditional music' (Folk Music Society of Ireland, Constitution, 1971). The first meeting was held in the Organ Room of the Royal Irish Academy of Music on 24 April 1971, at which Seóirse Bodley gave a talk on Irish harp music. Over the years, the society has established a precedent of academic publications, cassettes and recordings, and a yearly series of illustrated lectures and performance evenings on topics dealing with Irish traditional music and the folk music of other countries. Lectures and performances have continued to promote the Irish language by including some presentations in Irish and by working in conjunction with the Sean-nós Cois Life Festival. The society has also hosted seminars and conferences, such as the one-day seminar 'Performer and Audience', held in Dublin in April 1994, and the conference entitled 'Blas: The Local Accent', held in Limerick in conjunction with the University of Limerick in November 1995. Ongoing projects of the society include the editing and publishing of unpublished collections. The society meets once a month from September to May, and usually hosts one lecture or performance per month. It currently has an office at 15 Henrietta Street, Dublin 1. Its newsletter is *Ceol Tíre*, its journal, *Irish Folk Music Studies/Éigse Cheol Tíre*. (ELM)

**folklore.** See Roinn Bhéaloideas Éireann.

**Forde, William.** (1795–1850). Musician and antiquarian. He wrote about all kinds of music and devoted the last ten years of his life to that of Ireland. In 1845 he issued a prospectus for a printed collection of music, calling for 250 subscribers to pay one guinea each. This did not succeed; he was still collecting by the time of his death. Researcher Caitlín Ní Éigeartaigh has studied his MS and notebooks, and estimates the collection to have up to 1,900 airs, mostly of songs. She holds that half are from printed sources, 420 from other MSS, and 500 taken first-hand. The collection is unique for Forde's method of organisation whereby he brought together the available versions of each piece and had begun to compare them by rhythm and phrase-length. The work also includes jigs, 6/8 marches, Carolan tunes, a rince fada, reels, country dances, pipe pieces, Ossianic airs, caoineadh tunes, as well as English, Scottish, Manx and Shetland melodies.

Forde seems to have been particularly impressed by what he found in Leitrim when he visited the area. In an 1846 letter to John Windele (1801–65) the Cork antiquarian, Forde describes his experiences, and his encounter with Hugh O'Beirne, a piper, from whom he wrote down approximately 150 tunes. He acknowledged to Windele that his book on Irish music would be limited if he did not become 'intimate with our music as it is in Connaught'. He was enthused by the fact that he was staying in the room where Turlough Carolan composed his first piece *The Fairy Queen*. Forde's extensive collection of tunes, writings and lectures are today housed in the Royal Irish Academy. Patrick Weston Joyce included some of this work in his 1909 publication, including eighty-seven of the tunes Forde had transcribed from the playing of O'Beirne. (CET, BRM)

See also Leitrim, South.

**Fortune, Henry.** (*c.* 1870–1930s). Cape Breton Irish fiddler. His people came from Ireland to Cape Breton via Newfoundland, and lived in the Bras D'Or area of the Northside. He played with a long bow, separating notes with grace notes. He influenced both Johnny Wilmot and Joe Confiant (grand-nephew and nephew). His repertoire and style were uninfluenced by books and recordings or by the local Scottish tradition. He believed that it was not possible to play both Irish and Scottish styles and tried to discourage Johnny and Joe from playing Scottish tunes. (PAC)

**fox chase.** See programme pieces.

**Fox, Mary.** (1960–  ). Set dancer, teacher. From Maghery, Co. Armagh, she learned Irish dance as a child, then whistle and flute. At a Monaghan workshop in 1984, Joe and Siobhán O'Donovan inspired her in set dancing. This she went on to teach in Queen's University. She administers the All Set dance organisation, and Belfast Set Dancing Society, which oversees several hundred dance learners weekly in Belfast and Derry.

**Freeman, Alexander.** (1878–1959). Born in Upper Tooting, London. He studied at Oxford and married Harriet Eda Peoples from Donegal; she was attached to Gaelic organisations in London, playing fiddle in their concerts and spent many years working for the Irish Folksong Society, assisting Dónal Ó Súilleabháin with its journal. Alexander was also a musician. He joined the IFSS and was on its publishing committee from 1920 to 1939. He is said to have learned Old Irish under scholar Kuno Meyer. The Freemans spent time in Ballyvourney in 1913, returning for a term in 1914. He notated some 100 songs there, these published with words and music, translations and notes in the journal of the Irish Folksong society, nos. 23–25, in 1920–21. This collection was described by Donal O'Sullivan as 'Incomparably the finest collection in our time of Irish songs noted from oral tradition.'

**free reeds.** Generic name for harmonicas, accordions, melodeons and concertinas, the strongest melody instruments in Irish music all through this century. The origins of their kind of 'free reeds' lie in South East Asia as far back as 1000 BC, survivors from which era are the Thai and Chinese Shengs (tuned, bamboo, mouth-organ reed-pipes). These were probably known about in Europe for centuries – 'free reeds' were used in organ reed-pipes in the 1700s. In Berlin in 1821, Christian Buschmann (who also bred the Alsatian dog), in pursuit of the development of an organ-tuning device using free reeds, accidentally created the mouth-organ out of the sheng's principle. In 1822 a bellows was added, then paired reeds – fixed on opposite sides of the reed-plate – which would sound on press and draw, then buttons and keys. The device was first called 'Akkordion' by the Viennese Cyrillus Demian in 1829, piano-keys were applied by Bouton of Paris in 1852.

*operation.* The sound is produced by air-pressure-generated vibration of a long, slender slip of spring-tempered metal fixed at one end. Such is a 'free' reed (free to move at one end while attached to a reed-plate base at the other). The free reed is fixed in an opening of only minutely larger size than itself in a metal plate, but is free to move backwards and forwards through the opening. The reed practically blocks the opening in the base plate, but when air is forced against it, it yields at the free end and is pushed forward through the opening. It springs back, and the rapid recurrence of this motion produces vibration and sound. The pitch of the sound produced is related to 1. the thickness of the metal in the reed, 2. the shape of the reed (whether parallel-sided, tapered, etc), 3. the length of the reed. The reed will sound only when blown from one direction.

See accordion; bandoneon; concertina; harmonica; melodeon.

**French, Percy.** (1854–1920). Singer, songwriter. Born at Cloonyquin House, between

Elphin and Tulsk, Co. Roscommon, his father was High Sheriff of the county, his mother a daughter of Rev. William Alex Percy, rector of Kiltyclogher, Co. Leitrim. Percy and his eight siblings were educated by tutors, and through their 'big-house' library. He edited a family magazine *The Tulsk Morning Howl* as a youngster, and attended Kirk Langley school, then Windermere College (England), and Foyle College, Derry. He studied Civil Engineering at TCD where interest in theatre and music led him to purchase a banjo. His first song – 'Abdullah Bulbul Ameer' – was published hastily with a borrowed £5, its 200 editions sold out at 1s. 6d., but without copyright was bootlegged by a London publisher and became hugely popular all over the Anglophone world. Working later with Dublin publisher John Pigott he eventually restored copyright. In Trinity he scaled the walls to live the night-life, and on eventual graduation was employed by the Midland Railway, the idleness of the job leading him and fellow apprentice Charles Manners to practice duets with bones and banjo. Their first performance was busking on the train as Black and White Minstrels for Punchestown Races crowds in 1881. In the same year he became Inspector of Drains to Tenants for Co. Cavan Board of Works. Stopping at his friend Rev. James Godley's at Carrigallen, Co. Leitrim, the chance hearing of how a local flute player had paid his rent arrears led to the song 'Phil the Fluther's Ball'. Continued satirical correspondence with the Godleys about his 'appointment to the sewers of Cavan' created 'Inspector of Drains'; life in Cavan gave him 'Slattery's Mounted Fut'. A talented painter, he started a sketching club, and formed the Kinny Pottle Komics minstrel group (named after Cavan town's stream). He was first editor of *The Jarvey*, a Dublin satirical journal in 1889, writing as 'Willie Wagtail'. It collapsed in 1890 due to public preference for London publications, but not before he had used it to promote a musical, *Knight of the Road* (1891), which he had co-written with William Collisson; Ireland's first musical comedy. He started performing solo after 1892 with a programme of recitations, sketches, ingenious drawing of caricatures, and songs with banjo accompaniment. His humour was perceived as laughing with the plain people rather than at them. He was successful in England, was favoured by the monarchy, and moved there in 1906. He toured Ireland also, regaling the pomposity of royalty and blue blood. His most famous song 'Are you Right There Michael' concerned the engine driver Michael Talty of the West Clare Railway which ran from Ennis to Kilkee – it might stop to deliver a parcel, or reverse back to the station for a latecomer. Typically, on an Irish tour, he might do twenty-seven venues over a month. Such strain contributed to his early decease at age sixty-six.

His songs demonstrate a great play on place names, anecdotes overheard and incidents experienced; his people were ordinary people – never the gentry. Many of his songs have been adopted by traditional singers, his themes sometimes parodied in other songs (Dick Hogan's repertoire and *Wonders of the World* album have several). Percy French's best-known songs include 'The Darlin' Girl from Clare', 'Come Back Paddy Reilly', 'Gortnamona', 'Mountains of Mourne', 'Whistlin' Phil McHugh', 'Donegan's Daughter', 'The Four Farrellys'. Some 130 of these survive, most in Brendan O'Dowda's biographical *The World of Percy French*.

**fret.** Raised strip of wood or metal placed horizontally at intervals on the neck of guitar, banjo, mandolin, bouzouki, etc. to mark the finger-positions for the various notes, and to facilitate the playing of these with a bright sound. Such instruments used in Irish music have fixed frets, the concept being known since the sixteenth century. Movable frets (of tied gut) are used on instruments such as Turkish saz, etc., this to facilitate dealing with key and mode changes in music played in 'natural' tuning where notes will be slightly different depending on the key being played in. Fixed frets have been used on guitar and mandolin since the late eighteenth century. Older instruments like Appalachian dulcimer are fretted to play a diatonic scale, but guitars, etc. are fretted to play a chromatic scale. Frets are begun furthest from the instrument body, the first giving the semitone above the open string; the number of frets depends on the instrument.

Frets are critical in guitar playing – their height off the fingerboard is important to the style of music being played and also to the comfort or taste of the player. On Indian sitar and Asian zithers, a combination of high frets and varied finger pressure is used to 'bend' the note to produce the desired note colour; this technique is used to varying extent too by guitar players.

See banjo; bouzouki; guitar; mandolin.

**Fureys, The.** Group based in the multi-instrumental Furey family from Ballyfermot, Dublin: George Furey (b. 1951, song, guitar, accordion, mandola, whistle), Finbar (b. 1946, pipes, song, banjo, whistle), Eddie (b. 1944, guitar, mandola, fiddle, mandolin, harmonica, bodhrán, song), and Paul (b. 1948, accordion, melodeon, concertina, whistle, bones, song). Their father, Ted (fiddle), was a solid institution in O'Donoghue's bar for many years. Finbar and Eddie played as a duo in folk clubs and festivals in Scotland and England, played with the Clancys in 1969, and then in Europe. Paul and George formed the Buskers in 1971 with Scot Davey Arthur (b. 1954); Finbar and Eddie joined with Paul and Davey in 1980 as Tam Lin. When George joined them in 1981 they formally became 'The Fureys and Davy Arthur'. Specialising in a mix of ballad-style sentimentality, their music was unselfconsciously popular, but Finbar's flamboyant pipes solos represented the highest standard of music virtuosity yet in any of the popular ballad-song bands. Their *When You Were Sweet Sixteen* made Britain's Top 20 in 1981. They remain popular both live and recorded, and like the Clancys and Dubliners, have been the introduction point for many players into traditional instrumental music.

# G

**GAA.** See song, GAA.

**Gael Acadamh, An.** Begun in 1976, a music teaching scheme in Connemara, Co. Galway, which has aimed at developing interest among young people in all forms of music. Presently it operates from Spiddal as a 'hub', and as far as Carna and the Aran islands, with a total of twenty-four classes. Sean-nós song is taught by active singers, among them Treasa Ní Mhiolláin, Tomás Ó Neachtain (Spiddal), Pat Phádraig Tom Ó Conghaile (Spiddal), Máire Pheter (Indreabháin), Peatsaí Ó Ceannabháin (Rosmuc), Joe John Mac An Iomaire (Cill Chiaráin), Máire Chuilin (Cárna), Johnny Mháirtín Larry (Cárna). All instruments are taught, and while classical and traditional were taught side by side originally, classical is now self-sustaining.

**Gallagher, Joe.** (1913–79). Fiddler. Born at Cloonmurgal, Drumkeerin, Co. Leitrim. Started playing at sixteen, greatly influenced by Dan Murphy, Jimmy Horan and Dan McGowan. He also learned much of his fiddle playing from records of Michael Coleman sent over by relatives from America. He played first with the Black Diamond Céilí Band, then formed one of his own, and later still joined the County Leitrim Band. He also played with the Belhavel Céilí Group, with Joe Clancy, Michael O'Brien and, earlier, Kevin O'Brien.

**Galligan, Bernard (Dr).** (1920–79). Flute, whistle, accordion. Born at Corstruce, Ballinagh, Co. Cavan, he was a founder member of CCÉ in 1951 and president of that organisation from 1954–56. A colourful and warm personality, besides practising as a GP from the 1950s until the early 1970s in Cavan town, he was also a prime mover in the Cumann Rinceoirí Éireann and in the establishment of the Breffni historical society.

**Galvin, Ellen (Mrs).** Fiddle. Born c. 1870 at Moyasta, Co. Clare. A player with a complex, highly developed fiddle style, her music uniquely suggests the influence of piping. She used the effect of droning strings, dissonance and intricate ornamentation. By virtue of her age and relationship to pre-famine mentors she is an important musical link with the past, but not being widely broadcast on radio or making commercial recordings eliminated her from having significant stylistic influence on present-day fiddling and music-making. Her mid-1950s recordings are part of the RTÉ collection at the ITMA in Dublin. (HAB)

**Galway, East.** Roughly bounded by the Slieve Aughty Mountains to the south, the river Shannon, Lough Derg and the river Suck to the east, and an arc from Ballinasloe to Athenry and down to Gort on the west. Such geographical description is only approximate, but perhaps easier than defining the area's style musically. 'Regional style' suggests a stable musical region with a fixed boundary created by geographical obstacles, in which communities of musicians developed in isolation, inhaling the same air, exhaling the same style. In reality, regional style is a literate term imposed onto an oral tradition, often describing the music of only one musician, or a small group of musicians from an area who have gained national popularity and thereby are ascribed regional identity. More accurately, the term describes a cluster of local and individual styles centred on one area, but the similarity of these styles might as easily be accounted for by the influence of Coleman 78s as any locational or environmental factors.

*history*. Francis O'Neill said that Galway was more the 'Mother of Pipers' than Virginia was 'The Mother of Presidents'. This was particularly so during the nineteenth century when the area's music was associated with the older style of solo dancing. Blind piper Dinny Delaney, born in Ballinasloe in the mid-nineteenth

Kilnadeema band, Co. Galway (1917), at Eamonn de Valera's election rally in that year. (Joe Burke)

century, is one of the first East Galway musicians of whom cylinder recordings survive. The first musician from East Galway to make a commercial disc recording was however Patsy Touhey, who was brought from his birthplace in Loughrea to America at the age of four. He recorded his own Ediphone cylinders for sale, but moved on to make 78s in 1919, these released in 1923 after his death. The first commercial recordings to come out of East Galway and actually made in Ireland were the 78s made by the Ballinakill Céilí Band. Its sound is especially sweet and rhythmical, with a unison phrasing and flow which later became the standard for all céilí bands. But its melodious combination of flutes and fiddles, and absence of drums, gives it only a slight resemblance to what we now associate with the céilí band 'sound' (they did not adopt the title céilí band until well into the 1930s). The Ballinakill is available on recent 78 compilations and on *Ciarán MacMathúna Introduces Music from Galway and Limerick* (1988); *From Galway to Dublin, Early Recordings of Irish Traditional Music* (1993); *Irish Dance Music* (1995). The neighbouring Aughrim Slopes Céilí Band was formed in roughly the same period.

*key players.* Music was highly regarded in East Galway, and through the musicians of the Ballinakill and Aughrim Slopes, the area became equated with a richness of quality music. It attracted broadcasters, and collectors such as Breandán Breathnach, all solidifying an association between East Galway and traditional music. The region also boasts a large number of musician-composers – Paddy Kelly (fiddle), Tommy Whelan (flute), Tommy Coen (fiddle), Vincent Broderick (flute), the Mulhaires, Eddie Kelly and Fr Kelly. But perhaps the most famous of these for the area is fiddler Paddy Fahy from Kilconnell who has composed a large number of tunes, many of which have thoroughly permeated the national repertoire. He does not name his tunes, and has not to date published or recorded them himself. However they have now been transcribed and publication is imminent. Seven of them appear in the CRÉ series; several are widely played on a large number of commercial recordings. Flute player Paddy Carty is another prominent and original musician from the area.

*style*. The Ballinakill influenced all successive players from that area, but while the band may give one perception of East Galway style, the music of Paddy Fahy and Paddy Carty gives another, this strongly tied to repertoire. It favours minor keys over major ones, a significant factor in the overall Irish music tradition where 65 per cent of the repertoire is in major keys. The minor keys tend to be the more unusual keys of G and D minor and the major keys favour C, F and Bb major, which are not as bright (or as common) as D or G major. The music is typified by a roving modality within the tunes, modulating between major and minor without ever fully resolving into one or the other. It comprises tunes that are intricate and technically demanding to play, melodically rather than rhythmically situated, yet still maintaining a strong inner pulse within the melodic line. However, even in the playing of standard tunes, a distinctive East Galway feel is omnipresent due to the slighter slower tempo (than is usual for traditional Irish music) at which the tunes are played, this achieving a 'lonesome' and atmospheric quality. Another common feature of East Galway style is the tendency to convert standard tunes into a minor key, altering the feel of the tune and sometimes transforming them beyond recognition. This is exemplified in the reel 'Pigeon on the Gate' (on *Bridging the Gap* by Seán and Kevin Moloney). The standard setting of this tune is in E minor, but what has become known as the East Galway version sounds like it is in G minor, although the complete absence of the third (B flat or B natural) leaves the tune suspended in neither a major nor a minor key. The characteristic alternation of the leading note between F sharp and F natural and the overall combination of all these factors creates a completely different atmosphere within the tune. It is interesting to trace the lineage of this piece, particularly in light of how comfortably it sits within the East Galway repertoire. The unusual setting has two potential sources, both dating back to the 1930s – Frank O'Higgins, a fiddle player from Westmeath, and Donegal fiddle player Neilidh Boyle (who changed tunes from major into minor keys to achieve melodic colouring). But whatever its history, the variant on the tune has now been appropriated by the tradition.

There are many reasons for the decline in piping in Galway (and indeed nationally), but the accordion both played a part in this and has become the instrument's successor. And though there is a strong association between East Galway style and fiddle or flute music, significantly the region is also home to a number of highly regarded accordion players – Joe Burke from Loughrea, Joe Cooley from Peterswell, Raymond Roland from Castledaly and Kevin Keegan from Kiltormer. Of them, it is the B/C instrument played by Burke (and also Paddy O'Brien) along with the keyed flute, that is likely to have enabled the more unusual compositions of Paddy Fahy to enter mainstream Irish music. Some of the characteristics of what is regarded as East Galway style are also seen however in adjoining East Clare and nearby North Tipperary. Paddy O'Brien and Seán Ryan (from Tipperary) both composed, and a more emotional type of music and use of unusual keys (possibly an influence of the concertina) are heard strongly in Paddy Canny and Martin Rochford of East Clare.

East Galway style therefore must be regarded as a conglomerate of many individual styles, yet the term 'regional style' will continue to be used due to the vital role music has been given in people's locating of themselves. Through the popularity of his compositions, Paddy Fahy has become a 'star', the cultural icon seen as responsible for the popular idea of East Galway style. But the fact that he is not typical of the many musicians who have come from the area demonstrates deficiency in the concept. In the present day, as with all regional styles, its musical realisation is as likely to occur outside the area as within it. However, context and ethos are still important factors in the music performance, and locally 'East Galway' is well represented at sessions, in particular in the Hill Bar at Kylebrack. (VEC)

**Gannon, John Joe.** (1915– ). Accordion. Born at Ballybrown, Streamstown, Co. Westmeath, into a musical family. His house was the centre of many concerts which involved such figures as Felix Doran and his own uncles, Tom and Peter. He later joined Billy Whelan on banjo, mandolin and fiddle to play for dancers. In 1936 he joined the Moate Céilí Band which had William Adamson on fiddle and piano accordion, Bill Donnelly on piano and piano accordion, Eddie Egan on fiddle, Billy Whelan on the banjo-mandolin, and Willie Davis on concertina. Later Paddy Gavin, Paddy Donoghue and Michael Kinkeade (fiddles) and Willie Jordan joined up. The Moate travelled throughout Ireland and to London in 1938. Moving to Dublin in 1949 John Joe joined the Kincora Band, and is featured on Gael-Linn/CCÉ's *Seoda Ceoil 2* with Séamus Ennis, Seosamh Ó hÉanaí and Seán Keane.

**Garda Síochána, An.** (The Civic Guards). The unarmed police force of the original Irish Free State. The new force took over policing duties from the RIC in August 1922. Policing in Dublin remained the responsibility of the DMP – the Dublin Metropolitan Police – who were incorporated into the main force in 1925. From this division came the Dublin Metropolitan Garda Céilí Band, an ensemble of serving policemen which included musicians like Leitrim fiddle player Joe Liddy and Cavan-born accordionist Terry Lane. The band played at céilís, broadcast on Raidió Éireann and recorded 78s for HMV during the 1930s under the direction of Superintendent C. O'Donnell Sweeney. Individual members of the force throughout the country pursued their interest in traditional music in their own area. The Garda Band, a military-style marching band, was formed to supply music at formal occasions and was augmented by players from the céilí band. Like the RIC, garda members were posted to unfamiliar areas of the country and so acted as agents of style dissemination. The Garda Band's *75 Years* album includes a swing setting of reels by Garda Pat Fitzpatrick on traditional flute. (HAB)

John Joe Gardiner (MIO, CCÉ)

**Gardiner, John Joe.** (1892–1979). Fiddle, flute. He was born at Corhubber Ballymote, Co. Sligo, in an area intense with music. His father Séamus was a fiddler and fife and drum bandmaster; his mother Ellen was a dancer. Their home was a popular céilí house throughout the early part of the twentieth century. He cited flute player Willie Snee as his chief influence, but self-taught, he had begun playing flute and fiddle while still very young. Musicians of the locality and travelling players affected him too, playing and singing in the houses and streets of Ballymote. He himself has said that he had a hand in teaching three of the most significant emigrant fiddle players of this century – Michael Coleman, Paddy Killoran and James Morrison. He was involved in early Republican politics and before moving to Dundalk in 1929 he had worked as assistant to Northern nationalist politician Cahir Healy. In Dundalk he exerted an important influence both as teacher and performer, helping to set up the Dundalk branch of CCÉ in 1957, and initiating the Siamsa Céilí Band with his wife Maureen on piano. An inspirational musician, he continued to play until shortly before his death, and can be heard on *Ceol Tíre* and on *Fluters of Old Erin*.

**garland.** An eight-page, double-fold chapbook, often containing reprints of English songs and long recitations. The term was sometimes used to denote a broadside. For the better-off, these had a woodcut on the front page, and from two to six songs on themes running from patriotic to popular and topical. Chapbooks of songs were popular, and were being printed and sold as 'popular press' in Ireland by the 1760s, more so in Belfast, and were exported for sale to America.

See broadsheet; chapbook.

**Garvey, Seán.** (1952– ). Singer and musician, born in Cahersiveen, Co. Kerry. He attended primary and secondary schools there, worked in the Civil Service in Dublin, then lived three years in An Spidéal making musical instruments. There he came under the influence of sean-nós singers like Tom Pháidín Tom Ó Coisdealbha, Tomás Ó Neachtain, Johnny Mháirtín Learaí, Joe John Mac An Iomaire and others. In Dublin he took a BA degree in Modern Irish and Folklore in UCD. He can be heard on *Ón dTalamh Amach – Out From The Ground*, where he sings and plays banjo, mouth organ and flute. (LIM)

**Gavin, Frankie.** (1956– ). Fiddle, flute, whistle. Born at Corrandulla, Co. Galway, his father played fiddle, his mother fiddle and concertina. Frankie began playing whistle at the age of four, fiddle at ten, encouraged by his brother Seán who played accordion. Together the family played for John F. Kennedy at Salthill. A junior All-Ireland winner on whistle and fiddle, he is self taught on piano, pipes and accordion. He took up flute at fifteen, and shortly afterwards founded the group De Dannan in 1974 and has been central to its influential music style and arrangements since. This he describes as 'tightly percussive melody lines set against a flowing, contrapuntal background'. Solo albums include *Croch Suas É* (1983) with flute, fiddle, tin whistle and accordion; *Irlande* (1994) live with Arty McGlynn and Aidan Coffey; *Jigs and Jazz* (1993) CD and video with Stephane Grapelli; *Omós do Joe Cooley* (1986) with Paul Brock and Charlie Lennon; *Traditional Music of Ireland* (1977) with Alec Finn; *Frankie Goes to Town*; *Island Wedding* with RTÉ Concert Orchestra. In 1996 he presented RTÉ's *Miltown Sessions* series for television. He also has a compilation album, *The Best of Frankie Gavin*. Ever innovative, he has recorded with many different genres of music, including gospel, blues and jazz, with Keith Richards on *Wicked Angel* (1988) and *Voodoo Lounge* (1994), with Elvis Costello. (EDI, JOO)

Frankie Gavin (Nutan)

See also De Dannan.

**gender.** The influences on musical performance and reception have become a focus for attention in relation to traditional musics in the second half of the twentieth century. The impetus for such interest has been the feminist critique, a broadening of focus in Western musicology, and cross-cultural analyses in ethnomusicological studies. Gender is a culturally ascribed category (like 'class', 'caste' and 'ethnicity'), the breadth of which can vary greatly. Gender influences music-making on various levels and to different extents; in some cultures, specific musical genres (often those with ritual associations) are performed by and/or for one gender only. In the transmission of musical traditions various extra-musical aspects are communicated – such as behaviour expectations and evaluation processes. Some of these are gender-related. It is important too to differentiate between the conceptual level and the level of performance practice, for in Irish music these two are different. The Irish dance music is conceptualised as a male genre, but there is evidence of female performers and teachers at different points in history and at present. Such a 'male' conceptualisation is influenced strongly by that which pertains in the Western art music tradition. Gender concepts of the German classical period and those of the French upper classes are reflected in the eighteenth- and nineteenth-century Irish 'dancing masters', and so have contributed to gender-related images in the Irish musical tradition. Evidence of the transmission of gender-related concepts can be found in the historical status-change of musical instruments. Fiddle, accordion and pipes have all changed their gender associations over history. Fiddle, which was seen as a male instrument in its use in country dances in the sixteenth and seventeenth centuries, became regarded as 'suitable' for female performers with its change of gender associations in the Western art music tradition. Concertinas, which entered the Irish tradition in the nineteenth century as low-status 'women's instruments', have changed their status and gender associations since the mid-twentieth century with the inclusion of accordions in céilí bands. Uilleann piping is still predominantly male, although bagpiping is increasingly involving females.

Other major factors affecting male and female musical performance derive from Dance Halls legislation which by shifting music-making to public stage concentrated it in fewer hands, those of males for whom it was acceptable to be 'out'. At various points in Irish history too, condemnations of the clergy have had effects on the musical traditions, e.g. the nineteenth-century clerical discouraging of 'caoine' performance, a traditionally female song genre.

Underlying all of this has been the impact of first, suffragette and then feminist thinking in popular politics and the consequent changes in attitudes and legislation which in the latter part of the twentieth century have led to a much higher visibility of females in music performance. (RIS)

*aesthetics*. Standards – for both players and of listeners – in traditional music are male defined. Perhaps the dominance of that 'sound', however, obscures actual difference within the music – one involving aesthetics. Fleadh competition results, and showcased performers in the national media both suggest a preference for a male ethos. Some examples of public performance illustrate this:

1. Cork Folk Festival (1994). Its concert celebration of Seán Ó Riada had but one woman – the octogenarian Julia Clifford.
2. Fleadh, All-Ireland, 1994: 144 competitions, 1,246 instrumental soloists, 162 singers, 45 céilí bands, 99 duets and trios, 31 marching bands, 45 music groups and 28 set-dance teams. In age groups up to eighteen, 57 per cent were female, 68 per cent were male in all senior categories. Overall, 56 per cent of singers were female, 51 per cent of instrumentalists. Of (mixed) senior first prizes 72 per cent went to males.

**gentlemen pipers.** A category of musician identified by Francis O'Neill in his *Irish Minstrels and Musicians* (1913). He lists a sample of thirteen of these, variously so defined by title, wealth, profession and land, beginning with Lord Edward Fitzgerald in 1763, and including composers Walker Jackson (Limerick), Augustus Nicholls (Leitrim), and Lawrence Grogan (Wexford). While it may be that idleness or freedom from the pressures of earning a living gave these men the leisure time to practise and perfect, nevertheless they were intensely interested in the music. It also seems likely that it was still then held in some level of esteem all through society. Such is reflected in the cross-class interest in old Irish music that has resumed today, having waned through much of this century. The 'gentlemen pipers' indicate a continuity of engagement with that music dating back to before the demise of harping. Their adoption of it reinforces the idea that 'culture', and especially appreciation of and regard for music, requires education and sustenance, is learned, and involves choice and rejection. 'Traditional' music in the present day

## Untitled German

*(LID)*

[Musical notation in 4/4 time, key of D major]

is only beginning to emerge from class and political stigmatisation within this island, among the neighbouring islands, and in the western world as a whole.

**German.** A variant of the nineteenth-century popular continental 'schottische', the German schottische, was adopted as a couple dance in Co. Donegal. As with the Scottish version, the highland 'schottische', the term schottishe was eventually dropped within the local tradition and the dance and related tune came to be known simply as 'Germans'. Although the dance is no longer part of the Donegal tradition a number of Germans still exist within the instrumental tradition. These are in 4/4 time and are similar in tempo and articulation to the barndance. As is the case with many of the less common tune-types within the Donegal fiddle tradition these are referred to simply by their tune-type rather than by individual titles. (LID)

**Gillespie, Hugh.** (1906–86). Born near Ballybofey, Co. Donegal, his father played fiddle. Learning to play around the age of thirteen, the playing of his uncle James had the most influence. He emigrated to the US in 1928, there meeting Michael Coleman almost immediately and becoming close friends, with Coleman encouraging him, and teaching him Sligo technique. He worked with Edison, but also fitted in daily broadcasts with Coleman on sponsored programmes, and recorded first in 1937 (with guitarist Mark Callahan), in 1938 and 1939 (with guitarist Jack McKenna). He played club venues in bands, first with his accordionist cousin, Jim Gillespie, then with the Star of Erin Orchestra and the Four Provinces Orchestra. He returned to Ireland to farm in the 1970s. His style is described on his 1978 Topic compilation album as 'singing'; it is not Donegal but neither is it the Sligo of his mentor. He was coloured by playing in the US among Paddy Killoran, James Morrison, Frank Quinn, Dan Sullivan, John McGettigan and the Flanagan brothers.

**Glackin, Paddy.** (1954– ). Fiddle. From Maghery, Dungloe, Co. Donegal, his father Tom was a renowned fiddle player, teacher and motivator in traditional music. His maternal grandmother, also from Donegal, played accordion. Paddy began playing at the age of six, influenced by visits to Reelin Bridge, Ballybofey, with his father to record Johnny and Mickey Doherty. He studied music at the Dublin College of Music, learnt traditional fiddle with Jim Carroll and played in the Clontarf, Dublin CCÉ session and in the Pipers' Club. He won All-Irelands at the end of the 1960s, then the Fiddler of Dooney in 1971. He played with Ceoltóirí Laighean and in the early Bothy Band in 1975. A composer in his younger days, he worked in traditional music programming in RTÉ in the 1970s, was the Arts Council's first traditional music officer (1985–90), and presented several series of *The Pure Drop* television series on RTÉ. He has two solo recordings, first with Jolyon Jackson, the second with Donal Lunny, and he has recorded in duet with piper Robbie Hannon. He lectures on traditional music at the Willie Clancy summer school and is on the board of the ITMA. His brothers Kevin and Séamus are highly regarded fiddlers, they have recorded *Northern Lights* (1988). Kevin has recorded also with many other players, notably with Seán Potts in *Bakerswell*, with Desi Wilkinson, Seán Corcoran and Ronan Browne in Cran, and with Davy Spillane.

**Góilín Singers' Club.** Singers' club in Dublin, it takes the spelling of its name from the Irish 'góilín' (a small sea inlet), but its meaning originates in the Connemara expression for singing, 'gabháil fhoinn'. Begun at the Pembroke Inn, Dublin in 1980 by Tim Dennehy and Dónal de Barra as an effort to gain a weekly space for performance of song, which at that time was either tokenistic, or impossible in the instrumental-oriented sessions which had developed. The following year the Friday night event moved to Thomas House, Thomas Streeet, then to Corbett's of Werburgh Street, to the Four Seasons in Bolton Street, the Ferryman on Rogerson's Quay, and finally to the Trinity Inn on Pearse Street in 1996. The success of the club has generated others around the country, notably in Ennis and Nenagh. There is no formal organisation, and no programme, but once a month a guest singer attends, this financed by a nominal subscription charged to those in attendance throughout the year. The club has also promoted the production of song broadsheets and albums – two by Tim Dennehy, one by Barry Gleeson, one by the Four Star Trio, and a collection of 1798 songs from Jim McFarland, Sean Tyrrell, Frank Harte, Éamonn Ó Bróithe, Jerry O'Reilly, Seán Garvey, Áine Uí Cheallaigh, Tim Lyons, Róisín White, Barry Gleeson, Terry Timmons and Luke Cheevers.

**Goodman, James.** (1828–96). Collector. During his lifetime his collection of melodies remained unpublished, though not unknown. After his death, it was deposited for safe-keeping in the library of Trinity College Dublin, where it remains today. Goodman was written about, his musical labours were desired in print, and consulted by a few in manuscript. The first serious interest was shown in the 1960s by Breandán Breathnach who seems to have concluded that Goodman was way ahead of other nineteenth-century collectors of traditional Irish music. Unfortunately Breandán did not live to realise his edition. The work has now been undertaken by Hugh Shields, with

The Traveller

'The Traveller', from Shields' *Tunes of the Munster Pipers* (1998)

the Irish Traditional Music Archive as publisher, the first volume (1998) under the title *Tunes of the Munster Pipers*.

Goodman was born at Ballyameen, Dingle, Co. Kerry. Protestants of English extraction, his father and grandfather between them had been Church of Ireland curates in Dingle for some eighty years, and James himself declared that his family could claim to be more Irish than the Irish themselves ('ipsis Hibernicis Hiberniores'). His qualities and circumstances brought him close to the people who played and sang for him: an unusual thing in his day. He grew up speaking their native language, singing their native songs, and, probably, playing what he called the 'Irish' (now uilleann) pipes from earlier than has been supposed. Irish music for him was 'leisure'; several manuscripts formerly owned, and some written by him, now in the Library of University College, Cork, show that he had been early on the lookout for songs in Irish. Though his collection contains melodies of many kinds – classical, popular and foreign – for him Irish music was a special category which he not only admired but responded to at a deep emotional level.

From 1846 to 1851 he studied Arts and Divinity in TCD and was ordained in 1853. He worked for the Protestant Missions to Irish-speaking Roman Catholics (the movement later referred to as 'Souperism') in West Cork at Skibbereen, Creagh, and Ardgroom. In 1867 he became rector of Abbeystrewry parish, in 1875 Canon of Ross, and, while remaining rector in Skibbereen, he also occupied the Professorship of Irish at Trinity from 1879, dividing his time between Skibbereen and Dublin. In the college, his students of Irish were mainly ordinands preparing for the missions to Catholics as Goodman himself had done, but they also included Synge and Hyde. By all accounts he was not a coercive proselytiser – it is clear that he was motivated by strong personal belief in the benefits of voluntary conversion. His principal musical source was a convert: Tom Kennedy, a 'parish' piper who seems to have moved around but lived for some time at Ventry with its missionary 'settlement'. Kennedy is the only performer Goodman names in his music books.

Goodman's music is noted in three oblong volumes 1–3, dated 1860–66, and in one other volume in different format – numbered 4 – which is in fact the oldest. Features of this early volume suggest that his fiancée Charlotte King of Ventry entered material in it, mostly parlour music, but also some well-known traditional pieces, including a few also written by James. 'Siubhail a Rún' suggests collaboration between the spouses – Charlotte writing the music and James the title and words (his only song air with words) – making his usual elegant distinction between Gaelic and roman script for the two languages.

Vols. 1 and 3 have many items noted from oral sources, whereas Vol. 2 contains almost wholly copies taken from print or manuscript. In Vols. 1 and 3 he uses symbols to indicate the status of many items, whether from printed sources or musicians. Most of these refer to printed sources, but among the rest, the letter 'K' marks over 500 items which he transcribed from 'Munster pipers etc.' Piper Tom Kennedy is the source of some, but not all, of these 'K' tunes. Only in about half-a-dozen places is Kennedy named – three times, in Vol. 4, as a source of music (each time a song air). Goodman's notations are competent, written from performance, most often in the common major keys of D and G, or copied in more varied keys from sources already published. He counts note and rest values correctly as a rule, but he shows little concern to distinguish quaver and crotchet rests. His aberrations hardly disturb strictly measured dance music and marches, since these fall readily into a regular scheme. But with songs and slow airs – being less strictly measured – it is difficult at times to discern Goodman's metrical intentions. Most nineteenth-century collectors did not bother to represent rubato style or metrical peculiarities in their tunes, but Goodman writes some bars as if deliberately to show irregularities of metre. A 3/4 piece may suddenly develop a single 6/8 bar of like time value, for example, two dotted crotchets instead of a minim and a crotchet, as if a song of ambling gait momentarily became a jig. Such aberrations are too common to be just dismissed as errors. Goodman is ready to absolve the sinful bar, though his interpretation of what it does may surprise us. The musical variety in the collection reflects his own tastes, and for traditional musicians his 'K tunes' – representing native musical practice in Munster or perhaps preponderantly in Corca Dhuibhne – are of most interest. Songs in Irish seem to stir him most deeply, though they have no words beyond their titles any more than those in English. This bewildering fact conflicts with his preface to Vol. 3: 'When noting down an air I always made it my business to take down the original words as well.' And what follows shows that Goodman has the piper's concern to 'give that expression to the music which the words require' while also declaring himself 'possessed of a multitude of Irish songs' enabling him to remember the airs. In these volumes, however, he never matched the missing words he says he wrote with the surviving tunes, for no space is allotted for words. They were, most likely, rough copies which, like the rough copies of the music now preserved only in fair copies, no one bothered to keep. It is worth noting that few nineteenth-century Irish collectors of songs took down words for the melodies they collected. Goodman, though disappointing us, thus appears innovative in making even half an attempt.

The situation is in a sense reversed in the case of the Fenian and other narrative lays, for Goodman copied many verbal but no musical texts of the lays into his literary (not musical) manuscripts. Perhaps the musicality of lyric genres seemed more apt than the declamatory style of lays, just as the 'Irish cry' would seem dissonant and formless in a context of songs. Keening was certainly practised in the district, as Mrs Thompson, the land steward's wife, reported of a group of Catholic women raising the cry at a Protestant burial service for converts who had been brought up as Catholics. Goodman, on the other hand, collected formal death laments, some of them placed in historical context by naming the poets or those who were mourned. But the most abundant lyric category is certainly the love songs, sung to impressive tunes in varied strophic forms, most often in phrases AABA or with repetition AABA, BA. These songs often have a narrative or discursive support in speech which rarely finds its way into writing or print (*an t-údar*). Goodman does not include it any more than he includes the words of the songs.

The instrumental music is still more abundant, in Vol. 1: 'jigs, reels, hornpipes, marches or slow airs in endless variety'. Generally speaking, the shorter the dance forms, the better they are, whereas the thirteen parts of the 'Drogheda Jig' are, to say the least, a pity. He cannot resist comment (preface to Vol. 1) on the two descriptive pieces, the 'Fox Hunt' and 'that strange piece Allisdrum's March', few versions of which were then known. He writes out both of them from the mythical piper-figure 'K' at the end of Vol. 1, with a commentary in Irish, on sounds of the chase and of battle and lamentation respectively.

Goodman remains elusive to us partly because we know him little as a person. Facts most reliably recorded, like the prizes at College in Hebrew and Irish, are usually least informative. The photograph of him printed and reprinted shows a degree of seriousness heightened by the costume of his vocation. It is at variance with the word picture of his homecomings to Ballyameen with a musician, ready to set up a session of dancing; at variance also with the Goodman brothers' game of running and then leaping into a sitting position with their legs dangling over 'the Top of the Cliff' recalled in the title of one of his reels. A more recent rector of Abbeystrewry remarked that he imagined Goodman as 'a hearty evangelical type'. If he was, it hardly shows in his music. But music is not a medium for such display, nor was Goodman probably given to it. There is still a lot to learn about this versatile and unusual man. (HUS)

**grace note.** In its simplest form a grace note is a single note used to ornament and accent a main melody note. It may be above or below the main melody note. A double form of the grace note is also common. This involves sounding the main melody note before the grace note is introduced. Two specific types of grace note are popular:

1. A 'pat' or 'tip'. This occurs between two consecutive notes of the same pitch. The pat is a lower note sounded to separate these two pitches.

Tip/Pat

2. The 'cut' is an upper note sounded to separate two consecutive notes of the same pitch. (LID).

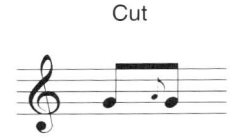

Cut

**Gradam an Phléaráca.** An award made annually in recognition of outstanding work in promoting the native culture and tradition of the Connemara Gaeltacht. Initiated in 1994 by 'Pléaráca Chonamara', part of the Connemara Community Arts Scheme.

**Gradam Shean-nós Cois Life.** An award of honour inaugurated by the Sean-nós Cois Life festival in Dublin. It is given annually to someone who has greatly contributed to the promotion of sean-nós singing. The festival was begun in 1992 and the award was instituted in 1993. Recipients have been: 1993, Mícheál Ó Ceannabháin; 1994, Áine Bn. Uí Laoi; 1995, Seán 'ac Dhonncha; 1996, Treasa Ní Mhiollán; 1997, Éilís Ní Shúilleabháin; 1998, Proinsias Ó Conluain; 1999, Dara Bán Mac Donnacha.

**Graham, Len.** (1944– ). Singer, collector. Born Glenarm, Co. Antrim, an area with which he has always had a close affinity despite family migrations in the course of his early life, he picked up local Derry and Antrim song initially from his parents. His mother Eveline Robinson – a cousin of hammer dulcimer player John Rea – sang and danced old set dances, she had been familiar as a child with the Irish language from the last of the Irish speakers in the Antrim Glens, and had heard keening women at funerals. Through his father, Len attended gatherings of the Cos. Derry and Antrim Fiddlers' Association, this introducing him to a wider repertoire. Hiking all over Ireland from his teenage years brought him into contact with all the music traditions of the island. In 1964 he met singer Joe Holmes, this beginning a friendship that was to last until the latter's death in 1978. Magilligan singer Eddie Butcher was another close associate in singing, as were eventually Geordie Hanna and Sarah Anne O'Neill from Co. Tyrone.

With Holmes he recorded *Chaste Muses, Bards and Sages* (1975) and *After Dawning* (1978), a solo *Wind and Water* (1976), *Do Me Justice* (1983) and *Ye Lovers All* (1985). He started the group Skylark with Gerry O'Connor, Garry O'Briain and Andrew McNamara in 1986 and now performs mostly with Mullaghbane, Co. Armagh storyteller John Campbell. His major collecting project has been a field-recordings series 'Harvest Home'. He has been the source of songs for many of the better known Irish groups and singers on the international scene – including Altan, De Dannan, the Chieftains, Battlefield Band, Boys of the Lough, Cherish the Ladies, Dick Gaughan, Andy Irvine, the Voice Squad, Lá Lúgh, Dolores Keane and Tríona Ní Dhómhnaill. In 1992 he was given the Seán O'Boyle Cultural Traditions Award, and in 1997, his and Padraigín Ní Uallacháin's contributions to the Irish song tradition were recognised in an award from the Feakle Traditional Singing Festival.

**gramophone.** See reproduction of music.

**Granard Harp Festival.**
See harp, conventions.

**graphic representation of music.**
See Three Ages of Music; transmission of music.

**Grattan Flood, William Henry.** (1857–1928). Writer, researcher, organist. Born in Lismore, Co. Waterford, he was educated in music by a private tutor and obtained a general education at Mount Mellary College. He played piano and organ, and became organist of St Peter's pro-Cathedral, Belfast at age nineteen. He attended All Hallows College, the Catholic University, then Carlow College where he studied for the priesthood. Returning to secular life he taught music in Clongowes, St McCartan's (Monaghan), St Kieran's (Kilkenny), becoming organist at Monaghan, Thurles and finally Enniscorthy cathedrals. A prolific and energetic writer with a wide range of interests, he researched and wrote on Irish and European musics, and on the local history of counties Wexford and Waterford. His major work was *A History of Irish Music*, published in 1905, with editions in 1906, 1913 and 1927, reprinted later. Other works were *Story of the Harp* (1905), *Story of the Bagpipe* (1911) and sketch of *Irish Musical History* (*c.* 1920). Among other works he edited *Moore's Irish Melodies, Spirit of the Nation* and the *Armagh Hymnal*. He wrote the contribution on Irish music to the 1905–10 edition of Grove's *Dictionary of Music and Musicians*, and was a composer of masses and hymns. He was given an honorary doctorate of music from the Royal University in 1907 (now National University of Ireland).

**Gray, John.** (1936–92). Fiddler. Born at Corglas, Co. Leitrim, he was taught by his father, and was part of a family band while a teenager. He played with John P. Reilly's band at céilithe throughout Leitrim, Cavan and Longford. With Dr Galligan of Cavan he set up the first Cavan CCÉ at Killeshandra. In 1958 he emigrated to Manchester where he played with Des Donnelly and Felix Doran. He returned to live in Drogheda in 1969, where with Roger Ryan, Br. Forrestal, Jim McGlynn, Andy Synnott, Paddy Joyce and Tom Kavanagh, he founded the local CCÉ branch.

**Green Linnet.** 1. One of the major Napoleonic songs. 2. Record label founded in 1973 by Lisa Null and singer-songwriter Patrick Sky in New Canaan, Connecticut. Like Shanachie, this 'independent' has been a prime mover in traditional music both in America and outside it. In late 1975, Wendy Newton, who had been an activist director of the World Affairs Center, joined the company and in 1978 she became sole owner. At that point, its two imprints, Green Linnet (Irish traditional) and Innisfree (usually folk), were consolidated into just Green Linnet. Redbird is the name of its singer-songwriter series, while Xenophile was founded in 1992 as an international music label. Based now in Danbury, Connecticut, Green Linnet has over 300 recordings in its catalogue. With a mailing list of some 125,000 names, mail order makes up about 20 per cent of sales; the rest is retail. Ryko Distribution Group handles US distribution. President and owner is Wendy Newton. Chris Teskey is chief operating officer. A large catalogue of Irish artists includes Martin Hayes, Moving Cloud, Patrick Street, Nomos, and Reeltime. (EAH)

**Greig-Duncan Folk Song Collection.** The major Scottish song collection, with more than 3,000 tunes and texts, this was amassed largely from sources in the north-east of Scotland in the decade before the First World War.

In 1903, the New Spalding Club, a historical publishing society of considerable importance (with royal patronage), whose Secretary, P. J. Anderson, was also the Librarian of Aberdeen University, approached Gavin Greig (1856–1914), an Aberdeen MA and a parochial schoolmaster in the northern Aberdeenshire village of New Deer. Anderson suggested that Greig undertake a survey of the musical culture of the north-east of Scotland to see if sufficient music and song remained to make a worthwhile volume in the club's series. The remit was wide – secular and religious, vocal and instrumental – and was to include (if any remained) folk-song. Greig was a nationally noted musician and writer of articles, books, plays and musicals. He lectured extensively on the glories of Scottish song as exemplified by the beautiful works of such as Robert Burns and Lady Nairne. In a lifetime in the neighbourhood Greig had only come across a couple of examples of 'folk-song', and doubted if much more remained. But when he set about investigating and collecting with his characteristic thoroughness, to his astonishment and chagrin, he rapidly collected several hundred tunes and texts within a few miles radius of his home. As the months progressed, the material flowed in at a similar rate, and he realised that he was in the midst of a treasure-house of folk-song of which he had been completely unaware, and which would clearly fill many volumes for the club. By 1905 he was contemplating how to deal with this amazing find. At the end of the year he intended to use his Retiring Presidential Address to the Buchan Field Club (a thriving north-east investigative and antiquarian society) both to announce his finds and his analysis thereof (the address was expanded, and published as *Folk-Song in Buchan* in 1906). But it was reading the fifth *Journal of the Folk-Song Society*, with its comprehensive thoroughness, editing and expert commentary, that convinced Greig that the day of the amateur antiquarian content to publish unannotated results in obscure local journals was over, and that he would have to meet this new gold standard of analysis and presentation.

He persuaded the New Spalding Club that he should indeed undertake to prepare a volume for them, secured the first of five large research grants from the newly formed Carnegie Trust for the Universities of Scotland, and sought the collaboration of his old friend and teacher, The Revd James Bruce Duncan of Lynturk. A superb musicologist, Duncan came from a folk-singing, farming family not far from Greig's school (which he had attended) and had a considerable body of folk-song available to him from this source, especially from his sister, Margaret Gillespie. The pair engaged on further field work, and increased their findings via lectures and correspondence, and by a series of weekly folksong columns which Greig ran in a local newspaper, the *Buchan Observer*, from 1907 to 1911. As a result their findings increased to an unmanageable stage, and although they attempted to make a start on at least one volume of 'classical' ballads (as categorised by Prof. Francis Child in his monumental *English and Scottish Popular Ballads* between 1882 and 1898) for the New Spalding Club, it was only half finished before Greig (who had been plagued by increasing ill-health during his last ten years) died in 1914, and Duncan in 1917.

P. J. Anderson had their material taken to Aberdeen University Library where it was reported on and carefully preserved. The club itself had suspended operations in 1916 (and was wound up in 1926 when Anderson died) but the Buchan Field Club initiated and funded the publication of the volume of 'great', 'traditional' or 'classical' ballads on which the collectors had started. It was completed and edited by the journalist Alexander Keith (1895–1978) under the close supervision of the Scottish ballad authority William Walker of Aberdeen (1840–1931), and published to international acclaim as *Last Leaves of Traditional Ballads and Ballad Airs Collected in Aberdeenshire by the Late Gavin Greig*, in 1925.

Despite the success of this publication – which comprised only 13 per cent of the whole – the university was unable to find funds and resources to publish the remaining material until the 1960s, when Duncan's grandson, Paul Duncan, interested the English Folk Dance and Song Society in providing an editor, Pat Shuldham-Shaw, for what was eventually to become a joint publication in eight volumes by the Universities of Aberdeen and Edinburgh (School of Scottish Studies). The first volume appeared in 1981 and the latest (number seven) in 1997.

*significance.* The importance of the collection lies not only in its sheer size and quality, but in the fact it was made by collectors who were themselves born and bred in the region, who had spent their lives there, who spoke the local Scots ('North-East Doric'), and who had the complete trust and confidence of their informants. Furthermore, these informants comprised an unusually wide range of age, sex, occupation and social class, from schoolgirls to pensioners, housewives to farmers, doctors to farm labourers. In keeping with the ethos of the times, Greig and Duncan initially hoped that their findings would enable them to present the world with a massive body of Scottish song, to equal any found in Europe (especially England, where Cecil Sharp was intent on replacing music-hall-driven popular song with 'true' English folk-song). To their surprise, as the material accumulated, they realised that they had uncovered a body of song which transcended local, national (Scottish and British) and even international boundaries – both European and North American. Although some songs, e.g. the 'bothy ballads' – were unique to their region (often with known composers and locations), the majority were not.

There was one other finding that astonished them. Greig had spent his lifetime in the neighbourhood extolling the virtues of 'Scottish song' as exemplified by Burns and Co.; indeed his operetta 'Robbie Burns' had famously moved his audiences to tears. But he found that not one of the 3,000 plus songs they collected was by the so-called National Bard or National Songbook composers, and rapidly came to the conclusion that genuine Scottish folk-singers would have nothing to do with the type of art song that the rest of the world (and the Scottish middle classes) regarded – and still regard – as 'Scottish Song'. The north-east of Scotland had been known since at least the seventeenth century for the considerable richness of its traditional song, especially the great 'classical' or 'traditional' ballads and this was thoroughly confirmed by Greig and Duncan. (It is ironic that many of these ballads became known as 'Border Ballads' following Walter Scott's publication of his *Minstrelsy of the Scottish Border* between 1802 and 1833, for Scott had gained most of the ballads in his famous Romantic section from Aberdeenshire informants.) They had, however, also taken the then unusual step of recording complete (as possible) repertoires from their singers and informants, and of transcribing their findings faithfully without any editorial interference. This was, however, to have serious repercussions, for when the collection was gone over by William Walker after Duncan's death (a ballad authority of the old school), Walker was appalled to find such a mass of what he considered to be worthless and trashy material. He firmly recommended that only the Child ballads should ever be published (as was to occur with *Last Leaves*) and the remainder was shelved in the Aberdeen University Archives until the 1950s' folk-song revival (and Duncan family pressure) led eventually to publication of the entire collection some sixty years later.

*Gaelic influence*. Both Greig and Duncan were puzzled by this mass of 'ordinary' songs (as opposed to the great ballads), for many of them gave the appearance of being quite recent (nineteenth century) in origin, and many had distinctly 'Gaelic' airs. They came to the conclusion that there must have been a lasting Scottish Gaelic influence (the north-east inter-digitated with the Highlands along its borders) despite the fact that the Gaels had been superseded in the region for some six hundred years by Lowland Scots and continental influxes (especially Flemish). But the bulk of their informants had learned their repertoires in the early nineteenth century, a period when the region was transformed by rapid massive construction of roads, railways, canals, bridges and harbours, carried out by a huge influx of labourers from the rest of Scotland, England (not forgetting Europe and North America), and especially Ireland. It cannot be doubted that the navvies left behind a rich legacy of songs and tunes which was enthusiastically assimilated by a population with a centuries-old vibrant and universal singing tradition. (IAO)

**Griallais, Nan, Nóra, Sarah.** From Muiceanach Idir Dhá Sháile, the Griallais sisters are from Connemara's most remarkable singing family of eleven sisters and one brother. They have lived and worked for many years in England and in America. Each has won Corn Uí Riada for sean-nós singing at the Oireachtas, a feat not equalled by any other family. Nóra is also the only woman ever to have won the trophy three times ('87, '89, '93) and is one of only three sean-nós singers ever to have done so, the other two being Josie Sheáin Jack Mac Donnchdha from Carna and the late Nioclás Tóibín from Ring, Co. Waterford. All are recorded by RTÉ. (LIM)

**Grier, Stephen.** (1824–94). Piper, fiddle player and collector. A native of Abbeylara, Granard, Co. Longford, he lived at Bohey, Gortletteragh, Co. Leitrim. His collection of over 1,000 tunes was compiled in 1883; sixty-four of these appear in *Ceol Rince na hÉireann 4*. Grier's work was passed on to his protégé William Mulvey, who with his son Edward and Michael McGuinness of Bornacoola, appears in a picture of pipers at the 1912 Dublin Feis Cheoil. A notable feature of Grier's collection is the wide variety of tune types and range of modes. The prominence of dance music, the absence of a bass clef, both indicate a musician of the 'folk' tradition. It includes approximately 300 reels, 200 jigs, 50 hornpipes and 40 slip jigs. Other dance pieces include 80 waltzes and some 160 tunes in other rhythms – primarily quicksteps and polkas. There are more than 40 marches, 70 and more instrumental pieces. As yet unpublished, it was brought to attention by Fr. John Quinn, PP Gortletteragh, Co. Leitrim who is also responsible for highlighting the unpublished manuscripts of Alex Sutherland. (BRM)

See *Ceol Rinnce na hÉireann*; Leitrim, South; Sutherland, Alex.

**groups.** Céilí bands and smaller ensembles like the Belhavel Trio established a significant popularity with the traditional music public all over Ireland. But the emergence of Ó Riada's Ceoltóirí Chualann in the early 1960s, paralleled with the extraordinary growth of interest in ballad groups, forged a new and enthusiastic different audience for folk and traditional music. The Clancy Brothers made their name in the United States in the folk underground of the Greenwich Village coffee-club scene at the start of the decade. Dublin was the site for a burgeoning music community centred on O'Donoghue's pub out of which the Dubliners emerged; they, along with the Clancy Brothers were to become leaders in the 'ballad boom' of the mid-1960s, introducing folk-songs to many people for the first time. Importantly, they also highlighted the idea of 'participation' – the songs they popularised often had choruses, simple story lines and listeners could join in enthusiastically.

Ceoltóirí Chualann's nation-wide popularity was established through influential radio broadcasts in the early 1960s; their formula was reflected in Paddy Moloney's development of the Chieftains, whose first LP was issued in 1963. These in turn were to be hugely influential in subsequent developments in ensemble playing of traditional music. Their international acclaim and commercial success up to the mid-1970s came as a result of a series of innovative arrangements, recordings and exposure through film soundtracks like *Barry Lyndon* and *The Purple Taxi*.

The McPeakes from Belfast had already established an audience for this approach to music through their radio and live work in the late 1950s and early '60s, while Finbar and Eddie Furey were among the many to leave Ireland and follow the demand to work in the folk clubs of Scotland and England. The Johnstons, Sweeny's Men and the Emmet Spiceland were among the more influential of the other groupings to follow into and put their own stamp on this commercial arena following such renewed public interest in traditional music. These new groups understood contemporary popular music and culture, and their arrangements and harmonies often reflected a cosmopolitan approach. Folk club audiences grew in response, this in turn creating greater demand for groups, ensembles and solo performers.

A new wave of semi-professional (and some professional) performers emerged in the early 1970s, many of whom had learned their trade either through the folk clubs or with earlier bands. Foremost among these was Planxty, formed around the charismatic presence of singer Christy Moore, with Andy Irvine of Sweeny's Men, Donal Lunny of Emmet Spiceland, and Liam O'Flynn with a background of serious piping tutored by Leo Rowsome and Séamus Ennis. Their music and image helped build a yet more extensive audience, drawing committed traditional followers, and many who were being introduced to traditional music for the first time.

The term 'band' was gradually coming to replace 'group' in the popular lexicon, and new Irish formations took their cue from the success of those in England – like Fairport Convention and Steeleye Span. They began to experiment with rock music and aspects of the Irish traditional music they had heard. 'Celtic Rock' – as the genre became known – was the creation of such bands such as Horslips, Spud, Cromwell and Mushroom. Of these, Horslips was by far the most popular, attracting a rock audience open to the possibilities that experimentation with traditional music allowed. *O'Neill's Cavalcade* was re-interpreted with a clarion-like electric guitar riff – tens of thousands of young people danced to it, and some were motivated to seek out Ó Riada's original recording of the same piece.

A brief enthusiasm for pan-Celticism saw Breton harper Alan Stivell attract largely the same type of audience as Horslips. Traditional music (or one version of it) was perceived as being trendy and hip. Influenced by British bands like Pentangle, and yet acutely aware of the richness of the music tradition that surrounded them, Skara Brae for instance were able to popularise a fresh approach to traditional Irish-language song; Clannad, from the Donegal Gaeltacht, incorporated jazz and other popular music idioms, like Planxty honing their skills on the road, and touring incessantly.

An international audience took to Irish music with enthusiasm. At approximately the same time groups like the Press Gang, MacMurrough, Munroe, the Sands Family and the Blacksmiths also helped expand the market for Irish bands.

The Bothy Band formed around a melodic core of solid traditional instruments (fiddle, flute, pipes), and incorporated the formidable rhythm section of Donal Lunny (bouzouki and guitar), Mícheál O Domhnaill (guitar) and Tríona Ní Dhomhnaill (clavinet). By 1975, music journalists were comparing them to rock ensembles, despite the fact that they were an acoustic band.

Through the early 1970s bands such as Na Filí, Aileach and Ceoltóirí Laighean issued recordings, but from the middle of the decade even more groups were to form and attempt to make some sort of professional living from music. The Boys of the Lough had established themselves in Scotland in the early 1970s, combining Irish and Scottish music while Frankie Gavin's young band De Dannan initially established their reputation in the mid 1970s. Inchiquin, Pumpkinhead, Stockton's Wing, Oisín, Shaskeen, General Humbert, Na Casadaigh, Any Old Time, Skylark, Altan, Buttons and Bows, Relativity, Dervish, Arcady, Bakerswell, Moving Cloud, Reel-time, the Sharon Shannon Band, Nomos, La Lugh, and Cran are the more prominent groups who have formed (and in many instances re-formed or disbanded) since the 1970s.

Another attempt at exploring overlaps of traditional and rock musics was made in the early 1980s by Moving Hearts – their piper Davy Spillane still continuing with that direction since their dissolution. Donal Lunny pursues this route in Coolfin with an orthodox rock rhythm section. US-based traditional musicians also formed bands, but these mostly reflected trends in Ireland. Chief among them were Celtic Thunder, Touchstone, Cherish the Ladies and, most recently, Solas.

Mary Black, Christy Moore, Dolores Keane, Sharon Shannon and many of Ireland's top selling artists of the 1990s have come from this kind of traditional and folk club background, that in thirty years has been a crucible of the traditional, the modern, the parochial and the international. (TOS)

**guitar.** Instrument of the lute family whose origins go back to fifteenth-century Spain. Its modern form, with six strings, flat waisted body with round soundhole and fretted neck, dates from the nineteenth century; strings were originally of gut, replaced in the twentieth century by nylon (for classical and flamenco guitars) and steel (for other types). Although long established in Iberian traditional music, the guitar is a relative newcomer to Irish music, and has yet to be completely accepted.

It was first used as accompaniment to Irish traditional music on recordings made in America in the 1920s. On these the guitar playing is clearly influenced by the swing band jazz style of the era: typically, the guitar is played with a plectrum, rather than the classical thumb-and-fingers, and there is some use of syncopation and passing chords. In Ireland, the guitar became popular for song accompaniment in the 1960s, in a thumb-and-fingers style influenced by the American folk music revival; it was used to a much lesser extent for accompaniment of Irish dance music, whose practitioners were not closely involved in the so-called 'ballad boom'. Later in the 1960s and 1970s, groups influenced by popular music appeared, and used the guitar in a more rhythmic, syncopated strumming style, played with a plectrum on steel-strings (despite the obvious example of flamenco music, contemporary players, with the exception of Stephen Cooney, rarely use the nylon-string guitar for Irish music). In this phase, the use of the guitar paralleled that of the bouzouki, and in some ways the playing styles are similar. (PAD)

*influences and development.* In spite of its use on some early recordings of Michael Coleman and Hugh Gillespie, the guitar did not make a significant appearance in Irish traditional music until the 1960s when the Clancy Brothers – themselves inspired by the guitar-based accompaniments of the American folk revival – inspired quite suddenly a new music scene in Ireland of folk or ballad groups using guitars. At first the instrument was used almost exclusively to accompany songs, and in general the playing was of a rudimentary nature. But by the late 1960s, a few Irish guitarists were developing new, more sophisticated styles in an attempt to attain some of the fragile beauty of the originally unaccompanied material. Most notable among these were Mick Moloney, Donal Lunny and Paul Brady. The interweaving of the acoustic (usually metal-strung) guitar with other plectrum instruments such as banjo, mandolin and bouzouki, in innovative bands such as the Johnstons, Sweeny's Men and Planxty, opened the ears of guitarists around Ireland to the possibility of new sounds and chordings that might complement the old songs and tunes, and render them more accessible to the uneducated listener of the day. The music of such musicians as the Beatles, Joan Baez and Bob Dylan, and of British guitarists such as Martin Carthy, John Renbourne and Bert Jansch, also influenced Irish musicians. In the 1970s the work of Mícheál Ó Domhnaill and Donal Lunny, both inside and outside the Bothy Band, and of Paul Brady in various combinations, set a new standard for the use of guitar in Irish music. Though their work has not resulted in any uniform style of playing in Irish music, they played a large part in creating an aesthetic for the instrument. They also popularised the use of non-standard tunings. Among these, the DADGAD, borrowed mostly from Bert Jansch's recordings, has become particularly common. The use of the acoustic guitar as a lead instrument has remained marginal, in spite of great work in this area by Dick Gaughan, Arty McGlynn and Paul Brady. (DAS)

*melodic use*. The guitar is less often used for melody playing, probably because its relatively small tone cannot compete with more traditional instruments. Guitarists such as Davey Graham, John Renbourn and others have adapted Irish melodies to create a solo finger-picking guitar style known as 'Celtic guitar'; the tempo at which Irish dance music is played, however, means that this style does not readily blend with traditional playing. The work of Paul Brady and Arty McGlynn has shown that Irish melodies can be played on the guitar in a traditional manner, using phrasing and ornamentation derived from the established tradition, as banjo players had done earlier.

*tuning*. The melodic nature of Irish music requires a flexible approach in accompaniment; some guitarists find that chords formed in standard tuning (EADGBE, from low to high strings) impose a harmonic rigidity which is unsuited to the melody, and prefer to use non-standard tunings such as DADGBE, DADGAD or DADEAE which they believe produce more appropriate chord voicings (Dennis Cahill has developed a unique style in standard tuning in his accompaniment of fiddler Martin Hayes). (PAD)

**Gunn, Tommy.** (1912– ). Fiddler, lilter, dancer and singer. Born near Derrylin, Co. Fermanagh, an area rich in music, particularly on fiddle and flute. These have been the main source of his style and repertoire; his father too played flute. In his early twenties Tommy moved to England for fourteen years, serving as a soldier in the Far East during World War II. In 1951 he settled in Belfast. During the 1950s he played at fleadhanna, was familiar with Co. Clare and met Paddy Canny on several occasions. In the 1960s and '70s he was a major figure in traditional music circles in and around Belfast where the Gunns' kitchen was a landmark among sessions. With Robin Morton and Cathal Mc Connell he was one of the founder members of The Boys of the Lough. A person of immense vitality and warmth, he contributed to three recordings: *Ulster's Flowery Vale*, *Good Friends – Good Music* and *Celtic Mouth Music*. A sign of the times, his son Brendan, also a fiddler, once observed that the last title shared the same advertising space in a Sunset Strip, Los Angeles music store with Snoop Doggy Dog, the Rolling Stones and Oasis. Since 1977 Tommy lives and plays in Killyleagh, Co. Down. (DEW)

# H

**Hamilton, Colin (Hammy).** (1953– ). Flute player and maker, singer, researcher and writer. Born Belfast, he was one of the many introduced to traditional music through the folk/ballad revival of the 1960s. Self-taught on tin whistle and flute, he studied Human Physiology at QUB, then did post-graduate studies in ethnomusicology under musicologist John Blacking. His MA study covered 'the session' in Irish music. He moved to Cúil Aodha, and in 1979 set up a workshop devoted to making flutes for Irish traditional music. He became flute tutor to the Music Department of UCC in 1983, in 1990 published the seminal *Irish Fluteplayer's Handbook*, and released the album *The Moneymusk*. He was a Fulbright Visiting Scholar at UCLA in 1995. His PhD thesis on the role of commercial recordings in Irish traditional music was completed in 1996. His research is in the history of traditional music, and organology. His publications include: *John Rea: A Profile of the Hammer Dulcimer Player* (1977); *The Irish Fluteplayer's Handbook* (1990); 'Designing a Flute for Irish Traditional Music', *Ireland's Musical Instrument Makers* (1990); 'The Simple System Flute in Irish Traditional Music', *Journal of the British Flute Society* (1991); 'Traditional Music – National Symbol?', *The Cork Review* (1992). *The Role of Commercial Recordings in the Survival and Development of Traditional Irish Music* (1994); 'Musical Connections – Tradition and Change', *Proceedings of the 21st World Conference of ISME*, Auckland, NZ; 'The Reinvention of the Simple System Flute', *The Woodwind Quarterly* (1995) vol. 8; forthcoming: *A Social History of Traditional Music in Ireland, Music in the Glen – Irish Traditional Musical Instruments*. He was one of the organisers of the 1996 Crossroads conference on traditional music and has given numerous papers at music conferences.

**hammer dulcimer (téadchlár).** A trapezoid, zither-like instrument with strings arranged in courses, stretched typically across two bridges (treble and bass), creating three playing areas. Courses consist of at least two strings tuned in unison, normally struck with hammers of wood, wire or, rarely, whalebone. The treble bridge divides the strings in the ratio 2:3, creating an extended diatonic system, based on fifths. The name, from the Latin 'dulce melos', was used first in the early Renaissance, but hammer dulcimer is known from at least the eleventh century AD in the Near East; it is presently found all over the northern hemisphere. Unlike the chromatic layout of the central European *hackbrett*, dulcimers used in Ireland are somewhat smaller in range. Dimensions vary, but the sound box was particularly deep on

Hammer dulcimer (EDI)

some old instruments found in Ulster. Instruments were frequently made locally or were of Scottish or English origin, while modern American models have appeared recently. The dulcimer is not common in Ireland, and is more associated with solo performance. Recent attribution of the term 'tiompán' is problematic, for this may have been a generic term for some fretted and percussion instruments. Dulcimer as we know it probably arrived in Ireland in the eighteenth century to counties Antrim and Down through trade and family links with Lowland Scotland; it is still chiefly associated with the north-east, particularly the southern glens of Antrim. Recorded examples of Irish players are scarce. Best known is John Rea (d. 1983) of Carnalbanagh, Co. Antrim. His repertoire was entirely traditional, including Scottish strathspeys and marches, and tunes by 'Piper' Jackson of Limerick. Other players like Jack Duffy of Lisburn, Co. Antrim, and Andy Dowling of Clonmeen, Rathdowney, Co. Laois, performed popular songs from the pre-war years when the dulcimer had something of a heyday. In recent years, players in the United States have drawn much of their repertoire from Irish dance tunes and eighteenth-century harp pieces.

Dowling's playing is in a tradition probably begun with the importation of dulcimers through Dublin in the nineteenth century – corresponding to a boom in the instrument in England. (BAC)

**Hammond, David.** (1928– ). Singer, raconteur, film producer. Born in Belfast of Derry and Antrim parents through whom he heard songs of the country. Their home was a calling house for relatives from the country, neighbours, workmen needing their tin cans boiled, street musicians. While in his teens Estyn Evans led him to recognise the one-ness in all this variety, influential friendships with collector Hugh Quinn and, a few years later, with Seán O'Boyle, added to this. Both were obsessive by nature and teachers by trade, they ably passed on information and skills: 'Both believed that songs and music had their origins in the heart, that it was in another heart they were intended to lodge'. A believer in the ordinary and the extraordinary, the wonder of the commonplace, Hammond has always been a collector and singer. He maintained these interests in the course of his years as a schoolteacher and later while a producer in radio, then television, first with the BBC, and then as an independent. His 1950s production *As I Roved Out* for BBC radio was an important groundbreaking series in the music revival. His short film, *The Boho Singers*, is a unique view of Fermanagh singers, musicians and dancers (BBC NI). He has produced several albums, including *Ulster's Flowery Vale*, *Green Peas and Barley-O*, a double LP of Johnny Doherty. In recent years he is best known for his Flying Fox Films which has produced city and country folklore related material, including *The Magic Fiddle* (C4). As a singer his recordings include *I am the Wee Falorie Man* (Tradition); *Belfast Street Songs* (Request); *Irish Songs of Freedom* (Request); *The Singer's House*, with Donal Lunny (Mulligan); *Songs of Belfast* (Mercier Press). He has compiled and presented many radio broadcasts for RTÉ and BBC on traditional music themes, all available for consultation in their archives.

**Hanna, Geordie.** (1915–87). Singer, raconteur. Born at Derrytresk, Co. Tyrone, on the southwestern shore of Lough Neagh, his father played fiddle and sang. His style adheres to no 'Ulster' standard, is a local and family inheritance (similar to that of his sister Sarah Anne O'Neill), but accentuated by a highly individual artistic intensity. Described by John Moulden (Topic, 1978) as entailing 'a breaking up of the tune and words into short phrases delivered with great force. It is also distinct in the placing and shape of the decoration. This results from the shortness of the phrases and allows a highly meaningful performance without any over-statement'. Repertoire and style were mutually influential between him and Sarah Anne. A winner of the John Player and Bellaghy song awards in the 1970s, with Sarah Anne he travelled to fleadhanna all over the island, was featured singer at such as Féile na Bóinne, and toured with CCÉ in the US. His early tragic death left a great void in Irish singing, he was recorded on Topic (1978) and an annual song weekend at Derrytresk commemorates his contribution to singing.

**Harbison, Janet.** (1955– ). Harper, teacher, organiser. Her father was originally a concert pianist and Janet and her sister were educated in music from an early age on piano at the College of Music, Dublin. Paddy Moloney, Éamonn De Buitléar and Seán Ó Riada were frequent visitors to the home. A year spent in the Ring Gaeltacht interested her in Irish music, and she began studying harp at Sion Hill school under Máirín Ní Shé who had taught Mary O'Hara and Kathleen Watkins. Sion Hill then used English-made Morley, or Dublin-made Quinn harps, neither suitable for dance music, this prompting Janet to take up one of the first of the Japanese Aoyama instruments (the backbone of harp revival). Ní Shé's students provided music for Jury's Cabaret; this led Janet to professional playing, eventually to tour in the US, and to play in Bunratty and Knappoge castle cabarets. In 1980 she took an honours music degree at TCD while resident pianist in the Shelbourne Hotel and a regular in a jazz club. Dissertation research on Ralph Vaughan Williams followed, this developing further interest in traditional music. She won All-Ireland, Isle of Man and Brittany major harp competitions, and toured with CCÉ. Composition with Mícheál Ó hAlúin (flute) followed, piece work in Hamburg, then postgraduate study in Irish music with Mícheál Ó Súilleabháin in UCC where she took an MA in 1984 with research on Bunting. So committed to harping, in 1984 she formed the Cláirseóirí na hÉireann organisation along similar lines to Na Píobairí Uilleann. She began the Ballycastle, Co. Antrim, harp summer school, and with Canon James McDyer initiated the Glencolmcille Harp Festival. In 1986 she began work as Curator of Music at the Ulster Folk and Transport Museum, Co. Down, where she remained until 1994. There she was involved in GCSE consultation on traditional music, and in 1992 she organised a World Harp Festival in Belfast which saw forty international players perform over eleven days. Other events around the two-hundred year anniversary of the 1792 Belfast Harp Festival followed, these leading to the formation of the Belfast Harp Orchestra, also in 1992. A 'fusion' player, her interests lie in mixing traditional with modern musics; her compositions are both large and small-scale.

**Hardebeck, Carl Gilbert.** (1869–1945) Organist, arranger, teacher, collector, publisher. Born in London and blind from birth, the son of a wealthy German, but naturalised British father, the early death of his mother intensified his passion in music and by age seven he was setting Shelly's poetry to music. From the age of eleven he spent thirteen years at the Royal National School for the Blind where he was trained in music. A Catholic, he came through a Methodist education to be provided for by a generous endowment from his jeweller father, this designed to develop his independence through music. By twenty-three he was an organist and pianist, and qualified as a teacher; this led him to open a music store in Belfast. Failure at that saw him teaching music from his home on the Limestone road, playing organ eventually in St Peter's Church on the Falls road. He won first prize for a composition at the first Dublin Feis Ceoil in 1897, and was influenced by Samuel Ferguson, James Clarence Mangan and Standish O'Grady. He had himself taught Irish in order to understand the music, mastering phonetic principles and poetry, obsessed with the antiquities of Gaelic culture. He collected songs in Donegal, working by repetition of phrase, much in the manner of contemporary collectors, but using a Braille board, frame and stylus. His training in plain-chant was of considerable value in this interpretation (Irish music used the same modes). He published *Gems of Melody* in 1908 to high acclaim, was eventually appointed to the Chair of Irish Music in UCC in 1918, and also as headmaster of the Cork Municipal School of Music. However, his Nationalist beliefs engendered local Anglo-Irish hostility, undermined his means and forced him to return to Belfast in 1923, then to Dublin. Reduced to poverty, he was rescued by the publishers of *The Capuchin Annual* who organised a pension for him. As a component of the Gaelic revival his influence was strong in Belfast where his Gaelic choir involved singers drawn from the Catholic middle class, so passing on an ideological passion linking national music and national identity. (Ref. *The Blind Bard of Belfast*, by Gregory Allen, in History Ireland, Vol. 6, No. 3; C. G. Hardebeck, by Sean Neeson, Sean O'Boyle, etc., in *The Capuchin Annual*, 1943,

'48 and '65; 'Traditional singing – its value and meaning', *Journal of the Ivernian Society*, Vol. 3, 1910; *Song Words for Irish Airs* – Alice Milligan, *Journal of the Irish Folksong Society*, Vol. VI, 1908).

**harmonica.** Known colloquially as 'mouth organ', and in blues music as 'blues harp' or 'harp', this is the simplest of the free-reed instruments. In its earliest versions the reeds were set in pipes, like tuning-pipes for guitar; later the familiar 'flat box' shape was developed. Based in the principles established by Buschmann in 1822, it was first manufactured by Hotz of Knittlingen in 1825, by Messner of Trossingen in 1827, Glier of Klingenthal, in 1829 – all eventually overshadowed and absorbed by clock maker Matthias Hohner of Trossingen (begun production 1857) who gradually built up a monopoly. Hugely popular in the last century, the instrument is also made on the German design in China. Modern harmonicas come in different types and keys in order to facilitate playing in blues or jazz. The longer the instrument the greater the range of notes, each hole in the blowing side has two reeds pitched to adjacent notes of the scale, one is sounded on blow, the other on suck. The 'chromatic' harmonica has two tiers of blowing holes, the upper row providing semitones which are activated by pressing a sprung knob with the thumb. The ten-hole mouth organ is similar to the ten-key melodeon – with bellows added; the chromatic harmonica is like a two-row accordion.

The system on a D diatonic illustrates:
Blow   D   F#   A   D   F#   A   D   F#   A   D
Suck   e   a   c#   e   g   b   c#   e   g   b

Diatonic harmonica                              (EDI)

Chromatic harmonica – note the slide mechanism operated by the button on the right          (EDI)

Of all the instruments used in traditional music, it is now probably the least popular, but up to the 1950s this was not the case. The instrument was an exceptional music-maker, testimony to that is the number of old people around the country who recall playing it (Templepatrick, Co. Antrim fiddler Kathleen Smith's grandmother played it up until her death in her nineties, in 1998). But where traditional music is concerned, 'harmonica' as a term covers several very different kinds of instrument:

1. Diatonic (or blue's harp) is the simplest construction. Playing it involves either having a selection of appropriately-pitched instruments, or bending or slurring notes to compensate for absent sharps and flats. The diatonic is pitched in different keys.

2. The Octave has the same scale set-up as the diatonic, but bending of notes is not possible. It has a double set of reeds for each note of the scale, these an octave apart (e.g. G and G'). This gives a very full, rich sound – rather like a melodeon.

3. The Tremolo also has a double set of reeds for each note of the scale, but the second set is tuned slightly sharp to the primary set – giving a 'tremolo' effect rather like an accordion sound. New models of these have a full scale.

4. The Chromatic has a button or slide mechanism which is used to get sharps and flats. This is the same as on diatonic melodeon.

Chromatic harmonicas can be played in any key, but they also are made in a variety of popular basic keys of G, D, A (and 'F# to G' by Hering only for traditional playing). The slide button is pushed in to achieve sharps and flats, these manipulated to make very effective rolls.

Tremolo and Octave harmonicas are fixed in key, so, for instance, playing on a D model will have C# only – therefore one has to pick one's tunes carefully. In addition, older models of the Tremolo have some notes of the scale missing and unavailable in the lower octave, but Suzuki and Tombo models have full scales, and in choices of keys. Hohner, Tombo, Suzuki, Hering and Lee Oskar are major makes of the instrument.

In the hands of a good player the Diatonic or 'blues harp' can be exciting for traditional music, for the playing will involve slurring and bending notes, a technique in itself. Tremolo and Octave remain the most popular in Irish music however, and instruments are chosen to match the key of a tune (i.e. a G tune will be played on a G instrument). Harmonica players in traditional music use all varieties of the instrument. Eddie Clarke (Chromatic), Brendan Power (Chromatic and Diatonic), Rick Epping (Diatonic and Octave), Joel Bernstein (Chromatic and Diatonic), Mick Kinsella (Chromatic), Mark Graham (Chromatic and Diatonic). John and Pip Murphy of Wexford, and their late father Phil, use Diatonic, Octave, and Tremolo; Phil played Tremolo, and also Chromatic in a vamping style. Phil's exploration expanded the melodic possibilities of this instrument by retaining one of the lower reeds, and to play in a lower octave, he sometimes used the larger 'chromatic'. For solo work, John Murphy also plays ten-hole, single-reeded diatonic 'harps' of the type favoured by American blues musicians. All-Ireland prize winners Austin Berry and Noel Battle use Tremolo as do Rory Ó Leoracháin and Tom Clancy. (MIK)

See Basker, Tommy; Clarke, Eddie; free reeds.

**harmony.** The decoration of melody, the idea of harmony dates to the ninth-century Christian church. Loosely it involves the simultaneous performance of 'parts' (sympathetic melodies accompanying and interwoven with the principal one – counterpoint), but strictly it involves the use of particular chords. Fundamental to orchestral and other forms of music, it has not been considered important to traditional musics, Irish in particular where melody has been dominant, in fact the hallmark of the genre. Yet such celebrated virtuosi as Michael Coleman and James Morrison frequently used harmony in various forms of 'backing' in the 1930s and '40s. And in recent times traditional music in Ireland has developed strong connections with harmonic structure through accompaniment.

Historically, much of Irish traditional music has been solo, and in the absence of evidence of the use of multiphonics, harmony did not play a part, particularly among singers. However, the development of certain instruments has introduced a harmonic element into what are seen as solo performances. The introduction of drones and regulators to the pipes is such a development. As to whether the early harpists employed a structured accompaniment to the tune is unclear, but taking the nature of the instrument, it seems likely that due to its resonance, some overtones were apparent, thus giving it harmonic qualities. So too the use of intentional and unintentional double stopping by fiddle players can give a similar harmonic effect. Octave playing employed by certain styles of fiddling is in itself a harmonic construction and one widely accepted and admired within the Irish music tradition. While sean-nós singing is viewed for the most part as being a solo performance, there are also examples of group activity within the song tradition of Ireland – in the form of work songs and *lúibíní*, for example – and in the wake tradition where there was wide use of group performance in the *caoineadh*. In all of these forms, while harmonic construction is rarely intentional, through variation, ornamentation, modulation and pitch and timbre differences in voice production, harmonic properties were introduced to the music.

As folk music could be classed as being part of a communicative process, text and melody could be seen to take precedence over harmony as a method of communication. In the modern world however, the use of harmony has become somewhat of a pre-requisite to most types of music presentation. Folk music is not exempt from this influence and today a traditional musician is as likely to – and be expected to –

utilise some form of harmony in performance as play a pure, melodic unaccompanied form. The refinement of 'Western Art Music' over the years has conditioned audiences, through the establishment of harmonic form and structure, who have come to expect certain criteria to be satisfied in all music to which they listen. In the case of Irish traditional music, while certain forms and measures are required – for particular dance forms for example – we also have come to expect a sense of harmonic grammar.

*pitch*. The establishment of pitch is perhaps one of the primary considerations taken for granted in the performance of many traditional musicians today. As to whether the 'primitive' traditional musician had any concept of pitch, be it A=440htz. or otherwise, we cannot be certain, but to expect all traditional musicians to possess perfect pitch would be unrealistic. This is borne out by older instruments still in existence which vary enormously with regard to pitch – the uilleann pipes in particular. Through this variation it could be presumed that pitch did not play such a primary role in the music of an earlier era, and furthermore, as instruments such as the pipes were susceptible to pitch variation due to climatic change and other conditions, the concept of fixed pitch becomes even more vague.

*tonality*. With an established pitch for a particular instrument, the concept of tonality then becomes relevant to the music being performed. While intonation and tuning may be considered today, it is again in relation to conditioning and the establishment of the diatonic scale. However – as in the case of many forms of folk music – traditional Irish music does not always comply with the requirement of the diatonic structure and there are many examples where the music presents features outside this formula. The frequent use of pitch-bending in certain notes, of micro-tonic ornamentation, or of glissando movement by sean-nós singers, all question the relationship of the music to the diatonic restrictions. Because present notions of harmony have developed primarily within the diatonic structure, the application of harmony to some traditional music can thus be somewhat confused.

*scales and modes*. We therefore can assume that the texture of Irish traditional music has altered through time due to developments in instrumentation, in musical form, and harmony – as well as other external influences. The music has been adapted to receive many of these features, and in doing so, certain facets of it must have been lost. It seems likely however that the fundamental construction of the music has remained intact, and evidence of this can be found in the retained closeness of the music to modal structure. While much of the music fits smoothly into the major or minor modes, there are also many examples which do not, and this calls for an alternative classification to that of the major or minor. To this end, we see that much of the music can be interpreted as belonging to an earlier modal system, this often comprised of the amalgamation of what we now know as the major and minor (both harmonic and melodic) modes. The ease with which many traditional tunes weave their way between major and minor is an important feature of the music. Some tunes classed in A minor for example can intermittently introduce the sharpened third, thereby causing confusion as to whether the piece is in A minor or A major.

A solution often used in the accompaniment of such a piece is to omit the third from the accompanying harmony. The tune is then free to change from major to minor without conflict with the harmonic accompaniment. To assist this process, alternative tunings are often employed to accompanying stringed instruments such as the guitar. The common use of 'open D', 'open G' or 'dropped D' tuning is employed by guitarists accompanying traditional music specifically to avoid the commitment to the third of either the major or the minor modes. This confusion is evidenced among many of the early piano accompanists on recordings of such as Michael Coleman, Denis Murphy or Paddy Cronin. Another feature of the earlier style of piano accompaniment is the conventional use of the 1-4-5-1 harmonic structure with the pianists generally using the simplest harmonic construction, that of, Tonic, to Sub-Dominant, to Dominant, and back to Tonic. With time however, keyboard accompaniment has developed a more imaginative harmonic phenomenon, again often largely influenced by the modal qualities of the music. Along with this, more elaborate harmonic constructions are being used today in the form of added sevenths, ninths, thirteenths, diminished and augmented chords etc., as distinct from the earlier restrictions of major or minor chords in root position or first or second inversion.

*part of the tradition.* Over the past twenty years or so the concept of harmony in the world of traditional music has become so much part of the tradition that it is now expected of performers. Groups such as Planxty, The Bothy Band, De Dannan and Clannad have all contributed to bringing the music to another level of presentation, one in which the concept of harmonic accompaniment is the norm. Today, not even the use of guitars and bouzoukis can fulfil the expanding harmonic horizons of some, thus the bass and drums have been re-introduced, so too orchestration – all of which gives the whole notion of harmony another dimension. While some may argue that harmony is the ruination of the music, it is possible that due to its adaptation many more are now willing to listen to the music who might otherwise have ignored it. This repeats a pattern begun in the 1970s when such groups as Horslips made the music attractive to new audiences. But while the acceptance of some form of harmonic accompaniment is unavoidable in the traditional music of today, it should be viewed as a feature of presentation or colour. Its application should not alter the fundamental true form, rhythm, melody or structure, and dance tunes should remain faithful to their specific dance types. Harmony in this music is accompaniment. (JMC)

## harp.

*introduction.* The National symbol of Ireland is the harp, it is on government stationery, Garda caps and coin currency, Ireland is the only county to have such a music instrument as its symbol. Yet it is almost two hundred years since Ireland's old harp tradition flickered out. The instrument's intense history has constantly motivated exploration, retrieval and ingenuity among harpers and harp enthusiasts through the twentieth century. It and its music have been painstakingly researched, instruments reconstructed and new harps based on models that survive from the eighteenth century have been made, music collected from the last of the

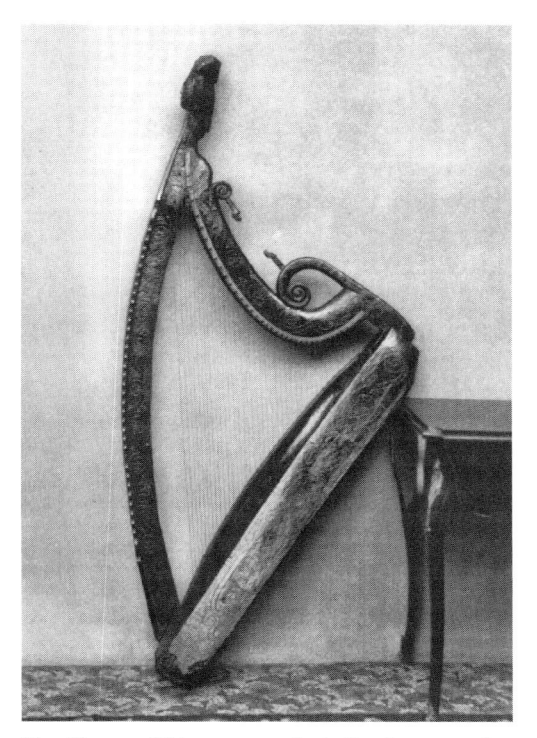

The 'Bunworth' harp, so called after its owner the Rev. Charles Bunworth of Baldaniel, Co. Cork (d. *c.* 1770), rector of Buttevant, five times umpire of the competitions of the Munster bards held at Charleville, Co. Cork and Bruree, Co. Limerick. The harp was made in 1734 by John Kelly, originally of Ballinascreen (Draperstown), Co. Derry. It passed from Bunworth to Thomas Crofton Croker and in 1854 was sold to a collector in London. It is now in the Museum of Fine Art, Boston. (CBÉ)

old order of harp players has been revived to suit these, and techniques of playing to suit the more modern dance-music repertoire have been perfected. Still, because the harp's tradition was broken, it suffers from that rupture in the passing on of skills, and players today are all in many ways also innovators, as each makes their own stamp on the instrument.

*eighth to tenth centuries.* Harps and lyres are not by any means restricted to the 'Celtic' countries. The instruments' oldest records date to the 2500 BC Mesopotamian graves of Ur, and various forms had travelled to Syria by 2000 BC, to Palestine where they were used in

Hebrew temple orchestras. In ancient Greece harp was played by males and females, finger plucked for ritual use, plectrum plucked (a harder sound) for dancing. Harps are still used all over North to Central Africa, in Burma and Afghanistan. Since lyres too are found from the Black Sea to the Atlantic it is likely that our early Celtic ancestors had adopted or become influenced by them. It is possible that the actual triangular harp may have had pre-Christian Celtic association in Ireland and therefore deliberately was not depicted in carvings – the psalterium may have been portrayed instead as a symbol of Christianity. Or it may be that the ninth-century-AD Danish incursions brought the actual triangular harp here.

*kinds of harp.* The present triangular shape of the Irish harp was set by the eleventh century, its particularly robust, heavy construction most likely developed to suit our climate. It has a soundbox of willow, metal strings, a T-shaped pillar and a string-bearer reinforced with metal. The instrument is smaller than other eighteenth-century harps, it was designed to be held on knee, as was the fourteenth-century Trinity college harp. Irish harps became gradually bigger, until by the seventeenth century they were large and floor-standing. Irish harping was highly regarded, and popularly favoured, leading a ethnocentric fourteenth-century Welsh poet to urge the youth of his day not to adopt the Irish fashion of metal strings. The harp on display in Trinity College Dublin – the model for the Irish emblem – dates to the fourteenth century and is used as a reference point for playing practice – it has brass strings strung so that it had to be held on the left shoulder. But in all there are three kinds of older Irish harp:

1. that of the fourteenth to early sixteenth century – 70 cm high, thirty strings, referred to as the 'small low-headed Irish harp';

2. the 'large low-headed Irish harp' with thirty-five to forty-five strings from the late sixteenth into seventeenth century. It has four survivors – The Otway and O'Fogerty harps have thirty-five strings, the Fitzgerald-Kildare instrument has thirty-nine, the Dalway (or 'Cloyne') has forty-five, with an additional seven which probably sounded sympathetically);

3. the high-headed Irish harp, used by later itinerant harpers – instruments like that of Turlough Carolan. Six of these survive – the Bunworth, Carolan, Mullagh Mast, O'Neill, Dounhill and Sirr. The most common harp played today is known as the modern or gut-string Irish harp. There are many different styles, some modelled on the low-headed, some on the high-headed older models, others use clairseach design. (EDI)

Twelfth-century triangular-frame harp carving from Ardmore Cathedral, Waterford (GRY)

*early history.* It is not known how or when the harp came to Ireland. Celtic crosses from the eighth, ninth and tenth centuries show stringed instruments of various shapes and sizes, but none of these could be called 'harp' in the technical sense. Two other depictions on stone show triangular frame harps. One is on the outside wall of twelfth-century Ardmore Cathedral, Co. Waterford, the other on a fifteenth-century tomb in Jerpoint Abbey, Co. Kilkenny (but this latter may possibly represent a harp of greater antiquity than the fifteenth century). However, the earliest Irish depiction of the familiar triangular frame harp is on the late eleventh-century shrine of St Meadóg (breac Maedóic). The depiction of a harp on such a shrine suggests that it was by then already well established as an important instrument.

*traditional wire-strung harp.* The earliest existing Irish harp is the so-called 'Brian Boru' (Trinity College Dublin), dating probably from the late fourteenth century. This is the instrument portrayed on Irish coinage. In form it is typical of the long line of wire strung harps produced over a period of at least 800 years until the early nineteenth century. These harps were made of high density wood, and featured a one-piece soundbox made by hollowing out a single block from below. Instruments varied in size from small knee-harps to those over five feet tall. The number of strings, of brass and steel wire, could be as high as forty-five, though the average number was thirty to thirty-six. It was a solid heavy instrument, often intricately carved and painted, sometimes inset with jewels.

*the harper* (an cruitire). The harper was an important figure in Gaelic society, second in stature only to the poet (an file). In a chief's household, poet and harper provided poetry and music as required; a performance could be a recitation of the chief's pedigree or his great deeds, the occasion a dinner entertainment, or the ritual mourning of the dead. Poet and harper were joined by the reciter (an reacaire) who chanted the poems to harp accompaniment. This kind of performance was still current in the early seventeenth century, though relatively rare. By then, for the most part, the harper performed alone, travelling between the great houses of both Gael and Gall, performing (and often composing) both words and music. The chanting of the poems eventually was transformed into conventional singing. By the end of the eighteenth century only a few travelling harpers remained.

*playing style*. In the early days harpers began studying in childhood, probably in harp schools similar to the bardic ones. Such schools certainly existed in Wales, and there were strong links between the Welsh and Irish harp traditions, particularly in the twelfth century. It is not known what music the early Irish harpers performed, because the tradition was wholly oral. They used long carefully shaped fingernails to strike the strings, using a complex technique of string damping, in order to combat the instrument's long-lasting resonance; without such damping, the music would sound distorted and confused. From the many comments written about the Irish harpers – ranging from Giraldus Cambrensis in the twelfth century to the German traveller J. G. Kohl in the nineteenth – we learn that the music was quick and lively, yet sweet and plaintive, with a strong contrast between the magical, bell-like sound of the treble and the booming resonance of the bass. Players used few harmony notes, but had a wide variety of ornamentation, and they could vary their sound from being barely audible to fortissimo.

*music of the wire-strung harp*. Irish music collections from 1724 on include harp tunes dating from the sixteenth century and later, but none were written down in any authentic way until Edward Bunting began to collect from harpers attending the Belfast Harpers Festival of 1792. He subsequently made several collecting tours, noting other harp tunes, but not for the most part writing down the bass line, a serious omission. Bunting also wrote down everything he could learn about traditional harp style and technique and listed many of the ornaments and musical terms used by the harpers. He noted that the harp was tuned in a basic Ionian (Doh) scale of G, with two strings tuned to tenor G. All this is preserved in his manuscripts and published collections. In spite of the efforts of Bunting and other collectors, much harp music has disappeared, but some went into the repertoire of other instruments, notably big melodies such as 'An Chúilfhionn'.

*harper-composers*. Ancient Irish literature abounds in tales of harpers and the magical power of their music, but more concrete references are to be found in the various annals kept by learned monks. These are usually about the deaths of prominent musicians, but there is nothing about their music.

1500s: Around this period lived the four Scott brothers. John and Harry wrote lamentations noted by Bunting in 1792. A third brother, Darby, was harper to King Christian IV of Denmark. Another court harper was Cormac McDermott, who was employed by Elizabeth I and James I. Ruadhrí Dall Ó Catháin travelled extensively in Scotland, and is best known for his piece 'Tabhair dom do lámh'. Another harper of the period, Nicholas Dall Pierse, was credited with 'compleating the harp with more strings than ever before his time were used'.

1600–1750: The harper Cearbhall Ó Dálaigh is said to have written the celebrated song 'Eibhlín a Rúin', while the best-known piece by Maelíosa Ó Riain is 'Marbhna Luimní' (Limerick's Lamentation). Cornelius Lyons, harper to Lord Antrim and a friend of Carolan, composed 'Miss Hamilton', and wrote variations to many other harp airs. He was unusual in being able to read music. Very unpopular among his fellow-harpers was Daithí Ó Murchadha, because of his self-important airs. A fine performer, he had played for Louis XIV and was harper to Lord Mayo, for whom he wrote the well-known song 'Tiarna Mhaigh Eó'. William and Thomas Connellan were credited with the composition of over 700 airs, of which only a few survive, including 'Máire Níc Ailpín' and 'Mallaí San Seoirse'. By far the best-known harper-composer was Turlough Carolan (1670–1738), whose music has become immensely popular internationally, nowadays played on instruments other than the harp. Over 200 of his airs survive, with, in many cases the words that went with them.

1750–1850: Most of our information about the later traditional harpers comes from the *Memoirs of Arthur O'Neill* (1734–1816), which were recorded by Edward Bunting. In these O'Neill names upwards of fifty professional harpers, as well as some amateur players. A good player himself, he gave much information and music to Bunting. He was principal teacher of the Belfast Irish Harp Society from 1808 to 1813. One of the finest players of this period was Charles Fanning, who played baroque style music, in particular pieces by Carolan. At the end of the eighteenth century, Rose Mooney was one of the few remaining female itinerant players. A fine musician, though often badly behaved, was Eichlin Ó Catháin, who spent much of his life in Scotland, where an account of his life was written and some of his tunes were noted. Also active at this period were Daniel Black, famous for his singing, and Dominick Mungan, noted for his 'whispering notes', while Thady Elliot was disgraced for playing Carolan's lively 'Planxty Connor' during mass in Navan cathedral. Unique was Denis Hempson, who lived in three centuries (1695–1807), the only player at the 1792 festival who still used the finger-nail technique. He preferred the old music, and had some unusual harp tunes and studies in his repertoire. He travelled widely in Ireland and Scotland.

1800s: There were just a few nineteenth-century harpers, mostly graduates of the harp schools set up in Belfast and Dublin after 1800. The only one worth noting is Patrick Byrne. While playing 'Brian Boru's March' in 1868, the sound of his harp was described in much the same terms as Cambrensis had used seven centuries earlier. The magical music had not changed, but the public now sang to a different tune; there was no longer an audience for the ancient wire-strung harp.

*the harp today.* From early in the nineteenth century the old wire strung harp faded, and was gradually replaced by the lightweight instrument of today, strung with gut (or nylon), fitted with semitone levers and played with the finger pads. This became the familiar Irish harp as we know it today, and which is now played all over the world, in countries as disparate as the USA and Japan. In the early 1970s, the US harp maker Jay Witcher began to make excellent copies of old Irish wire-strung harps, and since then there has been a revival of the instrument. The number of players and harp makers has steadily increased, particularly in the United States, but it is as yet little heard in its native land. (GRY)

*decline of harp.* The earliest stringed music accounts involve 'goltraighe', 'gentraighe' and 'suantraigh' or literally 'crying', 'laughing' and 'sleeping' time measure (possibly relating to poetic meter to which the crott/cruit and later cláirseach is intimately associated). Harpers enjoyed a privileged position, receiving land, stock and protection free of rent and military obligation from their chieftain patrons in return for helping the patron fulfil ceremonial, ritual and social obligations by accompanying the intoning of clan genealogy and praise, lament and heroic poetry in addition to performing instrumental preludes, laments and salutes. We learn from Scottish tradition that further duties included travelling with the chieftain on journeys, acting as envoy and playing the household to sleep. Growing English ambitions in the sixteenth century began to usurp land and power from the chieftains and to destroy the Gaelic social fabric, and the subsequent loss of support caused the filí to disappear rapidly; but in the late sixteenth and early seventeenth centuries some cláirseoirs found employment at English and Danish royal courts and received discernible favour from English nobility. The change in Irish land ownership meant that most harpers were forced to seek new patronage, adopt a new lifestyle and change their repertoire, adopting a new musical idiom – the playing and singing of folk and popular music. Ireland's famous harper-composer Turlough Carolan found much success basing many of his pieces on continental dance forms appropriate to each patron's generation. Nevertheless, musical tastes of the landed ascendancy continued to change throughout the eighteenth century, focusing on performing 'amateurs' of their own class and on other instruments that could better express the increasingly popular chromaticism – particularly keyboards and the violin. The cláirseach that was anachronistic at the end of the eighteenth century found itself in the early nineteenth century replaced by the harp known as the 'Irish Harp' today – one patterned after continental gut-strung models with semitone pitch-changing systems – and it passed into history as a museum-piece, a national symbol and a memory. (ANH)

*style and understatement.* Irish traditional music is orally transmitted, incorporating within it both the formal courtly traditions of the harp, and the 'music of the people'. No other instrument symbolises both the continuities and discontinuities of the Irish music tradition so thoroughly. It is the oldest instrument within it, having been played here for more than a thousand years, and therefore the one which appears to have changed the most. It is only through an understanding of the full, knowable gamut of Irish music since the earliest times that we can come to any just appreciation of that which is essential and immutable within the tradition: the Irish 'aesthetic' which informs both the harp and dance-music traditions.

From earliest times there seems to have been a distinctively Irish aesthetic, with a deep impulse towards ornament, and the exaltation of the subtle over the obvious, expressed in all art-forms. It would seem that the idea of 'art which conceals art' was as central to the approach of a twentieth-century uilleann piper such as Willie Clancy, or sean-nós singer such as Máire Áine Nic Dhonncha, as it was to the creator of an illuminated initial in the *Book of Kells*, or the art of the harpers as described by Giraldus Cambrensis in the twelfth century:

> The movement is not as in the British instrument to which we are accustomed, slow and easy, but rather quick and lively, while at the same time its melody is sweet and pleasant. It is remarkable how in spite of the great speed of the fingers the musical proportion is maintained. The melody is kept perfect and full with unimpaired art through everything . . . with a rapidity that charms, a rhythmic pattern that is varied, and a concord achieved through elements discordant. They harmonise at intervals of the octave and the fifth . . . They glide so subtly from one mode to another, and the grace notes so freely sport with such abandon and bewitching charm around the steady tone of the heavier sound, that the perfection of their art seems to lie in their concealing it, as if 'it were the better for being hidden. An art revealed, brings shame.' Hence it happens that the very things that afford unspeakable delight to the minds of those who have a fine perception and can penetrate carefully to the secrets of the art, bore, rather than delight, those who have no such perception . . . When the audience is unsympathetic they succeed only in causing boredom, with what appears to be but confused and disordered noise. (*Topographica Hiberniae*, 1185; trans. John J. O'Meara, 1982).

Although the musical forms favoured by the harpers in the construction of a number of those pieces which have been preserved for us by Edward Bunting were very different from those popular among most of the traditional musicians of today, the musical value-system has remained the same (see 'Scott's Lamentation').

Dance music dominates the current repertoire; its subtleties often escape the attention of the uninformed. The tunes will appear to the casual listener to be played at the same volume throughout, when this is not in fact the case. It may be illuminating to imagine first the music of Beethoven as a landscape painting, the main features shaped by broad-brush crescendi and diminuendi (macro-dynamics, to coin a phrase) stretching over several bars, melodic variation generally speaking being quite obvious to the listener. By contrast, imagine Irish music as the art of the miniature, where all dynamic variation takes place within the bar (micro-dynamics) and melodic variation is of a very subtle kind. The sean-nós singing and instrumental slow-air traditions, currently less prominent, are conservative in temper and have a direct stylistic connection with the music of the harpers. Many airs and 'pieces' preserved by

'Scott's Lamentation' from Buntings' *Ancient Music of Ireland*, Vol. III (1840)

the pipers show harp-like stylistic features and may have been learned by them directly from harpers. It is interesting to note that the uilleann pipes (like the harp, a gentleman's instrument, and expensive to buy) came to prominence at about the same time that the harp went into decline. Pipers have certainly inherited some of the prestige of the harpers within the tradition, and the most highly regarded of them tend to gravitate towards the performance of the older music in a consciously conservative manner.

The ancient Irish harp began its long decline in the seventeenth century; by the early nineteenth century it had practically disappeared, there being no longer any teachers competent to provide the long training in the complex and sophisticated techniques necessary to the performance of its demanding repertoire. By the late nineteenth century only the Neo-Irish harp was played, popular as accompaniment to the voice in suburban drawing-rooms and largely confined to that milieu. In the 1950s it was still played mainly by harpists with little knowledge of the old harp tradition (Gráinne Yeats was very much a lone voice crying in the wilderness at that time) and certainly no knowledge of, or interest in, the music of the oral tradition, a situation which still obtained in the early 1970s. Pioneer in this milieu was harper Máire Ní Chathasaigh, whose primary music influences were sean-nós singing and the uilleann pipes (from the Cork Pipers' Club), but who had an affinity with the harp. Challenged by the idea of establishing a style of harping which would be recognised by traditional musicians as 'authentically traditional' she sought to develop techniques – particularly in relation to ornamentation – which might lead to this. Her objective was to reclaim the music of the harpers for the oral tradition by re-interpreting their music in the light of her own knowledge of that tradition. Her workshops in Ireland, Britain and the USA from the mid-1970s onwards have passed on the techniques she developed; her arrangements and fingerings have been made available in book-form as *The Irish Harper* (1991). Those arrangements can be heard too on her 1985 solo album *The New-Strung Harp,* the first harp album to concentrate primarily on traditional Irish dance music (see 'Gander in the Pratie Hole').

The survival of Irish traditional music is dependent on the transmission of information and techniques from one generation to the next: performers of the past who have preferred to keep their technical secrets to themselves in order to maintain their own status have diminished themselves and deprived succeeding generations of their own particular acquired and self-generated pool of knowledge. The fact that hundreds of harpers have been influenced by Ní Chathasaigh's techniques and approach (learnt in many cases at fourth or fifth hand) is an immensely gratifying indication of the positivity of sharing accumulated and intelligently deduced instrumental technique. The harp's presence is now felt everywhere. It is a glue which binds together the Irish musical past and present. (MAN)

*Gaelic harp.* This is so designated because of its long and sole association with historical Gaelic-speaking areas. It was first known in Irish as 'crott' or 'cruit' and also since the late fourteenth century as 'cláirseach'. Featuring brass wire strings, this uniquely resonant harp is part of an oral tradition spanning well over a thousand years. The cláirseach's decline began with the seventeenth-century loss of Gaelic supremacy in Ireland, yet its voice continued to be heard until its disappearance in the early nineteenth century. Since then, there have been a few attempts to revive it, but none with lasting significance, until the 1970s. Though initially hampered by a lack of instruments and learning tools, players such as Gráinne Yeats in Ireland and Ann Heyman in the US have used modern and historical music traditions to develop technique, style and repertoire. While most harpers today use a neo-Irish gut strung harp, modelled after its European predecessor, there is a modest revival of the harp that is distinctly Irish involving notable Irish players such as Paul Dooley and Siobhán Armstrong. Playing and construction standards continue to rise and healthy differences in approach have emerged. Today the entire scope of Irish traditional music lies within the realm of cláirseach performance.

*construction of the cláirseach.* Traditionally the cláirseach's highly-tensioned brass wire strings are supported by a robust and heavy triangular frame.

/ HARP, CONSTRUCTION OF THE CLÁIRSEACH

# THE GANDER IN THE PRATIE HOLE

'The Gander in the Pratie Hole' as ornamented by Máire Ní Chathasaigh

Its quadrangular soundbox is hollowed and shaped from a solid log, leaving a soundboard ranging in thickness from ¼"-¾" on surviving instruments. Forepillar and neck are centred in the top and bottom of the soundbox so that strings run not completely vertical, but fan out slightly to one side. This alignment's added torque to the forepillar is countered by a broadening at the outside along most of its length to create in cross-section (looking from above) the shape of a thickened 'T'. Necks feature a metal band on each side through which the tuning pegs fit. The frame is joined by mortise and tenon joints and string tension alone holds it together. Strings varied in number from about thirty to thirty-six and they were secured in the soundbox by wrapping them around a wooden toggle. Throughout the seventeenth and into the early eighteenth century the frame size grew and necks were angled ever higher to accommodate a desire for stronger bass.

Traditionally the instrument rested against the player's left shoulder, the left hand sounding the shorter treble strings allowing right hand access to the longer bass strings. The fingernails were used as plectra, producing brilliant and sustained tones enhanced by specialised damping techniques. Tuning was diatonic except for two consecutive tenor G strings that were tuned first and formed a foundation for tuning the instrument by fifths. The Gaelic name for these tenor G strings was 'comhluighe', and their recorded usage spanned at least 750 years, from early twelfth-century glosses on the *Amhrán Colum Cille* in *Leabhar na hUidhre* to an interview with Patrick Byrne in 1849. Vocabulary collected from the harpers shows the cláirseach's primary scale to have been all natural, or G mixolydian mode, but at some undetermined time later the seventh scale step was sharpened and Bunting named the scale of one sharp, or G ionian mode, as standard at the end of the eighteenth century. Of course other modes accessible in these tunings were used.

*interpretation of the framework of the cláirseach and crott:* Information about the cláirseach tradition was collected by Edward Bunting between 1792 and 1802, most of it being published in his 1840 edition of *Ancient Music*

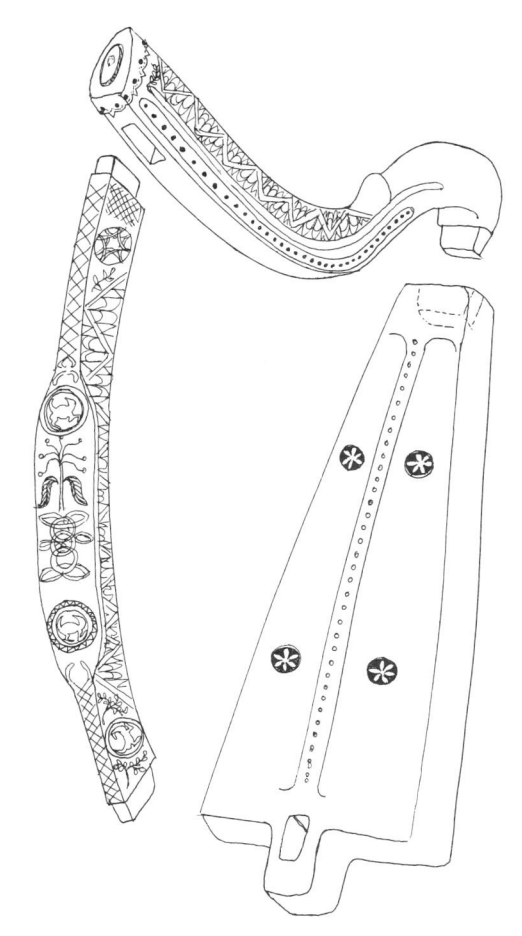

Cláirseach construction and jointing (ANH)

*of Ireland*, but little work has been done to collate and apply this legacy toward the goal of narrowing many wide gaps that remain in our knowledge and understanding of the instrument. His information has remained largely a list of 'facts', some of which are anomalies within the harp family. For instance, the cláirseach's mostly diatonic tuning included two consecutive tenor G notes named na comhluighe that were the first strings tuned and served as a tuning foundation. Bunting asked why they were used and received the reply 'We have always done it this way'. He probably would have received the same answer had he asked about performing orientation, which was on the left shoulder with the left hand in the treble and right hand in the bass, contrary to most other known harps. Practical answers to both curiosities have been offered: conventional wisdom explains that the length of the shortest strings, which fan out to the player's left, is insufficient to permit easy right hand access, so the left hand must be used in the treble. However Bunting recorded that harpers sometimes used their right hands in the treble and had a special name for when they did so. If that orientation was desired, the tuning pins need only have been inserted from the other direction. The difficulty of keeping long fingernails on the right hand has also been offered as a practical consideration for left-shouldered performance, but then why weren't other plucked stringed instruments such as early lutes, guitars, citterns, etc. not sounded with left-hand nails instead of with those on the right hand? Similarly, no satisfactory practical explanation has been offered for the over 750-years' tenure of na comhluighe strings in the cláirseach gamut. They definitely disrupt spacing and fingering patterns for the player, yet they are found on the harps of many if not all of the harpers at Belfast in 1792. In fact, the two anomalies are related in a manner that illuminates other elements of cláirseach tradition.

The first step in such an investigation is to realise that the failure to discover a satisfactory practical answer leads us beyond the boundaries of music performance to the realm of allegory and symbolism. Right and left in Gaelic culture were often equated with male and female. For example, the right side of the hearth was the man's and the left was the woman's. Men sat on the right side of the church, women on the left. If the cláirseach gamut was thought to encompass both a male and a female 'voice', then the harper's left (female) and right (male) hands sounded the appropriate voices. Such a gender-divided cláirseach gamut is implicit in the use of na comhluighe strings.

The term translates as 'lying/sleeping together' (conjugally), implying one of the strings to be 'male' and the other as 'female'. Bunting records that they 'neatly divided the instrument into bass and treble', so we may confidently group the female G with the female/treble voice and the male G with the male/bass voice. Observe, however, that we no longer see only two gendered groupings here, male and female, but have added a third, na comhluighe, that is at the same time androgynous and neuter ('it'), and whose function as a tuning foundation allows it to represent the entire gamut ('they'). Constant appearance of the number 'three' in Indo-European traditions led Georges Dumézil to identify a tripartite ideological construct made up of Sacred, Physical and Fertile functions, which has seen much use in social science since the middle of this century. Elements of cláirseach tradition such as construction, nomenclature, tuning and orientation are all consistent with such an interpretation. In fact, not only do they reflect his system, they broaden its scope both by emphasising the gender of each category and by illuminating a double identity and role for Dumézil's sacred function. Like comhluighe, not only is it an androgynous or neuter third gender but it may also represent the concept of the 'whole' triad or entity.

The cláirseach's construction utilised mortise and tenon joints to connect its three-part frame. The soundbox carries a female mortise at both top and bottom, giving it a Fertile identity. Likewise, the pillar's Physical masculinity is denoted by its male tenon at each end. Of course, this left only one possible configuration for the neck – a mortise at one end and tenon at the other, consistent with the androgynous Sacred category. Similarly reflected are the functions of these three parts and their nomenclature. The box's (*coim* or body, waist, belly, womb) Fertile role is to generate the harp's voice. The pillar's (*lamhchrann* or hand-pillar) physical strength permits use of highly tensioned metal strings that give the cláirseach's voice its proper character. The neck's Sacred role is filled through its regulating the tuning of these strings, though we are unsure of the precise spelling and therefore meaning of the name. One possibility is *cóir*, meaning propriety or harmony in the sense of being suitable, fitting or correct. Another, *cor*, has many meanings, including the act of putting, placing or setting up.

A third choice is 'corr', a white long-necked water bird such as crane or heron. Instead of trying to choose between the three spellings, they, their meanings and linguistic genders may be considered collectively, for all fall within the

Sacred domain. 'Cor' is a masculine gendered name, 'corr' is feminine and 'cóir' is neuter. Furthermore, all three can individually represent both the neck itself and the entire instrument, thereby fulfilling the dual condition established by na comhluighe. Cóir and cor may refer either to harpstring tuning or, allegorically, to a spiritual otherworld tuning of the earthly realm through harp music. Corr signifies the neck's resemblance to a bird, specifically the crane, that has ancient, widespread and intimate associations with both the harp and the heavens or otherworld.

*crott*. This is the older name for the brass-strung harp, but while the wire-strung crott and its traditions predate the ninth century (it appears in *Amhra Coluim Cille*, c. 600 AD), the earliest iconography in Ireland of a verifiable triangular frame harp isn't found until the eleventh century on the Shrine of St Mogue (Meadóg). This bronze plaque shows proto-typical cláirseach elements of a thickened, T-formation forepillar (shaped suspiciously like the zoomorphic figure on the Trinity College and Queen Mary instruments), metal bands on the neck, curved neck and bellied-up soundbox.

All of these characteristics suggest a long development and cultural entrenchment, but they cannot verify the form of the crott centuries before. Earlier stringed instruments associated with David are found carved on stone crosses in Ireland and Scotland. The Irish stones all portray various lyres or psalteries, correctly depicting the Middle Eastern idea of David's kinnor, while Scottish stones on the Christian Pictish fringe, where looser doctrinal conventions existed, portray triangular frame harps. In 1862 Eugene O'Curry used a passage in *Cath Maighe Tuired* to assert a quadrangular shape for the early crott, and every scholar of the passage since has agreed. We find encoded in that same story, which contains names, incantations, rhetoric and terms dating to the linguistic Old Irish period of 600–900 AD, allegorical information strongly implying the pertinent crott to be a triangular frame harp. *Cath Maighe Tuired* is an account of an epic confrontation between the Tuatha De Dannan and their enemies, the Fomoire. The following small section involves the crott and its music (edited and translated by Elizabeth Gray):

Then Lug and the Dagda and Ogma went after the Fomoire, because they had taken the Dagda's cruitire, Uaithne. Eventually they reached the banqueting hall where Bres mac Elathan and Elatha mac Delbaíth were. There was the crot on the wall. That is the cruit in which the Dagda had bound the melodies so that they did not make a sound until he summoned them, saying,

'Come Daurdábláo,
Come Cóircethairchuir,
Come summer, come winter,
Mouth[s] of crot and bolg and buinne!'
(Now that cruit had two names, Daur Dá Bláo and Cóir Cethairchuir.)

Then the crot came away from the wall, and it killed nine men and came to the Dagda; and he played for them the three things by which a cruitire is known: suantraigí and genntraigí and golltraigí. He played golltraigí for them so that their tearful women wept. He played genntraigí for them so that their women and boys laughed. He played suantraigí for them so that the hosts slept. So the three of them escaped from them unharmed – although they wanted to kill them.

Primary evidence for allegory is found in the name Uaithne. The fact that it represents both musician and instrument here and in the only other known appearance of the name (in *Táin Bó Fráich*) implies the two to be equivalent. Uaithne has many meanings and all can be organised into three categories, each representing a part of the cláirseach's frame: support pillar, post and suture identify the strong masculine forepillar; birthing pain and green indicate the fertile feminine soundbox; and union, concordance or harmony point to the neck's role in tuning. Furthermore, the crott's possession of two names is stressed. Modern scholarship edits 'Daurdábláo' as 'Daire Dá Bláo' (oak of two greens, meadows or fields) and 'Cóircethairchuir' as cóir (suitable, fitting or correct) and cethairchuir (four-angled, -cornered, or -peaked). O'Curry et al. concluded that the first name denotes an instrument made of wood and the second portrays its quadrangular shape, resulting in a wooden quadrangular lyre. However, the invocation's third line contains the year's two elemental parts – summer and winter. Because these two seasons make up the whole of a year, the preceding two crott names may be similarly interpreted as making up an entirety for the (whole) crott. A quadrangular meaning of Cóircethairchuir then refers not to the instrument's overall shape, but rather to the shape of one of its parts. On the cláirseach this is obviously the 'quadrangular' soundbox or belly named coim. Regarding Daurdábláo, the adjective 'two' in 'oak of two greens, meadows, or fields' implies the remaining two parts of a tripartite crott, lying in different or separate 'fields'. Thus, collectively, the names Cóircethairchuir and Daurdábláo describe a tripartite crott structure.

Names in the invocation's fourth line yield not only another triplistic entirety for the crott, but reveal attributes of these parts equivalent to those of the cláirseach, as did the name Uaithne. Crot (hump) literally names the cláirseach neck, where sacred regulation or tuning is performed. Bolg (bag, belly, womb) indentifies the feminine soundbox, and buinne (stalk, sapling, torrent) signifies the phallic masculine forepillar.

Dumézil's ideological structure has been heavily used by others analysing *Cath Maighe Tuired*, and it effectively collates the pregnant names in the Dagda's crott episode. The three meanings of Uaithne and the three parts of the incantation augment Dumézil's functions and may be easier understood by integrating them into the cláirseach tradition table (below). All linguistic clues to a tripartite/triangular crott in this passage denote a triangular frame harp in Ireland within or even pre-dating the Old Irish period.

*traditional cláirseach tuning.* Those familiar with the writings of Edward Bunting will no doubt find strange an investigation into cláirseach tuning, for he explicitly reports the harpers to have used a slight variation of the fully diatonic G major scale. However, such a tuning is not consistent with some of the vocabulary he collected from the harpers. The first step in the tuning procedure used by Gaelic harpers from at least 1792 through to the 1849 testimony of Patrick Byrne was to tune two consecutive strings to the pitch of tenor G – na comhluighe. The G pitch represented the ground tone upon which they based their scale. The harpers then tuned in fifths and octaves from na comhluighe G up to F#: G-D-A-E-B-F#. However they didn't complete their tuning in fifths, which would have yielded a C# for the last note and thus a key of two sharps or D major. Instead, after tuning F# they returned again to na comhluighe G and employed the interval of a fourth to produce a C natural. Tuning was then completed in octaves, yielding essentially a G major scale of one sharp that Bunting reported as the harpers' 'natural key'.

Bunting also recorded that on the harp of Denis Hempson, the last harper reported to use his fingernails and therefore presumably the most conservative and faithful to the tradition, the lowest note in this scale was CC, then DD, then EE, which was named 'téad leagtha' (fallen string), then GG, etc. The FF pitch was skipped and all other F strings were pitched at

| CLÁIRSEACH TRADITION TABLE |||
| --- | --- | --- |
| FERTILE | SACRED | PHYSICAL |
| female gender | neuter gender / androgynous | male gender |
| 'she' | 'it' / 'they' | 'he' |
| left | middle; entirety | right |
| treble strings ('female' voice) | comhluighe strings (both genders; tuning foundations) | bass strings ('male' voice) |
| soundbox (2 mortises) | neck (1 mortise and 1 tenon) | pillar (2 tenons) |
| coim | cóir, cor, corr | lamhchrann |
| Coircethairchuir | crott | Daurdablao |
| summer | year | winter |
| bolg | crot | buinne |
| Uaithne (labour pains; green) | Uaithne (union; concordance; harmony) | Uaithne (support; pillar; suture) |
| Goltraighe | Suantraighe | Gentraighe |

F#. When Hempson desired an all-natural scale, the F# strings were lowered to F and the EE string was raised to FF, becoming 'téad leagaidh' (falling string). Logically the name 'falling string' should denote the string's primary pitch, with 'fallen string' naming its secondary pitch. Certainly the implication is that the string is 'falling' or has 'fallen' from its primary position. If this were indeed EE as Bunting claims, then we might expect it to have been named 'rising string' and its secondary FF pitch to have been called 'risen string'. Bunting's recorded names indicate that the string's higher pitch (FF) must have been its original position at some earlier time, resulting in a 'natural key' of C major or G mixolydian mode.

Because there is no reason to doubt the accuracy of Bunting's report, this change was probably an indication of the tradition's decline. The replacement of modal music with the newly adopted system of 'keys' in seventeenth-century European music may have spurred such a change. This musical revolution favoured the sharped seventh and because the harpers didn't want to lose their G ground tone, they sharped the seventh (F) in their G scale. We've seen that the harpers tuned by fifths and one fourth. However, such practice doesn't exhibit the balance, symmetry and consistency one might expect from a highly developed art form. Consistently ascending or descending fifths, or use of na comhluighe as a focal point, ascending from them by fifths for three notes (G-D-A-E) and similarly descending from them by fifths for the last three notes (G-C-F-Bb) would all be reasonable. Such procedures are both consistent and symmetrical. Unfortunately, starting from G, none of them yield a scale of either all naturals or one sharp. The D string – the first scale note derived from na comhluige – is the clue we seek. Called by the harpers 'string of melody', it was named 'téad na [bh]feitheolach', meaning string (téad) of the (na) knowing, skilled, or guiding (eolach) sinews (feith). However the word 'feith' has an old and obscure meaning of 'melody' that exactly renders the harpers' English translation as reported by Bunting: 'string of knowing, skilled, or guiding melody'. The adjective 'eolach' implies a tuning centred around the D or 'string of knowing, skilled, or guiding melody' rather than around na comhluighe themselves. Thus after the first D string had been tuned, the harper would ascend from it in fifths for three notes (D-A-E-B), and then descend from it in fifths for three notes (D-G-C-F), yielding a scale of all naturals or G mixolydian mode.

A parallel may be found in the chanter scale of the great Highland (Scottish) bagpipe. As a music instrument it was second only to the harp in Gaelic regions, and its three-part construction closely resembles the cosmological construction of the cláirseach with a 'male' chanter corresponding to the harp pillar, a 'female' bag corresponding to the soundbox, and 'sacred' drones being a counterpart to the cláirseach neck. If the drones may be thought of as sounding na comhluighe G instead of the A or A# to which their modern pitch falls closest, its nine-note chanter sounds a scale of F-G-A-B-C-D-E-F-G, precisely matching the cláirseach's mixolydian G tuning. (ANH)

*symbolism.* The harp has featured in Ireland not only as a musical instrument but also as a symbol of national identity. From later medieval times the harp and its music were closely identified with Ireland, a thirteenth-century French roll of arms providing the earliest evidence for its use as a symbol of Ireland. The introduction of a harp on King Henry VIII's Anglo-Irish coinage in 1534 confirmed it as a national symbol, although the form depicted on these coins was not itself specifically Irish. It was incorporated into the English royal coat-of-arms in 1603, where it remains representing Northern Ireland, and continued to be used on Anglo-Irish coinage until the nineteenth century. As the symbol of Ireland under British rule, the harp appeared most often in the crowned 'winged-maiden' form first used in the seventeenth century and bearing little relationship to the Irish harp as an instrument of music. Harps of this type are found not only on coins but widely in other contexts including on public buildings of the eighteenth century, for example the Custom House, Dublin. The emergence of nationalism in the late eighteenth and early nineteenth centuries focused attention on the harp as an important emblem of Irish culture. Bunting's publications arising out of the Belfast Harp Festival (1792), a brief revival of interest in harp playing (although not of the true Irish harp) in the early nineteenth century, antiquarian interest in the early Irish harp, and its symbolic use by the United Irishmen which was echoed in Moore's *Irish Melodies*, combined to make the harp one of the major symbols of romantic nationalism. The crowned 'winged-maiden' harp of British rule was replaced in this context by images based on the early Irish harp, and by the mid-nineteenth century the Trinity College (or 'Brian Boru') harp was widely adopted as the model for the harp as a symbol of national aspirations. By the second half of the nineteenth century the harp, along with round towers, shamrock, and wolfhounds, became an ubiquitous symbol of national identity, appearing on buildings and monuments, publications and craftwear, and varying in form from the realistic to the most freely imaginative. Despite a revival in playing a modernised form of Irish harp, the early twentieth century saw a decline in the popularity of the instrument as a symbol. But following the foundation of the Irish Free State in 1921 the harp was officially adopted as the national symbol, being modelled directly on the Trinity College harp, and it has appeared on Irish coins and government publications since that time in a form which has remained substantially unchanged. It was first used as a commercial sign for Guinness stout in the 1850s (also modelled on the Trinity College harp, but facing right instead of left as it usually does as a national symbol), and it still forms the basis for the logo of a number of Irish companies and organisations. (BAB)

*harping conventions.* In the late 1700s, with a new awareness of language, folksong, music and dance as attributes of national distinctiveness, enlightened members of the upper classes set about trying to revive harping or preserve it for posterity. To this end in 1730 the 'Contention of the Bards' had been held at Bruree, Co. Limerick. In 1781 John Dungan, a wealthy Granard, Co. Longford businessman living in Denmark, affected by the awareness of 'national' music imparted through hearing of bag-piping festivals in Scotland, donated twenty-three guineas as prize fund to encourage participation and talent at a harp 'Ball' (festival) in his home town. Present at the first Ball were harpers Charles Fanning, Arthur O'Neill, Paddy Carr, Paddy Maguire, Rose Mooney, Charles Byrne and Hugh Higgins. The following year they were joined by Ned McDermott Roe and Kate Martin, in the final year by Laurence Keane and James Duncan. Thereafter the event was dormant for two centuries until revived in 1981. These festivals developed public awareness of the plight of the harping tradition and created an audience which valued the harpers' art. In July, 1792 the Belfast Harp Festival was organised by a committee which included Dr James McDonnell of Glenariff, and United Irishmen members Thomas Russell, Samuel Neilson and Henry Joy McCracken. Their aim was to 'revive and perpetuate the ancient music and poetry of Ireland'. The only recording facility available in their day was graphic representation of the music, and to this end Edward Bunting was commissioned to transcribe 'the most beautiful and interesting parts' of the harpers' performances. Fanning, O'Neill, Duncan, Higgins, Carr, Byrne and Mooney attended, as well as Denis Hempson, Donald Black and other harpers.

**Harp Foundation, The.** Formed in 1983, it arose out of summer schools organised in Kinsale and Cork and led to the establishment of the Irish Harpers' Association (Cláirseóirí na hÉireann) in 1986. Originally run under the auspices of the Pipers' Club in Dublin, in 1986 it moved with its mentor Janet Harbison to Belfast, where in 1993 the organisation became 'The Harp Foundation'. It covers all aspects of harping, organises educational and recreational activities (summer schools and festivals, concerts and tours for visiting professional artists). It has a harp bank to facilitate beginners and visiting harpers. The foundation runs the Belfast Harp Orchestra – a national harp ensemble – and the Glencolmcille Harp Festival in July each year. It also runs festivals in the Mournes and in Co. Antrim. It operates a certificate system of merit in teaching, and its teaching methods are oral.

**harpsichord.** Member of chordophone family of instruments whose strings are plucked with key-operated plectra rather than (as in piano) being struck with hammers. Technically a zither, it can most easily be visualised as a mechanised harp, with two or three strings sounded for each note. Its strings run away from the player, at right angles to the keyboard, like a grand piano. The oldest dating to Florence in 1515, this is in effect the same instrument as virginal and spinet. Seán Ó Riada initially played it along with Ceoltóirí Chualann as a sound close to that of the harp, Micheál Ó Suilleabháin has also recorded on it.

See chordophone; clavichord; dulcimer; piano.

**Harrington, Kathleen.** (*c*. 1903–84). Fiddle. A major figure in Irish music, she was born at Ballymote, Co. Sligo, into a musical family, the Gardiners. Encouraged by her father Séamus, her older brother John-Joe and sister Mary played first; after his death Kathleen, James and Lucy took it up. Throughout their youth in the Ballymote area the Gardiners were much in demand at house dances and céilís. At age fifteen Kathleen went to work in Kielty's drapers in Boyle, then to London and Liverpool where she and sister Lucy played music with the McNamaras. There too she joined Cumann na mBan and during the War of Independence organised music and dance fund-raisers, herself and Lucy playing in a highly regarded trio with Kerry player Kathleen Corcoran. She married volunteer Seán Harrington in 1923. The Free State silenced the fiddle and brought different work responsibilities that saw them live in Birmingham, Barnsley, Glasgow, Belfast, Lurgan and Boyle, settling eventually in Dublin in the early 1930s. In 1935 she took a trophy at the Fr Mathew Feis. She auditioned for 2RN with her brother John Joe on flute, impressing Séamus Clandillon and Vincent O'Brien; this led to many radio broadcasts with him, and they made several records with both IRC and HMV, many of which were for export. A popular and enthusiastic musician, she won other competitions – one, a duet with piper Seán Seery. Her home boasted visits from the major names in twentieth-century music – Paddy Killoran, James Morrison, Martin Wynne and his sister, Dick O'Beirne (brother of Lad), Batt Henry, Michael Anderson, Dick Brennan, Mickey and Tommy Hunt, Frank O'Higgins, Elizabeth Crotty, Joe Dowd, Fred Finn, Tom Horan, Séamus Tansey, Seán Maguire, Seán McAloon. A founder member of the Kincora Céilí Band in 1937, she was a proactive organiser and worker for the Dublin Pipers' Club, not missing a meeting in twenty years. One of her greatest achievements in the midst of a busy playing life was her role in the setting up of CCÉ, at the beginning of which she travelled all over the country, coping with a huge burden of voluntary secretarial work. Supportive to brother John Joe Gardiner, she worked with the Siamsa band in Dundalk, adjudicating too at fleadhanna. She was affectionately known in CCÉ as both 'auntie Kate' and 'the Queen'.

**Harte, Frank.** (1933–    ). Singer, collector. Born in Dublin and living at Chapelizod, he is an architect attached to Bolton Street College. Introduced to traditional song through a ballad-sheet seller in Boyle, he has amassed a large archive collection of song of all types and is consulted as a leading authority on the song tradition. Seeing himself as a 'story teller in song' he is an important figure in the Irish song revival. He has devised radio lectures and talks on songs and singing at song and music festivals in Ireland, Britain and the US. His albums include *Through Dublin City* (Ossian), *Dublin Street Songs* (Ossian), *We Shall Overcome* (Folkways*)*, *Daybreak and a Candle End* (Claddagh), *And Listen To My Song* (Hummingbird), *1798 – The First Year Of Liberty* (Hummingbird). *Songs of Dublin*, a book of songs, is also published by Ossian.

**Hayes, Martin.** (1962–    ). Fiddle. Born Feakle, Co. Clare, his father PJoe has been fiddler with the Tulla Céilí Band for fifty years. Martin began to play at the age of seven, absorbing the music of local céilí bands, and Coleman, Morrison and Paddy Cronin on records from a young age. He learnt much from such as Feakle concertina player John Naughton, radio programmes like *The Long Note*, and in Galligan's bar at Crusheen he had the opportunity to hear performers like Séamus Ennis. Fiddlers Kathleen Collins and Tommy Potts were an influence too, the latter often visiting the family home, uncle Paddy Canny was also inspirational. At fourteen he began playing with the Tulla band – in Ireland, England and America. Meeting Johnny McGreevy, Liz Carroll, Michael Flatley and Séamus Connolly there drew him to the US to play in 1984, first traditional, then Celtic rock with guitarist Denis Cahill. Reverting to traditional he recorded with Green Linnet and moved to Seattle in 1993, since then travelling constantly in Europe and the US. He considers fiddler and piper Martin Rochford as being intensely in touch with what music is about, and feels similarly about Junior Crehan, Micho Russell, John Kelly and Pádraig O'Keeffe. In his own music he minutely explores melody; his albums stick to one mood and his slow-fuse technique develops sensory structures in ornament, stylistic, melodic and dynamic variation. He teaches at the Willie Clancy summer school each year.

**Heaney, Joe.** See Ó hÉanaí, Seosamh.

**hedge schools.** Eighteenth-century 'unlicensed' schools, so called because of their clandestine nature, often held in the open air in remote places.

Irish higher, secular education took place in bardic schools, these lasting until the mid-1600s. In Christian time there were also monastic schools – these lasting from 450 AD until destruction by Danish invaders in 700 AD, but again established after 900 and surviving until Henry VIII's dissolution of the monasteries in 1539. In 1310 the Statutes of Kilkenny had also forbidden the educating of the native Irish, but this was not of great consequence in Gaelic Ireland outside the Pale. Despite legislation, monastic schools flourished in Ulster – Donegal, Tyrone and Fermanagh – but the Irish nobility sent their children abroad for university education all through the 1600s to some twenty universities (Irish Colleges), e.g. Louvain, Salamanca, Lisbon, Douai, Antwerp, Paris, Prague and Rome. However, students had to be of a certain standard to enter these institutions. Education for the native Catholic Irish in Cromwellian Ireland of the late 1600s was illegal, teachers being under pain of transportation to the Barbadoes. In the 1700s the ban was continued under the 'Penal Laws' and the 'hedge' school so evolved, its teachers heroes, education a political act. The schools were held in crude buildings, financed by the pupils' parents, and staffed by itinerant teachers, many of them educated on the continent: 'Popish Schoole Masrs., trayning . . . in Supersticion, Idolatory and the Evil Customs of the Nacion'. They taught the Classics, Latin, Greek, French, English, mathematics and other aspects of the humanities. Strongest in remote, mountainous areas – in Munster they had a high reputation – some were sophisticated, some crude, existing in towns too. They were most numerous up until 1782 when the Education Act then allowed for the licensing of schools but only at the discretion of the Protestant clergy. Hedge schoolmasters might well be poets too, and celebrated are Donnchadh Ruadh MacNamara, Cratloe, Co. Clare (c. 1740), Brian Merriman of Feakle (c. 1770), Eoghan Rua Ó Súilleabháin, Meentogues, Co. Kerry (b. 1748). Hedge schools continued until Catholic Emancipation in 1829, and were obliterated by cheaper education, under the National Board of Education, in the national schools which were to contribute decisively to the elimination of the Irish language (the teaching of which the hedge school teachers had championed). It is estimated that by 1824 there may have been 9,000 hedge schools in Ireland. (Ref.: Dowling, *The Hedge Schools of Ireland*, 1985)

See Ó Súilleabháin, Eoghan Rua; song, hedge school.

**Henderson, Hamish.** (1919– ). Folklorist, poet, translator, songwriter, political activist. Born Blairgowrie, Perthshire, Scotland. He served in the Italian and Western Desert campaigns of World War II, which inspired his 1948 cycle of poems *Elegies for the Dead in Cyrenaica*. Immediately after the war he worked as district secretary for the Northern Ireland branch of the Workers' Education Association. This brought him into contact with singers in places like Maghery, Co. Armagh. In 1950, Alan Lomax asked him to accompany him on his epic collecting tour for the Scottish leg of the Colombia world series of recordings. Through this he met Irish Folklore Commission worker Calum MacLean, and also Armagh song collector Seán O'Boyle with whom he travelled in the Scottish western isles. Joining the School of Scottish Studies in 1952, his fieldwork brought many magnificent but previously unknown singers like Jeannie Robertson to international notice. Known as the father of the Scottish Folk Revival he organised céilithe in Edinburgh and elsewhere from the early 1950s at which urban folk-song enthusiasts were brought in to contact with rural and traveller singers who were carriers of Scotland's ballad tradition. A champion of bawdy song, his *Ballads of World War II* (Glasgow, 1947) was far before its time in the history of the publication of unexpurgated folk-song. The broad sweep of Henderson's mind can best be appreciated in *Alias MacAlias: Writings on Songs, Folk and Literature* (Edinburgh, Polygon, 1992). His involvement with the revival continues actively as does his writing, notably his ongoing cycle, *Auld Reekie's Roses*. A collection of his work *Freedom Come All Ye: The Poems and Songs of Hamish Henderson* was published in 1977 by Claddagh. The eponymous songs and others from his pen like 'The 51st Highland Division's Farewell to Sicily' and 'John McClean's March' have themselves passed into the oral tradition. (TOM)

**Henebry, The Revd Richard.** (1863–1916). Born Portlaw, Co. Waterford to an Irish-speaking family of 'strong farmers', he was ordained in 1892, studied Celtic philology in Germany and was appointed Professor of Celtic at the Catholic University, in Washington DC. He was later Professor of Irish at University College, Cork from 1909 until his death in 1916. An ignored figure in the traditional music revival, his contribution has been important. A traditional fiddle player and a piper in later life, he was drawn to attempt to analyse the structure of the music, although he had no formal musical education. This resulted in two publications, a small work entitled *Irish Music* (1903), and the posthumous *A Handbook of Irish Music* (1928, Cork). Henebry's approach in these works is typically idiosyncratic, and yet they must be ranked among the earliest works of ethnomusicology which was only in its infancy at the time. Such analysis has fallen out of fashion among ethnomusicologists today, and few, even among Irish music academics, have read his works. One of Henebry's more important contributions to Irish music is the collection of wax cylinder recordings which bears his name and which is now housed in UCC. This collection consists of two distinct parts. First there is a series of cylinders, American in origin, recorded by Capt. Francis O'Neill in Chicago prior to 1905. Henebry and O'Neill had met in Chicago, and Henebry merits several mentions in O'Neill's own publications. The cylinders, sent to Henebry as a birthday present in 1907, consist of recordings of some of the best known of the Chicago-Irish musicians of the day, including the pipers Patsy Touhey and James Early and the fiddle player James McFadden. Some of them have been re-issued on the NPU cassette, *The Piping of Patsy Touhey* (1986). Secondly, there are the cylinders which Henebry himself recorded as part of a scheme which was funded by UCC in 1911 and seems to have been run in conjunction with the Music Department where Carl Hardebeck was professor at the time (his name appears on many of the boxes housing the cylinders). Almost all of this section of the collection was made in the Déise region of Waterford, and as such comprises what are in all probability the earliest field recordings of Irish traditional music and singing. These are in a bad state of preservation and almost none of the recordings of the Déise singers have survived in an audible state. The instrumental recordings are better, and are almost entirely of the Kilkenny-born, but Waterford resident, fiddle player Tom Higgins. Although few enough of the recordings are audible (they were transferred to tape by the British Sound Archive) they still represent a very important resource from several points of view. Firstly, the American material is all that survives of the extensive collection that O'Neill amassed, the remainder having been lost or destroyed. Secondly, they represent some of the very few non-commercial recordings of this period, from both Ireland and Irish-America. Finally the McFadden/Early duets are in all probability the earliest known recordings of ensemble playing in the tradition.

Henebry suffered from TB for almost all of his adult life and it was this that eventually led to his death at the age of fifty-three. Had he lived, we might have seen him amass a great collection of field recordings, since coming from the traditional background that he did, he was one of the very few academic researchers of the period who seems to have really understood the traditional player and singer. Henebry was eccentric and despite his undoubted linguistic and musical talents (he spoke thirteen languages and played many instruments, some of which, including his pipes, he made himself) managed to make many enemies in the course of his life. His outspoken nature and complete lack of diplomacy contributed to preventing him from reaching his full potential. (HAH)

**Hennelly, Patrick.** Uilleann pipe maker, Chicago. Born 1896 in Seefin, Co. Mayo, he emigrated to New York City in 1924, moved to Philadelphia in 1925 and to Chicago in 1928. Until the 1970s he was the only twentieth-century maker of uilleann pipes in North America. He experimented with exterior designs, materials and internal dimensions; he made many of his tools himself. As a child he had made simple reed whistles in the European shepherd-boy fashion, then played fife in a marching band in Castlebar where he served his time with a coachbuilder. There he learned to read music, studied wind instruments, wood-working tools, crafting and turning. Meeting pipers Tom Ennis, Billy McCormick and his son, Hugh, Edward Mullaney, Mike Joyce, Hughie McCullough and Charlie McNurney in Chicago developed his knowledge of pipes and piping lore; John Ennis (Tom's father), Joe Sullivan and John Flynn taught him reed-making. He used the Taylor model as his blueprint and began making full sets in the early 1930s. After World War II he continued making new sets and doing repairs, and teaching aspects of pipe making. In 1976 his work gained him a National Endowment for the Arts research project award, and he was a featured artist at the Smithsonian Festival of American Folklife. Examples of his work can be seen in *A Manual for the Irish Uilleann Pipes* by Patrick Sky (Silver Spear Publications, 1980). (LAM)

**Henry, Johnny.** (1922–97). Fiddle. Born at Doocastle, Co. Sligo, he began to play fiddle at age ten learning from Sarah Tuohy, she originally from Foxford, Co. Mayo. Later lessons came from locals Pat Kellegher, and P. J. Giblin of Charlestown. Sunday night sessions at Bartley Meehan's house in Curragh in the 1940s were his hey-day; memorable influences were Paddy Meehan (flute), Packie Batty Gallagher (flute), Paddy Jim Frank (flute), Pat Kellegher (fiddle), John Michael Cawley (fiddle) and Michael Joe Ryan (flute). His brother Kevin is a noted flute player in Chicago, his 1998 recording a window on younger days in Co. Sligo.

**Henry, Sam.** (1878–1952). Song collector and amateur polymath, Officer of Customs and Excise Office, Unionist Councillor in Coleraine, Co. Derry. He became interested in traditional songs through his contact with people whose old age pension claims he assessed when pensions were instituted in 1908. He instigated and was the principal editor of the *Northern Constitution* newspaper's series 'Songs of the People' and was the author of numerous articles (on natural history, topography, folklore and other subjects, many of which included his own photographs) in Irish and provincial newspapers. He lectured widely and was a pioneer broadcaster on the same subjects as well as upon his song collection. Enormously popular in these rôles – a person listed in *Who's Who in Ulster* (*c.* 1939) listed among his hobbies 'Listening to Sam Henry'. Enormously proud of his song collection he said his choice of epitaph would be 'He put an old song in their mouths'. Sam Henry left a substantial unpublished collection of songs and information relating to them and their singers and this is currently being edited. (JOM)

See also Sam Henry Collection.

**Hensey, Áine.** (1959– ). Radio presenter. Born in Dublin she began a career in journalism in 1978, first working for pirate radio in Galway. She joined RTÉ in 1979 to present traditional music programmes *The Heather Breeze* (1979–81) and *Sunday Folk* (1981–85). In the same period she was also a PRO for Gael-Linn, working with Slógadh and youth projects. In 1989 she began presenting traditional music programmes with Clare FM, with them producing *The Humours of Clare,* an album of

Clare musicians. She has been with Raidió na Gaeltachta since 1995 with the largely-traditional, weekend *Béal Maidine*. She was a host for RTÉ 1's *Sounds Traditional* (1996–98), and currently presents their Friday *Late Session*.

**Hernon, P. J.** (1951– ). Button accordion. Born in Cama, Connemara he now lives in Gurteen, Co. Sligo. His father played melodeon and he himself was influenced by Paddy O'Brien through neighbour, Mickey Berry. Playing two row accordion, he won senior All-Ireland solo accordion in 1973, played with Shaskeen from 1971–76, toured Canada, US and England 1974–75, and has also taught music since 1982. Shaskeen recorded albums in 1972 and '76, Hernon recorded a solo tape for Gael-Linn in 1978, later two duet albums with his brother Marcus (flute), and in 1985 a solo record *First House in Connaught*. He features on two set dancing tapes and co-produced two CDs for the Coleman Heritage Centre in 1994 and 1997. He has presented music programmes for Raidió na Gaeltachta between 1994 and 1995, and for Teilifís na Gaeilge in 1996. He plays presently with the Swallows Tail Céilí Band. (GRD)

**Hicks, Jerry.** (1916–95). Singer, songwriter, collector. Born in Cork, his family moved to the North and he was educated at St Patrick's College, Armagh from 1928. After graduation from Queen's University he took up teaching and was appointed to St Patrick's in 1942 where he was a colleague of Seán O'Boyle. Passionate about language and music, he was inspirational to many, including David Hammond and Tony McAuley (BBC). A schools broadcaster, he recorded a solo album of song in Irish – *Ceolta Uladh* (1971), and sang in English on *Dobbin's Flowery Vale* with Cathal McConnell, Seán McAloon and Tommy Gunn. He considered much of his satirical work private and it has not been published. 'Craigavon' is reputed to be the finest of this and 'Roving Sporting Blade' a significant parody that reflected his passion for hunting. He satirised local events such as the Armagh flood, even the fleadh cheoil and its absurdities, and, unusual for his era, accompanied himself on guitar. A few of his pieces appear with reminiscences in Irish and English in the booklet *Remembering Jerry Hicks* (1997).

**highland.** Properly called the 'Highland Schottische'. This is a couple dance introduced to Co. Donegal in the mid-1800s by migratory workers returning from Scotland. A local variant of the dance also emerged which was known as the Irish highland. The dance itself is no longer common, but the tune-type remains popular within the Donegal fiddle music repertoire. The highland is in 4/4 time with an accent on the first beat of the bar, which is usually of crotchet value. The tempo is more relaxed than that of the reel. The highland is characterised by the use of dotted rhythms articulated in a subtle manner

The Highland Man (Highland) (LID)

and not in the jagged fashion popular in Scotland. This, combined with the tempo chosen, creates the swing peculiar to the highland. While a number of new highlands were composed in Donegal it was also common for popular reel tunes to be broken down into highlands. Many highlands are based on existing Scottish strathspey melodies. Tunes such as 'Neil Gow's Wife', 'Maggie Cameron' and 'Brochan Lom' all exist as highlands in Donegal. In some cases the same title is retained; otherwise a new name is created e.g. 'Miss Lyall Strathspey' is known as the highland 'The Cat that Kittled in Jamie's Wig'. (LID)

*the dance*. Outside of Ulster, the highland is more commonly referred to as either a fling or a schottische. Older fiddlers believe the origin of the term 'highland' stems from its appearance in popular printed music collections describing tunes as a 'highland schottische'. Today, only one dance is generally done to a highland, this corresponding to what was called in Irish-speaking areas of North Donegal the 'highland beag' (little highland). Two other forms of the highland did exist and are now virtually extinct – the 'highland garbh' (rough highland, a couple dance), and the 'highland gaelach' (Irish highland), done with one boy and two girls. (CMA)

See fiddle, Donegal; German.

**Hill, James.** (*c*. 1814–60). Fiddler and composer. Born at Dundee, Scotland he moved with his family when he was ten to Newcastle. His years of prolific tunesmithing were between 1840 and 1850. His compositions include 'The High Level Bridge', The Low Level Bridge', 'The Bee's Wing', The Hawk' and 'The Steamboat' hornpipes, all played by Irish musicians.

**Hill, Noel.** (1958– ). Concertina. Born at Caherea, Ennis, Co. Clare, both his parents played concertina, as did both sets of grandparents and their siblings. He learnt from his mother at around the age of nine, and picked up the parental repertoire rapidly. His uncle Paddy introduced him to the playing of Paddy Murphy and Willie Clancy, his reputation and interest intensified, and by the age of seventeen he had already recorded the album *Inchiquin* with fiddler Tony Linnane, guitarist Tony Callanan and banjo player Kieran Hanrahan. The latter two's departure to form Stockton's Wing saw Noel and Tony play as a duo, recording the seminal *Noel Hill and Tony Linnane* in 1978 with Matt Molloy and Alec Finn. Another outstanding album followed in 1985 – *I gCnoc na Graí* – recorded in Dan O'Connell's bar with Tony MacMahon and a group of Clare set dancers. His solo album, *The Irish Concertina* (1988) is a definitive document in the instrument's playing; more recently he recorded *Aislingí Ceoil* with MacMahon and Iarla Ó Lionaird. He has played all over Ireland, Europe, the US and in China.

**Hitchner, Earle.** Writes on Irish and various musics for *The Wall Street Journal*, *Irish Echo*, *CTMS Journal*, and other publications. He has also written the liner notes for some thirty albums on such labels as RCA, Sony, Green Linnet and Shanachie, and been twice appointed to the nominating committee for the annual Association for Independent Music (AFIM) awards (USA). His radio show from 1984 to 1989 in the greater New York City area presented more than 150 musicians live in the studio, and he has consulted on or been featured in two highly praised documentaries on Irish traditional music that were broadcast on US public television.

**Hogans of Cashel.** A family of famous Tipperary musicians of the late 1800s. The father, Tom, and three sons were noted uilleann pipers; two other sons Michael and Larry were accomplished fiddlers.

**Holland, Jerry.** (1955– ). Cape Breton fiddler. Born and raised in the Boston area, he learned music from his father and from friends in both the Cape Breton and Irish music communities. Main early influences include Winston Fitzgerald, Angus Chisholm and Bill Lamey. He moved to Cape Breton in the mid-1970s and is a renowned composer and recording artist. (PAC)

**Holmes, Joe.** (1906–78). Singer, fiddle player. Born in Killyrammer near Ballymoney, Co. Antrim. He got a fiddle at the age of twelve from his brother Harry who had brought it home from France at the end of World War I in 1918. Two years later his first job was carrying the red danger flag in front of a steamroller for a north Antrim road contractor. This brought him around many of the Co. Antrim villages and towns and into contact with local musicians and singers. At that time the steamroller would also tow the wooden caravan in which the workers slept; Joe always brought the fiddle with him. His grandfather was also a fiddler as was his brother; his mother was a singer, and Joe inherited many of her songs. Their home was a popular 'céilí-house' frequented by travelling musicians such as fiddler and singer John McAfee, one of Sam Henry's contributors to the *Songs of the People* newspaper column. Other visitors to Joe's family home were Paddy McCloskey (who contributed to Peter Kennedy's *Folksongs of Britain and Ireland*) and Felix and Johnny Doran, the Wexford pipers, on their way to the Lammas Fair in Ballycastle. This sort of céilí-ing with song and dance was common to many houses in Co. Antrim regardless of religious background. Unmarried, most of Joe's social life was spent travelling around on a motor bike with the fiddle strapped on his back, sharing tunes and songs and playing for dancers. He played for quadrilles, four- and eight-hand reels, polkas, schottisches, lancers and mazurkas – this might account for similarities between his repertoire and that of Denis Murphy and Julia Clifford, this observed when he visited them with Len Graham in his latter days. Many of his tunes were the same but under different titles – for instance, Pádraig O'Keeffe's 'Farewell to Whiskey' was Joe's 'Neil Gow's Farewell to Whiskey'. Some of his music has passed on to a younger generation of fiddlers; Frankie Gavin recorded his 'Peacock's Feather'. Much of his wealth of music and song, including Child ballads, was recorded by his singing partner and friend Len Graham whom he met at an Antrim and Derry Fiddlers gathering in Dunminning near Ballymena in 1963 when Len was nineteen and Joe was fifty-seven. Holmes had stopped singing in the late 1940s just after the war, but contact with Graham got him involved again. They struck up a unique singing partnership which lasted until Joe's death. Unison singing, a common feature in the northern song tradition led to their recording two albums as a duo – *Chaste Muses, Bards and Sages* (1975) and *After Dawning* (1978). Joe can also be heard on the recordings: *Early Ballads in Ireland* (ed. Hugh Shields and Tom Munnelly, 1985) and on Graham's field recordings *It's of My Rambles* (1993). Joe Holmes' songs are now sung and recorded by many of a younger generation of singers including the groups Dervish, Boys of the Lough, Altan and the Voice Squad, and by solo singers like Tríona Ní Dhomhnaill and Len Graham himself. (LEG)

**Horan, Peter.** (1926–  ). Flute and fiddle. Born Killavil, Co. Sligo. He inherited a rich musical tradition from his mother, Margaret Davey (fiddle, melodeon, concertina), but due to a predominance of fiddle playing locally in his youth, his flute playing remained largely free of influence. Consequently he developed a unique style and technique but his fiddle style was much influenced by Michael Coleman and his tune selections are very representative of the South Sligo tradition. He began playing flute in duet with Fred Finn (fiddle) in 1959, their unaccompanied playing becoming legendary. He has also made many recordings for television and radio and toured America several times in the 1970s. Records include an LP with Fred Finn in 1988 (CCÉ), an LP with the Coleman Céilí Band (US 1972). He features on *Music from Coleman Country* (1972). An important link between past and present traditional music in Co. Sligo, he currently teaches flute at the Tubbercurry summer school and plays locally. (GRD)

**Horan, Séamus.** (1932–  ). Fiddle, button accordion. Born Creevalea, Killargue, Co. Leitrim. Early influences included his father, James (melodeon), and local players Joe Gallagher (fiddle) and Dan McGowan (flute). He played with the Shannon Star Céilí Band in the early 1960s which included James Early (fiddle) and Packie Duignan (flute). He partnered Packie Duignan on a fine fiddle and flute duet album (Topic 1978) and played with the Coleman Country Céilí Band in the early 1970s. His impressive North Leitrim fiddle style has influenced many younger local musicians. (GRD)

Humours of Tullycreen (hornpipe) (An Gúm)

**horn.** See trumpet.

**hornpipe.** 1. A primitive, double-reed instrument dating from the thirteenth century, examples described in eighteenth-century Scottish sources and in Wales where it is called a pibgorn. 2. A dance and related music originating around the middle of the eighteenth century and with maritime connections (through ship companies carrying a resident fiddler who provided music for dancing). The later, common time, version of the tune-type made its way to Ireland where it was adopted by the dancing-masters as a show piece. The heavy stepping involved deemed it unsuitable for female dancers and for a number of years it remained solely the domain of the male. The hornpipe today is used in solo dancing and also in certain set-dances. The tune-type is characterised by a relatively slow tempo and the use of dotted rhythms. It is performed in a deliberate manner with a definite accent on beats one and three of each bar. Three accented crotchet beats generally mark the end of a part. Hundreds of examples are contained in O'Neill's and Cole's collections. The hornpipe most likely came from England in the late 1700s. There it had taken its present form in the 1760s and was a figure dance, its older forms in 3/2 time and was performed between acts of plays usually by professional dancers. In Ireland it became the supreme display of intricate foot-work. Well-known composers of hornpipes known to us include Ed Reavy, Seán Ryan, James Scott Skinner, Paddy Kelly, Paddy Fahey and perhaps most notably James Hill of Newcastle. (LID)

**Horslips.** A 'Celtic Rock' band which combined traditional music melody instrumental principles with rock backing. Formed in 1970, it had Barry Devlin (bass, voice), Declan Sinnott (lead guitar, voice), Charles O'Connor (fiddle), Jim Lockhart (flute, fiddle, keyboards), Eamonn Carr (drums, voice). Their motifs were the heroes and tales of Irish mythology; hinting at traditional flavour, their 'Flower of the Flock' reached many ears on that account. Crossing between two worlds they perhaps were aliens in both, but while they made the British top 40 with the album, *The Book of Invasions – A Celtic Symphony*, they were regarded suspiciously by traditional music which, in the process of revival, tended to legitimate itself amidst hostility by damning the superficiality of what was seen as 'tune dabbling' and backing-supremacy – the reverse of the priorities of traditional musicians. Their albums continue to be re-released long after their 1979 break-up – the definitive collection being *Happy to Meet Sorry to Part* (1973), and compilations *Horslips History* covering the band's work from 1972 to 1979. Horslips were part of an interface between the brash popular-music dominated world and the small and often understandably embittered world of traditional music which was doggedly developing status and state recognition in the late 1960s and early 1970s. The band mediated traditional music spread by adopting its catchy pieces, dressing them in a music formula understandable to the children of generation which – especially in urban centres – had moved on from traditional music as its medium of entertainment. Broadcasting this to a huge audience through records and live performance resulted in further interest: many were drawn to 'the pure drop' (as others had been several years previously through the Clancy Brothers and the Dubliners) and ultimately began themselves to play.

**Howe, Elias.** (1820–95). Music publisher and fiddler. Born Framingham, Massachusetts, a member of the family who invented the sewing machine; another wrote 'Battle Hymn of the Republic'. He taught himself fiddle from a printed tutor, worked as a ploughboy and learned tunes from local players, noting their tunes in a copybook. Loaning this to his friends to help them learn tunes suggested the idea of a tune-book to him; he published it as *The Musician's Companion* in 1840, but he was obliged to sell it himself door to door as music stores resented the competition to their lucrative single-tune sheet music. Huge success led him to open a music shop; he collected more music and published a variety of popular tune and tutor books, among them *Howe's Accordeon Instructor* (1845, it sold 100,000 copies), *Accordion Without a Master* (1851), *Howe's School for the Flageolet* (1858), *Howe's School for Violin* (1860), *Howe's One Thousand Jigs and Reels: Clog Dances, Contra Dances, Fancy Dances, Hornpipes, Strathspeys, Breakdowns, Irish Dances, Scotch Dances, &c. &c., for the Violin, Flute, Clarionet, Cornet, Fife, Flageolet, or any treble instrument* (c. 1867), *Songs of Ireland* (1882). His business became centre to a large network of brass and dance bands who appear to have used it as a contact address. His contribution to Irish music however was the publication with William Bradbury Ryan of *Ryan's Mammoth Collection* of tunes.

See Ryan, William Bradbury.

**Hoy, Mick.** (1913– ). Fiddle player, raconteur, singer. One of Derrygonnelly, West Fermanagh's greatest cultural resources, a wit and authority on local tradition, his singing – like his air playing – has the finest artistry of glottal stop and variation. His music style is a blend of the very local, and of the Coleman legacy, biting and uplifting, his repertoire learned in part from his accordionist mother, and from renowned local flute player Eddie Duffy. As a youth he got himself hired as a labourer at Derrygonnelly Fair by a fiddle player in order to learn the instrument, eventually playing in céilí bands through the 1930s and '40s. Cathal McConnell plays many of his tunes with Boys of the Lough.

See Fermanagh.

**Hudson, Henry.** (1798–1889). While studying with Edward O'Reilly, at the age of fourteen he began his 'collecting' of Irish music when he transcribed his teacher's music manuscripts in 1812. The house in which he was reared – The Hermitage, in Rathfarnham, Co. Dublin – was later to become Pádraig Pearse's school, St Enda's. Hudson became a state dentist, and lived for many years at No. 24 Stephen's Green, Dublin. His collection comprises seven small books which became separated when the Hudson library was sold off *c.* 1901 to Nassau Massey, a bookseller in Patrick Street, Cork, who then sold them on. The Hudson Collection comprises some 870 tunes, songs and 'snatches', it ends with a version of 'Danny Boy' in five flats. One volume contains 113 melodies composed by Henry Hudson. The first three volumes contain 370 tunes. Of these, Vol. 3 was sold to Captain Francis O'Neill and is housed with the rest of the O'Neill Collection in the Hesburgh Library at the University of Notre Dame, Indiana. Vol. 2 became the property of piping enthusiast and bookworm, Séamus Ó Casaide and was purchased by the National Library of Ireland after his death. The other five volumes are housed in the Allen A. Brown Collection at the Boston Public Library and include Vol. 1 of the above set of three, as well as the volume exclusively dedicated to Hudson's original compositions, and another set of three volumes which contains the complete collection of 870 tunes rewritten as his *General Miscellaneous Collection*. Hudson's copying was begun sometime between December 1841 and January 1842 and a number of the tunes were published in *The Citizen* or *Dublin Monthly Magazine* in the early 1840s. To refute a statement by Edward Bunting to the effect that the 'last airs having any Irish character were Jackson's' (i.e. composed by Walker Jackson d. 1798), Hudson set about composing tunes and published thirty-eight of them, labelled as traditional airs, in *The Citizen*. He was delighted to hear of Bunting's jealousy of the music and when Bunting declared only one melody to be 'not Irish', Hudson took this as a tacit admission that the others had been accepted as genuine. However, Hudson never publicly admitted his trick, and some of the tunes have appeared in other collections such as Petrie's. As with many of his fellow amateur collectors Hudson thought nothing of borrowing tunes from published and MSS sources and so we find, along with his own field-work, tunes attributed to Walker's *Irish Bards* and Metzler's *Magic Flageolet* among the published sources, and 'from Miss Woodroofe's Book' and 'from F. M. Bell' among the manuscript sources. No doubt he continued to collect tunes for a number of years but there is no noticeable change in his handwriting towards the end of the manuscripts, suggesting that he did not do much after the 1850s. With the deaths of his older brothers, he inherited the family estate at Glenville where he remained until he died. (JIO)

**Hudson, William Elliot.** (1796–1853). Henry Hudson and his brother, William Elliot, with a certain degree of anonymity, embarked on the editing and presentation of music in *The Citizen* (later the *Dublin Monthly Magazine*). It is known that William certainly provided funding for the magazine and the following account suggests he made a literary and editorial contribution. However, it seems most likely that Henry was the music editor of *The Native Music of Ireland* from notes in his manuscripts. A number of his compositions survive, the best known of which is the music for *The Memory of the Dead* ('Who Fears to Speak of '98'). A brief synopsis of William's life can be derived from his obituary, written by John O'Daly, which appeared in Vol. 5 of the *Transactions* of the Ossianic Society in 1856. Having described William's very successful legal career O'Daly continues:

Amongst his other accomplishments, W. E. Hudson early displayed a taste for music and a musical talent of the highest order. That he had acquired a practical and theoretical knowledge of that science far beyond his compeers was often tested, and especially by Dr Russell, a highly gifted clergyman, and himself a great theorist. This gentleman, aware of the acuteness of W. E. Hudson's ear in distinguishing sound, put him to the severest proofs, without a single instance of failure; this induced him to test, through young Hudson, the accuracy of a theory which he held, that every natural sound, such as the roaring of a furnace, the howling of the storm, thunder, water falling in unison, were all one and the same note – the great 'A' of nature. Day after day for nearly three months Hudson accompanied Dr Russell from place to place to catch what he called 'natural sounds'; and so elated was he with the proofs given of the perfection of his own theory that it required the utmost vigilance of his physicians to prevent his intellect from becoming impaired.

In after years W. E. Hudson was the composer of a Te Deum and several chants, none of which were ever published; he likewise composed a variety of songs but his naturally modest and retiring habits prevented putting himself forward, and thereby caused his fame, either as a literary character or as a musical composer, to have a much more limited circulation than would be expected in the case of a person so highly gifted. When *The Citizen* was tottering in its fall, its publishers made a desperate effort to restore its vitality by bringing it out in a new form and under a new name, as the *Dublin Monthly Magazine*. In this struggle Mr Hudson lent the assistance of his purse and talents, and chiefly owing to his exertions, it revived for a while. Besides contributing to it in a literary way, he brought it out in a collection of Irish airs, the finest published since the days of Bunting.

Mr Hudson was the founder of the Irish Archaeological Society, and also the Ossianic Society for the preservation and publication of ancient Irish Manuscripts. Also the success of *Library of Ireland* and *The Spirit of the Nation*, are in a great measure due to Mr Hudson. His death, which occurred on the 23rd of June, 1853, may be truly regarded as a heavy blow and irreparable loss to the best interests of our Society.

William Elliot Hudson's name appears in many manuscripts and notices of the time and his circle of friends and acquaintances included Thomas Davis and James Clarence Mangan. (JIO)

**Hughes, Harry.** (1947– ). Born Foxford, Co. Mayo. Educated there and at University College, Galway, he undertook postgraduate study at Louvain, Belgium. Since 1970 he has taught English and history at St Joseph's Secondary School, Spanish Point, Co. Clare. His father played melodeon and the village had the Foxford Céilí Band in the early 1960s. He was the initiator of the *Dal gCais* annual, and has been its editor since 1972. The publication arose out of meeting piper Martin Talty who introduced him to the great names in West Clare music. Since 1973 he has been one of the main organisers of the annual Scoil Samhraidh Willie Clancy at Miltown Malbay, Co. Clare.

**Hummingbird.** Production company established in 1987 by Philip King and Nuala O'Connor to produce music documentary programmes. Now one of Ireland's leading independent producers of arts and music programming, its core activity remains documentary and studio Irish-music material. Its associated company Hummingbird Records has produced four programme-generated albums: *Bringing It All Back Home*, *River of Sound*, *Meitheal* and *Sult*. The company has succeeded in developing and sustaining relationships outside the domestic broadcasting market which have enabled the distribution of its material into the UK, the US and other territories. To date it has been nominated for a Grammy Award and won an Emmy Award for *Irish Music and America – A Musical Migration* in 1994.

See King, Philip; O'Connor, Nuala.

**Hunt, Michael.** (1904– ). Fiddle. Born at Lisananny, Ballymote, Co. Sligo, brother of flute and pipes player Tommy. Local fiddler Philip O'Beirne – one of Michael Coleman's first, and most important teachers – was an early influence on his playing and he played duet with his brother Tommy throughout his life. Michael recalls seeing Coleman playing and dancing in the family home, and he himself learned step-dancing from dancing master George Leonard (Dublin), giving many exhibition performances in the 1930s and '40s. Influenced by recordings of Coleman, his repertoire is typical of the South Sligo area, with many intriguing older versions of common tunes. He has recorded for radio, and still lives in the family home, a fund of knowledge on a century of local music and related matters. (GRD)

**Hunt, Tommy.** (1908–94). Uilleann pipes, flute, tin whistle. Born at Lisananny, Ballymote, Co. Sligo. His father Tom played flute, concertina and melodeon; neighbours included such people as flute player Mrs Doyle, Philip O'Beirne (fiddle), Paddy Killoran (fiddle), Jim Coleman (fiddle) and John Joe Gardiner (fiddle, flute). Introduced to pipes by local piper John Anderson who also made his first set, Tommy favoured the 'tight' style of piping and was much influenced by Patsy Touhey. Piper Johnny Doran was a regular visitor to the family home in the 1930s. Tommy played a simple-system concert flute for many years but changed later to the Böehm at which he excelled. He had an extensive repertoire of old and new tunes, these he added to up to his death. Together with Dick Brennan he recorded a 78 rpm disc at Jury's Hotel, Dublin in 1933, he recorded for radio and gave many concert performances but never entered any form of competition. (GRD)

**idiophone.** Self-sounding instrument. The term applies to cymbals, rhythm sticks and instruments such as bones, bass-drum woodblocks and castanets, but is also the generic term covering items as diverse as jew's harp, bells, xylophones, wind chimes, tambourine jingles, music-boxes, foot-stamping, hand-clapping, bottle-clicking and table-tapping with coins. Idiophones may be stamped on the ground, shaken, struck with a striker, struck against each other (bones), scraped (Latin music's 'guiros' scraper) or plucked (jew's harp). Idiophones play a part in ancient Irish music, but mostly in early Christian use, O'Curry noting crotals and clocca (religious bells), craebh ciuil and crann ciuil (possibly small, beater-played bells on a branched holder).

See bones; jew's harp; *Musical Instruments of the Ancient Irish*; wood block.

**IMRO (Irish Music Rights Organisation).** The collection agency for public performance royalties due to Irish composers, players and publishers, including those involved in traditional music. Through membership pledges, internal balloting and conferences it is owned and run, composed of and directed by, all its composer/publisher members, and includes many people involved in the playing, composing and publishing of traditional music. IMRO is run by an internally elected board through a full-time, paid staff and director; it is a non-profit organisation, limited by guarantee. It administers the performing rights of its members by the granting of licences to and the collection of royalties from, music performance venues and broadcasters; it then distributes such royalties to its members. IMRO is therefore only concerned with live, public performance, and with airwaves and PA broadcast of recorded performances. A member of CISAC (The International Confederation of Societies of Authors and Composers), IMRO was created in 1989 as a response to a growing need for a national society in Ireland to administer performing rights on behalf of Irish composers, authors and publishers. Until then, these rights had been administered by the UK-based Performing Rights Society (PRS). IMRO also represents foreign composers, authors and music publishers through reciprocal agreements with similar societies around the world. (ANM)

See copyright.

Sarah Anne O'Neill (right) with Róisín White and Joe Mulhearn at the singers' weekend at Inishowen, Co. Donegal, 1996        (EDI)

**Inishowen.** See song, Inishowen.

**Inishowen International Folk Song and Ballad Seminar.** The first weekend seminar was organised in March 1990 to promote the Inishowen song tradition and to bring it to a wider audience. Themes discussed to date have been the Scottish, Northern Irish and Donegal connections in the folk-song and ballad tradition, love songs of Britain and Ireland, songs of emigration, traveller songs, narrative songs in the Irish tradition, songs of the sea, songs of war and rebellion and humour in traditional song. The seminar – effectively a festival – presents about twenty singers and speakers annually from a wide spectrum of the song tradition at home and abroad. Dozens of singers from the local area and many others from all over the country attend, and several from Scotland and England, most singing in the informal sessions.

**innovation.** 1. A term loosely used to denote new direction or change, particularly in traditional music. 2. Described in Webster's (1971) dictionary as 'something that deviates from established doctrine or practice', and 'differs from existing forms'; to 'innovate' is to 'introduce as, or as if, new; to introduce novelties; make changes'. The concept of innovation can be interpreted as both contradictory and complementary to the dynamic idea of 'tradition' as expressed in the popularly-used term 'living tradition'. In essence social evolution, a battle between reverence for the past and the compulsion to explore and change, in traditional music it can be seen in two forms:

1. players draw on the past, but constantly move forward with history adopting and adapting other instruments and music genres within their experience (Davy Spillane, Donal Lunny, Eileen Ivers, Mel Mercier);

2. players search for artistic engagement within the established instrumentation, repertoire and melodic centre (Liz Carroll, Martin Hayes, John Carty).

However both approaches cannot avoid being informed by the varied cultural and economic experiences of their exponents. No clear lines can be drawn to confine artistic temperament or virtuosic skill. In the final analysis the matter is probably reduced to 'taste', with both categories recognised as having 'musicians' musicians'. This produces the view of traditional music as a mosaic or marl with many different colours and textures, skills and intuitive ability, each from its extremity gradually shading into the others, the whole mass interacting with other musics and cultures of the world which themselves are going through the same process.

See style and authenticity.

**instrument makers.** There are some 130 makers specialising in the manufacture of traditional instruments, most of these in Ireland, but many in the US, Britain and Germany. All supply to Irish traditional musicians both in Ireland and abroad. Some are highly organised, some are small-scale, craft workers producing instruments to a very high standard, most are professional and full-time. These makers are spread throughout the island, some towns have more than one maker:

   accordions – Co. Limerick and Co. Clare
   banjos – Clarinbridge and Castlemaine
   bodhráns – Thurles, Newcastle (Co. Galway), Ballingarry, Kilkenny, Belfast, Dublin, Doolin, Roundstone, Markethill, etc.
   bouzouki – Galway and Dublin
   fiddles – Belfast, Galway, Cork, Dublin, Navan, Ravensdale, Mayo, Carrigaline, Sligo, Donegal, Co. Down, Limerick (there is a violin-making course at Limerick School of Music)
   flutes – Kilmaley, Swinford, Bray, Coolea, Newry, Kinvarra, Ennis, Miltown Malbay, Belfast, Glencar (Sligo), Dublin
   guitars – Rathfarnham, Dundalk, Newtownards, Passage East, Castlegregory
   harps – Craughwell, Cork, Clonakilty, Limerick, Rathfarnham, Kenmare
   mandolins – Kilkenny
   uilleann pipes – Kenmare, Belfast, Daingean Uí Chúis, Glencar, Bray, Malahide, Miltown Malbay, Newcastle (Co. Down), Newry, Kinvarra, Dublin
   whistles – Ennis, Doolin, Finglas and Dublin.

**instruments, modern.** Irish music in the years since the sixteenth century has utilised bagpipes, fiddles, harps, uilleann pipes, whistles and flutes. Of these the oldest surviving instruments are harps; Jew's harps dating to the thirteenth century have been found. Uilleann pipes from the late 1700s still survive in playing order. Concert-style flutes are referenced as far back as the eighteenth century, and many of these survive; accordions and concertinas do not appear in Irish music until after the mid-nineteenth century. The major instruments used today for Irish music melody playing are fiddle, flute, tin whistle, uilleann pipes, accordion, concertina, melodeon, banjo, harp. Less popular are mandolin and harmonica. Dominant accompaniment instruments are guitar, bouzouki, and piano/keyboards. Mandola and cittern are increasingly used also, and synthesiser appears in many recordings.

Percussion used is drum kit and wood block in dance bands, bodhrán (and sometimes bones or spoons) in other situations. Occasionally Jew's harp is heard. African, Asian and Arabic portable instruments such as djembe (drum), tablas and úd (lute) are also creeping in.

See individual instrument names.

**Ionad na nAmhrán.** (The Song Centre). Based at University of Limerick's Irish World Music Centre, it began in 1995 with the purpose of promoting research and encouraging wider listenership in the area of songs.

**Ireland, provinces, counties.** These are important to understanding 1. organisation of the music and 2. the location of, and similarities between regional styles and instrumentation in traditional music. Most important is the historic spread of counties and provinces on the island of Ireland. Since partition of the island has only been in existence since 1921, regional differences based on the two political entities of 'Ireland' and 'Northern Ireland' have not formed, in particular because of (a) the intensified identification of Northern Catholic nationalists with traditional music, céilí and set dancing and (b) the distancing of the Northern Protestant/unionist community from traditional music.

*political states of Ireland and their counties.*

Northern Ireland: Antrim; Armagh; Derry; Down; Fermanagh; Tyrone.

Republic of Ireland: Carlow; Cavan; Clare; Cork; Donegal; Dublin; Galway; Kerry; Kildare; Kilkenny; Laois; Leitrim; Limerick; Longford; Louth; Mayo; Meath; Monaghan; Offaly; Roscommon; Sligo; Tipperary; Waterford; Westmeath; Wexford; Wicklow.

*historic provinces and their counties.*

Provinces: Ulster, Munster, Leinster, Connacht.

Ulster: Donegal; Derry; Antrim; Down; Armagh; Monaghan; Tyrone; Fermanagh; Cavan.

Munster: Clare; Limerick; Kerry; Cork; Tipperary; Waterford.

Leinster: Louth; Meath; Longford; Westmeath; Offaly; Laois; Kilkenny; Carlow; Wexford; Wicklow; Kildare; Dublin.

Connacht: Sligo; Leitrim; Roscommon; Mayo; Galway.

In addition, the smallest regional unit of the 'county' is further subdivided into 'townland'.

See map of Ireland (page ii); townland.

**Irish bars.** In the last two decades of the twentieth century Ireland's long dormant colonial aspirations have found expression in the export of national identity as cultural artefact. If Italian-ness in Ireland was expressed by chip shops staffed by high-status, specialised immigrant workers, Irishness in continental Europe, in a trend begun in the ethnic mosaic of the USA, is now demonstrated in Irish bars. These are, at the end of the twentieth century, a booming business all over Europe, some private, some financed by major European brewers, the majority franchised through deals with the supplier of their iconic, desired commodity – Guinness. Their exotic titles are harvested from existing romantic trend-setters in Ireland, and from among the populace of nineteenth-century Irish popular song and fable – Mulligan's, Dicey Reilly's, Kitty O'Shea's – these labels the secular equivalent of the fashion in pre-1980s Ireland to name houses and B&B establishments after Latin-titled saints – San Giovanni, Santiago, Sancta Maria. Critical to the 'Irish pub' is decor – hard benches, stressed pine furniture, caustic-dipped and worm-perforated, package-ornaments that include obsolete and valueless indifferent book-club editions, household and farmyard utensils – bricolage hoarded in anticipation of the boom by a thousand junk-shops nationwide. Often the factory-compiled, containerised product of an architect's central 'bar-bliss' master-plan, the 'Pub in a Box' is marketed as a concept, dressed as promoting 'Irishness', but of course of principal value to the beer producers' international market-share within business expansionism. Irish bars' drink prices can sometimes be – by Irish standards, and by local standards too – outrageously exorbitant: what is paid for Bush, Jameson, Powers, Paddy, Guinness and Smithwicks is the 'gatekeeper', prices designed to exclude the fighting classes. Yet these bars are still a cultural interface of some importance, for they are necessarily run by Irish personnel. And so they become sites of communication visited by both working exiles and the curious and imaginative non-Irish locals. With its 'authentic' ethos, 'traditional' music is very often the leavening in the institution's absurd image-mix. All permutations of tonal and melodic quality are perpetually peregrinating throughout mainland Europe – the good, the bad and the rowdy – Ireland's musicians on tour are very often the ambassadors who influence whether or not people from abroad will visit the island as tourists. Some of the wandering Irish troubadours are of the jigs and reels variety, more are Dubliners/Fureys/Clancys sound-alike balladeers, some are Christy Moore fans, others parade Horslips memorabilia, U2 impressions, mainstream pop and big-name rock covers. But all are part of the mainstream thinkers' experience of Ireland abroad. Each version of Irishness may have its own distinct and clearly defined constituency at home, but in Europe all can end up comfortable bed-partners in Ireland's uniquely imperial institution.

**Irish Music Academy of Cleveland.** This began with Seán Boland forming a CCÉ branch in Cleveland, Ohio in 1989. Rita Lally organised teaching workshops with such as Tom McCafferty, Tom Byrne, Rasa Chambers and Tom Hastings. Inside two years there were thirty students, and as a result of the demand IMAC was established, the first non-profit, community-based school for traditional Irish music in the US. IMAC offers tuition in fiddle, tin whistle, flute, piano and button accordion, uilleann pipes, harp, tiompán, bodhrán, guitar, piano and singing. Weekly lessons are supplemented by other educational programmes which involve band-work, master classes, workshops, summer programmes and a teacher training program. Funding is raised by trustees and volunteers, by the Pádraig Pearse Centre, 'Friends of IMAC', the Ohio Arts Council and the National Endowment of the Arts. In 1995 IMAC took over as the parent organisation for the local CCÉ branch. IMAC has now established links with Scoil Acla on Achill Island, Co. Mayo, in 1996 running an exchange programme with it. IMAC's 'Outreach Programming' – involving concert appearances by students and teachers – is of considerable benefit to its local and regional impact in the US.
  See USA.

**Irish Music Club.** See USA, Chicago.

**Irish Musicians' Association of America.** See Thornton, Francis J. (Frank); USA, Chicago.

**Irish Traditional Music Archive.** (Taisce Cheol Dúchais Éireann) This is a reference archive and resource centre for the traditional song, music and dance of Ireland. It is a public, not-for-profit facility which also promotes public education in Irish traditional music through its own activities and its support for the activities of others. Established in 1987, the archive is the first body to be exclusively concerned with the making of a comprehensive collection of materials – sound recordings, books, photographs, videos, etc. – for the appreciation and study of Irish traditional music. It now holds the largest such multimedia collection in existence, with coverage of the island of Ireland, of areas of Irish settlement abroad (especially in Britain and North America), and of non-Irish performers of Irish traditional music. A representative collection of the traditional music of other countries is also being made. The Archive is currently situated at 63 Merrion Square, Dublin 2. It includes public rooms for the study of materials, and an audio and video recording studio. The collection is open to the general public from 10.00 a.m.–1.00 p.m. and 2.00 p.m.–5.00 p.m., Monday to Friday.

*definition*. The archive interprets 'Irish traditional music' in the broadest possible terms, and always tries to include rather than exclude material. Items are collected if they could be considered traditional in any way – in origin, or in idiom, or in transmission or in style of performance, etc. – or if they are relevant to an understanding of traditional music. As well, therefore, as collecting music and song that is known to be centuries old, the archive also collects reels and jigs lately composed and recent ballads in traditional style. Its holdings contain the sean-nós singer and the solo fiddle player, along with heavy metal groups playing hornpipes and symphony orchestras performing arrangements of traditional airs. Printed collections of tunes and songs keep company with dissertations on traditional music and handbooks of ethnomusicology. Traditional music is regarded by the archive as being simultaneously a valuable part of historic Irish culture and a vigorous element of contemporary Irish culture which enjoys widespread popularity even outside Ireland.

*functions.*

Collection: Current and past commercial publications, unpublished material, and information about traditional music are acquired by donation, copying and purchase. The archive also records traditional performers in its audio and video studio in Dublin, and on location around Ireland and elsewhere.

Dissemination: The information held is made as widely available as possible, consistent with the preservation of material and with the limitations of resources. Personal callers have access to the collections, and a limited information service is given by phone and post. Assistance is given to record and book publishers and broadcasting organisations, the resource thus reaches large numbers of people. The archive is also involved in broadcasting activities on radio and television, and has a programme of intended publication.

Organisation: Organising the information and materials held by the archive is achieved by such library techniques as accessioning, classifying, cataloguing and indexing. This work is carried out on computer.

Preservation: All materials are preserved indefinitely for future generations by such techniques as binding, security copying, and archival and digital storage.

*history.* The archive arose directly from a proposal made by Harry Bradshaw and Nicholas Carolan to An Chomhairle Ealaíon/ The Arts Council in Dublin in 1987 to preserve historic sound recordings of Irish traditional music which they had uncovered while researching and producing an RTÉ radio series *The Irish Phonograph* (1983–86). The Council, which had earlier made a decision in principle to establish an archive of Irish traditional music, on the recommendation of a committee chaired by Breandán Breathnach, accepted the proposal, appointed a board to oversee its operations, and funded it first as a pilot project and then on an ongoing basis. Additional funding was later received from the Arts Council of Northern Ireland. Staff numbers have grown over the years. The archive was first situated in Eustace St, Dublin, and moved to larger premises in Merrion Square, Dublin, in 1991. It has assembled there the largest collection of Irish traditional music in existence, and is a premier research centre for this music. The operations of the archive are directed by a Board which includes members with performing, collecting, broadcasting and archival experience.

To help users find information contained in its collections, a programme of cataloguing and indexing all items on computer is constantly in progress. The archive provides photocopying, tape copying, and photographic services in accordance with its resources and the terms of copyright law. Since 1993 the archive has been involved in a programme of audio field recording and of audio and video studio recording of performers, some in multiple sessions. It is also involved in researching Irish traditional music collections in Ireland and throughout the world, with a view to having them copied.

*general collections.* The archive contains a very large and growing public reference collection of audio-visual materials relating to Irish traditional song, instrumental music, and dance. These materials exist in original or copied form, and in different formats:

Artefacts: Musical instruments, statues, badges, coins, trinkets.

Manuscripts: Music manuscripts, card indexes, research notes, letters, lecture scripts, typescript theses.

Printed items: ballad sheets, chapbooks, sheet music, song collections, instrumental music collections, dance collections, music studies, background studies, reference works, periodicals, and ephemera such as programmes, catalogues, postcards, leaflets, posters, and newspaper clippings.

Sound recordings: cylinders, 78s, SPs, EPs, LPs, reel-to-reel tapes, standard and DAT audio cassettes, CDs.

Visual items: Drawings, prints, photographs, microfilms, video cassettes.

The archive currently holds some 10,000 hours of sound recordings, 6,000 books, 3,000 ballad sheets, 3,000 photographs, a mass of ephemera, etc. All types of materials are continually being collected and preserved, and work on them is at different stages of progress.

*special collections and projects.* The archive values every donation of material, from a single photocopy to more substantial items, and it has several large collections of particular note which have been donated for public use. The archive also acquires copies of other notable existing collections and is engaged in ongoing long-term projects in the areas of field and studio recording, discography, bibliography, iconography, filmography, manuscript cataloguing and melody databases, etc. In addition, it is involved in various special projects which include: a co-operative radio project with RTÉ by which RTÉ's radio archive of Irish traditional music sound recordings, from the 1940s to the present, is being remastered and copied, catalogued and indexed by Harry Bradshaw; a co-operative television project by which RTÉ's television archive of Irish traditional music film and video recordings, from the 1920s to the present, is undergoing indexing by archive staff; a co-operative project of the archive and of the BBC and the National Sound Archive of the British Library in London by which the BBC's radio archive of sound recordings of Irish traditional music, over 1,500 performances from the 1940s to the present, has also been copied. (GLC)

**Irvine, Andy.** (1942– ). Singer, songwriter, bouzouki and guitar player. Born in London, his father was Scottish, his mother from an Irish background. Introduced early to stage and film, he pursued these up to 1964; his first music interest was for stage, and influenced by his mother, jazz. He learnt classical guitar and was playing skiffle at fifteen; this led to folksong and Woody Guthrie. Arriving in Ireland in 1962, he played with Ronnie Drew and Luke Kelly and in 1966 toured with multi-instrumentalist and singer, Johnny Moynihan and with Joe Dolan, eventually forming Sweeny's Men. He left again in 1968 to travel and busk in Bulgaria, Romania and Yugoslavia. Playing mandolin and harmonica, he developed an interest in Balkan rhythms. Returning in late 1970, he played solo and toured with Donal Lunny. With Christy Moore, Lunny and Liam O'Flynn he recorded the album *Prosperous* (1971) and formed Planxty (1972–75). He toured with Paul Brady (1976–78), and made a unique and influential album with Brady, Donal Lunny and Kevin Burke; he also toured solo and with Mick Hanly. They re-formed Planxty in 1978 and made three albums along with a solo album *Rainy Sundays* (Irish and Balkan rhythms/tunes plus his own compositions). Andy recorded *Parallel Lines* with Dick Gaughan. Mosaic, a band he formed with Donal Lunny and Declan Masterson, had players from Hungary, Holland and Denmark. They toured with Gerry O'Beirne, and with Kevin Burke and Jackie Daly. With Arty McGlynn, Burke and Daly he formed Patrick Street (1986, three albums). He recorded *Rude Awakening*, a solo album of his own material and *East Wind* (Macedonian and Bulgarian music) with Davy Spillane, Nikola Parov and Bill Whelan. He has been playing solo and touring with Patrick Street since 1992. (JOO)

**Isle of Man.** See Manx traditional music.

**Jackson, Walker.** (d. 1798). Uilleann pipes, fiddle. Born at Ballingarry, Co. Limerick he was a noted composer of high-quality tunes and airs. He was described in 1787 by Ferrar as: 'a native of the county of Limerick and a good musician, who has composed a number of excellent pieces of music, which are much admired for their harmony and expression. Most active in the latter eighteenth century, he has always been popularly confused with another Jackson – supposedly of Ballybay, Co. Monaghan – a 'linen lord', sportsman and benevolent landlord. That individual may be the Jackson referred to in the songs 'Jackson and Jane' and 'The Boys of Mullaghbane'. Many of Walker Jackson's tunes are still favourites among today's musicians, notably 'Jackson's Morning Brush' and 'Jackson's Coggie'. Thirteen of his pieces can be found in a volume entitled *Jackson's Celebrated Irish Tunes* first published in 1774, and re-printed in 1790. Interestingly, this features both treble and bass clef, as was customary for any music publication of the time. This arrangement for accompaniment indicates piano, and not as one might expect, the regulators of the pipes. Of the thirteen tunes which appeared in print over two hundred years ago, six are still very popular with musicians today and remarkably these have varied very minimally from the settings first published. Almost another seventy tunes are accredited to Walker Jackson in the oral tradition of Irish music. However there is not sufficient evidence to substantiate the claim that Jackson actually composed all the tunes bearing his name. Indeed, a slip jig called 'Cummillum' that features in his collection predates his time and is commonly known as 'Drops of Brandy'. On the other hand, a double jig in the same collection called 'Jackson's Nightcap' is played very widely but no reference is made to Jackson in its most frequently used name 'Strike the Gay Harp'. It is impossible to ascertain just what other tunes Jackson composed, given the oral tradition and very nature of traditional music. Jackson's importance lies in 1. the fact that in the oral tradition no other early musician has as many tunes associated with his name, 2. his collection was extremely important for featuring instrumental music only, and 3. for being the first such publication. Many Jackson tunes occur in other music collections of primary importance – e.g. O'Farrell's *Pocket Companion*, Bunting's, Goodman's, various of O'Neill's, Roche's, and the four Breathnach works. (SIN)

**Jacobite song.** See song, Jacobite.

**Jew's harp.** A metal frame idiophone played pressed between the teeth with one hand, sound made by plucking its free-reed-style blade with the other. The 1861 census of Ireland recorded nine makers of Jew's harps – two in each of Dublin and Cork, one in each of Limerick and Tipperary, and three in Belfast. Once reasonably common on account of its size and accessibility, the Jew's harp has declined almost to the point of obsolescence in traditional Irish music. Also known as the trump – particularly in Donegal – or by the misnomer the 'jaw' harp, it combines a flexible tongue or 'lamella' with a metal frame that is played cupped in the hand. Manual oscillation of the lamella with the instrument held to the mouth as a resonator produces a sound of

Jew's Harp (EDI)

constant pitch, rich in overtones approximating the harmonic series, and which can be varied by adjustment of the tongue, larynx and mouth cavity. It is made of resonant material which is made to sound by bending and release or by friction.

*early use*. Anne Buckley's research (*NMAJ*, 25, 1983) indicates that Jew's harp is 1. frequently found in post-medieval sites, 2. the great majority of finds date to the sixteenth and seventeenth centuries but some are from as early as the thirteenth century, 3. copious information from non-archaeological sources shows widespread social and commercial use from at least the late sixteenth to the late nineteenth century. Jew's harp came to prominence in Europe during the 1850s. In Ireland in recent years it has achieved a media presence through its prominent use in a Radio na Gaeltachta jingle; on the commercial, touring scene Tommy Hayes is a noted player. It is found throughout Europe, Asia and the Pacific, except Australia, and no traces have been found in the pre-Columbian Americas, or pre-European Africa. Materials of which it may be made include bamboo, ivory, bone, brass, iron, and steel. (ANM)

The term 'Jew's harp' is a subject of some academic discussion, for it has no history in Jewish music. One derivation holds that the term comes from corruption of the French 'jeu-trompe' (toy trumpet), but from a narrative in 1591 it is described as 'Jews-harp', 'trumpe' and 'Jews-trumpe' (*NMAJ*, 28, 1986). Many players today refer to the instrument as 'Jaw's Harp', which (from being played in the mouth) is considered could be the original name. But there does not appear to be musicological evidence to sustain this. That term is also preferred by those who wish to avoid accusation of political or racial insensitivity.

**jig**. The jig is first mentioned in Ireland in 1674, this in a condemnation of tavern frolicking by the Archbishop of Dublin who derides the dancing of 'Giggs and Countrey dances'. Four variants of the jig exist within the Irish music and dance traditions: the double jig, single jig, slide and slip jig. Most common among these is the double jig.

*double jig*. This is the tune-type implied when the term jig is not qualified by a more specific label. The most common dance tune after the reels, many of our traditional jigs are native in origin (unlike the reel which is often of Scottish descent) and date from the eighteenth and nineteenth centuries. The tunes are usually constructed in two parts of eight bars, each of which is doubled creating the form AABB. Exceptions to this include tunes where the parts are not doubled (AB) and tunes involving more than two parts (AABBCC etc.). The double jig is in 6/8 time and is characterised throughout by the rhythmic pattern of groups of three quavers. The final bar often ends with a crotchet, this allowing a quaver as the upbeat to the next part. While the jig tempo is generally lively when played solo, competitive dancers usually call for a greatly reduced tempo in order to execute their complicated footwork.

*single jig*. The single jig is in either 6/8 or 12/8 time. It differs from the double jig in that the predominant rhythmic pattern is crotchet followed by quaver. The single jig is associated with a specific soft-shoe solo dance still performed in competitions today, usually by female dancers. A fast version of the tune is referred to as a slide and is used in the dancing of sets.

*slide*. The slide is a tune type associated with the jig family, in particular the single jig. A slide is in effect a fast single jig. It is in 6/8 or 12/8 time and the predominant rhythm involves the alternation of crotchets and quavers creating the feeling of long and short. Slides are essentially dance music and the long-short rhythm of the tune is echoed by the movements of the dancers. The tune-type is used in the dancing of sets and, along with the polka, is particularly associated with the music and dance traditions of Sliabh Luachra, where it is the brisk tempo of 12/8 tunes that dominates.

Breandán Breathnach's rule of thumb was to identify the tune-end: 'a three-quaver group followed by a crotchet or dotted crotchet marked a tune as a jig, while an ending of two dotted crotchets indicated that it was a slide' (Moylan, 1994). Some double jigs lend themselves to being played at brisk tempo and can double as slides (and slides played more slowly as double jigs). It is how the tune is played that matters. The most notable

**Scatter the Mud (double jig)** (O'Neill, 1907)

**Christmas Eve (single jig)** (O'Neill, 1907)

collection of Kerry slides appears in the Terry Moylan edited collection *Johnny O'Leary of Sliabh Luachra* (1994).

*slip jig.* In 9/8 time, the slip or hop jig is distinct from the other types. It is usually in single form i.e. the 8 bar parts are not repeated. The slip jig continues to be danced in competitions usually by females and in soft shoes. (LID)

**Jigtime Programme.** This arose from the convergence of discussions, reports, challenges, handbooks, suggestions and, most importantly, a pilot study in schools in the Belfast area that was financed by the Arts Council of Northern Ireland. Jigtime was conceived in 1990 with the aim of introducing to children at the upper end of the NI primary school cycle an appreciation of the enjoyment, accessibility, diversity and informality of the traditions of music, song and storytelling. Intended as a key component of the Cultural Heritage theme of the schools' curriculum, it had its own support material, was class based, and involved the teacher in preparation and follow-up work. Surveys of teachers and others in the educational field tended to confirm the view that the schools' music curriculum by itself, with its very limited traditional music content and uneven application, could not meet the challenge of providing schoolchildren with a broad, positive view of their musical and oral traditions. Similarly, most teachers acknowledged their own lack of expertise in the area and supported

### Pádraig O'Keeffe's Slide (Moylan, Lilliput)

*[musical notation in 12/8]*

### Whinny Hills of Leitrim (slip jig) (An Gúm)

*[musical notation in 9/8]*

the idea of a group of accomplished traditional performers bringing live music and song to the classroom.

The group consists of a singer, a storyteller, a fiddler, a piper and a flute player. Performance takes one of two forms, depending on the wishes of the school. Most common is an hour-long group performance for a class or year group of sixty to eighty. More advanced is a series of four, hour-long, weekly visits by the individual performers. Music and song from the various regions, styles and eras are represented, while instruments, history and development, folklore and the wider European and American context of the music are discussed. Particular emphasis is placed on the local regional music, notably song, and fife and drum music. Students are involved in song learning, beating time to the various rhythms, and tuning instruments. They are encouraged to ask questions. The programme is aimed at children across the religious spectrum; by 1999 it had been done in more than 600 school groups of all kinds, these including many paired Catholic and Protestant schools under the Education for Mutual Understanding scheme. Other groups are also working in this area, most notably the Derry-based Different Drums, the Armagh Rhymers and All Set, a Belfast-based set dancing group. All receive their funding from a variety of sources – European support programmes such as the PSEP and the Peace and Reconciliation Fund, the Department of Education for Northern Ireland, Co-Operation North, the Cultural Traditions Programme, the Arts Council of Northern Ireland and its National Lottery fund, Belfast City Council and the Northern Ireland Community Relations Council. Jigtime is administered by uilleann piper Tom Clarke, All Set by dancer and flute player Mary Fox, Different Drums by Roy Arbuckle. (TOC)

**Job of Journeywork, A**. Title of a Raidió Éireann bilingual traditional music radio programme run from 1957–*c*. 1969 and presented by Ciarán MacMathúna. It took its name from the set dance of the same name. Like its sister programme *Ceolta Tíre*, it made the names of many top-class players, notably Fred Finn and Peter Horan. A series of *Job of Journeywork* recorded in the US in 1962 was titled *American Journeywork*; it popularised such names as Andy McGann and Larry Redican. A journeyworker is the equivalent of a skilled labourer.

See *Ceolta Tíre*; MacMathúna, Ciarán.

**Joe Mooney Summer School.** Held annually in Drumshanbo, Co. Leitrim, this is built around the legacy of flute player John McKenna. Sponsored by CCÉ, it offers classes in accordion, concertina, fiddle, flute, whistle, uilleann pipes, banjo, harp, piano accordion, bodhrán, traditional singing and set dancing. It has afternoon lectures on history and research topics in traditional music, evening recitals, concerts and céilís.

The school was established in 1989 upon the death of Senator Joe Mooney, chair of the Connacht Council of CCÉ, who had been involved in music organisation and cultural activities all his life. Having begun with eight teachers and eighty pupils in 1989, by its tenth year it had twenty-four teachers and some five hundred pupils. It is funded by the Arts Council, Leitrim County Council, local businesses and students' fees.

**Jordan, Tadhg.** Cork songwriter responsible for many urban comic songs, including 'Johnny Jump Up'.

**jongleur.** 1. Medieval strolling or itinerant musician who played for hire. 2. Twelfth or thirteenth-century accompanist for a troubador.

See song, sean-nós, origins; troubador; trouvère.

**Joyce, Patrick Weston.** (1827–1914). Recognised as a major collector of traditional music, Joyce was a native of the Ballyhoura mountains in Co. Limerick, an area rich in music and song. His interest in collecting the music with which he was familiar was sparked when on moving to Dublin he became aware of the Society for the Preservation and Publication of the Melodies of Ireland, of which George Petrie was President. Encouraged by Petrie, he noted tunes which he remembered from his youth, and, according to himself, a considerable number of these manuscripts remained among Petrie's papers at the time of his (Petrie's) death. Petrie used them extensively in his own publications.

Joyce published his first collection, *Ancient Irish Music* in 1873, but is mainly remembered for his work, *Old Irish Folk Music and Songs* which appeared in 1909; a large collection, not only of material which he had collected himself or recalled from his early days in Limerick, but also taken from many manuscript sources, including almost 300 from the Goodman collection and around 100 from the Forde and Pigot collections. Another earlier publication which is less well known is *Irish Music and Song*, a collection of songs in Irish, which appeared in 1888. Importantly, this was the first published work to match the Irish words syllabically to their airs.

Joyce also published several other works in the related area of folklore, and history including *Old Celtic Romances* translated from the Gaelic in 1879, and R. A. Child's *History of Ireland* in 1916. (HAH)

# K

**Keane family of Caherlistrane.** From the townland of Laragh, Caherlistrane, Co. Galway, this family have been strongly influential in Irish traditional singing. Matt Keane played Jew's harp, his wife, May Costello, was from a family of singers and musicians and collected song; her large repertoire included 'Lord Donegal', an obscure version of an old ballad 'Lord Lovell' not found in Child's collection or in Irish sources. Of their children, Rita (accordion) and Sarah (fiddle) are best known as singers; unusually for the Irish tradition they perform in unison. Son Pat played whistle and flute, and together with brothers Matt, Tom, John and Joe made up the Keane Céilí Band through the 1940s–50s (it continued in the next generation as a group up to the 1980s). Matt's wife played fiddle, and all of their children, born at Castlehackett, played music from an early age. Best known of these nationally are singers Dolores and Seán, while Matt jnr. and multi-instrumentalist Noel are well known in Connacht. Raised with music, Dolores (b. 1953) also plays flute and whistle, taught by uncle Paddy. Her singing and repertoire were picked up through the family and in the locality, developed by performing at fleadhanna ceoil in the late 1960s when her reputation was initiated with a series of All-Ireland awards for song in both Irish and English languages. She sang with De Dannan from 1974–75, before moving to England to work as a song-sourcer and consultant on the Canada-emigration documentary *Passage West* for BBC. In 1975 she and John Faulkner were regular guest-hosts at the Singers' Club in London, at this time playing in Reel Union with Monaghan piper Eamonn Curran, Dublin fiddler Ciarán Crehan, and Terry Yarnell. Returning to Ireland in 1981 the band continued, but with Máirtín O'Connor, then Jackie Daly and brother Seán Keane. With O'Connor the band reputedly holds a record for the longest between-gig, motor-car drive: while on a five-month tour of North America they travelled from Santa Monica to Edmonton, and Winnipeg to Vancouver. Dolores performs solo and with her own band; many of her recordings making a profound impact on singing style and repertoire in Ireland. Such is 'Rambling Irish Man', learned from Len Graham, and 'May Morning Dew' learnt from aunts Sarah and Rita. Recorded first on *Once I Loved* in 1978, Sarah and Rita have a 1994 album *At the Setting of the Sun*. Dolores, like Seán, has many recordings of both traditional and contemporary song.

**Keane, Seán.** (1946– ). Fiddler. Born in Dublin, but parentally influenced by Clare and North Midlands traditions. He attended the Municipal School of Music in Dublin and became a teenage member of the Castle Céilí Band. On winning a Fleadh Cheoil an Radio competition at seventeen he was recruited by Ó Riada into Ceoltóirí Chualann. He joined the Chieftains in 1968 and has recorded three solo albums. (BIM)

**Kearney, Patrick ('Packeen').** (1870–1941). Uilleann pipes, war pipes, tin whistle. Born at Shanbally, Williamstown, Co. Galway. A stonemason, carpenter and general handyman, for most of his adult life he was a popular musician and entertainer at all social functions in his area.

**Keenan, Paddy.** (1950– ). Piper, whistle player. Born Trim, Co. Meath, son of piper John Keenan from Longford-Westmeath and banjo and accordion player Mary Bravender from Cavan. Among Paddy's neighbours growing up was fiddler Ted Furey, father of Finbar. Music was an important part of their lives, John playing for both recreation and in pubs for a living. All the children played. Drawn to the pipes a couple of years after starting whistle, Paddy was bought a Matt Kiernan practice set, by the age of ten or eleven had a full John Clarke set and at age twelve in 1962 he was given a new Rowsome set – the chanter of which he still plays. He played in his younger years with Finbar Furey, prior to his departure for Scotland in 1966; in this period travelling piper Felix Doran, winner of three Oireachtas competitions, was a regular visitor to the home. Like his father and Ted Furey, Paddy busked with his brother Johnny before teaming up with singer Liam Weldon and singer/guitarist Johnny Flood in 1966 to form a band to play clubs like the Swamp. Joined by their father, he took it over to become the Pavees Club, an institution of the 1960s' revival in Slattery's of Capel Street. Paddy played blues in London, then part of a busking skiffle band – the Blacksmiths – and with them made an album, and another, solo, with Gael-Linn. Gigs with Tony MacMahon, Paddy Glacken and Tríona Ní Dhómhnaill led to Seachtar, which became the Bothy Band with Matt Molloy, Tommy Peoples and Donal Lunny, this lasting only four years. Disillusioned by the lack of artistic space, Paddy spent time in Brittany, lived quietly in Clonakilty, eventually going on tour to the USA in 1991 where he has been based since. A strong individual, with a definite idea of his music, he is a particular, charismatic and wildly energising player. *Na Keen Affair* is his 1996 CD.

**Kelly, James.** (1957–   ). Born in Dublin, the son of Carrigaholt fiddle and concertina player John. Playing from a young age, he was also taught classical music at Dublin School of Music. With his father and brother John he was a regular in 1970s' Four Seasons bar sessions in Dublin, and played with Paddy Glackin, Mick Allen, Éamon de Buitléar, Aileen McCrann, Mary Bergin and Peter Phelan. He went to the US in 1979 as Bowhand with Dáithí Sproule (Altan) and Paddy O'Brien, and recorded two albums with them. He has appeared with the Chieftains and has played with Jackie Daly, Dolores Keane and John Faulkner as Kinvarra, also with Planxty and Patrick Street. He now lives in Miami, Florida.

**Kelly, John.** (1912–87). Fiddler, concertina player, raconteur. Born Rehy West, Loop Head, Co. Clare, John got his music from his mother, Elizabeth, and uncle Tom Keane's family of Kilclogher, both concertina players. At age nine he began to play on a cheap, half-crown instrument bought in a draper's shop, then he began playing fiddle. His brother Miko played button accordion, sister Nora played fiddle. Local musicians Timmy Griffin and Mikey Callaghan of Lisheen were his contemporaries, as were Ellen (Mrs) Galvin of Moyasta – an outstanding player and friend of travelling piper Garret Barry – Delia Crowley of Moyadda, Mary (Houlihan) Naughton and Tim Griffin of Ross – all concertina players. A professional fiddler who lived there, Patsy Geary from Tipperary, tutored John, eventually they often played together for house dances. Working on the Bog of Allen in Kildare brought him to Dublin on occasions, there in 1945 he married Frances Hilliard from Ballisland, south of Shillelagh, Co. Wicklow, an accordion player with siblings who played flute. The 'Horse Shoe' shop in Capel Street beside the (now) Four Seasons pub was purchased then, so beginning a rendezvous point and hub of debate that was critical to music confidence in its time, and to the revival process in the years that followed. Piper Andy Conroy, and flute player Dessie O'Connor were neighbours, fiddlers Tommy Potts and Tom Mulligan, Jimmy Brophy and accordion player Bill Harte were regular callers, Willie Clancy too, and in 1946 nineteen-year-old Seán Maguire visited, later piper Johnny Doran who was known to John from Kilrush in 1942. It was at John's insistence that Kevin Danaher of the Folklore Commission recorded Doran. Through Éamonn de Buitléar at the Church Street Club John met Seán Ó Riada as part of a 1960 play which also involved Paddy Moloney, Ronnie McShane and Seán Potts. All continued playing together for the Raidió Éireann series *Reacaireacht an Riadaigh*, this led to the formation of Ceoltóirí Chualann which 'went public' in a Shelbourne concert during the 1961 Dublin Theatre Festival. John played too in the Castle Céilí Band with Bridie Lafferty, Paddy O'Brien (younger), Seán Keane, Mick O'Connor and Michael Tubridy. All this was the melting pot out of which emerged the Chieftains in 1963. Growing up in a breac-Ghaeltacht, John Kelly's language was Irish in idiom, striking in the visuality of his turn of phrase, his interest in history and lore of music made him a great storyteller, inspiring and enabling company. A collector of '78 records, he admired Coleman and his variations in dance tunes, yet he never changed from his Geary style, instead he simply learnt an additional repertoire. He acquired one of the earliest tape recorders in 1956, travelling and recording hundreds of performances from people like Johnny Doherty, Seán McAloon and Willie Clancy. He adjudicated at fleadhanna ceoil and played for two decades with Joe Ryan in O'Donoghue's of Dublin. He was in at the founding of CCÉ, and taught fiddle at the Scoil Samhraidh Willie Clancy. He supplied and did minor repairs on fiddles from his emporium, sold Clarke whistles, banjos, and sometimes flutes. All of his children played fiddles, John regularly in Dublin sessions, James professionally in the USA. He is recorded on a CCÉ album *Seoda Ceoil 1*, on CCÉ's *Ceol an Chláir* with Joe Ryan, Bobby Casey, Junior Crehan and Patrick Kelly, and can be seen on RTÉ archive tapes and on one commissioned by CCÉ.

**Kelly, Patrick.** (1905–76). Fiddle. Born at Cree, Co. Clare. In his parish of Kilmacduane, musicians included Stack Ryan, Elizabeth Crotty and Solus Lillis. His childhood was the heyday of house dancing and 'American wakes'. The plain set and a jig set were the dances, the Caledonian came in 1910. An outstanding fiddle player, his style was influenced by blind Kerry fiddler George Whelan who had taught his father Tim, and also Danny Mescall – from both of whom Patrick learned. Tim himself taught in the locality, passing on Whelan's music with its Kerry flavour in 12/8 pieces. It is from Patrick Kelly that the Foxhunters reel has been passed on, *c.* 1963, later popularised by the Chieftains. He tuned his fiddle AEAE to make use of double stopping and droning, and to 'lift' the music. He can be heard on CCÉ's *Ceol an Chláir*, with Bobby Casey, Joe Ryan, Junior Crehan and John Kelly.

**Kennedy, Frankie.** (1955–94). Flute player. Born in Andersonstown, Belfast, one of the new traditional music world's more exuberant personalities. Singer and fiddle player Robert Cinnamond was a regular caller to the family home, his daughter was married to Frankie's uncle. But Frankie did not become interested in the music until age eighteen, then through listening to Horslips and Planxty, the Chieftains and Boys of the Lough. His early association with fiddler Mairéad Ní Mhaonaigh both motivated and identified him strongly with Donegal, the two of them marrying, teaching in national school together and eventually starting the group Altan. Their first recording as a duet was *Ceol Aduaidh* (1983). They played in Brittany and regularly in Dublin, in the 1980s running the Tradition Club at Slattery's. Frivolity coloured Kennedy's personality, but his music integrity was tough, and his determination was a key ingredient in Altan's success – some of which had begun to be realised by the time of his early death. An unquenchable conversationalist with an addictive compulsion to ply the acid humour typical of his native city, he was a great asset to Altan on their exhausting tours in Europe, Britain and the USA. He can be heard on *Ceol Aduaigh*, on Altan's early recordings, *Horse with a Heart*, *Island Angel* and on their early collections.

**Kennedy, John.** (1928–  ). Singer, flute, whistle, fife, accordion, mandolin. From near Cullybackey, Co. Antrim, at fourteen he was self-taught on fife and whistle, learning repertoire from Hughie Surgeoner while employed with him at Hillmount. He fifed with Surgeoner in marching bands and with the Lambegs over thirty years, played in his dance band for country hall dances from the age of sixteen, and played Bb flute in Duneaney 'First Flute' band *c.* 1939. A teacher of flute, fife and whistle, he has trained and played in many marching flute bands and is an authority on fifing. He has broadcast on radio and television, has a large repertoire of local tunes and song, is a highly regarded music teacher and is an All-Ireland winning singer.

**Kennedy, Peter.** (1922–  ). Singer, collector. A child of the first English folk song revival, his father, Douglas Kennedy, was director of the EFDSS and his aunt, Maud Karpeles, was secretary to the song collector Cecil Sharp. He began collecting songs in 1947 when he joined the EFDSS staff. In 1950 he joined with Alan Lomax (head of the Archive of American Folk

Song at the Library of Congress, USA) in collecting traditional songs, and in 1952 the BBC Sound Archive was persuaded by them to initiate the Folk Music Custom and Dialect Survey. As a result thousands of songs and hundreds of singers were recorded in England, Scotland, Wales and Ireland on a project which employed also Séamus Ennis and Seán Ó Baoill. He left the EFDSS in 1967 and runs Folktracks Publications (Gloucester) issuing cassettes of traditional music and song. (JOM)

**Kennedy, Rory.** (1925–93). Piano accordion. One of the founders of the Siamsa Céilí in Dundalk, Co. Louth. A long-time associate of Sligo flute and fiddle player John Joe Gardiner, he was an important organiser in CCÉ and initiated its Dundalk branch in 1958.

**Kennedy, William.** (1768–1833). Pipemaker and innovator. Born at Tandragee, Co. Armagh, he was blind from the age of four. First apprenticed as a musician to Armagh piper and fiddler John Moorehead in 1781, he then began repairing pipes at fifteen through meeting the celebrated piper Downey in the Scarva, Co. Down home of harpist Mrs Reilly. By the turn of the century he had made thirty sets; later he is reputed to have improved on the regulators and developed chanter keys to enable the playing of sharps and flats. A cabinet-maker, watchmaker and repairer too, he made all his own tools and is most fittingly remembered by the survival in playing order of a few sets of his uilleann pipes, one of them brought to life at the 1996, Co. Armagh William Kennedy Piping Festival – after a silence of perhaps a hundred years.

**Kerr, Alex.** (b. 1888). Fiddler, singer. Born near Newtowncrommelin, Co. Antrim, he learnt fiddle from his father. As a child precentor he led the hymns in his local church, in later years leading the Larne Male Voice Choir. Also as a child he played for local dances. His older brothers played bagpipes, the younger the fiddle too. At twenty-three he worked his passage to New Zealand, where he worked in mines, as a sheep-herder and studied violin. He returned to marry in 1916, worked as a cement factory stoker for twenty-three years, then at the Ballylumford power station where he was a trade union official. In the 1960s his home was a focal point for local singers and musicians. With Mickey McElhatton and Charles O'Curry he often adjudicated competitions, and was a founder of the Antrim and Derry Fiddlers' Association. He also acted as its liaison officer with CCÉ.

**key.** 1. The notes (note levers) on piano and piano accordion; 2. the bright-metal, semitone levers on wooden flutes and keyed chanters; 3. 'key' is used to refer to the scale in which a tune is played. A great number of Irish tunes are in the keys of D and G, some are in C, fewer in A, some others in Bb. It is the rule of thumb practice to assign a tune the key corresponding to its ending note. Fiddle and accordion players have, and often use, the facility to play in other keys not conveniently available on pipes, flute, whistle, melodeon.

See chromatic; diatonic; scale.

**Kilmore carols.** See Wexford carols.

**Kilroe, Peter.** Flute, bagpipes, saxophone. From Ballinamona, Durrow, Co. Laoise, he began playing flute at eleven, and was in St Colmcille's pipe band, Tullamore for many years. With the Ballinamere Céilí Band – formed by his uncle, Dan Cleary, in the 1940s – he toured Britain several times and broadcast regularly on Raidió Éireann's Céilí House programmes. He was involved in the inaugural meetings of CCÉ at Mullingar in 1951 and was closely involved with the organisation throughout his playing career.

**Kimmel, John.** (1866–1942). Accordion. Born in Brooklyn, New York of German immigrant parents. He played vaudeville in his own bar (opened in Brooklyn, 1906) as The Elite Musical Four with pianist Joe Linder. The group performed skits and popular music and song, he playing piano, cornet, xylophone and saxophone; they practised in an undertakers on nights off, when other performers were hired to keep his saloon busy (these included Joe Schenk, Gus Van and Mae West). Prohibition ruined his business, closing down the final bar he owned, the Accordion – so called after the instrument he preferred. He played accordion accompaniment to silent movies, and recorded from the beginning of cylinder technology onwards, his best material being from 1908 to 1918. His style is still admired for its flamboyant virtuosity. Kimmel exploited everything possible in producing his characteristic sound. He used four fingers of his melody hand, using that too to control bellows pressure, he used bass notes slightly, and played out of the instrument's accustomed D key in different keys – G, Em, A, Bm.

His repertoire was an equal mix of Irish traditional with German, patriotic and contemporary popular music. He also composed. His most impressive music is the technically complex, much of it Irish – 'Cuckoo's Nest', 'Bonnie Kate', 'Rights of Man', 'The Blackbird'. Considering that his hornpipes are played always in strict dance tempo he obviously knew Irish musicians and the music and was also possibly used to playing for dancers. He recorded on 'novelty' and comic albums too, and on a Victor demonstration record for dealers, *The Irresistible Accordion*. His first recording was a popular song, 'Bedelia', made in 1903, released on both 7" and 9" flat discs by Zon-o-phone. He went on to record two discs of Irish reels and jigs. On all of these and on subsequent discs he was accompanied by Joe Linder who – unlike many other accompanists for Irish music – is reported as being absolutely familiar with the material. Kimmel recorded with Edison from 1906 until they closed in 1929; with them and Columbia he produced forty cylinders and 78s. He also recorded for Victor, and for the small firms Regal, Emerson, Silvertone, Perfect, Velvet Tone. His recordings were popular – *Geese in the Bog* and *Stack of Barley*, released in 1917, were still sold in 1933. A classic selection of his playing is on Smithsonian Folkways.

See accordion; Derrane, Joe; melodeon; reproduction of music.

**Kincora Céilí Band.** Formed in 1937, its first engagement was for a Céilí organised by the Scottish brigade of the Old IRA at the Round Room in the Rotunda, Dublin. Originally it had Kathleen Harrington (fiddle), Tom Liddy (accordion), John Egan (flute), Pat O'Brien (fiddle), John Brennan (flute), Benny Carey (drums) and Kathleen O'Connor (piano). It was highly popular, successful too over the years, winning both All-Ireland and Oireachtas competitions, and making many broadcasts for Raidió Éireann over twelve years. 'Dancing on the radio', pioneered by 2RN, had the Kincora play for step dancer Rory O'Connor.

**King, Philip.** (1952–   ). Singer, songwriter, broadcaster, producer. Born in Cork, he has been involved with Irish music since the early 1970s, and is best known as a member of Scullion. In 1987 he set up Hummingbird Productions with Nuala O'Connor and wrote and produced the series *Bringing It All Back Home* which won a Jacobs Award in 1991. A documentary film on Daniel Lanois – *Rocky World* – was nominated for a Grammy award in 1993. He directed *The Juliet Letters*, *Christy*, *River of Sound*, *Sult*, two studio-based music series for Telefís na Gaeilge and three documentary films also for TnaG. He produced the music soundtrack for John Boorman's 1998 film *The General*. An energetic performer and motivator, he has recorded seven albums, five with Scullion and two with the piper Peter Browne.

See *Bringing It All Back Home*; Hummingbird; *River of Sound*.

**Kinnaird, Alison.** (1949–   ). Harper. She began playing Scottish harp at age fourteen with Jean Campbell. She has made a study of Scottish harp music and made the first recording of this in 1979, *The Harp Key* (Temple). She has an MA in Celtic studies and archaeology and has published a collection of Scottish harp music, also *The Harp Key* (Kinmor), a tutor for the small harp and a number of other collections. In 1992 she was co-author, with Keith Sanger, of the first history of the harp in Scotland, *Tree of Strings* (Kinmor). Her recordings include *The Harper's Gallery*, *The Harper's Land* (with Ann Heymann) and *The Quiet Tradition* (with Christine Primrose). She is well known as a performer, teacher and lecturer and is married to Portadown born musician and collector, Robin Morton. In 1997 she was awarded the MBE for services to art and music.

# L

**Lafferty, Bridget (Bridie).** (1923–86). Piano. Born Dublin, her father was from Derry and her mother from Donegal, and both had a keen interest in traditional music. She lived all her life in Dublin, where she was a popular and accomplished piano accompanist to traditional musicians from all parts of Ireland. Over the years she played with many leading musicians including Paddy Canny, Peter O'Loughlin and P.Joe Hayes, and in the Kincora, the Brophy, the Castle, the Green Linnet and the Fodhla Céilí Bands. She ran a boarding house at Home Farm Road, Drumcondra, where she was landlady to many of her musician friends. Her house was sometimes used by Ciarán MacMathúna for making recordings for his radio programmes. (MIT)

**Lambeg drum.** Developed from eighteenth-century 'Long Drum', it had reached its present size by the late 1800s (3' diameter, 2'4" wide, 30 lb weight, volume +/− 120 decibels). It is played in accompaniment to fife and sometimes played in combination with snare drums. It is associated with processions of Orange Order and Ancient Order of Hibernians. It is made of oak and goatskin, rope tensioned, with painted decorations on shell and hoops. Originally played at low tension with ball headed sticks, canes were introduced around the 1870s and rhythms speeded up; tension, volume and size all increased, motivated by competitions where drum was matched against drum, and greater volume was needed to rise above opponents. Importance of competitions meant its role as an accompaniment to fife in processions was marginalised. Drumming associations now arrange matches throughout the year. Styles changed accordingly from 'single time' (slow single beats in a set tune), to 'double time', with rolls added, then to fast, loud, repetitive rolling, 'competition time'. Lambegs are found in counties Antrim, Down, Armagh and Tyrone. With old styles of playing, and AOH tradition largely moribund, it is now played with fifes only in the mid-Antrim area. Largely superseded by flute bands since end of the 1800s, it is now perceived as being old fashioned and rustic although it regained a political iconicism in the late 1990s. An instrument unique to Ireland, it is possibly the only European traditional drum music and is most likely the oldest Irish music of that kind. (GAH)

*Late Late Show.* A weekend magazine-style chat show presently on RTÉ television which has constantly achieved high audience ratings since it began in 1964. Presented, and for most of its run produced by Dubliner Gay Byrne, it often dealt with socially challenging topics. Its music policy is non-specific, often including traditional, but on occasions it did specialist, dedicated tributes to major professional traditional performers. These have included the Chieftains, Sharon Shannon, the Dubliners, Donal Lunny and Michael Flatley. It was on

Richard Sterrit of Markethill, Co. Armagh 'rattling the tibby' for his father (EDI)

this programme in 1995 that RTÉ television producer, Tony MacMahon, as an invited audience speaker, doubted the 'Irishness' of Mícheál Ó Súilleabháin's 'River of Sound' composition, thereby catalysing a polarisation of opinion about the defining of traditional music. This debate was carried forward by the Crosbhealach an Cheoil conference in April 1996 where both MacMahon and Ó Súilleabháin were keynote speakers. (HAB)

See Crosbhealach an Cheoil (Crossroads Conference).

**launeddas.** Triple, mouth-blown reed-pipe having two melody pipes played by the hands, and one drone. In Ireland a similar instrument is depicted on the tenth-century Cross of the Scriptures at Clonmacnoise, Co. Tipperary; in Scotland on tenth-century stones on Iona, in Argyllshire and Perthshire. Its earliest representation in Europe is a bronze statue from the eighth or ninth century BC. A figure playing a double-pipe version is found on a bas-relief in St Antioco catacombs (Italy), this dating to the late Byzantine period. The first graphic sign is found in a thirteenth-century miniature by Juan Gonzalez. Considered the 'national' instrument in Sardinia, there it is taught formally in a dedicated school at Villaputzo – where the instrument is found in several different keys. A sculpture of a player stands outside the archaeological museum at Cagliari. In its Italian form it can be heard solo and in accordion duet on the re-issued, mid-century 78 recordings of Efisio Melis.

**lay.** Epic or heroic songs, many being narratives relating to the adventures of the warrior band, the Fianna, and the Ulster Cycle, the legacy of an ethnically unified early Gaelic culture among Ireland, Scotland and Isle of Man. These and prose storytelling were, objectively, an oral expression of, or passing on mechanism for, historical data, while actual song and music were used for celebration. The tales of Fionn Mac Cumhaill and those who figured in them are of the early Middle Ages and their origins apparently pre-literary, though they only first appear in texts of the twelfth century. In the context of song it is the verse narratives in the form of lays (*laoithe*) which are of interest and have long been chanted, and perhaps recited, whether from manuscript books or from memory. The orally transmitted music, which survives from the late eighteenth century down nearly to the present, sometimes with verbal texts, is regrettably varied, so giving an impression that tunes have been altered or replaced during their poetic history, or that those who wrote them down had a very different understanding of what they heard. Some suggest plain chant, for example, '*Laoi na Mná Móire*' (The Lay of the Big Woman, as sung by Mícheál Ó hÍghne). The same song sung by Séamus Ó hÍghne has the tunefulness of lyric song, and ('*Laoi an Amadáin Mhóir*' (The Lay of the Great Fool) is sung to a dance tune at a slow pace by Seán Bán Mac Grianna. Like the last of these, a number of the Northern tunes use a five-tone scale.

But it may perhaps be asked whether the *Laoi Fiannaíochta* (Fenian, or Ossianic, lay) should be called a 'song' at all. The term tends to be avoided, probably on the grounds that the lay was syllabic, with seven syllables to a line – not in the common stressed metre called *amhrán*, the ordinary term for 'song'. Strangely, the lays are thus associated in early centuries with scholarly literature, rather than with popular song. They seem moreover to

Luigi Lai of Sardinia plays the launeddas (BRV)

have a history of recitation, not just of chant. Modern survivals, without becoming accentual in metre, as modern Irish poetry is accentual, tend to lose their syllabic exactitude. The influence of ballads in English, which are also in quatrains with even lines in rhyme, may well have made itself felt in the lays (whether consonantal or assonantal rhyme is unimportant).

Celtic scholarship, perversely enough, usually calls these chanted or recited poems 'ballads', though the narrative examples which have gone into popular tradition lack the lyric input or the domestic context of ballads. Lays are on the contrary concerned with warfare, battles and hunting. Action focuses on the Fianna led by Fionn, his son Oisín – fictional author of many of the lays – his grandson Oscar, and other familiars who by their reappearance in different lays make up the personae of an exclusive community. Often the action concerns the defence of Ireland against an invader or hunting, which provides in time of leisure useful physical exercise for subsequent battles. This kind of poetry is called epic, and the poems, though each is less than epic in scope, belong to a heroic *ambiance* that predates ballads. Forms of magic are not excluded from this *ambiance* and sometimes provide comic motifs, chiefly by hyperbole. As spoils of conquest, Airgheann King of Lochlainn sought 'Ireland of the green hills . . . to take away with me in my boat'. '*Laoi an Bhruit*' (Lay of the Cloak) shows the wives of the Fianna to their disadvantage, competing for success in a chastity test by trying on a cloak which will not cover the body of an unchaste woman. Yet supernatural motifs are present to be believed in, and this lay, though bringing in some trivial magic and a new set of characters, relates the women to the commoner themes by having them carouse like their husbands.

Humour is no more out of place in heroic poetry than the supernatural, but a certain respect for heroes is also required. Some may find the Ossianic lays harder to regard seriously since Flann O'Brien satirised their heroes in *At Swim-Two-Birds*. But traditional generations treated them seriously, and could describe the lays – in a context mentioned by Breandán Ó Madagáin – as being 'ever quoted by the ancients in urging the youth to deeds of manliness and heroism'. Ó Madagáin also cites an allusion to the Teelin storyteller Condaí Phroinseais as one who 'firmly believed in the adventures and events he related [in lays].' The stories of the lays are framed in 'commentary' dialogues between Oisín and St Patrick on the pagan and Christian cultures which they respectively hold dear. Late texts in oral use have tended to omit this element, deemed unsuitable in a popular tradition. Some lays not of the Fionn cycle have been handed down to the late twentieth century, and two may be cited in conclusion for their popularity. In *Laoi an Amadáin Mhóir* (fragment), dated to the later Middle Ages, an Arthurian source is suggested, the Big Fool identified with the naive knight Perceval. In Deirdre's *Caoineadh Chlainne Uisnigh* (Lament for the Sons of Uisneach), she laments the killing of her lover Naoise and his brothers before joining them in death. The latter-day version of this story of native origin is also late medieval, though it goes back much further. These two lays were recorded respectively in the 1970s and in 1985. They are probably the last texts of (sung) lays from an oral tradition now extinct. (HUS)

**Lee, Frank.** Born Bayswater, London, son of a Kerry father and a Portlaw, Co. Waterford mother. His father played concertina. Working in London he frequented the Sarsfield Club at Notting Hill (Douglas Hyde was one of the founders) – a venue at the centre of Irish cultural activities at the time – where dance master Padraig O'Keane taught old Irish reels. The occasion of a St Patrick's Day 'céilí mór in 1918 at the Argyle Hall, Notting Hill, London led Frank to organise a group of musicians which eventually became known as the Tara Céilí band. Its members were Harry McGowan (fiddle, Galway), Paddy and Richard Tarrant (fiddlers, Ballydesmond, Co. Kerry), Pierce Power (piccolo, Mayo), Joe Hann (flute, piccolo, saxophone, Dublin) and Jerry Hartigan (piccolo, Dublin). Up to the time of the band's formation, music groups had been titled 'Ballinakill Traditional Dance Players', 'Paddy Killoran's Pride of Erin Orchestra' and such; it is likely therefore that Frank Lee coined the term 'Céilí Band'. They played for several EFDSS festivals in Britain – influencing contemporary

English country dance bands – they recorded forty-odd records, some of which were issued in Australia. Frank's brothers Joe and Eddie played music too, and in the USA recorded in Philadelphia where they had a weekly radio show, Eddie having the Four Provinces Orchestra and playing piano on some of William J. Mullally's (concertina) and Michael Coleman's recordings. Frank himself met Coleman in the US when in New York on the run in 1919. Key to the Tara's particular attraction were tight arrangements and a synergistic rhythm worked out between piano and drums; their albums were sold all over the world. In 1932 they recorded on acetate discs for 2RN. After WW1, Frank Lee moved away from Irish music, playing popular music on piano in pubs and clubs around Shepherds Bush.

**Leitrim, South.** The region takes in the parishes of Aughavas, Cloone, Gortletteragh, Drumreilly, Carrigallen, Fenagh, Mohill, Bornacoola and Ballinamore, an area concurrent with the ancient Magh Réin. It is credited as having its own regional style; flute, fiddle and uilleann pipes were the predominant instruments there in the early part of the century. Local repertoire includes a wide variety of different types of tunes, with the standard national repertoire here having its own local models. In reels, four-bar parts predominate in contrast to the standard eight-bars per part model. This phrasing evokes the fife playing of former times, itself an important part of local tradition. The music's 'brightness' and definite, short phrasing is referred to as a 'lifty' style. Fiddle-playing was particularly strong in the area, characterised by a 'slur and cut' style which can be traced to the early years of the nineteenth century. Piping stretches back even further – gentleman piper Augustus (Gusty) Nicolls had his estate there. A contemporary of his was piper Hugh O'Beirne (late 1700s–mid-1800s), who was described by collector P. W. Joyce as a fiddler too. James Quinn (1805–90) from Cloone – better known as 'Old Man Quinn' – learned piping from Nicolls, and passed on the same staccato style of piping to Aughavas musician Sergeant Early (late 1840s–early 1900s) while the two were resident in Chicago. The region is also the source of a number of manuscripts by local musicians and collectors who transcribed the tunes played and taught there. Such collectors include Stephen Grier and Alex Sutherland. A 1998 recording by the McNamara family (*Leitrim's Hidden Treasure*) features twenty tunes from the Grier and Sutherland MSS, and other South Leitrim material passed on in the aural tradition by such as John Blessing, Pee Fitzpatrick and the Reilly family from Drumreilly. (BRM)

See Blessing, John; *Ceol Rince na hÉireann*; Forde, William; Grier, Stephen; McNamaras of Leitrim; Nicolls, Augustus; Reillys of Leitrim; Sutherland, Alex.

**Lenihan, Tom.** (1905–90). Born Miltown Malbay, Co. Clare. Singer. From a music family, in the last century the Lenihan farmstead was frequently visited by the blind piper, Garret Barry. Throughout the 1930s and 1940s there were weekly sessions there attended by musicians from miles around, including Junior Crehan and Paddy Killoran. Although Tom was a fine lilter and dancer, it was as a traditional singer that he became best known. In line with West Clare style, his singing is relatively undecorated and his delivery understated. Phrasing and timing are impeccable. This is particularly noticeable in narrative songs wherein he captures the listener's attention with the ability to engage unhistrionically with the story. Deceptively simple to the unaware, this singing is a perfect example of song taking precedence over singer. Here was not a large voice, but one used with great narrative and melodic skill. Over the years collectors from Ireland and abroad visited Tom and his wife Margaret. Towards the end of his life he appeared on radio and television and travelled Ireland attending singing festivals, for sixteen years the anchor of the singing event at the Willie Clancy Festival. He had a huge amount of folklore, much of which he dictated, from 1971 to 1989, to Tom Munnelly of the Department of Irish Folklore in UCD. These hundreds of pages and tapes of song and lore constitute a valuable insight into the folklife of Clare for most of the twentieth century. Some of this material was published in *The Mount Callan Garland: Songs From the Repertoire of Tom Lenihan*. (TOM)

**Lennon, Ben.** (1938– ). Fiddle. Born at Kiltyclogher, Co. Leitrim, one of four sons of fiddler Jim Lennon and Sally McGriskin. A tailor, his father had learned much from travelling Donegal players the McCaffreys, and in Ben's younger days North Leitrim had some fifty fiddlers. Dancing master Seán O'Donoghue taught him the rudiments of his music, he learned much from nearby Fermanagh fiddlers John Timoney and John Gordon, and from pipes, fiddle and flute player John McGovern. Following his father's trade Ben studied the clothing trade in London, then worked in Limerick, Cork and finally Donegal. In these places he played with local musicians, including the Russells, Paddy Canny and Francie Donnellan in Clare. His biggest influence remains the music of Coleman, Killoran, Morrison and Gillespie, but he was influenced strongly by his own Leitrim, Fermanagh and Donegal proximity and experience from childhood. He teaches regularly, and tutors annually at the Drumshanbo and Willie Clancy Summer schools.

**Lennon, Charlie.** Youngest brother of Ben, he began piano at age seven with teacher Teresa Gilmartin, and by fourteen he had worked his way through the grades. From seven he was also taught fiddle by Ben, learning from the 78s. At twelve he played with the Blue Haven Dance Band, at fourteen he was in Michael Shanley's Seán McDermott Céilí Band, and from seventeen he toured professionally for five years, first with the Richard Fitzgerald Band on fiddle, then with the Assaroe Céilí Band on bass and fiddle, also with the Emerald Valley Dance Band. In his late teens he studied classical violin, and jazz harmonies. In 1960 he went to England to study physics at Liverpool University; there he played with the Liverpool Céilí Band until 1968, during which time they won two All-Ireland titles, recorded two albums with Decca, played in the Royal Albert Hall, on ITV's *Sunday Night at the London Palladium*, and toured the USA. He married sean-nós singer Síle Ní Fhlaithearta of Spiddal in 1966, and in 1969 they returned to Ireland. His first composite piece 'The Emigrant Suite' was released by Gael-Linn in 1984, this was followed by 'Island Wedding' – with orchestra and traditional musicians – and was given its European premiere in Moscow in 1993. 'The Famine Suite' (*Flight From the Hungry Land*) followed in 1995. Accompanist on twenty-five albums over the decades since the 1950s, he is one of the best-known names in current traditional music tune-smithing. His tunes are published in *Musical Memories*.

**Liddy, Joe.** (1916– ). Fiddle, melodeon, fife and accordion. Born Killargue, Co. Leitrim, his parents and brothers played accordion, one of his sisters the fiddle also, another was a step dancer, another a singer. Beginning on melodeon and fife he moved to accordion, then fiddle, the family's loft became a dancing centre for the townland and adjoining Creevelea. He played with James Coleman (Michael's brother), the Gardiners of Ballymote (with all of whom he was a life-long friend), Leitrim piper Michael Gallagher, and flute player John McKenna. In 1924 he joined the Garda Síochána and the Garda Céilí Band. With brother Tommy, and Collinstown, Westmeath piper Ned Gorman in 1933 he formed the Belhavel Trio who recorded three 78 records and did numerous broadcasts on Raidió Éireann up until mid-century (a track is on CCÉ's *Ceol Tíre* album). The three also played in the Kincora Céilí Band with Kathleen Harrington. Joe composed many tunes, earliest of which was 'The Black Road', in 1936; most of them were made in the 1960s and '70s. He was for many years involved in teaching and playing at sessions of the Booterstown CCÉ, later in Monkstown, Co. Dublin. In 1981 a book of 103 of his tunes – *The Leitrim Fiddler* – was published as a tribute by CCÉ.

**lilting.** Lilting is one of the terms used in Ireland for a musical style known as vocalisation. Its typical sound-structure has been adopted as the colloquial term 'diddley-dee' to denote (and often trivialise) traditional music. 'Vocalisation' is found in many musical cultures throughout the world, referring to the use of what has been termed 'nonsense words', 'meaningless syllables', 'non-lexical syllables' or 'obsolete words'. In Ireland, the terms diddling, dydilling, puss music, mouth music, gob music, humming and jigging are some of the other terms used, though lilting is the most common term. An example from another Western musical culture is scat singing in jazz music, where syllables are used to communicate a melodic and/or rhythmic pattern, the choice and placing of syllables reflecting tone, colour, rhythmic pattern and other features of musical instruments. These functions are also present in lilting.

In Ghana, onomatopoeic syllables are used by drummers to communicate rhythm and pitch of a particular beat. Players of the tabla in Indian classical music use syllables to represent a stroke executed in a certain way. Successive strokes which make up standard rhythmic patterns are represented by syllables grouped together. Within the piping tradition in Scotland, a system of sung syllables or vocables was used, called 'canntaireacht', as an alternative to written notation. Within this, each syllable had a specific musical meaning. Non-lexical syllables are also used in musical cultures as diverse as Cantonese opera and Navajo ceremonial music.

Lilting has been largely overlooked in the consideration of Irish music, perhaps because it has been so widespread. Indeed, a common colloquial term used to describe Irish instrumental music is 'diddilee-eye music' which refers to lilting. Lilting may be identified in four main forms:

1. A memory aid for musicians. This is one of the most common uses of lilting. It can be used between musicians when they are talking about a tune, or in the teaching of a traditional tune. A teacher may encourage a pupil to learn to lilt a tune before learning to play it on an instrument, or during the learning of a tune, the teacher may lilt it along with the hesitant playing of the pupil to encourage her or him along.

2. To supply music for dancing. Musicians often ascribe the origin of lilting to the need for music for dancing. Although lilting probably existed in itself previously, there is no doubt it had much importance in providing music for house dance, particularly in rural areas. It may also be that a shortage of musical instruments, or difficulty in getting repairs done to instruments would mean the services of a lilter would be called on to provide music. Whistling could also be used for this purpose.

3. A novelty item, e.g., so-called nonsense syllables as a refrain within a song, or in conjunction with an instrumental performance. Many examples exist of lilting as a refrain within a song text, as a chorus or otherwise both in Irish and English language texts. An excellent example in the collection of the Irish Traditional Music Archive, Dublin was performed by Colum Ó Ciabháin in Connemara in the 1940s, and was recorded for the BBC by Séamus Ennis. Entitled 'Port na Gibóige', this comprises a spoken text in Irish which relates a story interspersed with lilting.

4. A refined recital form. As the social function of lilting as a means of providing music for dance has declined through time, there has been a rise in popularity of lilting as a form in itself. It may be used by a singer as an alternative for songs, or by a musician in a session as a novelty item. Comhaltas Ceoltóirí Éireann has a separate competition for lilting in its annual fleadhanna.

Although listening might give an initial impression of abstract use of syllables, analysis of features such as type of syllables used and their place within a particular phrase of music suggests that lilting conforms to an unconscious set of rules. It is an area awaiting further academic investigation. (AMA)

Lilting sounds are very much the speciality of the individual. Thus there may be 'Dubbley-dam', 'rupptley-tam', 'Row de doh', 'Dum de doodley dum', 'dithery-didle', 'dahm-tee-damtery', 'Hoor-ee-diddley', and so on. Some lilters will mimic instruments – such as banjo (dinker-danka, dinka-diddely) or bodhrán (rupp-buppety, buppety-bup), or in slower tunes the flute/fiddle by using vowel sounds only. Lilting may well have come from a functional substitution for instrument, but while there are many expert lilters who address themselves to particular tunes as conscientiously as an instrumentalist, today there are also many who treat it as a high-novelty performance. Bobby Gardiner's *The Clare Shout* takes most of his signals from skin-tensioned bodhrán, applying melody to a percussive interpretation of the tunes. This is not remarkable, considering his expertise is on dance-rhythmic melodeon. He also bends, stretches and slurs notes in the manner of a sean-nós singer. Tim

Lyons of Co. Cork is a fine lilter of complex ornamentation akin to instrumental music. This talent stems from his expertise both as a singer and accordionist, and may relate to the fact that he played harmonica in his younger days. Rhythmically, the syllabic structure of lilting follows the course of a tune's time-signature: Die-dlee-iye, die-dlee-iye corresponding to a bar in 6/8 time, Dump-tee-dith-ery, dan-tee-dith-ery corresponding to a bar in 4/4 reel time.

**Linnane, Kitty.** (1921–92). Fiddle, piano. Born in Ballygannor, Kilfenora, Co. Clare, she was involved with CCÉ locally since its beginning in 1953. She was a founder member of the Kilfenora Céilí Band, playing with it from 1940, and in its prize-winning All-Irelands of 1954, '55, '56. The band played in Britain too, becoming one of the household céilí band names.

**Loch Lurgan Céilí Band.** Formed in the late 1950s in Galway with leader Mícheál Ó hEidhin (piano accordion), Eddie Moloney (flute), Aggie White, Tommy Cohen (fiddle), Brendan Mulcaire (button accordion), Eamon Ryan (drums), Larry Kelly (piccolo, C-flute).

**Lomax, Alan.** (1915–   ). Collector, singer, archivist, academic and film maker. Born Austin, Texas, son of another famous collector, John Lomax (1867–1948) with whom he collaborated and recorded for the Library of Congress in Washington, e.g., *American Ballads and Folk Songs* (New York, Macmillan, 1934). He recorded a great number of legendary American singers and musicians including Muddy Waters, Leadbelly, Woodie Guthrie and Fred McDowell. From the 1940s he expanded his fieldwork to include the Caribbean, Europe, Britain and Ireland, and collaborated with Séamus Ennis and Hamish Henderson. With Ennis's assistance he wrote a ballad opera *The Stones of Tory* (1951). In Ireland he recorded scores of the best traditional performers of the period. A good sample of this was published on *The Columbia World Library of Folk and Primitive Music, vol. 1, Ireland* (AKL4941). He also developed cantometrics, a system for measuring song style on a global scale. The results of this work are documented in *Folk Song Style and Culture* (New Jersey, Transaction Books, 1968). In the 1980s he produced a series of documentaries, *American Patchwork. The Land Where The Blues Began* (London, Methuen, 1993) gives an overview of his American field work and describes vividly the often harrowing situations in which this work was carried out. Rounder Records are currently engaged in publishing a major portion of his recordings on CD. Samples of these on the musics of Ireland, England and Scotland are presently available. (TOM)

**lonesome**. See draíocht.

***Long Note***. Title of a reel, it is best known as the name adopted for a ground-breaking RTÉ radio series on traditional music begun with Tony MacMahon as producer in 1974. Upon his move to television, Harry Bradshaw produced it after 1978. The weekly programme took a serious view of the traditional musician and delved into archive and other material for its research. Under Bradshaw, for instance, through Jackie Small it gave a thorough history of dancing, and used documentary to cover the life of nineteenth-century uilleann piper and composer, Johnny Patterson, and the mid-nineteenth-century piper, Johnny Doran. It used various presenters, including Mairéad Ní Mhaonaigh. It concluded in 1990.

See Bradshaw, Harry; MacMahon, Tony.

***Lord of the Dance***. An Irish step dance spectacular drama with a rock and roll approach. Its premier performance was at the Point Theatre, Dublin, in June, 1996. Star performer was Michael Flatley (of *Riverdance* fame), together with Bernadette Flynn, Daire Nolan, Gillian Norris, and Helen Egan. *Lord of the Dance* has an Irish folk-legend storyline which tells of a little spirit who has a dream. Characters involved are the Lord of the Dance, the Evil Warlord, two heroines – Erin the Goddess (the love interest of the story), and Gypsy (the temptress). As in the folk-tale idiom, good triumphs over evil, and the Lord of the Dance emerges supreme in the end. Michael Flatley, choreographer, set out to express the 'drama, power, and passion of the Irish people, a people with a colonial history'. In reclaiming this passion, *Lord of the Dance* works on sexual energy and chemistry between the male and female dancers. As in *Riverdance* the use of contrastive techniques are employed in the dances, dance types, performances, costumes, and energy. Strong, percussive, serious, 'masculine' movements are performed by the men in contrast to the more air-borne, light, playful, and 'feminine' movements of the women. Solo performances are contrasted with strong, unison line-ups, as are the music metres with performances in 9/8, 4/4, and 6/8. In effect, *Lord of the Dance* promotes and reinforces traditional constructions of gender roles through movement, facial expression, costume, lighting, and storyline. Contemporary Irish step dance movements are immersed in the dances with older movements, rocks and cross-heels, while spatially, circular and linear patterns predominate, as they do in both Irish céilí dances and set dances. It is a complete Irish step-dance stage-show, using Irish solo singing, and Irish traditional music performances. Musically, Ronan Hardiman, composer of *Lord of the Dance*, concentrates on Irish traditional topline melodies with eclectic percussion and rhythmic patterns from other cultures. Like *Riverdance*, *Lord of the Dance* has succeeded in both popularising and commodifying Irish step dance and has presented the experienced Irish step dancer with a choice of alternative employment in theatre. (CAF)

See *Riverdance*.

**Lowry, Dan.** Comic singer and clown, born in Roscrea, went from rags to riches through Leeds and Liverpool Musichall. He set up 'The Alhambra' musichall in North Street, Belfast in 1857, but not finding the city's wit to his taste, in 1878 he purchased Dublin's first musichall – the 'Monster Saloon' in Crampton Court – which had been opened by Henry Connell in 1855. This he demolished. On the site he built 'Dan Lowry's Star of Erin Music Hall' which eventually became today's Olympia Theatre.

**Lunny, Dónal.** (1947– ). Bouzouki, guitar, bodhrán, composer and arranger, record producer. Born in Newbridge, Co. Kildare, his early music performance was in the duo the Rakes of Kildare with Christy Moore, and Emmet Spiceland, a soft-centred ballad group of the late 1960s. In the 1970s and early '80s, he was a key member of three of traditional music's most influential groups – Planxty, the Bothy Band and Moving Hearts. Planxty, which emerged from Christy Moore's 1972 album, *Prosperous*, gave him scope for experimentation with arrangement and instrumentation. The Bothy Band, with whom he played from 1975 until its demise in 1979, became the template for many traditional bands in the succeeding decades. His next project, Moving Hearts, pitted uilleann pipes and saxophone against a background of guitar, keyboards, bass and drums. Musically, Moving Hearts attempted to carry the Bothy Band concept a step further, mixing traditional music, jazz and rock within a complex instrumental style.

He is regarded as a leader in the development of the 'Irish' bouzouki. To compensate for what he considered the awkwardness of the Greek bouzouki (Andy Irvine had introduced him to the instrument in 1970), he had a version made with a flat back and a shorter neck – this having now become known as the Irish bouzouki. As his musical career developed, so did his technique. The gentle understated style of his early bouzouki work with Planxty contrasts with the percussive, rhythmic approach that became his trademark with the Bothy Band. Later, he experimented with the blarge (a large bouzouki with five pairs of strings in place of the usual four), and with electric bouzouki.

In other musical spheres, he has collaborated with Van Morrison, Mark Knopfler, Elvis Costello, Kate Bush and Rod Stewart. He has produced more than 100 albums and has contributed to countless more. His television work includes the series *Bringing It All Back Home*, *A River of Sound* and *Sult*; he served on the latter as presenter, performer and musical co-ordinator. (PAA)

**lúibíní.** Literally 'stitches'. The term used to describe a kind of improvised or set duet (in sean-nós song) that takes a dialogue form in which singers perform alternating verses.

See sean-nós.

**Lyons, John.** (1934– ). Accordion, singer. Raised at Drumtarriff, Millstreet, Co. Cork, in his younger years he absorbed music at the local cross-roads 'platform' dance and picked up melodeon. Interested in song, much was learnt from RÉ's *Balladmakers' Saturday Night* on which Albert Healy accompanied song on piano accordion – Joe Lynch, Seán Ó Síocháin and Eamon Kelly were contributors. Apprenticed as an electrician in Wolverhampton at sixteen he played harmonica also, and in 1955 returned to Co. Cork. There the cross-roads dances continued and he played in the Duhallow, Seán Lynch and Tommy Doocey céilí bands, and collected song. He worked as an electrician on trains with CIE at Inchicore, but went to Wales with flute player Mick Kelly to work on nuclear power plants in 1960. He moved to live in Newmarket, Co. Clare in 1961, by then renowned as an exceptionally lyrical singer also. He recorded *May Morning Dew* in 1971, and *Troubled Man* in 1992.

**Lyons, Tim.** (1939– ). Singer, accordion, lilter, songwriter. Born in Cork city, his mother sang, her own father played melodeon. Tim moved with the family to Wolverhampton at the age of twelve, was apprenticed as a die-caster, and with brother John he took up harmonica at fourteen, then melodeon. RÉ programmes and Jimmy Shand's '208-Luxembourg' fifteen-minute radio show were influences, developing his interest in ballad-singing. He played céilithe with Roscommon fiddler Tommy Rogers around Wolverhampton, these organised by Mayoman 'Blondie' Walsh. In search of repertoire while home on holidays, he and John bought 78 records of such as Malachy Sweeney's céilí band. In 1959 he returned to live in Co. Cork where he played accordion in the Duhallow band. Influenced by Paddy Tunney and Joe Heaney he studied sean-nós singing, and, back in England by 1962 his community became the Irish of Kilburn. He sang in the Singers' Club in London at Cecil Sharp House, toured folk clubs all over England from Devonshire up to the Watersons' venue in Hull, and played in CCÉ sessions in the Greyhound, Fulham Palace, the White Hart, and Fulham Broadway with such as Raymond Roland (accordion) and Liam Farrell (banjo). He settled in Newmarket on Fergus, Co. Clare in 1970, recorded his LP *The Green Linnet* in 1971, toured Europe with Micho Russell in 1973. Another LP *Easter Snow* followed in 1977, and with De Dannan he toured the US in 1978. In 1985 he began writing satirical song in traditional style, his 'Fast Food Song' and 'Murder of Joe Frawley' being hugely popular. Since 1987 he has toured English and Scottish folk clubs and festivals both solo and with Fintan Valley as Schitheredee, recording an album of satirical song and music *Knock, Knock, Knock* in 1988. His dozen or so compositions reflect on the absurdities of life, his lilting is superb, and his traditional song style and repertoire are highly regarded among aficionados in both in Ireland and Britain.

# M

**Mac An Iomaire, Joe John.** (1934– ). Sean-nós singer. From Ros Dugáin, Cill Chiaráin, his mother was a sean-nós singer, and was daughter of the celebrated Maoinis shipwright Máirtín Ó Cathasaigh who built some of the most famous Galway hookers. He won the men's competition at the Oireachtas in 1968 and 1978, and Corn Uí Riada in 1975 and 1977. He is married to Dublin traditional singer Rita Devine. (LIM)

**macaronic song.** See song, macaronic.

**MacColl, Ewan.** (1915–88). Singer, songwriter, playwright and collector. Born Jimmie Miller in Salford, Lancashire, he was considered a playwright of genius by George Bernard Shaw. With Joan Littlewood in the 1940s he specialised in agit-prop theatre. Much of his songwriting was political. With Charles Parker and others he did a series of 'Radio Ballads' for the BBC from the late 1950s. Songs from these programmes (e.g. 'Shoals of Herring', 'Freeborn Man') are still in oral tradition in Ireland and Britain. He and fellow Marxist A. L. Lloyd were the most dominant figures in the British Folksong Revival and recorded scores of LP records. With his wife, Peggy Seeger, he published many works including collections of their own compositions and traditional songs, most importantly, *Traveller's Songs From England and Scotland* (London, Routledge & Kegan Paul, 1977), and *Till Doomsday in the Afternoon; the Folklore of the Stewarts of Blairgowerie* (Manchester University Press, 1986). A love song he wrote for Seeger, 'The First Time Ever' was recorded by Roberta Flack in 1971 and was a number one hit in the USA. The financial security this brought him allowed him time to write even more political songs. His autobiography was published posthumously, *Journeyman* (London, Sidgwick & Jackson, 1990). (TOM)

**Mac Con Iomaire, Liam.** Sean-nós singer. Born Casla, in the Connemara Gaeltacht, he lives and works in Dublin. He has been a primary teacher, journalist, lecturer and broadcaster, chairs Raidió na Gaeltachta's *Leagan Cainte*, is author of *Ireland of the Proverb*, *Conamara: An Tír Aineoil*. He has translated Tim Robinson's *Mapping South Connemara* into Irish (*Conamara Theas – Áit agus Ainm*) and has translated seventeenth- and eighteenth-century Irish poems into English in *Taisce Duan*.

**Mac Donnacha, Máirtín Tom Sheáinín.** (1955– ). Sean-nós singer. Born at Sruthán Buí, Leitir Caladh, Leitir Móir, Co. na Gaillimhe, he is a presenter and broadcaster with Raidió na Gaeltachta. He won Corn Uí Riada in 1983 and 1988, the Pan Celtic Song Contest in 1983 and teaches sean-nós singing. His paternal grandmother, Máire Ní Mháille from Eanach Mheáin, was a singer and song writer and An tAthair Tomás Ó Ceallaigh collected a number of songs from her at the turn of the century for his collection *Ceol na nOileán*. His songs can be heard on *Bláth na hÓige*.

**Mac Donncha, Máirtín.** (1946– ). Sean-nós singer. Popularly known as Máirtín Chóil Neaine Pháidín after his sean-nós singer father, he comes from a long line of singers, poets and musicians. His parents were one of twenty-seven or so Irish-speaking families (182 people) transplanted to Co. Meath in 1935, thereby laying the foundation of the Ráth Cairn Gaeltacht. A singer, he is also a story-teller and an award-winning sean-nós dancer. He composed a lament for sean-nós singer Darach Ó Catháin in 1991, and has a repertoire of the lesser-sung songs of Raiftearaí and of lesser-known poets like Tomás Ó Lochlainn, Beairtlí Ó Cuanaigh and Aindí Ó Ceallaigh.

**Mac Donnchadha, Dara Bán.** (1939– ). Sean-nós singer. Born third youngest of twelve children, all singers, at Aird Thoir, Carna, Co. na Gaillimhe, to Seán Choilm 'ac Dhonnchadha, a famous singer himself. He was reared next door to Joe Heaney, who once asked him to sing a song for the Clancy Brothers who were visiting there. Upon finishing, Heaney remarked 'This man is better than myself!' He sang in public first only in 1985 and was discovered, as it were, by Meaití Jó Shéamuis Ó Fátharta and Máirtín Jaimsie Ó Flaithearta from Raidió na Gaeltachta. Dara Bán has won many prizes for his singing and some of his great repertoire of songs are available on cassettes *An Meall Mór* and *Máire Rua: An Sean agus An Nua*.

**Mac Donnchadha, Johnny Mháirtín Learaí.** (1937– ). Sean-nós singer. From Leitir Ard, Carna, Co. na Gaillimhe, he won Corn Uí Riada in 1985 and now adjudicates at competitions. His mother, Nan Cheoinín, was sister of the renowned helmsman Pat Cheoinín and the late Seán Cheoinín, poet, raconteur, and composer of many sean-nós songs. Johnny remembers, as a child, hearing a neighbour, Feichín Ó Loideáin, tell the singer's father that he had stayed awake the previous night counting his songs and that he had counted fifty-eight. Another neighbour, Colm Ó Caoidheáin from nearby Glinsce, gave the collector Séamus Ennis 212 songs. Some of Johnny's own songs can be heard on the CD *Contae Mhaigh Eo*. (LIM)

**Mac Donnchadha, Josie Sheáin Jack.** (1943– ). Sean-nós singer. Born in An Aird, Carna, Co. na Gaillimhe, birthplace also of Seosamh Ó hÉanaí, Seán 'ac Dhonncha and many other well-known singers. A celebrated helmsman too, he is one of only three sean-nós singers to have won the Oireachtas Corn Uí Riada three times. (LIM)

**MacDonnells of the Glens.** Glenariff, Co. Antrim. Patrons to many famous harpers down through the centuries, this family had itself also several harpers. James MacDonnell was the major organiser of the Belfast Harpers' Assembly of 1792.

**MacGabhann, Antoin.** (1945– ). Fiddle. From Mullahoran, Co. Cavan, he learned to play from a neighbouring fiddle master, Terry Smith and later, from Sr Brigid in the Convent of Mercy, Granard. He grew up with music in the home; his mother played melodeon and had a gramophone and records that she brought from America where she worked before her marriage. An agricultural scientist, he spent his student years in Dublin's music scene, and since living in Co. Meath has been teaching fiddle locally, and also at Mullahoran in Cavan. Each year since 1970 he organised 'The Mullahoran Concert', this bringing outside players regularly into the area as a great stimulus to local music. He teaches workshops and adjudicates, notably for the Antrim and Derry Fiddlers' Association competitions since the 1970s. He worked with Fr Pat Ahearn on the first Fleadh Nua in Dublin in 1971, was producer of CCÉ's sponsored programme on Raidió Éireann, and was chosen as 'Cavan Person of the year 1986' by the Cavan Association Dublin, for his work in traditional music. He has played in Cape Breton and the US and with wife Bernie from Co. Clare is to the forefront of set dancing and revival of house-sessions in Co. Meath.

**MacMahon, Tony.** (1939– ). Accordion player, television producer, commentator. Born at The Turnpike, Ennis, Co. Clare, his father P. J. was a builder, of Irish-speaking parents from Kilmaley. His mother Kitty (née Murphy), from Connolly, was a first cousin to concertina player Paddy Murphy and a neighbour of fiddler Hughdie Doohan. Hugely influenced by Joe Cooley (who was a regular visitor to the family home) from age ten, it was the master who gave him his first accordion (a small piano model), and later piper Seán Reid provided a button instrument. His brothers Brendan and Christy played accordion too, and sister Ita (mother of Mary and Andrew McNamara) danced. Training as a teacher in Dublin from 1957 introduced him to Sonny Brogan, Bill Harte, John Kelly and Breandán Breathnach. Sharing Séamus Ennis's apartment in Bleecker Street, New York in 1963, he was coached by the master in air-playing. He played sessions at O'Donoghue's in Merrion Row, met Seán Ó Riada and singers from Coolea at An tOireachtas in the RDS, and played for the BBC sound recording of *The Playboy of the Western World*. In 1966 MacMahon played with Bobby Casey, recording with him and others on the Topic record *Paddy in the Smoke*. Busking in France and Morocco led him back to Dublin where he ran a weekly session of traditional music and poetry at Slattery's of Capel Street in aid of the ANC. From 1969 he was a freelance TV presenter with RTÉ for traditional music programmes *Aisling Geal*, then *Ag Déanamh Ceoil*; in 1974 he joined the RTÉ staff as radio producer, and initiated *The Long Note*. An exceptional performer on accordion – particularly in his interpretation of airs – he nevertheless considers that instrument inappropriate to the ethos of traditional music, is unimpressed by modern trends in traditional music, and strongly believes that the art of the older traditional musicians is dying. This is reflected in the choice of musicians for his later television series *The Pure Drop*. The flashback series *Come West Along the Road,* drawing on television archive material, is his most recent traditional music work. His earlier presentation of music and his later production complemented an intense rigour in music expression and a personality which created and maintained an active consciousness of the artistic understatement involved in traditional music. His work gave expression to this, and his highly articulate intelligence has been a vital sound-post through the final three decades of the twentieth century. He retired from RTÉ in 1998 and has been engaged in an archival-ethos TV recording project since then.

**MacMathúna, Ciarán.** (1925–   ). Broadcaster, collector. Born in Limerick city his father was immersed in Conradh na Gaeilge, and as a national school teacher was involved in Irish language song and 'claisceadal' (unison choir). At school at CBS, Sexton Street, Ciarán sang with his peers in musicals. A degree in Irish from UCD in 1947 led to an MA there in which his research was 'themes of Irish folksong'. Some months of temporary teaching in Castleknock was followed by a few years in the new placenames commission – then seeking to arrive at a standardised version of spellings, this related to the memory of the oldest local Gaelic speaker in all areas. The experience gained in the country led him to step into the shoes of Séamus Ennis and Seán MacRéamoinn, joining Raidió Éireann in late 1954 as scriptwriter, with special responsibilities to collect music and song for broadcast. Three weeks spent in Clare in 1955 with such players as Elizabeth Crotty led to similar collecting and organising of gatherings, house sessions and field recordings with the OBU all over the island, and among emigrant communities in Britain. Out of this material was put together perhaps fifteen years of the fifteen-minute *Ceolta Tíre* programme he had inherited, and then, from 1957, the bilingual *A Job of Journeywork* Sunday afternoon series. His relaxed microphone style built a radio following in what was the key period of revival of interest in traditional music. These shows, and other short-run, studio material like *Pléarácha na hAoine* became the voice of traditional music revival, the link between all parts of the country and with emigrants, a source of comparison and inspiration. Utterly different as they were to the céilí band broadcasts after 1926, they picked up the 'solo-instrumental', non-glamorous integrity implied in the fleadh cheoil principle, thus both servicing and generating a listenership. 'Miltown Malbay', 'Killavel', 'Kilrush', 'Loughrea' became familiar names, creating an important part of the mythology that still sustains the music. While this may have contributed to an association between Co. Clare and 'proper' music, and so marginalising the importance of other regions, it also hugely encouraged the playing of music by demonstrating that it could sustain continuity, community and exceptional practice in the modern age. At a time of one radio station voice only, this was public broadcasting strongly contributing to the scale of awareness of traditional music that was to produce its sizeable professionalism through the 1980s and 1990s.

*The Humours of Donnybrook* followed with the advent of television, in short-run series that placed traditional musicians in 'big houses' like Dunsany and Bunratty Castles. *Reels of Memory*, on radio, with Padraigín Ní Uallacháin in the 1970s drew on his and earlier collectors' archives; *Mo Cheol Thú* was begun on Sunday mornings in 1970 (still running). A member of the Cultural Relations Committee of the Department of Foreign Affairs, and for all of its thirty years a figurehead in the Merriman Summer School in Co. Clare, MacMathúna (officially only) retired from RTÉ in 1990, in that year receiving honorary doctorates from the National University of Ireland at Galway and the University of Limerick. He is married to Dolly MacMahon, prominent as a singer in the 1960s–70s; their son Pádraig is a well-known piper, daughter Deirdre plays flute as does son Ciarán. Although more specialised programmes have followed, it was his broadcasts – particularly in the 1960s – that developed by education the listening audiences which re-patterned the music community as complimentary to Ó Riada's model.

**Mac Mathúna, Séamus.** (1939– ). Flute, singer, organiser. Born at Geamhair, Cooraclare, Co. Clare, Elizabeth Crotty's home area. Cousin Jack McMahon, a bagpiper, got him interested in music and taught him whistle. Taught through Irish locally, a good memory aided learning the language and songs. In his younger years the visits of charismatic Kilmihil flute player and singer Paddy Breen were of fiesta proportion, and music was played at American wakes, on flutes, fiddles and on concertinas by players of renown like Solas Lillis, Patrick Kelly, Bernard O'Sulllivan and Stack Ryan. Music and set dancing went on in Mrs McInerney's shop, there were sessions there on Sunday nights. His first songs were learned from Joe Cooney of Clooneena. The Miltown fleadh of 1957 introduced him to names heard on radio like Willie Clancy, Paddy Canny. Working in Clare Co. Library in Ennis involved him with older players such as Seán Reid, Sonny Murray, the Sullivans, the Byrnes, Paddy Donoghue, Peadar O'Loughlin and Gusty Evan. His ability with words made him CCÉ county board secretary from 1959–61. The 1961 Clare fleadh broadened his vision of music from the parish to the professional with the McPeakes, a ritualistic Séamus Ennis, Aggie White, the Rowsomes, Brodericks and Seerys. He oversaw the publication of Breathnach's first collection, *Tacar Port*, in 1962. They had Seán Ó Riada and Ceoltóirí Chualann play in Kilrush in 1963, and in 1966 he was appointed Conradh na Gaeilge regional organiser for Cork and Kerry, through this getting in contact with Coolea singers, Pádraig Ó Tuama and Diarmuid Ó Riordáin. Living in Coolea, he organised Conradh concerts with Willie Clancy, Seosamh Ó hÉanaí, Nioclás Tóibín and Séamus Ennis. Full-time with CCÉ in 1969, he moved to Cork city, then Dublin in 1977, his role demanding constant travel, recording for their archive, and a weekly commercial radio programme (1970–80). For these he recorded such as John Joe Gardiner, Patrick Kelly, Joe Cooley, Willie Clancy, Julia Clifford and Denis Murphy. He was involved with Tony MacMahon in RTÉ's television programme, *Ag Déanamh Ceol*, a 1970s series which in some eighty programmes focused on regions, age-groups and localities. Now primarily singing, as CCÉ's timire cheoil he remains one of the organisation's most highly regarded musicians, personalities and communicators.

**Mac Suibhne, Toirdhealach (Turloch McSweeney, An Píobaire Mór).** (*c*. 1829–1920). Uilleann pipes. Born in Luinneach, Gaoth Dobhair, Co. Donegal, he was reputedly as much a figure of folklore as a piper, claiming to be one of the 'good people' whom he on occasion involved in his music to the great curiosity and sometimes distress of his audience (O'Neill, 1913). Descended from Donnchad Mór, last of the MacSweeney chieftains, with the dignity of the descendant of a dispossessed chieftain that he was, he took his profession seriously and wore tall hat and tails. One night in his sportier days he found himself playing in the home of a Protestant clergyman. So impressed was the daughter of the house that she eloped with him and 'turned' Catholic, until the wedding stopping with the great grandmother of Altan singer Mairéad Ní Mhaonaigh – Róise Mhór Ní Bhraonáin. An Píobaire is also reputed to have introduced the Boortree (elderberry) to the area in order to have a supply of cane for making his pipe reeds. He played at the World Exhibition, Chicago in 1893, claiming the title of world champion piper.

**Magee, Johnny.** (1923– ). Dancer. Born at Beleek, Co. Fermanagh, he began dancing at

Johnny Magee and his granddaughter of Beleek, Co. Fermanagh, doing the 'clap dance'  (EDI)

the age of five, learning from his uncle who, being too stiff to dance, would demonstrate the steps with his fingers. His father had been a drum major in a military band (conscripted while working in Scotland in WWI), his mother sang and lilted for dancing in country houses. 'Battering' was a fashion in step dancing in his childhood; their neighbour's house had a flag floor with a number of old pots buried beneath a slab to facilitate this. Music and dance were hugely popular in the local Callagheen and Glenalun townlands in those years, the dance moving then to Brallagh AOH Hall, but still involving reel dancing (two facing two, women and men, solo dancing on the spot – the 'sean nós' style). The Fermanagh set was danced too – a jig set danced straight through, and usually done in cramped country houses as a half set. Lancers and two-hand dances were performed and singing was a popular and important part of the entertainment – Johnny can recall a night when each of several singers sang twenty-six songs each. His younger brother Paddy is also a dancer, and plays whistle, bagpipes and mouth organ. He learnt accordion too from Mrs Dick of Roscor who played concertina; another neighbour, Fanny Dundas, who played melodeon also taught him tunes. Local entertainment nights were focused around 'shillingy raffles' and 'sixpenny raffles' – house dances to raise rent money, or to trample in the 'blue till' damp-proofing clay in house floors. The Magee brothers' speciality, the 'clap dance', was taught to them by their uncle Johnny.

**Maguire, John.** (1902–76). Singer. Author of *Come Day, Go Day, God Send Sunday* (ed. Robin Morton). He was born and lived most of his life in Roslea, Co. Fermanagh though he also worked at mining and labouring in Scotland. Introduced to Morton by Paddy McMahon and Cathal McConnell, he was then introduced to folk clubs, concert halls and television performance. He was a gentle, precise performer and engaging storyteller with great presence and authority. His CD album is *For the Sake of Old Decency*. His book provides the fullest available description of the life of a singer and the part that songs and singing played in his life. (JOM)

**Maguire, Johnnie.** (b. 1892). Tin whistle, piccolo, flute, fiddle. Born at Callanagh Kilcogy, Co. Cavan, his father played fiddle, his mother (a niece of the uilleann piper Mahon of Finea) sang, but his greatest music influence was fiddler James McInerney whose son James was a contemporary of Coleman in the US and made at least one commercial recording. Other players influencing Maguire were flute players from the Co. Cavan Doyle and Donaghy families. He moved to Belfast in 1918 and while his main instrument was whistle, he played piccolo in several céilí bands. *Ceol* (No. 1, 1967) carries transcriptions of his music.

**Maguire, Seán.** (1924– ). Fiddle, uilleann pipes. Somewhat legendary in Irish fiddle-playing over half a century, his style borrows from classical and Scottish – he describes it as 'progressive traditional'. He was born in Belfast (son of Johnnie Maguire) and began learning violin at the age of twelve, his opportunities for playing limited by working as an apprentice machinist. He studied under Dr George

Vincent in Belfast first, then was taken up by May Nesbitt who put him through rigorous bowing practice for several months, to which application he dedicates his bow-hand. Then playing traditional music, he first broadcast on BBC Overseas Radio at the age of fifteen, and won the Oireachtas in 1949, playing professionally ever since. He also plays flute, guitar, piano and whistle, but also uilleann pipes – his set made by Belfast man Frank McFadden – these a feature of his numerous stage performances all over the world. He played with the Malachy Sweeney Céilí Band in the company of his father, and with accordionist and fiddler Johnny Pickering. With his own céilí band he toured England and made several solo and group recordings. He toured the US, playing in Carnegie Hall and guesting on the popular Ed Sullivan and Arthur Godfrey magazine shows. His playing prowess however extends far outside traditional music, this providing him with the opportunity to play the iconic Stradivarius and Guarnerius violins held in the Wurlitzers' trust in New York, thereby adding his name to a list which includes Fritz Kreisler and Yehudi Menuhin. His playing is regarded by some as being outside what can be regarded as traditional music, by others as the finest fiddling. Breathnach (*Ceol* 1, 1967) describes him as 'gifted with amazing powers of execution . . . able to toss off reel after reel in riotous variations'. Surviving serious and debilitating illness he continues to play professionally, usually with accompaniment, something often frowned upon by traditional music aesthetics, yet he remains respected as a grand virtuoso.

**Máire Bhuí (Máire Bhuí Ní Laoghaire).** (1774–1849). Lyricist, songwriter. Born in Tuairín na nÉan in the Mountain Parish of Ballingeary in West Co. Cork. At the age of eighteen, she eloped and married Tomás de Búrca from Skibbereen. They took possession of a substantial holding of 150 acres in Inse Bheag and Inse Mhór. Though formally uneducated, Máire was inspired to write poetry and songs. Despite the moderate prosperity of her circumstances, she identified with the disadvantaged rural poor of her locality, composing pieces that reflected their hardships and the injustices of the times. In these she expressed a passionate indignation that has rarely been equalled, and which has assured her songs a lasting place in West Cork's song tradition. Most celebrated is her 'Cath Chéim an Fhia', about clash in 1822 between the men of the parish and the Yeomanry. Among others still to be heard are 'A Bhurcaigh Bhuí ón gCéim' (*c*. 1819), a light-hearted advice to her son Mícheál concerning marriage; 'Maidin Álainn Ghréine' (*c*. 1829) a late example of the aisling or 'vision' genre, celebrating Catholic Emancipation; the haunting 'A Mháire Ní Laoghaire', a dialogue between Máire and the Ballyvourney poet Donnchadh Bán Ó Loinsigh concerning Repeal – in it is ably illustrated the social responsibility of the Gaelic poet both to give expression to the community's hopes and to boost morale. (EAO)

**Makem, Jack.** (*c*. 1920–*c*. 1990). Singer, pipes, whistle, fiddle. Born Keady, Co. Armagh. First a mill-worker locally, then a small farmer in his home townland of Derrynoose, he inherited the music legacy of his mother, Sarah Makem, and the lively tongue of his father Peter. Brother to singer Tommy, he also played church organ, providing a total spectrum of music for his neighbours. Later he formed a touring band which included his sons. Devoted to his native place, its history and folklore, he was passionately involved with traditional music and was keenly observant of his community. Once, after a long Saturday night's music session where he had been playing the pipes, he is reported as having arrived in the organ loft in Derrynoose chapel just in time for the first Sunday mass. Before he slipped seamlessly into something more formal, the first music the congregation heard were the opening bars of 'Rakish Paddy'.

**Makem, Sarah.** (*c*. 1898–1985). Singer. Born Keady, Co. Armagh, her family inheritance was songs. Keady was a market town, a cultural confluence of the Irish, English and Scots, a community of small farmers. Her repertoire reflected those separate traditions in over 500 items, which, while mainly traditional, also drew freely on the music hall, gramophone, wireless and popular song as sources; she loved songs and plucked them out of the air. Her singing style was effortless and fluent, paying careful attention to the words, laying out the phrases like a storyteller, aware of the inherent drama. Beyond singing at local dances in her youth she never became a public performer but she came to the attention of a wide audience in 1950 when she sang the introductory song 'As I Roved Out' to the radio programme of the same name. Following this popularisation, her songs were recorded by generations of visiting scholars and younger singers who beat a path to her door. She made an LP record, *Sarah Makem* and a short film of her life and times for BBC Northern Ireland, also entitled *Sarah Makem*. She also sings one track on the Clancys' *Bard of Armagh*, and on Topic's *Irish Voices*. (DAH)

**Malone, Molly.** The tragic heroine of the popular song 'Cockles and Mussels', commemorated by a well-known, endearingly kitsch statue in Dublin's Grafton Street, near Trinity College. The lyrics of the song inform us that she 'was a fishmonger' in Dublin's 'fair city', who wheeled her barrow 'through streets broad and narrow', ultimately succumbing to 'a fever'. Sung by rugby crowds and sometimes soccer fans at international matches, it is a kind of sing-along anthem-cum-football/drinking ditty. Over the years Molly has become the subject of a classic urban myth, and the commissioning of her statue was inspired by improbable 'historical' revelations in 1988. These asserted that her baptism and burial records had been discovered in a seventeenth-century register, and that she had been a part-time prostitute catering to licentious Trinity College students. The ascertainable facts of the case are less colourful. In his booklet *The Mystery of Molly Malone* (Dublin, 1992), Seán Murphy shows that far from being a centuries-old folk song, 'Cockles and Mussels' appears to have been composed in the late nineteenth century. The earliest-traced published version, dated 1884, describes the piece as a 'comic song' written and composed by James Yorkston of Edinburgh. Molly therefore was in all likelihood a Victorian 'type' rather than a real person, and the song's widespread popularity and Dublin associations are probably the principal reasons for its evolution into the city's unofficial anthem. (SEM).

**mandocello.** Second largest of the mandolin family of instruments.

**mandola.** A larger version of the mandolin using four sets of double strings tuned GDAE. Known as 'octave mandolin' because it plays a full octave below mandolin, its short neck, like that on cittern, facilitates articulation of melodies.

See mandolin.

**mandolin.** A small pear-backed lute using four sets of double-strings and a short, fretted neck. Earliest references to this instrument date to 1583 at which time it was customarily carved from one piece of wood. Known by the 1760s as the 'Neapolitan mandolin' it has been most popular in the late 1800s all over southern Germany and Italy where it was played in orchestras using instruments of different size – Mandolin (smallest), Mandola, Mandocello and Mandobass (similar to violin, viola, cello and bass in the violin family). In the late nineteenth century a flat-back model was developed in the USA, where ensembles were also popular. Tuned GDAE (like the fiddle) it adds a

Mandolin (EDI)

brightness to ensemble playing. The instrument today is extremely popular in flat-back and electric versions used for Bluegrass music. The pioneering Irish maker is Joe Foley, in Britain Stefan Sobell is the innovator; Martin Murray has enhanced mandolin's artistic profile considerably in traditional Irish music, as has Pádraig Carroll whose tutor is published by Waltons (1991). Murray is one of today's best-known exponents.

**Mann family.** From Drumraney, Co. Westmeath, these were noted as instrumentalists at the beginning of the twentieth century. Pat Mann played bass drum in the original Drumraney fife and drum band, brother Jack was a fifer, Billy and his sister Katie both played concertina, brother Ned was a fiddler.

**Manx traditional music.** Generally defined as the material contained in the manuscript notebooks of the collectors of the late nineteenth and early twentieth century. Although limited to about 300 tunes, there is a wide variety of styles and content. The collections reflect the Isle of Man's political and social history, with examples showing the influence of Ireland, Scotland, Northern England, Wales and Norway. However, the early collectors were seeking out music that they felt was Manx and therefore Celtic, often ignoring other aspects of the island's traditions. For not only were the Manx bilingual to some degree for some centuries, they were also bi-musical, drawing on both their Gaelic origins and the cultures that were inevitably filtering in through strong economic links with the north of England, south-west Scotland and further afield. In addition, the principle of compulsory elementary education had been established by the Manx church by the seventeenth century, although enforcement was sometimes spasmodic, and the evidence of the early nineteenth-century manuscripts of church music strongly suggest that many Manx were also musically literate, a factor which may have speeded the decline of the Gaelic oral tradition. Commentators from the mid-seventeenth century noted with some surprise the absence of harps and pipes; this was probably due to the lack of wealthy courtly or military patrons. Even in the 1600s the Manx were said to be 'much addicted to the violin' and this strong fiddle tradition, which probably owed much to the Scandinavian influence, seems to have survived in spite of the influx of Irish and Scottish fiddlers in the eighteenth and nineteenth centuries. The move to the towns and the growth of tourism during the nineteenth century heralded the disappearance of the traditional fiddler, whose services at country 'hops' and harvest and Christmas celebrations, assembly balls and church worship was no longer needed.

The Manx have always been enthusiastic singers and this too is reflected in the nineteenth-century collections. The earliest printed selection was *Mona Melodies* (London, 1820), which featured thirteen songs with anglicised Manx Gaelic titles and English texts. This was followed by a spate of publications of new songs which entered the tradition and arrangements of old songs, notably 'Mylecharaine' which was early identified as 'the Manx national song' and appeared in two forms, both in triple time; the minor version was always sung. The major tune was instrumental and described, rather oddly, as a march. Like many other popular tunes, this appeared in many variants. In 1907 it was arranged by W. H. Gill (1839–1922) and later adopted as the national anthem.

One of the most distinctive Manx forms was the 'carval', a type of religious song, with origins in European medieval carol-forms. Although the tradition is probably much older, the earliest surviving carvals date from the seventeenth century and have parallels with the Welsh 'plygain'. The form was as popular with the literate as the ill-educated. Traditionally performed at the 'Oiell Verrees' on Christmas Eve, subjects were taken from the Old Testament and often dealt with the dreadful consequences of sin. Another popular theme was the story of the prodigal son. A few interpret the Christmas story and are Marian in content, surprisingly surviving the introduction of Methodism in the late eighteenth century. Carvals continued in the popular tradition well into the nineteenth century and a fine collection was published in the Isle of Man in 1891 by J. C. Fargher and A. W. Moore under the title *Carvalyn Gailckagh*.

By the end of the nineteenth century there was a determined effort by a number of scholars and enthusiasts to record and preserve the language, folklore, customs, oral literature and music. Foremost collectors of music were A. W. Moore (1853–1909), Dr John Clague (1842–1908) and W. H. Gill. In 1896 Moore published *Manx Ballads and Music*, a scholarly work which focused on the texts but contained some tunes simply arranged for piano and voice. In the same year Gill published fifty-two reworkings and arrangements of tunes in *Manx National Songs* (London, Boosey and Co.). This popular volume remained in print for almost a century and for many decades was the only source of publicly available printed material. Gill adapted many of the melodies to conform to contemporary taste and many new texts were composed, some of them by A. P. Graves. For many the music and language revival went hand-in-hand. Sophia Morrison (*c*. 1859–1917) collected and published songs and children's rhymes and taught the rudiments of music to the young Mona Douglas, who was to become the most important figure in the revival of music and dance in the twentieth century. The first significant studies of Manx music were in the 1920s, when A. G. Gilchrist published a series of major articles in the *Journal of the Folk Song Society*, nos. 28–30 (London, *JFSS*, 1924–26); P. W. Caine and C. I. Paton contributed substantial papers on carvals to the *Proceedings of the Isle of Man Natural History and Antiquarian Society* in 1926.

Performance styles are difficult to assess. Some of the earliest recordings were initiated by Sophia Morrison but these wax cylinders have disappeared, probably neglected after her death. Documentary descriptions suggest that there were two singing styles: that of the mainstream in the European 'art' tradition, while the 'old style' lingered on in country districts until the 1970s, when it was usually regarded as eccentric and unmusical. An account by Canon John Quine in his novel, *Captain of the Parish*, of the singing at a religious camp meeting in the mid-1800s sounds remarkably like Gaelic psalm-singing and Hall Caine's descriptions of carval singers brings vividly to mind the Irish sean-nós.

Leading the performance revival in the twentieth century was Mona Douglas (1898–1987). From her great-grandfather's notebook and from the memories of elderly fishermen and farmworkers she managed to recreate a dance tradition. Working with teachers such as Philip Leighton Stowell, who was to prove an equally potent force, Manx dance took root in elementary schools. A team from Albert Road Elementary School, Ramsey took the Albert Hall by storm with their performance in 1930, accompanied by Arnold Foster's orchestral arrangements. The real renaissance had to wait until the 1970s when Mona Douglas revived the Chruinnaght, a competitive festival which had flourished during the inter-war years. It was re-launched as an interceltic event, and has grown from strength to strength. The new festival coincided with the publication by Colin Jerry of the nineteenth-century collections, giving, for the first time, easy access to the largely unedited traditional material (*Kiaull Vannin*, Isle of Man, 1987).

The new groups of instrumentalists and dancers which were formed gradually worked towards a new Manx voice, encouraged by their growing awareness of the traditions of other countries and by their increasing confidence in a sense of 'Manxness'. By the 1990s audiences at the Chruinnaght were flocking in for the music and not simply because the event was 'Manx'. Not only had the music and dance been integrated into the schools' activities but a number of adult groups were injecting a new vitality into the old songs and dances. Many of these groups of dancers, singers and instrumentalists appear regularly at festivals in Europe and further afield. New ideas have been adopted, further enriching the living tradition. As in the late nineteenth century, there have been parallels with the language revival. Manx Gaelic is now officially taught in schools, initially jointly funded by the Manx Heritage Foundation and the island's Department of Education and now solely by the Department. Meanwhile, the country cruinnaghts and eisteddfods continue, with their mix of Manx music (largely drawing on Gill's publication), non-Manx songs, story-telling and dialect recitations, usually highly satirical in nature.

*recording*. The increasing accessibility of

technology has enabled an steady increase in the production of tapes and CDs by Manx groups and soloists, encouraging the development of a distinctive modern Manx style. The most influential recording has been *Mactullagh Vannin*. By the mid-1990s styles ranged from the 'mystical' traditional of Emma Christian (*Beneath the Twilight*) to the Manx rock sound of Greg Joughin and The Mollag Band. Work in primary and secondary schools has been fostered by a number of dedicated teachers; representative recordings include *Kiaull Vannin*, *Paitchyn Vannin* and *Kiaull yn Aeglagh* (cassette, no catalogue number). Central to these developments has been composer and performer Charles Guard (*The Secret Island*), whose role as producer and sound recordist has been instrumental in raising the standards of performance and presentation. Examples of the variety of styles can be found on *The Best that's In!* Bob Carswell's bilingual *Claare ny Gael* and John Kaneen's *Folk Hour* are long-running programmes on Manx Radio which present the island's music to a wider audience. Fenella Bazin's *The Manx and their Music* (Isle of Man, Manx Heritage Foundation, 1997) is the first comprehensive account of the history of music in the Isle of Man. Manx harp can be heard on Emma Christian's *Beneath the Twilight*. (FEB)

**Maoin Cheoil an Chláir (Clare Music Education Centre).** Set up in 1993, by 1998 it had 500 students, with twenty teachers offering between them over thirty courses of study. Traditional and classical lessons take place side by side, with specialist teachers for each discipline. No diluting of one form or another is entertained, but many students find no trouble in crossing between the styles. Based in Erasmus Smith House in Ennis – a large college building dating from the 1770s with an auditorium in the form of a modern, acoustically fine chapel – it was financed by a grant from the European LEADER scheme (designed to combat rural decline), as a model for a new style of music school suitable for areas where there is an existing local music culture. The initiative for such an all-inclusive music school was taken in 1992 by Fr Harry Bohan of Shannon, Co. Clare, who in consultation with Mícheál Ó Súilleabháin set up planning and development committees. The school opened in 1993 with Andrew Robinson as director; he was succeeded in 1998 by Colette Moloney, author of a major eighteenth-century Irish harp music study on Bunting.

The school provides supplementary short courses in piping, harp, flute, recorder, banjo and traditional fiddle. It has a traditional music recital series, Fidil Beo, and has hosted many Co. Clare and visiting performers. It promotes regular orchestral, choral and soloist concerts, and runs student concerts which take place throughout each term. First-prize-winning groups in the National Slógadh competition have been produced by the school, as well as high results in Leaving Certificate and other music examinations. A model for future such developments, Maoin Cheoil an Chláir is a limited company and a registered charity. Its four shareholders are Rural Resource Development Ltd, Clare County Council, the Sisters of Mercy and County Clare Vocational Education Committee. The Board also includes representatives of various musical interests in the county including CCÉ and the Willie Clancy Summer School. Its traditional music teachers in 1998 included Siobhán Peoples (fiddle); Joan Hanrahan (fiddle); Claire Keville (tin whistle); Niall Keegan (flute); Conor McCarthy (accordion and concertina); Marcus Moloney (banjo and mandolin); Deirdre Stephenson (harp). (ANR)

**march.** Among the most ancient music forms in any country, this tune type is originally related to military activities and was incorporated into dance in Ireland to utilise the great number of tunes so called. Designed for, or arising out of the need for military companies to cover distance efficiently despite adverse conditions, by improving humour and overcoming exhaustion, the march might be functional to speed travel, celebratory to mark victory, or slow and funereal to evoke death or defeat. Military marches are described as 'slow', 'parade' and 'quick', the last of these used in popular early-century dance as the 'quickstep'. Some old Irish examples are in 9/8 time, and tunes like 'O'Sullivan More's March', 'O'Donovan's March' are found in 3/4 time.

MARCH

Allistrum's March (Roche, 1927)

O'Donovan's March (Roche, 1927)

But generally, as in other cultures, in the Irish tradition they are most common in 4/4, and 2/4. 6/8 time is also popular, as in the 1647, 'Allistrum's March'. During the céilí band era many common song melodies were recruited as march tunes – 'Dawning of the Day', 'Roddy McCorley', 'Who Fears to Speak', etc. – mostly patriotic tunes, their zeal drawn upon in the context of the desired Irish-Irishness of céilí dancing. The march is one figure in the well-known 'Waves of Tory' céilí dance. Some bands prided themselves in the complexity and sophistication of the marches they played, others were content to provide the basic rhythm. 'The Triumphal' is an example of the former. Because of the redundancy of the bulk of traditional music in dancing entertainment, the march has fallen out of popularity and will almost never be heard played – except in a limited fashion in céilí dances. The older of the tunes however are of great interest musically, particularly the clan marches, some of which date to the sixteenth century. The location of marches in Irish music history has a bearing on instrumentation, for while in sixteenth-century Germany such tunes were reported as played on fifes with drums, in Ireland the bagpipes were used – as with Derricke's 'Irish piper'.

**Triumphal March** (Roche, 1927)

*[Musical notation for Triumphal March]*

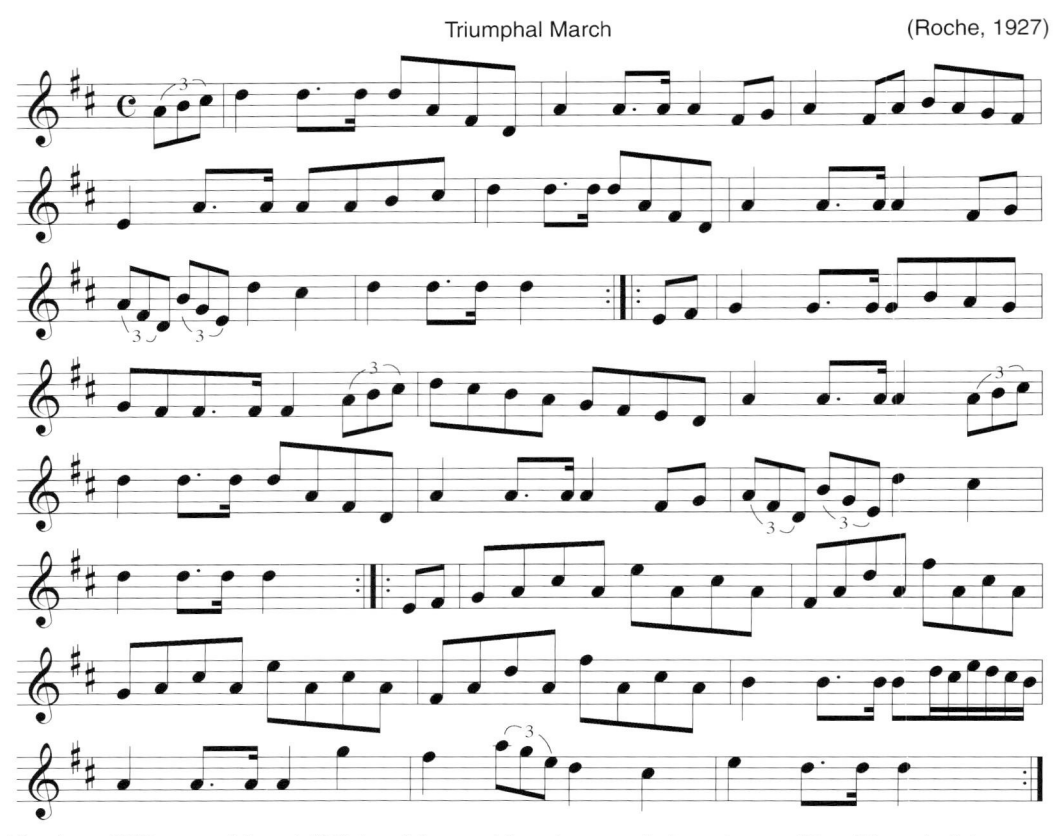

Marches. 'O'Donovan's' and 'Allistrum's' are older clan-march type tunes; 'The Triumphal' is more modern and associated with céilí dance and brass bands

**Martin, Tony.** (1917– ). Fiddle-maker. Born near Barr na Trá, North Mayo, now living near Charlestown. In 1932 he began as an apprentice carpenter in Belmullet. He went to England in 1935, working as a shopfitter in London. In 1947 he by chance visited a violin workshop run by the then-famous Czech maker George Rost, and was invited to learn the trade. He stayed there for only a few months before he began repair work on his own, earning a living by day as a joiner. After thirty years in London he returned to Mayo in 1987. He has made fiddles for Seán Maguire, Danny Meehan, Michael Gorman and Kevin Burke and says that 'A good restoration job will extend a fiddle's life by a hundred years, it will long outlive the restorer'.

**Mayglass Céilí Band.** (Wexford) Formed in 1927, one of the first bands to broadcast on 2RN. It had Tommy Mallon (piccolo), Jim Shiel and Paddy Hayes (accordions), Jim Cullen, Murt Doyle, Nick Kinsella, Tom Harpur (fiddles), Jimmy Cassidy, Pat Fortune (banjos), Mrs Harpur (piano). With the Kincora and Athlone bands it tied for first in the 1954 All-Ireland Fleadh at Cavan, and toured Irish dance halls in London and Leeds in the early 1960s.

**Maypole.** First introduced into Ireland in the 1930s in Goldsmith country, Tubberclaire, Co. Westmeath. It was a forum for dancing done in the open air on a timber or concrete floor. Most 'Maypoles' remained open throughout the summer months and people paid a small admission fee. Such dances were very popular during the 1930s and early 1940s with Maypoles situated in many areas. They were gone by 1945.

Sonny's Mazurka (EDI)

**mazurka.** A sung 'national' dance-form in 3/4 time, traditional in Poland, originating in the Mazovia province, this became popular in the fashion-setting Germany and Paris of the mid-1700s, arriving in Britain by 1830. In its dance form it was a round dance done by four couples, implemented more vigorously than the sensuous waltz.

Adopted into the Donegal tradition the mazurka was one of the many local couple dances. Today it is no longer commonly danced although a small number of mazurka tunes still form part of the repertoire of fiddlers such as Vincent Campbell and Francie Mooney. The mazurka is in 3/4 time with an accent falling on the second beat of each bar. Mazurka tunes are usually referred to by tune-type rather than having individual titles.

**McAloon, Seán.** (1930–98). Piper, pipe maker. Born at Altawalk, Roslea, Co. Fermanagh, his father played accordion and sang, and introduced Seán to the whistle. Moving to flute, then fiddle, he was influenced by Coleman recordings. He became interested in pipes on hearing Kilturk player Phil Martin at a feis in Roslea, and ordered himself a Crowley (Cork) set, later acquiring a flat set by O'Mealy. He emigrated to the US in 1964, but returned, working first in Dublin, then Belfast in 1966. He recorded *Drops of Brandy* with dulcimer player John Rea in 1976. He became a respected pipes repairer and highly-regarded reed-maker, and produced some twenty sets of the instrument in his lifetime.

**McBurney, Billy.** See Outlet Records.

**McCarthy, May.** (*c.* 1890–1961). Uilleann pipes. Born in Cork city of Tipperary parents. A member of the Cork Pipers' Club from an early age, she and her brother were taught uilleann and war pipes by Seán Wayland. An accomplished dancer, whistle player and pianist too, she played all over Ireland and in Wales and England. She was a member of Cumann na mBan, intensely interested in the promotion of Irish culture, and led a céilí band.

**McCarthys of London and Clare.** Piper and concertina player Tommy McCarthy was born at Shyan, Kilmihil, West Clare in 1939. His aunt played fiddle, his mother concertina, sets were danced in their house. Tommy began to play tin whistle at the age of nine following a visit by a flute player Miko Dick Murphy on 'the wren'. He learnt fiddle from Malachy Marrinan, picked up tunes from local blacksmith, concertina player Solas Lillis, and by the age of fourteen he was visiting Elizabeth ('Mrs') Crotty's in Kilrush. He played at farmhouse dances, 'wrens' and exile wakes where rhythm and swing were critical to the sets danced. His mentors were Michael Downes, Junior Crehan, Bobby Casey and flute player John Joe Russell.

Staying in Dublin once weekly introduced him to John Kelly, through whom he was directed to Leo Rowsome to purchase his first set of uilleann pipes. He moved to London in 1952 with his wife, dancer Kathleen Connaughton; their four children – Jacqueline, Marion, Bernadette and Tom – all played music. His associates there were Roger Sherlock, Bobby Casey, Martin Byrnes, Séamus Ennis, Kit O'Connor, Michael Gorman, Margaret Barry, Seán Maguire, Paddy Taylor, Raymond Roland and piper Michael Falsey from Quilty. Willie Clancy was also there from 1952–54, as a carpenter, playing in the Laurel Tree in Camden Town.

Tommy joined NPU in 1968, co-founding the London Pipers' Club in 1980; he played on CCÉ's first American tour in 1972 with Paddy Glackin, Séamus Connolly and Joe Burke, and with Bobby Casey played folk clubs all over Britain. He taught daughter Jacqueline to play concertina at the age of nine, Marion the tin whistle, then uilleann pipes. Bernadette played piano, Tommy jnr. eventually took up fiddle, and now runs a music-pub in Boston. Bernadette married Tennessee fiddler Henry Benagh and lives in Miltown Malbay, Marion lives in Oranmore, Jacqueline is married to Waterford city piper Tommy Keane, living also in Co. Galway where she teaches concertina. Tommy McCarthy's music has embraced diverse challenges, such as playing in the film score for *Young Guns*, with Jacqueline in *Three Wishes for Jamie*, in *The Playboy of the Western World*, with all of the children with The Chieftains. Jacqui and Tommy Keane recorded *The Wind Among the Reeds* in 1995, Tommy himself made a solo album *Sporting Nell* in 1997.

**McCollum, Frank.** Fiddler, song and music collector, composer. One time 'master' of the Ballycastle, Co. Antrim Orange Lodge. His best-known and widely recorded piece is 'The Home Ruler' hornpipe, usually presumed to have been named in honour of James Brown Armour (a nineteenth-century Antrim Home Rule champion), but in fact written for his wife.

**McConnell, Alec and Mickey.** Fiddle. Born *c.* 1880, these brothers were extremely influential musicians and tinsmiths who travelled around south-west and central Donegal, centring their activities around Ardara. In-laws of the Dohertys, they would have regularly played and traded tunes and techniques with them. Alec was considered the better musician, but Mickey also played bagpipes, these for outdoor performances at harvest and hiring fairs, the two rarely ever playing without each other. (CAM).

See also fiddle, Donegal.

**McConnell, Cathal.** (1944– ). Song, flute, whistle. Born in Ballinaleck, Co. Fermanagh, his father, Sandy McConnell, played whistle and accordion and sang. His grandfather and great-grandfather played flute. Sandy had a large repertoire of song and stories, and greatly encouraged the children in music. Like his brother Mickey (singer and songwriter), Cathal played whistle, then took up flute, learning not only from the 78 record 'masters', but through local fiddler and whistle player Peter Flanagan. Cathal played in various céilí bands, and met and played with the older age-group of players all over the island. Flute player John Joe Maguire was an inspiration, local players John McManus, Tommy Maguire, Tommy Gunn, Eddie Duffy and Mick Hoy important too. In 1967 he was a founder member of the Boys of the Lough with Robin Morton and Tommy Gunn.

**McConnell, Mickey.** (1947– ). Singer, songwriter. Of the McConnell family of Ballinaleck, he is the youngest of five. Brothers Seán, Cathal, Cormac and sister Maura are all well known in music and writing. He is also a journalist. His best-known songs include 'Only Our Rivers Run Free', 'Peter Pan and Me', 'Supermarket Wine' and 'Tinkerman's Daughter'. He plays guitar, banjo and mandolin. He recorded a solo album *Peter Pan and Me* in 1991; his songs have been recorded by Niamh Parsons, Cilla Fisher and Artie Tresize, Benny Sands and Christy Moore. 'Only Our Rivers Run Free' was taken up by orchestral arranger James Last. A perceptive writer, his lyrics are subtle yet uncompromising, and his 'GUBU Song' is an outstanding feat of the satirist's art. (JOO)

Brendan McCusker of the McCusker Brothers Céilí Band (EDI)

**McCusker Brothers' Céilí Band**. From an intense family environment of music in Kilcreevy, Co. Armagh, their mother played melodeon and concertina, their father played piccolo. Eight brothers among the children played instruments, sisters Mary and Teresa both sang. The fiddle was taught to them by local man Bill Lenagh, a fund of local music style and repertoire who had picked up his music from travelling musicians heard on fair days in the town of Keady. The band began in the 1930s at house dances and in halls, the boys travelling by bicycle with the instruments strapped on their backs. By day all had jobs, yet they managed to travel to all parts of the country, by the beginning of the war already famous, witnessing on their return home one night the sky lit up with the German bombing of Belfast. Later travel was done by car, when petrol was available, otherwise by train. From 1945 onwards they played in England in all the major Irish halls of Liverpool, London and Birmingham. By then with fiddler Kevin Vallely, and using banjo (Francie), electric and American fiddle (John), fiddle (Brendan), piano (Barney) and button accordion (Tommy, Benignus), piccolo (Kevin), drums (Malachy), they made their name with the swelling Irish population there. At home in the same decade they broadcast often on Raidió Éireann's *Céilí House*. In 1962 they played in the US in Boston, Chicago and Philadelphia, in New York they played in Carnegie Hall. Changing dance styles in the '50s and '60s saw them playing 'old-time' as well as 'céilí' dances, helping them make their name with tunes like 'The Cuckoo Waltz'. Their regular venue was Armagh City Hall for the Céilí Mór where song collector Seán O'Boyle frequently acted as 'fear an tí'. They broadcast on RÉ and BBC, and performed live from the Gresham Hotel on the opening night of RTÉ. They did a special St Patrick's Day issue of BBC's *As I Roved Out*, and played for BBC's first NI TV broadcast *Come Dancing*. Most recently the band played on RTÉ TV's *Pure Drop*. They recorded several 78 records and LPs.

**McDermott, Josie.** (1925–92). Flute, saxophone. Born at Coolmeen, Co. Sligo, near Ballyfarnan, Co. Roscommon, his mother sang and played concertina. His greatest influence growing up were neighbours the Butlers whose home was a céilí house, the mother a fine lilter; local fiddler James Flynn influenced him too. By the age of six he was able to play trump (Jew's harp) and Clarke tin whistle. With a broad taste in music Josie McDermott played what he liked, from whatever source – tunes from gramophone records or the radio. By the age of fourteen he was singing in a local, 'modern' jazz-style dance band, took up trumpet, then tenor and alto saxophones. In later years he might alternate nights céilí-ing on flute and whistle with cycling sixty miles to hear the Jimmy Compton Jazz Band. He played in perhaps ten modern bands in his time, blindness from eczema in 1962 barely slowing him down. He spent two years with Sonny Flynn's Céilí Band, his final group was the multi-genre 'wedding' band Flynn's Men which he joined in 1967. All this paralleled his traditional whistle, fife and flute playing which earned him considerable reputation throughout the country, gaining him a 1964 All-Ireland on whistle, and another on alto sax. He was placed in ballad singing, won the lilting competition in 1967, and in 1974 the flute.

**McDonagh, Sonny.** (1926–91). Flute. Born at Bunninadden, Co. Sligo, he began music at the age of six, influenced by his mother Kate, a melodeon player. He picked up music naturally from the various players he came in contact with, in particular Master Bartholomew Henry (fiddle) and Willie Mulligan (flute). A highly regarded player locally and nationally, in the 1960s he played with the Sonny Flynn Band, in 1977–78 he toured the USA with Eddie Clarke (harmonica) and Maighréad and Tríona Ní Dhómhnaill. Later he played with the Liffey Banks band, and is commemorated by a monument in his home town.

**McEntee, Patrick.** (1939–86). Fiddler. Born at Corragarry, Co. Cavan. He joined CCÉ on its foundation in 1951 and helped Dr Galligan, the President, establish it in Co. Cavan. He frequently played for dancers and was a member of the first group who were awarded the Teastas i dTeagasc Ceolta Tíre (TTTC) certificate. He was county chairman of CCÉ from 1978 until his death.

**McFadden, Frank.** (1911–76). Piper, pipe maker. Born off the Springfield Road, Belfast, his father, Peter McFadden, was a pipe maker, principally of warpipes, but also uilleann pipes. Peter was friendly with Francis Joseph Biggar MRIA, one of the editors of the *Ulster Journal of Archaeology*, and keenly interested in traditional music. The 'house piper' to F. J. Biggar, Peter named his son after him. With the retirement from pipe-making of both his father, and R. L. O'Mealy, Frank took on the business, becoming adept at reed-making. His matching of reed to chanter was superb and he enjoyed a huge reputation. He played regularly for the BBC on *Piping, Fiddling and Singing* for almost twenty years. McFadden's style was very tight, reminiscent of R. L. O'Mealy's; this, he maintained, was the old style of piping, and the particular style of Ulster. He started many pipers off, supplying and perfecting instruments and teaching technique. (WIG)

**McGann, Andy.** (1928– ). Fiddle. Born in West Harlem, New York, one of the most important Irish-American fiddlers, famed for his distinctive Sligo-style of playing. His father, Andrew, came from Ballymote, his mother (née Margaret Dwyer), from Tubbercurry, Co. Sligo; they met and married in New York City. Andy took step dancing lessons from Kerry teacher Seán Murphy in the Bronx, where the McGann family lived, and at the age of seven he began fiddle lessons with American-born teacher Catherine Brennan Grant. Informal teaching followed with Michael Coleman, from whom he learned many tunes and with whom he played privately up until Coleman's death in 1945. He formed another, more public fiddling partnership with Ballinamuck, Co. Longford, fiddler Paddy Reynolds, with whom he performed in the New York Céilí Band; this also featured Paddy O'Brien, Larry Redican, Jack Coen, Jerry Wallace, and Felix Dolan. McGann's discography includes *Joe Burke, Andy McGann and Felix Dolan Play a Tribute to Michael Coleman* (reissued as *A Tribute to Michael Coleman* in 1994), a classic recording that featured 'Andy McGann's' jig, his own composition; *Andy McGann and Paddy Reynolds*, with Paul Brady on guitar; *Andy McGann and Paul Brady* which was Andy's solo debut at age forty-nine; *The Funny Reel*, where he was reunited with Burke and Dolan; and *My Love Is in America*, a live recording taken from an Irish fiddle festival held at Boston College, Massachusetts, in 1990.

Frank McFadden

Jimmy McGettrick     (Noel Kilgallon)

**McGettrick, Jimmy.** (1909–98). Tin whistle. Born at Aughris, Rathmullen, Ballymote, Co. Sligo, he began to play music at the age of fifteen. Early influences were Tom Shields (fiddle) and Michael Gardiner (accordion, fiddle and flute). Through the 1930s and '40s, céilís in Mc Dermott's Hall in Bunninadden had fiddlers Frances Scanlon, Charlie Scanlon, James Henry Scanlon, and Edward Healy as regular performers. Bernard Flaherty's book *Trip to Sligo* speaks of Jimmy's description of fiddlers Nora O'Gara, née Hunt, and Margaret Horan, née Davey, whom he knew from the old schoolhouse at Killavel during his youth: 'This was excellent music, and the fiddles hummed an internal rhythm which he never heard before or since.' One of Matt Molloy's main musical touchstones, he also played with fiddlers Willie and John Joe Coleman.

**McGinley, John (Mhósaí).** Fiddle. Born during the famine at Loch Uinshe, Co. Donegal between Carrick and Glencolmcille – he was the youngest of ten children, most if not all of whom played fiddle. His father Moses was a blacksmith and a noted fiddler, and his oldest brother Maurice (an RIC officer) was also highly regarded as a fiddler. John, however, is fixed in folklore as the greatest, his travel circuit as a fish-seller taking him all over South-West Donegal. He travelled regularly to Scotland, playing at stopping points on the journey across counties Derry, Tyrone and Antrim. Known to have had a rare, old and diagnostic Glencolmcille repertoire, his style has been passed down partially through the Dohertys – with whom he was quite familiar – as well as through numerous fiddlers in the Glencolmcille, Carrick and Teelin area. John Doherty constantly remarked that his father, Mickey Mór, had considered John Mhósaí to have been the most exceptional player he ever encountered. The 'Mhósaí' repertoire can be heard presently in James Byrne of Meenacross, Glencolmcille. (CAM).

See also fiddle, Donegal.

**McGinley, Martin.** (1961– ). Fiddle, presenter. Born Raphoe, Co. Donegal, he inherited a fiddle tradition through his St Johnston mother. Initially learning classical violin, he turned to traditional music in his late teens, at the time a journalist with the *Derry People* and *Donegal News*. He played for a year with the band Ferdia, writing also for the *Derry Journal*, then as a news reader with the BBC in Belfast. Now running a music bar in Killybegs, he presented the 1995 *Pure Drop* RTÉ television series and RTÉ Radio 1's *Sounds Traditional*.

**McGlinchey, Brendan.** (1940– ). Fiddle, composer. Born in Armagh city, his Forkhill mother had played melodeon. He took fiddle lessons at the age of twelve in response to his mother being told by a fortune-teller that the family would have a gifted musician. Entered in Dungannon feis by his competitive Portadown teacher William Collins (a tunesmith), his victory portrait in the local paper attracted céilí band leader Malachy Sweeney to recruit him at the age of sixteen. In the company here of such players as Johnny Pickering and Bobby Gardiner he sessioned all over the country in 1956–57 with Seán Maguire, Paddy Canny, Seán Ryan, Leo Rowsome, Paddy O'Brien,

Willie Clancy and Kevin Collins. The J. Scots Skinner music then in vogue was picked up by ear from records, and from BBC Scotland radio programmes; RÉ's *Ceolta Tíre* and *A Job of Journeywork* were important too. His playing in competition at the first Ennis fleadh of 1956 was broadcast by Ciarán MacMathúna, creating a reputation enhanced by winning all levels of All-Ireland competition, and tying with Aggie White in the Oireachtas. He tied too with Séamus Connolly in the 1961 Swinford fleadh, then winning in 1962 at Gorey. The excitement of the times led to CCÉ's inauguration of the Champion of Champions event which he won at Clones in 1964. In England at eighteen he played for two years at the Hibernian Club on Fulham Broadway with Roger Sherlock, Liam Farrell and Raymond Roland, with whom he toured Ireland as the Hibernian Céilí Band. An associate too of Bobby Casey, Máirtín Byrnes and Joe Burke, he was later in Johnny Pickering's band from 1960–64; the leader's death prompting his return to London where he has lived since. He has composed many tunes, sixty of which he rates highly, he has broadcast on radio and television, and recorded in 1974 with Finbar Dwyer's Silver Hill label. He dropped out of playing in 1977, but came back in 1993, presently teaching and giving workshops, and a regular at the Willie Clancy summer school.

**McGowan, Harry.** (1937– ). Flute. Born at Carrowdore, Co. Sligo. His father John taught Harry marches on a band fife when he was young; Jim Henry (fiddle and flute) was his music partner in later years. With James Murray (flute), Joe Fallon (button accordion) and James Murphy (fiddle) he formed the Countryside Céilí Band in 1972, and also played with the South Sligo Céilí Band. He plays with Tubbercurry flute player Peter Walsh, and sons Éinrí and Shane are also flute players.

**McGowan, Ted.** (1933– ). Fiddle, bodhrán, band manager and promoter. Born in Culfadda, Co. Sligo, he was active in the London Irish music scene in the 1950s and '60s. He managed the famous London-based céilí band, the Glenside which won an All-Ireland title in 1966. He returned to Ireland in 1973, where he and his wife Teresa opened the Roisín Dubh in Gurteen, Co. Sligo. This has become one the best-known venues in the country for traditional music and as a meeting place for musicians. It also houses a fine collection of photographs of musicians. Always involved in all aspects of music in the locality and one of its most ardent supporters, in 1998 his bar celebrated a quarter-century of its weekly session. (GRD)

**McGrath, John.** (1900–55). Fiddle, accordion. Born at Rossport, Co. Mayo he emigrated to the USA in the late 1920s and was taught music by James Morrison while working in New York. From the early 1930s until his death he worked as a musician, teaching and playing in the New York area. He was involved in the Irish Music Club there throughout the 1930s and played music with Michael Coleman and Hughie Gillespie. A creative musician, he is credited with the composition of many fine tunes now in the standard session repertory.

**McGrath, Peig.** See Needham, Peig.

**McGreevy, Johnny.** (1919–90). Fiddle. Born in Chicago of Irish parents, it was 1959 before this highly regarded musician ever came to Ireland – on a tour with sixteen Chicago-born Irish musicians, singers and dancers organised by Frank Thornton. He grew up in a period when some of the most influential Irish fiddlers of the century were in their prime. He listened to Coleman, Morrison, Killoran and Sweeney recordings, based himself in the Sligo style, and was taught in his late teens by James Neary, James Giblin, Martin Wynne and Tom Fitzmaurice. He recorded with Pat Roche's Harp and Shamrock Orchestra for Decca in 1938, then again in 1974 with flute player Séamus Cooley on *McGreevy and Cooley*. Feis and private session playing were his outlets until a new audience emerged in the 1970s. Then he played with piper/flute player Kevin Henry and piper Joe Shannon. President of the Chicago Irish Musicians' Association in 1974–75, he was 1975 Chicago Irishman of the Year. He was a featured artist at the Smithsonian Festival of American Folklife in 1976 and plays on the recordings *Irish Traditional Instrumental Music in Chicago*,

*The Noonday Feast*, *Sop'n up the Gravy*, *Hollow Poplar* and *Chicago Irish Musicians*. (LAM)

**McGurk, Jim.** (1904–78). Singer, poet, fiddler. Born at Creevagh Lr, Carland, Donaghmore, Co. Tyrone. A mason by trade, he was intensely interested in local history and wrote satirical songs, praise-poetry and sketches. Of these 'The New Curate', and 'Banks of Sweet Lough Neagh' are sung by Sarah Anne O'Neill, the latter specially written for her.

**McHugh, James Josie.** (1917–79). Fiddler. Born at Kentucky, Ardara, Co. Donegal. He learned to play the fiddle from his father and from John Gallagher with whom he spent his earlier playing days. He joined the Forthill Céilí Band, formed in 1948, with other local musicians playing informally. After it broke up in 1954 he took up playing again with John Doherty and they went on to record for television and radio on both sides of the border. Literate in music, a large percentage of his repertoire came from the Scott Skinner collections.

**McKenna, John.** (1880–1947). Flute. Born Tents, Tarmon, Co. Leitrim. Highly regarded and influential flute player who through his recordings established the flute as a major instrument in traditional music. He worked in the Arigna coal mines and in 1911 emigrated to the US, settling at East 97th St, New York. He worked initially for the New York City's fire department and his first records, made in 1921, describe him as 'Fire Patrolman McKenna'. He recorded thirty discs from 1921 to 1936, and through this was responsible for bringing many local Leitrim tunes into the standard Irish music repertoire. These include 'Lucky in Love', 'Leitrim Town', 'The Corry Boys' and 'Arigna's Green Vales'. He recorded many polkas, particularly on his duet recordings, and he is renowned for the breathy, rhythmic style of North East Connacht. James Morrison, whose maternal grandfather Jack Dolan came from Drumkeerin, was his most celebrated recording partner. In 1980 a memorial in his honour was unveiled at Tarmon, Co. Leitrim. (HAB)

**McLaughlin, Dermot.** (1961–  ). Fiddle. Born in Derry city. Both his parents were interested and active in music and culture. His father played harmonica, accordion, whistle and fiddle, his mother played piano. Dermot learnt to play classical piano, taking part in the school orchestra and céilí band. He and brother Joe were taught fiddle by Tony Blace – once a member of David Curry's band; Joe now plays uilleann pipes. Maternal relations Denis Heany and Paddy McCafferty were influences, but Dermot's main inspiration has been the music of Donegal, particularly the fiddle playing of John Doherty. He has also studied the repertoire and style of such as Con Cassidy, James Byrne, Francie Dearg O'Beirne and Mickey Golly. He has recorded on Fiddlesticks, and on James Byrne's solo album. From 1986 until 1998 he was first traditional music officer, then music officer with An Chomhairle Ealaíon in Dublin.

**McMahon, James.** Flute. From Roslea, Co. Fermanagh, he lived in Belfast and was an important figure during the revival at CCÉ's Belfast Derryvolgie Avenue sessions. He played on an ivory flute (there is a tune named after it, 'The Ivory Flute') and composed several tunes, best known of which is 'McMahon's Reel'. His pieces are anonymously part of the music's repertoire all over the island. Several of the tunes appeared in print in *Fonn* magazine and many in the Liam Donnelly collection. His father Mick was a renowned flute player in the 1920s.

**McMenamin, Joe.** (1911–85). Seanchaí, piper and accordionist. Born in Tyrone, he and Charles O'Reilly organised music classes in 1974 in conjunction with The West Tyrone Culture Club and Kiltyclogher CCÉ (now Cappagh). A music teacher and organiser, he played in house sessions and was associated with the Loughmacrory Band.

**McNamara's Band.** A busy and popular Armagh dance-band of the 1940s led by button-accordionist Jimmy McNamara, with Frank Donnelly on the same instrument, and Jimmy Murphy on drums.

**McNamaras of Leitrim.** The family of Michael McNamara of Carrickavoher, Aughavas, Co. Leitrim (exponent of local flute-playing style) and his wife Mary, children Brian and Ray (uilleann pipes), Ciaran, Enda and Deirdre (flute, fiddle and concertina respectively). Their music consciously incorporates the style and repertoire of their native south Leitrim, some assimilated aurally over generations, more the result of a reviving forgotten tunes sourced in old local MSS. Their recording, *Leitrim's Hidden Treasure*, features music from John Blessing, the Reilly family, Grier and Sutherland MSS and other South Leitrim sources.

See also Leitrim, South.

**McPeakes of Belfast.** The oldest member of this family grouping of musicians was Frank, born 1885 in Belfast of a local mother and a Ballymacpeake, Curran, Co. Derry father. He left school at age thirteen to work in a linen mill, then at fifteen was a tram conductor, eventually a photographer. Interested in Irish history, the visit to Belfast city in 1907 of blind uilleann piper John O'Reilly from Galway involved him in pipes, O'Reilly staying with him for six weeks in order to teach him the instrument. In 1909 Frank McPeake won a Belfast piping competition, and with harper John Page represented Ireland at the Pan-Celtic Congress held in Brussels in 1911. Frank McPeake is photographed in O'Neill's IMM (1913). His son Francis was born in 1917, took up the pipes in 1945, and performed on radio in 1949. Recorded by Peter Kennedy in 1952 he and his father were invited to perform at the Royal Albert Hall in London in 1956. Francis's son James was born in 1936, took up fiddle at age nine, later piano accordion, and eventually a Belfast-made McFall harp upon which he played in the family trio which became known as 'the McPeakes'. With this unique (for its time) combination of pipes and harp (echoing Frank and Page's performances) the group made their name through such as their version of 'Jug of Punch' and 'Will Ye Go Lassie Go' (a derivative of the Scottish 'Braes of Balquiddhar'). The McPeakes are best known in Belfast still as teachers of traditional music on the Falls Road, many of their former pupils well-known and respected players.

**McWilliams, Hugh.** (*c.* 1783 – *c.* 1840). Song maker and poet, schoolmaster. Almost uniquely for a nineteenth-century Irish poet McWilliams is credited with being the author of at least ten songs which have become traditional; of these 'When a Man's in Love' and 'The Trip over the Mountain' have been recorded by Len Graham, the Voice Squad, Andy Irvine and others. Born Glenavy, Co. Antrim, he conducted 'hedge' schools in north Down and mid-Antrim and wrote in the styles of both the Irish and the Scots who lived in that area. His work is covered in John Moulden's *Songs of Hugh McWilliams, Schoolmaster, 1831.* (JOM)

**Meagher, Ned.** Flute and tin whistle, singer. Born at Mallow, Co. Cork, he was involved in all levels of CCÉ – Craobh Phrionsias Uí Néill, Cork city, co-founder of Cork County Board and Comhairle na Mumhan, of which he became Honorary President. Munster representative on the Ardcomhairle of CCÉ for a number of years, he was instrumental in introducing CCÉ scholarships for students entering the B. Mus faculty at University College, Cork.

**Mechanical Copyright Protection Society Limited (MCPS).** The right to record a piece of music is known as the mechanical right. By law, whoever records an in-copyright musical work is obliged to have the composer's (or their representative's) permission to do so (this is distinct from public performance, and from broadcast performance). Such a permission is treated as a 'licence', it must be purchased, and is normally given in return for a recording royalty being paid to the owner of the tune or song. MCPS is the main organisation representing the recording rights of Irish composers, including traditional composers; it sells licences to individuals and companies who wish to record its members' musical works, and it distributes the payments to its members. (ANM)

See copyright.

**medieval Ireland.** The history of music in medieval Ireland represents a fusion of all the cultural elements which comprised that society, some aspects of which were unique to it, others shared with international European culture. Irish narrative literature abounds in allusions to social occasions of performance, patronage, roles and status of musicians, types of instruments, perceptions of the power and effects of music. From this, we gain a good impression of the ubiquity and importance of music in social life, as well as a range of technical terminology. But more precise information on instruments and repertories has to be carefully assembled through extensive searching and cautious interpretation of other types of data, such as iconographic and archaeological materials, and not least, with reference to what is known of the wider European context. Music-iconographic sources reveal information about the symbolic meanings, and perhaps realistic images, of music-making in medieval Irish society. The recovery of actual instruments from archaeological excavations attests to musical activity in a particularly direct way while liturgical manuscripts containing music notation also inform considerably on local practices.

*music at the Gaelic Courts*. The most common characteristics of music alluded to in Irish sources are weeping music (*goltraige*), laughing music (*geanntraige*), and sleeping music (*suantraige*). In addition to the high-status *crot*, another stringed instrument was the *timpán*, in its earlier history a lyre plucked with the fingernails, which was later also bowed. A twelfth-century commentator on the Brehon Law Tracts notes that a *timpán* player who suffered a blow and lost his nail 'from the black upwards' was entitled to a compensatory 'wing nail', presumably a quill plectrum, while his assailant was fined. Players of flutes and whistles, though of lower status, are frequently referred to as providers of entertainment, often in the company of string players. Terms for wind instruments include *cuisle ciúil*, *feadán*, *píopaí*, *corn* (horn), *stoc* (war-trumpet).

It was customary for a *ríg* ('king' or leader of the household) to employ an official poet, *file*, whose duty was to compose poetry in praise of his patron and to be the oral repository of historical events, presented in a way that would uphold the excellence of the king's line of descent. The *file* often combined these duties with the office of *brithem*, or judge. He held the highest position at court next to the king and was also an *ollam*, one who had pursued an approved course of training in a particular discipline, such as law or poetry. In the performance of court poetry, the poem made by the *file* was recited, probably in a declamatory fashion, by a *reacaire*, accompanied by a musician, or *oirfidech*, who was usually a *cruit(t)* – a player of a lyre or harp. This court musician also had professional standing, recognised in law as equivalent to the highest grade of independent commoner or freeman, that of a superior *bó-aire* (i.e. entitled to an honour-price compensation for injury of four cows). Regarding identities of actual musicians and their patrons, some information may be gleaned from eulogistic poems, and from collections of annals dating from the sixteenth century onwards but incorporating materials from considerably older sources. They record obituaries of a handful of musicians associated with ruling families, mostly players of *cruit*, but some *timpán*-players are also named.

*Hiberno-Norman society*. Following the formal establishment of English administration in Ireland under Henry II, the new settlers also engaged in patronage of local harpers and poets. But there are also examples of imported music practices such as the texts of Latin songs, Anglo-Norman *chansons de geste*, and evidence for the presence of English harpers in Ireland from the twelfth century onwards. The main source materials are in the form of liturgical manuscripts from post-conquest cathedrals and monasteries, among them evidence for the performance of liturgical drama. From the sixteenth century survives detailed documentation of the protocol for the elaborate annual pageants which were great public spectacles in Dublin up to the time of the Reformation. The Corpus Christi pageants were an important civic occasion in which the city guilds (bakers, cordwainers, butchers etc.) each had an assigned function. Altogether eleven plays survive from the fifteenth-century Dublin cycle of Corpus Christi plays, together with details of the pageants, which appear to have been very elaborate. Musicians were required for these: for example, four trumpeters had to participate in the pageant for St George's Day. A music society was founded in Dublin in 1465 with responsibility for the night watch. It also provided the music for mystery plays and moralising theatre pieces. Up to the seventeenth century these musicians also served the pageants until they were superseded by organists in the second part of the century. The City Music association was established in 1590 and in the following year its members were accorded a fixed income by the city magistrate.

*iconographic sources.* Stringed instruments on ninth- and tenth-century Irish high crosses tend to be lyres rather than harps. They occur in three forms: 1. with one curved and one straight arm, 2. round topped, and 3. oblique. Their strings are fixed in both parallel and fan formation except for type 3 which has only fan formation. Type 1 occurs on the crosses at Ullard and Graiguenamanagh. Examples of type 2 are found on the Cross of the Scriptures, Clonmacnois, Co. Offaly, on the West Cross at Kells, Co. Meath, and on the Cross at Castletown and Glinsk, Co. Offaly. Oblique lyres may be seen on the Cross of Muireadach, Monasterboice, and on the Cross at Kells. Parallel strings occur on Ullard; a fan disposition is evident on Clonmacnois and Kells, with a ridge clearly visible at the base of the Clonmacnois example, which probably represents the string holder, while the Durrow lyre shows a six-stringed example particularly clearly: the strings are attached to the top of the curved arm, pass over a bridge and converge at the base. Other sources of iconographic information include the Shrine of St Maelruain's Gospel (also known as the Stowe Missal) which depicts a small figure crouched between two clerics, plucking a lyre similar in shape to that on the Durrow Cross (though with only three strings where Durrow has six). This may be a unique representation of the three-stringed *timpán*. The round-topped six-stringed lyre was the most common court instrument of north-west Europe from at least the fifth to the tenth centuries (the early seventh-century Anglo-Saxon instrument from Sutton Hoo being perhaps the best-known example). And whereas no West European material evidence is known to exist for oblique lyres, the consistency of this form in Irish iconography is suggestive – we can be reasonably confident that whatever inaccuracies they may contain in matters of technical detail, the Irish carvings are largely based on local knowledge.

Little is known about the use of harps in Ireland or Britain prior to *c.* 1000. (They are found in manuscript iconography from *c.* 800, and on Pictish stone carvings of the eighth, ninth and tenth centuries.) The earliest Irish image is found on the eleventh-century *Breac Maedóic*. It has about eight strings but twelve tuning pins, and is thus somewhat inaccurate. Another occurs on the Shrine of St Patrick's Tooth (*Fiacail Phádraig*), *c.* 1100, but refurbished *c.* 1376; the harp dates from the latter period. Both instruments have a distinctly lighter frame than the 'Brian Ború' harp now preserved in the library of Trinity College Dublin, which dates from the fourteenth/fifteenth century. The latter type is nowadays generally regarded as the 'Irish harp', and is distinguished by a heavy, monoxylous soundbox, deep-curved neck and sturdy rounded forepillar (often with zoomorphic carving). But there may well have been a variety of lighter-framed instruments in use before, and indeed during, this time. A unique twelfth-century carving of a bowed six-stringed lyre survives among the ruins of St Finan's Church, Lough Currane, Co. Kerry. The curved bow held in the player's right hand is typical of the period.

Both literary and iconographic sources abound with imagery of not only singing monks but monks who play musical instruments. According to numerous literary references, travelling clerics sang sacred music to the accompaniment of an *ocht-tédach* or eight-stringed instrument which they carried attached to their girdle. This is likely to have been a lyre in the early medieval period; it may be that small harps were also used.

Depictions of wind instruments are rare when compared with the relatively rich variety of stringed examples. Although in some cases they may represent the sounding of the Last Trumpet, in others they seem to be part of a musical ensemble, as in the Day of Judgement scene on Muireadach's Cross, Monasterboice, where a choir of monks is led in singing by two instrumentalists, one playing a lyre, the other a horn. Triple pipes are found also on Muireadach's Cross and on the Cross of the Scriptures, Clonmacnois.

*material evidence.* The contribution of excavation to Irish music archaeology has been especially significant in recent years. Urban archaeology, most notably in Dublin, Cork and Waterford, has yielded objects for which no other evidence exists. One particularly important find from medieval Dublin is a bow made of dogwood, dating to the early or mid-eleventh century. It is unique not only in Irish but also in European terms: no other medieval bow is known to exist. Other materials relating to stringed instruments are tuning pegs from sites in Dublin, Cork and Waterford. They include longer examples from harps as well as shorter models from fiddles or lyres. Flutes and whistles have been recovered from all three sites, and fragments of ceramic horns from Dublin and Waterford. Such objects were well known all over western Europe, serving both as signalling instruments (for hunting, keeping watch etc.) and as pilgrim's horns, purchased as souvenirs at pilgrimage centres. Over seventy ecclesiastical bells of Irish provenance survive – the number is high because preservation was ensured by the importance attached to them as sacred relics. They were the essential pre-requisites of a church: a large bell in the tower, and handbells for summoning the monks to prayer and meals. Bells are also depicted on stone carvings, usually in the hand of an ecclesiastic, and accompanied by other symbols of office such as a book and a crozier.

*liturgical music.* According to the Rule of Columbanus, psalms formed the main component of the Divine Office, and were sung in threes (*chori*), the first two straight through, and the third antiphonally, i.e., with the singers in two groups, one intoning the psalm verse, the other the response. According to Jonas, Columbanus's biographer and a member of his community in Bobbio, the saint was reported to have set out instructions for the performance of chant, but no record has survived.

Hiberno-Latin hymns make up the largest body of material from any Celtic-speaking region, as well as being among the most unique and striking aspects of early Irish liturgy. They attest to a new fusion between Latin poetry and indigenous Irish verse forms. Some hymn texts refer to the performance of hymns which, as with the psalms, were sometimes accompanied by a lyre or a harp. Colmcille was said by Admonán, his biographer, to have written a book of hymns for the week (*Hymnorum liber septimaniorum*). They were considered a particular source of indulgence and grace, and also used as a protective charm, as were certain prayers, indicating an absorption of Christian doctrine within the older pre-Christian culture.

There are eighteen surviving liturgical manuscripts of Irish provenance containing partial or complete music notation. Dating between the twelfth and fifteenth centuries, they include six Missals, a Gradual, a Breviary, two Psalters, five Antiphonals, one Troper, two Processionals. Though mostly containing plain chant for Mass and Office, there are also a few examples of polyphony in these sources which may indicate a more widespread practice.

*notation.* Liturgical music was probably orally transmitted in Ireland until the twelfth century – the oldest notation is found in the Drummond Missal, dating from the first half of the twelfth century, though incorporating older material. Its neumes were previously thought to be indecipherable, but recent work indicates the contrary. We are thus beginning to reconstruct some of the characteristics of pre-Norman chant usage in Ireland, a heritage which had long been assumed to have disappeared without trace. Similarly, the text of a hymn in honour of St Patrick, '*Ecce fulget clarissima*', in the late eleventh-century *Irish Liber Hymnorum*, is found with its melody in the fifteenth-century Kilmoone Breviary. The Sarum (or English) rite predominates in Irish liturgical manuscripts (mainly from the fifteenth century), yet while attesting to the direct importation by the new settlers of established English (particularly western English) and Norman-Welsh customs, they also reveal continuity in the veneration of Irish saints long after the Celtic liturgies were suppressed at the Synod of Cashel in 1172. Complete notated offices survive for Patrick, Brigid and Canice. And while there are no Irish sources with notation prior to the twelfth century, some Irish or Celtic regional melodies seem to have survived in later sources. The texts of a number of antiphons known to have been used in the Irish and Scottish Celtic church display the Irish characteristics of assonance and alliteration; and their melodies reveal features not found in Sarum or Gregorian chant, this strongly suggesting regional distinctiveness. (ANB)

**Meek, Bill.** (1937– ). Writer, singer. In childhood he was influenced by the East Down music of fiddlers and singers, learning the rudiments of most instruments from an uncle, playing whistle, accordion, guitar and uilleann pipes. From 1963–64 he lived in the US and became involved in the civil rights movement there in Mississippi and in Tennessee (where his name features in the Nashville Civil Rights Museum); these experiences were reflected in his music-based programmes on Raidió Éireann. In 1963 he recorded an album of songs for the Folk Legacy label and in 1971 he commenced twenty-one years as traditional music correspondent for the *Irish Times*, scripted a television documentary on Edward Bunting whose collection includes tunes donated by a Meek ancestor who was a brother of Henry Joy McCraken. In 1975 he became the second presenter of RTÉ radio series *The Long Note*. His eight published works include three song collections (*Land of Libertie*, *Moonpenny*, *Irish Folk Songs*) and a biography of the Chieftains.

**melismatic ornamentation.** A form of ornamentation (particularly sean-nós) in which a syllable is maintained over several different notes.

**melodeon.** See accordion.

**melody.** The 'tune'. This is supreme in traditional music, on all non-accompanying instruments. It may be augmented by a drone effect, and/or by the use of harmonic accompaniment on instruments like harp, piano, guitar, accordion, concertina, etc.

**membranophone.** An instrument the tone of which is produced by a sounding a stretched membrane. In this category are not only all kinds of drums, but also technically related cross-category items like banjo (the 'head' is a membrane of skin or plastic) and 'mirlitons' such as 'kazoo' (a tone generated by the voice is slightly amplified and modified by a buzzing, tightly stretched membrane). A Chinese flute also uses this principle – a rice-paper covered hole near the embouchure modifies flute sound to a reedy buzz; children play with comb and paper to get the same effect.

The pitch of the note produced in striking membranophones is in proportion to 1. the thickness of the membrane, 2. the diameter of the drum head, and 3. the tension of the membrane. The thicker, broader and looser the membrane, the lower the pitch of the note. The major Irish membranophone is the bodhrán.

See bodhrán; Lambeg drum; snare drum; tambourine.

**Mercier, Mel.** (1959– ). Born in Dublin, the son of original Chieftains bodhrán player, the late Peadar Mercier. He plays bodhrán, bones and a range of international percussion instruments. A composer and arranger he lectures in the Music Department of University College, Cork, on Irish, African, Indian and Indonesian musics. He has featured on albums like Mícheál Ó Súilleabháin's *The Dolphin's Way*, on *A River Of Sound* as well as with Alan Stivell, Stockton's Wing, John Cage, Bobby Gardiner and Áine Uí Cheallaigh. (PAD)

**Mhic Choisdealbha, Eibhlín Bean.** Song collector. Born in England, she collected song in north-east Galway at the beginning of the twentieth century. These were published in 1918 as *Amhráin Mhuighe Seola*.

**Mhic Dhonncha, Mairéad.** (1945– ). Sean-nós singer. One of eight children born in Baile Reo, west of Dingle in the Kerry Gaeltacht, to Séamus Mac Gearailt from Baile Reo and Máire Ní Shúilleabháin from An Blascaod Mór (Blasket Island). She got most of her songs from her mother and though now living among the Connemara tradition in the transplant-Gaeltacht of Ráth Cairn in Co. Meath since 1974, she retains Kerry style and repertoire. She is married to Pádraig Mac Donncha, son of singer Cóil Neaine Pháidín. She has won the women's competition at the Oireachtas, and the 1987 Pan-Celtic competition. Twelve of her songs can be heard on *Mairéad Mhic Dhonncha – Up Cuas!* (LIM)

**minstrels.** The essence of minstrelsy was black-face caricature which became increasingly popular toward the end of the eighteenth century, leading to fully fledged black-face skits and songs on stages throughout white America by the middle of the nineteenth century. A great number of the performers in minstrelsy were Irish. It was during this time that the banjo, in all probability, was introduced to Ireland, when the Virginia Minstrels toured in England, Ireland and France in 1843, 1844 and 1845. A famous member of the Virginia Minstrels was Dan Emmet, who is given credit for writing 'Dixie'. It is ironic that a Yankee, and an Irish American at that, should be the man who introduced the nation to the anthem of the Confederacy. The leader of the Virginia Minstrels was Joel Walker Sweeney who was born in Buckingham County, Virginia in 1810. Sweeney, whose antecedents came from Co. Mayo, has become one of the most controversial characters in the history of the banjo, having been credited widely with introducing the fifth string, or chanterelle, to the instrument. But in fact, there are watercolour paintings well before Sweeney's time showing the fifth string on plantation banjos. He did, however, extend the popularity of that banjo to an enormous audience all over the United States and Europe. In Ireland Percy French's early music performance was as a blackface minstrel. (MIM)

See banjo.

**Mitchell, Kevin.** (1940– ) Singer. Born in Derry city, he was inspired to sing by local Irish-language singer Seán Gallagher, eventually acquiring much of his repertoire. Competition awards – Derry feis (1959), John Player ballad competition (1965), Bellaghy song competition (1966) – led him to perform on the folk club circuit in Belfast, and to recording for BBC's *Come Listen here a While* programme. In Glasgow since 1969, he sang in folk clubs and at folk festivals. He is recorded on *Free and Easy* (1978) and *I Sang that Sweet Refrain* (1996).

**modes.** A variety of different modes or scales were in general use in European music from the early middle ages until about 1600, when they fell largely into disuse in art-music – with the exception of the Ionian mode, which became the modern major scale, and the Aeolian, which with the addition of a sharpened seventh became the modern minor scale. However, they continued to flourish in plainsong (Gregorian chant) and much folk music. Irish traditional music has continued to use four of these modes.

The simplest way of understanding how modes work is to play a scale upwards from each of the white notes of the piano in turn, using only the white notes. Each corresponds to a mode. Note that although all of the modes are constructed from five intervals of a tone and two of a semitone, the semitones are placed differently in each mode; this gives them a different flavour. The four which concern traditional music are:

C-C  (Ionian)
D-D  (Dorian)
G-G  (Mixolydian)
A-A  (Aeolian)

Thus a tune in the Dorian mode will end on D: this note is the finalis. Although in the middle ages this type of scale was linked directly to the actual pitch of the scale, this no longer applies to Irish music as we know it, and the modes can be transposed to any pitch. For example, a tune with its finalis in A may actually be in the Dorian mode, e.g., 'The Star of Munster' and a tune with its finalis in E may be in the Aeolian mode, e.g., 'The Fermoy Lasses'.

It must of course be remembered that since folksong in many countries is modal, modality alone is not enough to account for the distinctive sound of Irish music, and a number of additional factors have to be examined. Some authorities find a method of tune-analysis based on note-frequency more illuminating than one based on modality, but for the average musician, a knowledge of modes is a more useful tool.

The use of these modes, together with the practice common in dance music of switching between one mode and another in the course of a tune, help to give Irish music its characteristically plaintive undercurrent, even in such a rapid musical form as the reel. The constant movement of the C between natural and sharp in 'Corney is Coming', for example, is found in a large number of dance tunes. It can be explained as switching between the Mixolydian and Ionian modes while retaining the same finalis, D; it can also be explained as the existence of a 'mobile' seventh degree of the Mixolydian mode, one capable of having an accidental applied to it or not, at will. Another mobile note in many tunes is F. The reason for this mobility may be that it is these two notes,

C and F, which are lacking in the pentatonic scale (if one thinks of a pentatonic scale starting on G and consisting of the notes G, A, B, D and E). Such an interpretation would seem to point towards the possible antiquity of the tunes in question, or of that type of tune. (Interestingly, in this connection, Gráinne Yeats points out in *The Harp of Ireland* that since the nature of the old traditional Irish wire-strung harp is such that it was almost impossible to play accidentals in any satisfactory way, the pentatonic scale was very useful, enabling a harper to play in several different modes with minimal retuning. He could sing a song with passing accidentals, while avoiding those particular strings of the harp).

For the practising musician, the value of a knowledge of modes lies solely in its practical application. Players of melody instruments such as the fiddle or flute may not need detailed theoretical knowledge of modes, but they do need enough to make sound judgements about the appropriateness of certain types of variation. Knowledge of modes is however essential for uilleann pipers (to ensure tasteful use of regulators), harpers and guitarists. Immersion in the oral tradition from an early age often ensures an instinctive understanding, but just as often, does not. Those who come to traditional music from a classical and romantic art-music background may need to give their concentrated attention to the harmonic implications of modal melodies, as otherwise what they 'hear' as correct tends to be different to what a traditional musician 'hears' and the results of their arranging labours will be stylistically incorrect. Interestingly, guitarists without formal theoretical knowledge but with a background in blues or related popular music forms tend to have an instinctive understanding of what is appropriate.

Accompaniment of tunes such as 'Corney is Coming' needs to be approached with care: chords need to be as 'open' as possible so that the 'mobile' notes can move about unimpeded. Some dance tunes such as 'The Old Bush' have a different type of complex modality which is hard to pin down: here again the constituent notes of chords must be carefully chosen to leave space for ambiguities suggested by the melody.

The harmonic revolution which has taken place in both art and popular music in the last hundred years has paradoxically been of immense benefit to those wishing to develop a suitable form of accompaniment to Irish traditional music, one of the oldest oral traditions in Europe. The vastly expanded harmonic palette now available to us has facilitated the development of a neo-modal form of harmony, which enhances, not destroys the distinctiveness of the music. It is probably no accident that the current worldwide popularity of Irish music has been preceded by the development of its own harmonic language with its roots deep in a musical past. (MAN)

**Molloy, Matt.** (1947– ). Born in Ballaghaderreen, Co. Roscommon. Influenced by whistle player Jim Donoghue, by the time he was eighteen he had won several awards, and went to Dublin where he worked with Aer Lingus as an engineer. He played with Liam O'Flynn, Tommy Peoples and Paddy Moloney three nights a week in the Old Sheiling Hotel in Raheny, Dublin, and with Donal Lunny and others in sessions, as well as with Comhaltas Ceoltóirí Éireann. He joined the Bothy Band in 1974 and then the Chieftains in September 1979. He recorded his first solo album *Matt Molloy* in 1976 and *Heathery Breezes* in 1978, but the album was not released until 1981. He recorded a TV special with James Galway, *Galway and Molloy in Studio 1* in 1977, and with Paul Brady and Tommy Peoples recorded *Molloy, Brady and Peoples* in 1978. His solo *Stony Steps* came out in 1988, and *Shadows on Stone* in 1997. He is highly regarded internationally, both for his work with the Chieftains, and in his own right as an exceptional player. While his style could be said to be of his home area, it is also highly personal and well-developed. His popularity – like that of Michael Coleman in an earlier era – has been inspirational to younger players, so much so that competition adjudicators have long been critical of 'Matt Molloy clones' in their judgement standards. This is a considerable, if inverse, tribute to any player in his or her lifetime. Still a member of the Chieftains with whom he delivers formidable unaccompanied solos, Molloy runs a music-bar in Westport which is internationally famous.

**Moloney brothers.** (*c.* 1800). Andrew, a carpenter and Thomas, a blacksmith were highly regarded as pipe-makers in the first half of the nineteenth century, at Knockerra, near Kilrush, Co. Clare. They initially began as pipe-repairers but eventually moved on to make complete sets. One of these – now in the National Museum, Dublin – is made of ebony, ornamented with ivory. The metalwork – tubes, ferules and keys – are all of solid silver. The set has only two drones (tenor and bass), but has five regulators one of which has five keys. Another has three keys, and the remaining three have four each. The two principal regulators are connected independent of the stock. It is thought that the set was made by the Moloneys around 1835 for a local landlord. They made instruments for the local market, and it is known that John Carroll of Miltown Malbay played one of their sets in the late 1800s.

**Moloney, Mick.** (1944– ). Singer, banjo player, writer, researcher, commentator, teacher. Born in Co. Galway, he was a moving force in the ballad group movement in Ireland of the 1960s. He played in the Emmet Folk, and in the Parnell Folk with Dubliners Dan Maher and Tony Butler; their venues were pubs like Dublin's Castle Inn (Christchurch), and Maher's of Moore Street. He played often in Dublin's folk clubs – the Old Triangle in Leeson Street, the Universal in Parnell Street, the 95 Folk Club in Harcourt Street. With Drogheda collector and singer Seán Corcoran, and Paddy McEvoy, he played as the Rakish Paddies and ran the 95 Folk Club. He joined the Johnstons group, emigrating to live in the US in 1973. There he has been involved in an array of performances and projects as a college lecturer, arts administrator, presenter and advocate, professional musician, and radio and television personality. He holds a PhD in folklore and folklife from the University of Pennsylvania, his dissertation was titled 'Irish Music in America: Continuity and Change'. He has published numerous articles in journals including *Pennsylvania Folklife*, *Keystone Folklore* and *New Hibernia Review* and has written liner notes for more than fifty recordings of Irish American music. He has served as the artistic director for several major arts tours including The Green Fields of America – an ensemble of Irish musicians, singers and dancers in America – and Cherish the Ladies, the first all-women's Irish music ensemble. He has also run tours of American traditional musicians and dancers to Africa and South and Central America for the United States Information Agency. He has worked as an advisor and produced concerts and festivals for scores of cultural organisations including Davis and Elkins College in West Virginia where he has served as co-ordinator of Irish Week for seventeen years. In 1977 he founded the Folklife Center of International House of Philadelphia for the presentation of traditional ethnic arts. He has been twice named one of the 'Top 100 Irish Americans' by *Irish America* magazine. In 1991 he was voted into the Fiddlers Green Festival Hall of Fame (Rostrevor). He has appeared as a performer on television shows in Europe and America including *Great Performances* on PBS in 1994. He has hosted three nationally syndicated series of folk music shows on PBS, produced by WNBC in Fairfax Virginia. In 1980 he produced the documentary movie *Did Your Mother Come From Ireland?* He was a consultant, performer and interviewee on *Bringing it All Back Home*, was participant, consultant and the music arranger of the 1994 PBS documentary film *Out of Ireland* and a performer and music researcher for the 1998 PBS Special, *The Irish in America: The Long Journey Home*. He has performed also on hundreds of radio shows in Europe and the United States, including *Morning Edition*, *All Things Considered* and *Fresh Air*. In 1978 he co-produced, wrote and narrated *Across the Western Ocean* – a thirteen-part series on Irish music in America – for National Public Radio. He has recorded and produced some forty albums, and through arts advocacy and consultation has played a major part in the revival of Irish music in the United States. On four occasions *Frets* magazine readership polls voted him best tenor banjo player in America. His performance partners have included Robbie O'Connell, Jimmy Keane, The Green Fields of America and long-time Philadelphia-based musical colleagues Eugene O'Donnell and

Séamus Egan. He also tours with Tommy Sands, fiddler Eileen Ivers, uilleann piper Kieran O'Hare, guitarist and bouzouki player Zan McLeod and top Irish American step dancers.

**Moloney, Paddy.** (1938– ). Uilleann pipes, tin whistle. Leader of the Chieftains. Born in Dublin, his maternal grandfather was a flute player from the Slieve Bloom area of Co. Laois. As a child he studied uilleann pipes with Leo Rowsome at the Leinster School of Music and through musical get-togethers his early influences included pipers Peter Flynn, Séamus Ennis, Jack Wade, Tommy Reck and others. In 1960 he joined the Ó Riada group which was to become Ceoltóirí Chualann, and three years later founded the Chieftains. He managed Claddagh Records for some years from 1968, and since the band went full time in 1975 he has lived a life of constant touring. He has collaborated with artists from a wide musical spectrum, and has written scores for theatre, cinema and ballet. He was awarded an honorary Doctorate of Music, by the University of Dublin in 1988. (BIM)

**Moloneys of Ballinakill.** Associated with the music of East Galway, the earliest Moloney antecedent, James, was a tailor, flute player and opera singer from East Limerick who emigrated to England, then America. In England he learned much of his traditional music from other members of a working men's club in Leeds. Returning to Ireland in the late 1800s he settled at Ross, Kylebrack in the parish of Ballinakill between Loughrea and Woodford, Co. Galway. His son Stephen, born in the 1880s (d. 1963) was a step dancer and played flute, uilleann pipes, war pipes and fiddle; his practice was, like neighbour Tommy Whelan, to play outside during the summer. They were the key members of the Ballinakill Traditional Dance Players (referred to also as the Ballinakill Céilí Band), who recorded nine 78s between 1928 and 1938, disbanding only in 1943. Stephen's daughters Alice, Lucy, Lily, Evelyn and Carmel were all singers and dancers; his sons James, Eddie and Ambrose played flute, Kevin played fiddle.

Of them, Eddie is best known, for fiddle playing also, and in duet with Aggie White. He broadcast on radio and TV, for Raidió Éireann and the BBC between the 1940s and his death in 1980. He went on to play with the new Ballinakill Céilí Band of the 1950s, and with them played for the 1951 BBC-produced ballad opera *The Story of Tory*. In Galway city he played in the Loch Lurgan Céilí Band during the 1960s, and on their LP in the 1970s. He played with, and was mentor to the Shaskeen Céilí Band also. His brother Ambrose also played with the new Ballinakill, and with the Leitrim Ramblers who came from around East Galway. Stephen, Ambrose and Eddie contributed tunes to Breandán Breathnach around 1960 for his *Ceol Rince na hÉireann* collection. Kevin was taught by the travelling fiddle-teacher Jack Mulkere, and played with the old Ballinakill band in the 1930s, with whom in 1938, while still a teenager, he played in the Olympia Theatre, Earls Court, London. He recorded with nephew Seán (Eddie's son) in 1996 on *Bridging the Gap*, an east-Galway style album, and still teaches fiddle in Balla, Co. Mayo. The fourth generation of Moloney descendants play still, some at home, some in the US; they are involved in different kinds of music and instrument repair. A fifth generation is now playing.

See Ballinakill Traditional Dance Players; céilí bands; piano.

**Moore, Christy.** (1945– ). Singer, songwriter. Born in Newbridge, Co. Kildare, to Andy Moore from that town, and Neans de Paor of Yellow Furze, Navan. From his mother he learned to sing, and became absorbed in rock 'n roll initially, then was deeply moved by the Clancy Brothers. He learnt guitar in 1961 from Donal Lunny, and while still in his teens he formed with him a duo the Rakes of Kildare. He worked briefly in the Bank of Ireland, but left during the strike of 1966 to tour folk clubs in England, during his stay there recording his first album *Paddy on the Road* with Dominic Behan as producer. Out of Ireland he was influenced by music heard in pubs in Fulham, Camden Town, Cricklewood, Moss Side, Glasgow and Blairgowrie. Singers John Reilly, Luke Kelly, Ewan McColl, Martin Carthy, Hamish Imlach, Joe Heaney and Annie Briggs also influenced him. He returned to Ireland in

1971, and recorded *Prosperous,* released in 1972. With three of the musicians who played on that album – Liam O'Flynn, Donal Lunny and Andy Irvine – he formed the group Planxty, the most interesting and popular band of the 1970s. When they split in 1975 he pursued a solo career; they re-formed in 1978, but within a few years Moore and Lunny had left to form Moving Hearts. He left after that band's second album and developed a highly successful solo career, playing to huge audiences at home and abroad. An uncompromisingly political singer, Moore has espoused such causes as the Carnsore Point Anti-Nuclear protest, H-Block hunger strikes and the lot of the ordinary worker. His lyrics are intense, rhythmical in a 'talking blues' style, and when not (as sometimes), bitingly sarcastic, moralistic, sentimental or angry, can radiate an intense humorous understatement. Other members of the Moore family are involved in music. Brother Barry performs as 'Luka Bloom', nephew Conor Byrne plays flute (album *Wind Dancer*). Christy Moore retired from public performance in 1998.

Moore performed on all of Planxty's recordings and on *Moving Hearts* (1982) and *The Dark End of the Street* (1982) with Moving Hearts. His solo albums include: *Paddy on the Road* (1969); *Prosperous* (1972); *Christy Moore* (1975); *Christy Moore Folk Collection* (1973–78); *The Iron Behind the Velvet* (1978); *Live in Dublin* (1979); *Christy Moore and Friends* (1981); *The Time Has Come* (1983); *Ride On* (1984); *The Spirit of Freedom* (1985); *Ordinary Man* (1985); *Nice'n'Easy* (1986); *Unfinished Revolution* (1987); *Christy Moore* (1988); *Voyage* (1989); *The Christy Moore Collection* (1981–91); *Smoke and Strong Whiskey* (1991); *King Puck* (1993); *Christy Moore – Live at the Point* (1994); *Graffiti Tongue* (1996); *Collection Part 2* (1997). (PAA)

**Moore, Thomas.** (1779–1852). Born Aungier St, Dublin, the son of a grocer. Encouraged by his mother he developed a talent at recitation and was frequently called upon to entertain in the family home. He would appear to have acquired his piano-skills while eavesdropping on his sister's lessons. Preoccupied with writing, he had his first poem published at age fourteen.

He was one of the few Catholics to enter Trinity College Dublin, and there began a translation of *Anacreon* which was eventually published in 1800 to instant acclaim. In TCD he associated with many of those involved in the 1798 rebellion, and although never actively involved himself, these friendships – particularly that with Robert Emmet, whom he greatly admired – consolidated his already nationalistic leanings. One particularly important friendship made here was with collector Edward Hudson with whom he shared not only a common interest in the politics of the day but also in music. Hudson got many of his airs from harpers and would play them for Moore on the flute, this influencing Moore's ultimate work. Moore moved to London in 1799, and there his convivial nature and gifts as an entertainer endeared him to polite society, with whom his reputation as a fine conversationalist and after-dinner singer guaranteed him invitations to all 'high-quality' gatherings. Through connections made in this company, in 1803 he was appointed Registrar of the Admiralty Court in Bermuda, travelling there to appoint a deputy and returning via America and Canada. In 1808 he began publishing the first of his *Irish Melodies*, which along with the 1817 Byronic poem, *Lalla Rookh,* were so phenomenally successful, both critically and financially, that they should have provided Moore with lifelong security. But by 1819 he was virtually bankrupt, blaming his embezzling Bermuda deputy for his troubles. These difficulties caused his and his wife's removal to the continent from 1819–22, during which period he renewed his friendship with Lord Byron (each for some time had been ardent admirers of the other). After Byron's death Moore was appointed his literary executor and wrote his biography, the first of many. In 1822 he returned to his wife's home in Wiltshire where he was to spend the rest of his life having survived his five children. There he continued writing both a personal journal and commercial literature of every type, this eventually halted by mental illness. He was granted a government pension in 1835. His *Irish Melodies* appeared between 1808 and 1834 in ten successive volumes with a final supplement, these containing 124 original songs which used 126 airs. The tunes themselves were drawn principally from other printed collections with only minor alterations being made, Bunting was his primary source. An 'appeal for material' made in a number of the volumes also ensured that Moore became the owner of a variety of manuscript collections from which he also drew. *Irish Melodies* was widely and immediately celebrated, its songs' popularity waxing and waning with political climate, but nevertheless lasting to the present day and ensuring his place as Ireland's 'National' poet. Often criticised for pandering to the tastes of a London society far removed from the reality of eighteenth- and nineteenth-century Ireland, Moore still holds a revered place in the popular political cultural imagination. Some of his songs have gone into or are popularly perceived as part of the traditional repertoire. James Flannery's 1998 *Dear Harp of My Country* (Wolfhound) is a valuable text and audio document of his life and music. (GLC)

**Morris, Henry.** (1874–1945). Gaelic scholar, song collector. Born Coolfure, Farney, Co. Monaghan. Essay cash-prizes financed his early acquisition of music and history works. He was influenced by Eugene O'Growney and inspired to collect by collector J. H. Lloyd (Seosamh Laoide). Graduating from St Patrick's, Drumcondra, he taught Irish classes in Lisdoonan from 1895, later at Laragh and Cornanure. While teaching at St Malachy's Dundalk he was secretary to the local Gaelic League, and a founder of the Louth Archaeological Society. Married to harpist Alice Reilly in 1907, she and their son died a year later; he married again in 1912. A schools-inspector from 1921, he moved to Skerries, then Mountshannon, and to Dublin as Deputy Chief Inspector of National Schools. A tireless worker for the Gaelic traditions of Ulster, he was a prodigious editor and publisher. He is known for the song collections *Céad de Cheoltaibh Uladh* (1915), *Amhráin Airt Mhic Cubhthaigh* (1916), *Duanaire na Midhe* (1933), *Dhá Chéad de Cheoltaibh Uladh* (1934) and *Dánta Diadha Uladh* (1936). Although seldom with notated music, these have become standard reference works for singers in the Northern Gaelic tradition. (EDI/LIO)

**Morrison, James.** (1893–1947). Fiddler. Born at Drumfin, near Riverstown, Co. Sligo, the spot is now marked by a subtle memorial on the main Dublin–Sligo roadside. One of the leading mentors and stylistic proponents of the Sligo style of fiddle playing in the first half of the twentieth century, he learned music from his brothers and others locally, in an area where flute and fiddle were the favoured instruments. He was taught dancing by his uncle and as a teenager he learned to read and write music from a local priest Fr Bernard Creehan, a skill rarely found among traditional musicians at that time. The Gaelic League employed him as a dancing and Irish language teacher before he left to join five members of his family in the Boston area in 1915. Within three years he had won the fiddle competition at the New York Feis and later settled in that city where he married in 1919. He began recording in 1921, this continuing over the following fifteen years with a large output of solo fiddle records, duets with leading Irish musicians of the day, and band recordings. A natural teacher, he developed an extensive music teaching practice in New York and also gave private tuition in academic subjects. Recent years have seen a renaissance of interest in Morrison's music led by players like Frankie Gavin, Séamus Quinn and Charlie Lennon, and in July of each year a weekend commemorating Morrison's contribution to Irish music is held at Riverstown, Co. Sligo. (HAB)

**Morton, Robin.** (1939–   ). Singer, bodhrán. Born at Portadown, Co. Armagh. His early interest was in jazz, but he became involved in traditional music while at Queen's University in 1962–64 where he started the Folk Club in 1963 and later the Ulster Folk Music Society, along with John Moulden, Dave Scott and others. He started the group Boys of the Lough with Cathal McConnell and Tommy Gunn in 1966, he managed and played with it until 1979. He has written *Folksongs Sung in Ulster* and is the editor of John Maguire's biography, *Come Day, Go Day, God Send Sunday*. He has produced many records of traditional musicians such as Seán McAloon, John Rea and Séamus Tansey. He was director of the Edinburgh Folk Festival 1985–88. He founded Temple Records in 1979 and now runs this recording company and manages the Battlefield Band. He is married to Scottish harper Alison Kinnaird.

**Moulden, John.** (1941– ). Concertina, singer, researcher, and publisher. Founder member and organiser of the Belfast Folk Song Club (1963), Ulster Folk Song Society (1965) and Down Coast Folk Society (1973), he is currently involved with the Singers' Club in association with Glens Cultural Traditions Group (1991). He is a member of the English Folk Dance and Song Society, is a committee member of Folk Music Society of Ireland and is on the board of the Irish Traditional Music Archive. He lectures on traditional music and on Ulster song. Articles and essays have been published in *Canadian Folk Music Journal*, *Éigse Ceol Tíre*, *Folk Review*, *Folk Song Research*, *Fortnight*, *Honest Ulsterman*, *Journal of the Wesleyan Historical Society*, *Living Tradition*, *Slow Air*, *Treoir*. Sleeve notes and research for records have been published by Mercier, Leader, Ossian and Topic. His major achievement is the editing and geographical indexing of the *Sam Henry Collection* (Blackstaff, 1979). He is the author of *A History of Methodism in Portrush*; *The Trim Little Borough* (1992); *Songs of Hugh McWilliams, Schoolmaster* (1992) and *Thousands are Sailing* (1994).

**mouth organ.** See harmonica.

**Moving Hearts.** Formed in 1981 by Christy Moore and Donal Lunny it started with a line-up of Declan Sinnott (guitar), Eoghan O'Neill (bass), Brian Calnan (drums, percussion), Davey Spillane (uilleann pipes) and Keith Donald (saxophone). Mixing traditional music with rock, jazz and contemporary songs, some with political overtones, the band toured Ireland in 1981 and recorded their first single 'Landlord'/'Category' for WEA Ireland. The debut album *Moving Hearts* entered the Irish charts at No. 1. The band became a massive live attraction and their gigs displayed a penchant for improvisation. They supported various causes including H-Block hunger strikers and Nicky Kelly. Matt Kelleghan (drums) replaced Calnan for the second album *Dark End of the Street* which went unreleased in the UK. Moore was replaced by Mick Hanly in November 1982 and *Live Hearts* was recorded at London's Dominion Theatre in early 1983. Noel Eccles (percussion) and Declan Masterson (uilleann pipes) joined late in 1983 and Hanly was replaced by Flo McSweeney in 1984. Anto Drennan (guitar) replaced Sinnott and their final single 'State Music'/'May Morning Dew' was released in 1984. 'May Morning Dew' became the theme tune for 2FM radio show *Night Train*. The band broke up in late 1984 after 'Last Reel' concert at Dublin's National Stadium. Their last recording, *The Storm*, was released in the summer of 1985. An all-instrumental album, it was an amalgamation of traditional music, rock and jazz. They played at 'Self Aid' in 1986 and in later concerts as an instrumental line-up. (JOO)

**Mulcaire, Jack.** (1900–82). Fiddler. Born in Crusheen, Co. Clare, son of an ardent Gaelic League organiser who was an associate of scholar Eugene O'Growney and Lady Gregory. Through visits to such as Coole House, Gort, Jack was aware that pipers then played for the gentry. With the encouragement of his teacher – Miss Barry of Kiltartan NS – and the local Minister he taught himself fiddle as a young teenager, and joined Gort's fife and drum band in 1922. He began teaching in 1923 at Peterswell, then at Kiltartan, then at Ballinakill where he taught Aggie White, and gave Lucy Farr her grounding in slow air playing; by the early 1930s he was teaching throughout Galway. He played for Republican Club dances all over the area – Dunirey, Loughrea, Ballinasloe – his pupils included Jack and Mick Cooley, later Joe. He taught often with Sligo dance master Mick Coleman. An associate of both Paddy Kelly and Jack Fahy, he began playing with Kelly and Joe Mills at Kilconnell in 1925, broadcasting on 2RN in 1927 as the Aughrim Slopes Trio with which they won first prize at the Thomond Feis of Limerick in 1934. They expanded into the Aughrim Slopes Céilí Band (one of the first) in 1932, becoming a household name throughout the country. From the 1930s to the mid-1950s his classes had spread to North Clare, one of his better known students being Patrick Deveney. Mulcaire was one of the principal figures involved in the expansion of CCÉ in Clare and often adjudicated at fleadhanna ceoil. He married singer Angela Fogarty – winner of the Cavan All-Ireland in 1954 – and moved to live in Crusheen. He greatly influenced his sons Des, Enda, Brendan (who teaches and plays in London) and Ciarán, but in particular music teacher Frank Custy.

**Mullally, Katherine (née McCarthy).** (1907–94). Singer and concertina player, she was the youngest and only girl in a Doonogan, Co. Clare music family of eleven. Orphaned at a young age, she was educated as a boarder in Loreto Abbey in Rathfarnham. In 1932 she opened a private school for four- to seven-year-old children and worked there till her retirement in the late 1980s. In 1937 she married Phil Mullally from Owel, Mullingar, Co. Westmeath and they lived in Mullingar. In 1968 Mrs Mullally was the first female chair elected to the Leinster Council of CCÉ, a position she held until she stepped down in 1972. She worked tirelessly promoting the organisation, held every possible office with it in her own county, and was delegate to its Ard Chomhairle from 1967 to 1988. Her family home at Clounlaheen, Miltown Malbay, which included a small bar and a grocery store, is still known as McCarthy's pub and is a prized venue for music making during the Willie Clancy summer school. It is particularly favoured by singers. (MAO)

**Mulligan, Tom ('T. P.').** (1915–84), Piper, fiddler. From Currycramp, Bornacoola, Co. Leitrim, one of the great motivating personalities of music revival. Séamus Ennis, Tommy Reck, Seosamh Ó hÉanaí, Tommy Potts, Breandán Breathnach – household names of the music in the mid-twentieth century – were his compatriots. He was the third generation playing, his grandfather played concertina at age ninety-six, his mother and aunt played melodeons and all his family learnt fiddle. Tom was taught by local fiddle master Jack Conboy, his first experience of uilleann pipes was hearing Leo Rowsome at Mohill in 1932. Working in Dublin in 1935 he bought his first pipes from Phibsboro-based Abbeyshrule maker James Mulcrone, this leading to friendship, music performances and feis duet awards with piper Tommy Reck. Interest in the future and survival of the music involved him too with the Dublin Piper's Club in the 1940s. Married in Cabra he was neighbour to pipe maker Matt Kiernan, the Mulligan home having such a constant parade of musicians that Séamus Ennis dubbed it 'the Rotary Club'. His family spent summers in the Gaeltacht – Coláiste Lurgán was a meeting ground then for other enthusiastic figures in music, among them dancer, singer and flute-player Paddy Bán Ó Broin. Dublin sessions were an exciting source of learning and listening in those years. Mulligan's associates were legends of a passé era – singer Larry Dillon, fiddler Jack Howard, box player Mick Grogan. All-Ireland fleadhanna were other important rendezvous, as well as impetuous, whirlwind trips to visit renowned players – Lad O'Beirne, Willie Clancy, Tommy McCarthy, Felix Doran, Seán Ac Donncha, Packie Duignan, Joe Heaney. Mulligan's friendship with Séamus Ennis was motivating and important in this highly charged, organisational, pedagogic social scene – Ennis might spend a fortnight in the Mulligan home between trips. The Mulligan children carry on the music – Alfie, Néillidh (who plays Séamus Ennis's Brogan pipes) and Tom (who inherited Felix Doran's Rowsome-made set and runs the Cobblestone traditional music pub in Dublin's Smithfield). Néillidh alone has recorded, his 1991 album a tribute to T. P., and the 1997 *Leitrim Thrush* featuring T. P. playing fiddle.

**Mulqueen, Anne.** (1945–   ). Singer. Born at Castleconnell, Co. Limerick her interest in singing began with her grandmother. Her uncle favoured sporting songs and her father favoured recitation – he could deliver forty verses of Tennyson. Her mother was a set dancer, she knew tunes and used to lilt for Anne and her other daughters' dancing at home. A chance entry in a touring talent competition with the song 'Falls of Dunass' in 1956 gave her confidence, and in 1959 she won the senior song competition at the fleadh in Thurles, adjudicated by Séamus Ennis and Seán Ó Síocháin. A repeat of this in the following two years at Boyle and Swinford made a name for her, and with céilís as the popular social dance she was in demand to sing in waltz time. This led to her joining at the age of fourteen the touring Gallowglass Céilí Band, which caused difficulties with competition judges. Favouring ballads, she sang in concerts with Willie Clancy and Joe Heaney and subbed for Dolly McMahon with the Dubliners. She sang too in the Bunratty Castle cabaret and toured England, playing weekends for two years with Roger Sherlock, Kevin Taylor, John Bowe, Oliver and Raymond Roland, Seán Maguire and Josephine Keegan. In 1967 she returned to Ireland, singing cabaret at Cruise's of Limerick, in 1969 moving to Ring, Co. Waterford. She learnt to speak Irish, developing a repertoire in the language from such as the Tóibín family, and is currently on the board of TnaG.

**Mulvihill, Charlie.** (1917–75). Accordion. Born in New York, his father Tom, from Miltown Malbay, played concertina; his mother came from Shanagolden, Co. Limerick. He began playing with his father in Irish clubs in New York through the 1930s – with Michael Coleman, James Morrison and Ed Reavy. In the Air Corps at the end of World War II, he spent much of his life playing music; his friends were Lad O'Beirne, Denis Murphy, Paddy Killoran and Paddy Reynolds. He established contact with Ireland in 1964, meeting family musicians and bringing back tunes from Kerry, Dublin and Clare. He composed tunes, and recorded with Paddy Reynolds and James Keane. His son Tommy is also well known as an accordion player.

**Mulvihill, Martin.** (1919–  ). Fiddler. Born at Ballygoughlin, Co. Limerick, he was taught fiddle by his mother first, then by a teacher in nearby Glin. He played the fiddle during his period in the army, then took up accordion and played with the local Meade's Dance Band. He emigrated to England in 1952 settling in Northampton, playing mostly dance band music in England with Dubliner Tommy Murray. He moved to the USA in 1965 where he took up fiddle again, playing in his West Limerick/Kerry style. A popular teacher since 1970, he has students throughout New York, in New Jersey and Philadelphia. He has one LP recording and has been heard on many broadcasts, particularly on Ciarán MacMathúna's *Job of Journeywork*. His music collection published in 1986 has 513 tunes, these mostly reels and jigs, with hornpipes, polkas, slides, marches, set dances and slip jigs, of current provenance. The music was drawn from his maternal and childhood repertoires, and from session tapes of his associates, these including Larry Redican and Paddy Taylor, and players from his home area of west Co. Limerick.

**mummers.** 'Mummers' plays' as we know them in Ireland are closely related to similar plays in England. They appear to be medieval in origin and are performed predominantly in the east and north of Ireland around Christmas time. They are basically a form of folk drama which involves the death and resuscitation of a hero, usually followed by music and dancing. Frequently the play itself also involves music and dancing and may also, as in Wexford, for example, include a type of sword dance.

The plays are always in verse form and the characters vary. Some of these may be historical, such as Napoleon Bonaparte, the Tsar of Russia or Mussolini. Others are more specifically based in Irish history, including St Patrick, Brian Boru and Daniel O'Connell, while other characters are of a more imaginative nature such as Jack Straw, Devil Doubt or Beelzebub. The plays often include references to local and topical events. Mummers are also known as Christmas Rhymers and the following verse is typical of the introduction to the play by the first character:

> Here I come, Rim Rhyme,
> Give me room and give me time
> For myself and many more
> Tired of the road, and all footsore,
> We fought our journey, every inch.
> Prepared to murder, at a pinch
> He who tries us to oppose
> We'll split his skull and punch his nose
> If you don't believe what I have said
> You may take it from me you'll soon be dead.
> The one above all I'd hate to be,
> Is that white-wigged man from o'er the sea
> The Sasanach who'd raise my gorge
> So, enter in my brave Prince George.

(RIO)

See wren, the.

**Munnelly, Tom.** (1944–  ). Collector, archivist, singer. Born in Dublin, this field worker has made traditional song his life and has uniquely imprinted its society. With an intense interest in song and folklore he emerged from no academic background to produce by 1998 a prodigious volume of research, analysis and presentation. Beginning in 1964 he recorded traditional song in the field, from 1969 to 1971 he was research assistant to D. K. Wilgus, Professor of Anglo/American Folksong, UCLA, noting, cataloguing and describing narrative song materials (English and macaronic) in the Main MS Collection of the Irish Folklore Commission, covering some 1,750 manuscripts page by page. In 1970, with Breandán Breathnach, Prof. Seóirse Bodley and Dr Hugh Shields, he founded the Folk Music Society of Ireland (Cumann Cheoil Tíre Éireann) and still serves on its committee. In 1971 he became the first song collector for the new National Traditional Music Collecting Scheme then initiated by the Department of Education under Breandán Breathnach. In 1975 this merged with the Department of Irish Folklore at UCD, so leading him to lecturing on traditional song. In 1976, at the request of the Smithsonian Institute, he and Ciarán MacMathúna selected the twenty-five traditional performers to represent Ireland in the American Bicentennial celebrations, and was spokesperson and lecturer there. In 1978 he moved to Co. Clare, and from 1984 until 1991 was chairman of the Willie Clancy Summer School. In 1981 he was appointed to the Arts Council's Irish Traditional Music Archive Advisory Committee. In 1982 he founded An Cumann le Béaloideas agus Ceol Tíre an Chláir (The Folklore and Folkmusic Society of Clare), organising its lectures over nine years. Between 1983 and 1985 he was the Arts Council nominee to the board of Mid-West Arts, and in the same year, with Dr Hugh Shields of TCD and Nicholas Carolan organised the fifteenth International Ballad Conference of the Kommisssion fur Volksdichtung (Société Internationale d'Ethnologie et de Folklore). From 1985 to 1988 he was a member of the Arts Council of Ireland and from 1988 to 1993 was chairman of the Irish Traditional Music Archive (re-elected to its board 1995 and 1998). In 1990 he was chairman/founder of the Ennistymon Festival of Traditional Singing and is presently still on its board, and in 1990 was chairman/founder of Scoil Leacht uí Chonchúir (Lahinch Folklore School). Between 1990 and 1994 he also indexed all oral poetry (lyric and narrative, English and macaronic) in the first 2,000 vols. of the Main Manuscript Collection of the Department of Irish Folklore, generating some 18,000 cards in a self-developed system of cataloguing. Since 1971 he has recorded some 1,500 tapes of folksong (mainly) and folklore, the largest and most comprehensive collection of traditional song ever compiled in Ireland by any one individual. This is transcribed, indexed and catalogued using Irish, British, American and European systems of identification. He has lectured to practically every folkmusic and folklore body in Ireland, has talked in all Irish universities, and continues to give papers abroad every year.

His publications include: 'The man and his music – John Reilly', *Ceol*, vol. IV, no. 1, 1972; 'Lord O'Bore and Mary Flynn – a unique ballad survival', *IFMS*, vol. 1, 1972–3; 'The singing tradition of Irish travellers', *FMJ*, vol. 2, no. 6, 1975; 'Tom Lenihan, traditional singer', *Dal gCais*, vol. 4, 1978; 'Collecting folksong', *Sinsear*, 1980; 'Joe Mikey McMahon', *Dal gCais*, vol. 3, 1977; 'Folktales and folk music', vol. 7, *The Irish Travelling People*, resource collection, Ulster Polytechnic, 1981; 'Scots ballad influences in Ireland' (with Hugh Shields), *Ceol Tíre*, no. 15, 1979; 'Songs of the sea' 1, *Béaloideas*, vol. 48–49, 1980–81; 'Songs of the sea' 2, *Béaloideas*, vol. 50, 1982; 'The nature of Ireland's traditional song', *Dal gCais*, vol. 6, 1982; 'On the Wran in Dingle', *Ceol Tíre*, vol. 25, 1984; 'Seosamh Ó hÉanaí', *Dal gCais*, vol. 7, 1984; 'Breandán Breathnach – a personal memoir', *An Píobaire*, vol. 2, no. 28, 1986; 'The long song singer – Martin Reidy of Tullaghboy', *Dal gCais*, vol. 8, 1986; 'Narrative songs in west Clare', Ballad Research, *Proceedings of the 15th Int. Conf. of the Kommission für Volksdichtung*, ed. Hugh Shields, 1986; *Ennistymon – local songs*, 26 pp. booklet; The decline of narrative song in Anglo-Irish tradition, 1990; *Recent Ballad Research*, 1990; *Micho's dozen – traditional songs from Micho Russell*, 1991, 34 pp. booklet; 'They're there all the same! Supernatural elements in narrative songs in the English language in

Ireland', *Béaloideas,* vol. 60–61, 1992–93; 'Scientists, amateurs and antiquarians – folklore collectors in county Clare', TUI, *Annual Congress Journal,* Ennis, 1993; *The Mount Callan Garland – Songs from the repertoire of Tom Lenihan,* 1994, book and audio cassettes (CBÉ 003); 'Black pudding and bottles of smoke', *Crossroads Conference Papers,* 1996; 'Comic voyages in Irish song tradition: Islanders and water dwellers', *Proceedings of the Celtic-Nordic-Baltic Folklore Seminar,* 1996; 'Junior Crehan of Bonavilla' (pt. 1), *Béaloideas,* vol. 66, 1998, pp. 59–161; 'Oh, what a falling off was there – A survey of collections of, and attitudes to, English language folk song in Ireland, 1789–1972', in *Essays in Honour of Breandán Breathnach,* ed. Nicholas Carolan, IAP, forthcoming; 'Women in traditional song in Ireland' (with Ríonach Uí Ógáin), *The Field Day Anthology of Irish Writing,* Vol. 4, forthcoming.

Audio publications include *The Bonny Green Tree – songs of an Irish traveller* (12T359, 1978, 5 pp notes); with Jim Carroll and Pat McKenzie, *Paddy's Panacea, Songs from the repertoire of Tom Lenihan* (12TS363, 1978); *John Reilly – Irish come-all-ye* (Folktracks FSA-60-175, 1981); *Songs of the Irish travellers, 1967–75* (EEOT, 1983, cass. and 24 pp. notes); *Early Ballads in Ireland* 1968–85 (with Hugh Shields, EEOT, 1985, cass. and 26 pp. notes).

**Murphy, Delia.** (1902–71). Ballad singer. Born at Ardroe, Claremorris into a modestly wealthy family she attended national school at Roundfort where she was taught music by Miss Sweeney. As a child she spoke Irish – but this was not permitted in school – and sang local and national songs. She was taught singing, violin and piano by Sr Fursey at the Presentation convent in Tuam, her repertoire including such as 'Carraigdoun', she sang songs from musicals and took part in the choir. While at UCG she met Padraig Ó Conaire and learnt ballads around the Claddagh. She led a sit-down during the playing of 'God Save the Queen', and graduated with a BComm in 1922. County-house dances with step and set dancing were the stuff of weekend recreation in her teenage years, she herself singing at every opportunity. Married to diplomat Tom Kiernan, while posted in London she developed this, and was to record 'The Spinning Wheel' and 'Three Lovely Lassies From Bannion' with HMV in 1939. In the years that followed she covered almost a hundred songs, her consciously-uncompromising, passionate ballad style – particularly on 'Dan O'Hara' for which she was famous – a total contrast to her lifestyle. Throughout her life she broadcast and sang in concerts, most famously at a céilí in the Ulster Hall in Belfast during the 1941 German bombing raid there. She put her singing career second to that of her husband though, breaking off and renewing sporadically in response to his moves to London, Rome, Canberra, Bonn and Ottawa where her final concert was to a folk-festival audience at Camp Fortune. She moved to Strawberry Beds, Dublin in 1969, appearing on the *Late Late Show* in 1971, and died shortly afterwards. She is commemorated by a memorial at Annefield crossroads, near her childhood home Mount Jennings House. This is inscribed 'Delia Murphy, Ballad Queen'. RTÉ documented her in the television programme *The Ballad of Delia Murphy,* and Aidan O'Hara minutely describes her life in *I'll Live 'til I Die* (Drumlin, 1997).

**Murphy, Denis.** (1910–74). Fiddler. From Lisheen, Gneeveguilla, Co. Kerry he was one of the famous pupils of Pádraig O'Keeffe and came from a large musical family all of whom played the fiddle. He played in the local dance halls as a youth and recorded for Raidió Éireann before making the first of a number of lengthy visits to work in the USA. He was friendly with some of the famous exponents of the Sligo style of fiddle playing – Lad O'Beirne, Andy McGann and Paddy Killoran. He returned to Ireland in 1965 to live at Lisheen and played locally in Sliabh Luachra especially in Dan O'Connell's pub in Knocknagree, Co. Cork. His recordings can be heard on *Denis Murphy – Music from Sliabh Luachra.* Two forty-five minute radio documentaries (RTÉ Radio 1, 1995) tell his full life story. (PEB)

**Murphy, Jimmy.** (1938– ). Fiddle. Born Meelick, Swinford, Co. Mayo, he was influenced by his aunt's melodeon playing, and neighbour Bill Kelly (fiddle). Later he was drawn to the playing of Fred Finn (fiddle), who was to become his main inspiration. He played with the Countryside Céilí Group which included James Murray (flute), Harry McGowan (flute), and Joe Fallon (button accordion). He toured the US in 1972 and '74. He has played duet with James Murray (flute) for many years and their playing is in the forefront of Sligo style fiddle/flute music. He has also recorded for radio and television. His style reflects that of South Sligo and he plays many of the older, more unusual versions of well-known tunes. (GRD)

**Murphy, Maggie (Chambers).** (1923– ). Singer. Born Tempo, Co. Fermanagh, as a young girl she was obsessed with song, a reputation added to by the sound of her voice often heard over the fields as she returned from work in the evenings. Her repertoire contains much that is local; her style is straight-out and unaffected. She sings with a rare joy, her repertoire embracing the old and the modern without prejudice and uncluttered by idealism. A significant and empowering contributor to many of the singers weekends she attends each year, she was recorded – and described vividly – by Peter Kennedy in the 1960s, and can be heard on his *Folksongs of Britain and Ireland* from the mid-1960s. Her solo album is the 1996 *Linkin' O'er the Lea*.

**Murphy, Michael J.** (1913–96), Collector, poet and playwright. Born in Liverpool, reared in Dromintee, Co. Armagh, he spent most of his life there. He left school at fourteen to labour on farms, but started writing at an early age, encouraged by Maud Gonne MacBride and others. He wrote articles and stories for *The Bell* and *Hibernia*. From 1938 he began broadcasting with the BBC and soon after with Raidió Éireann. His collection of folklore *At Slieve Gullion's Foot*, which was published in 1941, brought him to the attention of Séamus Delargey of the Irish Folklore Commission for whom he worked until 1983. His published output consists of some ten books, mainly on folklife and the folklore he gathered for the commission. A classic among these is *Tyrone Folk Quest* (Belfast, Blackstaff Press, 1973). As well as short stories and poetry he penned six plays, several being produced by the Group Theatre, Belfast, who staged one of them, *Men on the Wall* in Dublin's Abbey Theatre in 1959. His vast collection of folklore, including many songs, is now in the Department of Irish Folklore, UCD. His extremely detailed diaries are a remarkably intimate record of Ulster life from the 1940s to the 1980s. (TOM)

**Murphy, Paddy.** (d. 1992). Concertina. An influential musician from Connolly, Co. Clare, he began learning the concertina at age thirteen, initially taught by uncle, Martin Meehan, later influenced by fiddler Hughdie Doohan, by Jacko Cahill, Mick Tom Doohan, Tom Eustace, Mickey Hanrahan and the Bolands. In 1953 he won an All-Ireland; later, in 1955, he formed and led the Fiach Rua Céilí Band. He has two tracks on *Irish Traditional Concertina Styles*.

**Murphy, Rose (née Conlon).** (b. 1900). Fiddle, accordion. Born at Bellmount, Milltown, Co. Galway. Her father John James Conlon came originally from Foxford, Co. Mayo, he played fiddle, flute and bagpipes. Her mother was Maria Dwyer from Killasser, Swinford; she played melodeon, was a dancer and was a pupil of master Alfie Tuohy. Rose's siblings were all musical: Tommy played flute, John sang, Delia played fiddle and melodeon, P. J. (Peteen) played melodeon in a childhood filled with music. She was a prize-winning dancer and left school at age ten to go into service with a family at Dunmore. There she taught dance, and up to her early twenties taught fiddle, melodeon and dance all over Connacht. She performed in Langtron and Bailey's Roadside Hippodrome as 'The Irish Colleen', leaving it when it migrated over the then-new border. She emigrated to England in her twenties, married miner Paddy Murphy and lived in South Yorkshire at Maltby. She played for and taught dancing in the mining villages all through the depression years of the 1930s until arthritis crippled her. She was brought out of retirement in 1975 to record.

Her brother P. J. emigrated to the US and was to be one of the major figures in Irish music recording of the Coleman/Morrison era. A player with an unpretentious, early-century, Connacht style, Rose was a composer too – she made 'Ladybower's Reel' and 'The Lonely Maid', both on her Topic album.

**Murphys of Bannow.** Harmonica. Phil Murphy (1917–89) of Ballygow, Bannow, Co. Wexford, his sons John and Philip ('Pip'). Phil began playing at the age of eight and, in the decades that followed won local acclaim for performances with mummers' groups, at house dances and in informal sessions. His artistry came to national attention through 1969, '70 and '71 All-Ireland awards; John won in 1973 and Pip on two occasions in the 1980s. The Murphys brought a previously unknown standard of technical accomplishment and sophisticated group arrangements to the tremolo-tuned, double-reeded, diatonic mouth organ, the model most commonly played by Irish traditional musicians. Phil's exploration expanded the melodic possibilities of his harmonica, sometimes using the larger, chromatic models, while John explores the use of the ten-hole, single-reeded 'diatonic' type. The Murphys were recorded on *Traditional Music from South Wexford*, and on Kevin Burke's *Up Close*. Three weeks before Phil's death in 1989 the trio recorded their definitive *Trip to Cullenstown*. Redundancy from his lighthouse employment led John to running Colfer's bar at Carrick-on-Bannow in 1995, a music house; this became the focus in the same year of the annual Phil Murphy traditional music festival in Carrick-on-Bannow. (DOM)

**Murray, James.** (1947–  ). Flute, fiddle, tin whistle. Born at Ougham, Tubbercurry, Co. Sligo, he taught himself to play whistle at the age of eleven. Early influences were his uncle Joe Murray (flute), local musicians Peter Walsh (flute), Burke brothers (fiddle) and John Feely (fiddle). He played with Jimmy Murphy (fiddle), Harry McGowan (flute) and Joe Fallon (button accordion) in the early 1960s. He formed the Countryside Céilí Group in 1970, and toured the US in 1972 and '74. Has played flute and fiddle duet with Jimmy Murphy for many years. A great exponent of Sligo flute playing style particularly regarding tone and control, he has recorded for television and radio. (GRD)

**Murray, Martin.** (1955–  ). Mandolin, fiddle. Born at Carrick on Suir, Co. Tipperary, he first played guitar and sang at the age of seventeen. Influenced by piper Tommy Keane and fiddler John Dwyer he moved to banjo and fiddle, by 1993 recording a solo album of mixed musics, *Dark Horse*, this involving Séamus Maguire, Frankie Gavin, John Dwyer and others.

**muses.** The nine mythological Greek muses, daughters of Zeus and Mnemosyne: Calliope (epic poetry), Clio (history), Euterpe (flute playing, music), Erato (love poetry, hymns), Terpsichore (dancing), Melpomene (tragedy), Thalia (comedy), Polyhymnia (song, mime), Urania (astronomy). These are often recruited or appealed to, particularly in nineteenth-

The God Apollo surrounded by the nine muses portrayed with sixteenth-century clothes and instruments

century place-praise song. Darby Ryan's 'Shades of Ashgrove' opens: 'Ye bright Helliconian maidens, your favours I humbly implore'; in 'The Town of Mullingar' the poet beseeches too: 'Ye nine inspire me, with rapture fire me, to sing its praises both old and new'; 'Ye muses nine with me combine' are invited in 'The Maid of Craigienorn'; 'Ye followers of the nine, Apollo's tuneful line, residing in the Valley of Glenelly' addresses 'The Pride of Glenelly' to a sophisticated audience. The source of the allusion is the Classics education imparted by hedge schoolmasters.

See aisling; song, place-praise.

**music.** Sound structured scientifically and artistically according to various sets of cultural codes and experiences. Although dictionaries all give 'musics' as the plural of music, it is assumed that because music (like disease) is also a collective noun, that 'musics' is inaccurate. 'Music' has both singular and plural – all music is collectively 'music', but there are many different kinds of music – as in 'disease' being a general term, yet there are many different diseases. The attitude is possibly rooted in the (assumed) notion that there is only one music, of which Western orchestral music is the pinnacle. Within this century, with the elimination of colonial and supremacist thinking, it has become apparent that there are thousands of different genres of music, often fundamentally at variance. Hence the validity – and importance – of the use of the term 'musics'. In this context the term 'world music' (under which Irish music is often found abroad) is used to denote, collectively, the non-Western and non-classical musics of the world. While being undoubtedly a useful shop-shelf, broad classification category, it is nevertheless profoundly unscientific and patronising, if not racist in its implication.

**music notation.** The oldest evidence of notation in music in Ireland is religious, this is in the Drummond Missal dating to the twelfth century. Many of today's traditional musicians are musically literate and use the standard Western staff notation system. Breathnach's *Ceol Rince na hÉireann* has a particular usage of notation to indicate complexities relating to rolls etc., on different instruments. Documentors of fiddle-music will use additional markings to indicate bow direction, so too with 'up or down' plectrum on plucked strings, 'push and pull, suck and blow' in free reeds, where to take a breath on flutes and whistles, etc. But individual teachers, faced with young beginners, very often employ their own specialist devices, some of them totally confusing to the outsider. Most common and simplest among these systems is 'ABC' notation, using alphabetic letters to represent the notes. Duration and grouping of the notes is done in the same way as on the staff (see examples). This is particularly useful for tin whistle, flute and pipes. The latter also use a graphic black-out system to indicate closed and open holes, but this is of practical use only to absolute beginners. Alternatively a simple numbering system which takes account

'Ancient Irish music notation with a translation into the modern scale' (O'Neill, 1910)

MUSIC NOTATION

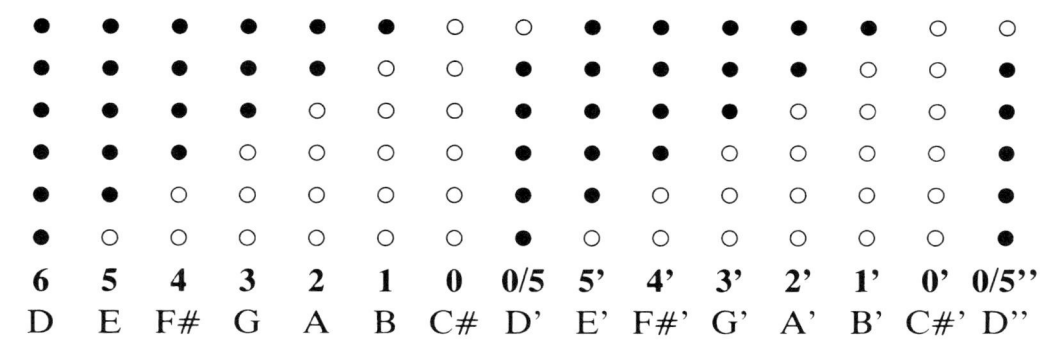

Depiction of the scale on a 'D' tin whistle or flute (Waltons)

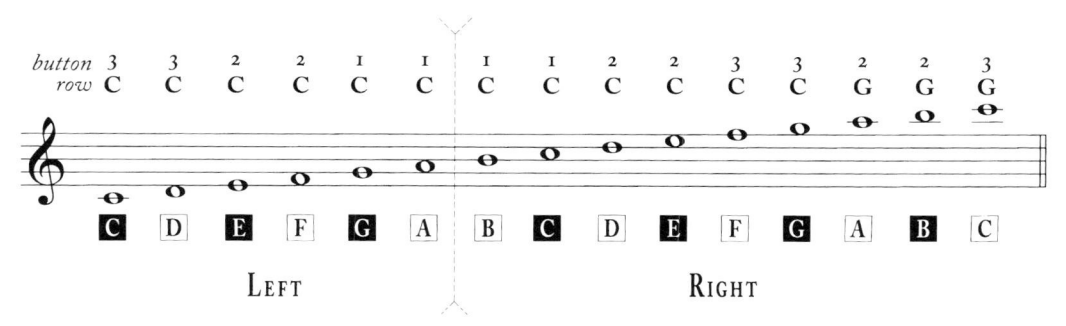

Concertina fingering chart: the black notes indicate pushing in the bellows, the white indicate drawing it out (Mick Bramich)

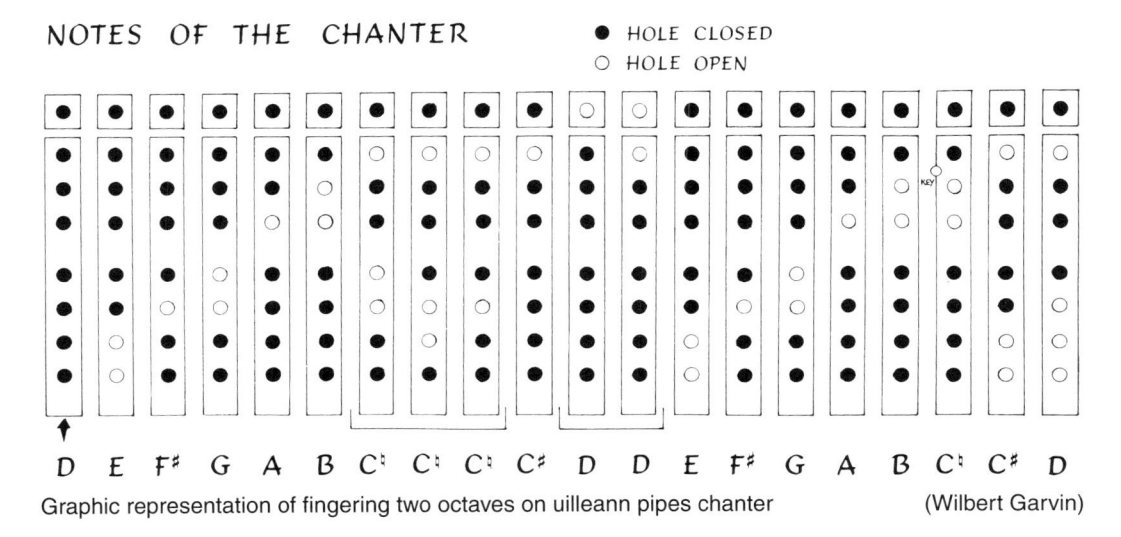

Graphic representation of fingering two octaves on uilleann pipes chanter (Wilbert Garvin)

of the 'circular' nature of the octaves on those instruments, counts the fingers from the top down, as the player sees them, 1, 2, 3, 4, 5, 6.

Staff notation, in simple form, remains the most widely used graphic representation system for traditional music. For all players, however, it is only a means to learning the notation of the tune, an aid to working out difficult 'turns' or variations. Notation is never regarded as a set of instructions – as it may be in classical music – rather it is a map to which the player must travel by their own taste, ingenuity and communally derived aesthetics in order to play the piece 'properly'. Regional musics may well use similar notation, but interpret it differently. Listening remains the way to understand how to play the music. Irish music has been using graphic representations since the early eighteenth century, but these have only become of any widespread practical use since the publication of O'Neill's collection. This, in fact, was available to musicians in the regions from a library address in Dublin in the 1920s and '30s; individual players (like Lucy Farr, Angela and Ita Crehan, etc.) learnt from it, and then aurally passed on the tunes so learnt to family, friends or neighbours. In this way tunes from other eras have been preserved for reconsideration by future generations, and have (perhaps confusingly) fed into repertories gathered by collectors in the nineteenth and twentieth centuries. O'Neill's books in the early part of this century undoubtedly coloured the repertoires of the céilí bands of the following decades, just as surely as Breathnach's *Ceol Rince 1* became the agenda for 'The Revival'.

See O'Keefe, Pádraig; scales; Three Ages of Music; transmission of music.

**musical.** 'Of or relating to music, its notation or performance'; 'having the qualities of music'; 'having an interest in or a talent for music'; 'skilled at music'; 'accompanied by music' (hence the term 'musical' – short for 'musical drama'). 'Musical', however, as commonly applied to instruments, literally denotes something which is of itself musical, and clearly an instrument is not, although a person may be so. A 'music instrument' is 'an instrument of music' as is a 'gardening implement' an 'implement of gardening'.

***Musical Instruments of the Ancient Irish.*** Part of Eugene O'Curry's monumental, 1873, three-volume lecture series. Some 180 pages relate to history of the development of music, music in early Ireland, song-verse structure and description, analysis, derivation of and possible forms of: 1. stringed instruments played with the fingers – the cruit, the psalterium, the nable, the organum, the ochttedach; 2. stringed instruments played with a bow – the timpan, the fiddle; 3. wind instruments – bennbuabhal, corn, cuisle feadan, buine, guthbuine, stoc, sturgan, pipai; 4. percussive instruments – crotals, clocca; 5. undetermined instruments – craebh ciuil and crann ciuil.

The instruments are dealt with in relation to earlier civilisations. Detailed too is analysis of scales and modes, heavily footnoted and side-indexed. O'Curry targeted two kinds of subject for this material: the musical archaeologist whom he expected to reproduce every note faithfully, and the artist, who he saw as using the melodies to build out of in the manner typical of 'art' music. However, he was critical of both categories at the time: 'It is unintelligible how Irish musicians should neglect such a pure fount of original melody as exists in the unpublished airs of Ireland'. He attributed a 'peculiar sweetness and beauty of melody' to Irish and Scots Gaelic airs, something he did not find in English music.

See aerophone; chordophone; crwth; idiophone; O'Curry, Eugene.

**musichall.** Performances of music and song in concert as we know it date to the seventeenth century in Britain, beginning as the prelude to theatre productions, and being recognised as pay-in events in 1672 when one John Bannister opened his house in London to commercial performance. Earlier than that, during the seventeenth century Puritan regime in England, organs were banished from churches and were bought by innkeepers who used music to woo customers. An account by a French traveller from 1659 says:

> That nothing may be wanting to the height of luxury and impiety of this abomination, they have translated the organs out of the churches to set them up in taverns, chaunting their dithyrambics and bestial bacchanalias to the

tune of those instruments which were wont to assist them in the celebration of God's praises (Scholes, *Oxford Companion to Music*, 1977)

Through the eighteenth and nineteenth centuries pubs kept up the practice, advertising with notices on the door. By law, the variety of acts was restricted, and full freedom was not achieved until the 1843 Theatre Act gave publicans more flexibility. In 1866, restrictions on and prosecutions against the 'saloon theatres' were dropped with a wink and a nod until the Act was repealed in 1912. In these premises the show was run by a 'chairman' in regal attire who introduced the acts, and the audience sat at tables. The staple bill of fare was ballads to which the audience were invited to contribute – rather like modern-day folk clubs. Later the chairman was replaced by printed programmes. The musichalls proper began when an entrance fee was charged at the door, and the landlords ceased to aim at making all their money from drink and food. This is the popular variety period of the musichalls, and dates from the mid-1800s. Being the entertainment of the lower classes, and frowned upon by the upper, these institutions were powerful transmitters of songs:

> singers of vocal and histrionic talent who popularised in a few nights some song that came to be hummed or whistled by every errand-boy in the kingdom and played on street pianos on every west-end street and every slum. (Scholes, 1977).

The demise of the musichalls was brought about by first the Vitagraph (cinema) and then the Phonotoscope (gramophone) at the end of the 1800s – both of which had ironically been introduced as stage acts, the latter boasted as:

> This wonderful Machine stands in the centre of the Stage, talks as a Human Being, Sings Comic and Sentimental Songs, Plays Piccolo and Cornet Solos, also a Full Brass Band Selection – a modern miracle. (Scholes, 1977).

Dublin and Belfast had such institutions, as well as 'Catch' clubs, and 'Glee' clubs. Many Irish songwriters turned their talents to writing for the singers, and many songs in the current repertoire come from that stage, remoulded in the style of traditional unaccompanied song. 'Football Crazy' was written by James Curran, born in Moville, Co. Donegal and brought to Glasgow at the age of four in the late 1800s. He wrote possibly hundreds of songs, few of them traceable to him today. Musichall songs led seamlessly therefore from the broadside street balladeering into the era of recorded music and cinema performance, which in turn lead us to popular music of the present day.

See Lowry, Dan; popular music.

**Muskerry Gaeltacht (Gaeltacht Mhúscraí).** Múscraí or that part of it which covers the parishes of Baile Mhúirne, Uíbh Laoghaire, and Cill na Martra – was well known for its prolific poets. Their compositions took in songs of purely local interest as well as some of the 'amhráin mhóra', or 'big songs', which came to be known to a wider audience throughout the country. 'Amhráin mhóra' might be defined as songs with an eight-line verse and an air of great range which demands a lot of skill from the singer. Much of the output of poets from before the middle of the eighteenth century has been lost, or survives as words without airs. But that of later poets is still often performed today, having been passed down largely by word of mouth. There follows a list of some twenty major, local Irish songs, in roughly chronological order, with notes on their texts, and on their composers where known.

*'An Goirtín Eornan', 'Ar Bhruach na Laoi'*. These two songs are amongst the oldest still current in Múscraí, both are compositions of Seán Máistir Ó Conaill, originally from Kerry, and related to the O'Connell family of Derrynane. He was well educated and spent most of his life teaching in Cill na Martra, where he is buried. 'An Goirtín Eornan' is a song of lost love, in which the poet says he loves the lady, not for her land and riches, but for the sweetness of her kiss, and since he has lost her, his whole world has deteriorated into a storm-tossed, snow-covered wasteland, and even the birdsong which might have consoled him is silent. 'Ar Bhruach na Laoi' is an aisling, a vision song, though unusual for this type. Normally in an aisling the poet is alone, meets a beautiful lady, asks her who she is, she tells him she is 'Éire' in one guise or another, and leaves him with a message of hope for the future. In this song the poet does indeed meet with the spéirbhean (beautiful lady), and asks her name,

but receives no reply; the second half of the song is in fact a hymn of praise to the flora and fauna by the river Lee. In Múscraí, the song is sung to the music of 'Táimse Im' Chodladh'. However it has now migrated to the Déise where it is sung to a totally different air.

'Cath Chéim an Fhia', 'A Mháire Ní Laoghaire'. Máire Bhuí Ní Laoghaire, born 1774, lived in Béal Átha an Ghaorthaidh. Though she might by present-day standards be considered illiterate, she nevertheless had a great store of learning, not just Irish, but Greek and Roman as well, and could handle with ease the most difficult of rhyming schemes. She died shortly after the Famine. 'Cath Chéim an Fhia' is perhaps the best known of her songs. It was composed shortly after the battle of Céim an Fhia, near where she lived, in 1822. It was very personal to her, as two of her sons and her brother were involved, and while they were not killed, they were on the run for a long time afterwards. The song is a description of the battle as she saw it, and she also includes encouragement to the people to overthrow the oppressor, a motif which is found in most of her songs. The song 'A Mháire Ní Laoghaire' was probably her last great composition, and was in fact a joint effort with Donncha Bán Ó Loinsigh, from the neighbouring parish of Baile Mhúirne. It was he who started the ball rolling by sending a verse to Máire Bhuí to enquire why she had been so silent of late – she was then quite elderly. She replied – again condemning the oppressor to hunger and banishment – saying that because of old age, this was her final work, and she was now passing the poetic flame on to Donncha Bán himself. Of the ten verses now sung, nos. 1, 3, and 10 are by Donncha Bán, the rest by Máire Bhuí.

'Amhrán Phead Bhuí' (also known as 'Níl Mo Shláinte ar Fónamh'), 'An Cailín Aerach'. The composer of these was known as Pead Buí Ó Loinsigh. An unusual man, he was a native of Baile Mhúirne, but lived most of his life in neighbouring Kilgarvan where the family moved a few years before the Famine. Pead was a musician (he played whistle and pipes), a healer (with cures for toothache and burns), a poet whose sharp-tongued satire did not endear him to his neighbours, and a drinker of infinite capacity which did not endear him to the clergy of the day. 'Amhrán Phead Bhuí' was composed at a time when he was under clerical pressure to mend his bibulous ways, under pain of eternal damnation. Pead gives as good as he gets and better, accusing his tormentors of being interested only in money, and foretelling that it is they who will end up being damned, while he and his like will feast in Heaven. 'An Cailín Aerach', on the other hand, is a charming love song written to a girl who worked as a servant in the house of Máire Ní Thuama. The lady of the house disapproved of Pead and seems to have done her best to break up the romance. In the song he keeps a rein on his blistering tongue, out of deference to the loved one, it seems. 'Amhrán Phead Bhuí' is sung by Diarmuid Ó Súilleabháin on *Bruach na Carraige Báine.*

'Abha an tSuláin', 'Céide Ghlas Laoi na Seol'. Pádraig Ó Crualaoich (1861–1949), was one of the most prolific of the Múscraí poets of all time. A tailor from Baile Mhúirne originally, but living most of his life in Macroom, he was better known by his pen name 'Gael na nGael'. He published two books of poetry, much of it designed to be sung to traditional airs. Some of his songs have become classics, none more so than the majestic 'Abha an tSuláin', a song in praise of the Sullane river which flows through Múscraí, joining the Lee near Macroom. It is in fact a reply to an earlier song on the same theme by Donnchadh Ó Laoghaire which attests to a somewhat sketchy knowledge of the Sullane. Pádraig, who knew every twist, turn, tributary and townland on the river, sets out in his piece to educate his brother poet. Pádraig Ó Crualaoich was also known to compose new airs for his songs as well as using traditional ones, 'Céide Ghlas Laoi na Seol' is one such. This is also a song in praise of a river – the Lee – which flows past his adopted town of Macroom.

'Aisling Gheal'. Composer unknown. This song came to light when collected by A. M. Freeman from Peig Ní Dhonnchadh, Baile Mhúirne, in 1914. It had been almost forgotten until revived by Seán Ó Riada in the 1960s. An aisling of the type known as 'reverdie', it was first recorded by Iarla Ó Lionáird on *Ceol agus Cibeal Chúil Aodha* in 1978 (repeated on *Seacht gCoiscéim na Trócaire*). It is also to be found on Diarmuid Ó Súilleabháin's *Bruach na Carraige Báine*, and on Eilís Ní Shúilleabháin's *Cois Abhann na Séad*.

'Bruach na Carraige Báine'. Composer unknown. There are many versions, the one most usually sung in Múscraí comes from the Béara district of Co. Cork, and has become macaronic. It is believed that when the Irish language was waning, people began to compose English versions of popular songs and combine them to be sung as one. It is a love song in which the young man describes a meeting with his loved one, praises her beauty, and proclaims to her his own worth as a worker. She then signals her acceptance of him and suggests that they travel across the sea together. The 'Carraig Bhán' may be on the river Lee near Inchigeela.

'Faiche Bhreá Aerach An Cheoil'. Composer unknown. A song in praise of Kinneigh, near Bandon, Co. Cork and an area of great scenic beauty with a church where the sick are healed and the lame miraculously cured, its people warm and welcoming. A. M. Freeman collected a version of this song from Conny Coughlan of Baile Mhúirne. It was also collected from Elizabeth Cronin by Séamus Ennis for the BBC. The air is the same as that of 'The Green Linnet'.

'Carraig Aonair'. Composer unknown. Gaelic name for the Fastnet Rock off the coast of Co. Cork, it is a lament by a father for his three sons and son-in-law, who were drowned in its vicinity. Probably from the late nineteenth century, there are differing opinions on who the victims were. According to Amhlaoibh Ó Loinsigh of Cúil Aodha (1872–1947), from whom Seán Ó Cróinín collected the words, they were a Quill family from Dromaclaraigh near Kilgarvan. In *Ár gCeol Féinigh*, the 1920 collection by an tAthair Pádraig Breathnach, there are two versions, one titled 'Luan Dubh an Air', another 'Carraig Aonair', collected from Caitlín Ní Shéaghdha of Adrigole, West Cork. The music has some similarities but differs in all three. The Cúil Aodha song is on Danny Maidhcí Ó Súilleabháin's *Carraig Aonair*.

'An Chúil Daigh Ré'. In praise of Gaortha, south of Macroom, along the course of the Lee, this was collected by Freeman from Conny Coughlan in Baile Mhúirne about 1914. Seán Ó Riada's Cór Chúil Aodha had it in their repertoire, and the air, related to 'Róisín Dubh', was used by him as theme music for the film *Mise Éire*. It is sung on Ó Suilleabháin's *Carraig Aonair*.

'Na Gleannta' (also known as 'An Gleanntáinín Aoibhinn'). Almost forgotten, this has recently been relearned from the singing of the late Elizabeth Cronin. A song in praise of a place around the Lee and Bandon rivers, a kind of guided tour of the Múscraí district that names places such as Macroom, Gougane Barra and Ballyvourney. Each is praised for a particular virtue – the southern glen for the excellence of its timber, the Macroom glen for its flora and fauna, the Gougane Barra glen for its spiritual peace and tranquillity. The Ballyvourney glen with its poets, writers and patron saint Gobnait is described as the most fragrant of all – leading one to suspect that the author hailed from there. It is on *Cois Abhann na Séad*.

'Baile Mhúirne'. Composed in 1900 by Donnchadh Ó'Laoghaire and Mícheál Ó Murchú, both natives of Cúil Aodha. In praise of their native place, it describes the majestic mountains, rivers, and trees, the beauty of its maidens, the generosity of its people, ending with a plea to St Gobnait for lifelong protection. It took first in Feis Bhaile Mhúirne in 1900. Fluent in Irish, Donnchadh Ó Laoghaire taught Irish and French at St Peter's College, Wexford. Mícheál Ó Murchú lived in Cúil Aodha, and wrote for journals like *An Claidheamh Solais* and *Fáinne an Lae*. The song is on *Bruach na Carraige Báine*.

'Cois Abhann na Séad'. Of the aisling type known as 'reverdie', similar to 'Aisling Gheal', in this the poet extols the beauty of his loved one and praises the sweetness of her singing. He has been pursuing her for more than two years with no commitment on her part, and has come to the stage where he feels that unless she provides him with some tangible evidence of affection, he may have to make plans to leave the country. Collected by Jean Ritchie from Bess Cronin, a version was given to Seán Ó Cróinín also by Diarmuid Ó Duinnín, a seanchaí, also from Baile Mhúirne. Recorded by Máire Ní Cheocháin in Alan Lomax's *Columbia World Library of Folk and Primitive Music 1* and his 1998 *Ireland* album.

'*Réidh-Chnoc Mná Duibhe*'. There are two versions collected by Freeman from Conny Coughlan, and a third from Peig Ní Dhonnchú. The order of the eleven verses varies with the singer, this making the subject matter of the song rather difficult to determine. Some of the verses are sung by the woman, making reference to 'slua sí na gréine' (fairies) who have abducted her from her people. The man's verses refer to her beauty, and to his sense of loss at being parted from her. It was probably imported, with words changed to suit a Co. Cork setting, e.g. 'Glaise na Tuaithe' (the Finglas river) has become 'geataí na tuaithe'; 'bruach na Máighe' changes to 'bruach geal na trá'; and 'tír' has been altered to 'Laoi'.

'*An Gamhain Geal Bán*'. The bright white calf, a term of endearment for the loved one. A love song in which the poet rhapsodises about the beauty of his lady and her scenic surroundings, which judging by place-names is in West Cork, around Bantry. He swears that were he to meet with any misfortune, such as at card-playing, which would result in a rift between himself and his lady love, he would throw himself in the river, and never be seen again. Collected by Freeman from Peig Ní Dhonnchú, Baile Mhúirne. Bess Cronin also sang it, having learned it from Seán Ó Muirithe; Séamus Ennis recorded it from her in 1947. It is on *Cois Abhann na Séad*.

'*Bean Dubh an Ghleanna*'. One of the great songs from the Gaelic love-song tradition, demonstrating all that is best in the 'amhráin mhóra' (big songs) of the Munster tradition, with its wonderful soaring melody, though paradoxically with a dark and sombre mood generated by the loss of the beloved. There are versions of this song in Connemara, and in Donegal where it is known as 'Mall Dubh an Ghleanna' and is sung to a faster tempo. The Múscraí version sung by Iarla Ó Lionáird is on *Aislingí Ceoil*. (EIN)

# N

**Na Píobairí Uilleann.**
See Píobairí Uilleann, Na.

***Nation, The.*** Founded by Charles Gavan Duffy, John Blake Dillon and Thomas Davis in 1842. The newspaper of the Young Ireland Movement, it became the main disseminator of 'national' song in the nineteenth century.
See song, political; Young Irelanders.

**nationalism.** Irish music has associations at two levels: direct involvement with the popular republican balladry, and sympathetic interest in traditional Irish music from those with a vision linking Irish nationality and 'culture'. The beginnings of the latter were implicit in the titling of post-1700s' song and music collections e.g., 'National music of Ireland'. It gathered momentum throughout the nineteenth century, paralleled, if not inspired by similar thinking in Britain and elsewhere. The process became established with the formation of the Gaelic League in 1893 when Irish music was usually the music for dance at its social events. Comhaltas Ceoltóirí Éireann's linking of 'culture', language, national identity and music reflects the same process, highlighted by their cancellation of the 1971 All-Ireland Fleadh on the introduction of internment in Northern Ireland in that year. (Ref. Martin Stokes, 'Place, exchange and meaning' in *Ethnicity and Identity*, 1994).

**Naughton's, Galway.**
See Tigh Neachtain.

**Neale, John and William.** Father and son, these were eighteenth-century music publishers, instrument makers and suppliers in Dublin. Located in the centre of Dublin's music-activity area at Christ Church Cathedral, they made flutes, fiddles and recorders (Carolan, *FMSI*, 1986), and began publishing in 1723. Their *Collection of the Most Celebrated Irish Tunes*, with some fifty pieces, became in 1724 the first collection of Irish music in print. Researched by Nicholas Carolan of the Irish Traditional Music Archive, it was republished as a facsimile edition by the Folk Music Society of Ireland in 1986.

**Neary, Eleanor Kane.** (1915–93). Piano. Born of Irish parents in Chicago, she learned piano with nuns at the age of six. Her mother played melodeon; this and listening to records on the Victrola making her able, by by the time she was eleven, to pick tunes from O'Neill's collections. She played publicly first in 1934 at the World's Fair with Pat Roche; she recorded several Decca 78s with Roche's band and also with fiddler Jim Donnelly and accordionist Packie Walsh. From 1930 to the early '60s she was popular at functions in Chicago, her powerful, swinging style a favourite of dancers, her repertoire making her popular at sessions. Influenced by fiddlers and flute players, she developed a style around in Sligo melody. Her husband James, a fiddler, came to Chicago from Swinford in 1929, their contemporaries were Martin Wynne, James Giblin, Jim Donnelly and John McGreevy; their home was popular among visiting musicians. Her left-hand accompaniment style is unique among keyboard performers of Irish dance music. She used the basic vamping pattern of a single note in the bass on the strong beat followed on the off-beat by a chord in a higher register, she frequently introduced syncopation in this pattern to highlight the melodic activity in the right hand. Phrase cadences were emphasised with a series of successive block chords on each beat in the cadential measure; this alteration of the normal harmonic rhythm added an entirely different dimension to the tune when coupled with a highly embellished and fluid right-hand line. Eleanor appeared on the albums *Irish Traditional Instrumental Music in Chicago* and *Chicago Irish Musicians*; her 1934 recordings with the Harp and Shamrock Orchestra have appeared on *Irish Dance Music* (Folkways) and other anthologies. (LAM)

**Needham (McGrath), Peg.** (1948–95). Flute player, teacher. Born near Boyle, Co. Roscommon, she learnt her music among the great players of south Sligo and north Roscommon. She was an All-Ireland Champion at senior level in 1976, and slow air winner in 1993. Taught by Josie Mc Dermott from Keadue, she appeared several times on television, once on *The Pure Drop*. She was actively involved in CCÉ, touring America with the organisation in 1974 and later with the Coleman Country Céilí Band. She was also a member of the Green Linnet Céilí Band in Dublin, and a member of the Dundalk, Siamsa Céilí Band which won All-Irelands in 1989 and '90. She later made television appearances with the Táin Céilí Band, and performed too with a Dundalk group at the Inter-Celtic Festival in Lorient, France. With fiddler Kathleen Smith she recorded a fiddle/flute album, *Cherish the Ladies*, and was a fleadh adjudicator at county and provincial level. A teacher too, she taught regular classes in whistle at Coláiste Rís, Dundalk, at the Willie Clancy school over several years and at other flute and whistle workshops up to the time of her tragic and untimely death.

*Newcomers' Hour.* A programme competition begun in the early 1940s by RÉ. Like a talent show, musicians would compete on stage, the prize was to get the opportunity of broadcasting from the station.

**Ní Chathasaigh, Máire.** (1956– ). Harp player. Born Bandon, Co. Cork into a music family, she played harp from the age of eleven. She won major awards such as the Pan Celtic Harp competition and the Oireachtas, junior and senior All-Irelands, throughout the 1970s. She was the first harp player to teach at CCÉ's Scoil Éigse in 1976, subsequently she adjudicated for several years. She played on many CCÉ tours, with them recording on various 1970s albums. With Gráinne Yeats she featured on a harp-centred edition of *The Pure Drop*, and also on *The Long Note*. Highly regarded for her ground-breaking approach to interpreting

Máire Ní Chathasaigh

dance-music on harp, she is seen as a unique bridge between the old world of harping and modern-day expression of traditional music; her technique is the leading influence on the instrument. A contributor to all the major harp summer schools, she has been associated with many top harp exponents internationally. An honours graduate in Celtic Studies from UCC, this informs her understanding of harping and its culture, her book *The Irish Harper* (1991, Old Bridge Music) illustrates her technique with simple precision; she has several recordings.

**Ní Cheannabháin, Treasa.** (1951– ). Sean-nós singer. Born in the Cill Chiaráin area of Connemara, she is a graduate of St Catherine's College, Sion Hill, Dublin and teaches in Coláiste na Coiribe, Galway. She won the Oireachtas Women's Competition in 1995 and was second in Corn Uí Riada in the same year. She teaches sean-nós song to children in Barna, outside Galway where she lives and, with the assistance of Coláiste na Coiribe and Raidió na Gaeltachta, organises an annual sean-nós competition for primary school children. Together with 'An

Gaelacadamh' in An Spidéal, she organises sean-nós workshops before the Oireachtas festival each year. Her daughter Róisín Elsafty is also a prize-winning sean-nós singer. (LIM)

**Ní Chearna, Eilín.** (1956– ). Sean-nós singer. Born Muiríoch, of Blasket Island parents Caitlín and Pádraig who moved to the mainland in 1948. Her father was a sean-nós singer and with Eilín and her uncle Seán Sheáin Uí Chearna can be heard on *Beauty an Oileáin*. Her present interest in sean-nós singing arose through working as a teenager in Begley's pub at Baile na nGall. She won the Women's Singing Competition at the 1992 Oireachtas, and can be heard on *Forever by Dingle Shore* and *Mighty Session*. (LIM)

**Ní Cheocháin, Máire.** (1925– ). Sean-nós singer. Grew up in Cúil Aodha, Co. Corcaigh, in the house that was later to become home to Seán and Ruth Ó Riada. Her father, Dónall Ó Ceocháin, a teacher of Irish from Ros Ó gCairbre, encouraged her from an early age to sing in the Cúil Aodha tradition and her mother, Caitlín Ní Arrachtáin from Oileán Bhéarra, was a fine singer. She was also influenced by Máire Bean Uí Chonaill, daughter of Connie Coughlan, from whom Alan Freeman collected songs. She was educated through Irish at Clochar Lughaidh, Monaghan, and graduated in pharmacy in Dublin. She won the Gold Medal at the Oireachtas in 1951 and married the late Caoimhín Ó Crualaoi in 1961; her three daughters and two sons are traditional singers and musicians. The words and music of many of Máire's songs have been documented by Carol Ní Chuimín from Inis Eonáin as an MA project entitled 'Traidisiún Amhránaíochta Mhúscraí' (Traditional Singing of Muskerry) in the Modern Irish Department of UCC. (LIM)

**Nic Dhonnchadha, Máire.** (1937– ). Sean-nós singer. Popularly known as Máire Choleman, An Cheathrú Rua, Co. na Gaillimhe. She won an Oireachtas Gold Medal in 1964, recorded for Gael-Linn, CCÉ and RTÉ labels and teaches sean-nós singing. Her father and mother were singers but it was her paternal grandmother, Bríd Choilm from Ros a' Mhíl, who gave her most of her songs. (LIM)

**Ní Dhomhnaill, Maighread.** (1952– ). Singer. From Kells, Co. Meath, her father Aodh (singer, flute player and song collector) came from Rannafast, Co. Donegal, her mother (singer, melodeon player) from Gurteen, Co. Sligo. Childhood summers were spent with the Ó Domhnaill family in Rannafast where Aodh taught in the Coláiste Gaeilge, collected for the Folklore Commission and so immersed the family in Gaelic language and song that learning was subconscious. Through the winter months their home was centre too to her father's and mother's singing, intensifying a musicality that saw Maighréad as a schoolgirl perform and record in 1972 with Daithí Sproule, sister Tríona and brother Mícheál as Skara Brae. Equally at home in Irish or English, she had a solo album in 1976, another in 1991, and she featured on the best-selling 1995 *A Woman's Heart* compilation. Married to Belfast man Cathal Goan (now director of TnaG) her years in Dublin saw her perform at the Tradition Club in Slattery's of Dublin; she studied the singing of Joe Holmes, Eddie Butcher and Geordie Hanna. In 1980 she supported the Chieftains in the Sense of Ireland concert in London. In 1997 JVC licensed her Gael-Linn album; she performed with Donal Lunny's band through 1998 and has sung all over the world.

**Ní Dhomhnaill, Neilí.** (1907–84). Singer. Born in Rannafast, Co. Donegal, she was one of the outstanding traditional Irish singers, storytellers, and song composers of this century. From early childhood (due to poor eyesight and, eventually, total blindness) she spent much of her time indoors in the company of older women, from whom she learned the majority of her songs. Her extensive repertoire – which consisted of songs in both Irish and English – represented a wide range of folksong genres, including ballads, lullabies, laments, and love songs. Late in life she began composing songs, two of which ('Aoibhneas na Maidine' and 'Aisling an Deoraí') won awards in Raidió na Gaeltachta songwriting competitions during the 1970s. Her singing was chiefly recorded for archival purposes (most notably by Mícheál Ó Domhnaill and Cathal Goan), but she also appears (along with her sister Annie) on *Rann* *na Feirste*. Her style was deceptively simple, marked by subtle variation and nuance which she used to remarkable effect in her understated but highly expressive singing. Her involvement with the songs themselves – and with the human stories behind them – was reflected in the lively comments she made about them and in the descriptive narratives with which she frequently preceded them. Despite her physical disability, Neilí remained active and cheerful throughout her life. Her nieces Tríona and Mairéad and nephew Mícheál learned many of her songs, performing them solo and with such groups as Skara Brae, the Bothy Band, and Touchstone. She can be heard on the compilation album *Ireland* produced by UNESCO.

**Ní Dhonnchadha, Máire Áine.** (1919–91). Sean-nós singer. Youngest of nine children, she was born in Cnoc na hAille, west of An Spidéal in the Connemara Gaeltacht. Both parents were singers and were rich in songs and stories, as were many of their neighbours. After Sailearna National School she spent a year in the Convent of Mercy Tuam, won a scholarship to Coláiste Mhuire Tourmakeady and qualified as a primary teacher in Mary I. Training College, Limerick in 1941. She was awarded 'Bonn Óir' at the Oireachtas in 1950. She taught in Dublin and Galway and while on pilgrimage to Knock Shrine in the early 1950s was heard singing 'Caoineadh na dTrí Muire' by Mairéad Piogóid from Raidió Éireann who invited her to sing regularly on national radio. She performed at the Edinburgh Festival in 1958 where she recorded for the School of Scottish Studies. She also performed at the Irish–French Society's thirteenth anniversary festival of St Fiacre (Naomh Fiachra) in Meaux, France. A frequent radio and television broadcaster, she played in *Riders to the Sea* on RTÉ in 1978. Some of her most famous songs, including her unusual version of 'Úna Bhán', were learned from Máire Bean Uí Scanláin (Máire Coffey) in Ros a' Mhíl. She collected songs from Pádraig Ó Ceannabháin in Bóthar Buí, Aille, Indreabhán, the most important of which is 'Neilí an Bhrollaigh Ghil' (1957). Resident artist in 'An Tobar Glé', Dublin in 1970, she featured in the 1984 edition of *Who's Who*. She recorded with Claddagh Records – *'Deora Aille': Irish Songs from Connemara*; *Traditional Music of Ireland* (old traditional songs of Connemara and Clare from Máire Áine, Seán 'ac Dhonncha and Willie Clancy) and *Claddagh Choice: An Anthology of Irish Music*. (LIM)

**Ní Fhlaithearta, Síle.** (1939–   ). Sean-nós singer. From Baile an tSléibhe, An Spidéal, she learned her first songs from her mother, Lizzy Nic An Iomaire, and grew up with fireside céilí in song and storytelling. She trained as a teacher in Birmingham and in 1957 won the singing competition at the feis there. She won the women's sean-nós at the 1964 Oireachtas, and in the same year first place in singing both in Irish and in English at Fleadh Cheoil na hÉireann in Clones. She is married to Charlie Lennon and can be heard on *The Lennon Family*, *Lucky in Love*, and *Deora an Deoraí*. (LIM)

**Ní Ghráda, Máire.** (1959–   ). Uilleann pipes. Originally from Cork city, she now lives in Clonlara in East Clare. A pupil of Mícheál Ó Riabhaigh's at the Cork Pipers' Club, she was influenced by Liam O'Flynn, Willie Clancy and Séamus Ennis. She can be heard on the 1978 album *The Pipers Rock*. She has played in Germany, on Music Network Tours in Ireland, in the NPU's Ace and Deuce of Piping Concert, on Donal Lunny's *Sult* series on Teilifís na Gaeilge, and on RTÉ's *High Reel*. (PAD)

**Ní Mhaonaigh, Mairéad.** (1959–   ). Fiddle, song. From Gweedore, Co. Donegal, her father Francie is a fiddler, his mother had played concertina. She learnt the songs of north-west Donegal from a young age, and began music at the age of eight. She was influenced by weekly sessions of reels and highlands with her father at fiddler Joe Jack Curran's in Magheragallon. Influenced too by the song repertoire of Jimmy Dinny Ó Gallachóir, she picked up songs in English and Irish, and by ten she was playing fiddle too, taught by her father. In 1973 hearing Paddy Glackin and Tony Smith at a Dublin CCÉ concert she became obsessed with the music; Buncrana fiddler Dinny McLoughlin gave her technique and repertoire. Fleadhanna and the Gaeltacht brought her into contact with Belfast and with Dermy Diamond and Tara Bingham (fiddle and flute), Gerry

McCartney (banjo), and fiddler Andy Dickson. Other music came from the radio, particularly from RnaG. In Dublin at college from 1979-80 she played with Nollaig Casey, and with Belfast flute player Frankie Kennedy whom she married in 1981. Teaching for ten years they played constantly, recording the album *Ceol Aduaidh*, and in 1983 *Altan*. Touring in America on a career break in 1987 led to the formation of their group Altan. For her, dance is central to music: 'My mother dances, my father dances. I'm able to dance highlands, I'm able to dance Mazurkas. So when we play highlands, I'm playing the dance.'

**Ní Mhiolláin, Treasa.** (1943– ). Sean-nós singer. From Árainn, largest of the Aran Islands, she won Corn Uí Riada at the Oireachtas in 1972 and 1979, and was recipient in 1996 of 'Gradam Shean-nós Cois Life'. Her mother, Bairbre Ní Dhireáin, was in great demand in her youth for singing at house-weddings and house-dances, called 'times' in Connemara and in Aran. She travels frequently to singing festivals all over Ireland, England, Scotland and the European mainland. She lived for some years in London and in Dublin, but returned to Aran in 1984 where she has been teaching sean-nós singing to schoolchildren on each of the three islands. Some of her songs can be heard on *An Clochar Bán*. (LIM)

**Ní Riain, Nóirín.** (1951– ). Singer, writer. Born Lough Gur, Co. Limerick and raised at Caherconlish. Her 1980 MA study 'Traditional Religious Song in Irish' heralded a performance career, bringing her as guest to spiritual music festivals among diverse religions in Sarajevo, Rotterdam, Bruges, Oxford, Findhorn, Catalonia and many other places. She has represented Ireland culturally at UN summits in 1989, '92, '94 and '95 and has sung with John Cage. Author of *Im Bim Baboró* and *Gregorian Chant Experience,* she writes also on women, song, spirituality and healing. Perhaps best known for her 1989 *Vox de Nube* chant performance with the monks of Glenstal Abbey, Co. Limerick, her numerous recordings include *Caoineadh na Maighdine* (1979), *Good People All* (1982), *Stór Amhrán* (1991), *Soundings* (1994) and *Celtic Soul* (1996). Her book *Stór Amhrán,* an outstanding collection of eighty-five traditional songs in Irish, many from the Déise region, and a selection of airs, is dedicated to the memory of mentor Pilib Ó Laoghaire.

**Ní Shúilleabháin, Éilís.** (1943– ). Sean-nós singer. Born in Cúil Aodha, the eldest of seven children of Nóra Ní Éalaithe from Kilgarvan and Maidhcí Ó Súilleabháin from Cúil Aodha. Both parents were musical and Maidhcí sang and played fiddle. Their house was a meeting place for singers, musicians, poets and story-tellers for social nights – 'scoraíocht'. The family were educated in the local Scoil Bharr d'Inse, made famous in the song of the same name, where they came under the influence of sisters Cáit and Máire Ní Chuill, who were well versed in local songs. From there Éilís won a scholarship to Clochar Lughaidh, Monaghan, where she sang in the choir and played viola in the orchestra. She won the women's competition at the Oireachtas twice and was awarded Gradam Shean-Nós Cois Life in Dublin in 1997. She now runs an Irish-language pre-school in Parteen, Co. Clare and teaches traditional singing in the performance module of the B.Mus. course in UCC. Fifteen of her songs can be heard on *Cois Abhann na Séad*. (LIM)

**Ní Uallacháin, Padraigín.** (1950– ). Singer, researcher. Born in Co. Louth, of a Cullyhanna, Co. Armagh mother, and Dundalk father, her childhood was immersed in lore and song in the Irish language. In 1926 her father, Paddy Weldon, had been with the first group ever to be brought to learn Irish in the environment of the Gaeltacht at Rannafast, Co. Donegal. By dint of his profession as school inspector, her younger life was spent in counties Mayo, Donegal, Monaghan, and Dublin. She listened to and studied sean-nós song in Dublin in the end of the 1960s, and worked for Comhdháil Náisiúnta na Gaeilge before taking Irish studies at Coleraine University in 1973. She researched and presented RTÉ radio's *Reels of Memory* between 1979 and '81, and was the first woman to read the news in Irish for RTÉ TV. Now teaching in Gaelscoil Dhún Dealgan, and living in South Armagh with its legacy of eighteenth-century poets, she researches, performs and records. Her albums include a children's song collection *A Stór 's A Stóirín* (1994), a solo collection of sean-nós and accompanied songs, including own compositions, *An Dara Craiceann* (1995), and a children's album of traditional song with husband Len Graham *When I Was Young* (1996).

**Nic a' Luain, Anna.** (1884–1954). Singer. Born Nic a'Bhaird, and known locally as Anna John Chiot, she was a monoglot Irish speaker and a noted carrier of traditions of all kinds. She lived all her life in the townland of Cruach Thiobraid at the foot of the Blue Stack mountain in central Donegal. Her repertoire, which included 250 songs in Irish, was collected by Seán Ó hEochaidh in 1947–48. (LIO)

**notation.** See music notation.

**NPU.**
See Píobairí Uilleann, Na.

# O

**O'Boyle, Seán.** (1908–79). Collector, teacher, broadcaster. From Belfast, he spent his working life teaching in St Patrick's College, Armagh. An Irish language enthusiast with a particular love for songs, he combined these interests in his 1944 collection *Cnuasacht de Cheoltaí Uladh*. He was the prime Ulster advisor and colleague to Peter Kennedy and Séamus Ennis between 1952 and 1954 when material was being recorded for the seminal radio series *As I Roved Out*. In 1971 he was a founder member of the Folk Music Society of Ireland. His great gift was his ability to pass on enthusiasm for the music, song and language he loved. Unfortunately, he is not well served by his later publications, *The Irish Song Tradition* (1976) and the posthumous (1980) *Ogham, the Poet's Secret*. (TOM)

**Ó Briain, Donncha.** (1960–90). Tin whistle. Born in Dublin, he was both a specialist performer and popular teacher of the tin whistle. He compiled a comprehensive collection of tunes – *The Golden Eagle* – aimed at all learning levels. Reissued by CCÉ (Cluain Tarbh, 1993), it includes a piece specially written in his memory by Charlie Lennon, 'The Flying Wheelchair', this a tribute to his stubborn battle against nature. Working by day in the Department of Labour until his untimely death in 1990, he was an important and proactive member of Clontarf CCÉ where he taught whistle. He recorded *Donncha Ó Briain* in 1979.

**Ó Briain, Garry.** (1949– ). Guitar, mandocello, keyboards, úd. From Dublin city, he learnt piano from the age of nine and became familiar with dance music through his grandfather's O'Neill and Bunting collections. Playing guitar by fifteen, he was impressed by Ó Riada's *Fleadh Cheoil an Raidió*. He played rock and classical while in UCD, then, introduced to mandocello in his early twenties he began playing tunes, working also with blues and country music. He experienced French Canadian music while in Canada during the 1970s, and with Jackie and Tony Small he recorded *Aengus* in 1976, studied fiddle-making with Arthur Grayson at Limerick College of Music, ultimately setting up a workshop in north Clare and making his own instruments. He formed Buttons and Bows with Séamus and Manus Maguire and Jackie Daly in 1984, this covering Irish, Shetland, Quebecois and Scandinavian material. Since 1989 he has partnered Máirtín O'Connor in Chatterbox, has played with Gerry O'Connor and Len Graham in Skylark, with Boys of the Lough and with John Carty's At the Racket. A skilled and sensitive arranger, he has worked with the singing of Padraigín Ní Uallacháin, Len Graham and Tim Dennehy, and has accompanied many of the major professional players.

**O'Brien, Paddy.** (1922–91). Accordion, fiddle. Born at Newtown, Co. Tipperary, his grandfather Pat played fiddle and concertina, uncles Paddy and Mick were celebrated fiddle and concertina players; his father Dinny was a fiddler and the leader of the Bridge Céilí Band. Dinny got much of his repertoire from Mick Quinn who had learned from uilleann pipers Matt Seymour and Darby Kennedy of Portroe. The family home was a meeting place for musicians, and Paddy began to play fiddle at age seven, but subsequently came to concentrate on accordion. His first influence and teacher on this was local Garda Sergeant John Kelly of Aughrim, Co. Galway. At fourteen, with his father and flute player Bill Fahy of Puckane, Paddy formed the Lough Derg Céilí Band. A noted composer, the three records he made before going to America in 1953 made him the role model for two generations of accordion players. Like Coleman, and later, Joe Burke, his tune selections have been widely copied; so too his style which he related to his

Patrick's Night  (Paddy O'Brien, courtesy Eileen O'Brien Minogue)

close association with many fiddlers down the years and his observations of their variations. In his career he played with the Tulla, Aughrim Slopes, New York and Ormond Céilí bands. He was leader of the Ormond Céilí Band and composed much of its material. A collection of his work is published in *The Compositions of Paddy O'Brien*; this also available in an Ossian CD. His daughter Eibhlín, a fiddler, continues the family tradition.

**O'Brien, Paddy.** (1945– ). Accordion player, collector. Born at Daingean, Co. Offaly. In his youth he travelled his area seeking out older players, these including Joe Delaney and Dan Cleary of Offaly, Donegal fiddler John Doherty, Paddy Fahy, Eddie Kelly from Galway, Frank McCollum of Antrim, Seán Ryan from Tipperary, and Johnny Henry from Mayo. In Dublin by 1969 he played with fiddlers John Kelly and Joe Ryan – an apprenticeship of a sort with informal lessons on settings, stories about the music and the players. He has played in many céilí bands: 1966–69, Ballinamere, with Peter Kilroe, Dan Cleary, Seán Monaghan, Seán Conlan, and Michael Lynam; 1968, Seán Ryan Trio, with Seán and Kathleen Ryan; 1969–78, Castle Céilí Band, with Michael O'Connor, John Kelly, Seán Keane, Michael Tubridy, Joe Ryan, John Dwyer, Bridie Lafferty and Benny Carey; 1971–78, Ceoltóirí Laighean, with Éamonn de Buitléar, John Kelly, James Kelly, Paddy Glackin, Peter Phelan, Mary Bergin, Mícheál Ó hAlmhain, and Aileen McCrann; 1978–82, Bowhand, with James Kelly and Dáithí Sproule; 1983–84, Hill 16, with Seán O'Driscoll and Tom Dahill; presently in Chulrua with Tim Britton and Pat Egan. In 1978 he returned to the United States to record for Shanachie Records with fiddler James Kelly and guitarist Dáithí Sproule as Bowhand. He settled in Minneapolis in 1983, since then playing all over the US, becoming one of the anchor artists for John D. McGurk's Bar in Saint Louis, the only US venue with Irish traditional music seven nights a week. In his forty years of playing he has collected more than 3,000 jigs, reels, hornpipes, airs and marches – including many rare and unusual tunes. A careful listener (this archive is retained in his memory), his 1994 National Endowment project committed some 500 pieces to tape as *The Paddy O'Brien Tune Collection*, the first published oral collection of traditional music. Regarded as a generous teacher, he is often consulted for source material on tunes, and some twenty of his tune notations appear in Breathnach's *Ceol Rince na hÉireann*, vols. 2 and 3. He has won numerous awards at all levels, most notably the 1969, '70, '73 and '77 Oireachtas accordion;

1969 Oireachtas with the Castle Céilí Band; 1970 and '77 All-Ireland senior accordion. He received Minnesota State Arts Board's Master Artist Folk Arts Apprenticeship Grants in 1989, '93 and '96. His 1978 album with James Kelly and Dáithí Sproule, *Is It Yourself?* is a classic as is the 1982, *Spring in the Air* with the same line-up. His solo album is *Stranger at the Gate*.

**O'Brien, Patrick.** (*c*. 1773–1855). Piper. Born in Labasheeda, Co. Clare. He went blind in his twenties, and after failing to find a sponsor in Limerick, he become a street musician. Usually positioned at the corner of Hartsonge and the Crescent, he was the subject used for the painting 'The Limerick Piper' by the artist Joseph Patrick Laverty.

**O'Brien-Moran, Jimmy.** (1957–   ). Uilleann pipes, saxophone. Born at Tramore, Co. Waterford, his interest in Irish music, and piping especially, was awakened through Planxty whose sleeve notes prompted his listening to Séamus Ennis and Willie Clancy. At age seventeen he began playing on a Matt Kiernan chanter and home-made bag and bellows. Lessons from Tommy Kearney, tips from Donncha Ó Maidin and Pat Mitchell's classes at the Willie Clancy Summer School in 1975 and 1976, at Liam O'Flynn's in 1977, all developed his playing, placing him on *The Piper's Rock* showcase album of young pipers in 1977. He played with Scullion from 1979–80, learning too the saxophone. In the jewellery trade for a number of years, he then took a music degree in 1992, now teaching music part-time at Waterford Institute of Technology. His postgraduate study at UL is on the Hudson Collection. He plays a pre-1925 Colgan B set, this 'loaned for life' by the late Seán Reid. He played at the 1980 London Sense of Ireland and the French 1996 L'Imaginaire Irlandais festivals, has toured Europe, and USA and New Zealand. He gives workshops, lectures and writes in the field of piping, and also plays saxophone in a ten-piece dance-band. He can be heard solo on *Seán Reid's Favourite*.

**O'Callaghan, Seán.** Early twentieth-century Cork songwriter who sang the praises of the triumphs of his locality: hurling matches, drag hunts and bowling tournaments, this in songs like 'The Boys of Fairhill', 'The Kileens Hunt', 'The Armoured Car' and 'Lloyd George'. These were popularised in particular by Jimmy Crowley.

See Crowley, Jimmy; song, Cork, urban ballads.

**Ó Canainn, Tomás.** (1930–   ). Uilleann piper, composer. He was born in Derry, and while working in England he was a founder member of the Liverpool Céilí Band. Later he formed Na Filí, and working in Cork as Dean of Engineering at UCC, he also lectured there in music for some years and taught uilleann pipes at Cork School of Music. Author of several books, including the general study *Traditional Music in Ireland*, he has also two albums. He also published a selection of his own tunes and a book and CD collection of 100 slow airs.

**Ó Caodháin, Colm.** (1893–1975). Singer. Born in Glinsce, Carna, Co. Galway and lived there for most of his life. The eldest of nine children, he received little, if any, formal schooling. He learned many of his songs from his father and from local people. He spoke little English, although he could probably understand it. Séamus Ennis, then a full-time collector with the Irish Folklore Commission, visited him in 1943, discovering in him a rich source of music, song and lore. A deep, lifelong friendship ensued during which Ennis collected over two hundred items from the singer, comprising songs for the most part, some of which Colm composed himself, and also tunes, airs, and a vast amount of other lore. Other collectors – including Alan Lomax – also recorded him, using many methods including manuscript, wax cylinders, photographs, audiotapes and film. He can be heard on UNESCO's *Ireland*. (RIU)

**O'Carolan.** Goldsmith called him 'Carolan' (1760, twenty-two years after the harper's death); Walker (1786) referred to him as 'O'Carolan'; Bunting, who dealt with harpers in 1792 referred to him as 'Carolan', as does, more recently, Donal O'Sullivan (1958).

See Carolan, Turloch.

**Ó Catháin, Darach.** (1922–87). Born in Máimín, Leitir Móir, Co. Galway. Seventh in a family of twelve children, five boys and seven girls, he acquired his songs and his love of singing from his mother. In 1935, as part of a government scheme for improved conditions, the family sold their home and land in Connemara and relocated to the newly established Gaeltacht in Ráth Cairn, Co. Meath. He married Bríd Ní Chonaire, originally from Ros Muc in Co. Galway, who had moved to Meath in 1937. They emigrated to England where he worked as a builder in Leeds. An LP of his singing, *Darach Ó Catháin*, was issued by Gael-Linn in 1975. (RIU)

**Ó Ceannabháin, Mícheál.** (1936–    ). Sean-nós singer, accordion. Better known as Michael Mháire an Ghabha after his famous mother, he lives in An Aird, west of Carna with a highly musical family. He was the first recipient in 1993 of 'Gradam Shean-nós Cois Life'. His songs can be heard on *Cruach na Caoile*. (LIM)

**Ó Ceannabháin, Pádraig.** (1933–    ). Sean-nós singer. Better known as Pádraig Tom Phaits, from Coill Sáile, Cill Chiaráin, Connemara. A singer and, after his mother, an accordion player, he became involved in Carna CCÉ, and has won many prizes for singing in Irish at fleadhanna ceoil. He was the first recipient of 'Gradam an Phléaráca' in 1994. (LIM)

**Ó Ceannabháin, Peadar.** (1956–    ). Sean-nós singer. Born and reared at Aill na Brún, Cill Chiaráin near Carna, Co. Galway, he comes from a long line of poets and singers: the celebrated poet Jeaic Bacach Ó Guairim was his maternal grandmother's grandfather; singer, seanchaí and athlete, Cóilín Sheáin Dhúdara Ó Cualáin, was his uncle. Both his father, Maidhcil Phíotair a' Ghabha and his grandfather, Peadar a' Ghabha were singers. Most influenced by Joe Heaney, he lectures in Irish in St Catherine's, Sion Hill, Dublin. He edited *Éamon a Búrc: Scéalta* (An Clóchomhar, 1983), and his songs are available on various compilations. His first solo album *Mo Chuid den tSaol* is probably the first sean-nós CD to be featured on the worldwide web at: http://www.GrafxSource.com/MCS/Cuid_den_tSaol.html. (LIM)

**Ó Ceannabháin, Peatsaí.** (1943–98). Sean-nós singer. Fourth of a family of nine children from Ros Muc where his mother Kate, and aunts Agnes and Sadie were well-known singers, and his granduncle. Tomás Choilm, composed songs. Guest singer at community festivals like 'Pléaráca Chonamara' and teacher and singer at 'Sean-nós Cois Life', he taught sean-nós to children, and worked with Údarás na Gaeltachta. Some of his songs can be heard on *Tógfaidh Mé Mo Sheolta*. (LIM)

**Ó Cearbhaill, Pádraig.** (1956–    ). Sean-nós singer. Grew up in an Irish-speaking family in south-west Limerick where spoken English was still greatly influenced by Irish. He learned his songs initially from his father, but feels a great affinity to the songs of the Déise area of Munster, especially those of Sliabh gCua in north-west Waterford. Nioclás Tóibín, Tadhg Cúndhún, Labhrás Ó Cadhla, Bríd Ní Núnáin and Pádraig de Faoite from Déise Mumhan in Waterford and Seán Ó Donaíle from Uíbh Ráthach in Co. Kerry have all been influences. A placename researcher by profession, his songs can be heard on *Seachrán Sídhe*. (LIM)

**Ó Conluain, Proinsias.** (1919–    ). Born near Benburb, Co. Tyrone, an area of importance in Irish history and rich in the variety of its cultural traditions. At boarding-school in St Patrick's College, Armagh, he was fortunate to find on the teaching staff there such influential figures as the Gaelic scholar, Pádraig Mac Giolla an Átha (Paddy Forde), Seán O'Boyle and Jerry Hicks. The two last-named he was to record on many occasions later as contributors to various series and documentaries which he compiled for Raidió Éireann and RTÉ Radio from 1947 onwards. Those series had such titles as *The Ballad Tree*, *The Singer and the Song*, *Between the Jigs and the Reels*, all featuring traditional music and song, their provenance and performers. As scriptwriter and producer over a period of almost forty years he was responsible for numerous documentaries featuring such collectors as Carl Hardebeck, Henry Morris (Énrí Ó Muirgheasa), Sam Henry. Capt. Francis

O'Neill, and such as Robert Cinnamond from Glenavy, Mrs Eileen Keaney of Glenelly and Belfast, Eddie Butcher ('By the Strands of Magilligan'), John Maguire ('The Rosslea Pad') and John Rea ('The Dulcimer Man from Glenarm'). Since his retirement he has, as founder-editor of *Dúiche Néill*, the journal of the O'Neill-Country Historical Society, contributed many articles thereto about his collecting experiences and the people he has met. His 1997 article, *Cuimhní Cinn ar an Oireachtas*, published by Conradh na Gaeilge, deals largely with the development of the sean-nós style of singing through the festival's hundred years of competitions and performance.

**O'Connell, Connie.** (1943– ). Fiddler and composer. Born at Kilnamartra, West Cork, his father's family had a history of fiddle playing, his mother played single-row melodeon. Growing up, he was influenced by Sliabh Luachra musicians Pádraig O'Keeffe and Denis Murphy. He featured on a CCÉ recording *Ceol Go Maidin* in the late '80s, along with Séamus MacMathuna and Jimmy Doyle. His solo album (*The Torn Jacket*) on Shanachie came out in 1999. He teaches fiddle at University College, Cork.

**O'Connell's, Dan.** Pub, Knocknagree, Co. Cork. The revival, and survival, of traditional music is very often associated with particular friendly 'houses' in the licensed trade. Such a spot in the Sliabh Luachra music area is 'Dan Connell's'. Bought by the present owner in 1964, on St Stephen's Night of that year he invited Johnny O'Leary and Denis Murphy, two of the best-known Sliabh Luachra players, to host a regular session there. Denis died in 1974; Johnny has continued ever since. The bar has seen many noted musicians and media visitors over the years – Séamus Ennis, Willie Clancy, Ciarán Mac Mathúna and Eileen Ivers have all been through its doors. Julia Clifford often played there during her regular trips home from England. As set dancing activity expanded, so did the pub, with a middle bar and, later, a dance area added to the rear. Despite the fact that it has never advertised, the pub has attracted musicians and dancers from all over the world, and has featured in many television programmes. The album *I gCnoc na Graí* by Tony MacMahon and Noel Hill, was recorded there, as was *Dance Music from the Cork/Kerry Border* by Johnny O'Leary. Since 1988, the pub has been run by Dan's daughter, Mairéad, and her husband, Tim Kiely, who is Johnny O'Leary's guitar accompanist. Sessions in Dan O'Connell's are still held regularly at weekends. (PAA)

**O'Connor, Máirtín.** (1955– ). Accordion. From Barna, Co. Galway, he was raised in Galway city, and encouraged in music by his paternal grandparents who played melodeon. Beginning at the age of nine, he picked up repertoire too from 78s of groups such as the Flanagans (a favourite of his mother); later he learnt through radio and television. A planned career in electronics was interrupted in 1976 after a request to play with singer Thom Moore. He played with the band Midnight Well from 1978–79, with Boys of the Lough in 1980, and toured USA and Europe with Dolores Keane's Reel Union in the early 1980s. He then played with De Dannan from 1983–87, with fiddler Gerry O'Connor, then Skylark from 1992–96. He recorded the solo *Connachtman's Rambles* in 1978, *Perpetual Motion* in 1990, and *Chatterbox* in 1993. He has played with Frankie Gavin and Carl Hession, and was the first accordionist with *Riverdance*. He has guested on many recordings, has done several pieces of film music, and plays the theme for the TnaG series *Ros na Rúin*.

**O'Connor, Nuala.** (1953– ). Researcher, producer, writer. Born in Dublin, she was a founding member of Éigse na Trionóide, traditional music festival in Trinity College Dublin (begun in 1974), and later of the Dublin Folk Festival. She joined RTÉ Radio in 1979 as a researcher, from 1984 worked as a producer. She then moved to television, but left to set up Hummingbird Productions in 1987. Assistant producer to Philip King on *Bringing It All Back Home* she is the author of the book of the same name which accompanied the series. She was series editor, researcher and writer on *River of Sound*, on *Christy, Meitheal, Bláth gach Géag dá dTig* and *Laoi na Píbe* – documentary films for Teilifís na Gaeilge. From

1992 to 1997 she was the traditional music album reviewer for the *Irish Times*.

**O'Connor, Rose.** (1920– ). Fiddler, teacher. Born at Shancarnan House, Moynalty, Co. Meath, her father John played fiddle, her mother Elizabeth (née Smith) played fiddle and concertina. Learning first from her father, she was taught too in Kells by Leonard Cantwell of the Silver Star Céilí Band with whom she played before emigrating to London in 1946. In 1951 she settled in Dundalk, there playing in brother-in-law Joe Dunne's Cuchulainn Céilí Band until 1958. In 1962 she began teaching her sons Brendan, Peter and Gerry fiddle, later daughter Eilish. She taught junior members of Dundalk CCÉ, their band won an All-Ireland in 1967. Her former pupils have won many awards and many play professionally in Ireland and abroad. Her son Gerry (fiddle) is, with Eithne Ní Uallacháin in the group Lá Lugh, one of the better known Irish players in Europe.

**O'Curry, Eugene.** (1794–1862). Antiquarian, researcher, chronicler of manuscripts, author of *Musical Instruments of the Ancient Irish*. Born at Dunaha West, south of Kilkee, Co. Clare, his father was Owen Mór O'Curry, a respected oral historian, seanchaí and farmer. Eugene grew up in an Irish-speaking culture in which the story-telling and the tales of Finn were still valued. At age sixteen he was helped learn English by Fr Meehan of Carrigaholt but poverty dictated that he remain working on the land. He taught for a few years at Kilferagh, then moved to labouring in Limerick city in 1824. He became an overseer, then got a position as warden in the Mental Home. From youth he had an obsessive interest in the Irish language and he collected old manuscripts, thus acquiring a scholarly reputation which, through a chance meeting with George Smith (of Hodges Smith publishers), led him to a position with the Ordnance Survey in Dublin in 1835.

The founding of the Royal Irish Academy in 1795 for the study of improving literature and antiquities had helped to develop a basis for exploring Gaelic culture. Its patrons were politically ill-equipped to understand the import of this, but its premises did house a jumbled turmoil of ancient manuscripts. George Petrie had joined the society in 1827, and two years later as a council member put in train a nationwide manuscript collecting process. In this connection George Smith had travelled to Limerick, met with O'Curry and encouraged him into the Academy. John O'Donovan of Kilkenny had already joined in 1832, and the triumvirate of he, Petrie and O'Curry succeeded in establishing a solid foundation for Irish studies and linguistics. In 1826, Capt. Lorcom, director of the then land survey and valuation, decided to chronicle history, antiquities and social conditions. The task was deputised to Petrie, who involved O'Donovan and O'Curry. O'Donovan worked in the field, investigating placenames, O'Curry supplied him with manuscript backup. Their work continued until 1842, producing 193 volumes of Survey Letters – still in the RIA – these containing the names of 62,000 investigated townlands, and 144,000 names on maps. Despite these successes, funding was withdrawn because of the emotional and cultural sustenance the research implicitly provided for the Young Ireland movement.

During this time the *Nation* newspaper was founded by Thomas Davis and Charles Gavan Duffy, and scholarly societies were set up – the Irish Archaeological Society in 1840, the Celtic Society in 1845 and the Ossianic Society in 1854. The *Nation* published material compiled by O'Curry and O'Donovan, as well as an Irish grammar and the *Annals of the Four Masters*. In 1842 O'Curry was employed by the RIA to research and catalogue their material, and this he did in painstaking detail. His work involved copying tattered texts of up to 1,000 years vintage, translating them, and explaining their references, this done on meagre and precarious wages. In 1849 O'Curry catalogued the British Museum's Irish MSS, almost hitting penury in the process. O'Curry and O'Donovan – married to sisters from Broadford, Co. Clare – were eventually given good salaries in 1852 with the setting up of the Brehon Law Commission, but their work there was frustrated by ignorance, their task never since completed. O'Curry was eventually recognised by Cardinal Newman and was given the chair of Irish History and Archaeology at the new Catholic University in Dublin. He helped Petrie with his music collection, and from 1857–62 he delivered in the college his famous lecture series 'On The Manners and Customs of the Ancient Irish', dying of a heart attack soon after the last of them. O'Donovan died six months later. It is these lectures, edited by W. K. O'Sullivan, published in 1873 in three volumes, which are the source of much information on music in Early Ireland. The detail of investigation of both instruments and scales rates O'Curry's rigours as among the first works of what today would be termed 'ethnomusicology'.

**O'Donnell, Brian.** (d. 1980). Organiser, producer, fiddle. A native of Co. Donegal, he lived most of his life in Belfast. Chairman of the Ulster Council of CCÉ, he was recognised as an authority on traditional music in Ulster and played a vital part in the making of many radio and television programmes. Highly regarded as a fiddle repairer, he was well known all over Ulster. and was constantly in demand in this field. He was one of the great personalities of the Revival who made the early years exciting, and involvement in the music compelling and meaningful.

**O'Donoghue's.** In 1959 'the widow O'Donoghue's' was an unassuming pub in Merrion Row, frequented by the occasional civil servant from government offices in Merrion Street, and enlivened in the evenings by students from the adjacent National College of Art and the University in Earlsfort Terrace. Friendly with the art students and recently returned from Spain was Ronnie Drew, then admired as a classical/Spanish guitarist and hilarious raconteur. Among the other habitués were art student Joe Dolan who had played rhythm guitar with The Swingtime Aces showband. Architecture students and traditional music enthusiasts, Eamonn O'Doherty and Johnny Moynihan (who had recently re-established the University Folk Club) and agriculture student Ciarán Bourke were part of this milieu. Ronnie Drew and Bourke were to be the nucleus of the Dubliners and the other three later formed Sweeny's Men with Andy Irvine. Music was in those days prohibited in the pub, but by 1961–62 it had become the major centre in Dublin for the traditional music revival.

Important early concerts in the Hibernian Hotel and the Grafton Cinema (following the success of Ó Riada in the Gaiety) were organised from O'Donoghue's by Peggy Jordan, John Molloy and Joe Pilkington. Luke Kelly returned from England in 1961. Barney McKenna, Séamus Ennis, Joe Heaney, Liam Weldon and Tony McMahon were regulars along with family groups like the McKennas, the Grehan sisters and the Fureys (including their father Ted). These overlapped with musicians from the 'ballad' end of the revival like Danny Doyle and Anne Byrne/Paddy Roche duo. The mood of the pub was further invigorated by many from literary and theatrical Dublin who came to enjoy the music. The general mood of '60s' optimism prevailed, and one notable effect was the breaking down of social barriers and differences between town and country engendered by a common appreciation of the music. By the mid-'70s however, O'Donoghues was foundering under the weight of its own success with great musicians like John Kelly and Joe Ryan, regulars in the front section, often drowned out by noisy and unappreciative crowds engaged in communication with tourists or joining in crude renditions of 'rebel' ballads to the accompaniment of guitar and bodhrán. It has since changed hands and music sessions continue. (EAO)

**O'Donovan, Joe.** (1918–   ). Dance teacher. Born in Cork city, both his parents came from the west of the county. His mother played whistle, concertina and melodeon, his father ran a dance school. Joe himself played whistle, piano and button accordions, melodeon and warpipes. He was taught whistle first by Neilus Cronin, then by Fr O'Flynn, and learned warpipes from Tadhg Crowley (a pipe-maker who supplied uilleann pipes and had a large export business in warpipes). He played with the Cork Volunteers pipe band, and, an all-Ireland dance champion at fourteen, he played for a number of years with the Blarney Jimmy McNamara céilí band through the late 1930s and 1940s. His step dance style is that of his father (d. 1972 at age 94), learned by the latter from a local Dunmanway master in pre-Coimisiún times. Joe was a founder member of Cork CCÉ in 1951 and began teaching with them then, this practice growing as interest in dance expanded in tandem with the revival of the music. With the Willie Clancy summer school's revitalisation of set dancing he was well placed and in great demand to teach the sets. In his working life he had spent time in practically every county in Ireland, picking up dance steps and sets wherever he went – much like a musician accumulating tunes. This gives him the rare breadth of knowledge which has been backbone to the revival of set and step dance. His steps are archived on CCÉ's video *Old-Style Traditional Step Dancing, 1700–1930*, and he continues to teach set dance with his wife Siobhán at schools and workshops in Ireland and abroad. He also teaches dance in UCC's music department, lectures on the subject and has begun work on a major historical survey of dancing in Ireland.

**O'Dowd, Joe.** (1914–87). Fiddle. Born at Knocknaska, Gurteen, Co. Sligo, he was taught fiddle by his older brother while in his early teens. 'O'Dowd's Favourite', a reel recorded by Michael Coleman in the 1920s, is named after his uncle John, also a fiddle player. Joe was influenced by Coleman recordings in his early life, but in the mid-1930s moved to London where he played professionally until 1940 in a céilí and old time band which had Martin Wynne (fiddle) and Paddy Taylor (flute). In 1942 he returned to Ireland, playing little in public until he formed the Owenmore Céilí Band in 1954. When Irish music's public performance began to shift to the pubs in the 1960s, with Carmel Gunning he took a leading role in Sligo CCÉ playing all over that area. His wife Sheila is a well-known fiddle player and teacher, son Séamus plays fiddle and guitar with the group Dervish.

**Ó Duibheannaigh, Aodh (Hiúdaí Phadaí Hiúdaí).** (1914–84). Sean-nós singer. From Rannafast, Co. Donegal he was a fine exemplar of the Donegal sean-nós singing tradition. During his lifetime he worked as (among other things) a schoolteacher, a civil servant, and a collector for the Irish Folklore Commission – this last position being especially consonant with his love of and interest in traditional music and culture. Educated and articulate, Hiúdaí was also a knowledgeable local historian. Despite the prevalence in his youth of songs in English, his repertoire consisted almost entirely of songs in the Irish language. His singing was relatively understated, but his distinctive legato phrasing and unerring use of subtle rhythmic and melodic variation and ornamentation reflected a musicality of the highest order. He won the Bonn Óir at the 1958 Oireachtas. While he made a number of recordings (including a 1976 solo album, *Aodh Ó Duibheannaigh*, and an anthology of the songs of Seán Bán Mac Grianna), some of his best singing can be heard on *An Cailín Gaelach*, recorded in 1953. He had definite and articulately expressed ideas about traditional singing, which he believed, should always convey the singer's personality as well as the emotional and poetic content of the song. A gracious and hospitable man, he was always ready to impart knowledge and songs from his large store to anyone who came to seek them. (LIO)

**Ó Faracháin, Antaine.** (1959– ). Sean-nós singer, fiddler, song writer, teacher and broadcaster. Born in Dublin, with a wide repertoire of traditional songs in Irish and in English, he has taught Gaeltacht songs to Dublin schoolchildren and to older singers. An active member of the Góilín Club in Dublin, he has been influenced by the traditional singing in English of the late Liam Weldon. A founder member of 'Sean-nós Cois Life', he researches and presents programmes for Raidió na Life. He has also presented traditional singing programmes on Teilifís na Gaeilge. Some of his songs can be heard on *Seachrán Sídhe*. (LIM)

**O'Farrell, Patrick.** Compiler of *O'Farrell's Pocket Companion for the Irish or Union Pipes* (four volumes *c*. 1805, '06, '08 and '10). Volumes one and two have 197 tunes, volumes three and four have 177. Reputedly born in Clonmel, Co. Tipperary, Grattan Flood deduced his Christian name as 'Patrick'. A piper of some renown in his time, one of his boasted engagements was playing the pipes for a 1791 Covent Garden production of William Reeve's *Oscar and Malvina* along with harpist John Weippert. Patrick Sky's 1995 meticulously researched reproduction of O'Farrell's 1804 tune collection gives some detail of this.

**Ó Fátharta, Meaití Jó Shéamuis.** (1947– ). Sean-nós singer, piper, flute-player, music collector and broadcaster. Born in Cois Fharraige, his mother, the late Nan Phaddy Nic Diarmada, was a fine sean-nós singer. Taught to play by his uncle Máirtín Shéamuis Ó Fátharta – who composed and plays Raidió na Gaeltachta's signature tune on the 'trumpa' (jew's harp) – he is best known as a presenter with Raidió na Gaeltachta. (LIM)

**Ó Flatharta, John Beag.** Singer. Sometimes seen to represent a recent development in singing in Irish, he is from Connemara and is deeply involved in the world of boats and boat-racing there. From 1980, for a period of about ten years, he was the principal singer with the music group Na hAncairí, which was extremely popular in Connemara and beyond. The group performed songs with Irish-language lyrics, in a highly rhythmic, accompanied, 'country and western' style. Many of the songs, composed by John Beag's contemporaries, mostly men, addressed current social problems and issues in Connemara, such as unemployment and emigration and also document traditions of boats and boat-racing. An indication of the modernity of these songs is the use of certain words in English: words such as 'pothole', 'grant' and 'dole' are used constantly, rather than their Irish language equivalent. These recently composed C&W style songs are sung with modern dance-band amplification on highly public occasions. John Beag also sings in the older, individual, unaccompanied, ornate style identified with sean-nós singing in Connemara. Numerous recordings of Na hAncairí and of John Beag have been released by Cló Iar-Chonnachta. (RIU)

**O'Flynn, Liam (Liam Óg).** (1945– ). Piper. Born Kill, Co. Kildare. His father, also Liam, plays fiddle; his mother, Maisie Scanlan, had links to Co. Clare music through her cousin, Junior Crehan. He was introduced to uilleann pipes by Garda Tom Armstrong who had won prizes at Oireachtas and Fleadh Cheoil in his early teens. Liam studied initially under Leo Rowsome, and later was influenced by Willie Clancy and Séamus Ennis (who bequeathed his pipes to him). A solidly traditional player, he has also been involved in many imaginative projects. He was a founder member of Planxty in 1972, with Christy Moore, Donal Lunny and Andy Irvine, and played on all their recordings. In 1980, he recorded *The Brendan Voyage,* a work for solo uilleann pipes and orchestra, written by Shaun Davey. He also worked with Davey on *Granuaile, The Relief of Derry Symphony* and *The Pilgrim.* His film score credits include collaborations with Mark Knopfler and Elmer Bernstein. He has appeared and recorded with John Cage, and with popular musicians Kate Bush, Enya and The Everley Brothers, and has also performed with Nobel Laureate, Séamus Heaney.

**Ó Gráda, Conal.** (1961– ). Flute. Born in Cork, now living in Baile Mhúirne, his earliest influence was hearing Jackie Daly, Séamus Creagh and others playing in his parents' house after CCÉ sessions in the Country Club. A pupil of Mícheál Ó Riabhaigh's at the Cork Pipers' Club, he initially played flute, uilleann pipes, banjo, fiddle and accordion. He has a solo album *The Top Of Coom*, is on *Eavesdropper* with Jackie Daly and Kevin Burke, and on Eoin Ó Riabhaigh's 'tribute' album. (PAD)

**O'Hannigan, Thomas.** (b. 1806). Piper. Born at Cahir, Co. Tipperary, he lost his sight while in his teens. He served an apprenticeship with various Munster pipers and subsequently went to Dublin where he performed at the Adelphi and Abbey Street theatres. He later played for Queen Victoria and at the Oxford University Commemoration. He died in Bray, Co. Wicklow.

**Ó hÉanaí, Seosamh (Joe Éiniú/Joe Heaney).** (1919–84). Sean-nós singer. Fifth of seven children, he was born in Carna, in the Connemara Gaeltacht. Of Irish-speaking parents, his songs and storytelling reflect their culture. Encouraged to sing and learn old songs in Irish by teacher Bríd Ní Fhlatharta in Aird National School. He won a scholarship to preparatory college for teachers (where he spent only two years) and won first prize at the Oireachtas in Dublin in 1942, where he met Séamus Ennis. He laboured on building sites in Scotland and England, married Mary Connolly in Clydebank, Glasgow in 1947 and with her had two sons and two daughters. He drifted to

London and Southampton in the mid-1950s and sang with piper Willie Clancy, fiddler Martin Byrnes and many other Irish musicians in the pub music scenes, frequently performing in the Singers' Club. He won the gold medal at the Oireachtas in Dublin in 1955 and performed in Damer Hall, Dublin during 'Oícheanta Seanchais' (traditional nights), Gael-Linn's contribution to 'An Tóstal' (National Tourism Festival) in 1958. Riobard Mac Góráin of Gael-Linn brought him back from England during 1959, 1960 and 1961 to make a series of records for Gael-Linn. He returned to Dublin during the ballad boom in the early 1960s and took up residence together with his old friend Séamus Ennis and the newly formed group 'The Dubliners' in O'Donoghue's Singing Pub in Merrion Row, across the road from the then Irish-speakers' pub, Leo O'Neill's. Tom Clancy, home from USA with the Clancy Brothers, brought Joe to perform at the Newport Folk Festival in 1965 where his singing made a big impression. He emigrated permanently to the USA in 1966, working for years as an elevator operator in Manhattan, New York before coming to prominence on the *Merv Griffin Television Show* one St Patrick's Night. In 1980 he was appointed part-time teacher in Irish folklore at Wesleyan University in Middletown, Connecticut and was later appointed to similar position at the Ethnomusicology Department of the University of Washington, Seattle. He performed at festivals and concerts, captivating audiences everywhere. In July 1982 in Washington DC he was presented with the National Heritage Award for Excellence in Folk Arts by the National Endowment for the Arts. He visited Ireland regularly and performed in the National Concert Hall on his last visit in Autumn 1982. Emphysema weakened his health and he died in 1984. Máire Davitt, formerly of Gael-Linn, with the help of Aer Lingus, arranged for his remains to be brought home to Maoras cemetery. 'The Joe Heaney Collection', an index to the songs and stories of Joe Heaney compiled by Seán Williams in the Ethnomusicology Archives of the University of Washington, Seattle, has been presented to the NUI Galway (UCG) and to the School of Scottish Studies in Edinburgh. (LIM)

See *Féile Chomórtha Joe Éiniú*.

**Ó hEidhin, Mícheál.** (1938–   ). Accordion, concertina, schools music inspector. Born in Baile na hAbhann, Ros a' Mhíl, Connemara. His father played fiddle and concertina, his mother melodeon – they played regularly on 2RN (Tommy Coen filled in for her on the night that Mícheál was born). Mícheál studied science at UCG 1956–59, and while there was the leader of the Loch Lurgan Céilí Band. He entered music education only after sitting a scholarship exam as a bet that he couldn't get it. Passing it led to him studying music at UCC under Prof. Aloys Fleischmann, later working as Timire Cheoil (Music Organiser) for Co. Galway VEC. In college he was a contemporary of Fr Pat Ahearn of Siamsa Tíre, and worked throughout Co. Cork on choirs with he and Pilib Ó Laoghaire for four years. He organised the first traditional music concert in Cork City Hall in 1961, and in this period (from 1959–63) played with Donal O'Connor's Brosna Céilí Band. He later started the group, the Connemara Quartet. CCÉ's TTCT diploma was developed by him in 1980, with a view to improving the quality of traditional music teaching. Since 1988 he has brought a dozen such teachers to tutor at the Festival Interceltique at Lorient each year and while chairman of An Gael Acadamh in 1980 he initiated sean-nós singing classes. He has composed for drama and screen, and has published books relating to schools music education: *Cas Amhrán, Lúrabog-Lúrabog, Amhráin do Choláistí Gaeilge, Déan Rince*, and *Ceoi don Chór*. He believes that music must 'develop or die, but must never lose track of the true music', and that music is of equal worth throughout the island, north and south. He has worked as music director for traditional programmes such as *Guth na nÓg, Bring Down the Lamp, In Song and in Story, Comórtas-Cabaret*, and has done *A Man and his Music* slot for RTÉ. He has adjudicated with Slógadh since its beginning in 1968, and at the Oireachtas from age sixteen until recently. His most recent intervention is setting up a 'grades' syllabus for young traditional musicians, this project sponsored by CCÉ and the Royal Irish Academy of Music.

**Ó hEidhin, Risteárd.** (1944–   ). Sean-nós singer. Born at Cill Chiaráin where he learned singing from his mother, Áine Geraghty in Cill Chiaráin NS. He was influenced by prominent local sean-nós singers Dara Bán Mac Donnchdha, Nóra Ghriallais and Johnny Mháirtín Larry. His sister Máire Ní hEidhin won Corn Uí Riada in the mid-1960s, Risteárd won the Oireachtas men's competition in 1988 and 1996, that at Féile na hInse and at Fleadh Cheoil na hÉireann in 1988. (LIM)

**Oifig an Cheoil.** Dingle, Co. Kerry. A contact and information centre set up in 1994 with LEADER funding to assist musicians in finding employment within the tourist-driven entertainment industry in Co. Kerry. It has information on venues, recording, taxation and promotion, encourages new composition and exchange of ideas, and holds a register of musicians. It is funded by musicians' £30 p.a. subscriptions and commission fees.

**Oireachtas, An t-.** Annual competitive, celebratory and social festival run by Conradh na Gaeilge to celebrate the arts among the Irish-speaking communities and within the Irish language movement. Begun in 1897, as part of this it promotes competitions in music and song, most prestigious of which today are those in sean-nós singing, these involving separate male (corn na bhfear) and female (corn na mbean) categories, and also, the prestigious Corn Uí Riada, open to men and women. The solo music and group competitions have declined in popularity and competitive significance with the rise of the fleadhanna ceoil since the early 1950s, but the piping event still carries prestige. An tOireachtas was wound down in 1924 due to a lack of funding and a fall-off in interest in the Gaelic cultural movement in the distressing early days of the Irish state. It was revived in 1939, and has been heavily promoted in recent years. As with the All-Ireland fleadh An tOireachtas involves many people, and rotates its venue between the Irish speaking areas from year to year. The music and song competitions are held in late October.

**Oisín.** Late 1970s Dublin-based traditional band consisting of Geraldine McGowan (vocals, bodhrán), Shay McGowan (guitar), Mick Davis (fiddle), Brian McDonagh (mandolin) and Tom McDonagh (bouzouki). Their first album *Oisín* was released in 1977 on ID records. Produced by Paul Brady it also featured Darach De Brún (pipes, whistle) and Brady playing guitar. A second album *Béaloideas* was recorded in 1977 and also produced by Brady; it was released in 1978 on ID records. The band toured Europe and were popular in Germany, Holland, France and Italy. Gerry Phelan (flute) joined for *Over The Moor To Maggie* on Tara records in 1980. The 1982 line-up featured Geraldine McGowan, Shay McGowan, Mick Davis with Anne Conroy (accordion), Noreen O'Donoghue (harp) and Mícheál Ó Briain (pipes) – as featured in *The Jeanie C* album from 1982. Later line-ups included Steve Cooney, Gerry O'Connor, Brian O'Connor and Davey Spillane. A final album *Winds Of Change* was released in 1987 and Geraldine, Shay and Mick relocated to Germany. Geraldine McGowan has recorded two solo albums *Reconciliation* and *Till the Morning Comes* on Magnet Music. Mick Davis formed Stuttgart-based band Bachelors Walk and Brian McDonough plays with Sligo band Dervish. (JOO)

**O'Keeffe, Pádraig.** (1887–1963). Born at Gleanntán, approximately mid-way between Ballydesmond, Co. Cork and Castleisland, Co. Kerry. One of the most important figures in the history of traditional music and an example of how one person can be central to the development and continuity of the musical tradition of an area. His father was master in the local school, and the family lived across the road in the house which remained Pádraig's home until his death. His mother, Margaret O'Callaghan, one of a music family from Doon, near Kiskeam, Co. Cork, played the concertina and fiddle. At an early age Pádraig displayed an aptitude for music, and he learned to play the fiddle, accordion and concertina. A major influence was his uncle Cal O'Callaghan, another fiddle-player. He succeeded his father as principal teacher in Gleanntán school in 1915 but in 1920 lost this post and became a full-time fiddle teacher, known as the 'last of the fiddle-masters'. He also taught accordion.

*teaching methods.* His method was to travel up to twenty miles a day on foot calling at the houses of his pupils and writing out tunes for

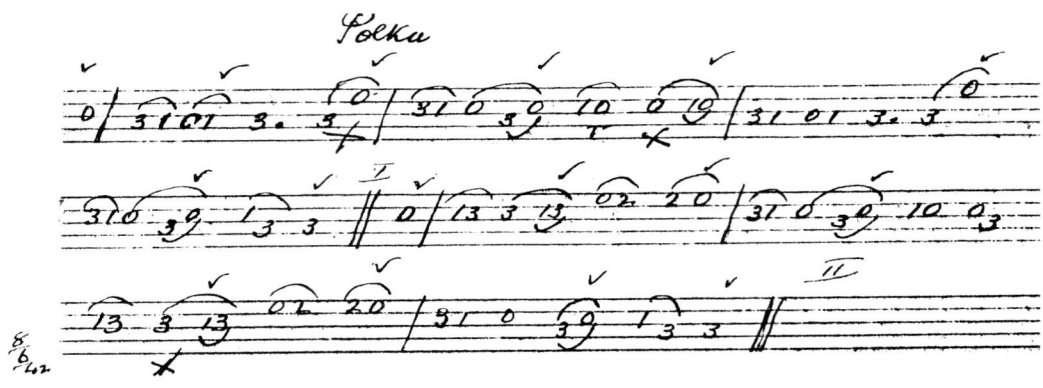

Polka in Pádraig O'Keeffe's fiddle 'code'. (Matt Cranitch)

them in a system of notation which he had developed himself. In his teaching, he used two different systems of tablature, one for the fiddle and one for the accordion. In the accordion 'code', numbers and symbols were used to denote the keys, or buttons, to be pressed and the direction in which the bellows was to be moved. In the fiddle 'code', the four spaces of the standard five-line music staff were used to represent the four strings of the fiddle, with numbers, 0 to 4, being placed in the appropriate spaces to indicate the fingers required to play particular notes (see illustration).

As time progressed, his reputation as a musician and teacher became established both within the Sliabh Luachra area and outside. Séamus Ennis made a large number of recordings of his playing for Raidió Éireann and the BBC. Some of these have subsequently been issued on CD. *Kerry Fiddles*, which also includes Denis Murphy and Julia Clifford, features music recorded in Castleisland, Co. Kerry, in 1952 for the BBC. It was issued on LP by Topic Records in 1977 and on CD by Ossian in 1993. A selection of the music recorded for Raidió Éireann in 1948 and 1949 was issued by RTÉ in 1993 on the CD, *The Sliabh Luachra Fiddle Master* (containing extensive notes on his life).

*repertoire and influence.* He had an extensive repertoire of tunes including many of the local slides and polkas and was also a sensitive player of slow airs. All the famous musicians of the Sliabh Luachra area were pupils of his – Denis Murphy, Paddy Cronin, Julia Clifford, Terry McCarthy, Johnny O'Leary, Mikey Duggan –

and it is no exaggeration to say that every session of music which takes place today in Sliabh Luachra will have O'Keeffe's imprint on style, musical technique and repertoire. Many tales and anecdotes have come now to adorn what was undoubtedly a colourful life and it is noteworthy that even today in Sliabh Luachra his name is frequently mentioned with respect. Many an hour's conversation at any social gathering could be occupied by humorous descriptions of his sayings and adventures from people, most of whom never knew him personally. It was the lifestyle of a committed bachelor, he never married and indeed he said that the fiddle was his 'only wife'. He lived to the age of seventy-five, but having become ill during an exceptionally cold winter in 1962–63 he died in St Catherine's Hospital, Tralee. (PEB, MAC)

Matt Cranitch's *The Sliabh Luachra Code* gives fuller details of O'Keefe's system.

**Ó Laoghaire, Donnchadha.** (1877–1944). Uilleann pipes, flute, harp. Best known as the piper featured in the portrait in Capt. Francis O Neill's collection *1001 Gems of Irish Music*. Born at Doire an Chuiling, Cúil Aodha, from an early age he was an active member of Conradh na Gaeilge, and a regular participant in Oireachtas and Feis competition. At twenty-two he moved to Cork to work for Beamish and Crawford, and there learnt piping from Seán Ó Faoláin. After a year he was appointed 'timire' (Irish language organiser) by Conradh na Gaeilge for Co. Roscommon. Spells in Cork and then Clare followed; there he met Capt. O'Neill and acquired a Moloney brothers set of pipes made *c.* 1837 (now in the National Museum). In Louvain next, he studied French and started a branch of the Gaelic League, returning to spend his life organising and teaching in Waterford and Wexford. He is best known for his many books, poems, songs and articles in the Irish language. (POR)

**Ó Laoghaire, Pilib.** Singer, fiddle, arranger. Brought up with plain chant and sixteenth-century polyphonic church music from an early age, and educated in classical, he learned traditional fiddle and song as a teenager. His interest in Irish song led to analysis and interpretation of this through his formal training. A believer in the centrality of the text in song, he brooked no deviation from the 'authentic'; his mentors were Déise sean-nós singers Labhrás Ó Cadhla and Mícheál Ó Foghlú. His analysis of sean-nós style was intense, his application meticulous, thus according him a personal style which was regarded as being neither strictly traditional nor strictly classical. Interested in choral singing, he founded the Cór Cois Laoi and Kilumney choirs and was expert at training and conducting, specialising in arrangements of Irish song and the work of Irish composers. Perhaps his enduring legacy is his work as Co. Cork VEC's music-scheme organiser which led to the formation of choirs all over the county. Later music inspector with the Department of Education, he was an important contributor to Fleischmann's *Sources of Irish Music* project. A selection of his work is published in Nóirín Ní Riain's *Stór Amhrán* (1988).

**Ó Laoire, Lillis.** (1961– ). Sean-nós singer. He grew up in the Donegal Gaeltacht but it was only when studying Irish at University College, Galway in the late 1970s that he became interested in sean-nós singing. He lectures in Modern Irish at the University of Limerick where he is also director of Ionad na nAmhrán. He is currently researching songs on Tory Island, this taking him for the year 1996–97 as Fulbright Scholar to the Ethnomusicology Department at UCLA. He won Corn Uí Riada in 1991 and in 1994, and a dozen of his large repertoire can be heard on *Bláth Gach Géag dá dTig*. (LIM)

Johnny O'Leary (Topic)

**O'Leary, Johnny.** Accordion. (1923– ). Born in the Sliabh Luachra area on the Cork–Kerry border, this highly regarded player picked up his first tunes from his uncle, Dan O'Leary, a pupil of Tom Billy Murphy, but learned much of his music from the Sliabh Luachra fiddle master, Pádraig O'Keeffe. In the mid-1930s, he struck up a musical partnership with the fiddle player Denis Murphy at Thade Willie O'Connor's dance hall in Gneeveguilla, which lasted until the latter's death in 1974. With Murphy too, in 1964 he became a regular feature of music in Dan O'Connell's Bar in Knocknagree where they played for set dancers. He is still a house player there. He is the subject of the 1994 book and tune collection *Johnny O'Leary of Sliabh Luachra*, edited by Terry Moylan. (PAA)

**Ó Líatháin, Donal.** (1934– ). Singer, songwriter. Born at Cúil Aodha, Co. Cork. Annual attendance at the Dábhscoil made him extremely interested in local song and composition. This could be an intense and moving experience. There he first heard 'An Poc Ar Buile' from D. Mullins: 'I was hooked, and had to have a go.' A teacher locally, he wrote the comic songs 'An Ancient Priceless Horn', 'An Pósadh', and 'An Péint', and most of 'Bímis Ag Ól' (all verses except the first and chorus). A composer of serious song also, Cór Cúil Aodha have recorded his piece 'Im Long Mé Measaim'.

**Ó Lionaird, Iarla.** (1964– ). Sean-nós singer. Born at Cúil Aodha into a sean-nós singing family, he is a grand nephew of Elizabeth (Bess) Cronin. He was recorded first at age seven, was a member of Seán Ó Riada's Cór Chúil Aodha, and later was one of the various presenters of RTÉ's *The Pure Drop*. With Tony MacMahon, Noel Hill and John Gibson he made the 'live' Gael-Linn album *Aislingí Cheoil*; he has recorded and performed internationally with the band Afro-Celt Sound System, and in 1997 recorded an 'experimental' solo album *The Seven Steps to Mercy*. (PAD)

**O'Loughlin, Peadar.** (1929– ). Fiddle, uilleann pipes, flute. Born at Cullen, Kilmaley, Co. Clare. Influenced by his father, who played fiddle, flute and concertina, his growing up was among local and visiting musicians, including fiddler Ellen Galvin. Beginning on whistle, he moved to flute, then fiddle, then pipes. Solo playing for solo set dancers was common practice in his youth, making his first experience of attempted group playing odd enough to be memorable. Inspired by flute player Mickey Hanrahan, this led to the Fiach Rua Céilí Band in 1940 which Peadar joined in 1948. In later years he played in the Tulla and Kilfenora bands, and recorded with Aggie White, Willie Clancy and Elizabeth Crotty. With Paddy Canny, Bridie Lafferty and P. Joe Hayes he recorded *All-Ireland Champions*. Much local music was originated in 'O'Neill's' (learned and transmitted by fiddler Hughdie Doohan), but travelling players were also a major source: Jerry O'Shea introducing 'The Blooming Meadows', dancing master Paddy Barron (who taught regularly in Peadar's home) bringing 'The Drunken Gauger'. Seán Reid introduced him to piping – via the Tulla Céilí Band – giving him Bro. Gildas O'Shea's flat Egan set of pipes for a wedding present. From the early 1950s he is best known for his playing in Fleadh and Oireachtas competitions with concertina player Paddy Murphy. He plays presently with Paddy Canny, and teaches annually at the Willie Clancy Summer School.

**Ó Madagáin, Breandán.** (1932– ). Singer, researcher. Born in Limerick, he lectured in Irish first at UCD, then UCG where he was professor of Irish from 1975–97. There he established song as an integral part of degree programmes in Irish. Elected a member of the Royal Irish Academy in 1992, his primary research interest has been Irish song. His publications include *Gnéithe den Chaointeoireacht* (1978), 'Irish Vocal Music of Lament and Syllabic Verse' (*The Celtic Consciousness,* 1981), 'Ceol a chanadh Eoghan Mór Ó Comhraí' (*Béaloideas 51,* 1983), 'Functions of Irish song in the nineteenth century' (*Béaloideas* 53, 1985), 'Amhráin Bheannaithe: an Ceol Dúchais' (1987), 'Limerick's heritage of Irish song' (*North Munster Antiquarian Journal, 28,* 1986), 'The Gaelic lullaby: a charm to protect the baby?' (*Scottish Studies,* 29), 'Gaelic Work-Songs' (*Ireland of the Welcomes,* 40, 1991), 'Echoes of Magic in the Irish Song Tradition' (*Proceedings of the Second North American Congress of Celtic Studies,* Halifax, 1992), 'An ceol a ligeann an racht' (*Léachtaí Cholm Cille* xii, 1992), 'Song for emotional release in the Gaelic tradition' (*Irish Musical Studies 2,* 1993).

**Ó Maonaigh, Proinsias.** (1922– ). Fiddle. Gaoth Dobhair, Donegal. His mother played concertina – it was popular in her locality – and the area had competitive fife-and-drum band music. In his youth, travelling pipers the MacSuibhnes would set up each winter at Húidí Beag's pub. He attended Coláiste Éinne where he learned fiddle, and trained as a primary teacher in St Patrick's College, Drumcondra. Author of a number of songs, most famous being 'Gleanntáin Ghlas' Ghaoth Dobhair', he is predominantly responsible for the revival of instrumental music, particularly fiddling, in north-west Donegal. Presently he teaches music in the area between Dungloe and Falcarragh. (LIO)

**Ó Méalóid, Colm.** (1935– ). Sean-nós singer. From Camus, Connemara, but moved with his family to Ráth Cairn in 1956, he presently lives in Ashbourne, Co. Meath. Third oldest of a large and famous family of teachers, musicians, singers, dancers and footballers, an accomplished box player and fine traditional singer, he got his music from his father, Sonaí Shéamuis Ó Méalóid, and his singing from his mother, Nóra Ní Shúilleabháin, also from Camus. He can be heard on *Céad Slán le Camus: Ceol agus Amhráin*. The recording includes two of his compositions 'Ráth Cairn na Mí' and 'Céad Slán le Camus'. (LIM)

**O'Mealy, Richard Lewis (R. L.).** (1873–1947). Uilleann piper. Born at Templecross, near Ballynacarrigty, Co. Westmeath, the fourth generation of pipers which passed back through father Larry, grandfather Charlie, and great-grandfather, Tom, who originally came to the midlands from Co. Mayo. On leaving school, R. L. lived first in Boyle, Co. Roscommon, then Cork, finally settling in Belfast c. 1900 where he lived first in Edinburgh Street, then Rugby Avenue. A renowned pipe-maker, O'Mealy was influenced by the style of the Taylor brothers of Drogheda and Philadelphia, particularly in his regulator-key work. His preference was for making sets pitched in C-sharp with one regulator. At the Oireachtas in 1901 and 1902 he won prizes for the quality of his workmanship, and his instruments were displayed at the Irish Industrial Exhibition at the St Louis World Fair in 1904. O'Mealy was also an accomplished piper, and newspaper reports from the early 1900s show that he was in big demand for various music and cultural events. In the first Feis Cheoil held in Dublin in 1897 he was placed second in 'unpublished airs'. Examples of his piping can be heard on a number of recordings made for the BBC in August 1943. These, made at age seventy, show him as an exemplar of close, or staccato, fingered piping. These suggest that in his younger years he was most likely a remarkable musician. (ROH)

**Ó Miléadha, Pádraig.** (1877–1947). The last of the Sliabh gCua, Co. Waterford, poets and one of very few writers of the Irish Language Revival to leave a lasting impression on the folk-song repertoire. Born in Sceichíní, near Cill Brien in Co. Waterford, he emigrated to Wales in 1903 where he composed his most popular song 'Sliabh Geal gCua na Féile' (1912). He was an energetic trade-unionist, Labour Party activist and participant in various Irish cultural and political movements in Wales and England. After returning to Ireland in 1922, he was employed as an Irish teacher by the Waterford Vocational Education Committee. Other songs of his still popular in the Waterford Gaeltacht include 'Mo Thig Beag Aerach' (1923), 'Na Tincéirí' (1911) a witty and eloquent account of an encounter with travellers, and 'Cearta Mhichíl de hÓra' (1913) an affectionate evocation of that once central institution of rural social life, the forge. (EAO)

**Ó Móráin, Dónal.** (1923– ). Founder of the Gael-Linn organisation, one of the earliest recording companies to specialise in traditional music and song. This was founded in 1953 as a result of a proposal made by him to an inter-university organisation *An Comhchaidreamh* which had a common agenda of promotion of the Irish language. They developed a self-help promotion deal with the then government which gained grant aid matched pound for pound with Gael-Linn's own promotions. First of these was a football pools, until the advent of the Nation Lottery the major casual-gambling structure in Ireland. Gael-Linn's other major project was the (then new) introduction of three-month, Gaeltacht scholarships for children. In 1957 it began making short films, these aimed at the pre-television cinema-going Irish public. Early items were *Mise Éire* and *Saoirse* directed by George Morrison with soundtracks by Seán Ó Riada. Louis Marcus directed later works including such as *Capallogy* (about the horse business) and *Peil* (on hurler Christy Ring). Their busiest output however was weekly newsreels in the Irish language from 1959, produced by Colm Ó Laoghaire, these achieving ratings of 0.25 million viewers by virtue of distribution by the Rank organisation. They were rendered redundant however by television in 1962 with the setting up of Raidió Telefís Éireann. Gael-Linn's music performance involvement began in 1959 with the setting up of *Cabaret Gael-Linn*, a Dublin-based touring ensemble built around harpist Kathleen Watkins which offered cabaret-style performance to regional hotels during the tourist season; it also organised major concerts. Recordings began in 1957, the first of these being of Seán 'ac Dhonncha, 45 rpm singles. Earliest of the LP catalogue (CEF 1) featured accompanied singer Tomás Ó Súilleabháin on side A, with the Raidió Éireann Light Orchestra – *Ceolfhoireann Eadrom Raidió Éireann* – on side B playing arrangements of Irish slow airs and such by Seán Ó Riada and Seoirse Bodley. CEF 2 was the *Mise Éire* soundtrack on 45 rpm, CEF 3 featured singer Seán Ó Síocháin; other albums had Martin Dempsey (all songs were in Irish). Gael-Linn gradually increased their involvement in the traditional, producing such as Ó Riada's work with Ceoltóirí Chualann (*Playboy of the Western World, Ceol na nUasal*, etc.), by 1970 recording Clannad's second album (CEF 041). Their Irish language policy dictated that they recorded many of the great Irish-language singers such as Seosamh Ó hÉanaí, Darach Ó Catháin and Caitlín Maude; this policy continues to be their ethos, broken finally in 1997 with the introduction of the Fonn label on which Len Graham and Padraigín Ní Uallacháin became their first English-language singers with *When I Was Young/Nuair a Bhí Mé Óg*. In addition to a hundred pieces from their earlier 78, 45 and EP period, Gael-Linn's catalogue now has in excess of 180 albums, plus another fifteen compilations drawn from these.

**Ó Murchú, Seán.** (d. 1982). Radio broadcaster, for many years presenter of Raidió Éireann's hugely popular Saturday programme *Céilí House*.

**Ó Murchú, (Senator) Labhrás.** (1939–   ). Organiser. Born at Cashel, Co. Tipperary, Director General of Comhaltas Ceoltóirí Éireann since 1968. Growing up in an atmosphere of dances in his family home generated a commitment that led him to change his name to the Irish by deed poll, and in the 1950s to form a local cultural body – Cumann an Phiarsaigh – built around Irish language, music, dance and drama. This was subsumed into the local CCÉ branch when that was formed in the late 1950s – during which time he also taught céilí dance in the county – and in 1960 he became CCÉ Co. Tipperary Secretary. In the early part of that decade he was made PRO of the organisation's Munster Council, became a national Ard Comhairle member in 1968, and in the same year was elected president, first of two, three-year terms. In the late 1960s, negotiations with the government resulted in the provision of state funding, this, CCÉ applied to the provision of full-time staff. He was appointed to the major post of director – a full-time, permanent position which he still holds and which he has held (controversially) concurrent with the office of president for two terms. He is also the organisation's main spokesperson, and editor of its journal *Treoir*. His editorials therein, and public statements, emphasise a tradition-based, 'national cultural' commitment, this is expressed mostly through music-related issues, but also embraces the Irish language and, sometimes controversially, religion, abortion, the family, and national politics. Interned himself at the Curragh under the Offences Against the State Act in the 1950s for failing to give an account of his movements, in 1971 he defended his organisation's decision to postpone the All-Ireland Fleadh Cheoil as a reaction to internment in Northern Ireland.

Educated at CBS, Cashel, his career began as a law clerk, then he was a clerical officer in Tipperary Co. Council. An organiser for Conradh na Gaeilge at Harcourt Street, Dublin from 1965–68, he ran CCÉ's affairs from their building while spearheading CCÉ's move to present headquarters at Monkstown in 1974. In CCÉ debate, and through *Treoir*, he has been to the forefront of ideological dispute with the Arts Council over funding and policy on traditional music particularly in the later 1980s.

In 1998 his wife Úna Uí Mhurchú, was appointed to the Arts Council. She is the director of Brú Ború, CCÉ's flagship, tourist-oriented performance venue in Cashel. He was elected Senator (to the Culture and Education Panel) in 1997 and is a member of Oireachtas committees on education, heritage and Irish language, he is deputy government spokesperson on these matters in Seanad Éireann. National chairman of the Irish Family History Foundation – a North/South genealogy network – he has been recipient of both the

Dublin Civic Honour Award and Tipperary Person of the Year Award. He was rapporteur for the (controversial) 1999 Joint Committee report on traditional music.

**O'Neill, Arthur.** (1734–1818). Harp player and chronicler. Born Drumnastrade, Dungannon, Co. Tyrone, he lost his sight after an accident in childhood and was sent to learn harp under Owen Keenan of Augher. Thus began an itinerant musician's life at age fifteen, which in the course of several years took him on a first 'tour' over Antrim and Down, to Meath, Munster and back to Donegal. In the course of his stay in Limerick he re-strung the 'Brian Ború' harp and played it at the head of a procession through the streets of Limerick. Most of his life story was dictated to a scribe appointed by Edward Bunting during the harper's stay in Belfast between 1808 and 1813 when he was master of the Irish Harp Society there. Therein O'Neill relates anecdotal and colourful tales of harpers like Charles Byrne, Arthur Short, Cornelius Lyons, Rory Dall Ó Catháin and Turloch Carolan. He recalls the players at the harp 'Balls' at Granard, Co. Longford (1781–83), and otherwise gives a thorough account of the social life of the times in which the harper was immersed, the dying years of the harp tradition. Particularly interesting are his accounts of the other instruments being played: in the 1750s there were 'plenty of pipers and fiddlers' in the Rosses, Donegal; around 1782, in the home of Jones Irwin of Streamstown, Co. Sligo, attending a music night he records, 'in addition to the daughters of the house playing piano, Gentlemen flutes 6, Gentlemen violoncellos 2, Common pipers 10, Gentlemen fiddlers 20, Gentlemen clarionets 4'. His memoirs can be read in Donal O'Sullivan's *Carolan*.

**O'Neill, (Captain) Francis.** (1848–1936). Flute, fiddle, pipes, collector. Born Tralibane near Bantry, Co. Cork. At the age of sixteen he left home and embarked on an adventurous life: sailing the world's oceans as a cabin boy, working at various jobs across the US, then marrying an Irish emigrant and settling in Chicago where he joined the city's police force in 1873. He advanced steadily through the ranks and from 1901–05 was General Superintendent or Chief of Police. Along with other like-minded enthusiasts in Chicago he collected and documented a large body of dance tunes from immigrant Irish musicians and began publishing the material in book form in 1903. As well as his collecting and publishing work he also had the foresight to photograph numerous players and in 1902 he equipped himself with an Edison cylinder phonograph on which he made some of the earliest recordings of Irish music. (HAB)

A musician himself, O'Neill took an active role in the traditional music scene in Chicago which was flourishing among the large Irish immigrant community there. The importance of his involvement was recognised in 1901 when he was elected president of the Chicago Irish Music Club. O'Neill became aware of the fact that many of the tunes he recalled from his childhood in Co. Cork were not known to musicians from other parts of Ireland whom he encountered in Chicago. This led to the broader realisation that there was in fact a substantial body of Irish music which had not yet been collected. With the initial view of committing his own repertoire to print O'Neill embarked on a notation project recruiting a colleague, James O'Neill (1863–1949), to assist in transcribing. Originally from Co. Down, James O'Neill was a fiddler himself, had a good ear and was literate in music. He committed to written form the tunes which Francis would play for him and would then play back from the written version to check for errors. As word of the project began to spread throughout the music community in Chicago, others became interested and began to contribute tunes, both from memory and from manuscript and printed collections.

*publications.* In 1903 the largest ever collection of Irish music, *The Music of Ireland* was published, financed by O'Neill himself. The 1,850 tunes presented were classified according to tune-type (airs and songs, Carolan compositions, double jigs, slip jigs, reels, hornpipes, long dances, marches and miscellaneous). In 1907 the first of four editions of *The Dance Music of Ireland – 1001 Gems* appeared. Including many tunes from the previous collection this publication focused entirely on the dance music repertoire. The most popular written source of Irish dance music until Breathnach's *Ceol Rince na hÉireann*, this collection was, up to the 1970s, referred to by musicians simply as 'the book'. In 1908, *250 Choice Selections Arranged for Piano and Violin* appeared. Again based on material from previous O'Neill publications, the provision of piano arrangements by James O'Neill was intended to attract an audience beyond Irish musicians. An enlarged 400-tune edition of this with piano arrangements by Selena O'Neill (also no relation), a student at the Chicago Music College, appeared in 1915. Selena's involvement in Francis' projects dates from 1910 when she arranged *Popular Selections from O'Neill's Dance Music of Ireland* for piano. *Waifs and Strays of Gaelic Melody*, again including piano accompaniments arranged by her, was first published in 1922, with a later edition appearing in 1924, this including historical and descriptive notes on the tunes by O'Neill himself. He also published two important text-books. *Irish Folk Music – A Fascinating Hobby* (1910) contains much personal information about the author, reflects his interest in piping and comments on various aspects of the Irish music tradition. *Irish Minstrels and Musicians*, from 1913, is a substantial directory of musicians, again with an emphasis on t hose involved in piping. The 1987 reprint of this book has a valuable assessment of O'Neill by Breandán Breathnach.

The published collections of Francis O'Neill represent a remarkable contribution to the Irish music tradition. The volume of material involved is considerable. It is also significant that this was the first collecting and publishing project to be undertaken by and aimed primarily at Irish music practitioners.

*reservations*. While the collections of Francis O'Neill remain invaluable to Irish musicians, there are a number of problems with them. 1. The tunes represented are those played by O'Neill and his fellow musicians in the Chicago area, supplemented in part by tunes obtained from visitors to the area. Therefore, the music of all the counties of Ireland, particularly the north-west, is not represented equally. 2. Titles of tunes are often the invention of O'Neill, who was quite candid about naming tunes after the individuals from whom they were obtained. 3. Given the wealth of material involved, it is inevitable that duplication of tunes might occur, and in a number of cases the same tune appears within a single collection, identical but for the title. 4. When considering the transcription methods involved, the scope for error is wide and so the O'Neill collections show errors in key signatures and rhythms, and inconsistencies in repeat markings and ornamentation. 5. One round of the basic melody is given in the case of each tune. While it is common for O'Neill to include more than one setting of a particular tune, no account of variation and style is mentioned. 6. O'Neill also confessed to creating parts of melodies where memory lapses occurred.

In 1931 O'Neill donated a substantial part of his library to the University of Notre Dame, Indiana. While his collections have been used primarily as source material for traditional musicians – as he originally intended – they have also been the focus for considerable scholarly attention. Miles Krassen published a new and revised edition of *The Music of Ireland* in 1976. Breandán Breathnach compiled a thematic index of the tunes collected by O'Neill which is currently housed in the Irish Traditional Music Archive, Dublin. In 1997 Nicholas Carolan's biography of O'Neill – *A Harvest Saved: Francis O'Neill and Irish Music in Chicago* – described his work and life in full, and in 1999 Ossian published a complete edition of the works of O'Neill. Edited by Liz Doherty of University College, Cork, this work has edited versions of all 2,500 tunes and a complete revised version of the thematic index. (LD)

**O'Neill Centre, Chief.** (Smithfield, Dublin).
See Chief O'Neill Ceol Centre.

**O'Neill Irish Music Collection.** Archive holding the collection of Capt. Francis O'Neill. Located in the Hesburgh Library at the University of Notre Dame, South Bend, Indiana, USA. It has more than 1,500 Irish music books and recordings of Irish traditional music as well as O'Neill's personal correspondence. Breandán Breathnach considers O'Neill's bequeathing of the collection to an American university to have been 'a silent condemnation of the indifference of the Irish race towards its native culture'.

**O'Neill, Sarah Anne.** (1919– ). Singer. Born at Derrytresk, Co. Tyrone, sister to Geordie Hanna. Her father played fiddle and sang, lilted and danced a sean-nós style. Travelling musicians and neighbouring players were regularly entertained in her home and music and song could be heard in local 'céilí houses'. Sarah Anne sang from a young age, like most others of that generation she had all kinds of material, local and popular. Consciousness of and concentration on traditional song came in the 'revival' years, through the programming on Raidió Éireann and local sessions in Mackle's Hotel in the 1950s. Through the 1960s her home was a major Tyrone venue for 'sessions', bringing together players and singers from all the northern counties, including Joe Holmes and Len Graham, Jeannie McGrath, the Comacs and John Loughran. She can be heard on Topic's *Irish Voices* with Geordie Hanna and others. Local songwriter Jim McGurk – a singer, poet and fiddler – composed one of Sarah-Anne's best known songs for her, 'Banks of Sweet Lough Neagh'. This was tailored specially to incorporate the placenames of her locality. The words were sent to her on paper via 'the breadman'.

**oral tradition.** The passing on of music, song, storytelling, etc. from generation to generation by a process of performance and absorption. This may or may not involve active teaching, but ideally it does not use written music or song lyrics. Melodies and words are committed to memory by listening repeatedly to the same tune or song. In the absence of the use of written music or words, even without access to tape or other recordings, a good young musician/singer can develop a scientifically rigorous alertness and memory, and might be inclined, and able, to reproduce exactly what has been taught, but a poorer student may have inaccurate recall. In the former case the musician may develop, or build upon what has been learnt and in the latter they might forget, and improvise, perhaps destructively. Either way, music in the oral tradition changes slowly, but inevitably.

See traditional music.

**Orange Order.** Founded in Co. Armagh in 1795, as a secret, Protestant, self-defence society. It spread rapidly in the next few years to include many landowners and aristocracy in its ranks, achieving favour and respectability not shared by other contemporary peasant organisations. Through emigration it spread to Canada, Australia, Africa, New Zealand and became very strong in Scotland which had a similar, associated culture. With secret rituals and passwords based on Freemasonry and the Old Testament, it organised in Lodges, Districts and Counties. The Order conducts an annual spectacle of processions, with marching bands, banners and flags and uniforms of collarette or sash, sometimes white gloves and bowler hats.

Shanghai March (EDI)

A popular Orange-band marching tune. The air is that of 'The Shearing', a song popular in Scotland.

Ceremonial swords and pikes ('deacon poles') are also carried. The main processions are at commemorations of the Battle of the Somme on the 1st of July, and on 12th of July in commemoration of the Battle of the Boyne (1690), but also include church parades throughout the year and political demonstrations in times of crisis. Sister Unionist organisations include the Royal Black Preceptory and the Apprentice Boys of Derry. The Ancient Order of Hibernians is a Catholic, nationalist equivalent but in Ireland is largely irrelevant. The Orange Order is significant in NI as a politico-cultural catalyst, providing unity amongst Protestants divided by denomination. Musically the Order is important due to the association of fife and Lambeg drum as accompaniment to the main annual processions, and also (since the 1870s) due to a very strong marching band tradition, especially flute, but also accordion, silver, brass, and pipe. There are possibly more than 10,000 people associated with these bands, though not necessarily with the Orange Order. The conservative nature of the organisation meant that dance traditions, largely moribund in the wider area were preserved in some Orange Halls, e.g., step dancing, lancers, etc. especially in east Co. Down. A strong singing tradition is evidenced in the large amount of printed material (broadsides etc.) but is also largely moribund now. Many of these older songs are published by the Ulster Society. By the late 1960s membership was dropping, but the Troubles brought a new relevance and strength based on defending the union of Northern Ireland with Britain. (GAH)

**O'Reilly, Edward.** (1765–1830). Collector. A well-known Gaelic scholar and lexicographer who around 1810 established a small school with Edward Farmer in which they gave instruction in the Irish language. He also was a collector of songs, seventy-eight of which from his MS were reportedly copied into collector Henry Hudson's notebooks (Hudson was studying with him in 1812). O'Reilly's original MS does not survive. (JOM)

See Hudson, Henry.

**Ó Riabhaigh, Mícheál.** (1911–76). Uilleann piper and noted teacher, he learned his playing from Tadhg Crowley of Crowley's Music Shop in Cork. In 1963, he revived the Cork Pipers' Club, the oldest Pipers Club in existence (founded 1898), and his pupils, many of whom are now established traditional musicians, won a succession of All-Ireland and Slogadh titles. One of the outstanding pipers in the country and known for his radio programmes *Journey through Munster* and *Irish Music Collected in America*, Mícheál's children, Mícheál, Nora and Eoin all play uilleann pipes. Best known is Eoin, a former All-Ireland winner who features on albums by Dolores Keane, Jimmy Crowley and Stokers Lodge. A solo album, *Tribute*, named in honour of his late father, was released in 1998. (PAD)

See Cork Pipers' Club.

**Ó Riada, Seán.** (1931–71). Composer, arranger, academic and musician. Born in 1931 in Cork, while his father, Seán Reidy of Kilmihil, Co. Clare, a sergeant in the Garda Síochána, was stationed in Adare, Co. Limerick. His mother was Julia Creedon from Kilnamartra in the Barony of West Muskerry. Both parents came from a farming background with a high level of cultural awareness, she a concertina and melodeon player with many of the songs of her area, and he having once studied the fiddle with Patrick Kelly. Ó Riada's cradle songs were 'Codhlaigí Éiníní' from his father and 'Cois an Ghaorthaidh' from his mother. At age four he went to CBS, Adare where his first teacher, Br Long from Dingle, set the foundation for his strong passion for the Irish language. At seven he got his first violin lesson from Granville Metcalfe from Limerick, a year later he began to study the piano, also studying theory, counterpoint and harmony with Prof. Van de Veld. At ten he joined the Limerick Club, performing with them until he left to board at Farranferris Seminary School, this on a scholarship won in 1943. He matriculated in 1947, and too young to enter university, he spent a year at St Munchin's in Limerick where he took his Leaving Certificate. He entered UCC in 1948 on a scholarship, studying Arts, with Music (with Prof. Aloys Fleischmann), Greek, Latin and Irish. He read widely, this with talk and debate was oriented towards the ancient and modern cultures of Europe; he graduated with honours in music. He married Ruth Coghlan in 1953; in the same year, he was appointed assistant director of music in Raidió Éireann along with Dr Arthur Young with whom he dismissed many traditional fiddler hopefuls who presented for audition. Ó Riada resigned from Raidió Éireann in 1955, and, in a logical extension to all of his classical reading and studies, took off to experience intellectual life in Paris, here meeting artists and musicians through RDTF (French radio), but finally confronted by the *Aisling* – which had been hovering over him all his life – to whom (through the persona of his wife) he addressed: 'I'd rather be breaking stones in Ireland than be the richest man living in Europe.' Back in Dublin his most prolific period began, arranging for the Raidió Éireann Singers and Light Orchestra; writing original compositions for Symphony Orchestra and Chamber Orchestra as well as for solo voice and for piano. During this time he also worked as music director of the Abbey Theatre, this allowing him time to do many radio broadcasts and work on film music.

Parallel with the European classical creativity of these years, a traditional Irish theme emerged, first expressed in the music for the 1959 film *Mise Éire*. He studied traditional music, the radio series *Our Musical Heritage* (also published as a book) the result. He experimented with combinations of musicians, finally evolving the group Ceoltóirí Chualann. It was first presented to the public as a folk or traditional orchestra providing music for Brian McMahon's *The Honey Spike* at the Abbey Theatre, its first formal appearance as a stage group was at the Shelbourne Hotel. The summer of 1959 spent with his family in Brú na Gráige (Corca Dhuibhne, Co. Kerry) was Ó Riada's first contact with the Gaeltacht. Deeply impressed, he and his wife began a salon-style céilí at their home in Galloping Green, Dublin, this bringing together all the strands of the composer's interests – muintir na Gaeltachta, traditional and classical musicians, poets, diplomats, tradesmen and business men.

He resigned from the Abbey in 1962 and moved to Corca Dhuibhne for a year doing freelance work for RTÉ, and writing for the *Irish Times*. In 1963 he was appointed assistant lecturer in music at University College, Cork. The family moved to An Draighean, Cúil Aodha to live, ten miles from where Seán's mother was born. He made 16 mm films, wrote music, fished, studied Indian and Oriental music, sat on national commissions and committees, and was deeply involved in the local community. He formed a local choir – Cóir Chúil Aodha – and wrote his first Mass for them. His fascination with things spiritual produced two others – for Glenstal, and an Irish government-commissioned Requiem.

*arrangements and compositions.* Ó Riada made more than 700 arrangements of songs and dance music for traditional group, some twenty-five orchestral arrangements of traditional Irish tunes and 120 chorale arrangements of Irish songs. He did various lecture series too: the early-1960s, Raidió Éireann broadcasts titled *Our Musical Heritage*, and those on Irish music in general delivered at UCC some weeks before his death. He also wrote a play (*Spailpín a Rúin*), articles, essays and some songs. He composed a body of original Irish melodies, these made with the express purpose of letting them drift into the mainstream of Irish music – best known is 'Mná na hÉireann' (text from Ó Doirnín). He composed two masses as well: 'Cúil Aodha' (1965) and 'Glenstal' (1968). (PEO)

*traditional music.* In 1960 Ó Riada was commissioned by Gael-Linn to arrange the score for the film *Mise Éire,* and subsequently *Saoirse* (George Morrison's cinema documentaries on events surrounding the foundation of the Irish Free State). In 1961 he scored the music for the film version of *The Playboy of the Western World*. On record these made a huge impact in the country, and coming as they did at the fiftieth anniversary of the 1916 Rising were extremely influential in re-fashioning Irish cultural self-identity.

*Ceoltóirí Chualann.* While still associated with the Abbey, Ó Riada gathered together this group of largely traditional musicians and singers, some of whom were to use his model to form the Chieftains and later Ceoltóirí Laighean. In reaction to the practice of contemporary céilí bands who always performed in unison, he developed an approach which highlighted individual musicians, permitting them to play passages in various combinations; he also introduced an element of harmony. In addition to dance tunes and slow airs, he included pieces from the corpus of the harper/composers. Originally playing the bodhrán, he himself went on to lead the group on harpsichord. Although they made few concert appearances, Ceoltóirí Chualann gained a wide following during the early 1960s due to two radio programmes – *Reachaireacht an Riadaigh* and *Fleadh Cheoil an Raidió* – and from recordings. The group had a major influence on the direction of Irish traditional ensemble thereafter. (BIM)

**ornament.** A general label applied to specific techniques involved in traditional music performance. Irish traditional music depends largely on individual creativity; thus a single player may never play a given tune in exactly the same way twice, and two players will rarely play a tune identically. One way in which this individuality and fluidity is maintained is through the use of ornaments, and the process of ornamenting a tune. The player is free to choose from the common stock of these (cuts, tips, rolls, trebles, cranns and triplets) and to apply them to the melodic outline where they are considered appropriate. (LID)

See cran; double stopping; grace note; roll; tip; treble; triplet.

**Ó Róchain, Muiris.** (1944– ). Born in Dingle, Co. Kerry. His family are from the Gaeltacht, and he was reared bilingually; in younger years he was involved with music, song and local traditions such as the wren. He collected folklore for UCD from the last of the Gaelic storytellers while teaching in Cahersiveen and Waterville, and was involved in setting up Ballinskelligs local development co-op in 1968. He taught in Dublin from 1967 where he was an associate of Breandán Breathnach, John Kelly, and other major figures in traditional music revival. Married to Úna Guerin of Miltown Malbay in 1970, he moved there to teach at Spanish Point. A contributor to CCÉ's *Treoir* magazine and involved in *Dal gCais* magazine from its inception, he played a leading part in the making of three short films – *My Own Place* (RTÉ, 1980, prod. Tony MacMahon), *Cur agus Cúiteamh* (RTÉ, 1990, prod. Cathal Goan), *Up Sráid Eoin – The Story of the Dingle Wren* (RTÉ, 1991, prod. Ríonach Uí Ógáin). The original proposer of the Willie Clancy Summer School, he drew up its first programme in 1973 with Séamus MacMathúna of CCÉ and has been its director since.

**Ó Sé, Seán.** (1936– ). Singer. Born at Ballylickey, Co. Cork. His family had a long tradition of singing, particularly on his father's side. He studied singing for a time at the Cork School of Music under John T. Horne, until Seán Ó Riada advised him that 'too much training might spoil his voice'. He won the traditional singing competition at Feis na Mumhan in 1959 and made many radio broadcasts in subsequent years, during this time singing with the Blarney Céilí Band. In 1961, he was invited by Seán Ó Riada to join Ceoltóirí Chualann, and he remained with the group until their final performance at Cork City Hall in 1969. He presented a number of programmes for RTÉ, including *An Ghaoth Aneas*. He taught as a national school teacher in Baltinglass, Co. Wicklow, and Bandon, Co. Cork. Later he was principal at the Cathedral School and at Knocknaheeny, both in the northside of Cork city.

**Ó Seighin, Mícheál.** (1940– ). Sean-nós singer, whistle. Born Gleann Bruachán (Glenbrohane) in the Ballyhouhra mountains, Co. Limerick, an area with a strong music tradition, he has been teaching in Erris, Co. Mayo since 1962. Singing from an early age, he specialises in older songs of Erris, many of which he has revived. He was a pioneer teacher of traditional music in Co. Limerick in the 1950s. (LIM)

**osmosis.** A scientific term often applied to the process of a child or newcomer learning music or song aurally.

See transmission of music.

**Ó Súilleabháin, Béara.** See Ó Súilleabháin, Eoghan Rua.

**Ó Súilleabháin, Diarmuid.** (1948–91). Born into the Muskerry song tradition of the Irish-speaking area of Cúil Aodha, West Cork. Third in a family of seven, his father Maidhcí was a well-known singer, and his mother, while not a singer herself, had a great store of song lyrics and was an expert on their history. Influenced by his father, Diarmuid owed much to neighbours Diarmuid Ó Ríordáin and Pádraig Ó Tuama. He was educated at Coláiste Íosagáin in Baile Mhúirne, and St Patrick's College, Drumcondra, Dublin. He began teaching school in the late 1960s at Passage West. In 1974, he joined Cork Local Radio, moving in 1977 as newsreader to RTÉ's Irish language newsroom in Dublin. In the early 1980s he joined Raidió na Gaeltachta in Baile na nGall, West Kerry, where he remained until his death in a car accident. With his father and brothers, Eoin and Danny, he was a member of Cór Chúil Aodha, initially under the direction of Seán Ó Riada, later under Seán's son Peadar. *Bruach na Carraige Báine*, a collection of his songs drawn from RTÉ, Raidió na Gaeltachta and private sources was issued in 1995. He may also be heard on Ceoltóirí Laighean's recordings *An Bóthar Cam/The Crooked Road* and *The Star of Munster*. Diarmuid is commemorated by an annual weekend of song, music and dance held in Cúil Aodha in early December each year. (PAA)

**Ó Súilleabháin, Eoghan Rua (Béara).** (1748–84). A disconcerting aspect of the oral tradition is that examples of tenaciousness can be matched by examples of a most fragile transience. The most popular and widespread tradition, for all its vigour, has only a most precarious foothold and its very existence can soon be forgotten. Such has been the fate of Eoghan Rua 'An Bhéil Bhinn' who, in his short life enchanted Gaelic-speaking Munster with his songs, and for several generations held a place uncontested in the popular imagination as the greatest song craftsman ever to live in their midst. And so today a verse from 'The Sweet Mouth' will be rarely heard, and the writer's memory rarely invoked.

Eoghan was born in 1748 in the townland of Na Mínteoga about seven miles east of Killarney in the heart of Sliabh Luachra. He received a hedge-school education which afforded him fluency in English, as his verse in that language testifies, some knowledge of the classics, literacy in Irish and familiarity with the Gaelic literary tradition. He spent the first ten years of his adult life (*c*. 1767–77) as a 'spailpín' or migrant labourer working in various districts mostly in North and East Cork. There he came into contact with what remained of literary circles, and amongst them his reputation was quickly established. Around 1777 he seems to have been press-ganged into the British navy and served as a marine. During this spell in the King's service he composed some of his most memorable verses: 'I Sacsaibh na Séad', 'Ar Maidin Inné Cois Cé na Slímbharc'. He seems to have been in Ireland again around 1779–80, but was in the navy again when it defeated the French fleet near Fort Royal in the West Indies in 1782: Ó Súilleabháin's ship, *The Formidable*, saw some of the severest fighting which is ably described in his song 'Rodney's Glory'. The poet died aged thirty-six at Knocknagree in June 1784 from a wound on the head inflicted in a pub-brawl in Killarney. We have fifty poems and songs in Irish from his pen of which twenty perhaps are written to convention of the Aisling or Political Vision.

While conventional in theme, the distinctive genius of Ó Súilleabháin's songs are their luxurious eloquence and musicality: words artfully combined with rhythm and music in the most difficult assonantal and rhythmic patterns that flow with amazing ease and fluency. Lyricality and eloquence were always admired in Gaelic society and thus the supremacy of his popularity was ensured for over a hundred years after his passing. Ironically, this is also the reason for his subsequent disappearance from the traditional repertoire. Given the relative impoverishment of vocabulary in contemporary colloquial Irish, the simplification of grammar, and the current widespread unfamiliarity with Gaelic myth and poetic history (with which Ó Súilleabháin's songs are replete), his songs present a formidable challenge to singer and listener alike and the scarcity of a discerning and appreciative audience must discourage the effort involved. Ó Súilleabháin remained in folklore as a womaniser and a romantic, silver-tongued rover whose ready wit and clever poetic retorts provided entertaining fire-side anecdotes. (EAO)

**Ó Súilleabháin, Mícheál.** (1950– ). Piano, composer, Professor of Music at the University of Limerick. Well known for his integration of traditional and classical musics while lecturer in the Music Department of University College, Cork between 1975 and 1993, he has nine albums of music. He produced a further five recordings with Donegal, Shetland, Irish America, Cape Breton Island and England-Irish musicians on the Nimbus and Real World labels. He established the Irish World Music Centre at the University of Limerick in 1994, scripted and presented the 1995 television series *River of Sound*, and set up the traditional music archive at Boston College while visiting professor there in 1990. His doctorate on the music of Tommy Potts is from Queen's University, Belfast where he studied under John Blacking. He was assistant editor to the late Aloys Fleischmann's *Sources of Irish Traditional Music* project, published in 1999. Currently he is chair of the board of the Irish Traditional Music Archive and of Clare Music Education Centre (Maoin Cheoil an Chláir); he is a member of the board of directors of the Irish Chamber Orchestra and is a frequent performer of his own work with them. Five of his recordings have been released since 1987, most recently *Becoming* features a film score for the 1925 silent film *Irish Destiny*.

**O'Sullivan, Donal.** (1893–1973). Born in Liverpool, his father James was a civil servant; his mother was Mary Hudson. Both were from Kerry, and his first interest in music came from summer holidays there. He worked in the civil service in London and attended Gaelic League activities in the city. At age eighteen he was secretary to An tAonach, an Irish trade fair in London, 1911; in World War I he worked in signals for Royal Navy convoys. After the war, he was transferred to Ireland, was called to the bar in 1922 and later became a clerk in the Senate. From 1920, he was editor of the *Journal of the Irish Folklore Society*, and in it published the first two volumes of the Bunting collection (1927–39). In 1940 he published his controversial *The Irish Free State and its Senate,* and *Study in Contemporary Politics*. He lectured in foreign affairs at Trinity College, Dublin from 1949 to 1965; from 1951 to 1962 he was director of the Folklore Department in UCD. He wrote articles in many journals including *Éigse, Studies, Journal of the Royal Society of Antiquaries of Ireland, Journal of the English Folk Dance and Song Society*. He also wrote the entry on Irish music for the 1954 *Grove's Dictionary of Music and Musicians*. He published *Songs of the Irish* in 1960, his own translations of some of the major songs in the Irish language. His great work was *Carolan – Life and Times of an Irish Harper*, in 1958. Under the name Outis he also wrote essays in the *Times Pictorial* and *Irish Monthly*. As vice-president of the *International Folk Music Council* in 1949 he led an Irish delegation to an international Folk Festival in Venice. He is criticised by some for being snobbish towards traditional music – for instance, Breathnach noted that Francis O'Neill, the greatest collector of traditional music, went unmentioned in his *Grove*'s article, 'Irish Folk Music, Song and Dance'. His papers are held by the Folklore Department in UCD.

Mícheál Ó Súilleabháin

**Ó Tuama, Mícheál (George Curtin).** (1877–1927). Born Michael Twomey at Lacka (Lackanastooka, Leaca na Stuaice), Millstreet, Co. Cork. His mother Ellen was a widow by the time the birth was registered, this possibly giving rise to rumours that he was illegitimate. He lived with his mother at Liscarrigane (Lios Carragáin) Cross, Clondrohid, and briefly attended Carriganima (Carraig an Ime) school. He inherited the gift of poetry from his mother, a sister of the poet Tadhg na Toinne Ó hIarlaithe. Conchubhar Ó Deasmhúna, one of the Ballyvourney Four Masters, was Mícheál's maternal first cousin. He worked locally as a farm labourer, was fond of a drink and consequently never accumulated wealth. He briefly rose to national prominence between 1901 and 1903 when an tAthair Peadair Ua Laoghaire came across his song 'An Gandal' and quoted some lines from it at Feis na Mumhan, with lavish praise for the poet whom he compared favourably with Burns. An tAthair Peadair later acquired the entire song from his cousin Diarmuid Ó Laoghaire, and published it with translation in *St Patrick's* in 1901. Publication of other songs in this journal followed: 'Na Cleaganna', 'Ar Airiúir an Ghároid a bhí ar an gCáitigh', the bilingual 'The Pup came Home from Claeideach', 'Bhí slua 'gainn lá gímhre ar fhíora Chnoc na nUllán', and finally 'A Dhiarmuid is dóigh liom nach ionadh me brónach', a response to two verses from Diarmuid Ó Laoghaire. An tAthair Peadair also praised him in 1903 in articles in *The Leader*, presenting him as a young native speaker with great linguistic riches to share with the rest of the country. These articles were later gathered together in the book *Sgothbhualadh*. George Curtin's most popular English songs are probably 'Mick Sullivan's Clock', 'The Man who Came Home from Prétoria', 'Jer Foley's Boat', and 'The Siege of Port Arthur'.

'Mick Sullivan's Clock', by George Curtin
This clock of Mick Sullivan's, down in the bog
It gave up keeping time when he started on grog
It got into the habit of drinking strong wine
And it often struck eight when it should have struck nine
Rally, fal, da, la, lah, rally fal, da, lah roh

He occasionally visited his father's sister in Cardiff and upon her death he was obliged to go over to collect some money she left him. He drank the entire legacy, arriving home via Dundalk around Christmas 1900, and composed 'The Man that Came Home from Prétoria' – pretending that he was returning from the Boer war. Almost all of his songs are humorous, and local. His wit and masterful Irish made him briefly worthy of national interest, but essentially he composed for his local audience. In spite of his happy humorous songs he became affected by depression towards the end of his life and committed suicide on the banks of the Danganasillagh (Daingean na Saileach) river. (SEO)

**Outlet Records.** Founded in Smithfield, Belfast in 1967 by Billy McBurney, owner and manager of the Primary Records Shop in Smithfield market, following his 1962 purchase of Irish Studios International from Peter Lloyd. In the late 1960s and 1970s Outlet grew rapidly to become the largest self-financed record production and distribution company in Ireland. It catered to popular, Irish-based genres, including country, show-band, gospel, republican and Orange music. It also had a massive output of traditional music, with important early recordings of, for example, the street singer Margaret Barry, Seán Maguire, Séamus Tansey, Finbar Dwyer and Joe Burke. Outlet has a backlist of 2,700 LPs, totalling over 17,000 tracks and continues to release CDs in a wide variety of genres (fifty-three issued in 1998). Although the majority of these are reissues and repackages, the Outlet recording studio remains active, still using the same Studer multi-track recorder it acquired in the 1960s. (MAD)

# P

**pat.** A form of ornamentation which involves playing the note below the main melody note. Sometimes called 'tip'.

See grace note.

**Peoples, H. E.** See Freeman, Alexander.

**Peoples, Tommy.** (1948– ). Fiddle. From Killycally, near St Johnston, Co. Donegal he began playing at the age of seven helped by cousin Joe Cassidy. He moved to Dublin while still in his teens where he became well known through playing in city sessions, notably in O'Donoghue's bar; in 1970 he moved to Co. Clare. He became known internationally with his iconic membership of the Bothy Band, and he recorded on their first album. His own collections include *A Traditional Experience with Tommy Peoples, Tommy Peoples, The High Part of the Road, The Iron Man,* and *The Quiet Glen/An Gleann Ciúin* (1998). A sensitive and intense player, he received the TnaG National Traditional Music Award in 1998 for his contribution to music.

**Percy, Bishop.** His *Reliques of Ancient English Poetry* (1765) awakened widespread interest in English and Scottish traditional songs, which had formerly been ignored in literary circles. The basis of Percy's collection was a tattered fifteenth-century manuscript of ballads (known as the Percy folio) found in the house of a friend when it was about to be used to light a fire. To this nucleus Percy added many other ballads, songs and romances, supplied by friends who, at his request, rummaged in libraries, attics and warehouses for old manuscripts. The judgement with which the ballads were edited, despite some sacrifice of authenticity to readability, influenced concern for original sources and collation of texts. Publication of the *Reliques* inaugurated the 'ballad revival', a flood of collections of ancient songs, that proved a source of inspiration to the romantic poets. Samuel Johnson praised his 'minute accuracy of inquiry'. Living 'in a polished age', Percy felt obliged to apologise for the 'artless graces' of his reliques, and to atone for their rudeness he introduced 'a few modern attempts in the same kind of writing'. Johnson ridiculed contemporary ballad-writing, but applauded Percy. 'Percy's attention to poetry', he wrote, 'has given grace and splendour to his studies of antiquity.' (ANM)

**Petrie, George.** (1790–1866). Collector, antiquarian. One of a group of scholars and antiquaries who from the late eighteenth and into the nineteenth centuries began to take an interest in indigenous music in Ireland, initially as a remnant of ancient culture, and eventually as a symbol of the uniqueness of Irish culture. Professionally employed by the Ordnance Survey, Petrie had a life-long interest in music of all sorts, and it is known that he played several instruments, including the violin. His collection took shape from his habit of jotting down any tune which caught his fancy, and his travels throughout Ireland with the Ordnance Survey offered him many opportunities to hear new material. In common with other collectors who were eventually to publish on their own behalf, he began by offering his pieces to the recognised experts in the field at the time – in Petrie's case this was Edward Bunting, and, to some extent, Thomas Moore, to whom Petrie offered airs between 1807 and 1808. Petrie began to write and publish on the topic of Irish music in the second decade of the nineteenth century. He later became involved in the production of the *Dublin Penny Journal*, which brought articles on Irish culture and history to a very wide readership, to which he contributed numerous articles on ancient Irish musical instruments, as well as other aspects of Irish music. On Bunting's death in 1843, Petrie, who had to some extent been in his shadow, helped to form, and became president of, the Society for the Preservation and Publication of the Melodies of Ireland, formed in 1851. The society's only publication was the 1855 Vol. 1 of *The Petrie Collection of the Ancient Music of Ireland*. The society disbanded shortly afterwards and an incomplete second volume was published posthumously as *Music of Ireland*, in 1882. Another posthumous work was *Ancient Music of Ireland from the Petrie Collection* which appeared in 1877 – piano arrangements of the previous material, but without any notes or other commentary originally made by Petrie. The most important manifestation of Petrie's collection was however *The Complete Collection of Irish Music as noted by George Petrie* which was edited by Sir Charles Stanford, and published in three volumes between 1902 and 1905. This contains almost 1,600 tunes and is currently re-published in facsimile by Lanerch (1994).

Among present-day traditional musicians, Petrie's work, like Joyce's, has tended to be overshadowed by that of O'Neill, and latterly Breathnach, who produced collections which were, and are, of more use to the practising musician. As a musicologist Petrie made an important contribution to the study of Irish music. Whereas Bunting maintained that traditional airs never varied, Petrie saw that this was not so, and insisted that variation invariably led to a dilution and denigration of the original 'pure' form. Yet he also advocated some remarkably advanced ideas, such as proposing a comparative study of the folk musics of the world. (HAH)

**piano.** Member of chordophone family of instruments whose strings are struck with key-operated hammers. It is therefore a mechanised dulcimer. Its invention is credited to harpsichord maker Bartolomeo Cristofori in the late seventeenth century. Its lower notes use a single string, the middle register two, the higher register three. The various pitches of strings are an accommodation between string length and thickness. When a piano key activates a note, the note will be sustained until the sound dies away naturally. This can clash destructively with the following note played, so a damping device automatically 'kills' each note as soon as it is produced. But a sustained note can also be desirable, and harnessed to produce many interesting sympathetic resonances, therefore control of the damper is an essential part of playing, particularly in airs. The damper can be on/off controlled by a pedal operated by the right foot, the 'sustaining' or 'loud' pedal. If a quieter note is required, another pedal at the left foot – the 'soft' pedal – either moves the hammers closer to the strings, or moves them sideways so only one string of a pair is struck, thus giving a quieter note. On modern pianos there may be a third, middle pedal, the practice pedal, which mutes the strings. The keyboard on a grand piano produces seven and a half octaves, that on an upright fewer. Piano is normally encountered in Irish music in its upright model where the strings run vertically from the floor. But players like Mícheál Ó Súilleabháin and Antonio Breschi play on grand piano – with strings running away from the player horizontally – which has a richer sound and greater octave span.

See chordophone; clavichord; dulcimer; harpsichord.

*accompaniment*. The piano has been used for this purpose for almost 100 years, yet only some people openly welcome it; others dismiss it and more are indifferent. Irish music was conceived as essentially melodic, this has meant that piano has never been viewed as necessary, except in céilí bands. This is not surprising, in light too of the piano's strong ties with the Western art music or 'classical tradition'. It has been associated with the upper echelons of society, the 'big house', such imperial links imbuing it with political undertones. Also, it is bulky and heavy, and for a long time was financially prohibitive to most people. But if it is less costly at the present time, it is still a relatively immobile instrument and tainted by its original symbolism.

And yet today the piano has a strong voice in traditional music's commercial life, this the result of a view that in order for Irish traditional music to 'sell', it must have harmony. Few contemporary recordings avoid piano, keyboards or stringed accompaniment – this a reversal of the earlier emphasis on solo melodic music. The fact that 'accompaniment' signifies a difference between the commercial and non-commercial stems from piano's inception as an accompaniment instrument: it has always been bound up with commercialisation and commodification in music. (AID)

Geraldine Cotter with brother Eamonn on flute (EDI)

*céilí band use.* Many factors from the 1920s onwards induced musicians to play in bigger groupings. The opening of dance halls, the availability of 78 recordings, the radio broadcasts from 1926 – all laid the foundation for change and the creation of the céilí band. Emigration led to many of these being formed abroad – more famous are Dan Sullivan's Shamrock Band in the US, the Tara Céilí Band in London. Piano was important to them and led by piano player Frank Lee, the 1930s' Tara was one of the earliest to have a drums and piano line-up, now considered essential to such a band. A group from Ballinakill, Co. Galway, with piano-player Anna Rafferty was one of the first ever to broadcast on Irish radio (2RN). Another player Kitty Linnane led the Kilfenora Céilí Band with her own very unique style of introduction. The Tulla Band too has had some fine piano players, the most famous being Seán Reid and George Byrt (Jim Corry today). The renewed interest in set dancing today has generated new bands to satisfy demand – such as the Templehouse (with Mary Corcoran), the Moving Cloud (with Carl Hession), Shaskeen (with Geraldine Cotter). (GEC)

*dance music.* The popular term for piano accompaniment to Irish music is 'vamping', this was first heard on Irish music recordings made in the US up to 1940. Those in power in the recording industry were often not musically discerning; the piano simply helped unacquainted listeners make sense of an essentially foreign sound. At the beginning of the twentieth century piano was already a familiar part of American life – at once a symbol of Victorian-era social class and prestige, and a factory-produced machine epitomising America's modernity, one that produced a familiar and comforting sound. In pursuit of maximum record sales, the inclusion of piano accompaniment invested the music with pan-American feel, prestige and modernism. But Irish musicians themselves may have wanted the piano. America was now their new home, and to them it may have been desirable that the sound of Irish music there should reflect the new urban environment and cultural experiences. They were aware that they were now playing for more diverse audiences, and probably believed that they needed a more cosmopolitan feel, as provided, arguably, by the piano.

A less positive reason might be that the various recording companies had piano players on contract in their studios, whose unions would have insisted on securing their members a minimum amount of work. On occasions Irish musicians were obliged to record with the available piano-vampers – who in some cases seem to have possessed little or no foreknowledge of the music – for no better reason than fulfilling work quotas.

Another aspect of the use of piano is that, on being committed to record, Irish dance music had essentially lost its primary function – its relationship to the dance. At that point it existed in a purely 'listen-to' context (even though these records could be danced to). Perhaps the addition of accompaniment, with its percussive element, was a replacement for the absent constituent of steps sounded and viewed in dance. Such a lack of visual accompaniment could also suggest a need to keep the record 'interesting' – this the act of piano accompaniment could provide. Whatever the reasons, piano was added to Irish music, and many piano players emerged in the new American scene. The better-regarded played with the big names like John Kimmel, Michael Coleman, Packie Dolan and James Morrison.

*decline and change.* Between 1910 and 1945 with the influence of 78s, the piano spread to Ireland. Musicians imitated the American line-ups, the 'céilí band' modelled itself on the likes of the American Pride of Erin Orchestra or Packie Dolan and His Melody Boys. Piano was vital to this set-up, for both its harmonic and percussive elements. In a time before amplification, the piano's volume was vital too, especially for the beat which dancers needed to hear above the social din. From the 1960s the 'group' format in traditional music favoured lighter stringed accompaniment – guitar, mandolin and then bouzouki and cittern – reflecting the trend in folk revivals elsewhere. In this, piano presented a dull image; it hinted at formality, classicism and snobbery and so it faded almost to oblivion. The keyboard gained ground once more in the 1980s – in its electronic manifestations – and by the end of the 1990s it is a combination of these and strings that are favoured both in studios and on stage. Within Ireland there have been iconic players. Bridie Lafferty and Kitty Linnane with the Castle and Kilfenora bands moved from their parlours to the podium at a time when very few females were seen to play; their accompaniment styles are regarded by many as the essence of traditional vamping. Contemporary accompanists Carl Hession and Charlie Lennon explore the harmonic and percussive in vamping quite differently – Lennon light and delicately counter melodic, Hession employing a full harmonic vocabulary with tasteful seventh and distinctive rhythmic skip. (AID)

*piano in Irish music.* There have been references to this since the eighteenth century when Jackson's *Celebrated Irish Music* was arranged to suit piano in 1774. Edward Bunting's first *Ancient Music of Ireland* in 1796 had piano arrangements of tunes he had collected from harpers such as Carolan, Hempson, and Rory Dall Ó Catháin. In 1855 George Petrie also arranged airs for the piano in *The Ancient Music of Ireland*, published for the Society for the Preservation and Publication of the Melodies of Ireland. In the 1920s, Capt. Francis O'Neill published Selena O'Neill's piano arrangements of tunes in *Waifs and Strays of Gaelic Melody*. In Dublin, Waltons published arrangements by T. M. Crofts and P. M. Levey, Carl Hardebeck arranged many of his pieces for piano. Later publications in America included *The Dance Music Of Ireland* by John J. Ward, Ed Reavy's *Where the Shannon Rises*. More recent is fiddler and composer Charlie Lennon's *Musical Memories* – his own compositions with accompaniment for piano.

Piano playing instruction for traditional music is given in Geraldine Cotter's *Seinn an Piano: Playing the Piano Irish Style* (1996). Albums of piano-based solo music have been produced by Mícheál Ó Súilleabháin, Antonio Breschi and Carl Hession. Harpsichord and clavichord have been recorded by Mícheál Ó Súilleabháin and Seán Ó Riada. (GEC)

*modern changes.* The introduction of an accompaniment – tionlacan – competition in the fleadh cheoil has increased interest in piano today, as have the demands of a large recording industry, but while Irish piano style's 'open' sound is immediately identifiable, many vampers would feel that a truly Irish sound has yet to emerge – considering for instance the distinctiveness of the Cape Breton playing style. In that tradition, piano is an integral part of the process, playing fiddle without the piano for many is unthinkable (and often musicians can play both). The style is quite dense, and uses full keyboard, syncopation and imitation to drive the music, it retreats and swells in complement to the fiddle creating a constant relocation of focus. Through players like Tracy Dares this is influencing Irish style, as is popular and contemporary music, even jazz – Mícheál Ó Súilleabháin has his own style of piano playing and piano vamp which he dubs 'Hiberno-Jazz'. In the 1960s Seán Ó Riada's new form of ensemble playing in Ceoltóirí Chualann introduced harpsichord; this because of a similarity in sound to the Irish harp. But while players like Arcady's Patsy Broderick give outstanding solo performances of reels and jigs, few are recording melodies on the instrument. (AID/GEC)

*standards and styles.* From *c.*1900–40 these vary hugely. With no precedent to copy, accompanists drew on sources within their own experience. Some did not seem to understand Irish music, others complemented it beautifully. Styles varied in the rhythmic and harmonic constituents of the vamp. Some of the recordings feature tight, fluid ensembles; others hint at seeming indifference towards the accompanist who will lag behind, or drive ahead, or even be in a completely different key to the soloist or group. Many were non-Irish, best known of these was Joe Linder (probably German) who accompanied accordionist John J. Kimmel. His vamping showed a keen sense of harmony and good rhythm. Dan Sullivan, leader of the Dan Sullivan Shamrock Band, used the full register of the piano, with an earlier vaudeville style with hints of contemporary ragtime. Edward (Ed) Lee recorded with concertina player William J. Mullally in a remarkably restrained way, with a delicate sound from the upper notes of the keyboard, also using counter-melody. Tom Banks's vamping style with fiddler James Morrison and guitarist Martin Christi has a jazzy feel; John Muller's playing with James Morrison, Tom Ennis and John McKenna is rhythmically bouncy with tasteful chord progressions that propel the music forward. Ed Geoghegan was one of the more popular, he recorded sometimes with Michael Coleman, as did Kathleen Brennan, she very much at odds with Coleman harmonically and rhythmically. Eileen O'Shea was popular, with an uncomplicated sound which masked well worked-out technique. There are, however, so many un-credited players that one must conclude that piano accompanists were held in low esteem. (AID)

*recordings.* In the US, fiddlers Michael Coleman, James Morrison and Paddy Killoran, accordionist John Kimmel, concertina player William Mullally, flute players John McKenna, the Flanagan brothers, accordion player Joe Derrane, etc. have all been accompanied by great piano players. These included Clare Reardon, Ed Geoghegan, Eileen O'Shea, Seán Frain, Charles Bender, Della McMahon, Paddy Muldoon, Frank Fallon, A. P. Kenna, Ed Lee, Tom Banks, John Muller and Joe Linder. Dan Sullivan, leader of the Shamrock Band, is considered to have influenced many piano players, especially those in America, and in Cape Breton. He recorded not only with his band, but also solo on two 1920s–30s' 78 discs of reels and airs. Eleanor Kane from Chicago was highly regarded too as both a soloist and accompanist, recording mostly in the 1930s. Many of these musicians' recordings are now re-issued on CD. One of the outstanding players of the modern period is Bridie Lafferty who played with the Castle Céilí Band. She also played with Joe Cooley, Peadar O'Loughlin, Paddy Canny and PJoe Hayes on the album *All Ireland Champions.* Seán Maguire has been accompanied by many fine players over his playing career – Josephine Keegan, Seán O'Driscoll, and Eileen Lane. The album *Ceol Tíre* includes music by Rose O'Connor, Brendan MacEachrain and some unique work by Moya Achesan.

*technique.* A good piano-accompanist enhances others' playing, and to achieve this, an understanding of tunes is needed. 'Vamping' is the popular term used to describe the style of piano accompaniment used in Irish music. In its simplest form it means the playing of chords – a single note played by the left hand on the beat, chords played by the right hand on the off beat. Basic to this is a knowledge of keys and chord progressions. The approach to accompanying depends on whether it is being done for a group like a céilí band, for a single musician, or a small grouping. In band playing, the most important factor is keeping a steady rhythm, avoiding syncopated effects or heaviness in the right hand. Strong rhythm is not as vital when accompanying smaller groups, when tunes will be chosen for melodic appeal rather than rhythmic qualities. Highly melodic tunes may not be good for dancing, for quite often they will be complicated, in order to accompany them well, with appropriate chords: the piano player must therefore know them well. It is the ability to interpret particular tunes with a mixture of the different hand-techniques – choice of chord progressions, use of the right hand, etc. – that creates the distinctive personal styles. Additional players to listen for are Brian McGrath, Felix Dolan, Maureen Glynn, Bríd Cranitch, Tríona Ní Dhomhnaill, Jim Higgins, Séamus Quinn, Donna Long and Helen Kisiel. (GEC)

*electric*. This must be regarded as a substitute for the acoustic piano, usually in a situation where it is not available (or if available most likely not in tune). Few piano players would use or record on an electric piano when the 'real' instrument can be obtained. Strictly acoustic players find it very difficult to adapt to the electric version. Conversely a regular electric piano user always finds it pleasant to move over to the response of the 'real' piano. The touch of electric piano lacks response, depth and tone, models with weighted keys sometimes can be heavy to the touch. Technically, most such instruments are linked to a module which has a 'sampled' piano sound (e.g. sample Steinway etc.), and will be at their best in the recording studio, yet still a poor second to the acoustic. The earliest electric piano in use in Ireland was a Hohner model, this strictly an 'electric piano' (many players will use keyboard synthesisers, upon which 'piano' is only one of many sounds available). Popular among proper electric pianos is the Yamaha with a full range of keys (unlike the usual five-octave electric pianos), but it is not particularly portable. The popularity of electric piano is influenced by the acoustic piano and so its main users are céilí bands, especially those playing for set dancing. It is considered by them to be a vital rhythmic instrument, in most cases used along with drums. (CAH)

**pibgorn.** See Wales, pibgorn.

**piccolo.** A small, side blown flute sounding one octave higher than the concert flute, having the range D–D". With the same fingering as flute, tin whistle and uilleann pipes, this became popular in céilí bands where, as in its orchestral use, when played in its top octave, could (like fife with Lambeg drum) be heard clearly above the general music sound and dance-hall noise. Today made of metal, in Irish music the earlier wood version was most often used, sometimes keyed, sometimes not. It can be heard played by Kevin McCusker on recordings of the McCuskers' Céilí Band, and also on *Flutes of Old Erin*.

**Pigot, John Edward.** (d. 1853). Music collector. His work includes ninety-two airs copied from an MS by barrister William Elliot Hudson.

See Hudson, William.

**Píobairí Uilleann, Na.** (Lit. 'the uilleann pipers'). A body representing and composed of uilleann pipe players. It was set up in October 1968 out of An Tionól Píobaireachta at Bettystown, Co. Louth which had been organised by Breandán Breathnach and Séamus MacMathúna (then Oifigeach Ceoil of CCÉ). Fifty pipers took part, they engaged in formal discussions and casual music-making. Seán Reed proposed setting up a formal association of pipers; this was unanimously agreed. Shortly afterwards, a meeting in Dublin adopted a constitution as an organisation. By request, Labhrás Ó Murchú of CCÉ addressed this meeting, urging the pipers to disband the association, instead to promote piping as individual members of CCÉ branches. His offer was debated at length, but rejected. Instead, CCÉ was invited to send an observer (who should be a piper) to all future meetings of the new organisation, 'Na Píobairí Uilleann'. NPU's aims were set out as: promotion and encouragement of the playing of the uilleann or union pipes; collection and preservation of pipe music; assembling of material about pipes and pipers; issuing of publications about piping and the affairs of the association; spreading of knowledge of reed-making and the promotion of pipe-making.

Fundamental to the NPU was that all full members should be pipers. Leo Rowsome and Séamus Ennis were made its first patrons. Its first council members were: chair, Breandán Breathnach; secretary, Brian Vallely; treasurer, Dan O'Dowd; committee, Pat Mitchell, Paddy Moloney, Finbar McLaughlin and Seán Reid. In March 1969 the publication *An Píobaire* was

Piccolo (EDI)

The pipers of Ireland at Ballyfarnan, Co. Longford, NPU tionól, 1969 (EDI)

circulated as a newsletter, and the processes of sourcing reed-making materials, initiating an archive, gathering publications, classes in piping and pipe-making were all begun. NPU eventually established a base in the Plasterer's Hall, Essex Street, Dublin in 1975, moving to its present base at Henrietta Street (on long lease from Dublin Corporation) in 1979. This premises was refurbished under various grants, AnCo and private labour schemes, funding raised by appeal, benefit concert and promotion touring. The large premises has meeting, office, recording, archive and practice space, and a performance area. A series of piping recitals and an annual Concert Hall showcase 'The Ace and Deuce of Pipering' promote the uilleann pipes. An instrument loan scheme is in operation, piping classes are organised throughout the country on a regular basis, teachers are organised to facilitate summer schools and exhibitions are held throughout the country. Pipers travel abroad to a network of international festivals; 'tionóil' are held in Europe, USA and Australia. Facilities have been provided for classes in other instruments and in set dancing, and the building is home to the Brooks' Academy set dancers. There are some 500 pipers registered as members of the NPU in Ireland, 300 abroad. There are now fifty pipemakers at work (compared to five in 1968) and there is now a very high level of literacy in music among pipers. The body has a full-time organiser and An Chomhairle Ealaíon/The Arts Council has been aiding its funding; its grant in 1998 was £36,000.

**pipers' club.** See Armagh Pipers' Club; Cork Pipers' Club; Dublin Pipers' Club; Walderstown Uilleann Pipers' Club.

**pipes.** See bagpipes; uilleann pipes.

**planxty.** A type of tune written in honour of a patron, particularly associated with seventeenth-century harper Turlough Carolan. The term may derive from the Irish 'sláinte' (meaning health). Carolan's handful of 'planxties' are in 6/8 time, with one – 'Planxty O'Rourke' – also appearing in a variant, 3/4 time.

**Planxty.** Emerged from a group of musicians who contributed to Christy Moore's 1972 album, *Prosperous*, named after the Kildare village where the recording was made. The original Planxty line-up consisted of Christy Moore (replaced in 1974 by Paul Brady), vocals, guitar, bodhrán; Liam Óg O'Flynn, uilleann pipes, whistle; Donal Lunny (replaced in 1973 by Johnny Moynihan), bouzouki, guitar; and Andy Irvine, mandolin, bouzouki, harmonica, vocals. The group was unique for its mix of high-quality traditional dance tunes with ballads and contemporary folk ethos. Their instrumentation and arrangements were exhilarating for the time and spawned many imitators. The group split in 1975, but re-formed with the original line-up in 1978 on the initiative of Christy Moore. They recorded three further albums, bringing in musicians such as Matt Molloy, James Kelly, Nollaig Casey, Noel Hill, Tony Linnane and Bill Whelan. Planxty performed 'Timedance' – composed by Bill Whelan and Donal Lunny – during the interval in the 1981 Eurovision Song Contest. The band split for the second, and final, time when Moore and Lunny left to concentrate on Moving Hearts. (PAA)

**political song.** See song, political.

**polka.** A popular dance form which was developed in Bohemia in the early 1800s, gained popularity and spread epidemically all through Europe. It reached England by the middle of the century, and there it was called the 'German Polka'. One version popular in 1840s' Paris was the 'Schottische bohème'. So popular was it that Scholes (OCM, 1970) reports that streets and pubs were named after polkas. Introduced to Ireland in the late 1800s, two distinctly different kinds are now found – the simple polka of Sliabh Luachra music, and the 'double' polka associated with the playing of such as John McKenna. Polkas are most commonly found originally in counties Cork, Kerry and Limerick, and in Sliabh Luachra music, but recordings have spread them throughout the Irish music world.

**polska.** Unrelated to the polka, this is a Scandinavian dance derived from the Mazurka. It dates to the unity of Polish and Swedish crowns in 1587.
See mazurka; polka.

**Potts, Tommy.** (1912–88). Fiddler, improvisational composer, born in the Coombe, Dublin. From Bannow, Co. Wexford, his father played uilleann pipes and flute, his reputation drawing a constant stream of music visitors from all over the country throughout Tommy's childhood. Tommy Potts so developed a select taste, and an aesthetic sense which while similar in many ways to his contemporaries, nevertheless from his beginning playing at the age of fifteen differed in that he was compelled to explore alternative routes in setting and key. He favoured improvisation, the players influencing him most having a similar interest – his brother Edward, Luke Kelly, a Mrs Sheridan and Séamus Mahoney. Séamus Ennis's father, Jem Byrne of Mooncoin, Johnny Doran, and John Kearney of Longford impressed him on pipes. Through his life he built his music around this attitude – constant re-exploration and alternative routings of basic tune structures. His 1972 *Liffey Banks* recording has been used by Mícheál Ó Súilleabháin who compares (FMSI, 1988) his playing in the twentieth century to that of Turloch Carolan. Contrary to the standard practice of his contemporaries, Potts recorded and notated his versions. Ó Súilleabháin has made a thorough study of his music ('Innovation and Tradition in the Music of Tommy Potts', QUB, 1987). But while Carolan's music may have borrowed from contemporary European or Italian melodies and structures, and has left a body of work that is mostly readily identifiable, is attributed to him and was (in large part) popularly accessible in its time and since, Potts' creation has been in the field of personal interpretation which frustrates popularisation and challenges comfortable acceptance by the dominant (nineteenth-century Romanticism-conditioned) conservative aesthetic of traditional music.

See style and authenticity, Tommy Potts.

**PPI (Phonographic Performance Ireland).** 'Recording-performance' rights for compositions are nothing to do with the original composers, but are an invention of and the property of the recording companies who have issued the records. Recording-performance rights regard the album or track as itself a performer. Charges for these rights are levied on public-broadcast users of music. Wherever a sound-recording (tape, CD, video etc.) subject to PPI's control is broadcast on the public airwaves or in a shopping centre, etc., a PPI licence is required. Established in 1968, PPI centrally administers and controls such broadcasting-performance rights by issuing licences to Irish public-performance users and broadcasters on behalf of its member record companies. PPI is run by and on behalf of the Irish record industry; it differs from IMRO which is run by and on behalf of member songwriters, composers, and music publishers. Phonographic Performance (Ireland) Ltd., PPI House, 1 Corrig Avenue, Dun Laoghaire, Co. Dublin. (ANM)

See copyright.

**practice set.** An uilleann pipes bellows, bag and chanter, the essentials for melody to be played on the instrument, so-called only in relation to the practising of control over bellows, bag and chanter pitch. As an introduction to the pipes, a practice set need not always be of high quality, but in order to sustain music interest it is better that it should be so.

**programme pieces.** Descriptive music in one or more time signatures. Designed for listening, these include such as 'The Fox Chase', 'O'Farrell's Return to Limerick', etc. The former, also called 'The Fox Hunt', is reputed to have been developed from the air 'An Maidrín Rua' by nineteen-year-old Edward Keating Hyland (1780–1845), of Cahir, Co. Tipperary. This performance piece involves the use of the regulators to mimic the sounds of the chase and associated zoological utterances. Henry Hudson included it in his 1842 manuscript, and O'Neill included it in his *Music Of Ireland* collection, 1903. The composer was commanded to play for the reigning monarch – George IV – in 1821; the music first appeared in print in *O'Farrell's Pocket Companion for the Irish Union Pipes*, 1806.

***Pure Drop****.* Euphemism for un-cut whiskey, poitín, etc., so implying 'undiluted' and 'unpolluted'. The term was used by RTÉ television producer Tony MacMahon for his series on traditional music begun in 1989. Over its seven years it covered a huge spread of players from all parts of Ireland. It also dealt with Irish musicians abroad and devoted editions to Scotland, Breton music, and the US. Notably it gave importance to such performers as Micho Russell, Junior Crehan and Con Greaney. During its years it used musicians such as Noel Hill, Seán Potts (sen.), Seán Potts (óg) and Fintan Vallely as its researchers, and it had various presenters including Dolores Keane, James Kelly, Paddy Glackin and Martin McGinley.

See MacMahon, Tony.

**purist.** A person dedicated to maintaining the purity of a specialised, usually artistic, pursuit. While the term may be used genuinely by those lacking more appropriate terminology, it usually indicates criticism rather than compliment. Used in relation to traditional music it often reflects reluctance on the part of the user to accept the artistic integrity of a person so described. It is generally applied to those players, organisers or aficionados who are cautious about or abhor commercialism, fusion and borrowing between music genres, adulteration of the centrality of melodic line, and popular or classical music ethics and instrumentation. During the 1960s revival period when there was active hostility to the music, use of the term indicated intolerance, if not abusiveness. US writer H. W. Fowler challenged its implicit derision in relation to literature with the remark: 'readers who find a usage stigmatised as purist have a right to know the stigmatiser's place in the purist scale'.

# Q

**'Quill, Bold Thady'.** (b. 1860). The Muskerry Sportsman. Title and hero of a song composed by Johnny Tom Gleeson. The sporting, carousing subject of this song in fact had never felt the shaft of a hurley, smoked cigarettes, drunk porter or courted women. Thady Quill was born to *seanchaí* Mary Golden, in a small-farming family in Glounagloch South near Rylane in the barony of Duhallow, Co. Cork in July 1855. Displaying a literary bent at an early age, he seemed to be forever lampooning. No local personage of any rank or station was exempt from his caustic wit. He displayed no love for agronomic vocation, but it is rumoured that he studied for the priesthood. Of eccentric disposition, habits like sleeping with his clothes on contributed to his failure to settle in any profession. Somewhat diminutive, he was a 'dealer' at horse fairs and the like, a 'jobber' too, and a competent road-bowl player.

Once, having cut a field of corn for farmer Johnny Tom Gleeson, when remuneration was slow in coming, Thady traded his labour for his employer's poetic efficacy – Thady persuaded Johnny Tom to eulogise him in a ballad. So was born 'The Muskerry Sportsman' in 1888. Locally it became an instant hit, but it wasn't until 1940, sixteen years after Johnny Tom Gleeson's death, that it reached the nation at large. Seán Ó Síocháin heard it on a visit to Wiseman's pub in Ballinagree in the 1940s and went on to sing it many times on Raidió Éireann. Joe Lynch took it up in the late 1950s, recording it with Waltons' Glenside label, making it a popular radio hit. Thady's Aunt Kit was greatly taken by the song: 'isn't it little we know about Tim [her pet name for Thady] when he walks out!' Among Gleeson's works are patriotic effusions like 'The Battleship Sinn Féin', 'The Aughabullogue Feis', a poem to the Muskerry Hounds 'The Wild Bar-a-Boo', and a song in Irish, 'Foley the Tailor'. He worked to great effect that most sarcastic of literary devices – singing the subject's praises most eloquently, whilst simultaneously exercising disdain. (JIC)

**Quinn, Hugh.** (1885–1956). Born in Belfast 1885, his society was the mill and factory workers of the linen industry who had recently swarmed to Belfast from the shores of Lough Neagh. Quinn became a schoolmaster, working all his life in his home area of the Falls Road. A playwright, he drew his themes from his immediate world, producing works like *Mrs McConaghy's Money* and *The Quiet Twelfth*. These were performed by the Group Theatre in Belfast and the Abbey in Dublin. A songwriter himself, he also collected street songs, children's rhymes and games. His songs were occupational – of weavers, doffers, tenters, watchmen – and the children's anthology included jokes, riddles, irreverent parodies, sectarian chants. Some of the verses collected were tender versions of narrative songs that were as old as time. Other people have drawn freely on his work, but he never published a collection of his own. The Linen Hall Library, Belfast and BBC Northern Ireland both have copies of his written articles and examples of his broadcasts of his own songwriting. (DAH)

**Quinn, Seán.** (1942– ). Accordion, writer. Born Newcastle, Co. Down. Began playing on button, later moving to piano-accordion. Played in various céilí bands consecutively from 1956 – the Dundrum, the Blackthorn (Co. Down), the Inis Fail (Co. Tyrone), the Ard Rí, Eddie Fagan's (Belfast) and the McElroy Bros (Co. Down). He cites the influence of Paddy O'Brien (Nenagh), Ciaran Kelly (Athlone) and James McElheran (Antrim). A founder in 1990 of The Antrim Glens Traditions Group which promotes singing, set-dancing and traditional instrument classes. Founder too of Glens Music which produces recordings of local traditional music and songs. He has written extensively for CCÉ's *Treoir* journal.

# R

**Radio Programmes, Northern Ireland.** From its inception in 1924, BBC Northern Ireland Radio carried programmes of traditional music and song and frequently used music or song in documentaries or as atmosphere, while Arts programmes carried brief talks or single performances. To choose a few examples: in the 1930s and '40s, Sam Henry scripted programmes of songs on themes such as 'Songs of the Fair', 'The Ballad Seller' or 'The Music of County Londonderry' and David Curry presented *Irish Rhythms*. More recently there have been profiles of Eddie Butcher, Mary O'Hara and the Chieftains, while pipe and flute band music, Festivals of Traditional Singing and the Ulster Fleadh Cheoil, have had programmes devoted to them. In the 1970s, weekly 'folk magazine' programmes, and others which featured concert performances by groups such as Planxty, began to be produced. Broadcasts for schools started in 1960, and featured Sarah Makem, Paul Brady and the Sands Family and described the singing town and the singing townland. In the 1950s and '60s a series called *Ulster Band* presented music for marching bands and featured mostly flute bands (playing in parts), silver bands and pipe bands: in the late 1990s a programme entitled *Pipes and Drums* presented pipe bands, solos on the Scottish and Irish pipes and performances by Scottish and Irish music groups. The independent radio station, Downtown Radio has had a two-hour *Country Céilí* each Saturday evening from its foundation in the 1970s and an hour-long more general programme, initially presented by Jackie Dixon and now by Jane Cassidy. Regular programmes of traditional music and song have also been heard from the Derry-based BBC Radio Foyle. Presently, traditional music and song commands few specialist programmes; perhaps this reflects its absorption into the mainstream of music rather than a significant drop in popularity. The BBC Radio Archive at the Ulster Folk and Transport Museum has examples of many of the programmes. (JOM)

**Raidió Éireann.** Ireland's state radio service. It began broadcasting from a studio in Little Denmark Street, Dublin on 1 January 1926 using the call sign 2RN. Séamus Clandillon, the station's first director, had a keen interest in Irish music and song and so the programme schedules frequently included what is now known as traditional music. Part of the Department of Posts and Telegraphs, the service was relocated to the third floor of the General Post Office building in Henry Street where the name Raidió Éireann was adopted in the late 1930s. A period of expansion followed the Second World War when mobile recording units equipped with disc-recording facilities were acquired to enable programme makers to collect broadcast material throughout the country. The music held in the station's sound archive dates to this era with recordings made by Seán Mac Réamoinn, Séamus Ennis, Proinsias Ó Conluain, Pádraig Ó Raghallaigh, and later Ciarán MacMathúna and Seán Ó Riada. Raidió was complemented by the new television service, Telefís Éireann, in 1961 and both were combined in 1966 as Raidió Telefís Éireann. In 1972 the service moved to a custom-built radio centre in Donnybrook. (HAB)

**Raidió Éireann, Outside Broadcast Unit.** The national radio station changed hugely in 1947. Among many significant innovations were the establishment of a Mobile Recording Unit (MRU) and the appointment of scriptwriters and Outside Broadcast Officers. These could now record *in situ* material from all over Ireland and thus assemble radio programmes which up to then could only have come live from studios in Dublin or Cork, or wherever there was a land line available. The broadcasters were in place before the Mobile Unit was fitted out and road-worthy, and it thus came about that the first MRU was in fact Séamus Ennis's Ford 14.9 car, into the back of which the

Raidió Éireann OBU team in Casla, Connemara, L–R Séamus Ennis, Proinnsias Ó Conluain, Terry O'Sullivan (*Sunday Press*), Dermot Maguire (technician) (RTÉ)

necessary recording equipment was packed before the two OBOs – Ennis and Seán Mac Réamoinn – with Joe Lacey as sound engineer, set out on their pioneering expedition. The first recordings done were of a group of Spanish sailors singing their own songs on Valencia Island, Co. Kerry, and an interview with Peig Sayers. The recording apparatus itself was a disc-cutting machine recording on acetate disc at 78 rpm. This was to be replaced by the tape recorder.

Earlier recording apparatus was heavy and cumbersome, particularly so in the days before rural electrification, when wet batteries supplied the MRU with power. The first recording car was a Ford V8 of the type then in use by the Department of Posts and Telegraphs, fairly unstable when all the machinery, transformers, microphones and stands, cables, boxes of discs and a supply of batteries were on board, particularly so in winter conditions or on potholed roads. Quite a number of recording expeditions in early days ended up in mishap, being rescued by a tractor and a meitheal of strong men. The invention of the tape recorder provided the facility for much more efficient editing of material for broadcast, and the portable tape machine allowed the radio producer to work completely independently of the Mobile Unit in certain circumstances – to travel in his or her own car and to carry all the equipment needed. The first such machine used by Raidió Éireann was the EMI British-manufactured L2, a box-like affair, heavy by today's standards, but producing good-quality sound. Since its only playback facility was an earphone which gave little indication of the actual quality of the tape, one had to play it in a studio machine before making a judgement as to the quality of the sound. Improved versions of the L2 followed, soon superseded by the Uher and other smaller and lighter machines, all capable of providing material of broadcasting standard. For longer recording sessions in the early 1950s the transportable EMI TR50 was invaluable. One of its earliest uses, and the first on an off-shore island, was in 1953, when the recording engineer Jimmy Mahon and Proinsias Ó Conluain brought it to Arranmore Island to record about sixty songs, in Irish and English, from Róise Bean Mhic Ghrianna (Róise na nAmhráin), then seventy-four years of age. A selection of these songs, re-mastered by Harry Bradshaw and transcribed, with translations from the Irish and notes by Cathal Goan, was issued on both cassette and CD by RTÉ in 1994. (PRO)

**Raidió Teilifís Éireann.** See Raidió Éireann.

**Raiftearaí, Antaine.** (1784–1835). Lyricist, singer. Raiftearaí was born at Cill Liadáin near Kiltimagh in Co. Mayo, a place made famous by his song 'Contae Mhaigh Eó'. Blinded by smallpox in early childhood, he spent his adult life wandering about Co. Galway, playing the fiddle, singing and composing songs. During the distressing and often violent decades before the famine, his intriguing and fearless personality and extraordinary poetic ability made a deep impression on the people of the West. Ever since, he is commonly regarded as the greatest Gaelic folk-poet of that region. His reputation was greatly augmented by Dr Douglas Hyde's anthology of his work, first published in 1903, one of the most widely read books in Irish ever published. Raiftearaí's most ambitious work was *Seanchas na Scéiche*, a folk-history of Ireland based on oral Gaelic tradition, apparently derived from Seathrún Céitinn's *'Foras Feasa ar Éirinn'*. His song 'Anach Chuain' concerning a boating disaster in Lough Corrib (1828) is justly famous. Other songs of his still heard in Co. Galway and elsewhere include 'Caoineadh Thomáis Uí Dhálaigh', a lament for a piper from Cashla, 'An Táilliúir Drúisiúil', an uncompromising criticism of adultery, and songs in praise of women 'Peigí Mhistéal', 'Brídín Bhéasaigh' and 'Máire Ní Eidhin'. Versions of the latter were collected as far away as Co. Waterford. (EAO)

See sean-nós.

**Rea, John.** (1922–83). Dulcimer, fiddle. Born at Carnalba, near Glenarm, Co. Antrim, he came from a family of ten, all of whom played fiddle. His father taught them, but in the absence of an instrument for John, he had a dulcimer made on the pattern of a model then popular in the area. Proximity to the sea possibly brought the instrument there in the first place, via boats from the Baltic. A labourer initially, he went to sea working on coal-coasters when in his twenties, later on tug-boats in Belfast harbour when, living on board during the week, he would play dulcimer on deck for recreation. He is recorded with Seán McAloon on *Drops of Brandy* (1976), and *Traditional Music on the Hammer Dulcimer*. His repertoire incorporates that of his father, including tunes attributed to eighteenth-century piper Walker Jackson, and also many of Scottish origin.

**Réadoirí, Na.** Competition series run by the (Catholic) Pioneer Total Abstinence Association of the Sacred Heart (temperance organisation). It mixes all kinds of music, regarding music as music, song as song. But many young traditional musicians take part, particularly in the set dancing competitions. Regional events take place in November, diocese-based in December, provincial in January, All-Irelands at the end of February.

**Reavy, Ed.** (1898–1988). Fiddler, composer. Born at Barnagrove, Maudabawn, Co. Cavan, his Monaghan-born mother Sarah (née Dawson) was a champion lilter. In 1912, he emigrated to the US and eventually settled in Drexel Hill, a suburb of Philadelphia, Pennsylvania, where he worked as a plumber. One of the greatest and most prolific composers of Irish music during the twentieth century, his first recordings date to the 1920s when he cut some 78s for the RCA Victor company. He also made many six-inch 78 rpm discs of his compositions at home. 128 of his tunes have been saved from over 400 he wrote. In 1971, *Where the Shannon Rises* collected in book form many of his most popular melodies, and all of those, plus many others, were later published in *The Collected Compositions of Ed Reavy* assembled by his nephew Joseph. Still another book, *Music of Corktown*, named for what was once considered the most Irish section of Philadelphia, offered 100 dance tunes picked by Reavy, including seven of his own. In 1979, a tribute album entitled *Ed Reavy* featured such musicians as Liz Carroll, Martin Mulvihill, Mick Moloney, Paddy Cronin, and Armagh-born friend Louis Quinn performing his tunes, with Ed featured on six tracks of his own. A medley of six Reavy tunes set to a tribute poem can be heard on *The Green Fields of America: Live in Concert*. 'The Hunter's House', 'Maudabawn

John Rea plays hammer dulcimer with ivory flute player James MacMahon at Belfast CCÉ session in Derryvolgie, *c.* 1966 (APC)

Chapel', 'Never Was Piping So Gay', and 'The Wild Swans at Coole' are among his tunes played every day as part of the traditional repertoire. A memorial plaque was unveiled at the former Reavy home at Maudabawn, in 1990. (EAH)

**recording of Irish traditional music.**
See reproduction of music.

**Redican, Larry.** (1908–75). Fiddle. Born in Boyle, Co. Roscommon. His family moved to Dublin when he was young, his father from Co. Roscommon, his mother, a whistle player (née Kielty), from Sligo. In Dublin Larry took fiddle lessons from Arthur Darley before emigrating in the 1920s to Toronto, and then settling in New York city. For more than thirty years he worked in a Long Island factory for Elizabeth Arden cosmetics, but his spare time was spent playing fiddle, often at home in Brooklyn and later in Queens, New York. From the 1950s to the 1960s, he played for the Bronx-based McNiff Irish Dancers and also for dancing at the weekly Gaelic League céilíthe, where he met many of the musicians who would go on to form the New York Céilí Band. In 1960 he won the All-Ireland senior trio competition with New York Céilí Band colleagues Jack Coen and Paddy O'Brien. In America, in 1962 and 1966, Ciarán MacMathúna made a number of field recordings of Redican (and other musicians). Broadcast by Raidió Éireann these helped to spread his reputation in Ireland. Several of those tracks appeared on the cassette *A Job of Journeywork* issued by RTÉ in 1989. Redican also composed tunes, including the well-known 'Redican's Reel'. Adept on the tenor banjo as well, Larry Redican suffered a heart attack while playing the fiddle in Mineola, New York, and subsequently died. Tracks can be heard on RTÉ's Ciarán MacMathúna albums. (EAH)

**Redmond, Leo.** (d. 1982). Founder and conductor of the Austin Stack Céilí Band. A pianist, and composer of 'The Tostal Hornpipe' and 'The Duckpond', he arranged his band's music for broadcasting.

**reed.** All pipes use some form of 'beating reed' – either a single or double. The sound of a

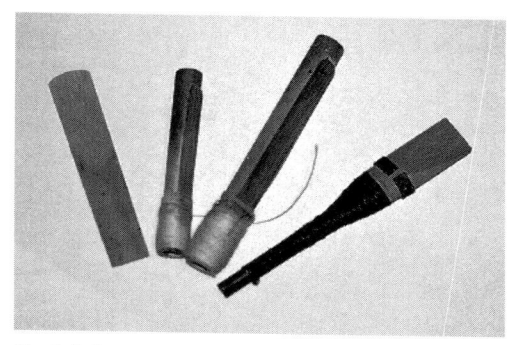

On left is a one-piece clarinet reed, centre are two 'single' reeds (note the binding at the base of the cut), on the right is a 'double' uilleann pipe chanter reed.

single reed (also called idioglot) is softer and bleating, a double reed is harsh and commanding. Breton 'bombardes', medieval 'shawms' and 'oboes', Italian 'ciaramella' and Bulgarian 'zurna' all use double reeds. Bulgarian 'gaida' bagpipe, Mediterranean 'Aulos' double pipes, Sardinian 'launeddas' triple pipes all use single reeds. Simplest is the single reed, which is made by making a slice in a piece of hollow cane or reed (hence the name). A double reed is formed by two 'lips' of cane being spliced together. All reeds sound when air is passed into them from the outside: the air causes the adjacent faces of thin wood to vibrate, so generating a sound. This sound is modified by the length and diameter of the pipe it is inserted into, the note is changed by means of the fingering holes.

See pibgorn; pipes; uilleann pipes.

**reel.** 1. A variety of solo or group step-dance, done to the music of a tune-type of the same name. 2. The most popular tune-type within the Irish tradition. In 4/4 time it consists largely of quaver movement with an accent on the first and third beats of the bar. Most reels follow the standard AABB form where the first eight-bar part of the tune is repeated before the second eight-bar part – the turn – is introduced and repeated. This thirty-two-bar 'round' is repeated usually two or three times before a second reel is introduced. The grouping of two or more tunes together in this manner is typical. It is likely that the reel originated in

REGIONAL STYLE

### Ravelled Hank of Yarn (Reel)

[musical notation]

### Doctor Gilbert (Reel)

[musical notation]

Note the different note-structure in these tunes. Such makes reels a particularly-expressive section of the tune body.

(CRÉ 1, An Gúm)

France in the early 1500s as the haye. It was being played as 'reill' in Scotland in 1590 and its modern form was brought to Ireland from there in the late 1700s. Many of the older reels in the tradition are borrowings from the Scottish tradition and the tunes are often found in more than one variant in different parts of the country. Today, the many Irish reels are supplemented with new compositions and by tunes from other traditions which are easily adapted as reels. (LID)

**regional style.** The varying ways in which music is played from region to region. There are several possible ingredients involved in the establishment of regional difference.

1. Choice of instrument. Most basic is the voice, totally flexible within any culture, it can be trained to spread itself across many cultural 'sounds'. Among instruments, the fiddle too is universal to all our regions since like the voice it possesses unrestricted variety of intonation; everything about it is bendable – note creation, attack, tuning, loudness, ornamentation, timbre. The accordion too is a biddable universal and has abundant access to subtlety. Its features and dynamics can be manipulated by skilled players in many different cultures to present different

local 'attacks' so well that Irish music played by a German player can be perceived within Irish music culture as quite different to that played by an Irish player. Styles associated with the accordion in this country are in fact named after individual mentors. The uilleann pipes too have a fairly universal sound within Ireland, but their technology encourages players to aspire to technical perfection, rendering variation mostly personal. The history of piping within the last century – cycles of commercial popularity, decline, rescue, revival, and now again commercial popularity – has led to a piping practice which quite logically dismisses or bypasses the notion of regional styles, instead incorporating idiosyncrasies of former local styles as piping 'technique'.

2. Way of playing is definitive; how one blows, bows, pushes the bellows, plucks the string, holds the instrument are all critical to sound and appearance.

3. Tune types. Regions have created their own tunes, and usually favour some repertoire from other places, but many tunes are simply not suited to adoption by players from a different stylistic background.

4. Repertoire is another characteristic. Donegal is associated mostly with reels and 4/4 variants; Sliabh Luachra/Cork Kerry have slides and polkas associated with a strong segment of their popular culture, these linked with body movement and dance. Actual tune selection is also important, for at some (unspecified) time in the past, each area would have had a limited number of available pieces (whether local or imported does not matter). Before the availability of recorded music the only people with a wide variety of tunes were the travelling people, by virtue of their constant moving on to new places. Their circular routes meant that they could, theoretically, keep learning new material, bringing difference to all areas. Modern transmission media render that role redundant.

5. Use to which the music is put is another differentiating factor. For instance the Sliabh Luachra rhythm is still bound up in dancing, while most urban music is for listening, and may or not accompany life rituals like weddings and other celebrations.

6. Demeanour of the performer. 'Letting go', 'getting into' the music, the shoulder-twitch of Sliabh Luachra players versus the often stoic demeanour of northerners are significant. While such may be extremely personal idiosyncrasies, they can also become fashions, if not – like the sympathetic head movement of the guitarist/bouzouki player – obligatory.

7. Attack on tunes is another variant, how the player 'goes at it'. Compare the playing of Paddy Canny with, say, Liz Carroll, Joe Cooley with Paddy O'Brien, Séamus Tansey with Peadar Ó Lochlainn, Micho Russell with Mary Bergin.

8. Local interaction and familiarity with the repertoire and instrument also define the music: feedback is ultimately a strong determinant in the quality and consistency of the music produced. (EDI)

*effects of the famine.* In pre-famine society in Ireland, music-communities were linked by migrant and seasonal workers. They also had a system of continentally-influenced dancing-masters who introduced new steps (and tune-forms) to rural Ireland (perhaps a standardising influence?). Pre-famine music therefore had a connection with the popular music practices of continental Europe. Further, if one accepts that musical expression is bound to the economic and social history, then economic regionalisation and the marginalisation of rural communities in Ireland following the worst years of the famine would have fostered a more insular system of music-making and music transmission. In a time of marginalised communities and difficult communication, the continuity of musical tradition would logically also become more locally based. Repertoire and performance would change at different rates as a result of these isolating trends – in some cases not changing at all.

The traditional process in music preserves individual nuance and character in performance. A master of traditional playing passes on his or her repertoire and approach to pupils and admirers. If barriers to widespread communication exist, it is reasonable to expect that the dissemination of a unique style of playing would be local. Extending this idea, the innovations of a single player or a few like-minded players may persist over many years, and be recognised long afterward as the hallmarks of a regional or local style of performance. (SAS) *influence of recordings*. Most players today adopt personally favoured combinations of different techniques which individually may have originally characterised particular local styles. They also play tunes drawn from the repertoire of other instruments and from all of the style-centres. In the session social scene, players hold onto, or lose, music accent in proportion to any individual's ability or desire to hold on to speech accent in a different social environment. Yet however strong the pressure to conform exerted on local styles by the compelling influence of others' tastes and by flawlessly engineered and absolutely unreal recordings, all evidence suggests that, almost paradoxically, but by dint of artistic quest for difference and uniqueness of expression, regional styles are strengthening, and will persist. This is also the case because their initial development has had a strong link with personal styles of playing, going back to an age when there were fewer musicians and instruments, before the levelling format of the session came into vogue. If dancing masters exercised a strong influence on dance steps and figures, then the better players also defined something in music. Thus the ultimate variant among regional styles is the 'personal' style, attached to an individual regardless of where they were born and ultimately settle. Witness Tommy Peoples (Donegal–Clare), Séamus Creagh (Westmeath–Cork), Mary Bergin (Dublin–Galway), Tom Treanor (Armagh–Kerry), Brendan Begley (Kerry–Dublin), Kathleen Smith (Antrim–Meath), Lucy Farr (E. Galway–Britain), Séamus Tansey (Sligo–Armagh), etc. If regional styles have become scattered, they also remain located in the playing of these individuals.

*the revival process*. The major outside influences on regional styles have perhaps come about since the 1960s. Revival produced our central 'standard of perfection' (broadcasts, recordings and competition). This undoubtedly has contributed to the undermining of regional identities. Competition adjudicator comments, results and demand for conformity have not favoured Donegal-style fiddling, Ulster-style singing, or Sliabh Luachra fiddle style. On the other hand the revival has preserved the techniques and repertoire which all local styles collectively draw upon. But it has also marginalised song in live music sessions. While sean nós is still a strong regional style in everyday use in the west, other vocal styles struggle for context, and so survival. There is also much ambiguity about what is acceptable as traditional song.

The revival process is built on a new ex-rural, comparatively wealthy middle class. Migration of the 'traditional' rural culture and values associated with its pre-1970s growing up, have altered the composition of the bourgeois 'centre' of Irish society, and thus its formal notion of what is 'proper'. In an age of emblems and icons – visual, culinary and tonal – where traditional music has simultaneously taken on and been ascribed an identity as the distinct cultural badge of 'Irishness', it has become extremely important within the scale of the European and world-wide field of regional identities. For Irish people in England, or the US, and among scattered emigrant groups on the European mainland, consuming Irish music is as important as socialising with people with Irish accents. This is in spite of the fact that due to education system deficiencies the majority of such people often don't know the difference between one tune-type and another, let alone different tunes

*sense of local place*. A strong element within the idea of regional style is that of specific local meaning. Johnny McCarthy (*Irish Music Studies*, 1996) gave evidence of deep-seated local relevance for a way of playing – suggesting that the achievement of ritual trance was the original objective of the playing of simple, repetitive but engaging melodies and rhythms in West Cork. Tony MacMahon (*Bringing it All Back Home*) voiced a belief in a relationship for music with non-urban, remote, spiritual place. Peadar Ó Riada suggests that older music was slower, free from the constricts of dance time, reflective of spirituality, and, by inference from his work, also of place. These ideas suggest a view of music as an alternative form of communication, transmitter of spirituality, a kind of 'songlines', or umbilical cord to the ancient past. The intensity experienced in listening to particularly fine players has perhaps much to do with musicianship, with a suitable instrument driving a player capable of seemingly limitless refinements of style and technique.

That same emotional power, when brought on by technically weaker musicians, may be related to the listener's pre-disposition to 'let go' – empathy, occasion and context are important in this.

*identity.* Regional style is a reassuring landscape for a returned migrant, pleasantly different for a music tourist. It is also that which people in a particular area feel most comfortable with, like relaxing among the accents of a home place, within a parish accent in a county setting, or any Irish accents at all when abroad. Outside of the music voyeur and the academic, a regional style is of most meaning to local identity wherein it can be invested fully with the experience of its people's earlier lives. However, like the 'beauty spot' in tourism, regional styles make music particularly interesting to discerning consumers – the record-buying and concert-going, dancing public – and provide their exponents with a distinct economic niche. The totality of styles represents all the technical expertise, the possible and the favoured ways of doing things. They are, collectively, the bible, the stylistic manual of traditional music. They may also be a kind of 'songlines', but while no longer useful as a route by which to identify locality within Ireland, they may be, for individuals, a path back to the ancestors for those compelled to invest the playing of music with personal or collective spirituality. On another level, regional styles may also be 'songlines' in the sense that their differences, their interfaces and their overlaps chart a great weft and warp of history, change, variety, ingenuity and possibility within the music genre.

See fiddle; flute.

**Reid, Seán.** (1907–78). Fiddler, piper, organiser. Born Castlefin, Co. Donegal. His father, and uncle John Reid played fiddle; the family home was a meeting place for musicians throughout his childhood. This listening was supplemented by 78 recordings and he learned fiddle and was taught 'classical' piano. School life involved Irish dancing; local fiddler Eddie Toland provided music for this. Raised by his mother, in 1927 he went to Queens University Belfast to study civil engineering and science; while there he learnt to play bagpipes in the Officer's Training Corps, and was a committed

Seán Reid (EDI)

and successful athlete. Interested in literature, his regular browsing in the city's famous Smithfield market yielded a Tom Ennis 78 rpm record and kindled his passion for the uilleann pipes. Competing in an athletics event at Feis na nGleann in Cushendun soon after brought him into contact with Meath-born piper R. L. O'Mealy. A period in Dublin brought him in contact with John Potts' family and friends, a circle which included Breandán Breathnach and Tommy Reck. In 1937 he began work with Clare County Council as a civil engineer. A friendship with fiddler Martin Rochford of Bodyke resulted in the two of them working together at learning uilleann pipes. Leo Rowsome was one of their mentors, as was Johnny Doran whom Seán visited regularly. Joe Leyden, who worked with Seán, was another invaluable contact in those years. Seán Reid's presence in Clare was to have an important influence on the music and its players. From his house in Ennis he was a catalyst and voluntary co-ordinator for many of the musicians in the county and he played an important role as musician and leader in the Tulla Céilí Band. He brought players together at a time when transport was scarce and communication difficult, often taking them to competitions as far away as Dublin. Humorously described as one of the 'driving forces' in Clare (one of the few who had a car), he frequently endured personal sacrifice and expense supporting issues in which he believed, never afraid to speak out where he it felt necessary. His application and commitment to traditional music as an Irish art, as a bridge across political division, and to piping in particular marks him as critical in the traditional music revival. He was involved in the early CCÉ, in 1956 a key figure in introducing it into the north-eastern counties through the Derry and Antrim Fiddlers' Association, and he was the proposer of setting up Na Píobairí Uilleann in 1968. His work in the field of piping has been extremely valuable. In the years when pipes were held in little regard he collected several sets, passing them on to pipers when interest had revived, thus ensuring that players would have good instruments with which to continue the tradition. A gentle personality, a careful researcher and collector, a tireless organiser and a humble, caring, scrupulously honest man, he impressed and succeeded by conviction and discussion: one of music revival's fondest-remembered mentors. (JIO, EDI)

**Reilly, John ('Jacko').** (1926–69). Singer. Born to a travelling family at Carrick on Shannon, Co. Leitrim, both his parents were singers, his childhood night-time entertainment was of songs and singing around the fire in the open. Their repertoire was eclectic – popular songs, music-hall pieces and classic ballads – but from his father he learnt songs of the status of 'Lord Baker'. The family's route was Leitrim, Sligo and Roscommon, a routine peregrination that denied regular formal education, but was intensely involved with practical survival, bearing ostracisation from settled community labour. Time served as a tinsmith, he moved the family to Belfast, but returned to the Leitrim area in 1953. He settled in Boyle in 1962, spent some time in nearby Gurteen, Co. Sligo, both strongly associated with traditional music. Poverty dominated his existence despite his skills; ill health diminished his chances of employment, and the introduction of mass-produced enamel household and farm utensils undermined his livelihood further. Collector Tom Munnelly brought him to Dublin to sing at the Tradition Club in Capel Street, but otherwise in those years his talent was unrecognised: the 'folk' world did not respect unaccompanied singers, his lustre was not of the hue favoured by competition aesthetics. With the co-operation of D. K. Wilgus, Professor of Folksong at the University of California, LA, Munnelly recorded some thirty-six songs and ballads from John Reilly in Grehan's pub in Boyle. Six weeks later, at age forty-three, he died from pneumonia, bought on by cold and malnutrition. He was buried in an unmarked grave in Ballaghaderreen cemetery. His songs are available on *The Bonny Green Tree*, a selection archaic and mesmerising, loaded with all the more importance because of the indifference with which his world dismissed this transmitter of the art of past centuries. (TOM)

**Reillys of Leitrim.** Fiddle players of renown from Toome, Carrigallen, Co. Leitrim, they were very important to their area's music. Terry learnt from master player Peter Kennedy (b. 1803), and passed this on to his three sons Michael, Hughie, and Pat. The style is taken to be that still extant, notably in the playing of the McNamaras.

See Leitrim, South.

**religion.** See song, religious.

**reproduction of music.**
*history.* Up to 1877 music was passed on by one of three means: orally, graphically and by mechanical simulation. Oral processes involved learning by ear in community situations. Graphic methods used some kind of written representation of music notes which indicated melody, time signature, key signature, tempo and accenting. Mechanical simulation was used in music boxes and player pianos. In the 'music boxes', a 'comb' of tuned metal teeth was activated in sequence by a series of melodically patterned protrusions on the surface of a rotating cylinder or disc. In 'player pianos' a moving cardboard belt punctured with holes in

melodic sequence engaged pins that activated the piano keys. In 1857 E. L. Scott's phonautograph could trace sound patterns on a moving plate, but the idea of playing back such physically represented sound was mooted by Frenchman Charles Cos in 1877, his speculated device named Paléophone. American research overlapped with his thesis however and Edison was the first to realize the machine. (EDI)

See Three Ages of Music, The.

*ediphone*. In New Jersey, 1877, Thomas Edison succeeded in recording, and playing back, 'Mary had a Little Lamb' through a cylinder 'talking machine'. This was achieved by capturing vocal sound waves in a funnel, the vibrations thus caused were picked up by a sensitive diaphragm connected to a fine needle which then scored their impression progressively in up-and-down, 'hills and valleys' fashion on a four-inch, rotating, soft, metal-foil-coated cylinder which moved forward, lathe fashion, on a fine screw-thread. In its varying amplitude, this 'sound-groove' was a physical representation of the fluctuations in volume and tone of the recorded sound. So was born sound recording and reproduction. Wax-coated cylinders were then used to improve reception. As the technology improved not only was it possible to record/replay the spoken word, but the notion was then applied to the singing voice. While early acoustic recordings of musical instruments sounded feeble and withdrawn, the human voice, being able to project into the acoustic horn, reproduced more strongly. For collectors of folklore and music the machine was a revolution. By 1890 the

Ediphone

Tadhg Ó Murchú recording for Roinn Bhéaloideas Éireann on the ediphone in Spuncán, An Coireán, Co. Chiarraí, 1936 (CBÉ)

available four-inch Ediphone cylinders gave three to four minutes of recording time, a six-inch gave nine minutes. These could be slowed down or speeded up, collectors could analyse and transcribe for posterity 'in peace and quiet'. In 1896 machines became available for domestic use, blank cylinders were withdrawn from the open commercial market in 1913 due to competition from other means of reproduction, but were still in demand, and so were still manufactured up until the 1930s. The Ediphone cylinder recorder was relatively expensive and was not commonly found in Ireland. It was used however by individual enthusiasts and by the Irish Folklore Commission to record music, song and folklore for transcription. Folklore collectors tended to record, transcribe and scrape clean – in much the same way that radio and television stations often did with tape in the years since. This means that comparatively few cylinder sound recordings survive in the Irish Folklore Department at UCD. (EDI)

*pre-recorded cylinders*. These offered everything from minstrel songs and opera to stage-Irish sketches. They were sold in large quantities to an audience for whom the main interest was amazement. But people like uilleann piper Patsy Touhey recorded and sold their own cylinders for commercial sale. Competition from flat recording discs spurred Edison to continue refinement of the cylinder, and his four-minute, Blue Amberol introduced in 1912 was the peak of the cylinder's capabilities, with a frequency response of 200–3,000 cycles per second. By 1914 the cylinder's battle with the flat disc had been lost and Edison ceased cylinder production in 1929. (HAB)

*flat discs – the 'record'*. In 1887 a German immigrant to the US, Emile Berliner, filed a patent for a 'gramophone' player using a flat disc rather than a cylinder (from the Greek 'gramma', writing and 'phone', voice). The disc was coated in a material called shellac, and on this, sound-grooves in concentric circles were gouged in a spiral in a lateral 'meandering river' motion. The process was developed to permit the pressing of multiple copies from such a 'master' disc. From its public availability in 1897, this became known as the 'gramophone' in Europe, 'Victrola' in the US. Because such playback machines involved a mechanical apparatus with a wound spring, it fell to bicycle shops to market and service them, and also their successors, radio and then television; this pattern is still obvious in smaller towns. Branches of this company were opened in Europe also: the Gramophone Company in London; Deutsche Grammophon AG in Berlin and Compagnie Francais du Gramophone, France. Berliner's brother opened a disc-pressing plant in Hamburg. In the US the Berliner company grew into the giant Victor label. The recording process was constantly improving – developing to electroplated wax and leading in 1902 to Victor and rival Columbia pooling their patents to capitalise on newer methods. Columbia issued ten-inch diameter discs, and shortly after this the Victor company began issuing three-and-a-half-minute, twelve-inch discs.

The first electric gramophone recording was made at Westminster Abbey in 1920; by 1925 this method had replaced the mechanical recording process.

European companies manufactured double-sided discs, these used by Victor in 1923. The relationship with Deutsche Grammophon was broken with the outbreak of World War I, after which Deutsche Grammophon Gesellschaft (DGG) started as an independent label. The 78 revolution per minute (rpm) records were made from shellac but synthetic materials soon replaced this. Technologies developed during World War II led to Columbia Records (CBS) in 1947/8 perfecting the flexible, vinyl, 33.3 rpm record which could play for up to thirty minutes a side. The seven-inch, single, 45 rpm and EP, which could play for up to eight minutes a side was developed by RCA, leading eventually to the twelve-inch, Long Player (LP) microgroove (reportedly the result of pressure put on RCA by the conductor Toscanini in 1951). For most Irish music the three or four minutes of the 78 rpm was adequate, but larger symphonic works had to be put on five or more discs and bound in an 'album' – so creating the term we still use today. The grooves on the LPs were much finer and detailed than on the 78s, this demanding slower play speeds. Turntable decks therefore came with $16\frac{2}{3}$, $33\frac{1}{3}$, 45 or 78 rpm; originally they were driven by a wound-spring, eventually electric motors became standard. Sound reproduction too moved from being purely mechanical to electronic; volume control followed suit, originally having used horns – an ingenious systems of doors and deflectors on old 'parlour' machines. Seventy-eight records however were rugged, the machines easily maintained and improvisable, they stood up to dusty conditions well. This gave them a much longer life in hotter and poorer countries like India where vinyl was too delicate, its machinery too expensive. (AOO)

*acetate discs*. The acetate disc, or 'soft record', was the standard recording medium in radio and recording studios when recording and immediate playback was required. Acetate discs revolved at 78, and later $33\frac{1}{3}$ rpm, and were named after the chemical make-up of their acetate/shellac base which was moulded on an aluminium core. Acetates provided a 'direct cut' unlike the factory-made 78 disc which required an elaborate factory-pressing process to manufacture. Basic home-recording machines with supplies of blank discs became available but their cost and availability limited their use among Irish musicians. Ed Reavy in Philadelphia recorded on such a machine, and small numbers of his and others' acetates survive. Acetates were intended to have a short life span and were recommended to be replayed about ten times before deterioration of the playing surface became evident. (HAB)

*wire recorder*. In 1897 the Dane Vlademar

Poulcen invented the 'Telegraphone' wire-recorder which could record for one hour, and is the ancestor of the modern tape-recorder. The phonograph's basic principle was the inscription of a linear sound-wave pattern on a moving surface. With a needle it scored this physically on a moving, wax-covered cylinder or flat, shellac disc. The wire recorder used the same principle, only it traced its sound-wave electronically on a wire being pulled across a recording 'head'. Wire recorders were used by folklore collectors and in business as dictaphones. They recorded through a small electric microphone, playback was through earphones. They were in use up until the 1940s. Because of poor sound quality they were of no commercial significance after 1910, but were modernised by Pfleumer of Dresden using paper tape instead of the wire reel. Steel tape was then used, and finally plastic. (EDI)

*tape recording*. The principles of recording sound magnetically had been understood for a considerable time but the technology to produce a workable system did not exist. During the late 1930s, two German companies co-operated in the development of a magnetic recording system. A quarter-inch wide ribbon of plastic tape, coated on one side with ferric oxide particles, was magnetised by a processed audio signal as tape passed across the heads of the Magnetophon recording machine. On replay, the spool of tape retraced its path and a playback head reproduced the magnetically stored audio signal which was then amplified. Magnetic tape had important advantages over disc recording. The system provided high fidelity recordings, tape was robust, could be erased and re-used and allowed longer recordings to be made. Perhaps the greatest advantage of tape was the ease with which a recorded performance could be cut and edited. Magnetic recording machines were in use in German radio stations during World War II and these were copied and further developed by the Allies. By 1947, magnetic tape and recording machines were in production by English and American manufacturers and in 1952 Raidió Éireann took delivery of its first machines. Tape running speed was originally thirty inches per second (ips) but constant development produced machines with ever improving performance specifications which allowed speeds to be reduced to fifteen and then 7.5 ips. Home tape recorders were on the market in the 1950s and valuable collecting work was done locally by music enthusiasts who acquired them. Despite the recent advances by various forms of digital recording on tape and hard disc, there are, within the recording industry, those who prefer the sonic qualities of magnetic analogue recording. (HAB)

*records, LP, long-play, vinyl*. The appearance of vinyl as a material for records in the late 1940s led to several technological advances in the recording industry. The material allowed a much finer groove to be used, this gave a much better sound quality, and also allowed more than one track to be recorded on each side of the record. In Ireland, the first vinyl recordings of traditional or folk music did not appear until the mid-1950s, and the first reliably dated recordings are two made by Patrick Galvin, the Cork playwright and poet, for the Riverside company in 1956, entitled *Irish Street Songs* and *Irish Humour Songs*. David Curry's Irish Band, and singer Margret Barry both recorded albums around the same time. Seventy-eight rpm recordings were still being produced in Ireland after this date, since many of the consumers would still have been using the old 'phonograph' equipment. The series of 78s produced by Gael-Linn around this time are highly significant, competing as they did with vinyl LP recordings.

Although the new format allowed up to around twenty minutes of uninterrupted music to be recorded, in the fields of popular music and folk music the three-minute standard, which had been established by the physical restraint of the 78 continued to be the normal length of recorded pieces, thus allowing normally twelve tracks to appear on one recording. This in turn allowed an expansion in the type of material, and the number of performers that could be accommodated on one recording. Thus we see the appearance of the compilation album, where artists from any number of instrumental or stylistic backgrounds can be accommodated. This facility was and is commonly used by recording companies to produce 'samplers', which contain a selection of their various artists.

*Irish companies.* The first of the vinyl long playing records (LPs) to appear in Ireland in the mid-1950s were produced by English or American companies such as Folkways, but by the late-1950s two very important Irish companies, Ceirníní Cladaigh, and Gael-Linn had appeared. These two, along with the English company Topic were of exceptional importance in the early revival period. Run by individuals who were mainly culturally, rather than financially, motivated, many recordings of authentic traditional music were made available to the public. Vinyl recordings were also the first to feature stereo sound. This began to appear on records on the Irish market in the 1970s, but its relevance to many of the records that were being made at this time was limited, and mono recordings of Irish traditional music were still being made after stereo became the industry standard in other genres. The complex technology associated with the production of vinyl records meant that it was an expensive process and as such traditional musicians were denied access to it except via the medium of recording companies. The advent of the cassette tape in the 1960s was the beginning of a gradual opening-up of the access to the recording medium for the traditional musician, and the demise of the vinyl recording (*c.* 1991) coincided with a significant increase in the number of independent recordings. (AOO)

*new technologies.* Ireland, and indeed Europe, was much slower in changing from the 78 to the newer, slower speed, but LPs were being issued here by the late 1950s. In 1958 the RCA-Victor label in the US issued stereo LPs and introduced a cartridge-format, stereo tape player. In the same year Aindreas S. Ó Dubhghaill launched Comhlucht Céirníní Éireann, issuing two ten-inch LP records – *Seán Maguire* (fiddle and uilleann pipes) and *Seán Ó Tuama with An Claisceadal* – both of which were pressed by Deutsche Grammophon Gesellschaft (DGG) in Germany. Shortly afterwards the twelve-inch LP became the norm.

*cassettes.* Between 1962 and 1964 the Phillips company of the Netherlands perfected the Compact Cassette, a portable tape recorder using a small cartridge with a 0.15 inch (3.8 mm) tape. But in 1965 the Ford and Mercury Company, in conjunction with Motorola and RCA-Victor records, introduced the 'Eight-Track' or 'Stereo-8' tape and players. This became the first successful form of tape-playback music in the US; the format lasted until 1980 and only a very small quantity of Irish music was issued on it. In 1969–70 DuPont and BASF began offering chromium dioxide recording tapes, this improving quality and durability in cassettes.

*Dolby, Walkman.* The introduction in 1969 of Dolby Noise Reduction which reduced tape 'hiss' aided cassette popularity, and it took over as the popular in-car system. Its position was further advanced by Sony's 1979 introduction of the flexible and convenient 'Walkman'. By 1984 audio cassettes sales were exceeding those of LPs. But cassettes' easy-record facility invited copying of LPs, pirating of albums and 'bootleg' recordings of concerts. Countries where copyright laws are not as stringent as those of Western countries – such as Thailand – still market cheap, pirated, cassette versions of popular music, including the Chieftains.

*CD technology.* This was introduced in Japan in 1982, becoming available in the Europe and the US the following year. The extremely high quality of its digital reproduction gradually led to its taking over from cassettes. Originally non-reproducible, cheap, recordable digital technology now makes it simple to copy CDs also. CD technology uses a revolving, 4.75 inch (12 cm) digital disc that is 'read' by a laser beam that makes no physical contact. Compared to the needle-in-groove 78s and LPs and the abrasiveness of tape-heads, there is almost zero wear and tear. Nor can their clear resolution and wider dynamic range be matched by cassette. For recording studio use, Digital Audio Tape (DAT) was introduced in 1987 and has gradually come to almost totally replace quarter-inch, reel-to-reel tape. Cassettes are still the most inexpensive way to acquire and play music, but CDs dominate the pre-recorded market. The Digital Compact Cassette tape (DCC) by Philips and the Mini Disc (MD) by Sony are currently challenging CDs and cassettes for domestic use – both offer digital (CD quality) recording. Now too there is the recordable video disc, CDR (recordable CDs), CD+ or CD enhanced – all representing industry battles for control of the domestic music market. (AOO) *discography.* Thirty years ago this would have been a simple undertaking and perhaps superfluous, for the simple reason that there were few albums available. This affected airplay of material – a radio producer could exhaust the record supply in a week. But the revival of traditional music since the 1950s, paralleled by economic changes, created a new domestic market, new albums, and an export market. Native demand was filled first by Gael-Linn, later by Claddagh Records, by Topic and Shanachie, added to since then by Green Linnet and dozens of 'mé féin' and other labels. Up until the mid-1980s new traditional material was released on LP, CD and cassette, but since then LPs have progressively disappeared. Used record players are inexpensive and there is a huge amount of Irish material available on second-hand recordings, but many of the more renowned albums have been re-issued on cassette and/or CD, often by different companies. (AOO)

*Irish recordings.* From the earliest days of commercial recording, Irish material was available, but usually restricted to parlour songs, Moore's melodies and arrangements of stock Irish airs. It was not until the early 1920s that performances of what we now know as 'traditional' music became widely available, mainly from American and English record companies eager to exploit large immigrant markets. English companies came to Ireland to record traditional material from the late 1920s, HMV, EMI setting up an Irish branch in Dublin in 1936. Most Irish country towns had shops which sold records, and houses which had a gramophone and a supply of records were often the centre of attraction for local musicians. (HAB)

*phonograph archives.* Throughout the nineteenth century folklorists and musicologists had collected and published written transcriptions of music, information on instruments and documents on playing practices. The invention of recorded music made it possible for the first time to preserve also the sounds from the past, and so folklorists and antiquarians moved to set up sound archives. First of these was the Phonogramm Archiv in Berlin in 1900. It was followed by the Archive of Folksong in the US Library of Congress (1928), and the Archive of Folk and Primitive music, Indiana (1948).

*standards and democracy.* The phonograph made available the repeated reproduction of music performances. Initially it was seen as of value to collectors – they recorded an informant, took away the cylinder, played it back and noted the words/music. Another person could also cross-check this for accuracy. Prior to this, performances had to be repeated over and over until the transcriber was satisfied that they had got it all down, and no checking of accuracy might be possible. The Ediphone cylinders were primarily a recording machine, the cylinder could be smoothed over and re-used. But they provided both recording and playback. Gramophones did not have this flexibility – the recording process was specialised and vastly expensive; recording and playback were separated – the concept of the 'studio' was created to provide for this. The public purchased pre-recorded records in order to listen only, to consume. The idea of a music performance as a 'product' was born. This remained the standard until the availability of domestic tape recorders – reel-to-reel – which from 1949 made recording as well as playback possible for the public. Cassette tape machines further revolutionised – or democratised – this position, making it possible to record selected, or exceptional, performances – or indeed one's own performance – for personal analysis, learning or pleasure; it gave personal and local choice in listening. This 'democratic' quality of domestic recording has been a major factor in the post-1950s' spread of traditional music learning in Ireland and other countries. In its own time, this new impact of tape and cassette on traditional music appreciation is as significant as was the introduction of the phonograph. In the music they make available, 78s and LPs provide a fixed and limited reference-point, they are 'colonial'; cassettes have repatriated old recordings, preserved ephemeral radio performances, and undermined the dominance of radio station and record-company choices in style – they are 'democratic'. All of these factors have implications for the idea of authenticity and taste in traditional music.

**republican songs.** See song, political.

**revival.** The totalling of attitudes and events in and about traditional music, song and dance since the setting up of Comhaltas Ceoltóirí Éireann in 1951, but having been set in motion by the political and cultural movements from the late 1700s onward, particularly after the setting up of the Gaelic League at the end of the nineteenth century. The phenomenon is not restricted to Ireland: it has been a huge force in Britain where folk music revival has pervaded the entire twentieth century. It has been of major significance in the United States where analysis suggests that revivalism is an ongoing phenomenon in all 'people's' musics. Revivalism – or 'revitalisation' – is a cocktail of awareness of value, politics, reaction to technology, conservatism, nostalgia, music and commitment. Essentially it involves much more than music, for it can build sub-cultures and new myths which may eventually so obscure the vision of some of its passionate creators that sight is lost of the object of central importance – the art of music.

**Reynolds, Willie.** (1916–  ). Piper. Born in Athlone, he was influenced by his father's concertina playing and began playing it at age seven. He was later helped on melodeon by neighbour Kate Kerrigan, and was self-taught on the uilleann pipes by twenty-two. He began on a Crowley practice set, directed by Harry Bryan. He founded the Walderstown Pipers' Club in 1934, and others in Lissdoughan and Moyvore. These led into the setting up of CCÉ (of which he was one of the founding members). He played with Leo Rowsome and Johnny Doran, and has been teaching music all his life throughout Westmeath, Roscommon, Offaly and Longford under the local Vocational Education Committees.

**RIC.** The Royal Irish Constabulary. Ireland's police force under the British administration up until the founding of the Irish Free State in 1922. The Irish Constabulary, founded by an Act of Parliament in 1836, united earlier local forces which had policed the country prior to that time. In 1867 Queen Victoria decreed that the title Royal be added to the force's name. The force recruited young men from all parts of the country, many of whom played music. As a matter of course, recruits were not stationed in their home area and in this way 'musical policemen' inadvertently helped cross-pollinate repertoires and playing styles. (HAB)

**Rimmer, Joan.** Ethnomusicologist and organologist, she has conducted much research into the history of instruments. Her work on the harp in Ireland has been particularly valuable, her 1969 book *The Irish Harp* is an important contribution to Irish music studies.

**Ritchie, Jean.** (1922–  ). Singer, collector, writer, dulcimer player. Born in Viper, Kentucky, she grew up in a traditional Applachian family where singing was a part of daily life. This is described in her *Singing Family of the Cumberlands* which has been kept in print since it first appeared in 1955. She has collected in Ireland and Britain as well as in America. Material gathered in Ireland in the 1950s is well represented in the LP *As I Roved Out*. This contains recordings of Elizabeth Cronin, Sarah Makem, Séamus Ennis, Máire Áine Ní Dhonncha and others at their peak. In the past four decades she has published a myriad of recordings, singing solo or with others such as Doc Watson. Whereas the majority of her songs have been traditional and frequently sung unaccompanied or with her mountain dulcimer, she has proved that she can adapt gracefully to modern settings with electric backing on discs such as *None But One* (London, Sire Records, 1977). On this she also highlights her consider-

Willie Reynolds demonstrates to a pupil    (CCÉ)

able talent as a songwriter. Her husband, photographer George Pickow, has been documenting the singers, musicians and folklife they have encountered over the years. The sound recordings and an extremely valuable photographic record of their fieldwork in Ireland in the 1950s has recently been donated to the archive of University College, Galway. (TOM)

***River of Sound.*** A seven-part television series on contemporary Irish traditional music broadcast on RTÉ and BBC in 1995. Presented by Mícheál Ó Súilleabháin, it generated an ongoing debate around the issues of change and continuity in traditional music. Performance-led, and involving 130 musicians, it set out to portray Irish traditional music under several categories: the voice, dancing, traditional instruments, the classical influence, repertoire, structure, etc. It introduced many young musicians to a popular TV audience for the first time. Central to it was specially commissioned music by Ó Súilleabháin and Donal Lunny, including 'River of Sound' with chamber orchestra, bodhrán, harp, keyboards, saxophone, harmonica, bouzouki, fiddle and kora (African harp).

See King, Philip; *Late Late Show*; O'Connor, Nuala.

***Riverdance.*** A spectacular Irish step-dance stage-show, with traditional-ethos orchestra and Irish choral group, Anúna. Initiated as an intermission piece of seven minutes during the Eurovision Song Contest, 1994, it was extended into a ninety-eight-minute stage show due to critical acclaim on the night. According to producer, Moya Doherty, *Riverdance* was an attempt to promote a more modern image of Ireland. Its theme is one of seduction; the river (symbolised by American step dancer, Jean Butler) seducing with a graceful, flowing slip jig the land (symbolised by American step dancer, Michael Flatley). It works on contrastive elements in both the dance movements and dance types in emphasising male/female gender roles. The pacing and momentum mounts from the solo entry of Jean Butler's slip jig in 9/8, to the fast, percussive performance of Michael Flatley in 2/4, to the final line-up of the full company with its hard percussive unison performance in 6/8. The show has a cast of eighty, including Irish step dancers, American tap dancers, a Flamenco dancer and a Russian dance company. All these explore visual, percussive, and auditory elements of their respective genres, all belonging to a percussive dance community. *Riverdance* is post-modern in its spectacular, patchwork, and image-oriented appeal, and is located within the world of popular culture. From Radio City Music Hall, New York, to broadcasting stations and use in homes, it has had a transcultural mass appeal. The Irish step-dance element of the show uses motifs from Irish step dance vocabulary, but in a different way to that used within the competition; the strictness of 'hands to the sides' is relaxed too. A primary reason for this is due to the influence of the lead dancer, Michael Flatley, who in response to his cultural environment had already taken artistic licence with the genre prior to *Riverdance*. The music's composer, Bill Whelan, did not confine himself to the usual eight-bar structural accompaniment of Irish traditional music, but introduced irregular, East European phrasing, this allowing for alternative choreographic possibilities. Therefore, although foot movements are those already known within the Irish step dance world, it is the phrasing and repetition of these movements, faster and harder, functioning in a more spectacular and dramatic way, which has contributed to its success. *Riverdance* has already been anticipated in the work of Siamsa Tíre (the National Folk Theatre in Tralee) with its production of *The Seville Suite*, also composed by Bill Whelan, and performed in Seville in 1994. It also draws much from developments in competition step dance, particularly that in the US, out of which Michael Flatley comes. The *Riverdance* success was therefore determined by economic, temporal, and dance/music developmental structures already in place. But it is its particular combination of dance, music, sound, lighting, and costume – all on a 'big stage' – which has assisted in bringing Irish step dance to a level acceptable to popular culture. Like *Lord of the Dance*, *Riverdance* is currently divided into several touring shows, providing work in theatre for Irish step dancers on a previously unimaginable scale. Hitherto, step dancers had few options, but to teach or retire; the big shows have supplied an alternative. (CAF)

**Roche, Frank.** (1866–1961). Dancing master, collector. Born at Elton, Co. Limerick, son to dancing master and classically trained violinist John. Frank was sent to Cork city by train each Saturday for piano and violin lessons. The family opened a dance academy at Charles Street (now Clontarf Place) in Limerick *c.* 1900, the sons playing music, the father teaching ballroom dance. The school declined after the father's death in 1913. Frank and Jim returned to Elton from where they taught dance in a wide circle ranging as far as Kanturk and Herbertstown. Gaelic League interest in music led Frank to learn Irish, this leading him to stay in Kerry where he collected tunes. Friendship with a Fr Brennan in Millstreet led to the priest writing the foreword to Roche's collection. Frank spent his life adjudicating at feiseanna and writing for the *Limerick Leader* newspaper. Interested in collecting, he was friendly with such as Mairéad Ní Annagáin, Séamus Clandillon and Carl Hardebeck. His 1911 collection was an attempt at avoiding material already published, and excluding 'pieces of doubtful national origin'. Among Gaelic League enthusiasts of the time, in the preface to his book he was different by his defence of set dancing: 'It may be objected to by some that the work contains matter foreign to a collection of Irish music, such as Quadrilles, or "Sets", as they are popularly called . . . The objection may be admitted as regards their origin, but they have become Irish by association, and so long as the people dance Sets, etc., it is better they should do so to the old tunes in which their parents delighted rather than be left depending on those books from across the water containing the most hackneyed of Moore's Melodies mixed up with music hall trash, and, perhaps, a few faked jigs and reels thrown in by way of padding.' He believed that music should be committed to print in order to be used. His dream, as evidenced in the 1927 notes to vol. 3 of the collection, that 'Our policy and ambition for the future should be to make full use of the great store already in our possession, and to found and equip a truly national School of Music which may yet give us a Chopin, a Grieg, a Sarasate, a Weber or a Wieniawski to bring to fruition the seed that has been garnered by the

John Roche's Favourite (Fling)

From the Roche Collection (compare with 'Here Anna' from Cole's collection

devotion of the collector.' His 'Notes on Irish Dancing' are an interesting document of his way of thinking and the nature and intensity of his involvement in music and dance life of the new Irish State. Therein he favoured social dance, and criticised the outlawing of quadrilles (sets), lancers, valse, polka, schottische (barn dance), two step and mazurka: 'These were all banned and nothing put in their place but a couple of long dances . . . A few years later, however, the "Bridge of Athlone", "Siege of Ennis", and an incomplete form of "Haste to the Wedding" were introduced, but, as might have been expected, these simple contre dances proved inadequate as substitutes for all those that had been prohibited. The showy and intricate four and eight-hand jigs and reels of the Revival, although interesting to the spectator, were generally looked upon as designed only for competition or display . . . and, consequently, had no appeal as social dances.' However, he remained hostile to the then-modern music and dance forms: 'Pernicious and degrading foreign influences must be combated and suppressed if our dancing and music are to be restored to their rightful place in the social life of our people.' His three collections of music are unique for their variety of tune-type, they contain airs, reels, double, single and hop jigs, long dances, old dances, hornpipes, set dances, quadrilles and marches. These have been re-published by Ossian (Cork, 1982) in one volume.

**Rochford, Martin.** (1916–    ). Fiddle, whistle, pipes. Born at Ballinahinch, Bodyke, east Co. Clare. The concertina was very popular in his childhood, had many fine players, and could be purchased for seven shillings and sixpence in local shops. Preferring fiddle, he took this up on a borrowed instrument at the age of ten, getting his own in 1927 for a pound from Solons of Whitegate through fiddler and step-dance teacher Margaret Malone. His interest in fiddle was whetted by experience of players such as Johnny Allen of Laccaroe, near Feakle, Michael Touhey and Patrick Moloney of Feakle, and Pat Canny of Glendree, all of whom had learned from blind fiddle master Paddy McNamara. Local dance in his teenage years was the four-figure reel set; step dancing was popular, and 'battering' with nail-tipped shoes was fashionable. Locally the 1935 prohibition of country house dances provoked the ploy of 'gamble dances', where a card game or a raffle was going on in one room, the prize being a gramophone or valuable item, while people danced in the kitchen. Legally the event was above board. On one occasion Martin recalls prosecution by plainclothes police, and on another, a Bodyke Sunday afternoon dance was sabotaged by the PP 'reading it out' from the pulpit with the words: 'The vultures will sweep down on Kilnoe and pick up the last of the bones.'

In the 1930s he began playing whistle, then developed an interest in pipes in 1936 after hearing Galway travelling piper Tony Rainey (1880–1958) playing in the square in Ennis. He met Felix and Johnny Doran playing for local dances, and in 1937 he got his own practice set from Johnny. Meeting Seán Reid and then Willie Clancy furthered his interest up to 1940. His first full set came from Leo Rowsome, and with Reid he played all over the area. The precursor of the Tulla Céilí Band was formed by them in his home as 'The Ballinahinch Céilí Band'. Still playing, Martin Rochford is a fund of keen observation and memory, an acerbically intelligent commentator on traditional music and life. He is interviewed at length in vol. 4 of *Dal gCais* (1978).

**Roinn Bhéaloideas Éireann.** The Department of Irish Folklore, University College Dublin 4, is the successor to Coimisiún Bhéaloideas Éireann (The Irish Folklore Commission), which was established in 1935 to collect and preserve the folklore of Ireland. One of the founder members of the commission, Séamus Ó Duilearga, was first professor of Irish Folklore in University College Dublin. The commission was disbanded in 1972. During the lifetime of the commission, full-time, part-time and special collectors worked throughout Ireland, documenting all aspects of folklore and folk tradition in many forms, including manuscripts, illustrations, ediphone cylinders, acetate discs, wire recordings, tapes, photographs and film. Seán Ó Súilleabháin, archivist with the commission and later with the department, was author of *A Handbook of Irish Folklore*, which was written primarily as a guide book for field collectors, and which is also used as a basis for indexing the material. Two full-time collectors of music and song, Liam de Noraidh and Séamus Ennis, spent a total of seven years in the field.

In 1972 Comhairle Bhéaloideas Éireann (The Folklore of Ireland Council) was established to index and publish material from the collections. Its publications to date include the audio-cassettes *The Bunch of Keys* (1988), which consists of recordings of the piper Johnny Doran made by Caoimhín Ó Danachair in 1947, *The Gravel Walks* (1990), which comprises recordings of the fiddle player Mickey Doherty, made by Caoimhín Ó Danachair and Seán Ó hEochaidh in 1949, a book *Binneas thar Meon* (1994), containing music and song collected by Liam de Noraidh, and a book and audio-cassette, *The Mount Callan Garland* (1994), consisting of the music and songs of Tom Lenihan recorded by Tom Munnelly.

The department offers undergraduate and postgraduate courses in Irish and Comparative Folklore. There are ten staff members including one full-time collector, Tom Munnelly, who lives in Clare. Other staff members also undertake occasional field work. The department is open to the public on week-days, 2.30–5.30 p.m. The Folk Music Section of the department, which is situated in Earlsfort Terrace, Dublin 2, includes a library as well as manuscript, sound, photographic and video archives, documenting various aspects of traditional music, song and dance. As director of the section, the late Breandán Breathnach instigated a number of collecting schemes in various parts of Ireland, and also acquired donations of manuscripts, broadsheets and other items. Among the collectors appointed under these schemes were Mícheál Ó Domhnaill, Proinsias Mac an Leagh, Seán McCann, Seán Corcoran, Angela Bourke and Fionnuala Carson. (RIU)

**Róise na nAmhrán (Róise Bean Mhic Grianna).** (1879–1964). Born on mainland Donegal, she spent most of her life on Arranmore Island. Her teenage years were spent working 'in service' in Tyrone and 'The Laggan'; harvesting took her 'tattie-hoking' in Scotland. This, and visits by US exiles, gave her a mixed Irish and English song repertoire. Fifty items from this were recorded by Proinsias Ó Conluain for Raidió Éireann in 1953, and were subsequently consigned for dumping but retrieved by him and eventually issued in 1994 as a CD. This includes 'Bacach Síol Andaí', a song about Napper Tandy's landing on nearby Rutland Island in 1798. Pádraig Ua Cnáimhsí has produced a biography of the singer, *Róise Rua* (1988).

**roll.** One of the most common ornaments used in Irish traditional music. It exists in two variants, the long roll and the short roll. In each case a single melody note is being decorated. The long roll consists of five notes and is played in the time value of a dotted crotchet.

Long roll

Within this the main melody note is sounded three times. An upper grace note is sounded between the first and second of these, and a lower grace note between the second and third. The first note is lengthened, thus the remaining notes must be played quickly to be contained within the given time value.

E and F short rolls on fiddle

The short roll involves the time value of a crotchet.

It follows the same pattern as the longer type but does not sound the main melody note first, starting instead on the upper grace note.

E and F long rolls on fiddle

Long rolls on flute and whistle

The roll is popular with players of most instruments, the extent of its usage differing according to regional styles and personal tastes. Its execution differs from pitch to pitch and from instrument to instrument. (LID)

**Rooney, Brian.** (1951– ). Fiddle. Born at Kiltyclogher, Co. Leitrim, his father played fiddle and flute; Co. Fermanagh fiddle player John Timoney was another influence. He emigrated to London in 1970 where Donegal fiddler Danny Meehan made a deep impression. He became very much part of the Irish music scene there, playing with the group Sliabh Luachra which had John Carty (banjo), Michael Hynes (flute) and Mick Casey (guitar). An important figure in music in London and source of much inspiration to a younger generation of players, his bowing style has a moving delicacy. He has played duet for many years with Paddy Hayes (button accordion) and with Gregory Daly (flute). He is featured on the 1994 album *Across the Waters*. (GRD)

**Rooney, John.** (1955– ). Pipes. Born in Drogheda, he spent his younger years in Crossmaglen, Co. Armagh where he began playing the whistle at the age of twelve, then pipes, inspired by and under the direction of his father's uncle, Felix Doran, a regular visitor to the home. With the family's move to England, John played there with Doran, and in partnership with Felix's son, Michael. His style has a legato drive and percussive, rhythmic regulator work similar to Doran's.

**Rowsome, Leo.** (1903–70). Uilleann pipemaker and player. The third generation of pipers, son of William, he inherited the family pipe-making and repair business. A dedicated teacher and organiser, through his pupils he re-initiated the Dublin Pipers' Club in 1936, became its first president, and with brother Tom he was a founder of Cumann Ceoltóirí Éireann in January 1950. The brothers were also key to the planning that led to the first national music gathering at Mullingar in 1951 and the inauguration of CCÉ. A master craftsman, Leo was also a professional musician and took great care to present the pipes with dignity, to help the instrument overcome the beggared image it had come to have. Like his uncle Tom before him, he won a first in the Dublin Feis Cheoil, in 1921, and was a part-time teacher of the pipes in the Dublin Municipal School of music in Chatham Row from the age of seventeen for fifty years. He produced a tutor for the instrument in 1936, which was reprinted often in the years since and was re-issued as a new edition in 1999. His playing took him to many places – notably before an audience of 6,000 in Carnegie Hall in New York in the 1960s, and on to television there. He made many recordings – from the early days of 78s up to his vinyl LP on *Claddagh King of the Pipers*, and the Topic two-volume compilation set *Classics of Irish Piping*. Living in the age before recognition of traditional music as an art, Leo's economy of concerts and teaching was precarious, but made viable by his wife Helena's working as a national school teacher. All his family are musically talented; his grandson Kevin is a 1996 Oireachtas winner and a pipe maker. His son Leon (d. 1994) was a talented musician and pipe maker who took over the family business; daughter Helena was a piper and tireless worker for CCÉ and contributor to *Treoir* magazine through the 1960s and '70s. Leo Rowsome practised both his art and his craft in the difficult years of Irish music's transition from necessity of life through practical redundancy into revival. He has been one of the architects of that comeback. He died suddenly at age sixty-seven – having just adjudicated Paddy Glacken in the Fiddler of Dooney competition at Riverstown, Co. Sligo. The book *The Man I Knew* by his son Leon (1996) details his life.

**Rowsome, Samuel.** Born Ballintore, Co. Wexford in the 1820s. Huguenot by origin, he was well-respected locally as a formidable recreational piper who, Francis O'Neill relates, once 'gave eighty four couples dancing enough' at a ball in the Harrow, Wexford. He may have developed a taste for the pipes from Wexford's 'gentlemen pipers' – the Brownriggs of Norrismount. Sam was taught by the professional Carlow piper Jemmy Byrne jnr, and was both patron to and associate of the great travelling piper John Cash. He became a Catholic, and married dancer Mary Parslow of the adjoining Ballyhaddock townland, whose own brother also played pipes. Skilled at pipes maintenance, Sam passed both this and musicianship on to his three sons John, Thomas and William whom he also had taught more formal music by a German music professor who lived then in Ferns. Tom went on to become a renowned piper all over these islands, winning first prize at the 1899 Feis Cheoil; William moved to Dublin with no resources beyond his skills, and rapidly became a well-known instrument maker and repairer, earning recognition too as a piper. He had one daughter, May, and five sons – Samuel, John, Harry, Tom and Leo, all of whom had music. John played pipes, but Samuel was the early talent on them by age sixteen, photographed with and quoted glowingly by Francis O'Neill, ultimately to follow him to America where he died young. Tom was an accomplished piper too, he ran a drapers' shop in Thomas Street and was a vital link in the Pipers' Club and early CCÉ with one of the few cars available at the time.

**RTÉ.** See Raidió Éireann.

**Rushe, Hugh.** (1895–1979). Tin whistle. Born at Clonee House, Ederny, Co. Fermanagh, he was also a song collector, his first source those sung by his mother. In early youth he played in the Ederny flute band with Frank Maguire and Johnny Mc Pheliny. In later years he was close to, and influenced, singer and flute player Cathal Mc Connell, Pat Gallagher (fiddle), Len Graham and Joe Holmes.

**Russell, Micho.** (1915–94). Flute, tin whistle, song. Born at Doonagore, Doolin, Co. Clare, overlooking the island of Iniseer, an area then still suffused with folk custom. Influenced in his youth by his mother Annie (née Moloney) and aunt, as well as Patrick Flanagan and Jack

Micho Russell (centre) with Eamonn McGivney (left) and Tony MacMahon (EAO)

Donoghue (all 'German' concertina players). His father, Austin, was a sean-nós singer – indeed about a third of the people in his locality spoke Irish when he was growing up, and there was constant contact with Irish-speaking Iniseer. House-dances introduced him to tin whistle; his father purchased a Clarke model for him at a fair, and at age eleven he began to teach himself to play. Flute player John Darcy was an influence too, the remoteness of the area from gramophone technology gave him a strong local repertoire to learn from. At fourteen he left school to farm, an uncle got him a wooden flute and brothers Packie and Gussie began playing concertina and flute too. They played music for house dances locally and further afield, in later years in O'Connor's pub in Fisher Street, Doolin, then McGann's and McDermott's. The 1960s revival brought new attention and demands – playing in Slattery's, Dublin, led to other performances, to radio and TV work – the freshness of Micho's style both startling and captivating. His melodies were neither cluttered with ornament nor driven by beat. Instead he had a rudimentary tune-line – deceptively simple but rhythmically complex. A thoroughly individual player – subtlety was his hallmark – he was influenced by 'push and pull' concertina style and kept double time with both feet. He played with the Johnstons in London, and with Tim Lyons in Europe in 1972. Winning the All-Ireland whistle in 1973 led to playing in Germany over many years; he played in Holland, Scandinavia and Austria, at the Smithsonian Institution's Bicentennial festival

**The Swallow's Tail (Reel)**

The popular tune as played by Micho Russell

(Micheál Ó hÁlúin)

in Washington in 1976. Tales of his travels are legendary; he survived by his wits, and often by miracle, with a surprising, calm and straight-forward intelligence. Through him and his brothers the external world of Irish music colonised Doolin. An engaging and charismatic performer, Micho Russell's performance typically involved lore of the tune, tales about its source performers and references to where it had been played. A natural and unaffected performer he was as much at ease with a festival audience of thousands in Germany as with a handful of listeners in a pub corner at home. His best-known songs were 'John Phillip Holland' and 'The Well of Spring Water' and his repertoire included satirical and place-praise lyrics. He had a large collection of local dance tunes and was a source of many for Breathnach's collections. He can be heard on *Ireland's Whistling Ambassador*, and on video PWV 80001; on both his life is chronicled by Bill Ochs.

**Ryan, Connie.** (1939–97). Set dancer and dance teacher, the central figure of his era in set dancing. Born at Clonoulty, Holycross, Co. Tipperary he learned to dance from his parents who were the main dancers in the area. He developed his skills by acting as fear an tí at local céilithe. Passionately interested in set dance, his name is synonymous with its revival.

Throughout the 1950s he organised classes and dances at Cappaghmore, Co. Tipperary, often bussing in participants. Expanding his influence to Dublin, his first workshop was given at Churchtown in 1969; others followed at such as the 1977 Cork Folk Festival, in Ennis, Dingle, the Aran Islands and Tory Island. His charismatic personality expanded this work, resulting in huge demand for his talents. Unimpaired by serious eyesight deficiency and, later, chemotherapy, his workshops continued up to the time of his death at which time he had a full year's teaching programme planned at home and abroad. He took awareness of set dance to social circles and places where it might have been otherwise unknown – to the annual Merriman Summer School, the Irish communities in Britain, in the US, Canada and Australia. A student of his art, he was responsible too for reviving and encouraging research on many old sets.

**Ryan, Darby.** (*c*. 1777–1855). Lyricist, singer. Author of 'The Peeler and the Goat', he began life as Diarmuid Ó Riain, son of well-to-do farmers, at Ashgrove, near Bansha, on the brink of the Glen of Aherlow, Co. Tipperary. Educated in the hedge-school, Ryan was an avid reader and had access to 'big-house' libraries. Involved in land agitation, 'The Peeler' was written in revenge after his unjusti-

**Reel of Rio** (Reel)       (Seán Ryan, Brian Ryan)

*[musical notation]*

fiable arrest. It was performed off the back of a horse a week later and spread like gorse-fire throughout the country in the tinder-dry political climate of the times; its town-name – originally Bansha – was adjusted to fit different places such as 'Bantry'. His most dramatic piece, 'Ireland's Lament' survives printed in *The Tipperary Minstrel* (now in the British Museum). He wrote many florid recitations, in glowing praise of place, notably 'Shades of Ashgrove'.

See song, comic and satirical; song, place-praise.

**Ryan, Seán.** (d. 1985). Fiddle, composer. Born Nenagh, Co. Tipperary. His father was a noted local fiddle player, and as a child Seán learnt fiddle and flute. He also sang and was a champion step dancer. In later years his fiddle playing and compositions brought high standing among traditional musicians. Between 1949 and 1956 he won numerous awards in solo and duet competitions, the latter with Galway flute player P. J. Moloney. During the 1960s he appeared frequently on television and radio broadcasts and toured the USA in 1968 and 1969. His playing was marked by a steady and relatively unsyncopated rhythm, long and controlled bow strokes, with an emphasis on crisply fingered embellishment. He composed more than 250 tunes, many of which had already become standards of the traditional repertoire by the 1970s, eighty-two of them published in 1991 by Brian Ó Riain. Included in this collection are such tunes as the jig 'A Thousand Farewells' and the reel 'Glen of Aherlow' which, though widely played, had not previously been widely associated with their composer. (MAD)

**Ryan's Mammoth Collection.** See Ryan, William Bradbury.

**Ryan, William Bradbury.** (1831–1910). Collector, Publisher. Born at Lyndon, Vermont, USA. He worked for his uncle's grocery in Boston in 1850 and enlisted in the Union army as a musician in 1861. Involved in the first battle of Manassas, or Bull Run, he was captured by Confederates but released after a year, taking up employment with publisher Elias Howe in 1865, working with him for thirty years. In 1883, with Howe, William Ryan published *William Bradbury Ryan's Mammoth Collection, of more than 1050 Reels and Jigs, Hornpipes, Clogs, Walk Arounds, Slip Jigs, Essences, Strathspeys, Highland Flings and Contra Dances with Figures*, this drawing on previous Howe publications such as *Howe's 1000 Jigs and Reels*, which in turn had borrowed from others such as *Playford's English Dancing Master* (1716), and *Riley's Flute Melodies* (1814). The collection credits thirty-nine composers; many were minstrel performers, banjo players, fiddlers or clog dancers. It remained in circulation for more than fifty years as *Ryan's Mammoth Collection*. Through the 1890s and early 1900s the book was offered for sale through the mail-order Sear's catalogue, therein described in 1897 as 'A very popular collection of lively music arranged for the violin'. Since Sears' customers numbered millions, and it only dealt with top-selling items – including banjos, guitars and many other music instruments, music for zither, violin, harp and dulcimer – it is likely that Ryan's collection sold hugely all over the USA. The book was released again – without credit to the original compiler or publisher – in 1940 by the MM Cole Co. as *One Thousand Fiddle Tunes*. *Ryan's Mammoth Collection* (referred to sometimes as 'Cole's collection', and reprinted in a mass, cheap edition up to the 1980s as *1000 Fiddle Tunes*). In 1995 the Mel Bay company re-issued it yet again, with a new copyright, and a thorough, scholarly introduction to its history by US uilleann piper Patrick Sky. After Howe's death, Ryan published on his own for five years with collections of music and some twenty personal compositions.

Patrick Sky sees Ryan and Howe as 'the most important collectors of Irish dance music in America before Francis O'Neill'. He considers the *Mammoth Collection* to have been a substantial portion of the surviving written records of the mid-nineteenth century, and: 'one of the most important repositories of nineteenth-century American music created for or by blackface minstrel shows, songwriters, instrumental musicians, singers, and dancers, trained or traditional – the music that eventually developed into such twentieth-century forms as blues, country music, ragtime, etc.' Of the period of its production, he quotes Kenneth Goldstein's opinion that: 'the 1860s was a musically creative and turbulent period. Songsters "sold by the truck loads" . . . The minstrel show had reached its popular zenith, and road shows of every description were travelling all over the United States . . . a music boom took place in the middle of the nineteenth century that included not only song and dance but also instrumental music and especially music for the violin and for the banjo'. The importance of Ryan's collection to Irish music is that, in compiling his own tune collections, Francis O'Neill was undoubtedly aware of or familiar with it, Patrick Sky noting that some tunes – for instance 'The Cameronian Reel', and 'Miss Johnston's' – would appear to have been taken directly from it. It seems likely too, that some of O'Neill's informants would have been playing tunes originally sourced in the earlier Ryan's collection, and absorbed by the oral tradition.

# S

**Sam Henry Collection.** From 1906, or before, until his death, Sam Henry collected songs. About 500 of these appeared first in the *Songs of the People Collection* and have been published in book form. The rest remain in typescript or manuscript, though they have been listed and systematised and are eventually to be published. This remainder contains about 500 more songs and song fragments but has a lot more information about singers and the song tradition, some of it contained in letters from singers themselves. Sam Henry made lists: of the repertory of a few singers (many more titles than the songs he collected); of the singers in the north Co. Derry/Co. Antrim area (many more names than those from whom he collected); of the collections of other people in his area, some whose collections, like that of Mrs Houston of Coleraine, are now lost. He investigated the stories and origins of songs; he recorded information about singers, in a few cases he took their photographs. He collected books of songs and noted versions of songs or the name of the person who, in his experience, sang that song. He kept his correspondence with other collectors: with Archie McEachren of Kintyre, Scotland; with Francis Collinson, music editor of the BBC radio programme *Country Magazine* and later a Fellow of the School of Scottish Studies; with the English collectors, Walter Pitchford and Harry Albino; and the Americans, Alan Lomax and Helen Hartness Fanders. He kept his BBC contracts and scripts; cuttings of his newspaper articles and lectures. He retained the books he learned fiddle music from. Altogether the collection amounts to a tantalising, but incomplete (unfortunately, it is likely that a lot of paper was sacrificed to be pulped when it ran short during the Second World War), series of glimpses into the singing and living tradition of a fairly small area (within about twenty miles of Coleraine) in the first half of the century. However, given that Mrs Houston's collection is from the late nineteenth century, that both Len Graham and Hugh Shields' collecting and much of John Moulden's researches have been in or near this area, coverage is extensive if less than comprehensive. (JOM)

See Henry, Sam.

**Sands, Colm.** (1951– ). Born in Mayobridge near Newry, Co. Down one of the multi-talented Sands Family. His own songs are minutely observant, humane and cleverly written. Three solo albums *Unapproved Road*, *The March Ditch* and *All My Winding Journies* demonstrate him as a songwriter of great lyric melodic power and integrity. Best-known songs include 'The Man with the Cap', 'The Last House on Our Street', 'Almost Every Circumstance' and 'Whatever You Say Say Nothing'. A radio presenter on BBC Radio Ulster he presents *Folk Club* and *Sands of Memory*. Also an accomplished record producer he runs Spring Studios in Rostrevor which has recorded much traditional music. (JOO)

**satire.** See song, comic and satirical.

**scale.** A note progression or 'octave' of eight notes, e.g. C D E F G A B C

The intervals between these notes are not equal, and – in Western music – some of them are half notes – semitones. Thus each note can have two different pitches – 1. the normal, or 'natural' note, and 2. the 'sharpened' note, this indicated by the '#' symbol placed after it.

Music systems over centuries have determined the interval between E and F, and between B and C on the basic 'scale of C-Major' are semitones:

C D E_F G A B_C

i.e. the interval between third and fourth notes (E_F), and seventh and eighth notes (B_C) are semitones. This is represented overleaf, and is indicated at the beginning of the staff by the absence of # symbols.

SCALE

*Scale of C Major*

C D E F G A B C

*Scale of D Major*

D E F# G A B C# D

*Scale of G Major*

G A B C D E F# G

*Scale of A Major*

A B C# D E F# G# A

The other 'Major' scales are derived from this, each starting on a different note – but always keeping the 3rd–4th interval, and the 7th–8th interval a semitone. Thus the scale of D-Major runs:

D E F#_G A B C#_D

This is indicated at the beginning of the staff by # symbols on the uppermost C and F positions.

The scale of G Major runs
G A B C D E F# G
The scale of A Major runs
A B C#_D E F'# G#_A

This is indicated at the beginning of the staff by # symbols on the uppermost C, F and G positions.

*Irish scales, Henebry's research.* However, while this generally applies to much Irish music, for many tunes it is an inadequate explanation. Listening to the music being played throws up contradictions. These are described by Richard Henebry in his 1903 'Irish Music – Examination of the matter of Scales . . .' as the F# often demanding to be played a quarter tone flat, the C# played flat: The Irish C natural, three-quarters of a tone above B, and three-quarters of a tone below D. He revised the basic D-major scale of Irish music, using Gaelic letters 'F' and 'C' to indicate replacements of the modern; in this the F# and C# are a quarter tone lower than standard F# and C#. These two notes of difference are not achievable on fixed-note instruments like accordion or concertina (unless the player has them specially tuned so), but in slow airs, and such contemplative playing, are achievable on pipes, flute and whistle by partially covering a hole, and on the fiddle by altering tuning and finger position, with the voice by adjustment. Awareness of the implications of this scale gives some idea of where the 'sound' and 'feel' of older music and playing stem from. Henebry asserts that 1. most Irish airs are based in this scale, 2. F# and C natural are normal values of F and C employed in them – F-nat. and C# occurring as mostly unaccented, 'passing' or 'slid' notes. Translating this into other keys, and deriving modes from this scale, Henebry produces D, G and A modal scales with different intervals, this different to the modern tempered scale. This idea has implications for the overall sound of Irish music, and, theory aside, reinforces the belief of all older players that the music can only be properly learned by listening. Henebry develops this further, pointing to a set of tunes of all kinds which end in G, but follow none of the modern temperament rules, producing instead a different tone and colour:

> But here the airs are of a piercing clang that is ineffable. They reveal a closeness of suggestion and an almost awful directness of appeal, with a complaining reproachful calling to mind of something we never knew or remembered.

'Táimse 'mo Chodladh' is one such air, as is the jig 'Strop the Razor'. In these tunes Henebry identifies (Irish) F and C natural, and Bb, as critical. He points out that in each of these cases the only notes that diverge from the standard scale are those with two values, the others utilise no semitones.

**Scanlon, Batt.** Fiddle, collector. A pupil of Kerry master George Whelan, he emigrated to San Francisco. There he notated Whelan's tunes and published them in *The Violin Made Easy and Attractive* (1929), an instructional collection.

**schottische, highland.** See highland.

**Scoil Acla.** Summer School on Achill Island, Co. Mayo, involving John McHugh, John McNamara, Séamus McNamara, Tom McNamara and Paddy Lineen. It runs through the first fortnight of August each year and draws its teachers from among the country's top musicians.

**Scoil Éigse.** CCÉ's annual summer school covering traditional music, song, dance and language. Aimed at younger and improving players, it is held each year in the week preceding Fleadh Cheoil na hÉireann in the Fleadh host town. Initiated in 1972, the school has some four hundred students, many on scholarships awarded at the provincial Fleadhanna Ceoil. Classes run from 10 a.m. to 4 p.m. Monday to Friday, and are offered in two-row button accordion, concert flute,

Biddy Barry (Schottische) (Roche, 1927)

concertina, fiddle, harp, piano accordion, sean-nós singing, set dancing, tin whistle, singing in English, uilleann pipes and Irish language. Classes are followed by an organised session, this lending the event the feeling of a music festival.

**Scoil Samhraidh Willie Clancy.** A week-long summer school in traditional music and set dance held annually at Miltown Malbay, Co. Clare. The first and biggest of such events, it commemorates the town's best-known uilleann piper, Willie Clancy, and has been running since just after his death in 1972. The idea was initiated by Clancy himself, and implemented within six months by teacher Muiris Ó Róchain in collaboration with CCÉ's timire ceoil Séamus Mac Mathúna and local musicians Martin Talty, Paddy Joe McMahon and Junior Crehan. Now independent, the school is focused around the teaching of instruments and set dancing in formal classes, but stresses the value of the oral/aural tradition. In its fleadh-style volume of music-making in bars it has become something of a Mecca in the music, its retinue of up to a hundred teachers, and hundreds of improving and competent musicians, dancers and singers drawing in thousands of listeners. The school addresses the cultural and intellectual side of traditional music by the inclusion of daily workshops on singing and the tradition, afternoon lectures and evening recitals. The 'Breandán Breathnach memorial lecture', given by various authorities in traditional music, opens the school, a music tribute at Clancy's grave, launch of albums and publications in traditional music follow. Scores of impromptu sessions accompany these organised activities, nightly set dance and céilís complement a routine of morning classes given by top players on uilleann pipes, flute, tin whistle, concertina, fiddle, button accordion and set dancing.

## Scotland

*music links.* There are many of these within and beyond their common Celtic background. Harpers and poets crossed back and forth from at least the thirteenth century, some having patrons in both countries. Later, celebrated harpers such as Rory Dall Ó Catháin and Denis Hempson of Derry spent considerable time in Scotland whereas Scots counterparts like Ruadhrí Dall Morrison are reputed to be buried in Ireland. The Jacobite cause gave rise to a vast body of poems and song with mutual sympathies. Following the Plantation of Ulster in the seventeenth century the influence of Lowlands Scots became more pronounced. English or Scots-speaking Lowlanders brought with them cultural innovations such as balladry which differed from the non-narrative Gaelic songs. Instrumental traditions shared by Ulster and Scotland are particularly evident in the fiddle music of Donegal and musical exchanges, facilitated by ease of travel, are even more common nowadays. For more than a century navvies and seasonal migratory workers have gone from Ireland harvesting and tattie-hoking (potato picking). The extent to which Scots farm workers absorbed the songs of the Irish, and vice versa, can be seen in such major collections as *John Ord's Bothy Songs and Ballads* (Edinburgh, John Donald, 1930). (The Bothy Band took their name from an illustration in this book.) Scores of Irish songs in this collection will be familiar to Scots singers and many of the Scots songs will be found in the Irish repertoire. Though the balladry of Scotland has received scholarly attention for centuries, recent research in the Irish field has discovered many ballads once believed to be known only in Scotland. A factor in this is the interchange between Scots and Irish travellers. Celebrated singers and musicians such as Davie Stewart and Jimmy McBeath travelled the Irish roads. Sheila Stewart of Blairgowerie was even born here. (TOM)

*history.* Scotland originally takes its name from the Irish who migrated from Co. Antrim between 300 and 400 AD to the west coast area known today as Argyll ('Earraghail', 'coastland of the Gaels'). By *c.* 500 AD the Kingdom of the Scots was established under Fergus Mór mac Eirc of Ireland's royal dynasty, Dalriada. Their language was Gaelic and they adopted the Christian religion after the Irish missionary, Columba, had established the centre of Christianity in Iona in 563. In 843, Dalriada was united with its Celtic neighbours to the north and east, the Picts, under one king, Kenneth Mac Alpin, whose people, by that time, had also converted to Christianity. This new kingdom, which took the ancient name, Alba (Scotia, as the Romans called it), extended south to the Forth-Clyde line. The Latin designation for the people, Scoti, anglicised to Scots, ultimately gave the name Scotland to the entire country.

Historically united and connected, rather than divided, by a highway of sea, Ireland and Scotland shared a common language until the seventeenth century. It is understandable, therefore, that they shared a common culture which continues to be reflected in many aspects of the way of life to this day. The area of Galloway in the south-west of Scotland was also Gaelic-speaking until at least 1700, and though the traditions of the Scottish Gael have been rooted for several centuries in the Highlands and Islands, their language, sgeulachdan (stories), songs, music and art have more in common with Ireland than with the rest of Scotland lying to the south and north-east of the demographic divide known as the 'Highland line'.

In the twentieth century the boundary of spoken Gaelic has receded to the point where, in the 1990s, it no longer includes Perthshire. The stronghold of the Scottish Gael is now in the Outer Hebrides, since its cradle in Argyll has largely been taken over by non-Gaels who are increasingly populating the Highland mainland and Inner Hebrides. While a few learn the language, most do not, thus Scottish Gaels still regard Ireland as the home of their closest cultural connections.

*canntaireachd*. In Scottish Gaelic usage, these refer to the complex syllabic notation used in teaching the Highland bagpipe. Throughout the history of the instrument, both tunes and techniques of the playing were handed down via this traditional method. The learner not only picks up the tune but also acquires the fingering of it on the pipe chanter. Even today in Scotland, skilled pipers sing canntaireachd versions to their pupils while teaching them to read the printed musical notation that has become second nature to every twentieth-century piper.

*highland pipes*. See bagpipe.

*Gaelic lyrical song*. These post-date the rare Ossianic ballads. Vast numbers were composed by both literate poets and non-literate 'folk-poets', all strictly conforming to the dictates of complex metrical styles. Many have choral refrains of meaningless vocables which fit the chosen metre and remain true to the style. Some of the motifs in them are traceable to literary origins (the Scoto–Irish inheritance of Classical Gaelic), and specific songs that continue in oral tradition can be dated, some approximately, some accurately, by the central theme of the song. For example, variants of 'Seathan mac Rígh Éireann' (Seathan son of the King of Ireland), were first written down from singers in the late 1800s by Alexander Carmichael (*Carmina Gadelica*, vol. 5, pp. 60–83). 'An Brón Binn' (The Sweet Sorrow), which survives both in manuscript and oral tradition, sings of King Arthur and his Knights of the Round Table. While its roots are in Ireland, it has Scottish influences from Clan Campbell bards, who trace the lineage of their chiefs to King Arthur with his court at Dunbarton. More precise dates can be attached to songs such as 'Griogal Chridhe', the lament for Gregor MacGregor of Glenstrae, beheaded in Perthshire in 1570.

*Ossianic ballads*. Called 'heroic' ballads, because many are attributed to Ossian, son of Fionn, these are the most ancient songs to be found in Gaelic Scotland. Composed in a distinctive syllabic form, they recount and celebrate the feats of ancient warriors such as Fionn, Oscar and Cú Chulainn. Some of the themes can be identified as having a literary origin, traceable to twelfth-century Irish sources, though they have been popular in Scottish oral tradition from at least the fifteenth century. Now very rare among singers, they were traditionally regarded as having the highest status in any repertoire. Fragments of Ossianic ballads inspired James MacPherson to produce his collection of poems which he claimed to have been composed by Oscar. Misleading as the claim may have been, translations of the work became world famous (Napoleon is said to have kept a collection in his pocket) and must be credited with influencing subsequent generations of composers, writers and travellers.

Ossianic ballads are outside the corpus of international balladry (Child Ballads) that can be claimed by North-East and Lowland

Scotland as the 'jewel' of their oral tradition – the 'classic ballads' known in Scots as the 'muckle sangs'. Nevertheless, they too have a strong link with Ireland, which could be regarded as travelling in the opposite direction, for, since the sixteenth century, political and historical events account for the wealth of Scots balladry that exists in the North of Ireland.

Recordings: Mrs Archie MacDonald of South Uist singing 'Latha dha'n Fhinn am Beinn Iongnaidh' (A day when the Fenians were in the Mountains of Marvels), 1960, School of Scottish Studies; *Music from the Western Isles*, Scottish Tradition, Vol. 2, Greentrax Recordings.

*panegyric.* 'Praise songs and poems', these were the stock in trade of every clan and district in Gaelic Scotland, even after the breakdown of the clan system (1746). Composed by both literate and non-literate song-makers alike, subjects ranged across a wide spectrum while retaining ancient themes and motifs. From the 'high age of vernacular poetry' (approx. 1645 to 1800) are countless compositions which are still sung. For example, the songs of the phenomenally productive, non-literate Duncan Bán MacIntyre may be as highly valued among Gaels as those of the eloquently literate Alexander MacDonald (*c*. 1700–70), and compositions of both remain vibrant in oral tradition to this day.

*psalms.* Sung in iambic pentameter metre, these date from the Reformation of 1560, as they were part of the Genevan order of service. They were introduced into Gaelic Scotland when the Synod of Argyll proposed the first translation in 1653 and, though 50 psalms appeared in print in 1658, the first complete edition was published by The Revd Robert Kirk of Aberfeldy and Balquhidder in 1684. (Kirk also published the Irish Bible in Roman type in 1690, the basis for the Scottish Gaelic Bible, though he may be better known for his treatise on fairies, 1692.) The striking quality of Gaelic congregational psalm-singing grows out of a complexity of features: there is no instrumental accompaniment to the pan-European tunes which make up the Scottish psalter. While very few are actually Scottish in origin, all the tunes are in ballad meter, and thus they are interchangeable from psalm to psalm. The minister announces the chosen psalm 'to the tune of [named]' then a precentor leads the singing. He 'lines out' (in chant-like melody) and, after each line, is followed by a surge of congregational singing that seems to defy the metre of the set tunes which are standard to the English-speaking churches. Because 'ballad metre' is not part of Gaelic tradition, each congregation elongates notes and ornaments lines according to local tradition, thus producing the unique sound of Gaelic psalm-singing.

*puirt-a-beul.* Scottish Gaelic mouth music, this has two functions: to provide music for dancing, and to facilitate learning or teaching tunes for the bagpipes or fiddle. All have texts, usually catchy, comic, witty, clever, often tongue-twisting ditties, and many have lines or choruses of meaningless vocables. All require vocal agility, as they are composed in strong, often complex rhythms, which precisely fit the notes of a reel, strathspey or jig. Most are very ancient, and there is no basis whatsoever for the common, but senseless, notion that they were 'invented' post-Culloden. Most are by unknown composers; titles and texts may vary from area to area, and several melodies can be identified as sharing a common history with tunes popular in Ireland.

*waulking songs* (Scottish Gaelic: 'orain luaidh'). These are work songs for keeping the rhythm steady during the 'fulling' of hand-made woollen cloth, cló mór (heavy tweed). The aim is to shrink and thicken newly woven tweed to make it warmer and more wind-proof. In Scotland the process was exclusively done by women rhythmically beating the wet cloth on wooden boards till it attained the required width and texture. Though the prime function of waulking songs was work, the social aspect allowed women to get together and express themselves through singing. The songs are by unknown women composers, and while some can be dated to the end of the sixteenth century, collectively they are more ancient. Floating lines and motifs are characteristic; some can be identified as borrowings from rowing songs, entering the repertoire as 'men's songs', and adopted for their suitable rhythm. Waulking songs form the largest body of Scottish Gaelic song in existence and are known as 'milling songs' in Eastern Canada where it became the custom for men to join in. (MAB)

*harp.* The harp has been played in Scotland for more than a thousand years. The first indisputable representations anywhere in the world of three-cornered pillar harps occur on Pictish stones on the east coast of Scotland. These include the eighth- or ninth-century stone at Nigg in Easter Ross, the stone at Dupplin in Perthshire which has a pre-820 date, and ninth- or tenth-century stones at Monifeith and Aldbar in Angus. Some of these show players with their harps, and depict large, floor-standing instruments, apparently lightly built, with a straight string-carrier and a straight or slightly curved pillar. They do not appear to be sufficiently strongly built to sustain the pull of high-tension metal strings, and thus may have been strung with another material – possibly horsehair. Between the sixth and ninth centuries, waves of emigration from the Picto-British tribes of south-eastern Scotland, which carried their poetry and language to Wales, may also have taken with them their harps, which, until the tenth to twelfth centuries, were strung with horsehair (from the tails of Eriskay ponies). This material was superseded in Wales by gut strings, and it is likely that Anglian influence pushing up into south and eastern Scotland had the same result in that area.

The literary references and pictorial representations appear to show a movement of the three-cornered gut-strung harps south and eastwards through England and the continent, while the Scottish stones also show a movement westwards to the areas of Gaelic influence. Here the harps become smaller and sturdier and of the typical construction which was necessary to withstand the high tension of metal strings. Metal was a material known to be favoured by the Gaels, but Irish representations until the eleventh century show only four-cornered harps or lyres of various shapes.

In Scotland, the metal-strung harp was referred to as a 'clarsach'. A distinction was made between the two different harps, as in the Treasurer's accounts of payments to harpers at the court of James IV:

> 1501, April 13, Pate harpar on the harp, Pate harpar on the clarsach, James Mylson harpar, the Ireland clarsach and English harpar, each received . . . xiijs.

The first player named in a contemporary context was Adam of Lennox *c.* 1260. He was porter at Melrose Abbey and subsequently abbot at Balmerino in Fife. He had a great reputation for holiness and would spend 'the greater part of the winter nights in playing the harp (in citharizando) and singing songs which are called "Motets", written in honour of the holy virgin-mother.' He is likely to have played a small gut-strung instrument. The small gut-strung harp was widely used in the Lowlands by travelling harpers and harpers attached to families of Norman or Flemish origin, such as the Fitz-Alans (later Stewarts), whose harper held the 'Harperland' at Kyle-Stewart near Ayr in 1373. The music played on gut-strung harps is likely to have reflected the classical music of the European aristocracy, both solo and in consort. There are fine ceiling paintings dating from the sixteenth and seventeenth centuries, along with lute, viols and other instruments, at Dean House and Crathes Castle. As well as this music, travelling harpers, often mentioned in the great Scots ballads, played the indigenous music of the Lowlands.

> And by there cam a harper fine
> Wha harped tae the King at dine . . .

The reign of James VI, with its shift of cultural emphasis to England, marked the end of any appearance at the royal court of the Scottish harp. The last specific reference to a Lowland harper was in the accounts of Campbell of Cawdor in Glasgow on 1 October 1591: 'giffen to the Lowland harper – 6s 8d'.

The metal-strung clarsach was played in the Highlands, in the hands of aristocratic amateurs, sometimes women, or by professional harpers attached to clan chieftains. Some families held the post as a hereditary office, such as the MacGhille Sheanaichs, who served the MacDonald Lords of the Isles, and held lands in Kintyre from the fifteenth to the eighteenth century. The harper's declining status may be followed in the family's economic decline. Other families who employed harpers include the Campbells of Argyll, served by the MacVicars in the sixteenth century, and the Lamonts, who employed the MacEwen family of harpers. One of these MacEwen harpers apparently moved to Atholl with a member of the Lamont family and settled there, serving the Robertsons from the fifteenth to the seventeenth century. Other clans associated with harpers include the Campbells of Breadalbane, and of Auchinbreck, and of Cawdor; the Mackenzies of Applecross; the Frasers of Lovat; the Grants, the MacLeans of Coll; the MacDonaids of Sleat, and of Keppoch; and the Gordons of Huntly. There appears to have been a great deal of harping activity in the Highlands until the seventeenth century.

*Irish harpers.* Irish harpers, such as Ruairi Dall Ó Catháin, travelled to Scotland 'where there were great harpers' (Arthur O'Neill). Ó Catháin seems to have settled in Atholl in the first half of the seventeenth century and died there. The O'Connellan brothers, Lawrence or William, and Thomas, travelled to Scotland where Thomas was made a burgess of Edinburgh, apparently for his harp playing. Tunes such as 'Killiecrankie' and 'Lochaber no More' are associated with him. An Irish harper was executed for the murder of Angus Óg of the Isles in 1490. Other players are recorded in the Royal Accounts as attending court in the 'tail' of Irish chieftains, while some, like Jago McFlaherty, were employed in aristocratic households such as that of the Duke and Duchess of Hamilton in the 1680s. Denis Hempson toured Scotland in the mid-eighteenth century, as did Echlin Ó Catháin, some of whose repertoire was taken down by Scottish collectors before his death around 1790. In the opposite direction, Scottish harpers such as Ruaidhri Dall Morison apparently travelled to Ireland to train as musicians. Ruaidhri Dall Morison, the most famous Highland harper bard, was born *c*. 1656, and was blinded by smallpox while a child. After returning from Ireland where he apparently went to expand his musical knowledge, he was employed by Iain Breac Macleod at Dunvegan on Skye. He composed many songs for his patron such as 'Oran do Iain Breac MacLeod', 'Creach na Ciadaoin', and 'Oran do MhacLeoid Dhun Bheagain', which have survived in the oral tradition. His Jacobite sympathies, voiced in 'Oran mu Oifigich Araid', may have led to his banishment to Glenelg in 1688. After Iain Breac's death in 1693, he travelled in Scotland, and found another patron for some years in John MacLeod of Talisker. Morison apparently returned to Skye at the end of his life, where he died around 1714.

The social upheaval of the Jacobite Risings in the mid-eighteenth century marked the demise of the Highland harp, though it had been in decline for a century or so, probably because of its association with the old formal orders of bardic poetry. The defeat of the Highland clans, some of whom had been patrons of harpers, meant that there were no longer households of the old style in which a harper would have been employed. The clarsach survived in the hands of versatile musicians such as William McMurchy until the end of the eighteenth century. After this, its music was occasionally played on gut-strung harps by classically trained harpists who had an antiquarian interest in the ancient harp repertoire, such as the MacLean-Clephane sisters of Mull, Elizabeth, Lady D'Oyly, or Joseph Elouis, a French harpist who taught in Edinburgh in the late nineteenth century. Travelling harpers were still occasionally heard, such as Padraig O'Beirn, a blind Irish harper, who visited Edinburgh in the 1840s and William ap Pritchard in Llandegai of North Wales, who frequented south-west Scotland in the early nineteenth century.

The Celtic revival of the late nineteenth and early twentieth centuries led to the commissioning by Lord Archibald Campbell of harps to be made, so that a competition for self-accompaniment might be held. Several harps were made by Robert Glen, copied from the Queen Mary Harp, and strung with wire. Other harps were also made by Robert Buchanan and H. D. Harnaack (later taken over by J. Morley) which were strung with gut. In 1831, Comunn na Clarsaich (The Clarsach Society) was formed and included in its members Mrs Hilda Mary Campbell of Airds, Heloise Russell-Ferguson and Patuffa Kennedy-Fraser Hood (daughter of Marjory Kennedy-Fraser), and Jean Campbell who was particularly active in teaching small gut-strung harps during the next thirty years. This harp has seen a tremendous revival since then in Scotland, and a revival of the wire-strung clarsach is also showing signs of gaining momentum.

The music played on harps was never written down by any harper. In the areas of Scots influence, it played its part in the European-style classical music of the day, as well as the native traditions shared with other instruments. It was used for song accompaniment – one of the major functions of the Highland clarsach. The harper would originally have accompanied the 'file' poet, or been a bard himself, able to compose lesser forms of poetry and accompany his performance of them. During the sixteenth century the general trend towards instrumental music grew. 'Ports' – a type of harp tune also popular with lute players who wrote them down – may be dated to this period. The clarsach also played a form of music comparable to the 'ceol mor' of the bagpipes. This is a series of variations on a theme, which are constructed by formalised decoration of the main melody notes. Laments, salutes and marches are the main categories of clarsach music. Dance music was not a feature of the repertoire until recent years, when several players took a particular interest in it. A large number of recordings were made in the 1960s by players such as Alison Kinnaird, Wendy Stewart, Isobel Mieras, Patsy Seddon, Mary Macmaster, Savourna Stevenson and Bill Taylor, representing different approaches to the music. These along with harp festivals, summer schools, mods and feisean, as well as the availability of harps made in Scotland, continue to encourage the revival of both gut-strung harp and wire-strung clarsach. (ALK)

**sean-nós.** Literally 'old style', refers most often to style of song. Also indicates freer, old style of solo step-dance.

See step dance, sean-nós.

*song*. A singing style developed over the centuries in Irish-speaking Ireland and Gaelic-speaking Scotland. The term is somewhat misleading. As the line of singing has never been broken the style is as modern as it is old. It has been passed on from generation to generation, hence the term 'traditional'; it is the traditional way of singing a song in Irish in Ireland and in Gaelic in Scotland. The Scottish poet Somhairle MacGill-Eain (Sorley MacLean) describes this singing on his Gaelic-speaking island of Raasay as 'that ineffable fusion of music and poetry, in which the melodies seem to grow out of the words and be a simultaneous creation'. The style is deeply rooted in the rhythms of the Gaelic language and in the metres and rhythms of Gaelic poetry. In Ireland it has survived wherever the Irish language itself has survived, in areas in Donegal, Mayo, Galway, Kerry, Cork, Waterford and Meath; it is at its most vibrant in the Connemara Gaeltacht in West Galway. Outside the Gaeltacht some Irish speakers from various parts of the country have learned the craft and are fine traditional singers. Songs in English are also sung in this style but, while there are similarities between traditional singing in English and traditional singing in Irish, they are two different traditions and are generally celebrated as such. The songs in Irish reflect an outlook on life and a view of the world that is quite different to the songs in English. (LIM)

*composition*. Relatively little is known of composers of traditional song in Irish-speaking Connacht until the demise of the formal Bardic schools in the seventeenth century. Although 'folk' songs must have existed before that time, they were held in poor regard by the trained bards who composed in highly structured, formal metres. For this reason, there is very little documentation on folk songs from the period of the Bardic schools. Most of the songs heard in Connacht today were probably composed some time between 1700 and 1850, and most of them are anonymous. They include lyrical love-songs such as 'Bean an Fhir Rua' (The Red-haired Man's Wife), 'An Draighneán Donn' (The Blackthorn Bush), or 'Bríd Thomáis Mhurcha'. One of the best-known poets, Antaine Ó Reachtaire or Raiftearaí (1779–1835), composed songs which are still widely sung, such as the love-song 'Máire Ní Eidhin', and the lament about a drowning, 'Eanach Chúin'. Many composers depict aspects of social history as did the Mayo poet Riocard Bairéad (1740–1819), whose mock lament about a bailiff, 'Eoghan Cóir' is still sung. The names of some other song-composers are also known and these are, for the most part, local poets who made songs for their immediate audience, some of which have survived. Poets of this kind whose songs have survived include Seoirse Osborne, from Moycullen, composer of 'Sicíní Bhríd Éamoinn', and Colm de Bhailis, composer of 'Cúirt an tSrutháin Bhuí', for example. However, it is probably true that many songs, particularly those documenting matters of immediate local relevance only, were never recorded and have now disappeared. Song airs were and still are, to a high degree, transmitted orally. It is not possible to trace the origins of many of the song-airs, and, in any case, a song is often sung to an air which is already well established. Indeed, this kind of transference occurs in both the English- and Irish-language song traditions. (RIU)

*context*. It is a personal, ornamented and usually unaccompanied style of solo singing. Its natural habitat, as it were, is an Irish-speaking situation where the listeners not only know the words of the song but also know the background story, especially of the great love songs and laments. There is a communal sense of place and a shared sense of social history which often moves the listeners to utter words of approval and encouragement to the singer. The profound and intimate feelings of love and of sorrow expressed in the lyrics, together with subtle embellishment of the airs with delicate forms of ornamentation, create a strong emotion and form a bond of sympathy and affection between singer and listeners. The audience refrain from singing along with the singer however, except sometimes in chorus verses or in repeated last lines. Otherwise, the 'one voice' rule is nearly always strictly observed. (LIM)

*performance*. Like story-telling, the context most conducive to the performance of sean-nós singing is a quiet, intimate one, with an attentive and sympathetic audience. Historically, sean-nós singing was almost entirely confined to community gatherings, such as house céilís, dances, wakes and weddings. With the decline of these traditional contexts, the performance of sean-nós singing has become increasingly common in pubs, at traditional music festivals and schools, at singing competitions, and at specially organised singing sessions. Despite the more public nature of most of these, much of the interaction between singer and audience found in the older, more intimate settings, still obtains. For instance, one still finds in these settings the practices of 1. vocal encouragement (in which a listener interjects a phrase such as 'Maith thú' into the song at an appropriate moment), 2. 'helping' the singer by joining in on a verse or phrase of the song, incidental commentary by a singer or audience member, and 3. the rhythmic squeezing, swinging, or rotating of the hand by a listener (a practice most common in Connemara). Sean-nós singers often assume an air of detachment when performing (as indeed do traditional singers in many cultures). Some close their eyes, some sing with their heads raised or thrown back; others lower their heads or even turn towards the wall. Still others, however, keep their eyes wide open, engaging specific audience members much as though they were narrating a story. Some singers prefer to sit while singing; others to stand. The singer is not usually demonstrative, however, and hand gestures or conspicuous body movement are rare in sean-nós singing, although sometimes employed in the performance of certain occupational songs. Speaking rather than singing the final line or phrase of a song is a not infrequent device in sean-nós performance, signalling the song's completion. Since traditional Irish songs are primarily lyric rather than narrative in composition, sean-nós singers also often give the narrative background of a song, or 'údar an amhráin' (source of the song), before singing it, even when they can assume that the audience is already familiar with the story.

*regional difference*. Certain regional differences can be identified regarding the use of stylistic and performance practices in sean-nós singing. For instance, the kind of pronounced melismatic ornamentation and attenuation of phrases often found in Connemara sean-nós is not characteristic of the Donegal tradition, where rhythm tends to be more regular and melodic ornamentation more restrained. On the other hand, some Connemara singers also use only a limited amount of melodic and rhythmic ornamentation. Differences should thus be spoken of in terms of tendencies rather than hard-and-fast distinctions: there are too many exceptions in matters of style (and still too little known historically about the subject) to make dogmatic statements on the matter tenable. While individual variation has probably always made such generalisations problematic, this is even more the case in recent times, when competitions, radio broadcasts, and recordings have exerted an increasingly powerful influence on singers throughout the country, complicating not only the issue of regional style but also the entire nature of the tradition. *Amhráin ar an Sean-nós*, an anthology of field recordings made between 1948 and 1965, before such influences were prevalent, illustrates a broad range of regional and individual styles and offers a well-documented introduction to the sean-nós tradition. (JUH)

*revival.* Not until the foundation of Conradh na Gaeilge (The Gaelic League) in 1893 and of its national festival of Irish music and song 'An tOireachtas', in 1897, did any appreciation emerge in English-speaking Ireland of these old, unaccompanied Irish language songs. With the decline in the traditional means of transmission of the songs from parents to their children, voluntary organisations such as 'An Gaelacadamh' in An Spidéal in Connemara and 'Sean-nós Cois Life' in Dublin have seen the need to bring sean-nós singers to teach in the Gaeltacht schools and to organise sean-nós singing classes for adults in the capital city. Whether one approves of competition or not, it is generally agreed that the annual Sean-Nós Singing Competition at the Oireachtas over the years, especially since its revival in 1939, has done much to promote this vocal art form, as has Raidió na Gaeltachta since its foundation in 1972 and Gael-Linn Records (Ceirníní Ghael-Linn) since the late 1950s. There has been a renewed interest in traditional singing in Irish in the last quarter of a century and a measure of its popularity in Ireland at the moment is that Cló Iar-Chonnachta in Connemara, publishers and distributors of books, CDs and tapes, have produced some fifty 'sean-nós' titles in the last ten years, fifteen of which are on CD.

*style and influence.* There are many types of traditional songs in Irish, from the fast, the topical, the humorous, the bawdy, to the slow and emotional laments and love songs. Each of the Gaeltacht areas tends to have its own repertoire but some of the so-called 'amhráin móra' (big songs) are found in all the areas in differing versions. Similarly, each of the Gaeltacht areas has its own distinct regional style. These styles, however, should not be defined by region alone, as many styles, ranging from an elaborate ornate style to a more simple subtle form of ornamentation, are to be found in each region. Some of the airs of traditional songs are the oldest surviving form of Irish traditional music. It is believed by some traditional musicians that no aspect of Irish music can be fully understood without a deep appreciation of traditional singing. Tomás Ó Canainn expresses it thus: 'It is the key which opens every lock. Without a sound knowledge of the sean-nós and a feeling for it a performer has no hope of knowing what is authentic and what is not in playing and decorating an air.' (LIM)

*technique.* 'sean-nós' includes a range of traditional Irish singing styles whose diversity reflects both regional and personal preferences. Performance technique in sean-nós consists of a number of interrelated elements: tone quality, vocal registration, ornamentation, phrasing, and rhythmic variation.

1. Tone quality, or 'timbre', may vary from extreme nasality, to a hard or constricted tone, to a relaxed, 'open' one.

2. Registration may exclusively use chest voice, or have a preference for the highest register, or head voice.

3. The technical feature most frequently associated with sean-nós singing, particularly in Connemara is melodic ornamentation or variation. This includes melismatic ornamentation and intervallic variation. In melismatic ornamentation, a single syllable is sung to several notes, as in rolls or turns (in which the main melody note alternates with adjacent notes above and below it), 'shakes' or mordents (in which the melody note is interrupted by a grace note a step or half-step above or below it), and appoggiatura (the use of one or more grace notes to lead into a melody note). Intervallic variation involves the varying of intervals between specific notes of a melody.

Many other stylistic techniques are available to the sean-nós singer, however, including the use of glottal stops (in which the singer briefly interrupts the flow of air through the windpipe); the act of subtly sliding into a melody note – often involving microtonal changes in pitch; manipulation of the vocal break (as in the more exaggerated yodel); and the 'sigh and sob' technique. This last effect, which is more commonly associated with Scottish singing (where it is more pronounced), is executed by 'leaning' on a grace note leading into a melody note a step or half-step below it.

Marked attack or accentuation of specific notes is also sometimes employed as a means of conveying emphasis, as are subtle variations in dynamics.

4. Rhythmic variation is another important aspect of sean-nós, especially the use of rubato – a designation which includes the varying of the value of notes within a musical phrase, the holding or lengthening of notes beyond the mathematically available time, or the use of breaks or pauses within or between phrases. Rallentando, or the gradual slowing of tempo, is also occasionally used in sean-nós, usually at the ends of songs.

5. Of particular importance is the management of 'phrasing' – the way in which the musical phrases are presented, both individually and in relation to each other – and, connected with this, 'line', or the ability to convey not only the notes of the melody but a sense of continuity and of the melody's over-all shape and feeling. In both instances, rhythmic and melodic considerations are so intertwined as to be two aspects of the same musical phenomenon.

*variation.* A sean-nós singer may vary the ornamentation – both melodic and rhythmic – of a song from performance to performance, or even from verse to verse within a single performance of a song, responding not only to the song's exigencies, but also to his or her own mood, as well as that of the audience. Variation is, like other stylistic features of sean-nós singing, a highly individual matter, and its use or nature depends on a number of factors, including regional tendencies and personal taste or facility. It is thus dangerous to place undue stress on this or other technical aspects of the tradition. (This is particularly true of melismatic ornamentation, whose use as a hallmark of sean-nós singing has often been overemphasised.) Ultimately, the good sean-nós singer uses technique not as an end in itself, but as a vehicle for artistic and emotional expression. The late Donegal singer Aodh Ó Duibheannaigh stressed the importance of communication – as well as self-expression – in sean-nós singing when he remarked (1979):

> The way I had it was the theme of the song, whether it was a sad one or otherwise, I'd try to put that feeling into it – my own feeling about the words and the song and the theme – I tried to put that into my singing, and tried to convey that to my listeners . . . There's some sort of story attached to every song, and you must put that story across in your singing – and put your own personality into the singing of it.

Expressivity in sean-nós singing is paramount, though it is achieved not by means of melodramatic or 'emotive' singing but through an understated, relatively restrained presentation in which conspicuous dynamic variation and other features of art and popular singing (such as pronounced vibrato and glissandi) have no place and the song is allowed, in essence, to 'speak for itself'. Because of the importance of allowing for spontaneous variation – and hence, self-expression – instrumental accompaniment is generally avoided in sean-nós; and although some instances of duet or group unison singing in the tradition exist, it is primarily a solo form. (JUH)

*speculative origins.*

1. Seán Ó Tuama's analysis. Popular Irish love-poetry began to surface in great quantity in the early seventeenth century. Most Irish folksongs collected in the nineteenth and twentieth centuries are love-songs, composed perhaps between 1600 and 1850, and on models dating to medieval times. Medieval scholar W. P. Ker suggests that the twelfth century holds the main sources and models of western European poetry and song, that '. . . an old civilisation with an elaborate literature of its own came to an end in the eleventh century . . .' and that there is '. . . great difficulty in understanding the transition. Modern poetry, including the ballads, begins about the year 1100' (*Form and Style in Poetry*, 1928). The man's love-lyric in particular seems shaped by popular versions of French *amour courtois* (courtly love) as practised by poets and entertainers after the Anglo Norman invasion.

One form of the love song from French, and associated with dance, is the *carole*, hugely popular all through western European society among all classes. Singing and dancing of caroles is reported at New Ross in 1265, clerics are known to have been disseminators of the fashion. High society in England had begun to abandon the love-song form – as distinct from the later devout carol form – by about 1400. Today the love *carole* is absent from collected English folksong, but common in the Irish. Ó Tuama analyses the structure of *carole*, comparing its French metrical form as:

> ... chiefly A + C (one line with refrain), 2A + C (two rhyming lines with refrain), or 3A + B + C (three rhyming lines with coda and refrain). The refrain or burden often contained nonsense words such as *haro, derin din, ding ding dong, avec la tourloura*, etc.; such nonsense words are found in medieval English songs as well as in Irish folksongs, and in origin were sounds used by dancers, and possibly onlookers, to imitate the sound of pipes and other musical instruments (sometimes played as an accompaniment to the dance).

The A + C and 2A + C metrical forms, Ó Tuama suggests, seem linked to the most primitive type of carole which has been traced back by French scholars to archaic women's dances at May-time.

It is noteworthy that many of the examples of the A + C form extant today in Irish folksong are also linked with the coming of summer: *Thugamar Féin an Samhradh Linn* is a widespread motif.

The form 3A + B + C, however, mostly became identified with the *carole* in the high *amour courtois* period (*c.* 1200–1400), when this type of entertainment became an elitist court activity for both men and women. Well-known troubadours and *trouvères* cast their *chansons à dancer* in this mould.

Ó Tuama holds that Irish folksong and traditional Irish poetry in general utilise versions of 3A + B + C, among them simpler songs like 'Beidh Aonach Amárach', 'Is Trua gan Peata an Mhaoir agam', and 'An Páistín Fionn'.

He breaks the first of these down as follows:

Song:
Beidh aonach amáireach i gCondae an Chláir
(A x 3)
Cén mhaith dhom é, ní bheidh mé ann (B x 1)

Refrain:
'S a mháithrín an ligfidh tú 'na aonaigh mé?
(x 3)
A mhúirnín ó, ná héiligh é.

Such practice of casting the refrain in the same general mould as the verse, he argues, had become common already in medieval times:

> My lady is a prety on,
> A prety, prety, prety on,
> My lady is a prety on
> As ever I saw

He cites other songs still sung as having typical *carole* verse and refrain, essentially dance music:

> Is trua gan peata an mhaoir agam,
> Is trua gan peata an mhaoir agam,
> Is trua gan peata an mhaoir agam,
> 's na caoire beaga bána.
>
> Is ó goirim, goirim thú
> Is grá mo chroí gan cheilg thú
> Is ó goirim, goirim thú
> 'S tú peata beag do mháthar

Another form of *carole* to be established in Ireland was *rondel*, commonly used in many folk and literary songs in Irish (e.g. 'Eibhlín a Rún'), and in medieval French verse. The form seems close to that used for the making of Latin hymns by Bishop Ledrede in Kilkenny in the fourteenth century. Ó Tuama concludes that the deep rooting of the *carole* form in Ireland is supported by the fact that the present-day Irish words for dancing – 'rince' and 'damhsa' themselves derive from either English or Norman-French. He suggests that the foreign rounds, or ring dances, in this way became the models for our subsequent older Irish dance forms.

But it is the opening up of all kinds of literary channels between Ireland, England, France and Provence that Ó Tuama considers as important as setting the tone and substance of Irish love-lyrics. The Provençal convention of the 'man's love-lyric' is found throughout Irish folksong literature collected in the nineteenth and twentieth centuries. This means that many songs held faithfully in the folk-memory were originally literary forms; in the words of Alexander Krappe:

> In periods of intense literary activity, literary products will sink from the classes for which they were intended in the first place, to lower levels of the common people. When the songs of the medieval troubadours had charmed the knights and ladies, and even after they had ceased to charm them, they still appealed to the peasants.
>
> (*The Science of Folklore*, 1930)

J. M. Cohen adds that

> The vernacular literature of the twelfth century was not designed for reading. The epic poems were composed to the simple music of the

primitive fiddle, and the lyrics for singing to more complicated tunes, sometimes with refrains, or as a voice and fiddle accompaniment to a dance. There was, consequently, a very close relationship between the metre used and the traditional dance steps; and since most of the dances were popular in origin it was at this point that the cultivated lyric touched the folksong with the result that in some districts . . . poems began to be devised on less sophisticated subjects by the *jongleurs* (strolling performers) themselves, independently of the *trouvères* (lyricists), to be sung at the festivities of the common people. It was the dance that bridged the gap between the art-forms proper to each caste.

(*A History of Western Literature*, 1956)

A large amount of popular Irish love-song is in the Provençal mould of the love-lyric set to elaborate music. Dominant in the man's love lyric is the concept of courtly love, and a high lyric quality, but generally effusive, eulogistic, lacking in poetic structure and owing some of its tone to the rhetoric of praise poetry as composed by professional bards and other poets, perhaps, in the medieval periods (1200–1650). Ó Tuama sees lyric utterances as appearing at random, but, nevertheless, astonishing:

When my lady moves towards me on her path
the moon awakens and the sun shines forth
A honey mist spreads by night or day
On each side of the road as she makes her way

Such thematic material, he deduces, when taken together, can be seen to correspond most accurately to that of French and Provençal *chansons d'amour*, both literary and semi-popular of the thirteenth and fourteenth centuries. He points out that there are changes in it in response to Irish background and native literary traditions, notably praise poetry, and he notes that the images are often of a non-courtly, non-philosophic rural environment. As in the medieval prototype, the object of the man's love is sometimes married, thus making secret fantasy of the matter. Special names for the loved one like 'Little Dark Rose', or 'Pearl of the White Breast' are created, the man imagines her rescuing him from his love-sickness by a kiss, or by sleeping with him; there is no fear of sin in this. 'Non-courtly' motifs also appear in some of these songs – the lovers may contemplate marriage, poverty may be an issue – and the woman is addressed as the poet's equal (unlike the prototype with its feudal subservience). But present in the Irish lyrics is the *amour courtois* tenet that without woman's love God is unattainable, and only through woman's love can God be fully experienced.

The *Pastourelle* is also found in Irish folk-literature, a form cultivated by Provençe troubadours or northern French *trouvères*. This twelfth/thirteenth century French/Provençe theme is the opposite of the *amour courtois* ideal love: here the poet is of knightly social standing, meets a young girl, generally a shepherdess and attempts seduction; a love-debate ensues, she either yields to his advances or else resists and is raped, either way boosting the poet's macho prowess. This is the aristocratic prototype of the 'As I Roved Out' model of song both in French and in English, but in the latter the scene is modified to conclude safely in marriage. While many such songs may have entered Ireland in later centuries, a significant core appear to reflect closely the twelfth/thirteenth century French examples, no prototype for which appears to be extant in the English language. These songs in the Irish language include 'Seoladh na nGamhan', 'An Binsín Luachra', 'Eochaill', 'Risteard Ó Bruineann'. In such the Irish girl is likely to be plucking rushes or herding calves, in the French she is a shepherdess, but the general structural and verbal similarities between modern Irish examples and the medieval French texts are striking:

(a) The poet names the location where the adventure takes place:
*Antre Aras et Douai/*Between Arras and Douai.
*Sor la rive de Seine/*On the bank of the Seine.
*Idir Caiseal agus Dúrlas/*Between Cashel and Thurles
*Ar maidin inné cois Féile bhíos/*Yesterday morning by the River Feale I walked

(b) The poet makes physical advances to the girl he encounters, but she demurs:
*N'atouchies pas a mon chainse/*Do not touch my chemise
*Is é dúirt sí 'stad is ná strac mo chlóca'/*She said 'stop, don't tear my cloak'
*Alleiz vostre chamin/*Go on your way.
*Is dúirt sí liomsa, 'imthigh uaim'/*She said to me 'be on your way'

(c) The poet invites her to sleep with him – giving the lambs/calves the freedom of the meadows in the meantime:
*Que nous dormons lez a lez*/So we will sleep side by side
*si lessiez voz aigneaux pestre aval les prez*/and let your lambs graze down on the meadow
*. . . cead síneadh síos led' bháinchnis*/leave to stretch out by your white body
*Agus gheobhaimid na gamhna amáireach*/and we will find the calves tomorrow

(d) She says she is too young; she fears her parents:
*Trop per je sui jonete*/Because I am too young.
*Mar is maighdean mé ná táinig mh'aois*/Because I am a virgin, too young yet
*je n'os por mo pere*/I dare not for my father
*Och mo dhaidí féin go dúch insa mbaile*/Och my own daddy, disconsolate at home
*ní fhéadaimse teacht ina láthair*/I cannot appear in his presence

(e) The poet promises her the life style of a chatelaine:
*Dame seras d'un chastel*/You shall be chatelaine of a castle
*robes et biaux joiaus assez vos donrai*/dresses and a lot of fine jewels I shall give you
*Tá caisleáin gheala im choimeád 's teacht iarlaí im chúirt*/I own bright castles and earls visit my court
*Gheobhaidh tú athrú den fhaisiún sin a rún go fóill*/You will get a change of fashion yet, my love
*Gúnaí geala, sciortaí breaca, síoda agus sróill*/Bright gowns, dappled skirts, silk and satin

(f) When refused finally, the poet forces her violently into the sexual act:
*Couchai la a terre*/I laid her on the grass
*tout maintenant*/immediately
*levai li le chainse*/lifted up her chemise
*lou jeux d'amors sens atendre*/The game of love, without delay
*le fix per delit*/I engaged in with delight
*Lors me sembla que fusse en paradis*/Then it seemed to me I was in paradise
*In éineacht chun tailimh a treascradh sinn*/We both tumbled to the ground
*Rug mé greim gúna uirthi is leag mé ar an drúcht í*/I seized her dress and brought her to the dewy ground
*D'imríos cluiche den chleas nach neosfad ...*/I played a game of a business I'll not describe
*Do shaoil an ríoghain gurbh í tír na nÓg í*/The princess thought it was paradise

(g) She, exceptionally, wants him to repeat the sex act:
'*Faites le moi encor amis*'/Do it to me again, my love
*lors recomensai san demor*/at which I recommenced without delay
*le jeu k'elle m'avoit requis*/the game she had asked of me
*Shin agat cead saor, agus déin é arís*/You have my full permission, do it again
*Arís gan mhoill nuair d'éirigh liom do rinneas an scéal d'athnuachan*/Again, quite soon when I found it possible, I renewed the whole business

(h) The poet, exceptionally, declares (despite her pleadings) that he will never return to her again:
'*Revenés arier, biaus sire*'/'Come back fine sir'
*mais por tot l'or de l'empire*/but for all the gold of the empire
*ne fuisse tornes vers lors*/I would not return to her
*Is é dúirt mo stór liom filleadh arís*/My love declared I should return again
*Agus siúd mar a thréigeas féin mo bhuíon*
*Agus nár chastar im shlí go brath í*/And that's how I abandoned my loved one, and may we not meet again

The other major song type examined by Ó Tuama is the *Chanson de la Malmariée*, a women's monologue on the unsatisfactory state of the marriage, and her desire for some younger man. She typically tells her own story, is young, blames her parents for marrying her off to an older or unsuitable husband (humped, crippled, coughs, impotent, etc.), she declares her intention to run off with a young lover, she curses him and wishes him an early death. This was also a literary genre in France, composed by male trouvères. It is found in fifteenth- to sixteenth-century English broadsides, in sixteenth-century Scots, and in English and Scots folksong. Examples in Irish literary and folk composition (in the style of Merriman's *Midnight Court*) could date to anywhere between the thirteenth and eighteenth centuries.

The young woman's love lament, believed by some scholars to be the oldest type of love-song extant in the romance languages, was possibly the most popular song type before the advent of the *amour courtois* type, and was directly opposed to the sentiment portrayed by *trouvère* and troubadour who placed the man in anguish from unfulfilled love. The theme was used by the Normans in *carole* themes, versions of such song were sung in English and in French to dance-tunes in Kilkenny in the early fourteenth century. Already in Ireland however, before the Normans, was a highly-conscious and artistic tradition of the young woman's lyric – possibly the only type of love-lyric cultivated between 600 and 1200 AD – thus it is possible that a fusion of styles took place, but from a thematic analysis, it would seem that the Norman-French models had a large influence on the lyric in Irish folksong as it survives today. As distinct from the man's bawdy *chanson d'aventure* type song, amatory lingua franca is delicately deployed as a rule in the young woman's love-lament: images and metaphors referring to gardens, flowers, fruit-trees, dew, birds, music, musical instruments, nearly always have sexual connotations. There are innumerable examples of such in late medieval French and in English and Irish folksong:

(a) My garden is over-run, no flowers in it grew.

*Tá an gáirdín seo 'na fhásach, A mhíle grá bán, agus mise liom féin.*

This garden is a waste-land/dear loved one and I am alone.

(b) *A ce poyrier y a ung fruict/de le cueiller il est temps.*

On this pear-tree there is a fruit/it is time to pick it.

*Tá crann amuigh sa gháirdín le a bhfásann air sú craobh/Má baintear barr an bhlátha de ní fhásfaidh sé go héag.*

There is a tree outside in the garden on which raspberries flourish/if its flower is picked it will never grow.

(c) A maid again I shall never be, till an apple grows on an orange tree. (English folksong)

*I mo mhaighdean óg ní bheidh me go deo, nó go bhfásfaidh úlla ar adharca bó.*

A young virgin I shall never be/until apples grow on the horns of cows.

(d) The music motif is common to both the man's and woman's son

*jouns nous deux de cette cornemuse.*

Let us both play on this bagpipe.

*Tiocfaidh mo ghrá-sa le bánú an lae, is seinnfidh sé port a's is tig leis é*

My loved one will come with the dawn of day/ and he will strike up a tune, as well he is able.

Despite the fact that it seems quite likely that songs on the model of the young woman's love-lament were mostly composed (as in other countries) by male poets, the woman's voice is vividly represented in them. The best of them have a poetic quality of rare distinction. In these generally one finds a dramatic stance, and a tendency to develop the poem creatively from situation to situation (which is perfectly in accord with our oldest literary tradition of the dramatic monologue). These songs are frequently tense, nearer to life as lived, more assured in style, more finely structured than our other folk-lyrics. Douglas Hyde's *Love-songs of Connaught* has some remarkable examples of this type of song, supreme among them 'A Ógánaigh an chúil cheangailte':

Ringleted youth of my love
with thy locks bound loosely behind thee,
you passed by the road above,
but you never came in to find me;
where were the harm for you
if you came for a little to see me;
your kiss is a wakening dew
were I ever so ill or so dreamy...

So too is 'Dónall Óg' known throughout Ireland and in Gaelic Scotland, emphasising that the line between folksong and learned lyric can be fine:

'Dónall Óg', if you cross the ocean
take me with you, and don't forget,
and on market day you'll get your present:
a Greek King's daughter with you in bed!

Last night late the dog announced you
and the snipe announced you deep in the marsh.
You were ranging the woods, out there by your self.
May you lack a wife until you find me!

Other European love-song types found in Irish folk music are the *reverdie* (e.g. 'Fáinne Geal an Lae'/Dawning of the Day), *complainte*, and *chansons dialoguées*, fragments of *aube* (verse of 'Tá 'na Lá') and *serenade* (e.g. the opening verses of 'Éamonn an Chnoic').

The conclusion Seán Ó Tuama is led to from this analysis is that the models for presently known Irish folksong probably became established in Ireland after the Norman period (1200–1600). It is likely that the thematic material was transmitted directly from the French, and not via English, this before 1400. Irish love-song as we have it today emanates ultimately from the aristocratic medieval period, the models for much of our folk song may ultimately date to the thirteenth and fourteenth centuries, most of the songs sung, or in archives, today, were most likely composed between the sixteenth and eighteenth centuries by professional poets or poet-harpists of lower rank than bards. Compositions mirror aristocratic values, and are fusions of material shaped by French, English and Irish literary classes, predominantly the former. In Irish-speaking areas today many of these songs are considered to be 'na hamhráin mhóra' (great, or 'big' songs) representative of the high artistic point of Irish literary and musical culture, their rhythms have contributed to our dance music. This fulfils the comment by Richard Greene that many of our best love-songs are 'popular by destination' rather than 'popular by origin'. [This material is entirely sourced in, quotes at length and acknowledges Seán Ó Tuama's study *An Grá in Amhráin na nDaoine* (Love in Irish Folksong), originally published in 1960, reprinted in *Repossessions*, Cork University Press, 1995).

2. *Bob Quinn's thesis. Atlantean* was the title adopted by Bob Quinn for a 1984 series of three films and an accompanying book. The book was subtitled *Ireland's North African and Maritime Heritage* (1986). The *Atlantean* thesis argued against a narrow 'celtic' explanation for Ireland's distinctive culture, music and language. Using Connemara sean-nós singing as a starting point, it postulated a shared maritime culture on the Atlantic coasts of Europe beginning in Megalithic times and extending to the apex of European colonial divisiveness, the mid-nineteenth century. It suggested at least an affinity between Irish traditional music and those styles of music practised in Spain and the North African Mediterranean areas which were occupied by Islam for 700 years. Support for this view has been quoted from Seán Ó Riada and Charles Acton among others.

The thesis involved a broad survey of many disciplines and sources including: historical (Siege of Baltimore); linguistic (Heinrich Wagner's sub-stratum concept); religious (gnosticism in early Irish Christianity) etc. A fourth and concluding part of this film thesis, called *Navigatio – Atlantean 2* was completed in 1998. In this, the original speculation was developed into an overview of the relationship between central Europe and its peripheries. Quinn held that written sources were of limited value in unearthing the truths of history, certainly so in the middle ages where writing was not representative of the broad experience of humanity. Archaeology, though increasingly essential, was also limited in the sense that unearthed objects constitute a 'silent movie'. Quinn described language and music as providing a 'soundtrack' for history, thus introducing sean-nós singing.

First he demonstrated that the only difference between Connemara sean-nós and the singing of the Volga Bulghars (Tatarstan) is language, this opinion being supported by practitioners of each style. However, while it was clear that both were grounded in pentatonic form, it was conceded by the Tatars that the Connemara style was a little more adventurous: 'It goes for a walk', they said.

Quinn also postulated that the popular concept of the 'Dark Ages' was a Eurocentric fiction. It ignored the fact that, though the 'darkness' for 400 years after the demise of the Roman Empire (approx. 400 AD) may have applied to England, France and Germany, it did not apply to Arabic Spain or Ireland in their respective Golden Ages (711–1492 and 600–1000 AD). Using the Russian river and Black Sea exploits of the Vikings in combination with the music of the Volga Bulghars he argued that during this critical period, culture and civilisation had unceasingly flowed like a river round the edges of Europe (a fundamental concept of early Arab geographers). Quinn relied heavily on the original researches of Professor Sture Bolin (*Mohammed, Charlemagne and Ruric-Lund*, 1939) and the supportive ideas of Hodges and Whitehouse (*Mohammed, Charlemagne and the Origins of Europe*, 1989). These opposed the popular idea that Charlemagne 'rescued' civilisation. Using numismatic evidence Quinn showed that the Vikings became the agents for Muslim silver, samples of which can be found in Ireland and England but the main incidence of which is on the Baltic island of Gotland. An analogy was made between the cultural impact of the Arab 'dirhem' currency on the Europe of the eighth, ninth and tenth centuries and the cultural baggage that accompanies the equally pervasive American dollar today. Quinn's conclusion was that sean-nós singing is a cultural artefact and piece of evidence from this period as significant as, say, the *Book of Kells*, and should be treated with the same respect. (BOO)

**Sean-nós Cois Life.** See Ghradam Shean-Nós Cois Life.

**sean-nós dance.** See step dance, sean-nós.

**session.** A loose association of musicians who meet, generally, but not always, in a pub to play an unpredetermined selection, mainly of dance music, but sometimes with solo pieces such as slow airs or songs. There will be one or more 'core' musicians, and others who are less regular. It has become such an all pervasive form of traditional music performance that it has led many to believe that it has a much longer pedigree than is actually the case.

Irish dance music was performed solo in the past, a single instrument playing with no accompaniment, and this was the case up until the late nineteenth century. Playing together seems to have happened first largely among emigrant musicians in America, who in many cases were playing dance music for their own amusement or for theatre audiences, and not for dancers. The development of non-solo playing had two phases. Firstly an essentially solo musician playing with an accompanist, and secondly two or more melody musicians playing together. While there is some evidence of the bodhrán being used as accompaniment as early as the 1830s the concept was strongly reinforced when Irish music began to be recorded in America in the early 1900s. Accompaniment, normally piano, but occasionally guitar, very quickly became a standard feature of all 'solo' recordings. Genuine ensembles begin to feature around 1922, and they became one of the major features of recorded Irish music in the 78 era.

At home the development of ensemble playing was focused in the céilí band after the 1920s; this provided music for the newly developed céilí dances. These commercial forms of ensemble playing do not seem to have had much of an effect on amateur performance at this stage; that was still based on musicians playing individually, and still normally for dancers. The association with pubs is important, and it seems that the session developed at the same time as the pub became an important feature in Irish social life, this essentially a post-WW2 phenomenon.

It is almost impossible to give a precise date of birth for the pub session. In some areas, notably the Sliabh Luachra region of the Cork/Kerry border, there was traditional music in some pubs by the late 1930s, but within the country as a whole, this seems to have been ahead of its time by several decades. The concept was given a great boost by the music revival, where the idea of playing music for listening and not for dancing became important. An input from returning emigrants, particularly from England where sessions were a feature in Irish pubs from the late 1940s, also had a role to play. The fleadh cheoil from the early 1950s also helped to reinforce the importance of the session as musicians from different parts of the country met and swapped tunes.

Thus the session is essentially a phenomenon of the revival. Initially, sessions were a purely amateur event, and the most the musician could hope for was a complimentary drink. As the session became a standard aspect of Irish musical life, publicans, keen to have their bars known as centres of good music, began, from around the middle of the 1970s, to pay one or two musicians to turn up on a regular night, to ensure that a session would happen. If this 'seeding' worked, the publican was guaranteed a regular core of perhaps half a dozen musicians at a small cost. Almost all of the current regular sessions are based on this principle, but at festivals and other like events, sessions are still normally impromptu and non-commercial control.

Although to the outsider, a session appears to be a random event, where the instrumentation, the location, the duration, the number of musicians present, the music played etc., all seem to be highly variable, in fact there are controlling factors. The musical behaviour in a session is largely controlled by the relative status of the people playing, with the higher status musicians exercising more control over the way the session develops. Status is conferred by such factors as instrument played, ability, reputation, and age. The way in which musicians react to this is largely unconscious, but it is a useful tool in making sense out of what can seem to be a confusingly random series of events. The term 'session' seems to have been derived from the jazz-based term 'jam session' and was not originally applied to what we now call a session. Newspaper reports dating from before the 1970s tend to refer to 'impromptu concerts' but even by the mid-1960s fleadh musicians were already using the term 'session' freely among themselves in Ireland and Britain. (HAH)

**set dance**. A type of dance-tune composed or arranged by dancing masters to display to greatest advantage their own or their finest pupils' footwork skills. Such tunes were often in 2/4 time ('The Blackbird', 'King of the Fairies'), sometimes 9/8 ('Is the Big Man Within', 'The Barony Jig'), but generally resembled 6/8 double jigs ('Orange Rogue', 'St Patrick's Day') or 4/4 hornpipes ('Garden of Daisies', 'Job of Journeywork'). Typically the set dance might have a doubled first part, with a second part which leads back into repeating the first and is played only once. Some of them ('The Blackthorn Stick') have but one part, 'The Downfall of Paris' has four.

**'set' dance.** The term used to denote, literally, 'a set of quadrilles' and comprises a combination of Irish dancing steps and French dance movements, danced to Irish music. The dances were developed by eighteenth-century dancing-masters who travelled in various parts of Ireland. They originally had taught solo step dancing and created group or figure dances for their less talented pupils. In time they also included new dances such as the minuet, cotillions and quadrilles. These were brought from France, first to England and later to Scotland and Ireland by military personnel and other travellers of the time. The dancing-masters first taught

In the 'set' at Dan O'Connell's bar at Knocknagree, Co. Kerry, 1996 (EDI)

them to the upper classes in the big country houses and later to the ordinary people, in kitchens, barns or at the crossroads in summer. They taught the new dances to the music of their area, using steps already familiar to themselves and their pupils. In this way, sets danced to polkas, slides, reels, jigs and hornpipes evolved where those music forms were popular.

The movements of the sets can be traced back to 1723, to French folk dances called cotillions. These reached England by 1770 and were seen in Ireland by traveller and writer Arthur Young between 1776 and 1779. Many variations of the cotillion declined, but one variation, the quadrille, developed separately to become the most popular dance of its time in Paris. Described by a dancing-master named Hänsel in 1775 as a 'Minuet en quatre' or 'Minuet en huit', it reached England, Scotland and Ireland around 1816. Dozens of quadrilles existed. At popular dances, a selection of any four, five or six quadrilles were chosen by the MC for each dance and certain favourites became fixed into sets of quadrilles.

The most popular set of quadrilles became known as the 'first set' of quadrilles. It is similar to many of our quadrille sets of today, the Down quadrilles, the plain sets (Clare), the Corofin set (Clare), the Fermanagh quadrille set, the Valentia set (Kerry) and the Newmarket plain set (Cork) being closest.

The second set of quadrilles was the Lancer quadrilles (1820), said by historian Curt Sachs to have been composed for a Lancer Regiment based in Dublin. Many of the Lancer sets danced in Ireland today bear a close resemblance to this original, most notably the Down Lancers and the Clare Lancers. Most other Lancer sets have some typical Lancer features, such as a line up, grand chain and dancing in the corners.

The third set of quadrilles is called the Caledonian, found in Clare and Down, but different in each. The Clare example was brought by nineteenth-century Scottish military or workers and is found also in Scotland. In all of these the original footwork and body carriage has been substituted by Irish step dance practice.

Irish sets have most likely evolved from these or from other quadrilles that are no longer popularly danced. Today, most of the sets are named after their local town or area. An exception is the 'Jenny Lind', or 'Ginnie Ling' set, various versions of which are danced throughout Cork. It is named in honour of Swedish singer Jenny Lind.

Historically, 'set' dancing has been frowned upon by religious authorities of all denominations. Set dancing had been banned too by the Gaelic League in the early twentieth century and new 'céilí' dances were taught by the Dancing Commission, and promoted at local community dances. Set dancing therefore declined, but survived, particularly in the Munster counties. It has enjoyed a remarkable revival all over Ireland throughout the late twentieth century, attributable to the work of individual set-dance teachers, and also to CCÉ and the GAA network of set-dance competitions since the 1970s. The pioneering dancing-masters since the 1970s include Connie Ryan of Tipperary (who travelled the world teaching sets) and Joe and Siobhán O'Donovan of Cork, the first set-dancing teachers at the Willie Clancy Summer School. Along with the local people who passed on the revived sets, these have greatly inspired the present dancing generation, which is now catered for by summer schools, festivals, workshops, céilís and classes worldwide. Set dance has many organisers and teachers in Ireland and in Britain, foremost among these are Brooks' Academy in Dublin, and the Belfast and District Set Dancing and Traditional Music Society. (PAM)

Recordings of music for set dancing include Na Píobairí Uilleann's *Music for the Sets* and Scadna's *Set Dances of Ireland*. Set dancing is heard vividly on Tony MacMahon and Noel Hill's album *I gCnoc na Graí*. Terry Moylan, Pat Murphy, Eileen O'Doherty, Joe O'Donovan and Willie Hammond have all published detailed instruction on set dance.

**set-dance bands.** Demand for live music for dancing grew in the wake of the set-dancing renaissance of the late 1970s and early 1980s. Many musicians had never before played for dancing, and some adapted better than others to this demand, particularly in the matter of pace and tune type. Céilí bands such as the Tulla and the Kilfenora, which had been in decline for some time, received a new lease of life. In other cases, bands were formed with the express purpose of providing music for set dancers. Among these were the Temple House and the Moving Cloud. The céilí band format remained largely unchanged, with 'traditional' instruments, such as fiddle, accordion, flute and banjo accompanied by a rhythm section of piano and drums, the upright piano of old generally being replaced by its electronic counterpart. However, with developments in amplification technology, large bands were no longer essential. Smaller outfits, such as the accordion/guitar duo Begley and Cooney, were accepted with enthusiasm by dancers. Fees ranged from complimentary drinks for local musicians to perhaps £1,000 for one of the bigger bands. The relative decline in set dancing activity which began in the mid-1990s led to a corresponding reduction in demand for live bands. However, the more established bands still remain popular. (PAA)

See céilí bands; céilí dance.

**Shanachie.** Record label founded in 1972 by Daniel Michael Collins and Richard Nevins. American based, it has played a key role in promoting Irish traditional music. Shanachie started out in the Bronx, expansion prompted relocation to Ho-Ho-Kus and then to Newton, New Jersey. It has distributed all kinds of Irish material, but has made many important original recordings of present-day traditional musicians including James Kelly and Paddy O'Brien. Its catalogue presently features over 500 recordings, ranging from Irish music (its founding speciality) to traditional blues, 'world' music (Yazoo, bought in 1975), to contemporary jazz (Cachet, an imprint), and singer-songwriter. Today the company is co-owned by Collins, Nevins, and Koch International, which handles distribution. Irish artists include Solas, Tommy Makem, Phil Coulter, De Dannan, Séamus Egan, Joe Derrane, Cathie Ryan, and the Wolfe Tones. (EAH)

**Shannon, Joe.** (1919– ). Uilleann pipes. Born near Kiltimagh, Co. Mayo, he and seven older brothers played music; they were cousins of piper Eddie Mullaney whom Joe first heard shortly after the family moved to Chicago in 1929. Mullaney's encouragement, and the loan of a practice set from flute player Paddy Doran, led Joe to take up pipes while still in primary school. 'I was so small I had to stuff books around my stomach to keep the pipes from falling off me!' Pipe maker Patrick Hennelly made him his first full set, and in 1934 Joe played with Pat Roche for the Chicago World's Fair. He played all over the city until family and work pressure as a fireman forced him to retire but he was lured back by Mullaney's gift to him in 1967 of his 1880 Taylor set of pipes. Patsy Touhey and Chicago-born Tom Ennis were Shannon's stylistic models, vaudeville piper Charles McNurney advised him on Touhey's technique which he can reproduce note-for-note, chord-for-chord, yet, he is closest in style to Tom Ennis. He was impressed by Leo Rowsome too. Considered as having an 'American' style, typically his playing has frequent staccato triplets interspersed with single rolls, double-cut rolls, trills, crans and single and double grace notes rendered with generally legato phrasing. His articulation of jigs is more staccato than with reels and hornpipes. He uses regulators occasionally to heighten contrast; each tune is approached differently. He appears on the recordings *Irish Traditional Instrumental Music in Chicago* and *The Noonday Feast*. He was a featured artist at the Smithsonian Festival of American Folklife in 1976 and received the National Heritage Fellowship Award in 1983 from the National Endowment for the Arts. (LAM)

**Shannon, Sharon.** (1968– ). Accordion, fiddle. Born in east Co. Clare, her brother Garry (flute) introduced her and her sisters Majella and Mary to music when she was six. Her father played Jew's harp, he and her mother danced; both sets of grandparents played concertinas – her father's parents from Wellbrook, Corofin, her mother's from Ballinacally, near Kildysart. Sharon was taught whistle by Tony Linnane, later moving on to accordion. Frank Custy's Friday night céilís in Toonagh were the academy – dancing sets and playing for dancers. In her early teenage years she gigged with showband-style groups for sets, jiving and waltzes, and was in school with the Custys (fiddlers), Siobhán Peoples and singer Maura O'Connell. In college at UCC she played with Aidan Coffey, Matt Cranitch and Dave Hennessy, and took up fiddle. She moved to Doolin, Co. Clare for gigs where Micho Russell was a great friend. She began touring with the music for Behan's *The Hostage* at the Druid Theatre in Galway, joined Johnny Ringo McDonough in Arcady, and sessioned weekly with Seán, Breda and Cora Smith at Winkles' Hotel in Kinvarra. Playing with the Waterboys (modern music) brought her to festivals all over Europe and led to her solo recording in 1990. Rooted in a steady, contemplative and highly rhythmic traditional style, she branches into swing, Cajun, French Canada, Cape Breton. Her own band in the late 1990s had sister Mary (banjo, fiddle, bouzouki), Galvin Ralston (guitar, son of Kerry singer Jós Begley), and Sligo bass player James Blennerhassett.

**Sherlock, Roger.** (1932– ). Born at Cloonfeightrin, Co. Mayo, close to Gurteen, Co. Sligo. Encouraged by his grandfather, he began playing Clarke whistle while still at school, absorbing repertoire from such fiddle players as Pack Spellman, John Henry, Pat Kelleher, and particularly flute player Paddy 'Jim Frank' Hunt. He emigrated to London in 1953, there playing with all the great names of Irish music exile of the 1950s–60s – in particular Michael Gorman and Margaret Barry, Jimmy Power, Paddy Taylor, Bobby Casey and Willie Clancy, Máirtín Byrnes. He recorded with accordion player Kit O'Connor for Raidió Éireann's *Job of Journeywork*, this introducing his name, and original style back in Ireland. He worked at fitting out bars for Kerry entrepreneur John Byrnes, often performing in his halls by night with the Dunloe, Hibernian and Thatch céilí bands. He played too in The Favourite bar with such as Raymond Roland (accordion), Vincent Griffin, Seán Maguire, Liam Farrell and Brendan McGlinchey (fiddles). He returned to live in Ireland at Balbriggan in 1996.

**Shields, Hugh.** (1929– ) Singer, collector, researcher. Born in Belfast, he studied Medieval French and taught at TCD. He has collected and studied traditional music in Ireland and in France from the 1950s and has published many articles and sound recordings. His best-known works are *Shamrock Rose and Thistle: Folk Singing in North Derry* (1981), *Old Dublin Songs* (1988) and *Narrative Singing in Ireland* (1993). His major work has been the editing and selection of the Goodman collection, published as *Tunes from the Munster Pipers vol. 1* (1998).

**singing festivals.** See song, festivals.

**Sky, Patrick.** (1940– ). Singer, uilleann piper, writer. Born at College Park, Georgia, USA, he began singing and playing five-string banjo, guitar, bouzouki and uilleann pipes in 1959, making solo albums with MGM and Vanguard and performing throughout the 1960s. With Lisa Null he founded Green Linnet records in 1972, now a leading label in popular Irish music. For that label he produced *Séamus Ennis – Forty Years of Irish Piping; Tommy Reck – A Stone in the Field*; *Tim Lyons – Easter Snow*; *Joy Ryan and Eddie Clark*, and many others. He has produced another fifty albums for other labels also. He has an MA in Cultural Studies and Folklore, from the University of North Carolina, his thesis became the introduction for the re-release of the nineteenth-century tune book *Ryan's Mammoth Collection*. In 1980 he published *A Manual for the Uilleann Pipes* and in 1997 he republished and re-constructed the 1804 *O'Farrell's National Irish Music for the Union Pipes*.

**Slattery's (Paddy).** Capel Street, Dublin bar which from 1968 hosted 'The Tradition Club', in the process becoming a major centre for traditional music in Dublin.
　See Tradition Club.

**Sliabh Luachra.** Literally 'the rushy mountain', this is a definitive style of music, 'a state of mind' (Con Houlihan) and a loose geographic area found on both sides of the Cork–Kerry border. Its centre could be said to be between the towns of Killarney, Rathmore, Millstreet, Ballydesmond and Castleisland. It had a noted literary tradition (Aodhagán Ó Rathaile, Eoghan Rua Ó Suilleabháin) and its most famous music personality was Pádraig O'Keeffe – the last of the fiddle-masters. Nowadays it takes in a large part of east Kerry, north Cork and west Limerick and is identified with those places where the Sliabh Luachra musical style is prevalent.
*style*. This style has certain hallmarks – local tunes played and danced to in a particular way including slides (jigs in 12/8 time) and polkas. There is a large body of local tunes not played elsewhere except where they may have spread from Sliabh Luachra, and there are distinctive local versions of tunes well known nationally. The fiddle and accordion are by far the most common instruments and a common practice was for one fiddle in a duet to play an octave lower than the other (bassing). Lightness, liquidity, rhythmic, warmth, are some of the descriptions which have been applied to this style in relation to the dance music and there was also a strong and vibrant tradition of slow-air playing. Some of the famous players in what has been called a 'golden era' of Sliabh Luachra music are Pádraig O'Keeffe, Denis Murphy, Julia Clifford, Paddy Cronin, Johnny Cronin,

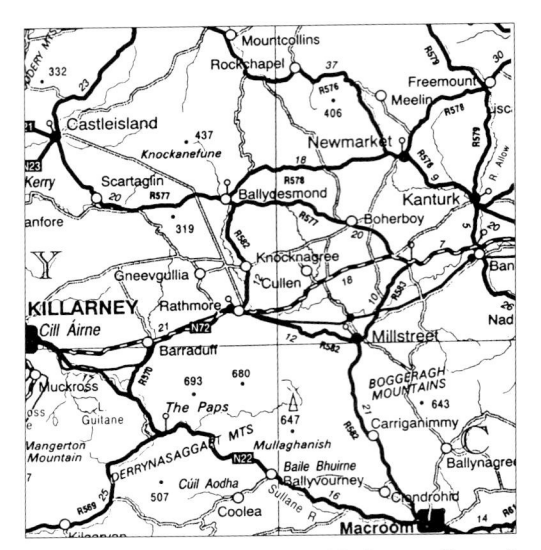

The Sliabh Luachra area    (Ordnance Survey)

Jerry McCarthy, Mickey Duggan and Maurice O'Keeffe (all fiddle players) as well as Johnny O'Leary and Dan O'Herlihy (accordion). Sets have been danced here since the end of the last century. Particularly strong is the stylistic legacy of fiddler and teacher Pádraig O'Keeffe. Already having guru status by the time of his death in 1963, he himself had been more fond of reels and airs, more fastidious about melody and detail, and had invented his own form of staff notation to teach tunes. Two of his best-known fiddle pupils from the late 1920s were Julia Clifford and Denis Murphy, of Lisheen, Co. Kerry. They carried his music abroad to London and New York respectively, and at Séamus Ennis's instigation in 1952 recorded with their mentor the material which was eventually wound on to the seminal *Kerry Fiddles* Topic album in the 1970s (available now on Ossian). Claddagh's *Star above the Garter* is the other symbolic album from the area, and CDs of Denis Murphy, Pádraig O'Keefe and accordionist Johnny O'Leary complete the music testament of this major style-region. Festivals of music commemorate these iconic figures annually. (PEB)

**slide.** See jig.

**slip jig.** See jig.

**Slógadh.** A performance/competition series done through the medium of the Irish language, begun by Gael-Linn in 1969. It includes music ensembles and set dancing. As a performance format it has contributed significantly to inspiring young people all over the island, and its competition series is, along with the Fleadh Cheoil, regarded as an important focus for achievement rating among young groups.

**slow air**. A piece of music in various metres, but generally adhering strictly to none, the slow air is an 'open-ended' melodic formula which has great similarity to the performance of sean-nós song. Often a slow air will be simply the air of an existing song (e.g. 'Dear Irish Boy', 'May Morning Dew', 'Wounded Huzzar', 'Anach Chuain' etc.), but a large number of classic pieces (including 'Lament for Staker Wallace', 'O'Donnell's Lament', 'Gol na mBan san Ár') appear independent of any original song. Many players and competition adjudicators insist that to impart correct phrasing, one must listen to the sung version of the air (if it exists), but players will often adjust even that to suit either their own hearing of the piece, or the qualities of their instrument. Harp players have the facility for harmonic accompaniment, pipe players likewise use regulators to great effect, accordion and concertina players explore similiar harmonic possibilities afforded by the absence of hurry. The slow air is played solo, is executed differently on different instruments and individual players' interpretations of it vary considerably too. Pipes lend themselves to a peculiar vibrato which is unacceptable on fiddle, flute can use a varying pulse related to use of diaphragm and embouchure, accordion can utilise its technical facilities and variance in pressure to great dramatic effect. Harp demands another set of characteristics since its notes are separate and diminishing. But the basic aesthetic is absence of regular metre, vibrato, ornament and excessive trills. Variation is acceptable if not desirable; this may be in tempo, ornament, metre, dynamics or may involve minute pitch change (on flute and fiddle). Some players favour great, florid rushing passages; others are minimalist. One is not complimented for fingering and ornamentation in slow air playing; it is emotion, or mediation of it, which is the desirable quality.

Mo Mhúirnín Bán  (Tomás Ó Canainn, Ossian)

The slow air is eminently suited to uilleann pipes, and is usually part of the piper's repertoire, much less often is it found in that of the fiddler, demanding, as the air's qualifications do, a steady, unwavering tone. Circumstances, venue, audience attention and empathy are all vital ingredients. Context is important too, and so many players simply do not bother with this type of tune. The slow air remains the least practised of the tune-types, this is as much a product of the inclement conditions of much session playing as it is of the impatience and/or technical levels of younger players. Slow airs can be heard on a large number of albums, and while by their nature, they are acquired orally, many, however, appear in print, the most ambitious collection being Tomás Ó Canainn's *Traditional Slow Airs of Ireland* which backs transcriptions with played examples of a hundred tunes on cassette.

While this type of tune is self-contained, players have become accustomed to following it immediately with a dance tune. This may indicate a lack of confidence in the slow air as a vehicle for expression of instrumental expertise, or it may be that the player wishes to demonstrate another level of expertise – especially if the playing occasion affords only a single set. This fashion of hitching on a jig or reel is noted by commentators both within and without traditional music. Reviewing Paddy Tunney's *The Mountain Streams* album in *Irish Folk Music Studies* 3 (1981), Tom Munnelly says:

> An idiosyncracy of Paddy's is 'tacking on' pieces of lilting to many songs. Frequently, as with 'The Blackbird' and 'Ballinderry', this has the effect of completely destroying the mood created by the foregoing song. Perhaps this intrusive habit has been acquired from instrumental performers who follow slow airs with a fast reel or jig, almost by way of apology.

**Small, Jackie.** (1946– ). Set-dance, pipes, fiddle, accordion. Best known as a radio broadcaster, Jackie Small has had a wide-ranging career as a researcher, collector, and performer. Born in Galway of Irish-speaking parents, his grandfather, Seán Rua Ó Beaglach, was a noted seanchaí. His father was a country tailor who sang in Irish and in English, and played melodeon, mouth-organ, and Jew's harp. In his late teens Jackie was taught tin whistle by Pádraig Ó Carra; in Dublin in the early 1970s he studied uilleann pipes with Pat Mitchell with whom in 1986 he was co-author of *The Piping of Patsy Touhey*. Introduced to NPU, he collaborated with its founder, Breandán Breathnach, on the collector's thematic index of Irish dance tunes. Currently he is editor of Breathnach's dance music series *Ceol Rince na hÉireann* (vol. 4 in 1997, vol. 5 due in 1999).

From 1983–91 he was an archivist and music collector with the folk music section of the Department of Irish Folklore at University College Dublin. There his projects included commercial releases of the music of uilleann piper Johnny Doran and of Donegal fiddle-player Mickey Doherty. His broadcasting work has largely been in association with Harry Bradshaw for RTÉ Radio 1: his 1987 radio documentary *The Dance Music of Ireland* outlined in sixteen parts the historical and cultural background of Irish dance music; from 1988 to 1990 he was the weekly presenter of *The Long Note,* this series including a two-part documentary on Johnny Doran. In recent years Small has worked for many bodies and institutions, among them An Gúm, and the Irish Traditional Music Archive where his work has included music collecting and consultancy, computer notation and setting. His publications include detailed sleeve-notes for many commercial sound releases.

**snare drum.** A small, metal-frame drum some 25 cm deep and 35 cm diameter, it has a skin on both heads, with the addition on the bottom of a (lever-controlled) stretched, multiple-wire, 'snare', which, when engaged, gives a buzzing quality to the music. It is played in a combination of single, double, triple and ornamented beats with two knobbed-end sticks, sometimes with brush-end sticks, its purpose in céilí bands was to develop rhythm. Older drums (for instance that in the Rising Sun Céilí Band in Killavel) were often locally made with plywood shells, mostly however the snare shell is of metal. The drum's origin is probably in 400–500 AD Syria, Egypt and Iraq arriving to Europe through military use, but it has been for almost a century part of the standard jazz/dance-band drum kit adopted by Irish céilí bands.

**song.**
The major song types found in Irish music are 1. historic 'lays', 2. fictional 'ballads', 3. documentary 'come-all-yes' and 4. 'lyric song' in Irish (sean-nós).

*metres.* While undoubtedly very much older, Gaelic song metres come to the fore in popular song, and as a literary medium for Gaelic poetry from the sixteenth century onward. An understanding of its metre and rhyming conventions is essential for the authentic performance or appreciation of Irish folksong or for the competent instrumental rendition of song melodies. The determining principle is the number of stresses in each line. However, rather than rhyming line-ends, the distinctive characteristic of Gaelic song is that vowel sounds on some or all of the stresses in a line are repeated in corresponding lines in the same verse. Thus simple or more complicated assonant (i.e. rhyming vowel sounds without rhyming consonants) patterns are created and are very musical in effect when sung. While the metres and assonant rhyming used in Gaelic song are many and various, the following verse from 'Sliabh Geal gCua' is offered as a simple illustration. If the unstressed syllables are represented by X and the following broad vowels:

(aw) as in str**aw**
(ow) as in c**ow**
(ay) as in d**ay**
(ee) as in m**ee**t,

The verse scheme could be illustrated as follows:

X/(aw)X/(ow)X/(ay)X/
X/(aw)X/(ow)X/(ay)X/
X/(aw)X/(ow)X/(ay)X/
X/(ay)X/(ee)
X/(aw)X/(ee)X(ay)X/
X/(aw)X/(ee)X(ay)X/
X/(aw)X/(ee)X(ay)X/
X/(ay)X/(ee)

Mo ghrá-sa th**a**ll na D**é**ise
Idir b**á**nta gle**a**nnta sl**éi**bhte
O sh**á**mhas an**o**nn thar tr**éa**nmhuir
Tá c**éa**sta gan bhr**í**
Ach o b'**á**il le D**ia** mé ghla**o**ch as
Mo shl**á**n-sa s**ia**r go hÉireann
Is sl**á**n le Sl**ia**bh na F**éi**le
Le s**ao**rghean óm chr**oí**

(Pádraig Ó Miléadha)

There is a tendency among some traditional singers to emphasise the assonant stress very strongly; this probably contributed to frequent attempts to compose songs in English according to the native conventions to which the ear had become accustomed:

X/(ee)X/(oo)X/(ee)X/(oo)X/
X/(ee)X/(oo)X/XX/(i)

The sw**ee**t impr**o**ve**me**nts they would am**u**se you
The tr**ee**s are dr**oo**ping with fruit all k**i**nd
The b**ee**s perf**u**ming the f**ie**lds with m**u**sic
Which y**ie**lds more be**au**ty to Castleh**y**de

In the literary song, assonant music can become very rich and complex. In the song 'Im Aonar Seal' the poet Eoghan Rua Ó Súilleabháin employed the very straightforward, though ambitious, scheme of eight stresses in every line where every line is a song of eight verses and follows the assonantal pattern:

ay, a, oo, ee, oo, ee, ay, o

Im **ao**nar s**ea**l ag si**ú**l a bh**í**os i dt**ú**s o**í**che i ng**ao**rthaibh c**eo**
Lem th**ao**bh gur dh**ea**cas f**io**nnr**í**on ag **io**nsaí go s**éi**mh ar s**eo**l
A c**éi**bh ar f**u**d ina b**ú**chla**í**bh ag t**á**irt s**í**os ar sc**éi**mh an **ó**ir
Go cr**ao**bhach c**a**sta ci**ú**mhais-bhi**ú** ina f**ú**nnsa**í**bh go b**é**al a br**ó**g

*regional singing style*. Although this is often mentioned and its demise frequently predicted or lamented, it has seldom been described and never fully defined. While it is reasonably easy to recognise the vocal styles of the major regions of Donegal, Connemara and Munster, it is much easier to recognise an individual voice than to place an unknown one in a regional context. The topic is so complex that present understanding could quickly be transformed by a researcher in possession of an adequate set of analytical tools. It is possible that the easiest to recognise of Irish singing styles is that of travellers – those without a region. Typically high-pitched and hard-edged, placed far back in the throat and with a slightly nasal tone, perhaps the most obvious features are tone and accent and what Tom Munnelly has called the 'exaggerated glottal stopping at phrase endings'. At the same time it is possible to find settled singers with some or all of the same characteristics. However, regional styles must exist, just as do regional accents and dialects, and these latter, together with personal habit, temper every performance in advance of any consideration of regional singing style.

Comparisons are most often made from the single perspective of 'melisma' – the amount of melodic ornament used. In these terms, regional differences of style in sean-nós singing have been described by Tomas Ó Canainn: 'a very florid line in Connacht, contrasting with a somewhat less decorated one in the south and, by comparison, a stark simplicity in the Northern songs'. However this ignores other stylistic factors, especially, in the north, the artistic effect produced by variations of tempo and by stops – rhythmic rather than melodic ornament. Vocal quality may be altered too, and melodic changes – structural rather than decorative – sometimes substitute one note for another, or split a single melody note into two or more notes. Some use of these dimensions has been attempted by Janice Maloney-Brooks and Julie Henigan in order to describe Donegal singing in general and that of Neilidh Ní Dhomhnaill in particular, but their application to practise elsewhere has been slight, though Seóirse Bodley mentions vocal quality and rhythmic variation in describing Connemara singing. Hence, no firm comparisons can be made. Although the examples and articles cited have drawn their data from singing in Irish, regional singing style in English is similar to that of Irish singing in the same region. At present, due to a variety of factors, especially modern communication methods and the fact that singers no longer learn songs mainly from their own regions, distinctions may become blurred. This is not as threatening, however, to the continuance of regional style as the tendency for singers to adopt the styles of the American singer of country music or of the conservatoire. (JOM)

*hedge schoolmaster song*. This is a species of Anglo-Irish folksong most conspicuously characterised by its use of classical and biblical allusion, Latinate and sometimes florid or hyperbolic vocabulary, and often by the use of certain Irish verse forms – particularly ochtfhochlach, which is marked by its metrically distinctive assonantal rhyme scheme. The songs are so called because of their initial association with the hedge schoolmasters of the eighteenth and nineteenth centuries. An example of a hedge schoolmaster song in ochtfhochlach is 'The Boys of Mullaghbawn':

Now to end my lamentation, we are all in
    consternation,
For want of education, I now must end my
    song,
Since without hesitation, we are charged with
    combination,
And sent for transportation from the hills of
    Mullaghbawn.

The songs are also typified by their exploitation of certain Irish and continental poetic genres, such as the aisling, or 'vision poem'; the reverdie, a French form in which the narrator describes the delights of springtime, and usually of a woman encountered among them; the conflictus, a medieval Latin form in which two parties debate the virtues of their respective religious or moral perspectives; and the geographical encomium, celebrating the glories of a locality or property. An example of the hedge schoolmaster reverdie is 'Lough Erne's Shore':

One morning as I went a-fowling, bright
    Phoebus adornèd the plain,
It was down by the banks of Lough Erne I met
    with this wonderful dame,
Her voice was so sweet and so pleasing, these
    beautiful notes she did sing.
The innocent fowl of the forest their love unto
    her they did bring.

Some of the songs in this category display genuine poetic skill, subtlety, and erudition; others, revealing negligible skill and only the trappings of learning, give way, in their use of pedantic verbiage and over-indulgence in classical allusion, to what, as in 'The Colleen Rue', Frank O'Connor termed 'Babu English':

Oh, were I Hector that noble victor who died a
    victim to Grecian skill,
Or were I Paris whose deeds are various an
    arbitrator on Ida's hill,
I'd range through Asia, likewise Arabia,
    Pennsylvania seeking for you,
The burning raygions like sage Orpheus to see
    your face, my sweet Colleen Rue.

The term may be applied with equal validity, however, to any song which exhibits the stylistic features common to the genre, whether composed by an actual hedge schoolmaster, a broadsheet hack, or a latter-day parodist. 'Moorlough Mary', 'Old Arboe', 'Castlehyde', 'Erin's Green Shore', and 'In Praise of the City of Mullingar' are some of the better-known examples of the genre. (JUH)

*macaronic song*. In the Irish experience this is song with every other line, group of lines or verse in Irish and English. John Addington Symonds called the macaronic song 'a spavined Pegasus, a showy hack stumbling on the bypaths of Parnassus'. He was referring to maccaronea, a sub-species of the genre, which came into fashion in Italy in the fifteenth century with the writings of Odassi, Fossa and especially Teofilo Folengo. Symonds described this Italian macaronic verse as follows:

> The jargon must consist of the vernacular, suited with Latin terminations and freely mingled with classical Latin words . . . The name by which it was known indicates its composition. As macaroni is dressed with cheese and butter, so the macaronic poet mixed colloquial expressions of the people with classical Latin, serving up a dish that satisfies the appetite by rarity and richness of concoction. At the same time, since macaroni was the special dish of the proletariat and since a stupid fellow was called a maccherone, the ineptitude and vulgarity of the species are indicated by its title.

Folengo's word was, after his day, applied to verse in which one finds a mixture of languages or dialects, correctly used in accordance with the prevailing rules of grammar and syntax. This kind of macaronic verse is ancient and belongs to bilingual communities. It was prevalent too when scholars decided to have a little fun with both the vernacular and the language of the learned. Lucretius was mixing his languages and his dialects in ancient Rome:

> Nigra melicrus est, inmunda et fetida acosmos,
> caesia Palladium nervosa et hgnea dorcas,
> parvula, pumilio, chariton mia, tota marum sal,
> magna atque inmanis cataplexis plenaque
>     honoris . . .

The Gildian Lorica is to a large extent a collection of as many obscure foreign and archaic words as the author could scrape together. Hebrew, Greek and Latin are mingled in a curious mishmash and are so corrupted that their meaning can only be divined with the help of the glosses.

The macaronics of the cloister are one of the glories of early English poetry, a poetry influenced by Irish monks who were composing beautiful hymns in honour of saints, and loricas against disease, since the seventh century. This is a part of a lorica against the yellow fever, attributed to St Colmán (*c.* 644). The American scholar, W. O. Wehrle, thought that Cynewulf may well have modelled the concluding lines of the Phoenix on it:

> Regem regum rogarnus in nostris sermonibus,
> anacht noe a luchtlach diluui temporibus
> Melchisedech rex salem incerto de semine
> ron soerat a airnighe ab onmi formidine.
> Soter soerus loth di thein qui per secula habetur
> ut nos omnes precamur liberare dignetur
> Abram de ur na galdai snaidsium ruri ronsnada
> saersum soerus in popul limpa fontis ingaba

This type of macaronic verse persisted in the literatures of western Europe until the decline of Latin in the seventeenth century. It gained impetus from the compositions of the *scolares vagantes*, 'those irresponsible college graduates and lighthearted vagabonds who were equally at home in alehouses, in hall, in market-place or in cloister ... if they compelled the rude folksong to conform to the metres of the Latin hymns they compensated for this by reducing to these same simple metres the artistically fashioned stanza of highly-wrought spiritual songs, as well as by introducing the popular refrain into lyrics of every kind'.

Seán Ó Tuama has shown in *An Grá in Amhrán na nDaoine* how strong the influence of medieval France was on folksong in the Irish language. The influence likely persisted too in the macaronic songs of the nineteenth century; the striking echoes of the medieval in the construction of the macaronics of the later period simply cannot be ignored or dismissed as mere coincidence. We find in both periods:

(a) The line in which two languages lie side by side:
> Dieu qui fustes coronné cum acuta spina
> De votre peuple eiez pitie, gratia divina,
> Que le siecle soit aleggé de tali ruina!

> My reed was out of order is do tháinig as mo bheilteanna
> And then she said 'my darling, ná fág anois le feirg mé;

(b) The song in which the language changes in alternate verses:
> Tho Judas Jesum founde
> donque ly beysa;
> He wes bete ant bounde,
> que nus tous fourma;

> I am a young fellow that ran out of my land and means,
> Seanamhná an bhaile ná tabharfadh dom bean ná spré
> I placed my affections on one who had gold and store,
> Is gur gheallas don ainnir go leanfainn léi féin go deo.

(c) The lines in regular patterns – 2A + 2B; 4A + 4B etc.:
> L'en puet fere et defere,
> Ceo fait-il trop sovent;
> It his nouther wel ne faire,
> Therefore Engelond is shent.
> Nostre prince de Engletere,
> Par le consail de sa gent,
> At Westminster after the feire
> Made a gret parlement.

> Tá fleet bhreá Fhrancach ag teacht faoi ardbhrat
> Anall thar sáile do chabhródh linn,
> Our Catholic boys will, without alarm,
> Break the cursed laws of old tyranny.
> Béimid go dílis inár suí i dtábhairní
> Ag ól fíon Spáinneach, ag glaoch na dí;
> Those cruel demons we will de-feat them,
> And our loyal heroes will have liberty.

(d) The macaronic coda:
> This freyer began the nunne to grope
> Inducas, inducas,
> was a morsell for the pope,
> In tentationibus

> Aréir cois na habhann ag taisteal do bhíos,
> In silence I rambled in raptures of glee,
> Is ea do dhearcas an ainnir chiúin mhaiseamhail mhín,
> Agus fágaimís siúd mar atá sé

(e) Songs in which words or phrases are scattered in a seemingly haphazard fashion. But the phrases in the second language become an ornament rather than a detriment to the songs:
> Onmes gentes plaudite,
> I saw many birds sitting on a tree;
> They took Right and flew away,
> With ego dixi, have a good day.

> Lá breá gréine is mé ag dul go hEochaill,
> With locks and curls upon the way,
> I met a comrade, a handsome buachaill
> Ba é Muiris Óg Mac Dáith Uí Shé
> 'O Kate,' says he, 'a chailín álainn,
> Bímis páirteach and never say
> Go bhfaigheadh do mháthair cliamhain níos breátha
> Ná Muiris óg mac Dáith Uí Shé'

(f) The macaronic paraphrase:
>    Amor est quedam mentis insania
>    Que vagum hominem ducit per deuia,
>    Sitit delicias et bibit tristia
>    Crebris doloribus commiscens gaudia.
>
>    Amur est une pensée enragée
>    Ke le vdif humme meyne par veie deueye
>    Ke a soyf de defices e ne beyt ke tristesces
>    Ed od souuens dolurs medle sa ioliesces.
>
>    Loue is a selkud wodenesse
>    That the idel mon ledeth by wildemeese,
>    That thurstes of wilfulschipe and drinketh sorwenesse
>    And with lomful sorwes menget his blithnesse.
>
>    Cois leasa do thógas bord go beacht
>    Um nóin roimh threascairt gréine,
>    Gan beatha dom shróin ná coróin im ghlaic
>    Ná cóir ar bha le haoireacht:
>    Is ea do theagmhaigh im threo bean chórach dheas
>    Ar an móta glas ina haonar,
>    Gur bhinne a guth beoil ná nótaí an bhand,
>    Ná an ceol do spreag Orphéus.
>
>    By an ancient fort reposed I sat
>    As the sun's resplendent beam shone;
>    To supply my nose no store I had,
>    Nor cattle to take care of
>    A beauteous nymph I chanced to spy
>    On a lonely green band seated;
>    Than Orpheus's harp or a tuneful band
>    Her voice was far superior.

The bilingual song of the nineteenth century is a product of a period when people other than song-makers were happy to use a foreign tongue. The sudden flowering of the macaronic song coincides with the period in which a variety of pressures led to the gradual dominance of English. The reduced economic condition of the people, and the terrible disasters of the century, gave rise to a situation in which many saw emigration as the only alternative to dire poverty; a dependence on English was seen as the means of salvation. The national schools and their clerical managers were conspirators with the majority of Irish parents in bringing the bilingual situation into being.

In those places where the people were comfortable in both Irish and their new English, a certain pride was shown both by the makers of the bilingual songs and those who sang them; the same sort of pride that led to the clever linguistic mixes heard in medieval taverns from the lips of the wandering scholars. Connie Coughlan from Baile Mhúirne in West Cork stopped his macaronic song to alert the collector, Freeman, in the early days of this century; 'Éist', he said, 'Ard-Bhéarla anso!' (Listen: great English here!)

Spavined Pegasus? Perhaps. But it is worth remembering that Yeats thought otherwise, and that both Ernst Curtius and Anthony Burgess saw their influence in the greatest macaronic work of this century, Joyce's *Finnegans Wake*. (DIO)

*regional song.*

*Clare.* The vibrant instrumental tradition of Clare has overshadowed a robust song tradition which flourished there until very recently. Manuscripts of the Folklore Commission collectors working in that county are liberally scattered with songs in both languages. The spread of song in Irish for the first three-quarters of this century is outlined in Marion Gunn's *A Chomharsain Éistigí* (Dublin, An Clóchomhar Tta, 1984). Less well known is that a very extensive range of classic and broadside ballads in English, along with a broad sample of local songs, were also in the repertoire of Clare singers. Field work in the 1970s and '80s, mainly by the Department of Irish Folklore, UCD, resulted in several hundred songs and ballads from Clare being added to the Archive of that department. As in other counties, the poorer land of the western seaboard has been more fruitful for the song collector than the richer land of East Clare. Song style is relatively unornamented, a factor not uncommon in areas with a preference for narrative song. Younger singers in the county today mainly seek outside their county for repertoire and ignore (or are unaware of) Clare's rich song heritage. Ennistymon and Feakle both host festivals of traditional singing annually. (TOM)

*Cork city.*

The Proletarian Perspective: Between the wars, due to the increase of the industrial proletariat, the urban Cork ballad begins to show signs of individuality. Being rich in indigenous sporting pastimes, this milieu inspired the ballad-making process which diverted occasionally to sample the bitter-sweet fodder of local and national politics. With the plantation of Gurranebraher, Churchfield, Togher and Ballyphehane by Cork Corporation, the working-class voice gained in ambience:

> They came from the Marsh, they came from Knapp's Square
> They came from Fair Lane and the devil knows where
> And now they're in Churchfield, it's ever so high
> Like the angels in heaven far up in the sky

This new voice represented a fresh agenda and a world-view at variance with the earlier Cork bards such as John Fitzgerald, Denny Lane, Richard Milliken and Daniel Casey who had sported the bourgeoisie's new-found affection for romantic nationalism. Didactic songs of revolution like Patrick Galvin's 'James Connolly' are scarce; songs of class-defiance and irony emerge most strongly:

> Now 'twas when the Gas Restrictions came in force
> Sure it didn't trouble us in Gurrane of course
> Montenotte got a glimmer, up in Gurrane we got the shivers
> All for one and one for all above in Gurrane.

Common and native ground: The pervasive influence of Tin Pan Alley flavoured Cork's urban representation too. New comforts like 'the wireless' permeated the cultural process. Shades of Al Jolson's *Sit Upon my Knee, Sonny Boy*, for instance, are difficult to ignore in Tadhg Jordan's proletarian paean, 'Come back Henry Ford to our Land':

> Oh come back, Henry Ford to our land
> When you were there you gave us a helping hand
> Now we're out of labour, we got no cheques of paper
> That you used to dish out, Henry Ford.

The emigrant Cork workers who made up the masses at Henry Ford's Motor Foundry in Dagenham, Essex, took with them their ways, sporting pastimes and songs aboard the *M.V. Innisfallen* across the Irish Sea. Several accounts of local people being terrorised by 'flying cannon-balls' are attested to, because to the uninitiated, the Cork game of road bowling must have proved a terrible sight in that new cultural milieu, as the 'Dagenham Yanks' (as the Cork Ford workers were called) 'scored' along the Essex boreens. One of Cork's fine contemporary writers, Gus McLoughlin, captures the Second World War period from this perspective in the song 'The Foundry Man':

> Half-hour on and half-hour off, it's how they worked the shift
> Till your eyes were red and your feet they bled and your lungs ne'er came adrift
> But Paddy from Cork could handle the work and though hard he handled his pay
> 'Tis little he spent for most of it went across the Irish sea.

Female voice. Cork ballads give several perspectives. The song 'Salonika' provides a rare female perspective on the First World War, being a diatribe between a 'sepera woman' (receiving separation pay from the British Government) and a 'slacker woman' (married to the equivalent of a modern day draft dodger):

> And when the war is over what will the slackers do
> They'll be all around the soldiers for the loan of a bob or two
>
> But when the war is over what will the soldiers do?
> They'll be walkin' around with a leg and a half
> And the slackers we'll have two.

Recalcitrant females emerge in two other songs. An interesting piece 'The Gaol of Sunday's Well' projects an earlier female voice above the walls of the prison at Sunday's Well now serving as a heritage centre:

> The magistrate next morning called me a Jezabelle
> I told him that I wasn't and that he could go to hell
> 'You cannot speak to me like that, you cause me to compel
> To send you back to prison up in Sunday's Well'.

The heroism and idealism of the War of Independence was not confined to men and there's a song celebrating the famous Mary Bowles of Clogheen who rode on horseback up Blarney Street, a machine gun slung over her shoulder:

> Never yet was known a lady, not yet was known a queen
> To match the deeds of Mary Bowles, the Pride of sweet Clogheen.

Seán O'Callaghan emerges strongly in Cork's Northside during this period, with a gift of versification which he practised with great dexterity after every hurling match, drag hunt or bowling tournament. Songs like 'The Boys of Fairhill', 'The Killeens Hunt', 'The Armoured Car' and 'Lloyd George' are among his work. Typically, he conveys in 'Lloyd George' a swaggering defiance of the Catholic clergy's refusal to grant absolution to republicans during the War of Independence:

> Now the Bishops they tell us, you won't be forgiven
> Unless you're a Free Stater you can't get to heaven

Urban renewal: From the 1970s onwards a new coven of writers emerged, confident enough to mediate contemporary events in the local style. Pat Daly is every bit as fond of Cork, apparently, as John Fitzgerald, the bard of the Lee and in his song 'As I went a Walking', the dinnseanachas or topography of cultural urban hot-spots is invoked to great musical effect:

> As I went a-walking out in Blackpool
> Huddlesome, Ruddlesome, Rancy-O!
> I heard the song of shuttle and spool
> Huddlesome etc.
> Weaving and spinning we pass the day
> Working and singing our worries away
> It's the reel and the loom, the wool and the tow
> With me Ruddlesome Rancy-O.

The present state of ballad-making presents a hopeful picture where a localised cameo is still represented despite the vicissitudes of global culture. The sporting songs of Denis McGarry immortalise bowl-playing legends like Mick Barry almost to heights reserved for Connie Doyle and Christy Ring:

> When he travelled North to Armagh Town
> He met those sportsmen all
> Who shook that mighty hand of steel
> Mick Barry from Waterfall

Jerry O'Neill and John Maguire represent a coming-of-age of the Cork ballad, where intrinsic subaltern elements are embraced but sifted though the sieve of philosophy:

> We don't need budget tourists or botanic cranks
> What we want are full busloads of opulent Yanks
> (Jerry O'Neill)

> As the shamrock-laced shroud was torn down by the crowd
> And our vigour and confidence bubbled,
> Back in June '63, ah sure how could we see
> That our world and our country were troubled
> (John Maguire)

(JIC)

*West Cork.* The Sullane Valley and the upper Ruachtaí Valley contain the parishes of Ballyvourney and Cluain Droihid, the lowlands of Inches and Grousemount, and Tooreen in the parish of Kilgarvan. These are recognised as an important source of poetry and music. Though isolated and mountainous, the area is however just off the main Kenmare–Cork road, often travelled when Kenmare was an important port. With St Gobnait's shrine it has also been an important place of pilgrimage. The Irish language survived in the area partly because of its isolation, but more so because of its rich cultural heritage which surpassed anything the English language had to offer. Because of the Famine, the introduction of national schools, and church and state policies, it began to decline towards the end of the nineteenth century. With cultural revival and the growth of nationalism it got a new lease of life however. The poet and the seanachaí were important people; a very strong oral tradition existed, this nurtured by the custom of scoraíochting – congregating in certain houses where stories, songs and poems were performed and which supplied artists with an appreciative audience. The Gaelic tradition did begin to wane however, when fewer people were proficient enough in Irish. And so, as English became more fashionable, the poets, storytellers and singers were obliged to compromise. The result of this was, first, bi-lingual song, and then – as at present – mostly songs in English.

The area has many well-known songwriters whose work is still sung. From Cluain Droihid came George Curtin in the first half of the twentieth century. An able composer in Irish and English, he is credited with 'Na Cloganna', 'The Pup Came home from Claidach', 'The Man that Came Home From Prètoria', 'Mick Sullivan's Clock', 'The Gander', 'Ger Foley's Boat', 'An Gandal'. Then from Tooreen, Kilgarvan came the Cronin brothers Patsy and Johnny, who wrote 'That Beauty Spot Glanlea'. John Twomey – Johneen Norah Aoidh (*c.* 1880) – wrote 'Connie's Big Campaign', 'The Tailor Bán', 'Boduram's Ball'. An Irish poet from Grousemount, Kilgarvan around 1880 was Pead Buí (Padraig Ó Tuama), who wrote 'Gleann Carn', 'Tureaill Pheig a' Bhreatha', 'Amhhrán Phead Bhuí'. In the same period, from Soreathan na nGabhann came Dónal Ó Mulláin (who composed 'An Poc Ar Buile' and 'An Budget'). Seán Eoin Ó Súilleabháin of Doire An Chuillinn wrote 'Táimse 'gus Máire', 'An Laca Bacach'. Padraig Mac Suibhne (b. 1900) (pen-name 'An Suibhneach Meann'), wrote 'An Peidhleacán', 'An tEmergency Léine', 'An Mhóin', and 'Bogfadh-saRód'; Padraig Ó Crualaoi (pen-name 'Gaedhail na nGaedhal', c. 1870) wrote 'An Cruach Tuí', 'Abha an tSulláin', 'Cat Dhiarmuid na Béarnan' and two books: S*aothar Dhámh Scoile Mhúscraí*, and *Filíocht Phádraig Uí Chrualaoi*. Diarmuid Ó Tuama, Screathan (b. 1934) wrote 'Maidin Aiseach', 'The Pedigree Chum'. Danny Tom Lehane (b. c. 1920) wrote 'The Mountain Rover', 'The Hole Below Kilgarvan', 'The Sow That They Failed to Kill', 'Krudger's Mare', 'The ESB', and 'Bat Connell's Grand New Stall'. Amhlaoíbh Ó Loinne ('Free Connai', b. c. 1870), Chúil Aodha, wrote 'A Tháilliúr na Déise' and 'Nuair a Casadh mé Suas go dtí 'n Town Hall'. Diarmuid 'ac Coilir wrote 'Mo Theaghlach'. Donal Ó Líatháin wrote 'The Ancient Priceless Horn', 'An Pósadh', and 'An Péint', 'Im Long mé Measaim Tránn an Taoide', 'Bóthar na Síochána', and most of 'Bímis Ag Ól'. From Ballingeary Máire Bhuí Ní Laoghaire wrote 'Cath Céim an Fhia', 'A Bhúrcaigh Buí ár gCéim', 'Maidin Álainn Gréine'. Seoirse Sheachtar wrote 'An Capaillín Bán'.

The area was remarkable for its poetry and song, in schools, in houses and pubs. Central to the tradition was An Dáibh Scoil (the Bardic School, first meeting in 1926) which is held every year and where many poets have a chance to air their work. 'An Poc Ar Buile' was heard first here. The Bardic school generated a huge interest in songs and in composition. Competitions at the Oireachtas have also been an incentive. Many of the songs are Dialogue – 1) Amhráin Saothair (work songs); 2) Lúibíní, and 3) Ceapoga. These songs are written by a group together. For instance, Paití Thaidhg Phéig Ó Tuama (b. 1890), Donal Ó hEalaíthe (b. 1934), Diarmuid Ó Riordáin (b. 1900), Maidhcí Ó Súilleabháin (b. 1910), Johnny Eoin a' Bhab Ó Súilleabháin, Seán Ó Duinnín (b. 1922) made between them 'An Cruach Tobac', 'An Poitín', 'An Rasúr', 'An Muileann', 'Tig mór Ard', 'De Bheatha's a' Pháití' and others. (DÓO)

*Donegal South West*. The strands of song tradition in south-west Donegal reflect the historical demography of the area, and so old ballads of Scottish and English origin exist side by side with Ossianic lays. These are the few extant examples of sung lays in Ireland, they were collected in the 1940s from Séamus Ó hIghne of Mín na Saileach, and from Mícheál Ó hIghne of An tAtharach. The Irish language and its traditions had a vigorous existence through the nineteenth century. Condaí Phroinnsís Mac Cuinneagáin (1832–1920) is remembered as one of the outstanding Teelin singers of that period, particularly so for his edification of the community in the 'ceartú ceoil' song competition, held in the neighbouring Kilcar parish. A weekend Éigse has been held in his memory, the location of his grave in Carrick graveyard recovered and marked. Máire Johnny Johndy Ní Bheirn and, more recently, Anna Ní Dhonnagáin are other locally acclaimed Teelin singers. Local teacher Alphonsus Mac a' Bhaird exercised great influence on the repertoire during his years in Teelin and subsequently in Carrick school. His children, Dónall, Máire and Fionnuala are also singers although not living locally. Others are Christine, Deirbhile and Yvonne Ní Churraighín and Anna Nic Bhriartaigh, while Kitty Seáin Mhic Cuinneagáin is regarded as a fund of older songs and airs. In Taobh istigh de chnoc – known as 'Glen' – today's singers are John 'Ac Uidhir and his wife Teresa who sings an unusual version of the well-known 'Pill Pill a Rún Ó'. The area had several poets in the eighteenth and nineteenth centuries, and among the more impressive of them was the Kilcar man Séamus Ó Doraidheáin. His eulogy for Sliabh Liag, in nine eight-line verses, a *tour de force* of mythical hyperbole, superiorly challenges that of Eoghan Óg Mac Niallais's shorter 'An Mhaoineach', which praises Ard a' Rátha. More famous yet was Bríd Bhán Ní Eochaidh, from Teelin, whose song of longing for the 'teach mór' of her home place, and of blunt rebuttal of her husband's overtures for compromise, is the most popular song in the area today. It is closely followed by Pádraig Ó Beirn's 'Mo Mháire'. Gaelic songs and singing survived decline, and have been boosted since the mid-1980s by Oideas Gael, whose courses and workshops draw language- and song-lovers from diverse parts.

*Donegal, central – An Ghaeltacht Láir.* The Croaghs mountain area is hugely symbolic here, but with a population of more than two hundred in 1911, today they are almost deserted. Once a storehouse of Gaelic language, lore and song, and frequented by the travelling fiddler tinsmiths, the Dohertys, the Croaghs' best-remembered song stylists were, Anna Nic a' Luain, Johnny 'Ac a' Luain from Éadan Ionfach, Eoghan Phádraig 'Ac a' Luain (collected by Seosamh Laoide) and his children Pádraig, Conall and Máire. Other singers are Máire Rua Uí Mhaí (née Nic a' Luain) and her daughter Bridie Mhic Fhloinn. Among the local poets was Tadhg Ó Tiománaí – Tadhg na mBan as he was known, because of his romantic exploits around the turn of the eighteenth century. The author of many fine songs, their sexual explicity led to their gradual exclusion, and they were either amended or omitted in Énrí Ó Muirgheasa's 1915 collection. Another poet was Peadar Breathnach (1825–70), author of the locally well-known and often-commer- cially recorded 'Amhrán Pheadair Bhreatnach'. Fiddlers Vince and Jimmy Campbell's mother is from the Croaghs, and indeed traditional music and song are still strong locally. (LIO)

*Inishowen.* This is the peninsula in North-East Donegal where a strong folksong and ballad singing tradition exists. Until the very recent past many older singers gathered regularly to sing. Many of them have now passed on, but some of their songs have been recorded and preserved. Local, narrative, love, humorous, historical, rebel and Child Ballads, were the most common. Corny McDaid, Jimmy Grant, Jimmy C. Doherty, Maggie McGee, Mary Anne Canny, Jimmy Houten, Denis McDaid, Paddy McCallion were among the best known of the older singers. Dan McGonigle, Margaret McEleney, Mack Devlin, Charlie, Michael, Roseanne and Pat McGonigle, Bridie and Joe Doherty, Annie Hirrell, Mary Gill still meet to sing songs. They provided a large body of song, recorded by several collectors including Tom Munnelly of the Folklore Department, UCD, but mainly by Jimmy McBride of Buncrana. He formed the Inishowen Traditional Singers' Circle, thus providing a forum for these old singers where they could meet regularly to exchange and discuss their varied repertoire. The formation of the annual seminar on folk song and ballads in 1990 gave the older singers an added interest. The McBride collection, with more than 500 songs, is currently being prepared for inclusion in the Irish Traditional Music Archive, Dublin. One hundred hours are already submitted.

Publications: *My Parents Reared Me Tenderly*, Buncrana, McBride/McFarland (1985); *The Flower of Dunaff Hill*, Buncrana, McBride, 1988 (130 songs). (JIM)

*Dublin street song.* The 'popular' music of the day, these are characterised by sarcasm and irony, satire and humour. They come from various sources – some are broadside ballads, others from the music hall, still more are adaptations of other song. There is a political repertoire relating to national politics, another to trade union politics, much of the material is of the twentieth century, much has been spread by recordings and song sheets or books. Perhaps most famous is 'Molly Malone', almost equally so Séamus Kavanagh's 'Biddy Mulligan', popularised on record by comedian Jimmy O'Dea:

> I'm a buxom fine widow, I live in a spot
> In Dublin they call it the Coombe
> My shop and my stall is laid out on the street
> And my palace consists of one room

In the songs the lives of the poor and the grafting workers are invested with a private dignity, they ridicule their own absurdities, tongue-in-cheek glamorise wretchedness, and obstinately hold on to a political identity 'agin' the authorities. Peadar Kearney (author also of 'Amhrán na bFiann', the national anthem) wrote the perennial 'The Liffeyside', with all these hallmarks, still sung by Dublin ballad groups:

> Oh ''Twas down by Anna Liffey, my love and I did stray
> Where in the good old Liffey mud, the seagulls sport and play
> We got the whiff of ray and chips, and Mary softly sighed
> Yerra John, come on, for a 'one-and-one', down by the Liffey side

Harry O'Donovan's 'Charladies' Ball' is a classic music hall-style work:

> We had one-steps and two-steps
> And the divil knows what new steps
> We swore that we never would be done again, be dad
> We had wine, porter and lemonade
> We had cocktails and cocoa and all
> We had champagne that night
> But we had real pains next morning
> The night that we danced at the Charladies' ball

The canals of Dublin – built as major commercial routes, the Grand opened in 1791 as a link to the Barrow after 35 years of work, to the Shannon in 1805; and the Royal, begun in 1789 – proved the object of much ridicule, the minute scale, placidity and slowness of their endeavour a source of amusement in 'the Cruise of the Calabar':

> Now when huggin the shore of Inchicore
> A very dangerous part
> We ran aground on a lump of coal
> that wasn't marked on the chart

'Dicey Reilly' is one of the more popular pieces to survive well into the twentieth century, promoted by the 1960s ballad boom. In living memory incomplete, it was given three extra verses by Tom Munnelly who rehabilitated it, the Dubliners and Luke Kelly in particular having much to do with its subsequent popularity. 'Finnegans Wake' has been made internationally famous by both James Joyce and the Dubliners, but pieces like 'The Forgetful Sailor', with the structural hallmarks of Gaelic ancestry remain superb pieces for solo performance:

> She calmly watched the neighbouring ship
> then suddenly became exclaimant
> For there upon the gilded poop
> Stood Mister Doyle in gorgeous raiment

The political song is strong on satire, sending up the police force in particular with such as Louis Tierney's 'Are you there Moriarity', and, earlier, in Brian O'Higgins' 'The Limb of the Law' wherein the force's attempts to learn Irish are ridiculed:

> 'Mo lámh' is 'my foot' and 'mo chluas' is my hand
> 'Tá mé ag foghlaim' – I'm learning, you see
> If I keep on like this an Inspector I'll be . . .
> I'm getting so big that I don't know the cat
> My head is two sizes too big for my hat

Trade union leader James Connolly, defender of the rights of the worker, is revered in the repertoire, 'James Connolly, the Irish rebel', and Cork poet Patrick Galvin's 'Where oh where is the citizen army?', Brendan Behan's 'The Oul' Triangle' reflects on life in Mountjoy prison, Peadar Kearney's 'Whack Fol the diddle' is bitingly sarcastic about English opposition to Irish independence, his 'Sergeant William Bailey' scorns the recruiting sergeant; 'Mrs McGrath' scorns war:

> Oh Mrs. McGrath!, the Sergeant said
> 'I'll make a soldier out of your son Ted
> With a scarlet coat and big cocked hat
> Now Mrs. McGrath, wouldn't you like that?'

'The Dublin Jack of All Trades' lists city occupations, 'Monto' mixes prostitution, the drinking classes and politics. Much of what we know as Dublin 'street song' is modern – Sylvester Gaffney's parody 'Three Lovely Lasses from Kimmage', writer Pete St John's 'Do you want your old Lobby Washed Down' carrying on this kind of 'traditional pop song' in a traditional style. The presence of Walton's music shop in the city cannot be ignored in this. It has always published scores of cheap, chap-book-style song books: songs of Thomas Davis ('Clare's Dragoons', 'A Nation once Again'), Leo Maguire ('Kevin Barry', 'The Foggy Dew'), Francis Fahy's 'Galway Bay', Johnny Patterson ('Shake hands with your Uncle Dan', 'Good-bye Johnny Dear') Moore's songs, Sylvester Gaffney's classic parodies, Robbie Burns' 'Flow Gently Sweet Afton', TP Keenan's 'Hello Patsy Fagan' – these mixed with such pieces as 'Nell Flaherty's Drake', 'The Star of Slane', 'Lowlands of Holland'. Post 1960s singers and groups, among them the Wolfe Tones, Danny Doyle, the Clancys, the Dubliners, laced their ballads with those from elsewhere – such as Sean McCarthy's 'Step it out Mary', 'Highland Paddy', 'Shanagolden' – blending Dublin street song into the *mélange* we know today as simply 'ballads', still popular among the old Dublin working class, and still with a currency both for them and tourists in pub-performances. Frank Harte's 'Songs of Dublin' (1978, Gilbert Dalton) lists a popular selection, his 'Through Dublin City' (Oss 44) and Barry Gleeson's Góilín 001 are examples of the 'head-thrown-back' singing style in the unapologetically Dublin accent which is vital to the ethos of the genre.

*Jacobite song.* This is political song concerned with the claims to the British throne of king James II (deposed in 1688), his son (claiming to be James III), and the latter's son Charles (who died in 1788). These three belonged to the Stuart dynasty, and the term Jacobite derives from 'Jacobus', Latin for James. During that hundred years the London government of king William and the Georges strengthened its political and cultural grip on Ireland, so that the Irish language continued to be displaced by English. It is therefore not surprising that the Gaelic majority supported the Stuarts, and, consequently most Irish 'Jacobite' song is in Irish.

Since there are very few Irish songs that we can confidently date before *c.* 1750, it is difficult to trace when this kind of song began. There were of course Jacobite songs from the 1690s, but not being the work of the literate class, most were not written down and therefore lost. The best-known kind of Jacobite song is the *aisling* (pl. *aislingí*), in the earliest surviving examples of which the 'messiah' is James III. The three earliest *aislingí* we have (the work of Aogán Ó Rathaille, *An Duanaire*, pp. 151–60) relate to the hoped-for return of James III around 1715. Because we do not have surviving tunes, the *aislingí* must be treated as poetry only, even if some once were set to melodies. Munster (where the *aisling* apparently originated), south-east Ulster and north Leinster were the main areas of production of the *aisling* poetry in the eighteenth century. Ulster's best-known example, 'Úirchill an Chreagáin', identifies no messiah (*An Duanaire*, 176), for once the Stuart cause was finally overthrown at the battle of Culloden in 1746, the northern poets gave up on them as potential saviours. In Co. Armagh Peadar Ó Doirnín (d. 1769) mocks both sides, Prince Charles' Gaelic Highlanders and William, Duke of Cumberland, the government leader:

> Adeir Iain is Eachann is Gilleaspaic mac Raghnaill
> Nach bhfuil boinéad nó bearád nó hata dubh lása
> Nó giolla breá fearúil dár cailleadh an lá sin
> Nach n-íocfaidh Sir Wully go huile le Cathal iad, is iombó!

Here the words 'is iombó!' tell us that this was to be sung. Reputedly a popular song in Ulster, this piece serves to illustrate that Jacobite song was not confined to the *aisling*. One well-known Jacobite song which is not an *aisling* is 'Bímse buan ar buairt gach ló', the enthusiastic welcome to Prince Charles by Seán Clárach Mac Domhnaill (1691–1754) in Co. Cork, one of the earliest songs known to the tune 'An Cnota Bán' (the Scottish 'White Cockade'). Today it is probably more popularly set to a more modern tune.

But many of the Munster poets still hoped for a Stuart return after Culloden. Eoghan Rua Ó Súilleabháin (1748–84), born in Co. Kerry when Stuart hopes were in reality over, is the most famous of the *aisling* makers. His are set to beautiful tunes, and use highly complex metrical ornament giving minute attention to detail in describing the woman's beauty, justifying John Jordan's 1982 remark made about his poetry in general that he 'often expires in a morass of loveliness'. His 'Im aonar seal ag siúl bhíos', set to the tune of 'An Binsín Luachra', is a triumph by a master of words:

> Im aonar seal ag siúl bhíos
> I dtúis oíche i ngaortha ceoigh;
> Lem thaobh gur dhearcas fionn-ríon
> Im ionnsaí go séimh ar seol,
> A céibh ar fad 'na búclaíbh
> Ag tabhairt síos ar scéimh an óir
> Go craobhach casta ciumhs-bhuí
> 'Na fonnsaíbh go béal a bróig.

Pádraig Ua Duinnín, his 1902 editor, credits this writer with fifteen *aislingí*, including 'Ceo Draíochta' and 'An Spealadóir'.

It was eventually accepted towards the end of the eighteenth century that national salvation did not lie with the Stuarts, but the *aisling* remained popular, and, as English tightened its grip on the land in the same period, we find examples of the *aisling* in English – though not always up to Gaelic standards of metrical precision:

> Are you any of these dames who agreed to strip,
> For Paris to view them on Ida's hill,
> Where Vulcan's fair bride obtained the golden prize,
> Which caused jealousy, spite, and dire revenge?
> (Zimmermann, 1966)

The *aisling* is an allegory, and allegories were popular in the eighteenth century, and not only in Ireland. Art Mac Cumhaigh holds a political discussion with a little bird in his lovely song 'Aige Bruach Dhún Réimhe', and he is not the only poet to do so. The English (or Scottish) song 'The Blackbird' is an allegory where James III is 'my Blackbird, wherever he may be'; it first appeared about 1718 and quickly became popular in Ireland. We must take it that songs of this kind in English first arrived on the English-speaking east coast, and gradually spread westward as the Irish language receded. This is a useful reminder that the Stuarts most certainly had considerable support among English-speakers, especially around Dublin.

Another English song which became popular in Ireland is 'When the king shall enjoy his own again', first printed to support king Charles II in his exile from Britain in 1651–60; but this was easy to rework in support of any exiled Stuart king. Around 1715, some students at Trinity College, Dublin, were brought to court for whistling its tune (Ó Buachalla, *Aisling Ghéar*, 1996), and in 1745 Denis O'Hampsey, the Co. Derry harper (1695–1807) was presented to Prince Charles in Edinburgh and sang to him:

'. . . I hope to see the day
When the Whigs shall run away,
And the king shall enjoy his own again.'

The English-language Jacobite songs that are still sung today are mostly recent Scottish imports. After Culloden the Stuarts and the Highlanders no longer threatened the establishment, the tartan and the pipes became symbols of Scottish national identity, and a literary industry arose to manufacture much of what now passes for Jacobite song. Robert Burns (1759–96) played his part, but probably the greatest romanticisers were James Hogg (1770–1835) and Walter Scott (1771–1832). A dramatic example of the produce of this literary industry is 'Speed, bonnie boat, like a bird on the wing . . .', in fact composed by an Englishman and published in 1885 (Donaldson, 1988).

The story of Jacobite song in Ireland involves close links with Scotland and England, but it is primarily the story of Gaelic song during the last century in which there were still considerable enough numbers of Gaelic speakers to have cultural confidence. (COO)

*Ulster.* The Ulster style of singing is well attested over many years, a definite entity, but difficult to describe, wraith-like in defying three-dimensional location. Its definitive exponents range from the insatiable repertoire and passionate, celebratory, glottal melodicism of Paddy Tunney's 'Mountain Streams where the Moorcock Crows', to the parsimonious abruptness of 'The Tamlaght Stone' from Matt O'Hagan on Len Graham's collection *It's of my Rambles*. Singers like Joe Holmes are well recorded and documented, Eddie Butcher of Magilligan is legend, Len Graham himself their repository: for him these and their contemporaries were the soundscape of childhood and coming of age. John Moulden makes some attempt at describing Ulster style: for him it is 'syllabic', 'rubato', Angular', 'each syllable carefully enunciated', with fluctuation in tempo. Such aural characteristics have caused problems in adjudication at fleadhanna outside the province – Comber, Co. Down singer Jackie Boyce once being notoriously criticised by a Co. Mayo adjudicator in an All-Ireland competition: 'We have to break this "Ulster Style" . . . it's not singing at all. It should be kept to the back rooms of pubs'. Moulden describes the song style more definitively however by repertoire. The strength of the tradition until recent times, the current deep value placed on it compared to English-language song in other parts of the island, the fact of the repertoire's meaning for place (shared also with Connemara?) – more than half of the song sung in Ulster is either local, or localised Irish song. (Seán O'Boyle (*Ulster Folklife*, vol. 5, 1959) identified, as early as 1955, three strains in Ulster folksong – Irish, originating in the form of Irish language poetry, English and Scottish from planters and other long- and short-term migrants. John Moulden in *Songs of the People* put the proportions at 70 per cent Irish (much of it local), 20 per cent English and 10 per cent Scottish in origin. There are many fundamental recordings, a lot made by Robin Morton – Archie McKeegan of Cushendall, Co. Antrim, Robert Cinnamond from the Co. Armagh shore of Lough Neagh, John Maguire from Fermanagh, Peter Donnelley, Co. Tyrone. Peter Kennedy recorded much of this too, for his 1+950s' BBC radio series *As I Roved Out* (named after, and signatured by, Sarah Makem's song) and in his 1975 collection *Folksongs of Britain and Ireland*. He collected songs for this from the Belfast McPeakes, themselves a vivid combination of song and traditional music, a forerunner of the ubiquitous 'group'. Love of melody, often in dance time, is demonstrated by today's Ulster singers still, this utilising expert articulation of syllable and words in a style akin to lilting: Tunney's 'Rollicking Boys of Tandragee' (jig time) has been taken up by Kilkeel, Co. Down singer Róisín White; Derrygonnelly, Co. Fermanagh singer Rosie Stewart sings 'Don't go to the Funeral' (reel time), this learnt from her father Packie McKeaney. Fermanagh retains singers and songs, these strongly part of community in several areas still, documented in Seán Corcoran's *Here's a Health* collection, its notable representative being Gabriel McArdle of Enniskillen. South Armagh values its legacy of song and eighteenth-century Gaelic poets in the annual Forkhill singers' festival, all now enshrined in a purpose-built cultural centre 'Tí Chulainn' at Mullaghbane, the rich timbre of whose local singer Patricia Flynn is highly regarded at singing festivals in Ireland and Britain. Tyrone singer Catherine McLoughlin of Drumquin contrasts with songwriter Damien Molloy of Dungannon, both are different from satirical/ comic writer Seán Mone of Keady, Co. Armagh. Brian Mullins of Derry has an altogether different gentle interpretation, Kevin Mitchell high and intense, Rita Gallagher of Killygordon, Co. Donegal is different again with an exceptional lyricism. John Moulden of Portrush has made this song territory his career – collecting and documenting, distributing recordings of local singers unavailable elsewhere. The Antrim Glens traditional group's Caitlín McElheron from Co. Antrim is also involved in such local promotion, Maurice Leyden has written on song in Belfast, David Hammond is a long-standing authority. In Lurgan, Co. Armagh, the Ulster Society promotes singing of old Orange song, and many Orange Halls retain a tradition of singing, although this is usually private, and therefore outside the remit and society of traditional singing elsewhere. Perhaps the most striking singer to emerge from the Ulster milieu is the late Geordie Hanna, whose family were singers from Derrytresk, Co. Tyrone on Lough Neagh, and whose sister Sarah Anne O'Neill still sings. He exhibited, as David Hammond has described, a profoundly rich personal intonation and considered 'way' with a song which, while it draws heavily on the unique antiquity of the English spoken locally, made him his own singer. 'Ulster style' is a unified concept, but an eclectic mix. Today it is undermined perhaps by the pressure to learn repertoire which is universally identifiable, this restricting the singing of the local material to where it is geographically relevant – but often without the necessary, sustaining community base.

*South Ulster*. An area covering North Monaghan, North Louth and South Armagh with considerable poetic legacy, its best-known classical writers have been Séamus Dall Mac Cuarta (17–18th century), Peadar Ó'Doirnín (d. 1769), Art McCooey (d. 1777). McCooey's songs in particular have filtered into the local folksong repertoire, best known of these is Úirchill an Chreagáin. Its leading exponent and researcher in the present day is Pádraigín Ní Uallacháin. (EDI)

*Wexford*. The county has a varied culture mix – from hillside farmers on the slopes of the Blackstairs Mountain, through the fertile tillage and grassland of the Model county, to the coastal fishing villages. All have great variety of song associated with them, little of it known about or appreciated outside the South East. Such was the pride of song repertoire in Wexford that Ranson (1937) could report a tradition of song challenges, in one of which a Kilmuckridge singer was victorious with sixty-four pieces. This strong tradition of ballad writing/singing and storytelling generated two books of song in the 1980s alone: Paddy Berry's *Wexford Ballads* (1982) and *More Wexford Ballads* (1987), these with some 300 pieces. Early references to the county in song begin with the construction of ramparts round the town of New Ross in 1265 on account of a feud between Maurice Fitzmaurice, Chief of the Geraldines, and Walter de Burgo, Earl of Ulster. 'The Ballad of the Entrenchments of New Ross', composed in Norman French, was translated by Mrs (George) McShane in 1831, and first appeared in Crofton Croker's *Popular Songs of Ireland* (1838):

> But on Saturday the stir
> Of blacksmith, mason, carpenter
> Hundreds three with fifty told
> Many were they, true and bold
> And they toiled with main and might
> Needful knew they 'twas, and fight.

Still older is the 'Song of Dermot', composed at the time of the Norman landing of 1169. More recent history has produced a great volume of song in the county relating to the 1798 rising, most of these penned in the generations since, with only a dozen or so contemporary accounts surviving. Historian Nicky Furlong relates that the details of the rising were of such profound impact that they were not discussed or sung about locally for some time – the folk memory developed a blind spot. An explosion of song relating to it took place in the mid-nineteenth century however, this producing a song for every incident, most popular having been 'The Croppy Boy'.

The study of hurling in the county surprisingly throws up song from an era before the county's modern-day GAA fame including 'The 1910 Hurlers' and 'The Bold Shelmalier' (1890) ballad of the county's defeat of Cork. Further back in 1805 a ballad commemorates a celebrated hurling game played between Duffry and the Barony of Bantry, and in 1779 Paddy Devereux tells his son about hurling at Carrigmanen:

> Hurling we may from greatest authors find
> To be of two Olympian games combined
> Where strength of body swiftness in the race
> These qualities in hurling still take place.

Peeling back the years in song reveals the great antiquity of the game locally through a the 'Yola' dialect song of a hurling game played in the 1680s in the parish of Our Lady's Island at the Cross of Lough:

> A cluttering gathered all in pile and in heap
> Tumbled over each other like flocks of wild sheep
> 
> (Translation Conchubhair Ó Cuileanáin, 1958, *Our Games*)

P. J. McCall, the ballad maker involved in the setting up of the Feis Cheoil of 1897, and well known for his 1798 songs 'Boolavogue', 'Kelly from Killane', 'Follow me up to Carlow', etc., also wrote numerous place praise songs: four books of his material were published between 1894 and 1911. His work has been described as 'martial in the hills, plaintive in the valleys, pathetic in the glade, rollicking on the hillside and sentimental in the groves'. Another ballad maker of the 1800s was Michael O'Brien who termed himself 'the Wexford Bard', familiar at fairs, race meetings and chapel gates, singing and selling his ballad sheets for a penny. 'Ballyshannon Lane', 'The Alfred D. Snow' and others, universal in the Irish song tradition, are his work.

But perhaps it is the maritime folksong of Wexford which, compared to other counties, is its other strong bardic legacy. Seventy-seven items of this were gathered together, notated and published in the decade after 1937 by Fr Joe Ransom as 'Songs of the Wexford Coast'. These document a deep involvement with the sea, its treacherous waters, the drama of sea travel and transport.

> They launched their boat at Fethard Quay
> And outwards they did go
> For to save the shipwrecked sailors
> On board the Mexico

'The Hantoon', 'The Tinaberna Fisherman', 'Bannow's Lonely Shores' and 'The Fethard Lifeboat Crew' are songs sung and appreciated locally, others were known on the south coast too. Ransom considered that the songs that had currency from east coast Arklow to Curracloe were all local, those from the barony of Forth were often of English origin, and many from the Hook peninsula were American. New maritime songs are still being written, but the passé era of the sailing ship and the wreck-strewn Wexford coast shipping lane was the song genre's prolific breeding ground. (PHB)

*political.*

*nationalist/republican.* When one considers the history of resistance to British domination of Ireland over some 830 years, it would be surprising if a large number of the songs did not reflect this. Statutory discrimination, particularly in the seventeenth to nineteenth century period of the Penal Laws (designed to discourage the Presbyterian as well as the Catholic) foddered the politico/religious cocktail of nationalist/Republican, and, derivatively, Orange/loyalist song we have inherited today.

It is very difficult to identify just where a song oversteps the simple social expressions of love, tragedy, and laughter and becomes 'political'. Often 'the lovers' have been thwarted because he or she is of 'a low degree', without land, or of the wrong religious persuasion; many such conditions can be traced to oppression/ disaffection. The 'tragedy' often tells of those who were shot down by government forces, evicted by the landlord with the assistance of the forces of law and order, or transportation to the penal colonies of Australia where the inhumane treatment of the prisoners would have been seen in the same context as that of a concentration camp today. Among the songs of 'humour and laughter', there are many which were used in a political context as a means of reducing those in positions of power to objects of ridicule. Laughter and sarcasm have always been used by the downtrodden who had no other means of protesting against the injustice under which they lived, and so the songs were written as a means of lampooning the posturing and pomposity of those in power, quite often with devastating effect. For instance, in the 1800s, Darby Ryan's 'Peeler and the Goat', or in the early 1900s, Brian O'Higgins' *Wolfe Tone Annual*'s reaction to a fawning proposal in March 1911, to collect subscriptions from all the women in Ireland named 'Mary', for the purchase of a coronation gift for the new British queen, one of whose names was Mary:

> O, then, fill the hat, with pence or pounds, and sure if famine comes
> When your loving England steals your loaf, And hands you back the crumbs
> 'Twill ease the hunger pangs to think that once when you were green
> You bought a poplin hobble skirt to decorate your queen!

Poetry, recitation, and song and even the slow airs are in many cases so closely linked together as the political expression of the people that they cannot be separated and should possibly all be classified as 'political song'.

This poetry and song refers back romantically to Cú Chulainn, to Fionn and the Fianna, the victory of Brian Boru over the Danes at the battle of Clontarf in 1014, and to the laments for Red Hugh O'Donnell and Eoghan Ruadh O'Neill:

> 'Did they dare, did they dare, to slay Owen Roe O'Neill?'
> 'Yes, they slew with poison him they feared to meet with steel.'

In the form that we still know them, there were anonymous ballads written at the time of the Battle of the Boyne (1690) telling of this most important event in Irish history, one such is 'The Boyne Water':

> July the first in Oldbridge town, there was a grievous battle
> Where many a man lay on the ground by the cannons that did rattle
> King James he pitched his tents between the lines for to retire
> But King William threw his bomb-balls in,
> And set them all on fire.

After the defeat of the native Irish and the signing of the Treaty of Limerick (October 1691), many of the soldiers left Ireland to serve under men like Patrick Sarsfield in the 'Irish Brigades' which fought with the armies in France against the English. Known as the Wild Geese, they gained fame on the battlefields of Ramillies, Fontenoy and Landen where Sarsfield himself was killed. Their deeds were celebrated in poetry by Thomas Davis and published from 1842 in the Young Irelander newspaper *The Nation*, which was set to music and widely sung:

> When on Ramillies bloody field,
> The baffled French were forced to yield,
> The victor Saxon backward reeled
> Before the charge of Clare's dragoons.

The rebellion of 1798 was to inspire a great number of political songs: laments from the insurgents and triumphalist songs from the Orange yeomanry. Many were written at the time or shortly after, songs such as the sad 'The Croppy Boy' and the triumphalist 'Croppies Lie Down'. The more popular of these which are still sung today – 'The Rising of the Moon', 'Boolavogue', 'Who Fears to Speak of 98' – were written almost a hundred years later to commemorate the rising.

The songs of the famine time, the evictions, the emigration and the shooting of landlords all tended to take on a political aspect, in that many of the landowners were absentee landlords living in England. In 1842 it was estimated that £6m left the country to absentee landlords, consequently the forces of law and order were seen as protecting their property by enforcing eviction notices. In many of the ballads such as 'Skibbereen' the final verse calls for revenge for the injustice meted out to the tenants, and the influence of the Fenians (from 1858 onwards) is evident.

> Oh, father dear the day will come when in answer to the call,
> Each Irishman with meaning stern will rally one and all,
> I'll be the man to lead the van beneath the flag of green,
> And loud and high we will raise the cry, 'Revenge for Skibbereen'.

Many songs were written in favour of the Fenians, and again, many are still sung today, 'Allen, Larkin, and O'Brien', and 'The Bold Fenian Men'. The Land League (from 1879 onwards) was originally set up by Michael Davitt and Charles Stewart Parnell to secure the rights of the tenant farmer but eventually became part of the 1880s' Home Rule movement. It too produced its own collection of songs against evictions and land grabbing, 'The Wife of the Bold Tenant Farmer' as well as those in praise of Parnell who was referred to in song as 'The Blackbird of Avondale':

> Near to Rathdrum in the County Wicklow,
> This brave defender of Grainuaile,
> First tuned his notes on old Ireland's freedom,
> In the lovely woodlands of Avondale.

After this period the political songs focused on the anti-recruiting campaign during the First World War, the Rebellion of 1916, the Black and Tan War, and the terrible Civil War, where brother fought against brother – although almost of the songs of this period were sympathetic to the republican rebels who refused to accept the treaty:

> Four Republican soldiers were dragged from their cells
> Where for months they had suffered the torments of hell,
> No mercy they asked from their pitiless foe,
> And no mercy was shown by the thugs of Drumboe.

Political songs are still being written today about the 'Civil Rights March', the 'Battle of the Bogside', 'Bloody Sunday', the 'Hunger Strike', right up to Drumcree in 1996:

> Ah, them people of Garvaghey, sure you couldn't keep them happy,
> With all of them shouting 'chuckey' though they never saw a hen,
> But with the RUC before us and their batons waving o'er us,
> We will all join in the chorus, 'happy days are here again'.

(FRH)

See *Nation, The*; Young Irelanders.

*World War I (1914–18)*. Irish songs of the Great War reflect the various (and changeable) political groupings and forces which existed at the time. Republicans expressed their resistance to recruitment in bitter songs like Peadar Kearney's 'Sergeant William Bailey', or those of Brian O'Higgins (Brian na Banban). Unionists and republicans, who had a few weeks previously stood ready to fight one another, and the British Army, shelved their quarrel and voluntarily (there was no conscription in Ireland), joined up and went to war taking with them books of songs produced especially to encourage their morale and sang either the popular songs of the day or bitter parodies of them. One detachment of troops, unwilling to leave without making a statement, left Dublin to the strains of 'God Save Ireland', the unofficial anthem of Ireland. In the trenches and on the march they sang the songs most closely associated with the war such as 'Hanging on the Old Barbed Wire' and 'Tipperary' (parodied as an anti-recruiting song: 'It's the wrong way to Tipperary'). The unionist and republican recruits were, for most of the war, segregated in the 36th (Ulster) Division and the 16th (Irish Division) and each tended to sing also songs sympathetic to their predominant political tradition. Those left at home sang songs such as 'Salonika' which condemned men who failed to join up as 'slackers' or songs in praise of particular regiments like 'The South Down Militia' or 'The Dublin Fusiliers'. Large numbers of songs and verses appeared in local newspapers – some of them urging joining the army or condemning those who didn't and many others presenting a very graphic and local or personal view of the war, its casualties and of local heroes, such as the VCs, Michael O'Leary and Robert Quigg; very few of these survived in tradition. The words of a very few songs about the battles of the war, whether composed by those at the front or those at home, survive in the diaries of serving soldiers or on scraps of paper – most of those appear to be about the Battle of the Somme. Only a few songs, such as 'Neuve Chappelle', 'Bonny Woodgreen' and 'The 1st of July', from the northern tradition, and 'Salonika', from the south, are still known. During the war, Ireland itself was relatively safe: only one place, Portballintrae, Co. Antrim was shelled from the sea and this episode is mentioned in a song, probably written later, about the 'Giant's Causeway Tram'. After the war many who returned found no work while the health of others had been shattered. Their discontent found expression in sets of verses on postcards, some of which may have been sung. At least 50,000 Irishmen, about equal numbers of Protestants and Catholics, died during this war, while many more were injured, and the war still evokes powerful images of waste and sacrifice. This is shown by the popularity of recently composed songs, especially Eric Bogle's 'The Green Fields of France' and 'The Band Played Waltzing Matilda'. At least one such song has its impulse in the need of loyalist paramilitaries for historical heroes: 'The Ballad of Billy McFadzean' praises 'Private Billy McFadzean of the UVF' (that is the UVF of 1912–14), who on the first morning of the Battle of the Somme, 1 July 1916, earned a posthumous VC. A box of hand grenades was being moved within the trench, was dropped, some of the safety pins were dislodged. McFadzean smothered the explosion with his own body, was blown to bits but saved his companions. The tune which carries his praise is also used for Patrick Galvin's song 'James Connolly, the Irish Rebel'. (JOM)

*famine*. The 'Great Famine' lasted approximately from 1845 until 1855. More than two million people were forced to leave the country; another million died from starvation and disease. Many songs deal with the effects of this, but few tell of 'the great hunger' itself, this explained by the contemporary comment: 'even the birds were silent with grief'. Lyric comment focuses on the sufferings of the Irish people at that time. 'Skibbereen' and 'Lone Shanakyle' record the injustice of landlord to tenant in badly affected West Cork, and Clare. 'The Shamrock Shore' and 'Slieve Gallen Braes' describe the abuse of the system of land tenure by the absentee landlord. 'Lone Shanakyle' observes the physical manifestations of famine:

Dark, dark is the night cloud o'er lone Shanakyle,
Where the murdered lie silently pile upon pile,
In the coffinless graves of poor Erin

Many songs tell of the forced emigration to Canada and America, the hardships encountered on what came to be known as the 'coffin ships'. In 'Edward Connors':

Nine more days we were at sea and our sea stores were all gone
But for our captain's kindness when he freely gave us more
We would all have died of hunger ere we reached the other shore.

The *Quebec* which left Derry in 1847 was wrecked with the loss of 228 passengers. On the *Ceylon* out of 257 passengers 117 had died on the voyage and 115 landed, infected with typhus. There is comment too on the mass-evictions of families throughout the country, in reaction to which many landlords were shot ('The Shooting of Lord Leitrim', 'Pat Maguire'). The topic is also viewed from a distance in a number of pieces by the recognised poets of the time – Sir Samuel Ferguson ('Inheritor and Economist'), Aubrey De Vere ('Weal in Woe'), James Clarence Mangan ('The Famine'). A poem by Lady Dufferin, 'The Lament of the Irish Emigrant', generally known by its first line as, 'I'm sitting on the stile Mary where we sat side by side', became one of the most popular sentimental songs of the period both in Ireland and abroad in America. (FRH)

*emigration*. Emigration from all parts of Ireland, by members of all religious groupings, to Britain, Europe, Canada, USA, South Africa, Australia and New Zealand, has been common since the late seventeenth century. The experience of emigrants is reflected in hundreds of songs (mostly in English), a few reflecting the eighteenth-century migration of northern Protestants (the Scotch–Irish) but most date from 1820–1900 and almost all are about going to North America. They were made by local song makers or professional writers, in

Ireland and to an extent abroad, and spread on ballad sheets, in small song books and by word of mouth. Many, for example, 'Thousands are Sailing', 'The Green Fields of Canada' and both of the songs called 'The Rambling Irishman', are widely sung today. The theme is also found in the popular song tradition with songs like 'Good-bye Johnny Dear' (Johnny Patterson) and 'Cutting the Corn in Creeslough' (Percy French). Songs showing a modern perception of emigration are still being made. Although songs tend to show what people *thought* happened rather than what actually *did* happen, they survive to illustrate almost every feature of emigration: the conditions which served to push the emigrants away from the land of their birth, the factors and beliefs which led them to choose any particular destination; the 'American Wake'; the journey to the port of departure; the emigrants' treatment at the hands of shipping agents or captains looking for fares; the shipboard experience; the dangers of the crossing; the welcome or lack of it on the other side.

> I remember the time when our country did flourish,
> When tradesmen of all kinds had both work and pay
> But our trade all has vanished across the Atlantic,
> And we, boys, must follow to America.
> No longer I'll stay in this land of taxation,
> No cruel task-monster shall rule over me;
> To the sweet land of liberty I'll bid good morrow,
> In the green fields of America we'll be free.
>
> ('The Green Fields of America')

Though most emigrants are shown to become prosperous, some songs show the hardship and rejection many suffered in the new land and some even relate their return home.

> No prospect of employment that caused me for to mourn
> I had what would enable us again for to return
> When on board of an Irish vessel we did embark once more
> And thank God we soon arrived safe upon the Shamrock Shore.
>
> ('Edward Connors')

Songs also show that even when well established, the emigrant felt anger at having been forced to leave and this attitude affected many of the political views recorded in the songs. They also show a strong wish to return home. The money which emigrants sent home, to help support their families or to help pay for the passage of other members, became an important part of the Irish economy and this is mentioned in song. By the 1870s emigration, once an escape, was more an aspect of growing up.

> It is God help the mother that rears up a child
> It is now for the father he labours and toils
> He tries to support them, he works night and day
> And when they are reared sure they will go away
>
> ('Thousands are Sailing')

The dominant image of the voyage given by songs of emigration is of people being crammed into unsafe, easily wrecked, disease-ridden coffin ships run by brutal captains, crewed by villains and preyed upon by pirates. Nevertheless, in some songs the worst that is reported is seasickness, while a few thank captains for safe passage and kindly treatment.

> Next morning we were all seasick – not one of us was free
> Quite helpless on my bunk I lay, no one to pity me
> No friends were near but strangers drear, to lift my head when sore
> None of my own to hear me moan far from the Shamrock Shore.
>
> ('The Shamrock Shore')

At the height of the Irish emigration, between 1840 and 1860, exploitation was widespread, indifference to hardship common and attempts to regulate the trade half-hearted or subverted. During the Famine many passengers, already fevered, were allowed through a cursory medical examination to infect whole ships.

> We hadn't been long sailing till fever it seized our crew,
> Falling like the autumn leaves and overboard were threw
> The Ocean waves they rolled o'er our graves our bed's the ocean foam,
> Our friend may mourn but we'll ne'er return to Erin's lovely home.
>
> ('Erin's Lovely Home')

The most serious abuses were practised in small ships, unsuitable to start with, which left small, unsupervised harbours or small inlets, overloaded, underprovisioned and without any medical checks at all. However, ships leaving the larger ports earlier, and all official ports later in the century were better regulated, better run and emigrants better treated (particularly in ships of regular lines). Wrecks of ships were much less frequent than the songs suggest and capture by pirates almost (if not absolutely) unknown while disease was a feature mainly of the period around 1845–49, the years of the Great Famine. The great danger was of contrary winds. Journeys to America, normally of about six weeks, occasionally took over 100 days and led to starvation of crew and passengers alike. Once steamships became common, journey time became predictable, food was provided and the journey much less hazardous. Songs – as would be expected – tend to emphasise extremes. (JOM)

*sport*

*GAA.* Songs have been written about hurling, Gaelic football and handball since the 1700s, and continue to be composed up to the present day. This material finds expression in vocal renderings in pubs, in various GAA publications or in local newspapers. The songs have traditional airs, national airs and those borrowed from popular Irish song; not all airs are traditional but the mode of singing is. Some airs are deliberately more jocose than others, and any one song can be sung to different airs depending on rhythm and metre, the singer usually adopting an air suited to their own style of singing.

> A tonic for all 'tis surest and best
> Good for the arms, the legs and the chest
> If you're nausey or needy or sickly or seedy
> A cure that is speedy – the ash and the ball
>   (From 'Game of the Gaels', by 'Sliabh Rua')

Songs are usually sung locally. The authors would have different literary backgrounds and some would be influenced by the pattern of language of a local area that has survived from earlier times. This can be attractive and noble, enriching, refreshing, original and eloquent. Sporting texts can be approached in five different ways: 1) The historical, starting from before the foundation of the GAA in 1884, until the end of the Civil War in 1923; 2) identity or wedding of territory to kin, creating a new voice for self-esteem; 3) the cultural, or the learned ways of feeling and thinking; 4) the values expected and admired in a GAA society; 5) the hero. The GAA had a stormy beginning in the climate of agitation for Home Rule and such discomfort lasted until the end of the Civil War in 1923. The association was, and is, nominally non-party political, but its members were and are free to join any political organisation; therefore it harbours all strands of nationalist political opinion. There were those who wished to gain independence through constitutional means, and also the physical force side which wanted a republic free from constraints, and a united Ireland. The ballad-makers followed the progress of the association with interest and the texts reflect all political developments of the early years.

> Don't talk about soccer or rugby or cricket
> Or such foreign games for they're not on my ticket
> With our old-fashioned-pastime, their best we can lick it
> For all their amusements are lazy and lame

The GAA fulfilled three very different aspirations: it encouraged local patriotism, it inculcated among its members an uncompromising hostility to foreign games, and it revived local and national pride. Its philosophy is that love of country draws its strength and vitality from love of neighbours, fellow-parishioners and fellow countrymen and women. Its strength comes too from love of the scenes, traditions, culture and way of life associated with one's home and place of origin, and a club or county provides a sense of importance, belonging and identity, a pride and a purpose.

> No more shall lime-white goalposts soar tapering and tall
> Above the greatest goalman that ever clutched a ball
> Nor yet he'll rouse the echoes of ash in native air
> Nor heed the throbbing thousands tense with pride of Clare
>   ('Lament for Dr Thomas Daly', by Bryan MacMahon)

All song-texts are equally charged with such values and aspirations. The ballad-makers write about hurling and the ash, the glory of Munster final day as a symbol and inspiration to the Irish nation, about hurling, camogie and football and their association with the land, the sea, the plough and the spade charging the atmosphere of All-Ireland day. They write about the grief of emigration and the strong links that bind the country with the exiles. There is description of victory and despair, the joys of celebration in music and drinking, sometimes to excess. They write sometimes with religious zeal, the role of the priest, the transience of life, the belief in a resurrection, in a hereafter, a God and the power of prayer. All these assumptions are woven into a complex web of a shared understanding. While there are ballads about the supreme spiritual pleasure that playing the games can give, there are others that say that hostile aggression is an accepted fact in Gaelic games, that playing conventions condone aggressive acts. There are writers also who applaud the warlike skills and 'do or die' attitude of players and teams, an appreciation which may encourage players to push the rules of the game and perhaps generate a willingness to hurt. But there is also the view that there is more to play than this, that competition is at its best when it works as an occasion of friendship: alienation is seen as a defective mode. Shame can be levelled at a player, a team and a community when right is pushed aside and illegitimate tactics or misconduct are condoned. The images given to the GAA heroes in the ballads are persons of renown, held in respectful awe, existing in the imagination as the highest and the best. They coincide to a large extent with the images given to the heroes of Irish folk culture and tell a story of strength, humanity, elegance and determination. The authors give players both human and divine qualities.

> When we were young we read at school that in the days of old
> The young Setanta showed his worth with shield and spear of gold
> As hurling hard on Royal sward he'd Red Branch heroes fling
> But Slaney's plan must find a man to equal Christy Ring
> ('Christy Ring', by Bryan MacMahon)

There is hero status attributed to those who are considered to have given special service to the GAA outside of the playing fields. But a hero is not necessarily one who has lineage, or moral or physical attributes – the vulnerable and solitary loner is sometimes cast as unbeatable, courageous, skilled, generous, human and earthy, in control of surrounding forces. These ballads have an instinctive sense of what is apt and give a clear picture on a broad canvas. They give emphasis to the games as a special ingredient in the make-up of Irish nationhood and point to a specific entity not so specifically celebrated by other nations. They strive to use their subject as a means towards a deeper understanding of the nature of Irish society and the national personality; they reveal the contentment, independence and satisfaction that the games bring into the lives of interested Irish people at home and abroad. The GAA songs heighten and enhance experience of the real world in their own way – joy and sadness, serenity and tension, humour and tragedy. They are well satisfied with their great games, great heroes, great people and great places. (JIS)

*horse racing*. 'Jackson's Grey Mare' illustrates a fine historical, documentary, sporting ballad. The scene is set by appealing to those from whom most loyalty would be reasonably expected, the pedigree is established, the nature of the challenge set forth, the drama of the chase unfolds through the medium of a discourse between horse and jockey, victory is achieved, and local dignity upheld.

> You Monaghan sportsmen I pray you draw near,
> To a few simple verses you quickly shall hear,
> It's the deeds of a hero that lives near Ballybay,
> And they call him Hugh Jackson, I hear people say.
>
> His mill, kilns and barns, they cut a great show,
> His cloths to the north and the city doth go,
> For bleaching and lapping he exceeds them all,
> And his cloth's first approved of at the Linen Hall.
>
> And more of his praises I'm going to explain
> If you will assist me, I will sing about Jane,
> Search Ireland all over from Cork to Kildare
> You'll not find a match for Hugh Jackson's grey mare
>
> He went to the stable, these words he did say,
> 'The hour is approaching and we must away,
> For a cup at Cootehill you have twice won with fame
> And this day I am challenged, you must run again.'

She turned in the stable, 'Kind sir, don't you
    know,
The cup is my own and I won't let it go,
For twice I have won it and I mean to do still,
And we'll roll it in splendour from the plains of
    Cootehill.'

The jockeys were mounted and all in a row,
If you'd been there when away they did go,
The bets were a-making ten guineas to four,
That the cup back to Crieve would return no
    more.

When Jane she heard this, her mettle did rise,
Over hedges and ditches like lightning she flies,
And with a loud 'neigh' these words she did
    say,
'You Bellamont sportsmen, I'll show you the
    way.'

When Jane and her jockey were half round the
    course
Miss Jane and her jockey began to discourse,
Said Miss Jane to her jockey, 'Kind sir
    let me know
Where are my opponents and are they in view?'

He turned in the saddle and he cast an eye
    round
'As for Squire Adams, he lies on the ground
I'm afraid that poor Corry by Spankers is threw
And the rest of your opponents, they are not
    yet in view.'

When Jane heard this, she went in at a race
And into the scales the balance was laid,
The hall was surrounded, for Jackson and Jane,
And the cup went with honours to Crieve back
    again

*hunting*. Most hunting songs in Ireland tell of local men's sport, each with his own dog, pursuing the Irish hare (a mountainy beast, related to the Arctic hare and the Scottish blue hare, not the more placid English brown one) on foot, enjoying the chase for its own sake, honouring the hare and regretting its death – which seldom occurred – often the hare is referred to affectionately as the 'puss', a name used in England too. Stag hunting is mentioned in few songs while hunting the fox on horseback, or at all, does not feature much. Occasionally, as in 'Farmer Michael Hayes', the hunt for a political fugitive is described as if it was a fox hunt. Most of the hare hunts seem to have taken place in the north and were organised locally, mainly spontaneous affairs; there were few formal hunt clubs and consequently these songs are intensely local and personal (many of them little known outside their own area) and, like 'The Granemore Hare', by local song makers, in this case Owen McMahon of Tassagh near Keady, Co. Armagh, who names himself in the song. They were sung in the pub after a hunt, or, less often, where regular hunts were organised, at formal hunt suppers. Some of the songs at these events were imported from North-West England where, especially in Cumbria and Westmorland a similar style of hunt existed, still on foot, though after foxes. Sam Hanna Bell, in *Erin's Orange Lily*, describes a Boxing Day hare hunt in Co. Down and quotes snatches of some songs. There is a recently compiled typescript of hunting songs, again from Co. Down in the ITMA. (JOM)

*religious* (in Irish). Religious songs in Irish belong to the private and domestic, not the commercial world. Their themes come from the elaborate Christian narrative tradition of medieval Europe, on which so many painters drew, and from the stirring sermons given by travelling preachers. They include material from the apocryphal gospels (unofficial, medieval narratives of the life of Christ), such as the blind man said to have pierced Christ's side with a lance as he hung on the cross, whose sight was restored by his blood, or the roasted cock that crew to announce Christ's resurrection.

Most religious songs in Irish focus on the crucifixion, unlike, say, Christmas carols in English, many of which deal with the nativity. There are exceptions, like 'Seacht Sólás/Suáilce na Maighdine', which has been adapted from the English-language 'Seven Joys of Mary', but in general the songs are sorrowful or repentant, and draw heavily on the diction of lament-poetry. A whole cycle of songs is called variously, 'Caoineadh na Páise', 'Dán na Páise', 'Caoineadh Mhuire', 'Caoineadh na Maighdine', or 'Caoineadh na dTrí Muire': variations on the idea of the Virgin Mary's lamenting her son at his crucifixion. They depict the grieving Mary not as the stoical, silent woman of the Latin Stabat Mater Dolorosa, but as a furiously angry and eloquent Irish *bean chaointe* or keening-woman, her hair streaming behind her as she runs barefoot through the desert to reach her son.

Religious songs were sung at wakes and funerals, as well as during Lent, often by women who stood clasping each other's hands above the head and shoulders of the dead person; they seem to have supplied an acceptable alternative when clerical opposition put an end to the custom of keening. Although invariably sung in a spirit of great devotion, the songs of Mary's lament also contain a note of defiance, for their last lines often promise a blessing to anyone who will lament Christ's death on the cross; singer after singer has told folklore collectors that this blessing means it is right and proper to keen the dead, as Mary keened her son. Many of them wept as they sang, and listeners were regularly moved to tears by the pathos of the words and music: what Patrick Pearse called the 'low, sobbing recitative' he heard when Máire Ní Fhlannchadha sang at Feis Chonnacht in Moycullen in 1904. Seosamh Ó hÉanaí (d. 1984), who grew up only yards from Máire an Ghabha in Carna, brought several of these songs to a wider audience through his recordings; Máirtín Ó Cadhain compared his singing of 'Caoineadh na Páise' to a Fra Angelico painting

The songs themselves are sacred, and earn special blessings for those who remember and sing, or even say them. In this they belong as much to the tradition of praying in Irish as to that of singing. Older singers who specialised in them often knew many prayers and religious legends as well, and a considerable number of song-texts have been collected from non-singers, notably Irish-language versions of 'The Cherry-tree Carol' (Child 54), only one version of which has been published with music (*Éigse Cheol Tíre/ Irish Folk Music Studies* 3, 1981, 36–39).

This special category of oral poetry in Irish was recognised by revivalists as early as 1906, when Douglas Hyde published his *Amhráin Diadha Chúige Connacht/The Religious Songs of Connacht*. Like Énrí Ó Muirgheasa's *Dánta Diadha Uladh* (1936, Ulster's Religious Poetry), it contains both songs and prayers, but unfortunately gives no musical notation. The version of 'Caoineadh Mhuire' written down by Patrick Pearse in 1904 appeared in print at least four times during his lifetime (also without music). After his execution in 1916, and the foundation of the Irish Free State in 1921, it was regularly included in anthologies of Irish poetry for use in schools, usually under the name 'Caoineadh na dTrí Muire'. It has acquired the authority of print and prescription, so that other religious songs, and other versions of this song-type, were almost forgotten until the 1960s, when the Catholic church's adoption of liturgies in vernacular languages inspired a revival. Meanwhile the recordings made by Seosamh Ó hÉanaí in the 1970s have ensured that his have become the standard airs for more than one of these songs, which are now often heard at funerals, sometimes with harp or other accompaniment. Versions collected from oral tradition can be up to and over a hundred lines long, sung slowly, and with a refrain after each line, but modern liturgies use quite short versions of traditional religious songs, and confine themselves to those which conform to orthodox religious teachings.

In a broadcast on Raidió na Gaeltachta in 1976, Séamus Ennis referred to such material as song 'ná raibh riamh go coitianta ach ag fodhuine thall is abhus': (songs that only a few people here and there ever sang). A woman of his acquaintance in Co. Donegal had known five of them, he said, and told him that people used to sing them at the fireside long ago, during the days leading up to Easter and Good Friday. This may have been Nóra Ní Ghallchobhair, of An Sruthán, Gort an Choirce, from whom Ennis collected several prayers and religious songs in 1944, but she was not unique: in every Gaeltacht area, for much of the twentieth century, there have been women, and sometimes men, who made a point of learning and transmitting traditional religious material, including songs. Máire Ní Ghríofa (d. 1918), of An Aird Thoir, Carna, Co. Galway, was known as a singer of such songs; her daughter Nan, Mrs Gilmartin, also sang for Séamus Ennis in the early 1940s, and Nan's daughter, Máire an Ghabha, Mrs Canavan (b. 1905), recorded several religious songs in the 1970s, together with prayers she learned while sharing a bed with her grandmother as a child. Máire's son, Michael Mháire an Ghabha, and his children, are noted singers and musicians too, who carry on the rich Carna tradition; one of them, Caitríona Ní Cheannabháin, was heard on the soundtrack of Cathal Black's film *Korea* (1995).*Caoineadh na dTrí Muire: Téama na Páise i bhFilíocht Bhéil na Gaeilge* (Dublin: An Clóchomhar, 1983) by Angela Partridge (Bourke) is a full-length study of the songs about the crucifixion. See also Angela Partridge and Hugh Shields, 'Amhráin Bheannaithe as Co. na Gaillimhe agus as Tír Chonaill,' *Éigse Cheol Tíre/Irish Folk Music Studies* 3 (1981) 18–44; Hugh Shields, *Narrative Singing in Ireland: Lays, Ballads, Come-All-Yes and Other Songs* (Dublin: Irish Academic Press, 1993), has several references to religious song. For sound recordings see Seosamh Ó hÉanaí; Nóirín Ní Riain's *Caoineadh na Maighdine* (Gael-Linn, 1980) is a compendium of religious songs from different Gaeltacht areas, sung by Ní Riain with choral accompaniment by the monks of Glenstal Abbey, while Lasairfhíona Ní Chonaola, Breda Mayock and Katie McMahon sing religious songs in Irish on Hector Zazou, *Lights in the Dark* (Warner/Detour 1998). (AND)

*place-praise*. Every spot has generated its praise songs, most likely originating with the leisured classes who had time to reflect. But the principles embedded in the practice of 'praise-poetry' were established in earlier times, and the concept is common to all cultures, like boasting, a part of the human condition. In nineteenth-century Ireland one did not normally travel far; the beauties of other places may not have been witnessed, but could be visualised through written or spoken description. Graphic song was an important herald in this, the lyric effort of place-praise songs not unlike the exhortations of today's travel agents. Particularly in the Romantic period, they provided an alternative image to bleak life in grimy industrial towns.

Typically the subject region is praised for its beauty and any special features or reputation. The people are inevitably hospitable and gentle, the history proud and resilient, the lands productive. Those pieces created by the hedge-schoolmasters or their pupils might often use the English language as they would have the Irish; the rhyming structures can be similar to older Irish song. The songs could be important to the spirit of the local community, and may have acted as a lure to visitors, but certainly are still popular with many modern examples such as the mildly country-and-western, ballad style 'Bailieboro' in the 1970s, or 'Doonaree' (about Kingscourt, Co. Cavan) in the 1940s. Darby Ryan's 'Shades of Ashgrove' gives the picture:

> Gay Flora with exquisite favour, on her fields in all seasons bestows
> The lily, the violet, the daisy, the tulip, carnation and rose
> Here all kinds of flowers grow spontaneous, in each sunny glade and alcove
> In abundance without cultivation, all along by the Shades of Ashgrove.

Today, the eulogised area may have been long obliterated by modern development, the song serving as historical record:

> Have you been to Killarney, to Causeway or the Quay
> The proud bay of Dublin, Loop Head or Kinsale?
> The City of Cobh's but a shadow on glass
> Compared with the proud rolling Falls of Doonass

In fact the Falls of Doonass were rendered empty by the Ardnacrusha hydro-electric scheme of 1927.

There is a deeper significance however behind this type of song in all cultures. Various 'senses of place' are reflected:

1. Home place. A special reverence for this is found in all cultures, poets tend to regard the childhood location as perfect paradise. Since cities in Ireland are historically associated with and are seen as the creation of hostile invaders, it is not difficult to appreciate an historically based sense of alienation between the rural and the urban. Seán Ó Tuama relates this to the decentralised nature of Irish society up until the recent past (*Repossessions*, 1995). Eoghan MacNéill (*Early Irish Laws & Institutions*, 1935) speaks of ancient Greek civilisation being 'organised like the Irish in small political communities', but these based on walled towns, while 'the Irish state remained a rural city, a city of the fields'. Pre-Elizabethan Ireland was divided into up to two hundred of such 'states', chieftains of them regarded as being 'of' that land.

2. Family name and place. Regions of Ireland are still associated with these – McCarthy and Cork, O'Doherty and Donegal, O'Neill and

Tyrone, O'Byrne and Wicklow. Town and family name are often synonymous, townlands retain family name associations over centuries, sometimes being one and the same thing – for example the name Soley and Artasooley townland (in Co. Armagh), where the family of that name were traditionally sacristans, and in earlier times, lamplighters in the church (Solely, from *solas* = light).

3. Historic places are associated with mythic and heroic figures, flora and fauna, and scenic beauty. Ó Tuama relates this to the *dinnsheanchas* of early medieval Ireland: its discipline informed 'the finest Irish literary works of medieval times'. Once the high literature of the later middle ages (and, as lays, a major popular entertainment in the eighteenth and nineteenth centuries) this resonates with place-names. Its pre-Christian values are embedded with symbolism: 'hill' connoting freedom, all wild nature, this opposed to 'cill' (church, graveyard), Christianity, controlling and hostile. Saints' feast-day 'patterns' and ancient fertility festivals such as Lughnasa which survived into this century reflect such lore (Máire Mac Neill numbers 195 of these in *The Festival of Lughnasa*, Vol. 1, Dublin, 1985). Despite the clerical rooting out of pre-Christian values, these remain embedded in present-day Christian veneers.

4. Burial place of the ancestors is fundamental too to reverence for place, this heightened by emigration to the USA and Britain and migration to cities within Ireland.

5. Past as ideal place. This has become of relevance through the progress of industrialisation and consequent alienation. It is invoked by religious, whole-earth, environmental, cultural and political awarenesses. The legacy of the nineteenth-century romantic movement and the Victorians are its enduring evidence today. Associated with this kind of long-standing tie is a mythological, environmental, historical and familial 'sense of place', but while this may fade over time, 'passion for place' remains, evidenced for instance in the writings of Patrick Kavanagh, Máirtín Ó Direáin and Nuala Ní Dhomhnaill (Ó Tuama, 1995). Such writing was rarely applied to urban place until modern time.

*comic and satirical.* The use of satire is often dated to the times of the bards, when one might fear the lash of their cryptic tongue in revenge for wrongs done or perceived to be done. For instance, a fifteenth-century report sent back to England on the state of things in Ireland had this to say on song: 'There are other SEPTES or professions, namely of BARDES, which are in manner of POETS or RHYMERS, which do nothing but sit and compose lies'.

The fourteenth-century poet Gofraidh Fionn Ó Dálaigh could explain this as:

In poetry for the English we promise that the Gael be banished from Ireland
While in poetry for the Gaels we promise that the English be hunted across the sea.

As far back as the 1830s the genre was exercised in service to political agitation. Darby Ryan's 'Peeler and the Goat' is a prime example:

The Bansha peeler went out one night on duty and patrolling-O
He spied a goat upon the road, who seemed to be a strolling-O
With bayonet fixed he sallied forth and seized him by the wizen-O
Swearing out a mighty oath he'd send him off to prison-O
'Oh, mercy! Sir,' the goat replied 'Pray let me tell my story-O
I am no rogue or Ribbon man, no croppy, Whig, or Tory-O
I'm guilty not of any crime ne'er petty nor high-Treason-O
And I'm sorely wantin' at this time, for 'tis the rantin' season-O.'

The genre survives up to the present day, having had an active life in service to the national movement until well after the setting up of the Free State. From 1915–25 satirical political song on broadsheets and postcards was being issued under the authorship of such well-known figures as Peadar Kearney ('The Row in the Town') and Seán O'Casey ('The Grand Ould Dame Britannia'), these often parodies of old national songs or then-recent music-hall songs. Brian O'Higgins composed satirical song verse prolifically, this appearing in his *Wolfe Tone Annual* up until the 1940s. Satirical political song is still indulged in, for instance John Maguire's exhortation on the US president Ronald Reagan's visit to Ireland:

Hey Ronnie Reagan, I'm black and I'm pagan
I'm gay and I'm left and I'm free
I'm a non-fundamentalist environmentalist
Please don't bother me.

Christy Moore's older lyrics provide the listener with the facility to laugh at themselves by making the plain and ordinarily seem positively hilarious. Tim Lyons' satire on the EEC takes a tongue-in-cheek swipe at a major political institution over which he has no control:

We expected cheap whiskey from Scotland
Cheap wine from the depths of the lake
Thick slices of beef off the mountain
Olive oil, goose paté and cake
Cheap Chateau Margaux from the Bordeaux
Cases of gold Avocaat
All we got was free love from Stockholm
And you all know the price paid for that.

Not all comic song is political. But it does permit the writer to criticise objects of derision, providing release for listeners, mediating unspoken exasperation, defusing frustration, as in Mícheál Marrinan's 'Night Club Song':

Well I'll sing of the capers of the rockers and shakers
That are out all the night 'til the break of the day
Some just of the cradle and more hardly able
In every night club sure they boogie away

Tim Lyon's 'Murder of Joe Frawley' parodies the classic 'murder ballad' in order to drive home observations on music and the bar trade:

When the week it starts
He has cards and darts
On Tuesdays there's nothing much
On Wednesdays there's a disco bar
With flashing lights and such
The local Comhaltas meeting
Goes wild on Thursday nights
But it's when the weekend comes around –
Man, it's really out of sight

Crawford Howard challenges the sanctimonious and sacred in the parody on sentimental ballad 'The Green Fields of France':

But still I don't know now – I'm glad that you're dead
With the green Fields of France piled up over your head
For the trouble you've caused since the day that you died
Oh, shootin's, too good for you, Willie Mac Bride.

The misery of one's neighbours is often a topic for release, as in Brian McGuinness' 'Rangy Ribs':

He was tubered for a fact
Pig-mouthed and humpy-backed
The warble fly had paid a visit too
Had there been a sale for lice
Sure I'd have doubled up the price
On that Rangy Ribs I bought from Mickey Dubh

Patsy Cronin of West Cork wrote not out of direct experience, but from things overheard, books or magazines read. Song for him was a fantastic escape, not unlike cinema, which draws in the listener to experience it with him in 'Beauty Spot Glanlea':

The Lebanon mountains' highest peaks
Were like McGillicuddy's reeks
And from their summits you could see
The lakes of Galilee
And likewise the river Jordan, and
The province of Samaria, and
Though it sounds contrary – Ah!!
The fairest was Glanlea

Nothing is sacred in this song genre. All the classic ballad types are mined for the worth of parody, or perhaps an air which matches a particular sentiment. The 'place-praise' song, a noble genre established through use of 'Hiberno-English' in the transition from Gaelic to English, is typical of the comic satire. Therein the singer has the freedom to criticise, but is exempted from judgement. Brian O'Rourke's 'Drumsnot'

Our hedge-master died, in eighteen-o-five
And since then we have had no school
And for all we see, of C I E
We might as well be in Kabul

This of course mimicking the effusion of Glaswegian W. J. Rankine who composed the ultimate praise of Mullingar in 1874:

And then there's Main Street
That broad and clean street
With its rows of gas lamps that shine afar
I could spake a lecture in the architecture
Of the gorgeous city of Mullingar

*festivals.* The major singing festivals (singing weekends) are held outside the summer or tourist season.

February: Mike Donoghue Weekend, Ballyvaughan, Co. Clare; Rosslare Singers' Weekend, Rosslare, Co. Wexford

March: Inishowen Folksong and Ballad Seminar, Inishowen, Co. Donegal

April: Geordie Hanna Weekend, Coalisland, Co. Tyrone; Sean-nós Cois Life, Dublin, Co. Dublin

May: Clare Festival of Traditional Singing, Ennistymon, Co. Clare; Feakle Singers' Weekend, Feakle, Co. Clare; Féile Chomhórtha Joe Éiniú, Cill Chiaráin, Co. Galway

October: Éigse Dharach Uí Chatháin, Rath Chairn, Co. Meath; Sliabh Gullion Festival of Traditional Singing, Forkhill, Co. Armagh

December: Éigse Dhiarmuid Ó Shúilleabháin, Coolea, Co. Cork

**song collectors.** Song collectors are those who preserve words and music in a way which allows a succeeding generation to perform the song. While without the slightest doubt all the collectors are of considerable value, in reality collectors approached their task with differing agendas. Some collectors, interested in 'ancient Irish music', mainly preserved song airs without texts, or provided airs of their collection with new 'poetic' words; others, who were primarily interested in Irish language, noted words without music. None of these collected adequately, though what has been preserved may be used to 'mend' what is unclear in current tradition or to construct songs anew. Edward Bunting employed Patrick Lynch to notate texts; some words proper to the airs noted by George Petrie were preserved by Eugene O'Curry. First to give words and airs (without harmonies) was John O'Daly's *Poets and Poetry of Munster*. The *Journal of the Irish Folk Song Society*, London, started in 1904, and contained the work of some otherwise unpublished collectors: Charlotte Milligan Fox, Edith Wheeler, Patrick Cairns Hughes. Some of them give airs only, but little in Irish until a full issue was devoted to the work of Eileen Costello (Eibhlín Bean Mhic Choisdealbha) whose *Amhráin Mhuighe Seóla* (1919) contains songs collected around Tuam, Co. Galway when Tuam was the centre of an Irish-speaking area (reissued 1990). Under Donal O'Sullivan's editorship the *Journal* published mainly Irish songs and between 1927 and 1936, the larger part of the Bunting Collection, some with texts. Martin Freeman, giving the words in an odd and not very satisfactory phonetic style, printed the results of his collecting in Ballyvourney, West Cork in the *Journal of the Folk Song Society*, Nos. 23–25 (London, 1920–23). Máighread Ní Annagáin and Séamus de Chlanndiolúin presented words and music from Waterford and Galway in *Londubh an Chairn* (1927). Many of the songs in the archive of the Irish Folklore Commission from 1935 are airless texts – though substantial collections of complete songs were made in Munster by Liam de Noraidh and Séamus Ennis in Ulster. Douglas Hyde and Éinrí Ó Muirgheas gave words only but more recent collections by Nollaig Ó hUrmoltaigh, Lorcán Ó Muireadach and Seán Ó Baoill have presented text and tune more often now in recorded form. Among the first to collect English songs was John Hume, from south Antrim. The Lancashire poet Edwin Waugh, visiting north Antrim in the 1860s, noted some scraps and perhaps the first oral text of the 'True Lover's Discussion'; John McCall and his son P. J. McCall left the words they had noted to the National Library of Ireland; Patrick Kennedy had song texts in his book *Banks of the Boro*. P. W. Joyce's volumes presented words and music only in sporadic unity, some unpublished material is in the National Library of Ireland. Herbert Hughes and his collaborators only sometimes gave the proper words. Miss Honoria Galwey presented her collections and recollections with fragmentary or no text. The earliest presentations of numbers of singable songs were the newspaper articles of Sam Henry and the books of Fr Ranson and Colm Ó Lochlainn. Since the advent of the tape recorder, the presentation of complete songs has become the norm: Alan Lomax, Diane Hamilton and Jean Ritchie, Peter Kennedy, Séamus Ennis, Seán O'Boyle made recordings – some of which were transcribed – in the late 1940s and '50s, for themselves, or for BBC or RTÉ. In the 1960s and recently, Robin Morton, Hugh Shields, Tom Munnelly, Seán (Vincent) McCann, Séamus MacMathúna, Seán Corcoran and many others made recordings with documentary intent, some of which have been issued; while many singers, initially in the interests of their own repertory have made collections; among them Paddy Berry, Frank Harte, Len Graham, Paddy Tunney, Jim Foley. Almost all singers now collect songs, mostly however from one another, though there are still songs unknown to archivists and new songs being made. Video recorders now allow performance and ambience to be collected together. Much of the fruits of the work of all these collectors is available at the ITMA though some must be sought at the Department of Irish Folklore at UCD or at the Headquarters of CCÉ in Dublin. (JOM)

In anything approaching its modern meaning, the collecting of song in Ireland began with Cavan woman Charlotte Brooke (c. 1740–93). She translated the songs she collected into English for her *Reliques of Irish Poetry, Consisting of Heroic Poems, Odes, Elegies and Songs* (1789). Musical antiquarian Edward Bunting (1773–1843) saw himself as rescuing an old tradition, that of the harpers, from oblivion. George Petrie (1790–1866) was a fastidious and enthusiastic collector of music but had little regard for the English language texts he encountered. The writings of Patrick Kennedy (1801–73) are sown liberally with texts of traditional songs and ballads he heard in the Wexford of his youth. This is particularly true of his *The Banks of the Boro* (London, 1867). His work seems to have inspired John McCall (1822–1902) to jot down whatever songs he remembered from his own boyhood in Clonmore on the Carlow/Wexford border a decade or so later. More than 150 complete songs and fragments make up McCall's unpublished manuscript which is held in the National Library of Ireland. Among the thousands of tunes collected by William Forde (1759–1850), Henry Hudson (1798–1889), and James Goodman (1826–96) we find airs to hundreds of ballads and songs. Regrettably, in these collections there are many songs whose existence is now known only from their tune titles as their lyrics have vanished forever. Patrick Weston Joyce (1827–1914), a prolific collector and publisher, also had a lofty attitude to much of the material he collected in English. Nevertheless, of his many publications, *Old Irish Folk Music and Song* (Dublin, Hodges, Figgis, 1909) remains a rich and diverse sampler of the music and song of nineteenth-century Ireland. (TOM)

**'Songs of the People.'** A series of articles which ran from 1923 to 1939 in the Coleraine weekly newspaper *The Northern Constitution*. Instigated by Sam Henry, who edited the series for all but the years 1928–32, the other principal editors were James Moore (for about a year) and Willie Devine (three years). This series comprised the contributions of singers mainly from within a twenty-mile radius of Coleraine – over 500 songs – and was enormously influential in sustaining a singing tradition in its area of circulation and among singers and researchers who quarried the scrapbooks Sam Henry presented to libraries in Belfast, Dublin and Washington DC. The contents of the scrapbooks have now been combined in a volume published by the University of Georgia Press: *Sam Henry's 'Songs of the People'*. The collection of James Moore, part of which was made in north Donegal, and that of Willie Devine, who was one of Sam Henry's contributors but whose edited contribution was mostly plagiarised, are presently being edited for publication. (JOM)

**Sources of Irish Traditional Music Project.** Compilation in one collection of all pre-1855 tunes recorded in Irish manuscript and printed collections, together with related materials. It opens with the first sources from c. 1583 and runs forward to Petrie's *Ancient Music of Ireland*. Proposed by Aloys Fleischmann, professor of music in UCC, the project was begun in the 1950s by one of his graduate students, Anette de Foubert. In the 1960s Fleischmann involved Seán Ó Riada and Pilib Ó Laoghaire. Later Mary Neville assisted, then Mary Bollard and Nóirín Ní Riain in the 1970s. In 1975, Mícheál Ó Súilleabháin was brought in as deputy editor as the compilation expanded. Helen Walsh and Sarah Collins were involved in the 1980s, and Nicholas Carolan, director of the ITMA acted as consultant after 1988. All these brought the selection of material to completion by the time of Fleischmann's death in 1992. However, an inflexible layout resulting from necessary, constant sub-sectioning and additions over the years, frustrated by changes in computer technology, rendered the mass still unpublishable. In the same year, the major task of organising it was undertaken by Paul

McGettrick (a post-graduate student of Prof. Ó Súilleabháin). His re-entering of all of the material in database format on computer rendered it suitable for printing, and its indexing, bibliography and accession compatible with electronic publishing systems. A profound memorial to the Professor Fleischmann, this finally appeared in print in 1998. The project also benefited from FÁS trainees, UCC computer department staff, individual members of the British Library and National Library of Scotland, School of Scottish Studies, the Irish departments of UCG, UCD and UCC and the music department of University College of North Wales. Support grants toward publication were given by the Ireland Fund, UNESCO and ACÉ; it is published by Garland Inc., New York.

*collection structure*. Within the collection, the tunes are presented chronologically with, for each of the sources, details provided about the source followed by the tunes taken from that source. For each tune the following information is provided: Tune No. and Title, Location in Source, Tune Category, Tonality, Structure, References to Concordances and Variants, Composer/Arranger. The indexes are a very important part of the publication. There are four: an index of Incipits (opening words), an index of Titles, an index of First Lines, and an index of Categories. Prof. Fleischmann considered the alphabetical index of incipits to be its most useful component. In creating it he adopted an approach which he discovered in use at the Institute of Folk Music in Ljubljana in the former Yugoslavia in 1967. It is not altogether dissimilar from the approach adopted by Barlow and Morgenstern in their book *A Dictionary of Musical Themes*. The first twelve notes, excluding ornamental notes, are taken into account. Each tune is entered in the index as commencing with the note G above middle C and the next eleven notes are then transposed automatically. Two incipits are created for all tunes with upbeats (*c.* 70 per cent), because of the variable nature of the anacrusis lead-in notes. (PAM)

*use of electronic media*. Because the collection now exists as a corpus of tunes or computer files an electronic version of the 'Sources' project either on CD ROM or the Internet is now possible. An electronic corpus teamed up with a library of musical pattern-matching functions and user-friendly interface becomes an incredibly useful and powerful resource. All of the following become possible:

1. Powerful text and music searches (including Boolean) e.g. for motives of any length in any position (not just incipits) over the whole corpus perhaps revealing further links between tunes that escaped the printed version;

2. identifying all tunes having a certain structure or in a certain mode;

3. perhaps analysis/comparison based on studying just accented notes, etc.

This offers a huge advantage over printed indexes. It will incorporate playback and print facilities; updating, changing, adding information can be done very easily on an Internet version; it will become a true multimedia project combining sound, image, music notation and text; hyperlinking cross-references. A demonstration of what's possible can be seen on the World Wide Web where Peter Flynn of the Computer Bureau, UCC has made the titles index searchable on the Internet (http://imbolc.ucc.ie/fleischmann/). It functions in a similar way to the CELT project for Irish manuscripts. With an electronic version in mind Mikael Fernstrom of the Interactive Design Centre, University of Limerick, is currently working on a graphical user-interface. (PAM)

**South Sligo Summer School.** Held in Tubbercurry, Co. Sligo, this is based in the hinterland of Coleman Country. It offers classes in fiddle, flute, button and piano accordion, banjo, concertina and traditional guitar, uilleann pipes, set dancing, traditional singing, bodhrán, harp and traditional music heritage. Classes are held each morning, lectures on aspects of the music are delivered by prominent figures in the afternoon, and céilithe, recitals and concerts occupy the evenings.

The school was initiated in 1987 by Marie Flannery, and she now runs it with Michael Severs and Geraldine Murtagh. Beginning with ten teachers and a hundred pupils it expanded rapidly, and its 1999 sitting had some thirty teachers and six hundred students. In addition to student fees, funding is provided by the Arts Council, the County Council and local businesses, while the local VEC pays teaching fees.

***Spirit of the Nation.***
See Young Irelanders.

**step dance.** A precise technical, rhythmic, performance genre danced by either male or female, with kinesthetic activity occurring predominantly in leg movements. Particular dance contexts, categorisations, stylistic features and aesthetics, distinguish and define this dance genre as Irish step dance. Irish step dance may be performed either solo or in a group. The primary solo Irish step dance types are the reel, jig and hornpipe. Other dance types include the treble reel, slip jig, single jig, light jig, and the solo set dances which are specific dances choreographed to specific pieces of music such as, 'The Blackbird', 'St Patrick's Day', 'The Job of Journeywork', etc. With the exception of the solo set dances, all the above mentioned Irish dances are choreographed to tunes within the reel, jig, and hornpipe categories. The reel is in 4/4 time; the double jig is in 6/8 time; the hornpipe is in 4/4 time; the slip jig is in 9/8 time; the single jig is in 12/8 time; and the light jig is in 6/8 time. The treble reel, jig, hornpipe and solo set dances, are performed with hard shoes enhancing the percussive nature of these dances, while the reel, slip jig, single jig, and light jig are danced with soft shoes (pumps) emphasising the graceful, airborn nature of these dances. Although similar movements and motifs may overlap between the different dance genres other movements may be specific to particular genres. Each step dance consists of an eight-bar choreographic structure which is assymetrically repeated for another eight bars of the music. Thus a complete performance of a step takes sixteen bars. A dance performance consists of a number of these choreographed step dances performed sequentially, which may be commenced and concluded with a specifically choreographed lead step.

References to Irish step dance date back to the closing decades of the eighteenth century. Arthur Young, in his *Tour of Ireland 1776–79*, is the first to mention the existence of dancing-masters. These dancing-masters travelled around rural regions of Ireland teaching step dance and other contemporary social dances such as the minuets, country dances, cotillions, and later sets (quadrilles), to the agricultural community. From references to step dance we find that the performance practice was one which was earthy in style, confined to personal space, and dominated by men. References to performances on half doors, flag stones, and tops of barrels is evident of this confinement of space. Indeed it was an aesthetic value that step dancers have the ability to perform within a confined space, thus requiring a neat performance directly under the dancer's centre of weight. Contexts for the performance of dance, both solo and group, up to the early decades of the twentieth century would have included house dances, weddings, fairs, patterns, pilgrimage days, feast days, holy days, and crossroads. From the 1920s, step dance schools emerged in the cities and larger towns of Ireland. Dance competitions gradually became the primary context for the performance and assessment of step dance. The age group of performers fell to include children from five to young adulthood. Also, a gender shift in performers, female dancers predominating, effected the development in Irish step dance choreography and performance. Further, in lieu of the prior confined spatial movements, larger stage platforms required a greater use of space; a factor which contributed also to choreographic choices. With the Irish diaspora, Irish step dance is presently taught also in Wales, Scotland, England, United States of America, Canada, Australia, New Zealand, and Africa.

*competition rules.* An Coimisiún le Rincí Gaelacha (The Irish Dancing Commission), under the auspices of the Gaelic League, is the primary organisation for Irish step dance. Since its emergence in 1929 An Coimisiún centrally controls Irish step dance and Irish step-dance competitions on a global basis. Irish step dance is taught by teachers registered with the organisation, and only those step dancers registered with these teachers may compete in the Coimisiún's network of competitions. Competitions are organised on a local, regional, national, and international basis, and in turn are organised according to dance type, dance competence, age group, and gender. Currently, registered teachers exist in Ireland, England, Scotland, Wales, the US, Canada, Australia, New Zealand, and Africa. Competition is both the primary step dance event and motivating factor in Irish step dance. Step dancers, teachers and adjudicators are required to follow the rulings of the Coimisiún both in the classroom and in competition. Concerning the latter, the rulings are explicate regarding registration of competitions, syllabi of competitions, grades, adjudication, prizes and musical accompaniment. For instance, registered competitions need to be adjudicated only by current registered adjudicators with the Coimisiún. Also, for registered competitions, organisers 'must not without the prior consent of the Regional Dancing Authority use a record-player or tape recorded to provide musical accompaniment for competitors.' Experienced musicians capable of playing the required accompaniment for every competition to the satisfaction of the adjudicator is the requirement. Indeed, when required, the Coimisiún may issue guidelines relating to issues such as music speeds, fees payable for registration of competitions, the level of difficulty of steps in lower-grade competitions, types of steps not permitted in any grade or dance, and footwear and types of costume and ornamentation permitted or forbidden. In these registered step dance competitions the rulings of the Coimisiún are paramount. The repertoire in Irish step dance is determined largely by competition requirements and standards. Since those team or céilí dances in *Ár Rinncídhe Fóirne* (the official text book of the Coimisiún) are the only permissible dances in the céilí dance competitions, these dances make up a large part of the group dance repertoires in the schools. Céilí dances other than those in the official book are inadmissible in competition thus effectively marginalising some regional dances while institutionalising those selected in *Ár Rinncídhe Foirne*. However, within the World Dancing Championships, the dance drama competition allows for choreography outside the prescribed text book dances. It is a requirement that these choreographies, especially choreographed for the competition, represent some aspect of Irish culture. Within the solo dance competitions, a repertoire which is constantly developing, familiar, traditional movements are combined with more innovative ones. It is the creative balance of these two factors – tradition and innovation – which allows for the gradual development of this art form. The 'step' within these genres is the basic dance choreography: a choreography which consists generally of eight bars. Although similar motifs and elements may be found in all step dances of a particular genre, no two step dances are the same. It is the unique creative combination of motifs – within a step dance – both visually and auditory, which differentiates it from other step dances in the repertoire. Each teacher choreographs his/her own step dances. Thus, the repertoire within particular dance genres constantly, but subtly, changes and develops over time. Being placed high in competition awards recognition to the dancer, the school of dance, the country of the dancer, and the technical movements within the dance. The actual prizes come in the form of cups, shields, belts, plaques, statuettes, or medals. Although no ruling regarding clothing is specifically stated, the concept of a school costume and a solo costume per dancer is the norm. Hand in hand with the technical development in step dance is a gradual development in dance clothing and footwear as dancers and teachers alike look for different ways of expressing themselves both visually and/or percussively. Other organisations of Irish step dance exist for example, An Comhdháil, and An Cumann Rince Náisiúnta. However, the Coimisiún has a current monopoly on numbers of step dancers, and registered teachers worldwide. (CAF)

*competition structure, Ireland and overseas.* Although competitions vary very much in size, the basic structure is extremely similar in all countries. Dancing competitions are referred to as feis (pl. feiseanna) and larger more prestigious events as an Oireachtas. Competitions can vary from small local events lasting a few hours to All-Ireland Championships/Oireachtas lasting 110 hours over six days and World Championships/Oireachtas lasting eight days. Competitions are held in: solo reels, light jigs, single jigs, hop or slip jigs, heavy jigs and hornpipes and in solo set dances; couple or two-hand dances and three-hand dances; céilí or figure dances; newly composed figure dances and in dance drama/choreography. The majority of competitions are for teen ages but range from under five years to 'adult competitions' with no upper age limit. The latter, very popular in America, are confined to those who commenced dancing as adults. A large majority of competitors are females. Males and females usually compete within their gender except at major events where separate solo championships are held, and céilí and figure competitions are divided into mixed (male and females on the same team) and unmixed. Individual competitions vary in size from two or three to over 200 competitors in solo competitions and up to sixty céilí teams with some 500 competitors. A single competition can take up to six hours to complete. Non-championship competitions are usually for a single dance. Solo championships consist of two or three dances including one light and one or two heavy dances of which one is usually a solo set dance piece. Solo dancers may perform two or three (but not more) pieces at a time, usually to prescribed metronomic speeds. Solo set dances, due to preference for different speeds, are performed individually. Non-championship events may utilise a single judge but championships must have a minimum of three judges (or as much as seven at the World Championships). The team of three to seven judges may judge either a single dance or all dances in the championship. The final result is achieved by each judge awarding points (first 100 points, second 75 points, third 65 points etc.), eliminating discrepancies between marking standards by different judges. Competitions are usually divided into three or four categories. Terminology varies geographically but they approximately correspond to: beginner, non-prize winner or novice, and open or championship level (bun grád, mean grád and ard grád).

Feiseanna, featuring Irish dancing competitions, were instigated in 1898. The All-Ireland Dancing Championships were first organised by the Irish Dancing Commission in 1933 and are held annually since. Other major, prestigious events include the Great Britain Championships, British Nationals, Australian Championships, and North American Championships. The latter have been held annually since 1969 in a different city in North America on the Fourth of July weekend. They run for three days, utilising four different halls in the same hotel and attract some 2,500 dancers from various countries. The World Championships were instigated in 1969. They are held annually in Ireland and attract around 2,000 competitors. Entries are strictly limited. Dancers must qualify at their own regional Oireachtas in the four provinces in Ireland and at other major designated 'qualifying Oireachtaisí' in England, Scotland, Wales, Canada, USA, Australia and New Zealand. Regardless of the location the prerequisites for qualification to the 'Worlds' are strictly legislated for and numbers of qualifiers are rigidly controlled in an effort to contain the event.

*teachers and registration.* The Irish Dancing Commission (IDC), established by the Gaelic League in 1929, produces an annual register of qualified céilí dance teachers (TMRF), céilí and step dancing teachers (TCRG) and adjudicators (ADCRG). Since 1943 qualifications are obtained by examinations, held at varying intervals in Ireland, England, Scotland, Australia, New Zealand, and North America. The TCRG exam consists of: written examination of thirty céilí dances, published in *Ár Rinncídhe Fóirne*; practical teaching of solo step dancing and céilí dancing; execution of variety of solo dances; music test on identification of solo dances and set dances by name, time signature and bar structure. ADCRG candidates must be qualified teachers and undergo an additional judging session and oral interview. Once qualified, teachers and adjudicators pay an annual fee, register with and agree to abide by the rules of the IDC.

*history of examinations.* The IDC commenced registration in 1933 with thirty-two teachers and twenty-seven adjudicators in Ireland only. Prior to 1943 qualification was by achievement in competition; the IDC introduced an examination system in Ireland in that year. The first exams held in America were in 1967, England and Australia in 1969 and New Zealand in 1973. Subsequently the IDC changed from a national to an international body. In 1997 the IDC registered some 1,200 teachers and forty-four adjudicators; 370 teachers and 110 adjudicators were from North America. At present the numbers registered in

North America are approximately the same as in Ireland, with teachers in thirty-eight different states and in every Canadian province. Teachers' circuits can be very large. A single US teacher may teach in up to seven different states. Qualified teachers reside in Ireland, England, Scotland, Wales, USA, Canada, Australia and New Zealand with 'occasional' teachers in Holland, Germany, Belgium, Brazil, South Africa and Kenya. Teachers reside as far south as Invercargill, South Island, New Zealand and as far north as Fort McMurray in Alberta and Fort St John in British Columbia. Dance teachers' associations existed in Cork since 1895 and Dublin since 1925 and they registered teachers prior to 1933. Since 1969 a separate teachers' organisation, An Comhdháil, also organises examinations and conducts registration. Its activities however, are largely confined to Ireland, England and Scotland. The IDC and An Comhdháil co-operate with each other and recognise each other's qualifications. (JOC)

See dance costumes.

*sean-nós.* The term sean-nós ('old style') step dancing is used to refer to the traditional style of solo step dance mainly performed in the Connemara Gaeltacht (Irish-speaking area) of West Galway. Unlike the style of the modern dancing schools there is freedom of arm movements, the steps do not follow a prescribed pattern and the stepping is close to the floor. The use of the term as applied to step-dance in Ireland is relatively recent. It derives originally from an initiative based in Connemara in 1975 when local activists held a series of fringe events during An tOireachtas. One of these was an exhibition of 'old-style' solo step-dancing by local people. The term 'damhsa ar a' sean-nós' ('dance in the old style') was first used at this event. Sean-nós had been accepted as a term to describe the intricate local style of solo unaccompanied singing and its connotations would be readily understood both inside and outside the Gaeltachtaí. The presentation of sean-nós dancing at the 'alternative Oireachtas' was an important element in the organisers' desire to highlight one of the distinctive features of Connemara culture which was unrecognised by and possibly even unknown to the authorities of the Gaelic League. The programme of the official Oireachtas had never allowed for the inclusion of this type of popular dance, even though it was to be commonly found at social gatherings in Connemara. Prior to the 1970s the local term for the indigenous dance style was simply *an bhatráil* (the battering) and it was on the verge of extinction. Such was the enthusiasm engendered by its new public presentation that many local people began to see the sean-nós dance as a badge of cultural identity and a source of pride.

*learning.* Central to an understanding of the local attitude to sean-nós dancing is the notion that it is not formally taught. A dancer in this style will always say in reply to the question 'Where did you learn to dance?' '*Phioc mé suas é*' (I just picked it up.) Counterposed to this is the concept of what they call *damhsa foghlamtha* (formally-learnt dance) – which means the costumed, dancing school form – ever-more athletic and balletic solo dance which is nowadays the 'official' style promoted by the extensive international network of Irish dancing organisations. The emphasis placed by dancers in the sean-nós style on the individuality of each dancer's performance is the key-note to its practice. The process by which a dancer acquires the necessary skills in the sean-nós style can be compared to the development of a singing style in an area where the song tradition is strong. The learner will consciously or unconsciously abstract, absorb and mentally process the distinguishing elements of the local style and will go on to practise and perfect the art through performance, whether public or private.

*the dance.* By far the most popular dance-tempo in Connemara is the reel, and most dancers will ask the musician to play 'Miss McLeod's reel'. The most distinctive and characteristic sean-nós foot-movement is called *timeáil* (literally, 'timing'). This percussive effect, which is produced by using the heel, takes up four quavers or half a bar of the reel and is the basic element in many sean-nós step patterns. Each count takes one quaver in 4/4 time.

Start with feet together, side by side, heels slightly raised.

Count
1. Strike the tip of the right heel on the floor.
2. Step down onto ball of right foot.
3. Strike the tip of the left heel on the floor.
4. Step down onto ball of the left foot.

The weight or balance of the body shifts from the ball of one foot to the other. On count 1, it is on the ball of the left foot; on count 2 it moves back to the right then back to the left on count 4. The form or structure of the dance is not rigid. Many dancers start with a *gabháil timpeall* (a lead around) for eight bars, then the steps begin. The custom in other areas of dancing – a step first off the right foot for eight bars and repeating the step off the left foot (doubling) – is not followed in the Connemara area. Some typical step elements are 'kicking' the floor with the tip of the right or left toe once or twice to the rear of starting position, 'stamping' with either foot in an emphatic fashion, 'side-step' movements in which the dancer moves to left or right, a 'shuffling' movement in which the ball of the foot 'brushes' the floor whilst the dancer moves the foot forward and 'brushes' it again whilst returning it to the starting position.

Any or all of the movements detailed or referred to above may be used in any combination by an individual dancer. The repertoire of a dancer will not remain static and steps will be created as inspiration strikes, whether in the privacy of the dancer's own home or in the heat of a competitive performance.

The use of arm movements is not subject to prescriptive direction. Some dancers maintain the arms by the sides where they move slightly as the body changes position. Flamboyant arm movements, where the arms are raised to shoulder height or even higher, are relatively rare and are used more commonly by male dancers who still outnumber female dancers in this tradition although the gap is closing in recent times.

The dancer in the sean-nós style does not attempt to 'cover the floor'. Most steps are danced 'in place'. Traditionally, good dancers were said to be able to 'dance on a plate/dance on a sixpence'. A recent Oireachtas champion has been known to dance on a dartboard. Although well-known dancers will still be called on to perform during a night out in a pub or at a social function whether public or private, it is undoubtedly the case that the main dance-arena is now the *comórtas ar a' sean-nós* (sean-nós competition.) The highlight of the sean-nós dance calendar takes place during the *Pléaracha* festival each September in An Cheathrú Rua. (HEB)

**Stewart, Trevor.** (1948– ). Pipes, singer. From Bushmills, Co. Antrim, his father sang, his mother's Magherafelt, Co. Derry, family played in pipe and flute bands. His interest in music was initially ballads and guitar. A Belfast concert of the Dubliners led him, via the Chieftains, to such as Séamus Ennis, and to taking up uilleann pipes in 1967. Journalist Joe Crane introduced him to Belfast pipe-maker Frank McFadden from whom he got a basic set, and to whose grandson he gave his guitar. His singing of local songs with the group, the Country Four, gained attention from A. L. Lloyd and Peter Bellamy's Young Tradition in England. This resulted in a Topic recording which included such as 'P stands for Paddy', culled from Sam Henry's collection, and other ballads from his father.

**Stewarts of Blairgowrie.** There has always been a strong sense of kinship between Scotland and Ireland and many songs and tunes are held in common or have gone back and forward between the two countries. This is particularly true of the West of Scotland, where many people have Irish family connections. The Scottish travelling people also tend to have links with Ireland. For example, in the early 1900s, members of the famous Blairgowrie, Perthshire Stewart family of singers, pipers and storytellers intermarried with Irish travellers. In 1915 when conscription was introduced, they, like many Scottish travellers, did not want to go to war for the country that did not recognise their place in Scottish society, although they were descended from its aboriginal inhabitants.

*visits to Ireland*. Consequently, they crossed to Ireland for the duration of World War I and continued to visit frequently through the 1920s and 1930s. Their traditional culture found them many friends among Irish travellers, with whom they mixed everywhere they went, and their songs, stories and piping helped to earn them a living on the roads in Ireland. They have many accounts of céilís at crossroads, good crack around the fire at fairs and markets, weddings and funerals. Old John Stewart played his pipes both on St Patrick's Day, and on 12 July. They learned many Irish songs and stories which became an important part of their repertoire and after the war they also encouraged squads of Irish workers to come to

Perthshire for the berry-picking and potato-lifting harvests, when this cultural exchange would be continued. Songs brought over to Scotland by Irish berry- and tattie-squads in the 1940s and 1950s include, 'There was an Old Man on Kellyburn Braes', sung by Harry Duffy, 'The Penitentiary Song', and 'Mo Bhuachaillín Donn'. Belle Stewart (1906–97) came to Ireland with her brothers Donald and Andy Macgregor and their uncle Jimmy Jack Stewart, at the invitation of their cousins the Stewarts, and she was married to Alec Stewart in Ballymoney in 1925. She did not take so happily to life on the road in a bow-topped wagon – she had grown up in Blairgowrie, where her mother settled after the death of her father in 1907.

The Stewarts had also led a croft-based existence in Perthshire, but they found the fresh-water pearl-fishing in the Irish rivers excellent, and even after the Troubles started, they continued to travel among the Irish people. Belle went backwards and forwards between Blairgowrie and Ireland for quite a number of years, before she and Alec settled permanently. The Irish songs in her repertoire included 'The Banks of the Foyle', 'The Rambling Irishman', 'If I Were a Blackbird', 'The Galway Shawl', 'The Dawning of the Day', 'The Maid of Culmore', 'John Mitchell', 'The Lonely Banna Strand', 'Ballyjamesduff', 'Glen Swilly', 'Terence's Farewell', 'The Real Ould Mountain Dew', 'Blue Bleezin Blind Drunk', 'The Bonny Irish Boy', 'The Blarney Roses', 'Master McGrath', 'Kathleen Mavourneen' (a comic bawdy song, not the well-known love song) 'Blackwaterside', and 'Mary on the Banks of the Lee'. From this selection it is clear that the Stewarts sang songs because they liked them as songs, not because of their political associations. There was also in their repertoire a broadside ballad called 'Blooming Caroline', which seems to be popular in Ireland among old singers. Since 'Caroline' belonged to Edinburgh, it might be that the Stewarts took it to Ireland. It is also possible that Belle might have passed on her version of the ballad 'The Twa Brothers', for it has been collected in Ireland in the area where the Stewarts travelled, yet in Scotland it has been recorded only from their family.

Another song which found its way into the Stewart repertoire from that of their Aberdeenshire cousin Jeannie Robertson – 'Jock Stewart' – seems to be adapted from the Irish, 'A Man You Don't Meet Every Day' which they claim was written about Alec's father, John Stewart, a noted piper and storyteller. 'The Mountain Streams Where the Moorcocks Crow', which Belle also sang, has been recorded from Irish singers such as Paddy Tunney. Belle passed on many of these songs to her daughters Sheila and Cathy. She used the tunes of Irish songs for one or two of her own songs, for example, 'The Banks of the Foyle', for 'The Canty Auld Wife', a song about a Blairgowrie mother who lost three sons in the war and 'Down by Glenside', for 'Down by the Sheiling', a song about her two brothers.

Recordings of the Stewart family's songs, stories and tunes are contained in the Sound Archive of the School of Scottish Studies, 27 George Square, Edinburgh, recorded by Maurice Fleming, Hamish Henderson and Sheila Douglas. They were also recorded by Topic and Lismor and these recordings have been re-issued by Ossian in Cork. Perhaps the most remarkable piece of Irish tradition found in the Stewart family repertoire was a version of the ancient Irish immram 'The Voyage of Mael Duin' told by Alec Stewart's brother John as 'Jack and the Seven Enchanted Islands'. This his father learned in the 1920s from a Donegal storyteller called Mosie Wray. John, born in 1910, remembered this story and recorded it in his seventieth year. The Stewarts can be heard on *The Stewarts of Blair* album. (SHD)

**St Mary's Music Club, Church Street.**
See Church Street Club.

**strathspey.** Originating in the valley of the river Spey in Inverness-shire, Scotland, the strathspey evolved from a hybrid dance-tune form known as a strathspey-reel. The first printed strathspey proper appeared in an edition of *The Caledonian Pocket Companion* by James Oswald in 1745. The strathspey was introduced to south Co. Donegal along with other tunes which became popular from the late nineteenth century onwards, although it never functioned for the dance there. The strathspey is in common time

### The Iron Man (Strathspey)      (J. Scots Skinner)

with each beat of a bar being accented. The tune-type is particularly noted for its dotted rhythms, especially the 'Scots snap', where the short note precedes the long note. In Scotland these dotted rhythms are articulated in a particularly exaggerated manner, facilitated by the use of the up-driven bow in fiddle-playing. Donegal fiddlers tend to articulate the same rhythms in a less jagged fashion. In Cape Breton music the combination of strathspeys and reels is central to the repertoire of the fiddler and the mainstay of the step-dance tradition. Strathspey tunes popular in Donegal (which have all come from the Scottish repertoire) often include triplet passages towards the end of parts. Slow strathspeys, popular in both Scotland and Cape Breton, are not common within the Donegal tradition. (LID)

**Stroh fiddle.** Invented by Augustus Stroh in the late 1800s, this is a fiddle in which the bridge is connected to a corrugated, light-metal diaphragm, and the resonating body has been replaced by a metal flared horn. Loud in volume, it was suited to early recording and was also used by street players. The late Julia Clifford (Sliabh Luachra and London) played on such an instrument, and while it enjoyed a certain fashion in Britain and the US, it has never become a feature of traditional music instrumentation.

**Stubbert, Robert (Bobby).** (1923– ). Fiddle. Cape Breton Irish fiddler who introduced many of the Irish tunes presently played by Cape Breton players. Influenced by Johnny Wilmot, Joe Confiant and Winston Fitzgerald. His daughter, Brenda Stubbert, is a well-known fiddler, composer and recording artist. (PAC)

**style and authenticity.** 'Authenticity' in music has always had an agenda, and what might be considered traditional by one set of ears may be heard quite differently by another. Traditional Irish music has a distinctive 'sound' that resonates even with listeners just beginning to appreciate its nuance. That 'sound', though collectively acknowledged, may be selectively applied by different players, or groups of players. Uninitiated listeners may complain that traditional music 'all sounds the same', but the music in reality differs greatly in the hands of different players, in different parts of the country. 'Traditional music' has often been thought of as a body of tunes held in common by members of a national group, or by those possessing affinity for the music if not the ties of nationality. It is not, therefore, primarily a music associated with individual composers, or performers. Without losing sight of the quality that makes the music identifiably traditional, individual musicians inevitably make tunes their own, imbuing melodies with their own rhythmic or melodic variations, and their own ornamentation. This questions the view that there is only one 'correct' form of a tune. And if the manner in which a tune is decorated or modified is passed on to other musicians along with the basic melody, then this constitutes change to which newer players can also be expected to contribute in time.

The evolution of traditional Irish music can thus be viewed as a series of interconnected stylistic lineages, traceable to different locales and master players within those locales. The styles are likened to dialects of a single language. If one is concerned with musical authenticity, and with tradition (and its evolution), one must consider the origins of these different regional styles of traditional practice. Prior to the 1950s, Irish music was presented as a pan-Irish means of expression, and not one immediately associated with specific locales or regions. It may be that, at the time of the great nineteenth-century music collectors George Petrie and P. W. Joyce, such differences as existed regionally were as yet too slight to be distinguishable. It may also be because some collectors (Capt. Francis O'Neill for instance) gleaned material from very disparate sources as it came to them, that regional or local styles were diluted in the process.

*limits to personal innovation in style.* There are limits to the amount of change acceptable as 'traditional'. While such limits may call into question whether or not a newly composed tune will enter the traditional repertoire, they are more applicable to the playing style in which a tune is presented, its 'setting'. Traditional music thrives on the creation of new tunes, so long as they conform to accepted patterns of structure and content. Breandán Breathnach observes: 'If a piece has been composed in traditional form by one totally immersed in the tradition, and if it is accepted and played by traditional players as a part of their repertoire, it has a claim to admittance which cannot be refused. Meeting the first condition implies that the piece conforms in content and structure to the body of native folk music; fulfilling the second condition (in which the first is implied) confirms the approval of the piece by the community.'

Community standards, as Breathnach implies, may be rigid in their application of the strictures of traditional form; hence it has been reported that some traditional composers have couched a recent effort in the mists of traditional past by reporting that the tune was learned from a distant relative rather than admitting it as their own. In this way, traditional music of Ireland has utilised 'newness' and personal contribution to render the music forever different, progressively more interesting. When such limits are accepted by a community, or by consensus of traditional musicians, they may be referred to as 'standards' for acceptable traditional practice. By keeping necessary variation and change within prescribed limits, community standards maintain the continuity of the tradition and direct its evolution. For most traditional musicians, standards represent not only a lesson in how to play 'correctly' but also a means of initiation into the traditional culture. Blind adherence to a strict traditional standard is, therefore, more a hallmark of musicians not born into the culture (and therefore anxious for acceptance) than of natives who learn and play the music as a portion of their heritage.

Michael Coleman and Tommy Potts represent significant departures from the standardised norm of playing styles, it is instructive to examine not only their diverse approaches to the music, but also the acceptance of their contributions by the traditional community.

*Michael Coleman.* Change is most often only obvious in hindsight. Occasionally, however, there occurs an event so stunning in its impact that it rapidly changes the course of evolution. In the recent history of Irish traditional music, such was the experience following the release of the recordings of fiddler Michael Coleman. His technical prowess alone would have been influential, but it was the wide dissemination of his recordings in Ireland and in America which made that influence so pervasive. In *The Northern Fiddler* Feldman and O'Doherty contend that few older fiddlers in Tyrone in the late 1970s played in any style but that which was derived from Coleman. 'Such', they say, 'was the combined power of Coleman's virtuosity and of the new technology of recording on the isolated musical culture of Tyrone.' Harry Bradshaw concludes: 'No other musician in the history of traditional music has been so imitated. His influence pervades the entire Irish tradition today'. Many saw in the success of Coleman's recordings the death knell of local and regional fiddling styles in Ireland and in Irish-American communities. But Coleman's influence, while monumental, did not – and has not – obliterated the local or individual approach to the music. In practice, players can – and will – play 'Coleman' medleys and 'Coleman' ornamentation, but will return to a more personal or regional style and repertoire afterward.

*Tommy Potts.* One of the finest examples of the persistence of individual voice despite the influence of Coleman is the music of this Dublin fiddler. To ears accustomed to the Coleman fiddling, Potts's music sounds at once familiar and yet extraordinarily different. His tunes were often recognisable as part of the traditional repertoire, but were changed either subtly or more dramatically by the exploration of slightly different sounds with the familiar traditional intervals. Caoimhín MacAoidh describes Tommy Potts' approach to the music:

> He [Potts] felt there was a cycle in the music. Its started with the player hearing and becoming interested in a tune. The next step in the sequence was to learn it . . . At this point, the piece was very stable . . . and could possibly become stale and even boring . . . Here is where the magic lay for Tommy. When the player was being lulled into disinterest with the tune he or she would, at some unexpected time, hear the same piece played by another player who, by simply altering a note or two, completely transfixed the complexion of the tune and the fiddler's delight with it . . . He described it as 'the hidden note'. It was there all the time waiting to be discovered and when all around was like a tedious drone it struck the ear and the imagination like a peal of thunder.

The music of Tommy Potts is a personal music; it could not easily be made to blend with that of fellow musicians in the local playing-circle. The fact that few players could play along with Potts suggests that he may have breached the limits of acceptable innovation in traditional Irish musical forms. Certainly he was aware of his outsider status: in an interview broadcast on RTÉ in 1988, he is quite open about his impatience with the propensity of most traditional players to follow standard settings of tunes. He heard something different in the music, something that called for quite different settings.

*Ó Súilleabháin's observations.* Mícheál Ó Súilleabháin, in his dissertation on Potts' music, notes that Potts placed himself outside of the mainstream of traditional music in Ireland due to his conscious inclusion of influences from classical, jazz, and other traditional musics. Ó Súilleabháin does not predict, however, whether or not Potts' music itself is peripheral to the stream of Irish tradition. But considering the strength of Michael Coleman's impact on the tradition through his recordings, the music of Tommy Potts would indeed seem peripheral. Ó Súilleabháin notes that at the time of the release of Potts' *The Liffey Banks* album, classical reviewers were more enthusiastic about its merits than were traditional musicians. The local playing-circle, and its standards, would seem to have wanted little to do with the innovations offered by this musician. And yet, the influence of Potts, although largely uncaptured by recording technology, has remained a part of traditional fiddle-playing in Ireland and in America. If not as broad as Coleman's impact, it is deep. It is heard in Martin Hayes, acknowledged in the fiddling of Joe Ryan and Paddy Canny, and in the accordion of Paddy O'Brien of Co. Offaly. In this sense, Potts' music shows traditional transmission changed by a personal vision which has been given the imprimatur by masters.

Limits to innovation are conditioned by awareness that: 1. the music must inevitably change and be changing, as individual players hear, interpret, and teach the traditional sound in their communities; 2. though the traditional process of transmission may normally be slow and gradual, radical departures from the traditional stream may be incorporated into the mainstream through the acceptance by local playing-circles; 3. future trends can be expected to be centred about the individuals whose playing sounds attractively different. (SAS)

*geography, landscape, topography.* Traditionally, the seasonal round of rural life was an important influence on the development of rural culture, with spring, summer, harvest and winter marking critical phases in the lives of the people. Vernacular landscapes reflected the pre-eminence of locality in the lives of people, personal mobility was low and restricted. Ways of living and doing things were influenced by local custom, conditions, materials and resources. Thus local styles of housebuilding were handed on, ways of farming, cures for ailments, accents and dialects – are all related to landscape diversity. Local styles of singing and playing music are essentially part of the same vernacular tradition. Fiddle-playing, piping, ways of singing, styles of dance, tempo of tunes all reflected the supremacy of the local in the lives of the people. Fathers, mothers, sons and daughters, handed on music and song from generation to generation, with occasional varied inputs from outsiders who passed through the community, or from returning migrants.

Development of these music landscapes probably mirrored broad topographical features in the sense that the landscape's physical features and settlement patterns conditioned the flow of people and traditions in it and through it. Tunes and songs and styles of playing flowed through the countryside, through the market hinterlands of towns, along the well-worn tracks of travellers, hucksters and broadsheet balladeers, beggars and tramps, journeymen, tinkers, seasonal migrants, leave-taking and returning emigrants. Remoteness, peripherality and isolation also ensured the survival of the oldest traditions. Rural life, farming, fishing, hiring fairs, military service, national and local politics, weddings and funerals combined to colour the music's canvas. Today the surviving regional differences are a residue of a much more extensive musical geography that may have been affected by interruptions of people's lives by injustice, industrial opportunity and emigration, but most importantly, nature's distinctive breaks and boundaries in the physical landscape have been hugely determining. (PAD)

**summer schools, winter schools**. Effectively these are the universities of aural music skills. Several have been running for many years and are an established part of individual, family, visitor and town lives. The schools vary in size – some may have a couple of dozen participants only, others may have more than a thousand.

May: Michael J. Murphy School, Mullaghbane, Armagh; Scoil Leacht Uí Chonchúir, Lahinch, Clare

June: Cúirt Chruitreachta, Termonfechin, Louth

July: Blas Summer School, Plassey, Limerick; Ennis/IMRO Composition Summer School, Ennis, Clare; Joe Mooney Summer School, Drumshanbo, Leitrim; Maoin Cheoil an Chláir Summer School, Ennis, Clare; Michael Davitt Summer School, Ballaghaderreen, Roscommon; O'Carolan Harp and Trad. Music Festival, Keadue, Roscommon; Scoil Samhraidh Willie Clancy, Miltown Malbay, Clare; South Sligo Summer School, Tubbercurry, Sligo

August: Cairdeas na bFhidléirí, Glencolumcille, Donegal; Cláirseóirí na hÉireann, Glengariff, Antrim; O'Carolan Harp Summer School, Keadue, Roscommon; Scoil Acla, Achill, Mayo; Scoil Éigse, Fleadh Cheoil na hÉireann, Ballina, Mayo

October: Scoil Samhna Shéamuis Ennis, Oldtown, Dublin

November: Scoil Shliabh gCuillinn, Mullaghbawn, Armagh; William Kennedy, Piping Festival, Armagh; Tionól Tommy Kearney, Kilkenny

December: Scoil Gheimhridh Frankie Kennedy, Derrybeg, Donegal

**Surgeonor, Hughie.** (b. 1907). Fife, whistle, mandolin, fiddle. Born in Scotland of parents from Tully, Portglenone, Co. Antrim who brought him back to Moyasset at age six. Having left Ahoghill national school at fourteen he worked in a textile factory, twice a week cycling to visit his uncle Willie McCullough at Rasharkin to learn and play fiddle. He played at dances, concerts and weddings and house-dances not only in Antrim and Derry but throughout the country. He played for step dancers on the occasion of Queen Elizabeth's visit to the New University of Ulster at Coleraine in the 1970s, and on radio and television. A fifer for Lambeg drumming for many years he was an active member of the Counties Antrim and Derry Fiddlers' Association. He taught and provided music for marching and dancing in his locality. In his 'country dance band' he played banjo and drums; the repertoire of the day covered music for quickstep, fox-trot and waltz, Scottish and Irish céilí dances.

**Sutherland, Alex.** (1873–1967). Fiddle player and collector. Of Scottish ancestry, he lived at Toome, Carrigallen, Co. Leitrim and like his neighbour, Terry Reilly, was a local 'fiddle master'. He collected many tunes during the first half of the twentieth century; much of this was accidentally destroyed, but a small portion which he sent to the Irish Folklore Commission survives. This includes approximately 240 tunes, with some 100 reels, 40 jigs, 25 hornpipes, 10 slip jigs, and more than 50 instrumental pieces which include airs and O'Carolan compositions.

See Grier, Stephen; Leitrim, South.

**Sweeny's Men.** Group formed in June 1966 by Joe Dolan, Johnny Moynihan and Andy Irvine. Dolan had studied art and played guitar with the Swingtime Aces Showband. Moynihan had renounced the study of architecture in favour of music some years before, and Irvine had moved from an early acting career to concentrate on his instrumental and vocal skills. They combined a broad knowledge of the various strands – Irish, Scottish, English, and American – which made up the folk music revival, and under the management of artist Eamonn O'Doherty, organised this material in arrangements and programmes which were intelligent and new to Ireland. A picaresque tour of Ireland in the summer of 1966 heralded a financial crisis which led to management by Des Kelly and the production of a single 'The Old Maid in the Garret' which went to No. 4 in the Irish charts.

Dolan left the group to return to painting and song writing. Many of his songs have been recorded by Christy Moore. He was replaced by Terry Woods (later of the Pogues) and then by guitarist Henry McCullough who had played with Joe Cocker and with Wings. The style of Sweeny's Men had a seminal influence on the make-up of future groups such as Planxty, De Dannan and the Bothy Band. The complete Sweeny's Men recordings have been re-released on CD. (EAO)

**synthesiser.** This instrument is used in a large number of Irish music recordings, the major reason for its use is its potential 'sounds'. Its role is very often to create atmosphere, especially in slow music. It crosses over into the style of vocal music and is generally used to layer sound. The earliest example of synthesiser playing in traditional music was Jolyon Jackson's recording with Paddy Glackin; this used both melody and accompaniment. Likewise, Tríona Ní Domhnaill of the Bothy Band (mid-1970s) used a harpsichord-style sound. Each was revolutionary in their own way, as the synthesiser in the 1970s was at an early stage of development. Early synthesisers were much less sophisticated than the keyboards of today which have almost unlimited individual and combined melodic to percussive tones. The modern 'synth' covers a wide range of possibilities. It has keyboard, instrumental, string, layer, orchestral, chorus and gimmick sounds, many of them specific to each particular instrument. In Irish music it is combined with most traditional instruments and voice, for instance on *Sult*, Liam O'Flynn's *The Piper's Call*, and more so on Declan Masterson's *Deireadh an Fhómhair*, where it is used to give colour to the music. Synthesiser playing style is generally chordal with very little movement. It can also be used in a percussive way – as with Donal Lunny – but the selected sound is always critical. Because it has more of a function in the overall setting of tunes, the synthesiser is considered more useful by bands in Irish music, performers choosing from a wide range of models, each with its own range of possibilities. Personal sounds can be programmed into these instruments and recorded on multiple tracks. Unlike early electric pianos, most keyboards are 'touch-sensitive' – the player can control the amount of pressure placed on the keys. (CAH)

See also harmony; technology, future projections; Three Ages of Music.

# T

**Taisce Cheol Dúchais Éireann.** See Irish Traditional Music Archive.

**Talbot, William.** (b. 1781). Piper. Born at Roscrea, Co. Tipperary, blinded by smallpox at age fifteen. He travelled all over the country but eventually opened a tavern in Little Mary Street, Dublin, and played in another in Capel Street. He was invited to play before King George IV and entertained audiences at several London theatres. His experimentation is credited with the addition of the two final regulators to the uilleann pipes.

**Talty, Martin.** (1920–83). Uilleann piper and flute player. Born Glendine, Miltown Malbay, Co. Clare. A founder member of CCÉ in Clare in 1954, and a close associate of Willie Clancy, he helped organise the first Fleadh Cheoil in Ennis in 1956, and those in Miltown Malbay of 1957 and 1961. With piper Seán Reid and accordion player Paddy Joe McMahon he served on CCÉ's executive for several years and was a regular adjudicator at fleadhanna and at an tOireachtas. An active member of Na Píobairí Uilleann, and in the Fleadh Scoil Éigse, he and Séamus Ennis were two of the stylistic father-figures of the Scoil Samhradh Willie Clancy.

**tambourine.** A small frame-drum, with loose, metal 'jingles' fitted in slots in the rim, usually shaken, struck against the knee, and played with the back of the fingers, but in Islamic-influenced cultures (Southern Spain, etc.) also in a friction fashion with fingertips. Likely called 'Tympanum' in ancient times the instrument is referred to in the Bible, and is depicted in images of ancient Greece and Rome, usually played by women. In Calabria, southern Italy, tambourine playing is a virtuoso art, sometimes the 6/8 Tarantella time for dancing being played out on it alone using gracings and ornaments similar to those employed presently by Irish bodhrán players. Sometimes a 'snare' will be used under the skin, or in models from China, rings will be suspended loosely around the inside of the frame to give a rustling effect. In Portugal a square, double-sided tambourine-style drum is used in folk music with beans or other 'rattles' loose inside – it is played suspended in the palms with both sets of fingers. In some parts of Ireland – notably Sligo/Roscommon – the bodhrán is referred to as 'tambourine' and older models have jingles attached.

See bodhrán.

**Tansey, Noel.** (1940– ). Flute, drums. Born at Cuilmore, Co. Sligo, he started tin whistle at age five, his earliest mentor was John Henry of Doocastle. In the late 1950s he played flute, whistle and drums with a variety of céilí bands – the Doocastle, the Rising Sun, the Martin Wynne Céilí Group and the Coleman Country Céilí Band – last of which he toured North America with in 1972.

**Tansey, Séamus.** (1943– ). Flute player, raconteur. One of traditional music's most colourful and outspoken personalities, he was born at Gurteen, Co. Sligo, his father a classical-style singer, his mother – née Gardiner – a fiddle player and first cousin of Kathleen Harrington and John Joe Gardiner, from 'fiddle' country around Keash. His father encouraged him on tin whistle, and he picked up much first from local labourers working around the house: 'there were a lot of spailpíns [migrant labourers] around this area, so with coming and going to England they were in the way of getting flutes and tin whistles. While they were waiting for their dinner at the table they might take out a whistle and play'. These were also 'wren boys', and on Stephen's Day they played together with flutes, whistles and tambourine. The area was noted for its flute and whistle players. Séamus got his first flute in 1961, won the All Ireland at Thurles in 1965, and Ó Riada's 'champions' Fleadh Cheoil an Raidió award the same year. In 1970 his first album *Séamus Tansey and Eddie Corcoran* (Leader) was released, in 1971 came *Best of Séamus Tansey*, in 1976 *King of the Concert Flute*, in 1980 *Reels and Jigs*, in 1997 *Easter Snow*. His book *The Bardic Apostles of Innisfree* was published in 1999.

See flute, Sligo style.

**Tara Céilí Band.** Director Frank Lee. The band recorded in the 1930s with fiddle, flute and piccolo, piano accordion, piano and drums. They played for a céilí-style dance at the Sarsfield Club, Notting Hill, London, on St Patrick's Day, 1918. This was the first large-scale 'céilí'-style dance.

**Taylor, Billy.** (1830–91). Piper, pipe maker. From the Alleys, Drogheda, Co. Louth, his father was a pipe-maker and piper also. He and step-brother Charles emigrated to New York in 1872 where they set up a workshop in piper Tom Kerrigan's basement. They moved to Philadelphia, setting up a pipe-repairing business. Performance conditions in noisy and large US venues prompted them to develop a louder instrument, raising it to concert pitch, this too making it more suitable for playing with fiddle, piano and flute. Although successful, their generosity guaranteed them many fair-weather associates who dissipated their fortunes in celebration. Charlie was a skilled craftsman, Billy tested the instruments and had a substantial collection of written music. The Taylors made highland pipes too, and medals were awarded to them for their work at the 1875 Philadelphia Centennial Exposition. The brothers' work was a major revolution in the instrument, and in piping practice, in continuum with that of Talbot and Kennedy of the previous century.

**Taylor, Paddy.** (1914–76). Flute. Born at Loughill, Co. Limerick, his immediate environment was one of music. His father sang, and his mother Honora played concertina, her brothers flutes. His most definitive early musical influence was maternal grandfather, Patrick Hanley, a flute player. Widowed, in 1932 his mother moved the family to Hammersmith, London where Paddy worked as a TV/film lighting engineer which brought him all over the country. He played music in London into the 1940s, notably with the Garryowen band along with Joe O'Dowd and Martin Wynne. With them and Leo Rowsome he made a recording for HMV studios in Hampstead in 1939. Never released, this was lost during the war but he subsequently recorded *The Boy in the Gap* for Claddagh. A fleadh prize-winning player too, with his wife May and other family members he helped to set up the west London branch of CCÉ in the 1950s; the playing of his son Kevin (1944–98) and daughters Nora and Katie is also highly rated. A lyrical and emotive player, Taylor's influence on the Irish music scene in London in his lifetime was profound. He played all over Britain at folk clubs and festivals.

**Teahan, Terry ('Cuz').** (1905–89). Accordion, composer. Born Castleisland, Co. Kerry. Exposed to music at house and crossroads dances in that district from earliest years, by his own account he wasn't seriously involved in music, even though his social life was saturated by it and he had taken a number of concertina lessons from master fiddler Pádraig O'Keefe. He emigrated to Chicago in 1928, married in 1938, and from 1936 until his retirement in 1970 worked for the Illinois Central Railroad. In the 1940s his daughters began to learn Irish step dancing and he acquired a one-row Baldoni accordion in order to accompany them. After winning an amateur radio music competition in 1942, he began to play publicly for weddings and dances in the Chicago area, earning $5 a night at the Sarsfield Limerickmen's Club, and from 1943–66 he played for dances, bars, and dance-schools. In the 1960s he put away his accordion for nearly ten years. In the 1970s he resumed a public profile, influencing a new generation of musicians with his style, repertoire and compositions. This style was rooted in the demands of the house dances of his youth: driving, unsyncopated, and with a minimum of embellishment. He searched out new tunes from manuscripts, and was a prolific composer of polkas, slides, jigs, hornpipes, highlands and reels; unusually these were often crafted for instruments other than his own. Many of them are among the sixty-three that were published along with samples of his poetry and textile artwork in *The Road to Glountane*, a tunebook he co-wrote with folklorist Josh Dunson in 1980. Teahan appeared on the albums *Terry Teahan and Gene Kelly: Old Time Irish Music in America*, *Irish Traditional Instrumental Music in Chicago* and *Chicago Irish Musicians*. (MAD)

**Teastas i dTeagasc Ceolta Tíre.**
See TTCT.

**technology.** Music has always reflected and exploited developments in technology. In performance, instruments such as the piano, flute and violin have evolved and improved over the centuries. The invention of the printing press led to improved music notation. In the more recent past the most significant developments have taken place in the fields of recording, electronics, and computing. The arrival of tape recording enabled the manipulation of recordings of natural sounds resulting in the *musique concrete* of Pierre Schaeffer and Pierre Henry in the 1940s. In the following decade Karlheinz Stockhausen pioneered the use of electronics and synthesis techniques where sounds are both produced and modified by purely electronic means. But possibly most significant in recent times are 1. the widespread use of computing technology and 2. the early 1980s' advent of MIDI (Musical Instrument Digital Interface) – a communications language for electronic musical instruments.

*future projections.* The future impact of technology on music is theoretically predictable, but music and musicians are not. However, one can speculate that 1. there will be increasing use of the Internet and World Wide Web. More and more music material will go online, whether music content, information about music, or music software etc. Traditional musicians will increasingly use the Internet for making contact with other traditional musicians as a source for tunes, information about traditional music, session locations etc. 2. There will be improved musical character recognition enabling the scanning of existing printed scores into electronic format. 3. There will not only be speech recognition and output but music recognition enabling for example automatic scoring. 4. There will be more powerful, useful, user-friendly, and interactive music software in the areas of music education, history, sequencing, notation, audio editing, synthesis and algorithmic composition. 5. The technological resources available to the individual composer/arranger will continue to increase. S/he will have all the tools necessary to move an idea from conception to realisation to CD. Compositions will increasingly explore sound and move further away from notation towards what Trevor Wishart calls 'Sonic Art'. 'Visual music' will also be popular where there is a direct link between the sound and graphics generated. 6. There will be new performance instruments and interfaces, many involving no actual physical contact with the instrument. 7. Hopefully there will be a greater acceptance of standards for music and sound encoding. Just one group that this would benefit greatly would be musicologists as it would enable the creation of more 'toolkits' such as the Humdrum toolkit for musicological research.

In fact, in every sphere of musical activity, technology will have something to offer. But 'technology is just a tool'. While it will make life easier and more productive for the musician it is only when technical know-how is teamed with genuine creativity that its full potential will be realised. Technology is just technology. Art is just art. Unity of the two can be revolutionary. Traditional musicians have only begun to experiment.

*MIDI and contemporary music.* For many people 'Music and Technology' suggests electric guitars, synthesisers, equipment and cables, but the reality is very different. Technology's impact on music activities is far broader and more varied. For many composers the composition process has changed radically. Rather than the compositional chain beginning with the conception of an idea and moving through scoring to performance, today many composers sit in the centre of a music studio, the heart of which is a computer and synthesiser. Through these devices they can communicate to a large number of MIDI instruments, creating music of extraordinary range and power. Sequencing software used in conjunction with sound modules provides orchestration and playback facilities, and editing capabilities. A full printout of the score is instantaneous. The actual act of physically writing down music, which used to slow the process down, is increasingly becoming a thing of the past. With technology it is now almost possible to notate musical ideas as fast as they are conceived.

Many composers now find that technology lets them accomplish their task with fewer things to clog the creative flow. Consider how many more symphonies and piano concertos Beethoven might have written with such resources. Rather than writing music for say a pianist, quartet, or orchestra, composers now have total control over the composition and the performance as they have the tools, such as software synthesis programs, which allow them start with a 'bare canvas' and actually create and manipulate the sounds themselves. More often than not there is no score, for much music being composed today provides only an aural experience. There is no visual performance element as there are no performers.

*music education.* In music education there is a plethora of software, of varying quality, principally in the field of aural-training and music theory. There are also a variety of initiatives being undertaken such as the CALMA project at the University of Huddersfield, and Computers in Teaching Initiative in Music at the University of Lancaster. The number of interactive hyper-media applications (i.e. combining voice, music, still pictures, full-motion video and text) opens new horizons for music history and analysis. Where music technology is concerned, disability is no handicap. The design of new performance interfaces has released a well of previously untappable musicality.

*storage and research.* Music is increasingly being stored in electronic format too, and the Irish Traditional Music Archive is just one of many archives transferring all its printed music material on to computer. There are searchable databases of tunes and songs on the World Wide Web such as the digital tradition folk-song database. In the field of musicology a scan of the annual journal *Computing in Musicology* reveals the myriad uses that technology is being put to in the investigation of many musics and musical issues. And all the time further advances are being made in music technology research

centres such as IRCAM in Paris, the Massachusetts Institute of Technology's Media Lab, Stanford's Centre for Computer Research in Music and Acoustics and Centre for Computer-Assisted Research in the Humanities, and STEIM in the Netherlands. In addition music technology is increasingly becoming a component in second and third-level music curricula. (PAM)

*traditional music implications.* Many Irish traditional musicians find it difficult to relate technology to their music, feeling that theirs is acoustic music. But the peripheral effects of technology are unavoidable, and are of immense, and everyday, benefit to it in research, analysis, archiving, storage, recording, broadcasting and performance. In particular, technology's impact on instruments and instrument making; the impact on the recording process: recording studios, microphones, mixers, multi-track recording hardware, effects units, improvement in recording media e.g. wax cylinder vs DAT or CD. Overdubbing facility allows a multi-instrumentalist to produce a 'group' recording. Home studios are becoming commonplace and there is much improved portable recording equipment for fieldwork. Technology is used in instructional material, e.g. cassette-based tutors for instruments. It has an impact through radio, television, video, newspapers, books, periodicals on Irish traditional music. Electronic instruments, sequencing/scoring software and computers are increasingly being used in arrangements of Irish traditional music and in the compilation of private tune collections and creation of tune archives. Sound processing software is used in the restoration of old recordings (e.g. ITMA-RTÉ project). Improved classification and searching of archive material is possible through the use of databases with powerful search features, and CD-ROM and Web-based tune collections and information about traditional music (combining sound, notation, text and video). (PAG)

**television programming, Northern Irish.** Both Northern Irish TV channels UTV and BBC have presented traditional music. In black and white, the Dubliners were first seen on *The Hootenanny Show* broadcast nationwide on BBC. Locally, the pioneer producer of BBC 'folk' programmes was John Whitehorn, whose *Sing North, Sing South* and *Folk Meet Folk*, combined performances from all over Ireland and juxtaposed the Johnstons, the Dubliners and Tommy Makem with traditional performers. However, local BBC productions have been dominated by Tony McAuley, himself a singer, whose work, some leaning towards the 'folky side', has included *Folkweave, One Night Stand, In Performance* and *The Gig in the Round*. The last of these had a 'new talent' policy; Mary Black, the Bothy Band, Planxty and De Dannan all made their television debuts on *The Gig in the Round*. More traditional in flavour were *As I Roved Out* and *The Corner House*. McAuley also presented profiles of traditional musicians and singers, Paddy Tunney and Cathal McConnell in *Schools' Broadcasts*, while, for the same service, David Hammond's *Dusty Bluebells, Sarah Makem and the Boho Singers* were justly praised. More recently the concept series *Bringing It All Back Home* and *A River of Sound* have been joint commissions of RTÉ and BBC, but since then, little traditional music has been featured. UTV's output was produced almost entirely by Andy Crockart, and, advised by Brian O'Donnell (chairman of Belfast Comhaltas) and later by Len Graham, had a somewhat more traditional flavour. His titles included *Glen to Glen, A Drop in Your Hand, A Fiddle and a Flute, The Half-Door Club* and *Session Folks*. These featured many of the North's best-known singers and musicians in fairly informal settings. (JOM)

**tenor banjo.** The standard banjo used in traditional music. With a pitch equivalent to viola, it is generally tuned GDAE (as fiddle) and sometimes will have a 'resonator' back of polished wood, this giving a deeper sound.

See banjo.

**Thornton, Francis J. (Frank).** (1908–97). Flute, Chicago. Born five miles from Listowel, Co. Kerry, Frank started on the flute at age eight, learning from a cousin named Hanrahan who was prominent in the local flute band and from a local player named Furey. Frank's uncle, Miles Thornton, also played the flute and was a dancing teacher and All-Ireland step-dancing champion. At the American wake held in his honour the night before he left for Chicago in 1929, Thornton recalls sixteen musicians playing, all local. On a visit home in 1936, the realisation that the music was disappearing led him to devote a major portion of his next forty years to teaching and promoting it. For eighteen years he taught children flute and tin whistle and formed a popular marching band. In August, 1956, he called together Irish musicians from Chicago, New York and Philadelphia to a convention that led to the foundation of the Irish Musicians' Association of America. He served as its first president and later was involved in the Chicago Irish Musicians' Association. In 1959 he organised the first tour of American Irish musicians to Ireland, and in 1969, he was instrumental in bringing musicians and singers to the US from Ireland, among them Paddy O'Brien, Seán Ryan, Peadar O'Loughlin, and singer Eibhlín Begley. The group also toured seven US cities and simultaneously raised funds for the American Congress for Irish Freedom. This became the model for future CCÉ tours of North America. Frank is on *Irish Traditional Instrumental Music in Chicago* and *Chicago Irish Musicians*. His son Jimmy plays flute and accordion. (LAM)

**Three Ages of Music, The.** The first age of music was the age of oral transmission. The second, which began for Europe only a thousand years ago, was the age of written music. We are now in the third age, which began about a hundred years ago with sound recording. The effect on musical style wrought by the medium of transmission is enormous. In the first age, the greatest virtue of the method of storage – human memory – was faithful conservation; so the plainsong of the church was passed on unaltered for perhaps thousands of years. We know that it was unaltered, by comparing the versions written down when notation was invented; they are remarkably faithful over a wide geographical spread. In the second age, that of written music, faithfulness is no longer a virtue; ink doesn't wander on a page, and conservation is easy. Instead the challenge, quickly exploited, was to use the method invented for *recording* melodies as a method for *composing*. 'Composing' in its early sense means not so much writing down a tune you have heard in your head, as fitting together a counterpoint with an existing tune. Within a few hundred years of the invention of staff notation, counterpoint reached a stage of incredible complexity that has been reducing gradually ever since. In the third age, the age of sound recording, complexity of counterpoint is no longer a problem, and musical invention moves into other areas of interest.

The effect on music education of all this is that teachers are finding it hard to discard the inflated values of the second age, the third still being so young. We see mistaken values everywhere, the most extreme perhaps being the kind observed by the ethnomusicologist, Bruno Nettl, in a dance band in what was then Persia – a band playing traditional Persian music, but with empty music stands in front of the players, so that they looked 'western'. The same value is persisted in by teachers and examiners who make their pupils pretend to read music they know by heart, often taking into an exam a book they have never actually handled before. The absurdity of this is demonstrated by the fact that a concerto soloist gets no kudos for bringing a score on stage. The reason for the pretence is the belief that reading is valuable in itself. It has value, certainly, but it is the value of convenience, the antithesis of aesthetic value. Staff notation is good at clarifying counterpoint, but not good at showing the details of phrasing and rhythm that constitute the living communication – the energy, the taste of music. Compared with painting, staff notation is painting by numbers. All music is learnt by ear; yet some teachers still use 'playing by ear' as a disparaging phrase. Why? Because it is a value inimical to the (recently superseded) age of written music.

One age does not die out when another succeeds it – like the Tuatha De Dannan, it goes underground. The oral tradition, disowned by Gregory the Great for church music when he decreed that the notation of all plainsong become the property of the professional dance musicians, became the realm of 'folk music'. A curious anomaly of 'folk music' is that it has strong professional roots. Each past age remains current as a constant critique of the new; a counter-culture. Thus no sooner had counterpoint reached its heights of artifice than artificiality became a dirty word and composers were asked to bring a more 'natural expression' into their work. The history of western music from 1500 to 1900 is (broadly) a series of revolutions, each claiming to make music that is more natural and more expressive. After Bach, counterpoint was despised as 'dry' (Bach's music was studied but unplayed for a hundred years) and after Beethoven 'form' was subjugated to 'content'. An apogée of 'expressive' music was reached in the late nineteenth century, when suddenly the forest of 'expression marks' on the musical page was rendered obsolete by the advent of sound recording.

Sound recording is good at filling in the details of rhythm, nuance and accent that notation cannot cover, and which make for regional or personal difference. The opposite of the oral age's virtue of uniformity, this celebrates diversity. Good news for 'folk' musics; indeed without sound recording, ethnomusicology could not exist. Now it is the written music which is the counter-culture, standing on high moral ground as a critique of the new musical values. It is most important to see and understand that the culture of recording and electronic transmission has not the same values – is not the same – as the oral culture. Recording has freed 'ethnic' music from the haughty dominance of written music, but only by, to some extent, devaluing both oral and written music. There is no longer any friction between 'composers' music' and 'people's music', because both are fair game for exploitation in the new medium; equally grist to the electronic mill. (ANR)

**Tigh Neachtain.** Cross Street, Galway, first established in 1894 by Seán Ó Neachtain from Spiddal who had been a successful business man in Australia, in the mid-1880s. It had a grocery shop at one end and bar at the other end. In the early days there was very little Irish music in Galway apart from a dockers' band and a fife and drum band around the Claddagh, but by the late 1950s and early '60s, Tigh Neachtain had gradually become known as a venue for traditional music. Ó Neachtain's grandson Jimmy Maguire remembers that the early visitors to the premises were pipers Paddy O'Connor, Mick Hession and Michael Padian. By the mid-1970s Tigh Neachtain was a mecca for traditional musicians. De Dannan, Séamus and Manus Maguire, Jackie Daly and bouzouki player Brendan O'Regan were regular visitors and in 1989 Gael-Linn recorded a live album of musicians who played there regularly (*Ceol Tigh Nechtain*). Among those featured were the Smith family, Patsy Broderick, Maureen Fahy, Eilish Egan and Chris Kelly. The album's success contributed to immortalising the venue. (MAO)

**times.** Expression used in Connemara and in Aran (island) for house-weddings and house-dances.

Boy playing on home-made, sycamore whistle at Glenariffe, Co. Antrim, *c*. 1950 (CBÉ)

**tin whistle.** A simple fipple-style flute where the sound is made by blowing air through a channel against a sharp edge. Without doubt the most popular instrument in traditional music today. Its simple construction and ease of playing make it cheap, almost disposable, yet equally suitable as an introduction to music for beginners, and for playing the most sophisticated airs and dance music. The principle of the whistle has been around for a long time, in many cultures, world wide, but the antiquity of the whistle as an instrument of Irish music dates only to the nineteenth century. Yet whistle-like instruments have been found on archaeological digs in Viking Dublin, and as in other cultures, children are recorded as making small whistles from corn stalks, elder (boor tree) and sycamore branches. The precursor of the tin whistle is the 'flageolet', often with a full compliment of chromatic keys, which appeared in the late 1700s. The earliest tin-plate whistles were being made in Britain from 1825, they appear to have been used in Irish dance music within the following twenty years.

Only with mass production was their cost reduced sufficiently to give the instrument mass popularity, and among the first such manufacturers was the Clarke company in 1843 (still making whistles). Later the instrument was made of white celluloid. Known as the 'penny' whistle, these appear to have been relatively expensive for their time – 2 shillings in the 1960s, but up to three pence ha'penny (possibly £10 today) at the beginning of the century. Evidence suggests that all whistles in use in Ireland up to the beginning of the 1980s were British made. Tin whistle fortunes were boosted hugely by the traditional music and folk revivals of the 1950s onwards, as it became the doorway into traditional music for many. Although still thought of as a beginner's instrument, the appearance since the revival of some virtuoso players creates for it also a reputation as a serious instrument. Recent classic recordings by players like Mary Bergin and Seán Ryan for instance show that the instrument is as serious as the player can make it.

*materials*. Such new-found popularity has led to some developments in the detail of the instrument's construction. The older Clarke whistle was a long, narrow, rolled tin-sheet cone with a wooden fipple (plug). This was normally available in just one pitch, and its construction was copied in cast, light metals for children's band use. Running parallel with the Clarke, after the 1950s the brass-tubed, cylindrical-bore, plastic top 'Generation' type whistle appeared, made also in England. This had both brass and nickel finishes, it was made in several pitches and was more musically true than its ancestors. Its form has been the basis of dozens of brands since the 1970s, many of these made in Ireland – Walton's of Dublin have made them of lacquered aluminium, brass alloys, and high-impact plastics. Other makers like Feadóg have

Whistles in a selection of keys and materials. On the right is a simple piccolo of wood. (EDI)

produced them in aluminium, stainless steel and bored synthetic woods. Today indeed there is a bewildering range of whistles in all pitches, colours, and materials. Culturally, the most significant among these is the low whistle, which plays a full octave below the standard D instrument. Easier to play than the concert flute which it mimics – and in some sense has tried to replace – it has become a fashionable sound in contemporary traditional music. However its necessarily large holes, wide finger spacings and great demand for wind tend to give it, in inexpert hands, colourless tone and render dynamic expression difficult. The D whistle (Shaw) is also produced in a conical, nickel-plate format. Whistles range in price today from £2 through to the expensive ultimate contradiction – the 'wooden tin-whistle'. Manufactured first in the USA, this can cost up to £200, and indeed completes the circle of progress back to its expensive eighteenth-century ancestor, the wooden flageolet. (HAH/EDI)

See flute.

**tip.** A form of ornamentation which involves separating two like notes by a note below. Also known as 'pat'.

See grace note.

**Tobar Glé, An.** A traditional music and singing club founded by Séamus Ennis in Slattery's of Capel Street, Dublin, 1970.

**Tomas, Otis.** (1952– ). Fiddle, luthier, composer ('The New Land'). Born Providence, Rhode Island, he has lived in Cape Breton since 1976. His music has been recorded by Touchstone, Jerry Holland, Cherish the Ladies, Máire O'Keeffe and Séamus Egan. His playing and composition style is predominantly Irish but reflects Cape Breton and Appalachia. He makes violin, mandolin, guitar, cello and harp which are stylistically original but based on traditional design. (PAC)

**Tory Island.** An Irish-speaking island off North-West Donegal, nine miles from the nearest point on the mainland. Habitation dates from the Neolithic period. Among the substantial early Christian remains is the impressive Tau (T-shaped) cross which stands at the head of the main pier in the Western village. A considerable body of myth and history clings to such sites, notably there are the tales of Balor of the Evil Eye and Colm Cille (St Columba). Tory has a vigorous tradition of music and dancing, it is rich in song in both languages – most famous songs include 'An Chrúbach', 'Thug mé Rúide', 'Amhrán na Scadán', 'Is trua nach bhfuil mé in Éirinn', 'Na Buachaillí Álainn' and 'An Cailín Gaelach'. Favoured instrument is accordion – Pól Mac Ruairí, Patsy Dan Mac Ruairí, Dennis Duggan and Éamonn Mac Ruairí among its senior players, Bernard Ó Tuatháláin, Mairtín Ó Dúgáin and Hugo Ó Baoill somewhat younger, Jimí Antoin Mac Fhionnaile plays fiddle and banjo. Early twentieth-century hotel-keeper Séamus Mac a' Bhaird – a highly regarded dancer – greatly influenced music and dance. He also made a number of songs, including the comic music/song/dance performance *An Maidrín Rua*. Éamonn Dooley Mac Ruairí, also a poet, made 'Amhrán na Scadán', which has become an island anthem. Singers of the recent past include Kit and John Tom Ó Mianáin (d. 1960s), their cousin Jimí Shéamuis Bháin (1897–1991) and his brother, Pádraig na Faiche Mac Ruairí. All are still vividly remembered. Today's older singers include

Éamonn Mac Ruairí, Séamus and Willie Ó Dubhgáin, Teresa Mhic Claifeartaigh and sisters Gráinne Uí Dhubhgáin, Hannah Mhic Ruairí, Sorcha Uí Bhaoill, Kitty Gray. They and their cousin Mary Meenan have a large repertoire of songs in both languages and strongly characteristic styles. Younger members of the community Nábla Uí Bhaoill, Máire Mhic Giontaigh, Mary John Rogers and Anne Marie Nic Ruairí continue the singing tradition. Public policy in the 1970s led to a decline in services and morale, with ten families settling in mainland Falcarragh in 1981. Lobbying turned the process around, and at present the island's future seems assured. Tourism, with an emphasis on the island's uniqueness, is now being developed as a mainstay of local economy. The effects on the music are not yet clear. (LIO)

**Touhey, Patsy.** (1865–1923). Piper. Born Cahertinna, Bullaun, near Loughrea, Co. Galway, his grandfather Michael was a piper, as was his father, James, professionally so, in service to Lord Dunsandle (an ancestor of whose was a noted patron of Carolan). Emigrating to the US in 1875 when Patsy was three, James died at thirty-five just seven years later, but not before the young Patsy had begun piping. Working in a timber yard at age eighteen, observing piper John Egan on stage in a Bowery, New York musichall led Patsy to professional playing, first touring with Egan in 1886 in 'Jerry Cohan's Irish Hibernia' show. Playing at the West 42nd Street 'Pleasant Hour' tavern owned by piper Thomas Kerrigan followed (Kerrigan's pipes were the first set made by the Taylors in the US). In 1893 he played at the World's Fair in Chicago to great acclaim, and for a hefty fee at the Louisiana Purchase Exhibition of 1903 where he socialised in the company of Lily Foley, wife of John McCormack. It was 'vaudeville' music halls however which gave him his bread and butter. There he not only played, but did sketches and was a comic, particularly involved with Charles Henry Burke's material up to 1918. His wife, Mary Gillen, was always included in these – Patsy playing pipes to her dancing. He had contact with other noted musicians of his day, and had met the Kerry piper Micí Cumbá O'Sullivan in Worcester, Massachusetts. Having witnessed the Edison phonograph at the World's Fair in Chicago, Patsy began using its commercial potential, selling his cylinders mail-order to complement his stage performances. He advertised himself from 1901 as the 'Best Irish Piper in America', sold his wares for $1 each, $10 for the dozen, and had a catalogue of 150 tunes.

These recordings were made sitting in a sound-proofed cubicle with his loud Taylor set, each cylinder recorded individually. A thorough account of the piper's life is given in *The Piping of Patsy Touhey* by Pat Mitchell and Jackie Small (NPU 1986). This also includes transcriptions of fifty-eight of the tunes he played, and 'Touhey Hints to Amateurs' (on uilleann pipes) dictated to Francis O'Neill by Touhey and included in *Irish Folk Music* (1910). Six of his cylinders are in the Department of Music at UCC. Two tracks can be heard on *Wheels of the World*, also a full album of revamped 78s, *The Piping of Patsy Touhey*.

**townland.** The smallest local sub-division of the county, these areas range in size from just a few to hundreds of acres. The island of Ireland has some 51,000 of them. Like counties, they often have rivers and streams as natural boundaries, but their huge variety in size relates to former clan power and occupation, to fertility, topography, political loyalty, etc. Their names may be taken from some local feature, industry, vegetation, occupation, past battle, lover's name or family name. In almost all cases the townland name is a translation (sometimes crude) from the Irish. Like counties and major towns of Ireland, the townland names are of great significance in the naming of tunes, and thus we have – among hundreds of examples – 'Knocktoran Fair', 'The Humours of Ballymanus', 'Kate of Garnevilla', etc.

See Ireland, provinces and counties; style and authenticity; tune names.

**tourism.** Ireland's entry into the European Economic Community in 1973 helped to open new tourist interests from the European mainland. Included were folk music-lovers from Europe, lured by the attraction of sessions and the fleadh cheoil. This traffic also created a market for Irish music in France, Germany,

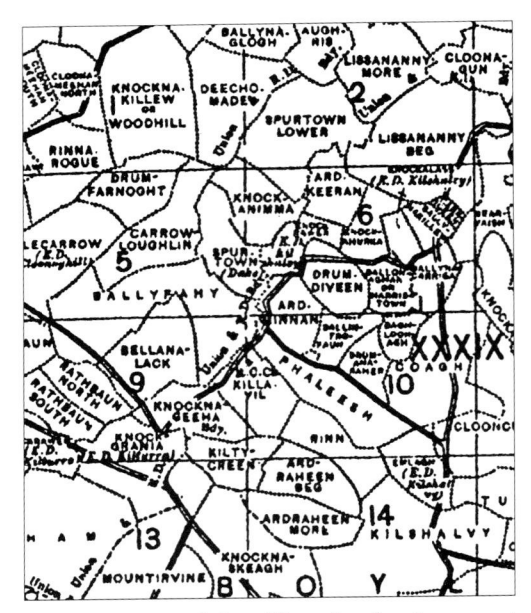

Townland map of Co. Sligo showing large and small townlands. The area has Knockgrania, where Michael Coleman was born, centre to much of the South Sligo music tradition.

(Ordnance Survey)

Belgium, Italy, the Netherlands and Scandinavia. Heading the resultant export of Irish talent were groups like the Sands Family, Clannad and the Chieftains, smaller bands like the Wild Geese and Oisín, and solo performers like Micho Russell found their own niche of support there too. Complementary to this was the development of Irish music communities in European cities, particularly in France. Throughout the 1980s, Irish music and dance were promoted there through for instance, L'Association Irlandaise, with music and set dancing classes at La Mission Bretonne in Montparnasse. A Parisian branch of Na Píobairí Uilleann promoted uilleann piping. Currently there are scores of all-French bands playing Irish and Irish-style music, among them are many outstanding musicians – Vincent Blin, Patrick Ourceau and Michel Ferry, flute player Herve Cantal, piper Denis Kersual. Brittany has many individuals (e.g. Patrick Molard and Jean Michel Veillion) and groups playing Irish music also, several Irish musicians playing professionally there, and in the region the Irish-style, wooden flute has been adopted for local music use. Like the many French and German intellectual 'revolutionary tourists', who, weary of their intense, native commodity-cultures, regularly or voyeuristically visited the scenes of high political action in Belfast and Derry in the 1960s–70s, the European 'music tourists' of the 1970s–90s have often made several trips to Ireland to learn directly from masters like Paddy Murphy, Bobby Casey, Paddy Canny and Junior Crehan. Today 'music tourists' come from all parts of Europe, the US and Japan.

See Irish bars.

**tradition.** Webster's dictionary gives the word many meanings and inflections, all of them illuminating and applicable in different ways to traditional music: 'act of handing over', 'an act of delivering and surrendering something to another', 'an inherited or established way of thinking, feeling or doing', 'a body of doctrine or practice preserved by oral transmission', 'a cultural feature preserved or evolved from the past', 'a literary or artistic rule or standard (as of theme, style, symbolism) or a body of such conventions normative for a period or group', 'a practice or pattern of events of long standing', 'a technique or set of habits used in making the artefacts characteristic of a period or culture', 'a line of historical continuity or development marked by distinctive characteristics', 'cultural continuity embodied in a massive complex of evolving social attitudes, beliefs, conventions and institutions rooted in the experience of the past and exerting an orienting and normative influence on the present', 'the force exerted by the past on the present', 'cultural inertia', 'inherited reputation or memory', 'something existing only in popular belief'. The term 'traditional' as applying to music draws on all of these.

See traditional music.

**Tradition Club.** Begun in 1967–68 by singers Tom Crean, Seán Corcoran and Kevin Coneff in Slattery's Bar, Dublin out of the Press Gang, a singing group that originally involved Crean and Corcoran, Greg O'Hanlon and Niall Fennell. Earlier, Crean and Coneff had run the Listeners' Club, also in Slattery's bar, in 1965–66. Operating on a Wednesday night, the

Tradition Club gave a platform to singers and musicians from all over the country. All the major names in present-day, professional traditional music and song played there, often to capacity audiences, but the club more importantly was a bridge between them and older artists. Joe O'Dowd of Sligo, Josie McDermott, Phil Murphy, Fred Finn, Peter Horan, Jim Donoghue, Willie Clancy, Packie Duignan, Solas Lillis, John Kelly, Joe Ryan, John Joe Forde and Paddy Fahy. Séamus Ennis performed many times, and it is for singing that the venue became particularly well known: Joe Heaney, Joe Holmes, Kevin Mitchell, Ewan MacColl & Peggy Seeger, A. L. Lloyd, Máire Áine Nic Dhonnchadha, Caitlín Maude, Darach Ó Catháin, Sarah and Rita Keane, Geordie Hanna, Sarah Anne O'Neill and Nioclás Tóibín were among these. Regular performances were made by Siney Crotty, Seán Ó Conaire, Seán 'ac Donncha and Paddy Tunney. Club policy was to charge an entrance fee to listeners, this partly to ensure attentiveness, but also to provide reasonable expenses for performers. The surplus from well-supported nights was used to subsidise those more poorly attended. 'Silence!' was the radical, and legendary, rule of the house. Corcoran worked with the club until the mid 1970s, Dundalk singer Finbar Boyle was involved from 1972 until its demise. In 1985 Tom Crean stepped down, Frankie Kennedy and Mairéad Ní Mhaonaigh became organisers *c*. 1985, and the club finished in 1988 having run twenty years, undermined by the commercial music scene which it had been instrumental in building.

**traditional music.** The term used to denote the older dance music and song in Ireland, this distinct from both modern 'folk' music, nineteenth-century 'national' and 'popular' music, and early nineteenth-century 'parlour' national songs – although all of these have exerted influences on it. The term meant much more to 'revival' period musicians in the 1960s than it does today; then it was felt necessary to distinguish 'authentic' Irish music from both popular 'folk song' as performed by commercial artists like Bob Dylan, Irish 'ballad-groups' and copies of that style, and political ballads. The term 'folk' may also have been considered trivialising, for instance, because of the prevailing academic attitudes to 'folk' musics – that they are essentially 'peasant' music: the 1970 *Oxford Companion to Music* puts forward: 'Every form of vocal and instrumental music we possess has developed out of folk song or dance ... folk music represents the culture of the countryside and art music the culture of the city'. This suggests an inferiority for 'folk' music – an 'undevelopment', socially and intellectually speaking – a notion which has come to be embedded in the term. When this attitude is coupled with the awareness of past active suppression of native 'art' music in Ireland – notably of the harp, and of song via undermining of the Irish language – and if one believes that that music tradition was absorbed by 'the folk', then it can be understood how, historically, Irish 'folk' music can be interpreted as the container of an ancient music heritage, Irish 'folk' musicians its 'keepers'. Since 'classical' musics have been historically identified with the Anglo Irish upper classes too, it is not difficult to see how 'folk' music of the Irish can be experienced strongly (however regrettably) as an opposition to the 'classical', and, particularly, in light of the pre-1921 prevailing balance of political power, vice versa.

It can be strongly argued, in addition, that considering the overwhelming volume of traditional music played currently, and the high class and artistic merit of many of the top exponents, that – like the centuries-dormant poppy seed sprouting in newly turned soil – the native music now, in the sympathetic climate of a distinctly Irish state and favourable economic climate, has merely resumed, via new instruments and technologies, its artistic course. For this reason, many traditional musicians find the term 'art', as applied to traditional music, elitist and arrogant. Terminology is never innocent of partiality; 'traditional' as a term has political and artistic implications.

As to the origins of its use in Ireland, one may profitably look at the terms used by collectors and publishers over the years. Before and during the time when the island of Ireland was politically part of Great Britain, Neal used 'Irish' to identify the music in 1724, Bunting used the terms 'Ancient', 'Irish' and 'Native' and referred to 'traditionary' stories, and

'National' airs (1796), O'Farrell titled it 'National Music' (1804), Moore talked of 'National' and 'Irish' melodies (1818), Conran used the term 'National' (1846), Petrie used 'Irish', *The Spirit of the Nation* preface (1858) speaks of 'old Irish' airs. In 1878, Carl Engel, writing in the *Musical Times* (1878) said: 'The difference between a national song (German 'volkslied') and a merely popular song (German 'Volksthümliches Lied') is not always distinctly observed by the English musicians, and the two terms are often used indiscriminately'. But English collector W. Christie used the title 'Traditional Ballad Airs' for a collection in England in 1876, and Frank Kidson there also had 'Traditional Tunes' in 1891. In 1910 O'Neill used the term 'folk' music, but in 1913 used 'traditional' without explanation: 'Traditional music unlike any form of modern composition is not the work of one but of many. Indeed it can hardly be said to have been composed at all. It is simply a growth to a certain extent subject to the influence of heredity, environment, natural selection, and the survival of the fittest'. This is similar to most definitions of 'folk' music. The terminology changes with the political climate, but the meaning remains roughly the same: like the expression 'Irish culture', everybody thinks they know what it is.

*ITMA definitions.* The Irish Traditional Music Archive explained 'traditional' as it is interpreted by Irish musicians in the pamphlet 'What is Irish Traditional Music':

> as a genre it includes many different types of singing and instrumental music, music of many periods, as performed by Irish people in Ireland or outside it, and occasionally nowadays by people of other nationalities. The different types however do have in common an essentially 'oral' character, that is, they belong to a tradition of popular music in which song and instrumental music is created and transmitted in performance and carried and preserved in the memory, a tradition which is essentially independent of writing and print. The necessity of being widely understood and appreciated and the nature of human memory govern the structures of the music and its patterns of variation and repetition. It is impossible to give a simple definition of the term. Different people use it to mean different things; the music shares characteristics with other popular and with classical music; and, as traditional culture changes, traditional music changes also, showing varying features at varying times.

The ITMA lists generally agreed characteristics:

1. It is music of a living popular tradition. While it incorporates a large body of material inherited from the past, this does not form a static repertory, but is constantly changing through the shedding of material, the reintroduction of neglected items, the composition of new material, and the creative altering in performance of the established repertory.

2. It is nevertheless music which is conservative in tendency. Change only takes place slowly, and in accordance with generally accepted principles. Most new compositions are not accepted into the tradition, and only a relatively small amount of variation takes place. Elements of the repertory perceived as old are held in esteem.

3. Being oral music, it is in a greater state of fluidity than notation-based music. Versions of songs and tunes proliferate, skilled performers introduce variations and ornaments as the mood takes them, and the same melody can be found in different metres.

4. It is European music. In structure, rhythmic pattern, pitch arrangement, thematic content of songs, etc., it most closely resembles the traditional music of Western Europe.

5. The bulk of it comes from the past, and is of some antiquity. Much of the repertory is known to have been current in the eighteenth and nineteenth centuries. Some is earlier in origin, and it is likely that some very old melodies and lyrics survive adapted to modern forms.

6. It is handed down from one generation to the next, or passed from one performer to another, more by example than by formal teaching. The traditional learner normally acquires repertory and style through unconscious or conscious imitation of more experienced performers. But nowadays learning also takes place in groups organised for teaching, and occasionally within the formal education system. Printed and manuscript song and music has had an influence on the tradition since at least the eighteenth century. Throughout this century books, sound recordings, radio and television have played an important part in the transmission of the music, and there are always

traditional performers with experience of popular and classical music.

7. Although items of the repertory are initially produced by individual singers and musicians, they are changed as they pass from performer to performer, and they eventually become the production of many hands, music 'of the people'. There is a community of taste between composer, performer and audience. The original producer normally receives no financial reward, and is forgotten. Words of songs are often written to existing tunes.

8. Repertories and styles have originally evolved in given regions, but natural processes of diffusion and especially the modern communications media have spread them more widely.

9. It is music of rural more than urban origins, a reflection of earlier population distribution, but many items and forms of the repertory have come from towns and cities, or through them from abroad. Much traditional music is now performed and commercially produced in urban areas.

10. It is performed, almost entirely for recreation, by people who are normally unpaid. There are relatively few full-time professional performers.

11. Solo performance, in which subtleties of style can best be heard, is at the heart of the tradition, but group performance is common. Singing is normally unaccompanied. Unison singing, in duet especially, is heard. Instruments are played in unison in combinations of any number. Counterpoint is not employed, and harmonic accompaniment, when possible on an instrument, is generally of a simple kind.

12. It is played in the home, in the public house and at other social gatherings – parties, weddings, dances, festivals – and latterly at concerts, and on radio, television and record.

13. Written words or music are only used as an aid to memory, if at all, and never in performance. Most singers cannot read music, but many players make some use of staff or other kinds of notation.

14. It is a small-scale art form and its structural units are typically symmetrical. Within them are found variations and embellishments of text, rhythm, phrasing and melody, but rarely of dynamics.

15. Songs are performed in Irish and English, but those in English, the more recent, are the more widespread. Songs can be quick or slow, strict or relaxed in rhythm.

16. The bulk of the instrumental music played is fast isometric dance music – jigs, reels and hornpipes for the most part; slower listening pieces composed for an instrument or adapted from song airs form only a small proportion. Melodies are generally played in one or two sharps, and belong to one of a number of melodic modes, which have mostly seven notes to the scale, but sometimes six or five. Their range does not frequently exceed two octaves, and they end on a variety of final notes. The dance music has associated solo and group dances.

17. String, wind, and free-reed melody instruments predominate – especially fiddle, whistle, flute, uilleann pipes, concertina and accordion, and percussion instruments are of minor importance. Certain timbres are considered traditional, and certain stylistic techniques are used which arise from the nature of the instruments. All are forms of instruments found in Western Europe. (Courtesy of the ITMA)

**Traditional Music Archive.** See Irish Traditional Music Archive.

**transmission.** 1. The process of passing on music style and repertoire within a player's peers and lifetime, and/or to another generation. The most fundamental method of transmission is referred to as 'oral' – 'by way of mouth' (as in song transmission). Complimentary to this is the 'aural' – relating to the ear. Before the advent of, and in the absence of any form of written notation or recorded sound these were the transmission mechanisms in Irish music. The earliest graphic representation of music in Ireland occurs with church music, this dating to the twelfth century. Graphic representation of music on paper (notation), accompanied by education in that, made it possible to pass music on to people remote in place or time. However, particularly in the case of traditional music, this can only indicate notes to be played, and only so if originally noted, and eventually read, accurately; it can not communicate rhythmic subtlety. Therefore notation is usually

Johnny Doran, in cap, with Pat Cash and his son, c. 1940 (John McCaffrey)

seen as an aid to memory, and to be utilised in tandem with an aural process. The cylinder recorder and the wind-up gramophone effectively 'stored' sound which could then be fairly clearly and repeatedly reproduced. More modern methods of music transmission – records, tape and CD – provide an accurate reproduction of the original music, and make it accessible, theoretically, almost indefinitely. In the Irish traditional music scene all four transmission methods are utilised: oral, graphic, mechanical and electronic. 2. The conveyance of music sound to audiences through radio, television, recordings, PA systems, etc.

See music notation; Three Ages of Music; oral tradition.

**Travelling People.** Also called tinkers or itinerants, their preferred appellation today is traveller. Though nomadism is (or was) a prime factor in their lifestyle, as with gypsies, they have separate ethnic identities. Opinion on their origins vary, the most common explanations being that they are descended from very ancient mendicant metalworkers or that they represent the remains of the dispossessed small farmers and tenants who were forced on to the road at the time of the Great Famine. Invariably Roman Catholic with a very strict moral code, they also have a complex structure of traditional beliefs and familial infrastructures regimenting their lifestyle, belying the chaotic superficial impression given to settled people unacquainted with their ways. It is widely believed that travellers have a secret language. Known as 'Shelta' by academics, travellers themselves refer to it as 'Gammon' or 'Minker's Torri'. However, it is a cant rather than a full language, its primary use nowadays being to obscure the meaning of what is being said to those not privy to its secrets. As literacy was not common among travellers until recently, this helped the conservation of their oral traditions of storytelling and singing. Lack of access to the electronic media meant that long after the majority of rural people were dependent on radio for their entertainment and the seanchaí had been rendered redundant, the traveller's camp-fire was still acting as a focus for the dissemination of tales, songs and news. The coming of the portable radio and, later, television, had the same effect on the travellers as it had on the settled community, though the traveller's social isolation played its part in keeping groups in closer contact than might otherwise have been. This enhanced proximity maintained a fertile environment for the diffusion of oral literature and other traditions. Work on the collection of the folklore of travellers in Ireland has been minimal when compared with the enormous body of lore and song recorded from Scottish travellers by the School of Scottish Studies, notably by Hamish Henderson. Most collectors for the Irish Folklore Commission would have some materials on or from travellers but very few worked in depth with them. Of those who did, Pádraig Mac Gréine of Ballinalee, Co. Longford, is the most diligent. Of his informants there is no doubt that Nora 'Oney' Power (1861–1937) was the most abundant source of tales. The foundation of the centre for traveller's rights and studies, Pavee Point, in Dublin, fills a long overdue need for a focus for traveller culture. The style of singing preferred by older travellers is commonly high pitched and nasal. It is more declamatory than most forms of traditional singing found in this country. Even if this style was not specifically formed to suit the trade of the street-singing ballad-seller, it was certainly an advantage to those travellers who were broadsheet peddlers. The use of a high pitch and full voice was an excellent method of drawing the attention of passers-by on busy, noisy streets and fair greens. Elements which appear frequently in traveller singing are exaggerated glottal stops and liberal use of supplementary syllables. The glottal stop is used as a form of audible punctuation. These devices may seem obtrusive when presented on the printed page, but in actual performance they are hardly noticeable as their function is to assist the flow of the song. Song texts which appear disjointed in print can come across as perfectly good narrative to the listener. Whereas a garbled song remains unintelligible, it should be remembered that there is a process in the oral transmission of songs whereby they are reduced to their 'emotional core'. That is, in their being passed from mouth to mouth, superfluous material is jettisoned over time until only the dramatic nucleus remains. So it is with many travellers' songs, particularly narrative songs. They may lack end-rhymes, lines or even complete verses and yet, in performance, retain perfect intelligibility for the singer and listener. The most celebrated Irish traveller singer was Margaret Barry. Little known in his short lifetime, the Roscommon traveller John Reilly's songs heavily influenced Christy Moore and have been recorded by many more performers, some as unlikely as the Waterboys. Traveller musicians have made their greatest mark on the uilleann pipes, favouring an open or legato form of fingering. The legendary Wexford musician and horse dealer, John Cash (1832–1909), is still much remembered in piping circles. The influence of his great-grandson, Johnny Doran (1908–50), is inestimable, having inspired many musicians such as Willie Clancy, Seán Reid and Martin Talty to take up the uilleann pipes. Even today, elements of Doran's fiery style are evident in the music of traveller or traveller-inspired musicians such as Paddy Keenan, Finbar Furey or Davy Spillane. Examples of traveller music and song are not numerous but the following are cited as being representative of the genuine tradition: *The Bunch of Keys; the complete recordings of Johnny Doran* (CBÉ, 1986); John Reilly, *The Bonny Green Tree: Songs of an Irish Traveller* (Topic Records, 1978); *Songs of the Irish Travellers* (European Ethnic Cassette compilation, 1983). A good comparative anthology of the vocal traditions of the travellers of Britain and Ireland is on the CD *Songs of the Travelling People* (Saydisc, 1994). (TOM)

**Traynor, Rena.** (1955–95). Concertina. Born 1955, Co. Clare, a relative of the late Mrs Elizabeth Crotty, she was involved in Clontarf CCÉ, then Leixlip, and Trim, for twenty years. She taught tin whistle and concertina, and was mentor to many highly regarded and prize-winning players. A competition commemorates her since her death.

**treble.** A treble is an ornament which involves the division of a long note (usually a crotchet) into three shorter note values of the same pitch.

Trebling

It is a technique particularly favoured by Northern-style fiddle players, and executed using short, accented bow-strokes. It has however increasingly been adopted by players on other instruments. (LID)

*Treoir.* The internal magazine of CCÉ. Begun in 1968 it has been edited since then by Labhrás Ó Murchú. Of hugely varying content over the years, it has published much written by, among many others, Séamus MacMathúna, Tomás Ó Canainn, Seán Quinn, Helena Rowsome, Mick O'Connor, Micheál Ó hÁlúin and Gearóid Ó hAllmhuráin. A strong photographic record, it carries material relating to CCÉ's major activities, branch events, instrumentation, and personalities (differing hugely to the strong commercial emphasis of *Irish Music* magazine). Its strongest feature has been the inclusion of notation of tunes and songs not found in published collections, and in this has been a valuable disseminator of new and rare pieces. Its literary style is anecdotal, but eclectic, and while it does not pitch itself at an academic reader, nevertheless it has carried some valuable analytical material. Its editorials adopt a detached, overseeing, pastoral, homily-like tone, sometimes patronising, often sentimental, appealing to a sense of duty and common bond. At times these are political, sometimes directly, often cryptically so; on occasions repeated in espousal of a similar idea in later years. They address the music in relation to the nation, and reflect the broad cultural remit of Irish identity that is CCÉ's ethos. While the magazine is mostly in English, it also carries material in Irish. Its format has changed from simple folded sheet in the beginning, to a large-scale colour magazine at present. It is not sold commercially, but is available by subscription, and in bound annual editions. In this format it is an outstanding kaleidoscope of the progress of traditional music through CCÉ over thirty years.

**triple pipes.** See aulos; laueddas.

**triplet.** The triplet is an ornament common to all instruments and all styles. It simply involves three consecutive notes, in either upward or downward motion, played in the value of a single beat. The notes may move in articulated, legato or staccato fashion. (LID)

Triplet

**troubadours.** 1. Lyric poets or poet-musicians, often of knightly rank, flourishing from the eleventh to the end of the thirteenth centuries mainly in Provençe, southern France and also in northern Italy. They developed a romantic, lyric poetry with intricate metre which through the Norman invasion in Ireland can be deduced as having had a major impact on Irish song style, particularly sean-nós. 2. Casual or strolling minstrels or singers, dating to eleventh-century France.

**trouvères.** Eleventh- to fourteenth-century school of northern French poets.
See song, sean nós, origins; troubadour.

**trumpet.** No such instrument is employed in traditional music, although in ancient times various kinds were used, most likely for hunting, signalling, civic or ceremonial purposes. O'Curry (*Musical Instruments of the Ancient Irish*) lists several instruments which are likely to have been trumpets – bennbuabhal, corn, buine, guthbuine, stoc, sturgan. 'Buine' is some kind of wind instrument, possibly (from the Irish meaning of the word) a reed pipe, or horn pipe, but derived by O'Curry's examination of its playing context, and deduced by Breathnach (1971) to be a horn trumpet like those still found on the African continent. More certainly trumpet is 'corn' (in one of its meanings a drinking horn); this has surviving long, curved metal examples with a flared end. One of these, part of the bronze age, Loughnashade trumpet hoard found in a lake of the same name near Eamhain Macha (Navan fort) on the western side of Armagh city, is used as the ITMA's logo. It is believed that the three trumpets were deposited there as a religious offering at the beginning of the Christian era. Stoc and sturgan are taken by O'Curry to be indigenous Irish, or Celtic, trumpets.

One hundred and twenty-two bronze age horns have been found in many locations in Ireland – these concentrated in Munster and north-east Ulster, with examples in the Midlands and in the upper Shannon area. One hundred and four survive in the National Museum of Ireland. An arc-shaped horn, made of bronze, originally side-blown, and modelled on an example from the Ulster Museum, has been re-constructed by Simon Dwyer of Dublin. With this he has evolved various potential methods of blowing, applying a didgeridoo-style of circular breathing and articulation, using various extended mouthpieces. However, since the old instruments produce their notes by overblowing (this, in the end-blown variety giving a maximum potential of five) it is unlikely that they were used for recreational purposes. Yet their sound is a reproducible effect dating to at least 3,500 years ago on this island. Simon Dwyer's music on 'adharc' and other horns can be heard on the cassette album DORD. A previous attempt to play on one of the National Museum's horns in 1857 resulted in the death of the collection's curator Sir

Robert Ball from a ruptured blood vessel. The instrument's distribution in Ireland, Britain and continental Europe is documented by John M. Coles in *Journal of the Royal Society of Antiquaries of Ireland*, vol. 97, part 2, 1967.

**TTCT. (Teastas i dTeagasc Ceolta Tíre).** Teachers' course, Comhaltas Ceoltóirí Éireann. Minutes of first CCÉs meetings from 1951 indicate a desire among the founders to have a training course for traditional music teachers. TTCT, a week-long diploma course for music teachers was initiated in 1980. Designed and directed by Mícheál Ó hEidhin, Music Inspector with the Department of Education and himself a traditional musician. By 1999, 400 had gained diplomas, these successful out of some twenty or so applicants selected for it each year.

**Tubridy, Michael.** (1935– ). Flute, whistle, concertina. Born in Kilrush, Co. Clare, his parents had an interest in traditional music; his mother played concertina. His maternal uncle played fiddle. He grew up with music and set dancing, playing Clarke's tin whistle. After secondary school in Kilrush, he took a degree in civil engineering at UCD and settled in Dublin. From the mid-1950s he frequented the Pipers' Club, Thomas Street, and John Egan's Club in Church Street. He played with several small groups including a quartet with Paddy Moloney, Anne Walsh, and Jack Dervan. In the 1960s he played flute with the Castle Céilí Band, was a member of Ceoltoirí Chualann and a founder member of the Chieftains. He has a solo album *The Eagle's Whistle* and is involved in set dancing. His *A Selection of Irish Traditional Step Dances* (1998), is the first tutor book in traditional step dancing. This contains his original and unique method of graphically notating step dance.

**Tulla Céilí Band.** One of the more famous of the old céilí bands, dating to 1945/6. Difference of interpretation cloud its origins, but in *Dal gCais*, 1978, Martin Rochford states that the Tulla band germinated with his and Seán Reid's piping and playing at house dances around east Clare in the early 1940s. Impressed by the 'beautiful blend of fiddles, flute and

Early Tulla Céilí Band with (L–R): Seán Reid, P.Joe Hayes, Joe Cooley. At back right is Tony McMahon. (CCÉ)

piano in the old Ballinakill Céilí Band', they formed a band, borrowing drums from the Bodyke fife and drum band. Reid, Rochford, Jim and Jack Donoghue, Mike Doyle, Jimmy Long, Paddy Canny and Jack Murphy came together in 1944 as 'The Ballinahinch Céilí Band', named after Rochford's home townland. The following year he says they changed the name to Tulla, because of a local wit's suggestion that the name fitted more easily on the bass drum. Chris Keane's 1998 history picks the story up at this point, with the band's re-formation in 1946 in Minogue's pub at Tulla, to take part in a Féile Luimní competition. With pianist Teresa Tubridy the inspiration, the other players then were fiddler Bert McNulty, a Foxford garda stationed at Ballinakill, Co. Galway, fiddlers Paddy Canny, P.Joe Hayes and Aggie White and Seán Reid, Joe Cooley on accordion, Jack Murphy, Paddy and James O'Donoghue on flutes. They won the award in that year – as 'St Patrick's Amateur Band' – and also, with Willie Clancy, in 1947 and '48, in '48 the Oireachtas Corn na Mumhan also. Under Seán Reid's direction now, they broadcast with Raidió Éireann, their signature tune 'The Humours of Tulla'. They added drummer Jack Keane in 1953, went on to become one of the best-known bands in the country, playing Irish emigrant venues in England and in America (first in 1958). This continued into the 1980s, the set-dance revival bringing them back in demand. They won an All-Ireland in 1957, the first of three, and recorded with HMV, later EMI. Over the years the personnel has changed – the band has had Paddy O'Brien of Tipperary, the McNamaras of Crusheen, Martin Mulhaire, Dr Bill Loughnane, Peter O'Loughlin, Francie Donnellan – P. Joe Hayes alone remaining constant up to the band's fifty years' celebration in 1996.

The band is an important exemplar of the development and maintenance of groups around recognition of talent and common style, mutual friendships, and adherence to a 'sound'. It shows too the dialectical relationship between demand for entertainment in a cosmopolitanising country (post-war 1940s Ireland), the recognition of that demand, its fulfilment (provision of group music for dancing), and the consequent cultural influence that the method of fulfilment (the formation of the Tulla) was able to exert on its public. Therein too is the commercial exploitation – and development – of traditional music, the incorporation of commercial recordings into the music's culture, the construction of local (Clare) image and status within traditional music society. It demonstrates the power of radio in moulding and confirming aesthetic taste and national confidence. Above all, it demonstrates the power of 'tradition' itself, and the process of its creation: 'the Tulla's own members believed in the band, the county believed in it, the exiles looked to it as a beacon of familiarity and comfort – even the country knew it well enough to permit comic writer Frank Kelly to coin the popular caricature 'The Ayatulla Céilí Band'.

The band is documented thoroughly in *The Tulla Céilí Band*, by Chris Keane (1998).

**tune names.** These are in great variety and follow no particular pattern. Older tunes tend to be recognisable by reference to various places, people and happenings. They might be usefully broken down to 1. place (area, county, town or townland, etc.); 2. particular people (especially the composer of a tune or the person who was associated with playing it); 3. incident, observation or domestic happening; 4. political aspiration or event; 5. aspects of nature; 6. domestic situation or object; 7. sport related; 8. work related; 9. various women, 10. sexual allegory and courting.

Thus we have 1. The Dublin Reel, The Maids of Mount Cisco (a town in New York State), The Sligo Maid, The Killavel Jig, The Sally Gardens, The Spike Island Lasses; 2. Garret Barry's, Eilís Kelly's Favourite, Patsy Touhy's, Tom Ward's Downfall; 3. Ask My Father, The Geese in the Bog, The Lark on the Strand; 4. The Rights of Man, Repeal of the Union, The Congress, The Connacht Rangers, The Peeler's Jacket; 5. The Sunny Banks, The Blackthorn, Long Hills of Mourne, The Bird in the Bush; 6. The Upper Room, Wallop the Potlid, The Blackthorn Stick, The Pipe on the Hob, The Frieze Britches, The Connemara Stockings, The Gold Ring, The Ravelled Hank of Yarn; 7. The Foxhunters, The Hurler's March, Curragh Races; 8. The Maid Behind the Bar, The Jolly Clam Diggers, Tom the Fisherman, The Woman of the House; 9. The Blackhaired Lass, The Lady on the Island, Charming Molly Brallaghan; 10. Toss the Feathers, The Ladies' Pantalettes, Come with Me Now, Behind the Haystack, Kiss the Maid Behind the Barrel, Rolling on the Ryegrass, Give the Maid her Fourpence, Boil the Breakfast Early.

Modern tune types often do not display the same poetic ring. This is because with modern travel, communications, everyday vocabulary and media informing people's lives, society is less umbilically attached to local place and happening, has new priorities and the player/composers are often of urban provenance. Today's names also indicate a shift from the familiar and community to the personal. Modern tune names thus usually sound modern.

See counties of Ireland; townland.

**tune types.** See barn dance; fling; German; highland; hornpipe; jig; march; mazurka; planxty; polka; reel; schottische; slide; slow air; strathspey; two-step; waltz.

**Tunney, Paddy.** (1921– ). Singer, lilter, dancer, raconteur and author. Born in Glasgow, he was reared at Rusheen, Templecarron, Pettigo, Co. Donegal. He lived in Co. Fermanagh for part of his youth. His mother was Brigid Tunney, herself a highly regarded source singer for Paddy and many others. Perpetually energetic, 'a dedicated hater of pop and cant and shamrockery, a lover of old ways and rare songs and raving poetry', his velvet articulation of big, serious songs has hugely affected repertoires of many new singers. His 'Moorloch Mary', 'Mountain Streams Where the Moorcock Crows', 'Highland Mary' are all gems. During four years in a Belfast jail for political activities this indefatigable singer turned to academic work, studying Irish history and language. He trained as a health inspector in Dublin and was later transferred to Donegal, Kerry, Letterkenny and finally to Galway. His eventful life has exposed him to a wide variety of styles and repertoire which he has, in turn, moulded and adopted in both his singing and writing. He is the author of several publications – the autobiographical *The Stone Fiddle – My Way to Traditional Song*, a selection of songs with anecdotal stories (*Where Songs Do Thunder*), and two volumes of poetry. *A Wild Bee's Nest* is his definitive recording, and he can be heard on *Where the Linnets Sing*, with his mother, sons and daughter.

**tutor-books.** 'Teach Yourself' manuals for the learning of instruments. These have existed in some form for more than a century and a half, but the earliest with relevance to Irish music is Charles Egan's *Harp Primer* (1729, reprinted 1822). Then there is John Geoghan's *Complete Tutor for the Pastoral or New Bagpipe*, which was issued *c*. 1745. The first tutor for the uilleann pipes proper was O'Farrell's *Collection of National Irish Music for the Union Pipes* (1804), with useful and clear instructions for playing the instrument, then his *Pocket Companion for the Union Pipes* (*c*. 1806). Henry Colclough's *Instructions for Playing the Bagpipe* was published *c*. 1809.

The fact that the *Pocket Companion* – although obviously aimed at musically-literate readers – contains many traditional tunes as examples, makes it the first Irish traditional music tutor. While accordion and other tutors appeared in the US and Britain during the nineteenth century, for Irish music it is the harp which leads the twentieth century, with the Loreto Sisters' 1903, London-published *Tutor for the Irish Harp* by 'MAC' (Mother Attracta Coffey). *The Violin Made Easy* was the title of Bat Scanlon's instructive 1923 collection published in San Francisco, then follows Kerr's *Violin Instructor* (still being published), and in 1936 Leo Rowsome's *Tutor for the Uilleann Pipes* (Walton's, reprinted many times, new edition 1999). The first accordion tutor with relevance to Irish music seems to be Gerry O'Brien's 1949 *Accordion Instructor* published in Massachusetts.

But as we presently know it, the 'tutor-boom' began with the publication of the Armagh Pipers' Club *Learn to Play the Tin Whistle* series which was initiated in 1972 purely as an internal teaching aid, but in all of its editions, bootlegs and offshoots has by now probably influenced more than half a million players world-wide. The 'whistle' has scores of tutors, some of limited service, but all potentially introductory to the broader field of traditional music. Beginning to match its numbers are bodhrán tutors, these involving rather slight books, but also audio cassettes, CDs and videos. More specialised instruments like harp, pipes, flute, fiddle, accordion and concertina have fewer books, possibly reflecting their non-beginner status (tin whistle is often recommended as a first instrument to achieve a grasp of the music structure).

Step dance and set dance are well serviced by video tutors, and by various publications, but singing alone remains ignored: one can blow an 'A' on a flute, or approximate it on a fiddle – but how can one be told how to sing it? Singing remains the last bastion of the truly oral tradition, and for this reason is little documented.

Orality of course is stressed in the majority of serious instrumental tutors, most state that the book is only a guide, that the learner's most important ally is the ear. Tutors have moved apace with technology through the years, and the 'Tin Whistle Pack' devised by Armagh Pipers' Club and owned by Appletree Press, was the first to include a flexible 45 rpm instruction disk. Tutors progressively used cassette, then CD and video as teaching supplements, the latter, and soon its successors CD ROM and the Internet, bringing the teaching process close to actual teacher–learner communication.

**two-step and quick-step.** Social dance-form popular in the first half of the twentieth century. These used 4/4, 'swung' marching time, and could be danced to such as 'The Sally Gardens'.

# U

**Uí Cheallaigh, Áine (McPartland).** (1959– ). Sean-nós singer. Born Belfast, 1959 to Póilín Nic Craith, a native Irish speaker from Ring, Co. Waterford and actor and singer Joe McPartland from Belfast. Her mother's and Nioclás Tóibín's singing were her earliest influences. She sang in English from an early age, in school choirs and learned classical violin and piano. She graduated in music and Irish from UCD, and went to teach in Ring in 1982. She won Corn Uí Riada in 1990 and 1992, sang in *Riverdance* in 1995, in concerts with the RTÉ Concert Orchestra at the National Concert Hall, with Hugh Tinney and with Anúna. Her recordings include her solo album *Idir Dhá Chomhairle/In Two Minds*.

**Uí Mhaitiú, Áine (Ní Fhlaithbheartaigh).** Sean-nós singer. Born at Tóin an Chnoic, Ros a' Mhíl. Local poet Paddy Beag Ó Conghaile composed the song 'Mná Spéiriúil Ros a' Mhíl' (The Winsome Women of Rosaveal) about her maternal aunt, Nan Rua Malone, a singer and accordionist now living in America. At eleven, Áine remembers seeing three neighbouring women 'keening' her paternal grandfather at his wake in their house in 1950, clapping their hands and singing his praises aloud while walking around the coffin. She learned songs from both her parents, and also in primary school from teacher Tadhg Ó Séaghdha who did much to preserve local song. Her family migrated to Co. Kildare in 1958 where Áine now teaches in Kill. She won the women's competition and Corn Uí Riada at the 1966 Oireachtas. (LIM)

**Uí Mhuineacháin, Cáit Bean.** (d. 1994). Mullingar, Co. Westmeath. Founder-member and first president of Comhaltas Ceoltóirí Éireann in 1951.

See CCÉ, history.

**Uí Ógáin, Ríonach.** (1950– ). Archivist/collector with the Department of Irish Folklore, University College, Dublin. She has lectured widely on traditional song and music. Among her publications is an edited compilation audio album of archive recordings entitled *Beauty an Oileáin: Music and Song of the Blasket Islands* (1992), an article entitled 'Music Learned from the Fairies' (*Béaloideas* vol. 60, 1992–93), and the books *Clár Amhrán Bhaile na hInse* (1976), consisting of an index of traditional songs collected in the West Galway area, and *Immortal Dan: Daniel O'Connell in Irish Folk Tradition* (1995).

**uilleann pipes.** Bellows-blown bagpipe with chanter, three drones and keyed melody pipes capable of providing harmony simultaneous with the melody. Evolved from the simple bagpipe in the early 1700s, the instrument had taken its present structure by the beginning of the nineteenth century. Originally known as the Irish Union bagpipe (as in O'Farrell's 1804 and 1806 books) this instrument is the most complex of its kind. Essentially indoor pipes – being relatively quiet compared to most other bagpipes – they are to be found in a variety of pitches, from concert pitch (D), and 'flat' pitch, by semitone down through C, to B and A. Such 'flat pipes' have a characteristically sweet and mellow tone.

*construction*. The pipes are constructed from hardwoods, the most common being African blackwood, ebony or boxwood. Keys are generally made of brass or silver, and mounts, previously made from ivory, are now turned from artificial ivory. The bag is made from a variety of materials but leather is preferred. A full set of pipes consists of a bag, bellows, chanter, three drones and three regulators. The player plays while seated, with the bag under the left arm (right-handed players), this which is linked to a bellows fixed under the right arm (hence the term 'uilleann' pipes, uilleann meaning elbow). The chanter rests on the player's right knee while the drones and

# UILLEAN PIPES, CONSTRUCTION

1. Bag (usually covered in cloth or velvet with trimmings)
2. Bellows
3. Bellows valve
4. Arm belt
5. Waist belt
6. Bellows outlet tube
7. Blowpipe
8. Blowpipe valve
9. Blowpipe stock
10. Main stock cup
11. Main stock
12. Drone key
13. Tenor drone     A. Butt piece
                          B. Tuning piece
14. Baritone drone    A. Butt piece
                          B. Tuning piece
15. Bass drone    A. Butt piece
                          B. Tuning piece
16. Drone reed
17. Tenor regulator
18. Baritone regulator
19. Bass regulator
20. Regulator reed
21. Chanter stock
22. Chanter top piece
23. Chanter reed
24. Chanter

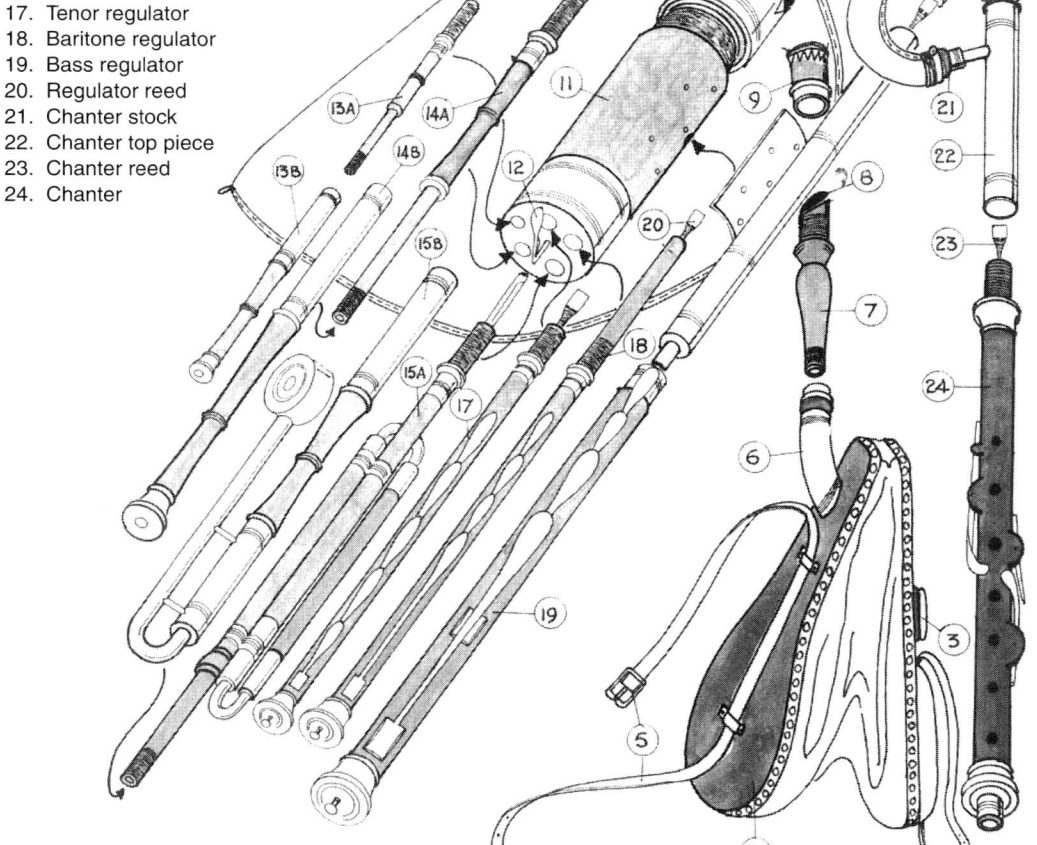

Arrangement of uilleann pipes parts

regulators, arising from a common stock, sit across the top of the player's legs.

*chanter.* The chanter has a range of two octaves and, unlike the mouth-blown bagpipes, can be 'overblown', due to the fact that it can be stopped by closing the end of the chanter on the knee. This also enables the player to play notes staccato or legato. Its scale of D, E, F#, G, A, B, C#, essentially limits playing to the keys of G, D, E minor and A minor (the main keys of traditional Irish music), but the chanter is often made with keys which enable semitones to be played, some chanters being fully chromatic. The chanter reed is a double reed made from cane rather like that in oboe. It is delicate and fine so that it can be readily overblown; it has to be prevented from getting wet since it would warp on drying. Hence the need for dry air to be supplied by bellows.

*drones.* The three drones, which can be turned on or off with a drone key, consist of tenor, baritone and bass, each tuned to the bottom note of the chanter and each an octave below the other. Each drone consists of two parts, the lower part sliding in and out for tuning purposes. The drone reeds (guills) are single with a tongue slit in the stem of fine lengths of cane or elder.

*regulators.* The three regulators lie on top of the drones and consist of tenor, baritone and bass. They possess keys which sound particular notes only when they are opened. They are played with the side of the hand and give a simple harmony to the chanter. The tenor regulator has five keys while the baritone and bass have four keys each. The keys lie in banks across the regulators so that three of them (one on each regulator) can be played as a chord. They can be played as held notes, vamped on the accent notes, or used in syncopation with the rhythm of the tune on the chanter. If the right hand is free individual notes can be played on the regulators.

The regulator reeds are double reeds, similar to the chanter reed. They are tuned by a

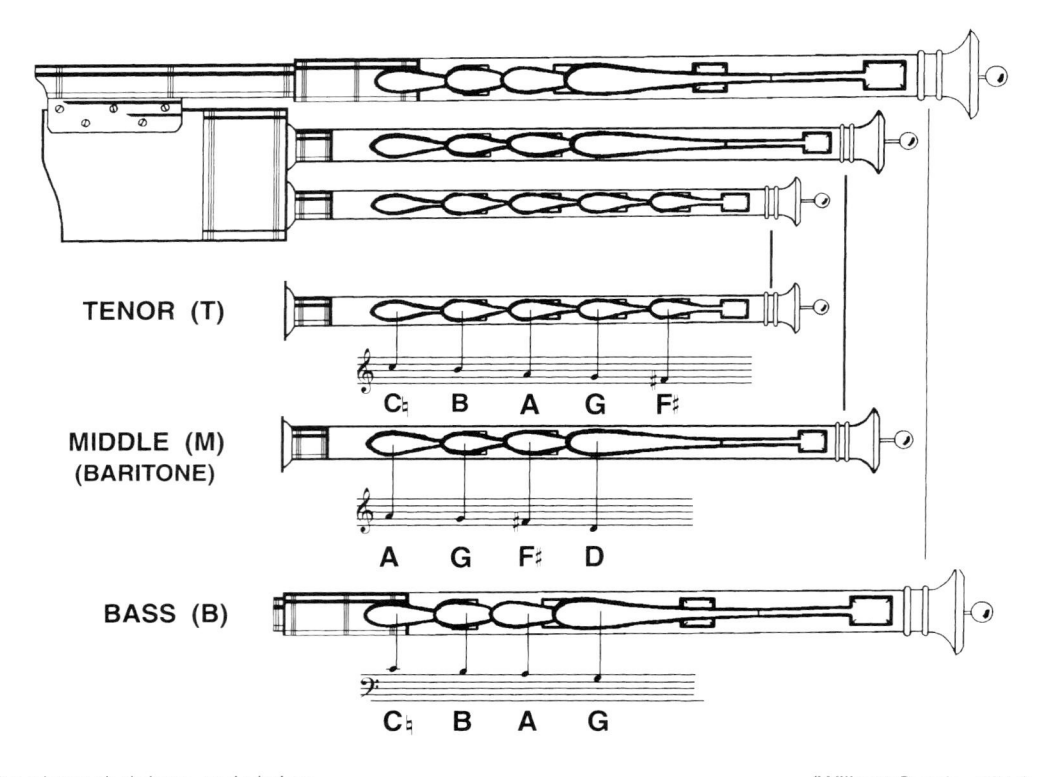

Regulator, their keys and pitches (Wilbert Garvin, NPU)

tuning-stop on their ends. The bass is furthest from the player, it has four notes, from top to bottom, low C, B, A, G. The baritone is in the middle, it has four notes A, G, F# and D in the same octave as the chanter. The tenor has five notes C B A G F#, also the same as the chanter. Together the regulators give the notes G A B C – D F# G A – B C. This effectively extends the range of the pipes down to the G below middle C. (WIG)

*playing style*. This is decided mainly by the chanter fingering, but the use of regulators can also have a profound effect. Chanter techniques include popping (lifting the chanter off the knee to accentuate a note), slurring or sliding of notes, playing with chanter off the knee, ornamentation, cranning, vibrato, 'tight' (staccato) or closed articulation and loose, open (legato) flute-style fingering. The regulators can be used melodically, harmonically, or crudely-harmonically in a percussive effect like older accordion players' method on bass buttons. Opinions differ as to the value of the regulators. Most see them as a unique feature that can be utilised to great advantage.

*history*. Like other pipes, the Irish uilleann pipes has three single-reed drones, but it is the only bagpipe to have a chanter geared to the full 'concert' scale. Using a double reed, the 'concert' chanter can produce two full octaves, this making even its use in symphony orchestras feasible (Liam O'Flynn etc.). Originating probably in the early 1700s, the first actual written reference to the uilleann pipes – then called the 'Irish pipes' – places them fully operational by the early 1770s. In the mid-1700s the third drone is believed to have been added to the uilleann pipes, along with the first 'regulator'. The regulators made it possible too for some Protestant clergy to use the uilleann pipes as a church organ. By the turn of the nineteenth century William Kennedy had developed chanter keys to enable the playing of sharps and flats, and the two final regulators were added to the instrument by William Talbot (b. 1781). Various modifications, notably the development of the concert-pitch chanter, were made by the Drogheda-born Taylor brothers in Philadelphia, *c.* 1875. All of this gave us today's instrument; the 'concert' uilleann pipes is the strongest colouring in modern Irish dance music. The pipes' idiosyncrasies – ornament, 'yelping' and cranning – are mimicked on fiddle, accordion and flute. This is similar to the way in which Scottish music on fiddle and piano accordion reflects the shape and colour of the bagpipes' music.

*in paintings*. This medium provides evidence for the use and development of the instrument, especially during the nineteenth century when scenes of Irish rural life attracted the attention of both Irish and foreign artists. Joseph Haverty's 'The Blind Piper' (oil, *c.* 1844, National Gallery of Ireland) shows Pádraig O'Brien, who played in Limerick, in an idealised rural setting, but his pipes are clearly depicted. Haverty also painted a second portrait of O'Brien (University of Limerick). Other portraits of pipers include examples by Frederick William Burton (water-colour, *c.* 1840, National Gallery), Thomas Bridgeford (oil, *c.* 1844, National Gallery), and William Charles Foster (oil, *c.* 1850, photo, Irish Traditional Music Archive). In the latter case the pipes are unusual in not having drones. Pipers are also found in genre paintings of rural life, both accompanying dancing and playing to an informal audience. Instruments are often shown with good detail. Pipers in nineteenth-century paintings are always male and often blind. Except when the piper is accompanying dancing, informal audiences are typically of women and children inside or immediately outside their cottages. Maria Spilsbury's 'Harvest Festival at Rosanna, Wicklow' (oil, *c.* 1813–20, sold at Philips, London, 1988) includes a piper accompanying straw men at a harvest dance. Examples of genre paintings include Alfred Fripp's 'Irish piper' (oil, *c.* 1846, City of Bristol Art Gallery) which shows an elderly piper playing to a group of women and children outside a row of cottages in a wild landscape, and Erskine Nichol's 'Over the Buckle' (oil, 1854, exhibited at the Corry Gallery, Dublin, May/June 1995) showing a couple dancing to a piper outside a cottage. Lisburn painter Samuel McCloy's *c.* 1880 work, 'The Piper', depicts the instrument in an unusual setting with a backdrop of the river Lagan and a Lisburn church steeple. The evidence from paintings emphasises the central role which uilleann pipes played in traditional music in nineteenth-century Ireland. (BRB) *piping-related manuscripts referenced under Hayes manuscript sources subject index in the National Library MSS Collection.*

1. Captain William Kelly collection (MS 13562, early nineteenth century): three pages from the piper referred to by Francis O' Neill in IMM. It references piper Mrs Jane Bailie, a granddaughter of Captain Kelly, and mentions TCD steward, piper John Kingston who was a music associate of Canon Goodman.

2. Séamus Ó Casaide collection (MSS 8116-81180): MS 8116 has pictures and some seventy letters relating to pipers and piping from the period 1901–29; MS 8117 has correspondence and postcards relating to music and piping, also Henebry's article on piping; MS 8118 has MSS and news clippings relating to pipes and pipers, including O'Farrell's *Treatise on the Union Pipes*, A. D. Fraser's *Reminiscences and the Bagpipe*, a typed copy of a *Programme Tutor for the Irish Bagpipes,* and programmes of Irish piping festivals and concerts between 1904 and 1914.

3. MS 10665 is a three-page document relating to the Irish Pipers' Club in 1921.

4. MS 1962: an alphabetical listing of some 300 contemporary and past pipers, pipe makers and Feis Cheoil pipes prizewinners, compiled by Cumann na bPíobairí *c*. 1914. This documents only five pipers in Ulster, four in Munster, twenty-two in Leinster, fourteen in Connacht and twenty-one in the US.

5. MSS 13063–13070: the papers of Thomas Ceannt relating his 1900–1916 activities with the Gaelic League and the Irish Volunteers, and including also documentation of his activities with the Pipers' Club. (SIN)

**Ulster.** See song, Ulster.

**Ulster Folk and Transport Museum.** At Cultra, near Holywood, Co. Down, this was established in 1958 upon the passing of the Ulster Folk Museum Act (NI) at Stormont, the original Northern Irish parliament. Its purpose is to collect and interpret materials relating to 'the way of life, past and present, and the traditions of the people of Northern Ireland'. The open-air museum consists both of a rural and urban area in which buildings representing both have been reconstructed from carefully dismantled originals. Galleries display various aspects of folk-life, and transport collections show road, rail and maritime transport. The museum collects non-material culture items too – folklore, local history and music. Its archive of traditional music dates to the early 1960s and collecting is ongoing. Collecting is done in the field and in studio, and utilises commercial recordings also. Traditional music and dancing feature prominently in the museum's events programmes, and includes classes, recitals, concerts, informal sessions, seminars and exhibitions. There is also a collection of music instruments. The present director of music is Belfast uilleann piper Robbie Hannon, his predecessor was Dublin harp player Janet Harbison. (ROH)

**Ulstersongs.** A small company, formed by John Moulden in 1993 which publishes small songbooks and cassettes and distributes, at singing festivals and by mail order, these and other books and albums mainly with the aim of promoting the social singing tradition of the north of Ireland. Most of the stock reflects unaccompanied singing styles or solo playing.

**universities.** See education.

**USA.** In the 1960s Irish emigration to America dwindled to a mere trickle following the abolition of the European immigrant quota. The halcyon years of Irish traditional music recordings in the United States had ended effectively just before World War II. The old Irish dance halls which provided a major social outlet for at least one aspect of the music were no longer to be found in urban America.

With diminishing immigration Irish traditional music was inexorably declining as a force in Irish American social and cultural life. By 1960 Irish traditional music had become ghettoised, played by a diminishing number of Irish immigrant musicians and appreciated by an even smaller group of aficionados. There were few places to play beyond the homes of the musicians themselves. Only a handful of American-born children showed any interest whatever in the music and indeed their parents rarely encouraged them to take it up, convinced that it could not serve any viable function in modern America.

Beginning in New York City in the mid-1970s a number of developments were to affect the future of Irish traditional music however. The television dramatisation in 1975 of Alex Haley's *Roots*, an epic saga of the search of African Americans for ancestral connections back in Africa set in motion a search for cultural roots and heritage among Americans of all ethnic backgrounds. *Roots* gave rise to a movement that intensified in the Bicentennial celebration of American Independence in 1976.

That year became an occasion for the celebrating of ethnic heritage on a national level legitimising ethnicity in a way that contrasted sharply with the abiding principle of Anglo-American conformity. In this climate federal and state funding benefited all through the 1980s. This began with the Smithsonian Institution's Bicentennial Festival of American Folklife in 1976 which brought together fifty-two Irish traditional musicians, singers and dancers, participating in a variety of concert and thematic workshop presentations.

Formal receptions for the performers were held by the Smithsonian Institution and also by the Irish Embassy – the first time that Irish traditional musicians from the United States had been so honoured. In the course of the week Irish musicians from different American cities met each other – in some cases for the first time – and numerous informal sessions took place throughout the week. A great sense of camaraderie was engendered; flute player Jack Coen, a native of Woodford, Co. Galway, who had lived in the Bronx since 1949, observing that for the American-based musicians it was the first time their music had ever been officially recognised. He maintains that the participation of the Irish American musicians in the Smithsonian Festival was a pivotal event in the validation of the music among the community of Irish musicians in his generation.

In 1976 the National Endowment for the Arts funded field recordings of Irish traditional musicians in the Midwest and East Coast and two long playing records with biographical notes were issued on Rounder in 1977. Remarkably these were the first field recordings of Irish traditional music in America ever issued on commercial recordings. By 1977 a separate Folk Arts Department had been established within the Arts Endowment. It funded several nationwide tours of Irish traditional artists over the next ten years, these named 'The Green Fields of America'. According to tour co-director Richard Shea:

> Four distinct groups can be identified as having been affected in one way or another by the tour . . . the touring musicians themselves, the local musicians . . . in each city, the local organizers and organisations . . . and finally the local Irish American communities who turned up in force at each of the concerts and witnessed, many for the first time, an evening of traditional Irish music and dance . . . The warm, often ecstatic reception that these audiences gave them, in turn, produced a heightened sense of self-esteem and self-confidence in the performers. Their years of practice and often lonely dedication to this music were finally being vindicated.

When the National Heritage Awards were instituted by the National Endowment for the Arts in 1982, Connemara sean-nós singer Joe Heaney, then a resident of Seattle, was among the first winners. According to Bess Lomax Hawes, Director of the Folk Arts Program, the awards were designed to:

> bring to public attention the range, the liveliness, and the continuing integrity of traditional artistic styles and practices throughout the United States, whether tribal, local, ethnic, occupational, religious, or regional in origin.

Five more Irish artists resident in America were to gain National Heritage awards in the next ten years: uilleann piper, Joe Shannon, in 1983; fiddler and teacher, Martin Mulvihill, in 1984; step dancer, Michael Flatley, in 1988; fiddler and composer, Liz Carroll, in 1991; step dancer and teacher, Donny Golden, in 1995.

During the 1980s there was a steady flow of federal and state funds for projects supporting Irish traditional folk artists in a variety of contexts. Several Irish American organisations also received federal or state public funds during this time for presentation or support of Irish traditional arts. These have included the Irish Fest in Milwaukee, the Irish Arts Center in New York and the Greater Washington Céilí Club for their festivals in Glen Echo and Wolf Trap. One of the most concerted efforts in the support of Irish traditional artists in America has been the Ethnic Folk Arts Center's sponsorship of the all-woman Irish music and dance group 'Cherish the Ladies'.

In all of these cultural efforts on behalf of Irish Americans one particular aspect of their culture was singled out for revitalisation – the older instrumental and singing traditions carried to America by immigrants and nurtured in Irish American communities. Only the folk or traditional aspects of the culture were chosen for regeneration and support. This orientation mirrored the definitions of folklife first articulated in the American Folklife Preservation Act of 1976:

> The term 'American Folklife' means the traditional expressive culture shared within the various groups in the United States: familial, ethnic, occupational, religious, regional; expressive culture includes a wide range of creative and symbolic forms such as custom, belief, technical skill, language, literature, art, architecture, music, play, dance, drama, ritual, pageantry, handicraft; these expressions are mainly learned orally, by imitation, or in performance, and are generally maintained without benefit of formal instruction or institutional direction.

This attitude encouraged a new generation of young Irish Americans to take up traditional music with the encouragement of parents from the last wave of Irish immigrants in the late 1940s and early 1950s. They all had direct living links to Ireland, positive attitudes to the homeland, links with living relatives and the opportunities for travel back and forth which had not existed for immigrants of past generations. They were in direct contact with an Ireland where the traditional arts were now flourishing and many emerged as accomplished musicians.

Typically the young Irish American musicians have undergone a rigorous process of enculturation into the ranks of Irish traditional musicians, learning appropriate style and repertoire from exemplary senior musicians. All live in a world of multiple musical cultures which are freely accessible. It is in the nature of young people to work with whatever is available and they meet musicians from other musical cultures in a variety of social circumstances: from Cape Breton, Quebec, Appalachia and Southern Louisiana. Sessions take place, tapes are made and swapped, invitations to visit are issued, friendships are formed. Ultimately music-making is mutually affected.

Competitive playing has also been crucial over the past twenty years. Many have achieved success early in their musical development in the regional and All Ireland Championships. With his or her cultural credentials so validated, the young musician often feels free to innovate outside the context of competition.

Sessions represent another key element. They ensure that change will take place in a relatively leisurely fashion and act as a brake, as it were, on the pace of innovation. Constant exposure to stylistic role models from Ireland is another factor encouraging stability and continuity. A constant flow of recordings, formal and informal, infuses the Irish American 'scene' as do sessions with musicians visiting or on tour from Ireland.

Irish music is typically performed in a variety of situations including various festivals, events sponsored by folk music societies, concert series sponsored by a variety of arts organisations and agencies, colleges, museums and historical societies. National public radio and television brings Irish traditional music weekly to millions of Americans – a situation that would have seemed impossible twenty years ago. This creates full- or part-time employment for Irish musicians in the process. Indeed some of the musicians, who earn a full- and part-time living playing Irish music, are non-Irish American. Non-Irish interest in the music creates an audience with quite a different make-up to that in Ireland. People these days are choosing what kind of Irish music they want to listen to and be involved in. (MIM)

*Chicago.* By 1900 there were 225,000 Irish in this city. These early emigrants congregated along the south branch of the Chicago River in housing developments around the brickyards, slaughter houses, rolling mills, lumberyards and other industries – Conley's Patch, Healy's Slough, McFadden's Patch, Canalport, Canaryville, Bridgeport, Brighton Park and the Back o' the Yards. Here Irish music, song and dance flourished most vigorously in the late 1800s. Occasional notices in *The Citizen* indicate that Irish music played a prominent role in the public life of the Irish community. Several dance halls featured Irish music and dance, some, like Finucane's Hall, were formal, others were impromptu, like the dances in the butcher shop on the northwest corner of Bonfield and Archer during the 1890s. Irish musicians and dancers were represented in the two Irish villages in the 1893 Chicago World's Fair, and many associations dedicated to political change in Ireland organised concerts, rallies and picnics that included a wide range of Irish musical entertainment. Several noted Irish musicians attached to minstrel troupes and vaudeville companies frequently passed through the city and often supplemented their income by performing in Irish-owned saloons; pipers John Hicks, John Moore, Eddie Joyce, and Patsy Tuohey were a few of the most frequent and popular of these visitors. Undoubtedly, however, then as now, the bulk of Irish musical activity in nineteenth-century Chicago was concentrated in private homes at occasions such as weddings, wakes, christenings and house parties.

*Irish Music Club.* A turn-of-twentieth-century outgrowth of frequent informal sessions held in the homes of Capt. Francis O'Neill and his friends. It involved pipers Barney Delaney, James Cahill, John Ennis, James Early, John Beatty, Adam Tobin, John Canners, fiddlers John McFadden, Edward Cronin, Timothy Dillon, James Kennedy, John McElligott, Abram Beamish, James O'Neill and flute players James Kerwin, Garrett Stack, Fr Dollard, Fr Fielding and Francis O'Neill himself. It was, in O'Neill's words, 'the most enjoyable, companionable and representative association of Irish musicians, singers and dancers ever organized in America'. A few wire and cylinder recordings of McFadden, Delaney, and Early still remain. In 1900, O'Neill was concerned with the growing indifference with which music was being treated by the Irish in America; the contemporary Irish-American press verifies this. O'Neill viewed the lack of proper patronage, appreciation and respect for the Irish musician as the chief problem and held misdirected social reformers, over-zealous clergy and greedy entrepreneurs as the three groups mainly responsible for the debased state of musical and cultural sensibility among the American-Irish of the day. Other significant factors were: the decline of Irish emigration to Chicago, the breakup of Irish neighbourhoods, the modification of cultural values and priorities that accompany the emigrant's successful transition from 'foreigner to native', and the chronic instability of American urban society in the post-industrial age. Despite the admonitions of O'Neill and other cultural commentators, Irish music, song and dance continued to recede for the next half century.

*recording.* The period between the two world wars saw a flurry of Irish musical activity in Chicago as several musicians made 78 rpm records for labels like Decca, Victor, Celtic and Columbia. In the 1920s pipers Eddie Mullaney, Tom Ennis and Joe Sullivan, fiddlers Tom Cawley, Paddy Stack, Billy McCormick, Francis Cashin, Selena O'Neill and Michael Cashin, flute players Paddy Doran and Tom Doyle and pianist Frances Malone appeared on commercial recordings in an assortment of styles and repertoire. This declined during the Depression – the last commercial recording of Chicago-Irish musicians before the 1970s was done for Decca in 1938 with Eleanor Kane, fiddler Jim Donnelly and accordionist Packie Walsh. In 1934 Pat Roche, a dancing teacher from Co. Clare, presented the Pat Roche Harp and Shamrock Orchestra at the Irish Village section of the Century of Progress World's Fair. The band was one of the first American ensembles modelled on the Irish céilí band and went on to make several records for Decca. Included were Jimmy Devine and John McGreevy, fiddles; John Gaffney, accordion; Pat McGovern, flute; Joe Shannon, uilleann pipes; Eleanor Kane, piano; Pat Richardson, drums; and Pat Roche, step-dancing. The efforts of McGreevy, Kane and Shannon had a big impact over the following forty years or so. So too did Pat Roche, whose radio programmes and organisational work influenced the city's Irish music and dancing activities into the 1980s.

*dance.* Irish music could still be heard at benefit dances for the Irish Independence movement in the early 1920s and during the Depression musicians played for open-air dances and in private dance halls with specialised dancing: the hall at Madison and Sacramento had Kerry sets, that at Root and Wentworth did Clare sets, the one at Madison and California had the Mayo set, or plain set. Gaelic Park – the GAA stadium

– at 47th and California had separate outdoor platforms for Kerry, Clare, Mayo and American-style group dancing. At various times during the 1930s, '40s, '50s, and early '60s, Irish dances were held in halls or parks at 47th and Halsted, 51st and Halsted, 64th and Halsted, 69th and Wentworth, 69th and Emerald, 63rd and Kedzie, 79th and Aberdeen, Halsted and Diversey, the West End Ballroom at Cicero and Madison and McEnery Hall at Madison and Pulaski.

*players*. Musical stalwarts of the 1930s, '40s and early '50s included fiddlers Tom Fitzmaurice, Jimmy Neary, Jim Giblin, John McGreevy, P. J. Concannon (who hosted an Irish radio programme for many years), Martin Wynne, Ann Cawley Scully, John McGinley, Jim McCarthy, Anna McGoldrick, Dan Keogh, Tom Ryan, and Theresa Geary; accordionists Tom Rush, Tony Lowe, Paddy Kenny, Tim Gehene, Dan Shea, Willie Guerin, Jim Bresnahan, Tim Sheahan, Tom Treacy, Paddy Durkin, Packie Walsh, John Gaffney, Martin Hardiman, Tom Kerrigan, Mrs McLaughlin, Nell O'Hara and Terry Teahan; flute players Jim Rudden, Paddy Doran, Pat McGovern and Frank Thornton; drummers Pat and Tom Richardson; pianist Eleanor Kane Neary; and pipers Eddie Mullaney, Joe Shannon, Denny Flynn, Joe Sullivan, Mike Joyce and Mike Scanlon. Yet even though there was plenty of music to be heard, Irish music in Chicago was at a low ebb of esteem within the Irish community there. Remuneration for performances was slight and infrequent when steady engagements were available at all. Few young Chicagoans had taken up the music, and it seemed to retreat to the narrowing community of newly arrived emigrants.

*1950s emigration*. The mid-1950s witnessed a new influx of musicians emigrating to Chicago from Ireland in a wave that lasted until the early 1960s. Kerry fiddlers Paddy and Johnny Cronin, Galway accordionist Kevin Keegan and the Galway accordion player Joe Cooley and his brother Séamus (flute) were among the most widely acclaimed of the recent arrivals. Though only Séamus Cooley would remain in Chicago into the 1970s, each made a substantial impact on the city's Irish music community. Inspired by the rise in Ireland of CCÉ, the Irish Musicians' Association of America was founded in August, 1956 by sixteen musicians attending a meeting at the Midland Hotel in Chicago. Frank Thornton was the first president, and, by the time of the first 'Irish Musicians' Ball' held on 30 November 1957 at McEnery Hall, sixty musicians had become active members of the Chicago branch. The national US organisation expanded to twenty-two branches within the next few years but dissolved in 1964 due to an inability to resolve matters of organisational structure and procedure. The Chicago branch survives, now affiliated to CCÉ.

Active in the 1950s and early '60s were also fiddlers Tom McMahon, Phil Durkin, Frank Burke, Mike Boyle, Pat Burke, Mike Shanley, Mossie Foran, Maida Sugrue, Una McGlew and Jack and Eileen Fitzgerald; accordion players Pat Cloonan, Mike Madden, Martin Byrne, Jim Coyle, Tim Clifford, Tom Maguire, Tom O'Malley and Des O'Grady; flute players Noel Rice, Tom Masterson, Albert Neary and Kevin Henry; pianists Nancy Harling and Maise Griffith; banjo player Bert McMahon; piper Dave Page; and drummers Billy Soden and John Smith. Several native Chicagoans also joined the Irish music ranks around this time, including fiddler Bob Murphy, accordionists John Murray and John Lavelle, flute players John Murphy, Pat McPartland and Jim Thornton and drummers Pat Gilhooly and John Cook.

*venues and teaching*. Music activity took place in numerous Irish music bars on 79th Street and 63rd Street; these declined during the 1970s, dwindling to a handful of spots for weekend céilís and sessions – Flanagan's Tavern, Hoban's Tavern and Hibernian Hall (which served as the meeting place for the Irish Musicians' Association). A weekly Irish Hour broadcast live on radio station WOPA by Martin Fahey Snr provided another focus. The Francis O'Neill Music Club, also affiliated with CCÉ, became active during the 1970s, as did the Emerald Music Club and Chicago Gaelic Society, each sponsoring monthly céilís and sessions. Schools of Irish music instruction were begun, and Chicago became a frequent host venue for the Midwestern American Fleadh Cheoil competitions held each spring.

Chicago-Irish musicians began performing

often for non-Irish audiences at folk festivals, coffee-houses and college concerts locally and throughout the United States, including at the Smithsonian Festival of American Folklife in Washington, DC. American folk labels issued LP recordings of Irish music that included Chicagoans Joe Shannon, John McGreevy, Séamus Cooley, Terry Teahan, Noel Rice, Eleanor Neary, Kevin Henry, Frank Thornton, Jimmy Thornton, Maida Sugrue, Albert and John Neary, Frank Burke and James Keane Snr. Eighty-year-old Chicago uilleann pipemaker and Mayo native Patrick Hennelly was the subject of a National Endowment for the Arts research project in 1976–77. Most importantly, a number of talented young American-raised musicians emerged in Chicago during the late 1970s, several of whom went on to win All-Ireland championships and to have national and even international impact on Irish traditional music of the 1980s and '90s, as soloists or group performers – fiddlers Liz Carroll, Kathleen Keane, Kathleen Rice and John Cleland; piano accordionist Jimmy Keane; flute player/dancer Michael Flatley Jnr; tin whistle players Maggie Henry, Mary Mayer and Johnny Harling; button accordionist John Williams; pianist Marty Fahey; guitarists Dennis Cahill and Jim DeWan; drummer Tom Masterson Jnr; and percussionists Kevin Rice and Patrick Flatley among them. The local scene was also refreshed during the 1980s and '90s by 'new blood' from Ireland, with musicians such as Clare fiddler Martin Hayes, Fermanagh flutist Larry Nugent and Dublin guitarist Pat Broaders.

At the end of the twentieth century, Irish music is well represented in Chicago's public cultural life. There are two annual city-wide Irish music festivals (one sponsored by the City of Chicago Mayor's Office), two active CCÉ branches, two large multi-arts cultural centres (the Irish American Heritage Center and a revived Gaelic Park), nine weekly Irish music radio programmes, fourteen Irish step dance schools with forty-three branches and fifteen sessions and pubs featuring Irish music and céilí and set dancing. The annual Chicago Feis has been held continuously since 1945 and, at close to 1,600 participants, is North America's largest.

The 1990s have seen Chicago Irish musicians on scores of commercial recordings and in numerous Hollywood film soundtracks. Mark Howard's Trinity Dance Company pioneered a dance fusion that presaged the format of *Riverdance*; *Riverdance* star and *Lord of the Dance* creator Michael Flatley Jnr, along with Joe Shannon and Liz Carroll, have been recipients of the National Heritage Fellowship Award from the National Endowment for the Arts. The O'Neill Irish Music Collection is now archived at the Hesburgh Library at the University of Notre Dame, and indeed the collector's labours are commemorated in two new books by Ossian Press of Cork – Nicholas Carolan's *A Harvest Saved,* and *The Complete O'Neill Collection* edited by Dr Liz Doherty of University College Cork. Ref. James Walsh (ed.), *The San Francisco Irish, 1850–1976* (Irish Literary and Historical Society, San Francisco, 1978). (LAM)

See O'Neill Irish Music Collection.

*Native Americans.* By the early 1800s, French-Canadians, Irish and Scots who worked for the Hudson Bay Company had introduced fiddle music to the native peoples of Canada. Dance tunes like 'Haste to the Wedding', 'Soldier's Joy', 'Drops of Brandy', 'The Devil's Dream', 'The Irish Washerwoman' and 'The Fisher's Hornpipe' were played by Native Americans from the Mi'qmak in Nova Scotia, the Saulteaux, Algonquins and inter-racial Metis in Manitoba. By the end of the century, Orcadian fiddling (a composite of Norse and Scottish played in the Orkney Islands) enjoyed widespread popularity among the Athabaskan people in Alaska's Interior. During the Klondike Gold Rush in the 1890s Irish fiddlers and pipers played for fellow prospectors in Dawson City, Fort Yukon and Fairbanks and shared traditional tunes and dances with native Alaskans. A century afterwards, similarities still exist between Irish and Athabaskan dance music. Both genres are played for set dancing (quadrilles and contra dancing are popular in Athabaskan communities), and both are still passed on through a process of oral transmission. As well as favouring slides and double-stops to ornament their dance music, the Athabaskans use lilting techniques to memorise tunes before transferring them to instruments. Like many older set dancers in Ireland,

Athabaskan Indian fiddler, Bill Stevens (GEO)

Athabaskan dancers favour 'close to the floor' stepping styles. Fiddler Arthur Kennedy who lived in the Koyukon village of Galena regarded himself as 'an Irish-Athabaskan'. His repertoire included Irish dance tunes as well as American old-time music. Celebrated Athabaskan fiddler Bill Stevens, who has been a guest performer with the Chieftains, readily acknowledges a rich core of localised Irish tunes in his repertoire. (GEO)

*West Coast.* Although most Irish famine immigrants settled in urban centres on the east coast of America, others set up rural communities in the Ottawa River Valley in Ontario, and the Miramichi Valley in New Brunswick, Canada. More travelled west to Texas – Irish settlements San Patricio and Refugio were founded in the 1830s when Texas was still part of Mexico. Irish music, song and dance contributed to the social life of host communities – Canadian lumber camps, Texan farmsteads, frontier towns throughout the American West. Thousands of Irish came across the Sierras in 1849 after gold was discovered in California. Mining industries also brought Irish workers to Montana, Utah, Nevada and Washington. Butte's 'Little Dublin' had one of the largest Irish settlements in the western states. Its saloons and variety shows employed scores of Irish musicians, singers and comedians in the 1880s and 1890s. William Bonney, otherwise known as 'Billy the Kid', Butch Cassidy and Jesse James were all of Irish extraction. Despite their notoriety, their exploits were immortalised by Irish song writers whose verse helped mould the iconography of the outlaw in American popular culture.

The relative isolation of San Francisco from other centres of American industry lasted until the 1870s. By the early 1900s, however, it had the largest branch of the Gaelic League in North America, sponsoring Irish history and language classes, weekly dance classes, and Gaelic Athletic Field Days. Its céilís were promoted by the Gaelic Dancing Club, and Professor Batt Scanlan, the self-styled 'leading exponent of Irish music in the West', provided dance music. San Francisco had its own pipers' club by the end of the 1890s and an ample repository of music to prompt a collection of tunes by Dr M. C. O'Toole – unfortunately O'Toole's collection project and the city's pipers' club were eclipsed by the devastating earthquake of April 1906. Two months earlier, Douglas Hyde, founder of the Gaelic League, had visited San Francisco, where he applauded the interest in Irish culture among both 'lace curtain' Irish in Nob Hill, and the working class in the Mission. But in the wake of the earthquake, some Irish began to move out of the poorer areas of the city, yet those remaining had quadrilles and céilí dancing at the Knights of the Red Branch Hall. Picnics organised by Irish 'county' associations bonded communities and integrated new immigrants through Irish music and dancing. No Irish recording stars like Coleman were to emerge in San Francisco.

Clare concertina player Mary Gavin – who played for 'kitchen rackets' hosted by local hurling and football teams – was one of only a trickle of Irish players to arrive during the Depression, but post-World War II industry attracted a large number of Irish. The 1950s brought in Kerry fiddler Seán O'Sullivan and accordionists John Hickey, Con Dennehy and Tadhg Reidy, the latter a past pupil of Pádraig O'Keefe. Post-war expansion of the city dispersed tight Irish communities however, dismantling what had been a cohesive nucleus of Irish settlement in the Mission district for over a century.

A radical counter-culture emerged in San Francisco initially in the non-conformist literary group 'the Beats' ('Beatniks'), then in the 'hippie' movement of the mid-1960s. Joe Cooley's arrival in San Francisco during this era drew many non-Irish into the music, and after his death Kevin Keegan continued as a focus of Irish music. But with Keegan's passing, traditional music-making in Northern California passed to mostly non-Irish, many part of the hippie movement. These lacked exposure to mentors like Cooley or Keegan, and did not share a sense of cultural identity with established Irish communities. For them, traditional music was just one exotic art among alternative lifestyles and soul-searching escapism.

In the same period, Irish and Irish American communities in the Bay Area relinquished Irish music to modern popular culture. Ironically they retained Irish step dancing, which (unlike instrumental music) had an established institutional structure. With a myriad of associated artistic activities, feiseanna offered the prospect of full-family entertainment, while dancing schools instilled discipline, reinforced school-based learning, and strengthened neighbourhood affiliations within Irish communities. This social and cultural polarisation between step dancing and instrumental music was also affected by changes in Irish emigration in the 1970s. With a healthier economic climate in Ireland then, fewer Irish immigrants (traditional musicians included) came to California and many older Irish pubs turned to newer forms of entertainment to attract non-Irish patrons. By the mid-1970s, older session houses, like McCarthy's Pub in the Mission District (which had hosted frequent sessions by Joe Cooley and Joe Murtagh), had ceded their place to more folk-oriented pubs like the Starry Plough in Berkeley, and the Plough and Stars in San Francisco. These continue to be the focal points of Irish traditional music in the Bay Area today.

*North West*. At the present time, Irish traditional music has a huge consumer audience on the West Coast, from Alaska to Southern California. This owes as much to its accelerated commercial development as it does to the immigration of players to the West Coast since the 1980s. The adoption of Irish music and dance by countless non-Irish born performers has also extended its artistic matrix well beyond the cultural topography of its former homeland. Despite its geographic isolation, Alaska has an expanding traditional music scene centred on sessions in Anchorage, Juneau, Haines and Fairbanks. The annual Irish Festival in Anchorage, offering national and local performers, has fostered indigenous talent by exposing it to quality performers from out of state. Until recently, Irish music in British Columbia was confined to passive British-style folk-club audiences; however, a programme of interactive workshops, Irish language and dance classes offered by a dynamic branch of CCÉ makes Irish music more community-oriented in Vancouver; the music in Washington State is centred around Seattle, home presently to Martin Hayes. Sean-nós singer Seosamh Ó hÉanaí was an artist-in-residence at the University of Washington until his death in 1984, its department of ethnomusicology houses an extensive corpus of his material. Irish music also has considerable patronage in Portland, Oregon, not least as a result of Kevin Burke and Mícheál Ó Domhnaill who moved there in 1983; fiddler Randal Bays and flute player Mick Mulcrone are also based there. In Southern California, Irish traditional music is concentrated for the most part around Los Angeles, with occasional session gatherings in San Diego and Oceanside. But Northern California, and especially the San Francisco Bay Area, continues to be the nerve centre of Irish music on the West Coast. There are no organised classes or schools of Irish traditional music, but step and set dancing are well catered for. San Francisco has revived its pipers' club too; it meets for sessions, classes and an annual tionól. The influx of new immigrant musicians since the mid-1980s has replenished the quality of Irish music, and since the early 1990s, several cultural associations have developed it commercially with 'Celtic' festivals. (GEO)

# V

**Vallely, Brian** (1943– ) **and Eithne** (1945– ). Uilleann pipes and flute-player, teacher and organiser, Brian was born into an Armagh family with strong Gaelic associations in sport and language, and studied art in Edinburgh. He was influenced initially by *Ballad Makers Saturday Night* on RÉ, but hearing Ó Riada's music at a local Gaelic League function in 1959 inspired him to play. Access to recordings of Willie Clancy, Michael Gorman, Margaret Barry, Séamus Ennis and Leo Rowsome led him to whistle, then flute; Glasgow uilleann piper Pat McNulty introduced him to piping. The Comacs of Tyrone developed this interest further, and he became secretary of the Armagh branch of CCÉ. Disagreements about the nature of traditional music directed him to setting up the Armagh Pipers' Club in 1966. A highly-acclaimed painter, the theme of traditional music is dominant in his prolific output of some four thousand canvasses.

From a line of fiddlers in Co. Donegal, Eithne's grandmother played fiddle and concertina, her grandfather, father and uncles also played fiddle. Her mother's family has fiddlers also around Kilcar, these including Francie Dearg and Mickey Byrne. Taught whistle at national school by Seán Brady (father of singer Paul), Irish was her home language and she began on fiddle at nine. While studying Irish at UCD, the Dublin Pipers' Club introduced her to Séamus Ennis, Tommy Potts and Tommy Peoples. Through them she met Breandán Breathnach for whom she transcribed tunes for his CRÉ 1, and through Helena Rowsome, daughter of pipe-maker Leo, began piping, taking lessons from Dan O'Dowd. Living in Armagh since 1969 she has been central to the local Pipers' Club and the mentor of its many tutor books for whistle, pipes, fiddle and song since 1972. Teaching music locally inspired her to instigate in 1997 a training scheme for traditional music teachers, and through the 1990s she has also been involved in the NI National Curriculum Planning for Music Education.

**Vallely, Fintan.** (1949– ). Flute player, songwriter, writer. Born Tullygarron, Co. Armagh, both his parents sang. His father's mother was a member of Carl Hardebeck's Gaelic Choir in Belfast, his mother's father (a descendant of eighteenth-century harper Cormac O'Kelly) a fiddle player with the Ballinascreen (Co. Derry) Banba Céilí Band. He picked up whistle himself at age fourteen and was introduced to music in the local and Co. Tyrone circuit. He took up flute, the uilleann pipes, playing at fleadhanna and sessions throughout the country and attended the early tionóil of NPU. Since 1993 he has specialised in writing about traditional music, and lectures on Irish and international folk musics at the NUI, Maynooth and St Patrick's Training College in Drumcondra. He is the author of traditional music's first flute tutor, *Timber – the Flute Tutor* (1986, 1987, etc.) and has recorded two albums of flute music and one of satirical song. He was *The Irish Times* traditional music correspondent and reviewer from 1994–98, writes a weekly column in *The Sunday Tribune* and writes on the music for academic and music publications. He was the essayist on traditional music for the 1996 French *Imaginaire Irlandaise* festival's document on Irish culture 'Désirs d'Irlande', and for that of the 'Irland Diaspora' festival in Germany the same year. He is a major contributor to *The Blooming Meadows – the Soul of Traditional Music* (Townhouse, Dublin, 1998), and an editor of *Crosbhealach an Cheoil – The Crossroads Conference Papers* (Crosbhealach, Dublin, 1999). From 1995–97 he was programme consultant for RTÉ's traditional music productions *Pure Drop*, *High Reel* and *Willie Clancy Sessions*. His *Jigging at the Crossroads* (1999) documents and analyses Protestant attitudes to Irish music. He was an initiating organiser for the 1996 Crosbhealach an

Cheoil traditional music conference in Dublin, and was education consultant for the Coleman Heritage Centre, Gurteen (1997). He has been a contributor to many conferences and seminars on music and cultural affairs and is on the board of the Irish Traditional Music Archive.

**Vallely, Peter.** (1926– ). Singer. Born Derrynoose, Co. Armagh. Reared by his mother, a singer, he picked up songs at house sessions and dances in childhood, but particularly from aunt Kate McAtavey (née Mooney) – from whom he got 'The Banks of the Callan' – and uncle John Mooney from whom he got 'At the Foot of Newry Mountains'. Neighbour Sarah Makem was also a big influence. He recorded for RÉ with Ciarán MacMathúna in Clontibret, in 1956, and with Johnny Pickering's Céilí Band. His daughter Patricia plays fiddle and sings professionally.

**Victrola.** Brand name of an early gramophone popular in the US.
See reproduction of music.

**Vignoles, Julian.** (1953– ). Born in Co. Wicklow, he joined RTÉ as a producer in 1979 to work in Radio 2. He produced a traditional music programme, *The Green Groves*, with Philip King, which ran until 1981. He moved to Radio 1 in 1986, and his award-winning documentary *The Story of Woodbrook* involved Mícheál Ó Súilleabháin's reworking of *The Plains of Boyle* hornpipe as its theme music. Other radio work in the 1980s included *Dance Movements*, a history of dancing in Ireland, and *Call The Tune*. Four of these were presented by Séamus Ennis in the year before his death. With Peter Browne he produced the four-part series *The Séamus Ennis Story*. Since moving to television in 1994, he made the first *High Reel* series, presented by Mairéad Ní Mhaonaigh, and in 1997 the six-part *Willie Clancy Sessions*, presented by Frankie Gavin.

***Voice, The.*** Newsletter of Nenagh Singers' Circle. Informs on session nights, guests, functions, festivals, albums and other areas' venues and activities.

# W

**Wade, Jack.** (1913–67). Uilleann piper. Born in Dublin, the death of his father in World War I led his mother to move eventually to Gormanstown, Co. Meath. His stepfather introduced him to the fiddle and sight reading, but it was Greenanstown warpiper, uilleann piper, fiddler, piano, harp and dulcimer player Tom Matthews who led him to the pipes. Working in Customs and Excise on the border he had many opportunities to meet musicians and pipers in border counties. Manuscripts of the tunes he learned in his youth in Co. Dublin were contributed to Breandán Breathnach for his collections. A committed worker in music revival from the 1950s, he was instrumental in setting up Roslea CCÉ.

**Walderstown Uilleann Pipers' Club.** Formed by Willie Reynolds in 1943 in an effort to revive the playing of the pipes. It fused with the first local CCÉ branch in 1952. Among its more notable members were Tommy and John Healion, Pat Keegan, Michael Doyle, Seán McCormack, Tommie and Bonnie Green.

## Wales

*bagpipes*. First mentioned in the twelfth century. The Eisteddfdod in Cardigan organised by Yr Arglwydd Rhys had competing pipers among the other delights. Giraldus in the same century says that Wales plays the harp, pipe and crwth. Bagpipes are frequently referred to in bardic poetry in Wales from this period on, usually in a satirical context by poets who were also harpists and would not have been enthusiastic about pipers or their instruments. Down the years there have been melodies notated, of differing aesthetics but all very suitable for piping, referring to the pipes or pipers – Erddigan y Pibydd Coch, Conset y Peipar Coch, etc. These span the sixteenth century to the nineteenth. The sixteenth-century MS by Robert ap Huw has in it music of a very early period – probably contemporary with such as Giraldus, Iolo Goch. There is a great deal of iconographical evidence of pipes and pipers in Wales, ranging from eleventh-century carvings of pipers and chanter players (à la bombarde and biniou etc.) including a double-chantered bagpipe, through to nineteenth-century drawings of pipers playing on horseback at weddings. This was the most common context for bagpiping by this time and there are many written accounts describing the pipers and their music. The bleak, upland region of Bannau Brycheiniog in South Wales was the probable last stronghold of the bagpipes or pipa cwd, with two named pipers coming down to us – Evan Gethin and Edward Gwern y Pebydd. Both played at weddings, Evan played in Glyn Nedd around 1860, possibly later. The urban centre of Carmarthen was also associated with the pipes. In a thirteen-verse poem describing each of the old counties, Dafydd Thomas describes Carmarthen as 'fair, with great houses . . . and the bagpipes are most commonly heard playing here at the biggest weddings in Wales'.

There are no known surviving native-made bagpipes in Wales. All are either lost or destroyed. Hundreds or more instruments of all kinds were burned or buried in the fervour of the successive Methodist revivals in the country, culminating with the biggest of all in 1905. All iconographical evidence, written descriptions, surviving pipe music in MS, etc., are consistent with a typical north-west European bagpipe, of the gaita, veuze, biniou type. Some instruments had one drone, some two, some three. In the last two cases the drones were of unequal length and were probably tuned an octave below the six finger note and a fifth above that, although the possibility that drones were tuned to the five finger note as in Brittany cannot be ruled out, especially when the common repertoire of tunes is taken into account. We do not know about the internal bores on the chanters on the old pipes or therefore the possibilities of overblowing or crossfingering. Contemporary pipe makers such as Jonathan Shorland make pipes with different types of bore for different uses as is the case with most contemporary pipe makers on the continent. (CEM)

*crwth*. (crot or crowd). A bowed lyre with three or six strings, played in Wales from the Middle Ages until the end of the eighteenth century. Known in Cornwall as the 'crowd' – depicted in stone on the 1326 Melrose Abbey – it was still in use in Wales in 1770, but then almost extinct. In the early period, bowed lyres with and without fingerboards were in widespread use across Europe and were probably used to accompany the declamation of poetry. There is some evidence that similar instruments were also used in Ireland. One of the closest relatives of the crwth is the Finnish 'jouhikko', a bowed lyre without a fingerboard. The main characteristics of the instrument are as follows: it is constructed within a rectangular frame (sometimes carved out of a single piece of wood); it has a flat belly and back with a relatively short fingerboard; the bridge is flat or nearly so, and set at an angle; one foot of the bridge rests on the flat belly, while the other passes through one of the circular sound holes, making contact with the back of the instrument and acting as a sound post. Two of the six strings lie off the fingerboard where they may be bowed as drones or plucked with the thumb of the left hand. Held against the breast, the instrument is supported by a strap which goes around the player's neck. The six-string instrument was tuned in octave courses as follows: G-G'-C-C'-D-D'.

The crwth and the harp were the two principal musical instruments of bardic society in Wales. 'Crowders' are noted as early as the Cardigan Eisteddfod of 1176; in the Caerwys Eisteddfod of 1567, a number of 'croweders' are listed as having qualified to the various attainment levels of Cerdd Dant. By the sixteenth century, there appears to have been a distinction between players of the six-string crwth (crwth chwethant) and the three-string instrument (crwth trithant), the latter occupying a lower social status. The antiquarians Daines Barrington and Edward Jones published descriptions of the instrument during the late eighteenth century, both noting that the instrument had died out in most of Wales apart from on the Isle of Anglesey. The instrument is currently experiencing something of a revival: modern makers such as Bernard Ellis of Hereford and Gerard Kilbride of Cardiff have made accurate copies of the surviving instruments at the National Library of Wales, Aberystwyth and the Museum of Welsh Life at St Fagan's, near Cardiff. The most accomplished contemporary performer on the instrument is Robert Evans, based in Cardiff, who may be heard on the album *Ffidil*. (STR).

*pibgorn*. ('hornpipe'). A single idioglot-reed instrument played in Wales certainly to the end of the eighteenth century in Anglesey, and possibly until the late nineteenth century in Pembrokeshire. References to wind instruments occur in Welsh writings from the Middle Ages onwards, but the pibgorn was the one distinctively Welsh instrument that survived. Essentially a pastoral instrument, it was constructed from a wooden or bone tube (in round or square outside section) with six finger holes and a thumb hole, a short animal horn reed cap at the blown end, and a more extended curved animal horn bell at the bottom, often cut with serrated edges. The reed was made from a cylindrical tube of elder, similar to that used for bagpipe drones; nowadays more resilient cane is used.

The pibgorn belongs to a family of instruments found widely across Europe, Asia and North Africa; its relatives include the Basque 'alboca' and the Scottish 'stock-and-horn'. Large double hornpipes are also found in North Africa. There are three extant instruments in the Museum of Welsh Life at St Fagan's, near Cardiff, each playing a major scale beginning on C' or F'. In 1770, the antiquary Daines Barrington noted that the instrument was now played only in Anglesey, and that an annual prize for playing it was offered. In one such eighteenth-century event over 700 competitors performed. Although no record of performance technique has survived, a large painted panel in the National Library of Wales at Aberystwyth depicts a man playing the pibgorn with clearly distended cheeks. This may indicate that circular breathing was a common technique on the instrument; modern reconstructions certainly lend themselves to this mode of performance. Since the late 1970s upwards of fifty reconstructions have been made by Jonathan Shorland of Cardiff. (STR)

*song*. Traditional styles here are similar to those found elsewhere in Europe but the ways they are used may be called characteristically Welsh. The Mari Lwyd horse ceremony, a seasonal custom which survived in unbroken tradition until recently, has certain features which are Welsh, although it has elements in common with other European luck-visiting processions. The Mari Lwyd party would go from house to house at the period of the winter solstice, carrying a horse's head and seeking admission by singing a verse of the Mari Lwyd song. This was answered by the party inside singing another traditional verse or improvising one. The contest went on until one of the parties gave up. If the party inside gave up, the Mari Lwyd party could enter and enjoy wassail and an entertaining evening in return for bringing luck to the family. But if the horse-party outside gave up first they had to leave and try somewhere else. Some pubs hired a local poet to answer the Mari Lwyd party, for if they won the right to enter they could drink the pub dry in an evening. Poetic contention also played an important part in a Candlemas ceremony on 2 February, taking the form of feat songs to test memory, or songs with tongue-twisting words, or cumulative songs testing the ability to sing long sections in one breath and in some cases dancing at the same time. Other seasonal customs were the wren-hunt, with songs describing the hunt or praising the bird as king, the Shrove Tuesday pancake songs, and the Cadi ha or May-dancing.

There were May carols as well as Christmas carols, but these were serious in tone and doctrinal in nature. The melodies were often popular tunes of the day with words by Welsh poets, often local, and learned by heart. The only carol which survived the Protestant Reformation has very strong Catholic characteristics in both words and music and was collected in oral tradition in the twentieth century. Welsh ballads of the seventeenth and eighteenth centuries often shared the same tunes as the Christmas carols. Welsh poets revelled in assonance and alliteration and the ballads of that period are full of these poetic devices.

By the nineteenth century, the style of words and tunes was much simpler, and many ballad tunes were imported from England, Ireland and America. Love songs such as 'chansons d'aventure' and night-visit songs abound, occasionally with a reference to caru yn y gwely (courting in bed), a practice known in the United States as 'bundling'. In Welsh songs of sexual metaphor the theme is usually mowing the hay although one is based on the collier's work and his tools. Some love songs were macaronic, alternating lines of English and Welsh, and some poets would send a bird as a love messenger to their sweetheart, a device called llatai in classical poetry but also popular among folk poets. Songs of occupation include Welsh oxen songs, distinguished by a 'call' to the oxen at the end of each verse. These were sung by a boy with a goad who walked backward facing the oxen and were essential 'to keep the oxen in good heart'. The practice was known in the twelfth century and survived till the end of the nineteenth. Although many Welshmen went to sea, only one Welsh shanty has survived.

Other songs of occupation describe coalmining, work in the smithy, sheepshearing and fishing. The most characteristically Welsh form of traditional singing is connected with the harp and is known as cerdd dant (a medieval term meaning 'the craft of the string'). In this form the instrument is not used as accompaniment but is an equal partner with the singer who sings a kind of descant to the harp melody. In this traditional Welsh singing the harp begins and the voice enters later but the singer must choose their piece of poetry carefully for they have to enter at a point which will allow them to finish exactly with the harp. This style of singing was also used at other times and there are many references to singing May carols with the harp, as well as performing traditional Welsh poetry with the harp at social occasions. After a period of decline cerdd dant is now enjoying a considerable revival. (PHK)

*penillion singing*. 'Canu penillion', lit. 'singing stanzas', now also known as 'cerdd dant', 'the craft of the string', involves the singing of verses to harp accompaniment, and has been a unique feature of Welsh tradition at least since the eighteenth century, although its roots in the more ancient bardic tradition reach back to the Middle Ages. Under Eisteddfodic regulation as promulgated in the sixteenth century, bards could acquire specific titles such as 'Pencerdd' ('master musician') only after rigorous examination in the art of cerdd dant (harping or playing the crwth), or the composition (and performance) of poetry in the twenty-four strict metres, this last known as cerdd dafod ('the craft of the tongue'). The musical elements of the bardic crafts were passed on by oral tradition; only one major written source of this music is now extant, the harp tablature of Robert ap Huw (London, British Library, Add MS 14905), written down about 1613 but containing a much older repertory. While some of this complex music must have been intended for solo instrumental performance, it seems likely that certain pieces were intended as accompaniments for the declamation or singing of strict-metre poetry. The structures and networks of bardic patronage fell into decline during the sixteenth and seventeenth centuries; by the eighteenth century, the highly organised musico-poetic schemes of bardic culture had been forgotten.

However, the performance of verses by a solo singer to harp accompaniment (penillion singing) was by now a familiar genre in both North and South Wales: the harpist began by playing a recognised air to which the singer added an improvised line, often in counterpoint but sometimes more closely related to the harp melody. Gifted practitioners could also either improvise the short verses (penillion telyn or 'harp stanzas'), or select appropriate verses from their repertoire.

In the 1860s, John Jones (known as Idris Vychan), a cobbler originally from the Dolgellau area, was responsible for codifying the practice and for outlining the rules which performers should follow. The result was to remove the elements of extemporisation from penillion performance, and to limit the repertoire to precomposed settings. Nowadays, both harp 'accompaniment' and vocal melody may be newly composed, For competition purposes, a specific cainc (melody) is prescribed, and the gosodiad (setting) is made by the performer(s). Moreover, the genre has embraced duo, trio, quartet and choral performance, where precomposition is a necessity. The term cerdd dant is now commonly used for the genre in deference to the older, lost art, but the current genre is essentially an outgrowth and formalisation of the eighteenth-century tradition. Cymdeithas Cerdd Dant Cymru (The Cerdd Dant Society of Wales, formed in 1933) held its first festival in 1947, and publishes a journal, *Allwedd y Tannau* ('The Key to the Strings'). The annual festivals attract audiences and performers in large numbers; most Eisteddfodau have popular cerdd dant sections, and despite the current highly formalised performance context, the genre is undoubtedly one of Wales's most visibly thriving traditions.

*hymn-singing*. The stereotypical image of Wales as a nation whose main musical tradition is the singing of hymns has at least a basis in fact. Such was the fervour of the eighteenth-century Methodist revival that congregational hymn-singing within the context of nonconformist religious observance became the major musical outlet for a large proportion of the Welsh-speaking population. Most of the tunes sung in the eighteenth century were not of Welsh origin, but came to be regarded as such by adoption; this was aided by the composition of memorable Welsh hymn texts of considerable power by such eighteenth-century writers as Williams Williams and Ann Griffiths (1776–1805). The nineteenth century saw a considerable increase in hymn tunes by Welsh composers, fuelled by an improvement in musical education and the widespread adoption of Curwen's new sol-fa notation. The memory of this persists even today: staff notation is still known as hen nodiant or 'old notation' in Welsh. Few if any of these new tunes could be said to demonstrate specifically 'Welsh' musical characteristics, other than perhaps a propensity for strong tunes in the minor mode. Popular and traditional melodies were borrowed from outside and inside Wales, and current hymnbooks contain numerous harmonisations of tunes labelled simply Alaw Gymreig ('Welsh air').

The puritanical streak within Methodism – and the eagerness with which the Welsh embraced nonconformity – had an adverse effect on the maintenance of popular traditions of song, dance and ritual; but even by 1806, the stonemason, antiquary and poet Iolo

Morganwg commented unfavourably on 'the practice of singing religious songs in public houses', a practice which continues to this day. Despite the current decline in religious observance, the hymn still maintains its position as a genuinely popular musical genre in Wales, many examples having attained the stature akin to folksongs. (STR)

*harp (telyn)*. Wales is the only Celtic country to retain an unbroken tradition of harping since the Middle Ages. This is not to say that the instrument, the repertoire and techniques employed today are those of six centuries. But the harper has always occupied a special position within Welsh culture, both as accompanist to sung or declaimed poetry, and as an instrumental performer in solo music or in ensemble with the crwth. Moreover, the current apparent uniformity of harps and harp playing in Wales – nearly all harpists learn classical technique on the orchestral pedal harp – is a recent phenomenon.

Until the early twentieth century, there have nearly always been at least two distinct types of harp in use in Wales, sometimes more. References to the harp occur as early as the laws of Hywel Dda (*c.* 950), and also in the writings of Giraldus Cambrensis in the twelfth century. Although no instruments survive from the earliest period, it seems that by the late middle ages there were several types of harp in use. The fourteenth-century poet Iolo Goch criticised the new leather-covered gut-strung instrument, and professed to favour the older wooden harp with strings made from horse-hair. These were most likely single-row harps, and by the Renaissance period the single-row harp with bray pins was certainly in use in Wales. The harper's place within the bardic order was established by an orally transmitted and highly formalised set of structures which are most fully documented in the records of the Eisteddfodau held at Caerwys in North-East Wales in 1523 and 1567.

The unique harp tablature of the Robert ap Huw MS (London, British Library, Additional MS 14905), although not written until the early seventeenth century, provides the only significant written record of this sophisticated tradition, the music being quite unlike anything else in the extant traditions of notated Western music. Many of the pieces are based upon the repetitions of a two-chord ostinato in the lower hand while the upper hand performs increasingly complex variations, employing nail technique with forward and backward strokes and repeated note figures. The instrument used for this music would most likely have been a harp strung in gut with bray pins. Both Robert ap Huw's manuscript and other writings of the sixteenth and seventeenth centuries give often contradictory information as to the complex different tunings required; each is known by a name, qualifying its 'cywair' or 'key', such as 'bras gywair', 'lleddf Gywair', 'gogywair', etc.

The seventeenth century witnessed the virtual end of the formalised bardic order, despite attempts by scholars and the minor gentry to preserve in written form the oral traditions of poetry (and to a lesser extent music). One important remnant of this is the manuscript written by the recusant priest Gwilym Puw in 1676, entitled 'Trefn Cywair Telyn' (approximately translated as 'the manner of tuning the harp'). It supplies instructions for some of the 'cyweiriau' mentioned in Robert ap Huw's manuscript, although the descriptions diverge in important details. By the eighteenth century, all recollection of the music of the bardic order had been lost. Single-row diatonic harps were the norm, and instruments with brays (known as 'gwrachïod' in Welsh) were known well into the nineteenth century.

Eighteenth-century Wales witnessed the ascendancy of the instrument that came to be identified as specifically 'Welsh': the chromatic triple harp with its three rows of strings was an Italian import to England during the seventeenth century, but it survived in Wales long after, taking root first in the North, then South Wales. The triple harp proved a versatile solo instrument and was visually imposing. Many examples were more than six feet in height, although their lighter construction enabled itinerant players to carry them on their backs. It was played by all of the great harper-publishers of the eighteenth and early nineteenth century; Blind John Parry (*c.* 1710–82), Edward Jones (1752–1824, known as 'Bardd y Brenin' or 'The King's Bard'), and John Parry (1776–1851, 'Bardd Alaw'), although the instrument was increasingly supplanted by the modern pedal harp. All three of these musicians made their names primarily in London as executants, and were closely involved in the London-based Welsh societies, the Cymmrodorion and the Gwyneddigion. Beginning with Blind John Parry's *Antient British Music* of 1742, their volumes contain the first published repertories of harp airs from Wales. Despite the misguided attempts of both Blind Parry and Jones to prove the ancient lineage of Welsh pieces that are self-evidently baroque in phrase and tonality, their collections (particularly those of Edward Jones, beginning with *Musical and Poetical Relicks of the Welsh Bards* in 1784) provide a fascinating link between the fashionable music of polite society and tunes popular among country harpists and fiddlers.

The triple harp tradition continued to flourish throughout the nineteenth century, although the repertoire expanded to include the newly fashionable waltzes, polkas and quadrilles as can be seen from the music manuscripts of Thomas D. Llewelyn (1828–79, known as 'Llewelyn Alaw'), a harper from Aberdare in Glamorganshire. Many of the tunes in his collections were composed by known musicians, and the title tunes such as 'The Aberdare Railway Polka' reflect the changing times and society. Harping in Wales should not be seen as a uniform tradition: it possesses numerous individual branches, many of which have yet to be fully explored and researched, such as the repertory of the harpers of Llanerchymedd in Anglesey.

However, there is no doubt as to the strong Romany influence in fostering musical tradition within Wales. Welsh Romanies were said to be descended from the famous Abraham Wood (*c.* 1699–1799), and many of his descendants played the harp and fiddle. The best-known branch of the family in the nineteenth century was headed by John Roberts ('Telynor Cymru') who settled in Newton in mid-Wales. Roberts was a bastion of the harp tradition, teaching all his nine sons to play harp, fiddle or flute, and forming a band called 'The Original Cambrian Minstrels' which played for dances in the Newtown area and toured Wales. Nevertheless, harpists aspiring to a wider stage adopted the modern double action pedal harp. One such, John Thomas (1826–1913, known as 'Pencerdd Gwalia') created complex and technically demanding arrangements of Welsh melodies for this instrument in the 'grand manner' of nineteenth-century instrumental virtuosi. They are very much of their period, yet still retain a place in the repertoire of present day Welsh harpists.

In the face of the apparent demise of distinctively Welsh harping, one individual strove to reinstate the triple harp as the 'national' instrument of Wales. Augusta Hall, Lady Llanofer (1802–96) actively promoted the traditions of dance, song and harping, even employing a 'court' harpist at Llanofer Hall near Abergavenny in Gwent. The twentieth century saw the ascendancy of the pedal harp, almost to the extent of extinguishing the triple harp as a living instruments. However, Nansi Richards Jones (1888–1979), played the triple harp in the traditional manner, on the left shoulder, and taught a number of highly influential pupils such as the brothers Dafydd and Gwyndaf Roberts (of the group Ar Log), and Llio Rhydderch of Bangor. The continued vigour of the solo harping style inherited by Llio can be heard on her 1997 CD, *Telyn* (Fflach Tradd, CD 197H). The Romany harp repertory survived in the playing of Eldra Jarman of Cardiff (albeit on the concert harp), and this music has been researched and revived by Wales's only professional triple harpist, Robin Huw Bowen, on his recording *Hela'r Draenog/Hunting the Hedgehog* (Teires RHBCD 002, 1994). Other musicians, especially among the younger generation, are now rediscovering the potential of the triple harp, and the number of players is probably greater today than it has been since the 1920s.

While triple harpers have always exploited the double-note effect made possible by the two outer rows of diatonically tuned strings (seen in the many variation sets published by Blind John Parry, Edward Jones et al.), other aspects of technique are more difficult to quantify due to the small number of players who specialised on the triple harp during the twentieth century. One factor united the majority of traditional Welsh harpers, however: nearly all of them played the harp on the left shoulder, the left hand taking the upper register, as opposed to the 'right hand treble' now common to concert harpists and keyboard players alike. The heyday of triple making in Wales was epitomised by John Richards of Llanrwst (1711–89), a number of whose instruments still survive, and in the nineteenth century by Bassett Jones of Cardiff, whose heavier instruments had greater projection in line with the demands of larger performing spaces of the period, but were thought by some to lack the subtler response of the earlier, lighter types.

In the later twentieth century, a number of triple harps have been made by Myrddin Madog in Glamorgan and John Weston Thomas of Pembrokeshire. Neither maker specialised in historical copies, but sought to devise new solutions to constructional problems of the older triple harps. Because of the great tension created by the three rows of strings, soundboards were prone to distortion and upward convex curvature, and both pillar and neck tended to be pulled out of shape to one side. Madog answered this problem by incorporating strengthening technology based on new materials, while Thomas adopted a new string and tuning pin arrangement on the neck so as to counteract the unequal tensions. Triple harps on Thomas's model are still made by Bryan Blackmore, active in Pembrokeshire. Another maker, Phil Lourie of Denbighshire, has recently been experimenting with triples of smaller dimensions and of lighter construction.

The bray harp has been revived by several makers outside Wales, but special mention should be made of the historical reconstructions of harps by Robert Evans of Cardiff. He has worked closely with the American-born harpist William Taylor, and Taylor's recording of the music of the Robert ap Huw manuscript – the first to utilise an appropriate bray instrument together with contemporary fingernail technique – appeared on the Dorian label in 1998. The concert harp and its technique are taught widely in schools in Wales, the repertoire often including specifically Welsh airs and melodies for cerdd dant. Traditional instruments and techniques have not yet entered the educational syllabus to any great extent, but with the rapidly growing interest in the multi-faceted harping traditions of the country, it may be only a matter of time until the Welsh traditions of the triple and bray harps take their place alongside that of the classical concert instrument. Welsh harp can be heard on *Telyn* (Fflach Tradd CD **196H**) (STR)

**Wall-Fitzpatrick, Larry.** (1894–1955). Piper, singer, flute player and notable fiddler. Born to musical parents at the Commons, Slievardagh, Co. Tipperary, his brothers played pipes, fiddle and flute. Frequently playing reels and slow airs – but rarely jigs or hornpipes – Larry was recorded in 1955 for Raidió Éireann's *Ceolta-Tíre*. He and brother Thomas were well known as a duet who played for crossroads dancing throughout Tipperary. A thatcher by trade, and a member of the Commons Pipe Band, along with four of his brothers and several other relatives, he was a contemporary of fiddler Michael Ryan, flute player Martin Cooney, fiddlers Neill Cloore and Phil Delahunty. There is a plaque to his memory in Gortnahoe, and a commemorative music event is held annually.

**Walsh, Tommy.** (1880–1963). Accordion. Born at Rosbeg, Westport, Co. Mayo, he was particularly influenced by travelling musicians. He worked for a time in Scotland (a common destination for Mayo and Donegal people at the turn of the twentieth century) but returned to Westport, and later made a recording at Jury's Hotel Dublin for Parlophone records called *The Rakes of Kildare and Other Jigs*.

**Waltons of Dublin.** For many years Dublin's premier music shop. It sold instruments of all kinds, sheet music and records. Still thriving with a strong export, publishing and instrument-making business, its early popularity was boosted by an institutional 'sponsored' commercial programme on Raidió Éireann from 1952–81, presented by Leo Maguire (1903–85). Born in Watling Street, Dublin, Maguire began his singing career at ten at a Citizen Army rally, eventually becoming a full-time music teacher at the School of Music and conducting church and school choirs. A popular concert compère, he was involved also in the Dublin Operatic society, wrote songs and dramas, and broadcast with 2RN from 1927 onward. His honeyed slogans 'A weekly reminder of the grace and beauty that lie in our heritage of Irish song, the songs our fathers loved' and 'If you must sing a song, do sing an Irish song' are the iconic memory of the Waltons' programmes. Proprietor of the business Martin Walton (b. 1901, a feis ceoil winner on violin) was a member of na Fianna at fifteen, acting as courier between the GPO and Jacob's Mill during the Easter Rising of 1916. Interned at Ballykinlar camp with Peadar Kearney (composer of the National anthem and *Down by the Liffey Side,* etc.) he organised an orchestra there in the spirit of the Irish provisional government's policy of culture and education. Living then in Shanganagh Road, Dublin he began publishing Irish songs by such as Kearney, Joseph Crofts, Delia Murphy, Leo Maguire and others, and in 1932 published Leo Rowsome's uilleann pipes tutor. He also set up production of pipes and harps, republished Bunting and O'Neill collections, these part of a wider catalogue of Irish material. From 1924 his base was the Dublin College of Music at North Frederick Street, this premises developing into a music shop that became nationally famous, not least because of the commercial programme in later years. Emigration created an export market for Irish material, this giving the premises important status among those interested in Irish music abroad. Walton's Glenside record label first produced 78s, then 45s with such as Joe Lynch singing more popular Irish song like 'Bould Thady Quill'. Leo Maguire, Noel Purcell, Charlie Magee, Din Joe, Liam Devalley and Joe Lynch (of Glenroe) were the major artistes, between them cementing a particular romantic, nostalgic and sentimental identity of Irishness and style of performance that challenged the ethos of older unaccompanied song and lyrics. This was 'popular' Irish music, complemented by the recordings of the Glenside Céilí Band. Despite its 'light' taste in music and song (by today's traditional music standards) Waltons nevertheless provided a reference point for Irishness in music. By their supply of collections of dance music, fiddles, flutes and tin whistles by mail order, they contributed hugely to making music accessible throughout the island and in Irish communities abroad. Today Waltons is best known in traditional music circles for its catalogue of book and video traditional music tutors, its instrument supply business perhaps rendered less significant by the proliferation of small, independent 'craft' makers.

**waltz**. A dance-form in 3/4 time, particularly distinctive for the strong accent given to the first beat in each bar. Unrelated to the European minuet, it has two possible sources.

1. It may be derived from one of a series of southern German upland folk dances, most likely the Austrian 'landler'; these all round-dances involving couples in close embrace and dating to the fourteenth century. The tunes were sung, or played on fiddle, but their main function was as agricultural work-songs (Carner, *The Waltz, c.* 1946). The dances that developed from these were often erotic, degenerating sometimes to the point where they were considered the work of the devil, inspiring the words: 'Whoso the dance did first discover, Had in his mind each maid and her lover, With all their burning ardour'.

Urbanisation sanitised them somewhat in the form of the 'allemande', then upon its redundancy came the waltz's immediate ancestors, all named after the action of turning in the dance (Dreher, Weller, Soinner) or the area in which they were done (Steirer = Styria, or Landler, indicating Land ob der Enns = Upper Austria).

2. Alternatively the waltz may be derived from the old French valse or volta, also a turning dance in 3/4 time, considered in 1589 to be lascivious and wayward for its common exposure of the knees of the female dancers. Its nature indicated social class – the minuet was the upper class dance. In the mid-eighteenth century, South German composers incorporated movements and melodies from the country dance into the minuet, the popularity of this a result of some empathy between Austrian peasantry and upper classes. The introduction of English country dancing to France at the end of the seventeenth century resulted in the corrupted term 'contre-dance', their spread to Germany brought a classlessness to cross-society social dance. Mixing with German dance forms produced ballroom dance which, being in its homeland, became hugely popular by the late 1700s. Irish singer Michael Kelly wrote in 1786:

## Over the Mountain (Waltz)

> The people of Vienna were in my time dancing mad ... so notorious was it that for the sake of ladies in the family way, who could not be persuaded to stay at home, there were apartments prepared, with every convenience for their accouchement, should they be unfortunately required ... The ladies of Vienna are particularly celebrated for their grace and movements in waltzing of which they never tire. For my own part, I thought waltzing from ten at night until seven in the morning, a continual whirligig; most tiresome to the eye and ear – to say nothing of any worse consequences.
>
> (Carner, *c*. 1946)

Pamphlets raged against the dance, associating it with indecency: 'the main source of the weakness of the body and mind of our generation'. The dance craze complemented the egalitarianism of the French revolution, it accompanied the wage-earning and demarcation of leisure time of the industrial revolution.

It arrived in Paris during the Napoleonic Wars, reaching Britain in the first decade of the 1800s where it became so popular as to be slated by Byron in 'The Waltz – an Apostrophic Hymn': 'With thee even clumsy cits attempt to bounce, And cockneys practice what they can't even pronounce'. But otherwise the dance masters promoted the waltz as a 'promoter of vigorous health' and free from the immorality associated with it in France or Germany, superior indeed too to the forerunner of the 'sets', supposedly 'chaste in comparison with Country dancing, Cotilloons and other species of dancing'.

Some commentators consider that the fall-out from almost two centuries of the waltz's popularity in these islands is that its rhythm has modified all European sense of rhythm (Quirey, 1987), this because 'waltz' is fundamentally a work-rhythm complementary to a large variety of tasks. Waltzes were also taught in Ireland by the 'dancing-masters', but generally only to the children of the well-to-do. The fact that these dances were among those performed (to Irish airs) at the first ever Irish céilí dance held in London in 1897, suggests that the Catholic middle class night have seen their European provenance as 'improving'. Waltzes, and fox-trots (an English dance of the 1920s), became part of popular recreation in Ireland, challenging 'sets' dancing, the dance-form becoming incorporated gradually into what since the 1960s at least been known as 'céilí & old-time' – a mix of ballroom dances (predominantly waltz) with céilí dance. As is the case with marches, popular Irish songs ('Gentle Mother', 'Boston Burglar', 'Molly Malone', 'James Connolly', etc.) Moore's Melodies ('Oft in the Stilly Night', 'Believe me of all those Endearing Young Charms', etc.) and some traditional song-airs ('Flower of Magherally', 'Trip o'er the Mountain', 'Rocks of Bawn', 'Erin's Lovely Home', 'Shores of Amerikay', 'Sliabh na mBan', etc.) have typically been recruited for service as waltzes. Many continental and French Canadian waltz melodies have found a home among traditional musicians too, these, like the song-airs, converted to a distinctly Irish style in the process.

**Ward, Pat.** (1847–1928). Uilleann piper. Born at Drumconrath, Co. Meath, he and his brother were taught fiddle and were introduced to pipes by Nicholas Markey and Billy Taylor of Drogheda. He was remembered by Séamus Ennis for his pipes with a Taylor double chanter (these were eventually sold to R. L. O'Mealy). His home was a calling house for pipers from all over the country, among whom he was a noted reed-maker. His son Pat played pipes and fiddle; his granddaughter Nancy also played a double chanter set.

**wax cylinders.** See recording, Ediphone.

**Weldon, Liam.** (1933–95). Singer, songwriter. Born in Dublin, a passionate interest in songs, singing and singers was developed both from the travelling people who used lodge their horses and caravans in his parents' yard in Dublin's Marrowbone Lane, and also from the last of the street singers and broadsheet sellers. He went to England at age sixteen, returning to Dublin in 1955 where he sang at the Central Bar, Aungier Street, and through the 1970s he and his wife Nellie ran the Pavee's Club in Slattery's of Capel Street, a Saturday singers' club in the Tailors' Hall, Sunday morning sessions first in The Brazen Head, then in Mother Redcaps. A forthright defender of the rights of the poor and the unpropertied, particularly of the travelling people, this came through in his song lyrics, particularly in 'The Blue Tar Road' (an indictment of the eviction of traveller families by Dublin Corporation at Cherryorchard). Unsentimental too, 'Dark Horse on the Wind', from 1966, criticised the hypocrisy of the 1916 commemorations in the face of emigration and poverty: 'In the ashes of our broken dreams/We've lost sight of our goal/Oh rise, rise, rise, dark horse on the wind.'

Always insisting on respectful silence for singers, he is remembered too as an important collector of old song, Tom Munnelly regarding him as 'a most uncompromised source' of songs, his handed-on version of 'The Well Below the Valley' in particular being a unique, otherwise-unheard, survivor from the early nineteenth century. He was a member of the pre-Bothy Band group '1691' with Tony MacMahon, Tríona Ní Dhomhnaill, Peter Browne and Donal Lunny, his songs survive on the lips of many singers. He recorded solo, *Dark Horse on the Wind* (1976), and with Pol Huellou in 1984 and 1990. His collected songs were issued on CD in 1999.

**West Clare Céilí Band.** Specially formed in 1935 at Kilrush, Co. Clare by members of the Old IRA in order to revive music and dancing in the area. It was generated around the idea of a live radio broadcast which took place in February 1936, but continued to play at local céilís and in Mrs Crotty's pub. Band members were Micko Harrison (fiddle), James Conway (fiddle), John Lillis (fiddle), Jack O'Donnell (fiddle), Mick Ryan (concertina), Paddy Cunningham (flute), Paddy McInerney (flute), Micko Howard (drums), Frank McAuliffe (banjo, accordion) and Peggy Howard (piano).

**West Cork.** See song, West Cork.

**Wexford carols.** The term refers to a set of eleven Christmas songs published in 1684, two of which are still sung to the present day in the village of Kilmore, Co. Wexford. Issued in Ghent by Luke Wadding, in the first year of his office as Catholic bishop of Ferns, they appeared in a book entitled *A Smale Garland of Pious and Godly Songs, Composed by a Devout Man For the Solace of his Friends and Neighbours in their Afflictions. The Sweet and the Sower/The Nettle and the Flower/The Thorne and the Rose/This Garland Compose*. The book also contained some religious 'posies', some poems written for the disinherited gentry of Co. Wexford, and some verses relating to the Popish Plot. The carols were to become the foundation of a tradition of carol-singing in the county. A member of one of the principal Anglo-Norman families of Co. Wexford, Bishop Wadding was born in Ballycogley Castle, the family's principal seat. The Wexford Waddings were the parent family of the Waddings of Waterford who numbered among them the famous Franciscan Luke Wadding, the Jesuit theologian Michael Wadding, better known as Miguel Godinez, and Peter Wadding, Chancellor of the University of Prague. They lost their lands in the Cromwellian confiscation and were banished to the west of Ireland. Luke Wadding was educated at Paris, and tradition has it that he obtained a doctorate at the Sorbonne. He may have been in exile at the time of the carols' publication. Ferns was without a resident bishop between 1651 and 1684, and in 1668 Bishop Nicholas French, who had left Ireland but was refused permission to return, invited his first cousin Luke Wadding to go to Wexford to represent him as Vicar General of Ferns, and appointed him parish priest of New Ross. To avoid banishment Wadding deferred his consecration as bishop, and was able to remain in Wexford where, in 1674, he had built a public mass-house within the walls, a privilege that most certainly would not have been granted without the approval of the old Protestant families of the town, who respected him as a gentleman of the county. An old man, he was finally consecrated bishop in 1683 or early in 1684, the year he published his *Smale Garland* in Ghent. He bequeathed his excellent library to the priests of Ross and Wexford. While this had theological tracts by Gregory the Great, Aquinas, Baronius and Bellarmine, it also had many books of poetry: Dryden was represented, and so were George Herbert, John Donne and Richard Crashaw. The metaphysical poets had an influence on Wadding: it is impossible not to be reminded of Crashaw's conceit of 'Aeternity shutt in a span' when we read Wadding's 'Heaven's great treasures are now but small/Immensity no extent at all'. This conceit he develops further in his long carol for Christ's Nativity: 'Now infinite hight is low, and infinite depth is shallow,/The greatest length is short, the greatest largeness narrow.' Luke Wadding's carols became very popular, and the *Smale Garland* was reprinted in London in 1728 and 1731 for James Connor, a Drogheda bookseller. Wadding lived only a few years after the publication of his *Garland*. Not long after his death, his chapel fell and his successor was refused permission to rebuild it. Eventually carol-singing was given a new impetus by Fr William Devereux, who, on returning from the Irish college in Salamanca because of ill health in 1728, composed a 'garland' of carols. He was appointed parish priest of Drinagh, and since he had no chapel the Register of Popish Priests of 1731 reports that he said mass in the corner of a field. Afterwards he built a thatched mud hut at Killane to serve as a chapel and his carols were first sung there.

Fr Devereux incorporated his carols in a manuscript which he called *A New Garland Containing Songs for Christmas*, manuscript copies of these carols multiplied, and are still being transcribed in Kilmore where the parish has kept up the singing of them to the present day. Formerly they were sung in Piercestown, Ballymore, Mayglass, Lady's Island, Tacumshane and Rathangan, but they died out in these parishes due to the neglect of priests who preferred the formality, the chiasmi and the dogmatism of hymnody. The religion of the heart has lost out to what Yeats has called the 'dead hand of decorum'. Fr Devereux's *Garland* contains three of Wadding's carols, but it is impossible to say how many of the others he wrote himself. Certainly he did not write 'Song For Jerusalem', which is English; first printed in 1601, its author is known to us only as F.B.P., a Catholic priest under sentence of death, according to English tradition. The people of Kilmore believe that Fr Devereux wrote the rest, as it is clear that they were written by someone very familiar with the liturgy.

These carols are sung during Christmas in Kilmore by a choir of six men, who divide into two groups of three to sing alternate verses. It is no small boast for a parish to say that some of their carols have been handed down from generation to generation for almost 300 years. To hear them sung during mass can be a very moving experience indeed, most eloquently described in a letter to *The People*, a Wexford newspaper, in January 1872: 'I have stood within many of the grandest Cathedrals of Europe and under the dome of St Peter's itself, but in none of them did I ever feel the soul-thrilling rapturous sensation that I did as a boy listening to six aged men on a frosty Christmas morning sing the carols beneath the low straw-thatched chapel of Rathangan.' The attachment of the people of Kilmore to their very special tradition is still strong; its guardians have been generations of the Devereux family. Jack Devereux has just retired from it at age eighty-seven, his cousin presently keeps up the tradition that 'there must be a Devereux among the carol singers'. (Sourced in Diarmuid Ó Muirithe's *The Wexford Carol*.)

**Wexford song.** See song, Wexford.

**Whelan, Bill.** (1950– ). Musician, composer and record producer. Born in Limerick he studied law at UCD and King's Inns. In 1970 he wrote a film score for *Bloomfield*, then in 1979 he joined the folk group Planxty, playing keyboards, but almost a decade prior to that had already gained experience writing music for the cinema. As a record producer he was involved with artists such as Andy Irvine, Paul Brady and Stockton's Wing, as well as several internationally known singers and musicians unconnected to the traditional or revivalist folk fields. He became known to Irish television audiences while leading resident music groups on popular television series such as *Saturday Night Live*. His commissioned orchestral works and film scores include *The Ó Riada Suite* (1987), *The Seville Suite* (1992), *The Spirit of Mayo* (1993), and *Some Mother's Son* (1996). Although in no sense a traditionalist by background, Whelan was aware of the Irish musical heritage and incorporated elements of it in his composition. In 1994 this approach led to spectacular international recognition with the production of *Riverdance*. Whelan's music, abundant in thematic appeal and rhythmic drama, proved an ideal vehicle to carry what was a new concept in the presentation of Irish dancing, and to some extent dance traditions from elsewhere. (BIM)

**Whelan, George.** Fiddle. From Kerry, this blind player taught around Kilmihil, Cooraclare and Doonbeg *c.* 1880. His repertoire is reputed to have had flings, slides, set dances and reels, rich in 12/8 tunes and Kerry 'style'. Fiddler Patrick Kelly of Cree, Co. Clare inherited his style through his father, fiddle master Tim Kelly. Whelan's material was collected by Batt Scanlon.

See Kelly, Patrick; Scanlon, Batt.

**White, Aggie.** See Ballinakill Céilí Band.

**White Róisín.** (1952– ). Song, concertina. Born near Kilkeel Co. Down. Her mother sang ballads and Róisín heard song locally and on RÉ. She began performing following a Beleek, Co. Fermanagh event in the 1970s, and was hugely influenced by meeting Nioclás Tóibín, Darach Ó Catháin, Joe Holmes, Len Graham, Sarah Anne O'Neill and Geordie Hanna, at a 1977 Clogherhead, Co. Louth, singers' weekend. Through meeting Gerry Hicks, Seán O'Boyle, and collector Peter Kennedy, she developed a considerable repertoire of Ulster song, rendering her one of its distinctive voices today. Now singing increasingly in Irish, she is a popular contributor to folk festivals in Britain, and song festivals in Ireland.

**Wilkinson, Desi.** (1954– ). Born in Belfast, childhood friendships made him a regular caller to the guest-house of Fermanagh-born fiddler Tommy Gunn. There he regularly heard traditional music played by such visiting players as Aly Bain and Cathal McConnell. Playing whistle by the age of fifteen, he was taught tunes by Tommy, and attendance with him at sessions and concerts drew Desi to hear music in Fermanagh and Cavan. Training as a teacher in St. Joseph's, Belfast introduced him to yet more players; his associates were such as Gary Hastings, Gerry O'Donnell, Deirdre Shannon, Andy Dixon, John Hendry and Paddy O'Neill. Planxty and Chieftains recordings encouraged him to take up flute at nineteen and travel in Brittany began an association with that region which saw him play professionally there from 1992–95. His 1991 ethnomusicology MA dissertation dealt with flute styles, and his PhD research in UL is on the social world of the traditional music of Brittany. From 1988–91 he was the ACNI's 'Artist in the Community'. With Gerry O'Connor and Eithne Ní Uallacháin he recorded *Cosa gan Bhróga* in 1986, in 1987 he made his solo *Three Piece Flute*. *Crooked Stair* and *Black, Black, Black* were recorded with his group Cran in 1991 and 1998.

**Willie Clancy Summer School.**
See Scoil Samhraidh Willie Clancy.

**Wilmot, Johnny.** (1916–93). Fiddler. An exceptional Cape Breton fiddler who made 78 and LP recordings of both old style, Sligo-influenced Irish dance music and strathspeys and reels in the Scottish tradition. A nephew of Joe Confiant, his best-known composition is 'Hughie Shorty's Reel'. (PAC)

**wire recording.** See reproduction of music, wire recording.

**wood block.** Like a miniature of the African 'slit drum', an idiophone, this is a partially hollowed wood block some 18 cm by 8 cm typically seen mounted atop the bass drum, sometimes in the company of a cymbal, in céilí bands. Slots cut in the block give a variety of tones when it is struck in different places with a drumstick. The instrument was adopted into Irish bands along with the jazz/dance-band drum kit, and has become almost the clichéd opening signal for dancing: two 'clicks' – one per beat, in time – announce that reel music will, on the third beat, begin with no further introduction; three clicks indicate a hornpipe.

**World War I.** See song, World War I.

**'Wounded Huzzar, The'.** A classic of the melodramatic literary ballad which illustrates the mottled pedigree of tunes and tune names. The tune used is similar to that of 'Captain O'Kane', this probably written by Turloch Carolan for one Captain Ó Catháin, a member of a distinguished Antrim family, and a well-known sporting lad known as 'Slasher' O'Kane (described by O'Neill in *Irish Minstrels and Musicians*). The tune was regarded by Edward Bunting (1843) as 'The Wounded Huzzar' because the poem of that name (by Thomas Campbell) was sung to the air. Campbell would appear to have enjoyed popularity in Ireland in the eighteenth century since some of his poems appear in Bunting's collection – 'There Came to the Beach a Poor Exile of Erin', ''Twas the Hour when Rites Unholy', 'To the Battle, Men of Erin', 'A Chieftain to the Highlands Bound'. Donal O'Sullivan felt that the air, although not attributed to Carolan, had his distinctive stamp, and records that Hardiman claimed that it was composed by him for Captain O'Kane. Tony MacMahon plays the tune with a constant bass drone, piping style, extending it to over five minutes. Fiddler Pete Cooper says of the tune that it passed into both Irish and English folk tradition, and was played by nineteenth-century Shropshire fiddler John Moore. Donegal fiddler John Doherty (quoted by Peter Kennedy on a Folktrax recording) claimed that it was in his family also.

See Campbell, Thomas.

**wren, the.** The custom of 'hunting the wren' during the twelve days of Christmas was known throughout most of Ireland and elsewhere. It is still observed on St Stephen's Day in many areas in Ireland, especially in the south and west. Groups of people dressed in disguise go from house to house, singing and playing music and asking for money in return. In former times, the wren-boys carried a dead wren on a bush, usually a holly bush which was decorated with rags and ribbons, and they asked for money to 'bury the wren'. The following verse is a typical example of the verse recited by the wren-boys:

> The wren, the wren, the king of all birds,
> On St Stephen's day was caught in the furze,
> Although he is little, his family is great,
> So rise up, landlady and give us a treat.

Wrenboys in Dingle (CBÉ)

The verse is based on the traditional belief that the wren was responsible for indicating St Stephen's hiding place under a bush to the pursuing Roman soldiers by singing on that particular bush. Although any musical instrument can be played by the wren-boys, those which occur most frequently are the accordion, melodeon, tin whistle, mouth organ and bodhrán. In parts of Munster, a more formal, elaborate type of wren hunt existed and this is still a vibrant part of the tradition in the town of Dingle, Co. Kerry. Here, there are several groups of 'wrens', and each group is named after a street in the town. Many participants are dressed in straw costumes. Each group has an elected leader called a captain, and the group carries a 'lair bhán' (white mare) which is a wooden hobby horse. The musicians participating in the Dingle wren play fifes and drums for the most part. (RIO)

See bodhrán; mummers.

**Wright, John.** Jew's harp. Born in Leicester he developed an interest in folk music while studying art in Wolverhampton. He took up the Jew's harp after hearing a BBC archive recording of Angus Lawrie of Oban. Patrick Devane of Carraroe, Co. Galway, and Thomas McManus from Co. Fermanagh also influenced him. His interest in Jew's harps led him to live in Paris where he worked on a large collection of the instruments from all over the world.

**Wynne, Martin.** (1916–98). Fiddle. Born at Bunninadden, Co. Sligo, he spent two periods in England in 1937 and 1946, playing in London with the Johnny Muldoon Céilí Band in the Garryowen Club, Hammersmith and the Shannon Club, Kilburn with Paddy Taylor (flute) and Joe O'Dowd (fiddle) with whom he made a recording. He emigrated to the USA in 1948. A deeply sensitive player, knowledgeable on the origins and stylistic features of music and a careful analyst of repertoire, he learnt much from Michael Coleman, James Morrison, Paddy Killoran and Jim 'Lad' O'Beirne. He made a few non-commercial discs with O'Beirne, and with Sligo player Vince Harrison. He is best known for three outstanding reels, Martin Wynne's No. 1, No. 2 and No. 3, these the best of half a dozen composed back in the 1930s before he left home.

Martin Wynne's (Reel)

# Y

**Yeats, Gráinne.** (1925– ). Harp, singer, researcher. Born in Dublin and raised bilingually in Irish and English, she learnt her first traditional song from Kerry sean-nós singer Máighréad Ní Bheaglaíoch. She studied piano, singing and Irish harp at the RIAM in Dublin, and in extended visits to Gaeltacht areas she acquired a repertoire of traditional songs and music. She has developed a particular interest in wire-strung harp, and has written extensively on its history and music, and was the first professional musician to revive and record it. As a soloist she has broadcast on radio and television, has recorded with Gael-Linn, and played all over the world.

**Young Irelanders.** A major 'Repeal of the (1801) Union' political movement begun in 1842 which addressed and developed a model of Irishness that combined economics, history, and culture. Song, as a medium of news and ideas transmission in pre-popular-press times, was a central medium for them. The movement's leaders wrote prolifically, their works were published in their newspaper *The Nation*, and were released in the songbook *Spirit of the Nation* (1845) republished fifty-eight times, the last edition in 1934. One of its leaders, poet and editor of *The Nation*, Thomas Davis, bound song and political identity firmly in one dialectic package:

> National poetry shows us magnified, and ennobles our hearts, our intellects and our country and our countrymen – it binds us to the land by its condensed and gem-like history, to the future by examples and aspirations. It solaces us in travel, fires us in action, prompts our invention, sheds a grace beyond the power of luxury round our homes, is the recognised envoy of our minds, presents the most dramatic events, the largest characters, the most impressive scenes, and the deepest passions, in the language most familiar to us.

Of an 1840s' anthology of ballads and street songs by Charles Gavan Duffy, Davis said it was 'A propaganda worth a thousand harangues'. Davis himself wrote fifty or so songs and ballads, and *The Nation* was at one point receiving twenty or more in the post each week. A gauge of the popularity of *Spirit of the Nation* and ballad song in general is seen in the paper's claim in 1844 that the songbook had a larger sale than any book published in Ireland since the Union.

The process of song composition is of interest as Duffy describes Davis's method:

> A song or ballad was struck off at a heat, when a flash of inspiration came, – scrawled with a pencil, in a large hand, on a sheet of post-paper, with unfinished lines, perhaps, and blanks for epithets which did not come at once of the right measure or colour; but the chain of sentiment or incident was generally complete. If there was time it was revised later and copied with pen and ink, and last touches added before it was dispatched to the printer; but if occasion demanded, it went at once. (1844).

The Young Irelanders were surpassed by James Fintan Lawlor's assertion in 1847 that the land question was superior to that of the Union with Britain. (Not to be confused with the Young Ireland *Association*, September 1933, successor to the 1930s' fascist-style 'Blueshirts' movement, and who, on being banned, after three months changed their name to 'League of Youth' and were finally wound up in 1936.)

See song, political.

# Z

**Zimmerman, Georges-Denis.** (1930– ). Researcher. Born Lausanne, Switzerland, educated in Geneva where his PhD studies were based in Irish political ballads. From 1951 he was in Ireland annually, and in pursuit of his research he examined some 12,000 Irish broadside ballads, these in every major library in Ireland and England. His book *Songs of Irish Rebellion* is the classic work in this field. Illustrated with song texts it covers the theme under: 1. blind violence and vain hopes, 2. popular nationalism and unsuccessful risings, 3. political realism and blood sacrifice, 4. romantic patriotism and literary imitations of street balladry, 5. the form of the songs. He takes 100 song texts (eight of these are Orange songs), lists sources and alternative versions, printers of broadsides, garlands and songbooks. He gives an extensive bibliography of nationalist, republican and Orange song sources, and lists 1. nationalist newspapers which published songs, 2. books and articles on songs and ballad singers, and 3. other books and literature with political contexts.

**Zozimus.** (1794–1846). Singer composer and character, born Michael Moran at Blackpitts, The Liberties, Dublin. Blinded as a child by smallpox, he had a profound memory, and acquired his title 'Zozimus' from his ability to recite his adaptation of 'St Mary and Zozimus', this the tale of the latter's fifth-century conversion of St Mary in Egypt. The singer's platforms for the presentation of this and his own compositions were the present-day Grattan and O'Connell bridges, Grafton and Henry Streets and Conciliation Hall at Burgh Quay. His finest piece is 'The Finding of Moses':

> Bedad now says she,
> 'It was someone very rude
> Left a little baby by the
> river in his nude.'

His last public appearance was in the present South Great George's Street; his last hours were spent in a room crowded with his peers – the city's ballad singers. A memorial to his memory was erected in 1988 over his paupers' grave in Glasnevin cemetery, this carried part of a song written by singer Kevin Molloy of the Dublin City Ramblers ballad group: 'Sing a song for us oul' Zozimus, As always from the heart, Your name will live forever, As a Dubliner apart' – a piece somewhat inferior to the bard's own epitaph, and the circumstances of its erection unsought:

> My burying place is of no concern to me
> In the O'Connell circle let it be
> As to my funeral all pomp is vain
> Illustrious people does prefer it plain.

# CHRONOLOGY

*A chronology of mostly music items and related historic incidents.*

| | |
|---|---|
| 1571 | 'Execute the Harpers' (edict, Gerald, Earl of Kildare) |
| 1724 | *Most Celebrated Irish Tunes*, John and Wm. Neal (Coll.) |
| 1726 | *A Choice Collection of Country Dances*, Neal (Coll.) |
| 1729 | *Harp Primer,* Charles Egan |
| 1730 | *Aria di Camera*, Daniel Wright (Coll.) |
| 1730 | Contention of the Bards, Bruree, Limerick |
| 1748 | Burke Thomoth Collection (Coll.) |
| 1748 | *Carolan … The Celebrated Irish Bard*, John Lee (Coll.) |
| 1780 | *Jackson's Celebrated Irish Tunes*, Walter Jackson (Coll.) |
| 1786 | *Historical Memoirs of the Irish Bards*, Joseph Cooper Walker (Txt.) |
| 1789 | *Reliques of Irish Poetry*, Charlotte Brooke (Coll.) |
| 1790 | *Curious selection … Fifty Irish Airs*, J. Brysson (Coll.) |
| 1792 | Belfast Harp Festival |
| 1796 | *Ancient Irish Music*, Edward Bunting. (Coll.) |
| 1804 | Belfast Harp Society founded |
| 1804 | *Collection of National Music for the Union Pipes*, O'Farrell (Coll.) |
| 1804 | *O'Farrell's Pocket Companion for the Irish or Union Pipes* (Coll.) |
| 1809 | *Ancient Music Of Ireland*, Edward Bunting (Coll./Txt.) |
| 1818 | *Historical Memoirs of the Irish Bards*, reprint of 1786 (Txt.) |
| 1822 | *Harp Primer* (reprint of 1729), Charles Egan |
| 1831 | *Irish Minstrelsy,* Hardiman (Coll.) |
| 1840 | *The Ancient Music of Ireland*, Edward Bunting (Coll.) |
| 1842 | Dungiven Harp Society |
| 1845 | *Spirit of the Nation*, songs from *The Nation* newspaper (Coll.) |
| 1848 | *National Music of Ireland*, Michael Conran (Txt.) |
| 1851 | Soc. for the Preservation and Publication of the Ancient Music of Ireland founded (George Petrie) |
| 1852 | *Folk Melodies of Ireland*, William Allingham (Coll.) |
| 1855 | *Ancient Music of Ireland* (2 vols.), George Petrie (Coll.) |
| 1858 | *The Dance Music of Ireland*, R. M. Levey (Coll.) |
| 1873 | *Ancient Irish Music*, P. W. Joyce (Coll.) |
| 1873 | *Musical Instruments of the Ancient Irish*, Eugene O'Curry (Txt.) |
| 1873 | *The Dance Music of Ireland*, R. M. Levey (reprint) (Coll.) |
| 1877 | *Music of Ireland*, Francis Hoffman (Coll.) |
| 1883 | *Ryan's Mammoth Collection*, William B. Ryan (Coll.) |
| 1892 | Gaelic League formed |
| 1893 | *Amhráin Grádh Chúige Connacht*, Douglas Hyde (Coll.) |
| 1893 | Irish traditional music performed at World's Fair, Chicago |
| 1894 | *Irish Song Book*, Alfred P. Graves (Coll.) |
| 1895 | Irish Dance Teachers' Association formed, Cork |
| 1897 | First céilí held (London) |
| 1897 | First Oireachtas held |
| 1897 | Introduction of Gramophone |
| 1898 | Cork Pipers' Club founded |
| 1900 | Dublin Pipers' Club founded |
| 1901 | Patsy Touhey issues cylinder recordings |
| 1902 | *A Guide to Irish Dancing*, J. J. Sheehan |
| 1903 | *Complete Petrie Collection*, ed. Charles Villiers Stanford (Coll.) |
| 1903 | *Irish Music*, Richard Henebry (Txt.) |
| 1903 | *Tutor for the Irish Harp* Loreto Order |
| 1903 | *Music of Ireland, The,* Francis O'Neill (Coll.) |
| 1903 | John Kimmel's first recording of Irish music |
| 1904 | Irish Folksong Society founded |
| 1905 | *A History of Irish Music*, W. H. Grattan Flood (Txt.) |
| 1906 | *Irish Peasant Songs*, P. W. Joyce (Coll.) |
| 1907 | *Dance Music of Ireland, The,* Francis O'Neill (Coll.) |
| 1908 | *Gems of Melody/Seoda Ceoil*, Carl Hardebeck (Coll.) |
| 1909 | Dublin Feis Cheoil founded |
| 1909 | *Old Irish Folk Music and Song*. P. W. Joyce (Coll.) |
| 1910 | *Annals of the Irish Harpers*, Charlotte Millington Fox (Txt.) |

| | | | |
|---|---|---|---|
| 1910 | *Irish Folk Music, a Fascinating Hobby*, Francis O'Neill (Txt.) | 1939 | *Irish Street Song*, Colm O'Lochlainn (Coll.) |
| 1912 | *A Handbook of Irish Dances* (Txt.) | 1942 | Séamus Ennis collecting for Irish Folklore Commission |
| 1913 | *Irish Minstrels and Musicians*, Francis O'Neill (Txt.) | 1943 | First examination in Irish step dance held |
| 1914 | The Feis Cheoil Collection (Coll.) | 1947 | Introduction of tape-recording |
| 1915 | *Céad de Cheoltaibh Uladh* (song in Irish), Énrí Ó Muirgheasa (Coll.) | 1947 | Outside Broadcast Units initiated in Raidió Éireann |
| 1916 | *Amhráin Airt Mhic Cubthaigh* (Coll.) | 1948 | *Songs of the Wexford Coast*, Joseph Ranson (Coll.) |
| 1917 | Feis Cheoil Collection (Coll.) | 1950 | *Ceolta Tíre* radio programme begun on RÉ |
| 1918 | Frank Lee uses term 'céilí band' | 1951 | Comhaltas Ceoltóirí Éireann founded |
| 1919 | *Sketch of Irish Musical History*, W. H. Grattan Flood (Txt.) | 1951 | *As I Roved Out* programme begins on BBC |
| 1920–2 | *Irish Folk Songs from Ballyvourney*, Martin Freeman (Coll.) | 1952 | First Fleadh Cheoil |
| 1921 | New Republic Irish Recording Co., USA | 1955 | Vinyl LPs introduced |
| | | 1957 | *Job of Journeywork* begun on RÉ with Ciarán MacMathúna |
| 1921 | John McKenna recorded | | |
| 1921 | Michel Coleman recorded | 1958 | *Carolan* (2 vols.), Donal O'Sullivan, (Txt./Coll.) |
| 1922 | *Waifs and Strays of Gaelic Melody*, Francis O'Neill (Coll.) | 1958 | *The Dance Music of Ireland*, R.M. Levey, reprint of 1873 (Coll.) |
| 1922 | Okel label first US record company to issue an Irish series | 1959 | *The Dance Music of Ireland, 1* (O'Neill extracts) (Coll.) |
| 1922 | Gaelic Phonograph Co. set up, USA | 1959 | Claddagh Records set up |
| 1923–39 | Sam Henry's column in *Northern Constitution* paper | 1960 | Cáirde na Cruite founded |
| 1925 | Aughrim Slopes Céilí Group founded | 1960 | *Songs of the Irish*, Donal O'Sullivan, (Txt./Coll.) |
| 1925 | Irish Dance Teachers' Association, founded in Dublin | 1960 | *Songs of the People* (Sam Henry), Gale Huntington ed. (Coll.) |
| 1925 | *Ulster Songs and Ballads*, Richard Hayward | 1961 | *Geantraí na hÉireann* (Coll.) |
| 1926 | 2RN National Radio broadcasting Irish music | 1962 | *The Dance Music of Ireland, 2* (O'Neill extracts) (Coll.) |
| 1926 | Ballinakill Traditional Dance Players formed | 1963 | *Ceol Rince na hÉireann, 1*. Breandán Breathnach (Coll.) |
| 1927 | Aughrim Slopes band play on 2RN | 1963 | Chieftains formed |
| 1927 | *Roche Collection of Irish Traditional Music*, Francis Roche (Coll.) | 1965 | *Dance Music of Ireland* (2 vols.), R. M. Levey (reprint of 1873) (Coll.) |
| 1928 | *Handbook of Irish Music*, Richard Henebry (Txt.) | 1965 | Breandán Breathnach transferred to Dept. Education |
| 1929 | Irish Dancing Commission formed by Gaelic League | 1966 | Cassette technology available |
| | | 1966 | Armagh Pipers' club formed |
| 1929 | P. J. Conlon the first Irish accordion player to be recorded | 1967 | *Co. Fermanagh Dance Tunes*, Liam Donnelly (Coll.) |
| 1929 | James Morrison band records | 1967 | *Songs of Irish Rebellion*, Georges Denis Zimmerman (Txt.) |
| 1933 | *Céad de Cheoltaibh Uladh*, Énrí Ó Muirgheasa, reprint (Coll.) | 1968 | Na Píobairí Uilleann formed |
| 1935 | Public Dance Halls Act | 1968 | *Treoir* magazine initiated |
| 1935 | Irish Folklore Commission founded | 1969 | *Ancient Music of Ireland* (compilation of Bunting) (Coll.) |
| 1936 | *Dánta Diadha Uladh*, Énrí Ó Muirgheasa, ed. (Coll.) | 1969 | *Dánta Diadha Uladh*, Énrí Ó Muirgheasa, ed., reprint (Coll.) |
| 1936 | EMI recording co. opens in Dublin | | |
| 1939 | *Ár Rinncidhe Fóirne*, Irish Dancing Commission handbook | 1969 | *Dhá Chéad de Cheoltaibh Uladh*, Énrí Ó Muirgheasa, ed., reprint (Coll.) |
| 1939 | *Dhá Chéad de Cheoltaibh Uladh*, Énrí Ó Muirgheasa, ed. | 1969 | Split in dance movement – An Chomhdháil and An Comisiúin result. |

|  |  |
|---|---|
| 1970 | *A History of Irish Music*, reprint of 1905, W. H. Grattan Flood (Txt.) |
| 1971 | *Folk Music and Dances of Ireland*, Breandán Breathnach (Txt.) |
| 1971 | Folk Music Society of Ireland founded |
| 1971 | *Historical Memoirs of the Irish Bards*, extract from 1818 (Txt.) |
| 1971 | *Where the River Shannon Rises*, Ed Reavy (Coll.) |
| 1972 | Planxty formed |
| 1972 | Irish Folklore Commission disbanded |
| 1972 | CBÉ (Folklore Dept., UCD) inaugurated |
| 1973 | Initiation of Irish Folk Music Studies series, 'Éigse Cheol Tíre' |
| 1973 | *Irish Folk Music, a Fascinating Hobby*, reprint of 1910 (Txt.) |
| 1973 | Scoil Samhraidh Willie Clancy inaugurated |
| 1974 | *Music From Ireland* (vols. 1-3), Bulmer and Sharpley (Coll.) |
| 1975 | *Folk Songs of Britain and Ireland*, Peter Kennedy (Coll.) |
| 1976 | *Ceol Rince na hÉireann, 2*, Breandán Breathnach (Coll.) |
| 1976 | *Dance Music of Willie Clancy*, Pat Mitchell (Txt., Coll.) |
| 1976 | *The Irish Song Tradition*, Seán O'Boyle (Txt.) |
| 1978 | *O'Neill's Music of Ireland*, Myles Krassen ed. (Coll.) |
| 1978 | *Traditional Music in Ireland*, Tomás Ó Cannain (Txt.) |
| 1979 | *Northern Fiddler, The*. Eamon O'Doherty and Allen Feldman (Txt./Coll.) |
| 1979 | *Songs of the People* [Sam Henry selections] John Moulden ed. (Coll.) |
| 1979 | *Sully's Irish Music Book*, Anthony Sullivan (Coll.) |
| 1980 | *Collected Compositions* (reprint), Ed Reavy (Coll.) |
| 1981 | *Shamrock, Rose and Thistle* [North Co. Derry song] Hugh Shields (Txt.) |
| 1982 | *Our Musical Heritage*, Seán Ó Riada (Txt.) |
| 1982 | *Play Fifty Reels*, Armagh Pipers' Club (Coll.) |
| 1984 | *Complete Works of O'Carolan* (Coll.) |
| 1984 | *The Darley & McCall Collection*, reprint of 1917 Feis Cheoil (Coll.) |
| 1985 | *Ceol Rince na hÉireann, 3*, Breandán Breathnach (Coll.) |
| 1986 | *Dance Music of Ireland*, reprint of O'Neill 1907 (Coll.) |
| 1986 | *Most Celebrated Irish Tunes*. John, Wm. Neal, ed. Nicholas Carolan (Txt./Coll.) |
| 1986 | *Piping of Patsy Touhey*, Mitchell and Small (Txt./Coll.) |
| 1987 | *The Hidden Ireland*, Seán Ryan (Coll.) |
| 1990 | *Pocket Guide to Traditional Music*, Ciarán Carson (Txt.) |
| 1990 | *Songs of the People* (Sam Henry), Gale Huntington ed., new edition of 1960 (Coll.) |
| 1992 | *Compositions of Paddy O'Brien*, Eileen O'Brien Minoge ed. (Coll.) |
| 1992 | *Trip to Sligo*, Bernard Flaherty (Txt./Coll.) |
| 1993 | Ulstersongs research founded |
| 1994 | *Between the Jigs and the Reels*, Caomhín Mac Aoidh (Txt.) |
| 1994 | *Johnny O'Leary of Sliabh Luachra*, Terry Moylan ed. (Txt./Coll.) |
| 1995 | *Irish Music* magazine begun |
| 1995 | *Music for the Sets* (3 vols.), David J. Taylor (Coll.) |
| 1995 | *Music for the Union Pipes*, O'Farrell, reprint, ed. Patrick Sky (Txt./Coll.) |
| 1995 | *Paddy O'Brien Collection* (oral, on cassette). Paddy O'Brien (Coll.) |
| 1995 | *Ryan's Mammoth Collection*. W. B. Ryan, reprint, Patrick Sky ed. (Coll.) |
| 1995 | *Traditional Slow Airs of Ireland*, Tomás Ó Canainn (Coll.) |
| 1996 | *Ceol Rince na hÉireann, 4*, Breandán Breathnach, Jackie Small ed. (Coll.) |
| 1996 | *Collected Compositions*, reprint, Reavy ed. (Coll.) |
| 1996 | Croisbhealach an Cheoil [Crossroads Conference], Dublin |
| 1997 | LCM traditional music syllabus initiated |
| 1998 | *A Pocket History of Irish Traditional Music*, Gearóid Ó hAllmhuráin (Txt.) |
| 1998 | *Dear Harp of My Country* [reprint Thomas Moore] James Flannery (Txt.) |
| 1998 | *Exploring Irish Music and Dance*, Dianna Boullier (Txt.) |
| 1998 | *The Blooming Meadows* [biography] Vallely, Piggott, Nutan (Txt.) |
| 1998 | *Tunes of the Munster Pipers*, Hugh Shields ed. (Txt./Coll.) |
| 1998 | RIAM/CCÉ traditional music syllabus launched |
| 1999 | *Sources of Irish Traditional Music*, Aloys Fleischmann, Mícheál Ó Súilleabháin, Paul McGettrick eds. (Coll.) |

# SELECT BIBLIOGRAPHY

Books published after 1985 are first editions unless otherwise stated, and all reprints are by the original publisher unless otherwise noted. Place and date of publication are given where available. Some books have no date: 'n.d.' is given in place of the date. Many theses, for example, lack an exact place of publication as this has not been stated clearly on the work. Entries on specific instruments may be found in either/both 'Tutors' and 'Instrument related collections'. Within each section, the listings are organised alphabetically by author, and where the author is not identified, the entry is by title. Companion cassettes or compact discs are indicated – this is common practice with tutors in particular. University theses and dissertations are also listed separately. This bibliography is based on Maeve Gebruers' 1996 dissertation, and the dance listing is compiled substantially by John Cullinane.

## AUTOBIOGRAPHY, BIOGRAPHY

Audley, Brian, *Denis O'Hampsey the Harper c. 1695–1807*. Whisper Press, Belfast, 1992, 57 pp.

Bradshaw, Harry, *Michael Coleman, 1891–1945*. Viva Voce/Gael Linn, Dublin, 1991/93.

Brady, Margery, *The Last Rose of Summer: The Love Story of Tom Moore and Bessy Dyke*. Green Hills Publications, Kilkenny, 1993, 137 pp.

Carolan, Nicholas, *A Harvest Saved: Francis O'Neill and Irish Music in Chicago*. Ossian Publications, Cork, 1997, 80 pp.

Carson, Ciaran, *Last Night's Fun*. Blackstaff, Belfast, 1996.

Coady, Michael, *The Well of Spring Water: A Memoir of Packie and Micho Russell of Doolin Co. Clare*. Michael Coady, 1996, 40 pp.

Curtis, P. J., *Notes From the Heart: A Celebration of Traditional Irish Music*. Torc, Dublin, 1994, 180 pp.

Feldman, Allen and Eamonn O'Doherty (eds.), *The Northern Fiddler* (reprint of 1979 edn). Oak Publications, London, 1985, 251 pp.

Flaherty, Bernard (ed.), *Trip to Sligo*. Flaherty, Boyle, 1990, 184 pp.

Glatt, John, *The Chieftains: The Authorised Biography*. Century, London, 1997, 331 pp.

Hanafin, Dermot, *Padraig O'Keeffe: The Man and His Music*. Hanafin, Castleisland, 1995, 44 pp.

Hunter, Jim, *The Blind Fiddler From Myroe*. Danny Boy Trading Co. Ltd., Bangor, n.d., 21 pp.

McNamara, Christy and Peter Woods, *The Living Note: The Heartbeat of Irish Music*. O'Brien Press, Dublin, 1996, 160 pp.

Meek, Bill, *Paddy Moloney and The Chieftains*. Gill and Macmillan, Dublin, 1987, 141 pp.

Ó Canainn, Tomás, *A Lifetime of Notes*. Collins Press, Cork, 1996, 194 pp, and Gearóid Mac an Bhua, *Seán Ó Riada: A Shaol agus a Shaothar*. Gartan, Dublin, 1993, 286 pp.

O'Dowda, Brendan, *The World of Percy French*, Blackstaff, Belfast, 1981, 1991, 1997.

Phelan, Robert, *William Vincent Wallace: A Vagabond Composer*. Celtic Publications, Waterford, 1994, 125 pp.

Piggott, Charlie with Fintan Valley and Nutan, *The Blooming Meadows: The World of Irish Traditional Musicians*. Townhouse, Dublin, 1998.

Reynolds, Willie, *Memories of a Music Maker*. CCÉ, Dublin, 1990, 106 pp.

Tongue, Alan, *A Picture of Percy French: An Illustrated Life of the Irish Songwriter, Entertainer, Poet and Painter*. Greystone Books, Dublin, 1990, 99 pp.

Tunney, Paddy, *The Stone Fiddle: My Way to Traditional Song*. Gilbert Dalton, Dublin, 1979; *Where Songs Do Thunder: Travels in Traditional Song*. Appletree, Belfast, 1991, 191 pp.

## BIBLIOGRAPHY

Pickering, Jennifer M. (ed.), *Music in the British Isles 1700 to 1800: A Bibliography of Literature*. Burden and Cholij, Edinburgh, 1990, 419 pp.

Porter, James (ed.), *The Traditional Music of Britain and Ireland*. Garland Publishing, New York, 1989, 408 pp.

Roud, Steve (ed.), *Broadside Index: Electronic Index, 2*. Hisarlik Press, Middlesex, 1994, 28 pp. With floppy discs. *Folksong Index: Electronic Index, 1*. Hisarlik Press, Middlesex, 1994, 66 pp. With floppy discs.

Shields, Hugh (ed.), *A Short Bibliography of Irish Folk Song*. Folk Music of Ireland, Dublin, 1985, 39 pp. Reprinted 1987.

## BIBLIOGRAPHY

### DANCE

Ajello, Elvira, *The Solo Irish Jig*. C. W. Beaumont, London, 1932, 30 pp.

Anon, *An Coimisiúin le Rinnci Gaelacha – Liosta Oifigiúl*. CRG, Dublin. Produced almost every year from 1944 to 1999.

Anon, *Ár Rinncidhe Fóirne*. Part 1. CRG, Dublin, 1939, 21 pp.

Anon, *Ár Rinncidhe Fóirne*. Part 2. CRG, Dublin, 1943, 20 pp.

Anon, *Ár Rinncidhe Fóirne*. Part 3. CRG, Dublin, 1969, 23 pp.

Anon, *Ár Rinncidhe Fóirne*. Parts 1, 2 and 3 combined. CRG, Dublin, 1972, 64 pp.

Anon, *Cairde Rince Céilí na hÉireann, Ceiliúradh Náisiúnta*. CRC, 1997, 46 pp.

Anon, *Coiscéim. An Authentic Guide to Set Dancing for Instructors and Learners*. Includes 'history of the set dancing', CCÉ & GAA, Dublin, n.d., 44 pp.

Anon, *Comhairle Céilí. Parts 1–6*. Newsletter of Comhairle Céilí, Tipperary–Kilkenny, 1967–69.

Anon, *Feis Sligigh – Comóradh Caoga Bliain. 1929–79*. 1979, 80 pp.

Anon, *Irish Dancer Magazine*. Ed. Suzanne McDonough, Wisconsin. 1998.

Anon, *Irish Dancing Magazine*. Published monthly in Bristol, January–December, 1998.

Anon, *North American Feis Commission List of Feiseanna*. Produced annually, 1998, 4 pp.

Anon, *1964–94, Celebrating the Anniversary of Fedelma Mullan Davis – 30 years teaching Irish Dancing*. New Jersey, 1994, 25 pp.

Anon, *Rialacha na gComhairlí Réigiunacha. Rules for Regional Councils*. CRG, Dublin, 1996, 36 pp.

Anon, *Rince – Iris Oifigiúl An Coimisiún le Rinci Gaelacha*. Dublin, 1998, 24 pp.

Anon, *Rince – The Annual of Irish Dancing*. CRG, Dublin (nd), 1974, 32 pp.

Anon, *Rules of the Irish National Dancing and National Dress Promotion Association of Victoria*. Melbourne, 1932, 26 pp.

Anon, *Rules and Regulations of the Victorian Irish Dancing Committee*. Melbourne, 1944, 30 pp.

Anon, *Rules of the Victorian Irish Dancing Association*. Melbourne, 1937, 32 pp.

Anon, *1966–91 – McLauglin – Silver Jubilee*. Glasgow, 1991, 28 pp.

Breathnach, Breandán, *Dancing in Ireland*. Dal gCais, Co. Clare, 1983. 55 pp. Also serialised in *Céim*. Vols. 36–41.

Burchenal, Elizabeth, *National Dances of Ireland*. Barnes and Company, New York, 1924, 136 pp.

Burchenal, Elizabeth and Roche, Patrick, *Lord of the Dance*. Roche publications, Chicago, 1990.

Carty, Peggy, *My Irish Dance*. Carty, Galway, 1987, 118 pp.

Cullinane, John, *Notes on the History of Irish Dancing*. Cullinane, Cork, 1980, 30 pp; *Aspects of the History of Irish Dancing – in Ireland, England, New Zealand, North America, Australia*. Cullinane, Cork, 1987, 128 pp; *Further Aspects of the History of Irish Dancing – Ireland, Scotland, Canada, America, New Zealand, and Australia*. Ballineaspig, Cork, 1990, 148 pp; *Notes on the History of Irish Dancing in the New York Area*, Cullinane, Cork, 1991, 35 pp; *Short History of Irish Dancing in Australia*. Cullinane, Cork, 1994, 31 pp; *Irish Dancing Costumes – their origins and evolution*. Cullinane, Cork, 1996, 121 pp; *Aspects of the History of Irish Dancing in North America* (incorporates *Notes on the History of Irish Dancing in the New York Area 1991*). Cullinane, Cork, 1997, 98 pp; *The Contribution of the London Irish Migrants to Irish Dance*. Presented at 'The Scattering' Conference at UCC, 1997, 18 pp; *Aspects of the History of Irish Céilí Dancing – 1897–1997*. Cullinane, Cork, 1998, 80 pp.

Curran, Murt, *Memories Linger On*. Curran Publications, c. 1973. 52 pp.

Flynn, Arthur, *Irish Dance*. Irish environmental Library Series, No. 73, Folens, Dublin, 96 pp.

Long, Lucey, *To Dance Irish*. Bowling Green State University, USA, 1998, 45 pp.

Moloney, Leo, *Irish National Dancing in Queensland*. Brisbane, 1996, 32 pp.

Mulholland, Patricia, *Ulster Dances, Book 1*. Ed. Mary Kenny, ACNI, Belfast, n.d.

Orpen, Grace, *Dances of Donegal*. Wilkie, London. 1931, 31 pp.

Ó hEidhin, Mícheál, *Déan Rince*. Cló Chois Fharraige, 1976, 46 pp.

O'hAilpín, Seosamh, Ní hAilpín, Treasa & O'Cuirráin, Seán, *Rogha an Fhile*. Chomhlucht Oideachais na hÉireann, Dublin, 1922, 5 pp.

O'Keeffe, J. G. and O'Brien, Art, *A Handbook of Irish Dances*. First ed., O'Donoghue, Dublin, 1902), 98 pp.

O'Rafferty, Peadar, *The Irish Folk Dance Book One & The Irish Folk Dance Book Two*. Patersons, London, 1950, 38 pp.

O'Rafferty, Peadar, & O'Rafferty, Gerald, *Dances of Ireland*. Max Parish, London, 1953, 40 pp.

O'Shea, Geraldine, *The Geraldine O'Shea Academy Annual Report*. Melbourne, 1958–67. Ten annual reports.

Neal, John, and Neal, William, *A Choice Collection of Country Dances*. Dublin c. 1726, reprint by Country Dance Society Boston, 1990.

Robb, Martha, *Irish Dancing Costume.* Country House, Dublin, 1998.

Sheehan, J. J., *A Guide to Irish Dancing.* Denver, London, 1902, 48 pp.

Tubridy, Michael, *A Selection of Irish Traditional Step Dances.* Brooks Academy and NPU, Dublin, 1998, 72 pp + cassette.

Tucker, Henry, *Clog Dancing Made Easy.* Dewitt, New York 1874, reprinted by Chris Brady Moonlight Litho, UK, 1989.

## Set dance and céilí dance

Anon. *Cairde Rince Céilí na hÉireann, Ceiliúradh Náisiúnta.* CRC, 1997. 46 pp.

Burke, Stephen, *Set Dances for Fun.* Leo Publications, 1994.

Breathnach, Breandán, *Dancing in Ireland.* Dal gCais, Clare, 1983, 55 pp. (also serialised in *Céim*, vol. 36–41).

Cullinane, John, *Aspects of the History of Irish Céilí Dancing, 1897–1997.* Cullinane, Cork, 1998, 80 pp.

Ó hEidhin, Mícheál, *Déan Rince.* Cló Choise Fharraige, 1976, 46 pp.

*Céim* (magazine of An Coimisiún le Rincí Gaelacha).

Coghlan, Aruba, *Twenty Irish Dances*, 1994.

Coimisiún le Rincí Gaelacha. *Ár Rinncidhe Fóirne*. 1939 and editions.

*Coiscéim – An Authentic Guide to Set Dancing for Instructors and Learners.* CCÉ & GAA, Dublin, n.d., 44 pp. (includes 'history of the set dancing', pp. 6-7).

Hammond, William, *Call the Set*. vols. 1–3, Cork Folk, 1988, '90, '94.

Lynch, Larry, *Set Dances of Ireland, Traditional and Evolution.* Seadhna books, 1989.

McManus, John, *Irish Céilí and Set Dances.* McManus, 1992.

Moylan, Terry (ed.), *Irish Dances.* NPU, Dublin 1984–'92; *The Pipers' Set and Other Dances,* NPU, 1985; *The Quadrilles and other Sets,* NPU, 1988.

Murphy, Pat, *Toss the Feathers.* Mercier, Cork, 1995.

Neal, John and William, *A Choice Collection of Country Dances,* Dublin, 1726.

O'Doherty, Eileen, *Set Left, Set Right.* NPU, 1989; *The Walking Polka*, NPU, 1995.

Ó hEidhin, Mícheál, *Déan Rince.* Cló Cois Fharraige. 1976, 46 pp.

Power, Vincent, *Send 'Em Home Sweatin'.* Kildanore, Dublin, 1990.

Quinn, Tom, *Irish Dancing – A Guide to Céilí, Set and Country Dancing.* Harper Collins, Glasgow, 1997, 478 pp.

*Set Dancer, The.* Galway, 1990-98 (irregular magazines, six issues).

Uí Chathasaigh, A., *Gliogaram Cos – 1, A Collection of Traditional Sets of Co. Cork,* CCÉ, NPU, 1988.

### DIRECTORIES

Craig-McFeely, Julia (ed.), *Music Research Information Network Register of Music Research Students in Great Britain and the Republic of Ireland 1989: With Thesis Titles and General Areas of Study.* Music Research Information Network, St Hugh's College, Oxford, 1989, 65 pp. (Series continues annually to 1996.)

Gifford, Gerald (ed.), *Music Research Information Network Register of Music Research Students in Great Britain and Ireland 1997: With Thesis Titles and General Areas of Study.* Royal College of Music, London, 1997, 75 pp.

Gribben, Arthur and Marsha Maguire (eds.), *The Irish Cultural Directory for Southern California.* UCLA Folklore and Mythology Publications, Los Angeles, 1985, 145 pp.

Mulvenna, Catherine (ed.), *Irish in Britain Directory* (5th edn). Brent Irish Advisory Service, London, 1993, 111 pp.

Pye, Joyce, *Ireland's Musical Instrument Makers: Who They Are and Where to Find Them.* Salmon Publishing, Galway, 1990, 121 pp.

Swift, Ann (ed.), *Irish Music Handbook.* Music Network, Dublin, 1996, 266 pp.

### DISCOGRAPHY

Carolan, Nicholas (ed.), *A Short Discography of Irish Folk Music.* Folk Music Society of Ireland, Dublin, 1987, 24 pp.

*Guide to Recordings – BBC Sound Archives: The National Music of England, Ireland, Scotland and Wales.* BBC, London, 1989, 219 pp.

O'Connor, Liz (ed.), *Music Master Folk Music of the British Isles Catalogue.* Retail Entertainment Data Publishing Ltd., London, 1994, 210 pp.

O'Dubhghaill, Aodan (ed.), *Ceirníní (1986): A Guide to Irish Folk and Traditional Music on LP Records.* Raidió Teilifís Éireann, Dublin, 1986, 60 pp; *Ceirníní (1987): A Guide to Irish Folk and Traditional Music on LP Records.* Raidió Teilifís Éireann, Dublin, 1987, 10 pp.

Roud, Steve (ed.), *Discography of English-Language Traditional Song from Britain and Ireland, Version 2.* Roud, 1995, 60 pp.

Schaeffer, Deborah, L. (ed.), *Irish Folk Music: A Select Discography.* Greenwood Press, Connecticut, 1989, 181 pp.

Schuldes, Axel (ed.), *Irish Folk Series Band II: Das*

*Gosse CD – Buch Irland.* Fáilte Der Irlandversand, Germany, 1996, 142 pp.

Williams, Sean (ed.), *An Index to the Songs and Stories in the Joe Heaney Collection.* University of Washington Ethnomusicology Archives, Washington, 1985, 52 pp. Revised edition 1991.

INSTRUMENT TUTORS

### Accordion/Melodeon

Hanrahan, David C., *The Box: A Beginner's Guide to the Irish Traditional Button Accordion.* Ossian Publications, Cork, 1989, 32 pp. With audio cassette.

McCabe, Pat, *Tutors and Tunes.* McCabe, Roslea, Co. Fermanagh, 1990, 76 pp.

Watson, Rodger, *Handbook for Melodeon.* Wise Publications, 1981.

### Banjo, bouzouki, mandolin

Carroll, Pádraig, *The Irish Mandolin.* Waltons, Dublin, 1991, 63 pp. With audio cassette.

Grotewohl, Chris, *Celtic 5 – String: Playing Irish Dance Tunes.* Grotewohl, Roeland, Park, KS, 1993, 20 pp.

Loesberg, John, *Chords for Mandolin, Irish Banjo, Bouzouki, Tenor Mandola, Mandocello.* Ossian Publications, Cork, 1989, 20 pp.

Ó Callanáin, Niall and Tommy Walsh, *The Irish Bouzouki.* Waltons, Dublin, 1989, 48 pp. With audio cassette.

O'Connor, Gerry, *The Irish Tenor Banjo.* Waltons, Dublin, 1998.

Sullivan, W. A., *Easy Traditional Irish Banjo & Mandolin.*

*Teach Yourself Traditional Irish Banjo and Mandolin.* Coldwater Music, Cork, 1986, 35 pp.

### Bodhrán

Caswell, Chris, *How to Play the Bodhrán.* Andy's Front Hall, New York

Driver, Nicholas, *Bodhrán & Bones Tutor.* Hobgoblin Music, Sussex, 1985, 26 pp. Reprinted by Gremlin Musical Instrument Company, Crawley, West Sussex, 1988, 1994.

Gracy, Mance, *Playing the Irish Drum: Getting Started,* n.d.

Hannigan, Steafán, *The Bodhrán Book.* Ossian Publications, Cork, 1991, 96 pp. With audio and video cassettes; *Bodhrán Basics.* Ossian, Cork, 1994, 32 pp. With audio cassette.

Hayes, Tommy, *Bodhrán, Bones, and Spoons* (video), n.d.

Mercier, Mel, with Séamus Egan, *Bodhrán and Bones* (video). Interworld Music.

Murphy, Martin, *The International Bodhrán Book.* John Elison, Rathdrum, Wicklow, 1997, 52 pp.

Ó Súilleabháin, Mícheál, *The Bodhrán.* Waltons, Dublin, 1984.

Smith, Robin M., *Power Bodhrán Techniques: A New Approach to the Celtic Drum.* Memphis, n.d.

Sullivan, Tony, *Learn to Play the Bodhrán.*

Walsh, Tommy, and Jim Kelly, *The Walton Bodhrán Tutor.* Walton Manufacturing Ltd., Dublin, 1994, 23 pp. With audio cassette.

### Concertina

Bramich, Mick, *The Irish Concertina: A Tutor for the Anglo Concertina in the Irish Style.* Dave Mallinson Publications, West Yorkshire, 1996, 76 pp. With audio cassette.

Butler, Frank, *The Concertina,* Oak Publications, 1976.

Watson, Rodger, *Handbook for Anglo-Chromatic Concertina.* Wise Publications, 1981; *Handbook for English Concertina.* Wise Publications, 1981.

### Dulcimer, piano, harmonica, Jews' harp

Ashbrook, Karen, *Playing the Hammered Dulcimer in the Irish Tradition.* Oak Publications, New York, 1987, 90 pp.

Cotter, Geraldine, *Geraldine Cotter's Seinn an Piano: Playing the Piano Irish Style.* Ossian Publications, Cork, 1996. With two audio cassettes.

*Jews Harp Triple Pack* (book, instrument and cass.) Mallinson Music, Yorkshire, 1995.

Sullivan, Tony, *Traditional Mouth Organ.* Halshaw Music, Cheshire 1997, 21 pp. With CD.

### Fiddle

Cooper, Pat, *Mel Bay's Complete Irish Fiddle Player.* Mel Bay Publications, Missouri, 1995, 157 pp. With audio cassette.

Cranitch, Matt, *The Irish Fiddle Book: The Art of Traditional Fiddle Playing.* Mercier Press, Cork, 1988, 180 pp. Reprinted 1993. With audio cassette.

Lawlor, Úna, *An Veidhleadoir Óg.* Cló Iar-Chonnachta – Bord na Gaeilge, Dublin, 1996, 67 pp.

Mac Suibhne, Donnchadh, *An Fhidil Céim ar Chéim: Book 1 The First Twelve Notes.* Ceol Dal Riada, Antrim, 1995, 26 pp; *An Fhidil Céim ar Chéim: Book 2 Easy Marches, Polkas, Jigs, Slides.* Ceol Dal Riada, Antrim, 1995, 32 pp; *An Fhidil Céim ar Chéim: Book 3 Dress It Up.* Ceol Dal Riada, Antrim, 1995, 36 pp; *An Fhidil Céim ar Chéim: Book 4 Highways and Byways.* Ceol Dal Riada, Antrim, 1995, 25 pp.

Vallely, Eithne and Brian, *Learn to Play the Fiddle with the Armagh Pipers Club*. Armagh Pipers Club, 1977, 48 pp.

### Flute
Hamilton, S. C., *The Irish Flute Player's Handbook: A Comprehensive Guide to the Traditional Flute in Ireland*. Breac Publications, Cork, 1990, 215 pp. With audio cassette.

McCaskill, Mizzy and Dona Giliam, *Complete Irish Flute Book*. Mel Bay, 1997.

Vallely, Fintan, *Timber: The Concert-Flute Tutor*. Long Note Publications, Miltown Malbay, 1986, 44 pp. Second edn. 1987, as *Timber: The Flute Tutor*, Waltons, Dublin. With audio cassette.

### Guitar and accompaniment
*Accompaniment*. Coldwater Music, Cork, 1986, 35 pp.

De Grae, Paul, *Traditional Irish Guitar*. De Grae, Kerry, 1989, 97 pp. Reprinted with CD by Ossian, Cork, 1996.

Grossman, Stefan, *Mel Bay Presents Celtic Airs, Jigs, Hornpipes & Reels Arranged for Fingerstyle Guitar*. Mel Bay Publications, Pacific, 1990, 70 pp.

McQuaid, Sarah, *The Irish DADGAD Guitar Book*. Ossian Publications, Cork, 1995, 93 pp. With audio cassette.

Ralston, Gavin, *Irish Traditional Guitar Accompaniment*. Waltons, Dublin, 1998.

### Harp
Calthorpe, Nancy, *Begin the Harp*. Waltons, Dublin, 1987, 44 pp.

Cuthbert, Sheila Larchet, *The Irish Harp Book: A Tutor and Companion*. Mercier, Cork, 1985, 245 pp. Reprinted by Music Sales Corporation, New York 1993.

Heymann, Ann, *Secrets of the Gaelic Harp*. Clairseach Publications, Minneapolis, 1988, 128 pp.

### Tin whistle
*Geraldine Cotter's Traditional Irish Tin Whistle Tutor* (2nd edn.). Ossian Publications, Cork, 1989, 104 pp. First published 1983. With two audio cassettes.

McCaskill, Mizzy, and Dona Gilliam, *Mel Bay's Complete Irish Tin Whistle Book*. Mel Bay Publications, Pacific, 1996, 144 pp. With audio cassette.

Maguire, Tom, *An Irish Whistle Book*. Ossian, Cork, 1985, 40 pp. With audio cassette. Reprinted 1995.

Ochs, Bill, *A Handbook for the Clarke Tin Whistle*. The Pennywhistler's Press, New York, 1990, 80 pp. With audio cassette.

Ryng, Mary C., *Recorder Rules, Part II*. Ryng, Cork, 1987, 36 pp; *Whistle A While* (2nd edition). Ryng, Cork, 1986, 48 pp; and Julie Ryng, *Whistle-A-Way*. Ryng, Cork, 1991, 40 pp.

*Soodlum's Tin Whistle Book: Fully Diagrammed Enabling the Complete Beginner to Play Immediately*. Waltons, Dublin, 1988, 32 pp. With audio cassette.

Vallely, Eithne and John B., *Learn to Play the Tin Whistle Parts 1–3*. Armagh Pipers' Club, 1972, 1997.

Walsh, Tommy, *The Walton Tin Whistle Tutor: Book One*. Waltons Manufacturing Ltd., Dublin, 1994, 24 pp.

### Uilleann pipes
Brooks, Denis, *The Tutor: Irish Union Pipes*. Brooks, Washington D.C., 1985, 74 pp.

Clarke, Heather J., *The New Approach to Uilleann Piping*. St. Martin's Publications, Galway, 1988, 85 pp. With audio cassette; reprint with CD 1998.

Ennis Séamus, *The Master's Touch* (eds. Wilbert Garvin, Robbie Hannon), NPU, Dublin, 1998.

*Learn to Play Uilleann Pipes*. Armagh Pipers Club, 1975, 44 pp; reprint 1998 with cass.

Spillane, Davy and Tommy Walsh, *The Davy Spillane Uillean Pipe Tutor: Book One, Basic*. Waltons Dublin, 1996, 48 pp. With audio cassette.

Sky, Patrick (ed.) *O'Farrell's Pocket Companion for the Irish or Union Pipes* (London 1806); *O'Farrell's Collection of National Irish Music for the Union Pipes* (1804, London, reprint 1995, USA).

Rowsome, Leo, *Tutor for the Uilleann Pipes* (Waltons, 1936 & reprints; new edn. Waltons, 1999).

### INSTRUMENT-RELATED BOOKS AND COLLECTIONS
#### Bagpipes
Flood, W. H. Grattan, *Story of the Bagpipe*. Dublin, 1911.

Nicholson, Ailean, *Ailean Nicholson's Collection of Irish Tunes for the Bagpipe*. Ailean Nicholson, Surrey, 1985, 112 pp.

Rickard, Dave (ed.), *Traditional Irish Music for the Bagpipe*. Mercier Press, Cork, 1987, 36 pp. Reprinted by Ossian, Cork, 1995.

Tully, Terry (ed.), *Collection of Traditional Irish Music*. Tully, Kildare, 1991, 51 pp; (ed.), *Collection of Traditional and Contemporary Irish Music Book Three*. Tully, Kildare, 1997, 52 pp.

## Bodhrán

Kearns, Malachy, *Wallup! Humour and Lore of Bodhrán Making*. Roundstone Musical Instruments, Connemara, 1996, 84 pp.

McCrickard, Janet E., *The Bodhrán*. McCrickard, Somerset, n.d.

## Fiddle

Cranitch, M., *The Irish Fiddle Book*, Ossian Publications (in association with Mercier Press), Cork, 1996.

De Marco, Tony, and Miles Krassen, *A Trip to Sligo (A Guide to the Sligo Style)*. Silver Spear Publications, Pittsburgh, 1978.

Feldman, Allen and Eamonn O'Doherty (eds.), *The Northern Fiddler*, reprint of 1979 edition, Oak Publications, London, 1985, 251 pp.

Hanafin, Dermot, *Padraig O'Keeffe: The Man and His Music*. Hanafin, Castleisland, 1995, 44 pp.

Hunter, Jim, *The Blind Fiddler From Myroe*. Danny Boy Trading Co. Ltd., Bangor, n.d., 21 pp.

Keane, Sean (ed.), *Fifty Fiddle Solos*. Conway Editions, New York, London, Sydney, 1990, 48 pp. With audio cassette.

Lyth, David, *Bowing Styles in Irish Fiddle Playing Vol. 1*. CCÉ, Dublin, 1981; *Bowing Styles in Irish Fiddle Playing Vol. 2*. CCÉ, Dublin, 1996, 150 pp.

Mac Aoidh, C., *Between the Jigs and the Reels: The Donegal Fiddle Tradition*. Drumlin Publications, Leitrim, 1994.

Ó Broin, Seosamh, *Fidileirí: Mayo Fiddlers*. Dreolín Productions, Achadh Mór, Ballyhaunis, Co. Mayo, 1995, 50 pp.

Peoples, Tommy, *Fifty Irish Fiddle Tunes*. Waltons, Dublin, 1986, 48 pp. With audio cassette.

Ward, A., *Music from Sliabh Luachra*. Topic Records, London, 1976.

## Guitar

Billaudot, Gérard (ed.), *Guitare D'Irlande*. Bigo, France, 1987, 59 pp.

Gelo, Dan (ed.), *Fiddle Tunes and Irish Music for Guitar*. Mel Bay Publications, Pacific, 1985, 135 pp.

Grossman, Stefan (ed.), *Guitar Artistry Series: Music of Ireland*. Mel Bay Publications, Pacific, 1992, 28 pp; *Guitar Artistry Series: Irish Guitar Encores*. Mel Bay Publications, Pacific, 1993, 28 pp; Duck Baker and El McMeen (eds.), *Mel Bay's Complete Celtic Guitar Fingerstyle Book*. Mel Bay Publications, Pacific, 1995, 244 pp.

Hinchliffe, Keith (ed.), *Carolan's Dream: Music of the Harper Turlough O'Carolan, Arranged for the Guitar*. Dave Mallinson Publications, West Yorkshire, 1996, 44 pp.

Shields, Andrew (ed.), *Twenty Popular Irish Solos for Easy Guitar*. Waltons, Dublin, 1985, 42 pp.

Steinbach, Patrick (ed.), *Celtic Classics: Traditional Dances and Harp Pieces from Ireland Arranged for the Guitar*. G. Ricordi & Co., Munich, 1993, 40 pp.

Stevens, William (ed.), *Turlough O'Carolan for Finger Style Guitar: 21 Arrangements in Notation and Tablature*. Granger Publications, Minneapolis, 1995, 47 pp.

Van Hagen, Joshua H. (ed.), *Songs from Ireland for Solo Guitar*. Guitar Ed. (Int) Ltd., Dorset, 1986, 8 pp.

Weiser, Glenn (ed.), *Celtic Harp Music of Carolan and Others: For Solo Guitar*. Centerstream, LA, 1995, 111 pp.

## Hammer dulcimer

Ashbrook, Karen, *Mel Bay Presents Karen Ashbrook Hills of Erin: A Sweeping Sonic Travelogue of Ireland for Hammered Dulcimer*. Maggie's Music – Mel Bay, Pacific, MO, 1996, 32 pp.

Johnson, Sara Lee, *The Kitchen Musician's Occasional Mostly Irish Airs for Hammer Dulcimer*. Kitchen Publications, 1989, 52 pp; *The Kitchen Musician's Occasional Jigs for Hammer Dulcimer, Fiddle, etc, No. 6*. Kitchen Publications, 1989, 16 pp.

Stevens, Shelley S. (ed.), *Mel Bay's O'Carolan Harp Tunes for Mountain Dulcimer*. Mel Bay Publications, Pacific, 1993, 38 pp.

## Harp

Audley, Brian, *Denis O'Hampsey the Harper c. 1695–1807*. Whisper Press, Belfast, 1992, 57 pp.

Bolger, Mercedes, and Gráinne Yeats (eds.), *Sounding Harps: Music for the Irish Harp, Book 1*. Cáirde na Cruite, Dublin, 1990, 43 pp.

Bunting, Edward, *A General Collection of the Ancient Irish Music Vol. 1*. (Facsimile of 1796 edn). Linen Hall Library, Belfast, 1996, 36 pp.

Calthorpe, Nancy (ed.), *Complete Works of O'Carolan, The: Irish Harper and Composer*, 2nd edn. Ossian, Cork, 1989, 154 pp; *A Tribute to O'Carolan: Music for the Irish Harp*. Waltons, Dublin, 1993, 12 pp; *The Calthorpe Collection: Songs and Airs Arranged for the Voice and Irish Harp*. Waltons, Dublin, 1993, 94 pp.

Coffey, Mother Attracta, *Tutor for the Irish Harp*. Vincent, London, 1903.

Flood, W. H. Grattan, *Story of the Harp*. 1905.

Grossman, Stefan and John Renbourn (eds.), *Mel Bay's Deluxe Anthology of O'Carolan Music*. Mel Bay Publications, Pacific, 1995, 160 pp.

Heymann, Ann (ed.), *Off the Record: Arrangements for Wire Strung Harp*. Clairseach Publications, Minneapolis, 1990, 40 pp; *Legacy of the 1792 Belfast Harp Festival*. Clairseach Publications, Minneapolis, 1992, 36 pp.

Kilroy, Peter & Corry, *The Ogham Harp*. Ogham Harps, Kerry, 1988, 10 pp.

Loesberg, John (ed.), *The Celtic Harp*. Ossian Publications, Cork, 1988, 36 pp.

Loughnane, Kathleen (ed.), *Harping On: Irish Traditional Music for the Harp*. Reiskmore Music, Galway, 1995, 39 pp; *Affairs of the Harp*. Reiskmore Music, Galway 1998, 32 pp.

McGrath, Mercedes, Elizabeth Hannon and Mercedes Bolger (eds.), *My Gentle Harp*. Cáirde na Cruite, Dublin, 1992, 52 pp.

Magee, John, *The Heritage of the Harp*. Linen Hall Library, Belfast, 1992, 31 pp.

Maher, Tom, *The Harp's a Wonder*. Uisneach Press, Mullingar, 1991, 147 pp.

Ní Chathasaigh, Máire, *The Irish Harper Vol. I*. Old Bridge Music, West Yorkshire, 1991, 28 pp.

Porter, A. J. (ed.), *Two Carolan Tunes*. Wedderburn Music, Wicklow, 1996, 4 pp.

Rimmer, Joan, *The Irish Harp*. Mercier, Cork, 1969, '77, '84

Woods, Sylvia (ed.), *Forty O'Carolan Tunes for all Harps*. Woods Music and Books, California, 1987, 112 pp; *Irish Dance Tunes for all Harps*. Woods Music and Books, California, 1987, 54 pp.

Yeats, Gráinne, *The Harp of Ireland: The Belfast Harper's Festival, 1792 and the Saving of Ireland's Harp Music by Edward Bunting*. Belfast Harper's Bicentenary Ltd., Belfast, 1992, 71 pp.

## Piano

Moffat, Alfred A., *Irish Tunes for Piano*. Ossian Publications, Cork, 1991, 80 pp.

O'Donoghue, Nora (ed.), *Irish Concert Pieces for Piano*. Fentone Music Ltd., Northants, 1993, 19 pp; *Music of Ireland for Piano Solo*. Fentone Music Ltd., Northants, 1986, 12 pp.

Smith, Gail (ed.), *Mel Bay Presents Ancient & Modern Songs of Ireland for Piano*. Mel Bay Publications Inc., Missouri, 1993, 152 pp. With audio cassette.

Sweeney, Eric, *The Blackberry Blossom for Piano*. Contemporary Music Centre, Dublin, 1991, 10 pp.

## Piano accordion

O'Donoghue, Nora (ed.), *Collection of Irish Solos for Piano Accordion*. Fentone Music Ltd., Northants, 1986, 8 pp.

Walsh, Tommy (ed.), *Irish Piano Accordion*. Waltons, Dublin, 1989, 32 pp.

## Tin whistle

Coady, Michael, *The Well of Spring Water: A Memoir of Packie and Micho Russell of Doolin, Co. Clare*. Michael Coady, 1996, 40 pp.

Maguire, Tom, *An Irish Whistle Tune Book*. Ossian Publications, Cork, 1996, 39 pp. With audio cassette.

Russell, Micho, *The Piper's Chair*, reprint of 1980 edition published by Russell. Ossian Publications, Cork, 1989, 33 pp; *The Road to Aran*. Micho Russell, 1988, 16 pp.

Walsh, Tommy, *Irish Tin Whistle Legends*. Waltons, Dublin, 1989, 48 pp.

## Uilleann pipes

Britton, Tim, *My Method: A Step by Step Guide for Constructing Reeds for the Irish Uillean* [sic] *Pipes*. Pied Piper Productions, Fairfield, IA 1986, 27 pp; revised edition, 1994, 39 pp.

Climo, Eddie, *A Handbook for Uilleann Pipers*. South Western Association of Uilleann Pipers, 1996, 48 pp.

Garvin, Wilbert, *The Irish Bagpipes: Their Construction and Maintenance*, 2nd edn. Garvin Publications, Ballymena, 1988, 40 pp.

McNulty, Pat, *The Piper's Dream: A Selection of the Music and Poems of Pat McNulty*. Dragonfly Music, Northumberland, 1990, 24 pp.

Mitchell, Pat (ed.), *The Dance Music of Willie Clancy*. Ossian Publications, Cork, 1993, 136 pp.

Mitchell, Pat, and Jackie Small (eds.), *The Piping of Patsy Touhey*. Na Píobairí Uilleann, Dublin, 1986, 113 pp. With audio cassette.

Moylan, Terry, *The Regulators: Regulator Maintenance, Tuning and Use*. Na Píobairí Uilleann, Dublin, 1991, 30 pp.

Ó Canainn, Tomás (ed.), *New Tunes for Old*. Ossian Publications, Cork, 1985, 50 pp; *Tomás' Tune Book*. Ossian Publications, Cork 1997, 31 pp.

Sky, Patrick, *O'Farrell's Collection of National Irish Music for the Union Pipes*. Sky, Chapel Hill, NC, 1995, 53 pp.

Walsh, John B. (ed.), *The Collection of Pipe-Friendly Tunes*. Cumann na bPíobairí, Seattle, 1997, 165 pp.

**INSTRUMENTAL MUSIC COLLECTIONS**

Armagh Pipers' Club, *Play Fifty Reels*. APC, Armagh, 1979.

Ashbrook, Karen, *Mel Bay Presents Karen Ashbrook Hills of Erin: A Sweeping Sonic Travelogue of*

# BIBLIOGRAPHY

*Ireland for Hammered Dulcimer.* Maggie's Music, Mel Bay, Pacific, MO, 1996, 32 pp.

*Best of the Chieftains, The.* Wise Publications, London, 1995, 55 pp.

Billaudot, Gérard (ed.), *Guitare D'Irlande.* Bigo, France, 1987, 59 pp.

Black, Bill, *Music's the Very Best Thing: The Bill Black Irish Tune Collection Vol. 1.* Sunphone, Falmouth, MA, 1996, 196 pp.

Bolger, Mercedes, and Gráinne Yeats (eds.), *Sounding Harps: Music for the Irish Harp, Book 1.* Cáirde na Cruite, Dublin, 1990, 43 pp.

Breathnach, Breandán (ed.), *Ceol Rince na hÉireann I*, reprint of 1963 edition. An Gúm, Dublin, 1997, 108 pp; *Ceol Rince na hÉireann II*, reprint of 1976 edition. An Gúm, Dublin, 1992, 203 pp; *Ceol Rince na hÉireann III.* Oifig an tSoláthair, Dublin, 1985, 133 pp. Reprinted 1995; *Ceol Rince na hÉireann IV.* ed. Jackie Small, An Gúm, Dublin, 1996, 127 pp.

Bunting, Edward, *A General Collection of the Ancient Irish Music Vol. 1.* (Facsimile of 1796 edition). Linen Hall Library, Belfast, 1996, 36 pp.

Calthorpe, Nancy (ed.), *The Calthorpe Collection: Songs and Airs Arranged for the Voice and Irish Harp.* Waltons, Dublin, 1993, 94 pp; *A Tribute to O'Carolan: Music for the Irish Harp.* Waltons, Dublin, 1993, 12 pp.

Carolan, Nicholas (ed.), *A Collection of the Most Celebrated Irish Tunes Proper for the Violin, German Flute or Hautboy, by John and William Neal, Dublin, 1724*, Facsimile edn. Folk Music Society of Ireland, Dublin, 1986, 82 pp.

*Complete Works of O'Carolan, The: Irish Harper and Composer* (2nd edn). Ossian, Cork, 1989, 154 pp.

*Compositions of Paddy O'Brien, The*, Eileen O'Brien Minogue (ed.), JCD Publications Ltd., Ayrshire, 1992, 53 pp.

Deloughery, Paul (ed.), *Sliabh Luachra on Parade.* Deloughery, Kentucky, 1988, 104 pp.

Feldman, Allen and Eamonn O'Doherty (eds.), *The Northern Fiddler*, reprint of 1979 edition. Oak Publications, London, 1985, 251 pp.

Flaherty, Bernard (ed.), *Trip to Sligo.* Flaherty, Boyle, 1990, 184 pp.

Fleischmann, Aloys, Mícheál Ó Súilleabháin & Paul McGettrick (eds.), *Sources of Irish Music.* Garland, New York, 1998.

Fuchs, Cari (ed.), *Irish Sessions Tune Book: 317 Favourite Session Tunes.* Fuchs, Pittsburgh, January, 1995, 120 pp.

Gaimh, Caoimhín (ed.), *Smoke Gets in Your Eyes Vol I: Common Jigs and Reels.* Fish House Publications, Seattle, 1993, 79 pp.

Gelo, Dan (ed.), *Fiddle Tunes and Irish Music for Guitar.* Mel Bay Publications, Pacific, 1985, 135 pp.

Grossman, Stefan (ed.), *Guitar Artistry Series: Music of Ireland.* Mel Bay Publications, Pacific, 1992, 28pp; *Guitar Artistry Series: Irish Guitar Encores.* Mel Bay Publications, Pacific, 1993, 28 pp; Duck Baker and El McMeen (eds.), *Mel Bay's Complete Celtic Fingerstyle Guitar Book.* Mel Bay Publications, Pacific, 1995, 244 pp.

Grossman, Stefan and John Renbourn (eds.), *Mel Bay's Deluxe Anthology of O'Carolan Music.* Mel Bay Publications, Pacific, 1995, 160 pp.

Grotewohl, Chris (ed.), *Celtic 5-String: Fifty Irish Dance Tunes.* Grotewohl, Kansas, n.d., 25 pp.

Gunn, Douglas (ed.), *Irish Music by Carolan (1670–1738): Arranged for the Recorder Trio.* Ossian Publications, Cork, 1986, 23 pp. *Three Irish Tunes.* Poodle Press, Dublin, 1989, 11 pp.

Hardebeck, Carl G., *Gems of Melody/Seoda Ceoil.* Belfast, 1908.

Heymann, Ann (ed.), *Off the Record: Arrangements for Wire Strung Harp.* Clairseach Publications, Minneapolis, 1990, 40 pp; *Legacy of the 1792 Belfast Harp Festival.* Clairseach Publications, Minneapolis, 1992, 36 pp.

Hinchliffe, Keith (ed.), *Carolan's Dream: Music of the Harper Turlough O'Carolan, Arranged for the Guitar.* Dave Mallinson Publications, West Yorkshire, 1996, 44 pp.

Hoffman, Francis (ed.), *The Antient Music of Ireland from the Petrie collection.* Dublin, 1877.

Johnson, Sara Lee, *The Kitchen Musician's Occasional Mostly Irish Airs for Hammer Dulcimer.* Kitchen Publications, 1989, 52 pp; *The Kitchen Musician's Occasional Jigs for Hammer Dulcimer, Fiddle, etc, No. 6.* Kitchen Publications, 1989, 16 pp.

Jordan, Eamon (ed.), *Down By the Sally Gardens: Music for Little Bands.* Ashardan, Armagh, 1988, 52 pp; *Whistle and Sing, Books I and II*, reprint of 1974 edn. Ashardan, Armagh, 1988, 111 pp.

Joyce, Patrick Weston (ed.), *Ancient Irish Music.* Dublin, 1873.

Keane, Sean (ed.), *Fifty Fiddle Solos.* Conway Editions, New York, London, Sydney, 1990, 48 pp. With audio cassette.

Kilduff, Vinnie (ed.), *Fifty Irish Tin Whistle Solos.* Conway Editions Music Sales, New York, London, Sydney, 1989, 48 pp. With audio cassette.

Kisiel, Helen Rosemary (ed.), *The Music of Brendan Tonra.* Quinlin Campbell Publishers, Boston, 1988, 18 pp.

Lennon, Charlie (ed.), *Musical Memories Vol. 1.* Worldmusic Publications, Dublin, 1993, 88 pp.

Loesberg, John (ed.), *The Celtic Harp*. Ossian Publications, Cork, 1988, 36 pp; *An Irish Tune Book Vol One and Two*. Ossian Publications, Cork, 1988, 52 pp; *Musical Reflections of Ireland*. Ossian Publications, Cork, 1988, 32 pp; *More Musical Reflections of Ireland*. Ossian Publications, Cork, 1988, 36 pp.

Loughnane, Kathleen (ed.), *Harping On: Irish Traditional Music for the Harp*. Reiskmore Music, Galway, 1995, 39 pp.

Lyth, David, *Bowing Styles in Irish Fiddle Playing Vol. II*. Comhaltas Ceoltóirí Éireann, Dublin, 1996, 150 pp.

Maguire, Tom, *An Irish Whistle Tune Book*. Ossian Publications, Cork, 1996, 39 pp. With audio cassette.

Mallinson, Dave (ed.), *Mally Presents . . . 100 Enduring Irish Session Tunes*. Dave Mallinson Publications, West Yorkshire, 1995, 42 pp; *Mally Presents . . . 100 Essential Irish Session Tunes*. Dave Mallinson Publications, West Yorkshire, 1995, 42 pp; *Mally Presents . . . 100 Evergreen Irish Session Tunes*. Dave Mallinson Publications, West Yorkshire, 1997, 43 pp; *Mally Presents . . . 100 Irish Polkas*. Dave Mallinson Publications, West Yorkshire, 1997, 44 pp.

McCullough, L. E. (ed.), *120 Favourite Irish Session Tunes*. Skylark Productions, 1988, 44 pp. With four audio cassettes.

McGrath, Mercedes, Elizabeth Hannon and Mercedes Bolger (eds.), *My Gentle Harp*. Cáirde na Cruite, Dublin, 1992, 52 pp.

McNulty, Pat (ed.), *A Collection of the Dance Music of Ireland*, 4th edn. Ossian Publications, Cork, 1988, 29 pp; *The Piper's Dream: A Selection of the Music and Poems of Pat McNulty*. Dragonfly Music, Northumberland, 1990, 24 pp; *A Collection of the Dance Music of Ireland*, 5th edn. Ossian Publications, Cork, 1991, 30 pp.

Mitchell, Pat (ed.), *The Dance Music of Willie Clancy*. Ossian Publications, Cork, 1993, 136 pp.

Mitchell, Pat, and Jackie Small (eds.), *The Piping of Patsy Touhey*. Na Píobairí Uilleann, Dublin, 1986, 113 pp. With audio cassette.

Moffat, Alfred A., *Irish Tunes for Piano*. Ossian Publications, Cork, 1991, 80 pp.

Moylan, Terry (ed.), *Johnny O'Leary of Sliabh Luachra: Dance Music from the Cork–Kerry Border*. The Lilliput Press, Dublin, 1994, 213 pp.

Mulvihill, Martin (ed.), *Martin Mulvihill Collection*. Bronx, 1986.

Neale, John and William (eds.), *A Collection of the Most Celebrated Irish Tunes*, Dublin, 1724; reprint with introduction FMSI, Dublin, 1986.

Ní Chathasaigh, Máire, *The Irish Harper Vol. I*. Old Bridge Music, West Yorkshire, 1991, 28 pp.

Nicholson, Ailean, *Ailean Nicholson's Collection of Irish Tunes for the Bagpipe*. Ailean Nicholson, Surrey, 1985, 112 pp.

Ó Briain, Donncha (ed.), *The Golden Eagle*. Comhaltas Ceoltóirí Éireann, Dublin, 1988, 31 pp, *The Golden Eagle*, 2nd edn. Comhaltas Ceoltóirí Éireann, Dublin, 1993, 31 pp.

Ó Canainn, Tomás (ed.), *New Tunes for Old*. Ossian Publications, Cork, 1985, 50 pp; *Traditional Slow Airs of Ireland*, Ossian Publications, Cork, 1995, 100 pp. With two audio cassettes; *Tomás' Tune Book*. Ossian Publications, Cork 1997, 31 pp.

O'Connor, Gerry and David McNevin (eds.), *Fifty Solos for Irish Tenor Banjo*. Waltons, Dublin, 1986, 80 pp.

O'Donoghue, Nora (ed.), *Collection of Irish Solos for Piano Accordion*. Fentone Music Ltd., Northants, 1986, 8 pp; *Music of Ireland for Piano Solo*. Fentone Music Ltd., Northants, 1986, 12 pp; *Irish Concert Pieces for Piano*. Fentone Music Ltyd., Northants, 1993, 19 pp.

O'Farrell, Patrick, *O'Farrell's Pocket Companion for the Irish or Union Pipes*. London, 1806; *O'Farrell's Collection of National Irish Music for the Union Pipes*. London, 1804, reprint Patrick Sky 1995, USA.

O'Neill, Francis and James O'Neill, *The Dance Music of Ireland (1001 Gems)*, reprint of 1907 edn. Waltons, Dublin, 1986, 171 pp; *O'Neill's Music of Ireland: Eighteen Hundred and Fifty Melodies*, reprint of 1903 edn. Mel Bay Publications, Pacific, n.d., 349 pp.

O'Neill, Francis and Selena O'Neill, *O'Neill's Irish Music 400 Choice Selections arranged for Piano and Violin*, reprint of original 1915 edn. Mercier Press, Cork, 1987, 192 pp.

O'Neill, Francis (ed.), *O'Neill's Music of Ireland* (1903); *The Dance Music of Ireland* (1907); *Waifs and Strays of Gaelic Melody* (1922).

O'Sullivan, Donal (ed.), *Bunting's Ancient Music of Ireland [1840]*. Cork University Press, Cork, 1983; *Carolan: the Life, Times and Music of an Irish Harper*. RKP, London, 1958, reprint 1983, Louth (UK), Celtic Music.

Peoples, Tommy, *Fifty Irish Fiddle Tunes*. Waltons, Dublin, 1986, 48 pp. With audio cassette.

Petrie, George (ed.), *Ancient Music of Ireland 1*. Dublin, 1855; *Ancient Music of Ireland, 2*. Dublin, 1882; both reprinted in one vol. 1967, 1978, Gregg International; facsimile edn. 1994, 2 vols., Lanerch, Wales.

Porter, A. J. (ed.), *Two Carolan Tunes*. Wedderburn Music, Wicklow, 1996, 4 pp.

Reavy, Joseph M. (ed.), *The Collected Compositions of Ed Reavy*, reprint of 1984 edn. Green Grass Music, Drumshanbo, n.d., 152 pp. With audio cassette; *The Reavy Collection of Irish-American Traditional Tunes*, reprint of 1979 edn. Green Grass Music, n.d., 54 pp. With audio cassette.

Rickard, Dave (ed.), *Traditional Irish Music for the Bagpipe*. Mercier Press, Cork, 1987, 36 pp. Reprinted by Ossian, Cork, 1995.

Roche, Francis (ed.), *The Roche Collection* [3 vols.]. Cork, 1927; reprinted in 1 vol. 1982, Cork, Ossian.

Russell, Micho, *The Road to Aran*. Micho Russell, 1988, 16 pp; *The Piper's Chair*, reprint of 1980 edition published by Russell. Ossian Publications, Cork, 1989, 33 pp.

Ryan, Brian (ed.), *The Hidden Ireland: The First Selection of Irish Traditional Compositions of Sean Ryan*, 2nd edn. Brian Ryan, 1994, 43 pp.

Ryan, Danny (ed.), *Old Time and Irish Waltz Book*. DR Music, Tipperary, 1990, 20 pp.

Shields, Andrew (ed.), *Twenty Popular Irish Solos for Easy Guitar*. Waltons, Dublin, 1985, 42 pp.

Shields, Hugh, *Tunes of the Munster Pipers*. ITMA, Dublin, 1998.

Sky, Patrick (ed.), *O'Farrell's Collection of National Irish Music for the Union Pipes*. Sky, Chapel Hill, NC, 1995, 53 pp; *Mel Bay Presents Ryan's Mammoth Collection*. Mel Bay Publications, Pacific, 1996, 176 pp.

Smith, Gail (ed.), *Mel Bay Presents Ancient & Modern Songs of Ireland for Piano*. Mel Bay Publications Inc., Missouri, 1993, 152 pp. With audio cassette.

*Smoke Gets in Your Eyes Vol. II: Not the Jigs and Reels*. Fish House Publications, Seattle, 1994, 50 pp; *Smoke Gets in Your Eyes Vol. III: More Jigs and Reels*. Fish House Publications, Seattle, 1995, 75 pp; *Smoke Gets in Your Eyes: A Compilation of Irish Tunes Played in Seattle Sessions*. Fish House Publications, Seattle, 1995, 146 pp.

Spring, Edwin, (ed.), *Camden Breeze*. Edwin Spring, Somerset, 1987, 77 pp; *A Supplement to Camden Breeze*. Edwin Spring, Somerset, 1992, 67 pp.

Stanford, Charles Villiers (ed.), *The Complete Petrie Collection of Irish Music* [3 vols.]. London, 1902–5; (ed.), *The Complete Collections of Irish Music as Noted by George Petrie (1789–1866) Parts I–III*, reprint of 1902 edition. Llanerch Publishers, Felin Fach, 1994, 126 pp + 268 pp + 397 pp.

Steinbach, Patrick (ed.), *Celtic Classics: Traditional Dances and Harp Pieces from Ireland Arranged for the Guitar*. G. Ricordi & Co., Munich, 1993, 40 pp.

Stevens, Shelley S. (ed.), *Mel Bay's O'Carolan Harp Tunes for Mountain Dulcimer*. Mel Bay Publications, Pacific, 1993, 38 pp.

Stevens, William (ed.), *Turlough O'Carolan for Finger Style Guitar: 21 Arrangements in Notation and Tablature*. Granger Publications, Minneapolis, 1995, 47 pp.

Sullivan, William (ed.), *Traditional Irish Music: Tunes from the Repertory of William Sullivan*, 2nd edn. Sampler Records, New York, 1989, 34 pp.

Tarbatt, Henry and Jenny Smith (eds.), *The Tune Book Music Stand: Over One Hundred Cracking Good Session Tunes*. Merlin Music, Preston 1997, 108 pp; *The Tune Books Music Stand 2: More Cracking Good Session Tunes*. Merlin Music, Preston 1997, 107 pp.

Taylor, David J. (ed.), *Where's the Crack? Vol. I*. Dave Mallinson Music, West Yorkshire, 1989, 32 pp; *The Crossroads Dance*. Dave Mallinson Publications, West Yorkshire, 1992, 52 pp; *Music of Ireland: The Big Session*. Dave Mallinson Publications, West Yorkshire, 1992, 32 pp; *Through the Half-Door*. Dave Mallinson Publications, West Yorkshire, 1992, 52 pp; *Traditional Irish Music: Music for the Sets – The Blue Book*. Dave Mallinson Publications, West Yorkshire, 1995, 32 pp. With three audio cassettes; *Traditional Irish Music: Music for the Sets – The Yellow Book*. Dave Mallinson Publications, West Yorkshire, 1995, 38 pp. With three audio cassettes; *Music of Ireland: A Mighty Tune!* Dave Mallinson Publications, West Yorkshire, 1995, 32 pp; *Music of Ireland: Give Us Another*. Dave Mallinson Publications, West Yorkshire, 1995, 32 pp; *Music of Ireland: Fire Away Now*. Dave Mallinson Publications, West Yorkshire, 1997, 32 pp.

*Ted Furey Collection of Irish Traditional Tunes, Vol. I, The*. Banshee Music Ltd., Dublin, 1992, 64 pp.

Tubridy, Michael, and Méabh Ní Lochlainn (eds.), *Irish Traditional Music: Craobh Naithí*. Comhaltas Ceoltóirí Éireann, Dublin, 1995, 51 pp.

Tully, Terry (ed.), *Collection of Traditional Irish Music*. Tully, Kildare, 1991, 51 pp; *Collection of Traditional and Contemporary Irish Music Book Three*. Tully, Kildare, 1997, 52 pp.

Tweed, Karen (ed.), *Traditional Irish Music: Karen Tweed's Irish Choice*. Dave Mallinson Publications, West Yorkshire, 1994, 46 pp.

Tyrrall, Gordon (ed.), *Gordon Tyrall's Irish Choice*. Dave Mallinson Publications, West Yorkshire, 1996, 44 pp.

Van Hagen, Joshua H. (ed.), *Songs from Ireland*

*for Solo Guitar*. Guitar Ed. (Int) Ltd., Dorset, 1986, 8 pp.

Walsh, John B. (ed.), *The Collection of Pipe-Friendly Tunes*. Cumann na bPíobairí, Seattle, 1997, 165 pp.

Walsh, Tommy (ed.), *Irish Piano Accordion*. Waltons, Dublin, 1989, 32 pp; *Irish Tin Whistle Legends*. Waltons, Dublin, 1989, 48 pp.

Weiser, Glenn (ed.), *Celtic Harp Music of Carolan and Others: For Solo Guitar*. Centerstream, LA, 1995, 111 pp.

Woods, Sylvia (ed.), *Forty O'Carolan Tunes for all Harps*. Woods Music and Books, California, 1987, 112 pp; *Irish Dance Tunes for all Harps*. Woods Music and Books, California, 1987, 54 pp.

## MAGAZINES AND PERIODICALS

*Ceol: A Journal of Irish Music*. Vol. 8, nos 1 & 2, 1986. (Breathnach, 47 Frascati Park, Blackrock, Dublin.) Edited by Breandán Breathnach and Nicholas Carolan. Articles on music and song, melodies and song texts, in both Irish and English. Irregularly published. First issue 1963.

*Ceol na hÉireann: Irish Music*. No. 1, 1993, no. 2 1994. (Na Píobairí Uilleann, 15 Henrietta Street, Dublin 1.) Edited by Seán Donnelly, Seán Potts and others. Articles and reviews on music, song and dance. Irregularly published.

*Ceol Tíre*. No. 27, 1985–no. 33, 1989. (Folk Music Society of Ireland, 15 Henrietta Street, Dublin 1.) Edited by Hugh Shields. Newsletter of the Society. Irregularly published. First issue 1973.

*Éigse Cheol Tíre: Irish Folk Music Studies*. Vol. 4 1985. (Folk Music Society of Ireland, 15 Henrietta Street, Dublin 1.) Edited by Hugh Shields, Breandán Breathnach and others. Articles, reviews and a detailed bibliography and discography in each issue. Irregularly published. First issue 1973.

*Irish Music*. Vol. 1, no. 1, 1995. (Lacethorn Ltd., 11 Clare Street, Dublin 2.) Edited by Sean Laffey. A monthly folk and traditional music popular magazine containing reviews, articles and information on events in the Irish music scene.

*Ó Riada Memorial Lectures*. No. 1, 1986, no. 10 1995. (Traditional Music Society, University College Cork.) Edited by authors. Annual series of lectures on Irish music given in University College Cork.

*Píobaire, An*. Vol. 2, no. 24. (Na Píobairí Uilleann, 15 Henrietta Street, Dublin 1.) Edited by Seán Potts. A quarterly newsletter of the Uilleann Pipers' Society. First issue 1969.

*Treoir*. Vol. 17, 1985. (CCÉ, Cearnóg Belgrave, Baile na Manach, Co. Átha Cliath). Edited by Labhrás Ó Murchú. Quarterly house magazine of the Association of Irish Traditional Musicians. Articles, reviews, songs and music. First issue 1968. (MAG)

## MUSIC STUDIES, GENERAL

Acton, Charles, *Irish Music and Musicians: The Irish Heritage Series 15*. Easons and Sons, Dublin, 1978.

Barra, Boydell, *Music and Paintings in the National Gallery of Ireland*. The National Gallery of Ireland, Dublin, 1985, 100 pp.

*Boydell Papers '97, The: Essays on Music Policy in Ireland*. Music Network, Dublin, 1997, 32 pp.

Boullier, Dianna, *Exploring Irish Music and Dance*. O'Brien, Dublin, 1998.

Bradshaw, Harry *Michael Coleman*, Viva Voce/Gael Linn, Dublin 1991, 93.

Breathnach, Breandán, *Dancing in Ireland*. Dal gCais, Miltown Malbay, 1977; *Folk Music and Dances of Ireland*. Mercier, 1971, 1977; *Ceol agus Rince na hÉireann*. An Gúm, Dublin, 1989, 257 pp.

Carolan, Nicholas, *A Harvest Saved: Francis O'Neill and Irish Music in Chicago*. Ossian, Cork, 1997.

Carson, Ciaran, *Pocket Guide to Irish Traditional Music*. Appletree Press, Belfast, 1986, 72 pp. Reprinted 1994 as *Irish Traditional Music*.

Conran, Michael, *National Music of Ireland*. Dublin, 1848.

Cowdery, James R., *The Melodic Tradition of Ireland*. Kent State University Press, 1990, 202 pp. With audio cassette.

Devine, Patrick F., and Harry White (eds.), *Irish Musical Studies 4: The Maynooth International Musicology Conference 1995, Selected Proceedings: Part One*. Four Court Press, Dublin, 1996, 444 pp. See also Gillen, Gerard, for other volumes in the series.

Falc'her-Poyroux, Erick, and Alain Monnier, *La Musique Irlandaise*. Coop Breizh, Kerangwen, 1995, 116 pp.

Flaherty, Bernard (ed.), *Trip to Sligo*. Flaherty, Boyle, 1990, 184 pp.

Flannery, James, *Dear Harp of My Country*. Sanders, Nashville, 1998.

Flood, W. H. Grattan, *A History of Irish Music*. Dublin, 1905, 1906, 1913; Irish University Press, Shannon, 1970; *Sketch of Irish Musical History*, Reeves, London, 1919.

*Folk Music and Dances of Ireland*. Mercier, Cork, 1971, revised 1977, reprinted 1989, 1993; Ossian, Cork, 1996, 152 pp. With audio cassette; Ireland entry in the *New Grove*

*Dictionary of Music and Musicians*, Stanley Sadie (ed.). Macmillan, London, 1980.
Gillen, Gerard, and Harry White (eds.), *Irish Musical Studies 1: Musicology in Ireland*. Irish Academic Press, Dublin, 1990, 312 pp; *Irish Musical Studies 2: Music and the Church*. Irish Academic Press, Dublin, 1993, 354 pp; *Irish Musical Studies 3: Music and Irish Cultural History*. Irish Academic Press, Dublin, 1995, 236 pp; *Irish Musical Studies 5: The Maynooth International Musicological Conference 1995 Selected Proceedings: Part Two*. Four Court Press, Dublin, 1996, 409 pp. See also Devine, Patrick F., for other volume in the series.
Grimes, Robert R., *How Shall We Sing in a Foreign Land? Music of Irish Catholic Immigrants in the Antebellum United States*. University of Notre Dame Press, Notre Dame and London, 1996, 237 pp.
Hand, John, *Irish Street Ballads*. 1875 and Carraig Books, Dublin, 1976 reprint.
Hardiman, James (ed.), *Irish Minstrelsy*, 1831, and Irish University Press, Shannon, 1971 reprint.
Hayden, Jackie, *The Need to Know Guide to the Record Industry*. Foxrock Music Productions, Dublin, 1997, 48 pp.
Henebry, Richard, *A Handbook of Irish Music*. Cork University Press, Cork, 1928; *Irish Music*. An Cló-Chumann, Dublin, 1903.
Keane, Chris, *The Tulla Céilí Band, 1946-1997*. McNamara, Clare, 1998.
Kennedy, Peter (ed.), *Folk Songs of Britain and Ireland*. Cassell, London, 1975.
Lappin, Johnny, *The Need to Know Guide to Music Publishing*. Foxrock Music Productions, Dublin, 1997, 48 pp.
Lennon, Seán, *Lennon's Hits and Myths: A Rapid Music History From Carolan to U2*. Wolfhound Press, Dublin, 1993, 128 pp.
Mac Aoidh, Caoimhín, *Between the Jigs and the Reels*. Drumlin Publications, Co. Leitrim, 1994, 320 pp.
McNamara, Christy and Peter Woods, *The Living Note: The Heartbeat of Irish Music*. O'Brien Press, Dublin, 1996, 160 pp.
McNamee, Peter (ed.), *Traditional Music: Whose Music?* Institute of Irish Studies, Belfast, 1992, 115 pp.
O'Boyle, Seán (Seán Ó Baoill), *The Irish Song Tradition*. Gilbert Dalton, Dublin, 1976.
Ó Canainn, Tomás, *Traditional Music in Ireland*, reprint of 1978 first edn. Ossian Publications, Cork, 1993, 145 pp.
O'Connor, Nuala, *Bringing It All Back Home*. BBC Books, London, 1991, 176 pp.
O'Curry, Eugene, *Musical Instruments of the Ancient Irish*, in *'On The Manners and Customs of the Ancient Irish'*. Dublin, 1873.
Ó hAllmhuráin, Gearóid, *A Pocket History of Irish Traditional Music*. O'Brien, Dublin, 1998.
Ó Muirithe, Diarmuid (ed.), *An tAmhrán Macarónach*. An Clóchomhar, Dublin, 1980; *The Wexford Carols*. Dolmen, Dublin, 1982.
O'Neill, Capt. Francis, *Irish Minstrels and Musicians*, reprint of 1913 first edn. Mercier Press, Cork, 1987, 498 pp; *Irish Folk Music, a Fascinating Hobby* (1910 and 1975); *Irish Minstrels and Musicians* (1913 and reprints).
O'Sullivan, Donal, Ireland entry in *Irish Folk Music and Song*. Dublin, 1952; *Grove's Dictionary of Music and Musicians*. Macmillan, London, 1954; *Carolan: The Life, Times and Music of an Irish Harper*. RKP, London, 1958, reprint 1983, Louth (UK), Celtic Music; *Songs of the Irish*. 1960, Mercier, Cork, reprint 1981.
O'Tuama, Seán, *An Grá in Amhráin na nDaoine*. An Clóchomhar, Dublin, 1960, 1978; *Repossessions*. Cork University Press, Cork, 1996.
Potts, Seán, Terry Moylan, and Liam McNulty, *The Man & His Music: An Anthology of the Writings of Breandán Breathnach*. Na Píobairí Uilleann, Dublin, 1996, 163 pp.
Prendergast, Mark J., *The Isle of Noises*. St Martin's Press, New York, 1990, 315 pp.
Shields, Hugh (ed.), *Popular Music in Eighteenth-Century Dublin*. Folk Society of Ireland and Na Píobairí Uilleann, 1985, 37 pp.
Tansey, Séamus, *The Bardic Apostles of Innisfree*. Tanbar, Craigavon, 1999.
Walker, Joseph C., *Historical Memoirs of the Irish Bards*. Dublin, 1786; reprint 1818, and 1971.

MUSIC STUDIES, INSTRUMENTAL

Britton, Tim, *My Method: A Step by Step Guide for Constructing Reeds for the Irish Uillean* [sic] *Pipes*. Pied Piper Productions, Fairfield, IA 1986, 27 pp; revised edn. Britton, 1994, 39 pp.
Climo, Eddie, *A Handbook for Uilleann Pipers*. South Western Association of Uilleann Pipers, 1996, 48 pp.
Garvin, Wilbert, *The Irish Bagpipes: Their Construction and Maintenance* (2nd edn). Garvin Publications, Ballymena, 1988, 40 pp.
Hegarty, Dave, *Reedmaking made Easy*. NPU, Dublin, 1980.
Kearns, Malachy, *Wallup! Malachy Bodhrán Chats about the Humour and Lore of Bodhrán Making*. Roundstone Musical Instruments, Connemara, 1996, 84 pp.
Kilroy, Peter & Corry, *The Ogham Harp*. Ogham Harps, Kerry, 1988, 10 pp.

Magee, John, *The Heritage of the Harp*. Linen Hall Library, Belfast, 1992, 31 pp.

Maher, Tom, *The Harp's a Wonder*. Uisneach Press, Mullingar, 1991, 147 pp.

Moylan, Terry, *The Regulators: Regulator Maintenance, Tuning and Use*. Na Píobairí Uilleann, Dublin, 1991, 30 pp.

Ó Broin, Seosamh, *Fidileirí: Mayo Fiddlers*. Dreolín Productions, Achadh Mor, Ballyhaunis, Co. Mayo, 1995, 50 pp.

Yeats, Gráinne, *The Harp of Ireland: The Belfast Harper's Festival, 1792 and the Saving of Ireland's Harp, Music by Edward Bunting*. Belfast Harper's Bicentenary Ltd., Belfast, 1992, 71 pp.

## MUSIC STUDIES, VOCAL

Corcoran, Sean, *Here's a Health*. ACNI, Belfast, 1986.

Donaldson, William, *The Jacobite Song*. Aberdeen Univ. Press, 1988.

Graham, Len, *Harvest Home*. ACNI, Belfast, 1993.

*Legend of Danny Boy, The*. The Danny Boy Trading Co. Ltd., Bangor, Co. Down, 1995, 58 pp.

Murphy, Sean, *The Mystery of Molly Malone*. Divelina Publications, Dublin, 1992, 24 pp.

Ó Buachalla, Breandán, *Aisling Ghéar: Na Stíobhartaigh agus an tAos Léinn 1603–1788*. An Clóchomhar Tta., Dublin, 1996, 808 pp.

Ó Conchuir, M. F., *Úna Bhán*. Cló Iar-Chonnachta, Galway, 1994, 245 pp.

Ó Conghaile, Micheál, *Gnéithe D'Amhráin Chonamara Ár Linne*. Cló Iar-Chonnachta, Galway, 1993, 48 pp.

O'Rourke, Brian (ed.), *Blas Meala: A Sip from the Honey Pot*. Irish Academic Press, Dublin, 1985, 128 pp; *Pale Rainbow: An Dubh Ina Bhán*. Irish Academic Press, Dublin, 1990, 105 pp; *When I Grow Up*. Brian O'Rourke and Camus Productions, 1992, 101 pp.

Shields, Hugh, *Narrative Singing in Ireland: Lays, Ballads, Come-All-Yes and Other Songs*. Irish Academic Press, Dublin, 1993, 283 pp; *Oliver Goldsmith and Popular Song*. Folk Music Society of Ireland, Dublin, 1985, 11 pp; *Shamrock, Rose and Thistle* (1981).

*Where the Linnets Sing: Three Generations of the Tunney Family and their songs*. Comhaltas Ceoltóirí Éireann, Dublin, 1993, 32 pp.

Williams, William H. A., *'Twas Only an Irishman's Dream': The Image of Ireland and the Irish in American Popular Song Lyrics, 1800–1920*. University of Illinois Press, Urbana & Chicago, 1996, 311 pp.

## SONG COLLECTIONS IN IRISH

*Amhráin Rithimiúla/Lively Songs*. Comhaltas Ceoltóirí Éireann, Dublin, 1991, 15 pp.

Bowles, Micheál, *Claisceadal I*. Glendale Press, Dublin, 1985, 60 pp; *Claisceadal I, II*. At the Sign of the Anchor, Dublin, 1986, 60 pp.

*Comórtas Amhrán Nuachumtha 1995*. Coiste an Chomórtais, Galway, 1995, 56 pp.

Cussen, Cliodna (ed.), *Inniu an Luan*. Coiscéim, Dublin, 1987, 32 pp.

De Fréine, Seán (ed.), *Sing Along Linn*. Ababúna, Dublin, 1986, 51 pp.

De Noraidh, Liam (ed.), *Ceol ón Mumhain*. An Clóchomhar, Dublin, 1965.

Denver, Gearóid (ed.), *Amhráin Choilm de Bhailis*. Cló Iar-Chonnachta, Galway, 1996, 138 pp.

Freeman, A. Martin (ed.), 'Irish Folk Songs from Ballyvourney', in *Journal of the Folk Song Society*. VI (1920–2, nos. 23–25).

Goan, Cathal, *Róise na nAmhrán: Songs of a Donegal Woman*. RTÉ Commercial Enterprises, Dublin, 1994, 50 pp. With cd and audio cassette.

Gunn, Marion (ed.), *A Chomharsain Éistigí agus Amhráin eile as Co. an Chláir*. An Clóchomhar, Dublin, 1984.

Hughes, Herbert (ed.), *Irish Country Songs*. Boosey and Hawkes, London, 1909–36.

Hyde, Douglas, *Abhráin Grádh Chúige Chonnacht: Love Songs of Connacht*, reprint of 1893 edn. Irish Academic Press, Dublin, 1987, 158 pp; *Abhráin Diadha Chúige Chonnacht* (1906, London, Dublin) (ed.), *Abhráin atá Leagtha ar an Reachtúire* (1903, Dublin; 1933)

Kenny, Adrian (ed.), *An Caisideach Bán: The Songs and Adventures of Tomás Ó Caiside*. Greensprint Ltd., Ballyhaunis, Co. Mayo, 1993, 31 pp.

Laoide, Seosamh (ed.), *Fian-Laoithe* [heroic lays of Ireland and Scotland]. Dublin, 1916.

Mac Aodh, Ristéard Dónal, *Na Fonnadóirí: Taispeántas agus Anailís*. Cló Iar-Chonnachta, Galway, 1996, 95 pp.

Mac Cába, Éanna, *Loscadh Sléibhe: Tomás Mac Eoin agus Máire Uí Fhlatharta*. Cló Iar-Chonnachta, Galway, 1989, 128 pp.

Mac Coluim, Fionán (ed.), *Cosa Buidhe Árda* [dandling songs, lullabies, lilts]. 1922, 23.

Mac Seáin, Séamas (ed.), *Pléaraca Dhún Dealgan – Humours of Dundalk*, 2nd edn. Mac Seáin, Louth, 1985, 68 pp.

Mac Seáin, Pádraig (ed.), *Ceolta Theilinn*. QUB, Inst. of Irish Studies, Belfast, 1973.

Mahon, William (ed.), *Ceol na nOileán: An tAth Tómas Ó Ceallaigh a Chruinnigh*, 2nd edn. Cló

Iar-Chonnachta, Galway, 1990, 151 pp. First edition edited by Tomás Ó Ceallaigh, 1931; *Amhráin Chlainne Gael*, 3rd edn. Cló Iar-Chonnachta, Galway, 1991, 205 pp. First edition edited by Micheál and Tomás Ó Maille, 1905; *Amhráin Ghaeilge an Iarthair*, 2nd edn. Cló Iar-Chonnachta, Galway, 1992, 112 pp. First edition edited by Micheál Ó Tiomanaidhe, 1906.

Mhic Choisdealbha, Eibhlín Bean (ed.), *Amhráin Mhuighe Seóla: Traditional Folk Songs from Galway and Mayo*, reprint of 1923 Talbot Press edition). Cló Iar-Chonnachta, Galway, 1990, 150 pp.

Morris, Henry, see Ó'Muirgheasa, Énri.

Ní Annagáin, Maighréad, and Séamus Clanndiolúin (eds.), *Londubh an Chairn*. London, 1927.

Ní Chinnéide, An Siúr Veronica, *Salm Caintic Cruit: Sailm agus Cainticí le Ceol Cruite is Cláirsí*. Iníonachca Carthanachta, Dublin, 1992, 98 pp.

Ní Riain, Nóirín (ed.), *Ím Bím Babaró*. Mercier Press, Cork, 1997, 84 pp; *Stór Amhrán: A Wealth of Songs From The Irish Tradition*. Mercier Press, 1988, 118 pp. With CD and audio cassette.

Ní Shúilleabháin, Máire (ed.), *Amhráin Thomáis Rua Uí Shúilleabháin*. An Sagart, Maynooth, 1985, 82 pp.

Ní Uallacháin, Pádraigín, *A Stór 's a Stóirín*. (Casette, cd, booklet).

Ó Baoill, Mánus (ed.), *Ceolta Gael, 2*. Mercier Press, Cork, 1986, 100 pp. Reprinted 1990 and 1997 by Ossian publications, Cork.

Ó Baoill, Micheál (ed.), *Dosaen Amhrán do Leanaí*. An Gúm, Dublin, 1985, 38 pp.

O'Boyle, Seán (Seán Ó Baoill), *Cnuasacht de Cheoltaí Uladh*. Comhaltas Uladh, Newry, 1944.

Ó Baoill, Seán Óg, and Mánus Ó Baoill (eds.), *Ceolta Gael*, 5th edn. Mercier Press, Cork, 1993, 96 pp. Reprinted 1997, Ossian Publications, Cork.

Ó Ceallaigh, Proinsias (ed.), *Fáilte Uí Cheallaigh*. Oifig an tSoláthair, Dublin, 1985, 63 pp.

Ó Coigligh, Ciarán (ed.), *Raifteraí: Amhráin agus Dánta*. An Clóchomhar Tta, Dublin, 1987, 253 pp.

Ó Conaire, Breandán (ed.), *Amhráin Chúige Chonnacht 1-3: The Songs of Connacht*. Irish Academic Press, Dublin, 1985, 156 pp.

Ó Conchubhair, Liam, and Derek Bell (eds.), *One Singer Many Songs of the North of Ireland*. The Cultural Traditions Group, n.d., 211 pp.

Ó Conghaile, Micheál (ed.), *Croch Suas É*. Cló Iar-Chonnachta, Galway, 1986, 216 pp. Reprinted 1987, 1989; *Up Seanamhach*. Cló Iar-Chonnachta, Galway, 1990, 176 pp.

Ó Doibhlín, Diarmaid (ed.), *Duanaire Gaedhilge Róis Ní Ógáin*. An Clóchomhar Tta, Dublin, 1995, 136 pp.

Ó hEidhin, Míchéal (ed.), *Cas Amhrán*. Cló Iar-Chonnachta, Galway, 1990, 156 pp.

Ó hÓgáin, Dáithí (ed.), *Binneas Thar Meon, 1*. Comhairle Bhéaloideas Éireann, BÁC, 1994, 269 pp.

Ó Macháin, Pádraig (ed.), *Riobard Bheldon: Amhráin agus Dánta*. The Poddle Press, Dublin, 1995, 158 pp.

Ó Muireadhaig, Lorcán (ed.), *Amhráin Chúige Uladh*. Gilbert Dalton, Dublin, 1977.

Ó Muirgheasa, Énrí (ed.), *Céad de Cheoltaibh Uladh*, 1915, Dublin revised reprint 1983, Comhaltas Uladh; *Dhá Chéad de Cheoltaibh Uladh*, 1930, reprinted 1969, Dublin, Government Publications, Dublin; *Dánta Diadha Uladh*, 1936, reprint 1969.

Ó Néill, Eoin Rua (ed.), *Seoltóireacht Ghéar: Amhráin Sheáin Cheoinín*. Cló Iar-Chonnachta, Galway, 1988, 72 pp.

O'Regan, Susan (ed.), *Read and Sing* (2nd edn) Cumann Náisiúnta na gCór, Cork, 1989, 50 pp.

Shields, Hugh (ed.), *Scéalamhráin Cheilteacha*. An Clóchomhar Tta, Dublin, 1985, 82 pp.

Uí Chuill, Róisín (ed.), *Ceol Diaga do Chóracha*. Cumann Gaelach na hEaglaise, 1993, 70 pp.

### SONG COLLECTIONS IN ENGLISH

Allingham, William, 'Irish Ballad Singers and Irish Street Ballads' (1852), in *Ceol*, III (1967, pp 2–20), with notes and song index by Hugh Shields.

Berry, Paddy (ed.), *Wexford Ballads*. Berry, Wexford, n.d. *More Wexford Ballads*. Berry, Wexford, 1987, 254 pp.

*Best of Irish Music, The: Complete Sheet Music Editions*. Creative Concepts Publishing Corp., California, 1992, 160 pp.

*Best of Percy French, The*. EMI, London, 1985, 40 pp.

Bruckner, Karl, *The Minstrel Boy: Irish Songs and Ballads*. Universal Editions, Wien, Germany, 1995, 9 pp.

*Clannad Past, Present*. Wise Publications, New York, 1989, 35 pp.

*Collection of Irish Ballads Vol. I & II, A*. John Ellison, Co. Wicklow, 1993, 96 pp.

Connolly, Frank (ed.), *The Christy Moore Songbook*, reprint of 1984 edn. Brandon, Kerry, 1989, 142 pp.

Conway, Pat (ed.), *One Hundred Irish Ballads Vol II*. Waltons, Dublin, 1987, 112 pp; *Irish Songs for Harmonica*. Wise Publications, London, 1992, 48 pp; *The Favourite Songs of Ireland*. Wise Publications, London, 1993, 48 pp, *One Hundred Irish Ballads Vol. I*. Waltons, Dublin, 1985, 110 pp.

Coogan, Tim Pat, *Who Fears to Speak?* Canavaun Books, Dublin, 1985, 64 pp.

Corcoran, Seán (ed.), *Here is a Health: Songs, Music and Stories of an Ulster Community*. Arts Council of Northern Ireland, Belfast, 1986, 50 pp; *Harvest Home: It's of My Rambles. Songs and Crack from West Tyrone*. Arts Council of Northern Ireland, Belfast, 1991, 79 pp.

Corp, Ronald (ed.), *Folksongs From Ireland: Selected and Arranged for Voices and Keyboard*. Faber Music, London, 1993, 30 pp.

Crowley, Jimmy (ed.), *Jimmy Crowley's Irish Song Book*. Mercier Press, Cork, 1986, 112 pp.

Crowley, Lisle, *Creative Irish Guitar*. Creative Concepts Publishing, Ventura, California, 1997, 96 pp.

Cuellar, Carol (ed.), *The Book of Golden Irish Songs*. CPP/Belwin Inc., Florida, 1992, 100 pp; *The Chieftains: The Long Black Veil*. Warner Bros. Publications, 1995, 58 pp.

Cunningham, John F., *The People Turned to Stone*. First Friday Publications, Galway, 1989, 20 pp.

Dennehy, Tim, *A Thimbleful of Song*. Góilín Traditional Singers' Club, Dublin, 1989, 24 pp.

Donlon, Pat, and Maddy Glas (eds.), *Moon Cradle – Lullabies and Dandling Songs from Ireland with Old Childhood Favourites*. O'Brien, Dublin, 1991, 64 pp.

Donohue, Mike, *St Helena's Shore*. Camus Productions, Galway, 1987, 33 pp.

Doyle, Danny, and Terence Folan (eds.), *The Gold Sun of Irish Freedom: 1798 in Song and Story*. Mercier Press, Cork/Irish American Book Company, Colorado, 1998, 202 pp.

*Dubliners Songbook, The*. Baycourt Ltd. Editions, Dublin, 1994, 160 pp.

Duffy, Charles Gavan (ed.), *Ballad Poetry of Ireland* (1845, 1866)

Duke, Henry, *Let's Play . . . Songs of Ireland*. Fentone Music, Northants, 1994, 11 pp.

*Duncles 50 Great Irish Ballads Vols. I, II, III*. Ossian Publications Ltd., Cork, 1993, 40 pp.

Evans, Peter, Peter Lavender and Richard O'Mahony (eds.), *101 Irish Songs for Buskers*. Wise Publications, London, 1996, 101 pp.

Ferguson, Howard, *Five Irish Songs: Op. 17 for Voice and Piano*. Boosey & Hawkes, London, n.d., 24 pp; *Irish Folksongs: For Voice and Piano*, reprint of 1956 edition. Boosey & Hawkes, London, n.d., 24 pp.

*Fields of Athenry: Songs of Peter St John, The*. Soodlum (Waltons), Dublin, 1985, 10 pp.

*Fifty-One Lucky Irish Classics*. Warner Bros, New Jersey, n.d., 112 pp.

Fitzmaurice, Gabriel (ed.), *Between the Hills and Seas; Songs and Ballads of Kerry*. Oidhreacht, Kerry, 1991, 52 pp; *Con Greaney, Traditional Singer*. Oidhreacht, Kerry, 1991, 42 pp.

*Folkland. Songs, Music and Stories of Ireland*. Raidió Telifís Éireann, Dublin, 1985, 23 pp.

Foss, Peter (ed.), *Irish and Scottish Favourites*. International Music Publications, 1990, 69 pp.

Fox, Dan (ed.), *The Great Irish Songbook: International Passport Series*. Carl Fischer, New York, 1995, 128 pp.

Galvin, Patrick, *Irish Songs of Resistance 1169–1923*. Oak, New York, 1962.

Graham, Len, *It's of My Rambles . . . Field Recordings from the Irish Tradition No. 2*. Arts Council of Northern Ireland, 1993, 100 pp.

Greaves, Desmond G., *The Easter Rising in Song and Ballad*. Kahn and Averill, London, 1980.

Hammond, David (ed.), *Songs of Belfast*, reprint of 1978 first edn published by Gilbert Dalton. Mercier Press, Cork, 1986, 70 pp.

Hammond, David (ed.), *Songs of Belfast*. Gilbert Dalton, Dublin, 1978.

Hanvey, Bobbie (ed.), *Lilliburlero*. The Ulster Society, 1987, 106 pp; *The Orange Lark*. The Ulster Society, 1988, 95 pp.

*Happiness Is . . . Seventy Irish Songs*. Columbia Pictures Publications, Florida, 1985, 143 pp.

Harte, Frank (ed.), *Songs of Dublin*, reprint of 1978 first edition published by Gilbert Dalton. Ossian Publications, Cork, 1993, 92 pp.

Healy, James N. (ed.), *The Second Book of Irish Ballads*. Mercier, Cork, 1962; *Ballads From an Irish Fireside*. Mercier Press, Cork, 1986, 72 pp. Reprinted 1993 as *Ballads from the Pubs of Ireland Vol 2* and by Ossian, Cork, 1996; *Ballads from the Pubs of Ireland*. Mercier Press, Cork and Dublin, 1985, 80 pp. Reprinted 1988, 1992, and by Ossian, Cork, 1996;*Comic Songs of Ireland*. Mercier Press, Cork, 1986, 1978, 72 pp. Reprinted 1993 as *Ballads from the Pubs of Ireland Vol. 3*, and by Ossian, Cork, 1996; *Irish Ballads and Songs of the Sea*. Mercier Press, Cork, 1987, 80 pp. Reprinted by Ossian, Cork, 1995; *The Songs of Percy French*. Mercier Press, Cork, 1988, 80 pp. Reprinted by Ossian, Cork, 1996.

Hughes, Herbert (ed.), *Irish Country Songs: Highlight Edition*. Boosey & Hawkes, London, 1995, 100 pp.

Huntington, Gale, Lani Herrmann and John Moulden (eds.), *Sam Henry's Songs of the People*. University of Georgia Press, Athens, 1990, 632 pp.

*Ireland the Songs: Books I, II, III, IV*. Walton Music Inc., Westfield MA, 1993, 65 pp.

*John McCormack Song Album*. Boosey & Hawkes, London 1985, 38 pp.

Jones, Margery Hargest (ed.), *Songs of Ireland*. Boosey & Hawkes, London, n.d., 87 pp.

Klose, Carol (ed.), *Easy Piano Irish Favourites*. Hal Leonard Publishing Corporation, Wisconsin, 1993, 96 pp.

Koning, Henk De, *The Dubliners and Their Music: Ambassadors of Irish Folk for a Quarter of a Century*. Vierkan Drukkerij, [Norway] 1987, 123 pp.

Leniston, Florence (ed.), *Popular Irish Songs*. Dover Publications, New York, 1992, 149 pp.

Leyden, Maurice, *Belfast City of Song*. Brandon Books, Kerry, 1989, 178 pp; *Boys and Girls Come Out to Play: A Collection of Irish Singing Games*. The Appletree Press, Belfast, 1993, 152 pp.

*Little Irish Songbook, A*. Appletree Press, Belfast, 1992, 59 pp.

*Little Irish Songbook, A: Illustrated by Ian McCullough*. Chronicle Books, San Francisco, 1992, 59 pp.

Loesberg, John (ed.), *The Irish Pub Songbook*. Ossian Publications, Cork, 1993, 56 pp; *Folksongs & Ballads Popular in Ireland, Vol. 4*. Ossian Publications, Cork, 1989, 100 pp; *More Songs & Ballads of Ireland*. Ossian Publications, Cork, 1993, 56 pp; *Music From Ireland*. Ossian Publications, Cork, 1993, 56 pp; *Songs & Ballads of Ireland*. Ossian Publications, Cork, 1993, 56 pp.

Long, Jack (ed.), *The Joy of Irish Music*. Yorktown Music Press, London, 1997, 63 pp.

MacKenzie, Pat, and Jim Carroll, *Early in the Month of Spring: Songs and a Story from Irish Travellers in England*. Vaughan Williams Memorial Library, London, 1986, 23 pp.

MacMathúna, Séamus, *Traditional Songs and Singers*. CCÉ, Dublin, 1977.

Makem, Tommy, *The Songs of Tommy Makem*. Tin Whistle Music, New Hampshire, 1988, 74 pp.

McBride, Jimmy (ed.), *The Flower of Dunaff Hill*. Crana Publishing Company, Donegal, 1988, 155 pp; and Jim McFarland (eds.), *My Parents Reared Me Tenderly*. McFarland & McBride, Donegal, 1985, 96 pp.

McCrory, Frank (ed.), *Songs of Tyrone*. River Valley Print and Design, Dublin, 1993, 63 pp.

McDonnell, John (ed.), *Songs of Struggle and Protest*. Mercier Press, Cork, 1986, 140 pp.

McElgunn, Sean (ed.), *Songs of the Winding Erne Vol. I & II*. McElygunn, Keadue, 1993, 112 pp.

McGurk, Jim, *Where the River Tarrant Flows*. Dungannon, 1991.

McMahon, Sean (ed.), *The Poolbeg Book of Irish Ballads*. Poolbeg, Dublin, 1991, 188 pp; *Rich and Rare: A Book of Irish Ballads* (revised edition). Poolbeg, Dublin, 1991, 379 pp. First published 1984.

Meek, Bill (ed.), *Irish Folk Songs*. Gill & Macmillan, 1997, 96 pp, *Moonpenny*. Ossian Publications, Cork, 1985, 150 pp; *Songs of the Irish in America*. Gilbert Dalton, Dublin, 1978.

Moore, Thomas A., and Alan Hampton (eds.), *'We'll All Go A-Hunting Today': A Collection of Traditional Sporting Songs Sung at Hunting Parties in Ulster During the Years of the Twentieth Century*. Banbridge, Co. Down, 1992, 25 pp.

Morton, Robin, *Folksongs Sung in Ulster* (1970, Cork, Mercier) [double LP also]; *Come Day, Go Day, God Send Sunday*. RKP, London, 1973.

Moulden, John (ed.), *The Trim Little Borough: Songs of the Coleraine Area and the Causeway Coast*. Coleraine Borough Council, 1992, 12 pp; *Songs of the People* [Sam Henry selections], Blackstaff, Belfast, 1979; *Songs of Hugh McWilliams, Schoolmaster, 1831*. Ulstersongs, Portrush, Co. Antrim, 1993, 24 pp; *Thousands are Sailing: A Brief Song History of Irish emigration*. Ulstersongs, Portrush, Co. Antrim, 1994, 48 pp. With audio cassette; *British Bravery or the Irish Privateer*. Portrush, 1995, 16 pp.

Mulcahy, Michael and Marie Fitzgibbon (eds.), *The Voice of the People* [songs], O'Brien, Dublin, 1982.

Munnelly, Tom, and Marian Deasy (eds.), *The Mount Callan Garland: Songs from the Repertoire of Tom Lenihan of Knockbrack, Miltown Malbay, County Clare*. Comhairle Bhéaloideas Éireann, Dublin, 1994, 153 pp.

Murray, Anne Mulkeen (ed.), *There was Music There in the Derry Air: A Derry Songbook*. Guildhall Press, 1989, 62 pp.

Ó Broin, Seosamh (ed.), *Songs of the Past and People: Singers from East Mayo Vol I & II*. Byrne, Achadh Mór, Mayo, 1994, 37 pp; *Verses from the Woodlands: Songs, Poems and Lore from Willie Grady*, Loughlynn. Dreoilin Community Arts, Mayo, 1996, 54 pp.

Ó Brúdaigh, Seán (ed.), *Bliain na bhFrancach: Songs of 1798 The Year of the French*, reprint of 1981 edition. Cló Elo, Dublin, 1997, 74 pp.

O'Boyle, Carmel (ed.), *Cut the Loaf: The Irish Children's Songbook.* Mercier Press, Cork, 1986, 132 pp; *The Irish Woman's Songbook.* Mercier Press, Cork, 1986, 60 pp.

O'Boyle, Cathal (ed.), *Songs of Co. Down.* Gilbert Dalton, Dublin, 1979.

O'Boyle, Sean, *The Irish Song Tradition.* Gilbert Dalton, Dublin, 1989, 91 pp.

O'Brien-Docker, John (ed.), *Irish Magic.* Peer Music, Hamburg, 1991, 21 pp.

O'Dowda, Brendan (ed.), *The World of Percy French.* The Blackstaff Press, Belfast, 1991, 192 pp. Reprinted 1997.

O'Lochlainn, Colm (ed.), *Irish Street Ballads.* Dublin, 1939, Dublin, reprint 1978, Pan, London, 1965, reprint 1978; *More Irish Street Ballads.* Dublin, 1965, reprint 1978; *Complete Irish Street Ballads.* Pan Books, 1984; *Songwriters of Ireland in the English Tongue.* Dublin, 1967.

O'Sullivan, Donal (ed.), *Songs of the Irish,* 1960, reprint 1981, Mercier, Cork.

Olsen, David C. (ed.), *Fifty-Four Irish Melodies.* Columbia Pictures Publications, Florida, 1985, 127 pp; *World's Best Loved Irish Songs and Melodies.* CPP Belwin Inc., Florida, 1987, 96 pp.

*Orange Song Book, The: A Collection of Songs for all Loyal and True Orangemen and Protestants.* Cumber Claudy Loyal Orange Lodge 649, Claudy, 1986, 104 pp.

*Paddy Reilly Songbook, The.* Conway Editions (Music Sales), London, 1989, 64 pp.

*Pick of Irish Songs, The: Music and Lyrics to a Selection of Irish Pub Songs.* Appletree Press, Belfast, 1996, 48 pp.

*Pint of Irish Ballads, A: Thirty of Ireland's Favourite Songs.* Ossian, Cork, 1993, 30 pp.

*Pocketful of Irish Ballads, A, Vols. I, II, III, IV.* Wicklow Press Ltd, John Ellison, Co. Wicklow, 1995, 32 pp.

Power, Dermot (ed.), *The Ballads and Songs of Waterford from 1487.* Scolaire Bocht Publishing, Waterford, 1992, 193 pp.

Ranson, Joseph (ed.), *Songs of the Wexford Coast.*, 1948; reprint 1975. Norwood.

Robertson, Fleur (ed.), *Irish Ballads.* Bord Failte – Gill & Macmillan, Dublin, 1996, 93 pp.

Russell, Micho, *Micho's Dozen: Traditional Songs from the Repertoire of Micho Russell.* Ennistymon Festival of Traditional Singing, Clare, 1991, 34 pp.

*Selections from Moore's Irish Melodies.* Ossian Publications, Cork, 1986, 36 pp.

Shields, Hugh (ed.), *Shamrock Rose and Thistle.* Blackstaff, Belfast, 1981; *Old Dublin Songs.* Folk Music Society of Ireland, Dublin, 1988, 73 pp.

Shields, Hugh, and Tom Munnelly (eds.), *Early Ballads in Ireland 1968–1985.* Folk Music Society of Ireland, Dublin, 1985, 24 pp.

Silverman, Jerry (ed.), *Songs of Ireland.* Mel Bay Publications, Pacific, MO, 1991, 104 pp.

*Sing an Irish Song.* Dancmac, Dublin, 1985, 28 pp.

Sinnott, Declan (ed.), *The Mary Black Songbook: The authorised version.* Dara Records, Dublin, 1993, 96 pp.

*Songs and Recitations of Ireland, Book I* (An Brat – The Flag), Coiste Foillseacháin Náisiúnta, Cork, 1985, 48 pp.

*Songs of Ireland.* IMP, Essex, 1995, 47 pp.

*Thirty Favourite Songs in Ireland, Vols. I, II, III, IV.* Danmac, Dublin, 1987, 32 pp.

*Traditional Songs and Singers.* Comhaltas Ceoltóirí Éireann, Dublin, 1993, 74 pp.

*Ulster Songbook, The.* Causeway Press, Londonderry, n.d., 76 pp.

*Very Best of Foster & Allen, The.* Soodlum (Waltons), Dublin, 1987, 40 pp.

*Wolfe Tones Song Book, The, Vol. II.* Waltons, Dublin, 1990, 64 pp.

Woods, Armin and Stefan Kohl (eds.), *Famous Irish Songs with the Lyrics, the Score and Guitar Support.* Bergh Publishing, New York, 1991, 179 pp.

*Words of One Hundred Irish Party Songs, Vols. I & II, The.* Bookmark (Ossian Publications), Cork, 1992, 64 pp.

*Words of One Hundred Irish Songs and Ballads, The.* Bookmark (Ossian Publications), Cork, 1992, 68 pp.

Wright, Robert L. (ed.), *Irish Emigrant Ballads and Songs.* Bowling Green, Ohio, 1975.

White, Harry, *The Keeper's Recital.* Cork University Press, Cork, 1998.

Zimmerman, Georges Denis, *Songs of Irish Rebellion.* Allen Figgis, Dublin, 1967.

### THESES AND DISSERTATIONS
### Composers, Collectors and Teaching

Deasey, Marion. 1982. *A New Edition of Airs and Dance Tune from the Music* MS *of George Petrie.* Ph.D., University College Dublin.

Gershen, Paulette. 1989. *Francis O'Neill, Collector of Irish Music, a Biography.* Senior thesis, University of California, 68 pp.

Holohan, Maria. 1995. *The tune compositions of Paddy Fahey.* MA, University of Limerick.

Jardine, Stephen Cannon. 1981. *A Study Of Tunes and Their Assimilation In Irish Traditional Dance Music.* MA University College, Cork.

Kelly, W. N. 1978. Music in Irish Primary Education. MA, University College Cork.

Moloney, Colette. 1995. *The Bunting Manuscripts*. Ph.D., University of Limerick, 1181 pp.

Rogers, David. 1996. *The Music of the Irish Harper Turlough Carolan (1670–1738): Influence, Style and Reception*. MA, University of Oregon, 237 pp.

Uí Eigeartaigh, Caitlín. 1966. *A Thematic Index and Analytical Investigation of the Joyce* MSS, *National Library, Dublin, Nos. 2982–3*. Ph.D., National University, Dublin.

Veblen, Kari Kristin. 1991. *Perceptions of Change and Stability in the Transmission of Irish Traditional Music: An Examination of the Teacher's Role*. Ph.D., University of Wisconsin, 1991, 303 pp.

Willis, Anne. 1971. *Neal's Celebrated Irish Tunes: A Critical Edition*. Ph.D., University College Cork.

## Dance

Austin, Valerie Ann. 1993. *Influences on the Decline of Indigenous Irish Music in the 20th Century: The Dance Halls Act, 1935*. M. Mus., University of Florida, 148 pp.

Brennan, Helen. 1994. *Dancing on Plate, the Sean-Nós Dance Tradition of Connemara*. MA, Queen's University Belfast.

Cullinane, John. 1998. *History of Irish Dancing in Cork 1890–1940*. MA, University College Cork, 130 pp.

Danaher, Marie. 1991. *Irish Dance Costumes*. Dip. FD, LSAD, 59 pp.

Flanagan, Kathleen. 1995. *The History of the Development and Promotion of Irish Dancing in Chicago 1893–1953*. Ph.D. vol 1, 2. 112 pp + .k

Foley, Catherine. 1988. *Irish Traditional Step dancing in North Kerry*. Ph.D., CNAA. London, 356 pp.

Hall, Frank. *Irish Dancing – Discipline as Art, Sport, and Duty*. Ph.D., Indiana University. 1995. 210 pp.

Hall, Reginald Richard. 1994. *Irish Music and Dance in London, 1890–1970: A Socio-Cultural History, Parts I and II*. Ph.D., University of Sussex, 554 pp.

Neville, Andrea. 1996. *From Céilís to Riverdance, the Changing face of Irish Dance Costumes*. Dip. FD, LSAD, 42 pp.

Nic Ghabhainn, Aine. 1998. *The Dancing Master*. unpublished thesis for BA., University College Dublin.

Peake, A. 1996. *Post Colonialism and the Development of Irish Dance*. MA, De Montford University, 101 pp.

Robb, M. 1995. *Irish Dancing Costumes: elements of History and Design*. B.Tec.Des., National College of Art and Design, 104 pp.

Smulder, L. 1974. *De Ierse Volkdans*. Thesis for licentiate in de Lichamelijke, Katholieke, Universiteit, Leuven, Belgium, 152pp + i–viii.

Sorohan. R. 1977. *Irish Dancing: an Investigation into what it is, its Organisation and its Social Origins*. London.

## Performance, instrument and repertoire

Buckley, Ann. 1972. *The Tiompán*. MA, University College Cork.

Casey, Conor. 1994. *The Rise of the Didjeridu in Irish Traditional Music*. MA, Queen's University Belfast.

Culloty, Gerry. 1996. *The Role of the Drum-Kit in Traditional Irish Music*. MA, University of London, 40 pp.

Fairbairn, Hazel. 1993. *Group Playing in Traditional Irish Music: Interaction and Heterophony in the Session*. Ph.D., Corpus Christi College, Cambridge, 388 pp.

Hamilton, S. C. 1978. *The Session: A Socio-Musical Phenomenon in Irish Music*. MA, Queen's University Belfast.

Hutchinson, Patrick. 1991. *The Work and Words of Piping*. MA, Brown University, 67 pp.

Mitchell, Mary, *Repertoire and Style of Six Kerry Musicians*. MA, University of Limerick.

Ní Fhionghaile, Nollaig. 1990. *The Adoption and Transformation of the Greek Bouzouki in the Irish Music Tradition*. M. Mus., University of London, 73 pp.

Nic Suibhne, Damhnait. 1993. *Repertoire in the Donegal Fiddle Tradition*. MA, University College Cork.

Ó hAllmhuráin, Gearóid. 1990. *The Concertina in the Traditional Music of Clare, Parts I & II*. Ph.D., Queen's University Belfast, 482 pp.

O'Callaghan, Donal. 1978. *Trumpets of the Irish Bronze Age*. MA, University College Cork.

Schiller, Rina. 1995. *The Lambeg and the Bodhrán: A Comparative Organological Study*. MA, Queen's University Belfast.

Scullion, Fionnuala M. B. 1982. *The Lambeg Drum in Ulster*. MA, Queen's University Belfast.

## Recording and technology

Dunne, Denise and Edel Reilly. 1995. *The Influence of RTÉ Radio on Traditional Irish Music*. BA, University College Dublin, 26 pp.

Hamilton, S. C. 1996. *The Role of Commercial Recordings in the Development of Irish Traditional Music 1899–1993*. Ph.D., University of Limerick.

Ní Fhuartháin, Méabh 1993. *O'Byrne Dewitt and Copley Records: A Window On Irish Music*

*Recording in the U.S.A., 1900–65.* MA, University College Cork Cork, 180 pp.

Ó Maidín, Donncha Seán. 1995. *A Programmer's Environment for Music Analysis.* Ph.D., University College Cork, 284 pp.

Shields, Geraldine. 1991. *Graphic Design of Irish Traditional Music Recordings: From Wax Cylinder to Compact Disc.* Graduate thesis. Dublin Institute of Technology, Dublin, 56 pp.

## Sociology, politics and identity

Curtis, Bernard Francis. 1971. *Music in Belfast in the 19th century.* MA, Queen's University Belfast.

Hubbard, Jane Anne, 1993. *Children's Play, Songs and Games in Derry: A Social Anthropological Study.* Ph.D., Queen's University Belfast.

Jacobsen, Helle Eble. 1996. *Irsk Folkemusik – Tradition og Fornyelse.* Graduate thesis, University of Copenhagen, 127 pp.

Kearney, A. 1981. *Temperance Bands and their Significance in 19th Century Ireland.* MA, University College Cork.

King, Norah. 1977. *The Flute Band of Northern Ireland.* MA, Queen's University Belfast.

Lundh, Lise. 1991. *Music, Pubs and 'Crack' in Belfast: perspectives on revival of traditional music in Belfast.* MA, Queen's University Belfast.

McAuley, Marion. 1989. *Aspects of Stylistic Change in Irish Traditional Dance Music.* MA, University College Cork.

McCann May. 1985. *The Past in the Present: A Study of Some Aspects of the Politics of Music in Belfast.* Ph.D., Queen's University Belfast.

McCarthy, Marie F., *Music Education and the Quest for Cultural Identity in Ireland 1831– 1989.* Ph.D., University of Michigan, 1990, 492 pp.

McKeon, M. 1995. *The Construction of Performance, Place and Identity in Counties Antrim & Derry Fiddlers Association.* MA, Queen's University Belfast.

Moloney, Michael. 1992. *Irish Music in America: Continuity and Change.* Ph.D., University of Pennsylvania, 624 pp.

Ní Earcáin, Treasa. 1995. *Issues of Celtic Identity: A Study of the Festival Interceltique de Lorient.* MA, Queen's University Belfast.

O'Connor, Annie. 1934. *A Short General Survey of the History of Irish Folk Music.* MA, University College Cork.

Vallely, Fintan. 1993. *Protestant Perceptions in Traditional Music.* MA, Queen's University, Belfast, 166 pp.

## Song

Neilands, Colin Weston. 1986. *Irish Broadside Ballads in Their Social and Historical Contexts, Vol. I & II.* MA, Queen's University Belfast, 52 pp.

Ní Riain, Nóirín. 1980. *The Music of Traditional Religious Song in Irish.* MA, University College Cork.

## Style

Casey, Michael T. 1989. *Traditional Irish Flute Music from East Galway: A Regional Study.* MA, Chapel Hill, Virginia, 178 pp.

Cunningham, Órla. 1996. *The Development of Irishness in Art and Popular Music.* B. Mus., University of Wales, College of Cardiff, 116 pp.

Keegan, Niall S. 1992. *The Words of Traditional Flute Styles.* MA, University College Cork.

Ó Súilleabháin, Mícheál. 1987. *Innovation and Tradition in the Music of Tommy Potts.* Ph.D., Queen's University, Belfast.

Ring, Brendan. 1992. *Travelling Style: The Uilleann Piping of Paddy Keenan.* MA, University College Cork.

Sky, Cathy Larson. 1997. *'I'd Barter Them All' – Elements of Change in the Traditional Music of County Clare, Ireland.* University of North California at Chapel Hill, Virginia, 142 pp.

Smith, Graeme, 1990. *The Social Meaning of Irish Button Accordion Playing Styles from 1900–75.* Ph.D., Monash University, Australia, 505 pp.

Wilkinson, Desmond J. 1991. *'Play me a lonesome reel'. Factors relating to the building of a musical style and the social reality of performance in the Sligo/Leitrim region of north west Connacht.* MA, Queen's University, Belfast, 88 pp.

## Research in progress

Cranitch, Matt, Ph.D., Padraig O'Keeffe and the Sliabh Luachra Fiddle Tradition, UL.

Dillane, Aibhlín, MA, Harmonic Accompaniment in Irish Traditional Music, UL.

Higgins, Jim, MA, Contemporary Developments in Bodhrán Performance Technique, UL.

Joyce, Sandra, Ph.D., The Life and Music of Turlough O Carolan, UL.

Keegan, Niall, Ph.D., Communication Beyond Performance: Notation and Speech About Traditional Irish Music, UL.

McCann, Anthony, Ph.D., Copyright as a Key to Cultural Analysis: An Analysis of Copyright in the Context of Irish Traditional Music, UL.

McCarthy, Johnny, MA, A Trip to the City: Myth and Music in Sliabh Luachra, UL.

McGettrick, Paul, Ph.D., Tune Simulation and Performance in Irish Traditional Music, UL.

Mercier, Mel, Ph.D., The Development of Irish Popular/Traditional Music, UL.

Ní Chonaráin, Siobhán, *Sources of Irish Music*. Mary I.

Ní Shúilleabháin, Eilís, *Songs and Singers of Gaeltacht* Mhúscaraí. MPhil.

O'Brien-Moran, Jimmy, MA, The Henry Hudson Collection of Irish Traditional Music, UL.

O'Keeffe, Máire, Ph.D., A Journey into Tradition: The Position of the Irish Button Accordion, UL.

Randles, Shiela, MA, The Fiddle Music of Connie O'Connell, UL.

Trew, Johanne, Ph.D., Ethnicity and Identity: Music and Dance in the Ottawa Valley, UL.

Vallely, Fintan, Ph.D., Flute band influence on Traditional music in North Connacht, UCD.

Wilkinson, Desi, Ph.D., Traditional Music in Brittany and its Irish ingredient, UL.

# SELECT DISCOGRAPHY

This discography gives a sample of mostly currently available material, usually on CD. Some of the items have been issued on LP or cassette only, and some are not commercially available. Many of the items listed have also been released elsewhere, for instance Ossian have licensed a large selection of early Topic material, while Shanachie and Green Linnet both re-issue material already available in Ireland. Most of the major groups and soloists are covered. Information on early twentieth-century 78 recordings – few of which are listed here – can be found in Richard Spottswood's *Ethnic Music on Record* (vol. 5, 1990); further details of songs in Ulster are located in the appendix to the Sam Henry collection. Other discographies are listed in the bibliography section. The ITMA, which has a computer listing of performers and recordings from non-commercial as well as commercial sources, is probably the best source of information on older recordings. The best sources of information on currently available albums are the catalogues from the major Irish labels and distributors such as Claddagh, Gael-Linn, Shanachie, Green Linnet and Ossian.

### ACCORDION

Begley, Brendan, *Seana Choirce* (CEFC 123); *We Won't Go Home 'til Morning* (KM 9510)
Burke, Joe, *Galway's Own* (OLP 1015), *Traditional Music of Ireland* (SIF 1048), *A Tribute to Michael Coleman* [with Andy McGann] (SIF 3097), *The Bucks of Oranmore* [with Charlie Lennon] (GLCD 1165)
Byrne, Dermot, *Dermot Byrne* (HBCD 0007 & GLCD 3113)
Clifford, John, *The Humours of Lisheen* [with Julia Clifford] (12TS 311)
Coffey, Aidan, *Séamus Creagh and Aidan Coffey* (OSSCD 112)
Connolly, Johnny Óg, *Dreaming up the Tunes* [with Brian McGrath] (CICD 133); *The Bee's Wing* (CIC 026)
Cooley, Joe, *Cooley* (CEFCD 044), *The Bucks of Oranmore* [with Charlie Lennon] (GLCD 1165)
Daly, Jackie, *Jackie Daly* (12TS 358), *Jackie Daly agus Séamus Creagh* [with Séamus Creagh] (CEFCD 057); *Music From Sliabh Luachra* (GLCD 3065); *Eavesdropper* [with Kevin Burke] (LUNCD 039); *Domnach is Dálach, Many's A Wild Night* (CEFCD 176)
De Barra, Dómhnall, *Munster Sets and Things* (CEF 093)
Derrane, Joe, *The Tie That Binds* (Shanachie 78009), *Give us Another* (GLCD 1149), *Return to Inis Mór* (GLCD 1163)
Donohue, Martin, *Free Spirit* (CICD 89)
Doody, Denis, *Denis Doody Plays Kerry Music* (LUN 019)
Dwyer, Finbarr, *Pure Traditional Irish Accordion Music* (PTICD 1004); *The Best of Finbarr Dwyer* (OLP 1011); *Ireland's Own* (OLP 1016); *Star of Ireland* (PSH 106); *Ireland's Champion Traditional Accordionist* (SOLP 1032); *Pure Trad Accordion* (PTICD 1004)
Gardiner, Bobby, *The Best of Bobby Gardiner* (CCÉ CL 21), *The Clare Shout* (BG 007)
Hernon, P. J., *P. J. Hernon* (CEFCD 065); *First House in Connaught* (GTDHC 075); *The Floating Crowbar* [with Marcus] (GTDHC 097); *Béal a' Mhurlaigh* (CEFCD 141)
Keane, Conor, *Cooley's House* (CKCD 01); *Oidhreacht* (CKCD 02)
Keane, James, *The Irish Accordion of James Keane* (Rex 808); *That's the Spirit* (GLCD 1138); *Roll Away the Reel World* [with Seán Keane] (SIF 1026); *With Friends Like These* (Shanachie 78015)
Learaí, Choilm, *Accordion* (SC 2026)
Loughlin, Kevin, *All-Ireland Champion Traditional Accordionist* (SOLP 1039)
MacMahon, Tony, *Tony MacMahon* (CEF 033, Shanachie 34006); *Aislingí Ceoil* (CEFCD 164), *I gCnoc na Graí* [with Noel Hill] (CEF 114)
Marsh, Josephine, *Accordion Music* (JMCD 001)
McComiskey, Billy, *Makin' the Rounds* (SIF 1034)
Mulcahy, Mick, *Mick Mulcahy* (Gael-Linn 050), *Mick Mulcahy agus Cáirde* (CEFCD 143)
Mulvihill, Charlie, *Atlantic Wave* [tracks] (KM 9513) [with Paddy Reynolds and James Keane] (RIR 1000)
Murphy, Rose, *Milltown Lass* [fiddle also] (12 TS 316)
Ó Beaglaíoch, Séamus and Máire, *Plancstaí Bhaile na Buc* (CEFC 138)

O'Brien, Paddy [Offaly], *Is it Yourself?* (Shanachie 29015); *Spring in the Air* (Shanachie 29018) [both with James Kelly]; *Hill 16* (Meadowlark 101); *Stranger At the Gate* (GLCD 1091)

O'Brien, Paddy [Tipperary], *The Banks of the Shannon* [with Séamus Connolly] (GLCD 3082)

O'Connor, Máirtín, *The Connachtman's Ramble* (LUNCD 027); *Chatterbox* (DARACD 052); *Perpetual Motion* (CCF 26CD)

O'Leary, Johnny, *Music for the Set* (12TS 357, OSS 25); *An Calmfhear/The Trooper* (CEFCD 132), *Johnny O'Leary of Sliabh Luachra* (CRCD 01)

Shannon, Sharon, *Sharon Shannon* (ROCD 8); *Out the Gap* (ROCD 14, GLCD 3099); *Each Little Thing* (GRACD 226, GLCD 3116)

Staunton, Mary, *Bright Early Mornings* (FMCD 001)

Teahan, Mattie, *Trip to Sliabh Arda* (MC 001)

Teahan, Terry (Cuz), *Terry Teahan and Gene Kelly* (12TS 352); *Irish Traditional Instrument Music in Chicago* (Rounder 6006); *Chicago Irish Musicians* (IMA 82 513)

Whelan, John, *Fresh Takes* [with Eileen Ivers] (SIF 1075); *Pride of Wexford* (SOLP 1024); *Celtic Crossroads* (ND 61060)

Williams, John, *John Williams* (GLCD 1157)

**BALLADS**

Barnbrack, *Irish Folk Pub Sing Along* (CDHRL 199)

Clancy Brothers, *The Clancy Brothers and Tommy Makem* (TCD 1022), *The Men of the West* (SUMMIC 4073); *Reunion* (Shanachie 52038); *Story of the Clancy Brothers* (Shanachie V 201); *Reunion Concert* (Shanachie V 202)

Corrib Folk, *Best of Irish Folk Music* (CDBALLAD 006)

Dublin City Ramblers, *Best of the Dublin City Ramblers* (DOCDX 9005); *Festival of Irish Folk Music* (CHC 1035)

Dubliners, The, *Collection* (CHCD 1011); *20 Original Greatest Hits* (CHCD 1028); *Instrumentals* (CHCD 1052); *The Dubliners* (TRTCD 205)

*Forty Folk Ballads* (2DHXCD 806)

*Forty Irish Pub Songs* (CDPUB 026)

Furey Brothers, *Festival of Irish Folk Music* (CHC 1035); *Winds of Change* (Shanachie 52037); *Best of the Fureys* (TRTCD 137)

*Legends of Ireland* [compilation: Clancys, Dubliners, Johnstons, Sweeny's Men, Planxty]

Reilly, Paddy, *The Very Best of Paddy Reilly* (PTRV CD 1); *Festival of Irish Folk Music* (CHC 1035)

Wolfe Tones, *25 Years of Greatness* (Shanachie 52024/5)

**BANJO**

Carty, John, *The Cat That Ate the Candle* (CIC 099), *At the Racket* [with Christy Dunne] (RR001); *Pluckin Good* (MDLMCD 03)

Hanrahan, Kieran, *Plays Irish Tenor Banjo* (BDCD 001)

Hayden, Cathal, *Handed Down* (RBC 116)

Keenan, Johnny, *Dublin Banjos* [with K. Sullivan] (HM 309)

McGrath, Brian, *Dreaming Up the Tunes* [with Johnny Óg Connolly] (CICD 133); *At the Racket* [with John Carty and Séamus O'Donnell] (RR 001)

Moloney, Mick, *Strings Attached* (GLCD 1027); *Kilkelly* (GLCD 1072); *There Were Roses* (GLCD 1057); *With Eugene O'Donnell* (SIF 1010); *Uncommon Bonds* (SIF 1053); *Three Way Street* (GLCD 1129)

O'Connor, Gerry, *Time to Time* (LUNCD 051)

**BODHRÁN**

Conneff, Kevin, *The Week Before Easter* [with Paul McGrattan, Máire O'Keeffe] (CCF 23)

Davey, Junior, *Skin and Bow* [with Declan Folan] (SUNCD 23)

Hayes, Tommy, *An Rás* (LUNCD 055); *A Room in the North* (OPPCD 001)

Mercier, Mel, *Casadh* [item] (CDVE 904); *Oileán* (CDVE 10)

Morton, Robin, *Music From Co. Leitrim* (12 TS 339)

Murphy, Colm, *An Bodhrán/The Irish Drum* (CEFCD 175)

**BONES AND SPOONS**

Hayes, Tommy, *A Room in the North* (OPPCD 001)

McLoughlin, John, *Paddy in the Smoke* [spoons, item] (OSS 19)

Mercier, Mel, *Casadh* (CDVE 904); *Oileán* (CDVE 10)

Neylan, Paddy, *Lark in the Clear Air* [spoons, item] (OSSCD 13)

**BOUZOUKI**

Finn, Alec, *Alec Finn* [with Frankie Gavin] (Shanachie 34009); *Blue Shamrock* (CBM CD 011)

Lunny, Dónal, *Dónal Lunny* (CEFCD 133)

**CÉILÍ BANDS**

*Aughrim Slopes Céilí Band* [re-released 78s] (IAA 005)

Ballinakill, *Irish Dance Music* [with Moate, Siamsa Gael, Kincora] (TSCD 602)

Castle Céilí Band, *Irish Pub Music* (Artfolk SB 314); *Castle Céilí Band* (CCÉ)

Donal Ring Céilí Band, *Come to the Céilí* (HSMC 048); *21st Anniversary* (HSMC 18)
*Glenside and Kilfenora Céilí Bands* (MATMC 219)
Harp and Shamrock Orchestra, *Irish Dance Music* (FW 8821)
Kilfenora Céilí Band, *Kilfenora 1995* (HHCD 141); *Set on Stone* (TOLCD 1)
Kincora Céilí Band, *Ceol Tíre* (CCÉ CL 12); *Irish Dance Music* [with Ballinakill, Moate, Siamsa Gael] (TSCD 602)
Kips Bay Céilí Band, *Digging In* (GLCD 1130)
*Liverpool Céilí Band* (LPR 1001, LPR 1006)
Malachy Doris Céilí Band, *Irish Dance Time* (CG 006)
Matt Cunningham, *The Green Hills of Erin* (ARCD 020); *Memories of Ireland* (ARCD 021); *West of Old River Shannon* (ARCD 022)
*McCusker Brothers* (33ST 138)
Moate Céilí Band, *Irish Dance Music* [78 recordings] (TSCD 602)
Moving Cloud, *Moving Cloud* (GLCD 1150); *Foxglove* (GLCD 1186)
Pride of Erin, *Harvest Time in Ireland* (COX 1036)
Shaskeen, *25th Silver Jubilee* (CDFA 3509); *Live* [for set dancing] (CFA 3506, 07, 10); *Music for Set Dancing* (CDFA 350206)
Siamsa Gael, *Irish Dance Music* [with Moate, Ballinakill, Kincora] (TSCD 601)
Swallow's Tail, *Hell for Leather* (Sun CD 28)
Templehouse, *Music for the sets vol. 1* (LNMC 7024); *Crossroads Céilí* (CHCS 015)
Tulla Céilí Band (HMV 78 (1956), IP 1147, 1149, 1150, 1157); *Echoes of Erin* (SLP 903, 1958); *Tulla Céilí Band* (EP 1970); *The Claddagh Ring* (STAL 1 1002); *Ireland Green* (STAL 1 1029); *Sweetheart in the Spring* (ISLE 3004), *40th Anniversary* (GTDC 014); *A Celebration of Fifty Years* (GLCD 1178)

CÉILÍ DANCE

Cunningham, Matt, *Come to the Céilí* (ARV 004) video
Hurley, Olive, *Irish Dancing Step by Step* (ARV 003) video
Malachy Doris Céilí Band, *Irish Dance Time* (CG 006)
*Rince – Irish Dancing, Beginners' First Steps* (CL 501); *Rince 2* (CL 502)
*Twenty Irish Dances* (OP 132)

COMPILATIONS (MUSIC AND SONG – RADIO, TV, COMPETITION AND COMPANY SELECTIONS)

Alan Lomax Collection (1951), Vol. 1, *Ireland* [Máire Ní Shúilleabháin, Séamus Ennis, Seán Moriarity, Elizabeth Cronin, Kitty Gallagher, Maigí Ní Dhonnchadha, Mickey Cronin, Máire Seoighe, Colm Ó Caoidheán, Seán 'ac Dhonnchadha, Cáit Ní Mhuimhneacháin, Máire Ní Cheocháin] (Rounder CD 1742)
*Amhrán ar an Sean Nós* [song] (RTÉ 185)
*An Bóthar Cam* (CEF 035)
*Beauty an Oileán* (CC56CD)
*Blas* (RTÉ 161)
*Blas Meala/A Sip from the Honeypot* [from book of same title, 1 & 2] (GTDC 050 & 051)
*Céad Slán le Camus* [Colm Ó Méalóid] (CIC 002)
*Céilí House on the Road* (RTÉ 169)
*Céilí House Saturday Night* (RTÉ 128)
*Forever by Dingle Shore* (Sulán LNLP 1003)
*Ireland/Irlande* [Colm Ó Caoidheán, Cáit Ní Mhuimhneacháin, Nioclás Tóibín, Neilí Ní Dhomhnaill, Val Ó Flatharta] (Auvidis, UNESCO D 8271)
Mac Mathúna, Ciarán, *Job of Journeywork* (RTÉMC 124); *Mo Cheol Thú* (CEFCD 064); *Silver Jubilee* (RTÉMC 191); *Lark in the Clear Air* (RTÉMC 125)
*Mighty Session* (DB001)
*Orchiste Ceoil, Amhránaíocht 1/A Treasury of Irish Song* [Clannad, Maighréad Ní Dhómhnaill, Tríona Ní Dhomhnaill, Iarla Ó Lionáird, Dolores Keane, Mary Black, Deirbhile Ní Bhrolcháin, Áine Uí Cheallaigh, Mairéad Ní Mhaonaigh] (CDTCD 004)
*Pale Rainbow/An Dubh ina Bhán* [from book of same title, 1 & 2] (CP 006, CP 007)
*Seachrán Sídhe* (CICD 135)
*The Star of Munster* (CEF 035)
*Tógfaidh Mé Mo Sheolta* (CIC 088)
*Togha Agus Rogha* [2 CDs, selections of mixed-genre song, Raidió na Gaeltachta] (RTE 204 CD)
Ritchie, Jean, *As I Roved Out* (FW 8872, OSS 15)
*Seoda Chonamara* 1 (CIC 019)
*Traditional Music of Ireland*, Vol. 1 [Máire Áine Nic Dhonncha, Willie Clancy, Denis Murphy] (CICD 033)

CONCERTINA

Bingham, Terry, *Terry Bingham* (TBMC 001)
Droney, Chris, *The Fertile Rock* (CIC 110)
Hill, Noel, *The Irish Concertina* (CEF21 CD, 1988); *Aislingí Ceoil* (CEFCD 164); *I gCnoc na Grai* [with Tony MacMahon] (CEF 114); *Fiddle and Concertina* [with Tony Linnane] (TACD 2006); *Irish Traditional Concertina Styles* (Topic-Free Reed 506)
Kelly, John, *John Kelly* (Topic-Free Reed 504)
McCarthy, Tommy, *Sporting Nell* (MMCCD 52)
McNamara, Mary, *Traditional Music from East Clare* (CC60CD)

Mullally, William, *Concertina* [from 78s] (VV 005)

Ó hAllmhuráin, Gearóid, *Traditional Music From Clare and Beyond* (OWR 0046)

O'Sullivan, Bernard, Tommy McMahon, *Clare Concertinas* (Topic-Free Reed 502, GLCD 3092)

Russell Gussie, *The Russell Family* (Topic 1977)

Williams, John, *John Williams* (GLCD 1157)

**DULCIMER**

Carroll, Barry, *The Long Finger* [with Joe McHugh] (JMB 1991)

Dalglish, Malcolm, *Banish Misfortune* [with Grey Larsen] (June Appal, 1977)

James, David, *Tiompán Alley* (TAM 003)

Rea, John, *Traditional Irish Music on the Hammer Dulcimer* (12TS 373); *Drops of Brandy* [with Seán McAloon] (12TS 287)

**FIDDLE**

Boyle, Néillidh, *The Moving Clouds* (FSA 60 170)

Bradley, Paul, *Tuaim na Farraige/Atlantic Roar* (PTICD 1090)

Breatnach, Máire, *The Voyage of Bran* (SCD 394); *Angels' Candles* (SCD 593), *Celtic Lovers* (SCD 696)

Brown, Mick, *Fiddle Music of Donegal* (CNF 001)

Burke, Kevin, *If the Cap Fits* (LUNCD 021), *Sweeny's Dream* (OSSCD 18); *Promenade* (LUNCD 028); *Portland* (GLCD 1041), *Up Close* (GLCD 1052); *Eavesdropper* [with Jackie Daly] (LUNCD 039)

Burke, Kevin, Séamus Creagh, Paddy Glackin and Seán Keane, *An Fhidil 2* (CEFC 069)

Byrne, James, *The Road to Glenlough* (CC52CD) [with Francie Byrne]; *The Brass Fiddle* (CC44CD); *Ceol na dTéad* [with Mickey Byrne] (CIC 078)

Byrnes, Martin, *Martin Byrnes* (LEA 2004)

Campbell, Jimmy, *Fiddle Music of Donegal* (CNF 001)

Campbell, Vincent, *The Brass Fiddle* (CC44CD)

Canny, Paddy, *Traditional Music from the Legendary East Clare Fiddler* (CICD 129)

Carroll, Liz, *A Friend Indeed* (Shanachie 34013); *Liz Carroll* (GLCD 1092)

Carty, John, *Last Night's Fun* (Shanachie 79098)

Casey, Bobby, Junior Crehan, John Kelly, Patrick Kelly and Joe Ryan, *Ceol an Chlár 1* (CCÉ CL 170); [with Willie Clancy] (FSA 30 173); *Casey in the Cowhouse* (Bellbridge 001)

Cassidy, Con, *The Brass Fiddle* (CC44CD)

Clifford, Julia, *Kerry Fiddles* [with Pádraig O'Keeffe and Denis Murphy] (OSSCD 10); *Ceol as Sliabh Luachra* (CEFCD 092)

Coleman, Michael, *Michael Coleman 1891–1945* (Gael-Linn/Viva Voce CEFCD 161)

Collins, Kathleen, *Traditional Music of Ireland* (SHCD 34010); *Kathleen Collins* (Shanachie 29002)

Connolly, Séamus, *The Banks of the Shannon* [with Paddy O'Brien] (GLCD 3082); *Notes from my Mind* (GLCD 1087), *Here and There* (GLCD 1098); *Warming Up* [with Martin Mulhaire and Jack Coen] (GLCD 1135)

Conway, Brian, *The Apple in Winter* [with Tony De Marco] (GLCD 1035)

Cranitch, Matt, *Take a Bow* (OSSCD 5); *Give it Shtick* (OSSCD 6); *Sliabh Notes* (CBMCD 018)

Creagh, Séamus, *Jackie Daly and Séamus Creagh* (CEFCD 057); *Came the Dawn* (OSSCD 90); *Seamus Creagh, Aidan Coffey* (OSSCD 112)

Crehan, Junior, *Ceol an Chláir 1* [with Bobby Casey, John Kelly, Patrick Kelly and Joe Ryan] (CCÉ CL 17)

Cronin, Paddy, *Kerry's Own* (OAS 3002)

Custy, Mary, *Mary Custy and Eoin O'Neill* (Custy, Ennis)

Doherty, John, *Bundle and Go* (OSSCD 17); *The Floating Bow* (CCF31CD), *Taisce, The Celebrated Recordings* (CEFCD 072)

Dolan, Packie, *The Forgotten Fiddle Player* (VV 006)

Donnelly, Des, *Remember Des Donnelly* (Donnelly DD 01)

Donnelly, Desi, *Live in Hamburg* (MMRCD 1005); *Welcome* [with song] (MMRCD 1005); *Champions of the North* [with Michael McGoldrick] (MMRCD 801)

Dowling, Martin, *A Thousand Farewells* [with Christine Dowling] (CM 001)

Farr, Lucy, *Heart and Home: Irish Fiddle Music from Lucy Farr* (Veteran Tapes, Suffolk, 1992)

Finn, Fred, *Music of Sligo* [with Peter Horan] (CCÉ CL 33)

Furey, Ted, *Toss the Feathers* (OLP 1020)

Gardiner, John Joe, *Ceol Tire* (CCÉ CL 12); *Flutes of Old Erin* (VV 002)

Gavin, Frankie, *Frankie Gavin and Alec Finn* (Shanachie 34009); *Croch Suas É* (CEFCD 103); *Frankie Goes to Town* (BKCD 001); *Best of Frankie Gavin* (RTÉ CD 187); *Shamrocks and Holly* (Shanachie 78004); *Omós do Joe Cooley* [with Paul Brock] (CEFCD 115)

Gillespie, Hugh, *Classic Recordings* (12T 364); *Traditional Recordings of Irish Fiddle Music* (GLCD 3066)

Glackin, Kevin and Séamus, *Na Saighneáin/Northern Lights* (CEFCD 140)

Glackin, Paddy, *Paddy Glackin and Jolyon Jackson* (4TA 2009); *Paddy Glackin* (CEF 060); *Rabharta Ceoil* (CEFCD 153), *Paddy Glackin* and Robbie Hannan (CEFCD 171); *Flags of Dublin* (OSS 31); *Doublin* [with Paddy Keenan] (4TA 2007)

Gorman, Michael, *The Mountain Road* (FSA 60 174); *Irish Music in London Pubs* [item] (CIC 032)

Griffin, Vincent, *Fiddle Music From Co. Clare* (OSS 73)

Gunn, Tommy, *Ulster's Flowery Vale* [item] (BBC 28M, 1968); *Good Friends, Good Music* (Philo CD PH 105 1, 1997); *Celtic Mouth Music* (Ellipsis Arts CD 4070, 1997)

Hayes, Martin, *Martin Hayes* (GLCD 1127); *Under the Moon* (GLCD 1155)

Healy, Tommy, *Memories of Sligo* (OSS 46)

Ivers, Eileen, *Fresh Takes* [with John Whelan] (SIF 1075); *Traditional Irish Music* (GLCD 1139); *Eileen Ivers Wild* (GLCD 1166)

Keane, Seán, *Gusty's Frolics* (CC17CD); *Jig it in Style* (CCF25CD) (BLB 5005); *Roll Away the Reel World* [with James Keane] (SIF 1026); *The Fire Aflame* [with Matt Molloy, Liam O'Flynn] (CCF30CD)

Kelly, James, *Irish Traditional Fiddlers* [with John Kelly jnr.] (PTICD 1041); *James Kelly* (SLP 1006); *The Ring Sessions* (SPINCD 999); *Traditional Irish Music* (Capelhouse CD 896012)

Kelly, John (jnr.), *Irish Traditional Fiddlers* [with James Kelly] (PTICD 1041)

Kelly, John, *John Kelly, Fiddle and Concertina* (12TFRS 504); *Ceol an Chláir 1* [with Bobby Casey, Junior Crehan, Patrick Kelly and Joe Ryan] (CCÉ CL 17)

Kelly, Patrick, *Ceol an Chláir 1* [with Bobby Casey, Junior Crehan, John Kelly, Joe Ryan] (CCÉ CL 17)

Killoran, Paddy, *Paddy Killoran's Back in Town* (Shanachie 33003)

Larrissey, Brendan, *A Flick of the Wrist* (CBMCD 016)

Lennon, Charlie, *Lucky in Love* [with Mick O'Connor] (CCÉ CL 22); *Deoraí an Deoraí/The Emigrant Suite* [with Frankie Gavin] (CEF 112); *Flight From the Hungry Land* [with orchestra] (WOM 102); *Dance of the Honey Bees* [with Lennon family] (CEFCD 167); *The Bucks of Oranmore* [with Joe Burke] (GLCD 1165); *The Lennon Family* (CEFCD 167)

Liddy, Joe, *Ceol Tíre* [item] (CCÉ CL 12)

Linnane, Tony, *Fiddle and Concertina* [with Noel Hill] (TACD 2006)

Mac Gabhann, Antóin, *Ar Aon Bhuille* (CIC 105)

McGann, Andy, *Andy McGann and Paul Brady* (Shanachie 29009), solo (Shanachie 34016); *My Love is in America* (GLCD, 1991); *The Funny Reel* [with Joe Burke] (Shanachie, 1979); *A Tribute to Michael Coleman* [with Joe Burke] (GLCD, 1994); *Andy McGann and Paddy Reynolds* (Shanachie 34008)

McGinley, Martin, *Fiddle Music of Donegal* (CNF 001)

McGlinchey, Brendan, *Music of a Champion* (Silverhill PSH 100)

McGuire, Manus, *Carousel* [with Séamus McGuire] (CEF 105)

McGuire, Séamus, *The Wishing Tree* (GLCD 1151); *Carousel* [with Manus McGuire] (CEF 105)

McGuire, Seán, *Seán Maguire Plays* (VV 103); *Champion of Champions* (PTICD 1005); *The Best of Seán Maguire* (COX 1006); *Ireland's Champion Fiddler* (SOLP 1031); *From the Archives* (OAS 3017); *Portráid* (CEFC 137); *Sixty Years of Irish Fiddle, Celtic Music* (CM 043); *Hawks and Doves* (PTICD 1089); *Irish Traditional Fiddling* [with Roger Sherlock, Josephine Keegan] (PTICD 1002); *The Master's Touch* (ARCD 027)

McKillop, Jim, *Irish Traditional Fiddle Music* (PTICD 1045); *To Hell with the Begrudgers* [with Séamus Tansey] (SUN C30)

Morrison, James, *The Pure Genius of James Morrison* (Shanachie 33004); *The Professor* (Viva Voce 001)

Mulvihill, Brendan, *The Morning Dew* (GLCD 1128); *The Flax in Bloom* (GLCD 1020)

Mulvihill, Martin, *Traditional Irish Fiddling* (GLCD 1012)

Murphy, Denis, *The Star Above the Garter* [with Julia Clifford] (CC5CD); *Kerry Fiddles* [with Denis Murphy and Julia Clifford] (OSSCD 10); *Music from Sliabh Luachra* (RTÉ CD 183)

Ní Cathasaigh, Nollaig, *Nollaig Casey and Arty McGlynn* (TARA CD 3035); *Causeway* (TACD 3035)

O'Brien, Eileen, *Compositions of Paddy O'Brien* [with W. Fogarty] (CD 001)

O'Connell, Connie, *Ceol go Maidin* (CCÉ CL 43)

O'Donnell, Eugene, *Slow Airs and Set Dances* (GLCD 1015); *The Foggy Dew* (GLCD 1084)

O'Keeffe, Máire, *Cóisir, House Party* (CEFCD 165)

O'Keeffe, Pádraig, *Kerry Fiddles* [with Denis Murphy and Julia Clifford] (OSSCD 10, TSCD 309); *The Sliabh Luachra Fiddle Master* (RTÉ CD 174)

O'Loughlin, Peadar, *South West Wind* (CC47CD)

O'Maonaigh, Proinnsias, *Fiddle Music of Donegal* (CNF 001)

O'Shaughnessy, Paul, *Within a Mile of Dublin* [with Paul McGrattan] (SPINCD 1000); *Fiddle Music of Donegal* (CNF 001)

Peoples, Tommy, *A Traditional Experience with Tommy Peoples* (SOLO 7012), *Tommy Peoples* (CCÉ CL 13); *The High Part of the Road* (Shanachie 79044); *The Iron Man* (SHCD 79044); *Traditional Irish Music Played on the Fiddle*, GTD Heritage (TRAD HCD 008); *The Quiet Glen/An Gleann Ciúin* (TPCD 001)

Potts, Tommy, *The Liffey Banks* (CC13CD)

Power, Jimmy, *Irish Fiddle Player* (12 TS 306, OSS 81), *Fifty-odd Years* (TEMPO TP 001)

Queally, Michael, *The Trip Over the Mountain* (QOD 001)

Reavy, Ed, *Ed Reavy* (Rounder 6008); *The Music of Ed Reavy* [by US players] (CIC 047)

Reavy, Joseph, *The Collected Compositions of Ed Reavy* [3 vols.] (GGM 3)

Redican, Larry, *Larry Redican* (RTÉ MC 124) (RTÉ CD 191)

Reynolds, Paddy, *Atlantic Wave* (KM 9513)

Ryan, Joe, *Ceol an Chlár 1* [with Bobby Casey, Junior Crehan, John Kelly, Patrick Kelly] (CCÉ CL 170); *An Buachaill Dreoite* (CICD 113)

Smyth, Kathleen, *Cherish the Ladies* [with Peg McGrath, Mary Mulholland] (PTICD 1043)

Smyth, Seán, *The Blue Fiddle* (LUNCD 060)

FIFE/PICCOLO

Doonan, John, *Fenwick's Window* (1992); *At the Feis* [piccolo] (OSS 42); *The Lark in the Clear Air* [item] (OSS 13).

*Fluters of Old Erin* [fife and piccolo] (Viva Voce 002)

*Lambeg Drums with Fife and Rattlys* (PTICD 1088)

FLUTE

Broderick, Vincent, *The Turoe Stone* (OP 103)

Burke, Joe, *The Tailor's Choice* (SIF 1045)

Byrne, Conor, *Wind Dancer* (Newberry CB 001)

Cahill, Eddie, *Ah Surely* (Shanachie 29014)

Carty, Paddy, *Traditional Irish Music* (Shanachie 34017); *Traditional Music of Ireland* [with Conor Tully] (GTD, Galway 1986)

Clifford, Billy, *Flute Solos and Band Music* (12TS 337, OSS 11)

Coen, Jack and Charlie, *The Branch Line* (GLCD 3067)

Cooley, Séamus, *McGreevy and Cooley* (Philo PH 2005, CIC)

Cotter, Eamonn, *Traditional Irish Music From Co. Clare* (CDEC 001)

Crawford, Kevin, *D Flute Album* (KBS 77, GLCD 1162); *Raise the Rafters* (CCD 002)

Doonan, John, Doorley, Tom, *Danú* [in ensemble] (TM 002)

Duignan Packie, *Music from Co. Leitrim* (12TS 339)

Egan, Séamus, *Traditional Music of Ireland* (Shanachie 34015); *A Week in January* (Shanachie 65005)

Finnegan, Brian, *When the Party's Over* (ARAD CD 101); *Flook!* (SMALL CD 9405)

Flatley, Michael, *And Then Came Flatley* (Flatley 309070)

Gardiner, John Joe, *Ceol Tire* (CCÉ CL 12); *Flutes of Old Erin* (VV 002)

Gavin, Frankie, *Up and Away* (CEFCD 103)

Gavin, Mick, *Irish Traditional Music* (SOLP 1041)

Hamilton, Hammy, *The Moneymusk* (Hamilton, Coolea)

Healy, Dan, *The Wyndy Turn* (DHCD 001)

Healy, Tommy, *Memories of Sligo* (12TS 335)

Hernon, Marcus, *Traditional Irish Music Played on the Concert Flute* (GTDC 031); *The Floating Crowbar* (GTD 097); *Béal a' Mhurlaigh* (CEFCD 141)

Horan, Peter, *Music of Sligo* [with Fred Finn] (CCÉ CL 33)

Kennedy, Frankie, *Ceol Aduaigh* (CEF 102, GLCD 3090); *Altan* (GLCD 1078)

Kerr, Barry, *The Three Sisters* (SCD 1040)

Lee, John, *An Ríl Ar Lár, The Missing Reel* [with Séamus Maguire] (CEF 146)

Lyons, Donie, *No Boundaries* [with song] (CIC 114)

Madden, Joanie, *A Whistle on the Wind* (GLCD 1142)

Mayock, Emer, *Merry Bits of Timber* (KEYCD 121)

McConnell, Cathal, *An Irish Jubilee* (12TS 280, OSS 24), *On Lough Erne's Shore* (12TS 377, OSS 69)

McDermott, Josie, *Darby's Farewell* (12TS 325, OSS 20)

McEvoy, Catherine, *Scaoil Amach É Traditional Flute Music in the Sligo-Roscommon Style* (CIC 117)

McGoldrick, Michael, *Morning Rory* (AUGH 01)

McGrath, Peg, *Cherish the Ladies* [with Kathleen Smyth, Mary Mulholland] (PTICD 1043)

McGrattan, Paul, *The Frost is All Over* (CC58CD); *Within a Mile of Dublin* [with Paul O'Shaughnessy] (SPINCD 1000)

McKenna, John, *Original Recordings* (J. McKenna Traditional Soc., cass.); *Fluters of Old Erin* [tracks] (VV 002)

Molloy, Matt, *Matt Molloy* (LUN 004, SIF 3008, Shanachie 79064); *Heathery Breeze* (Polydor 2904 018); *Contentment is Wealth* (SIF 1058); *Stony Steps* (CCF 18); *The Fire Aflame* [with Seán Keane, Liam O'Flynn] (CCF30CD); *Shadows on Stone* (CDVE 930)

O'Connor, Mick, *Lucky in Love* [with Charlie Lennon] (CCÉ CL 22)

Ó Gráda, Conal, *The Top of Coom* (CCF27CD)
Ó Murchú, Marcas, *Ó Bhéal go Béal* (CICD 126)
O'Connor, Brian, *Come West Along the Road* (CD 307.2192.2)
Russell, Micho, *Traditional Music of Co. Clare* (FRR 004)
Shannon, Garry, *Lose the Head* (GTDHCD 135)
Sherlock, Roger, *At Their Best* [with Seán Maguire, Josephine Keegan] (SOLP 1088, COX 1008)
Tansey, Séamus, *The Best of Séamus Tansey* (PTICD 1007); *Masters of Irish Music* (LEA 2005); *King of the Concert Flute* (Silver PSH 1008); *Reels and Jigs* (Heritage); *Traditional Music of Co. Sligo* (SOLP 1022); *Séamus Tansey with Eddie Corcoran* (LEA 2090); *Easter Snow* (COMD 2063); *To Hell with the Begrudgers* [with Jim McKillop] (SUN C30)
Taylor, Paddy, *The Boy in the Gap* (CC 8); *Rolling in the Ryegrass* (FSA 60171)
Tubridy, Michael, *The Eagle's Whistle* (CC 27)
Vallely, Fintan, *Fintan Vallely* (Shanachie 29019); *Timber, the Flute Tutor* [instruction] (Waltons); *Starry Lane to Monaghan* (WHN 001)
Wilkinson, Desi, *The Three Piece Flute* (CSP 1009)
Woods, Mick, *A Tribute to McKenna* (Inch 7420)

## GROUPS

Altan [fiddles, accordion, flute, guitar, cittern, traditional song in Irish and English, Donegal base], *Harvest Storm* (GLCD 1177); *Horse with a Heart* (GLCD 1095); *Island Angel* (GLCD 1137); *The Red Crow* (GLCD 1109); *The Best of Altan* (GLCD 1177); *Blackwater* (CDV 2796); *Runaway Sunday* (CDV 2836); *The First Ten Years* (GLCD 1153)
Anam [accordion, bodhrán, guitar, bouzouki, contemporary song], *Anam* (CACD 001); *Saoirse* (CACD 002)
Arcady [accordion, fiddle, bodhrán, piano, flute, guitar], *After the Ball* (Shanachie 79077); *Many Happy Returns* (DARA CD 080)
Bakerswell [fiddle, pipes, flute, whistle, harp] *Bakerswell* (CCF 20)
Beginish [accordion, flute, fiddle, Kerry based], *Beginish* (INIS 001)
Begley and Cooney, *Meitheal* (HBCD 004)
Bothy Band [flute, fiddle, pipes, song in Irish and English], *The First Album* (GLCD 3011, LUNCD 002); *Old Hag You Have Killed Me* (LUNCD 007, GLCD 3005); *The Best of the Bothy Band* (GLCD 3001, LUNCD 041); *After-hours, Live in Paris* (GLCD 3016, LUNCD 030); *Live in Concert at the BBC* (GLCD 3111); *Out of the Wind, Into the Sun* (GLCD 3013, LUNCD 013)

Boys of the Lough [flute, fiddle, bodhrán, guitar, pipes, song], *To Welcome Paddy Home* (Shanachie 79061, Lough 001 CD); *Farewell and Remember Me* (Shanachie 79067, Lough 002 CD); *Sweet Rural Shade* (Shanachie 79068); *Live in Concert* (Shanachie V206); *An Irish Jubilee* (OSS 24); *The West of Ireland* (Lough 007 CD)
Bumblebees [harp, fiddle, piano accordion], *Bumblebees* (HBCD 0012)
Buttons and Bows [accordion, fiddle, guitar], *Buttons and Bows* (GLCD 1051); *First Month of Summer* (GLCD 1079); *Grace Notes* (CEFCD 151)
Calico [pipes, whistle, fiddle, guitar], *Celanova Square* (OSS CD 100)
Calua [flute, whistle, guitar, bodhrán], *Bóthar gan Briseadh* (CALCD 001)
Casadaigh, Na, *Fead an Iolair* (CEFC 108)
Celtic Thunder, *Celtic Thunder* (GLCD 1029); *Light of Other Days* (GLCD 1086)
*Ceol Tigh Neachtain* [session music] (CEFCD 145)
Ceoltóirí Chualann [under Seán Ó Riada], *Reacaireacht an Riadaigh* (CEF 010); *Playboy of the Western World* (CEF 012); *Ceol na nUasal* (CEF 015); *Ding Dong* (CEF 015); *Ó Riada sa Gaiety* (CEF 027); *Battle of Aughrim* (CCT 7); *Ó Riada's Farewell* (CC 12)
Ceoltóirí Laighean, *The Crooked Road* (CEF, 1975); *The Star of Munster* (CEF 047)
Cherish the Ladies [fiddle, flute, guitar, accordion], *Fathers and Daughters* (SHAN 79054); *Irish Women Musicians in America* (Shanachie 79053); *New Day Dawning* (GLCD 1175); *The Back Door* (GLCD 1119); *Out and About* (GLCD 1134)
Chieftains, The [fiddle, flute, pipes, harp, bodhrán, song in English and Irish], *The Chieftains* (CC2CD); *The Chieftains 2* (CC7CD); *The Chieftains 3* (CC10CD); *The Chieftains 4* (CC14CD); *The Chieftains 5* (CC16CD); *The Chieftains Live* (CC21CD); *Bonaparte's Retreat* (CC20CD); *The Chieftains 7* (CC24CD); *The Chieftains 8* (CC29CD); *Boil the Breakfast Early* [Matt Molloy debut] (CC30CD); *The Chieftains 10* (CC33CD); *The Year of the French* (CC36CD); *The Chieftains in China* (CC42CD); eight album series of re-issues on Shanachie (Shanachie 79019–21, 22, 23, 24, 25, 26, 27)
Cian, *Three Shouts from a Hill* (CIAN 001)
Clannad [song, synthesiser, guitar, mandolin, etc.], *Clannad 1* (1977001); *Clannad 2* (CEFCD 041, Shanachie 79007); *Dulaman* (CEFCD 058, Shanachie 79008)
Cran [flute, pipes, bouzouki, song], *The Crooked*

*Stair* (CBMM C002); *Black, Black, Black* (CC63CD)

Craobh Rua [pipes, fiddle, banjo, bodhrán, song, etc.], *The More That's Said* (CDLDL 1215); *Soh it is* (CDLDL 1259); *No Matter how Cold and Wet* (CDLDL 1237)

Danú [flute, bouzouki, accordion, fiddle] *Danú* (TM 002)

Déanta [flute, fiddle, harp, guitar, keyboards, song in Irish and English], *Déanta* (GLCD 1126); *Ready for the Storm* (GLCD 1147); *Whisper of a Secret* (GLCD 1173)

De Dannan [fiddle, flute, bouzouki, bodhrán, accordion, song], *The Mist Covered Mountain* (CEFCD 087, Shanachie 79005); *Star Spangled Molly* (Shanachie 79018); *The Best of De Dannan* (Shanachie 79047); *Ballroom* (GLCD 3040); *Jacket of Batteries* (GLCD 3053); *Half Set in Harlem* (GLCD 1113); *Hibernian Rhapsody* (Shanachie 78005); *Selected Jigs, Reels and Songs* (SH79001); *Anthem* (DARACD 013); *Song for Ireland* (SHCD 1130)

Deiseal [whistles, bouzouki, bass, etc.], *The Long, Long Note* (SCD 193); *Sunshine Dance* (SCD 596)

Dervish [flute, fiddle, whistle, accordion, bouzouki, guitar, song], *The Boys of Sligo* (SUNC 1); *Harmony Hill* (WHRL 001); *Playing With Fire* (WHRL 002); *At the End of the Day* (WHRL 003); *Live in Palma* (WHRL 004)

Dordán [whistle, harp, fiddle, song in Irish and English], *Dordán* (CEFC 150); Ceol na Gealaí, *Jigs to the Moon* (CEFCD 168)

Douglas Gunn Ensemble, *O'Carolan's Feast* (OSSCD 65)

Filí, Na, *Pure Traditional Music of Ireland* (PTICD 1010)

Fisherstreet, *Fisherstreet* [fiddle, concertina, flute, accordion, keyboards, mandola, guitar] (LUNCD 057)

Flanagan Brothers, The, *An Irish Delight* (OSS 80); *Tunes we Like to Play on Paddy's Day* (VV 007)

Four Men and a Dog [fiddle, banjo, accordion, bass, percussion, contemporary song], *Barking Mad* (CBMMC 01, TSCD 461); *Shifting Gravel* (CBMCD 005, SPCD 1047); *Long Roads* (TRA CD 273, 1996)

Four Star Trio, *The Square Triangle* (CRCD 02); *General Humbert* (CEFC 095); *Green Fields of America* [banjo, song, fiddle] (GLCD 1096)

Horslips, *Happy to Meet, Sorry to Part* [debut] (MOOCD 003); *Horslips Collection* (MOOCD 025); *Short Stories, Tall Tales* [finale] (MOOCD 019)

*Johnstons, The* [albums 1 and 2, re-release] (ESMCD 410)

Lahawns, The [fiddle, piano, accordion, guitar], *Live at Winkles'* (LM 001, 1996)

Lá Lugh {fiddle, flute, guitar, percussion, song in Irish and English], *Cosa Gan Bhróga* (CEFCD 111); *Lá Lugh* (CCF 29 CD); *Brighid's Kiss* (LUGCD 961, 1996)

*Lonely Stranded Band* [Piggott, Collins, Corcoran] (CIC 116)

Macalla, *Mná na hÉireann* (CEFC 010); *Macalla 2* (CEFC 122)

Macha Trio [small pipes, flute, piano, fiddle, drums], *The Bear Dance* (STCD 1001, 1995)

McPeake Family, *Traditional Songs and Music* (OSS 76)

Nomos [fiddle, concertina, bouzouki, bodhrán, contemp. song], *I Won't be Afraid* (ROCD 16, GLCD 3112); *Set You Free* (GRACD 230)

North Cregg, *And They Danced All Night* (MMR CD 1026)

Óige [flute, whistle, bodhrán, guitar, fiddle], *Live* (CDLDL 1225f); *Bang On* (CDLDL 1241)

Oisín, *Oisín* (OSSCD 37); *Béaloideas* (OSSCD 38); *Over the Moor to Maggie* (OSSCD 39); *Celtic Dream* (OSSCD 85)

Open House [fiddle, harmonica, guitar, contemp. song, etc.], *Open House* (GLCD 1122); *Second Story* (GLCD 1144, 1994); *Hoof and Mouth* (GLCD 1169, 1997)

Patrick Street [fiddle, accordion, guitar, bouzouki, song], *Made in Cork* (GLCD 1184); *All in Good Time* (GLCD 1125); *Corner Boys* (GLCD 1160); *Irish Times* (GLCD 1105); *No. 2 Patrick Street* (GLCD 1088)

Planxty, *Planxty* (Polydor 2383186, Shanachie 79009); *The Well Below The Valley* (Polydor 2383232, Shanachie 79010); *Cold Blow and the Rainy Night* (Polydor 238330 1, Shanachie 79011); *The Planxty Collection* (Polydor 2389397, Shanachie 79012); *After the Break* (Tara 3001); *The Woman I Loved So Well* (Tara 3005); *Words and Music* (WEA Ireland 240101 1, Shanachie 79035)

Raymond Roland Quartet, *Saturday Night at the Céilí* (OSS 61)

Reeltime [fiddle, accordion, guitar, keyboards], *Reeltime* (GLCD 1154)

Relativity [guitar, keyboard, accordion, song], *Gathering Pace* (GLCD 1076); *Relativity* (GLCD 1059)

Skylark [fiddle, accordion, mandocello, song, bodhrán], *Skylark* (CC46CD); *All of It* (GLCD 3046); *Light and Shade* (CC57CD); *Raining Bicycles* (CC62CD); *Sliabh Notes* [fiddle, accordion, guitar] (OSS CD 114)

Sliabh Notes [fiddle, accordion, guitar] (OSSCD 114)

Smoky Chimney [fiddle, accordion, guitar], *The Smoky Chimney* (Spin CD 1001)
Solas [flute, fiddle, accordion, guitar, song in English and Irish], *Solas* (Shanachie 78002); *Sunny Spells and Scattered Showers* (Shanachie 78010)
Stockton's Wing, *Stockton's Wing* (4TA 2004); *The Collection* (TACD 4)
Sult, *Sult* (HBCD 009)
Sweeny's Men [items] *The Irish Folk Collection* [3 CD set] (TBXCD 5091, 2, 3)
Tabache [flute, fiddle, guitar], *Are You Willing?* (CDLDL 1244); *Waves of Rush* (CDLDL 1283)
Tamalin [pipes, whistle, fiddle, flute, guitar, bouzouki, bodhrán, contemp./popular song], *Rhythm & Rhyme* (GRACD 227)
Trian [fiddle, accordion, guitar, song in Irish and English], *Trian II* (GLCD 1159)
Wild Geese [flute, whistle, banjo, guitar, accordion, mandolin, bodhrán], *Salute to Baltimore* (Ar Linn 4052)

### GUITAR
Brady, Paul, *Welcome Here Kind Stranger* (LUN 024)
Cahill, Denis, *The Lonesome Touch* [with Martin Hayes] (GLCD 1181)
Cooney, Steve, *Meitheal* [with Séamus Begley] (HBCD 004)
Feely, John, *John Feely* (CEFCD 109)
Gaughan, Dick, *Coppers and Brass* (12TS 315)
Lane, Frankie, *Dobró* (CEFCD 159)
McGlynn, Arty, *McGlynn's Fancy* (MCLD 19351); *Arty McGlynn* (MCACD 19351); *Nollaig Casey and Arty McGlynn* [with Nollaig Ní Cathasaigh] (TARACD 3035); *Causeway* [with Nollaig Ní Chathasaigh] (TACD 3035)
Morrison, James, *The Professor* [fiddle] with early-century guitar tracks (VV 001)
Ó Domhnaill, Mícheál, *Portland* [with Kevin Burke] (GLCD 1041); *Promenade* (GLCD 3010)
Trimble, Gerald, *Crosscurrents* (GLCD 1065); *First Flight* (GLCD 1043); *Heartland Messenger* (GLCD 1054)

### HARMONICA
Basker, Tommy, *The Tin Sandwich* (Silver Apple 7588 901932)
Clarke, Eddie, *Sailing into Walpole's Marsh* [with Maeve Donnelly and Seán Corcoran] (SIF 1004); *Crossroads* [with Joe Ryan] (SIF 1030)
Murphy, Phil, Pip and John, *The Trip to Cullenstown* (CC55CD); *Traditional Music from South Wexford* [items]; *Up Close* [Kevin Burke, item] (GL 1052)
Power, Brendan, *New Irish Harmonica* (SIF 3098); *Blow In* (HBCD 008)

Pepper, Noel, *The Lark in the Clear Air* [item] OSS 13

### HARP
Bell, Derek, *Carolan's Receipt* (CC 18); *Carolan's Favourite* (CC 28); *Music for the Irish Harp* (CC 59); *Derek Bell's Musical Ireland* (CC 35)
Cassidy, Patrick, *Cruit* (CEF 130)
Daly, Patricia, *Harping Daly* (PDCD 001)
Harbison, Janet, *O'Neill's Harper* (BHO 002); *The Wedding Album* (BHO 004); *Traditional Dance Music of Ireland* (UFTM, 1991)
Kelly, Laoise, *Just Harp* (LK 001)
Loughnane, Kathleen, *Affairs of the Harp* (Reiskmore Music 5 034167 039295)
McKenna, Antoinette, *The Best of Antoinette McKenna* [with Joe McKenna] (Shanachie 78012)
Ní Chathasaigh, Máire, *The New Strung Harp* (COMD 2019); *The Living Wood* (OBMCD 07); *The Carolan Albums* (OBMCD 04, 06); *Out of Court* (OBMCD 03) *Live in the Highlands* (OBMCD 08)
O'Farrell, Annemarie, *The Jig's Up* (CD 1903)
O'Hara, Mary, *Mary O'Hara sa Ghailearaí Náisiúnta* (CEF 118)

### HARP, WIRE-STRUNG
Ball, Patrick, *Celtic Harp I* (1983), *II* (1983), *III* (1985), *IV* (1989)
Dooley, Paul, *Rip the Calico* (PDCD 001)
Heymann, Ann, *Queen of Harps* (COMD 2057); *The Harper's Land* [with Alison Kinnaird on gut-string clarsach] (TP012)
Yeats, Gráinne, *A Rogha Féin* (CEF 096); *The Belfast Harp Festival 1792–1992* [two discs: I Music of the Irish Harpers, II Music of Carolan] (CEF156CD)

### HARPSICHORD, CLAVICHORD
Ó Riada, Seán, *Ó Riada's Farewell* (CC12CD)
Ó Súilleabháin, Mícheál, *Mícheál Ó Súilleabháin* (CEFCD 046)

### JEW'S HARP
Flanagan Brothers, The, *Tunes We Like to Play on Paddy's Day* (Viva Voce 007)
Hayes, Tommy, *An Rás* (LUNCD 055); *A Room in the North* (OPPCD 001)
*Irish Music Played on Small Instruments* (OSSCD 13)
Wright, John, *Happy to Meet, Sorry to Part* (ORBD 092); *The Lark in the Clear Air* [item] (OSS 13)

### KEYBOARD, SYNTHESISERS, ETC.
Jackson, Jolyon, *Paddy Glackin and Jolyon Jackson* (4TA 2009)

## LILTING

*Celtic Mouth Music, Lilting from many cultures* (Ellipsis Arts CD 4070)
Gardiner, Bobby [items] *The Master's Choice* (OSSCD 86); *The Clare Shout* (BG 007)
Lenihan, Tom [item], *Hurry the Jug* (CDORB 090)
Ó Caodháin, Colm, *Ireland/Irlande* [compilation item] (Auvidis, UNESCO D 8271)
Ó Maoldhomhnaigh, Aodh, *Ireland/Irlande* [compilation] (Auvidis, UNESCO D 8271)

## LAMBEG

*Lambeg Drums with Fife and Rattlys* (PTICD 1088)

## MANDOLIN

Murray, Martin, *A Dark Horse* (CBMMC 21)
Moloney-O'Donnell, *Mandolin and Fiddle* (CSIF 1010)
Rafferty, Paddy [item], *The Old Fireside Music* (LR 093098)

## MELODEON

Begley, Brendan, *Seana Choirce* (CEF C123); *We Won't Go Home 'til Morning* (KM 9510)
Brock, Paul, *Mo Cháirdín* (CEFCD 155)
Connolly, Johnny, *An tOileán Aerach* (CICD 63); *Drioball na Fáinleoige* (CICD 127)
Doherty, Tom, *Take the Bull by the Horns* (GLCD 1131)
Fledler, Andy [with John Kimmel] (Folkways RF 112)

## MUSIC COMPILATIONS

*Claddagh's Choice, Anthology* (CC40)
*Gaelic Roots, Boston Irish Studies* (KM 9514)
*Green Linnet 20th Anniversary Collection* (GLCD 106)
*Orchaiste Ceoil* [solo, duets] (CDTCD 005, 006)

## PIANO ACCORDION

Kelly, Alan, *Out of the Blue* (BBM 001)
Shannon, Séamus, *Séamus Shannon* (SOLP 1037)

## PIANO AND ACCOMPANIMENT

Arcady, *Many Happy Returns* (Dara CD 080)
Breschi, Antonio, *At the Edge of the Night* (ARNR 0594)
*Folk Music and Dances of Ireland* [companion to Breathnach book] (OSS 03)
Hession, Carl, *Echoes of Ireland* (RGMC 3); *Ceol Inné, Ceol Inniú* (CEFCD 173); *Trá, Water's Edge* (CEFCD 177)
*Irish Dance Music* (TSCD 602)
Lennon, Charlie [with Joe Burke], *Bucks of Oranmore* (GLCD 1165)
Ó Súilleabháin, Mícheál, *Irish Music on Keyboards* (CEFCD 046); *Cry of the Mountain* (CEFC 079)

## REGIONAL MUSIC AND SONG

### America, general

*Dear Old Erin's Isle* (NI 5350)

### California

*Off to California* [Joe Murtagh, Seán O'Sullivan, Milíosa Lundy, Larry Fitzpatrick, Maureen Murtagh, with Max Parsley, Marty Somberg, Peter Persoff] (Advent, La Habla, CA); *Out of the Woods* [Randal Bays] (FG9704CD); *Wind on the Water* [Nancy Curtin and the Strayaways] (FG9501CD); *Like Magic* [Bill Dennehy] (Aniar CD 101); *Dale Russ: Irish Fiddle* [Dale Russ] (FG9502CD); *Jody's Heaven* [Dale Russ] (FG9603CD); *The Fiddler's Friend* [Barbara MacDonald Magone] (CUL 103C); *Minding Mice at the Crossroads* [Vincy Keehan, Richard Morrison, Kenny Somerville, Colm Ó Riain, Jimmy O'Meara, Vinny Cronin, Orla McGowan, Cormac Gannon Dana Lyn] (OGM9801CD)

### Canada

*Irish and British Songs from the Ottawa Valley* (Folkways 4051)

### Cape Breton

*Traditional Music From Cape Breton Island* (NI 5383); *The Fiddlesticks Collection* [Jerry Holland] (GLCD 1156)

### Chicago

*Irish Traditional Instrument Music in Chicago* (Rounder 6006), *Chicago Irish Musicians* (Irish Musicians' Assoc. 82–513)

### Clare

*Clare Tradition* (GTDHCD O82); *Farewell to Lissycasey, Traditional Music of County Clare* (OSSCD 79); *Irish Music and Song From County Clare*, Vol. 2 (TRADHC 001); *Lambs on the Green Hills, Songs from Clare* (OSS 9; *Clare-Kerry* [collected by Ciarán Mac Mathúna] (RTE MC 102); *Sanctuary Sessions, from Cruise's Pub, Ennis* (CCD 001)

### Cork

*Small Island* (OSSCD 70)

### Donegal

*The Flower of Dunaff Hill* (ITSC 001); *An Hour of Song* [Maggie Magee & Dan McGonigal] (ITSC 002); *Fiddlesticks, Donegal Fiddle Music* (NI 5320); The *Fiddle Music of Donegal*, Vol. 1 (CNF 001), Vol. 2 (CNF 002); *The Brass Fiddle* [V. Campbell, C. Cassidy, J. & F. Byrne] (CC44CD); *The Donegal Fiddle* (RTÉ 196)

## Dublin
*Dublin's Fair City, A Musical Tour in Dublin* (DOCDK 111)

## England
*The Bird in the Bush* (TSCD 479); *English and Scottish Folk Ballads* (TSCD 480); *Bold Sportsmen All* [sporting ballads] (TSCD 495); *Round Cape Horn* [sailing-ship songs] (TSCD 499); *English Drinking Songs* (TSCD 496)

## Fermanagh
*Here's a Health* [collected by Seán Corcoran, with booklet] (ACNI 1986)

## Galway and Limerick
*Galway and Limerick* [collected by Ciarán Mac Mathúna] (RTÉ MC 113)

## Galway, East
*Bridging the Gap* [Kevin Moloney, Seán Moloney] (MOL 001); *Aughrim Slopes Céilí Band* [release of original recordings made in the 1930s] (IAA 005, 1995); *Heart and Home: Irish Fiddle Music from Lucy Farr* [Farr, Lucy] (Veteran Tapes, Suffolk, 1992); *Traditional Irish Music Played on the Fiddle and Flute* [McGreevy and Cooley] (Cló Iar-Chonnachta Teo.); *From Galway to Dublin: Early Recordings of Traditional Irish Music* (Rounder CE 1087); *The Dangerous Reel* [Rafferty, Mick and Mary] (Barrel, USA 1995); *The Branch Line* [Coen, Jack and Charlie] (GLCD 3067); *The Old Fireside Music* [Mike and Mary Rafferty] (LR 093098)

## Leitrim
*Leitrim's Hidden Treasure* (LHTCD 1)

## London Irish
*Irish Music in London Pubs* [old recordings] (CIC 32); *Across the Waters* (NI 5415, 1994); *Paddy in the Smoke* (TSCD 603)

## Isle of Man
*Kiaull Vannin* (MXCM1, 1992); *Paitchyn Vannin* (MHFC1, 1995); *The Best that's in it* (MHFCD1, 1996); Charles Guard, *The Secret Island* (MMC4, 1993); Emma Christian, *Beneath the Twilight* (EMCD1, 1994)

## Northumberland
Kathryn Tickell, *Borderlands* (CROCD 210); Pauline Cato, *By Land and by Sea* (TCCD 01)

## Sardinia
*Launeddas playing by Efisio Melis* (Silex Memoire Y225 106)

## Scotland
Jeannie Robertson, *Scottish Ballad Singer* (OSSCD 92); *The Stewarts of Blair* (OSS 96); *Scottish Voices* (TSCD 703); *Bothy Ballads* (CDTRAX 9001); *Music From the Western Isles* (CDTRAX 9002); *Waulking Songs From Barra* (CDTRAX 9003); *Shetland Fiddle Music* (CDTRAX 9004); *The Muckle Sangs* (CDTRAX 9005); *The Fiddler and His Art* (CDTRAX 9009); *Gaelic Bards and Minstrels* (CDTRAX 9016D); *Gaelic Psalms from Lewis* (CDTRAX 9006); *Calum Ruadh, Bard of Skye* (CDTRAX 9007); *James Campbell of Kintail/Gaelic Songs* (CDTRAX 9008); *Piobroch, Pipe Major William MacLean* (CDTRAX 9010); *Piobroch, Pipe Major Robert Brown* (CDTRAX 9011); *Piobroch, Pipe Major RB Nichol* (CDTRAX 9012); *Calum and Annie Johnston* (CDTRAX 9013); *Piobroch, George Moss* (CDTRAX 9015); *English and Scottish Folk Ballads* (TSCD 480); Hamish Moore, *Dannsa'air an Drochaid* (CDTRAX 073); *Heather and Glen, Scots Ballads and Tunes* (OSS 62); *Fhuair Mi Pog* Margaret Stewart, Allan MacDonald [Gaelic song, with bagpipes, small pipes, etc.]

## Sligo
*A Musical Trip to Coleman Country* (Coleman Heritage, CC 002); *The Sound of Coleman Country* (Coleman Heritage CC 0010); Coleman Country Céilí Band, *Jigs and Reels* (HSMC 020M)

## Ulster
*Harvest Home* [collected by Len Graham, with booklet] (ACNI 1993); *Ulster's Flowery Vale* [with Sarah Makem, Geordie Hanna, Seán McGuire, Jerry Hicks, Barney McKenna, Seán McAloon, Cathal McConnell, Tommy Gunn, Mickey McCann] (BBC 28); *Singing Men of Ulster* (GLCD 1005)

## Wales
*Sraith Rhyfeddod* [Welsh bagpipes] (Fflach C104 G); *Harp Music of Wales* (CDSD L412); *Fernhill, Ca' Nós* [song, pipes, accordion] (BEJOCD 14); *Ffidil* [fiddle and crwthi music] (Fflach TRADD CD 182H)

## Wexford
*Carols* [tracks] *Christmas Day in the Morning* (Revels Records CD 1087; choral), Voice Squad (SPIN 996)

### SAXOPHONE
O'Donnell, Séamus, *At the Racket* [with John Carty, Brian McGrath] (RR 001)

## DISCOGRAPHY

### SET DANCE MUSIC

*Call the Set*, vols. 1–3 (CFP 001, 2, 3)
*Dance Music of Ireland*, vols. 1–8 (GTD HC series)
*Magic of Irish Set Dancing, The*, vols. 1–9 (An Fáinne Rince Club, videos no. V001–V009; cass. no MS 001–009)
*Music For the Sets*, vols. 1–6 (NPU 2–NPU 7)
*Full Polka Set*, Johnny Reidy (JRK)
*Set Dances of Ireland*, vols. 1–5 (Séadna 001–005)
*Shaskeen Live*, vols. 1–3, Shaskeen (CFA 3506–8)
*Step it Out*, Pádraig Moynihan (KSUL 1113)
Templehouse, *Music for the Sets*, vol. 2 (LNMC 7024); *Crossroads Céilí* (CHCS 015)
*The Thresher and the Dance*, video, with Matt Cunningham (ARV002)

### 78s ON CD

Morrison, James, *The Professor* (VV 001)
Neary, Eleanor, *Irish Dance Music* [Harp and Shamrock Orchestra] (FW 8821)
Dolan, Packie, *The Forgotten Fiddle Player of the 1920s* (Viva Voce 1994)
Mullally, William, *The First Irish Concertina Player to Record* (Viva Voce 005)
Flanagan Brothers, *The Tunes We Like to Play on Paddy's Day* (Viva Voce 007)
*Fluters of Old Erin: Piccolo and Whistle Recordings of the 1920s and 30s* (Viva Voce 002)
*From Galway to Dublin: Early Recordings of Traditional Irish Music* (Rounder CE 1087)
Kimmel, John, *John Kimmel: Virtuoso of the Irish Accordion* (Smithsonian Folkways Records RF 112)
*Milestones at the Garden: Irish Fiddle Masters from the 78 rpm Era* (Rounder CD 1123)
*Wheels of the World, Classic 1920s–30s Recordings* (Vol. 1, Yazoo 7008, Vol. 2, Yazoo 7009)

### SONG IN ENGLISH

*Ancient Celtic Roots* [compilation, Heaney, Makem, Tunney, Robertson, etc.] (TSCD 704)
Barry, Margaret, *Margaret Barry* (COX 1029); [with Michael Gorman] *Her Mantle so Green* (TSCD 474); *Ireland's Own* (PTICD 1029); *Irish Music in London Pubs* [item] (CIC 032)
Butcher, Eddie, *Adam in Paradise* (FRR 003); *Harvest Home* [item] (ACNI, 1993)
Carolan, Mary Ann, *Songs from the Irish Tradition* (12TS 362); *Ireland/Irlande* [compilation] (Auvidis, UNESCO D 8271)
Casey, Karan, *Songlines* (Shanachie 78007)
Cassidy, Jane, *The Empty Road* (CCF 14)
Cinnamond, Robert, *Ye Ramblin' Boys of Pleasure* (12T 269, OSS72)
Cleary, Nora, *The Lambs on the Green Hills* [compilation] (12TS 369)
Conway, Ollie, *The Lambs on the Green Hills* [compilation] (12TS 369)
Cronin, Elizabeth, Alan Lomax Collection (1951), Vol. 1, *Ireland* [compilation] (Rounder CD 1742)
Crotty, Siney, *The Lambs on the Green Hills* [compilation] (12TS 369)
Crowley, Jimmy, *Jimmy mo Mhíle Stór* (CEFC 113); *My Love is a Tall Ship* (CDCR 006)
Dennehy, Tim, *A Winter's Tear* (CICD 87); *Farewell to Miltown Malbay* (SRCD 002)
Drew, Ronnie, *Dirty Rotten Shame* (COL 481 483 2)
*Emerald Grooves, Parlour Songs from Old 78s* [compilation] (OSS 55)
Flanagan, Michael, *Lone Shanakyle* (OAS 3013)
Flynn, Mick, *The Lambs on the Green Hills* [compilation] (12TS 369)
Flynn, Patricia, *Stray Leaves* (CSP 1031)
Garvey, Seán, *Ón dTalamh Amach/Out of the Ground* (HS 010)
Gleeson, Barry, *Path Across the Ocean* (Wavelength CD 1)
Graham, Len, *Chaste Muses, Bards and Sages* (FRR 007); *After Dawning* [with Joe Holmes] (12TS 401, OSS 78); *Wind and Water* (1976); *Do me Justice* (1983); *Ye Lovers All* (CC41CD)
Greaney, Con, *The Road to Athea* (CIC 082)
Hammond, David, *I am the wee Falorie Man* (TCD 1052)
Hanna, Geordie, *Geordie Hanna Sings* (Eagrán, MD 002); *On the Shores of Lough Neagh* [with Sarah Anne O'Neill] (12TS 372)
Harte, Frank, *Dublin Street Songs* (12T 172); *Through Dublin City* (12T 218 & OSS 44); *We Shall Overcome* (Folkways), *Daybreak and a Candle End* (SPINCD 995); *And Listen To My Song* (LUN 025, SPIN 994); *The First Year of Liberty* (HBCD 0014)
Hogan, Dick, *The Wonders of the World* (5 099386 028529)
Holmes, Joe, *After Dawning* [with Len Graham] (12TS 401)
*Irish Voices* [compilation includes the McPeakes, Sarah Makem, Willie Clancy, John Lyons, John Reilly, Len Graham, Paddy Tunney, Tom Lenihan, Sarah Ann O'Neill] (TSCD 702)
Irvine, Andy, *Rude Awakening* (CSIF 1114); *Andy Irvine and Paul Brady* (GLCD 3006); *East Wind* [with Davy Spillane] (TACD 3027)
Keane, Dolores, *Brokenhearted I'll Wander* (GLCD 3004); *Farewell to Eirinn* (GLCD 3003); *Sáil Óg Rua* (GLCD 3033); *Solid Ground* (Shanachie 8007); (CDTUT 72136) (OKCD 2) (FXCD 175); *The Best Of Dolores Keane* (TORTE CD 206)

Keane, Sarah and Rita, *At the Setting of the Sun* (FIENDCD 771); *Sáil Óg Rua* (CEFCO 101); *Once I Loved* (CC4); *Muintir Catháin* (CEFC 107)

Keane, Seán, *Turn a Phrase* (INDCD 001); *All Heart, No Roses* (CBMCD 007)

Kelly, Luke, *Collection* (CHCD 1041); *The Luke Kelly Album* (CHCD 1016)

Lenihan, Tom, *Paddy's Panacea* (OSS 77); *The Mount Callan Garland* (CBÉ 003)

Lyons, John, *The May Morning Dew* (12 TS 248); *Troubled Man* (1992)

Lyons, Tim, *The Green Linnet* (LER 3036); *Easter Snow* (SIF 1014)

Maguire, John, *For the Sake of Old Decency* (SNG 960601)

Makem, Sarah, *Mrs Sarah Makem, Ulster Ballad Singer* (12T 182); *Bard of Armagh* [track with The Clancys] (EXIN 28973); *Irish Voices* [item] (TSCD 702)

Makem, Tommy, *Songs of Tommy Makem* (TCD 1054); *Live at the Irish Pavilion* (Shanachie 52036); *Ancient Pulsing* (Red Biddy 3001); *Lonesome Waters* (Shanachie 52011)

McKeown, Susan, *Bushes & Briars* (ALU 1008)

McMahon, Dolly, *Dolly McMahon* (CC 3)

Mitchell, Kevin, *Free and Easy, I Sang that Sweet Refrain* (CD TRAX 108)

Moulden, John, *Thousands are Sailing* [songs from the book] (Ulstersongs USCASS 01)

Mulqueen, Ann, *Kerry's 25th* (COAS 3022); *Mo Ghrása Thall na dTéad* (CIC 080)

Murphy, Briege, *The Longest Road* (SCD 1034)

Murphy, Maggie, *Linkin' O'er the Lea* (VTI 34 CD)

*Nenagh Singers Circle* [various local singers] (NSCC 001)

Ní Dhómhnaill, Tríona, *Tríona* (CEFCD 043)

Ó Sé, Seán, *Ó Riada sa Gaiety* (CEF 027, CEFCD 027); *Babaró* [with Cathal Dunne] (CEF039); *Heritage* [with Dónal Lunny] (HM 10); *An Poc Ar Buile* (GL 2); *Táimse im' Chodhladh* (CES 003); *Bhí Bean Uasal* (CES 012)

Ní Uallacháin, Pádraigín, *When I Was Young* [with Len Graham] (FONN 001)

Parsons, Niamh, *Loosely Connected* (GLCD 3094); *Loosen Up* (GLCD 1167)

Quinn, Mick, Campbell, John, *A Whisper of Ballads from South Armagh* (OAS 3018)

Reilly, John, *The Bonny Green Tree* (Topic, 12T 359, 1978)

Roscommon South Singers Circle, *What Will We Do?* [various singers] (SRSC CD 001)

Ryan, Cathie, *Cathie Ryan* (Shanachie 78008); *Music of What Happens* (Shanachie 78024)

Sands, Colum, *Unapproved Road* (SCD 1001); *The March Ditch* (SCD 1014); *All My Winding Journeys* (SCD 1035)

Sands, Tommy, *The Heart's a Wonder* (GLCD 1158); *Singing of the Times* (GLCD 3044)

*Sea Songs and Shanties* [compilation] (CDSDL 405)

Shine, Noel, *Land You Love the Best* [with Mary Greene] (SGCD 1)

*Songs of the Irish Travellers* [compilation] (CDSDL 407)

Spillane, John, *The Wells of the World* (HBCD 0011)

Sproule, Dáithí, *A Heart Made of Glass* (GLCD 1123)

*Thousands are Sailing* [emigration] (Shanachie, 78025)

Tunney, Paddy, *The Irish Edge* (OSS 40); *A Wild Bees' Nest* (12T 139); *The Mountain Streams Where the Moorcock Crows* (12TS 264); *The Flowery Vale* (12TS 289); *Lough Erne Shore* (LUNA 334); *The Green Linnet* (SIF 1037); *The Stone Fiddle* (GLCD 1037)

Tyrrell, Seán, *Cry of a Dreamer* (HNCD 1391)

Voice Squad, *Many's The Foolish Youth* (Spin 996); *Hollywood* (HBCD 002); *Good People All* (Shanachie 79081)

Weldon, Liam, *Dark Horse on the Wind*

White, Róisín, *The First of My Rambles* (VT 126)

### SONG IN IRISH

'ac Dhonncha, Seán, *An Aill Bháin* (CC 9); *Seán 'Ac Dhonncha* (CIC 6); *An Spailpín Fánach* (CICD 006), Alan Lomax Compilation

*Amhráin ar an Sean-nós, 1948–65* (RTÉ 185)

*Blas Meala/A Sip from the Honeypot* [from book of same title, 1 and 2] (GTCD 050/051)

*Buaiteoirí Chorn Uí Riada 1972–96* [2 CDs] (RTÉ 207)

Caitlín Maude, *Caitlín* (CEFC 042); *Croch Suas É Aríst Eile* [item] (CIC 011)

Curtin, Eileen, *An Draighneán Donn* (GTDHC 065)

De hÓra, Seán, *Seán de hÓra* (CEF 063); *Ó Chorcha Dhuibhne* (CIC 016)

Hernon, Seán, *An Nóra Bheag* (CICD 123)

Johnny Mháirtín Learaí, *Contae Mhuigheo* (CIC 013)

Mac an Iomaire, Seosamh, *Bean an Leanna* (CEFC 078)

Mac Dhonnagáin, Tadhg, *Raiftéirí san Underground* (CICD 094)

Mac Donnacha, Máirtín Tom Sheánín, *Bláth na hÓige* (CICD 128)

Mac Donnchadha, Johnny Mháirtín Learaí, *Contae Mhuigh Eo* [compilation] (CICD 013)

Mac Ruairí, Éamonn, *Toraigh Ó Thuaidh* (CIC 023)

Meirbhic, Áine, *An Buachaillín Bán* (AMECD 001)
Mhic Dhonncha, Mairéad, *Up Cuas!* (CIC 015, 1989)
Mulqueen, Ann, *Mo Ghrása Thall na Déise* (CIC 80)
Na hAncairí, *Ar Bord Leis na hAncairí* (CIC 046)
Ní Bheaglaoich, Seosaimhín, *Taobh na Gréine* (CEFCD 170)
Ní Bhrolcháin, Deirbhile, *Smaointe* (CEFC 147)
Nic Grianna, Róise, *Róise na nAmhrán* (RTE CD 178)
Ní Cheocháin, Máire, Alan Lomax Collection (1951), Vol. 1, *Ireland* [compilation] (Rounder CD 1742)
Ní Cheocháin, Máire, *Columbia World Library of Folk and Primitive Music 1* (SL 204, 1952); Alan Lomax Collection (1951), Vol. 1, *Ireland* [compilation] (Rounder CD 1742)
Ní Dhomhnaill, Caitlín, *Bean an Fhir Ruaidh* (CIC 009)
Ní Dhomhnaill, Maighread, *Maighread Ní Dhomhnaill* (CEF 055); *Dhá Phingin Spré* (CEFCD 152)
Ní Dhomnhanill, Néilí, *Ireland/Irlande* [compilation] (Auvidis, UNESCO D 8271)
Ní Dhomhnaill, Tríona, *Tríona* (GLCD 3034)
Ní Dhonnchadha, Máire Áine, *Deora Áille* (CC 6); *Claddagh Choice* (CC 40)
Ní Fhearaigh, Aoife, *Aoife Ní Fhearaigh* (CEFCD 172)
Ní Fhlaithearta, Síle, *Lucky in Love* [item] (CCÉ CL 22); *The Lennon Family* (CEFCD 167); *Deoraí an Deoraí* [item] (CEF 112)
Ní Mhiolláin, Treasa, *An Clochar Bán* (CIC 022)
Ní Riain, Nóirín, *Caoineadh na Maighdine* (CEFCD 084); *Stór Amhrán* (OSSCD 7); *Darkest Midnight, Good People All* (STAA 322); *Seinn Aililiú* (CEFCD 067); *Celtic Soul* (LMUS 0031)
Ní Scolaí, Máire, *Máire Ní Scolaí* (CEFC 029)
Ní Shúilleabháin, Eilís, *Cois Abhann na Séad* (CICD 132)
Ní Uallacháin, Pádraigín, *A Stór 's A Stóirín* (1994, CEF 166); *An Dara Craiceann* (CEFCD 174); *When I Was Young* [with Len Graham] (Fonn 001)
Ó Caoidheán, Colm, Alan Lomax Collection (1951), Vol. 1, *Ireland* [compilation] (Rounder CD 1742)
Ó Catháin, Darach, *Darach Ó Catháin* (CEFC 040, Shanachie 34005)
Ó Ceannabháin, Peadar (RTÉ MC 145, 161) (CICD 102, 123); *Mo Chuid den tSaol* (CICD 131)
Ó Ceannabháin, Peatsaí, *Tógfaidh Mé Mo Sheolta* (CIC 088)
Ó Dochartaigh, Seoirse, *Oíche go Maidin* (SCD 005)
Ó Duibheannaigh, Aodh, *An Cailín Gaelach* (FSB 003); *Aodh Ó Duibheannaigh* (CEF 048) [Mac Grianna anthology] (CEF 049),
Ó Fathartaigh, John Beag, *Tá an Workhouse Lán* (IC 093); *An tAncaire* (CIC 025); *The Winds of Freedom* (CIC 106)
Ó hÉanaí, Seosamh, *Seosamh Ó hÉanaí* (CEF 028); *Come all you Gallant Irishmen* (CIC 020) (NWAR CD 001); *Joe and the Gabe* (GLCD 1018); *Ó mo Dhúchas/From my Tradition* (CEFCD 051)
Ó Laoire, Lillis, *Bláth Gach Géag dá dTig* (CICCD 075, 1996)
Ó Lionáird, Iarla, *Aislingí Ceoil* (CEFC 164); *The Seven Steps to Mercy* (CDRW 671)
Ó Mealóid, Cilm, *Céad Slán le Camus* (CIC 002)
Ó Riada, Peadar, *Aifrean 2* (CEF 081); *Ceol is Cibeal Chúil Aodha* (1977), *Go mBeanaíotar duit* (CEFC 125); *Seamuisín* (1988, with book)
Ó Súilleabháin, Danny Maidhcí, *Carraig Aonair* (MC 002)
Ó Súilleabháin, Diarmuid, *Bruach na Carraige Báine* (CICD 115); *An Bóthar Cam* (CEF 035); *The Star of Munster* (CEF 035)
Ó Súilleabháin, Eilís, *Cois Abhann na Séad* (CICD 132)
*Pale Rainbow/An Dubh ina Bhán* [from book of same title, 1 and 2] (CP006/007)
Roscommon South Singers Circle, *What Will We Do* [various singers] (SRSC CD 001)
*Seachrán Sídhe* (CICD 135)
*Skara Brae* (CEFCD 031)
*Togha agus Rogha* [2 CDs, selections of mixed genre song, Raidió na Gaeltachta] (RTÉ 204 CD)
Tóibín, Nioclás (CEF 062), *Ireland/Irlande* [compilation] (Auvidis, UNESCO D 8271); *Rinn na nGael* (CIC 104)
Uí Cheallaigh, Áine, *Idir Dhá Chomhairle* (CEFC 158)

SONG, POLITICAL

Cassidy, Jane, *Mary Ann McCracken* [with Maurice Leyden] (ASH 004)
*Croppy's Complaint* (CRCD 03)
Harte, Frank, *The First Year of Liberty* (HBCD 0014)
*Irish Songs of Freedom*, Vols. 1, 2 (DOCDS 2002, 2008)
*Men of No Property, Ballads from Behind the Barricades* (RES 1002); *England's Viet Nam* (RES 1001); *The Fight Goes On* (RES 1003)
Moore, Christy, *Ride On* (WEA 240 4071)
O'Moore, Cormac, *A Rebel's Heart* (IRB 1998 CD)

Sinnott, Art, *With Pike in Hand* [with family] (SFCD 001)
*Songs of Irish Civil Rights* (BOL 4008)
*Songs of Irish Labour, Bread and Roses* (BRP CD 001)
Wolfe Tones, *25 Years of Greatness* (Shanachie 52024/5)

SONG, SATIRICAL/HUMOUROUS
Howard, Crawford, *The Diagonal Steam Trap* (SLP 1002)
Lyons, Tim, *Knock, Knock, Knock* [with Fintan Vallely] (UMFA 001)
Mone, Seán, *The Transit Van* (SMRC 101)
O'Rourke, Brian, *When I Grow Up* (CP 010)

SPOONS
Neylan, Paddy, *The Lark in the Clear Air* [item] (OSS 13)

STEP DANCE
*Buntús Rince* (CEF 017)
*Feis, Musical Accompaniment for Step Dancing* (EI 803); *Feis 2* (EI 824)
*Irish Dancing Made Easy* (IDV 1) video
O'Donovan, Joe, *Old Irish Step Dancing* (CCÉ)
*Rince, An Dara Céim* (CEF 020); *An Tríú Céim* (CEF 025)
*World Irish Dancing Championships* (WIDV 001) video

TIN WHISTLE
Bergin, Mary, *Feadóga Stáin* (CEFCD 071); *Feadóga Stáin 2* (CEFCD 149)
Duignan, Eoin, *Coumineol* (CEFCD 163)
Hughes, Brian, *Whistle Stop* (CEFCD 178)
*Irish Tin Whistle Legends* [various] (OP 65a)
*Irish Whistles* [various] (TRADDHCD 07)
Kilduff, Vinnie, *The Boys From the Blue Hill* (LUNCD 050)
Madden, Joanie, *A Whistle on the Wind* (GLCD 1142)
McCullough, L. E., *St Patrick was a Cajun* (OSSCD 110 & 111)
McHaile, Tom, *All-Ireland Whistling Champion at Boyle* (OLP 1001); *Airs of Ireland* [compilation] (SOLP 1035); *Pure Irish Tin Whistle* (PTICD 1001)
Moloney, Paddy, *Tin Whistles* [with Seán Potts] (CC 15)
Nugent, Laurence, *Traditional Irish Music on Flute and Tin Whistle* (Shanachie 78001); *Two for Two* (Shanachie 78014)
Ó Briain, Donncha, *Donncha Ó Briain* (CEF 083)
Potts, Seán, *Tin Whistles* [with Paddy Moloney] (CC15)
Russell, Micho, *The Russell Family* [with Packie and Gussie Russell] (12TS 251 & SIF 3079); *The Limestone Rock* (GTDHCD 104); *The Man From Clare* (TRAD HCD 011); *The Wind that Shakes the Barley* (GTDHCD 133); *In Our Own Dear Land* (GTDHCD 134); *Micho Russell* (TRL 1009); *Ireland's Whistling Ambassador* (PWCD 80001)
Ryan, Seán, *Siúil Uait/Take the Air* (CEFCD 142); *Cliaraí Ceoil* (CEFCD 169)
*Totally Traditional Tin Whistles* (OSSCD 53)

UILLEANN PIPES
*Bagpipes of Britain and Ireland* (CDSDL 416)
Browne, Peter, *Rince Gréagach* (CEF 090); *Seacht Nóiméad Chun a Seacht* (CEF 097) [both with Phillip King]
Browne, Ronan, *The Drones and the Chanters, 2* [compilation] (CC61CD); *The South West Wind* [with Peadar O'Loughlin] (CC47CD)
Clancy, Willie, *The Drones and the Chanters* [compilation] (CC 11); *The Minstrel From Clare* (12T 175); *The Pipering of Willie Clancy* (No. 1, CC 32, No. 2, CC 39)
Clarke, Heather, *New Approach to Uilleann Piping* [instruction CD] (OSS CD91)
Doran, Felix, *Last of the Travelling Pipers* (12T 288, OSS 63); *The Fox Chase* (FSA 3 172)
Doran, Johnny, *The Bunch of Keys* [re mastered 78s] (CBÉ 001)
Ennis, Séamus, *The Wandering Minstrel* (12 TS 250, OSSCD 12); *The Bonny Bunch of Roses* (TCD 1023, OSS 59); *Forty Years of Irish Piping* (CSIF 1000); *The Best of Irish Piping* (TACD 1002–9); *The Return to Fingal* (RTÉ CD 199); *The Drones and the Chanters* [compilation] (CC 11); *The Séamus Ennis Story* [documentary] (RTÉ MC 115)
Furey, Finbar, *Prince of Pipers* (Polydor LP 2908023)
Hannan, Robbie, *The Pipers' Rock* [compilation] (LUN 023); *Traditional Irish Music* (CC 53); *Paddy Glackin and Robbie Hannan* [with Paddy Glackin] (CEFCD 171),
McLoughlin, Joe, *The Drones and the Chanters, 2* [compilation] (CC61CD)
Keane, Tommy, *The Pipers' Apron* (LUNCD 052); *The Wind Among the Reeds* [with Jacqui McCarthy] (MMCCD 51)
Keenan, Paddy, *Paddy Keenan* (CEF 045); *Port an Phíobaire* (CEF 099); *Na Keen Affair* (HCR 01 97)
Keenan, Brendan, *Brendan Keenan* (CEFC 106)
Lambe, Eugene, *Trip to Fanore* (GTDC 106)
Lavin, Jim, *Ceol an Mhála* (GTDC 010)
Mac Mathúna, Pádraig, *Blas na Meala* (CEFCD 157)

## DISCOGRAPHY

Masterson, Declan, *Deireadh an Fhómhair* (CEFCD 148); *Tropical Trad* (SCD 1093); *Fair Water-Fionn Uisce* (FRCD 961)

McAloon, Seán, *Ulster's Flowery Vale* (BBC 28); *Drops of Brandy* (12 TS 287); *The Gentlemen Pipers* (CDORBD 084)

McFadden, Gerry, *Drones from the Black Mountain* (OAS 3031)

McKenna, Joe, *The Best of . . .* [with Antoinette McKenna] (Shanachie 78012)

McKeon, Gay, *The Pipers' Rock* [compilation] (LUN 023); *Irish Piping Tradition* (CDGMK 001)

McPeake, Frank, *The Rights of Man* (FSA 60 176)

Moloney, Paddy, *The Drones and the Chanters* [compilation] (CC 11)

Mulligan, Neilidh, *Barr na Cúille* (SD 1022); *The Leitrim Thrush* (SCD 1037)

Ní Gráda, Máire, *The Pipers' Rock* [compilation] (LUN 023)

Nolan, Martin, *Travel'n Style* (MSN 001)

Ó Briain, Mícheál, *The Drones and the Chanters, 2* [compilation] (CC61CD); *May Morning Dew* (ACM CD 101)

Ó Canainn, Tomás, *With Pipe and Song* (PTICD 1035); *Uilleann Pipes* (PTICD 1093)

Ó Riabhaigh, Eoin, *The Pipers' Rock* [compilation] (LUN 023); *Traditional Slow Airs of Ireland* [edited, compilation] (cass. OSS 118, 1190)

O'Brien, Mick, *The Flags of Dublin* [with Paddy Glackin, Mick Gavin] (OSS 31); *May Morning Dew* (ACM 101)

O'Brien Moran, Jimmy, *The Pipers' Rock* [compilation] (LUN 023),

O'Dowd, Dan, *The Drones and the Chanters* [compilation] (CC11)

O'Flynn, Liam, *Liam O'Flynn* (WEA LOFI); *The Fine Art of Piping* (Celtic Music CM 054); *Out To An Other Side* (TARA 3031); *The Drones and the Chanters, 2* [compilation] (CC61CD); *The Given Note* (TARACD 3034); *The Piper's Call* (TARACD 3037)

O'Leary, Christy, *The Northern Bridge* (OBMCD 09)

O'Sullivan, Jerry, *The Gift* (Shanachie 78017); *The Invasion* (GLCD 1074)

Potts, Seán, *The Drones and the Chanters, 2* [compilation] (CC61CD)

Reck, Tommy, *The Drones and the Chanters* [compilation] (CC 11); *The Stone in the Field* (SIF 1008)

Rowsome, Leo, *Classics of Irish Piping* (12T 259, TSCD 471 & OSS 66); *Rí na bPíobairí* (CC 1); *King of the Pipers* (Shanachie 34001); *The Drones and the Chanters* [compilation] (CC11)

Shannon, Joe [with Johnny McGreevy] *The Noonday Feast* (GLCD 1023)

Spillane, Davy, *The Pipers' Rock* [compilation] (LUN 023); *East Wind* [with Andy Irvine] (TACD 3027); *Atlantic Bridge* (TACD 3019); *Out of the Air* (TACD 2017); *Shadow Hunter* (TACD 3023); *Pipedreams* (TACD 3026)

Touhey, Patsy, *Wheels of the World* [tracks] (YAZOO 7008/9); *The Piping of Patsy Touhey* (NPU 001)

### VIDEOS

*Celebration of Irish Music* (RTÉ VC 53)
*Come West Along the Road* (RTÉ VC 56)
*Late Late* Tribute Shows: *The Dubliners* (RTÉ VC 01); *Chieftains* (RTÉ VC 02); *Sharon Shannon* (RTÉ VC 46)
*Riverdance, The Show* (RTÉ VC 57)
*The Pure Drop, Music of Dreams* (RTÉ VC 48); *Pure Drop '91* (RTÉ VC 40); *Pure Drop, Set Dancing* (RTÉ VC 31); *The Pure Drop* [1] (RTÉ VC 04)